BIOLOGICAL PSYCHOLOGY

SECOND EDITION

FREDERICK TOATES

The Open University

PEARSON

Prentice Hall

Harlow, England • London • New York • Boston • San Francisco • Toronto
Sydney • Tokyo • Singapore • Hong Kong • Seoul • Taipei • New Delhi
Cape Town • Madrid • Mexico City • Amsterdam • Munich • Paris • Milan

Pearson Education Limited
Edinburgh Gate
Harlow
Essex CM20 2JE
England

and Associated Companies throughout the world

Visit us on the World Wide Web at:
http://www.pearsoned.co.uk

First published in 2001
Second edition 2007

ISBN: 978-0-13-197531-6

British Library Cataloguing-in-Publication Data
A catalogue record for this book is available from the British Library

Library of Congress Cataloging-in-Publication Data

Toates, F. M. (Frederick M.)
   Biological psychology / Frederick Toates. -- 2nd ed.
     p. cm.
   Includes bibliographical references and index.
   ISBN-13: 978-0-13-197531-6
   ISBN-10: 0-13-197531-5
    1. Psychobiology. I. Title.

   QP306.T632 2007
   612.8--dc22

                              2006050395

10 9 8 7 6 5 4 3 2
10 09 08

Typeset by 30 in 10.25/12pt Minion
Printed and bound by Rotolito Lombarda S.p.A, Milan, Italy

Brief contents

Chapter 1   Introduction   *1*

Chapter 2   Genes, environment and evolution   *21*

Chapter 3   The nervous and endocrine systems   *46*

Chapter 4   The cells of the nervous system: how they work   *81*

Chapter 5   The brain: basics of structure and role   *105*

Chapter 6   Development and plasticity   *145*

Chapter 7   Sensory systems: general principles   *177*

Chapter 8   Vision   *189*

Chapter 9   The other sensory systems   *218*

Chapter 10   The control of movement   *245*

Chapter 11   Learning and memory   *274*

Chapter 12   Emotion   *301*

Chapter 13   Stress and coping   *329*

Chapter 14   Pain   *353*

Chapter 15   Motivation   *371*

Chapter 16   Feeding and drinking   *397*

Chapter 17   Sexual behaviour   *423*

Chapter 18   Drugs and addiction   *445*

Chapter 19   Sleep and waking   *466*

Chapter 20   Cognition and action   *488*

Chapter 21   Brains, minds and consciousness   *516*

Chapter 22   When things go wrong   *533*

Contents

Preface xi
Guided tour xiv
Reviewers xviii
Acknowledgements xix

CHAPTER ONE
Introduction

Why should a psychologist be interested
   in biology? 2
The physiology of the body 6
Some sources of understanding 7
The way of thinking of biological psychology 12
Genes, development and learning 14
The comparative approach: psychology and ethology 16
Linking brains and minds 17
Bringing things together 19
Summary of Chapter 1 19
Further reading 19
Signposts 20
Answers 20

CHAPTER TWO
Genes, environment and evolution

Introduction 22
Principles of evolution 23
Processes controlling behaviour 25
Genes, replication and reproduction 29
The process of inheritance 32
Genes, brains and behaviour 34
Genes, learning and the environment 37
Evolutionary psychology 39
Depression: a case study 42
Bringing things together 44
Summary of Chapter 2 44
Further reading 45
Signposts 45
Answers 45

CHAPTER THREE
The nervous and endocrine systems

Introduction 47
What nervous systems do 48
Neurochemical actions at synapses 55
Neurons: development and learning 59
Terminology and organization of the nervous
   system 61
Hormones – the endocrine system 65
The autonomic nervous system 71
Bringing things together 78
Summary of Chapter 3 79
Further reading 80
Signposts 80
Answers 80

CHAPTER FOUR
The cells of the nervous system: how they work

Introduction 82
The neuron as a typical cell 83
The neuron: an excitable cell 86
Glial cells 91
The synapse and neurotransmitters 93
Alterations in synaptic strength 100
Bringing things together 103
Summary of Chapter 4 103
Further reading 103
Signposts 103
Answers 104

CHAPTER FIVE
The brain: basics of structure and role

Introduction 106
Describing the brain and finding your
   way around it 107
Relating structure to role: sensory and motor
   systems 115

Emotion, regulation and motivation   123
Cognitive processing, reasoning and anticipation   129
Comparative and evolutionary perspectives   130
Techniques for studying the brain   136
Bringing things together   144
Summary of Chapter 5   144
Further reading   144
Signposts   144
Answers   144

CHAPTER SIX
Development and plasticity

Introduction   146
Conceptual issues in understanding
    development   147
The basic biology of nervous system development   152
Development of neurons, neural systems and
    behaviour   158
Hormones and development   163
The brain: cognitive and social development   168
Atypical development and health issues   170
Ethology and a comparative perspective   173
Bringing things together   175
Summary of Chapter 6   176
Further reading   176
Signposts   176
Answers   176

CHAPTER SEVEN
Sensory systems: general principles

Introduction   179
Sensory systems and perception   179
General principles   183
Bringing things together   187
Summary of Chapter 7   187
Further reading   187
Signposts   187
Answers   188

CHAPTER EIGHT
Vision

Introduction   190
Within the eye   191
Basics of visual pathways   200
Functional specialization: perception and action   204
Functional specialization within perception   209
Bottom-up and top-down factors in close-up   213
Bringing things together   216
Summary of Chapter 8   216
Further reading   216
Signposts   217
Answers   217

CHAPTER NINE
The other sensory systems

Introduction   219
Hearing   219
The vestibular system   226
The somatosensory system   226
Chemical senses – taste and smell   236
Bringing things together   243
Summary of Chapter 9   243
Further reading   244
Signposts   244
Answers   244

CHAPTER TEN
The control of movement

Introduction   246
Basics of control   248
How stability is maintained   251
Muscles and motor neurons   255
The control of skeletal muscle   258
The control of movement by the brain   261
From brain to motor neurons   268
Motor imagery   270
Development of motor systems   271
Bringing things together   272
Summary of Chapter 10   272
Further reading   273
Signposts   273
Answers   273

CHAPTER ELEVEN
Learning and memory

Introduction   275
Basics of learning   277
Basics of memory   282
Studying the brain   285
Linking brains to evolution and function   292

Cellular mechanisms   294
Bringing things together   299
Summary of Chapter 11   299
Further reading   300
Signposts   300
Answers   300

CHAPTER TWELVE
Emotion

Introduction   302
The nature and function of emotion   304
Some emotions and their triggers   310
Feedback from the periphery   313
Role of brain regions   316
Neurochemicals   323
Some other effects of emotions   324
Bringing things together   327
Summary of Chapter 12   327
Further reading   327
Signposts   327
Answers   328

CHAPTER THIRTEEN
Stress and coping

Introduction   330
Characterizing stress   331
Two neurohormonal systems   333
Stressors, contexts and reactions   336
Stress and the immune system   339
Brain mechanisms   342
Depression   344
Stress and the cardiovascular system   345
Post-traumatic stress disorder   347
Influence of stress on the gut   348
Positive action for health   349
Bringing things together   350
Summary of Chapter 13   351
Further reading   352
Signposts   352
Answers   352

CHAPTER FOURTEEN
Pain

Introduction   355
Adaptive value of pain   355

The role of tissue damage and the sensory
   input side   357
The gate theory   359
Brain processes   361
Techniques of analgesia   363
Anomalous phenomena   365
Cognitive and social factors: theory and therapy   366
Bringing things together   369
Summary of Chapter 14   370
Further reading   370
Signposts   370
Answers   370

CHAPTER FIFTEEN
Motivation

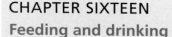

Introduction   372
Properties of motivation   374
The neuroscience of motivation   378
Temperature regulation   382
Social behaviour   385
Aggression   387
Exploration   392
Bringing things together   394
Summary of Chapter 15   395
Further reading   395
Signposts   396
Answers   396

CHAPTER SIXTEEN
Feeding and drinking

Introduction   398
Some physiology   400
The internal cue for feeding   402
The role of sensory factors, learning and cognition   405
Satiety   407
Brain mechanisms and eating   409
Abnormalities of feeding   412
Drinking and sodium ingestion   415
Bringing things together   421
Summary of Chapter 16   422
Further reading   422
Signposts   422
Answers   422

CHAPTER SEVENTEEN
Sexual behaviour

Introduction   424
An organizing framework   425
Control of the secretion of sex hormones   427
A comparative perspective   429
Human sexual desire   433
The human sexual response   436
Effects of chemicals on sexual behaviour   440
Sexual orientation   441
Bringing things together   443
Summary of Chapter 17   443
Further reading   443
Signposts   444
Answers   444

CHAPTER EIGHTEEN
Drugs and addiction

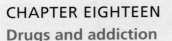

Introduction   446
Characteristics of drug-taking   448
Drugs and drug-taking   452
Non-drug-related activities   459
Trying to explain addiction   460
Bringing things together   464
Summary of Chapter 18   465
Further reading   465
Signposts   465
Answers   465

CHAPTER NINETEEN
Sleep and waking

Introduction   467
Rhythms of sleep-waking   468
The function of sleep and its link to causation   471
The motivation to sleep   475
Characterizing sleep   476
Brain mechanisms   478
Development   481
Dreaming   483
Issues of health   484
Bringing things together   486
Summary of Chapter 19   486
Further reading   486
Signposts   487
Answers   487

CHAPTER TWENTY
Cognition and action

Introduction   490
Modularity   491
Attention   493
Hemispheric asymmetry   497
Goal-directed behaviour   501
Language   506
Bringing things together   514
Summary of Chapter 20   514
Further reading   515
Signposts   515
Answers   515

CHAPTER TWENTY-ONE
Brains, minds and consciousness

Introduction   517
Conscious and unconscious information
   processing   519
Basis in the brain   521
Functional and comparative issues   526
Some philosophical considerations   528
Bringing things together   531
Summary of Chapter 21   532
Further reading   532
Signposts   532
Answers   532

CHAPTER TWENTY-TWO
When things go wrong

Introduction   534
Alzheimer's disease   536
Schizophrenia   540
Obsessive-compulsive disorder   549
Attention deficit hyperactivity disorder   552
Bringing things together   556
Summary of Chapter 22   556
Further reading   556
Signposts   557
Answers   557

Glossary   558
References   573
Index   615

Supporting resources

Visit www.pearsoned.co.uk/toates to find valuable online resources

Companion Website for students
- Interactive exercises and animations
- Multiple choice questions with Grade Tracker function to test your learning and monitor your progress
- 'Reflections' – enrichment activities to challenge and encourage development of deeper understanding
- Explanation of the 'test your knowledge' answers found in the book
- Research details
- Links to relevant sites on the web
- Online glossary

For instructors

- Instructor's Manual featuring teaching ideas, answers to 'test your knowledge' questions, essay and tutorials ideas and suggestions for discussion activities
- PowerPoint slides that can be downloaded and used for presentations

Also: The Companion Website with Grade Tracker provides the following features:

- Search tool to help locate specific items of content
- Online help and support to assist with website usage and troubleshooting

For more information please contact your local Pearson Education sales representative **or visit www.pearsoned.co.uk/toates**

Preface

When I produced the first edition of this book, I asked myself, what is the justification for yet another book on biological psychology? I noted that there already existed a number of excellent, well-established and frequently updated texts. In the meantime, still more have appeared. However, the time since the 1st edition has served to confirm my belief in the book. Based upon enormous amounts of feedback, this rather different and, I trust, improved second edition has appeared. So what is it about my prototypical reader that has motivated the long hours of work?

The present book sets out to put the emphasis in a rather different place from that of other texts. The rationale behind it derives from several closely related considerations. First, I believe that there is a need to present the biological material in a broader context of psychology. My guess is that you probably did not enter psychology in order to understand some of the favourite tools of the trade of biological psychology. These include the mechanism of the action potential of the giant axon of the squid and the nature of absorption of light by rhodopsin in the human retina. However, you are probably open to persuasion as to their relevance. Therefore, it seemed to be worth trying to show exactly why such topics are important in understanding broader issues of mind and behaviour. That is to say, material needs to be contextualized into a 'person-friendly' psychological picture. In so doing, I believe that, as a bonus, the subject demarcations between the biological and other perspectives, e.g. social, become less clear.

Psychology can sometimes seem more like a political election rally than a science. On one extreme wing, a type of 'nuts-and-bolts' physiological psychologist stands on a platform of reducing everything to neurons, while making disapproving noises towards such 'soft' approaches as social psychology. On the other extreme, social constructivists appear like a medieval French religious sect in the zeal with which they reject everything to do with the flesh, while placing their faith in higher things. This book is based upon a rejection of both extremes. It is based on the conviction that the fragmentation of psychology is to be regretted and that the future lies in reinforcing bridges rather than blowing them up.

In my opinion, an appreciation of biological psychology cannot be achieved simply by statements of the kind, 'This chapter is about learning and memory, which you study in courses on animal learning and human cognition'. Even if they have taken such courses, students will probably have forgotten what is meant by, for example, working memory or

taste-aversion learning, by the time that they get to do a biology course. Therefore, before describing the biology of an aspect of behaviour, I briefly review the basic psychology.

To emphasize its integrative role, I was tempted to call the book *Biological Psychology – a Social Sciences Introduction* but decided against this. It might suggest that there is something peculiarly social about the approach adopted, which would make it less applicable to the more biologically orientated student. This is not the case. In my view, the Janus-head nature of psychology, pointing in one direction to the social sciences and in the other to the traditional sciences of chemistry and biology, etc., should be seen as the subject's strength rather than as a weakness.

An author confronts a fundamental dilemma in writing of this kind. To what extent should the links between topics be emphasized, or should each topic be dealt with simply in its own right? For example, should the student be able to close the chapter on emotion when they move on to motivation, or should they be reminded constantly about the interactive nature of all things? The first edition went for the interactive approach but this edition allows more flexibility. The chapters are much more self-contained than in the first edition. This allows teachers to 'cut and paste' chapters as they wish. However, the integrative theme can be followed if you wish by going to the companion website. At various points in each chapter there are web reflection symbols.

This means that the section that you have read is now developed in more detail on the website. Links with other sections of the book will be found there.

I believe that we can only understand who we are by describing clearly the principles of evolution and function. These topics are introduced at the outset and reference is made to them throughout. Students often find evolutionary ideas difficult to grasp and they confuse causal and functional levels of explanation. However, I felt the need to confront these issues rather than avoid them. If they are not discussed, there is the risk that the student will apply their own homespun wisdom (not necessarily a bad thing) but without relating this to contemporary ideas. The book is based on the conviction that biological psychology should be presented in the context of whole functioning animals living in a 'normal' environment (whatever that might mean for either rat or human!).

I also felt the need to relate the biological material to a philosophical context. Again students will apply their own logic here but it needs at least to take cognizance of established thinking. For example, physiological accounts often leave students perplexed about issues of brain and mind, whereas a brief philosophical orientation can serve to clarify the issues and describe openly the gaps in our understanding.

In my experience, a fundamental problem with biological psychology is that students are often totally overwhelmed by the sheer mass of detail, isolated facts, technical terms and Latin and Greek words. Thereby, they fail to follow the story-line and details tend to get collected by rote. I have therefore tried to impose strict limits on the amount of detail, while expanding the space devoted to explanation and integration. I use a number of analogies to aid understanding. This unashamedly top-down approach might offend some of my more purist, reductionist ('hard-nosed') colleagues, who exhibit an insatiable appetite to present Latin names and microscopic dimensions. I make no apologies to them since the book is as much about the proverbial forest as the trees and leaves. It is not that details are unimportant; on the contrary. References are provided to allow the students to pursue these if they so wish. It is all a question of balance. In my view, psychology is about the coming together of detail and the broader picture.

It seems to me that the difficulties that students encounter in studying biological psychology are a mixture of two basic kinds: (i) those inherent in the natural world and (ii) the human-made kind. I can do little about the first contribution to difficulty, since some biological processes (e.g. the action potential or aspects of evolution) seem to be inherently complex to understand. However, in my experience, the 'natural-made' factor is the smaller of the two. I feel that we often blame nature as a cover for our own self-made failure to explain clearly. I have several times heard students, after being told the essence of something, respond: 'Is that the point of it all? I suspected it might be something vaguely like that but after struggling so hard I thought that there had to be more to it than that!' This book is unashamedly an attempt to hold the student's hand and tread very gently as they meet the difficulties. It tries very hard to avoid intellectual overkill.

Since psychology is about people, I have attempted to give a human dimension and story-line as much as possible. Each chapter starts with 'scene-setting questions', which relate to everyday human experience. It is not guaranteed that, after reading the chapter, you will have a convincing answer to these. For example, the mind–body problem might well remain a problem even after reading Chapter 21! However, I would be very disappointed if you were not able to make a better attempt at an answer than before reading it.

After years of teaching biological psychology in introductory courses, I have seen quite a range of conceptual misunderstandings. Also, in getting the response 'yes – I see', I have learned to distinguish the sentiment 'Please leave me alone', accompanied by a forced smile devoid of positive emotion, from genuine understanding. I hope that I have learned a thing or two about how students can go off the rails and alternative models of reality. In the present study, I have tried to exploit this experience by avoiding such confusion as much as is humanly possible.

Some students have a curiously ambivalent attitude towards the biological perspective. On the one hand, they seem unsure as to why they need to study a subject felt to be inaccessible to all but the scientifically gifted, more the domain of weird scientists in white coats, who like to inject rats with complex-sounding chemicals. On the other hand, there is a kind of distant admiration, a feeling that the secrets of life are most likely to be revealed by such things as PET scans and genetic analysis. If the present book serves to give some balance to such feelings it will have performed its role.

There are two types of boxed components throughout, marked 'Evolutionary psychology' and 'A personal angle'. The 'Evolutionary psychology' box points to the relevance of evolutionary psychology to the particular topic under discussion at that point. 'A personal angle' is designed on the basis that you are probably especially interested in the lives of individual humans. These examples range from sombre case studies of patients with damaged brains to insights into the more memorable and eccentric events in the lives of scientists. The latter will give you (I hope) a moment of light relief and distraction in an otherwise demanding text. I believe that 'A personal angle' box can give you a tag for forming an association with a substantial amount of otherwise less-memorable material.

The book is accompanied by an Instructor's Manual (available on the website) designed to assist lecturers who have adopted it for their courses. The book has an associated website (www.pearsoned.co.uk/toates), designed to serve a number of purposes:

1 On the 'noticeboard' will be found (a) details of significant new research advances and pointers to where they relate to the content of the book, and (b) feedback information on the book, e.g. (i) how something might be better understood, (ii) new cross-references between material and (iii) notification of any errors, which, in spite of all attempts to eliminate them, have crept through.
2 What are termed 'Reflections': a deeper look at certain selected material in the book as indicated by the web symbol in the text. This is designed to be slightly more interactive than the text and involves links between different chapters of the book.
3 Justifications of the answers to the 'Test your knowledge' questions found in the book.
4 Multiple-choice questions, with feedback.

There are a number of people whose influence and help I would like to acknowledge. The efforts of the Open University library staff are much appreciated. The enthusiasm and dedication of Pearson Education staff and freelancers, Melanie Beard, Sarah Busby, Tina Cadle-Bowman, Morten Fuglevand, Sue Gard, Mary Lince, Annette Musker, Alison Prior, Emma Travis, Janey Webb, Maggie Wells and Ros Woodward, amongst others, were invaluable, as was, in the Open University, Giles Clark's advice and Becky Efthimiou's help throughout. In addition to the reviewers listed (page xviii), one or more chapters were read by the following:

Kent Berridge, University of Michigan
Angus Gellatly, Open University
Graham Hitch, University of York
John Lazarus, University of Newcastle
Alison Lee, Bath Spa University
Carol Midgely, Open University
Ralph Mistlberger, Simon Fraser University
Daniel Nettle, University of Newcastle
Arne Öhman, Karolinska Institute
Jaak Panksepp, Washington State University
Jeffrey Schwartz, University of California, Los Angeles
Henry Szechtman, McMaster University
Lance Workman, Bath Spa University

I am very grateful to them for their tireless efforts to improve earlier drafts, which has made an immense difference. Of course, I do not hold them responsible for the final product.

My students have given me inspiration and useful feedback and have taught me how to teach. Finally, I would like to record my thanks to my wife, Olga Coschug-Toates, who encouraged the project, has been a source of strength and patience and has read and critically commented on at least four versions of each chapter. I would like to dedicate the book to her.

Should anyone have any comments, I would be delighted to hear from you, e.g. at F.Toates@Open.ac.uk

Frederick Toates
Milton Keynes, England
February 2006

Guided tour

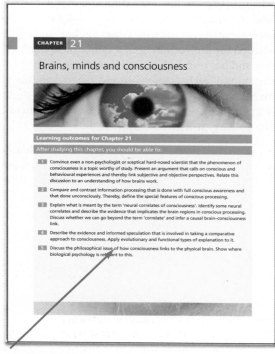

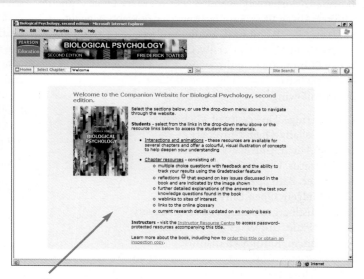

Learning outcomes give you a taste of what you'll be covering.

The access code packaged with this book allows you to explore the companion website at **www.pearsoned.co.uk/toates**. This contains a range of resources including questions, animations, interactions, further reflections on a topic and web links to help you consolidate and develop your understanding.

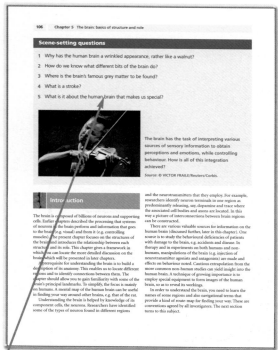

Scene-setting questions begin each chapter, encouraging you to engage with the main issues and concerns of the topic

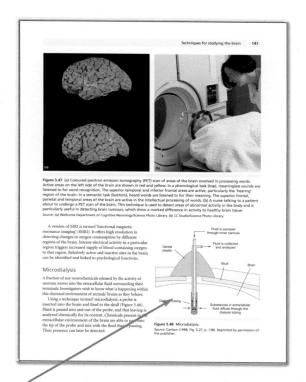

The new edition is richly illustrated with diagrams and photographs.

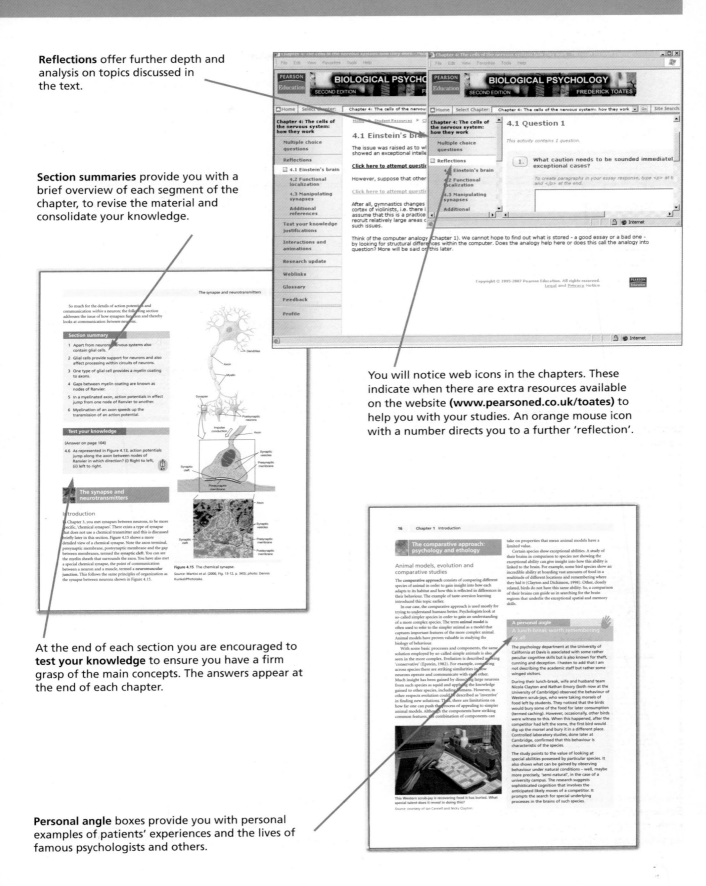

Reflections offer further depth and analysis on topics discussed in the text.

Section summaries provide you with a brief overview of each segment of the chapter, to revise the material and consolidate your knowledge.

You will notice web icons in the chapters. These indicate when there are extra resources available on the website (**www.pearsoned.co.uk/toates**) to help you with your studies. An orange mouse icon with a number directs you to a further 'reflection'.

At the end of each section you are encouraged to **test your knowledge** to ensure you have a firm grasp of the main concepts. The answers appear at the end of each chapter.

Personal angle boxes provide you with personal examples of patients' experiences and the lives of famous psychologists and others.

Bringing things together reminds you of the main issues explored in the chapter and highlights connections within and between areas of study to give you a broader understanding.

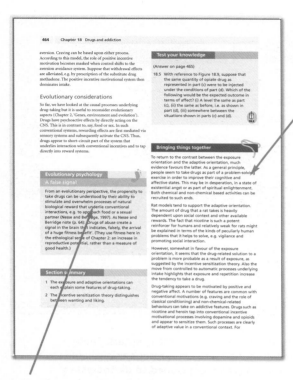

An annotated list of useful books at the end of each chapter allows you to explore the topic further.

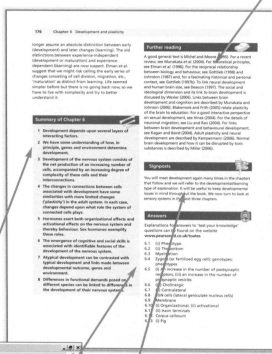

Evolutionary psychology boxes provide you with an insight into a psychological concept from an evolutionary perspective.

Each chapter has a summary giving you a comprehensive outline of the topics covered and the conclusions reached.

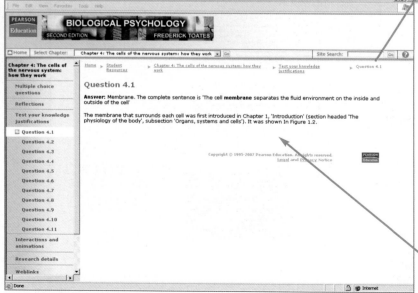

Signposts at the end of each chapter indicate where the issues raised relate to other chapters within the text.

Explanations to the answers provided for **test your knowledge** questions can be found on the website.

Colourful **interactions and animations** accompany several chapters. These offer a visual illustration of concepts to deepen your understanding. Details of these can be found at the end of each chapter.

Research updates on the website give you an insight into what is happening at the cutting edge of biological psychology.

Multiple choice questions can be found on the website to help you assess your progress and reinforce what you've learnt.

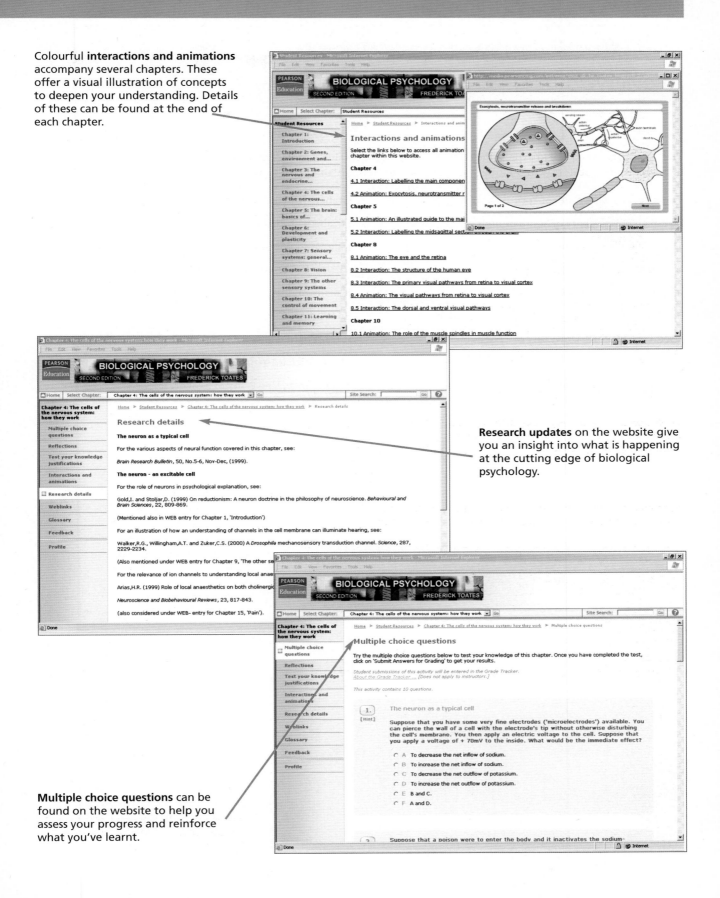

Reviewers

The publishers would like to express their appreciation for the invaluable advice and encouragement they have received for this book from educators within Europe, Scandinavia and New Zealand.

Tim Andrews, University of York

D.A. Baden, University of Southampton

Chris Chandler, London Metropolitan University

Gareth Davies, University of Glamorgan

John Duggan, University of Sunderland

Ingmar Franken, Erasmus University, Rotterdam

Jason C.G. Halford, University of Liverpool

Arvid Kappas, University of Bremen, Germany

Lisa Leaver, University of Exeter

Graham Mitchell, University of Northampton

Elizabeth Ockleford, University of Leicester

John Podd, Massey University, New Zealand

Patricia Roberts, University of Bedfordshire

Hakan Sundberg, University of Bergen, Norway

Ed Wilding, Cardiff University

Peter Wright, University of Edinburgh

Martin Richard Yeomans, University of Sussex

Tom Ziemke, University of Skovde, Sweden

Acknowledgements

We are grateful to the following for permission to reproduce copyright material:

Figures 1.2 and 18.10 from Biological bases of behaviour in *Psychology – An Integrated Approach* edited by M. Eysenck, reprinted by permission of Pearson Education Ltd. (Toates, F. M. 1998); Figure 2.4 from Biological perspectives in *Introduction to Psychology*, Vol. 1 edited by I. Roth, pub Lawrence Erlbaum Associates Ltd. in association with the Open University, © 1990 The Open University, reprinted by permission of The Open University (Toates, F. M. 1990); Figure 2.7 from *Behaviour and Evolution* in course SD206: Biology, Brain and Behaviour, Book 1, reprinted by permission of The Open University (Hall, M. and Halliday, T. eds 1998); Figures 2.8, 2.9 and 2.10 from *Behavioral Genetics*, reprinted by permission of W. H. Freeman and Company (Plomin, R. *et al.* 1997); Figures 3.2 and 3.3 from *The Senses and Communication* in course SD206: Biology, Brain and Behaviour, Book 3, reprinted by permission of The Open University (Halliday, T. ed. 1998); Figures 3.4, 7.1, 7.7, 8.13 and 9.16 from Sensory systems in *Psychology – An Integrated Approach* edited by M. Eysenck, reprinted by permission of Pearson Education Ltd. (Toates, F. M. 1998); Figures 3.16a and 5.12 from *Human Physiology*, reprinted by permission of The McGraw-Hill Companies, Inc. (Vander, A. J. *et al.* 1994); Figure 3.21 from Communication and control in *Growing and Responding*, course SK220, Book 2 edited by M. Stewart, reprinted by permission of The Open University (Toates, F. M. 1997a); Figure 4.15 photo Dennis Kunkel/Phototake; Figures 5.13 and 5.38 from OU course SD286, Module A, reprinted by permission of the Open University; Figure 5.31 adapted from *Biological Psychology, 6th Edition*, reprinted by permission of Wadsworth, a division of Thomson Learning (Kalat, J. W. 1998); Figures 5.34, 5.35, 11.1 and 11.18 from *The Cellular Basis of Behavior: An Introduction to Behavioral Neurobiology* by Eric R. Kandel. © 1976 by W. H. Freeman and Company. Used with permission. (Kandel, E. R. 1976); Figure 5.36 and 11.19 from Cellular mechanisms of learning and the biological basis of individuality in *Principles of Neural Science, 3rd Edition* edited by E. R. Kandel, J. H. Schwartz and T. M. Jessell, reprinted by permission of The McGraw-Hill Companies, Inc. (Kandel, E. R. 1991); Figure 5.37 from *Brain Size and the Evolution of Mind*, pub American Museum of Natural History, reprinted by permission of the author (Jerison, H. J. 1991); Figure 5.40 reprinted from *Trends in Neurosciences*, Vol. 18, D. J. Povinelli and T. M. Preuss, Theory of mind: evolutionary history of a cognitive specialization, pp. 418-424, Copyright 1995, with permission from Elsevier (Povinelli, D. J. and Preuss, T. M. 1995); Figure 5.41 from The Hippocampal complex of food-storing birds in *Brain, Behaviour and Evolution*, 34, reprinted by permission of S. Karger AG (Sherry, D. F. *et al.* 1989); Figure 5.43 courtesy of Professor M. Stewart; Figure 5.46 reprinted from *Fundamental Neuroscience* edited by M. J. Zigmond *et al.*, G. S. Aston-Jones *et al.*, Attention, pp. 1385-1409, Copyright 1999 with permission from Elsevier (Aston-Jones, G. S. *et al.* 1999); Figure 5.47a photo courtesy Wellcome Department of Cognitive Neurology/Science Photo Library; Figure 5.47b photo courtesy CC Studio/Science Photo Library; Figures 5.48 and 5.49 from *Physiology of Behaviour, 6th Edition*, reprinted by permission of Allyn and Bacon. Copyright © 1998 by Pearson Education (Carlson, N. R. 1998); Figure 6.1 from *The Evolution of Development*, reprinted by permission of Cambridge University Press (Bonner, J. T. 1958); Figures 6.7, 6.11 and 6.12 from *Neural Activity and the Growth of the Brain*, reprinted by permission of Cambridge University Press and the author (Purves, D. 1994); Figure 6.9 from Binocular interaction in striate cortex of kittens reared with artificial squint in *Journal of Neurophysiology*, 28, reprinted by permission of The American Physiological Society (Hubel, D. H. and Wiesel, T. N. 1965); Figure 6.19 photo courtesy Science Photo Library; Figure 7.2 from *Eye and Brain: The Psychology of Seeing, 5th Edition*, reprinted by permission of Oxford University Press (Gregory, R. L. 1997); Figure 8.1 from Form analysis in visual cortex in *The Cognitive Neurosciences* edited by M. S. Gazzaniga, reprinted by permission of The MIT Press (von der Heydt, R. 1995); Figure 8.6 from Visual pigments or rods and cones in a human retina in *Journal of Physiology*, 298, reprinted by permission of The Physiological Society and J. K. Bowmaker (Bowmaker, J. K. and Dartnall, H. J. A. 1980); Figure 8.7 from Perception in *Introduction to Psychology*, Vol. 2 edited by I. Roth, pub Lawrence Erlbaum Associates Ltd. in association with the Open University, © 1990 The Open University, reprinted by permission of The Open University (Greene, J. 1990); Figures 8.23, 9.21, 10.13 and 11.12 from *Neuroscience: Exploring the Brain, 2nd Edition*, pub Williams and Wilkins, reprinted by permission of M. F. Bear (Bear, M. F. *et al.* 1996); Figures 8.24, 8.25 and 8.26 reprinted from *Cognition*,

Vol. 67, M. A. Goodale and G. K. Humphrey, The objects of action and perception, pp. 186, 198, 199, Copyright 1998, with permission from Elsevier (Goodale, M. A. and Humphrey, G. K. 1998); Figure 8.27a from *Sight Unseen: An Exploration of Conscious and Unconscious Vision*, reprinted by permission of Oxford University Press and the authors (Goodale, M. A. and Milner, A. D. 2003); Figure 8.27b republished with permission of Nature Publishing Group and the authors, from A neurological dissociation between perceiving objects and grasping them by M. A. Goodale *et al.*, *Nature*, Vol. 349, No. 6305, 10 January 1991; permission conveyed through Copyright Clearance Center, Inc. (Goodale, M. A. *et al.* 1991); Figure 8.28 from Mechanisms of contour perception in monkey visual cortex. I. Lines of pattern discontinuity in *Journal of Neuroscience*, 9, Copyright 1989 by the Society for Neuroscience, reprinted by permission of the Society for Neuroscience (von der Heydt, R. and Peterhans, E. 1989); Figure 8.29 from Visual properties of neurons in a polysensory area in superior temporal sulcus in the macaque in *Journal of Neurophysiology*, 46, reprinted by permission of The American Physiological Society (Bruce, C. *et al.* 1981); Figure 8.30 from Associative visual agnosia in *Archives of Neurology*, 24, reprinted by permission of American Medical Association (Rubens, A. B. and Benson, D. F. 1971); Figure 8.31 republished with permission from Nature Publishing Group, from How the brain learns to see objects and faces in an impoverished context by R. J. Dolan *et al.*, *Nature*, Vol. 389, No. 6651, 9 October 1997; permission conveyed through Copyright Clearance Center, Inc. (Dolan, R. J. *et al.* 1997); Figures 8.32, 8.33, 8.34, 8.35 and 20.8 from Brain mechanisms associated with top-down processes in perception in *Philosophical Transactions of the Royal Society of London B*, 352, reprinted by permission of Professor Christopher D. Frith (Frith, C. D. and Dolan, R. J. 1997); Figure 9.2 from *Physiology of Behavior, 5th Edition*, reprinted by permission of Allyn and Bacon. Copyright © by Pearson Education (Carlson, N. R. 1994); Figure 9.14 from Intensity of sensation in *Journal of Physiology* (London), 300, reprinted by permission of Blackwell Publishing Ltd. (Knibestol, M. and Vallbo, A. 1980); Figure 9.15 from Intensive and extensive aspects of tactile sensitivity as a function of body part, sex and laterality in *The Skin Senses* edited by D. R. Kenshalo, reprinted by permission of Charles C. Thomas Publisher Ltd. (Weinstein, S. 1968); Figures 9.17, 9.19 and 9.20 from Touch in *Principles of Neural Science, 3rd Edition* edited by E. R. Kandel, J. H. Schwartz and T. M. Jessell, reprinted by permission of The McGraw-Hill Companies, Inc. (Kandel, E. R. and Jessell, T. M. 1991); Figure 9.22 from *Development and Flexibility*, course SD206: Biology, Brain and Behaviour, reprinted by permission of The Open University (Whatson, T. and Sterling, V. eds 1998); Figure 9.23 photos Copyright G. W. Willis/Visuals Unlimited;

Figure 9.26 from Odor/taste integration and the perception of flavour in *Experimental Brain Research*, 166, pub Springer-Verlag GmbH, reprinted by permission of the authors (Small, D. M. and Prescott, J. 2005); Figure 10.4 adapted from *Eye and Brain: The Psychology of Seeing, 5th Edition*, reprinted by permission of Oxford University Press (Gregory, R. L. 1997); Figure 10.6 from The neural basis for learning of simple motor skills, *Science*, 242, reprinted by permission of AAAS. Copyright AAAS (Lisberger, S. G. 1988); Figure 10.8 adapted from The control of movement in *Growing and Responding*, course SK220 Book 2 edited by M. Stewart, reprinted by permission of The Open University (Toates, F. M. 1997); Figures 10.10 and 17.3 adapted from *Human Physiology*, reprinted by permission of The McGraw-Hill Companies, Inc. (Vander, A. J. *et al.* 1994); Figure 10.14 reprinted from *Textbook of Medical Physiology* by A. C. Guyton, p. 597, © 1991 Elsevier Inc., with permission from Elsevier (Guyton, A. C. 1991); Figures 10.20 a, b and c from The cerebellum and the adaptive coordination of movement from *Annual Review of Neuroscience*, Vol. 15, reprinted by permission of Annual Reviews and W. T. Thach. © 1992 by Annual Reviews, www.annualreviews.org (Thach, W. T. *et al.* 1992); Figure 11.7 from The medial temporal lobe memory system in *Science*, 253, reprinted by permission of AAAS. Copyright 1991 AAAS (Squire, L. R. and Zola-Morgan, S. 1991); Figure 11.8 from Memory in *Introduction to Psychology*, Vol. 2 edited by I. Roth, pub Lawrence Erlbaum Associates Ltd. in association with the Open University, © 1990 The Open University, reprinted by permission of The Open University (Cohen, G. 1990); Figure 11.11 from Frontal lobes and working memory: evidence from investigations of the effects of cortical excisions in nonhuman primates by M. Petrides in *Handbook of Neuropsychology*, Vol. 9 edited by F. Boller and J. Grafman, Copyright 1994, pp. 59-82, with permission from Elsevier Science (Petrides, M. 1994); Figure 11.15 reprinted from *Neurobiology of Learning and Memory*, Vol. 76, D. S. Woodruff-Pak *et al.*, MRI-assessed volume of cerebellum correlates with associative learning, pp. 342-57, Copyright 2001, with permission from Elsevier (Woodruff-Pak, D. S. *et al.* 1991); Figure 11.17 from Repeated confocal imaging of individual dendritic spines in the living hippocampal slice: evidence for changes in length and orientation associated with chemically induced LTP in *The Journal of Neuroscience*, 15, Copyright 1995 by Society for Neuroscience, reprinted by permission of the Society for Neuroscience (Hosokawa, T. *et al.* 1995); Figure 11.20 from Mind the gap in *Medical Research Council News*, No. 74, reprinted by permission of Medical Research Council (Collingridge, G. 1997); Figures 12.3 and 12.4 from Introduction to brains, minds and consciousness in *From Cells to Consciousness*, course SD226: Biological Psychology: Exploring the Brain, Book 1, reprinted by permission of The Open University (Toates, F.

M. 2004); Figure 12.5 adapted from Attachment and separation distress in the infant guinea pig in *Developmental Psychobiology*, Vol. 12, Copyright © 1979, reprinted with permission of Wiley-Liss, Inc., a subsidiary of John Wiley & Sons, Inc. (Pettijohn, T. F. 1979); Figure 12.9 from Neuroanatomy: Text and Atlas, 2e, The McGraw-Hill Companies, (Martin, J. 1996); Figure 12.13 from Amygdala acticity at encoding correlated with long-term, free recall of emotional information in *Proceedings of the National Academy of Sciences of the USA*, 93, Copyright 1996 National Academy of Sciences, USA, reprinted by permission of the National Academy of Sciences (Cahill, L. *et al.* 1996); Figure 12.15 adapted from Analysis of aversive memories using the fear-pontentiated startle paradigm in *Neuropsychology of Memory* edited by L. R. Squire and N. Butters, reprinted by permission of The Guilford Press (Davis, M. 1992); Figure 13.5 reprinted from *Journal of the Autonomic Nervous System*, Supplement, D. von Holst, Vegetative and somatic components of tree shrews' behaviour, pp. 657-70, Copyright 1986, with permission from Elsevier Science (von Holst, D. 1986); Figure 13.8 from Neuroanatomy: Text and Atlas, 2e, The McGraw-Hill Companies, (Martin, J. 1996); Figure 13.9 adapted from The subretrofacial nucleus: its pivotal role in cardiovascular regulation in *News in Physiological Sciences*, 5, reprinted by permission of The American Physiological Society (Dampney, R. 1990); Figures 14.1, 14.7 and 14.8 from Pain in *The Human Condition*, course SK220, Book 4 edited by F. M. Toates, reprinted by permission of The Open University (Toates, F. M. 1997); Figure 14.6 from Pain mechanisms: Labeled lines versus convergence in central processing in *Annual Review of Neuroscience*, Vol. 26, reprinted by permission of Annual Reviews and the author. © 2003 by Annual Reviews www.annualreviews.org (Craig, A. D. 2003); Figure 14.9 from Empathy for pain involves the affective but not sensory components of pain, *Science*, 303, reprinted by permission of AAAS. Copyright 2004 AAAs (Singer, T. *et al.* 2004); Figure 15.2 from Sensory Pleasure in *Quarterly Review of Biology*, 54(1), published and reprinted by permission of University of Chicago Press and the author (Cabanac, M. 1979); Figure 15.3 reprinted from *Progress in Psychobiology and Physiological Psychology*, Vol. 11, edited by J. M. Sprague and A. N. Epstein, H. J. Grill and K. C. Berridge, Taste reactivity as a measure of the neural plasticity of palatability, pp. 1-61, Copyright 1985, with permission from Elsevier and K. C. Berridge (Grill, H. J. and Berridge, K. C. 1985); Figure 15.4 from Relation of consummatory responses and preabsorptive insulin release to palatability and learned taste aversions in *Journal of Comparative and Physiological Psychology*, Vol. 95(3), reprinted by permission of APA and K. C. Berridge (Berridge, K. C. et al. 1981); Figures 15.6, 18.2, 18.3 and 18.6 from Neuropharmacological mechanisms of drug reward: beyond dopamine in the nucleus accumbens in *Critical Reviews in Neurobiology*, 12,

reprinted by permission of Begell House, Inc. (Bardo, M. T. 1998); Figures 15.8a and 15.8b reprinted from *Cognitive Brain Research*, Vol. 25, M. X. Cohen *et al.*, Individual differences in extraversion and dopamine genetics predict neural reward responses, pp. 851-61, Copyright 2005, with permission from Elsevier (Cohen, M. X. *et al.* 2005); Figure 15.14 reprinted from *Biological Psychology*, Vol. 13, J. Panksepp, The biology of social attachments: opiates alleviate separation distress, pp. 607-13, Copyright 1978, with permission from Society of Biological Psychiatry (Panksepp, J. *et al.* 1978); Figure 15.15 adapted from Affective Neuroscience: A paradigm to study the animate circuits for human emotions in *Emotions: Interdisciplinary Perspectives* edited by R. D. Kavanaugh *et al.*, reprinted by permission of Lawrence Erlbaum Associates, Inc. and the author (Panksepp, J. 1996); Figure 15.16 from A single administration of testosterone induces cardiac accelerative responses to angry faces in healthy young women in *Behavioral Neuroscience*, February, Vol. 115(1), reprinted by permission of APA and the J. van Honk (van Honk, J. *et al.* 2001); Figure 15.17 from Curiosity in zoo animals in *Behaviour*, 26, reprinted by permission of Brill Academic Publishers (Glickman, S. E. and Sroges, R. W. 1996); Figure 16.2 from *Animal Behaviour – A Systems Approach*, Copyright 1980. © John Wiley & Sons Ltd. Reproduced with permission (Toates, F. M. 1980); Figure 16.3 from Role of lipostatic mechanism in regulation by feeding of energy balance in rats in *Journal of Comparative and Physiological Psychology*, July, Vol. 84(1), reprinted by permission of APA (Le Magnen, J. *et al.* 1973); Figure 16.4 adapted from *Physiology of Behaviour, 1st Edition*, reprinted by permission of Allyn and Bacon. Copyright © 1977 by Pearson Education (Carlson, N. R. 1977); Figures 16.5 and 16.6 adapted from *Human Physiology*, reprinted by permission of The McGraw-Hill Companies, Inc. (Vander, A. J. *et al.* 1975); Figure 16.10 from Habits and food intake in *Handbook of Physiology*, Section 6, *Alimentary Canal*, Vol. 1, used with permission of The American Physiological Society (Le Magnen, J. 1967); Figure 16.14 reprinted from *Physiology and Behaviour*, Vol. 62, M. R. Yeomans and R. W. Gray, Effects of naltrexone on food intake and changes in subjective appetite during eating: Evidence for opioid involvement in the appetizer effect, pp. 15-21, Copyright 1997, with permission from Elsevier (Yeomans, M. R. and Gray, R. W. 1997); Figure 16.20 from Inhibitory controls of drinking: satiation of thirst in *Thirst: Physiological and Psychological Aspects* edited by D. J. Ramsey and D. Booth, with kind permission of Springer Science and Business Media and the author (Verbalis, J. G. 1991); Figure 16.21 adapted from Clinical aspects of body fluid homeostasis in humans in *Handbook of Behavioural Neurobiology*, Vol. 10, *Neurobiology of Food and Fluid Intake* edited by E. M. Stricker, reprinted by permission of Springer-Verlag GmbH (Verbalis, J. G. 1990); Figure 17.4 from

Dopaminic influences on male sexual behaviour in *Neurobiological Effects of Sex Steroid Hormones* edited by P. E. Micevych and R. P. Hammer, reprinted by permission of Cambridge University Press (Hull, E. M. 1995); Figure 17.5 adapted from Features of a hormone-driven defined neural circuit for mammalian behaviour in *Annals of the New York Academy of Sciences*, 563, reprinted by permission of New York Academy of Sciences and the author (Pfaff, D. W. 1989); Figure 17.7 from Human sexuality in *The Human Condition*, course SK220, Book 4 edited by F. M. Toates, reprinted by permission of The Open University (Toates, F. M. 1997); Figure 17.8 bottom reprinted from *Fundamental Neuroscience* edited by M. J. Zigmond *et al.*, M. J. Baum, Psychosexual development, pp. 1229-44, Copyright 1999, with permission from Elsevier (Baum, M. J. 1999); Figures 18.4 and 18.5 from Role of dopamine in drug reinforcement and addiction in humans: results from imaging studies in *Behavioural Pharmacology*, Vol. 13, Nos 5 and 6, reprinted by permission of Lippincott Williams & Wilkins (Volkow, N. D. *et al.* 2002); Figure 18.7 from Chronic caffeine exposure potentiates nicotine self-administration in rats in *Psychopharmacology*, Vol. 142, No. 4, reprinted by permission of Springer-Verlag GmbH (Shoaib, M. *et al.* 1998); Figure 19.1 adapted from *Control of Behaviour*, reprinted by permission of The Open University (Toates, F. M. 1992); Figure 19.2 from *Biological Clocks*, © J. N. Brady, 1979, reproduced by permission of Edward Arnold (Brady, J. N. 1979); Figure 19.5 based on data in Physiology of sleep hormones and its circadian regulation in *Sleep Science: Integrating Basic Research and Clinical Practice. Monographs in Clinical Neuroscience*, Vol. 15, edited by W. J. Schwartz, reprinted by permission of S. Karger AG, Basel (Dijk, D.-J. 1997); Figure 19.6 from Normal human sleep: an overview in *Principles and Practice of Sleep Medicine* edited by M. H. Kryger *et al.*, reprinted by permission of W. B. Saunders Company (Carskadon, M. A. and Dement, W. C. 1994); Figure 19.7 from *Neuroscience, 1st Edition*, reprinted by permission of Sinauer Associates, Inc. (Purves, D. *et al.* 1997); Figure 19.8 from *Dreaming Brain* by Allan Hobson, ISBN: 0465017037, Copyright © 1988 by J. Allan Hobson, M. D., reprinted by permission of Basic Books, a member of Perseus Books, L.L.C. (Hobson, J. A. 1988); Figure 19.9 adapted from *Physiology of Behavior, 5th Edition*, reprinted by permission of Allyn and Bacon. Copyright © by Pearson Education (Carlson, N. R. 1994); Figure 19.10 adapted from Modeling states of waking and sleeping in *Psychiatric Annals*, 22, March, reprinted by permission of Slack Incorporated (Sutton, J. P. *et al.* 1992); Figure 19.11 from Ontogenesis of the states of sleep in rat, cat and guinea pig during the first postnatal month in *Developmental Psychobiology*, Vol. 2, Copyright © 1969, reprinted with permission of Wiley-Liss, Inc., a subsidiary of John Wiley & Sons, Inc. (Jouvet-Mounier, D. *et al.* 1969); Figures 20.4 and 20.13 from Specializations of the human brain in *Scientific American*, 241(3) September, International Edition, reproduced by permission of the illustrator, Carol Donner (Geschwind, N. 1979); Figure 20.5 reprinted from *Fundamental Neuroscience* edited by M. J. Zigmond et al., S. M. Kosslyn *et al.*, Hemispheric specialization, pp. 1521-42, Copyright 1999, with permission from Elsevier (Kosslyn, S. M. *et al.* 1999); Figure 20.6 from Anatomical study of the cerebral asymmetry in the temporal lobe of humans, chimpanzees and rhesus monkeys in *Science*, 192, reprinted by permission of AAAS. Copyright 1976 AAAS (Yeni-Komshian, G. H. and Benson, D. A. 1976); Figure 20.7 reprinted from *Neuropsychologia*, Vol. 24, L. C. Robertson and D. C. Delis, 'Part-whole' processing in unilateral brain-damaged patients: dysfunction of hierarchical organization, pp. 363-70, Copyright 1986, with permission from Elsevier Science (Robertson, L. C. and Delis, D. C. 1986); Figures 20.9, 20.10 and 20.11 reprinted from *Brain and Cognition*, Vol. 55, A. Bechara, The role of emotion in decision-making: Evidence from neurological patients with orbitofrontal damage, pp. 30-40, Copyright 2004, with permission from Elsevier (Bechara, A. 2004); Figure 20.12 from Language and the brain in *Scientific American*, 226 (4), reprinted by permission of Donald Garber, Executor of the Estate of Bunji Tagawa (Geschwind, N. 1972); Figure 20.14 republished with permission from Nature Publishing Group, from Positron emission tomographic studies of the cortical anatomy of single-word processing by S. E. Petersen et al., *Nature*, Vol. 331, No. 6157, 18 February 1988; permission conveyed through Copyright Clearance Center, Inc. (Petersen, S. E. *et al.* 1988); Figure 20.15 reprinted from *Cognition*, Vol. 92, D. Boatman, Cortical bases of speech perception: evidence from functional lesion studies, pp. 47-65, Copyright 2004, with permission from Elsevier (Boatman, D. 2004); Figures 20.17 and 20.18 from Language, tools and the brain: the ontogeny and phylogeny of hierarchically organized sequential behaviour in *Behavioral and Brain Sciences*, 14, © Cambridge University Press, reprinted by permission of Cambridge University Press (Greenfield, P. M. 1991); Figure 21.1 from The problem of consciousness in *Experimental and Theoretical Studies of Consciousness* edited by G. R. Bock and J. Marsh, Copyright 1993. © John Wiley & Sons Ltd. Reproduced with permission (Searle, J. R. 1993); Figure 22.4 from Mapping adolescent brain change reveals dynamic wave of accelerated grey matter loss in very early-onset schizophrenia in *Proceedings of the National Academy of Sciences*, 98, Copyright 2001 National Academy of Sciences, USA, reprinted by permission of National Academy of Sciences and P. Thompson (Thompson, P. *et al.* 2001); Figure 22.5 republished with permission from Nature Publishing Group, from A functional neuroanatomy of hallucinations in schizophrenia by D. A. Silbersweig *et al.*, *Nature*, Vol. 378, 9 November 1995; permission conveyed through Copyright

Clearance Center, Inc. (Silbersweig, D. A. *et al.* 1995); Figures 22.6 and 22.7 reprinted from *Brain Research Bulletin*, Vol. 25, M. A. Geyer *et al.*, Startle response models of sensorimotor gating and habituation deficits in schizophrenia, pp. 485–98, Copyright 1990, with permission from Elsevier (Geyer, M. A. *et al.* 1990); Figure 22.9 courtesy of Jeffrey Schwartz.

Figures 1.1, 3.17, 4.15, 5.1(b), 5.2, 5.3, 5.4, 5.5, 5.6, 5.7, 5.8, 5.9, 5.10, 5.11, 5.16, 5.18, 5.20, 5.21, 5.22, 5.23, 5.24, 5.25, 5.27, 5.28, 5.30, 5.32, 6.3, 6.4, 6.8, 8.3, 8.5, 8.17, 9.1, 9.5, 9.6, 9.10, 9.11, 9.13, 9.23, 9.24, 9.25, 10.7, 10.9, 10.18, 10.19, 12.8, 13.2, and 17.8 (top) have been used directly from the original source, and have been reprinted with the permission of Prentice Hall from Martini: *Human Anatomy*, 3rd edition. Copyright © 2000 Prentice Hall.

Figures 3.18, 3.19 (a, b and d), 3.20, 3.27(a), 3.29, 3.30, 3.33, 4.13, 5.15, 5.17, 5.19, 8.4, 8.20, 9.8, 10.5 and 10.15 have been adapted and modified in some way from the original source with the permission of Prentice Hall from Martini: *Human Anatomy*, 3rd edition. Copyright © 2000 Prentice Hall.

Pearson Education Limited would like to credit the renowned medical illustrators Bill Ober, M.D. and Claire Garrison, R.N., and the biomedical photographer Ralph T. Hutchings for the illustrations developed and drawn for Martini: *Human Anatomy*, 3rd edition. Copyright © 2000 Prentice Hall.

Photographs: p.2 reprinted with permission from H. Damasio, T. Grabowski, R. Frank, A. M. Galaburda and A. R. Damasio (1994) The return of Phineas Gage: clues about the brain from the skull of a famous patient, *Science*, **264** (5162) pp. 1102–1105, 20 May. Copyright 1994 AAAS; p.4 © Bettmann/CORBIS; p.10 Bundy Mackintosh; p.16 Ian Cannell and Nicky Clayton; p.22 Victoria and Albert Museum/Bridgeman Art Library; p.24 Professor Jerry Hogan; p.47 Empics; p.82 © Gallo images/CORBIS; p.91 US Library of Congress/Science Photo Library; p.106 © VICTOR FRAILE/Reuters/Corbis; p.146 Getty Images/Iconica; p.151 Alex Bartel/Science Photo Library; p.174 © Martin Harvey/CORBIS (top); p.174 © Ariel Skelley/CORBIS (bottom); p.178 Richard Gregory and Priscilla Heard; p.190 Salvador Dali Museum, St Petersburg, Florida, USA/Bridgeman Art Library, © Salvador Dali, Gala-Salvador Dali Foundation, DACS, London 2006; p.246 Getty Images/Altrendo; p.249 © Winfried Wisniewski/zefa/Corbis; p.266 Empics (top); p.266 Empics (bottom); p.324 © David Parry/epa/Corbis; p.330 Getty Images/Workbook Stock; p.337 Rod Williams/naturepl.com; p.339 Gerry Ellis/Minden/FLPA; p.354 Topham Picturepoint/Topfoto.co.uk; p.367 Ian Hooton/Science Photo Library; p.377 © Michael Keller/CORBIS; p.392 Getty Images/Photographer's Choice; p.398 Topfoto/Rachel Epstein/ImageWorks; p.413 © Ariel Skelley/CORBIS; p.424 The Advertising Archives; p.446 The Advertising Archives; p.449 Janine Wiedel Photolibrary/Alamy; p.451 Bruce Alexander; p.460 Luca DiCecco/Alamy; p.467 Topham Picturepoint/Topfoto.co.uk; p.483 John Anster Fitzgerald/Private Collection/Bridgeman Art Library; p.489 Getty Images/The Image Bank; p.496 Ethno Images Inc./Alamy; p.506 Empics; p.529 james andrew/Alamy; p.534 © Bettmann/CORBIS; p.536 © Julian Calder/CORBIS; p.537 Alfred Pasieka/Science Photo Library.

In some instances we have been unable to trace the owners of copyright material, and we would appreciate any information that would enable us to do so.

CHAPTER 1

Introduction

Learning outcomes for Chapter 1

After studying this chapter, you should be able to:

1. Justify why, in order to explain behaviour and mental life, psychologists need to understand some biology. In so doing, distinguish the four principal types of explanation involved: causal, developmental/learning, evolutionary and functional.

2. Outline a few of the general principles underlying the science of physiology and how it relates to the concerns of psychology.

3. Describe some techniques used in biological psychology to link brain and behaviour: (i) experimental intervention, (ii) looking at the effects of damage to human brains and (iii) imaging the activity of brains while people perform tasks. Outline some problems associated with the application of these techniques.

4. Justify the statement that the 'link between biology and psychology is a *reciprocal* one', meaning that information and insight are exchanged between the two disciplines. In so doing, describe some of the social implications involved in biological explanation.

5. Describe what is meant by the terms 'gene', 'development' and 'learning'.

6. Explain how investigators can gain insight into brain and behaviour by studying the ways that different species adapt to their environments.

7. Speculate on the nature of the relationship between the brain and the conscious mind and, in so doing, explain what is meant by identity theory.

Scene-setting questions

1　Are we no more than our biology?

2　Does brain damage provide valid grounds to plead 'not guilty due to diminished responsibility'?

3　Are we free and responsible for our own actions?

4　Can something be 'all in the genes'? If so, are criminals 'born not made'?

5　Is the brain really a computer?

6　Can a person's problems be 'all in the mind'?

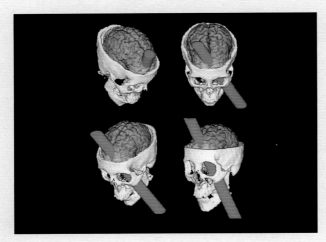

This is a reconstruction of a terrible accident suffered by Phineas Gage. An iron passed right through his head, following the trajectory indicated. What can such damage reveal about how brains normally work?

Source: Damasio *et al*. (1994).

Why should a psychologist be interested in biology?

Background

Why should psychologists study biology? Humans are undoubtedly part of the biological world and some of you might already be convinced that biology can provide the only secure base for psychology. Outside psychology, the public often seems to have little idea of what kind of subject psychology really is. Try asking your fellow students studying, say, French or chemistry what they think of it as a subject.

Psychology is at times depicted as not being really that serious. Psychologists are sometimes portrayed as the kind of people with fancy theories that are either banal or at odds with common sense. Quite in contrast, at other times we are depicted as all-knowing and thereby somewhat sinister. Even Frankenstein-like imagery is sometimes associated with us, on the assumption that we want to control the brains of others. Similarly, witness the familiar comment, 'Oh dear – you must have been reading my mind!'

To the public, biology has a certain unambiguous and accurate image as a true and serious science and has produced spectacular insights into the living world. It might seem a safe anchor for psychology and, at any party, provides an equally safe and uncontroversial answer to an enquiry, 'What's your job in life'?

Others of you might not share such enthusiasm for biology. You might not be clear why, as psychology students, you are asked to study another discipline. After all, biologists are generally not required to study psychology. You might have tried to avoid biology, or even all science, in school or feel that science forms an inappropriate basis for trying to understand mental life. Perhaps you consider that the human mind has peculiarities that cannot be captured by a traditional science, such as the possession of feelings, conscious awareness and free will.

Such tension within psychology is healthy and indeed forms an integral part of the subject. I will show where biology is essential to understanding the human psychological condition but will do so with respect for the reservations that some justifiably hold. First, it is necessary to consider what the subject-matter of biology is, as far as it concerns psychology, and how explanations within psychology can be guided by biology.

Types of explanation

Biology is the science of living things, animals and plants, and how they function in the natural world. How do we link biology and psychology in such a way that an understanding of biology can help us explain behaviour and our mental life? In doing this, there are various types of explanation within biological psychology. We will focus on four of these (Tinbergen, 1963), as follows.

1. The causal explanation

The first type of explanation to consider, the **causal explanation**, concerns how things work in the 'here and now', i.e. the immediate *determinants* of behaviour. This type of explanation is the principal concern of biological psychologists, as they attempt to link events in the brain to behaviour and mental life. Consider two simple examples:

1 A person treads on a thorn (i.e. a cause) and immediately afterwards yells (i.e. an effect). Information of some sort is conveyed from foot to brain, where it triggers the reaction of the yell. Scientists know the pathways that information follows in the body, which link such causes (in this case, damage to the skin at the foot) and effects (producing the yell).

2 A particular event within our body, a low body temperature (a cause) triggers action as behaviour, seeking a warmer location (an effect). Scientists understand something of how the body detects its own temperature and causes action.

Thus, the causal type of explanation consists of looking at behaviour and seeing how it arises in relation to the current state of the body's biology and the environment.

We are concerned with how identifiable biological processes contribute to behaviour. In so doing, the **nervous system** forms our primary focus. The nervous system consists, in part, of the **brain** and the **spinal cord**, which runs through the backbone (Figure 1.1). As another biological consideration, **hormones** are chemicals that are released into the bloodstream and that have effects at various sites in the body.

Particular hormones sensitize specific regions of the brain. This increases the probability that, in response to the presence of another animal, the brain will direct behaviour to, say, mating. In humans, such hormones sensitize our thoughts in the erotic direction. In this case, the biological psychologist investigates motivational processes that are

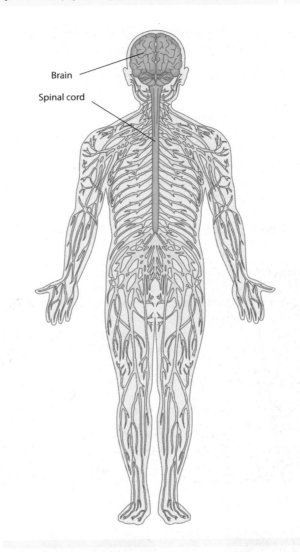

Figure 1.1 Brain and spinal cord.
Source: Martini *et al.* (2000, Fig. 13–1, p. 330).

organized in the brain. These processes depend upon internal factors (e.g. hormones) and external factors (e.g. potential mate) and help to determine the direction that behaviour and cognition take. These processes are said to have a physical structure (or 'embodiment') within the brain. The role of biological psychologists is to obtain insight into these processes, e.g. to try to understand how the brain is influenced by such things as hormones and how this relates to mind and behaviour.

Of course, not all behaviour can be understood in terms of causes as simple as treading on a thorn, the action of hormones or a low body temperature. Much behaviour arises from more subtle and hidden determinants within the brain and we also need to ask about how such processes operate.

Apart from this principal concern, there are three other types of explanation, as follows.

2. The developmental/learning explanation

The second type of explanation is what can be called the **developmental/learning explanation**. The compound of two terms 'developmental' and 'learning' emphasizes their common features. This type of explanation concerns events that occur over a lifetime or at least a much longer time than the fraction of a second normally involved in the causal explanation. For example, on studying the learning of a skill, events over weeks or months might be considered. These would be in terms of *changes* that occur in the brain and the corresponding *changes* in the behaviour that the brain directs.

As one feature of the developmental/learning explanation, psychologists try to account for how a living being proceeds from the moment of fertilization to the adult form. They attempt to answer how brain and behaviour develop over this period and this involves a consideration of genetics. We inherit **genes** from our parents and genes play a role in determining the development of the structure of our bodies, including the nervous system. Through this structure, genes indirectly play a role in behaviour. This type of explanation is involved in discussions of **nature** (what we inherit) and **nurture** (what we experience throughout life), as determinants of behaviour.

3. The evolutionary explanation

The third and fourth types of explanation arise from the theory that, over millions of years, we have evolved from a

Darwin's theory of evolution, as expressed in his book *The Origin of Species*, was met with some disbelief at the time of its appearance and triggered some ridicule. What is so challenging about its assumptions? *Source:* © Bettmann/CORBIS.

simpler form. The **evolutionary explanation** is in terms of the evolutionary history of the animal, its brain and associated behaviour. Looking back over countless generations, Darwin's theory of **evolution** has something to say not only about how the physical structure of our bodies has arisen but also about behaviour. Darwin suggested that species in existence today have evolved from a simpler form, i.e. they have been successful in the competition for survival. The term **phylogeny** refers to the history of a species over evolutionary time. We can gain insight into behaviour by considering how it relates to this process of evolution. Psychologists ask, where did present forms of behaviour come from in terms of evolution? What was the nature of the brain and behaviour of our evolutionary ancestors and how did these relate to the kind of demands posed by their environment?

4. The functional explanation

Closely related to the evolutionary explanation is the fourth type of explanation: the **functional explanation**. It asks – what is the function of behaviour? Certain behavioural strategies, as with physical characteristics, have been successful in the evolution of the members of a species and we see these today. We can ask *how* they emerged in evolution. The answer given is that they reflect what was **adaptive** to the animals' ancestors (Tooby and Cosmides, 1990). By 'adaptive' is meant something that evolved because it served a function that helped to promote the survival of the genes of the animal showing that characteristic. For example, an ability to react to danger by fleeing clearly serves a function that contributed to genetic survival.

Let's return to consider treading on a thorn. Apart from yelling, we quickly and automatically lift our foot from the thorn. What function does this serve? It protects the foot. If we did not lift it, we would risk more damage and infection. This seems clear. An animal not reacting would be at a disadvantage in terms of survival and reproduction. What is the function of yelling? This is not quite so obvious and often the functional explanation involves rich speculation. One possibility is that signalling pain alerts others of our distress. For instance, parents or mates might offer help.

Linking the four types of explanation

This section will give an example of behaviour and suggest how these four types of explanation can be applied to it and linked.

Suppose that your home is near to where a group of foxes lives. You decide to leave out food for them and observe their behaviour. Each night, one particular fox comes to your house and takes the food that you offer. Then, one night you notice that it declines to eat what was previously a very acceptable cut of meat. The *causal* type of question would be, what are the events in the brain of the fox at this point in time that cause it to decline the meat? It could be that it is not hungry but is simply following a routine of patrolling its environment. It might have fed well just prior to visiting you and the brain is detecting adequate nutrients in the body. However, you notice that the fox gets some of the food on its whiskers and then tries to remove it by wiping its mouth on the ground. So, on this occasion, something about the particular food appears to cause the fox to decline it. You offer a slightly different food and it quickly eats this, so it clearly is hungry. Between visits, it seems that it has formed an aversion to the particular food offered first. This *causes* it to reject the food.

You might then pose questions of the *developmental/ learning* type (with the emphasis on learning). What has happened to the fox in the period since you last offered it food of this kind? Something has changed in its brain, so that the reaction to this food has changed. What could well be the explanation is that the fox ate some of this type of meat but it had gone bad ('off') and it gave the fox gastrointestinal upset. So, it has learned to avoid this type of meat; so-called **taste-aversion learning**. The taste has become aversive to the fox.

You can then ask *evolutionary* type questions of this behaviour – such as at what stage in the evolution of foxes did the capacity for this type of learning first appear? How widespread is it among similar species? The answer is that the capacity is very widespread and is said to be evolutionarily old. You might well have experienced this effect, since humans have the faculty to do so.

You can also ask the *functional* type of question. What is the advantage in showing this behaviour? How does it enable foxes to survive and reproduce? The answer is clear: foods that cause gastrointestinal upset are dangerous and could even prove lethal. By rapidly learning to avoid them, foxes, as with humans, tend to live to see another day.

By bringing the evolutionary and functional types of explanation together, we gain a very powerful tool for understanding. We can compare species and their lifestyle. For example, in species such as humans, rats and dogs, the taste and smell of food are particularly easily associated with gastrointestinal upset. In birds, the visual characteristics of foods are particularly well associated. Birds normally discriminate foods by visual cues.

We can ask if there is a species that does *not* exhibit taste-aversion learning. If we were to find one, what might this tell us about the species' evolution and lifestyle? Very conveniently, in 2003 one such species did emerge to claim this so-far unique distinction (Ratcliffe *et al.*, 2003). It was the common vampire bat (Latin name *Desmodus rotundus*), perhaps not one's first choice of species to cultivate as either research subject or house guest. What does this species characteristic say about the functional value of taste-aversion learning and how to survive without the faculty? Vampire bats suck the blood of *living* animals and so are very unlikely ever to ingest a meal that has 'gone off'. Hence, they have little or no need for such a faculty. In the course of their evolutionary specialization for blood-eating, they have lost the faculty of taste-aversion learning. Other bat species, which are related but which eat fruit and insects, show taste-aversion learning.

Chapter 1 will discuss further the four types of explanation and show where each has something to contribute. Most of this book is concerned with the immediate determinants of behaviour, the causal explanation. Biological psychologists are most concerned with what causes behaviour in the here-and-now. This requires an understanding of the science of the physiology of the body, the topic of the next section.

Section summary

1 Understanding behaviour can involve a parallel consideration of four types of explanation:

(a) Here-and-now questions of what determines a particular behaviour, a causal explanation.

(b) Developmental/learning explanations. How events over periods within an individual lifetime affect behaviour, e.g. how the animal *changes* from a simple form at fertilization to a more complex form.

(c) The evolutionary history of the species.

(d) The functional value of behaviour.

2 The theory of evolution states that the species in existence today have evolved from simpler forms.

3 An adaptive characteristic is one that evolved because it helped to promote the survival of the genes of the animal showing that characteristic.

Test your knowledge

(Answer on page 20)

1.1 'The coughing was triggered by an irritant in the respiratory system'. Such a claim represents which of the following types of explanation? (i) Causal, (ii) developmental/learning, (iii) evolutionary, (iv) functional.

The physiology of the body

Organs, systems and cells

The science of **physiology** is concerned with the structure and function of the body, i.e. how its organs, such as the heart and kidney, work. There are various ways of dividing the body for the purpose of explanation. One is in terms of *systems* defined by the role that they serve. Thus, the circulatory system is responsible for moving blood around the body and consists of the heart and blood vessels. As psychologists, the nervous system, serving communication and control, is our principal focus.

To explain how the body works, another way of dividing it is based on the fact that it is composed of many millions of very small **cells**. Each organ (e.g. brain, heart or stomach) is made up of such cells. Cells are the fundamental building blocks of an organ and thereby the body. See Figure 1.2. The interior of each cell has a liquid composition and the cell is to some extent 'self-contained'. The cell has a membrane around itself and the chemical environment on the inside is different from that on the outside. However, like a person within society, the cell can survive only by its interaction with its immediate environment. Thus, energy and nutrients are brought into the cell and waste materials are carried away from the cell by the blood.

As just noted, all cells, whether in the brain, kidney or wherever, have certain features in common, e.g. each cell is surrounded by a membrane. However, cells also differ, in

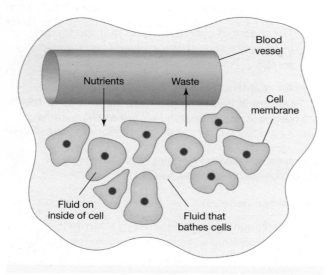

Figure 1.2 Some cells of the body, shown in association with a blood vessel (the latter is also composed of cells but for simplicity these are not indicated). Not to scale.

Source: Toates (1998b, Fig. 2.1, p. 25).

both their structure and function. As well as the general properties, cells are (again, rather like people) specialists, serving particular functions according to where they are located and to which organ they belong. For instance, red blood cells are specialists at carrying oxygen in the blood to be delivered to cells throughout the body. Nerve cells, termed **neurons**, are one of the types of cell that are specific to the nervous system and are specialized at transmitting and processing information. As one example of communication, it was just noted that a thorn in the foot triggers a signal that is transmitted through the body to the brain. This involves transmission of information by neurons.

Physiology and behaviour

A principal occupation of biological psychologists is to link physiology to behaviour and cognition. This section describes some forms that the link takes.

General principles

In achieving survival and optimal conditions within the body, a variety of different forms of information is conveyed to the brain. This concerns (1) internal events within the body and (2) events in the external world. For instance, a low or high body temperature is signalled to the brain. Information on the external world (e.g. presence of a source of warmth) is also signalled. This would be through such means as the sensations of heat or cold arising at the skin. Based upon this information, decisions are made and priorities of behaviour are established. For example, detection of cold within the body will make the sight of a warm location attractive to us.

In organizing reproduction, internal signals from the body (e.g. those arising from hormone levels) and external signals from prospective mates are integrated in the brain and decisions on courtship made. Decision-making involves establishing priorities, e.g. to mate rather than to feed.

Threats to the individual trigger emotions, such as fear and anger. The level of certain hormones in the body also affects these emotions. These emotions are associated with both behaviour, such as attacking or fleeing, and intrinsic changes to the body such as an accelerated heart-rate. During, say, feeding, the sight of a predator might trigger fear and cause prioritization to be instantly switched to fleeing.

Homeostasis

The inside of the body has an 'optimal condition', where it functions best. For example, as one feature of this, a body temperature of around 37 °C is optimal. Body temperature is regulated within close limits, with the help of behaviour, such as moving to a warmer or cooler location or buying a cold drink. Similarly, there is an optimal level of body water content. Maintaining the condition of the internal 'environment' of the body is therefore crucial to survival. As part of this, each cell requires a supply of energy and nutrients, obtained from outside the body with the help of the behaviour of ingesting food.

When internal conditions deviate from their optimal values, action is usually triggered to restore normality, a process termed **homeostasis**. In this way, homeostasis exemplifies the broadly used term **negative feedback**. Negative feedback is exhibited by the control of the temperature of a room with the help of a thermostat: when room temperature drops below that set at the thermostat, heating is switched on automatically. In other words, deviations from optimum tend to be *self-eliminating*, hence the adjective 'negative' before feedback. See Figure 1.3 and the minus sign, indicating negative feedback.

In the case of body temperature, homeostasis involves intrinsic processes, such as shivering and sweating, but also behaviour, such as emigrating to Florida. According to what is the internal feature of the body that deviates from optimum, we are *motivated* to seek sources of nutrients, water, heat or cold. The behavioural aspect of homeostasis will be one of the topics of the present book.

Given a basic introduction to physiology and behaviour, the following section will explore the application of this to the causal type of explanation.

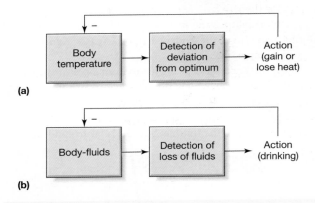

(a)

(b)

Figure 1.3 Homeostasis: (a) body temperature, (b) body fluids. The minus sign indicates that behaviour corrects the initial deviation that triggers behaviour, e.g. drinking corrects the loss of body fluids.

Section summary

1 The body can be divided into systems, our focus being the nervous system.

2 Another way of dividing the body is into its constituent cells.

3 Our principal focus will be a type of cell found within the nervous system, known as neurons.

4 The body possesses homeostatic systems that exhibit negative feedback.

Test your knowledge

(Answer on page 20)

1.2 Complete the following: 'Homeostasis means that deviations from a normal condition trigger action that tends to _____'. (i) correct the deviation, (ii) increase the size of the deviation.

Some sources of understanding

The methods employed

The task

The principal role of biological psychology is trying to understand what the brain does and how it does it. It is possible to identify different regions of the brain and to understand their contribution to behaviour and mind. For example, some regions (termed 'sensory regions') are responsible for processing information arriving at the eyes and others process auditory information from the ears. Some regions are involved in detecting the temperature of the body or the level of body fluids. Parts of the brain described as 'emotional' are responsible for the organization of fear and anger, and trigger changes in heart-rate, blood flow to the muscles and the flow of food along the gut.

This section looks first at some of the techniques that are employed in biological psychology in establishing 'what causes what'. It also looks at the implications associated with these techniques.

Experimental intervention

The causes of behaviour arise inside and outside the animal. Ideally, scientists would like to be able to make controlled manipulations of these external or internal factors under reproducible conditions and see what happens to behaviour. For example, a rat is injected with a drug and it starts to eat. What is the underlying cause of this? Feeding would normally be triggered by the sight of food or a fall in the level of energy available in the body, as detected by the brain. So, it could be that the drug stimulates the feeding control processes in the brain that normally detect a low energy level. Alternatively, the drug might alter how the rat's attention is directed, causing food to attract its attention. Detailed experimentation would be needed to find out exactly what the drug is doing.

For an everyday human example, researchers seek drugs to reduce appetite. Suppose such a potential drug has been developed and initial reports suggest that human participants lose weight while taking it. Researchers would need to know how it acts and on which brain regions. Does it target regions specifically concerned with appetite and suppress their activity, in effect fooling the body into not noticing that it is lowering its energy reserves? Alternatively, the drug might simply make people feel nausea and suppress a range of different types of behaviour. Subjective reports from the participants, in terms of their own sensations, need to be taken into account as well as objective biological evidence. Herein, a particular role of the biological psychologist lies in trying to link different sources of evidence.

Causal questions are of the kind 'If X occurs, then does outcome Y follow?' They might be: 'Does a new drug reduce pain?', 'Does alcohol cause deterioration in driving skills?' or 'How does brain damage disrupt emotional expression?' In some cases, one looks for a relationship in which cause and effect are close together in time, e.g. a drug reduces pain immediately. In other cases, experimentation involves manipulations that relate to the developmental/learning type of explanation. A relationship might be observed only over days or weeks, e.g. a drug improves the speed of learning a maze. In either case, in order to assess whether an effect is there, investigators need an experimental condition (e.g. injected with the drug) and a control condition (e.g. injected with a neutral substance) and they compare the two. Only then can they assess reliably whether there is a causal factor at work.

We now come to an area of biological psychology that causes controversy in the broader society. For non-human species, particular bits of the brain can be deliberately damaged by targeted surgery and the effects observed. The investigation of brain damage usually involves a form of causal explanation, i.e. what determines behaviour? In each case, investigators need some form of control: how does the damaged brain compare with one that is not damaged?

Consider Figure 1.4. In part (a), an experimenter presents an event (a 'stimulus') to an animal that does not have brain damage and notes what happens. In part (b) the same event is presented to a subject with brain damage and any difference in reaction from (a) is observed. Comparing the reactions in the two cases, experimenters can try to understand the role of the damaged brain region. Of course, such experimentation raises profound ethical issues, of which psychology is very much aware.

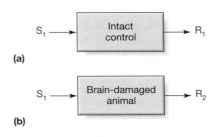

Figure 1.4 Testing for the effects of brain damage: (a) intact control reacts to event S_1 with behaviour R_1; (b) brain-damaged subject reacts to S_1 with behaviour R_2.

Human brain damage

In understanding what different regions of the human brain do, one source of insight is to look at damaged brains. Brain damage can arise in various ways. Sometimes the brain of a baby is traumatically damaged during birth. In other cases, damage, such as that from traffic accidents and gunshot wounds, happens later in life. Brain surgery on humans often involves removing parts of the brain that are diseased.

In the case of surgery, the comparison between intact and damaged brains can, at least in principle, be relatively straightforward. Scientists can look at the same human patient before and after surgery and compare behaviour. Of course, for there to have been surgery, there must have been some abnormality in the first place, so this creates problems of interpretation of the evidence. In other cases, rigorous control is impossible.

When the brain damage occurs to humans as an accident of birth or later injury, what do investigators use as a control? They can compare with other matched humans not having brain damage or with any records and memories of the individual prior to the trauma, but this is far from ideal.

A personal angle

Phineas Gage

Phineas Gage, who perhaps ranks as the most famous case in the history of biological psychology, appears to have been born in 1823 in East Lebanon, New Hampshire. He was a shrewd and well-respected foreman of a gang of railroad workers, blasting rock for the construction of a new line in Vermont.

In 1848, as a result of an explosion going disastrously wrong, a tamping iron, 3 cm in diameter, passed right through his brain, causing extensive damage to the front part of the brain on the left and some damage to the right (Damasio, 1996; Macmillan, 1986). It landed some 30 m away. Amazingly, Gage survived the accident and showed relatively little intellectual or linguistic impairment. However, he became more egocentric, obstinate and capricious than before and adopted foul language. This suggests that parts of the brain concerned with emotional expression based on the here-and-now were previously restrained by the damaged brain regions. Damage lifted the restraint. His doctor wrote: 'The equilibrium or balance, so to speak, between his intellectual faculties and his animal propensities, seems to have been destroyed' (quoted by Macmillan, 1986).

Phineas Gage died in San Francisco in 1861 but his skull was removed from the rest of his body and, together with the tamping iron, put on exhibition in a museum in Massachusetts.

Subsequently, other individuals with similar brain damage to the front part of the brain have been observed and the evidence tends to match that of Gage. Psychologists now understand slightly better the change in behaviour in terms of the interaction between regions of brain, damaged and intact. Of course, to be precise, brain damage reveals the working of the remainder of the brain, i.e. how it functions without the damaged region. Psychologists need intelligent speculation to get from this to understanding the normal role of the damaged region.

Such damage can be understood at a biological level and has clear consequences for behaviour. However, the cases call for caution in their interpretation. Accidents do not usually yield 'neat' damage, where investigators can specify exactly which brain region is affected. Neither, of course, do they occur under the control of the experimenter. Typically, they involve individual, often unique, cases. Researchers cannot be confident that they have eliminated all other factors that might have been involved. They do not have a control for Phineas Gage, to see the effect of the passage of time itself, etc. Nonetheless, the insight from such cases has been impressive and fits well into a broader picture. The biological psychologist can point to how the study of the structure and functioning of the brain provides insight into mind and behaviour.

As a second example, consider the patient known as DB. DB had surgery to remove a tumour in a region of brain concerned with processing visual information and exhibited a phenomenon known as **blindsight** (Weiskrantz, 1976). We are fortunate in his case; DB was studied in the 1970s using the methods of biological psychology, in Oxford. Experimenters were able to target visual stimuli precisely; the stimuli were carefully positioned relative to DB's eyes. In this way, DB's reactions could be compared between two conditions: processing that made demands on the damaged part of his brain and other processing that involved only the intact part. That is, DB served as his own control. When processing was triggered in the intact regions, DB reported seeing things as normal.

In certain positions, the location of the stimuli was such that detecting their presence would apparently require visual processing in the damaged region. At these locations, DB denied seeing anything. However, other evidence pointed to a rather subtle conclusion. It was demonstrated that, without DB's knowing it, he was extracting some appropriate information from the visual stimuli that he denied seeing. If the experimenter asked DB to *guess* what he saw, DB did so better than chance – implying something like 'the stimulus that I simply cannot see is vertical this time'. DB knew something but didn't know that he knew it. Such patients are blind to the stimuli as far as conscious awareness is concerned, hence the term 'blindsight'.

Dissociation of this kind, between behaviour and conscious awareness, is important for understanding the role of the brain in consciousness. A brain abnormality has radically changed a psychological system in ways that can be specified. Disturbances (if any) that occur following damage can give important insights into how the brain normally works.

Human brain imaging techniques

With the help of what are termed 'imaging techniques', investigators can examine the activity of particular parts of the brain while human participants engage in a specific task. For example, asking a participant to concentrate on a visual display increases the electrical activity within brain regions known from other evidence to be involved in processing visual information.

These techniques have generated immense excitement in biological psychology, with much hope for further insights to come. They have yielded some surprising and profound understanding that is of general interest in psychology and they are even shaping our ideas of what it is to be human. For example, investigators know that watching someone else

When we say that a person can 'feel' the suffering of another, does this have any identifiable basis in the brain?

Source: PhotoDisc, Inc.

in pain (the 'observed') can activate some brain regions in the observer that are active when the observer experiences pain directly from a noxious stimulus (Singer *et al.*, 2004). Thus, the notion of human empathy is given biological roots.

Consider also the following experiment. Without knowing exactly what was going on behind the scenes, participants were asked to engage in a game of virtual ball-tossing, while activity of their brains was examined (Eisenberger *et al.*, 2003). They were then abruptly excluded from the game. Anyone like the present author, who is seriously 'athletically challenged', might well have found exclusion to be a merciful escape but this did not appear to be so at all for these particular participants. Rather, following exclusion, activation was seen in the same brain regions as are activated by physical pain. So, in some real biological sense, social rejection appears to hurt and has an identifiable basis in the brain, surely an important message for society at large.

Can the biological psychologist see what is going on in your mind? In some as-yet very limited ways and with the help of imaging, the answer is a much-qualified 'yes'. When a person thinks of a human face, a specific brain region is particularly active. The region that is strongly activated is different from that activated when thinking of, say, a house (O'Craven and Kanwisher, 2000). In future, there could be unpredicted developments of such 'objective mind-reading'. However, although the results so far are certainly interesting, they do not yet have a sufficient degree of sensitivity to enable researchers to probe your inner thoughts. Indeed, despite the hype surrounding the technology, it might be

Does social exclusion have anything in common with 'real pain'?

Source: courtesy of Bundy Mackintosh.

seen as just one more tool among several that are available for gaining insight.

Putting biological psychology into context

Biological psychology assumes a lawfulness of behaviour, i.e. that behaviour can be understood in terms of some identifiable principles and that the place to look for these is in biological processes. This section shows how this biological approach can be put into a broader context.

The social link

Understanding behaviour can require an input from both biological and social perspectives. Thus, biological factors influence social behaviour and, reciprocally, social behaviour influences biology.

For a non-human example, consider the courtship behaviour of a male dove. Observing the male's courtship display alters certain hormone levels of the female. The change in the female's hormonal levels then changes her behaviour. This, in turn, changes the behaviour of the male. Similarly, in **primate** (this being the group that includes gorillas, chimpanzees and humans) males, levels of the hormone testosterone affect mating and competition. In turn, the outcome of interaction with receptive females and competitive males can influence testosterone level (Rose *et al.*, 1975).

In one study on primates, the drug amphetamine appeared to have no reliable effect on behaviour (Cacioppo and Berntson, 1992). However, that was before the animals' place in the social hierarchy was taken into account. Amphetamine increased the dominance tendencies of primates high in the hierarchy. It increased the submissive tendencies of those low in the hierarchy. No matter how sophisticated the analysis of physiological events, it might have missed the link that became apparent from looking at social context.

For an example in human social interaction, pain is determined in ways that are clearly the business of the biological sciences. There are detectors of tissue damage at the skin and elsewhere, and information on this is conveyed to the brain along pathways of neurons that can be identified biologically. However, pain can also be influenced by factors such as the nature of the interaction between therapist and patient and the confidence of the patient that this will bring relief. Here lies a meeting ground between biological and social approaches. Another area of interaction between social and biological factors that has come into the headlines in recent years is the effects of such factors as marital harmony or divorce on the body's physiology. Some evidence suggests that unhappiness has the effect of making us more disease-prone.

Human drug addiction (e.g. to morphine or heroin) depends not only on the chemical properties of drugs taken but also on social context (Peele and Degrandpre, 1998). A person's desire to take drugs arises from physiological factors (e.g. sensitivity of certain key brain regions, time since last taking the drug and state of withdrawal) and external factors (e.g. social context). Studying only one of these factors in isolation would miss the subtle nature of the determinants of addiction.

So, at times, the most effective way of understanding behaviour can be to include a study of social interactions. For example, if we were not to consider these interactions, we might be puzzled why hormone levels seem to be going up and down in a random way. Similarly, we might conclude that amphetamine has no reliable effect on dominance–submissive behaviour.

When correctly applied, a biological perspective can help to end fruitless and irrational debates of the kind: 'What is the most important factor determining behaviour? Is it biology or sociocultural context?' (Gilbert, 1998). Both need to be considered, together with their links.

The cognitive link

Within cognitive psychology, some influential theories of how the mind processes information are based on knowledge of the brain. For example, Rumelhart and Norman (1989, p. 17) suggest that it might: '. . . become a necessary exercise for those proposing particular memory representations to provide at least an argument to show that the brain could encode information in the way required by the theory'.

Similarly, suppose that, within the study of the psychology of perception, we generate a theory of how visual perception occurs. Any assumptions that go into this theory need to be compatible with a biological understanding of the visual system (Zeki, 1993). Suppose that we were asked to accept a psychological theory that seems to require structures that do not exist in the real visual system, as described by physiologists. Informed by biological psychology, we would surely have serious reservations about any such theory. Several psychological theories might equally well account for the psychological data, so how does one choose between them? One factor that would favour a particular theory might be the extent to which it is compatible with biological understanding (Cacioppo and Berntson, 1992).

A central concern in cognitive psychology is whether there are several systems of memory and, if so, how they differ (Schacter and Tulving, 1994a). Brain damage sometimes disrupts one class of memory while leaving another intact. This is evidence in favour of distinct classes of memory.

Evolutionary and functional explanations are also brought into the discussion of biology and cognition. For example, the issue of emotion has been considered in these terms. It used to be suggested that emotion is a hindrance rather than a help to sophisticated modern humans. The argument was that emotions might have served a useful function in our distant evolutionary past but we have now outlived this. Living in large urban centres, we have become creatures dependent on pure cool thought and rationality. Biological approaches have illustrated why such dichotomies between emotion and rationality are false. People with damage to brain regions involved in linking cognition and emotion have been found to make disastrous social decisions (Damasio, 1999). Rather, a contemporary position is that emotions are an integral part of our decision-making. We are somewhat protected from running serious risks because the mere prospect of doing so triggers negative emotion and this restrains us.

Having introduced the basics of the study of the immediate determinants of behaviour, the following section looks more closely at the way of thinking and explaining that is associated with biological psychology.

Section summary

1 To infer reliably a causal link, controlled experimentation is needed. Interventions into the biology of the body are made and the consequences observed.

2 Insight into behaviour can be obtained from studying individuals with brain damage.

3 Imaging of human brains reveals which regions are particularly active during specific tasks.

4 Understanding can sometimes be provided by considering biology in the context of social interaction.

5 For a suggested cognitive process to be viable, it needs to be compatible with a biological understanding.

Test your knowledge

(Answer on page 20)

1.3 Which of the following is true? (i) Testosterone affects behaviour, (ii) behaviour and social context affect testosterone levels, (iii) both (i) and (ii).

The way of thinking of biological psychology

The foundations

The biological psychologist tends to be a **determinist**, reflecting the belief that he or she can identify physical causes for behaviour. The central faith of biological psychology is that events within the nervous system cause behaviour and the task is to identify and characterize these causes.

The biological psychologist has some justification for a faith in **determinism** (the notion that for every event there can in principle be identified a cause). Not only is there evidence for the effects of accidental brain damage (discussed earlier) but, under some conditions, the researcher can take an experimental subject, e.g. rat, and determine its immediate behaviour. The rat can be injected with, say, a thirst-inducing drug and a prediction made at a much better than chance level: the animal will drink or learn to navigate a maze to obtain water.

Valuable insight can be gained at this level of analysis and some biological psychologists might well see no limits on how far this approach can be taken. However, I shall suggest that biological factors need to be *interpreted* within a context of rather subtle psychological principles.

A two-way street

Figure 1.5 shows that, in two closely related respects, the link between biology (brain) and psychology (behaviour) is a 'two-way street'. First, as in part (a), the brain controls behaviour. In turn, behaviour (e.g. social contact) influences events within the brain. Second, as in part (b), there is the relationship between biologists of the brain (e.g. neuroscientists) and psychologists. Psychologists need to look to the biological level to seek brain mechanisms that explain phenomena in behaviour. However, those researchers concerned primarily with the brain can get insight into its

working by looking to psychology. Knowing what the brain is doing at a psychological level can give vital insight into how it does it and the kind of brain structures involved. Thus, there is a regular exchange of information between biology and psychology.

A good example to illustrate the interdependence of biology and psychology is the **immune system** (Michel and Moore, 1995). This system consists of specialized cells, and it comes to the rescue when the body is invaded by bacteria or a virus, or cells become cancerous. So, it is clearly the business of the biological sciences. However, in the latter part of the 20th century, psychologists gave scientific respectability to what had been believed by folk wisdom for centuries: mood states can affect the disease vulnerability of the body (Ader and Cohen, 1985). Stress can lower the activity of the cells of the immune system that are recruited to fight invasion. The basic science of immunology had to assimilate a fundamental change: psychological events affect the immune system.

Reductionism

The term **reductionism** refers to a process of trying to explain events at one level (e.g. mind and behaviour) by looking at a 'lower' (i.e. 'smaller-scale') level (e.g. the activity of the cells of the brain). We make some use of this principle, as indicated in Figure 1.5(b). Indeed, the notion of *biological* psychology implies some kind of reduction to biology. For example, the most insight into the cause and possible cure of the movement and mood disorder Parkinson's disease has been obtained from reducing to the biological level. The disease is caused by the malfunction and death of certain neurons in a particular part of the brain. However, the disease cannot be understood *simply* in terms of the diseased cells. The whole brain needs to be considered in understanding why, for example, patients show a tremor of the hands and have difficulty in walking. The environment needs consideration in terms of the demands placed on the patient. So, we shall see where insight can be gained at a biological level but will need to put this information into a *psychological* context, as described in the next section.

Emergent properties

As part of the explanation of how psychological phenomena appear, properties are said to *emerge* at different levels. In other words, there are **emergent properties** at the psychological level. Phenomena (in terms of mind and behaviour) appear and these cannot be understood simply by considering the components of the brain in isolation. These psychological properties depend upon the parts that make up the brain but cannot be understood by *simply reducing* the explanation to their sum.

An **analogy** can clearly illustrate what 'emergent property' means. An analogy is an attempt to explain something that

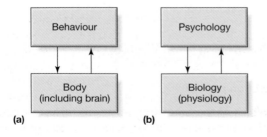

(a)   **(b)**

Figure 1.5 Links between levels of (a) the phenomena of behaviour and brain and (b) the disciplines studying them. The psychological level is shown above the physiological, since, as we go up, we get to a larger scale.

we don't understand in terms of a suggested similarity with (*an analogy with*) something that we do. The analogy illustrates the essential principle that we wish to explain.

For an example, consider two gases, oxygen and hydrogen, observed at room temperature. They each exhibit familiar general properties characteristic of gases and also some peculiar properties. In order for there to be life, oxygen is something that you need to breathe in. Hydrogen explodes when ignited. When these two gases come together and combine, their combination gives us water. Water exhibits a new property that was not evident in a study of either gas on its own: it is liquid. It flows downhill, among other things. The properties of the liquid are very different from those of the component gases.

We cannot take the property of oxygen, simply add it to that of hydrogen, and thereby hope to understand the properties of water. In other words, the property of liquidity of water cannot be reduced to the sum of the properties of the components but is said to *emerge* from the combination. However, this property, though said to be at a different level, i.e. at that of the combination, *depends upon* the properties of each gas. The peculiar properties of the component gases are necessary to give the combined effect. Take away the gases and the liquid vanishes. So, we need to understand the bits that make up the whole *and* how the bits act together.

If emergent properties are evident in something as relatively simple as this, just imagine how rich are the possibilities for unexpected psychological phenomena to emerge when millions of neurons combine their effects in making a brain. For example, biological psychologists assume that the conscious mind (discussed in a moment) emerges in this way from the properties of billions of neurons in combination, though none can explain how!

For another example, psychologists now have some success at associating complex disorders such as schizophrenia with disturbances in particular identifiable brain regions and in chemicals at particular neurons in known regions of the brain. However, we should not try to reduce the study of schizophrenia to *simply* these regions and chemicals. Rather, we need to see how the psychological phenomena of schizophrenia, such as apathy and hallucinations, emerge from a whole brain that contains such local disturbances.

Why biological psychology is so important to us all

The kind of consideration described so far in terms of linking biology and psychology is not just words of lofty academic discussion. (Not that you would ever have suspected that!) Rather, it is of fundamental practical significance to how we lead our lives, organize society and make decisions about human welfare.

Mental illness

Imagine that a patient who is suffering depression goes to his or her doctor. The doctor prescribes the drug Prozac, which has known chemical effects on particular neurons in specific parts of the nervous system. After a few weeks, the patient, mercifully, returns much better and the Prozac is assumed to have taken its effect.

There are at least three levels of relevant description here: (1) the biology of the drug's action, (2) the patient's observable reactions in terms of body and behaviour and (3) the patient's own reported subjective conscious experience. The last of these is described in such psychological terms as fears, feelings and hopes. It would be foolish to suggest that any one of 1–3 above is the most important. It would be equally foolish to try simply to substitute biological terms for the patient's subjective mental account. We need all the help that we can get in trying to understand phenomena such as depression, and no source of insight can be ignored or written out of the script.

Just imagine telling someone, 'it is only your neurons that are not acting right, so there's nothing more than that wrong with you'. Only a poor therapist would understand merely the biological level without having a corresponding familiarity with the way patients describe their feelings. The skill of biological psychology comes in relating these corresponding levels of discussion. That is to say, psychologists try to understand *how*, by their action on neurons in the brain, drugs change the patient's mental state. Some therapies favour use of biological means as in Prozac and others go for 'talking cures'. Some combine both, in which case we need insight into how these approaches might interact.

So, *in addition* to the more psychological level of approach there is also a place for the biological approach in understanding behaviour (Bolton and Hill, 1996). The types of description are not in competition for explanation. Rather, as the analogy to gases and water serves to illustrate, they refer to different aspects of the same complex system.

Social policy

Violence is a major social problem never far from the headlines. Discussions of the causes of violence need to be informed by current thinking in biological psychology. Psychologists have long held that aggression depends upon (i) such biological things as genes and levels of particular hormones and (ii) such 'non-biological' factors as social context and social deprivation, peer pressure, role modelling of aggressive others, etc. The argument is usually given along the lines of the need 'to understand aggression in terms of the *mix* between biological and social factors'. However, genes and hormones and social factors do not just mix as if they were parts of a fruit salad. Rather, there are complex rules of organization involved in linking genes, behaviour and social organization.

Aggression might be explained in part by an appeal to cognitive and social factors, in terms of self-esteem, expectation and frustration. The nature of such cognitive processing depends, among other things, on levels of particular hormones that affect activity of neurons in the brain. By their action on neurons, some hormones (e.g. testosterone) appear to tilt thinking and behaviour towards dominance seeking and conflict.

Personal responsibility

The combination of psychology and law forms an important academic area. In law, there exists the notion of responsibility versus diminished responsibility. One way of pleading diminished responsibility is to suggest that the accused has a biological abnormality in the brain. In Britain, when capital punishment was still used, such biological evidence could save the accused person's life. Evidence of abnormal brain activity could take the form of a brain tumour or an abnormal pattern of electrical activity recorded from the brain. These days, pleas of diminished responsibility have been made on the basis of an abnormal level of one of the brain's natural chemical messengers (Fenwick, 1993).

What exactly is such a claim saying? It might be as follows. We are normally guided in our behaviour by conscious goals that we set and for which we are responsible. We monitor our behaviour as we move towards these goals and adjust it to meet the goal. However, there can be a malfunction as a result of, say, a tumour. A person might set socially inappropriate goals (MacKay, 1974) or act abnormally strongly on impulse and against the goal. A biological disturbance dominates or at least distorts the control of behaviour. Under these conditions, such people might be judged to be sick and their behaviour outside their control. Where there is behavioural malfunction without evidence of biological abnormality, we might assume that the person is responsible for setting their own goals. In this case, when things go wrong, they might, to adopt a popular cliché, be said to be 'bad rather than mad'.

So, is it the case that, in the area of personal responsibility, we appeal to a biological level when things go wrong but are happy to accept that the normal principles of psychology (i.e. those of the 'person in the street') apply when everything works well? This is one possible approach (Bolton and Hill, 1996) and it more or less corresponds to law and folk psychology. However, any such discussion raises philosophical problems and more questions than it answers. There is always the possibility that such an argument can be informed by further discoveries in biological psychology.

The following section will turn to the role of genes, development and learning.

Section summary

1 Biological psychology is a deterministic approach, which assumes that behaviour is determined by events in the nervous system.

2 We shall seek insight by looking to biology but interpret what we find in psychological terms.

3 The expression 'emergent property' refers to new properties that emerge at increasing levels of complexity.

Test your knowledge

(Answer on page 20)

1.4 Complete the following 'In biological psychology, mind could be described as _____ the activity of the brain'. (i) a reduction in, (ii) an emergent property of, (iii) having nothing to do with.

Genes, development and learning

Genes

In bringing together the four types of explanation described earlier, genes play an important role. Genes form a component of the cells throughout our bodies, including neurons. See Figure 1.6. Lay logic has something to say about the role of genes too: 'It's all in the genes' and 'Criminals are born that way, not made' are expressions occasionally heard. Such claims have a strong feel of determinism, suggesting that the gene sets a course of action and the individual is a slave to this. They reflect implicit theories about the role of genes and suggest that phenomena at a behavioural and psychological level can be *simply reduced* to a small part of the biology.

Biological psychology suggests the more modest claim that genes play *a role* in determining behaviour. However, they do this in conjunction with many other factors that interlock with them in complex ways. By understanding something about genes at a biological level, the psychologist can formulate more precise questions about the control of behaviour. Thus, we can rule out certain ideas, for example, that genes can be either more or less important than the environment in determining behaviour.

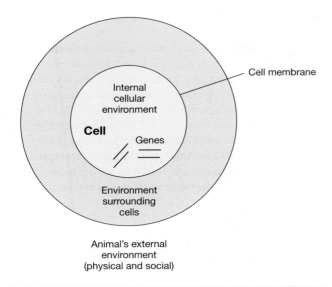

Figure 1.6 Genes within cells. Note the cellular environment surrounding the genes and the environment surrounding the cells and the whole animal. For simplicity just one cell is shown.

Genes trigger the production of chemical structures called **proteins** that are constituents of cells. These proteins form body structures and interact with their immediate environment in the cells of the body. Nervous systems, like other systems, are structures that are determined in part by genes. So, one link is (genes) → (nervous system structures) → (behaviour). However, life is more complex than this since behaviour tends to influence the structure of the developing body. See Figure 1.7. Already, subtle complexity appears. This cautions against a simple causal link, such as 'it's all in the genes'. We will look to the biological properties of genes but will interpret them in the context of a psychological account.

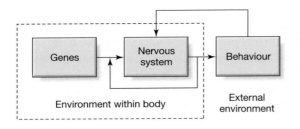

Figure 1.7 Behaviour is both caused by the nervous system and affects the nervous system. One site of this effect is where the genes affect structure.

Developmental/learning explanations

The process of change that starts at conception and continues until maturity is known as 'development', also termed **ontogeny**. This refers to the history of the development and growth of the individual and relates most obviously to the developmental/learning type of explanation.

The structure of the body changes as a result of the interdependence between genes and their environment. By 'environment' is meant both the internal environment of the body that surrounds the genes and the environment that surrounds the whole animal. Nervous systems grow and change as a result of protein synthesis. New connections between neurons are formed and some established connections get broken. As the nervous system changes, so behaviour changes. New possibilities for behaviour emerge while some behaviour drops out of the animal's repertoire.

Also within this type of explanation, learning represents a process of change but was traditionally discussed as something distinct from development. Alas, it is not easy to define the nature of this distinction, a topic discussed in Chapter 6, 'Development and plasticity'. Hence, there is the caution of the compound term 'developmental/learning'.

The next section considers the validity of trying to understand the behaviour of one species by studying that of another.

Section summary

1 Genes are a factor that helps to determine the structure of the body including the nervous system.

2 Behaviour cannot be 'all in the genes'.

3 Development refers to changes that are a function of age.

Test your knowledge

(Answer on page 20)

1.5 Complete the following: 'By their action on protein synthesis, genes _____' (i) play a role in determining the structure of the nervous system, (ii) trigger behaviour.

Animal models, evolution and comparative studies

The **comparative approach** consists of comparing different species of animal in order to gain insight into how each adapts to its habitat and how this is reflected in differences in their behaviour. The example of taste-aversion learning introduced this topic earlier.

In our case, the comparative approach is used mostly for trying to understand humans better. Psychologists look at so-called simpler species in order to gain an understanding of a more complex species. The term **animal model** is often used to refer to the simpler animal as a model that captures important features of the more complex animal. Animal models have proven valuable in studying the biology of behaviour.

With some basic processes and components, the same solution employed by so-called simple animals is also seen in the more complex. Evolution is described as being 'conservative' (Epstein, 1982). For example, comparing across species there are striking similarities in how neurons operate and communicate with each other. Much insight has been gained by dissecting large neurons from such species as squid and applying the knowledge gained to other species, including humans. However, in other respects evolution could be described as 'inventive' in finding new solutions. Thus, there are limitations on how far one can push the process of appealing to simpler animal models. Although the components have striking common features, the combination of components can

take on properties that mean animal models have a limited value.

Certain species show exceptional abilities. A study of their brains in comparison to species not showing the exceptional ability can give insight into how this ability is linked to the brain. For example, some bird species show an incredible ability at hoarding vast amounts of food in a multitude of different locations and remembering where they hid it (Clayton and Dickinson, 1998). Other, closely related, birds do not have this same ability. So, a comparison of their brains can guide us in searching for the brain regions that underlie the exceptional spatial and memory skills.

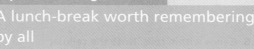

A personal angle
A lunch-break worth remembering by all

The psychology department at the University of California at Davis is associated with some rather peculiar cognitive skills but is also known for theft, cunning and deception. I hasten to add that I am not describing the academic staff but rather some winged visitors.

During their lunch-break, wife and husband team Nicola Clayton and Nathan Emory (both now at the University of Cambridge) observed the behaviour of Western scrub-jays, who were taking morsels of food left by students. They noticed that the birds would bury some of the food for later consumption (termed caching). However, occasionally, other birds were witness to this. When this happened, after the competitor had left the scene, the first bird would dig up the morsel and bury it in a different place. Controlled laboratory studies, done later at Cambridge, confirmed that this behaviour is characteristic of the species.

The study points to the value of looking at special abilities possessed by particular species. It also shows what can be gained by observing behaviour under natural conditions – well, maybe more precisely, 'semi-natural', in the case of a university campus. The research suggests sophisticated cognition that involves the anticipated likely moves of a competitor. It prompts the search for special underlying processes in the brains of such species.

This Western scrub-jay is recovering food it has buried. What special talent does it reveal in doing this?

Source: courtesy of Ian Cannell and Nicky Clayton.

Ethology and psychology

Ethology, a branch of zoology, is concerned with a particular approach to the study of animal behaviour. Both ethologists and psychologists study behaviour. Whereas psychologists have traditionally focused on a few species, mainly humans, rats and pigeons, ethologists have looked at a wider range. Ethologists place great weight upon functional and evolutionary explanations. They have also emphasized looking at animals within their natural environment. The rationale behind this is that, if we wish to understand how animals solve problems by their behaviour, it is necessary to consider them in relation to the environment in which they evolved.

The approach to doing research has been somewhat different between ethologists and psychologists. Traditionally, psychologists have looked at animals in a more restricted laboratory environment, such as a small cage or **Skinner box** (an apparatus in which an animal presses a lever or pecks a key and thereby earns a reward, such as a pellet of food). It has been remarked that the psychologists put their animals in a box and looked in at them, whereas the ethologists put themselves in a box and looked out at the animals.

There is now something of a welcome breakdown in the divisional boundary between these two sciences. Psychologists are showing an increasing willingness to relate their findings to the species' natural environment (Bolles, 1970; Garcia, 1989). Indeed, a number of psychologists have become very fired by ideas of evolution, discussed in the next chapter.

We now pick up again the issue of brains and minds and it will be shown where evolutionary thinking is relevant to this.

Section summary

1 Ethologists study a range of species in their natural environments and thereby suggest how behaviour has served a function in evolution.

2 Psychologists have traditionally focused on a few species, mainly rats, pigeons and humans.

3 There is now more of a coming together of ethology and psychology.

Test your knowledge

(Answer on page 20)

1.6 Fill in the missing words in the following: 'Complex behaviour can _____ from a combination of neurons of a kind that are common across species'. (i) not appear, (ii) emerge.

Linking brains and minds

Introduction

How do brain and mind relate? If only I knew! Biological psychology has much to contribute regarding how brains and minds *might* relate and even more on how they probably do not relate but there are no comprehensive explanations. It is sometimes said that 'the mind is what the brain does' or 'the mind is the brain in action'. How would we approach trying to assess the value of these statements? As one possibility, we will first consider an analogy that might just help us.

Is the brain a computer?

These days, a popular and persuasive analogy to brain and mind is with modern computers, though there is fierce debate on the extent to which even this analogy is appropriate (Dennett, 1993; Penrose, 1987). However, it is not essential to show that the brain is exactly like a computer for the analogy to be useful. Indeed, if two systems were identical, the word 'analogy' would be misleading. Where an analogy breaks down can be as insightful as where it works, by highlighting badly understood or unique characteristics of the system under study.

The computer might provide a useful first analogy in terms of the distinction between hardware, its physical structure, and software, the program that is run on it. As a first approximation, the hardware is analogous to the structure of the brain, as composed of neurons. The software is analogous to the mind and the cognitive operations that are performed by the brain, i.e. 'what the brain does'. The hardware and software each have their own principles and organization appropriate at each level. As part of the analogy, the hardware is also of interest in that it sets certain possibilities for the software operations and limits to what can be run.

Brains and computers each show phenomenal but different abilities. My simple computer humiliates me every time in terms of speed and the ability to spot spelling mistakes but, casting modesty aside, I do believe that I am more original and creative. You might not find an analogy with a computer particularly flattering. Why not? There seems to be something essentially human that is missing from a computer. You might well swear at your computer when it loses a file or crashes but surely you do not feel sympathy or guilt towards it afterwards (or do you?). Computers seem cold and mechanical in a way that a person or a cat just isn't. So, let us try first a more homespun approach to getting insight and this will lead us to a crucial aspect of mind – its consciousness.

The conscious mind

Introduction

Throughout recorded history, philosophers have been concerned with the relationship between the mind and the physical body. To be more precise, these days this concern is framed in terms of the *conscious* mind. Unconscious activity seems not that far removed from what computers do, but the peculiar property of consciousness is very problematic for attempts to explain the mind. For example, psychologists speculate about when consciousness first emerged in evolution – what sort of brain is necessary to support consciousness? Another question is, what functional advantage does consciousness confer?

Self-reflection

The issue can perhaps best be illustrated by your reflecting upon your own conscious mind and body, which you are asked to do now. Your reflection might lead you to suggest two different types of phenomena. First, consider your conscious mind. I assume that you experience a private conscious world of thoughts that are peculiarly *yours*. This is only my assumption since I do not know for sure that you experience this, or anything else for that matter. However, it would seem a reasonable assumption, since I know that I experience it. I would be narcissistic and arrogant in the extreme to think that only I do so.

Suppose that your conscious mind is now occupied with thoughts about the biological psychology of your brain and mind. The thoughts might be firmly focused on this topic or, of course, they might not be! However, you have the ability to switch these thoughts to something else, idiosyncratic and far removed from this topic. You might be wondering whether you will shortly go to the kitchen to make a coffee or not, or you might be thinking about some other subject known only to you. Go on – try switching your thoughts. This is a private world of your own and I have very little, if any, access to it except by means of what you might choose to tell me (though, as we saw, brain imaging might sometimes give a very crude measure). We might like to call it the 'software' but does this term really capture its essence? There is a raw subjective feel to this existence, that peculiar feel of *what it is like* to be you, a conscious human being (Nagel, 1974).

Now consider a rather different set of phenomena, those associated with the objective description of your brain. This seems like hardware, comprising many millions of neurons, i.e. structures, in turn made up from chemical components. Communication between neurons is by means of other specialized chemicals. Looking at the chemicals that make up the neurons and the messengers between them, investigators see nothing very special about their structure. These chemicals seem to have no properties that set them aside as

peculiar to the world of biological psychology, let alone the mental world. In principle, any scientist with the right equipment can observe this world of physics and chemistry. Indeed, it is only a scientist looking at your brain rather than you, the individual being observed, who can really see what is happening in this world.

The fundamental question of 'mind–brain', or to be more precise '*conscious* mind–brain', concerns the nature of the relationship between these two domains, the one private, with privileged access by you, and the other public, with privileged access by a scientist. There are various theories on this relationship, one of which is considered next.

Identity theory

These days, among neuroscientists and psychologists, the most popular model of the mind–brain relationship is a variety of **identity theory** (Gray, 1987b). Identity theory suggests that for every mental event there is a corresponding brain event. According to identity theory, a mental event cannot have an existence distinct from a corresponding brain event. The way that this is expressed is that the languages describing brain and mind are two different ways of talking about the *same underlying reality*. For example, I might use the alternative levels of description that 'I feel depressed' or 'There are abnormal levels within a cocktail of different chemicals in part of my brain'. One uses mental language and the other brain language but, to an identity theorist, they refer to the same reality. The depression could not exist without the abnormal chemical states. The two descriptions are obviously appropriate for different contexts of discussion.

For an analogy, it is a bit like French and English. The language chosen is appropriate to the context. One could use English and refer to 'the table' or French and refer to '*la table*' but there is only the one table that is being described. Using this analogy, the puzzle comes in trying to establish the rules of translation between the two languages. Alas, unlike English and French, we have no dictionaries or grammar texts.

A final thought

These days, philosophers, psychologists and neuroscientists (not to forget defence lawyers and priests) still passionately debate the nature of the relationship between brain and conscious mind. Although it is important to have some understanding of this, mercifully trying to solve it need not concern us too much. Rather, we need merely to keep it in focus and be aware of what we are claiming and the implications of muddled thinking. Remember the depressed patient at the doctor's surgery. According to the favoured contemporary model, the patient's problem is not '*all* in the mind' or '*all* in the body' but in both simultaneously.

Section summary

1 The relationship between mental and brain events is a hotly discussed issue.

2 A possible analogy for understanding brain and mind is to suggest that the brain is like a computer and the mind is like the software program.

3 It is particularly the *conscious* aspect of mind that creates problems in seeking an explanation.

4 A modern view informed by biological psychology tends to favour a version of identity theory, i.e. that languages describing brain and mind are different ways of referring to the one underlying reality.

Test your knowledge

(Answer on page 20)

1.7 According to identity theory, can something be 'all in the mind'?

1.4

Bringing things together

The present chapter points to the value of applying different types of explanation to a given behaviour or mental event. This can show where different insights can be mutually supportive. Subsequent chapters will build on the four types of explanation introduced here, i.e. causal, developmental/learning, evolutionary and functional, and will show their interdependence. Another message is the importance of taking the middle ground between the extremes of either regarding biology as the answer to everything or rejecting biological explanation. It will be argued that biology is of fundamental importance for understanding behaviour and mind. However, wholesale reduction of psychology to biology, in effect writing psychology out of the script, will not be attempted, for reasons developed in this chapter.

Summary of Chapter 1

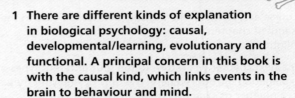

1 There are different kinds of explanation in biological psychology: causal, developmental/learning, evolutionary and functional. A principal concern in this book is with the causal kind, which links events in the brain to behaviour and mind.

2 The science of physiology is concerned with how the body works in terms of its organs and cells amongst other things. Our main interest is with an organ, the brain, and a type of cell called a neuron.

3 Biological psychologists draw evidence from (i) experimental intervention, (ii) looking at the effects of damage to human brains and (iii) imaging the activity of brains while people perform tasks.

4 The link between biology and psychology is a 'two-way street' with information and insight exchanged in each direction.

5 We develop and learn. Behaviour changes correspondingly.

6 We can get insight into brain and behaviour by studying how different species adapt to their different environments.

7 An unsolved problem is how the brain and the conscious mind relate. The favoured explanation of this is identity theory.

Further reading

For general considerations of the links between biology and psychological approaches, see Barkow *et al.* (1992). For links with social psychology, see Van Lange (2006). For links between biology and social development, see Johnston (1987). For ethology, see Greenberg and Haraway (1998). For different perspectives on the mind and consciousness, see Blackmore (2005) and the two journals: *Consciousness and Cognition* and (for a relatively gentle approach) *Journal of Consciousness Studies*.

Signposts

Of course everything in the introduction will be used in the subsequent chapters. However, it is worth particularly highlighting two topics:

- The next chapter will return to the four different types of explanation introduced here. It is only by applying these to a number of examples of behaviour that you can appreciate their full significance.

- I hope that the difficult issue of the relationship between the conscious mind and the brain will have fired your curiosity, rather than intimidating you. All of us find it hard to get our minds (!) around this issue. It will be discussed in much greater detail in Chapter 21, 'Brains, minds and consciousness'. For the moment, try not to lose sleep over it.

Answers

Explanations for answers to 'test your knowledge' questions can be found on the website **www.pearsoned.co.uk/toates**

1.1   (i) Causal
1.2   (i) correct the deviation
1.3   (iii) Both (i) and (ii)
1.4   (ii) an emergent property of
1.5   (i) play a role in determining the structure of the nervous system
1.6   (ii) emerge
1.7   No – anything in the mind is also simultaneously encoded in the body, to be precise the brain

CHAPTER 2

Genes, environment and evolution

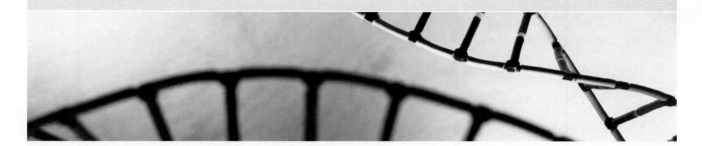

Learning outcomes for Chapter 2

After studying this chapter, you should be able to:

1. Understand how genes and environment act to influence behaviour and relate this to evolution.

2. Give an example to illustrate the principle that any behaviour is associated with both costs and benefits. Link this to an understanding of evolution.

3. In causal terms, describe some processes that underlie behaviour (e.g. reflexes, rhythms and motivation). Relate these processes to the functional significance of their role.

4. Outline the basic principles of genetics and define the terms 'gene' and 'allele'. Describe the role of genes, both within an individual and between generations.

5. Explain the link between genes and behaviour.

6. Describe the dynamic interaction between genes and environment and the subtle nature of this interdependence in so far as behaviour is concerned. In so doing, explain why dichotomies of the kind, 'which is most important – genes *or* environment?', are misleading.

7. Give the basics of evolutionary psychology in an informed and critical way. Explain why it stirs passion.

8. Using depression as an example, illustrate how the different types of explanation can be brought to a given phenomenon.

Scene-setting questions

1   Is nature basically selfish?

2   The popular image suggests that 'expectant fathers' pace up and down. Could we identify any biological basis for this?

3   Why is there such a liking for sweet tastes even in an epidemic of obesity?

4   Why do we reproduce sexually when the cost is so great and some species do not do so?

5   Why do we tend not to be sexually attracted to close relatives?

6   Why does evolutionary psychology stir such passion, for and against?

7   Can there really be a 'gene for' adultery or religious worship?

8   Why does natural selection not eliminate such apparently harmful features as depression?

Jealousy appears to have existed at all times and places. Is this evidence for a specially evolved brain process that underlies the characteristic?

Source: **Victoria and Albert Museum/Bridgeman Art Library**

Introduction

Consider how you got to where you are today. Your parents' initial contribution was a single fertilized cell, which was the start of you. Each parent contributed genes to this cell. Those genes were the product of a process of evolution spanning back over millions of years. Within the environment of early human evolution, some ancestor genes were obviously successful in that you are here today. The nervous system that you possess and the behaviour that you show are the outcome of this evolutionary process.

So, genes, environment and evolution are closely related and can best be considered together. To do this, the chapter will need to call upon the four types of explanation introduced in the last chapter: causal, developmental/ learning, evolutionary and functional. Given that our primary interest is in brains and behaviour, this topic will, of course, never be far from the discussion. We will see how genes and environment act to influence the form that brains take and, thereby, we can understand better how brains control behaviour.

Human evolution has not always been a smooth ride. Sexual reproduction brings many problems (e.g. jealousy, abandonment) and these also need to be understood in the context of genes, environment and evolution.

Figure 2.1 shows some means by which behaviour can contribute to passing on genes. Aggression, fear, feeding, drinking and temperature regulation maintain the integrity, stability and survival of the body, so that the animal (human or other) is around to pass on genes. Feeding, drinking and temperature regulation are rather obviously associated with the homeostasis of the body (Chapter 1, 'Introduction'). Sexual behaviour contributes to the continuation of genes by means of reproduction. Offspring share genes with parents and so caring for young helps to ensure that the offspring reach maturity and are themselves able to breed, and so on. The diagram should not be interpreted as if the individual *wants* its genes to be passed on to future generations or consciously strives to do so. It is simply that the genes of an animal (human or other) can be passed on only if the animal engages in a range of such behaviours, each finely tuned to conditions inside and outside the body.

All members of a given species are genetically similar but are, of course, not identical. A 'lion is a lion' and has 'lion genes' but within the species there are genetic differences. That is to say, a particular gene comes in different varieties or 'variants' when comparing individuals. Some variants are more successful than others. Those variants of genes that coded for successful strategies were perpetuated and their products represent successful animals that are here today (e.g. you and me!). Those that coded for less successful strategies tended to find themselves more often in such places as predators' stomachs. In this way, there is *selection* for those variants of genes that code best for their own transmission. In other words, evolution is said to occur through the process termed **natural selection** (Darwin, 1874/1974).

The next section looks in more detail at the principles of evolution and natural selection.

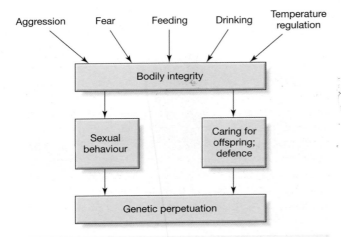

Figure 2.1 Means by which behaviour can increase the chances of genetic perpetuation.

Section summary

1 We can understand a range of behaviours in terms of their contribution to passing on genes.

2 Some behaviours contribute to passing on genes by helping to maintain the stability and integrity of the body (e.g. temperature regulation), whereas sexual behaviour contributes through reproduction.

3 Evolution is based upon 'natural selection' for variants of genes that code best for their own perpetuation.

Test your knowledge

(Answer on page 45)

2.1 Which of the following is/are involved directly with physiological homeostasis? (i) Feeding, (ii) drinking, (iii) temperature regulation, (iv) aggression, (v) sexual behaviour.

Principles of evolution

This section further develops the basis of the evolutionary and functional types of explanation.

Functional explanation, fitness and natural selection

In the present context, 'function' is used (in the ethological sense) in terms of reproductive success. The term **fitness** refers to the potential of an animal to reproduce successfully. Fitness is a measure of the animal's ability to pass on its genes, in terms of the number of viable reproducing offspring that arise. Thus, types of behaviour that increase fitness are favoured in the process of evolution by natural selection. (This sense of fitness should not be confused with its use to refer simply to bodily health.)

Closely related to the functional level of explanation is the notion of **adaptation** (Chapter 1). A physical feature or behaviour is said to be *adapted to* an environment in that it has been tested for its suitability to that environment. Those individuals that provide the best fit survive and pass on genes. However, there are some complications to this account (Buss *et al.*, 1998; Gould and Vrba, 1982), as follows.

A trait ('characteristic') that evolved by means of natural selection might no longer serve a useful function in the present environment. A good example of this is our excessive liking for sweet substances, which is associated with contemporary obesity. It is assumed that, in an early environment, our ancestors were more physically active and an attraction to rare ripe fruits would have been of enormous adaptive value. They provide energy in an environment where the supply of food is uncertain. However, we now have a relatively inactive lifestyle and an abundance of refined sweet items alongside the supermarket checkout, and so the same characteristic leads us into dangerous temptation.

Also, something might now be observed to serve a useful function but it evolved in the service of some different function. Noses and ears did not evolve because of their advantage as mechanical supports to those who wear spectacles! A capacity to read and write is doubtless advantageous in our society and there are identifiable brain mechanisms that underlie it. However, seen in evolutionary time, a written language and reading emerged recently. Reading and writing attach themselves to brain mechanisms that evolved much earlier than the appearance of written language. The combination of reading/writing and its biological bases has not had time yet to be tested by natural selection.

Of course, we do not have access to the environment of an animal's ancestors. Life on earth has been around for a very long time! However, psychologists have some insight based on extrapolation from the present (Tooby and Cosmides, 1990). They can be certain that (except in, say, the depths of the ocean) the environment was illuminated in an approximately 24 hour cycle of light–dark. They know about the magnitude of gravity that birds had to overcome in flying and the saltiness of seawater. Our species was probably subject to parasites. Psychologists can try to interpret the pressures for survival of present species' ancestors in terms of what they know about constant features of the environment and then speculate about different and past environments.

What can we expect adaptation to achieve? Suppose that an animal detects a predator and, predictably, responds by fleeing rather than carrying on with what it was already doing. It gets ambushed by an unseen fellow 'gang-member' predator and is then eaten by both predators. This might not seem beneficial to the fleeing animal's reproductive success! Natural selection cannot arrive at the perfect solution. It cannot possibly account for *every* instance of behaviour but can merely favour certain ranges of option over others (Tooby and Cosmides, 1990). Of course, animals cannot possibly inherit genes that tell them what to do under *every different circumstance encountered*. Rather, genes help to organize nervous systems that have certain general tendencies. Scientists assume that, in the ancestral history of the animal just described, a nervous system that played a role in the reaction of fleeing was of *overall advantage*, compared,

say, with carrying on regardless. The strategy worked more often than it failed.

A principle of ethology (the study of the behaviour of animals under natural conditions) is that no behaviour can bring pure gain. There is a mixture of costs and benefits involved in anything that an animal does, as is argued next.

Costs and benefits

The general principle can be well illustrated by the following example. When a jungle fowl is incubating eggs, it loses weight by staying on its nest and not eating (Hogan, 1980). How could this increase its fitness? Suppose that the mother leaves the eggs to obtain food. This increases the chances of the eggs cooling or being eaten by predators. Thus, in terms of the chances of passing on genes, there is a potential **cost** attached to leaving the eggs. There is also a potential **benefit** of doing so, i.e. to gain food and hence replenish reserves and strengthen the body. However, it appears that over evolutionary history, the actual cost of leaving the eggs has outweighed the benefit, and so there is a *net advantage* in staying. Investigators assume that the ancestors of jungle fowl were confronted with the problem of predation and cooling of eggs. Genes that coded for staying were placed at an advantage. However, rather as with fleeing and getting captured, evolution cannot guarantee that sitting on eggs will work in every instance. Both the sitting bird and its eggs may get eaten at the same time. It is merely that a strategy of staying has, over countless generations, been more successful than not, relative to the alternative of regularly leaving the nest. The example illustrates a number of issues associated with relating causation and function, as follows:

1 In terms of the homeostasis of her body, it is not to the female's *individual* bodily advantage to stay on the eggs. Individual survival of her body might be best served by

This fowl lets its weight fall as it incubates eggs. What are the costs and benefits associated with this behaviour?

Source: courtesy of Professor Jerry Hogan.

leaving them, to obtain food. However, the chances of passing on her genes are increased by incubation. She might have several eggs, each containing copies of her genes.

2   We should not suppose that the jungle fowl has knowledge in terms of function, i.e. she has no conscious intention to pass on genes (or even unconscious intention!). She just acts in such a way that this is achieved. Among her ancestors, jungle fowl that behaved in this way have been successful and their descendants are around today. Their genes have been favoured by natural selection. A gene coding for 'not incubating' has tended to perish.

3   Related to 2, in asking *how* behaviour is organized, we should not confuse causal and functional explanations. Claims that the bird acts this way because she *needs* to reproduce are misleading and can lead to the implicit assumption that she has conscious intentions. Birds do not read Darwin!

On a causal level, in the brain there is an inhibitory link from incubation to feeding. Natural selection will favour such a mechanism for restraining feeding.

4   It appears that natural selection acts on *individuals* via their genes rather than species as a whole, i.e. it acts to the relative advantage or disadvantage of passing on the genes of individuals within a given population. In this sense, the whole process is sometimes described as 'selfish', as in the term **selfish gene** (Dawkins, 1976).

Having described principles of function and evolution, in the next section we focus on the processes that control behaviour, involving the causal and developmental/learning types of explanation. In doing so, we look for links with functional and evolutionary considerations.

Section summary

1   Any behaviour has both costs and benefits.

2   Behaviour for which the benefits on average outweigh the costs is favoured. Genes that play a role in the production of behaviour with a net benefit are favoured by natural selection.

3   Natural selection acts in the interests of survival of the genes of individuals. Bodily survival is favoured since this serves the passing on of genes.

4   Animals (except, in some cases, humans) do not have conscious intentions to promote genetic survival.

2.2   Complete the missing word in the following: 'Natural selection favours solutions where the _____ outweigh the costs'.

2.3   Which of the following human capacities is assumed to have evolved by being tested in natural selection? (i) Hearing, (ii) reading, (iii) writing.

Processes controlling behaviour

Introduction

This section looks at some examples of the processes that underlie the control of behaviour. In this context, it will show how links can be made between (i) explanations of the causal kind and (ii) those of the developmental/learning, evolutionary and functional kinds. The discussion will exemplify where our understanding of brain mechanisms in causal terms can be enriched by a consideration of these other types of explanation.

Reflexes

A **reflex** forms the basis of the relatively straightforward and automatic **reaction** (or 'response') that is triggered by certain stimuli. Each reflex is found in all members of the species, unless there is malfunction. For example, every dog salivates to the presence of meat in its mouth. We automatically move a limb away from a damagingly hot object. We close our eyes when an object comes rapidly towards us. As a result of how the nervous system is constructed, reflexes just happen when an appropriate stimulus is presented. We do not need to think about producing them. The genes of an animal help to determine a nervous system that is equipped with a number of fitness-enhancing reflexes.

From functional and evolutionary perspectives, reflexes provide ready-made 'built-in' answers to solve common problems that have presented themselves throughout the evolution of the species. They are an economical means of operating. For example, all animals need to have a reflex that reacts rapidly to damaging stimuli, such as sharp objects touching the skin. We humans cannot afford to engage our sophisticated but very slow conscious processing with finding creative and original solutions to such a problem.

This would not be cost-effective. By contrast, other problems that are presented to us cannot be solved on the basis of 'ready-made' solutions and we need to engage our conscious processing in finding a solution.

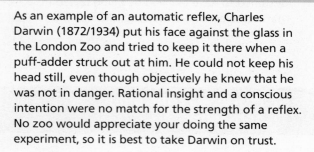

As an example of an automatic reflex, Charles Darwin (1872/1934) put his face against the glass in the London Zoo and tried to keep it there when a puff-adder struck out at him. He could not keep his head still, even though objectively he knew that he was not in danger. Rational insight and a conscious intention were no match for the strength of a reflex. No zoo would appreciate your doing the same experiment, so it is best to take Darwin on trust.

Reflexes are basically common to all members of a species. However, when comparing different animals within a species, reflexes are not entirely the same or triggered by exactly the same stimuli. Their form can vary to some limited extent with various factors. For example, all dogs have a reflex that triggers salivation to food in the mouth in much the same way. However, the range of stimuli that triggers salivation in an individual dog depends partly upon its learning experiences. Particular stimuli that have been associated with food (e.g. the sound of a can-opener) can act as a trigger for a particular dog. There is a fixed prescription, 'salivate to food', but there is flexibility for individual experience (based upon food type and context) to fill in the details of the trigger stimuli.

Actions

Whereas a reflex is triggered by external stimuli, what psychologists term an **action** is not tied so closely to a triggering stimulus. In the case of humans, action that takes the form of **voluntary behaviour** is associated with the internal factor of having a conscious intention (Baars, 1997). For actions, although no obvious external trigger stimulus needs to be present, of course, action commonly follows changes in external events.

Whereas the reflex is relatively stereotyped, voluntary behaviour is highly flexible and open-ended. Voluntary behaviour can be exploited in a multitude of ways according to the varieties of individual experience. Our brains have evolved with a capacity for such flexibility and learning by experience. The functional advantage of voluntary behaviour is our ability to exploit it even under novel circumstances and thereby to find a creative solution to a problem. There is

no way that we could be equipped with a preformed system for reacting to every situation, as in a reflex.

Although we can construct a dichotomy 'reflexes *versus* voluntary', behaviour normally depends upon both processes acting in combination, as discussed in the next section. Furthermore, the same muscles that execute reflexes are controlled by the brain in performing voluntary behaviour. The differences between these controls can be seen to match different functional considerations.

Complementary roles

To illustrate the point, consider the response to tissue damage, as in a burn. There is both (i) a reflex organized at the spinal cord, i.e. the limb is moved from the heat, and (ii) the conscious sensation of pain, which teaches us to be more careful in the future (Melzack and Wall, 1996).

Reflexes and voluntary behaviour serve different and complementary roles. For example, tissue damage that arises externally triggers an immediate reflexive reaction. Damage that arises internally triggers something rather different. Suppose that an animal damages its leg muscle. It behaves so as to favour the leg involved by, say, putting more weight on the intact ones. Alternatively, or in addition, the animal might be able to rest and thereby speed recovery. The example of tissue damage illustrates the functional value of joint control by (a) a reflex that is relatively simple and **hard-wired** into the nervous system ('ready-made') and (b) a more complex action system that is flexible and can find novel solutions.

Concerning withdrawal reflexes, all humans act in a similar way, since the pathway within the nervous system is the same for us all. By contrast, the system involving the conscious sensation of pain has flexibility and enables creative solutions to be found. This route is relatively slow. For such situations as treading on sharp objects, information would reach conscious awareness only after any local reflex action had already been initiated.

Tissue damage might require widely different solutions depending upon circumstances, and it would be impossible to specify all of these in advance. Suppose that a local withdrawal reflex fails, e.g. a thorn gets stuck in a foot. Other solutions might then be possible, e.g. to extract the thorn with the teeth. A sophisticated social animal, such as a human, can recruit the help of others. We learn how to solve such problems and this requires the emotional state of 'pain' and actions that are followed by its reduction. Pain serves as the arbiter ('judge') of how effective an action is. If behaviour reduces pain, the animal is encouraged to repeat this, an example of a developmental/learning type of explanation. For example, imagine yourself trying to lower the intensity of a back pain. You adopt various positions, determined by pain and its reduction. You learn strategies for coping.

Effects of behaviour

As part of a developmental/learning explanation, we can ask, how have the consequences of past behaviour influenced present behaviour, e.g. through this process of learning? The adaptive value of learning is that it gives flexibility to behaviour: an animal alters its behaviour according to its past experience.

There can be various consequences of behaviour. One possibility is **reinforcement**: the situation where behaviour is *more likely* to be repeated in the future as a result of its consequences on past occasions (Skinner, 1966). This principle applies to a whole range of different species.

In humans and based on subjective experience, behaviour is said to have **hedonic** consequences. This means that behaviour produces pleasure or pain (Cabanac, 1992). We could reasonably argue that at least some non-human species also experience this. Some behavioural choices seem to be made on the basis of trying to maximize their positive consequences and minimize their negative. So, how might such a subjective experience relate to the activity of the nervous system? If identity theory (Chapter 1) is correct, subjective pleasure and pain are features ('an alternative description') of the activity of certain brain regions.

The developmental/learning and functional types of explanation can be related. Thus, it is no coincidence that behaviours that are necessary for survival and passing on genes, such as feeding or mating, have consequences that encourage the animal to repeat them. An animal learns how to gain access to food and mates. If this were not so, the duration of advanced life on earth would have been rather short! However, the earlier caution can usefully be repeated in this context: in our present environment, not all immediate consequences described as positive serve fitness in any obvious way. Think again of the example of reinforcement associated with excessive sugar intake.

Considerable insight into one aspect of causation has been gained by studying motivation and homeostasis, described next.

Motivation

An internal process that gives direction and strength to behaviour is described by the term **motivation**. Motivation directs attention and behaviour to appropriate events in the environment and is at the basis of the selection of actions.

Link with homeostasis

Let us consider feeding, drinking and some other behaviour. In terms of the four types of explanation, by applying the principle of motivation, homeostasis and negative feedback (Chapter 1) we can gain understanding of these behaviours. Consider the homeostasis of body temperature. When body temperature rises, actions arise, such as switching on a fan or moving to the shade. These depend upon the automatic monitoring of body temperature and thereby the production of the appropriate motivation. The behaviour triggered in this way is also termed **regulatory behaviour** (or 'homeostatic' behaviour) since it regulates the internal environment.

This kind of behaviour can be understood in terms of its different aspects, such as:

- In causal terms, the activity of particular neurons controls this behaviour, which exhibits negative feedback.

- In developmental/learning terms, the immediate consequences of behaviour strengthen the tendency to repeat the behaviour ('reinforcement').

- In evolutionary terms, such behaviour can be seen across mammalian species.

- In functional terms, behaviour puts the body in an optimal condition and thereby contributes to fitness.

In relating causal, functional, developmental/learning and evolutionary explanations, behaviour 'makes sense'. Reflecting this, a water-deprived rat can be trained to perform a task to earn water; it is *motivated* to do so. For example, it can be taught to run through a maze or to press a lever in a Skinner box for reward (Figure 2.2).

Link with sexual behaviour

Not all motivation and behaviour is regulatory. For example, homeostasis does not lie at the basis of sexual motivation and behaviour, though these also depend on internal and external factors and exhibit a form of negative feedback. That is, after a while, sexual activity induces satiety, thereby lowering motivation and the tendency to engage in this activity. Sexual behaviour is not associated with the maintenance of optimal bodily conditions but, of course, it makes sense in terms of causation and function. This draws attention to different means by which behaviour contributes to fitness (Figure 2.1). On a causal level, such things as sex hormones and perception of a mate contribute to triggering sexual motivation and behaviour. Behaviour's immediate consequences are described as positively reinforcing (and in

Figure 2.2 Skinner box.

our case, pleasurable). That is, in terms of a developmental/learning explanation, the animal is encouraged to repeat the behaviour.

Understanding 'abnormal' behaviour

General principles

Behaviour sometimes seems self-defeating and contrary to the best interests of the individual showing it. In this sense, the behaviour is abnormal, though it might well not be abnormal in the sense of being uncommon in a population – just try glancing at the behaviour exhibited in a pub, burger bar or supermarket. In one meaning of the term, behaviour fails to make sense functionally. However, this should not cause us to abandon the functional type of explanation for such cases; rather, we can use it for intelligent speculation. We can ask how the behaviour is produced by brain processes that were once functionally matched well to their environment and indeed might still be so with a change of environment.

For example, evolution has not yet tracked the rapid environmental change of large amounts of refined sugar becoming available in our foods. This was a recent change in culture. Our excessive intake of fats tells a similar story. Given very many years of exposure to this environment, psychologists of the future might find that people with only a weak liking for either sugar or hamburgers are favoured.

Consider the intravenous self-injection of psychoactive drugs by humans. Of course, intravenous injection was not around to influence our early evolution – syringes and refined forms of drug did not exist. Drug-taking exploits mechanisms (tapping into positive reinforcement and pleasure systems) that evolved in a very different context from the one in which contemporary drug-taking behaviour is shown (Nesse and Berridge, 1997).

A central 'faith' of biological psychology is that *any* behaviour is determined by external and internal factors acting in interaction with the nervous system. Although some behaviour is difficult to interpret, scientists still ask: 'What nervous system events trigger it and what (if anything) is achieved as its immediate consequence?' (Würbel *et al.*, 1998).

Stereotypies and self-destructive behaviour

As another example of abnormality, animals in zoos or intensive agriculture often perform apparently pointless behaviour, such as rituals of chewing or pacing, termed **stereotypy**, plural stereotypies (and, yes, just in case you are wondering, that is the correct spelling, rather than 'stereotypes') or self-mutilation. Such behaviour is abnormal in not fitting an adaptive interpretation but not in the sense of being 'different from the norm', since, under intensive housing, most animals might exhibit it (Mason, 1991). Some human behaviour seems irrational and compulsive in a

similar way to that of domestic animals. Under stress, humans occasionally engage in self-mutilation, finger-chewing or hair-pulling. In severe mental retardation, there is an increased tendency to stereotypies (e.g. body-rocking) (Emerson and Howard, 1992).

The environment in which such behaviour of domestic animals is exhibited is very different from that in which the animals' ancestors evolved. Therefore, it would seem inappropriate to ask what advantage stereotypies have conferred in evolution. Evolution can only favour broad categories of behaviour as being those that on average were beneficial in the natural environment. It cannot account for behaviour shown in abnormal modern environments. Nonetheless, we might still ask a related question – how can processes that generate adaptive behaviour in a natural environment also generate aberrant behaviour in an abnormal environment? This is a similar question to that concerning human drug-taking.

In trying to understand the brain processes that trigger stereotypies, we can be guided by the observation that repetitive ('rhythmic') patterns are an important feature of some adaptive behaviour. Chewing, grooming and running exemplify this. As a cause of stereotypies, a type of such rhythm could become unmasked and uninhibited in an environment that offers no opportunity to exhibit flexible behaviour (Dantzer, 1986).

It remains an open question as to what is the immediate consequence of stereotypies. Stereotypies might provide, say, stimulation in a boring environment or lower the level of stress. However, it is possible that they have no beneficial consequence. It appears that there is a time-filling process where inactivity is not an option. In terms of a developmental/learning explanation, the fact that they increase in frequency over time suggests some kind of reinforcement process (Mason, 1991).

Whether describable in rational terms concerning immediate consequences (e.g. drinking following deprivation) or seemingly irrational (e.g. self-mutilation), behaviour reflects the activity of nervous system processes. So, how did we get the kind of nervous system the properties of which are described in this section? To start to answer this, the next section looks more closely at the role of genes.

Section summary

1 Reflexes provide rapid solutions. For a given species, reflexes are relatively stereotyped, similar in all individuals.

2 Action, as exemplified by voluntary behaviour, is characterized by its flexibility and variability between individuals.

3 Behaviour is influenced by the consequences of past behaviour, e.g. via reinforcement.

4 Abnormal behaviour can sometimes still make functional sense in terms of being a manifestation of processes that were adaptive under earlier conditions.

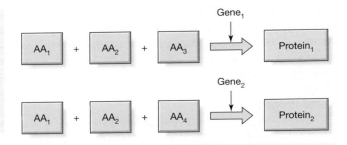

Figure 2.3 Two proteins formed from two different combinations of amino acids under the control of two genes. AA = amino acid. These show just a small sample of the many amino acids and combinations that are possible.

Genes, replication and reproduction

This section describes the gene, both as the unit of inheritance of information from one generation to another and as a source of information that plays a role in determining the form of the body throughout life. The section links genes and evolution.

Body structure

How does body structure, including the nervous system, form? The body is constructed in large part from proteins (Chapter 1), which are found in thousands of varieties within humans. They are analogous to the bricks, wood and mortar of a building. However, in addition to fixed structure, certain proteins serve as messengers and affect reactions. Some are **enzymes,** which speed up or slow down the body's chemical reactions. Of course, not all the body consists of proteins. In fact, most of it is water (Figure 1.2). However, proteins form an important part of the structures that hold everything together.

Proteins are made from substances termed amino acids. See Figure 2.3. A combination of different amino acids joining together in a particular form yields a particular protein. Genes are responsible for the construction of proteins. So, in coding for the construction of proteins from amino acids, genes have a role in the formation of structures.

Putting together the right combination of amino acids to produce the right protein at the right place and time is crucial to biological success. Who 'says' what is right? In effect, natural selection does and the 'right combination' means a viable one by the criterion of fitness.

The cells of the body, whether neurons or not, have features in common. Each has a **nucleus.** The nucleus contains the genetic material of the cell. The collection of all the genes within an individual constitutes its **genotype.** Each cell contains an identical set of such genes. The genotype represents a source of information, which, together with the environment, determines the current form of an organism. Genotype is determined at fertilization by the combination of genes that are contributed by the parents and it remains constant throughout life.

In terms of both physiology and behaviour, the form that appears as a result of the genotype interacting with the environment is termed the **phenotype.** Your phenotype is 'the you' sitting reading this book right now. Features of the phenotype change as a result of growth and experience. The genotype represents a source of information, a kind of potential for development into a number of different phenotypes. The end product depends also upon the environment experienced along the way.

In the process of development, the genes that you inherited interact with their immediate environment in the body and, if all goes well, you end up with a correctly functioning nervous system. This interaction of genes and their environment is a complex dynamic process. The mature nervous system does not exist in a miniature form at the start of life just waiting to expand. This and the next sections start to unravel this interaction.

Genes and evolution

The theory of evolution states that, over millions of years, complex species evolved from simpler precursor animals as a result of natural selection. How does this happen? First consider that, for a given species, the potential number of offspring that can be produced is usually greater than the number that can survive. The limitation on survival is due to such things as predation and competition for resources, such as food and shelter. As a result of their genes, among other things, some individuals will be better equipped than others in this struggle.

How is it that, within a species, individuals differ genetically? As will be explained in a moment, in coming together at fertilization new *combinations* of different variants of genes are produced and then, in effect, tested in the environment. Some combinations are more successful than others (they are '*selected for*') and some will be unsuccessful. A successful combination will, by definition, tend to reproduce at a relatively high rate. It will increase in numbers in the population. Less successful combinations will decline in numbers or even become extinct. That is, *evolution* will occur. For example, a combination might code for extra height so that taller trees can be exploited for food or a nervous system having a faster than normal capacity to learn. This particular offspring will have an advantage over others.

Also, occasionally, in producing either an egg or a sperm, a **mutation** occurs: the genes contributed to reproduction by one partner are changed slightly with respect to the parent genes. The altered phenotype that results from this change in genotype is termed a 'mutant'. Most mutant phenotypes are either of no increased benefit relative to their precursors or are less viable. However, suppose that a mutant version of a gene carries information that improves the offspring's chances relative to the precursor. This particular offspring will have an advantage over others, who do not share the mutation. The mutant form will tend to be copied in future generations and increase in frequency. The argument is that, over long time periods, the processes of (i) combination and (ii) mutation have contributed to the evolution of forms from the simple to the complex.

Now we need to look more closely at the gene.

Replication and reproduction

Consider the two roles that are served by genes:

1 We first come into being via genes inherited from our parents and we transmit genes to the next generation.

2 Within the individual, genes are responsible for protein synthesis.

This section looks at these interdependent processes. The biological inheritance of information by offspring from their parents is by means of genes that are located within sperm cells in the male and egg cells in the female. These two types of cell, which come together at fertilization, are collectively termed **gametes**.

Within each cell, whether gamete or not, genes are located in structures called **chromosomes**. These are shown as paired coloured lines in Figure 2.4. With the exception of gametes, the nucleus of a human cell contains 46 chromosomes. These 46 chromosomes come in two sets of pairs, i.e. 23 pairs. For simplification, only three such pairs are shown in each of the non-gamete cells of Figure 2.4. As represented in Figure 2.4, within each such cell, 22 pairs are termed matching or homologous chromosomes, meaning that the genetic material held by one chromosome of a pair corresponds to that held by the other (the 23rd combination will be described later).

In the process of forming gametes in the body, a division of chromosomes occurs such that each gamete contains only 23 *unmatched* chromosomes, shown in Figure 2.4 as three unpaired chromosomes. Note that the division of chromosomes is not random. One of each pair is represented within each gamete.

At fertilization, two sets of 23 chromosomes, one from the mother and one from the father, join, to give 46 chromosomes, a process termed **reproduction**. The coming together of individual chromosomes at reproduction is not haphazard (Figure 2.4). Rather, each one finds its match such that chromosome number 1 from the mother finds number 1 from the father, etc. In other words, chromosomes are divided at the formation of the gametes but then, at reproduction, they form new combinations with those from another individual.

Consider that an egg has been fertilized to produce a cell with 46 chromosomes, termed a 'zygote'. That we are now somewhat larger is due to the process termed **replication**. The initial cell, the zygote, divides into two and each then grows. These two then divide to give four cells and so on, until we are fully developed. Each time a cell divides, the genetic material in its nucleus is copied, so that both cells have the same genetic information as in the cell from which they were formed. With the exception of gametes (and some other cells that need not concern us), no matter what the role served by the cell is, it will contain a full copy of the original genetic material held in 23 pairs of chromosomes. In contrast to reproduction, replication is intrinsic to a given animal and the genetic material of each cell is an exact replica of that of the precursor cell.

Reproduction is a process involving two individuals, whereby a sperm and an egg come together to produce a new individual. Therefore, the genetic material of the new cell is *not an exact replica* of either that of the mother or the father. Bringing together cells from mother and father yields a *novel combination* of genes. Of course, the novelty is somewhat relative since the offspring often bear a close resemblance to one or other parent and yet they are not identical. Following the formation of the novel combination of genes in a new cell and then a long process of replication, we get the 'you or me' of the present.

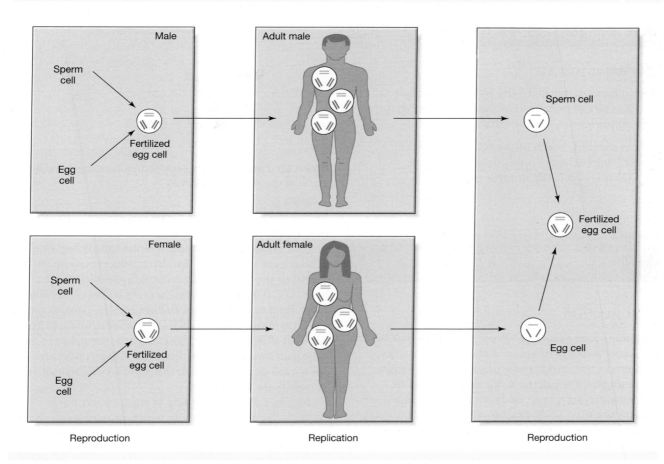

Figure 2.4 Replication and reproduction. Replication of the fertilized egg cell gives the adult human male and female. Reproduction is a coming together of gametes, a sperm cell and an egg cell. For simplification, each cell is shown with only 3 of the 23 chromosomes, or pairs of chromosomes.

Source: after Toates (1990, Fig. 5.12, p. 209).

Role of genes

From conception onwards, genes interact with their immediate physical environment in playing a role in development. At first this is the environment of the zygote in the womb. Subsequently, development is determined by the multicellular new organism interacting with its environment in the womb. After birth, the whole growing animal interacts with both the physical and social environments. Together with the environment, genes influence body structure and function, e.g. height, hair colour and the structure of the nervous system.

We now look more closely at the process of inheritance.

Section summary

1 Natural selection plays a role in the evolution of complex life forms from simpler precursor animals.

2 Sexual reproduction means that new combinations of genes arise.

3 New genetic material is tested in the environment.

4 Some combinations of genes are advantageous relative to others and will tend to increase in frequency in future generations. They will be 'selected for'.

5 In producing either a sperm or egg cell, mutations sometimes occur.

6 Genes are located in the nucleus of cells, including neurons.

7 Chromosomes in the nucleus are the physical base of genes.

8 The synthesis of protein structures is triggered by genes.

9 At fertilization, genes from the mother and father come together to give, in humans, a new cell containing 23 pairs of chromosomes.

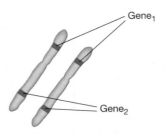

Test your knowledge

(Answers on page 45)

2.6 In humans, which of the following contain
     23 pairs of matched chromosomes? (i) Zygote,
     (ii) sperm cell, (iii) unfertilized egg cell.

2.7 In humans, which of the following contain
     23 unmatched chromosomes? (i) Zygote,
     (ii) sperm cell, (iii) unfertilized egg cell.

Figure 2.5 Two gene pairs each occupying corresponding places on paired chromosomes.

The process of inheritance

Introduction

Offspring acquire genes from their parents. We now need to look more closely at this process and thereby we will see some important implications for psychology. As will be discussed later, the pattern of inheritance of certain characteristics such as eye and hair colour in humans as well as some disorders (including some behavioural ones) can be followed from generation to generation and a picture of inheritance obtained.

Basics of genetics

Although investigators speak of *a* gene as the unit of inheritance of a characteristic (e.g. eye colour), genes exist in pairs, mainly located on paired chromosomes (Figure 2.5). As you saw, one of each pair of chromosomes (and its associated genes) is derived from the father and one from the mother. To be exact, a gene *pair* plays a role in determining a trait such as eye colour.

A gene for a characteristic such as eye colour is located at a specific region of a chromosome termed the locus (plural, loci) for that gene. The locus of a given gene exists in the same place for the two halves of a pair of chromosomes (Figure 2.5). At fertilization, the individual receives one of each of the pair of chromosomes from each parent (Figure 2.4). In the simplest examples, for a given phenotypic characteristic, there is just one pair of genes that need to be considered in its determination.

With caution, we may speak of a gene 'for' some phenotypic characteristic such as eye colour, meaning that (1) a particular gene at a particular locus on the chromosome is responsible and (2) this gene would normally exist twice, once on each chromosome. However, a gene 'for' a characteristic, at a particular locus, does not necessarily come in one standard

form. Rather, there can be different variants of a particular gene at a given locus (Figure 2.6).

Each variant of a given gene is termed an **allele** of that gene. For example, a gene that determines eye colour can be identified at a particular locus but different alleles of the gene exist. What colour the eye actually becomes (e.g. blue or grey) depends on the alleles. In Figure 2.6(a), $Gene_1$ comes in the form of two identical alleles, a_1. However, for $Gene_2$, two different alleles, a_2 and a_2', can exist at the two halves of the gene pair. Now imagine gametes from a given individual, as shown in Figure 2.6(b). Note that there are different alleles present in the two gametes.

Figures 2.4 and 2.5 can help to answer a very basic question. Surely few questions, whether described as 'evolutionary and functional' or not, could be more basic than this one – why bother with sex? Sexual reproduction is costly. Wouldn't it be simpler, even if (one imagines!) less

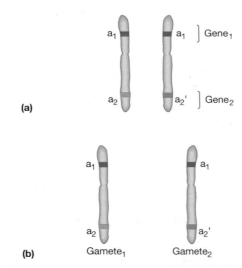

Figure 2.6 Schematic sketch of genes and alleles. (a) For $Gene_1$ the same allele a_1 occurs twice, whereas for $Gene_2$ different alleles, a_2 and a_2' exist. (b) Two gametes from the same individual shown to contain two different alleles of $Gene_2$.

pleasurable, to reproduce by replication? Well, it is doubtless too far down the evolutionary route of sexual reproduction to imagine us now switching to asexual reproduction. But how was it that evolution went down the sexual route at a very early stage? Sexual reproduction might be more fun but we also need to explain its appearance in functional and evolutionary terms. In principle, we might have evolved to reproduce simply by a process of replication. Some organisms do just this. Think what is avoided by reproducing without the help of sexual behaviour: problems of broken hearts, betrayal, jealousy, sexually transmitted diseases and injury suffered during fights over mates, etc. The list is a long and tragic one indeed.

Sexual reproduction offers a rich possibility for testing different solutions since different alleles from male and female are brought together to yield *novel combinations*. Also, the alleles provided by each sex show a rich variety. Consider just the alleles that make up Gene$_2$ in Figure 2.6. As shown in part (b), the allele that occupies this location can, in one gamete, take this form of a$_2$ and, in another gamete from the same individual, some other form, a$_2$'. By producing more than one form of allele, sexual reproduction in effect enables you to play safe ('hedge your bets'). Even if a$_2$ is not particularly successful when in combination with genetic material from the opposite sex, the slightly different a$_2$' might prove more successful.

Suppose that the environment changes. Given the enormous range of outcomes regarding alleles coming together at reproduction, it is possible that one of the combinations is put at an advantage in a new environment. To take the simplest example, suppose that suddenly, for a strange reason, blue eyes might become particularly favoured over all others in the new environment. We might speculate that opposite sex partners start to find them irresistible. The alleles coding for this colour would correspondingly be favoured relative to alleles coding for a different colour.

The advantage of testing novel combinations of alleles appears to provide a functional explanation for the universality of the avoidance of inbreeding, including a taboo against incest in human societies (Thornhill, 1991). Incestuous reproduction involves bringing genetically similar material together. This reduces the chances of novel combinations of alleles appearing. It also increases the chances of certain genetically determined disorders being transmitted (see Bateson, 1979), discussed shortly.

The biological basis of heredity

A complex molecule termed 'deoxyribonucleic acid' (DNA) constitutes the base of genetic information. As Figure 2.7 shows, different genes correspond to different segments of the DNA molecule. A single molecule of DNA contains thousands of genes. A molecule of DNA plus supporting protein constitutes a chromosome.

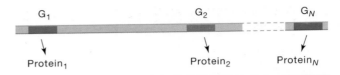

Figure 2.7 A section of a DNA molecule corresponding to three genes. Each triggers the construction of a particular protein. Not all the DNA molecule acts in this way.

Source: Hall and Halliday (1998, Fig. 3.2, p. 53).

In cell division, DNA replicates itself. A sperm or egg cell contains a copy of the DNA of a precursor cell. In such copying, occasionally the copied form of DNA is slightly different from the precursor form, i.e. a mutation.

How does DNA contribute to different characteristics? DNA codes for the synthesis of proteins. Proteins that form the basis of the cells of the nervous system are constructed at a time and in a form determined by particular genes at particular loci. Those that form other cells are constructed in a similar way. The genetic material is the same for each cell within a given individual. However, within a particular cell only a small subset of the genes is actually expressed in the form of protein synthesis. Thereby, the cell becomes, say, a part of the nervous system or a part of a kidney, as the case may be.

Sex-linked characteristics

So far, the chapter has described paired chromosomes and their alleles coming together at fertilization, without specifying which parent contributes which chromosome and thereby which allele. That is to say, it described inheritance of genes on the basis of a male and a female contributing with equal probability to any effect. Now we need to turn to a complication. It involves the 23rd of these chromosome pairs and means that, for some phenomena, we can no longer disregard the sex of the parent contributing the particular chromosome and alleles.

Considering humans, 2 of the 46 chromosomes are termed **sex chromosomes** because they are different between males and females. Also described as the '23rd pair' of chromosomes, females possess two X chromosomes and males one X chromosome and one Y chromosome. In spite of this difference from the other 22, the sex chromosomes appear in the gametes by a process of cell division just like the other 22. See Figure 2.8. Note that a daughter inherits two X chromosomes, one from each parent, whereas a son inherits an X chromosome from the mother and a Y chromosome from the father. In other words, the sex of children is determined by which chromosome they inherit from the father.

In the next section, we consider the role of genes in behaviour, as mediated by the nervous system.

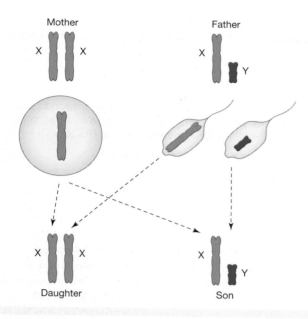

Figure 2.8 Inheritance of sex chromosomes.
Source: Plomin et al. (1997, Fig. 3.2, p. 20).

Section summary

1   Most genes come in pairs, one of each pair being found on each chromosome.

2   The site at which a gene is located is described as its locus.

3   A given gene can come in different forms termed alleles.

4   The biological basis of genes is deoxyribonucleic acid (DNA).

5   Some alleles are sex linked, associated with either the X or Y chromosome.

Test your knowledge

(Answers on page 45)

2.8   Complete the following: 'On a section of a DNA molecule a particular gene codes for a particular ____'

2.9   Who inherits two X chromosomes?

2.10 Who inherits one X and one Y chromosome?

Genes, brains and behaviour

By their effect on the synthesis of proteins, certain genes thereby play a role in the construction of the nervous system. In turn, nervous systems underlie behaviour, so there is a sequence of links (gene) → (nervous system) → (behaviour). This section considers the role of genes in constructing nervous systems and looks at how certain disorders of the brain can be linked to particular genes. In fact, since certain disorders give a particularly clear insight into the role of genes, we start with a consideration of them and then go on to consider some more complex gene effects.

Inherited disorders

There are some examples of human disorders that have behavioural manifestations and their chromosomal and genetic basis can be understood in terms of the principles just developed.

Phenylketonuria (PKU)

Phenylalanine is an 'essential amino acid', from which certain vital proteins are constructed. It is found in many foods. It is an essential component of our diet; otherwise these proteins cannot be constructed. In the 1930s, an abnormally large amount of phenylalanine was observed in the urine of some people with severe learning difficulties (Plomin *et al.*, 1997). Mental retardation associated with this condition is termed **phenylketonuria** (PKU). It appears that a failure to utilize phenylalanine results in its build-up in the body and causes damage to the brain.

The parents of PKU patients do not usually suffer from the condition, which might suggest that it arises from environmental factors. However, the pattern of inheritance reveals a genetic basis. See Figure 2.9. PKU can be traced to the influence of a particular allele (*p*). Note the possible combinations of alleles that can result in the offspring. On average, only 25% of the phenotypes develop PKU, i.e. those having the combination *pp*.

PKU can be described as a 'genetic condition', since the basic abnormality is 'solely due to a gene mutation' in a single gene (Plomin and Rutter, 1998, p. 1224). Although scientists do not need to look to the influence of the environment to understand how PKU arises, nonetheless the environment is important in coping with it. PKU can be managed successfully by environmental intervention, a qualification that needs to be made to any straightforward genetic determinism. The patient needs to avoid excessive phenylalanine in the diet.

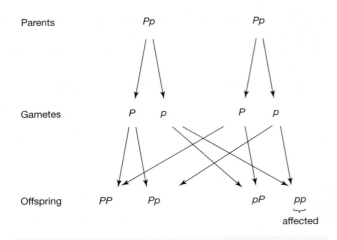

Parents   Pp   Pp

Gametes   P   p   P   p

Offspring   PP   Pp   pP   pp
                                     affected

Figure 2.9 Pattern of inheritance of phenylketonuria (PKU).

Source: Plomin *et al.* (1997, Fig. 2.5, p. 9).

Huntington's disease (HD)

Huntington's disease (or 'Huntington's chorea') also has a straightforward genetic basis. It is characterized by involuntary movements of the body, personality changes and forgetfulness (Plomin *et al.*, 1997). Normally it strikes in middle age, after the person might well have become a mother or father. Figure 2.10 shows its pattern of inheritance. Note that the combination *Hh* yields an affected individual but not the combination *hh*. Allele *H* is the problem and it dominates the influence of *h*.

HD is a good point at which to take stock of where we are with regard to genetic determination. Investigators can associate the disease or its absence with the forms that certain alleles take. According to their form, these alleles code for neural structures that either do, or do not, manifest HD.

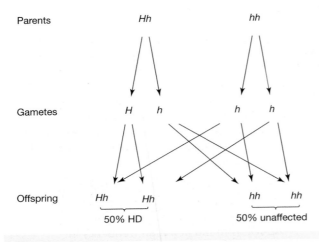

Parents   Hh   hh

Gametes   H   h   h   h

Offspring   Hh   Hh   hh   hh
             50% HD   50% unaffected

Figure 2.10 The inheritance of Huntington's disease (HD).

Source: Plomin *et al.* (1997, Fig. 2.4, p. 8).

The difference between individuals with or without the disorder can be traced to differences in the alleles at a particular locus. However, of course, the ultimate expression or not of the HD characteristics depends also upon all the other genes that code for normal neurons and other cells that underlie movement control. When focusing attention upon variation in the single gene, we can sometimes take for granted the role of these other genes.

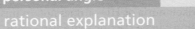

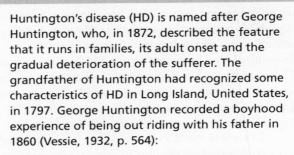

A personal angle
A rational explanation

Huntington's disease (HD) is named after George Huntington, who, in 1872, described the feature that it runs in families, its adult onset and the gradual deterioration of the sufferer. The grandfather of Huntington had recognized some characteristics of HD in Long Island, United States, in 1797. George Huntington recorded a boyhood experience of being out riding with his father in 1860 (Vessie, 1932, p. 564):

Driving with my father through a wooded road leading from East Hampton to Amagansett, we suddenly came upon two women, mother and daughter, both tall, thin, almost cadaverous, both twisting, bowing, grimacing. I stood in wonderment, almost in fear. What could it mean? My father paused to speak with them and we passed on.

Almost all sufferers from HD living on the United States East coast were descended from a small family group who emigrated to Boston Bay from Bures, Suffolk, in England in 1630.

In the 17th century, the abnormal movements of HD were commonly said to be triggered by demonic possession. Sufferers were lucky to escape execution by hanging for witchcraft, this usually being used against women. Clearly, the combination of a known genetic pedigree and a consequent dysfunction of parts of the brain is a radically different view. It gives a more accurate and humane account.

Down's syndrome

Down's syndrome consists of, among other things, short stature, a small round head and learning difficulties but often also an especially pleasant personality. Down's syndrome is caused by a chromosomal abnormality. Rather than inheriting two copies of one particular chromosome, the child inherits three copies. As a manifestation of the chromosomal abnormality, there are abnormalities in certain brain regions (Kleschevnikov *et al.*, 2004).

Complex characteristics

Introduction

To understand this section, recall the discussion of phenylketonuria and Huntington's disease, which are (a) in terms of their genetic basis, all-or-nothing phenomena and (b) linked to the effects of single genes. A person either suffers from phenylketonuria or HD or does not. In this regard, the population can be classified into two groups and family pedigrees can be worked out, both for individuals and most probable outcomes for populations. However, not all genetic influences are single-gene effects acting in this all-or-nothing way. The present section addresses these cases.

Characteristics such as height, weight and general cognitive ability have *quantitative dimensions* that we all exhibit to some degree. One cannot, of course, identify 'affected individuals' and compare them with normal individuals. People can be attributed a number and, if a variable such as height is plotted, it forms a bell-shaped distribution. In a similar way, cognitive abilities, as measured by, say, an IQ test, are something that we all possess to varying degrees and can be plotted on a graph (Plomin *et al.*, 1997).

Does this difference between, say, phenylketonuria and cognitive ability mean that genetic differences between individuals do not contribute towards differences in quantitative dimensions? No. The evidence suggests a role of a genetic factor here also. The genetic influence on a quantitative dimension such as general intelligence is mediated not by one, but by numerous, genes. In this way, a number of discrete components can, for a whole population, give rise to a smoothly varying effect.

Complex gene effects and behaviour

Although genetic determinants play a role in a number of psychiatric conditions (e.g. depression), genes represent only one contribution (Plomin and Rutter, 1998). Variables in the environment interact with genetic variables as determinants, as described by the developmental/learning type of explanation. In these cases, a particular combination of genes is more correctly seen as contributing a *certain probability* that a condition will appear, e.g. varying from highly likely, through some risk to not very likely. In other words, genes give a 'probabilistic bias' towards a condition appearing (more complex than a simple 0% versus 100%). Thus, combinations of genes can give a bias so that the probability of a disorder appearing varies almost smoothly, in a similar way to that in which it

varies as a function of the environment. A number of genes might contribute towards, say, chronic anxiety and their influence acts in combination with that of a smoothly varying environmental factor such as its stressfulness. The label 'genetic condition' would be inappropriate here but we should not ignore the genes' contribution.

For another example of this, the gene called *ApoE* is relevant to Alzheimer's disease (Plomin and Rutter, 1998), a form of cognitive decline (dementia). An allele of this gene, termed *ApoE4*, is found at a higher frequency in sufferers than in controls. Through the allele, one can identify people at increased risk of developing the disorder. This is a probabilistic, not deterministic, prediction; many people possessing the allele reach 80 years or more without developing Alzheimer's. The genetic relationship is found in some countries but not others. The allele might exert an effect such that the brain is more vulnerable to certain types of trauma under specific conditions.

There are still more possibilities of gene–environment interaction. A gene might bias a person to seek a certain environment and that environment might then exert a particular effect. For example, a gene might bias towards seeking novel, high-risk environments, which could then affect vulnerability to, say, drug-taking. Again, this illustrates why simple dichotomies – 'is it genes or environment?' – are misleading, a topic addressed in more detail in the next section.

Section summary

1 Certain conditions, e.g. Huntington's disease, are associated with a particular allele.

2 Characteristics that vary on a quantitative dimension are determined in part by multiple genes.

Test your knowledge

(Answers on page 45)

2.11 Complete the missing word here: 'Huntington's disease is associated with the combination *Hh* rather than *hh*. The letters *H* and *h* refer to different _____'.

2.12 Complete the two missing words in the following: 'The _____ called *ApoE* is relevant to Alzheimer's disease. An _____ of this gene, *ApoE4*, is found at a high frequency in sufferers'.

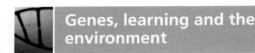

Genes, learning and the environment

Introduction

The language that we commonly employ can invite misunderstanding of genes and environment. Alas, discussions are commonly premised on misleading questions of the kind: 'Is it genes *or* environment?' or 'Is aggression *all* in the genes?' Of course, in reality, without genes, we would have no body. Similarly, without an environment, we could not exist. The nervous system depends upon genes and environment, and behaviour depends upon the nervous system in interaction with an environment (Figure 2.11). By feedback, the environment, in a broad sense, acts at each level in the production of behaviour, e.g. in the timing of when genes produce proteins (Gottlieb, 1998).

Neither one nor other is the most important

The question 'What is the most important – genes or environment?' is meaningless. It is like asking, 'What is the most important determinant of the area of a rectangle, its height *or* length?' Without either a height or a length, a rectangle cannot exist. Another analogy is baking a cake. Without ingredients or cooking, there can be no cake. Such analogies are an important first advance over naive polarizations between genes *or* environment.

Perhaps what people really mean is the more logical question of whether *differences* between individuals are due to *differences* in genes or *differences* in environment. To pursue the analogy, if two rectangles are different in area, this might be due to differences in height or length, or both. The degree to which differences in a characteristic are due to genetic differences is called the **heritability** of that

characteristic. By definition, the heritability within a population of genetically identical individuals would be zero.

Instinct and innateness

Before scientists had such a good understanding, behaviour was sometimes divided into one of two exclusive categories. Some was said to be 'instinctive' or 'innate' (i.e. genetically determined), whereas other behaviour was called learned (i.e. environmentally determined). Outside behavioural science, people still dichotomize in this way and it is not difficult to see why.

Think of watching a bird constructing a nest characteristic of its species in its first breeding season, which might lead us to suggest that this behaviour is innate. The bird seems not to have gone through a trial-and-error process; neither is it imitating another bird. Conversely, an animal showing clever circus tricks would seem to be revealing learning, rather than any 'circus-trick' instinct.

However, no behaviour is *purely* innate. From conception onwards, an animal reacts to events in its environment and thereby surely learns something relevant to each behaviour. The skills of a bird in constructing a nest doubtless owe much to earlier experiences with manipulating objects. Perceptual systems have a developmental history. Reciprocally, an animal exhibiting learning is employing nervous system structures that are partly determined genetically.

When we look closely at 'innate', it is not clear what exactly it means (Elman *et al.*, 1996). The term is used in a number of different ways and this adds confusion (discussed by Griffiths, 1997), which has led to calls for the term to be abandoned. Behaviour might be innate by one criterion but not by another.

If all members of a species exhibit a characteristic, does this mean that it is innate? The universal presence of something does not necessarily point in any simple way to its origins. Looking back to those grand and green days when

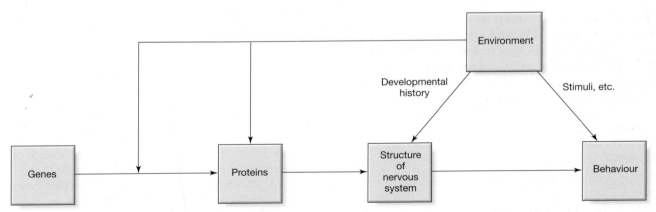

Figure 2.11 Genes and environment interacting in determining behaviour.

virtually everyone in the industrialized world showed considerable skill at riding a bicycle, it would have been absurd to describe this particular skill as innate. Apart from genetic similarity, another factor that gives constancy between individuals within a species is constant features of their environment (Hofer, 1988). During development, the infant mammal interacts with the mother's uterus and breast and the nature of this interaction might be very similar when comparing different individuals.

Most of the inhabitants of the United Kingdom speak English but that specific language could hardly be encoded genetically. The same population if raised from birth in France would presumably speak French.

Innate is sometimes used in the sense of being relatively insensitive to variations in the environment during development, given the presence of such basic necessities as heat, oxygen and energy (see Griffiths, 1997). However, a form of behaviour might normally be seen by all members of a species, have a clear evolutionary explanation and yet be very sensitive to changes in the environment during development (e.g. as revealed by experimental manipulation). For example, performance of sexual behaviour by adult rhesus monkeys counts as innate by the criteria of being seen by all normal members of the species and having an evolutionary explanation. However, it depends upon a social environment during development and early social deprivation severely disrupts later mating. Since some authors jump indiscriminately between these different meanings of innate, the word needs using with qualification if it is not to be abandoned.

Species-typical behaviour

The problems associated with the use of 'innate' might be avoided by employing instead the terms **species-typical behaviour** (STB) or 'species-specific behaviour' (Bolles, 1970). This means that the behaviour is exhibited by most, if not all, members of a species, given (1) normal development and environment and (2) the later presence of certain trigger stimuli. The existence of STB might be as closely associated with the identity of a species as are species-typical anatomical forms such as horns or antlers. It is probably best to consider a given behaviour to be on a continuum of more or less species-typical rather than either species-typical or not.

Strain differences

General

A **strain** is a subdivision within a species. It refers to members of a species who are similar to each other genetically but different from others of the same species, e.g. a high-anxiety strain of rat as opposed to a stable strain. Crossbreeding

between strains (e.g. high-anxiety and stables) results in viable offspring (i.e. offspring that can, in turn, reproduce).

By selectively breeding within a strain, one can strengthen a selected characteristic, something known to breeders of dogs and horses for a long time. For example, Tryon (1940) measured the ability of rats to learn a maze. Starting with a group of founding rats, Tryon bred within the brightest subgroup and within the dullest subgroup. Within the offspring of each subgroup, he then inbred among only the brightest and the dullest, respectively. Thereby he produced two strains, known as 'maze-bright' and 'maze-dull'. The result was a divergence of the two groups' scores on the maze task until there was little overlap.

Genes and environment – a caution

Consider two strains of mice housed under identical conditions in terms of space, diet and lighting, etc. (Southwick, 1968). Strain 1 has a high level of aggression, whereas strain 2 has a low level. Since the environment is said to be constant, it would seem to follow inevitably that differences in behaviour are due to genetically determined differences in the two strains. So far, so good, but now be very careful! The developmental/learning type of explanation calls for extreme vigilance.

To investigate, crossbreeding was done between strains. When a strain 1 female was mated with a strain 2 male, the male offspring had a high score for aggression. When a strain 2 female was mated with a strain 1 male, the male offspring had a low score. This suggests an effect linked to sex chromosomes, in which the male offspring acquire an allele for aggression from the mother. However, this does not exhaust the possibilities.

So, researchers tried cross-fostering, e.g. the product of a strain 1/strain 1 mating was raised by a strain 2 mother. The aggression score of the offspring followed that of the foster-mother rather than the biological mother. This suggests that something about the *social* environment of the young rather than their genotype determines the tendency to aggression. So, is it a genetic or environmental difference? The subtlety of genes and environment comes into focus here and precision of logic is crucial.

Suppose we accept that *certain differences* in genes between strains are apparently responsible for differences in aggression. To solve the puzzle, we need to probe further than this and to ask, whose genes are involved? Are the genes exerting their effect at the level of the mother's behaviour or that of the infant? Are they controlling aggression directly or via something else that in turn influences aggression?

Suppose that the nature of the maternal behaviour shown towards a pup has an influence on the subsequent aggressiveness of the pup. Figure 2.12 suggests that there might be a difference in degree of proximity between mother

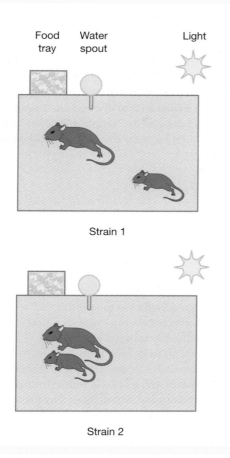

Food tray   Water spout   Light

Strain 1

Strain 2

Figure 2.12 Two strains housed under identical conditions.

Section summary

1 It is misleading to ask, 'What is most important, genes *or* environment?'

2 It is more valid to ask whether a given *difference* between individuals is due to genetic or environmental *differences*.

3 Heritability is a measure of the degree to which differences between individuals are determined by genetic differences.

4 We need to avoid describing behaviour as *either* innate *or* learned.

5 Genetic differences at the level of one individual can constitute environmental differences for another.

Test your knowledge

(Answer on page 45)

2.13 Imagine observing a society as it becomes more egalitarian and people are treated more equally. What happens to the heritability of characteristics over this period? (i) It increases, (ii) it decreases.

2.3

Evolutionary psychology

General principles

In recent years, a development of evolutionary thought has assumed great importance in suggesting explanations of human mind and behaviour. It is termed **evolutionary psychology** (EP) and its followers search for integrative principles linking evolution and psychology, in terms mainly of function (Barkow *et al.*, 1992). Evolutionary psychologists argue that, in order to understand mind and behaviour, we need to look way back to consider the environment in which we evolved and the nature of the demands that it imposed on our early ancestors.

EP employs the metaphor of **design**. For instance, a bird's wing looks *as if* a designer planned it with flight in mind. Similarly, it is as if our brains were *designed* so that behaviour fitted our early evolutionary environment. The environment in which we evolved was, of course, very different from that of modern London or Oslo. Our hunter-gatherer ancestors

and offspring but countless other differences could be suggested. Suppose too that genetic differences between strains underlie differences in maternal behaviour. This is still a genetically mediated difference but one for which the gene influencing *maternal* behaviour, not aggression as such, is responsible. Thus, the genetic difference between strains as revealed in the behaviour of the offspring does not reside in the offspring but rather in the mother. That is to say, what is a genetic difference at the level of the mother is an environmental difference at the level of the pup, since the mother is part of the pup's environment. The experimenter might be able to control the lighting and the cage size, etc. but this does not control the social behaviour of the mother.

This example has a message for the study of humans. Sometimes people explain differences between children not by genetic differences but by differences in environment, e.g. parenting styles. However, these styles might themselves be in part genetically determined (Plomin *et al.*, 1997).

The next section looks at an argument on genes and evolution that is powerfully influencing our view of ourselves as humans.

lived very different lives in that early environment, compared with ourselves. Yet we are still adapted for life in this older environment and our nervous systems were, in effect, 'designed' for solving the problems of life there. EP argues that it would be absurd to try to explain the workings of a car or a radio, or a heart or lung, without knowing what it was designed to do. By analogy, they argue that psychology also needs an evolutionary 'design' perspective. In this way, EP claims to have a unifying theoretical approach for all psychologists, including those concerned with causation and the brain.

Viewed in these terms, we can make sense of features of behaviour that otherwise might appear bizarre, e.g. our contemporary love of sweet foods even in the midst of an epidemic of diabetes, obesity and dental decay. Our behaviour reflects what was 'designed' for a life where there was not an abundance of sugars. For another example discussed by evolutionary psychology, why do symmetrical faces tend to be more attractive than asymmetrical ones (Perrett *et al.*, 1999)? One possible answer is that the symmetrical face is indicative of a younger age and a healthier developmental history. Thus, being attracted to such a stimulus would increase the chances of successful mating and is a factor that would be favoured by natural selection.

EP assumes that many features of human social life (e.g. worship), which might have been thought to be explained purely by cultural influences, are really to be explained at least in part in evolutionary terms. This is sometimes expressed uncritically by those who either promote or condemn a simple EP, as 'a gene for adultery' or 'a gene for religion' (note the singular 'a'). However, EP does not rest or fall on an assumption of single-gene effects. A combination of genes might give a bias towards, say, religious worship, since, by so doing, this combination has been placed at an advantage. Indeed, religion might still confer some adaptive advantages: as the cliché would have it 'families who pray together stay together'.

An immediate and well-worn qualification needs repeating: worship cannot literally be 'in the genes'. However, given certain genes, together with their social and learning contexts, worship might tend to emerge. By the same token, neither, for example, could physical height be determined simply by genes. Genes are a factor but for height to emerge also requires an appropriate environmental input, e.g. adequate food.

Such discussion has some important social messages. One of the reasons why EP is controversial is that it might at first seem to lend itself to rigid determinism. If something is 'in the genes', there appears to be little we can do about it. However, even if certain genes do exert a tendency in favour of, say, adultery, they represent only one contributory factor. The 'favoured' outcome is not necessarily inevitable.

The aspect of EP that has most fired the popular imagination and controversy is what it says about differences between the sexes. One point needs to be emphasized here. Though evolutionary theory might give insights into how behaviour has emerged in evolution, it cannot prescribe what humans *should* do morally. Such an unwarranted extrapolation is termed the 'naturalistic fallacy', and is a reason that doubtless turns some against evolutionary approaches.

Sex differences

Why do males appear to make more use of prostitutes and pornography and show a wish for greater indiscriminate promiscuity than do females? One might suppose that this reflects cultural norms and prohibitions ingrained in our institutions, i.e. 'social role theory' (see Archer, 1996). Change society, give enough time, and behaviour might change correspondingly. On the contrary, EP would suggest that such differences between the sexes reflect evolutionary history and different strategies of mating.

The optimal strategy for a human male (as with many species) to pass on his genes is different from that of a female. An instant and relatively indiscriminate sexual motivation and arousal, accompanied by promiscuity, might be to the advantage of the male since it maximizes his reproductive chances. There is relatively little to lose. The emphasis is on 'relatively' since, as always, there is not zero cost. For example, diseases can be caught and, since mating tends to focus the mind, genetic perpetuation might be rudely halted by an approaching tiger or jealous partner. However, for the female there is relatively much to lose. Some female inhibition and reserve ('coyness') might be to her genetic advantage, since in this way she can patiently wait to select the optimal male with whom to tie up her reproductive capacity for nine months or so and provide support.

Of course, few if any males visit prostitutes with the intention of passing on genes but no one is supposing that conscious intentions have had much to do with the evolution of sexuality. It is simply claimed that genes tend to code for those strategies that *in general* have served their own 'selfish' interests. In evolutionary history, a combination of genes that tended to promote male promiscuity via sexual motivational processes has been successful. Not all males are promiscuous. EP does not suggest that they should be, just as it does not suggest that all females should show coyness and fidelity. Genes give rise to tendencies not instructions carved in stone. It is simply that one can see a biological rationale in there being a difference between the sexes in this direction.

There is a point here many people misunderstand. Throughout evolution, rather than favouring desire for obtaining children as such, natural selection favoured sexual motivation. Of course, in the absence of a reliable technology of contraception, sexual motivation tends rather frequently to lead to children! This is not to deny that these days some people do desire to produce children as such but sexual desire was doubtless the driver in evolution. A casual glance at society today might suggest that this particular driver has lost none of its momentum over the course of human evolution.

While not denying the possibility that genetic differences might exert different degrees of tendency, explanations need to be framed in the broad gene–environment context discussed earlier. Biology is revealed within a cultural matrix (Barkow *et al.*, 1992).

Jealousy

EP makes testable predictions concerning sexual jealousy. What is the cost to an individual's chances of passing on his or her genes if the partner exhibits infidelity? The cost to a male partner could be large since it might be that his female partner produces offspring bearing another male's genes. Hence, the male partner misses his own opportunity of genetic transmission. The male partner could even unwittingly help with bringing up someone else's offspring. Thus, male sexual jealousy might involve a strong imperative against the sexual infidelity of his mate.

***

A personal angle

Some early intellectual roots of evolutionary psychology?

As a teenager growing up in Rockville, Maryland, Leda Cosmides (personal communication), a founder of Evolutionary Psychology, read – and reread – *Walden Two*, a Utopian novel by B. F. Skinner. She writes, 'Skinner, the most radical of the behavourists, claimed that by delivering rewards on just the right schedule, he could "engineer" people to do anything, e.g. mothers who were indifferent to whether they raised their own child or someone else's. I was skeptical – isn't there such a thing as human nature?' In your opinion, who was right?

***

In terms of the female's genetic perpetuation, the cost of a partner's infidelity might seem to be much less. The female can at least be sure that the offspring she produces are in part genetically hers. A male can recover his sexual potency relatively quickly, and with it, his capacity to contribute genes to reproduction with the female partner. However, there is a threat to the partner from other females, which

comes from the risk of being abandoned. The danger of this might be signalled by the male showing an abnormally large *emotional* interest in the well-being of another female, i.e. warmth and empathy. If that were to happen, the female might be put at a disadvantage in raising offspring. Therefore, one might expect some asymmetry in the trigger stimuli to jealousy, with males triggered more strongly by sexual infidelity and females by 'emotional infidelity'.

Working in the USA, Buss *et al.* (1992) invited people to imagine various scenarios and estimate the magnitude of the negative feelings that were evoked. These scenarios were of your mate (1) having sexual intercourse with another or (2) forming a deep emotional attachment to another. Eighty-five per cent of the women found the second to arouse more negative emotions, whereas 60% of the males found the first to do so. EP predicts a difference in this direction. A similar effect was found in the Netherlands, a country with a tradition of egalitarianism and more progressive culture.

Some argue that, rather than reflecting evolved differences, such differences are due to different perceptions of the respective roles of men and women in our culture. For example, society suggests that in women, sexual infidelity is not likely to occur without emotional infidelity – the so-called 'double shot'. By contrast, male *sexual* infidelity can be dismissed as being without emotional attachment (DeSteno and Salovey, 1996; Harris and Christenfeld, 1996). However, although not denying a cultural/cognitive factor, the EP researchers suggested that these different perceptions of sex roles are themselves to be understood in biological terms and directly capture the biological difference (Buss *et al.*, 1996). Cultural transmission of information might be expected to reflect and reinforce genetically determined differences.

Critiques of evolutionary psychology

Critiques of EP take many forms. Indeed, there now seems to be a small publishing industry dedicated to the polarities of claim and counter-claim. Few would argue against the notion that looking at evolution is essential for understanding current behaviour. The disputes mainly concern a particular interpretation of EP. This is sometimes termed the 'Santa Barbara school', named after the University of California location of its principal disciples (Tooby and Cosmides, 1990).

One point of criticism is that this school of evolutionary psychologists put their faith in what they term **modules**, special-purpose processors, each of which is dedicated to solving a particular problem. For example, the human brain would be described as being made up from such modules as a jealousy module, dedicated to detecting and acting upon threats as in sexual infidelity. Another such module is described as a cheating detection module. EP suggests that our mind is equipped with dedicated processes that alert us when someone is trying to cheat us, as in an unfair exchange of goods. Modules are something like cognitive equivalents of reflexes – fast, automatic and dedicated, with each solving just a single problem.

Tooby and Cosmides use the analogy of a Swiss army knife, a tool equipped with a number of components such as a knife and a can-opener, each serving just one particular function. You would have some difficulty in trying to use the can-opener to pull a cork from a wine bottle.

Critics of EP argue along two lines. First, they deny that we are quite as modularized ('compartmentalized') as EP suggests. Second, they suggest that, although some modularization of the brain does occur, EP has misunderstood its determinants. EP is said to put too much weight upon genetic factors and insufficient upon development. In fact, we turn out as we do as a result of the subtle dance between genes and environment. As noted earlier, a skill at riding a bicycle does not arise from *genes* producing a particular 'cycling module' – as one critic memorably expressed it, there were surely rather few bicycles around in our early evolution for this skill to be genetically encoded as a module! In reality, it emerges as the result of a combination of genes encoding for a brain with a *broad* capacity for controlling balance and early learning of the *particular* motor skills involved in balancing a bicycle. The behaviour becomes automatic ('modularized') with practice.

EP and the critiques of it are a particularly good demonstration of the need to bring together different types of explanation. EP is based firmly in the tradition of functional and evolutionary explanation. However, its conclusions need to match an understanding of the possibilities arising from the brain and its development.

Later chapters will explore the relevance of EP to such topics as emotion, feeding and sexual motivation. We now turn to a case study that will serve to bring together the different types of explanation.

Section summary

1 Evolutionary psychology suggests that many features of human social life that might be seen as purely socially constructed have, in reality, a biological basis in genes.

2 Evolutionary psychology makes some predictions regarding such things as differences in behaviour between the sexes (e.g. in triggers to jealousy).

3 Evolutionary psychology uses the metaphor of design. It is *as if* the brain were designed for certain functional roles by employing dedicated modules.

4 Critics of evolutionary psychology suggest that it underestimates the flexibility of behaviour and the extent to which the environment is involved in forming modules.

Test your knowledge

(Answer on page 45)

2.14 Complete the following: 'According to the analogy, the blade and bottle-opener of the Swiss army knife represent two different _____.'

 ## Depression: a case study

Introduction

This has been a long chapter and now it is time for an example that can bring some of the parts together. Depression serves well to do this.

Most people feel low at times but psychologists would not generally classify this as clinical depression. Depression is a serious disorder, characterized by a lasting feeling of negative **affect** ('negative hedonic feelings'), powerlessness, lack of motivation and an inability to influence events (Beck, 1967). The mental state is one of blackness, despair and fear, etc. Possible behavioural symptoms include early morning waking and withdrawal from social contact. Memory recall tends to be biased towards negative events. Evidence points to such disturbed mental and behavioural states as being associated with abnormalities in brain function.

Causes

Depression covers a number of different disorders and the present section can take only a simplified view. In some cases, depression appears to be a consequence of developmental/learning events, e.g. successive failures or repeated marital breakdowns. This is sometimes termed reactive depression and it can be understood in terms of external factors. However, such external events are experienced and interpreted by the nervous system and so we should not see their role as disconnected from the biology of the brain.

In other cases, there might be no obvious change in the external world associated with the onset of depression and one supposes that some internal change (e.g. abnormal hormonal level acting on the nervous system) is the trigger. However, such internal changes might be expected to change the patient's interpretation of events in the world, seeing things more negatively. Either way, it is safest to assume that depression depends upon the interdependence between (1) activity in basic brain regions that underlie emotions common to all people (Panksepp, 1994) and (2) the events within an individual lifetime and the way in which they are interpreted.

Genes and environment

Depression tends to run in families (McGuffin and Katz, 1993). This might reflect a social (developmental/learning) influence. Parents prone to depression might be remote in their interaction with offspring. This could affect the developing nervous system and hence the child might learn depressed ways of reacting. Also, differences between individuals in their tendency to depression might be due to genetic differences. Depression could result from a combination of a direct genetic contribution and exposure to a depressed social context, which itself might be partly genetically determined.

How could genes give a direct tendency towards depression? It is still uncertain exactly how this happens but we can speculate. Our mental states depend upon the structure and activity of the brain. Evidence shows abnormalities in the blood flow to a region of the brain in depressed individuals (Drevets *et al.*, 1997). In their case, this region might be smaller than that of controls with fewer incoming connections from neurons. Since neurons, like other cells, arise in part from the action of genes, particular forms of genes possessed by depressed people might bias towards abnormality within this region. In other words, genes are responsible for the synthesis of proteins (Figures 2.3 and 2.11) and nervous systems are constructed in part from proteins.

The fact that there is a tendency for depression to run in families is suggestive of a genetic factor but is not sufficient to prove this. One way of investigating is to compare identical twins (who are genetically identical) and fraternal twins (who are not genetically identical), though even this is problematic.

Investigators believe that there is a genetic contribution but estimates vary as to its size, depending in part upon the type of depression (McGuffin and Katz, 1993). Even though there might be a strong genetic contribution to depression, this does not mean that depression is 'written in the genes' as a predetermined property of the brain. Rather, a gene (or genes) could exert a tendency towards depression but this might only be revealed in combination with such developmental factors as the mother's exposure to stress or

alcohol. Even the emergence of an adult brain that is prone to depression does not mean that the disorder is inevitable. The environment might give a tendency towards mental health. By analogy, knowing that a piece of glass is brittle does not necessarily mean that it will break. Rather it means that, given an external 'stressor', the brittle glass has a higher probability of breaking.

Treatment

Treatments for depression include cognitive therapy (targeting how the patient views events in the world) and drugs. A biological psychologist would assume that, when a cognitive therapy works, in some way it changes the brain's operating characteristics. This might be the biological basis of the change in mental state and cognitive processing that comes with recovery. Drugs act on the neurons of the brain and thereby change their information processing, reflected in cognitive and mood changes.

Function

Would we expect to make sense of depression from a functional perspective? Using evolutionary psychology, theorists like to speculate. Taking one view and arguing by analogy, it would be absurd to ask, what is the evolutionary advantage of having a broken leg? However, we might reasonably discuss the evolutionary costs and benefits of constructing bones from material that is able to break. Similarly, we could ask about the advantage of having a nervous system constructed in a way that brings particular benefits but does so with an inevitable associated risk of depression. Chronic depression might be a *maladaptive exaggeration* of something that in smaller doses has served a useful function in our earlier evolution. Recall the example of our liking for sweet taste. It is possible that, similarly, a tendency to brief depression could have been an advantage in early evolution but has become a disadvantage now.

Some theorists go further and make the surprising suggestion that even full depression can bring real benefits to fitness. This is in terms of triggering adaptive change in both the depressed individual and those close to him or her (Watson and Andrews, 2002). One possibility is that withdrawal could be an appropriate temporary reaction to impossible circumstances, such as social rejection. This would enable energy to be conserved and attention focused on finding a solution to the current problems. Social conditions that are not working might then be able to be modified, with depression as the trigger for change. The depressed way of reacting might deflect aggression and, in social primates, help in accepting defeat and soliciting assistance from kin (Nettle, 2004; Price *et al.*, 1994).

Section summary

1 Depression is a mental and behavioural state of powerlessness and low affect.

2 It is logical to seek a disturbed biological basis in the brain underlying this disorder, whatever its cause.

3 There appears to be a genetic contribution to depression.

4 Depression could be a contemporary exaggerated expression of a behavioural tendency that was adaptive in small doses earlier in evolution.

Test your knowledge

(Answer on page 45)

2.15 Fill in the missing word from the following: 'The fact that depression tends to run in families _____ that differences between people in tendency to depression is genetically based'. (i) proves, (ii) suggests, (iii) disconfirms.

Bringing things together

Having its focus on functional and evolutionary types of explanation, this chapter has shown how the four types of biological explanation, including causal and developmental/learning (Chapter 1), are interrelated. It showed where we can gain a fuller picture of any one type, with at least some knowledge of the other types.

From now on, the focus of the book is very much on the nervous system and behaviour. Researchers who investigate this topic do not constantly feel a need to fit their ideas to the other types of explanation. However, it can be useful, for example, when trying to understand how the brain controls behaviour to be able to ask well-informed questions on functional aspects. Similarly, asking about the function that behaviour has served in evolution (what it has been 'designed' to do) can sometimes usefully inform causal explanations (Barkow *et al.*, 1992).

Researchers have gained much insight into the brain mechanisms of, for example, memory by asking a simple functional question: What was it 'designed' to achieve?

In our early evolutionary environment, what sort of information was it important for humans to remember? In the spirit of evolutionary psychology, it appears that there are different types of memory, each adapted to solving a particular type of problem.

Similarly, one can make better sense of the brain's role in sexual choice by considering the functional value of particular choices of partner in terms of reproductive advantage. We can better understand the dynamics of a colony of wild animals in terms of care for offspring and apparent altruism to kin, etc., if we can see a rationale for this in terms of the evolution of their ancestors. We can be informed of what kinds of process might be expected to underlie causation involving social dynamics.

Summary of Chapter 2

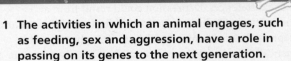

1 The activities in which an animal engages, such as feeding, sex and aggression, have a role in passing on its genes to the next generation.

2 Any behaviour has both benefits and costs. Natural selection favours strategies for which, on average, benefits outweigh costs.

3 The understanding of processes, such as reflexes, at a causal level can both help, and be helped by, an understanding of them in functional and evolutionary terms.

4 In sexual reproduction, different combinations of genetic material are formed and then tested in the environment.

5 A molecule of DNA forms the base for genetic information.

6 Genes code for the construction of proteins that form, among other things, the nervous system. Hence, as part of complex loops of influence, there is a sequence of effects: (gene) → (nervous system) → (behaviour).

7 Genes and environment act together as determinants of behaviour.

8 Evolutionary psychology suggests the controversial idea that the brain is composed of genetically determined modules, each adapted to serve just one function.

9 Depression is a good example to illustrate where causal, developmental/learning, evolutionary and functional explanations can be brought together.

Further reading

For a good account of genes and environment, undermining simple dichotomies, see Johnston (1987). For an introduction to evolution, see Stearns and Hoekstra (2000). For a discussion of adaptation, see Buss *et al.* (1998). For an excellent balanced approach to evolutionary psychology, see Workman and Reader (2004). For an argument for evolutionary psychology, see Buss (1999), for a challenging critique, see Buller (2005) and for a handbook, see Buss (2005). For a good account of depression from an evolutionary perspective, see Watson and Andrews (2002).

Signposts

The issues raised in this chapter will be with us throughout the book. You should try to get into the habit of thinking in terms of the four types of explanation when you encounter instances of behaviour in the subsequent chapters. Sometimes the relevance of the particular type of functional and evolutionary explanation summarized by the term 'evolutionary psychology' will be made explicit.

The principle of homeostasis will be described in Chapter 15, 'Motivation', and in Chapter 16, 'Feeding and drinking'.

Answers

Explanations for answers to 'test your knowledge' questions can be found on the website **www.pearsoned.co.uk/toates**

2.1 (i) Feeding, (ii) drinking, (iii) temperature regulation
2.2 benefits
2.3 (i) Hearing
2.4 (i) High speed, (ii) hard-wired, (iii) common to members of a given species
2.5 Stereotypy
2.6 (i) Zygote
2.7 (ii) Sperm cell, (iii) unfertilized egg cell
2.8 Protein
2.9 A daughter
2.10 A son
2.11 Alleles
2.12 Gene, allele
2.13 (i) It increases
2.14 Modules
2.15 (ii) suggests

CHAPTER 3

The nervous and endocrine systems

After studying this chapter, you should be able to:

1 Distinguish between the nervous system and endocrine system, while illustrating how adaptive behaviour depends upon their close cooperation and the integration of their activity.

2 Describe some of the ways in which the nervous system can be divided and classified for the purposes of explanation. Give a rationale for such classification and, on the basis of it, exemplify how information is transmitted within the nervous system.

3 Explain how information is communicated at synapses, thereby distinguishing excitation and inhibition. Compare and contrast neurotransmission and neuromodulation at synapses.

4 Compare and contrast the transmission of information *within* a neuron and *between* neurons.

5 Describe how the properties of synapses can change with development/learning and explain the significance of this for psychology.

6 Distinguish between (i) neurotransmitters and neuromodulators and (ii) hormones. Compare and contrast communication mediated by (i) and (ii).

7 Explain the origin of the term 'autonomic nervous system' and describe the ways in which its divisions can be classified.

1 How and why does fear make the heart beat harder?

2 Why do we have so little conscious control over the inside of our bodies? For example, why can't we stop ourselves blushing just by willpower?

3 How can mood affect the gut as in a 'tummy upset' following a traumatic event?

4 Do expressions such as 'gut feelings' and 'matters of the heart' have any real meaning in terms of biology? Is there a feedback route from periphery to brain?

5 Hormones are said to affect our mood, but what are hormones and how could they exert such effects?

How does our survival depend upon coordinated action between nervous systems and hormones?

Source: **Empics**

Introduction

Threats come in many forms, from floods to wild animals. There are some common features of your reaction to them. Imagine that you suddenly confront a situation of extreme emergency such as a large angry bear in a forest. Not a very pleasant prospect, I know, but one that serves to focus the mind of psychology student, author and bear alike. You react quickly by running away, to get back to your tourist bus before the bear gets to you (recalling that bears too can run). Your heart beats furiously as you run. This indicates that, as well as organizing running, the nervous system automatically accelerates the heartbeat. Your energetic behaviour requires a large supply of fuel to the body's muscles, particularly those of the legs, and the blood delivers it. This scenario exemplifies *coordination* between physiology (changes in blood supply) and behaviour (running). Nervous and hormonal systems are involved in producing such coordination.

By contrast, imagine yourself now relaxing on a sofa after a good meal, with thoughts far from angry bears. Your body is at rest and your brain has automatically lowered your heart-rate. There is now an automatic diversion of relatively large amounts of blood to the gut to facilitate digestion of your meal and relatively little blood is flowing to the muscles of the legs. Again, there is coordination between behaviour and physiology in the interests of efficiency and thereby survival.

These two examples introduce the organizing theme of the present chapter: adaptation involves coordinated action that is exerted simultaneously within the body's internal and external environments. How do we investigate such coordination?

As a convenience for explanation, the body is divided into systems. Chapters 1, 'Introduction', and 2, 'Genes, environment and evolution', introduced two of these briefly already: the nervous system and the system involving hormones. The present chapter examines coordinated action, by looking at the nervous system in the context of hormones. These two systems detect events at one location in the body, communicate information throughout the body and trigger action at another location.

The system involving hormones is known as the **endocrine system**. Hormones are chemicals that are secreted from what are termed **glands** (although there are also glands that do not secrete hormones, e.g. the salivary glands). The nervous system affects the release of hormones. On perceiving danger, for example, the nervous system would trigger release of hormones that facilitate an increase in the supply of fuel to the muscles. In turn, hormones affect the activity of the nervous system.

The action of the brain on the heart was just described as 'automatic'. By contrast, other features of the scenarios would be described as 'voluntary'. It might not feel as if you have much in the way of voluntary control or free-will when you confront an angry bear. However, at least in principle, you could have stood your ground and asserted your civil right to walk in the forest without menace. The action of resting after a meal surely illustrates the notion of voluntary behaviour – you might equally have chosen to go for a bracing walk.

So, a fundamental distinction is between what happens automatically and what is voluntary. In the examples just given, the brain's action on instigating behaviour in the outside world is voluntary, whereas its action on the inside environment is automatic. However, it is not only action on the internal environment that is automatic. Think again of the example of the reflex that protects you from tissue damage (Chapter 2). It 'just happens' automatically as a result of the stimulus, the construction of the nervous system and the activation of the muscles. As also observed in Chapter 2, such distinctions are not absolute. Although there are some rather clear instances of voluntary and automatic, some behaviour exhibits bits of each. (If there were not some complicating qualification to add immediately, it would surely not be psychology as we all know it!)

We will look first at the nervous system and then the endocrine system. We will then look at their interaction.

Section summary

1 The nervous and endocrine systems are involved in coordinating action between the internal and external environments.

2 These systems serve an adaptive function, which is also true of the interactions between them.

Test your knowledge

(Answer on page 80)

3.1 Within which of the following systems is communication mediated by chemicals being transported in the bloodstream? (i) Nervous, (ii) endocrine, (iii) both (i) and (ii).

What nervous systems do

Whether exhibiting reflexes, or feeding, fighting or fleeing, or whatever, the nervous system controls behaviour. Similarly, our internal feelings, such as fear, depression or joy, depend upon the neurons of this system. So, an understanding of the system and the cells that form it is fundamental. We will start with a description of the nervous system, then give some relatively simple examples to illustrate what neurons do. We then look at action exerted on the external environment, and at coordination between internal and external events. Finally, we consider emotions.

Basic division of the nervous system

The nervous system (Figure 3.1(a)) is made up of billions of neurons, which have different shapes and sizes. (The terms 'neural' and 'neuronal' are adjectives to refer to neurons, e.g. neural pathways.) There are also other cells located alongside the neurons but discussion of them will need to wait. The nervous system comprises brain, spinal cord and neurons located throughout the 'periphery' of the body.

The large concentration of neurons in the brain and the spinal cord makes up the **central nervous system** (CNS). The spinal cord is a column of neurons located within the backbone (Figure 3.1(a)). The CNS is sheltered from traumatic damage by bony structures: the skull for the brain and the backbone for the spinal cord. All of the nervous system that is not in the brain or spinal cord is called the **peripheral nervous system**.

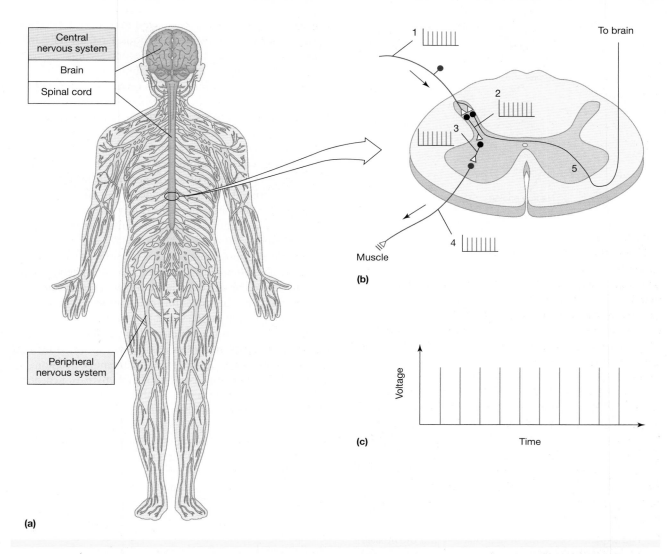

Figure 3.1 (a) Human nervous system, with brain and spinal cord shown in red. (b) A thin slice of the spinal cord with some of the neurons located there. (c) Graph showing action potentials.

How a reflex works

A simple reflex can be used to illustrate the principles of how collections of neurons work. These same principles can then be adapted so as to be applicable more broadly.

Have a look at Figure 3.2, which you might rightly feel has a rather ancient appearance. It does indeed, but please be patient: the logic underlying the age of the figure will be revealed in a moment. The figure shows two neurons marked in blue. Suppose that the 'Neuron ending' comes into contact with a noxious stimulus such as heat or a sharp object. This excites activity in the neuron indicated with the ending. Activity follows the ascending arrow and a message is thereby sent to the spinal cord. In response, a message

comes back from the spinal cord in the neuron indicated by the descending arrow, to the muscle of the leg. The leg is moved away from the noxious object, i.e. a reflex action. Now let us see in detail how this all happens.

Some of the neurons of the spinal cord and periphery are shown in Figure 3.1(b). (In reality, few neurons look anything like the 'typical' cells shown in Figure 1.2.) These are some of the neurons involved in the reflex of withdrawing the foot from a noxious object. Neuron 1 corresponds to the neuron with its ending indicated in Figure 3.2. The tip of neuron 1 is at the foot and this neuron extends to the spinal cord. Neuron 4 is that which takes the signal from the spinal cord in Figure 3.2.

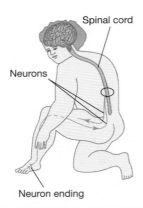

Figure 3.2 Two of the neurons that underlie a simple reflex.
Source: after Halliday (1998, Fig. 5.22).

Consider the sequence of neurons represented by the arrows (1 → 2 → 3 → 4) in Figure 3.1(b). Through such neurons, signals from the foot instigated by real or impending tissue damage (the noxious stimulus) communicate with the muscle of the leg to trigger a movement of the foot away from this stimulus.

The noxious stimulus very rapidly triggers electrical activity in neuron 1, which was previously inactive. This takes the form of a series of electrical pulses, termed **action potentials**. Activity in neuron 1 triggers action potentials in neuron 2. In turn, neuron 2 triggers activity in neuron 3, which triggers neuron 4. Action potentials in neuron 4 trigger muscle cells controlling the foot (muscles are made up of many such cells). So, the foot is moved from the noxious stimulus. Figure 3.1(b) is a simplification; in reality, there are many such parallel pathways of neurons acting simultaneously.

The sequence of events in neurons 1–4 and the muscle constitutes the basis of a reflex. A trace of action potentials is shown in Figure 3.1(c) and four such traces are included in Figure 3.1(b). This defensive action against damage to the body is local, organized at the spinal cord and termed a **spinal reflex.**

Reflexes, the spinal cord and the brain

Neuron 1 of Figure 3.1(b) is a member of a class of neurons termed **sensory neurons**, neurons that detect information on events in the external world or inside the body and transmit it to the CNS. The neuron's tip constitutes a **receptor**, not to be confused with a receptor molecule (described shortly). In the present example, it is sensitive to tissue damage, suffered either directly at the tip itself or in the near vicinity.

The reaction to the stimulus of Figures 3.1 and 3.2 has two aspects, both triggered by the type of sensory neuron that is sensitive to tissue damage, termed a **nociceptive neuron** (neuron 1 in Figure 3.1(b)). The expression

'nociceptive' refers to tissue damage and pain, and it derives from the same root as the word noxious. First, the reflexive aspect consists of quickly moving the foot. Second, nociceptive information reaches the brain, mediated by neuron 1 and then neuron 5, which carries the information up the spinal cord. This triggers pain. A nociceptive neuron would typically not be receptive to other stimuli such as harmless touch.

Sometimes investigators speak in abstract terms of 'information' conveyed along neurons and, at other times, in the more physical terms of 'action potentials'. Information and action potentials can be considered two different languages for describing the same reality: the brain is 'informed of a stimulus' or 'action potentials arrive at the brain'. By analogy, if you hear the sound of your doorbell, information on someone's presence is conveyed. Alternatively, you might speak about the same phenomenon in terms of electric currents and sound waves in the air.

Neurons communicate information, process it and trigger action. Information on the world (e.g. heat at the foot, sounds and lights) is communicated to the brain, where decisions are made. In the brain, the physical embodiment of our mental life – perception, emotion, memory, decision-making and all the rest – consists of the activity of neurons. For example, pain plays a part in labeling flames in memory as dangerous, therefore to be avoided.

As part of the spinal reflex (Figures 3.1 and 3.2), information travelling from tissue damage to the muscle does not go via the brain. Therefore, the distance that information needs to travel to trigger a response is relatively short. Removal of the foot from the noxious stimulus is correspondingly rapid. The reflexive response is well under way by the time you experience the pain. At your 'leisure', you can then think about your mistake in getting too near to the flame and experience the pain as a reminder.

The scenario illustrates how mind and behaviour relate to the underlying neural components. For example, how information arises from tissue damage and the speed with which it is conducted to the brain can be understood in terms of the properties of neurons. This can then be related to pain.

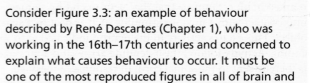

A personal angle

René Descartes

Consider Figure 3.3: an example of behaviour described by René Descartes (Chapter 1), who was working in the 16th–17th centuries and concerned to explain what causes behaviour to occur. It must be one of the most reproduced figures in all of brain and behavioural science. Now you can see the idea behind the historical flavour of Figure 3.2: to facilitate comparison. Descartes walked around the gardens of St Germain-en-Laye, near Paris, and observed automatons. These hydraulically activated statues of monsters were triggered into activity by a visitor stepping on a pedal. Descartes reasoned that all non-human behaviour (and much human behaviour) was like this: an automatic response to a stimulus.

Descartes wondered how heat triggers the reaction ('reflex') of limb withdrawal and the perception of pain. In those days, no one knew about neurons and Descartes speculated in terms of wires, pulleys and valves in the body. Now scientists look to neurons. Descartes suggested that information had to get to the brain to trigger action (Figure 3.3). Action *can* indeed be initiated by this route and the sensation of pain does involve such transmission to the brain. However, because of the distance of information transmission up to the brain and down again, this route is relatively slow. Scientists now know that the fast reaction of moving the foot from the noxious stimulus is the outcome of an automatic reflex organized by a collection of neurons at the leg and spinal cord (Figures 3.1 and 3.2).

Incidentally, it is not surprising that we can improve on Descartes, who was working with little to guide him.

Figure 3.3 Descartes' model of action. The foot touches a hot object, a message is sent to the brain and the person quickly withdraws the foot.

Source: after Halliday (1998, Fig. 5.21).

Coding of information

Information is coded in the nervous system by how *frequently* action potentials occur (other codes also exist but are beyond our scope here). Some neurons produce action potentials spontaneously and so a signal is carried by increases or decreases in frequency relative to the spontaneous rate. Other neurons are inactive until triggered into activity. For an example of how frequency conveys information, a sharp object that penetrates the skin would trigger action potentials at a higher frequency than one making only superficial impact. In Figure 3.1(b), a higher frequency of action potentials in neuron 4 would produce a stronger reaction by the muscle.

Figure 3.4(a) represents a different sensory system: that of detecting cold. We can now introduce some more of the terminology of neurons. Two components of neurons 1 and 2 that are very important for our purposes are the **axon** and the **cell body**. Their role will be described in more detail shortly. For the moment, consider just two of their fundamental properties.

- The axon is the long extension component of the neuron and along which action potentials are conducted. (This component also is shown in Figure 3.1 as serving this same role of communication.)

- The cell body is the site where the genetic material of the cell is located. Note the different location of the cell body in neurons 1 and 2, relative to the axon. (You can also see the comparable cell bodies in Figure 3.1(b).)

As shown in Figure 3.4, imagine that you put your hand in a glass of cold water. A series of action potentials is triggered by cold at the tip of a type of sensory neuron sensitive to cold. In Figure 3.4(b), trace (i) represents the response to a moderate cold, whereas trace (ii) is when the temperature at the skin is further decreased. Decreasing temperature is coded by an increase in *frequency* of action potentials. A still further decrease in temperature might be coded by an even higher frequency (trace iii).

Suppose cold (Figure 3.4) has initiated action potentials in neuron 1. Action potentials arise at the tip of the axon and are transmitted along its length by means of the following process. Action potentials at the tip influence the neighbouring region so that this region then shows an action potential. The action potential then invades the next bit of axon and so on. The effect is that the action potential moves along the axon from a region of stimulation to a neighbouring region.

In a given neuron, each action potential travels at the same speed. Also one action potential is exactly like another in shape and duration. Information is coded not by the form or speed of the action potential but by how many of them occur in a period of time. Information is carried to the brain by means of (a) *which* neurons are active and (b) the frequency of action potentials that they exhibit.

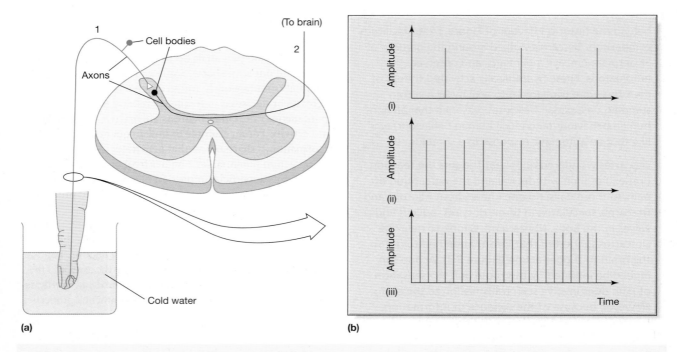

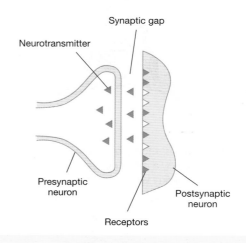

Figure 3.4 (a) Information on cold temperature is conveyed from periphery to the brain via neurons 1 and then 2. (b) The reaction of neuron 1. *Source*: after Toates (1998c).

At the brain, the arrival of action potentials in a neural pathway is interpreted in terms of the events that would normally trigger that pathway. Information arriving in the pathway mediated by neurons 1 and 5 in Figure 3.1(b) would be interpreted as pain. That arriving in the pathway of which neurons 1 and 2 in Figure 3.4(a) form part would be interpreted as cold. For another example, if you accidentally put pressure on your eye, you tend to 'see' visual objects even though they are not present physically. The mechanical disturbance triggers action potentials in neurons that normally convey visual information and this is interpreted as visual events.

Communication between neurons

In Figures 3.1(b) and 3.4(a), you can see that neurons almost make direct contact with their neighbouring cells, whether this is another neuron or a muscle cell. The region where one neuron almost touches another cell is known as a **synapse**, shown in Figure 3.5. This synapse represents any one of the links between cells of Figure 3.1 and 3.4. Details of communication involving synapses will be developed later. For the moment, we consider only one type of synapse, where activity in one neuron induces activity in another cell. The synapse consists of part of each cell and the small gap between them.

Communication at the point of contact between neurons is by means of a chemical termed a 'chemical messenger', 'transmitter' or **neurotransmitter**. In Figure 3.5, in response to activity, neurotransmitter is released at the terminal of what is termed the **presynaptic neuron**. This

neurotransmitter influences the activity of the **postsynaptic neuron**. How does this influence occur?

Embedded at the surface of the postsynaptic neuron, there are molecules termed 'receptors' (not to be confused with the earlier use of this term). They are receptors specifically for the neurotransmitter released at the adjacent neuron. The occupation of these receptors by neurotransmitter influences the electrical activity of the second neuron, so that, in the examples described so far, an action potential in one neuron will tend to trigger a further action potential in the next cell. Although this shows a

Figure 3.5 A synapse.

general principle, to help your understanding, you might like to consider the presynaptic neuron to be neuron 1 of Figure 3.4(a) and the postsynaptic to be neuron 2. The same sequence applies to the connections between neurons in Figure 3.1(b). A similar process applies to the link between neuron 4 and the muscle cell, where the latter is termed the postsynaptic cell.

The brain and action

Action within the external world

Apart from reflexes, movement can, of course, be commanded by a voluntary decision made in the brain, illustrated in Figure 3.6. Imagine that a person suddenly points his or her finger at an object. What is the sequence of events involved? A decision to move the finger is made in the brain and information conveyed down the spinal cord. The first neuron in the sequence (neuron 1 of Figure 3.6) transmits action potentials to the synapse between neurons 1 and 2. Action potentials are then instigated in neuron 2 and information transmitted to muscle cells, where mechanical ('motor') action by a finger is triggered. Neurons of the kind shown as neuron 2, termed **motor neurons**, carry information to muscles. The term 'motor system' refers to the motor neuron and the control exerted via it.

Most neurons are neither sensory nor motor. Rather, they are located somewhere between the input and output sides, wholly within the brain or spinal cord. They are called **interneurons**. Neurons 2, 3 and 5 in Figure 3.1(b) are interneurons.

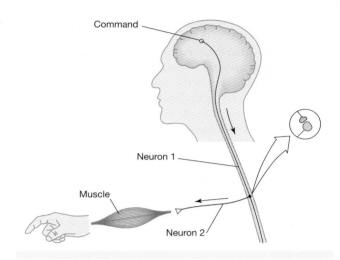

Figure 3.6 Motor action by a finger triggered by a conscious decision in the brain. (In the bubble, the synapse between neurons 1 and 2 is shown enlarged.)

We now look at the role of neurons in triggering coordinated action inside the body and outside.

Coordinated action inside and outside

Whether as part of voluntary behaviour or as a reflex, action that has an effect on the outside environment is exerted by means of what is known as the **somatic nervous system**. This system employs **skeletal muscles**, e.g. Figure 3.6 shows a skeletal muscle. The term 'skeletal' draws attention to the link

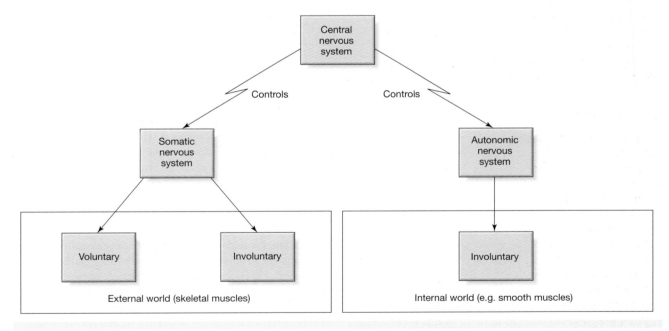

Figure 3.7 Distinction between somatic and autonomic nervous systems. Reflexes are under the category of involuntary action on external world.

between this type of muscle and the skeleton; most skeletal muscles are attached to the skeleton via tendons.

A division within the nervous system is between the somatic nervous system and the **autonomic nervous system** (described in detail later in the chapter). The autonomic nervous system (ANS) is automatic ('involuntary') and triggers action on the internal environment, partly through a class of muscle termed **smooth muscle**.

The distinction between controls exerted by the somatic and autonomic nervous systems is shown in Figure 3.7. A simplified version of a small part of each system is shown in Figure 3.8. A neurotransmitter is employed as a link between neuron 2 and the skeletal muscle that controls the position of

the leg. Neurotransmitter is also employed at the junction of neuron 5 and the muscle that controls the beating of the heart.

The somatic nervous system and the ANS normally work in a coordinated way in controlling action. Consider again the prospect of meeting a bear. The brain rapidly translates this into the emotion of fear, makes a decision – 'run!' – and triggers action. In Figure 3.8, the brain sends a command down the spinal cord (neurons 1 and 2) to the muscles that control the legs. This is the responsibility of the somatic nervous system. Simultaneously, the brain, acting through the ANS, accelerates the heart (neurons 3, 4 and 5) and triggers other internal changes to support the energized behaviour. Digestion is inhibited as the blood is needed elsewhere (Lisander, 1979).

In general, heart-rate is not under voluntary control, though there are techniques for gaining some voluntary control over it. There are many situations that cause the heart to accelerate. The anxiety of a nightmare or night terror can do so (Kellerman, 1987). However, there are more subtle stimuli. It is not just threats to physical integrity, real or in dreams, that excite the heart in this way. Challenges that require action do so, e.g. mathematical puzzles (Steptoe, 1993). For someone trying to give up drugs, the cognitive processing involved in seeing cues to drug-taking or even to imagine taking the drug can trigger activation of the heart (Weinstein *et al.*, 1997).

One change in the physiology of your body can sometimes be more obvious to others than to you: the changes in blood flow described as a blush (Darwin, 1872/1934). This is not under voluntary control and trying to resist it seems only to make it worse. If you are anything like me, you will still cringe as you recall some embarrassing incident that demonstrated just how little you can exert voluntary control over this feature of your internal environment. That's enough of that!

Deep within the brain – thoughts and moods

Connections between neurons at synapses, mediated by neurotransmitters, are fundamental to the control of behaviour and mental processes. There are billions of synapses in the nervous system, most being in the brain. (The term 'neurochemistry' describes the study of the effects of chemicals on nervous systems.) As an example of information processing, the emotions, e.g. fear, depression and elation, depend on the activity of many neurons in the brain and the properties of the synapses that link them (Panksepp, 1994). Just think what the image of the bear would do to those of your neurons that underlie fear.

One line of research consists of manipulating neural events to see what happens to behaviour and mental states, e.g. to excite large groups of target neurons in particular brain regions. It is possible to change artificially the activity

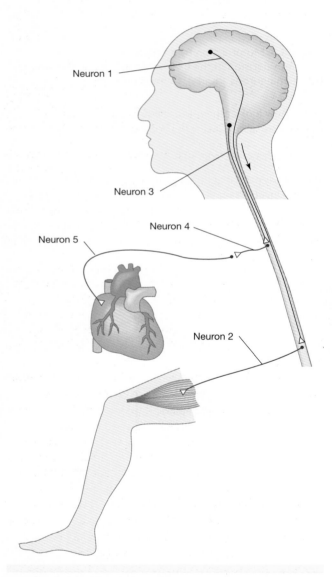

Figure 3.8 Part of the somatic nervous system (controlling a skeletal muscle in a leg) and part of the ANS (influencing muscle of the heart).

of groups of neurons by drugs that target particular classes of synapse in the brain, a branch of behavioural science termed **psychopharmacology**. That drugs, both legal and illegal, can alter mood indicates the interdependence between mental states and physical events, e.g. levels of chemicals in the body. For instance, a drug, e.g. Prozac, can boost activity at a type of synapse, change the activity of many related neurons and thereby affect mood. The rationale of much of the pharmaceutical and psychiatric professions is to enable us to change our neurochemistry, whereas the rationale behind much police and customs activity is to stop us from doing so.

The next section looks in more detail at chemical events at synapses.

Section summary

1 The nervous system contains billions of neurons, most being in the brain.

2 The nervous system is divided into the central nervous system (the brain and spinal cord; abbreviated as CNS) and the peripheral nervous system.

3 Information is transmitted in neurons as action potentials.

4 Systems of neurons organized in the spinal cord trigger local actions, termed spinal reflexes.

5 The region of communication between a neuron and another cell (neuron or muscle cell) is a synapse.

6 Neurotransmitter is released from one neuron (presynaptic neuron) and occupies receptors at a second cell (e.g. a postsynaptic neuron).

7 Neurons that are neither sensory nor motor but that convey information between other neurons are termed interneurons.

8 In the cases described so far, on occupying receptors, neurotransmitter excites the postsynaptic cell.

9 Both voluntary behaviour and some reflexes are produced via skeletal muscles.

10 The autonomic nervous system (ANS) controls the internal environment of the body.

11 The ANS employs smooth muscle.

12 The synapses of the brain are the target for drug interventions.

Test your knowledge

(Answers on page 80)

3.2 As described so far, information is transmitted between cells by which means? (i) Electrical or (ii) chemical?

3.3 A neurotransmitter conveys information from where to where? (i) Presynaptic cell to postsynaptic cell, (ii) postsynaptic cell to presynaptic cell.

3.4 Neurotransmitter conveys information between which of the following? (i) Neuron to neuron, (ii) neuron to skeletal muscle, (iii) neuron to smooth muscle, (iv) muscle to neuron.

3.1

Neurochemical actions at synapses

This section looks at some more details of how neurochemicals are able to act at synapses in the nervous system and the kind of information processing that this permits.

Classical neurotransmission

Excitation and inhibition

Figure 3.9 shows a collection of four neurons. Neurons 1, 2 and 3 form synapses with ('synapse on') neuron 4. Neurons 1 and 3 form 'excitatory synapses', i.e. they release neurotransmitter that occupies receptors at neuron 4 and thereby excite it. Activity in either neuron 1 or 3, or both, triggers activity in 4. This is the type of synapse described so far in the book.

In part (a) of Figure 3.9 there is no activity in any neuron. In part (b), neuron 1 is active, which excites neuron 4, indicated by action potentials in 4. In part (c), both neurons 1 and 3 are active. Note that the *frequency* of action potentials in 4 increases in (c) relative to (b); that is to say, more action potentials occur in a unit of time. Neuron 4 is increasingly excited on going from part (a) to (b) and to (c).

Rather than excitation, activity of a different type of neuron can *inhibit* the activity of another, a process mediated by a different combination of neurotransmitter and receptor. A neuron exerting such an effect is known as an **inhibitory neuron**. In Figure 3.9, whereas activity in neurons 1 and 3 tends to cause action potentials in neuron 4 (excitation), activity in neuron 2 suppresses them, i.e. lowers their frequency (termed 'inhibition'). Compare part (d) with (b).

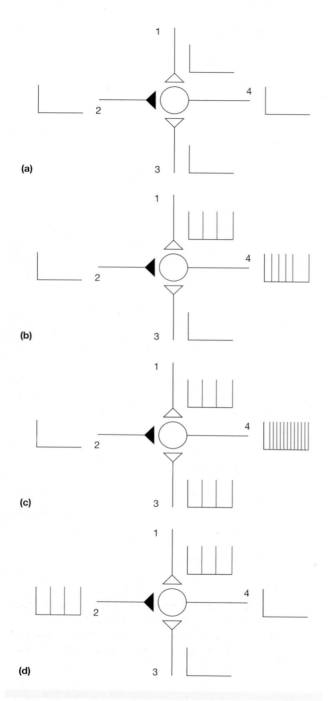

Figure 3.9 Activity in neurons: (a) no activity, (b) activity in neuron 1 excites 4, (c) activity in 1 and 3 add their effects in exciting 4, (d) the effect of 1 in exciting 4 is opposed by activity in the inhibitory neuron 2. △ = excitation, ▲ = inhibition.

The capacity to exert inhibition is fundamental to the control of behaviour and cognition, as some examples will illustrate. Let us revisit the example introduced earlier, part of which is shown in Figure 3.10. Tissue damage triggers

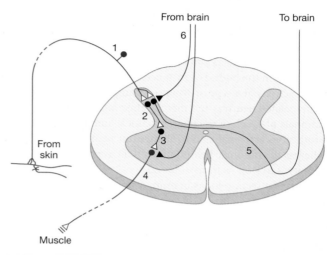

Figure 3.10 Inhibition. (As with the others, this figure is a simplification. In reality paths of neurons rather than single neurons would be involved in such processes.)

the withdrawal of a limb from an object and associated pain. There are pathways from the brain whereby inhibition can be applied to the activity of neurons in this system, represented by neuron 6. When inhibition is exerted, it is less likely that the reflex will be shown or that pain will be experienced. From a functional perspective, it might occasionally be an advantage *not* to respond to tissue damage. For example, animals in fight or flight show inhibition on the tendency to react to tissue damage (Rodgers and Randall, 1987). Attention to a wound mediated via pain would detract from fight or flight. Soldiers injured in battle have reported that they did not feel pain until they got away from the battlefield (Melzack and Wall, 1996).

The neurotransmitter action that you have met so far, whether excitation or inhibition, was the first to be discovered and is sometimes termed that of a 'classical neurotransmitter'. Blackburn and Pfaus (1988) use the expression 'detonating' to describe it (Figure 3.11). For as long as it releases neurotransmitter, one neuron produces a sharply defined action on one or more receiving cells, e.g. another neuron or a muscle. The second cell is a very small distance from the first. Following release of neurotransmitter from the presynaptic cell, there is a very slight delay (0.5 msec) as the neurotransmitter crosses the gap, attaches to receptors on the postsynaptic membrane and exerts an effect. This is termed the **synaptic delay**.

The effect of a classical neurotransmitter can sometimes be localized to one target neuron (one-to-one neuron–neuron links of the kind shown are not the most common but introduce the subject clearly).

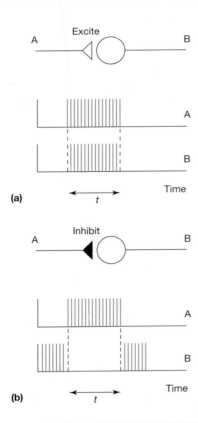

(a)

(b)

Figure 3.11 Two different types of connection between two neurons mediated by a classical neurotransmitter: (a) excitatory connection (a burst of activity in neuron A triggers B) and (b) inhibitory connection (neuron B is spontaneously active but is inhibited by activity in A).

Consider that, in Figure 3.12(a), synapse A is excitatory and synapse B is inhibitory. Typically, an inhibitory neuron employs a different neurotransmitter from that employed by an excitatory neuron. For example, the neurotransmitter represented by a triangular shape could be glutamate and that with a rectangular shape could be GABA (γ-aminobutyric acid). The shape of each neurotransmitter is drawn to correspond to the neurotransmitter's specific receptor at the surface of neuron C, analogous to a lock and key.

We shall meet various types of neurochemical in the subsequent pages. They are classified according to their chemical structure and function. Adrenalin and noradrenalin (known, respectively, as 'epinephrine' and 'norepinephrine' in the American literature), dopamine and serotonin (also termed 5-HT) are members of the class termed **monoamines**. Further subdividing, a subgroup of monoamines, consisting of dopamine, adrenalin and noradrenalin, is termed **catecholamines**.

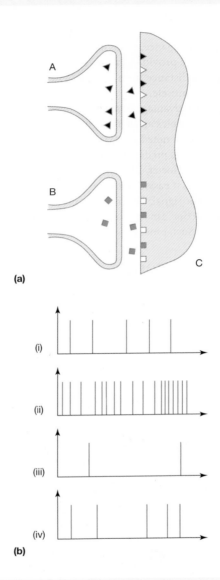

(a)

(b)

Figure 3.12 Two synapses, one excitatory (A) and one inhibitory (B), and the effects of activity in the presynaptic neurons A and B. (a) Synapses and (b) response of postsynaptic neuron C: (i) background activity; (ii) neuron A active (excitation); (iii) neuron B active (inhibition) and (iv) both A and B active (cancellation of effects).

Linking nervous system and function

How did synapses evolve? Let us try some armchair speculation. Take, for example, the system that reacts to a nociceptive stimulus (Figure 3.10). Speed often confers an important advantage, especially in reacting to tissue damage. However, as you can see, between sensory detection and the muscle, there are four neurons and four synapses, with an

inevitable slight delay at each synapse (Guyton, 1991).
Therefore, at first glance, it might seem more logical for
evolution to have provided simply a bundle of single neurons
that extend the distance from the site of detection of the
stimulus to the muscle.

The adaptive advantage of *flexibility* offers one answer to
why the more complex and very slightly slower system has
evolved. As was just noted, there is not invariably a
straightforward and predictable connection between stimulus
and response (cf. Floeter, 1999a). There is also some *processing*
of information as it passes along the route, e.g. inhibition can
be exerted on the signal. That is to say, the magnitude of the
withdrawal reaction can be modulated according to
circumstances. Such processing requires synapses.

Neuromodulators

Apart from classical neurotransmission, there is
neuromodulation in the CNS (Dismukes, 1979). A given
substance might serve as a **neuromodulator** in one context
but as a classical neurotransmitter in another. Like
neurotransmitters, neuromodulators are released from a neuron
and influence other neurons at receptors. However, compared
with the small distances travelled by neurotransmitters,
neuromodulators can diffuse relatively large distances within
the CNS from the site of release to that of action.

On occupying the receptor, neuromodulators do not have
a direct excitatory or inhibitory action. Unlike the sharp
detonating action of neurotransmitters (Figure 3.11),
neuromodulators have a smooth modulation role (i.e.
ranging from amplification to attenuation of strength of a
signal). Possibly they are something like the volume control
on a radio set, which makes the signal stronger or weaker but
does not change its content.

In some cases, acting via receptors at presynaptic neurons,
a neuromodulator can amplify the release of classical
neurotransmitter (Figure 3.13). In parts (a) and (b), the
frequency of action potentials in neuron 1 is the same.
However, the amount of neurotransmitter that is released is
different. Correspondingly, the postsynaptic neuron in part
(b) is more strongly affected than in part (a) as a result of the
influence of neuromodulator.

Alternatively, acting via receptors at the postsynaptic
membrane, a neuromodulator can make the neuron
occupied more sensitive to classical neurotransmitters. Other
neuromodulators inhibit release of transmitter or make a
neuron less sensitive to neurotransmitter.

So far the chapter has considered the structure of
connections between neurons as static. We now need to
consider briefly how connections between neurons can
change over time.

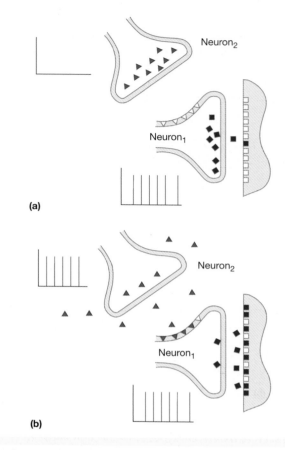

Figure 3.13 Classical neurotransmission and
neuromodulation at a presynaptic site. Presynaptic neuron$_1$
is active and neuromodulator (from neuron$_2$) is either
(a) unavailable or (b) available. Note increased release of
neurotransmitter and occupation of receptors in (b), which
increases the effect on the postsynaptic neuron. Note also
the diffusion of neuromodulator around the site of release.

Section summary

1   Comparing different synapses, neurotransmitter
has either an excitatory or an inhibitory effect,
depending upon the combination of transmitter
and receptors.

2   At an inhibitory synapse, activity in one neuron
inhibits the activity in another neuron.

3   The classical ('ballistic') action of a
neurotransmitter is to produce a localized effect
in a specified period of time.

4 The effects of classical neurotransmitters can be modulated. Neuromodulators are released from one neuron and, for example, make other neurons more or less sensitive in terms of generating action potentials.

Test your knowledge

(Answers on page 80)

3.5 In Figure 3.9, suppose that neurons 1, 2 and 3 are simultaneously active, each at the frequency shown by neuron 1 in part (b). Activity in neuron 4 would most resemble that shown in which part of the figure? (i) b, (ii) c.

3.6 In Figure 3.12, suppose that neuron C is active and then there is an increase in frequency of action potentials in neuron B. Which of the following effects on neuron C would this have? (i) Increase its activity, (ii) leave its activity unaffected, (iii) reduce its activity.

Neurons: development and learning

Introduction

Over the years, we grow and develop. Certain aspects of our behaviour change but in other regards our behaviour stays roughly the same. For example, we learn new skills but reflexes remain much the same. Reflecting these features of behaviour, nervous systems show both some changes and some constancy.

Concerning constancy, in some cases, connections between neurons at synapses seem to be fixed and clearly identifiable from animal to animal. This is exemplified by the connections underlying the reflex shown in Figure 3.1. Such systems are sometimes described as 'hard-wired', meaning that there is normally relatively little flexibility in their formation. The response of the system to its input is largely defined in advance. However, the term 'hard-wired' should not detract from the idea that adult nervous systems are the product of development. A developmental history underlies the formation of even straightforward sequences of neurons common to all members of a species. So, the developmental/ learning explanation comes in here. Nothing can be absolutely predetermined; neural circuits do not exist preformed in the genes.

Concerning the changing feature, over a lifetime or periods within it, there are changes in the structure and properties of the nervous system. More precisely, synaptic connections change and these underlie development and learning. Thus, the neural systems in which they are located are termed **soft-wired**. In other words, parts of nervous systems exhibit **plasticity**. Behaviour can show plasticity, which corresponds to that of its biological bases. In some cases, the apparent rigidity of the adult can be the outcome of processes that had flexibility when younger; alas some of us are at an age where we can almost notice any last signs of soft-wiring giving way to hard-wiring (try starting to learn a new foreign language at age 50).

Role of neurons and synapses

Functioning synapses, i.e. ones across which messages are regularly transmitted, can exert a self-reinforcing effect such that the connection gets stronger. With repeated occurrence of activity in the presynaptic neuron, there develops a greater effect on the postsynaptic neuron. Conversely, 'silent' synapses (i.e. those across which there is little or no traffic) can become ineffective.

Consider Figure 3.14. In part (a), the presynaptic neuron at the top is regularly active, indicated by action potentials. That at the bottom is permanently inactive. As shown in part (b), after a period of time and as a result of activity in the presynaptic neuron, the top synapse gets strengthened by means of increasing levels of neurotransmitter and receptors. The lower one becomes non-functional, indicated by loss of transmitter and receptors. Such changes in structure at the synapse involve changes in the formation of proteins at the presynaptic and postsynaptic sides (building in the case of the top synapse and breaking down in the case of the lower one).

For example, visual stimulation from a rich environment can activate and strengthen synapses in the visual system, with implications for subsequent perception. Conversely, if an eye is damaged or if it is covered for a period of time, the synapses in the pathway normally deriving information from that eye can weaken.

Learning represents plasticity in that the reaction changes with experience, e.g. Pavlov's study on salivation. All dogs tend to salivate to food in the mouth, owing to connections between neurons that are common to them all. Dogs do not normally salivate to ringing bells. In Pavlov's experiment, a bell was paired with food a number of times. After this, the dog salivated when the bell was presented on its own.

How might this be explained in neural terms? As a first approximation, one possibility is as follows. Imagine that food in the mouth activates a neuron and triggers salivation. See Figure 3.15(a). Suppose that the bell activates another neuron but normally does not trigger salivation (Figure 3.15(b)). In the procedure of conditioning, bell and food are paired. There might be a link formed by the parallel activation of the two neurons (Figure 3.15(c)) such that later the bell on its own is able to trigger salivation (Figure 3.15(d)).

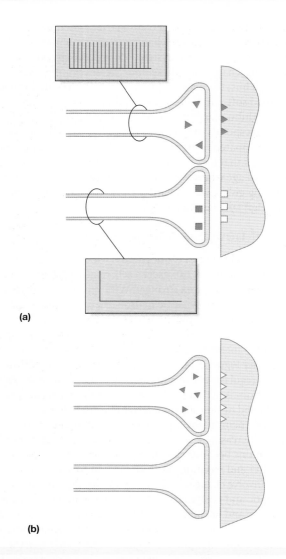

(a)

(b)

Figure 3.14 Changes in efficacy of synaptic transmission: (a) initial situation, showing two synapses, the upper regularly active and the lower permanently inactive; and (b) later situation: the upper is strengthened but the lower becomes ineffective.

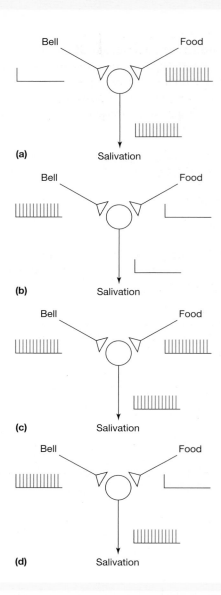

Figure 3.15 Simplified model of learning: (a) food triggers salivation, (b) bell does not trigger salivation, (c) bell and food are paired and (d) bell triggers salivation.

We described reinforcement earlier, as in a rat learning a task for food, an example of a developmental/learning explanation. The embodiment of this in the nervous system is assumed to be changes at certain synapses, e.g. those mediating links between the perception of the lever and the act of pressing it.

The discussion now starts to put some of the bits together in considering in more detail (a) how neurons are organized in forming a nervous system that contributes to coherent action and (b) the terminology used for describing the nervous system.

Section summary

1 Some combinations of neurons are hard-wired and others soft-wired.

2 Development and learning consist, among other things, of strengthening some synapses and weakening others.

Terminology and organization of the nervous system

This section takes a closer look at the nervous system both in its details and its overall construction; it considers how it is organized and classified.

Spinal cord organization

To discuss the nervous system further, it is necessary to get some anatomical orientation and we can start with the spinal cord. Figure 3.16(a) shows a short segment of the spinal cord and the protection that the bone of the vertebra offers to the neurons located therein. The term **dorsal** means towards the back, so the imaginary person represented in Figure 3.16(a) is facing out of the page. In humans, **ventral** means towards the belly, the front. Note the left–right symmetry. In sensory and motor terms, nerves to the person's left (the right-hand

side of the page) relate to the left side of their body and nerves to the person's right relate to the right side.

In the peripheral nervous system, a group of the cell bodies of neurons is termed a **ganglion** (plural, ganglia). In Figure 3.16(a), exemplifying this, a particular bulged area, termed the **dorsal root ganglion** (DRG), is indicated to each side. It contains the cell bodies of sensory neurons, two of which are illustrated in Figure 3.16(b).

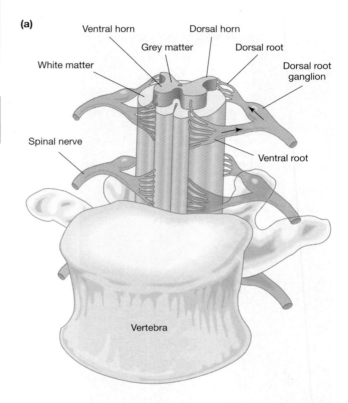

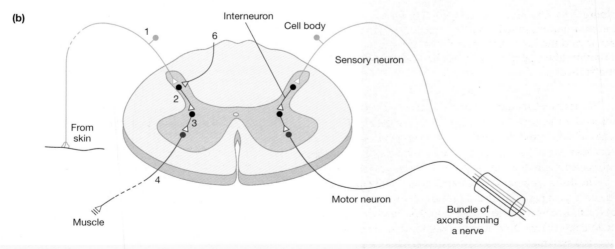

Figure 3.16 Spinal cord: (a) a section of spinal cord and (b) a thin slice of this section showing sensory, motor and interneurons. The bundle of axons corresponds to one of the nerves shown in blue in Figure 3.1(a).

Source of part (a): after Vander, *et al.* (1994) *Human Physiology*, Fig. 8.35, p. 215, reproduced with permission of The McGraw Hill Companies, Inc.

The ventral root is made up of the axons of motor neurons, two of which are shown in Figure 3.16(b). They convey information from the spinal cord to skeletal muscles. The cell bodies of motor neurons are located within the spinal cord and so the ventral root has no bulge comparable to the dorsal root ganglion (part (a)). The dorsal root and the ventral root converge to form a **spinal nerve** (Figure 3.16(a)).

The spinal cord and the associated spinal nerves are organized on a segmental basis (Figures 3.16 and 3.17). Each

segment of spinal cord is associated with a particular spinal nerve. The spinal nerves and the corresponding segmentation of the vertebrae (backbone) are shown in Figure 3.17. Figure 3.18 shows how the sensory surface of the body can be represented as a series of **dermatomes**. Each dermatome is associated with a particular spinal nerve such

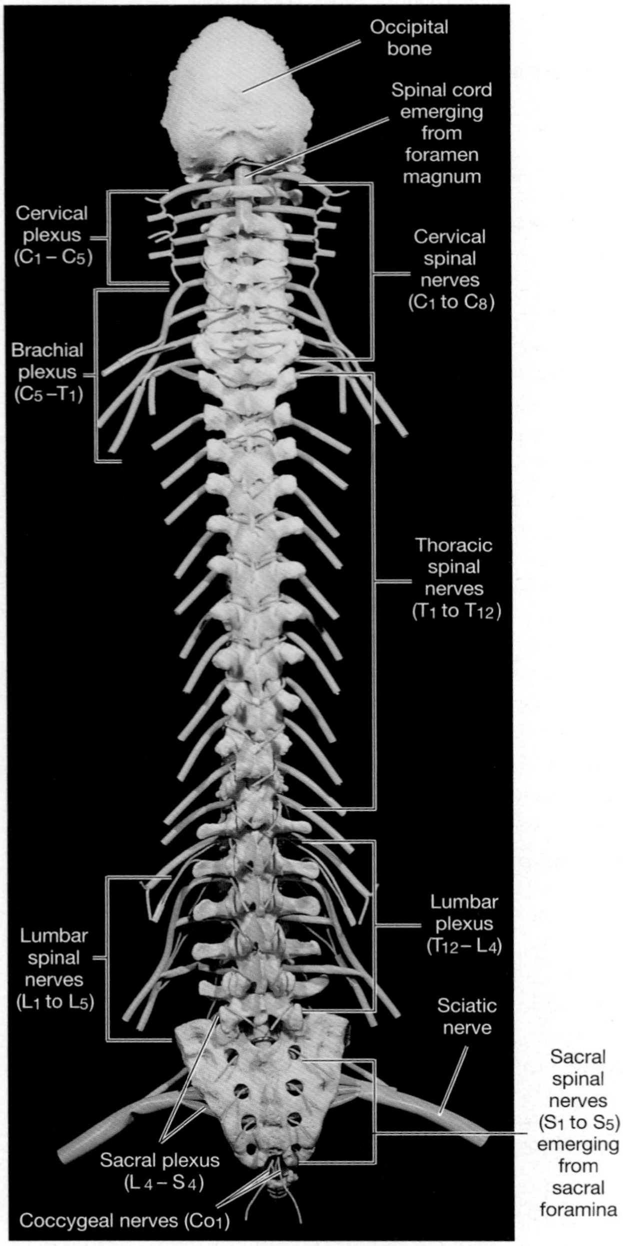

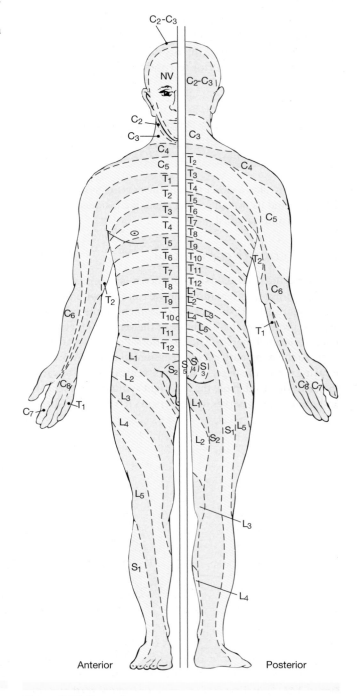

Figure 3.17 The backbone and spinal nerves.

Source: Martini *et al.* (2000, Fig. 14-3, p. 355).

Figure 3.18 Dermatomes.

Source: adapted from Martini *et al.* (2000, Fig. 14-8, p. 360).

that sensory information arising from within this dermatome travels to the spinal cord in the associated spinal nerve. For example, tissue damage arising at a toe would correspond to dermatome L5 and would be conveyed by axons that form part of nerve L5 (Figure 3.18).

The spinal cord comprises regions termed 'grey matter' and 'white matter' (Figure 3.16). Strictly speaking, white matter is pink rather than white (it is 'whitish' relative to the grey matter). The difference between these two regions arises from differences in the cellular constituents that are located there. Thus, the grey matter contains a relatively high density of cell bodies of neurons (e.g. those of the interneurons and motor neuron in Figure 3.16(b)).

The white matter consists of the axons of neurons the cell bodies of which are located elsewhere and associated cells described later. In Figure 3.16(b), for much of its length the axon of neuron 6 descends within the white matter of the spinal cord.

Neurons, nerves and tracts

Figure 3.16(b) shows part of the central and peripheral nervous systems. Neurons 2, 3 and 6 are located wholly within the CNS. Neurons 1 and 4 are partly in the CNS and partly in the peripheral nervous system.

Figure 3.16(b) also shows a bundle of axons of sensory and motor neurons. The light blue axons represent axons of neurons that detect events at the periphery (e.g. one neuron detects tissue damage and another detects cold) and the dark blue represent those that trigger action (e.g. muscular action). A bundle of axons in the peripheral nervous system is termed a **nerve**, the axons being physically located alongside each other and extending over the same distance (Figure 3.16b). By analogy, they are something like a bundle of wires in a cable of a telephone system.

An individual axon within any nerve can be classified according to its role: it *either* conveys information to the CNS (axons shaded light blue) *or* from it (axons shaded dark blue). Most nerves are composed of a mixture of both. The 'light blue' axons convey to the spinal cord information on events at a particular region of the body, in this case the foot. Each axon usually carries one specific type of information on, e.g., tissue damage, cold or harmless touch, at a particular region of the skin of a toe.

In the CNS, as in the periphery, a number of axons serving a common function would normally run in parallel transmitting information along the same route. Thus, alongside the axon of neuron 1 there would be others also carrying nociceptive information. In the CNS, a group of axons is termed a **tract** or pathway. A tract in the CNS is comparable to a nerve in the peripheral nervous system.

Neuron types

Neurons can be characterized by their structure or role. We shall look first at structure and then at role.

Structure

So far, neurons have been shown in a greatly simplified form. Some are shown more realistically in Figure 3.19, indicating that they come in different shapes and sizes. In each case, the neuron has a cell body, often termed a 'soma'. Among other things, the cell body contains the nucleus, which houses the genetic material. Some neurons have what are known as 'processes'. You have met already a particular type of process, a long structure termed an 'axon' or a 'nerve fibre' (e.g. Figure 3.16(b)). Another class of process is termed a 'dendrite', shown in Figure 3.19(a), (b), (d) and (e).

Neurons 2, 3 and 4 in Figure 3.16(b) are examples of the kind shown in Figure 3.19(a). In Figure 3.19(b), the cell body is out to one side of the axon. The sensory neurons of Figure 3.16(b) (e.g. neuron 1) are of this kind. Figure 3.19(c) represents a small neuron, without a process. It conveys information only a very small distance. This should be contrasted with the large distances that information is transmitted in neurons of the kind shown in Figure 3.19(a), (b) and (d).

Let us focus upon the type shown in Figure 3.19(a). The cell body is located at one end and the axon carries action potentials away from it. Figure 3.19(d) shows the same neuron again (neuron 1) but this time with some of its synaptic connections included. Neuron 1 can be influenced by means of synaptic contact at the dendrites (neurons 2, 3 and 4), the cell body (neuron 5) and the axon (neuron 6).

Synapses are classified according to where they are formed. For example, that between neurons 5 and 1 is an axo-somatic synapse, since it is between the axon of one neuron and the soma (cell body) of another. That between 6 and 1 is an axo-axonic synapse since it is from one axon to another. In turn, the activity of neuron 1 influences the activity of neuron 7. Figure 3.19(e) shows part of a neuron and a development of the dendrite known as 'dendritic spines', the site where synaptic connections are often made.

Most of the neurons that we discuss transmit information by action potentials, i.e. brief pulses of electricity. However, some transmit by means of smooth changes in voltage, rather than the pulses that characterize action potentials. For neural communication over anything but very short distances, action potentials are involved. The neuron of Figure 3.19(c) would communicate by smooth changes.

The speed at which neurons transmit action potentials varies between around 0.2 to 100 metres/second ($m\,s^{-1}$). If the diameter of the axon is large, the speed is higher. When they are transmitting action potentials, neurons are said to be showing 'activity'.

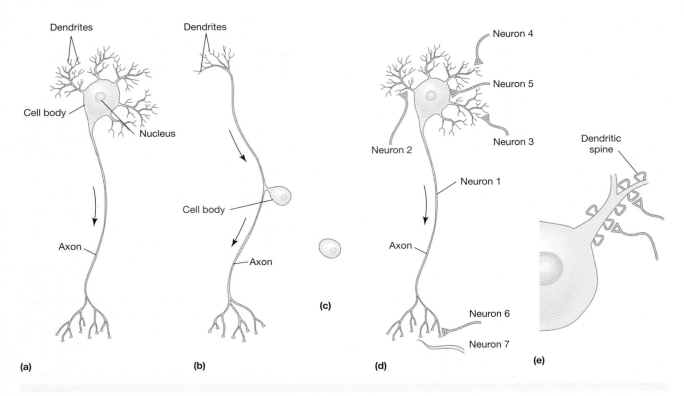

Figure 3.19 Neurons: (a) cell body to one end of the axon, (b) cell body to the side of the axon, (c) having no processes, (d) inputs and output represented and (e) with dendritic spines shown.

Source of (a) (b) and (d): adapted from Martini *et al.* (2000, Fig. 13-10, p. 340).

The role of neurons can be related to a classification based on their different types, as follows.

Afferent neurons

The term **afferent neuron** is often used to describe sensory neurons, though it can also be applied more broadly. Thus, every sensory neuron can be termed an 'afferent neuron' but 'afferent neuron' is used not only to refer to a sensory neuron. As the general definition, given a location forming a frame of reference within the nervous system, 'afferent' refers to a neuron conducting information *to* this location. For example, 'afferents' to a brain region conduct information to the region. Since the spinal cord is the frame of reference for Figure 3.16(b), afferents are sensory neurons that carry information to it (e.g. neuron 1).

Efferent neurons

A class of neurons, motor neurons, conveys information from the CNS to the periphery, where they trigger action through what are termed **effectors**. These are the muscles and glands that exert the *final effect* within an action.

Another name for motor neurons is **efferent neurons**. As with 'afferent', this term can also be used more widely. Efferent means neurons that carry information away from a structure that forms a frame of reference; in the present case, the spinal cord, e.g. neuron 4 of Figure 3.16(b).

Motor neurons are said to 'innervate' the muscle, which means that they supply the neural input to it. What triggers activity in a motor neuron? There are basically two types of trigger (Figure 3.16(b)). The motor neuron can be activated either as part of a local reflex (neurons 1, 2, 3 and 4) or as part of a descending pathway from the brain (neurons 6, 2, 3 and 4). It is through such a descending pathway that voluntary commands to move are put into effect.

How is an increase in the strength of activation of a muscle achieved? It is partly by increasing the frequency of action potentials within motor neurons. Imagine that you consciously exert an increasing force at a leg muscle to overcome some obstacle. The physical basis of this is an increasing frequency of action potentials in neurons that descend from the brain (e.g. neuron 6). In turn, this triggers increased activation of the motor neurons that extend to the muscles doing the work.

The cranial nerves

The spinal cord mediates information transmission between the brain and regions of body below the neck (Figure 3.16). However, as you might well have guessed already, communication between the brain and other regions of the head is not via this route. See Figure 3.20. Rather, information travels via a series of special nerves, termed **cranial nerves**. For example, the optic nerve transmits visual information from the eyes to the brain. In the opposite direction, neurons within cranial nerves transmit information from the brain to regions of the head, e.g. motor neurons activate the eye muscles. The vagus nerve and glossopharyngeal nerve carry afferent information from various regions of the body (e.g. heart and stomach), as well as taste information from the mouth. The vagus also carries efferent information to the heart and stomach.

The cranial nerves complete the introduction to the nervous system. The discussion now turns to chemical transmission of information by hormones. However, this is necessarily discussed in the context of interactions with the nervous system.

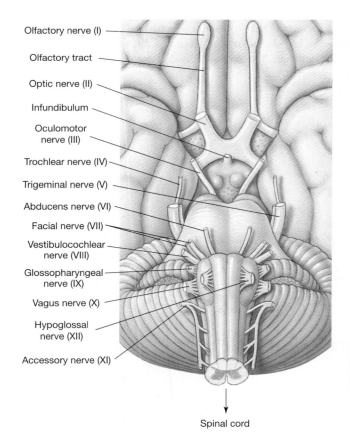

Olfactory nerve (I)
Olfactory tract
Optic nerve (II)
Infundibulum
Oculomotor nerve (III)
Trochlear nerve (IV)
Trigeminal nerve (V)
Abducens nerve (VI)
Facial nerve (VII)
Vestibulocochlear nerve (VIII)
Glossopharyngeal nerve (IX)
Vagus nerve (X)
Hypoglossal nerve (XII)
Accessory nerve (XI)

Spinal cord

Figure 3.20 The cranial nerves, shown cut away at the point of entry to the brain.

Source: adapted from Martini *et al.* (2000, Fig. 15-21(b), p. 405).

Test your knowledge

(Answers on page 80)

3.9 In Figure 3.19(d), relative to neuron 1 which of the following is post-synaptic? (i) 2, (ii) 3, (iii) 7.

3.10 In Figure 3.19(d), which of the synapses shown are axodendritic? (i) 6 → 1, (ii) 4 → 1, (iii) 5 → 1.

3.11 In Figure 3.19(d), which synapse is axosomatic? (i) 5 → 1, (ii) 4 → 1, (iii) 1 → 7

3.12 Which part of the neurons of Figure 3.19 would be housed within a dorsal root ganglion? (i) Axon shown in (a), (ii) cell body shown in (b), (iii) cell body shown in (d).

Hormones – the endocrine system

Introduction

The term 'endocrine system' describes the hormones of the body, the cells and glands that secrete them and the effects that they exert (Becker *et al.*, 1992). In some cases, a collection of neurons (not called a gland) secrete a hormone, a **neurohormone,** into a blood vessel. Hormones come in various types and examples of the more 'conventional' hormones are described first. More 'unconventional' hormones, which were relatively recently discovered, follow rather different principles of organization and are described later. They have been selected to illustrate different features of the collaboration between nervous and endocrine systems.

Chemically, a hormone and its receptors can sometimes be identical to a neurotransmitter and its receptors. Similar to the action of a neurotransmitter, when a hormone occupies a receptor, the target cell is affected. The neural and hormonal modes of communication are compared later.

Classical hormones

Hormones that were discovered relatively early in the history of studying the subject are termed here 'classical hormones'. They fit a well-understood pattern of action. Figure 3.21 shows some of the glands in the body that secrete hormones. This section gives some examples of classical hormones and illustrates their role in the adaptive function of the body.

Insulin

The pancreas secretes the hormone insulin, which influences a very large number of the cells of the body. It is released into the general circulation and distributed widely. Cells use a sugar, glucose, as fuel for their energy requirements and take this up from the blood. Insulin promotes glucose uptake. Neurons are an exception to this since their glucose uptake is not insulin-dependent.

If the glucose level in the blood increases, a control system detects this and triggers the release of insulin, so that cells take up glucose. See Figure 3.22(a). Conversely, when there are low levels of blood glucose, the secretion of insulin is reduced and insulin-dependent cells are unable to take it up. There is an important functional significance to this. Cells of the brain rely upon glucose as their fuel, whereas other cells can exploit alternative substances for energy. This means that, at times of low availability of blood glucose, any glucose is targeted for privileged use by the brain.

Consider an artificial situation of the injection of glucose into the blood, such that glucose levels in the blood rise sharply. After a time delay, there will be an increased secretion of insulin, which will increase the movement of glucose into cells. This shows that the insulin control system is sensitive to blood glucose. This much is regulatory physiology, so where is the interest of the psychologist in insulin?

To answer this, consider more natural circumstances; a rise in blood glucose level would be due to food arriving from the gut. The arrival of food is preceded by the sight and

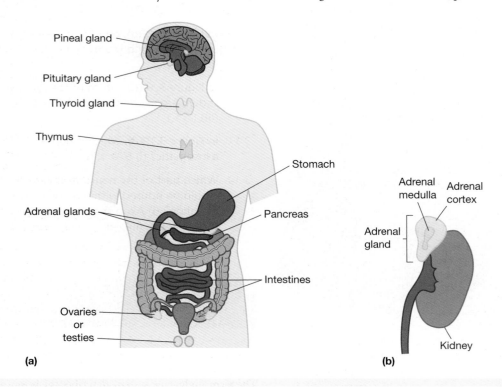

(a)

(b)

Figure 3.21 Hormones: (a) location of some of the glands that secrete them and (b) kidney showing adrenal gland and its divisions.

Source: adapted from Toates (1997a, Figure 3.1, p. 142).

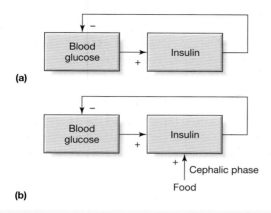

(a)

(b)

Figure 3.22 The insulin–glucose system: (a) control of insulin by blood glucose level and (b) addition of cephalic control. + = raises, – = lowers.

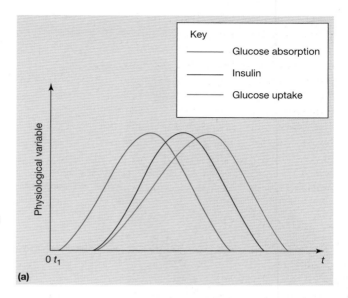

(a)

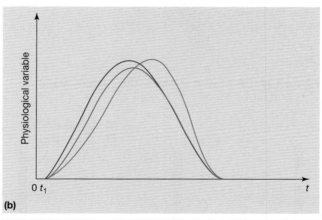

(b)

Figure 3.23 The control of insulin secretion. Absorption of glucose, insulin concentration in the blood and uptake of glucose by cells: (a) response in the absence of a cephalic phase and (b) response with cephalic phase functioning.

smell of food and its ingestion. The nervous system detects these stimuli and neural signals trigger insulin secretion, termed the **cephalic phase** of insulin release (Langhans and Scharrer, 1992). See Figure 3.22(b). Thus, under normal circumstances, an increase in secretion of insulin occurs before the glucose even gets to the blood. See Figure 3.23. The insulin response *anticipates* the arrival of glucose.

Thus, shortly after encountering food, cellular uptake of glucose from the blood and the **metabolism** of glucose (its chemical conversion and use as a fuel by the cell) can proceed, since replenishment of the blood glucose is on the way.

This illustrates how the nervous system (detection of food) and the endocrine system (release and action of insulin) act in a coordinated way to facilitate regulation of a vital parameter of the body.

Arginine vasopressin

The hormone arginine vasopressin (AVP) serves regulation of body fluids and illustrates neuroendocrine control, involving neurons that secrete hormones (Verney, 1947). (AVP is sometimes termed anti-diuretic hormone or ADH.) AVP is a hormone synthesized in neurons located in particular **nuclei** (singular, **nucleus**) of the brain. In this sense, a nucleus is a collection of cell bodies of neurons in the CNS and is not to be confused with the earlier meaning, as part of a neuron. A particular nucleus can provide a landmark when describing bits of the brain.

AVP is synthesized in the cell bodies of particular neurons and transported along their axons to the terminals at the pituitary gland, where it is stored. In Figure 3.24, neuron 2 represents one such neuron. When the body is deficient in water, neurons (e.g. neuron 1) detect this and excite AVP-containing neurons. Activation of AVP-containing neurons causes them to release AVP into the blood. AVP is transported

to the kidney where it slows the production of urine. Conversely, excess water in the body inhibits the secretion of AVP and the kidney excretes large amounts of urine.

The AVP–kidney system cannot gain water. In dehydration, it can only inhibit water loss, which is, of course, better than doing nothing. Water can only be gained by drinking and the AVP–kidney system acts alongside the behavioural system of thirst and drinking to regulate the level of body water. See Figure 3.25. The AVP–kidney system is made up of components of both the nervous and endocrine systems.

The example again illustrates how the nervous system (detection of fluid level) and the endocrine system (action of AVP) act together to preserve the homeostasis of the body.

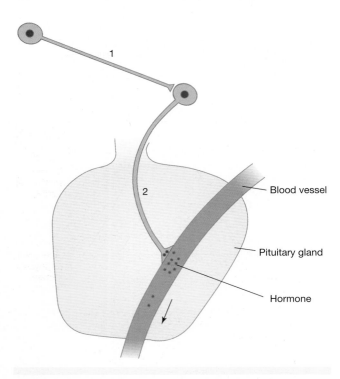

Figure 3.24 The control of AVP at the pituitary gland.

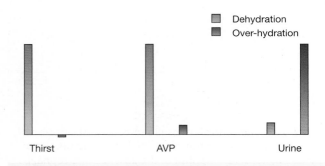

Figure 3.25 Regulation of body water level by control exerted over drinking and urine production.

Oestrogen

In many species, there is a distinct mating season or 'time-slot', i.e. period of time when sexual behaviour is most likely to occur (Beach, 1947). Hormones of the class termed **oestrogens** show cycles of activity within the female's body. A principal biological basis of the mating season is that oestrogens sensitize the female's sexual motivation. This makes the female sexually responsive and fertile at a particular part of the cycle. At a causal level, this can be understood in terms of a changed reaction to the male, depending upon the cyclic action of hormones on the brain and other organs of the body.

Consider Figure 3.26. The female rat's reflex reaction to the touch of a male depends upon whether a particular set of neurons in her brain has been sensitized by oestrogens. In a causal sense, the hormone does not *trigger* mating, since the touch does that, but the hormone makes a mating response to the touch more likely to occur. At a fertile point in her cycle, sensitization is evident. At infertile times, the hormones do not exert this effect and she is unresponsive to the advances of the male. Part (a) shows the situation when hormones have sensitized her. She reacts to touch by assuming the mating posture, termed **lordosis**. Such behaviour also makes functional sense: by biasing towards sexual behaviour at a time when the female is fertile, the chances of reproduction are maximized.

Testosterone

The hormone **testosterone** is secreted within the body of both sexes, though it is sometimes termed a 'male sex hormone'. In the male, it is secreted from the testes. In females, the adrenal gland is its principal source. Testosterone's secretion is controlled by other hormones which are secreted into the bloodstream at the pituitary gland at the base of the brain and then travel to the glands that secrete testosterone (Figure 3.21). Neural events within the brain determine the secretion of the 'trigger hormones', in a way somewhat similar to that for AVP.

After its release (e.g. from the testes), testosterone finds its way throughout the body to various target organs. These include certain nuclei in the brain, where it has effects upon particular groups of neurons (McEwen *et al.*, 1986). There is a reciprocal relationship between the level of hormone and psychological factors. In the direction (hormone) →

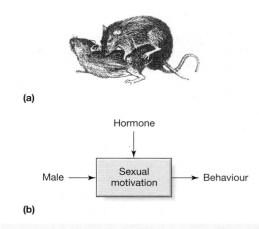

Figure 3.26 Rat mating: (a) the posture, showing the female lordosis response and (b) female sexual motivation, and therefore behaviour, depend upon both the trigger of the male and the effects of hormones on her nervous system.

(nervous system) → (behaviour), testosterone increases tendencies to sexual and aggressive behaviour. In the direction (behaviour) → (nervous system) → (hormone), defeat of male primates leads to a fall in production of testosterone (Rose *et al.*, 1975). The fall has an effect on behaviour, steering it away from challenging the dominance of other animals. There is functional significance to such steering of cognition and behaviour by hormones: defeat might be a time to readjust strategy away from confrontation and offence. The message from studying testosterone is the need to take into account the interaction of nervous and endocrine systems as well as social interactions.

So much for the action of the classical hormones – we now look at a type of hormone that does not fall into this classical pattern.

An 'unconventional' system

General

We can identify two clearly defined actions: classical neurotransmitters and classical hormones. However, scientists now see them not as two exclusive classes into which every example can be allocated. Rather, they are two cases on a spectrum of effects. In addition to unambiguous (i.e. classical) neurotransmission and hormones, there are shades of grey: a range of systems that have features of each, described with expressions such as **neurohormone** (Deutch and Roth, 1999). (Neither do neuromodulators, described earlier, fit into an entirely neat category.) For student and researcher alike, life might appear more and more to be a 'mess', as compared with the neat and simple elegance of the classical picture (Dismukes, 1979). You might feel that psychology students of the 1950s and earlier were lucky to have avoided all this.

As a generic definition, a hormone is carried in the blood from a site where it is released to a site where it produces action. However, there can be differences in how far different hormones are distributed. The distinction between hormones and neurotransmitters starts to break down here. Some neurohormones are not circulated in the whole bloodstream to influence distant targets. Instead, they are released from neurons into one particular vessel and transported a short distance within it to influence a local target.

Corticotropin releasing factor

Figure 3.27 illustrates an example of a local hormone, corticotropin releasing hormone (CRH), or 'corticotropin releasing factor' (CRF) (Akil *et al.*, 1999; Rivier, 1991).

CRF is synthesized, stored and released by neurons that have cell bodies in a region of the brain termed the

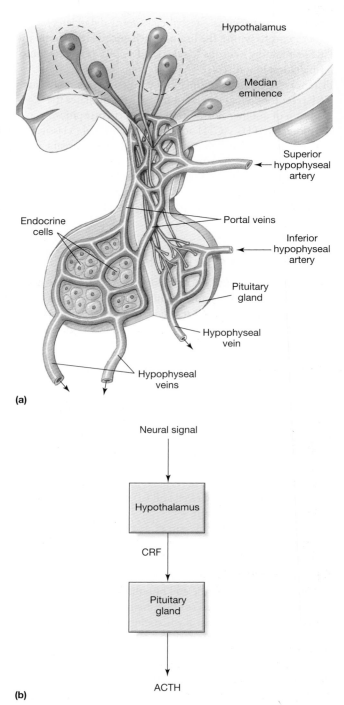

(a)

(b)

Figure 3.27 The pituitary gland. (a) Links to the brain region termed hypothalamus and blood flow to and from pituitary gland. (b) Hormonal sequence.

Source of (a): adapted from Martini *et al.* (2000, Fig. 19-6, p. 505).

hypothalamus. In part (b), this brain region is simply labelled 'hypothalamus' (described in more detail later). Other neurons within the brain, which encode fear, excite the CRF-containing neurons to release CRF. CRF is released into a small local blood vessel. Then it is transported the short distance to the region of the pituitary gland, where there are CRF receptors. Their occupation by CRF stimulates the secretion of another hormone, adrenocorticotrophic hormone (ACTH). ACTH acts as a conventional ('classical') hormone, i.e. it is distributed in the whole bloodstream and its distant target is the adrenal gland. At the cortex (meaning outer layer) of the adrenal gland ('adrenal cortex'), ACTH triggers the release of a class of hormones termed corticosteroids. These serve to mobilize the body for action, e.g. in recruiting fuels.

Classification and comparison

Neurotransmitters and hormones have an important feature in common: they communicate information from a cell that releases them to a cell *that has receptors for them*. A difference between neurotransmitters and hormones lies in the distance between the releasing cell and the cell with receptors: very small for neurotransmitters and relatively large for hormones.

Whether a substance is classified as neurotransmitter or hormone depends not on its chemical make-up but on its mode of release and transport. A substance acts as a hormone where it is (a) released at a distance from its target and (b) carried to the target by the blood. It acts as a (classical) neurotransmitter where (i) it is released by a neuron and occupies receptors at an immediately adjacent cell, e.g. neuron or muscle cell and (ii) has a sharply defined onset and end of its action.

There are possibly some substances that serve uniquely as neurotransmitters and others that act only as hormones. However, in several cases the same chemical substance can serve as either neurotransmitter or hormone. Adrenalin and noradrenalin (epinephrine and norepinephrine), for instance, can be classified as either neurotransmitters or hormones, depending upon where they are released and exert their effect. Evolutionary processes had some 'raw materials' (e.g. noradrenalin) available and have utilized them in serving different roles.

There are receptors at the muscles of the heart which adrenalin, circulating in the bloodstream, occupies. When they are occupied, the activity of heart muscle is accelerated (Dampney, 1994), a hormonal action. However, within the CNS, there are also receptors for adrenalin. These are at the membrane of neurons. Typically, adrenalin that is released from an immediately adjacent neuron attaches itself to such receptors. Acting in this mode, adrenalin is a neurotransmitter. See Figure 3.28.

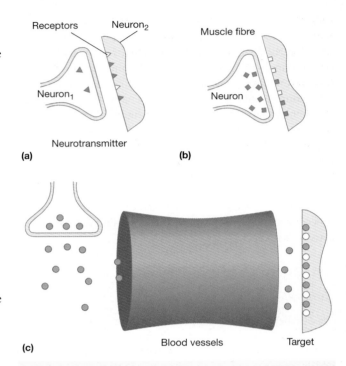

Figure 3.28 Classification of (classical) neurotransmitters and hormones: (a) a neurotransmitter, released from a neuron and influencing another neuron, (b) a neurotransmitter, released from one neuron and influencing a muscle and (c) a hormone.

In some cases, a particular hormone and a chemically identical neurotransmitter attach to the same set of receptors.

Why has nature evolved two means of communication: action potentials (with associated neurotransmitters) and hormones? They serve different but complementary roles. A hormone usually serves the general and broad transmission of information to sites in different locations throughout the body. By contrast, a neurotransmitter can be more specific and localized: for instance, one neuron might transmit information simply to a second neuron or to a muscle fibre (and to no other target).

For information transmission over relatively long distances, neurons have a clear advantage over hormones: speed. Time is involved in a hormone being released, circulating in the blood and finally influencing a distant location. Thus, neurons can transfer specific information at a relatively high speed.

There is a property of hormones that makes them more suitable for certain roles than neural connections. Although a hormone is slower, it solves the problem of how to transmit information to a large number of different distant sites all influenced in the same way. Hormonal action is typically broader than that of a classical neurotransmitter, affecting wide areas of influence and being more diffuse in time. (By analogy, a single television programme can be broadcast from one location to many different homes, whereas a telephone is suitable for one-to-one messages.) A good example of such 'broadcast' action is that of insulin. The same message, 'take up glucose', is clearly appropriate for a very large number of individual cells that are influenced by the single hormonal command. Only a hormone is able to broadcast this information throughout the body. It is impossible to imagine a network of neurons transmitting information to every cell outside the nervous system.

Occupation of a receptor by a hormone can have either a sharp and acute effect or a more long-term effect that is mediated via action at the gene of the target cell (Deutch and Roth, 1999; McEwen *et al.*, 1986).

Knowledge of both nervous and endocrine systems is essential in trying to understand the autonomic nervous system, which is the topic of the next section.

Section summary

1 The endocrine system consists of the sites of secretion of hormones in the body, the hormones and their targets.

2 A hormone is a substance released at one location and carried by the blood to cause action at a distant location.

3 The effect of a hormone is generally more wide-ranging and diffuse than that of a classical neurotransmitter.

4 A classical hormone is a chemical that is (i) secreted into the blood at one site and (ii) circulated broadly by the blood, and that (iii) exerts actions at more distant sites.

5 Examples of classical hormonal actions include (i) that of adrenalin (epinephrine) and noradrenalin (norepinephrine), (ii) insulin's action on cells taking up glucose, (iii) arginine vasopressin's action at the kidney and (iv) testosterone's action on the brain.

6 A given substance might act as either neurotransmitter or hormone. The difference lies in the mode of release of the substance and how it gets to its target.

7 Acting in their conventional ('classical') mode, hormones are an effective way of influencing multiple targets in different parts of the body at the same time.

8 Corticotropin releasing factor (CRF) is an atypical hormone. It is released from neurons in the brain and carried, in a local blood vessel, the short distance to the pituitary gland.

9 Neuronal communication is faster than hormonal communication.

Test your knowledge

(Answers on page 80)

3.13 Which of the following is involved in the homeostatic regulation of body-fluids? (i) Insulin, (ii) testosterone, (iii) AVP.

3.14 Which of the following are released from neurons? (i) AVP, (ii) testosterone, (iii) insulin, (iv) CRF.

3.15 Which of the following has the shortest distance from site of release to site of action? (i) AVP, (ii) CRF, (iii) insulin.

The autonomic nervous system

Introduction

When discussing the nervous system and action on the external world, it was emphasized that adaptation requires coordination between such activity and that of the internal environment. This section focuses upon coordination in so far as the internal environment is concerned.

Activity in the autonomic nervous system (ANS) determines such things as the production of saliva in the mouth and the state of the **viscera** (the internal organs) of the body, e.g. the beating of the heart, digestive activity by the stomach and intestine and adjustments of blood flow as in blushing. The ANS is also involved in energy exchanges between stores. Autonomic effects are mediated by special types of muscle and gland. The muscles that control internal actions have a different anatomical form from skeletal muscles. As noted earlier, many of these can be classified as smooth muscle. An exception is the muscle that controls the contractions of the heart, which is termed 'cardiac muscle'.

Whether we are asleep or awake, the ANS controls our internal environment, making adjustments to maintain optimal conditions. Examples of the activity of the ANS include (1) by its control of the stomach's churning action, digestion is facilitated and (2) by its control over blood flows, food in the gut normally triggers a diversion of blood to the gut in the interests of digestion. Under ANS control, such activities normally proceed at an unconscious, involuntary level, described as serving the body's 'housekeeping functions'. The ANS is sometimes termed the 'involuntary nervous system'. It is perhaps just as well that housekeeping is organized unconsciously (cf. Powley, 1999). Just consider some of the disastrous actions that we manage to inflict on our external environments through our conscious choices and the triggering of the somatic nervous system. In all probability, we would do an even worse job at trying consciously to organize the internal environment!

The ANS also controls the activity of certain glands that secrete hormones (e.g. some adrenal hormones, described earlier) and other substances. For instance, an increase in body temperature to above normal triggers parts of the ANS to promote the secretion of sweat from glands distributed over the surface of the body. Sweating cools the body.

Definitions

What is autonomic?

The ANS derives its name from the fact that it can operate with some *autonomy* ('automatically') from the rest of the nervous system, reminding us that its activity does not require conscious intervention. Thus, the functions that the ANS controls are clearly to be distinguished from those triggered by the skeletal muscles on the external environment.

Neurons that innervate the effectors of the body (muscles and glands) can be unambiguously identified as those of *either* the somatic nervous system *or* the autonomic nervous system. For example, a motor neuron controlling a skeletal muscle is part of the somatic nervous system and one innervating the heart is part of the ANS.

How autonomous?

Under various conditions, the ANS operates autonomously. However, conscious strategies can also influence its activity. As we have seen, parts of the nervous system outside the ANS normally exert an influence over it, so that the autonomic changes are functionally appropriate to behaviour (Hess, 1981). The bear incident illustrates this.

For another example, the blood flow to the genitals is under autonomic control. However, it can be affected by conscious mental strategies involving the use of sexual themes in the imagination, as some people appear to discover for themselves without the help of a textbook of biological psychology. Conversely, indicating the limitations of conscious control, the ANS sometimes 'goes its own way' in the face of our conscious commands. For example, in their courting days, many over-anxious men have found that, to their cost, they simply could not will the blood to flow to where they would most like it to flow.

Autonomic changes appear in anticipation of associated behaviour (Hilton, 1979). For example, the CNS perceives a threat and selects a defensive behavioural strategy and this then excites the ANS (Lisander, 1979). As a result, the ANS excites the heart to beat faster. This can be seen even in the absence of overt reactions as when we seethe with anger, the behavioural expression of which remains inhibited in spite of the triggering of autonomic effects on the heart and other organs.

Humans can sometimes learn to exert some control over the body functions that are part of the ANS, e.g. to reduce heart-rate (Lal *et al.*, 1998). This again underlines the fact that the ANS can only be understood in the context of its interaction with parts of the CNS concerned with conscious awareness and voluntary decision-making.

Divisions of the ANS

The ANS can be classified into two branches (sometimes termed 'systems' or 'divisions'): the **sympathetic branch** and **parasympathetic branch**. Figure 3.29 illustrates the sympathetic division. The roots of the term 'sympathetic' lie in the observation of its role in harmonization (coherence) between organs (Powley, 1999). Figure 3.30 shows the parasympathetic division (meaning 'lying alongside the sympathetic').

Note the organs innervated and, on comparing divisions, the different locations at which neurons of the ANS leave the CNS for the periphery. Sometimes the expression 'sympathetic neuron' or 'parasympathetic neuron' is used. This refers to a neuron that forms part of one or other of these divisions.

The two branches normally exert opposite effects as a 'push–pull' control. For example, activity in the sympathetic branch increases the vigour of the heart's pumping, whereas parasympathetic activity inhibits it (you saw the action of inhibition in Figure 3.12 and a similar principle applies here). There is normally some activity in both branches, so 'activation' or 'producing action' means increasing activity in one branch and decreasing it in the other (Polosa *et al.*, 1979). Under some conditions, one or other ANS branch dominates. This means that we can refer to 'sympathetic activation' or 'parasympathetic activation'.

Generally, the sympathetic branch is activated when the animal is engaging in (or about to engage in) active behaviour mediated via the somatic nervous system. This is particularly evident at times of fight or flight, e.g. the heart is stimulated to beat faster. Under sympathetic control, mobilization of energy reserves from stores is instigated, so fuel is available for the muscles. Adrenalin (epinephrine) and noradrenalin (norepinephrine) secreted from the adrenal

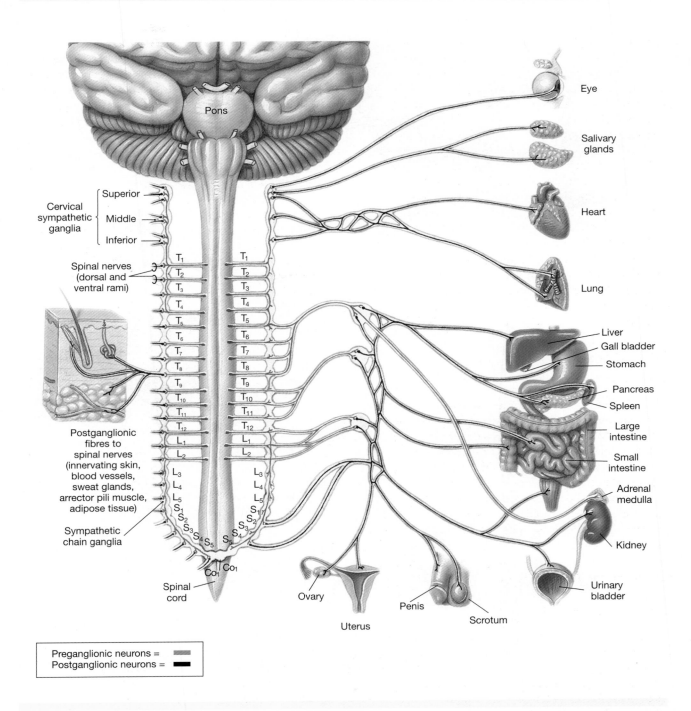

Figure 3.29 The sympathetic division.

Source: adapted from Martini *et al.* (2000, Fig. 17-5, p. 449).

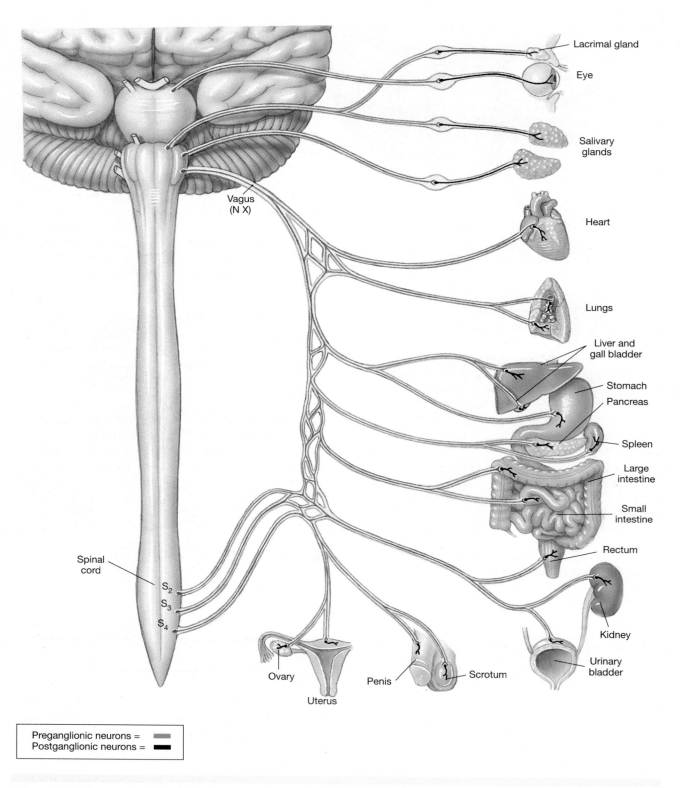

Figure 3.30 The parasympathetic division.

Source: adapted from Martini *et al*. (2000, Fig. 17-9, p. 454).

glands exert this effect. Sometimes the term 'autonomic activation' is employed with no specification as to branch. This would mean sympathetic activation.

The parasympathetic branch is activated and the sympathetic relatively inactivated at times of relaxation, e.g. the heart-rate is slowed. At rest, as a result of the autonomic state, blood is diverted from the skeletal muscles to the gut to assist digestion. In terms of function, at rest, blood does not need to be circulated so rapidly. However, there can be situations of emergency in which the parasympathetic branch is activated. These depend upon the species and situation. Parasympathetic activation tends to occur at times when there is no active behavioural strategy that can be switched in (Vingerhoets, 1985). For example, in rabbits, detection of a predator can be associated with immobility and a slowing of heart-rate (Jordan, 1990).

Within the ANS, there are two ways in which control is exerted over the internal environment, described in the section that follows.

The effectors of the system

Muscles

At sites throughout the body there are smooth muscles, the activity of which is determined by the ANS, e.g. in the wall of vessels of the circulation (Figure 3.31) (Loewy, 1990). The diameter of blood vessels depends in part upon the contraction of this smooth muscle. In turn, contraction is determined by neural activity of the neurons of the ANS that innervate the muscle. Transmitter is released from autonomic neurons, attaches to smooth muscles and these change their contraction, comparable to motor neurons and skeletal muscles.

The activity of cardiac muscle that causes the heart to beat can be modulated by the ANS. It is either excited or inhibited, thereby either increasing or decreasing the vigour of the heart's activity and blood flow from the heart.

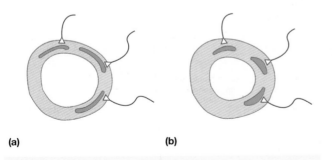

(a)   (b)

Figure 3.31 Smooth muscle in the wall of a blood vessel: (a) relaxed and (b) contracted.

Artificial stimulation of the vagus nerve (which innervates the heart) slows the heartbeat and this is chemically mediated, as part of the parasympathetic division of the ANS. How do we know this? In 1921, Otto Loewi working at the University of Graz in Austria had a famous dream about it (Kuffler and Nicholls, 1976). In his sleep, Loewi saw that a chemical released from the neuron endings mediated the effect. So if, as an experiment, Loewi were to bathe the heart of a frog, some of the chemical would be released into the bathing solution. Suppose that this solution were then applied to the heart of another frog. There might be sufficient chemical to cause a reduction in beat of the second heart. Loewi woke up and wrote down the idea for the experiment. Alas, the next morning, he was unable to read what he had written. Fortunately, the following night, he awoke with the same idea and this time did the experiment. The result of Loewi's experiment was as he dreamed it.

The chemical involved is acetylcholine, and Loewi's demonstration was highly influential in the development of neuroscience. To some, Loewi's experience exemplifies a broader creative aspect of dreaming. It is interesting that the role of acetylcholine, a substance having a profound effect on dreaming, should itself have been discovered by means of a dream (Perry et al., 1999). The moral of the story is to keep a pencil and paper by your bed and write clearly.

Secretions

The adrenal gland was shown in Figure 3.21. Although there are two such glands, the singular term 'gland' is commonly used. At this gland, activity within neurons of the ANS causes the hormones adrenalin and noradrenalin (epinephrine and norepinephrine) to be released into the bloodstream. These hormones are then transported around the body and influence multiple and distant sites. Receptors that are sensitive to adrenalin and noradrenalin are found at various sites, e.g. the heart.

At a time of emotional excitation, there is acceleration of the heart's activity mediated via two routes acting in parallel:

(i) neurons acting directly on heart muscle and (ii) neurons that trigger adrenal hormones that in turn act on heart muscle. The adaptive function of this link between nervous and endocrine systems is clear. It helps to prepare the body for fight or flight, e.g. in accelerating heart-rate and mobilizing fuels for use by the muscles.

Figure 3.29 shows one aspect of how the adrenal gland operates. A series of sympathetic neurons terminates at a part of the gland: the adrenal medulla. The adrenal medulla comprises a series of cells, which secrete their product, the hormones adrenalin (epinephrine) and noradrenalin (norepinephrine), into the bloodstream when the sympathetic neurons are activated. At times of emergency and exertion of effort, adrenalin and noradrenalin are released in large amounts. These effects help the body to cope. For example, metabolic fuel is mobilized from the liver and distributed along with oxygen at a high rate.

Cell bodies and axons

Figure 3.32 compares and contrasts the anatomy of part of the ANS and the somatic nervous system. In each case, neurons span the distance between the spinal cord and the effector in the body. However, a difference is also represented in Figure 3.32. In the somatic nervous system, single effector (i.e. motor) neurons, with cell bodies in the spinal cord, link the CNS and the skeletal muscles. In the ANS, combinations of two neurons span the distance from the CNS to the effector organ.

An **autonomic ganglion** (plural, autonomic ganglia) houses the collection of cell bodies of the second neurons, physically located together. In the figures, the axons of autonomic neurons are described as either 'preganglionic axon' or 'postganglionic axon'.

Try comparing Figures 3.29 and 3.30, looking at the location of ganglia, i.e. where preganglionic neurons contact postganglionic neurons. You can see that the site of the ganglia is different in the two branches of the ANS. Most of the sympathetic ganglia are located close to the spinal cord. In the parasympathetic branch, the ganglia are all in the periphery, at, or close to, the organ that the fibre innervates. For example, the cell body of the representative neuron that innervates the heart is located at the heart itself.

Figure 3.33 shows part of a chain of sympathetic ganglia and can be compared with Figure 3.29. A series of sympathetic ganglia lie close to the spinal cord and constitute the 'sympathetic trunk'. In Figure 3.33, it can be seen that sympathetic fibres leave the spinal cord as part of the ventral root.

Sensory feedback

Feedback is involved in control within the ANS. Not only does the CNS influence the ANS effectors but it is also informed of their state. The nerves within which autonomic effector neurons are located also contain sensory axons which carry information back to the CNS. As with other sensory neurons, their cell bodies are located in the dorsal root ganglia (Figure 3.33) and cranial nerve ganglia. Such information is used in feedback control, e.g. over heart-rate (Dampney, 1994).

For another example, the vagus nerve (Figure 3.30) is made up of both efferent and afferent neurons. The latter convey information to the CNS concerning such things as events within the liver and stomach. For example, the availability of fuel to the liver is signalled to the brain and this plays a role in the control of feeding.

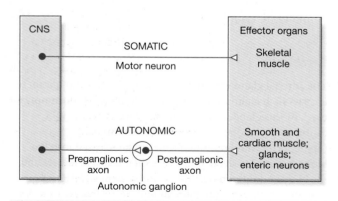

Figure 3.32 Part of the somatic and autonomic nervous systems compared. In reality, a ganglion contains many such cell bodies.

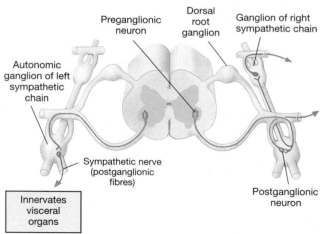

Figure 3.33 The sympathetic chain.

Source: adapted from Martini *et al.* (2000, Fig. 17-4(a), p. 447).

Global and local control

Introduction

There are two aspects of control by the ANS that illustrate a general feature of how the nervous system (both somatic and autonomic) operates: local and global control. Each component of the ANS has a capacity for local control based in part upon local feedback of information. For example, heart-rate and the strength of heartbeats can be adjusted as local actions involving only part of the ANS. Typically, this might occur in response to detection of events at the heart and blood vessels (e.g. blood pressure) by sensory neurons with tips located there. This information is fed back to the CNS and local corrective action instigated. Similarly, salivation can be triggered by substances in the mouth and might involve only a small part of the ANS.

Hierarchical control

Above local control, there is a global coordination of the ANS, controlled by **command neurons** in the brain. This ensures that autonomic activity matches the functional demands of the whole body. For example, acting globally in response to an emergency, the sympathetic branch can be excited and the parasympathetic branch inhibited. Comparable to control of the somatic motor output, such control is sometimes termed **hierarchical control**, meaning that a high level in the hierarchy determines events at lower levels. Anticipatory changes in the ANS in response to changes in posture and goals are examples of such hierarchical control.

The hierarchical control over the ANS has parallels with systems of government administration, where an action can depend upon both central decisions and local factors as responding to local conditions. Local decisions can be modulated or overridden in the interests of national coherence.

In attack or escape, a global signal is sent from the brain to accelerate the heart-rate and alter the diameter of blood vessels, among other things. As another aspect of the global command, blood is diverted away from such places as the gut and to the skeletal muscles.

The chemistry of the ANS

The 'classical pattern' of chemical neurotransmission is shown in Figure 3.34. Preganglionic neurons in both the sympathetic and parasympathetic systems employ acetylcholine. Postganglionic neurons of the sympathetic system usually employ noradrenalin. However, the sympathetic neurons that innervate the sweat glands employ acetylcholine. Also, more than one neurotransmitter can be employed by a given neuron (Loewy, 1990). Postganglionic neurons of the parasympathetic system employ acetylcholine.

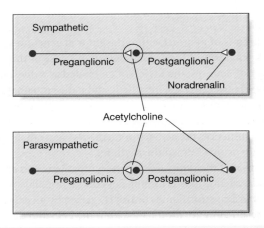

Figure 3.34 The neurotransmitters of the autonomic nervous system.

How do the two branches of the ANS normally exert opposite effects? This is achieved in part by different neurotransmitters being released by the end neurons within the branches (Figure 3.34). When noradrenalin attaches to receptors at the cardiac muscle, the muscle is activated more strongly. Within the parasympathetic system, when acetylcholine binds to receptors at the cardiac muscle, the heart's activity is reduced, i.e. inhibited (as in Loewi's dream-inspired experiment).

The enteric nervous system

Introduction

We divided the ANS into sympathetic and parasympathetic divisions. This is valid in so far as Figures 3.29 and 3.30 go; neurons fall into one or other category. The effectors of the ANS normally involve two such neurons between CNS and a muscle or gland (Figure 3.32). However, a complication can appear when we go beyond these figures, moving in a direction away from the CNS. At some organs, e.g. the gut, between these two neurons and the smooth muscles, there are specialized networks of neurons that organize the activity of the muscles (Wood, 1979).

The movement of ingested material through the stomach and along the intestine, i.e. the alimentary tract, occurs because of contraction and relaxation of its walls. This is caused by changing contraction within the muscles of the walls. Also, digestive fluids are secreted from the walls of the gut. There are various determinants of the neural activity of the gut and thereby its muscular and hormonal actions. For example, events intrinsic to the gut itself determine activity within local neural networks in the gut. The network of local neurons at the wall of the gut is known as the **enteric nervous system** (ENS). The extent of processing carried out by this system is witnessed by estimates that the human ENS contains as many neurons as the spinal cord.

Hierarchical control

Local circuits of neurons within the gut wall generate the rhythms that propel food along the gut. Because of this network of neurons, the ENS is often treated as a division of the ANS. However, the sympathetic and parasympathetic systems also exert control over the activity of this network of neurons. Thus, within the ANS but outside the ENS, neural activity influences the activity of the ENS (Figure 3.35). This speeds up or slows down the rhythms.

The role of the sympathetic, parasympathetic and enteric nervous systems in determining gut contraction illustrates hierarchical control. Some control is exerted by local factors (e.g. the rhythms are produced within the ENS and depend upon gut contents). However, over and above this, a layer of central control arises in the brain and is mediated via the sympathetic and parasympathetic systems. This allows the activity of the ENS to be excited or inhibited according to the broader context. For example, at times of emergency, digestion can be slowed down and blood diverted away from the gut.

Surely, most of us have had experiences demonstrating that factors outside the ENS can exert some control over it. At times of high emotion, we experience disturbances in our gut. This implies a route of information from CNS to ANS and so to ENS.

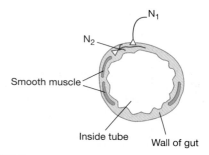

Figure 3.35 The enteric nervous system. There is an input from neurons of the ANS. N_1 = a neuron within ANS but outside ENS. N_2 = a neuron within the ENS.

Section summary

1 The ANS exerts control over the viscera, i.e. organs such as the stomach, heart and intestine.

2 Control by the ANS is produced by (i) glands, which secrete hormones or other substances (e.g. saliva) and (ii) smooth and cardiac muscle.

3 Conventionally, the ANS is divided into sympathetic and parasympathetic branches. These normally exert opposite effects on a target.

4 The adrenal gland secretes adrenalin (epinephrine) and noradrenalin (norepinephrine) into the bloodstream in response to activity in the sympathetic nervous system.

5 A division of the ANS that exerts control over the smooth muscles of the gut is the enteric nervous system, which is affected by activity in the sympathetic and parasympathetic divisions.

Test your knowledge

(Answers on page 80)

3.16 In Figure 3.29, which neurotransmitter is released from the neurons coloured red? (i) Acetylcholine, (ii) glutamate, (iii) noradrenalin (norepinephrine).

3.17 In Figure 3.30, which neurotransmitter is released from the neurons coloured black? (i) Acetylcholine, (ii) glutamate, (iii) noradrenalin (norepinephrine).

3.18 The cell bodies of preganglionic sympathetic neurons are located in which of the following? (i) Dorsal root ganglion, (ii) white matter of the spinal cord, (iii) grey matter of the spinal cord.

Bringing things together

You should now be in a position to appreciate the closely related reasons why nervous and endocrine systems were discussed together:

1 To emphasize their interdependence: the nervous system influences the endocrine system and is influenced by it.

2 To look at similarities and differences in their action. The nervous and endocrine systems convey information between the body regions, e.g. to and fro between the brain and the rest of the body. However, their speed of doing so and extent of their effects can be very different.

3 To underline that activity in either system can have implications for behaviour and mental state.

4 To emphasize that there is no clear-cut distinction between these systems (Blackburn and Pfaus, 1988).

5 To consider their function, which is best understood in terms of their interactions. These systems have evolved to serve a common end-point: survival and reproductive success. In this sense, the theme of Chapter 2, 'Genes, environment and evolution' is continued here.

To bring some of the story together, Figure 3.36 sketches a few interactions between the brain and other parts of the body. Note the *direct* link from the brain through the somatic nervous system to the skeletal muscles that execute behaviour. This action is supported by other factors, *indirect* effects, represented by two arrows marked 'alter sensitivity', which contact the 'skeletal muscle' box. These represent the effects of the ANS in making fuel available to the skeletal muscles, e.g. increased supply of blood. This effect is mediated by neurons of the ANS and hormones, hence one route through the box marked 'hormones'. Hormones influence the brain and the brain influences the release of hormones. These interactions work in a functionally coherent way in meeting challenges, e.g. increased flow of blood to skeletal muscles when we flee danger and decreased flow in relaxation.

Summary of Chapter 3

1 The nervous system, which contains neurons, and the endocrine system, which involves hormones, interact and thereby contribute to coordination of emotions, physiology and behaviour.

2 Nervous systems communicate information and process it. Information is transmitted to the central nervous system (CNS) and action triggered there.

3 Synapses are the region where one neuron influences another. They can be either excitatory or inhibitory.

4 The strength of connections between neurons at synapses can change, corresponding to development/learning.

5 Hormones are chemicals secreted into a blood vessel, transported in the blood to other sites where they occupy receptors, and thereby trigger action.

6 By means of specialized muscles and hormones, the autonomic nervous system controls the internal environment of the body.

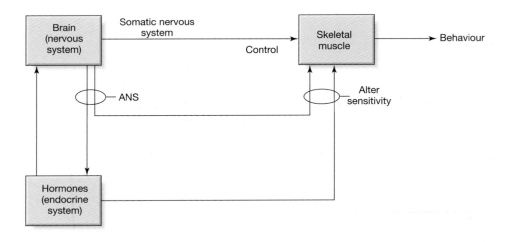

Figure 3.36 Some interactions between the nervous and endocrine systems.

Further reading

For details of neurotransmitters and hormones, see Deutch and Roth (1999). For the nervous system, see Hof *et al.* (1999) and Powley (1999). For neuromuscular control, see Floeter (1999b). For the ANS, see Powley (1999). For the control of insulin, see Woods and Stricker (1999). For hormones, see Pfaff *et al.* (2004) and, for a perspective that echoes the four types of explanation, see Adkins-Regan (2004).

Signposts

Having looked at the overall way in which information is transmitted in the nervous and endocrine systems, the next chapter takes a closer look at the details. It will ask how action potentials arise and how neurotransmitters convey information across synapses.

Answers

Explanations for answers to 'test your knowledge' questions can be found on the website **www.pearsoned.co.uk/toates**

3.1   (ii) Endocrine
3.2   (ii) Chemical
3.3   (i) Presynaptic cell to postsynaptic cell
3.4   (i) Neuron to neuron, (ii) neuron to skeletal muscle, (iii) neuron to smooth muscle
3.5   (i) b
3.6   (iii) Reduce its activity
3.7   (i) Excitatory
3.8   (i) More
3.9   (iii) 7
3.10 (ii) 4 → 1
3.11 (i) 5 → 1
3.12 (ii) Cell body shown in (b)
3.13 (iii) AVP
3.14 (i) AVP, (iv) CRF
3.15 (ii) CRF
3.16 (i) Acetylcholine
3.17 (i) Acetylcholine
3.18 (iii) Grey matter of spinal cord

CHAPTER 4

The cells of the nervous system: how they work

Learning outcomes for Chapter 4

After studying this chapter, you should be able to:

1 Describe neurons in terms of their general properties as cells, while highlighting the particular properties that they exhibit.

2 Summarize the processes that move ions across the cell membrane of neurons.

3 Explain how action potentials arise within neurons and are transmitted. Link this to how information is encoded by the nervous system.

4 Describe the properties of glial cells and link this to the role that they serve.

5 Explain the basis of how different types of synapse can be classified and the properties that are associated with this classification.

6 Describe the kinds of intervention that can alter the working of synapses and how the alteration occurs.

Scene-setting questions

1   Why is grey matter associated with the intellect?

2   How can degenerative diseases of the nervous system impair cognitive and motor function?

3   How do psychoactive drugs such as cocaine work?

4   How can a chemical such as Prozac alter mood?

5   Why do drugs have side-effects?

The speed of reaction can be vital to survival. What does a study of the cells of the nervous system tell us about how this is attained?

Source: © Gallo Images/CORBIS.

Introduction

In Chapter 3, 'The nervous and endocrine systems', we looked at communication by neurons, in the context of the nervous and endocrine systems. Now we need to look closer at the cells of the nervous system in their own right and how they function as individual units. By 'cells' is meant mainly, but not only, neurons. A principal concern will be how action potentials arise and travel in neurons. Another is how neurons process information and communicate information across the synapse. We shall need to ask how the properties of individual neurons and synapses contribute to the overall properties of the nervous system and thereby behaviour. How do the parts that make up the cells of the nervous system (with a focus on neurons) help us to explain how the cells work? How does similar insight help to explain how synapses work? Building on this, we can consider how it is

possible to manipulate events at neurons and synapses to change their performance and how this might affect nervous system properties, mood and behaviour.

The individual cell forms a fundamental building block of the body (Chapter 1, 'Introduction'). Neurons share some important properties with most other cells. For example, each neuron has a nucleus, a membrane that surrounds the cell and an internal fluid environment. Each cell is bathed by the external fluid environment that surrounds cells' membranes.

It is appropriate to consider first some general properties of cells and then to look at specific properties of neurons. An understanding of general properties of cells is necessary in order to explain how action potentials arise and are transmitted. We will then look at communication between neurons at synapses. The discussion of this and the preceding chapters then culminates in the next chapter, which considers how understanding of the whole brain can build upon knowledge of the properties of neurons and synapses.

Section summary

1 The neuron shares certain features with other cells.

2 Each cell is surrounded by a membrane and there is a different fluid environment on each side of the membrane.

Test your knowledge

(Answer on page 104)

4.1 Complete the following: 'The cell _____ separates the fluid environment on the inside and outside of the cell'.

The neuron as a typical cell

Structure

Figure 4.1 (developed from Figure 1.2, p. 6) shows a number of cells, the blood and interstitial fluid. The term **extracellular fluid** describes all the fluid that is not in the cells. It is made up of the interstitial fluid and the plasma, the fluid part of the blood. The interstitial fluid bathes the cells and is in close contact with the blood. By means of the interstitial fluid and the blood, energy and nutrients are brought to the cell and waste products are carried away. The fluid that is on the inside of the cell is termed **intracellular fluid** and has a different chemical composition from the extracellular fluid on the outside. The extracellular

and intracellular fluids consist of water and a number of other substances.

The cell is surrounded by a membrane, which forms a barrier of sorts between the inside of the cell and the interstitial fluid surrounding the cell. The membrane is not equally permeable (meaning 'allows substances to pass through') to all the substances that appear in the interstitial fluid, being permeable by various degrees to some but impermeable to others.

Figure 4.2 shows the difference in chemical composition between extracellular and intracellular fluids. For example, the concentrations of sodium (symbol Na^+) and potassium (symbol K^+) are different on either side of the cell membrane. This difference is crucial for the neuron to serve its role in communication, i.e. to produce action potentials.

Electrical events

Ions and voltages

In Figure 4.2, the symbols for sodium (Na) and potassium (K) have a plus sign associated with them. What does this signify? Each minute particle ('atom') of sodium and potassium has a particular sort of 'charge' (a positive or 'plus' charge) of electricity associated with it. Electrical charge will doubtless be familiar to you in terms of hair standing on end and sparking when we comb it or in static electricity associated with television sets, car doors, etc. That is, electrical charge produces action. Figure 4.3 illustrates charge and the action that this triggers: suspended spheres that carry electric charges. Charges of the same sign repel, so in part (b) the spheres are repelled from each other and move apart. Charges of opposite sign attract and so in part (c), the spheres are drawn towards each other.

To say that Na^+ and K^+ have an associated electric charge means that each such atom, termed an **ion**, is electrically active. The ions Na^+ and K^+ are active in a particular way, as described by their plus sign and are termed 'positive ions'. There are also negative ions in the fluid inside and outside of the cell, indicated by a minus sign. For example, Figure 4.2 shows one of these, chloride, represented as Cl^-. The minus sign indicates that a negative ion is electrically active in a way opposite to that of Na^+ and K^+. If you dissolve table salt,

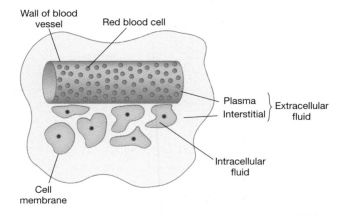

Figure 4.1 A group of cells, the interstitial fluid and blood supply. Not to scale.

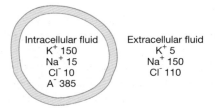

Figure 4.2 Concentration differences between extracellular and intracellular fluid (concentration in arbitrary units).

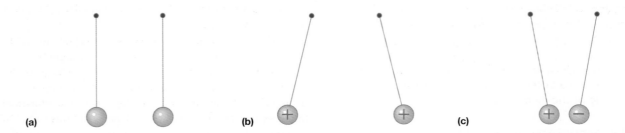

(a)   (b)   (c)

Figure 4.3 Hanging spheres: (a) no charge, (b) charges of same sign and (c) charges of opposite sign.

sodium chloride (chemical symbol NaCl), in water, each very tiny particle (termed 'molecule') of NaCl will split into two components, Na^+ and Cl^-. A type of large ion particle trapped on the inside of the cell and with an associated negative charge is indicated as A^- (Figure 4.2).

When, as in Figure 4.2, ions are in solution, they tend to move around according to the electrical forces that act on them. In turn, ions contribute to the electrical forces that exert effects on all ions. Whether an ion is positive or negative influences its tendency to move. Imagine a region of solution where suddenly there arises a surplus of negative ions relative to positive ions and another region of excess positive ions (Figure 4.4(a)). So-called 'like ions' repel whereas so-called 'unlike ions' attract (as in Figure 4.3(b) and (c)). So, in Figure 4.4(a) positive ions will be attracted to the negative region while negative ions will be

attracted to the positive region. The effect of such attraction and repulsion is that, if there are no other, counteracting, factors operating to move them, electrical charges become evenly distributed within a solution (Figure 4.4(b)).

The membrane potential

Figure 4.4(a) shows an *imbalance* of ions, more of one sort than another in a location. If you had a measuring instrument you would be able to detect an electrical voltage between the two ends. A voltage tends to move ions. Where an imbalance of ions exists, so does a voltage. In part (b), a voltage no longer exists and there is no net movement of ions.

Biology is no exception to this principle: there is an unequal distribution of positive and negative ions comparing one side of a cell's membrane to the other side. Thus, a cell is like a miniature battery (Figure 4.5(a)). (Don't worry about how nature got constructed this way. For your sake, and especially for the author's, please just take it on trust!) That is, there exists a small electrical voltage across the cell's membrane or, as it is sometimes called, a **membrane potential**. It is also said that there is an electrical 'polarity'

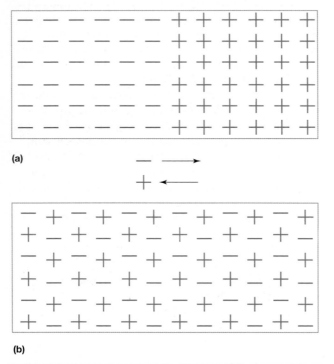

(a)

(b)

Figure 4.4 Ions in solution: (a) initially and (b) after distribution.

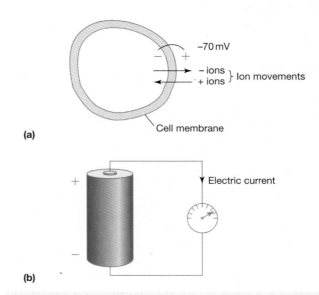

(a)

(b)

Figure 4.5 Comparison between (a) a cell and (b) a battery.

across the cell; it is 'polarized'. This voltage is normally of magnitude some –60 mV to –70 mV (mV = millivolt or one-thousandth of a volt). Remember: where a voltage exists, there exists also a force tending to move ions. In the case of the cell, the voltage tends to cause a movement of ions across the cell membrane. By analogy, a battery will cause an electric current to flow between its terminals if a wire is placed there (Figure 4.5(b)).

Electrically, the interior of a cell is negative with respect to the outside. What does this mean? 'Positive' and 'negative' specify the polarity. As a result of the membrane potential (voltage), positive ions such as sodium and potassium will *tend to* move from the outside of the cell to the inside and negative ions will *tend to* move out (Figure 4.5(a)).

Note the qualifying expression 'tend to'. Sodium and potassium move across the membrane to the extent that: (a) there is *not* a stronger force (something other than voltage) tending to pull them in the opposite direction and (b) the membrane is permeable to them. Another force, which also acts on these ions, is described next.

The concentration gradient

As just implied by the qualification 'tend to', the voltage is not the only force present across the membrane. Considering Na^+ and K^+, there exist chemical **concentration gradients**, which also tend to move them. The term 'gradient' usually refers to a slope, as in the gradient of a hill being 1 in 5. Gradients tend to cause things to move down them from a high point to a low point, as in when you cycle with no effort down the gradient of a hill. The force moving you is greater for a 1 in 5 gradient than for a 1 in 10. By analogy, a concentration gradient refers to a tendency to cause movement that arises from different concentrations of a substance.

To understand this, think of a comparable situation: two rooms that are totally segregated by a barrier in the form of a membrane. They are completely isolated from the outside world and there are no air currents blowing through either room. One room contains pure air but the other room has a high concentration of cigarette smoke uniformly distributed throughout. Imagine now that the membrane is suddenly made slightly permeable.

There exists a 'concentration gradient for smoke', which refers to the difference in concentrations of smoke in the two regions. What is the effect of making the barrier slightly permeable? In response to the smoke concentration gradient, smoke will move from a high concentration area to a low concentration area. Given time, smoke will distribute itself evenly between the two rooms.

That smoke tends to become evenly distributed depends upon the random activity shown by its molecules. For substances in air or liquid, where a difference exists between two regions, the difference tends to disappear, i.e. the substance becomes evenly distributed. A similar principle is at work in the distribution of dust. Any mud dropped from shoes will tend to become dust. This dust will then tend to distribute itself evenly over surfaces such as a table-top.

If you examine Figure 4.2, you will see the concentration gradients for sodium (150 versus 15), which acts from the outside of the cell to the inside, and for potassium, which acts in the opposite direction (150 versus 5). In response to the Na^+ concentration gradient, Na^+ will tend to move into the cell. K^+ will tend to move out, down the K^+ concentration gradient. Note that concentration gradient is always specific to a given substance, e.g. a concentration gradient for *sodium*.

The net force

Voltages and concentration gradients

The *net* force tending to move an ion across a membrane depends upon both (i) the voltage and (ii) the concentration gradient for that ion. Figure 4.6(a) shows the voltage and concentration gradients that arise from the distribution of ions on the two sides of a cell membrane. Typically, cell membranes permit a slight flow of K^+ and Na^+; they exhibit some permeability to these ions. Normally, the permeability to K^+ is greater than that to Na^+. In response to the forces shown in Figure 4.6(a), Na^+ will tend to move into the cell, since the voltage and the concentration gradient for Na^+ act in this direction. However, the membrane normally has a relatively low permeability to Na^+, so only a slight inwards movement occurs.

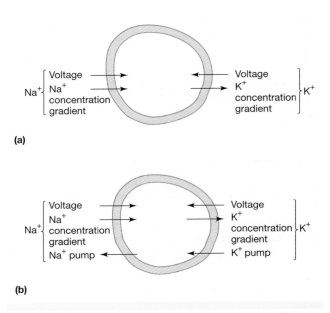

Figure 4.6 Ion movements across a cell membrane: (a) in response to voltage and concentration gradients and (b) representation that includes the role of pumps.

The concentration gradient for K^+ will tend to move K^+ out of the cell. However, the voltage will tend to move it in. In practice, the strength of the voltage is less than that of the K^+ concentration gradient. Therefore, as a result of the forces shown in Figure 4.6(a), there is a slow net movement of K^+ out of the cell.

Pumps

Suppose that the forces described so far (Figure 4.6(a)) were the only ones to be operating. What would be their effect? K^+ would be depleted from the cell and Na^+ would accumulate on the inside. So, how are the stable concentration differences (Figure 4.2) maintained in the face of these forces that are tending constantly to break them down?

As Figure 4.6(b) shows, there is an additional process involved in each cell, a so-called pumping mechanism, a **sodium–potassium pump**. Across the membrane of the neuron, the pump expels Na^+ from the cell and pulls in K^+. Over time, this pump will counter the tendencies to break down the segregation of ions across the cell. The differences in ion concentration between inside and outside shown in Figure 4.2 are normally well maintained. The pump helps to keep up the segregation of different types of ion and the imbalance in charge across the membrane, i.e. an excess of negative charge on the inside.

The term 'pump' should not suggest literally a mechanical pump, which is only a useful metaphor. In reality, it is a chemical reaction requiring energy. Enormous amounts of energy are devoted to maintaining the difference in ion concentration by pumping.

So far, what has been described is applicable to cells in general. However, neurons and muscle cells show certain peculiar properties and these form the topic of the next section.

Test your knowledge

(Answer on page 104)

4.2 With reference to Figure 4.2, what are the forces acting on the chloride (Cl^-) ions and where are they tending to move them? Hint. Think of membrane potential and chloride concentration gradient.

The neuron: an excitable cell

So far, the baseline electrical state of the cell has been described, in which a stable voltage of between -60 and $-70\,mV$ is maintained, a so-called **resting potential**. However, as you have seen earlier, neurons are dynamic in their performance – they do not just sit around doing nothing. Having understood the basis of the stable ('resting') condition of the neuron, you are now in a position to understand how the action potential arises.

Basis of the action potential

Action potentials were described as electrical impulses, which arise in a neuron and convey information by their transmission along an axon. That is, neurons and muscle cells have the property of *excitability*. To understand this, we need to view it in the context of the resting potential. See Figure 4.7. Note the series of action potentials, one of which is enlarged. To start, in the enlarged diagram, note the membrane potential from time zero through time 1 to time 2. This represents a voltage common to cells: the resting potential. It is shown as $-70\,mV$, the inside of the cell being $-70\,mV$ negative with respect to the outside. To remind you: the existence of a membrane potential depends upon the relative numbers of positive and negative ions on the two sides.

At time 2, a change starts to occur: a move to a less negative voltage. At time 4, there is a rapid move of the voltage across the membrane from a negative value, through zero to a positive value (at 6) and then a rapid return to the original negative value. This is the *action potential*; a peculiarity of neurons and muscle cells is that they can exhibit this reaction. We now need to consider how they can be triggered to do so.

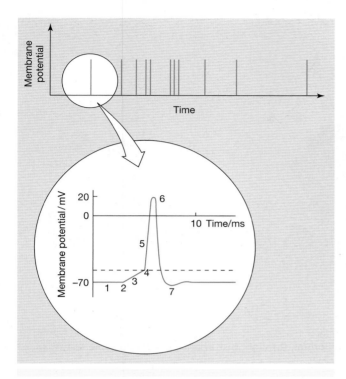

Figure 4.7 A series of action potentials, with one enlarged. (Note the different baselines in the two traces.)

Triggering an action potential

The membrane of a cell was described earlier as having a certain *permeability* to the movement of ions across it, to be 'semi-permeable'. The excitability peculiar to neurons and muscle cells depends upon the fact that the permeability of the membrane to K^+ and Na^+ is variable.

You have already met two different ways in which an action potential can be initiated: (a) at the tip of a sensory neuron as a result of stimulation (e.g. Chapter 3, Figure 3.1(b), p. 49) and (b) as a result of synaptic input to a neuron (e.g. Chapter 3, Figure 3.9, p. 56). We shall describe each of these means in more detail.

We first consider a sensory neuron that is sensitive to a tactile stimulus at the skin. It requires such stimulation before it will generate action potentials, i.e. it is not spontaneously active (Chapter 3). Suppose that a tactile stimulus is applied to the skin and pressure increased until it is sufficient to generate an action potential at the tip of a sensory neuron.

Let us consider again the action potential shown enlarged in Figure 4.7 and this time how the sequence of electrical changes occurs will be explained. Suppose a tactile stimulus starts to be applied at time 2. By deforming the membrane, the stimulus increases the membrane's permeability to Na^+ at the neuron's tip. See Figure 4.8. Both the voltage and the Na^+ concentration gradient tend to move Na^+ into the neuron.

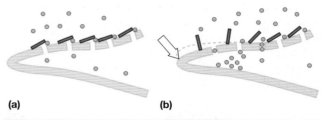

Figure 4.8 Tip of a sensory neuron: (a) resting condition with sodium channels almost closed (indicated by almost closed doors) and (b) deformation at tip as a result of tactile stimulus (arrow), triggering local sodium channels to open.

Therefore, when the permeability to Na^+ is increased by the tactile stimulus, Na^+ will tend to move into the neuron at a higher rate than normal. It moves in along sodium channels in the membrane. These are normally almost closed but are opened by the deformation of the membrane.

Movement of positive ions (Na^+) into the neuron moves the membrane potential in a positive direction, away from the negative resting potential, i.e. the stages marked 2, 3 and 4 in Figure 4.7. Since this is a move towards zero, away from the polarized value, it is known as **depolarization**.

At stage 4, a sudden change occurs, the voltage reaches the **threshold** and the action potential is triggered. This is an explosive depolarizing move of membrane potential, i.e. stages 4 and 5, through zero and then briefly to acquire a positive polarity (at 6). Over the period 4–6, incoming Na^+ makes the inside more positive, which increases Na^+ permeability, which brings in still more Na^+, and so on . . . , i.e. there is an explosive ('vicious circle' or 'positive feedback') effect.

The sequence 1–6 can perhaps be better appreciated with the help of an analogy (Figure 4.9). The ship is in equilibrium (part (a)) until something disturbs it (part (b)). A small disturbance is associated with a corrective force. However, if the disturbance is large enough (part (c), compare with point 4 in Figure 4.7), the ship will suddenly topple over.

Note that the move of membrane potential in a positive direction ceases at stage 6. What causes this? It is a property of the sodium channels in the membrane. Their opening is the basis of the movement of Na^+ into the cell and thereby the move in a positive direction. At stage 6, the channels slam shut, which prevents further Na^+ from moving into the cell and the movement of membrane potential in a positive direction ceases.

The voltage now moves in a negative direction, i.e. stages 6–7 in Figure 4.7. What causes this? It is the opening of K^+ channels, which occurs just after the opening of Na^+ channels. K^+ moves out of the neuron at a relatively high rate as a result of the concentration gradient for K^+. The movement of these positive ions out of the cell changes the voltage in a negative direction (6–7).

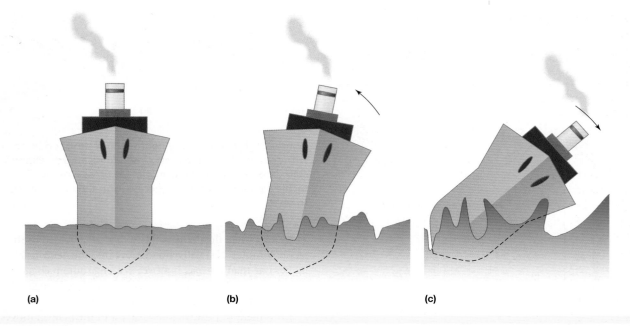

Figure 4.9 Analogy to the start of the action potential: (a) equilibrium, (b) slight disturbance and (c) unstable disturbance.

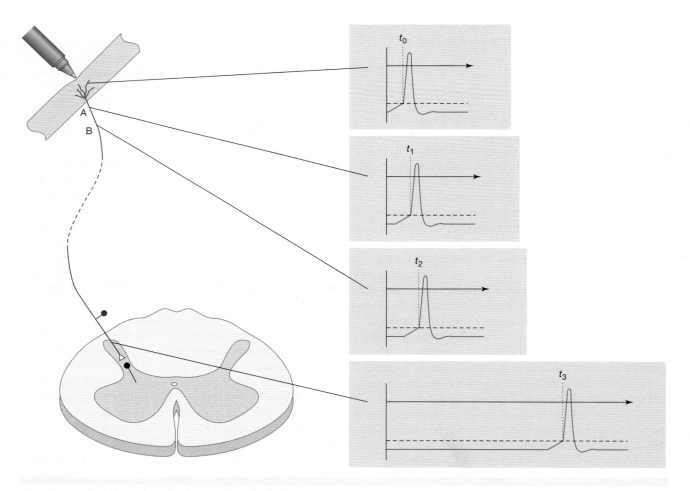

Figure 4.10 An action potential moving along an axon.

Movement of action potentials

So much for the generation of an action potential in a few milliseconds of time and at one location, but how does an action potential move along an axon? An action potential at one location of axon influences its neighbouring locations. This influence opens Na+ channels and changes membrane potential to a less negative value, and thereby tends to create a new action potential in a neighbouring location. This new action potential appears just as the instigating action potential is dying out. In effect the action potential moves along the axon. This property enables action potentials to communicate information.

Let us illustrate this with a familiar specific example. In Figure 4.10, tactile stimulation at the tip of the sensory neuron triggers an action potential there at time t_0. The action potential then travels smoothly from the tip. However, to explain this, it can be easier to think in terms of chunks of axon. So, consider that an action potential at the tip then tends to create an action potential at a region marked A, just away from the tip, at a brief instant of time later, t_1. In turn, when the action potential gets to A, it then tends to create a new one a moment later (t_2) at B. This means that, by the time the action potential at A has finished, there is a new one at B, and so on along the axon. At time t_3, it has almost reached the end of the axon in the CNS.

When the action potential gets to the end of the axon, it terminates. However, as was discussed earlier, information can be carried further by means of a synapse.

The frequency of action potentials

So much for the triggering of a single action potential and its transmission along the axon; we now need to ask further related questions. Information is carried by the frequency with which action potentials occur, so what determines this frequency? In posing such a question, we are, in effect, asking, after undergoing one action potential, how soon can a region of axon exhibit another action potential? The sooner it can recover and generate another action potential, the higher will be the frequency.

Look at Figure 4.11, which shows a 'snapshot' of an action potential travelling from left to right. At the time shown, the action potential has reached the region of axon labelled X_3. Note the disturbance to membrane potential at location X_3 and to each side of it. Region X_4 has yet to undergo the sequence of electrical changes. However, it is already showing the influence of events at neighbouring region X_3, in that the sodium channel is starting to open. Region X_2 has just exhibited an action potential. So, what sets the limit on how soon region X_2 can show a second action potential? Note that at X_2 the sodium channel is firmly shut, i.e. it is in the state immediately after having undergone an action potential. Such closure was noted earlier as the reason that the flow of Na$^+$ ions into the axon ceases and the membrane potential does not move any further in a positive direction.

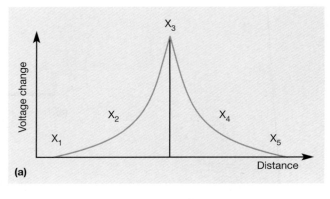

(a)

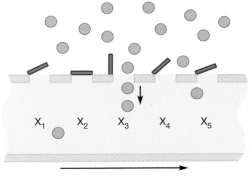

(b)

Figure 4.11 A 'snapshot' of a region of axon undergoing an action potential: (a) voltage change (i.e. disturbance from resting voltage) and (b) events at the sodium channels.

After a brief period of time, the closure relaxes slightly. Region X_1 is already showing recovery, so that, if the right trigger is applied, another action potential can happen there. In other words, following stimulation, what is termed a **refractory period** must elapse before a given section of axon can be stimulated again. So, why does the action potential that is now at location X_3 not trigger another at X_1? The action potential at X_3 is too far 'down the track' to influence events at X_1 sufficient to form another action potential (note there is only a slight disturbance of voltage at X_1). This explains why action potentials do not 'travel backwards'. It explains why, once one action potential is initiated, an indefinite series of them do not move chaotically along the axon in both directions. However, if the original tactile stimulus is still present, this will tend to instigate further action potentials, which again move from left to right. The whole sequence can then repeat itself. So long as the initiating stimulus is present, a series of action potentials occur.

Frequency of action potentials can be high or low. Frequency would normally depend upon the intensity of the stimulus. With the more intense stimuli, one action potential can follow very rapidly after another. Figure 4.12 shows the effect of increasing the intensity of stimulation, e.g.

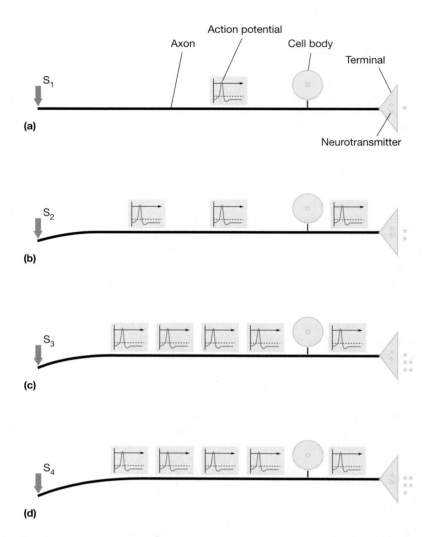

Figure 4.12 Different frequencies of action potentials in an axon as a function of increasing intensity of stimulation (S): (a) S_1, (b) S_2, (c) S_3 and (d) S_4.

increasing the magnitude of deformation of the tip of a sensory neuron. At first frequency goes up with increasing stimulation but then (part (c)) a saturation point is reached where frequency can increase no more. The refractory period sets this upper limit on frequency.

Section summary

1 The movement of sodium and potassium ions across the membrane of the neuron forms the basis of an action potential.

2 An action potential generated at one location tends to invade a neighbouring region of neuron when this region is in a state to support an action potential.

3 An action potential normally moves along an axon in only one direction.

Test your knowledge

(Answers on page 104)

4.3 In Figure 4.7, at which of the following times is the membrane potential at its resting potential? (i) 1, (ii) 5, (iii) 6.

4.4 Complete the following sentence: 'In Figure 4.8(b), the movement of sodium ions into the tip of the neuron as a result of the tactile stimulus, is caused by the _____ potential and the sodium _____ gradient'.

4.5 Complete the following sentence by stating the name of the chemical: 'In Figure 4.10, the sharp upwards move of the graph shown to start at times t_0, t_1, t_2, and t_3 is caused by the movement of _____ ions into the neuron'.

Glial cells

The nervous system consists not only of neurons. In addition, neurons are closely associated with another type of cell termed **glial cells** (or 'glia cells' or just 'glia'). There are many more glial cells than neurons in the nervous system. In the CNS, a major type of glial cell is described as 'oligodendrocytes', whereas in the peripheral nervous system glial cells are termed 'Schwann cells'.

What do glial cells do? That is, what does the half or more of brain tissue that is still relatively unexplored do? Traditionally glial cells were thought to play a supporting role in the maintenance of the nervous system, e.g. they help to regulate its chemical composition. However, more recent evidence suggests that they do much more than just this. They seem to play a role in the development of the nervous system, e.g. in the sculpting of new synapses. As another role, they appear to listen to the activity of their associated neurons and also influence the signalling properties of these neurons. Glial cells 'speak' to each other within networks of glial cells by means of chemical communication.

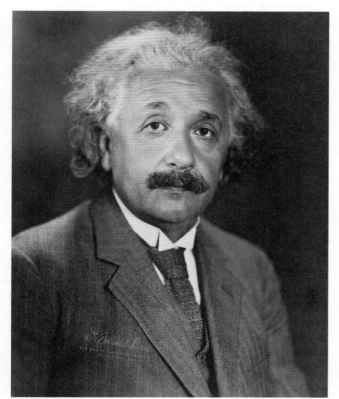

Can the study of the brains of people with exceptional abilities reveal anything interesting?

Source: US Library of Congress/Science Photo Library.

A personal angle
Einstein's brain

An extraordinary story surrounds the fate of the brain of the eminent physicist Albert Einstein, taken from his body following an autopsy in 1955. The pathologist Thomas Harvey took the brain home with him and preserved it for 40 years. He would occasionally take a small slice of brain and give it to people who wanted it for research. All were inspired by the wish to find something abnormal in its tissues that might reflect Einstein's genius. Researchers found no abnormality in the form or number of the neurons. However, an abnormal number of glial cells were found in brain regions associated with 'advanced' cognition. Of course, we cannot say that this proves a relationship between an aspect of brain and associated intellect but has provided a fruitful base for speculation.

Figure 4.13 shows one known role of glial cells: a neuron together with a part of some specialized glial cells that form an insulating coating termed **myelin**. Many axons are coated with myelin and are termed 'myelinated axons'. Sheaths of myelin cover the axon, the gaps between them being known as **nodes of Ranvier**. It is at nodes of Ranvier that ions can cross the membrane and action potentials occur. They do not occur elsewhere along the axon. However, action potentials still manage to travel along myelinated axons and do so at high speed relative to an unmyelinated axon of the same diameter. Myelin speeds up the rate at which action potentials are transmitted along the axon. The speed of some reactions, e.g. a motor response in escaping from a predator, can often be crucial to survival.

Myelin has a whitish appearance. Hence, where there is a high concentration of myelin, neural tissue appears 'whitish' or 'pinkish' (see Figure 4.10). The white matter of the spinal cord is where a large number of myelin-coated axons convey information up and down it. In the brain and spinal cord, grey matter consists of a high density of cell bodies. This is where information processing rather than 'simply' transmission occurs. Hence, in the popular imagination, there is an association of grey matter with cognition and the intellect.

How is myelin able to increase the speed of an action potential? As shown in Figure 4.14(a), an axon that is without myelin is known as 'unmyelinated'. Note the drop in strength of the influence of the action potential (disturbance from resting potential) to each side of the region directly experiencing the action potential. Now compare this with the less steep drop shown in Figure 4.14(b).

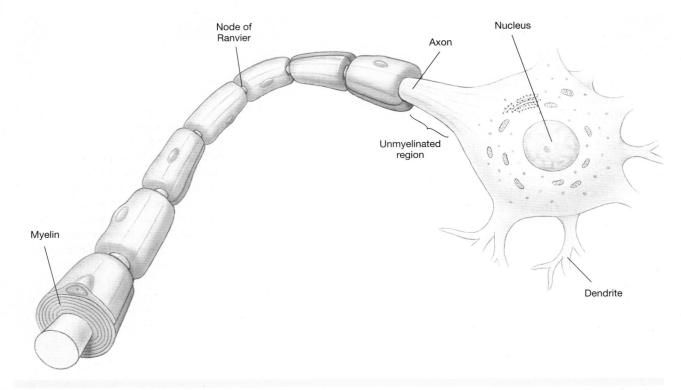

Figure 4.13 A number of glial cells contribute to the myelin sheaths that are formed around the axon of a neuron.

Source: adapted from Martini *et al.* (2000, Fig. 13-8, p. 337).

An action potential at one node of Ranvier creates a change in membrane potential in the axon at the next node such that a new action potential occurs there. The influence of an action potential at one region of a myelinated axon spreads a relatively large distance compared with the same axon but without myelin. Hence, there is the capacity for the action potential, in effect, to jump far ahead in a myelinated axon.

A consideration of myelination should help you to understand the destructive effect of degenerative diseases that destroy myelin. The action potential either cannot travel or is greatly reduced in speed. When the myelin that surrounds motor neurons is lost, there is disruption to motor performance. Loss of myelin within the CNS can also have effects on cognition.

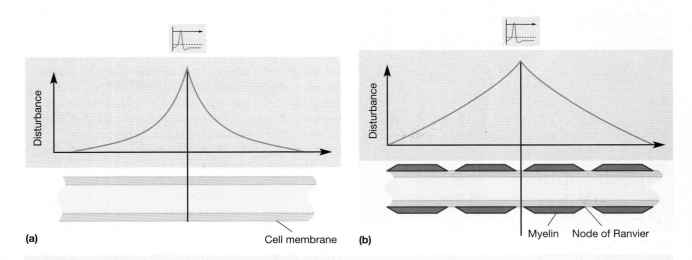

Figure 4.14 Myelination: (a) unmyelinated axon and (b) myelinated axon.

So much for the details of action potentials and communication *within* a neuron; the following section addresses the issue of how synapses function and thereby looks at communication *between* neurons.

Section summary

1 Apart from neurons, nervous systems also contain glial cells.

2 Glial cells provide support for neurons and also affect processing within circuits of neurons.

3 One type of glial cell provides a myelin coating to axons.

4 Gaps between myelin coating are known as nodes of Ranvier.

5 In a myelinated axon, action potentials in effect jump from one node of Ranvier to another.

6 Myelination of an axon speeds up the transmission of an action potential.

Test your knowledge

(Answer on page 104)

4.6 As represented in Figure 4.13, action potentials jump along the axon between nodes of Ranvier in which direction? (i) Right to left, (ii) left to right.

The synapse and neurotransmitters

Introduction

In Chapter 3, you met synapses between neurons, to be more specific, 'chemical synapses'. There exists a type of synapse that does not use a chemical transmitter and this is discussed briefly later in this section. Figure 4.15 shows a more detailed view of a chemical synapse. Note the axon terminal, presynaptic membrane, postsynaptic membrane and the gap between membranes, termed the **synaptic cleft**. You can see the myelin sheath that surrounds the axon. You have also met a special chemical synapse, the point of communication between a neuron and a muscle, termed a **neuromuscular junction**. This follows the same principles of organization as the synapse between neurons shown in Figure 4.15.

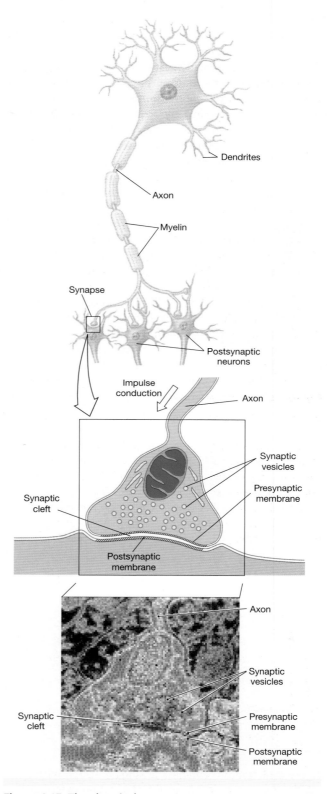

Figure 4.15 The chemical synapse.

Source: Martini *et al.* (2000, Fig. 13-12, p. 343); *photo*: Dennis Kunkel/Phototake.

As you have seen, neurotransmitter is stored at the terminal of a neuron and released by the arrival of an action potential there. A number of transmitter molecules are stored in packages, termed 'synaptic vesicles'. See Figures 4.15 and 4.16. (However, for some purposes, it is convenient to represent free molecules of transmitter, without the vesicles.) On arriving at the terminal, the action potential triggers the movement of calcium ions into the neuron, which, in turn, triggers the vesicles to fuse with the presynaptic membrane and release their contents into the synaptic cleft.

On release from neuron$_1$, transmitter rapidly moves across the gap between the two neurons and attaches to receptors on neuron$_2$. There is a slight delay (the 'synaptic delay'), of about 0.5 milliseconds (ms), between the arrival of the action potential at the terminal of neuron$_1$ and the start of electrical events in neuron$_2$. On attaching to neuron$_2$, the neurotransmitter changes the membrane potential at the local site of attachment in neuron$_2$. This change in membrane potential will typically make an action potential in neuron$_2$ more likely to occur (i.e. excitation) or less likely (i.e. inhibition), as will be shown shortly.

Neurotransmitter is commonly synthesized or partially synthesized in the neuron's cell body. It is slowly transported to the terminal and stored there until release. In some cases, synthesis occurs at the terminal.

Figure 4.12 showed the effect of increasing the frequency of action potentials in a neuron. Note that, as frequency increases, so does the amount of neurotransmitter released. Correspondingly, the effect on the postsynaptic cell increases with the amount of neurotransmitter attaching itself to receptors. For a specific example, you might like to imagine the postsynaptic cell to be a muscle cell, forming part of a skeletal muscle. The neuron would be a motor neuron triggering increasing degrees of force in the muscle as a result of increasing commands to do so.

Dale's principle and beyond

The principle

A neuron can be characterized by the chemical that it *synthesizes, stores and releases*, e.g. one that synthesizes, stores and releases serotonin is called 'serotonergic'. Note the ending '-ergic' which makes the adjective that characterizes each neurotransmitter and associated synapses. For example, a cholinergic synapse is one at which acetylcholine is released and occupies acetylcholine receptors on the membrane of the second neuron.

This classical picture, enshrined in what is known as **Dale's principle**, states that a given neuron synthesizes, stores and releases only one transmitter substance. Hence, a term like 'serotonergic' would uniquely label such a neuron. A neuron is labelled by this criterion, rather than by the transmitter(s) for which it has receptors. For example, Figure

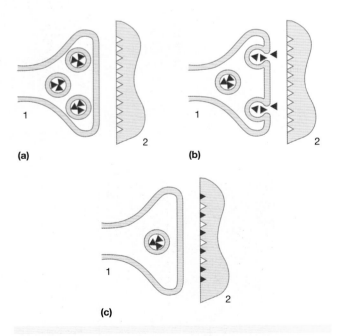

(a)   (b)

(c)

Figure 4.16 Neuron terminal showing neurotransmitter in vesicles: (a) unstimulated, (b) arrival of action potential and fusion of vesicles with presynaptic membrane and (c) reformation of membrane and occupation of receptors with transmitter.

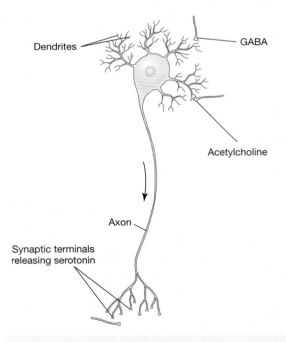

Figure 4.17 Serotonergic neuron with receptors for GABA and acetylcholine.

4.17 shows a serotonergic neuron, with receptors for GABA and acetylcholine on its surface. Although it contains multiple types of receptor, it is characterized as serotonergic.

Beyond the classical picture

As with other classical pictures, that of Dale's principle is now known to be only partly true (Dismukes, 1979). Although some neurons conform to it and can be uniquely described by a single neurotransmitter (Figure 4.17), others release more than one substance. A given neuron can contain different substances (termed 'colocalization') and can release them simultaneously or at different times according to its pattern of activity (Figure 4.18(a) and (b)). The associated postsynaptic sites can have multiple types of receptors. As an example, postganglionic neurons of the parasympathetic

system (Chapter 3) secrete both acetylcholine and 'vasoactive intestinal polypeptide' (Powley, 1999). This combination is involved in the swelling of blood vessels at the genitals in sexual excitement. Another mode of operation is shown in Figure 4.18(c): the same presynaptic neuron releases different transmitters from different sites.

The effect of synaptic inputs

Types of neuron

Chapter 3 noted that neurons come in different shapes and sizes (Figure 3.19). The location at which an action potential arises depends upon the type of neuron. It can normally be triggered in at least two different ways. The present chapter described earlier its initiation at the terminal of a sensory

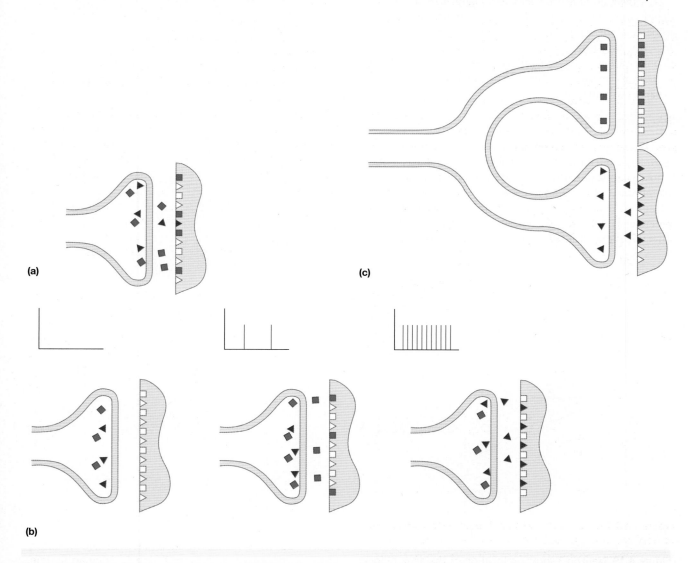

Figure 4.18 Colocalization: (a) co-release, (b) separate release as a function of the frequency of action potentials and (c) different transmitters stored and released at different locations in the presynaptic neuron.

neuron. Another way in which it can be triggered is at the 'axon hillock' of an interneuron or motor neuron (see Figure 4.19) by means of the activity of synapses, which is the topic of this section.

So far, as a simplification, the chapter described just a few presynaptic inputs to a postsynaptic neuron (e.g. Figure 4.19). Occasionally, such simple connections are found. However, what is more common, certainly in the human brain, is that very many synapses, up to 100 000, are formed on a single postsynaptic neuron. Typically, a large percentage of synapses are made on the neuron's many extensive dendrites. Unfortunately, discussion of the real situation is not easy, and so we shall describe just a few synapses formed on a neuron. The principles can be scaled up to consider the more realistic situation.

For the kind of neuron shown in Figure 4.19, if depolarization reaches threshold, action potentials are initiated at the axon hillock. Once initiated, they travel along the axon away from the axon hillock. What determines depolarization at the axon hillock? It is the effect of activity in neurons (in this case, 1 and 2) that form excitatory synapses with neuron 3.

Postsynaptic potentials

The arrival of an action potential at an axon terminal normally contributes only a small change in voltage, termed a **postsynaptic potential** (PSP) at the local postsynaptic membrane. See top trace in Figure 4.19 for this event at synapse 1. What is termed an 'excitatory postsynaptic potential' (EPSP) is, as shown, a brief move in a positive direction, i.e. a local reduction of the negative voltage

(depolarization). Local depolarization at the postsynaptic site extends away from this site, including to the axon hillock. However, as shown, between the site of the EPSP (location 1) and the axon hillock, there is a decrement in the strength of the change in voltage.

Suppose that two EPSPs occur in succession at synapse 1. Depending upon their timing, they can add their effects. This is shown in Figure 4.20. In part (b) the effect of the first action potential has not decayed to zero at the time that the second occurs and there is an addition of their effects, termed **temporal summation**. In distinction to events at a single synapse, the addition of EPSPs at different synapses is termed **spatial summation**.

Depending upon the nature of transmitter and receptor, there can be either an excitatory postsynaptic potential (EPSP) or an inhibitory postsynaptic potential (IPSP) (Figure 4.21). In other words, the arrival of an action potential at an inhibitory synapse causes an increase in negative voltage, an example of **hyperpolarization**.

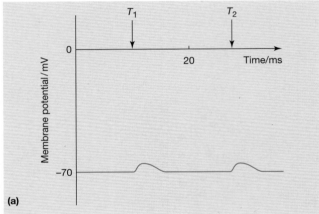

(a)

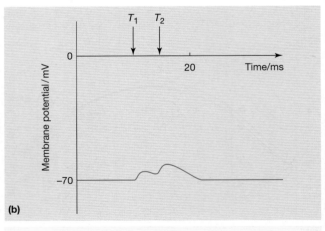

(b)

Figure 4.20 The effect at the axon hillock of two excitatory postsynaptic potentials at times T_1 and T_2: (a) apart in time, so that summation does not occur and (b) closer in time, so that summation occurs.

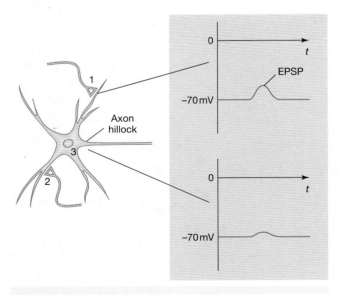

Figure 4.19 Neuron 3 showing location of the axon hillock, an excitatory postsynaptic potential (EPSP) at synapse 1 and its effect at the axon hillock.

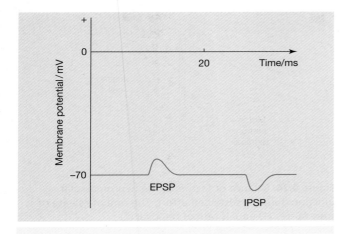

Figure 4.21 Excitatory (EPSP) and inhibitory postsynaptic potentials (IPSP).

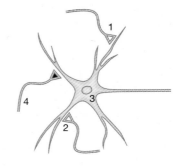

(a)

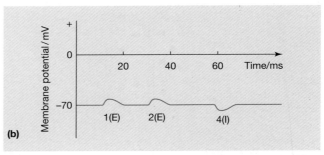

(b)

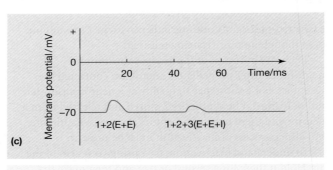

(c)

Figure 4.22 (a) Neuron 3 with two excitatory inputs (E; 1 and 2) and one inhibitory input (I; 4). (b) Effects of action potentials arriving in sequence at each of the three inputs, as measured at the axon hillock. (c) Integration of effects at the axon hillock when they occur simultaneously.

Inputs, whether excitatory or inhibitory, are *integrated* at the axon hillock. An action potential is triggered when the membrane potential reaches the threshold (Figure 4.7). Figure 4.22 represents another example of this: the neuron requires an excitatory input to trigger an action potential. The positive move of voltage needs to reach threshold at the axon hillock for an action potential to arise. Each postsynaptic potential extends a distance from the site where the postsynaptic receptors are located. Therefore, each contributes to just a very small voltage change at the axon hillock. The *net* summation ('integration') of many inputs, excitatory and inhibitory, determines whether a neuron generates an action potential or not (Figure 4.22 shows just a sample of inputs). Hyperpolarization caused by the inhibitory input acts in the opposite direction to the depolarizing effect of the excitatory inputs.

A large number of incoming action potentials at excitatory synapses triggers a high frequency of action potentials in the postsynaptic neuron. Conversely, activity at inhibitory synapses reduces the frequency of action potentials arising. This represents information processing, i.e. weighing up the relative strengths of excitation and inhibition.

Avoiding cross-talk

Considering the synapse, the receptor is like a lock and the neurotransmitter is like a key that fits just this one lock. This is termed the **lock and key principle**. It enables specificity of neural transmission between presynaptic and postsynaptic neurons. Figure 4.23 represents such specificity of transmitter and receptor between neuron 1 and neuron 2 and also between neuron 3 and neuron 4.

Suppose that a different neurotransmitter or hormone were to drift into the synapse that neuron 1 makes with neuron 2. For instance, as shown, the transmitter normally communicating from 3 to 4 might do so. This shape does not

fit the receptors at neuron 2, which means that the 'foreign' neurotransmitter cannot influence the synapse between 1 and 2. This allows different synapses to be close together and yet little cross-talk between them occurs.

Removal of transmitter from the synapse

Transmitter is released, crosses the synaptic cleft, attaches to receptors and, depending upon the synapse, either excites or inhibits the postsynaptic cell. Figure 3.11 (p. 57) showed that the effect on the postsynaptic cell can reflect very closely the duration of activity in the presynaptic cell. For example, when a burst of action potentials ceases, the release of neurotransmitter and its postsynaptic effect also cease. How is this achieved? Why does transmitter not remain attached

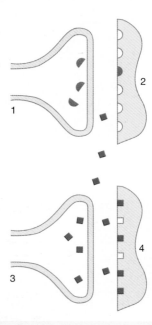

Figure 4.23 Avoidance of cross-talk.

to the receptors and continue either to excite or to inhibit, even though no more is being released?

There are processes at the synapse that remove neurotransmitter immediately after it has contacted the receptors. For a substance to qualify as a neurotransmitter, not only must it be synthesized, stored and released from a neuron and there must be receptors at a postsynaptic site, but also a process of inactivation must be present.

To understand inactivation, try raising your arm in the air. Hold it there for a second or two and then make the decision to lower it. The instant you put this decision into effect, contraction is relaxed in the muscles holding up the arm and the arm comes down. The state of contraction was maintained by occupation of receptors at the muscle by neurotransmitter. When the motor neurons cease activity, the effect of neurotransmitter also stops. The automatic removal of neurotransmitter means that the postsynaptic cell, whether neuron or muscle, can closely follow signals in the presynaptic neuron.

How then is a sustained activity in the postsynaptic cell maintained? For example, a muscle can be held in a contracted position over time (e.g. holding your arm in the air for minutes). To achieve this, there must be some occupation of the receptors at the muscle throughout. This is achieved by sustained activity in the motor neurons that innervate the muscle. Sustained activity in the postsynaptic cell (muscle cell, in this case) implies sustained activity in the presynaptic cell to produce neurotransmitter. This replaces the neurotransmitter that is removed from the synapse (Figure 4.24).

There are two different processes of removal, depending upon the type of synapse. At some synapses, a chemical (an

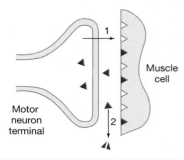

Figure 4.24 Balance of factors at the neuromuscular junction during a sustained effort. The rate of release of transmitter (1) equals rate of removal (2).

enzyme) that is present at the synapse literally breaks down the neurotransmitter, as in Figure 4.24. The fragments then waft away from the synapse. For constant activity at the postsynaptic cell, the rate of release and breakdown arrive at equilibrium. Breakdown is also shown in Figure 4.25(a). Another process is that neurotransmitter is taken back into the presynaptic neuron from which it was released, a process termed **reuptake**. Figure 4.25(b) shows such a two-way traffic of neurotransmitter across the cell membrane of the first neuron. Neurotransmitter is recycled.

Metabolites

When a neurotransmitter is broken down into components (Figures 4.24 and 4.25(a)), the breakdown products are termed its **metabolites**. Knowledge of metabolites represents more than just obscure biochemistry and is of interest to psychologists. Metabolites provide useful information to the investigator, since they will probably appear in the urine and can be measured. Knowing these metabolites, investigators have an idea of the transmitter that gave rise to them. For example, suppose that a particular class of neurotransmitter (e.g. dopamine) has been activated unusually strongly. This should be reflected in increased levels of secretion of its particular metabolites in the urine, which points the investigator to the neural activation giving rise to them.

Studying brain function in this way can be compared to trying to understand the events within a house by monitoring the contents of its rubbish bin. In each case, the method leaves something to be desired in terms of precision. However, as any detective knows, though less reliable than hidden video cameras, very useful insight can be gained from examining rubbish bins.

Second messengers

So far, the chapter has portrayed the classical picture in which a neurotransmitter occupies receptors on a postsynaptic cell and thereby immediately influences the cell,

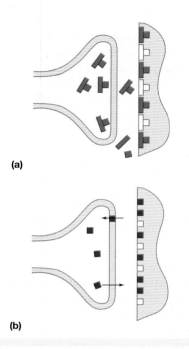

Figure 4.25 How transmitter is removed from the synaptic cleft: (a) enzymatic breakdown and (b) reuptake.

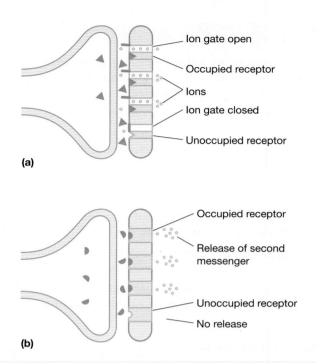

Figure 4.26 (a) Classical neurotransmission and (b) a second messenger system.

to excite or inhibit it. However, more complex effects are also found. To form a starting-point, Figure 4.26(a) shows the classical situation already described. When neurotransmitter occupies receptors, ion channels open and ions move through the channel. This has the immediate effect of either depolarizing or hyperpolarizing the cell, according to the nature of the ion channels that are affected. For example, opening sodium channels causes an inflow of Na+, which depolarizes the cell.

Figure 4.26(b) shows a different type of effect, involving what is termed a **second messenger**. On occupying receptors, neurotransmitter does not change ion channels but causes the release of a further substance, the second messenger, within the cell. (In these terms, the neurotransmitter assumes the role of a 'first messenger'.) The second messenger can have one of several effects depending upon the particular cell. As one such effect, it can open ion channels. In other cases, it targets the genetic material of the cell, influencing the activity of particular genes.

Electrical synapses

Finally, for the sake of completeness it is worth comparing the chemical synapse with a type of synapse that does not employ chemical transmitter, the **electrical synapse** (Figure 4.27). Note in part (b) that there is no synaptic gap: one neuron contacts directly another. Electrical events in neuron$_1$ trigger electrical events in neuron$_2$.

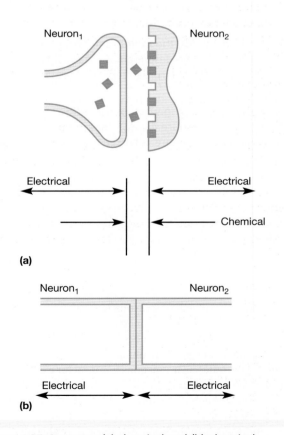

Figure 4.27 Synapses: (a) chemical and (b) electrical.

Section summary

1 A neuron forming a chemical synapse can be characterized by the neurotransmitter that it synthesizes, stores and releases at a synapse.

2 A given neuron can have receptors for several neurotransmitters.

3 Shortly after attaching, neurotransmitter is normally dislodged from the receptors and removed from the synapse (by enzymatic destruction or reuptake).

4 The breakdown products of a neurotransmitter are termed its metabolites.

5 Second messengers are released within certain neurons in response to neurotransmitter.

6 At electrical synapses, there is direct electrical communication from one neuron to another.

Test your knowledge

(Answers on page 104)

4.7 In Figure 4.20(a), what description is given to the membrane potential at time 20 ms?

4.8 In Figure 4.20(b), the membrane potential at time T_2 would be described as which of the following? (i) Hyperpolarized, (ii) depolarized, (iii) positive.

4.9 What is the missing word in the following sentence? 'In Figure 4.25(a), the green rectangle and square represent _____ of the transmitter'.

Alterations in synaptic strength

Introduction

Maintaining the strength of transmission at the different groups of synapses (e.g. dopaminergic and serotonergic) within a certain range is vital to behaviour, physical and mental health. For example, maintaining normal synaptic activity at neuromuscular junctions is crucial for exerting control in the somatic and autonomic nervous systems. However, the strength of synaptic connections of a particular class can vary both as a result of such things as physical interventions made in the interest of research or therapy, drugs such as nicotine, disease or as a result of genetic differences between individuals. There can be over-activity or under-activity in a particular neurotransmitter. This section will describe some of the implications of this for behaviour.

Consider again the sequence involving neurotransmitter: (1) release, (2) movement across the synaptic cleft, (3) attachment to receptors and (4) removal from the synapse. A change in any of 1–4 changes the strength of synaptic connection, i.e. for a given presynaptic activity, the postsynaptic activity will be different. 'Change' can mean, for example, those over time in a given individual as a result of a manipulation such as medication or genetically determined differences between individuals.

Naturally occurring changes

In a polluted and, to many people, an alienating world, it can be somewhat arbitrary as to what we label natural or artificial. This section will consider 'natural' differences in synaptic efficacy to be those that do not arise as a result of deliberate artificial manipulations.

For example, depression is associated with abnormalities in serotonergic, noradrenergic and dopaminergic synapses. There might be differences between individuals as a result of, say, genetics, which could contribute to depression (Chapter 2, 'Genes, environment and evolution'). It is possible that genes and/or environment play a role in producing synapses that are different, in terms of, say, the amount of transmitter stored or number of receptors.

How can disease alter the strength of synaptic connections? A possible source of malfunction is the loss of receptors at the postsynaptic membrane. In addition, consider events prior to neurotransmitter being released at the terminal of a neuron. Neurotransmitter is synthesized from precursor substances in the cell body and terminal. Neurotransmitter that is synthesized in the cell body is then transported to the terminal to be stored until its release. Inadequate amounts of transmitter might be synthesized.

Artificially changing synapses

Drugs (e.g. nicotine, alcohol, heroin and cocaine) have effects on mood because they exert action at particular classes of synapse. These, and other, drugs are commonly used as research tools by psychologists interested in probing their effects on the nervous system.

Agonists and antagonists

Certain unnatural substances that are different from the natural neurotransmitter nonetheless occupy its receptors after being introduced into the body. Such substances can be exploited as therapy and research tools. On occupying receptors, substances can have various effects. For example, the effect of the natural transmitter on the postsynaptic cell can be mimicked by drugs called **agonists**. If the natural transmitter excites the postsynaptic cell, by definition so does its agonist. If the natural substance inhibits, so does its agonist. Therapeutically, an agonist might be employed where there is a deficiency of natural transmitter.

Conversely, a drug might occupy receptors but not exert any effect on the second cell (i.e. it is inert), thereby blocking the natural neurotransmitter's occupation and action. A substance having this property is termed an antagonist. An **antagonist** would be used in a therapeutic role to lower the effect of a natural neurotransmitter.

For an excitatory synapse, Figure 4.28 shows the effects of agonists and antagonists, sometimes known as direct agonists and direct antagonists because of their site of action at receptors.

A natural neurochemical can interact with more than one subtype of receptor (Figure 4.29(a)). In this case, there are distinct D1 and D2 subtypes of dopamine (DA) receptor. Different subtypes are sometimes found in different brain regions. Figure 4.29(b) represents agonists or antagonists that target a specific subtype of receptor. For example, the D1 type of agonist fits the D1 receptor subtype but not the

D2 subtype. Note their unique configuration but the generic ('all-purpose') configuration of the natural transmitter.

Other substances are termed indirect agonists and antagonists. The term 'indirect' provides a contrast to the direct substance in terms of the difference in site at which they act. For example, an indirect agonist might trigger the release of neurotransmitter from a presynaptic neuron even in the absence of action potentials. An indirect antagonist might block its release.

Drugs can also affect synaptic efficacy by changing the rate of removal of neurotransmitter from the synaptic cleft. Neurotransmitter is removed in one of two ways (Figure 4.25). Some drugs block reuptake (Figure 4.25(b)) and this increases the amount of neurotransmitter at the synaptic cleft and hence increases that at the receptors (Figure 4.30). For example, cocaine acts in this way on the reuptake of dopamine.

Elevating dopamine levels by blocking reuptake with cocaine is experienced as 'euphoric', a 'high'. However, it comes at a price, both literally and metaphorically. The high has a limited duration, set by the length of time that elevated dopamine levels are available and before dopamine drifts from the synaptic junction. The effect is a powerful and dramatic one. Since dopamine is not being recycled by being taken back into the presynaptic neuron, the 'high' is followed by dopamine depletion and hence under-activity at the synapse. In the context of the whole CNS, this is felt as a

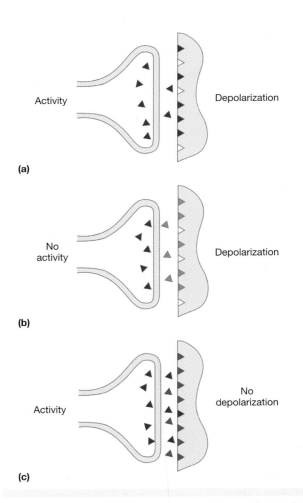

Figure 4.28 Agonists and antagonists: (a) normal situation, (b) addition of agonist and (c) addition of antagonist.

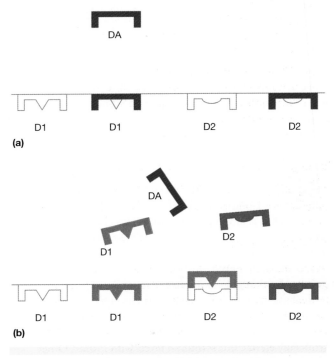

Figure 4.29 Dopamine exemplifying a neurochemical and subtypes of receptor: (a) natural situation and (b) addition of artificial chemicals that target only a subtype of receptor (either D1 or D2).

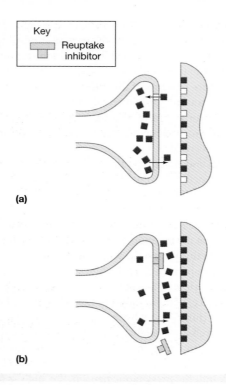

(a)

(b)

Figure 4.30 The action of a drug on blocking reuptake: (a) without drug and (b) in the presence of drug.

negative emotion and translates into a craving for more cocaine. In time, dopamine will be replenished at the presynaptic neuron.

Artificially altering synaptic function can trigger homeostatic-like changes at the synapse. For example, if a synapse is repeatedly excited there can be a compensatory loss of receptors at the postsynaptic membrane, termed **down-regulation**. Conversely, loss of transmitter can trigger a proliferation of receptors termed **up-regulation**.

Antidepressant medication

Mood-altering drugs, both legal and illegal, act in several different ways, one of which was shown in Figure 4.30. A number of legal antidepressant drugs also change the reuptake of neurotransmitters, though less dramatically than a drug such as cocaine. A drug, fluoxetine (Prozac), used to treat obsessive-compulsive disorder (e.g. compulsive checking or intrusive thoughts), inhibits the reuptake of serotonin. It is termed a **reuptake inhibitor**. Its reputation has now spread far. Some argue that happiness is everyone's birthright and, if we cannot achieve this by natural means, then we should artificially elevate our serotonin levels with Prozac. Other antidepressants reduce levels of the enzyme that breaks down a particular neurotransmitter, which increases levels of neurotransmitter at the postsynaptic membrane.

In time, drugs are broken down into their metabolites. Before metabolites appear in the urine, they wander around the CNS. In some cases, they influence neurons at receptors, having undesirable effects. Effects that are unintended in the prescription of the drug are termed **side effects**. For example, the drug clomipramine blocks serotonin reuptake and provides therapy for obsessive-compulsive disorder and depression. Logically, the efficacy might be attributed to its targeting of the serotonergic systems. However, clomipramine does not remain chemically unaltered in the body. It is metabolized and a metabolite is desmethylclomipramine, which blocks noradrenergic reuptake. See Figure 4.31. This has side effects, among others, of blocking orgasm.

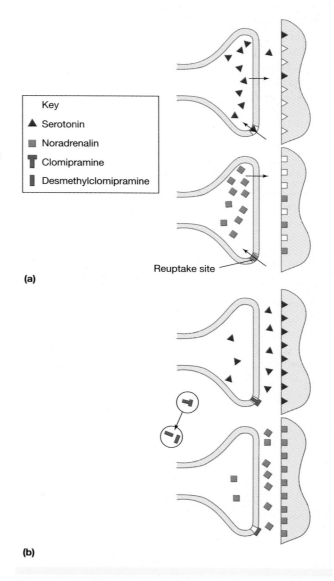

(a)

(b)

Figure 4.31 A drug that targets a natural neurotransmitter and the side effect of a metabolite on noradrenergic synapses: (a) without and (b) with the drug present.

Section summary

1 A direct agonist occupies postsynaptic receptors and mimics the natural neurotransmitter.

2 A direct antagonist occupies postsynaptic receptors and blocks the effect of the natural neurotransmitter.

3 Some drugs block reuptake and thereby elevate levels of natural neurotransmitter available at the synapse.

Test your knowledge

(Answers on page 104)

4.10 What effect does a direct agonist have on the membrane potential of a postsynaptic neuron at (i) an excitatory synapse and (ii) an inhibitory synapse?

4.11 Which of the following occupy dopamine D1 receptors? (i) Natural dopamine, (ii) a D1 agonist, (iii) a D1 antagonist, (iv) a D2 agonist.

4.3

Bringing things together

This chapter has given you enough detail to understand how information is transmitted and processed. Usually, for our purposes, knowledge gained at the level of individual neurons and synapses (the 'cellular level') needs to be interpreted in the broader context of the functioning of the whole nervous system, the topic of the next chapter. However, sometimes psychologists can understand rather straightforwardly how actions at the cellular level of the neuron and synapse affect our behaviour and mental states. Insights here can be vital. For example, side effects of medication are an important issue in dealing with patients who have psychological problems; a drug might be prescribed to target a certain part of the CNS but its metabolites have effects elsewhere, e.g. to induce sleepiness.

One sometimes sees an expression such as 'the dopaminergic hypothesis of depression' or 'the serotonergic hypothesis of obsessive compulsive disorder', implying that an abnormality in a particular neurotransmitter forms the basis of the disorder. In order to make sense of such ideas, you need to know

something about the classification of neurons, their release of neurotransmitter and removal of neurotransmitter from the synaptic cleft.

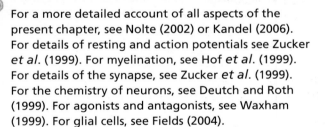

Summary of Chapter 4

1 **As a result of the distribution of electrically charged particles (ions), there is a small voltage across the membrane of cells, including neurons.**

2 **In neurons, a rapid change in the voltage (membrane potential) constitutes an action potential, this being their means of communication.**

3 **Apart from neurons, another type of cell found in the nervous system is the glial cell.**

4 **Signals are integrated at postsynaptic cells, by means of the effects that neurotransmitters have on these cells.**

5 **Both natural events and artificial manipulations can change the activity at synapses.**

Further reading

For a more detailed account of all aspects of the present chapter, see Nolte (2002) or Kandel (2006). For details of resting and action potentials see Zucker *et al.* (1999). For myelination, see Hof *et al.* (1999). For details of the synapse, see Zucker *et al.* (1999). For the chemistry of neurons, see Deutch and Roth (1999). For agonists and antagonists, see Waxham (1999). For glial cells, see Fields (2004).

Signposts

Chapters 1–4 have covered a large territory and different levels, ranging from evolutionary processes, nervous systems, neurotransmitters and ions. The scale has got smaller with each chapter. You might be wondering – now where? Do we consider the properties of subatomic particles and the world of quantum physics? You will probably be relieved to know that the book is not going in that direction. The next chapter looks at whole brains. Knowledge of how hormones, neurons and neurotransmitters work is invaluable in understanding how whole brains work.

Answers

Explanations for answers to 'test your knowledge' questions can be found on the website **www.pearsoned.co.uk/toates**

4.1   Membrane
4.2   Concentration gradient tending to move them into the cell; membrane potential tending to move them out of the cell.
4.3   (i) 1
4.4   Membrane; concentration
4.5   Sodium
4.6   (i) Right to left
4.7   Resting potential
4.8   (ii) Depolarized
4.9   Metabolites

4.10   (i) Excitation (depolarization); (ii) inhibition (hyperpolarization)
4.11   (i) Natural dopamine, (ii) a D1 agonist, (iii) a D1 antagonist

Interactions and animations relating to topics discussed in this chapter can be found on the website at **www.pearsoned.co.uk/toates**. These include

Interaction: Labelling the main components of a typical brain neuron

Animation: Exocytosis, neurotransmitter release and breakdown

CHAPTER 5

The brain: basics of structure and role

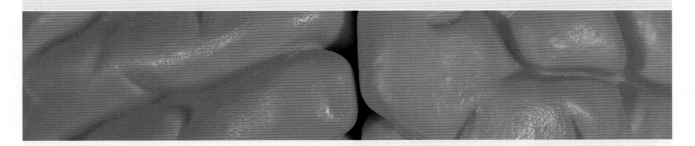

Learning outcomes for Chapter 5

After studying this chapter, you should be able to:

1. Understand the conventions for describing brain regions, locations and orientations within the brain. In this context, explain the meaning of such terms as ipsilateral, contralateral, gyrus and sulcus.

2. Describe the principal routes by which information is transmitted to the brain and motor information is conveyed from the brain to the periphery.

3. Give an account of the role of the brain in regulating the body's internal environment and in mediating links between the body and its external environment. Describe the special features of how the brain regulates its own environment.

4. Give an example of a link between brain structure and cognition.

5. Argue the case that our understanding of how nervous systems work can be aided by taking a comparative and evolutionary perspective.

6. Outline a number of the techniques employed to study the brain and relate this to the ways in which they can aid our understanding of how brains work.

Scene-setting questions

1 Why has the human brain a wrinkled appearance, rather like a walnut?

2 How do we know what different bits of the brain do?

3 Where is the brain's famous grey matter to be found?

4 What is a stroke?

5 What is it about the human brain that makes us special?

The brain has the task of interpreting various sources of sensory information to obtain perceptions and emotions, while controlling behaviour. How is all of this integration achieved?

Source: © VICTOR FRAILE/Reuters/Corbis.

Introduction

The brain is composed of billions of neurons and supporting cells. Earlier chapters described the processing that systems of neurons in the brain perform and information that goes to the brain (e.g. visual) and from it (e.g. controlling muscles). The present chapter focuses on the structures of the brain and introduces the relationship between each structure and its role. This chapter gives a framework in which you can locate the more detailed discussion on the brain, which will be presented in later chapters.

A prerequisite for understanding the brain is to build a description of its anatomy. This enables us to locate different regions and to identify connections between them. The chapter should allow you to gain familiarity with some of the brain's principal landmarks. To simplify, the focus is mainly on humans. A mental map of the human brain can be useful in finding your way around other brains, e.g. that of the rat.

Understanding the brain is helped by knowledge of its component cells, the neurons. Researchers have identified some of the types of neuron found in different regions

and the neurotransmitters that they employ. For example, researchers identify neuron terminals in one region as predominantly releasing, say, dopamine and trace where the associated cell bodies and axons are located. In this way a picture of interconnections between brain regions can be constructed.

There are various valuable sources for information on the human brain (discussed further, later in this chapter). One source is to study the behavioural deficiencies of patients with damage to the brain, e.g. accidents and disease. In therapy and in experiments on both humans and non-humans, manipulations of the brain (e.g. injection of neurotransmitter agonists and antagonists) are made and effects on behaviour noted. Cautious extrapolation from the more common non-human studies can yield insight into the human brain. A technique of growing importance is to employ special equipment to form images of the human brain, so as to reveal its workings.

In order to understand the brain, you need to learn the names of some regions and also navigational terms that provide a kind of route-map for finding your way. These are conventions agreed by all investigators. The next section turns to this subject.

Section summary

1 Understanding the brain requires an unambiguous description of its anatomy.

2 Identification of the brain's neurons, their location and the neurotransmitters that they employ is crucial for understanding the role of different brain regions.

Test your knowledge

(Answer on page 144)

5.1 In terms of cell bodies, axons and release of neurochemical, what is meant by saying that a tract of dopaminergic neurons projects from brain region A to brain region B?

Describing the brain and finding your way around it

Directions

Figure 5.1 shows how to orient with respect to the brain and, more generally, the whole body. For brain and spinal cord, the expression 'anterior' (also termed 'rostral') means towards the 'nose-end'. The expression 'posterior' (or 'caudal') means towards the 'tail-end'. The meaning of the term 'ventral' (Chapter 3, 'The nervous and endocrine

systems') is relative to context. In the case of animals which normally stand horizontal (e.g. rat or goat), it means towards the lower part of the body. So, a ventral brain region is one that is in a relatively low part of the brain. Similarly, a ventral region of the rat's spinal cord is on the side of the bottom of the body.

Because of the vertical posture of humans, the term 'ventral' needs some qualification. In humans, when used to describe the brain, it refers to relatively low parts of it. When used to describe the spinal cord, it refers to parts near to the front of the body. A similar qualification is needed for 'dorsal' (Chapter 3), which refers to the upper parts of the brain and body of the rat and the upper parts of the human brain. For the human spinal cord, it refers to the part towards the back.

The terms 'medial' and 'lateral' are unambiguous, regardless of species. With reference to the midline shown, medial refers to the centre of the body and lateral means 'away from the centre'. There are further terms in common use: 'superior' means in the direction towards the top of the brain and 'inferior' in the direction towards the bottom of the brain. Use of these terms is relative. Thus, the description 'superior' does not mean that the region is necessarily at the top of the brain, rather it is in that direction relative to a specific frame of reference. A given brain region might be divided into superior and inferior regions. A 'superior view' of the brain is one from above and an 'inferior view' is one from below.

Building on the term 'lateral', **ipsilateral** refers to the same side of the brain and **contralateral** to the opposite side. For example, if a neuron that originates in the left half of the brain projects to another region of the left half, it is an ipsilateral connection. If it crosses over and projects to the right half, it forms a contralateral projection.

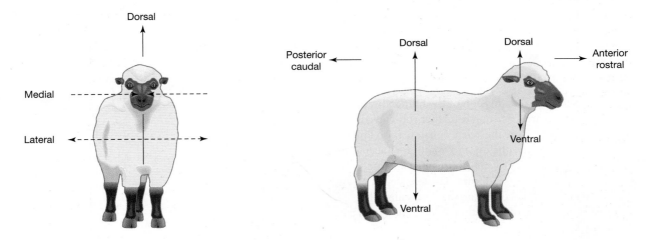

Figure 5.1(a) System of orientation: for an animal that stands horizontal.

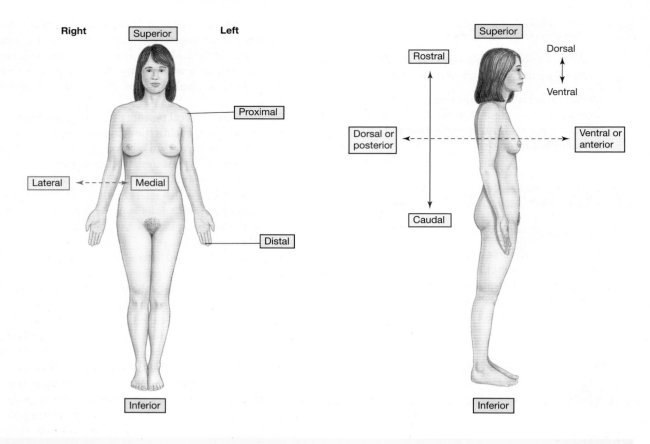

Figure 5.1(b) System of orientation: for humans.

Source of (b): Martini *et al.* (2000, Fig. 1-10, p. 16).

Figure 5.2 shows planes of reference, which you can imagine to be taking slices through the brain. The 'sagittal plane' either divides the brain down the middle or is parallel to such a line. A midsagittal section is one made through the centre-line. The 'horizontal plane' represents a real or imaginary cut made at the horizontal. The 'coronal plane' (or 'frontal plane') is at right angles to the sagittal plane.

Some landmarks

Figure 5.3 shows a gross division of the human brain into some of its structures. Of course, further sub-categorization of these is possible. Note the 'telencephalon' (also known as the 'cerebrum'), 'diencephalon' and 'midbrain' (also termed the 'mesencephalon'). The cerebellum, pons and medulla, together constitute the 'hindbrain'. The telencephalon and diencephalon together constitute the 'forebrain'. The medulla is the region of brain that links to the spinal cord. The term 'brain stem' refers to the combination of midbrain, pons and medulla.

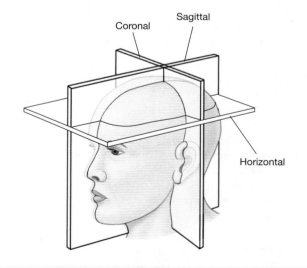

Figure 5.2 Planes slicing the brain.

Source: Martini *et al.* (2000, Fig. 15-13, p. 395 inset).

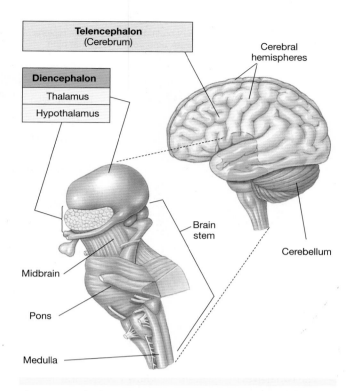

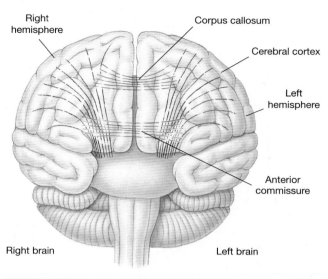

Figure 5.4 Anterior view of the brain.

Source: Martini *et al.* (2000, Fig. 15-10b, p. 391).

Figure 5.3 The human brain, showing its outer appearance and, relatively enlarged, some of its structures.

Source: Martini *et al.* (2000, Fig. 15-1, p. 379).

A brain can be divided into two, almost identical halves, along its midline. Figure 5.4 illustrates the outward aspect of the brain's near-perfect symmetry across its centre (midsagittal) plane. Note that, by convention, the terms left and right are with respect to the perspective of the individual represented. As a telencephalic structure, the outer layer of the brain is termed **cerebral cortex**. It is made up of folds and ridges.

Figure 5.5 shows, among other things, two paired structures of the midbrain (appearing as bumps on the dorsal surface): the 'superior colliculus' (concerned with vision) and the 'inferior colliculus' (concerned with hearing). These structures, of plural name 'colliculi', exemplify the meaning of the terms 'superior' and 'inferior'. Two paired structures termed the 'lateral geniculate nucleus' and 'medial geniculate nucleus' illustrate the meaning of medial and lateral. To remind you, the term 'nucleus' (plural: nuclei) refers to a collection of cell bodies in the CNS, analogous to a ganglion in the peripheral nervous system (Chapter 3). By convention, the single term 'nucleus' is sometimes used as a generic for paired nuclei, comparable to the use of 'gland' (Chapter 3).

Understanding the structure of the adult brain can be aided by an appreciation of how it grew into its adult form. It also enables the logic behind anatomical description to be better understood (Rosenzweig *et al.*, 1996). For example, as shown in Figure 5.3, not only is the part of the brain nearest the front termed the forebrain but so is that nearest the back. Why is this description used?

With increasing age up until maturity, bodies develop more and more complexity, derived from an earlier and simpler form. A human brain early in development is shown in Figure 5.6 (left) and a slightly more developed one to the right. The basics of the three divisions of Figure 5.3 are evident: forebrain, midbrain and hindbrain, defined by the location of swellings. To the right, the particularly extensive development of the forebrain is seen and, by now, its two subdivisions are also evident. Still further development ends with the adult structure. From these early forms, you can see why, in the adult, even the part of the brain nearest the back is termed 'forebrain'.

In Figure 5.5(b), note that the diencephalic structure termed the 'thalamus' consists of a left and right thalamus. (Again, the singular is used even though a structure is subdivided into halves.) This left–right pairing is typical of most brain structures. Located immediately under the thalamus is another paired diencephalic structure, termed the 'hypothalamus' (hypo means lower/less than) (Figures 5.3 and 5.7).

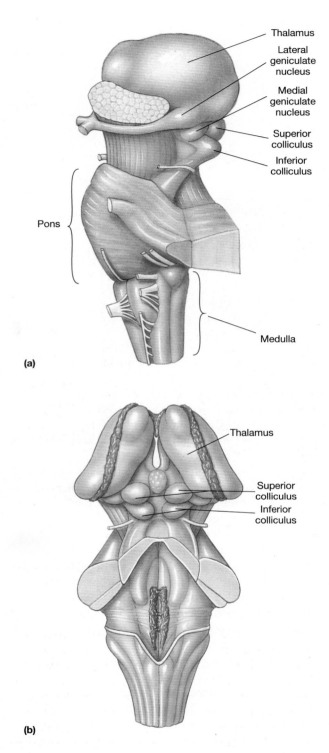

(a)

(b)

Figure 5.5 The brain stem and diencephalon in (a) lateral and (b) posterior views (note cerebellum is removed).

Source: Martini *et al.* (2000, Fig. 15-16(a) and (c), p. 400).

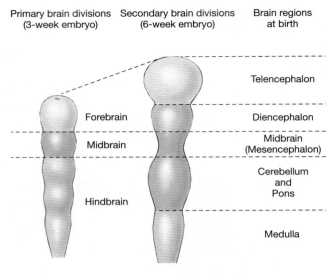

Figure 5.6 Human brain development.

Source: Martini *et al.* (2000, Table 15-1, p. 379).

The two halves of the brain are known as 'cerebral hemispheres' (Figure 5.4), which gives a classification into left and right half brains. A large bundle of fibres, termed the 'corpus callosum', links the left and right hemispheres (Figure 5.4). It is made up of axons of neurons that communicate information between one half of the brain and the other. A midsagittal view of the right half of the brain is shown in Figure 5.7. This reveals a section through the corpus callosum. A frontal section of the brain can also show the corpus callosum (Figure 5.8). Another means of communication, for anterior parts of the cortex, is a small bundle of axons termed the 'anterior commissure'. See Figures 5.4 and 5.8. In Figure 5.8, note regions of grey matter (high concentration of cell bodies) in the outer part of the brain and white matter (high concentration of myelin) at the inner part (cf. Chapter 3 and the spinal cord).

As you can see from Figures 5.4, 5.7 and 5.8, the exterior surface of the brain has a wrinkled appearance rather like a walnut. This arises because the cerebral cortex is folded. The word 'cortex' is Latin for bark, as in the bark that forms the outer layer of a tree, comparable to the cortex being the outer layer of the brain. Folding allows a large amount of the tissue that constitutes the outer layer to be packed into the space of the skull. The folds ('grooves' or 'furrows', depending upon which word conveys the best image) provide important landmarks (Figure 5.9). A generic term for these folds is 'sulcus' (plural, sulci). (Confusingly, a distinction is sometimes made between types of fold, in which a small one is termed a sulcus and a larger one a fissure.) The structure

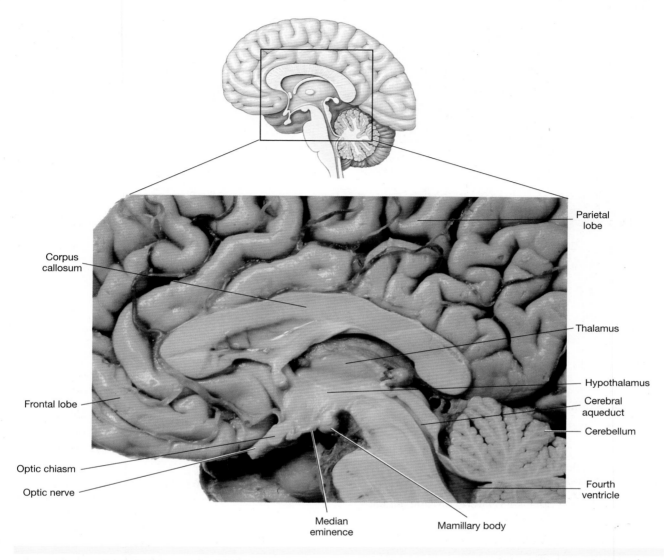

Corpus
callosum

Parietal
lobe

Thalamus

Hypothalamus

Cerebral
aqueduct

Cerebellum

Frontal lobe

Optic chiasm

Optic nerve

Fourth
ventricle

Median
eminence

Mamillary body

Figure 5.7 Midsaggital section through the brain, drawing attention to hypothalamus and thalamus. (Here, as elsewhere, the relevance of some labels will become apparent only later.)

Source: Martini *et al.* (2000, Fig. 15-15(a), p. 398).

between two sulci is termed a 'gyrus' (pl. gyri). The positions of the principal sulci on the cortex are not arbitrary but show a regular pattern from person to person and provide landmarks for locating particular cortical regions.

Based upon their outer appearance, the cerebral hemispheres are divided into lobes. Figure 5.9(b) shows these four lobes: the frontal, temporal, occipital and parietal lobes. Cortex is classified by the lobe within which it is located, e.g. occipital cortex. The lateral sulcus (sometimes termed the Sylvian fissure) provides a boundary between the frontal and temporal lobes. The central sulcus (central fissure) forms the boundary between the frontal lobe and the parietal lobe. Two landmark gyri are indicated in Figure 5.9(b), one to each side of the central sulcus: the precentral gyrus and the postcentral gyrus.

A more detailed classification of the cortex is in terms of numbered areas, named 'Brodmann's areas', after the person who first plotted them (Figure 5.10). Brodmann's areas give a system for finding a location within a lobe. There are other systems of description also employed. For example, posterior temporal cortex refers to that part of the temporal cortex near the back of the brain. Inferior temporal cortex refers to that forming the lower part of the lobe. The compound 'posterior inferior' means towards the back and low.

Figure 5.11 shows a midsagittal section through the brain. Some familiar regions are apparent from this perspective and also a new one, the cingulate gyrus. The cortex that comprises the cingulate gyrus is termed 'cingulate cortex'.

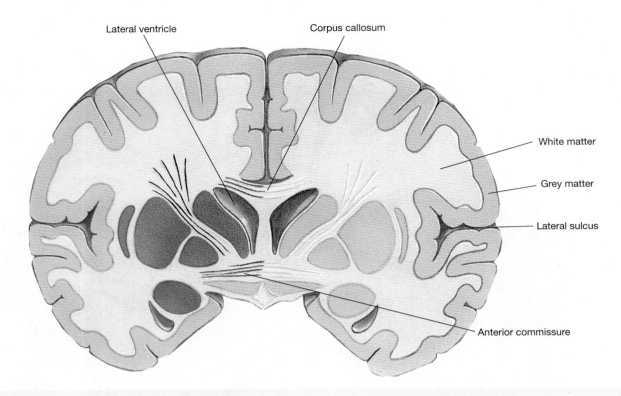

Figure 5.8 A frontal section of the brain.

Source: Martini *et al.* (2000, Fig. 15-11(a) and (b), p. 392).

Section summary

1 Terms such as dorsal and lateral provide a means of finding our way around the CNS.

2 The brain can be divided into forebrain, midbrain and hindbrain.

3 The cerebral cortex forms the outer layer of the forebrain.

Test your knowledge

(Answers on page 144)

5.2 Complete the following: 'With reference to Figure 5.4, axons that make up the corpus callosum would be said to project _____'
(i) Ipsilaterally; (ii) contralaterally.

5.3 Which is more caudal, (i) the superior colliculus or (ii) the inferior colliculus?

5.4 Figure 5.12 (p. 114) shows a segment of spinal cord.

(a) With reference to each set of paired letters (e.g. A_1, A_2), indicate the following:

(i)   Which is the most ventral? A_1 or A_2

(ii) Which is the most dorsal? A_1 or A_2

(iii) Which is the most lateral? C_1 or C_2

(iv) Which is the most medial? C_1 or C_2

(v)   Which is the most caudal? D_1 or D_2

(vi) Which is the most rostral? D_1 or D_2

(b) Which is (i) white matter (A_2 or B_2) and which is (ii) grey matter (A_2 or B_2)?

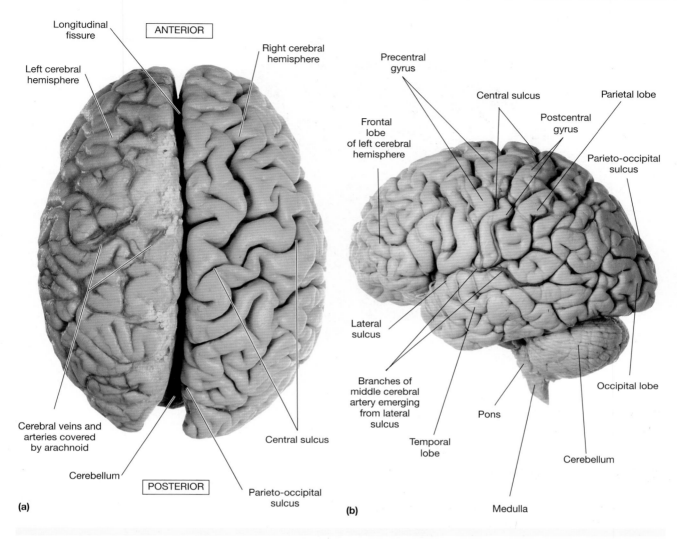

Figure 5.9 The brain highlighting some sulci and gyri: (a) superior view, (b) lateral view.

Source: Martini *et al.* (2000, Fig. 15-8(a), p. 388 and Fig. 15-9(a), p. 389).

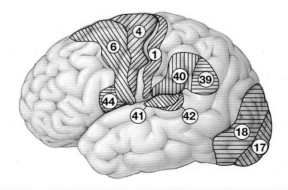

Figure 5.10 Lateral view of the left cerebral cortex showing some of Brodmann's areas. (In a full account, the entire cortex is numbered in this system.)

Source: Martini *et al.* (2000, Fig. 16-7(c), p. 435).

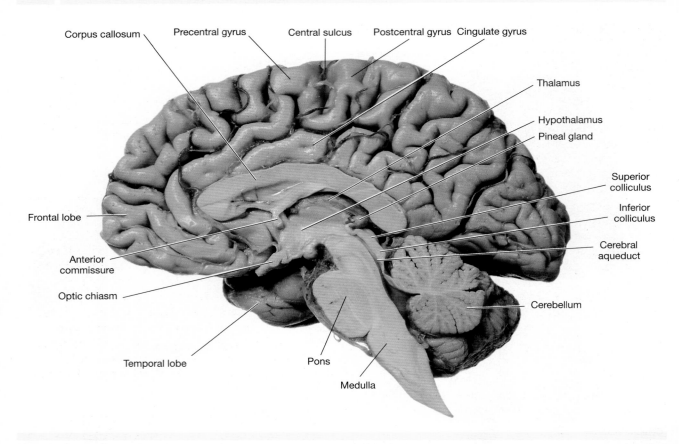

Figure 5.11 Midsagittal section through the brain. *Source*: Martini *et al.* (2000, Fig. 15-13, p. 395).

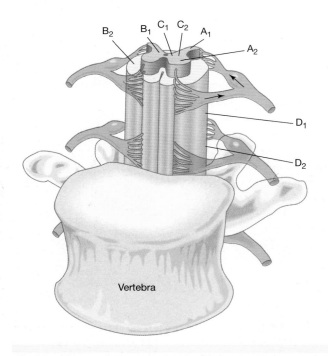

Figure 5.12 Segment of spinal cord.
Source: Vander *et al.* (1994) *Human Physiology*, Fig. 8-35, p. 215,
reproduced with permission of the McGraw-Hill Companies, Inc.

Relating structure to role: sensory and motor systems

Introduction

The brain makes decisions on what behaviour to perform. Making decisions is based upon events in the external world (e.g. presence of danger, food or a mate) and internal world (e.g. levels of nutrients, water or hormone). This section and the following two relate this information processing to some of the brain regions where it is performed. In this section, we start by considering some routes by which information gets to the brain, and how it is initially processed. We then consider how information leaves the brain and is used in motor control.

This section gives an embodiment to the brain processes involved in Chapter 3, where sensory inputs and motor outputs were discussed.

Sensory information

Introduction

This section discusses how sensory information is detected and information transmitted to the brain. It looks briefly at the initial stages of processing in the brain. In order to discuss the latter, some important landmarks in the brain are introduced in the context of what they do. That is, cortical areas are discussed in terms of the information that they process. Sensory information from the external environment is conveyed to the brain either via the spinal cord or via cranial nerves (Chapter 3).

Cortex – defined by role

For some of the cortex, it is possible to associate a region with a particular role in the initial stages of processing sensory information. See Figure 5.13. Visual information, derived from the eyes and transmitted via the optic nerve (Chapter 3, Figure 3.20, p. 65), arrives at the **visual cortex**, located in the occipital lobe (area 17 in Figure 5.10). Here, further analysis of visual information occurs. The visual cortex is also termed the striate cortex, because, on close inspection, striation (a striped appearance) of this region is evident. Similarly, auditory information, derived from the ears, arrives at the **auditory cortex**, a region of the temporal lobe. It is then processed further to extract meaning.

The information on touch arrives at the **somatosensory cortex** (soma: body, i.e. sensations from the body), a region of the parietal lobe. It is then further analyzed to extract information on the touch stimulus. More will be said later about the large areas that are not involved in the early stages of sensory processing (pink colour).

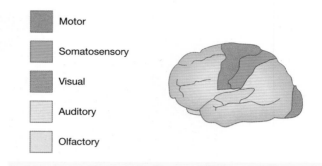

Figure 5.13 The cortex described by its role in information processing. *Source*: OU course SD286 (Module A, Fig. 22, p. 31).

Short tracts (Chapter 3), consisting of bundles of axons of neurons, convey information from one cortical area to neighbouring areas, whereas longer tracts convey information between distant cortical areas.

Within a given area of cortex, information is communicated between superficial and deeper regions. Figure 5.14 shows a typical section of cerebral cortex. The cortex is organized in six distinct layers of cell type (Northcutt and Kaas, 1995). Different layers are associated

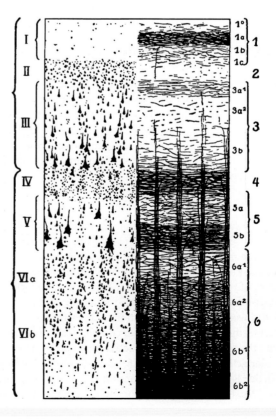

Figure 5.14 Section through cerebral cortex showing layered organization. *Source*: Fuster (1997, Fig. 2.2, p. 12).

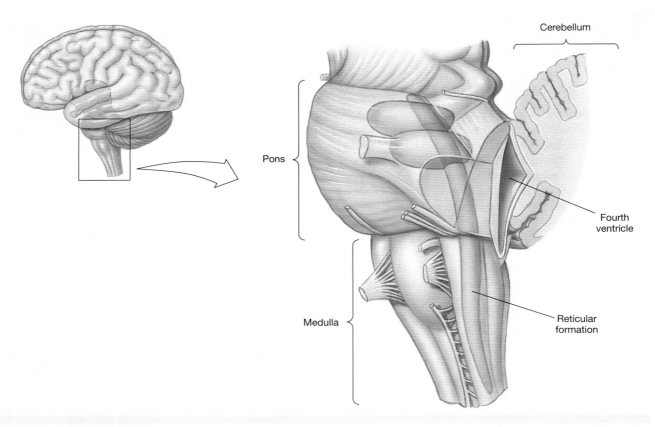

Figure 5.15 The pons and medulla, showing the reticular formation. *Source*: after Martini *et al.* (2000, Fig. 15-18, p. 402).

with different functions. For example, in parts of the cortex concerned with sensory processing, sensory information projected from the thalamus tends to arrive in layer 4. Information is communicated between layers.

The access of sensory information to the cortex is to some extent controlled by other brain mechanisms, the topic of the next section.

Controlling input to the cortex

Figure 5.3 shows some regions that are involved in the transfer of sensory information: (1) the hindbrain regions termed the medulla and pons, (2) the midbrain and (3) the thalamus. Running through the medulla and pons is a network of neurons termed the 'reticular formation' (Figure 5.15) (Moruzzi and Magoun, 1949). The name derives from the Latin word 'reticulum', which means network.

Part of the reticular formation contributes to a system termed the **ascending reticular activating system**, or just 'reticular activating system' (RAS) (Moruzzi and Magoun, 1949). See Figure 5.16. Sensory inputs trigger the RAS and, in turn, the RAS makes projections to the cortex and other higher levels.

Particular neurons carry information on specific sensory events such as visual events. Other specific neurons convey

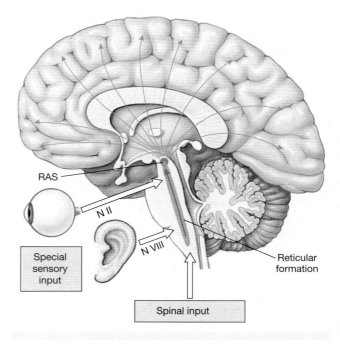

Figure 5.16 The reticular activating system.
Source: Martini *et al.* (2000, Fig. 16-9, p. 437).

information on other specific events, e.g. auditory events. Such specific neurons send branches to the reticular formation, where their effects converge. Neurons from the spinal cord also provide an input. Thus, the output of the RAS is non-specific to any given sensory channel.

The role of the reticular formation is, in association with other brain regions, a general one of modulating ('tuning') sensory processing and thereby exerting a control over waking, alertness and sleep. Output neurons from the reticular formation change the operating characteristics of neurons throughout large regions of the brain. They trigger states of high or low 'arousal'.

The RAS provides a non-specific gate for sensory information. We now look at some specific routes by which sensory information gets to the cortex. The first route of information processing discussed concerns information that is conveyed via the spinal cord. Vision is then employed to illustrate how information can be detected and transmitted to the brain via a cranial nerve.

Some specific spinal links to the brain

Earlier, the topic of information on tissue damage being transmitted to the brain was introduced (Chapter 3, Figure 3.1(b), p. 49). Figure 5.17 shows the equivalent of neurons 1 and 5 of Figure 3.1(b), indicated respectively as red and white. Within the spinal cord, the second ('white') neuron crosses from one side to the other and ascends to the brain in the cord's 'white matter', as part of a tract. The white matter is made up largely of axons of neurons that carry information up and down the spinal cord and the cells that provide support to these neurons (contributing to myelin). Information from the right side of the body arrives in the left half of the brain. In addition to the route shown in Figure 5.17, the white neuron would send a branch (sometimes termed a 'collateral') to the reticular formation. This would excite neurons in the reticular formation. The link via the reticular formation probably plays a role in the arousing and emotional aspects of pain. Pain can, of course, very effectively prevent sleep as you might have experienced.

In a number of sensory systems, the thalamus forms a relay station within the specific pathway. Figure 5.17 shows this for nociceptive information. At the thalamus, synapses are formed between neurons in the sensory pathway. Nociceptive information arrives at a particular nucleus of the thalamus. A set of neurons (indicated by black) conveys this information from the thalamus to the cortex. This route is specific to nociceptive information.

Similarly, for harmless (non-nociceptive) tactile information, there is a projection from the periphery to the thalamus and then to the somatosensory cortex (Figure 5.18). In anatomical terms, this region of cortex is the postcentral gyrus (Figure 5.9(b)). As you can see in Figure 5.18, information crosses from one side to the other but in this case

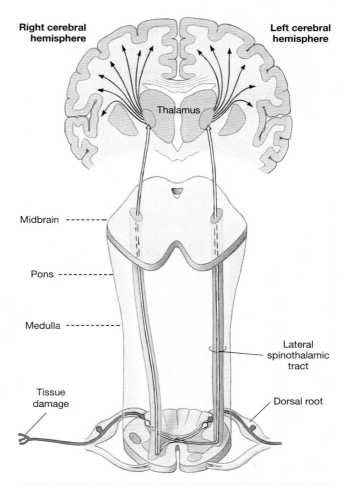

Figure 5.17 The transfer of nociceptive information (meaning, 'relating to tissue damage') to the brain.

Source: after Martini *et al.* (2000, Fig. 16-2(b) p. 426).

it occurs at a higher level than for nociceptive information, at the medulla. So again, information from the right side of the body arrives at the left side of the cortex and vice versa.

As represented in Figure 5.18, there is an identifiable relationship between particular areas of somatosensory cortex and the role of neurons located there: a given region of cortex is consistently associated with a given region of the sensory surface of the body. Tactile stimulation in a particular body region triggers neural activity in a particular cortical region. The body can be mapped across the surface of the somatosensory cortex according to the association between brain region and body region, and the result, a bizarre-looking person, is known as the **sensory homunculus**.

Figure 5.18 shows that, for their size, some body regions (e.g. fingers) are associated with relatively large areas of cortex. Other body regions (e.g. the back) are associated with relatively small areas. The relative sizes within the

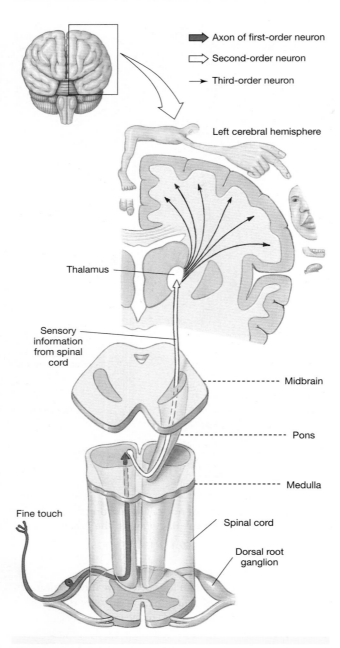

Axon of first-order neuron

Second-order neuron

Third-order neuron

Left cerebral hemisphere

Thalamus

Sensory information from spinal cord

Midbrain

Pons

Medulla

Spinal cord

Dorsal root ganglion

Fine touch

Figure 5.18 The route from periphery to brain for non-nociceptive tactile information.

Source: Martini *et al.* (2000, Fig. 16-2a, p. 426).

homunculus correspond to the sensitivity of resolution at the corresponding skin areas. For example, the fingers have a fine resolution, which enables them to discriminate detail, and a large cortical representation. The back has a lower resolution and correspondingly smaller cortical representation. The lips are associated with a relatively large

area of cortex. You might like to speculate on the functional significance of this in terms of passing on genes!

A specific cranial nerve link

This section is concerned with vision, an example of information that gets to the brain via a cranial nerve. Later chapters will look at other examples of how information gets to the brain via cranial nerves (e.g. auditory information). Figure 5.19 shows the eye: the cornea and lens bend light to form an inverted image of the world on the retinal surface.

At the retina, there is a layer consisting of a mosaic of millions of cells, which are sensitive to light (Figure 5.20). These are **receptor cells** (or just receptors) and they absorb light. Absorption changes their electrochemical state ('membrane potential'); thereby, in 'receiving' light, they register its presence. Although these cells change state, action potentials are not instigated in them. Rather, smooth changes in voltage are seen.

When receptors absorb light, the change causes information to be passed on to other neurons with which they form synapses. That is to say, a change in electrical activity at the receptors triggers a change in activity at the associated bipolar cells. Still no action potentials occur. In turn, the bipolar cells trigger further electrical events: the excitation or inhibition of action potentials in ganglion cells with which they form synapses. Information is transmitted to the brain in the form of a pattern of action potentials in the axons of ganglion cells. The optic nerve, one of the cranial nerves (see Figures 5.19, 5.20 and 5.21), is the bundle of millions of axons of ganglion cells. The bundle is termed the 'optic tract' after entering the brain.

There is something rather odd in the way that the eye is constructed and you might be able to spot it in Figure 5.20. It appears to be inside out: light passes through various cell layers before it reaches the receptors, at the back of retina. However, these layers are almost completely transparent.

Information is conveyed to the brain in the optic nerve (the 'optic tract' is often used to describe this pathway within the brain) and arrives at the lateral geniculate nucleus (LGN), a nucleus of the thalamus. The LGN then performs the next stage of information transmission (Figure 5.21). Apparently, to early anatomists, the LGN looked something like a knee, the Latin name of which is *genu*. As Kalat (1998) suggests, if you use a rich imagination, you might be able to see a knee there! (Try looking especially at Figure 5.5.)

Looking at the level of neurons, at the LGN, ganglion cells form synapses with other neurons (termed LGN cells). LGN cells carry the message further, their axons terminating in the visual cortex (Figure 5.21).

So much for information getting to the brain; the chapter now turns to how processed information leaves the brain to trigger motor action.

Figure 5.19 The eye.

Source: after Martini *et al.* (2000, Fig. 18-20 (a), p. 486).

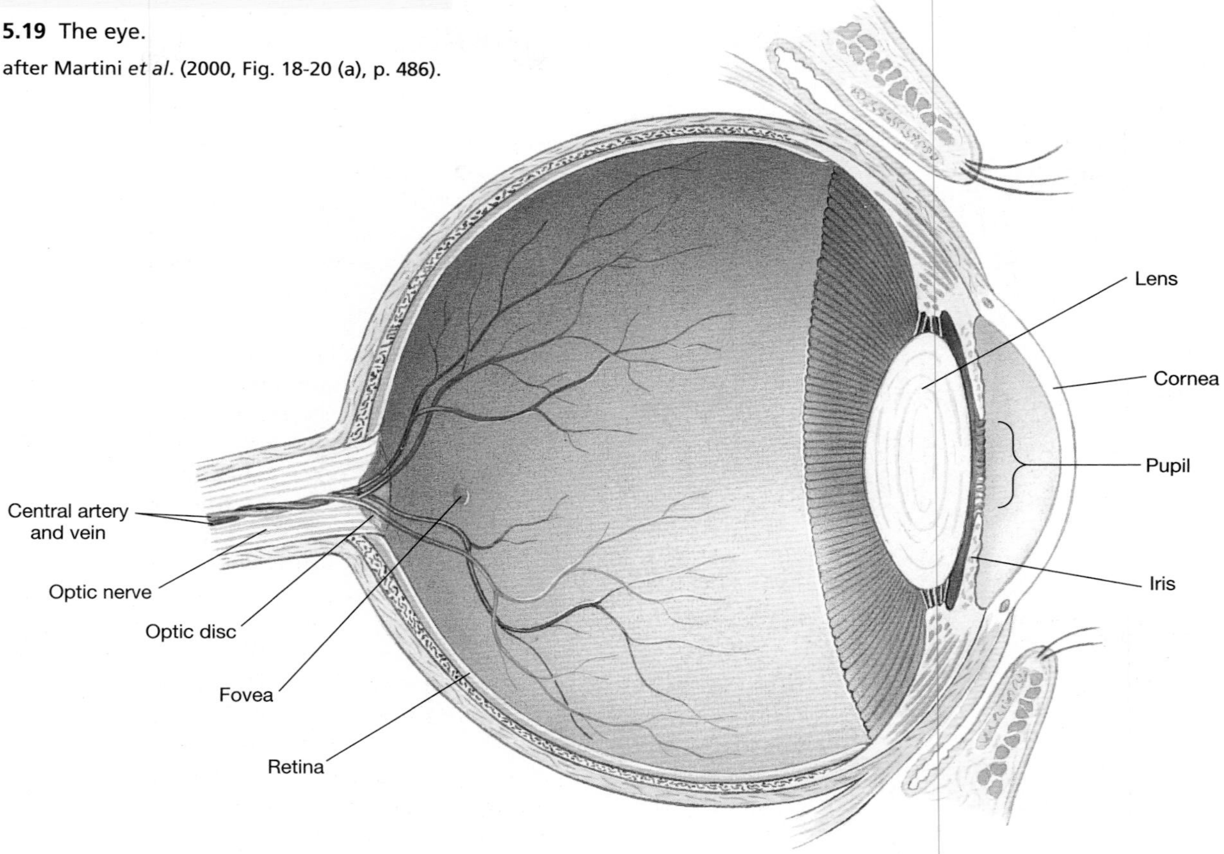

Lens

Cornea

Pupil

Iris

Central artery
and vein

Optic nerve

Optic disc

Fovea

Retina

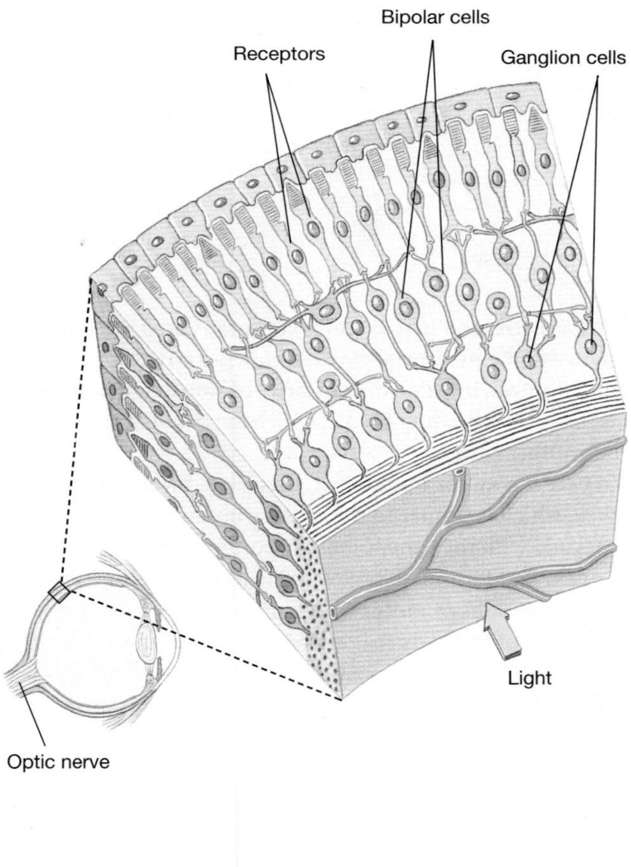

Bipolar cells

Receptors

Ganglion cells

Light

Optic nerve

Figure 5.20 A part of the retina shown in cross-section.

Source: Martini *et al.* (2000, Fig. 18-22(a), p. 490).

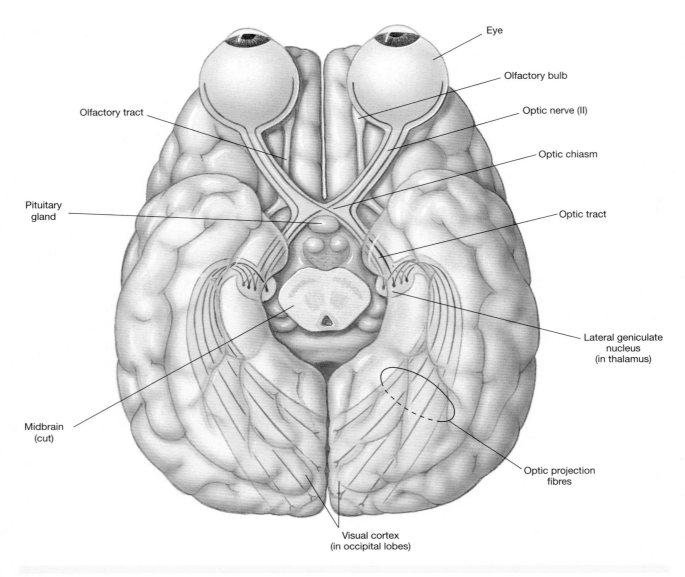

Figure 5.21 Pathway from eye to brain. *Source*: Martini *et al.* (2000, Fig. 15-23, p. 407).

Motor control

Chapter 3 described the control that the brain exerts over the motor neurons and thereby over the skeletal muscles of the body. There are many brain regions concerned with orchestrating this control. The present section considers some of these.

Motor cortex

Figure 5.9(b) showed the brain region termed, anatomically, the precentral gyrus. In terms of its role, this region is described as 'motor cortex'. Via sensory pathways, it is informed of such things as the current state of the body and, based on this, has a role in the generation of motor action. Information on touch is extracted at the somatosensory cortex (postcentral gyrus) and is communicated the short distance to the precentral gyrus, where it contributes to motor control. Imagine the dexterity of some manual actions such as reading Braille, which are based upon tactile information.

There is a **motor homunculus** associated with the motor cortex, which is similar to the sensory homunculus associated with the somatosensory cortex (Figure 5.22) (Penfield and Rasmussen, 1968). The motor homunculus identifies regions of motor cortex that exert control over those areas of the body that are represented in the homunculus. As with the sensory homunculus, some regions of the body have a relatively large amount of associated cortex. Regions with a large representation have a fine resolution of motor ability (e.g. fingers).

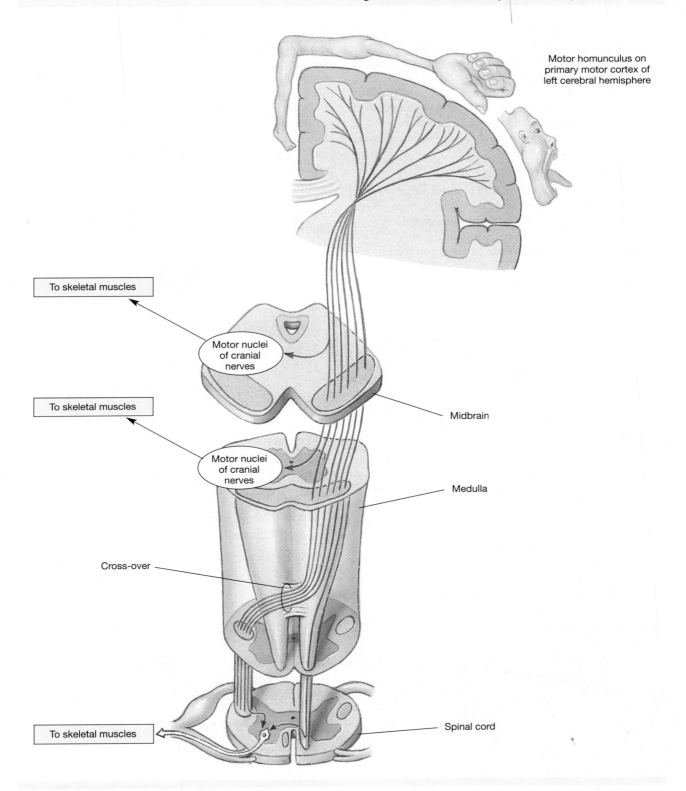

Motor homunculus on primary motor cortex of left cerebral hemisphere

To skeletal muscles

Motor nuclei of cranial nerves

Midbrain

To skeletal muscles

Motor nuclei of cranial nerves

Medulla

Cross-over

To skeletal muscles

Spinal cord

Figure 5.22 Motor homunculus.

Source: Martini *et al*. (2000, Fig. 16-4(a), p. 429).

Some neurons with cell bodies at the motor cortex have axons that extend down the spinal cord to contact motor neurons (or neurons in close proximity to motor neurons), as was represented in Chapter 3. You can see this in Figure 5.22. Other neurons (not shown) extend only so far as intermediate brain regions, which, in turn, perform further computation of motor commands, and then they project axons down to synapse with motor neurons, or further intermediate neurons.

Basal ganglia

The 'basal ganglia' are a collection of brain structures near to, and in close communication with, the cortex. Among other things, they process information on movement control. Figure 5.23 shows part of the basal ganglia, drawing attention to their proximity to the thalamus and cortex.

The cerebellum

Along with the motor cortex, basal ganglia and some other regions, the cerebellum (see Figures 5.3, 5.9(b) and 5.11) plays a role in computation of the commands sent to cause motor action. In humans, the cerebellum contains the largest number of neurons of any brain region (Courchesne and Allen, 1997). Traditionally, it was described as playing a role in the organization of balance and locomotion, which it does indeed do. However, the cerebellum is now associated with a broader

role, being concerned with sensory, motor and cognitive aspects of the organization of action, including such things as language production. Specifically, Courchesne and Allen (p. 2) propose that its role is: '*to predict internal conditions needed* for a particular mental or motor operation and *to set those conditions* in preparation for the operation at hand'.

The cerebellum has a large ratio (approximately 40:1) of afferent axons (bringing information to it) to efferent axons (carrying information from it). This gives pointers to its function: to integrate information. Thus the cerebellum integrates information from the external environment and from internal decision-making. It then acts to predict the future. That is, it appears to process and integrate sensory information within the context of the use of the information in motor action (Gao *et al.*, 1996).

Section summary

1 Sensory information reaches the brain via the spinal cord and cranial nerves.

2 Sensory cortex processes sensory information (e.g. visual or somatosensory).

3 The reticular activating system gates access of sensory information to the cortex.

4 The sensory homunculus represents how different regions of the body are represented in the somatosensory cortex.

5 At the retina, there is a mosaic of light-sensitive receptor cells.

6 Visual information is converted into electrical signals at the retina.

7 Different regions of motor cortex have a role in the motor control exerted over different regions of the body. The motor homunculus represents this responsibility.

8 The basal ganglia and cerebellum play a role in motor control.

Test your knowledge

(Answers on page 144)

5.5 What constitute (i) the afferent and (ii) the efferent sides of the lateral geniculate nucleus?

5.6 The cell bodies of motor neurons serving the lower parts of the body are located where? (i) Ventral horn of the spinal cord, (ii) dorsal horn of the spinal cord, (iii) white matter of spinal cord, (iv) medial geniculate nucleus.

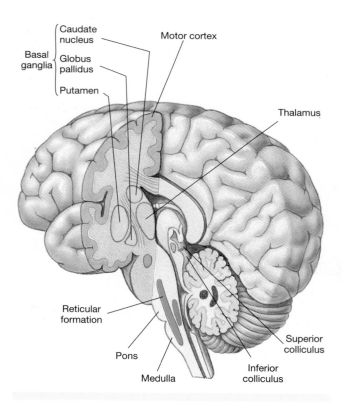

Figure 5.23 Cut-away view of part of the basal ganglia in relation to the thalamus and cortex.

Source: Martini *et al.* (2000, Fig. 16-5, p. 430).

Emotion, regulation and motivation

Introduction

The last section introduced the nervous system's input and output of information. The present section and the following one concern the processing of information between these sides of the system. The present section focuses upon how the brain makes certain decisions based upon both the external environment and the internal physiology of the body, as characterized by the terms 'emotion' and 'motivation'.

Emotion: cognition and action

Within the telencephalon beneath the cortex, other structures lie. Figure 5.24 highlights several: the amygdala, hippocampus (and the associated fornix) and mammillary bodies. Each of these is a paired structure, one half in each hemisphere.

Note the amygdala, just below the cortex of the temporal lobe. Amygdala means almond and the structure got its name from its resemblance to an almond. There are neural connections between temporal cortex and amygdala. The cortex performs cognitive processing concerning the world and conveys this information to the amygdala, where some emotional rating is attached to the information (Le Doux, 1989). The amygdala then passes this information to other brain regions, where further emotional processing occurs and emotion is translated into action by somatic and autonomic nervous systems. In addition to relatively highly processed information from the cortex, the amygdala receives, more directly from the sensory channels, raw information on threats (e.g. loud noises). Short-cutting the cortex, this provides an early-warning system to instigate such things as freezing. Short routes from sensory channels to the amygdala can be identified neurally.

The hippocampus is concerned with memory formation among other things. Hippocampus means sea-horse and to early investigators the shape of the structure bore a resemblance to this animal. It receives information on the world derived from sensory processing and appears to compare this with expectations. In this way, the hippocampus derives a measure of how well programmes of action are running (Gray, 1987a). Disparity between expectation and reality can serve as a trigger to emotion, e.g. in the frustration of when reality is less good than what is expected.

I am indebted to Kalat (1998) for pointing out that the term 'fornix', which means arc or arch, derives from an arch in ancient Rome. This was a meeting place for prostitutes (the link is with the term 'fornicate'). The fornix serves as an output pathway to link the hippocampus to the mammillary body, among other places.

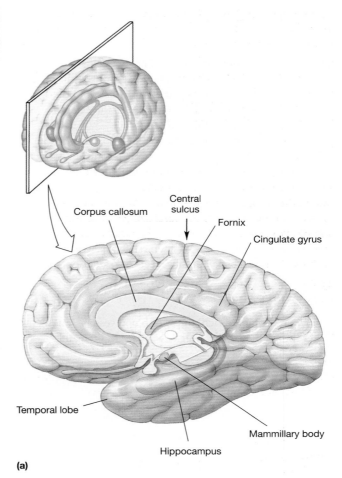

(a)

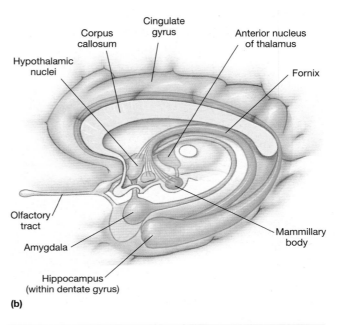

(b)

Figure 5.24 Some structures concerned with emotion.

Source: Martini *et al.* (2000, Fig. 15-12(a) and (b), p. 394).

Internal and external environments

Introduction

In making behavioural decisions characterized as emotional and motivational, the brain takes into account (a) its own immediate environment, (b) the environment of other parts of the body as relayed to the brain and (c) the external environment, e.g. availability of food.

The brain not only has a role in regulation throughout the rest of the body but it also has some responsibility for regulation of its own local environment. The brain, like the rest of the body, exists within a fluid environment and the neurons require a source of energy. This section describes some brain regions that are implicated in a complex 'juggling act' of regulation. First we look at the nutrient and fluid environment of the brain. We then relate this to general physiological and behavioural aspects of regulation.

The brain's environment

The brain contains a rich supply of blood vessels. Among other things, these bring nutrients, water, oxygen and hormones to it. Figure 5.25 shows the arteries that carry fresh blood to the brain. Note the paired 'internal carotid artery' that supplies the anterior part of the brain with blood and the arteries that derive from this, e.g. the anterior cerebral artery. Veins carry away the waste products of metabolism. A principal fuel for the CNS is glucose. Since neither glucose nor oxygen can be stored in significant amounts, a moment-by-moment unfailing blood supply is crucial.

The blood supply to different brain regions is of interest to psychologists, allowing links to be identified between structure and function. Suppose that an artery were to be blocked at, say, location X in Figure 5.25. This would result in a failure of blood supply. Thereby, it would deny oxygen and glucose to a region of the temporal lobe, causing death of neurons located there and the probable loss of some behavioural function. Modern techniques, discussed shortly, allow sites of such disruption to be identified.

The flow of blood to different regions is not constant but varies with their activity (Smith and Fetz, 1987). Variations in blood flow follow within a few seconds of changes in energy demands as a result of the changing activity of neurons. A change in blood flow is mediated by change in

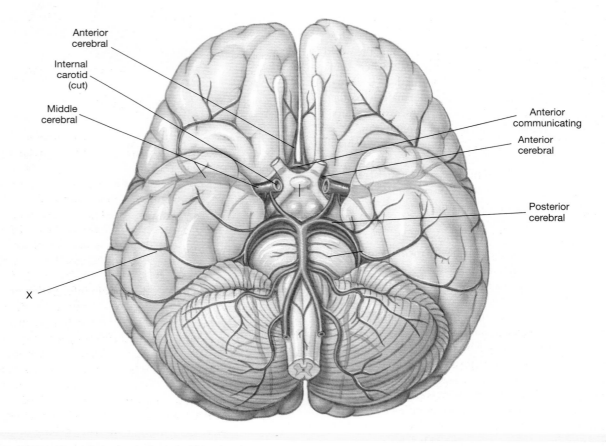

Figure 5.25 A view of the brain from underneath, showing arteries.

Source: Martini *et al.* (2000, Fig. 22-15(a), p. 578).

the diameter of blood vessels: high neural activity at a region promotes local dilation and thereby a relatively high blood supply. This is a local homeostatic process comparable to whole-body homeostasis (Chapter 2, 'Genes, environment and evolution'). The blood flow to a region is termed 'regional cerebral blood flow' (rCBF). A person can be asked to engage in a task (e.g. reading) and changes in rCBF monitored. Changes implicate a brain area as being involved in performing the task.

Figure 5.26 will remind you of some earlier material: some cells of the body, their immediate extracellular environment and blood supply. Some features of this general account apply equally to the brain and its constituent cells that are our principal interest: neurons. For example, red blood cells do not penetrate the spaces between cells, the interstitial fluid. Also, there is a difference in composition of ions in the cellular and extracellular environments of neurons (Chapter 4, 'The cells of the nervous system'). Cells acquire oxygen and glucose from the blood.

However, two special features of the fluid environment of the brain are as follows. As the imaginary view of Figure 5.27 shows, the brain contains large spaces, termed **ventricles**, which are filled with fluid. This fluid is a filtration from the fluid component of the blood (i.e. minus such things as the red blood cells) and is known as **cerebrospinal fluid** (CSF). This same fluid also fills the central canal that runs throughout the spinal cord. The cerebral aqueduct is a channel between the third and fourth ventricles. The CSF serves to cushion the brain against shocks. In some pathological conditions, the ventricles become enlarged. This can be due to a build-up of CSF pressure following hydraulic malfunction, which can damage surrounding neural tissue. In other cases, the ventricles enlarge as a result of filling the space that remains from the loss of surrounding neural tissue in degenerative disease.

The ventricles provide a rationale for some terminology of structures. The term 'peri' means 'surrounding' and so a periventricular structure is that surrounding a ventricle. More specifically, a midbrain structure called the 'periaqueductal grey matter', often simply termed

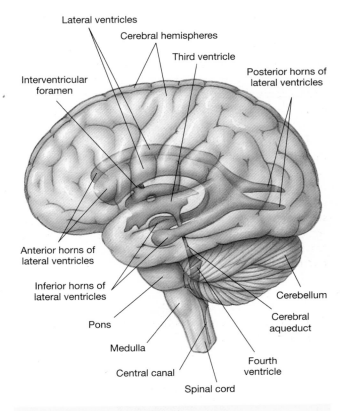

Figure 5.27 X-ray view of the brain that shows the ventricles.

Source: Martini *et al.* (2000, Fig. 15-2, p. 381).

'periaqueductal grey' (PAG), surrounds the cerebral aqueduct. So, the PAG refers to grey matter surrounding the aqueduct. See Figure 5.28.

In relation to the blood, the role of the brain represents a delicate compromise. The brain needs fluid and energy/nutrients from the blood. Indeed, relative to its weight, the brain is extremely energy-demanding (Aiello and Wheeler, 1995). Also, the chemical composition of the blood represents sources of information to be monitored, such as hormones and nutrients. This information is used in the control of behaviour. Detecting certain information on toxins can trigger vomiting and steer the animal to their future avoidance. However, in other respects, most neurons represent a delicate and sheltered environment. They are relatively protected against the toxins and swings in ion concentration that arise elsewhere and can be tolerated by the rest of the body. How is this conflict of interests resolved?

The ventricles are large spaces of fluid environment within the brain. A similar quality of fluid is also found in spaces between cells. Figure 5.26 showed a principle applicable to most cells of the body: cells are situated in such a way that the spaces between them and the boundary with

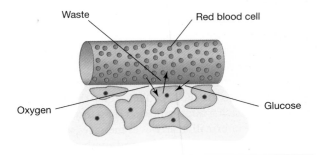

Figure 5.26 Some cells and their fluid environment.

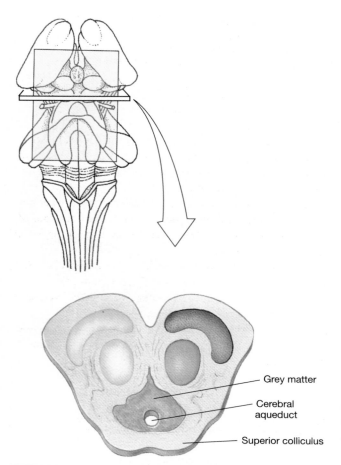

Figure 5.28 Section through the midbrain, showing PAG.

Source: Martini *et al.* (2000, Fig. 15-17(a), p. 401).

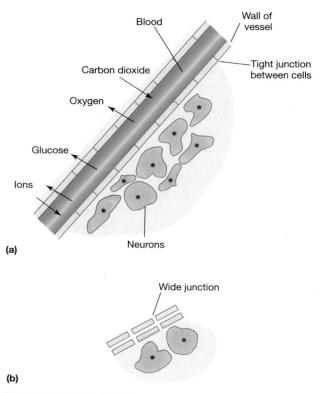

Figure 5.29 Blood–brain barrier: (a) links between neurons and blood across barrier and (b) relaxed barrier.

the capillary allow ready exchange of chemicals between plasma and interstitial fluid. However, this openness in general does not apply to the brain, where the pattern of cells forming the boundary of a capillary is tighter. This contributes to a selective barrier, termed the **blood–brain barrier**, between the brain's neurons and blood vessels. Figure 5.29(a) shows a simplified representation of this; note the tight junction between cells that form the wall of the blood vessel. The barrier protects the brain from potentially damaging contents of the blood. However, there are two ways in which the barrier can be crossed, each of which reflects adaptive considerations.

First, throughout the brain, there is a special mechanism that facilitates the transport of vital substances, such as glucose, into the neuron (Figure 5.29(a)). Second, in places, the barrier is relaxed allowing the fluid of the blood to gain access to special neurons in certain key regions (Figure 5.29(b)). These are the neurons that are specialized to detect such things as ion concentration and toxins, information

that is utilized by the brain to perform adaptive responses. Regions of brain consisting of neurons of this type are given the collective name of **circumventricular organs**.

Linking behaviour to internal and external environments

For the moment, we shall focus on two structures closely implicated in regulation. They *look in two directions*, their role being to integrate information on the internal and external world. Figures 5.3, 5.7, 5.11 and 5.24 showed one of these structures, the hypothalamus. Figure 5.30 shows a structure of the medulla termed the solitary nucleus, also known as the 'nucleus of the solitary tract' and, for those who prefer the more classical term, the 'nucleus of tractus solitarius' (NTS). Nuclei of the hypothalamus and the solitary nucleus act together in regulation.

Afferent neurons that detect various physiological events of the body project to the NTS. Figure 5.30 shows one example: processing information on substances at the tongue. Taste information arrives as messages at the NTS carried by part of the vagus nerve and another cranial nerve, the glossopharyngeal nerve (Chapter 3). Information on events deep within the body also arrives there. For example,

Information at the prefrontal cortex can then direct behaviour towards, say, food-seeking. Other projections from the hypothalamus appear to modulate information on taste that is available at the NTS. Such modulation presumably adjusts the signal so that its role fits the nutrient needs of the animal. For instance, at times of nutrient depletion, the animal tends to approach food and ingest it (Berridge, 1995).

Descending projections from the hypothalamus, via the NTS, adjust physiology in a way that fits nutrient needs. For example, according to internal nutrient availability (Chapter 3), adjustments are made to the secretion of the hormone insulin (Woods and Stricker, 1999). Efferent neurons of the vagus nerve are involved in such action. Efferent neurons of the glossopharyngeal nerve control the muscles of the throat involved in ingestion.

Regulation of the nutrient environment is only one role of the hypothalamus. Other nuclei have roles in other behaviour. For example, the hypothalamus and NTS are also involved in the circulatory and respiratory systems, conveying information for both psychological decisions and physiological adjustments. The next section looks at some other nuclei of the hypothalamus.

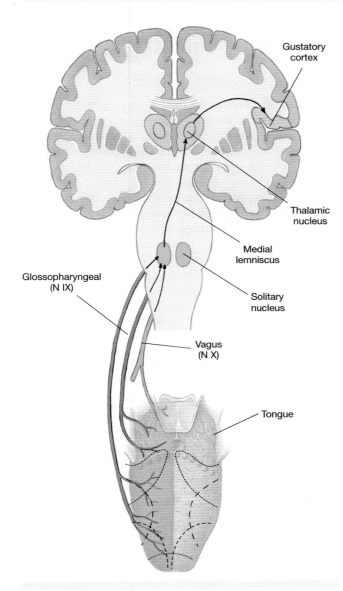

Figure 5.30 A focus upon the solitary nucleus.

Source: Martini *et al*. (2000, Fig. 18-8, p. 472).

at the liver, nutrients derived from the gut are detected by afferent neurons of the ANS (Novin, 1993). This information is conveyed to the NTS by axons that make up part of the vagus nerve (Chapter 3). Neurons with their cell bodies at the NTS project information to other brain regions, where it is further processed (e.g. thalamus and hypothalamus). This concerns particular events within the body. For taste, gustatory cortex continues the processing.

Nutrient-related projections *from* the hypothalamus affect both physiology and behaviour. In Figure 5.31, note the signals from the hypothalamus to the prefrontal cortex, which play a role in behavioural decision-making (see later).

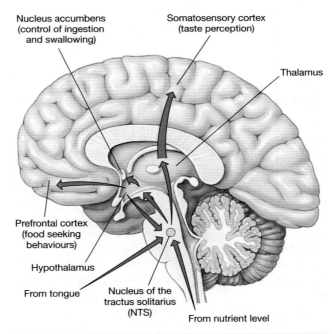

Figure 5.31 The hypothalamus as a link between nutrient state, food and behaviour.

Source: derived from Kalat (1998, Fig. 10.17, p. 288) and Carlson (1988, Fig. 7.30, p. 218). From *Biological Psychology*, 6th Edition by Kalat. © 1998. Reprinted with permission of Wadsworth, a division of Thomson Learning, www.thomsonrights.com.

Hypothalamic nuclei – broader aspects

Throughout the book, nuclei of the hypothalamus will be discussed in the context of their role in behaviour. Figure 5.32 shows some of these. It also shows the pituitary gland (Chapter 3), with which the hypothalamus is closely connected.

The term 'preoptic area' arises from the proximity of this region to the optic pathway (Figure 5.21). The term 'para' means alongside and so a paraventricular structure lies alongside a ventricle. The 'paraventricular nucleus' of the hypothalamus lies alongside the third ventricle. The suprachiasmatic nucleus derives its name from the fact that it is just above the optic chiasm.

As just exemplified by nutrient regulation, the hypothalamus plays a pivotal role in mediating between internal and external environments. Each one, among several of its nuclei, plays a distinctive role in organizing a particular behaviour. In so doing, they are informed of internal conditions, such as level of a particular hormone. Neurons in some nuclei are informed about the body's fluid level. When this falls, these neurons appear to be activated and to inform parts of the brain concerned with decision-making, so the animal is motivated to seek water. As an integrated part of homeostasis, they also play a role in triggering the secretion of arginine vasopressin at the pituitary gland (Chapter 3).

Other nuclei are concerned with the regulation of body temperature. The electrical activity of specific neurons in the hypothalamus depends upon local temperature. Thus, when body temperature is not at its optimal value, neurons detect this and action, both physiological (e.g. sweating) and behavioural (e.g. moving to another environment), is triggered.

Other nuclei of the hypothalamus play a role in the organization of sexual behaviour. For example, they contain neurons that are sensitive to the hormone testosterone taken up from the blood (Chapter 3).

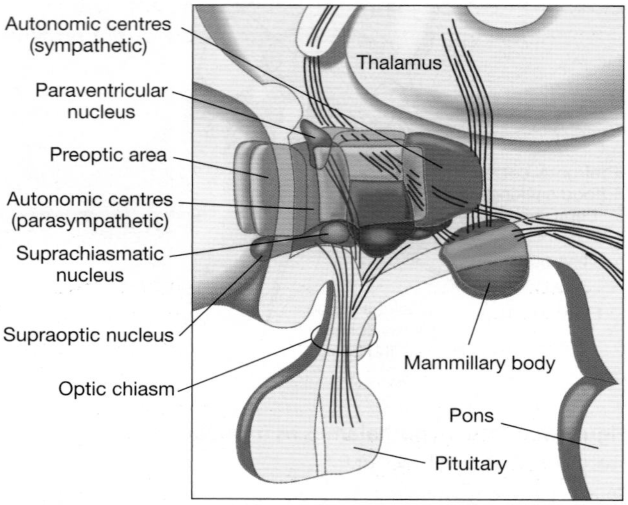

Sleep, waking and alertness

Adaptation requires that the animal's response to the environment varies. At times, the animal needs to engage actively with the environment, as in seeking food or a mate. At other times, it needs to withdraw and conserve resources, as in sleep. This section introduces a factor that underlies such variation.

You have already met a region of the brain stem, the role of which is triggering variation between sleep, waking and alertness: the reticular formation (Figures 5.15 and 5.16). Axons from here project to the cortex and other regions, where they synapse upon local neurons, i.e. the reticular activating system (RAS). Ascending pathways project information in a caudal → rostral direction. Activity by the RAS neurons changes the activity of the cortex between states corresponding to sleep, drowsiness and arousal (i.e. a state of being awake and alert). Breaking the connections between the RAS and the cortex causes a coma.

The activity of such ascending pathways has a broad influence over neurons in the forebrain. Large numbers of target neurons can all be influenced simultaneously by an ascending pathway. These pathways can be characterized by the neurochemical that they employ, and are cholinergic (i.e. employing acetylcholine), noradrenergic or serotonergic. The RAS and other brain regions, in interaction, control cycles of sleep and waking. The brain contains an intrinsic clock mechanism. An area that, in part, embodies this is the 'suprachiasmatic nucleus' of the hypothalamus (Figure 5.32).

Figure 5.32 Hypothalamus.

Source: Martini *et al*. (2000, Fig. 15-15(b), p. 398).

Section summary

1 The amygdala has a role in linking sensory input, cognition and emotion.

2 The blood–brain barrier protects the brain's neurons.

3 The hypothalamus and solitary nucleus have roles in linking the physiology of the body to behaviour. Both behavioural and physiological action depends upon monitoring internal and external events.

4 Different hypothalamic nuclei have different roles in motivation and behaviour, e.g. hypothalamic neurons are sensitive to nutrient level or testosterone, etc.

5 The reticular activating system participates in the regulation of states of waking, alertness and sleep.

Test your knowledge

(Answer on page 144)

5.7 With regard to Figure 5.28, complete the two expressions in the following: 'The cerebral aqueduct contains _____ whereas the grey matter consists largely of _____ '.

Cognitive processing, reasoning and anticipation

So far, the chapter has described various areas of cortex, e.g. those devoted to sensory and motor processing. It briefly mentioned the prefrontal cortex. This section continues the account of the role of different cortical regions (Figure 5.13).

Association areas?

A term sometimes given to areas of cortex that are not concerned directly with sensory and motor processing is 'association cortex' (or 'non-specific cortex') (J.H. Martin, 1996). This implies that they associate information available in more specific areas, e.g. to link visual and olfactory (smell) information in perceiving a rose or to link sensory and motor information in the control of action. However, it is misleading to suppose that all areas outside the primary sensory and motor areas can be defined by exclusion as associative in this way. Certain areas of cortex that are not primary sensory cortex continue the processing of one sensory input, e.g. vision (Preuss and Kaas, 1999). For example, such an area of processing for visual information, termed the 'prestriate cortex', is immediately anterior to the primary visual cortex. Further areas of purely visual processing are found in the temporal lobes. Considering such areas, some authors reserve the term association cortex only for areas where there is evidence that information from more than one sensory area is being associated (Fuster, 1997), e.g. portions of the frontal cortex, discussed next.

Prefrontal cortex

The essence of planning ahead is to be able to reach future goals by using information that is not physically present at the time, i.e. organizing motor actions ahead of their execution (Fuster, 1997). An important structure involved in this is the anterior part of the cortex of the frontal lobes (i.e. excluding regions directly concerned with motor control such as the motor cortex). It is termed **prefrontal cortex** (PFC). See Figure 5.33, which exemplifies that a named brain structure can often be subdivided. You should see the logic

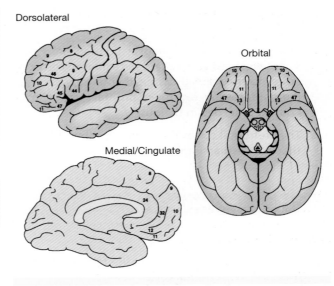

Figure 5.33 Prefrontal cortex showing its divisions as indicated by numbers.

Source: Fuster (1997, Fig. 6.5, p. 173).

for the name of one division: 'dorsolateral'. It refers to the dorsal side considering the dimension of dorsal–ventral and the lateral side in the dimension of lateral–medial.

When humans are engaged in planning, blood flow to the frontal lobes increases. At such times, the neurons of the region are particularly active and require a large supply of glucose and oxygen. One source of insight derives from the problems that patients encounter following damage to the frontal lobes. Luria (1973) found that patients were often unable to perform forward planning and were described as living in the 'here-and-now'. They were controlled by those stimuli that were currently physically present and had difficulty in extrapolating to situations that were not present.

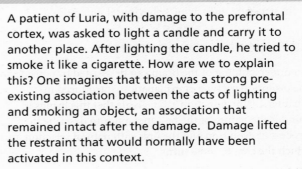

A personal angle

A patient of Luria

A patient of Luria, with damage to the prefrontal cortex, was asked to light a candle and carry it to another place. After lighting the candle, he tried to smoke it like a cigarette. How are we to explain this? One imagines that there was a strong pre-existing association between the acts of lighting and smoking an object, an association that remained intact after the damage. Damage lifted the restraint that would normally have been activated in this context.

Section summary

1 The terms 'non-specific' and 'association' are sometimes used with regard to regions of cortex not concerned directly with either sensory or motor processing, e.g. the prefrontal cortex. Caution is needed in their use.

2 The prefrontal cortex is associated with tasks that involve planning.

Test your knowledge

(Answer on page 144)

5.8 Complete the missing word in the following: 'Neurons in prefrontal cortex being "particularly active" means that they are exhibiting a high _____ of action potentials'.

Comparative and evolutionary perspectives

Introduction

Comparing nervous systems between different species and relating these to evolution and lifestyle can be an important means of understanding how nervous systems work. Some species are studied as a matter of convenience and convention, e.g. the rat. Rats are relatively cheap and simple to breed, and are unlikely to become an endangered species. In addition, strains can be 'standardized' across laboratories. Other species are brilliant with a particular skill, e.g. the hawk's use of vision. Examining how the nervous system of such species is different from species that are less developed at the particular skill can give insight. Some closely related species have found rather different solutions to a given problem, which makes it revealing to study divergence in brain structure underlying behavioural differences.

Evolutionary considerations

An understanding of the brain can be assisted by considering the evolutionary type of explanation, introduced in Chapter 1 ('Introduction'). One issue that this brings to mind is the nature of the best metaphor to describe the process of evolution and the link with natural selection, to which the chapter now turns.

Engineering or tinkering?

Evolution is more like an amateur tinkerer than a professional engineer. The tinkerer does not know what is going to emerge but tries various possibilities, working with whatever materials are to hand.

Evolutionary psychology
Evolution as design

Evolution is sometimes compared to an engineer in producing a design (recall the design metaphor of evolutionary psychology, described in Chapter 2). However, this analogy can be misleading (Jacob, 1977). Unlike evolution, an engineer has an idea in mind of a product and sets out to achieve it. Also an engineer can start from nothing, largely unconstrained by existing designs. Evolution has no design in mind (as far as we know!) and never sets out from nothing. Rather, evolution builds on what is there already.

The products of evolution are not necessarily optimal: they simply do the job sufficiently well. In some respects they might have design flaws when viewed from an engineering perspective. For example, Jacob suggests (1977, p. 1166) that attaching an evolutionary new cerebral cortex to the rest of the evolutionary older brain is an example of tinkering: 'It is something like adding a jet engine to an old horse cart. It is not surprising, in either case, that accidents, difficulties and conflicts can occur.'

Homology and analogy

In comparing characteristics of different species (e.g. the eye in providing vision), biologists employ the terms **homology** and **analogy** (Preuss and Kaas, 1999). Each term refers to a similarity in a characteristic but they distinguish between evolutionary origins. If something is 'homologous' between two species, it refers to a common evolutionary origin. Both species have a common precursor at an earlier stage of evolution. In the cultural domain, a similar logic applies to human languages where, say, similarities between Romanian and Italian can be traced to common roots in Latin.

In comparing two species, if a characteristic is 'analogous', this refers to the independent emergence of it in evolution. Common evolutionary pressures gave rise to the same characteristic. For example, insect vision and vision in humans have some common features but these cannot be traced in evolution to a common ancestor. This is comparable to the independent appearance of an idea, e.g. a new theory in science, at two different and unconnected places.

Vertebrates and invertebrates

Comparison

Animal species can be divided into **vertebrates** and **invertebrates**. Mammals (e.g. humans), birds, reptiles, amphibia and fish are vertebrates, defined as having a backbone. Our principal interest in this distinction is that a section of the nervous system, the spinal cord, is housed within the backbone (Chapter 3, Figure 3.16). Invertebrates, which include beetles, flies, worms, snails and slugs, lack a backbone.

Much understanding of the action potential (Chapter 4, 'The cells of the nervous system') was derived from recordings made from so-called giant axons (the diameter is giant relative to vertebrate axons) of the squid. The fundamental principles of how neurons work and communicate at synapses appear to be very similar, comparing vertebrates and invertebrates (Jerison, 1976). However, even by exploiting similar components, *assemblies* of these components can, of course, yield very different results when comparing species.

Because of the relative simplicity of their nervous systems, invertebrates permit us to understand how particular behaviours are organized. In some cases, the precise 'wiring diagram' of neural connections underlying behaviour can be mapped (Kandel, 1976). The neurons of such invertebrates as snails and leeches are often relatively large, few in number and able to be identified. This facilitates electrical recording (see later) from individual neurons within the sequence

(sensory) → (intermediate processing) → (motor output). Particular individual neurons can be relatively easily identified and are similar from one animal to another. By contrast, in vertebrate species, individual neurons can only rarely be identified and compared between animals.

There are also some important differences between invertebrates and vertebrates. For example, invertebrates have not 'invented' myelination (Chapter 4) as a means to speed up conduction of action potentials. Rather, speed is achieved by the large diameter of their axons.

Aplysia – *an invertebrate example*

Figure 5.34(a) shows an invertebrate, *Aplysia californica*, a member of a zoological group termed molluscs (by convention, the names of species are written in italics) (Kandel, 1976). It might not possess much in the way of beauty but has proved invaluable in understanding links between nervous systems and behaviour. Rather than having a brain as such in which information processing occurs and motor control is initiated, *Aplysia* has a series of ganglia, each containing about 2000 neurons. Projections from neurons link ganglia to each other and link ganglia to sense organs and effectors. For example, the eyes and tentacles are innervated by the cerebral ganglia.

As shown in Figure 5.35, in response to tactile stimulation, *Aplysia* can withdraw their gill (respiratory organ) and siphon (a 'spout' through which it expels waste). This occurs in response to even mild stimuli.

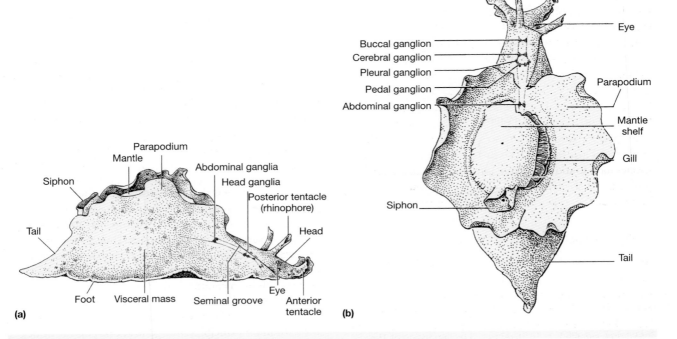

Figure 5.34 *Aplysia*: (a) side view and (b) dorsal view. *Source*: Kandel (1976, Fig. 4-4, p. 76).

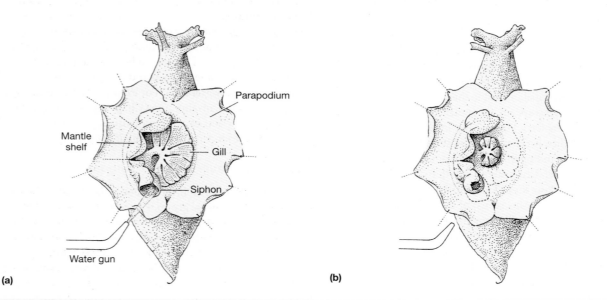

(a)

(b)

Figure 5.35 The reflex underlying defensive-withdrawal of the siphon and gill: (a) relaxed state and (b) following application of a jet of water, withdrawn state. *Source*: Kandel (1976, Fig. 9-2, p. 351).

Aplysia has relatively few neurons, which are large and individually identifiable. Figure 5.36 shows a simplified version of the system responsible for the withdrawal reflex. (In reality, there would be a number of parallel pathways of this kind.) The tip of a sensory neuron is embedded in the skin of the siphon. Tactile stimulation of the siphon excites this neuron. The sensory neuron makes synaptic connections with both the motor neuron that triggers the reaction in the gill and an interneuron. In turn, the interneuron also excites the motor neuron. By both routes, activity in the sensory neuron evokes a muscular response by the gill, i.e. withdrawal.

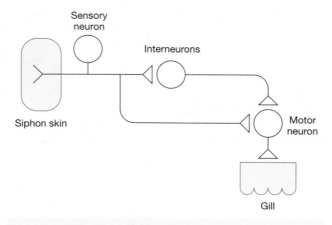

Figure 5.36 Simplified diagram of some neurons and their connections. *Source*: Kandel (1991) *Principles of Neural Science*, 3rd Edition, Fig. 65–1, p. 1010, reprinted by permission of The McGraw-Hill Companies, Inc.

Comparing vertebrate species

The area of study termed 'comparative psychology' compares the behaviour of different species and tries to link this to differences in their brains. Considering vertebrates, this section will compare brains between species, to see what insight can be gained.

Conservation and diversity

A comparison of the brains of different vertebrate species led to the principle of the *conservation of organization*, which states (Stebbins, 1969, p. 124):

Whenever a complex, organized structure or a complex integrated biosynthetic pathway has become an essential adaptive unit of a successful group of organisms, the essential features of this unit are conserved in all of the evolutionary descendants of the group concerned.

The implication is that most principles of brain organization are general rather than species-specific (Jerison, 1976). The same brain structures are to be found comparing various vertebrate species. Thus, psychologists can speak of a brain region, say, the amygdala and assume that, comparing rather widely across species, it reveals certain features in common.

Of course, the amygdala of a rat is not identical to that of a human, nor is its role. Rather, there are merely some common principles of organization. This illustrates the analogy that evolution can appear as a tinkerer or tuner, making slight changes to basic structures. For another example, fish, snakes and mammals all have a cerebellum, used for motor control. However, there are differences in the degree of specialization of such a structure. Certain species are adapted to show more flexible and nuanced locomotion, reflected in greater development of the cerebellum.

Although, on wide inter-species comparison, similar structures with similar areas of responsibility are found, the degree of responsibility associated with a structure can vary. For example, vision is organized in both cortical and brain stem regions. However, in fish, amphibians and reptiles a brain stem structure (comparable to the superior colliculus of the human, discussed earlier) has a greater role than in humans. In humans, the visual cortex has a relatively large responsibility for vision.

Brain size

Humans have an outstanding intellect and sometimes describe themselves as 'big-brained'. Indeed, brain size and thereby the size of the head causes problems with birth. However, all is relative and the 1.3 kg human brain is modest by comparison with the toothed sperm whale of brain size 5–8 kg and the Indian elephant which has a 5 kg brain (Harvey and Krebs, 1990).

Figure 5.37 compares various types of animal in terms of brain size and body size. As a general principle, brain size increases with body weight. However, the brains of primates are large relative to body weight (Northcutt and Kaas, 1995). This is especially true of humans. The term **encephalization** refers to the degree to which brain size exceeds what might

be expected on the basis of body weight (Harvey and Krebs, 1990). Humans are said to be strongly encephalized. Brain size depends on the factors determining the rate of development of neurons early in life and the length of time over which development occurs (Finlay and Darlington, 1995) (discussed in the following chapter).

For body weight, reptiles tend to have smaller brains than mammals. What might we expect to be the relationship between brain size and body size? Presumably in some respects a larger body requires more processing of information (e.g. the somatosensory surface is greater and muscles have more fibres requiring control). In other respects, the processing demands might be independent of body size. For example, we might expect that the need to detect odours and thereby the amount of brain devoted to olfactory processing would not vary with body size (Jerison, 1976). Somewhat surprisingly, olfactory bulb volume increases with body size. Some parts of the brain increase in proportion to brain mass (Jerison, 1991a). The hippocampus and cerebellum show this relationship.

Localization of function

Considering size of neural tissue, it is useful to take stock of some principles introduced earlier. We saw that, *within* the human species, differences in amount of tissue underlying control of something can reflect differences in information processing, e.g. large amounts of somatosensory and motor cortex are devoted to the fingers and are associated with high resolution. Can the principle of localization be extended to comparisons *between* species?

The issue of brain size raises the question of whether parts of the brain are relatively large in particular species (Harvey and Krebs, 1990). If so, can this be related to lifestyle? The **principle of localization** is that discrete parts of the nervous system are concerned with discrete roles. Based upon a comparison between species, the 'principle of proper mass' (Jerison, 1976, p. 24) states that: 'The mass of neural tissue controlling a particular activity is appropriate to the amount of information processing involved in performing the activity.'

Metaphorically speaking, the importance that a species attaches to an activity and the information processing involved in performing it tend to be reflected in the amount of neural tissue dedicated to its control. Thus, for example, a species that makes extensive use of vision, involving fine-grained discrimination, tends to have a relatively large visual cortex and superior colliculus. If this species makes little use of sound it tends to have a relatively small auditory cortex and inferior colliculus.

In the following sections, some examples of this principle are considered.

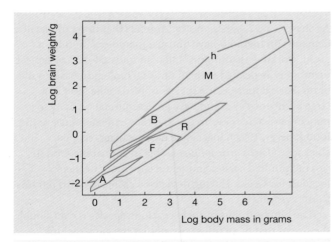

Figure 5.37 Brain size as a function of body size.
A amphibians, B birds, F bony fish, h humans, M mammals, R reptiles.

Source: Jerison (1991a, Fig. 15, p. 64).

The cortex

Among the vertebrate groups, a difference between mammals and the rest (e.g. reptiles and birds) is the extent of the six-layered mammalian cortex (Figure 5.14), sometimes termed neocortex ('new cortex', in evolutionary time) (Preuss and Kaas, 1999). The cortex of reptiles and birds is normally classified as three-layered. The cortex of mammals is enlarged as a percentage of brain mass compared with other vertebrates. In turn, within mammals, a feature of primates is the disproportionately large cortex, the size of which is increased by folding (Jerison, 1991b). A relatively large cortex is generally associated with the capacity to show flexibility in behaviour, a hallmark of primates.

Is the cortex of mammals analogous or homologous to that of other vertebrates? Is the mammalian cortex a completely new 'invention'? It is generally thought that the mammalian cortex derives from that of a non-mammalian precursor and that there exists homology (Preuss and Kaas, 1999). Figure 5.38 shows the cerebral cortex of some mammals. Note differences in size of the cortical regions that are concerned with particular sensory, e.g. visual and auditory cortex, and motor functions. As a difference between humans and other species, relatively little of the human cortex is either sensory or motor cortex. This remaining amount is sometimes termed 'association cortex' or 'non-specific cortex', though, as noted earlier, this is potentially confusing. There are some well-defined specific roles of areas outside the primary sensory and motor regions.

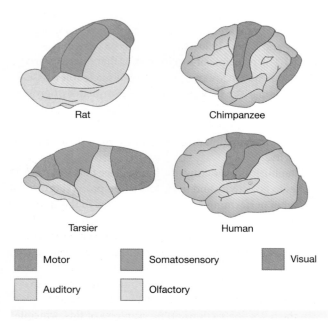

Figure 5.38 The cerebral cortex of different mammals.
Source: OU course SD286 (Module A, Fig. 22, p. 31).

Figure 5.39 also shows the brain of a number of mammalian species (Fuster, 1997). Two things are evident. First, the degree of folding is greatest in humans. Second, as a percentage of the cortex, the prefrontal region reaches a maximum in humans. To what use do primates put this enlarged prefrontal cortex (PFC)? The PFC, especially the dorsolateral PFC, appears to be involved in the primate specialization of advanced cognition involving extrapolation beyond current sensory input. Compared with non-primates, primates such as monkeys are good at performing special tasks that are guided by memory (Goldman-Rakic, 1987). For example, in one experimental design, one of two food wells is shown to be baited with food and then covered. After a delay, the monkey is given a choice of wells. The solution cannot be solved on the basis of current sensory input but requires a memory of a single event from the past (observing the baiting). Of course, the human skill at bridging such time delays hardly needs mention.

In certain primates (most obviously humans), the enlarged PFC might form a basis of a sophisticated extrapolation beyond sensory data: the utilization of a **theory of mind** of the self and others (Frith, 1996). That is, humans employ theories of the intentions of others, e.g. that they are using honesty or deceit.

Povinelli and Preuss (1995) ask whether humans are unique in employing a theory of mind. If so, the capacity emerged in evolution at a stage after our line diverged (Figure 5.40). Another possibility is that this capacity has an earlier origin and is shared with gorillas and chimpanzees. Some evidence is suggestive that these primates exploit a theory on the intentions of others.

The hippocampus

As Sherry (1992, p. 521) notes: 'Animals that make unusual demands on memory have unusual memories'. In turn, a useful working assumption is that an unusual species-typical memory is associated with an unusual biological basis in the brain. For example, some species of bird cache food in a large number of sites and have an exceptional capacity to remember where these are, so that they can later retrieve the food (Sherry, 1992). In a single day, the black-capped chickadee (*Parus atricapillus*) is able to contribute food to several hundred caches and retain a memory of their location for weeks. Having depleted a cache, the bird refrains from revisiting it.

The hippocampus of such a caching species is over double the size of that of an otherwise similar but non-caching species. Caching is disrupted by hippocampal damage. Evidence points to the hippocampus being associated with, among other things, spatial memory formation (O'Keefe and Nadel, 1978). This suggests that differences in the hippocampus of caching species can be associated with differences in their memory capacity.

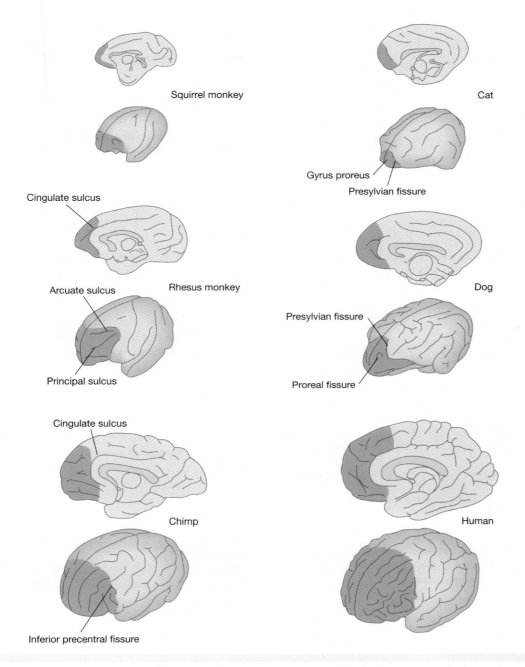

Figure 5.39 The brain of several mammalian species showing the prefrontal cortex (blue).

Source: Fuster (1997, Fig. 2.1, p. 10).

Figure 5.41 shows the relationship between volume of the telencephalon and the volume of the hippocampus for several 'families' (in zoological terms, closely related species) of bird (Sherry *et al.*, 1989). Three families of caching birds and ten families of non-caching birds are shown. In each case, hippocampal size increases with size of telencephalon but the disproportionately increased size of hippocampus in the caching families relative to non-caching is clear.

Differences in migratory or social behaviour between species cannot account for differences in hippocampal size.

The olfactory bulb

For their size of brain, primates (especially humans) have a relatively small olfactory bulb (Jerison, 1991a). See Figure 5.21. This suggests that, compared with, say, wolves, primates have made relatively little use of fine-grained olfactory

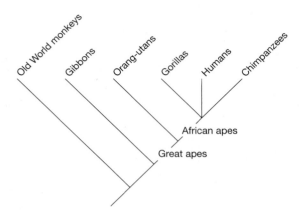

Figure 5.40 Evolutionary tree of primates. Note a common ancestor of gorillas, humans and chimps in African apes and a divergence of orangutans before this stage.

Source: Povinelli and Preuss (1995, Fig. 1, p. 419).

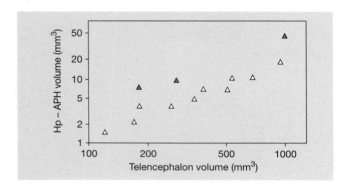

Figure 5.41 Relationship between hippocampal and telencephalic volumes for caching (filled triangles) and non-caching (open triangles) families.

Source: Sherry *et al*. (1989, Fig. 4, p. 314).

discrimination in their evolution. Comparing bird species, there are enormous differences in the size of olfactory bulb (Healy and Guilford, 1990). Olfaction might, to some extent, act as a substitute for vision in species that are active in poor illumination. Nocturnal birds might be expected to exhibit an enhanced olfactory capacity as compared with diurnal ('day-active') birds. Birds with high olfactory capacity might be expected to have relatively large olfactory bulbs. Olfactory bulb increases with brain size but an independent effect of activity is found, with a larger olfactory bulb in nocturnal species.

Section summary

1 Evolution can be compared to a tinkerer rather than a design engineer.

2 Similar characteristics can reflect either homology or analogy.

3 Certain invertebrates have relatively few, large and identifiable neurons.

4 In vertebrates, to some extent the size of a region of brain devoted to a form of processing reflects the amount of information handled.

Test your knowledge

(Answer on page 144)

5.9 Which of the following is a feature of the vertebrate but not invertebrate nervous system? (i) Axon, (ii) synapse, (iii) interneuron, (iv) node of Ranvier.

5.10 Supply the missing words in the following: 'Rather than being an _____, as in the design metaphor of evolutionary psychology, a comparison between species suggests that a better metaphor would be that evolution is a _____.'

 Techniques for studying the brain

This section looks at some of the techniques that are employed to gain understanding of how brains work. It considers both the activity of living brains and post-mortem analysis.

Defining neural connections

So far the chapter has discussed, on one level, individual neurons and, on the other, gross anatomy of the brain as revealed in its structures. It described neural pathways running from one structure to another, e.g. pathways from the lateral geniculate nucleus to the visual cortex. How have scientists been able to establish the route that such neural pathways take? This section introduces some of the techniques.

Tracing pathways

Imagine a particular nucleus in the brain (e.g. lateral geniculate nucleus) and the cell bodies of the neurons that are located there. To which locations do the axons of these ('efferent') neurons project? A technique for establishing this in non-humans is termed 'anterograde labelling'. Special chemicals are injected into the nucleus. These are taken up by the cell body and its associated dendrites. They are then slowly transported along the axon towards its terminal. The term 'anterograde' is because of this forward movement, i.e. in the same direction as the movement of action potentials in the axon. See Figure 5.42(a). The location of the chemical can be measured and hence the course of the trajectory established.

With reference to a nucleus, afferent neurons are defined as those that bring information to it. To establish the source of these, 'retrograde labelling' is employed. Chemicals are injected that are taken up by axon terminals. They are then transported away from the terminal along the length of the axon towards the cell body (Figure 5.42(b)). The term 'retrograde' relates to the direction of chemical migration being backwards relative to the movement of the action potential.

Since these techniques involve killing the animal and analyzing its brain tissue (see next section), they are obviously inappropriate for use with living humans.

Histology

A source of insight is provided by techniques that look at samples of brain ('tissue') taken from either deceased humans or rats killed in the laboratory. The term 'tissue' refers to collections of cells that make up a particular structure, e.g. kidney tissue is that which forms a kidney, consisting of millions of component cells. Of course, the tissue of most interest to us is neural tissue.

The science of 'histology' investigates the tissues that make up the body by preparing samples of them in a way that they are open to analysis. To study brain tissue, it is necessary to look at it under a microscope. Thin slices of tissue are cut shortly after death and preserved by chemical means so that they do not decay, and are hardened so that their structure is fixed. Slices are mounted on microscope slides, a procedure that facilitates their microscopic analysis.

Simply looking at slices of neural tissue under a light microscope reveals only a limited amount of information. Neurons are usually too small to be distinguished. Further histological techniques are employed to make the details of the sample more visible. One technique is **staining**, in which a chemical is applied which reacts with neurons in various ways. The chemical makes these neurons more visible by picking out and highlighting parts of them. A particular stain can have a special affinity for a part of a cell such as its membrane. The technique of forming a **Golgi stain** reveals the whole cell (Figure 5.43). The technique termed **Nissl stain** reveals the cell body. In some cases, a particular stain

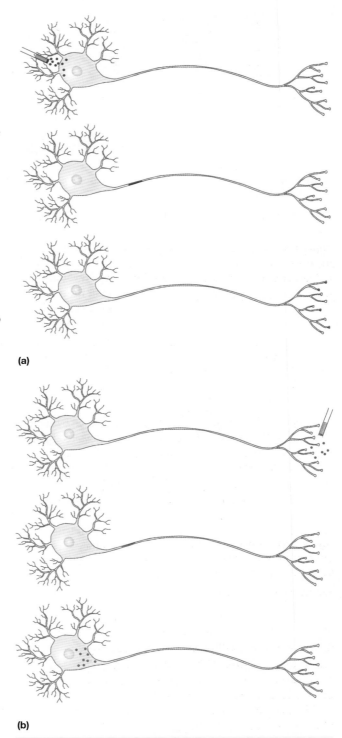

(a)

(b)

Figure 5.42 Labelling: (a) anterograde and (b) retrograde.

will target only neurons characterized by a certain type of neurotransmitter. A pathway made up of such neurons would then stand out against a background of neuron types that remained unstained. Some stains target myelin so that

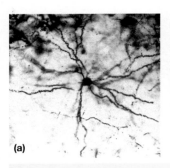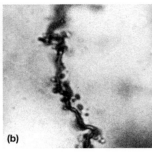

(a)   (b)

Figure 5.43 Golgi stain: (a) cell showing processes and (b) enlarged process showing spines.

Source: courtesy of Professor M. Stewart.

bundles of myelinated axons can be distinguished against a background of unmyelinated neurons.

For reasons not entirely clear, some stains target only a small fraction of all the neurons in a region but those neurons are stained throughout. Thus, in tissue containing large numbers of apparently identical neurons, only a small fraction becomes evident. This phenomenon can be exploited, since it enables just the trajectory of a few neurons to become visible against their background.

Electron microscopy

Although a certain amount of detail can be gained by such techniques as staining and the use of a high-powered light microscope, the resolution is limited. To obtain a magnification large enough to see more fine details, the technique of **electron microscopy** is employed. A slice of tissue is prepared on a slide and then a beam of electrons is projected at it. A film sensitive to their presence is placed on the other side of the tissue. Electrons in the beam tend to pass through the tissue. The degree to which they appear at the film and expose it depends on the physical properties of the material they are passing through. For example, the membrane of a neuron would stand out as different from the material on the inside and outside.

Measuring electrical activity

There are techniques for observing the electrical activity of the CNS, peripheral nervous system and muscles. These are sometimes described as 'non-invasive', where the technique does not involve breaking the skin (e.g. a surface electrode) or 'invasive' where the skin is broken (e.g. in implanting an electrode).

Electroencephalography

Electrodes (probes that detect electrical voltages), attached to the skin, detect electrical activity and recordings are made from the surface of the head. This study of the brain's

activity is called **electroencephalography** (EEG), the record being an electroencephalogram (also abbreviated EEG) (Figure 5.44).

The location of the electrode is necessarily some distance from the neurons that contribute to the signal. Therefore, voltage changes produced by individual neurons are too small to be detected. Rather, such electrodes give a picture of the brain's 'overall' electrical activity, i.e. the combined activity of millions of neurons. The activity of the brain's outer layer, the cerebral cortex, is particularly evident in such a record. Many of the brain's neurons are synchronized in their activity and thereby add their electrical effects. Because of this, the EEG can register coherent patterns of voltage change. Using this technique, signals characteristic of sleep or arousal are measured. Patterns characteristic of epilepsy (Hommet *et al.*, 2005) or the development of other abnormality, e.g. a brain tumour, can be detected.

Since it can detect only the averaged activity of the more superficial regions, the EEG cannot reveal what is happening in deeper brain regions. Implanted electrodes can do this for non-humans. Of course, it is not usually possible scientifically or ethically to perform similar studies on humans.

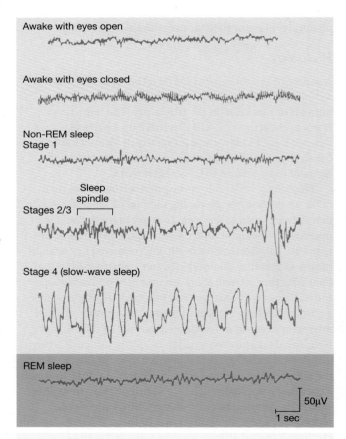

Figure 5.44 Electroencephalograms indicate different phases of sleep, e.g. that during which rapid eye movement (REM) is shown.

Evoked potentials

A stimulus triggers a change in electrical activity in the brain and this change is termed an **evoked potential** or, as it is also called, 'event-related potential' (ERP). Using EEG, the ERP is typically recorded by surface electrodes at the scalp. An 'idealized' example is shown in Figure 5.45. Note the background activity (termed 'noise') that exists before the stimulus is applied and after the stimulus is over. The signal that the stimulus triggers is clear against this background.

In reality, on a single observation, the difference between what is evoked (event-related) and what is background is not immediately obvious. However, by repeatedly presenting the same stimulus, and analyzing the electrical signal, a clearer picture of the consequence of the stimulus emerges.

The average electrical activity is taken over a number of trials. Averaging tends to cancel out the ups and downs of the noise, leaving the consistent event-related part clearly evident. Figure 5.46 shows such recordings. In the first (top trace) it is unclear what signal exists since there is a relatively high electrical activity even before presentation of the stimulus. As each successive recording contributes to an average (going from top to bottom), so an unambiguous signal progressively emerges from the background. For example, at time 550 ms, voltage X in trace 1, being negative, tends to cancel voltage Y in trace 3 and contributes to an average signal at this time that is near to zero in trace 5 (32nd recording).

Event-related potentials contribute to our understanding of such things as attention. If a person's attention is drawn to a stimulus, the change in potential that it evokes is typically increased.

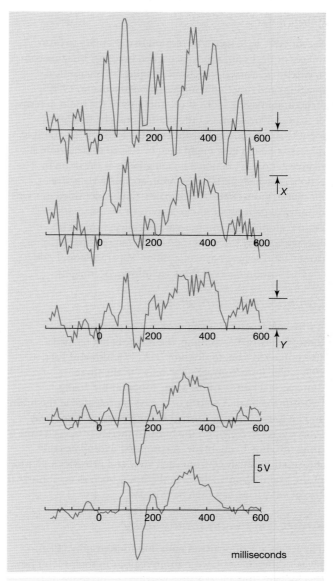

Figure 5.46 Event-related potentials in response to a stimulus at time 0. Response is averaged over 32 trials, 5 of these being shown from 1st (top) to the 32nd (bottom).

Source: Aston-Jones *et al.* (1999, Fig. 54.2, p. 1388).

Muscle activity

Chapters 3 and 4 described the contraction of muscle as a result of activity in motor neurons. Behavioural scientists need to be able to record the activity of muscles. Sometimes this is carried out by electrodes with their tips inside a muscle. At other times, rather like the EEG, it is done at a distance from the muscle, e.g. on the skin and picking up the activity of a muscle immediately below the skin. In either case, the recording is termed an 'electromyogram'.

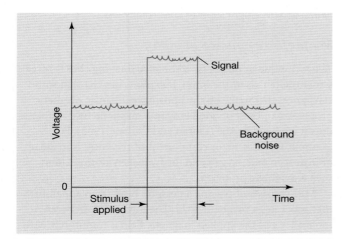

Figure 5.45 An 'idealized' signal against background.

Imaging

Recent years have seen a revolution in our ability to form images of the brain, a process termed **imaging**. Imaging comes in two broad classes: **structural imaging** (or anatomical imaging) and **functional imaging** (Papanicolaou, 1998). Structural imaging looks at the anatomy of the brain in terms of sizes and locations of different regions, etc. It helps to identify structural abnormalities in the form of, for example, diseased tissue. These might then be related to behavioural manifestations. Functional imaging looks at the brain in action, i.e. which parts of the brain are relatively active or inactive at given times. Abnormality can be identified in terms of unusual patterns of under-activity or over-activity in a brain region. For example, a case of epilepsy might be characterized by transient over-activity in regions of the frontal lobe, seen at particular times (Papanicolaou, 1998).

This section looks at three techniques of imaging.

Computerized tomography

A form of structural imaging is that of **computerized tomography** (CT) scanning, the image being termed a computerized axial tomogram (CAT) (Smith and Fetz, 1987). The term 'tomography' refers to the three-dimensional nature of the scan, 'topographic' being two-dimensional. A source of X-rays is projected at the brain and an X-ray image is formed at the detectors. The X-ray source is rotated around the brain in increments, each time a different 'shot' being made. A computer assimilates the information obtained from each view and provides a picture of the brain. Abnormalities in the brain, such as an abnormal size of ventricles, can then be revealed.

Positron emission tomography

The technique of **positron emission tomography** (PET) reveals differences between brain regions in their blood flow, metabolism of fuels (discussed earlier) or presence of substances, such as a particular neurotransmitter. Differences are seen both (i) within an individual but between brain regions and times and (ii) between different individuals.

Blood flow varies with activity of local neurons, which is a possible measure of the magnitude of local information processing (Smith and Fetz, 1987). PET consists of getting a radioactively labelled substance, a tracer, into a person, either by inhaling or injecting (Myers *et al.*, 1992). The location of that tracer is then examined. In one variety of PET, by inhaling radioactively labelled oxygen, the blood flow to different brain regions, termed regional cerebral blood flow (rCBF) (see earlier), can be measured.

The brain uses specific chemical fuels for metabolism. That is, each of its neurons has energy needs involved in transmitting information. Only a few types of fuel are able to be used by neurons, a principal one being glucose. A variety of PET exploits the properties of an artificial substance similar to glucose, 2-deoxyglucose (2-DG). This enters neurons as glucose does but, rather than serving as fuel, accumulates there. Brain regions in which neurons are most active, i.e. the highest frequency of action potentials, accumulate most 2-DG.

One variety of PET consists of first injecting some radioactive material (e.g. 2-DG) into the blood. The person's head is then placed in a scanning apparatus that detects the levels of injected radioactivity that arise from 2-DG accumulated in the different regions of brain. The level of radioactivity is detected and brain regions can be scaled according to activity level. Such a PET scan is shown in Figure 5.47. Different levels of activity are indicated by different colours alongside the representation of the brain. Whether oxygen or 2-DG, the radioactively labelled substance eventually leaves the neurons and is harmlessly lost from the body.

What kind of information can be revealed by a PET scan? There are various applications. For intact brains, researchers have had success in identifying what region does what. For example, a person can be asked to perform a response, e.g. clenching a fist. Regions of brain concerned with motor control of the hands will then be activated. Sensory stimuli in a particular modality can be presented and regions of brain associated with their processing identified.

Regions of brain that are diseased can be identified by their activity level being lower than normal. Recovery of function can be monitored in this way.

Chemicals that are employed by neurons to synthesize neurotransmitters ('precursors') are normally taken up by neurons and utilized. Labelled varieties of these precursors can be injected and their uptake monitored (Myers *et al.*, 1992). Their subsequent activity, in the form of release of the labelled neurotransmitter, can be tracked (Papanicolaou, 1998). If a type of neuron (e.g. dopaminergic) in a region is diseased, the uptake of labelled precursors and their activation as part of neural activity might show as abnormally low.

Magnetic resonance imaging

The technique of **magnetic resonance imaging** (MRI) reveals structural details of the brain. It exploits the fact that some substances that make up the body have intrinsic magnetic properties and respond to being in a magnetic field, rather as does a compass needle (Doran and Gadian, 1992). For example, water, a major component of the body, is made up of hydrogen and oxygen and the hydrogen atoms exhibit such a magnetic property.

MRI consists of placing a person's head in an apparatus that generates a magnetic field. The interaction between molecules and the applied magnetic field is monitored. MRI is able to detect different tissues on the basis of the kind of molecules that constitute it. Unlike the PET technique, it does not require that anything be injected into the person.

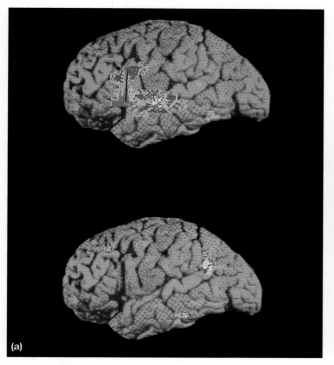
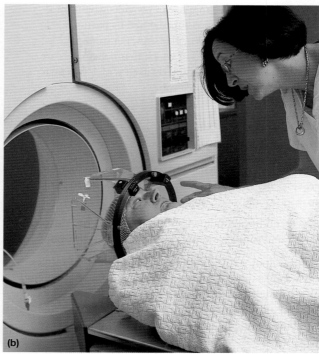

Figure 5.47 (a) Coloured positron emission tomography (PET) scan of areas of the brain involved in processing words. Active areas on the left side of the brain are shown in red and yellow. In a phonological task (top), meaningless sounds are listened to for word recognition. The superior temporal and inferior frontal areas are active, particularly the 'hearing' region of the brain. In a semantic task (bottom), heard words are listened to for their meaning. The superior frontal, parietal and temporal areas of the brain are active in the intellectual processing of words. (b) A nurse talking to a patient about to undergo a PET scan of the brain. This technique is used to detect areas of abnormal activity in the body and is particularly useful in detecting brain tumours, which show a marked difference in activity to healthy brain tissue.

Source: (a) Wellcome Department of Cognitive Neurology/Science Photo Library. (b) CC Studio/Science Photo Library.

A version of MRI is termed 'functional magnetic resonance imaging' (fMRI). It offers high resolution in detecting changes in oxygen consumption by different regions of the brain. Intense electrical activity in a particular region triggers increased supply of blood containing oxygen to that region. Relatively active and inactive sites in the brain can be identified and linked to psychological functions.

Microdialysis

A fraction of any neurochemicals released by the activity of neurons moves into the extracellular fluid surrounding their terminals. Investigators wish to know what is happening within this chemical environment of animals' brains as they behave.

Using a technique termed 'microdialysis', a probe is inserted into the brain and fixed to the skull (Figure 5.48). Fluid is passed into and out of the probe, and that leaving is analyzed chemically for its content. Chemicals present in the extracellular environment of the brain are able to pass into the tip of the probe and mix with the fluid that is passing. Their presence can later be detected.

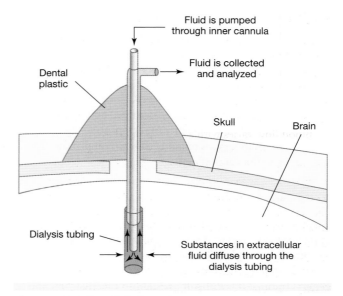

Figure 5.48 Microdialysis.

Source: Carlson (1998, Fig. 5.27, p. 138). Reprinted by permission of the publisher.

Therefore, this technique can provide insight into the timing of neuronal events defined by particular neurotransmitters at particular sites. For example, researchers are interested in which neurochemicals are activated when an animal injects itself with a psychoactive drug through an implanted tube.

Brain damage

Introduction

The observation of behaviour following brain damage provides insight into how the brain works. Brain damage can arise in several ways:

1   A result of gunshot wounds, traffic accidents, missiles in war and suicide attempts as in poisoning with gas.

2   A result of 'natural pathology' of the brain. Examples include a tumour and the disruption of neural activity associated with a **stroke**. A stroke can be caused by blocking an artery in the brain (Figure 5.25) or rupture of a blood vessel (Gardner, 1982).

3   Therapeutic interventions into the brain of humans in the form of surgery, e.g. cutting the corpus callosum to prevent disruption in one hemisphere influencing the other. The surgery in response to, say, a tumour can cause changes in brain function.

4   In the case of non-humans, experimental damage made to a specific region of the brain in order to study the effect on behaviour.

We normally assume that, if a type of behaviour is lost following damage to a brain region, then that region normally exerted a role in the control of the behaviour (Gardner, 1982). Understanding the effects of damage is rarely straightforward and needs subtle interpretation in the context of other results. The brain is an integrated system and a disturbance at one location will have influences elsewhere. Brain tissue other than the intended target might get damaged. Similarly, axons passing through the area might be damaged and there could be a disruption of their influence in regions some distance away. Other brain regions might be able to compensate and thereby mask the effect of damage.

Pathology, accidents and surgery

Regrettable as they are, strokes, tumours, wars, crime and accidents have produced a rich insight into how the brain functions. A complication for the investigator is that normally damage is to several regions and is associated with general trauma. It is difficult to establish exactly where the damage is. However, development of techniques such as PET is giving an increasing possibility of establishing localization.

The loss of function following brain damage in, say, a stroke is sometimes revealing in that relatively clear fracture lines of behavioural disruption appear (Damasio and Damasio, 1983). Thus, a patient might lose the ability to read and write while preserving speech intact. In other cases, reading is lost but writing remains intact. The writing of only certain classes of word, e.g. nonsense syllables, can be disrupted (Shallice, 1981). Examination of the brain regions associated with such specific losses can give insight regarding the normal flow of information and how this is disrupted.

Experimental lesions

In non-humans, damage can be made to the brain in order to investigate its effect. Specific parts of the brain, e.g. a particular nucleus, can be targeted. This damage is termed a **lesion** and the procedure is called lesioning (though 'lesion' can also refer to natural damage such as that caused by a blood clot). Surgical removal of part of the brain is a form of lesioning but here the more specific term **ablation** is also employed. A somewhat counter-intuitive terminology is used to describe such a subject: for example, an animal with the hippocampus removed is termed a 'hippocampal'. The means used to lesion the brain depend upon the intended target. Being on the outside of the brain, specific locations on the dorsal surface of the cerebral cortex can be identified and targeted with surgical knife cuts. Of course, deeper regions of brain require some form of penetration from the surface.

Under anaesthetic, an animal's head can be held in a fixed position in what is termed a 'stereotaxic apparatus' and 'stereotaxic surgery' performed. See Figure 5.49. A stereotaxic atlas is a three-dimensional map of the brain, which enables the exact coordinates to be located. With the help of a stereotaxic atlas, an electrode can be inserted into the brain until the tip is where the lesion is to be. By passing a particular electrical current through the tip, a region of brain can be selectively lesioned. Following the experiment, the animal is killed and its brain examined histologically to make sure that the lesion was at the intended site.

For an example of the difficulty of interpretation, suppose that a lesion is followed by excessive drinking. This suggests that regions of brain concerned with inhibition of drinking have been damaged. However, the effect might also be due to disturbance to urine production (as you saw in Chapter 3, hormones secreted at the brain play a role in urine production). In this case, excessive drinking is secondary to water loss. Further experimentation is required to tease apart these possibilities.

Another way of lesioning a brain region is to employ toxic chemicals that specifically target and damage cell bodies, sparing axons in the vicinity. This protects axons that are passing through the region. Using toxic chemicals, one particular class of neuron, as characterized by its

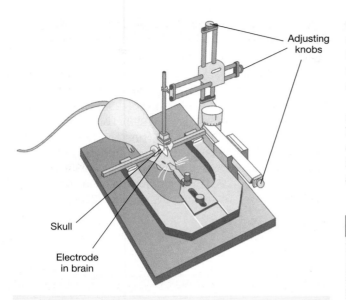

Adjusting knobs

Skull

Electrode in brain

Figure 5.49 Stereotaxic apparatus.

Source: Carlson (1998). Reprinted by permission of the publisher.

neurotransmitter, can be damaged. Thus, a toxin that selectively targets, say, dopaminergic neurons might be injected. This can either be applied generally or specific brain regions can be targeted.

Brain stimulation

Specific brain regions can be stimulated by chemical or electrical means. By the same stereotaxic surgery as just described, an electrode can be inserted and fixed in place. Wires can be joined to the electrode that is attached to the animal's skull and electric currents delivered to selected brain regions. The electrode and the magnitude of the current are such that neurons are stimulated. In the scientist's 'ideal case', stimulation of a site triggers behaviour whereas lesioning the same site disrupts it.

Recording through electrodes

In living animals (including humans), experimenters sometimes need to know what particular neurons are doing under particular conditions. Recordings can be made from a group of a few neurons or even from individual neurons while a non-human animal is stimulated with, say, light or while it explores its environment. An electrode with a very fine tip, capable of recording from single neurons, is termed a **microelectrode**. The technique of making recordings of this kind is termed 'single-unit recording' (Carlson, 1994).

The electrode is chronically implanted in the brain, i.e. fixed to the animal's skull and inserted until the tip is in the region of interest. Wires are attached to the electrode and

these are connected to an apparatus for recording electrical activity. A cat, for example, is anaesthetized and its head held in a stereotaxic apparatus. The experimenter then stimulates the retina with light and the activity of, say, a retinal ganglion cell is monitored on a screen.

Another type of investigation is where an animal is free to move within a cage and correlations are observed between behaviour and electrical activity in particular neurons. For example, by this means, O'Keefe and Dostrovsky (1971) identified 'place cells', neurons that fire when an animal is in a particular place in its environment.

Section summary

1 Techniques are available for tracing neural pathways in the brain.

2 Electron microscopy enables details of cellular form and connections within the nervous system to be revealed.

3 Electroencephalography (EEG) is a technique for recording the gross electrical activity of the brain with surface electrodes.

4 Positron emission tomography (PET) enables the activity of different brain regions to be monitored.

5 A valuable source of insight is brain damage, though results need to be handled with caution.

Test your knowledge

(Answers on page 144)

5.11 Suppose that a chemical is injected into the lateral geniculate nucleus of a living animal. (i) Suppose also that it is taken up by the cell body of neurons located there. By means of anterograde labelling, where might it be expected ultimately to appear? (ii) Suppose also that it is taken up by axon terminals. By means of retrograde labelling, where might it appear?

5.12 Complete the following sentence: 'Under conditions of artificial injection, brain regions that are particularly active tend to accumulate relatively large amounts of ____'. (i) Glucose, (ii) 2-deoxyglucose (2-DG).

5.1

Bringing things together

This chapter has shown how to start to find your way around the brain and to identify some key landmarks. You can now appreciate better how the brain serves its role in perception, motivation and emotion and in controlling both the somatic and autonomic outputs introduced in Chapter 3.

As the chapter has shown, ways of gaining insight include a detailed description of brains, looking at differences between brains in different species (comparative psychology) and manipulating the brain by lesioning and stimulation. Knowledge of neurons and their associated neurochemicals (Chapter 4) is valuable in plotting pathways and understanding what they do. Sometimes simpler systems, e.g. invertebrates, provide 'animal models' of more complex systems.

More recently developed techniques such as PET and fMRI have radically improved our ability to observe the working brain.

Summary of Chapter 5

1   An understanding of the nervous system requires universally agreed conventions of orientation within it and anatomical description of its parts.

2   Information is brought to sensory processing regions of the brain via various identifiable pathways. Distinct regions of the brain organize motor control and execute this via identifiable motor pathways to muscles.

3   In exerting control on the external environment, the brain processes and utilizes emotional and motivational information. The brain regulates the internal environment of the body and there is special regulation over the brain's own environment.

4   Based on extensive processing of information done beyond the dedicated sensory regions, the brain forms predictions of the future. A brain region having a role in the associated control of behaviour is the prefrontal cortex.

5   Insight into how nervous systems work can be gained by comparing different species, in terms of their brains and their solutions to the control of behaviour.

6   Techniques used in the study of the brain include tracing pathways, microscopic examination of brain regions, brain imaging, electrical recording of brain activity and studying the consequences of brain damage.

Further reading

For all of the material in this chapter, see Nolte (2002). For brain anatomy, see J.H. Martin (1996) or Martini *et al.* (2000). For a comparative perspective on the brain, see Butler and Hodos (1996) and on the basal ganglia, see Reiner *et al.* (1998). For the frontal lobes, see Fuster (1997). For a discussion of tinkering and the brain in the context of evolutionary psychology, see Buss *et al.* (1998), Gilbert (1998) or Prescott *et al.* (1999). For techniques, see Carlson (2003), Rosenzweig *et al.* (2004) or Kalat (2004).

Signposts

In the present chapter, only very brief reference was made to development of the brain, otherwise we dealt with adult brains. The following chapter describes the developmental processes by which nervous systems grow into their adult form. It will call upon knowledge gained in each of Chapters 1–5, looking at neurons and synapses, hormones and whole brains. Issues of function will be to the fore.

Answers

Explanations for answers to 'test your knowledge' questions can be found on the website **www.pearsoned.co.uk/toates**

5.1   Cell bodies of the dopaminergic neurons are located in region A, while a bundle of their axons (forming a tract) extend to region B, where dopamine is released

5.2   (ii) Contralaterally

5.3   (ii) The inferior colliculus

5.4   (a) (i) A_2, (ii) A_1, (iii) C_2, (iv) C_1, (v) D_2, (vi) D_1
      (b) (i) B_2, (ii) A_2

5.5   (i) The axons of ganglion cells that form the optic nerve; (ii) the axons of LGN cells ('optic projection fibres') that convey the message to the visual cortex

5.6   (i) Ventral horn of the spinal cord

5.7   Cerebrospinal fluid; cell bodies of neurons

5.8   Rate (or 'frequency')

5.9   (iv) Node of Ranvier

5.10 Engineer; tinkerer

5.11 (i) Their axon terminals in the visual cortex; (ii) at the cell bodies in ganglion cells in the retina

5.12 (ii) 2-Deoxyglucose (2-DG)

CHAPTER 6

Development and plasticity

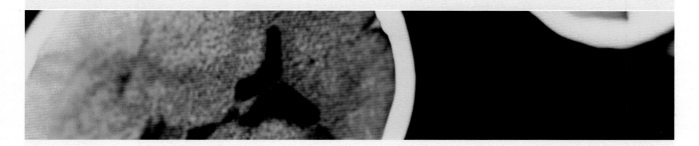

Learning outcomes for Chapter 6

After studying this chapter, you should be able to:

1. Describe how, in the study of development, the term 'environment' can mean more than one thing. In so doing, link the terms 'environment', 'cell', 'genotype' and 'phenotype'.

2. Outline some of the conceptual traps that await the unwary investigator who chooses to study development. Explain how these traps can be avoided by careful and rigorous use of language and analysis.

3. Describe the sequence of changes in the structure of cells and their connections, which constitutes neural development.

4. Explain, with examples, the role of hormones in development. Thereby, distinguish the terms 'organizational effect' and 'activational effect'.

5. Show how cognitive and social development can be linked to the development of underlying biological structures.

6. Give some examples of the types of influence that can disturb normal development and how the effects of these influences can be characterized in biological and psychological terms.

7. Illustrate how a comparison between different species can help our understanding of the principles of development. In so doing, discuss functional considerations.

Scene-setting questions

1   How did you develop from a single fertilized cell to the person you are today?

2   Are genes a 'blueprint', a plan for a future construction?

3   Are discussions of the role of 'genes *versus* environment' useful or fundamentally misleading?

4   What makes us male or female?

5   Can a bad upbringing damage the brain?

How does the social context affect the developing brain of an infant, involving its cognitive and emotional aspects?

Source: **Getty Images/Iconica.**

 ## Introduction

At fertilization, life begins as a single cell. This cell is a fertilized egg (a 'zygote') and thereby the genotype is formed (Chapter 2, 'Genes, environment and evolution'). In humans, starting from this single cell, there *develops* a body having a nervous system that ultimately contains some 100 billion neurons and probably even more glial cells. The present chapter is about how nervous systems and behaviour develop with time since fertilization.

In mammals, growth and change of the **embryo** (at times, also termed 'foetus') starts in the uterus. Development depends upon genes and environment. The term 'environment' means several different things: the chemical environment within each cell that surrounds the genes, the extracellular fluid environment surrounding the cells, the environment of the uterus or, in birds, the egg. Later there are the external physical and social environments.

When comparing members of a species, some features of the early environment are similar (Chapter 2). For a mammalian species, there is a similar origin in a uterus. Subsequently, feeding is consistently via the mother's breast and the early environment has some common social dimensions. Comparable to the influence of genetic similarity between individuals, environmental consistencies tend to give some common directions to early development (Hofer, 1988). Environments are similar but, of course, not identical.

Identical twins illustrate the interactive nature of development: they are genetically, but not phenotypically, identical. They commonly exhibit differences in, for instance, size at birth, suggestive of a different availability of nutrients prior to birth.

Because the development of the nervous system and that of behaviour are inextricably linked, the understanding of either needs some consideration of both. Looking at changes in the nervous system during development can provide insight into the bases of changes in behaviour. Different brain regions develop at different rates, corresponding to changing functional demands. Hence, the nature of the behavioural controls that are available to the developing animal and the possibilities for behaviour also change (Diamond, 1996; Prechtl, 1982).

Some biological measures (e.g. electrical activity of the brain) made at around the time of birth, or earlier, have predictive value concerning features appearing later (e.g. hearing defects) and can suggest therapies. Psychological indices, e.g. mental retardation, are important in diagnosis of developmental disorders, to be considered alongside biological indices such as abnormal levels of hormones. Disturbances to a baby's development, as a result of biological or chemical disruption (e.g. the mother drinking alcohol), are manifest in later disruptions of behaviour.

In rats, exposure to an enriched environment tends to enrich connectivity between neurons in the developing brain (Rosenzweig *et al.*, 1996). If this principle applies also to humans, its social implications in terms of the role of different environments are potentially enormous. For the developing child, inadequate social conditions, such as parental neglect, are manifest in abnormal development in certain brain regions (Teicher *et al.*, 2004).

The term 'plasticity' (Chapter 3, 'The nervous and endocrine systems') refers to the capacity to exhibit change. In other words, given a particular genotype, it represents the capacity for *variation* in the phenotypic characteristics that can emerge dependent upon different environments.

Those processes that exhibit plasticity during development are also sometimes capable of limited plasticity in the adult. For example, they can compensate to some extent for disturbances, such as neural damage, a property sometimes termed **malleability** (Cairns, 1979). This can be relevant to therapies designed to overcome the effects of neural damage. Conversely, knowledge of when underlying processes have become inflexible is relevant to the stubborn refusal of adult behaviour to show plasticity under some circumstances.

Early in the study of development, it is useful to try to clarify some conceptual issues that lie behind our understanding of it, the topic of the next section.

Section summary

1 Genes exist within a cellular environment, cells exist within an extracellular environment and whole animals exist within a physical and social environment.

2 Genes define a range of developmental possibilities, as revealed in the phenotype.

Test your knowledge

(Answer on page 176)

6.1 Complete the following sentence: 'Compared to being reared in an impoverished environment, rearing in an enriched environment might be expected to alter the ____ '. (i) Genotype, (ii) phenotype.

Conceptual issues in understanding development

This section looks at some of the issues that surround accounts of development. It will consider some very common pitfalls and how to avoid them. For example, confusion surrounds the interdependence between gene, developing biological structure and environment. Analogies, described next, are useful in getting a grasp of this complex issue.

Analogies

Analogies can capture certain important similarities with psychobiological processes and serve to organize our thinking. However, any analogy of development will doubtless also differ from real psychobiological development. Analogies can be seductive and misleading in subtle ways but recognition of where the analogy differs from psychobiology can also be an important guide to our thinking. This section looks at two commonly used examples.

One analogy is that development is like a ball rolling down grooves on a hill (Waddington, 1936, 1975). See Figure 6.1. At the top (fertilization), there are more possibilities for the ball's trajectory than when it is nearer the bottom

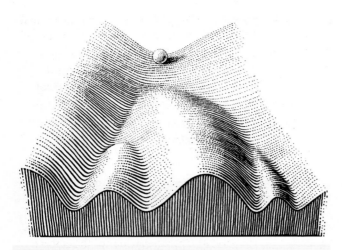

Figure 6.1 Analogy by Waddington.

Source: Bonner (1958, Fig. 10, p. 44).

(adulthood). As it descends, the future direction becomes more constrained. By analogy, development becomes less open-ended as it progresses.

Another analogy is that genetics is something like an architect's plan for a construction, whereas development is like the work of the builder (Rosenzweig *et al.*, 1996). So where does this analogy fit and where does it not? First, let us see where it fits. Neither the architect's plan nor the genotype can contain enough information to specify every local 'decision' in construction. Such plans would be impossibly complex and hopelessly inefficient in implementation (try asking any builder!). So, the builder's implementation of the plan is achieved by taking local circumstances and materials into account. Given two identical plans, some differences in construction are inevitable. Through biological evolution or architectural professional practice, plans ('genotypes') that are proven to work will survive.

Features of the analogy are useful but it suffers from a serious weakness: an architect's plan ('blueprint') describes the end-point of the construction – what the building will finally look like. By contrast, in spite of the common use of the term 'blueprint' in biology, the genotype does not specify an end-point (Gottlieb, 1998). Genes cannot provide a reference against which 'correct' or 'wrong' courses of development can be compared. There is not enough capacity in the genes to encode for all the details of an adult. The gene exerts effects on the course of development but the environment does the rest. Thus, we need caution even in an expression such as 'a gene for blue eyes'. Such a gene is different from one 'for' brown eyes but the gene acting in isolation does not create the blue eyes.

Learning and development

The study of development and plasticity raises the issue of learning. How do we distinguish development and learning? Can we or should we even try? Is learning a subdivision of development? I am sorry; I know that you have just had three rhetorical questions in a row. I would love to give some words of clarification and comfort here but I cannot put my hand on my heart and honestly come up with any.

There are cases that psychologists would unambiguously describe as learning, e.g. an adult learning a foreign language. However, although there are other situations, which psychologists would usually call 'developmental' but not 'learning', they can never eliminate the possibility that some learning is involved. For a young animal, aspects of change usually involve both development and learning, as traditionally understood.

The term 'learning' normally refers to change that is peculiar to a particular individual within a particular environment. For example, young children in France learn French and those in Britain learn English. That is, their linguistic behaviour changes over time. These different changes in behaviour are not to be explained in terms of initial differences within the nervous system of the two sets of children. Rather, the difference is in terms of the different environments to which they were exposed. Presumably, like any sort of learning, this has a biological basis in neurons somewhere in the nervous system.

As a first attempt at a definition, development refers to a sequence of general changes that are more dependent simply upon time since fertilization than of specific experiences peculiar to a given individual. Changes that occur in the nervous system corresponding to development are sometimes described as **maturation**, e.g. formation of a myelin coating around axons. Development proceeds in a way that is less subject to differences of personal experience of a given individual. However, development does not proceed independently of the environment, since an animal can only exist provided that it is within a certain range of environments. It is possible to define certain species-typical routes of development that are apparent within a range of different environments. For instance, developmental changes occur in the brain mechanisms underlying language. Provided that there is exposure to a language, some of these are similar whether it is, say, French or English to which the child is being exposed.

In some important respects, development is a process that cannot be reversed. We can hardly take a mature rat and reconstruct the infant form from it! By contrast, learning can, in at least some respects, be 'undone'. By exposing it to the right conditions, we can first teach a dog that food is to the left and no food to the right. By reversing the conditions, we can then undo this learning and teach it that food is to the right and no food to the left. However, as later chapters will show, the distinction between learning and development is becoming more blurred all the time.

Right from time zero

Starting from a consideration of the time of fertilization, there are subtle conceptual traps for the investigator. For example, consider the observation that more dominant mothers tend to give birth to sons rather than daughters. How could the status of the mother influence the sex of the child, since surely the male contribution of an X or Y chromosome determines this (Chapter 2)? The male indeed determines the sex but the hormonal condition of the female might determine whether sperm carrying an X or Y chromosome can more easily penetrate the egg cell and fertilize it (Grant, 1994a,b).

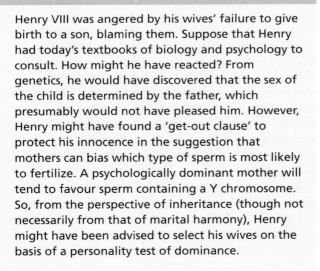

A personal angle
Henry VIII of England

Henry VIII was angered by his wives' failure to give birth to a son, blaming them. Suppose that Henry had today's textbooks of biology and psychology to consult. How might he have reacted? From genetics, he would have discovered that the sex of the child is determined by the father, which presumably would not have pleased him. However, Henry might have found a 'get-out clause' to protect his innocence in the suggestion that mothers can bias which type of sperm is most likely to fertilize. A psychologically dominant mother will tend to favour sperm containing a Y chromosome. So, from the perspective of inheritance (though not necessarily from that of marital harmony), Henry might have been advised to select his wives on the basis of a personality test of dominance.

Consideration of the determinants of sex raises the possibility that the uterine environment surrounding a male might on average be different from that of a female.

The dynamics of development

The developing nervous system influences behaviour and is influenced by behaviour. Throughout development, the growing animal is in dynamic interaction with its changing environment. Following birth or, in the case of birds, hatching, there is an abrupt change of environment. The

animal *influences* and is *influenced by* each environment that it encounters. This section looks at this interactive nature of biological and psychological development.

The embryo

In studying development, we need to be attentive to what can reach the growing embryo from the outside world. Elements of the environment such as the sound of television penetrate even to the human foetus. Now that really is something to worry about!

Does an embryo already *behave*? There is evidence for coordinated responses. The interactive nature of development can be summarized as (genetic activity) ↔ (structure) ↔ (behaviour), meaning that each is affected by the other (Gottlieb, 1998). Thus, behaviour of the embryo has implications for the structuring of the body including the nervous system and its links to the muscular system. Even very basic forms of response can be of significance for neural development.

Later stages

Development is influenced dynamically at different levels (Figure 6.2). Interactions occur between cells. Cells change shape and function and a combination of cells defines the physical form of the animal, which exists within an external environment. Consideration of the physical environment shows the interactive nature of development. For example, there is fine-tuning of connections within the visual system that can be done only following exposure of the eyes to visual stimulation (Blakemore, 1973). Considering the social environment, behaviour has consequences for the individual and for others.

In much of the literature, there is the assumption that there exist *distinct* inputs to development. In rejecting any such clear dichotomies, Michel and Moore (1995, p. 76) assert: 'It is not necessary – in fact, it may not be possible – to begin a psychobiological analysis by separating biological from psychological components'. Why is this?

As Michel and Moore (1995, p. 101) express it: 'The organism and its environment are in a reciprocal relationship. The environment shapes the organism and its behaviour, while simultaneously, the organism and its behaviour are shaping the environment'. For example, in understanding the development of a newborn mammal, the mother cannot be described as an independent entity since her reactions are affected by the offspring's behaviour (Stern, 1997). Reciprocally, developing biological structure is inevitably influenced by the social environment (Gottlieb, 1997a).

Let us now focus upon humans and their environment, termed 'culture'.

A human baby typically elicits such emotional reactions as smiling. In return, the mother's reaction of smiling or rejection affects the emotional reactivity of the baby. Comparing depressed and non-depressed mothers, differences

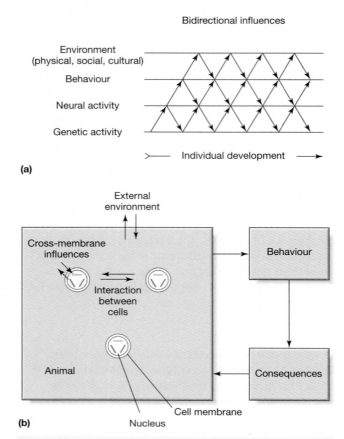

(a)

(b)

Figure 6.2 Determinants of development. (a) Model of Gottlieb (1997a, Fig. 5.4). (b) A cell interacts with its extracellular environment and thereby with other cells. The nucleus containing the genes influences, and is influenced by, the cell's intracellular environment. The whole animal interacts with its external world by behavioural and non-behavioural routes.

are also seen in their babies, mediated in part via differences in social interaction. These might have lasting effects on the infant's emotional development (Dawson, 1994).

Development of sex differences depends on how a social animal is treated, which depends in part on sexual characteristics (Grant, 1994a,b). Human mothers (not to forget fathers) behave differently towards sons and daughters. Differences might be prompted by sexually based differences in behaviour of the offspring or by the mother's perception of the sex of the offspring.

Consideration of interactions poses subtle problems for analysis of the role of genes and environment (Michel and Moore, 1995). For instance, siblings might be said to inhabit the same environment and this might be so in terms of such things as food intake and room temperature. However, genetic differences at the level of the child might manifest in,

say, personality, such that siblings are treated differently by parents and hence their social environment is not equal (Plomin, 1989).

This section shows the need to advance beyond simple analogies of genes and environment, e.g. these being like two sides of a rectangle (Chapter 2). Although such an analogy can improve upon certain fallacious assumptions, it does not capture the *dynamics of interaction*.

Determinants and developmental time

When psychologists look at development, how do they define age? It might sound simple but caution is in order. Development does not proceed as if driven by an inner clock regardless of the environment. In using age, is it time from fertilization or, when it concerns events following birth, postnatal age that should be considered (Schulte, 1974)? For some aspects, time from fertilization can provide a more reliable predictor of development than postnatal age, irrespective of whether the latter part of the time was spent *in utero* or not.

What measure can we use for when the nervous system has reached maturity? One possibility is myelination. Some neurons are surrounded by myelin, which facilitates the passage of action potentials (Chapter 4, 'The cells of the nervous system'). Different parts of the nervous system acquire myelin at different times (Bronson, 1982). The timing of such acquisition reflects the functional significance of the emerging neuronal systems. In humans, some myelination of sensory and motor pathways is evident at five or six months before birth. Subcortical regions start myelination next, with cortical regions myelinating last. Some myelination of pathways to and from the cerebellum still occurs up to three years of age, mirroring increasingly refined motor control.

Myelin can be necessary for the functioning of a brain region. For example, the capacity of the corpus callosum (Chapter 5, 'The brain') to convey rapidly information from one hemisphere to the other depends upon myelination of its axons (Salamy, 1978). However, we cannot assume that myelination proceeds regardless of information processing within the neurons concerned. The degree of myelination depends to some extent upon the activity of the neurons around which it forms its sheath. In turn, activity depends upon the capacity of other neural systems to perform information processing. Again, the interdependence of determinants needs to be emphasized.

Another index of development is the electrical activity of a given region of the brain (Chapter 5). If two animals are of the same chronological age but have differing degrees of myelination and electrical activity, this could alert us to possible developmental differences between them.

Functional considerations

Of course, an animal has to survive during development and move to sexual maturity as a necessary condition for passing on genes. Genes are selected because of the success of their role in the combination of development and beyond (Gottlieb, 1973). Some adaptations serve the here-and-now by their consequences at the current developmental stage. So, during development, behaviour both serves present needs and is a preparation for maturity.

Developing organisms find themselves in very different environments from adults (e.g. uterus, egg) and need adaptations to cope with them. For example, suckling is a technique by which mammals gain nutrients but the processes that organize it are different from those that underlie adult feeding (A.N. Epstein, 1990). Suckling cannot be understood as something that gets successively refined until the adult feeding pattern emerges. It is more like the first stage of a multistage space vehicle: necessary for survival and movement early on but which can be jettisoned when a later stage takes over.

Twin studies

Twins can provide a natural and well-controlled experiment. They attract attention from researchers, who try to tease apart the contribution of genes and environment. This section looks briefly at some of the issues that this research raises.

Types of twin

Twins come in one of two kinds: **monozygotic twins** (MZs) (or 'identical twins') and **dizygotic twins** (DZs) (or 'fraternal twins'). MZs derive from a single zygote and are genetically identical. Therefore, any differences between them in, say, cognitive ability can be attributed to 'environmental

differences' (considering environment in a broad sense). Each member of a pair of DZs derives from a separate zygote and so they are not genetically identical.

It is possible to measure the extent to which twins correlate in something, such as height or IQ score, known as their **concordance**. Thus, if genetic differences play a role in determining differences in behaviour, a higher concordance of MZs on a number of dimensions would be predicted. The concordance of MZs is indeed commonly found to be higher than that of DZs (Phelps *et al.*, 1997) and this is usually attributed to the influence of identical genes.

Twins that are reared apart are sometimes said to share no common environment. However, this ignores the womb and the fact that it must offer some common features as the environment for each of the pair (see Phelps *et al.*, 1997). Conversely, it might be assumed that twins, whether MZ or DZ, share an identical environment in the womb and differences in environment only start from birth. Take the case of MZ twins. Since they are genetically identical, differences can be attributed to differences in environment. If the environment of the womb is identical, then any difference in environments would start only after birth. However, it is difficult to imagine that the environment for the twins is absolutely identical, even though it is doubtless very similar. For example, one twin might be physically located in the womb more comfortably than the other.

Identical twins are identical genetically but what other factor is very similar when they are compared? How might we try to separate the influences of these factors?

Source: Alex Bartel/Science Photo Library.

Section summary

1 Analogies can capture certain features of how animals develop.

2 Calling genes a 'plan' or 'blueprint' implies a representation of an end-point, which is not how they operate.

3 Genes interact with the cellular environment that surrounds them and the whole animal interacts with the external environment.

4 Developing biological structure including that of the nervous system influences, and is influenced by, the environment. The infant's biological form and behaviour affect the social environment.

5 Stages of myelination give some indication of the development of part of the nervous system.

6 Some specific adaptations serve the here-and-now only during development.

7 A comparison of monozygotic and dizygotic twins can provide a source of insight into the factors underlying development.

The basic biology of nervous system development

Introduction

The nervous system does not exist in a miniature form in the zygote. Neurons and their connections are the products of growth and change. Over the course of development, neurons appear, grow and sometimes establish functionally appropriate connections with other cells (Grobstein, 1988). Sometimes all or part of them dies. Therefore, a problem addressed here is – how do developing neurons know where to go, what to extend and what form to take? For example, a frog darts its tongue out at a bug and has a good chance of hitting it. Such sensory-motor coordination implies that, during development, there occurs the formation of appropriate functioning connections between *particular* cells: sensory neurons, interneurons, motor neurons and muscles.

Gross structural changes

The human zygote, the first cell, is something like the size of the full-stop ('period') that terminates this sentence. Within 12 hours of fertilization, this cell divides (Chapter 2) into two cells. In turn, these also divide to give four cells and so on, such that the number of cells within the embryo rapidly increases. Figures 6.3 and 6.4 show part of the sequence of nervous system development (Martini *et al.*, 2000). If anyone needed persuasion that we do not start from a miniature preformed version and simply enlarge, considering this sequence should provide it.

The pattern of cell division is not even and the unevenness contributes to the formation of distinct structures. This can be seen in Figure 6.3 (at 21 days): the formation of neural folds and the neural groove. By 22–23 days, the neural folds come together to form the 'neural tube'. The neural tube is made up of 'stem cells', those that will form neurons and glial cells. The length of the tube defines the axis rostral–caudal of the developing CNS, e.g. the caudal 50% or so becomes the spinal cord and the remainder defines the brain. The cavity of the tube is destined to define the fluid-filled spaces of the CNS (Chapter 5): the cerebral ventricles and the central canal of the spinal cord and interconnections. As shown in Figure 6.3, the neural crest contains the cells destined to form the peripheral nervous system.

Figure 6.4 shows the development of the brain and cranial nerves from age 23 days. By 23 days, what will become the divisions of the brain emerge, e.g. the swelling that will become the forebrain. Behind it, two swellings are destined to become the midbrain and hindbrain. At a late stage of development, distinct and characteristic gyri and sulci are also evident.

Analyses suggest some increase in number of neurons at least up to age 6 years (Shankle *et al.*, 1998). The increase in weight of the brain seems to be due to an increase in the number of glial cells and neurons, as well as a growth of existing neurons.

The volume of the human cerebral cortex at birth is about one-third that of the adult (Huttenlocher, 1994). The main period of growth is in the first year. Synaptic density reaches its peak at around three years, at a level 50% higher than that at birth and puberty (Bruer, 1998). However, fine structural changes continue until adulthood, corresponding to the appearance of new cognitive capacities. The number of neurons in the cerebral cortex appears to double between the ages of 15 months and 6 years (Shankle *et al.*, 1998).

Development is not a one-way process of growth and increasing complexity. It is also associated with a loss of some neurons and neuronal connections (Edelman, 1987).

To understand the changes in gross structure (Figures 6.3 and 6.4), you need familiarity with the underlying changes that occur at the cellular level, the topic to which we now turn.

Changes at a cellular level

Considering development at the level of changes within, and between, neurons, theorists identify *stages* (Rosenzweig *et al.*, 1996). In humans, most changes occur prior to birth. There is some overlap and simultaneity between stages of development. Therefore, we might consider them as different processes of change rather than clear-cut events in a predetermined time-sequence. When things go wrong in these stages, adult behavioural pathology can result (Nowakowski and Hayes, 1999).

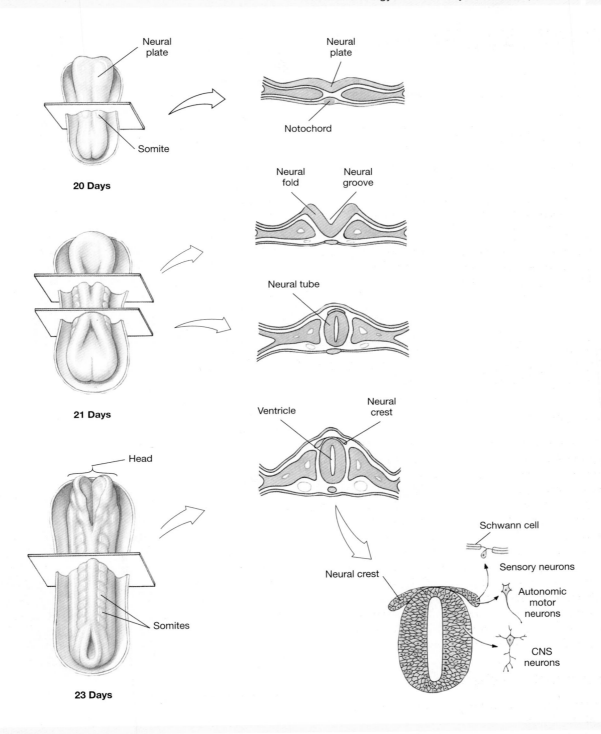

Figure 6.3 The development of the human nervous system up to age 23 days.

Source: Martini *et al*. (2000, p. 338).

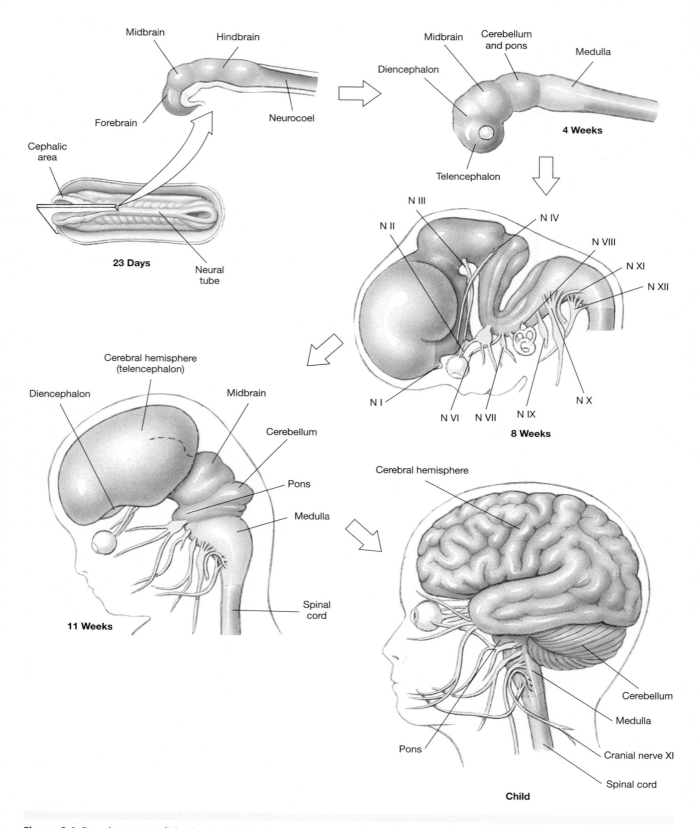

Figure 6.4 Development of the brain and cranial nerves. *Source*: Martini *et al.* (2000, pp. 416–417).

Figure 6.5 shows a summary of these changes. The stages, or processes, are as follows:

1 *Neurogenesis.* This consists of repeated cell division (Chapter 2) among the cells of the neural tube, so as to form new cells (Figure 6.5(a)–(c)).

2 *Migration.* There is a movement of neurons from their place of origin to another location. This is the stage at which the final anatomical location of neurons starts to be established (Figure 6.5(d),(e)).

3 *Differentiation.* Distinct types of neuron are formed from a standard precursor neuron (stages 2 and 3 can overlap considerably). Neurons start to produce extensions, termed neurites, which will form axons and dendrites (Figure 6.5(f),(g)).

4 *Synaptogenesis.* Accompanying the growth of axons and dendrites, synaptic connections between neurons form (Figure 6.5(h)).

5 *Selective death of neurons.* Neurons that fail to establish functioning synapses (stage 4) tend to die (Figure 6.5(i)). Contact alone may not be sufficient for survival, as represented here by the yellow cell.

6 *Synaptic reorganization.* Changes occur in the strength of synaptic connections. Some connections are strengthened and others weakened (compare Figure 6.5(i) and (j)). In some cases, if the outcome is weakening as a result of a failure to establish a functioning link, it can lead to cell death (compare Figure 6.5(h) and (i)).

As noted earlier, in humans, the full number of neurons that will finally be present has not been reached at birth. Thus, at a time that some brain regions are still at stage 1, others have reached stage 6.

We shall now look at these stages in more detail.

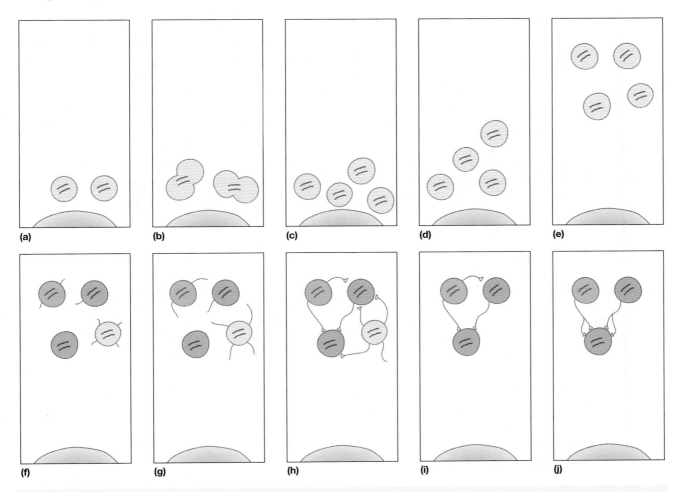

Figure 6.5 Development: (a) cells initially located by the ventricle, (b) cells starting to divide, (c) cells divided, (d) start of cell migration, (e) migration complete, (f) start of differentiation, (g) continuation of differentiation, (h) synapses formed, (i) death of some cells and (j) synaptic restructuring.

Neurogenesis

The process termed 'neurogenesis' (stage 1; Figure 6.5(a)–(c)) constitutes the formation of neurons from general ('precursor') cells. Of course, the diagram can represent only a very small part of this sequence of cells dividing and then these newly formed cells in turn dividing, and so on. When the process of repeated cell division ceases, this initial stage of early development has reached a stable point. This point in time represents the birth date of neurons. The neurons so formed then tend to migrate from the location associated with their birth.

Cell migration

By what means do cells migrate (stage 2; Figure 6.5(d), (e))? That is to say, how are cells caused to move from their location of birth to another location, where they will perform their role in the functioning nervous system? There exist chemicals that attract particular cells and guiding factors that influence the direction taken by them. For example, in some cases 'radial glial cells' already exist and these guide growing neurons (Rakic, 1971). The function of these radial glial cells is to act something like the wires that gardeners use to grow peas and other vegetables.

Differentiation

Different cells acquire different shapes and structures and serve different functions, a process termed **differentiation** (stage 3). This occurs because, among other things, genes exert different effects at different times. The initial trigger to this is termed **gene expression**. That is, various genes are switched on, meaning that they start to trigger the manufacture of proteins. Proteins form a physical base of the developing structure of neurons. For example, in a particular neuron at developmental age t_1, switching on $gene_1$ results in the production of $protein_1$, which might be part of the physical base of a dendrite.

In vertebrates, development of a particular neuron is generally determined by a *combination* of intrinsic factors and a range of possible immediate environments (e.g. hormones surrounding the cell or events at neighbouring neurons) (Gottlieb, 1997a).

A number of general and specific factors determine the environment of a neuron. In the development of mammals, one general factor is the current nutrient status of the mother. A deficiency of an essential component needed to make a protein will interfere with the ability of genes to express themselves in protein construction. An excess of a toxic element such as alcohol might similarly have a disruptive effect.

A 'specific factor' is one that applies particularly to the neuron(s) under consideration. For example, the timing of gene expression can be determined by chemical influences from neighbouring cells. An influence of one group of cells on events within a neighbouring cell is termed **induction** (Purves and Lichtman, 1985). For example, in some neurons of the autonomic nervous system, the neurotransmitter that a neuron synthesizes (e.g. acetylcholine) is determined only after it establishes contact with smooth muscle (Harris and Hartenstein, 1999). One consequence of induction is that, if a neuron gets damaged, others might be able to respond to the message and, to some extent, compensate for the role of the missing one, a phenomenon termed quite logically 'regulation'.

Neurons grow. They come to assume complex shapes and they form connections with other cells. Axons and dendrites grow out from the cell body (Brown *et al.*, 2001). Consider two closely related questions, as follows. What determines the final 'tree-like' shape that mature neurons commonly take, with their branches in the form of extending axons and dendrites? What determines the connections made between neurons? Interactions between what are initially relatively distant cells (e.g. two neurons) determine the direction that growing extensions take, their form and their connections. How do cells that are physically separated none the less manage to interact with each other in such a way as to determine their form and interconnections?

Central to such interactions is a feature of the growing neuron termed a **growth cone** (Raper and Tessier-Lavigne, 1999). See Figure 6.6. A growth cone is the swollen ending of an extending axon or dendrite, with fine extensions termed 'filopodia'. Consider the case of an axon. Filopodia attach themselves to their environment and then grow out, something like ivy growing over a building. In doing so, they pull the axon behind them. They are attracted towards chemical cues in their environment, termed **chemoattraction**. These cues are signals from other cells, some of which, the attractors, form targets for the axon with its growth cone serving as path-finder. As the growing axon gets nearer the target, the concentration of chemoattractive substance gets greater. The growth cone seems to ascend a

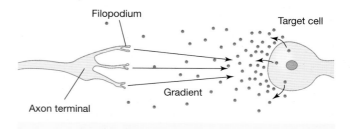

Figure 6.6 Growth cone.

gradient of chemical concentration (rather like a male moth ascending a gradient of chemicals released into the air by a female or like a heat-seeking missile maximizing infrared stimulation) (Whatson and Sterling, 1998).

Often the growing axon extends relatively large distances for which the chemical signals emitted by target cells might initially be too weak to direct it. How does it 'know' where to go? Again, interactions with other cells play a role. Along the trajectory of many axons, a series of 'guidepost cells' are found, like beacons crossing the countryside in former centuries. These are cells that space out the distance between the start and end of the trajectory. The growing axon is attracted to first the nearest and then the next guidepost cell until it nears its target. In many cases, several cues such as guideposts and chemoattraction by the final target act together to determine the trajectory.

Yet another guidance system is provided by 'pioneer axons' (Raper and Tessier-Lavigne, 1999), which start the journey first. Other developing axons then follow the trajectory set by the pioneers. This guiding process is termed 'fasciculation', meaning that functionally related axons that will come to form a neural pathway tend literally to stick together (Bear *et al.*, 1996). There are molecules termed 'cell-adhesion molecules' on the surface of growing axons and these bind axons together.

Cell life and death

During development, a relatively large percentage of neurons die (Edelman, 1987). This can vary from 20% to 80%, depending on the region of nervous system. Some compare this to evolution by natural selection (Chapter 2), with the fittest forms surviving and those neurons and connections that are less fit dying. For neurons, fitness is determined by their success at establishing contact with other cells and passing information, as was shown in Figure 3.14 on p. 60.

An abundance of cells accompanied by selective cell death represents competition, between one cell and its neighbour, for an influence over target areas. Something about making contact helps to protect neurons from destruction. What is it about the target cell that decides its new-found neighbour's life or death?

Physical contact itself might be enough to secure the fate of some neurons. A life-giving chemical, termed a **neurotrophic factor** (or 'chemotrophic factor'), is secreted by target cells and taken into cells with which they make contact (Purves, 1994).

In some neuron–target interactions, a specific neurotrophic factor termed **nerve growth factor** (NGF) has been identified (Purves, 1994). Among other places, it acts within the sympathetic branch of the ANS (Chapter 3). NGF

produced in target cells in smooth muscle is taken up by axons that innervate them and is transported to the cell body. It exerts survival-promoting effects on the presynaptic neuron.

In the absence of a neurotrophic signal, **programmed cell death** (PCD), also termed 'apoptosis', can occur (Oppenheim, 1999). The systematic death of large numbers of cells has functional significance for the establishment of an effective nervous system. In many cases PCD is the result of the expression of 'suicide genes' that initiate the cell's own self-destruction. It appears that they trigger the clearance of what amounts to the refuse of a non-functional cell and thereby allow recycling of its useful chemical constituents.

Damage to an afferent input during development is usually associated with atrophy of its target region in the brain (Purves, 1994). Development of sensory areas of the brain requires a minimal level of appropriate input.

Establishing physical contact can be a necessary, but not sufficient, condition for the continued existence of the extensions of the neuron that have made contact. A synapse might need to be operative, in conveying messages, for a survival-enhancing effect of contact to be felt (Figure 6.5(h),(i)).

Synaptic restructuring

As just noted, when a growing axon meets its target cell, it stops extending. Synaptic contact is made and this contact tends to consolidate the link in the form of structuring the synapse (Lichtman *et al.*, 1999). Rather as whole neurons live or die according to their experience during development, so synapses are strengthened or eliminated as a result of their connections and functioning in terms of transmitting messages (Chapters 3 and 4). Transmitting messages tends to strengthen, as a self-reinforcing effect.

Seen in a broader context of influences, the life or death of a synapse and thereby part or whole of a neuron can depend upon interactions between the animal and its external environment (Rosenzweig *et al.*, 1996), represented by Figure 6.2. Suppose that the survival of a particular neuron depends upon its establishment as part of a functioning neural circuit. Whether a circuit functions or not can depend upon the motor output side and behavioural consequences. That is, behaviour causes changing sensory stimulation, which provides an input to developmental processes. The fate of the individual neuron is locked into its role as part of the whole system (Grobstein, 1988).

So much for the general points. We now consider some representative cases of the development of neurons in the context of the neural systems of which they form a part and the behaviour with which they are associated.

Section summary

1 Viewed at a cellular level, there are six stages to development:

   (a) Neurogenesis: repeated cell division, the formation of neurons from general precursor cells.
   (b) Migration: the movement of neurons from their place of origin to their destination.
   (c) Differentiation: distinct types of neuron are formed from a standard precursor neuron.
   (d) Synaptogenesis: the formation of synaptic connections between neurons.
   (e) Selective death of neurons.
   (f) Synaptic reorganization: changes in the strength of synaptic connections.

2 The development of neurons is a function of intrinsic factors as well as their immediate environment.

3 Induction refers to the effect on one neuron of events in neighbouring neurons.

4 Growth cones have a role in 'navigating' the course of a growing axon.

5 Target cells attract axons.

6 Neuronal survival can depend upon a neurotrophic factor secreted by target cells, e.g. nerve growth factor.

Test your knowledge

(Answers on page 176)

6.5 Which two of the following suggest the strengthening of a synaptic link by the establishment of a functional connection? (i) An increase in number of postsynaptic receptors, (ii) a decrease in number of postsynaptic receptors, (iii) an increase in number of presynaptic vesicles, (iv) a decrease in number of presynaptic vesicles.

6.6 Which of the following classes of neuron is most likely to find itself attracted to a smooth muscle cell? (i) Dopaminergic, (ii) serotonergic, (iii) cholinergic.

6.2

Development of neurons, neural systems and behaviour

Introduction

Over the course of development, how do the changing properties of neurons and their interconnections give rise to changes in behaviour and cognition? How do feedback effects from behaviour and the environment act upon neural structures? This section addresses these issues.

According to contemporary understanding, developmental changes in behaviour and cognition are *bound to be* associated with changes in the brain. So, can psychologists demonstrate the nature of psychological development and *how* this depends upon the changing biological process? Non-invasive technologies (Chapter 5) for studying the brain permit a picture of the changing activity of its different regions (Fischer and Rose, 1994). Psychologists can try to relate this to both changing neural interconnections and to cognitive and behavioural changes. In some cases, changes in gross electrical activity in regions of cortex can be related to changes in synaptic growth and pruning and to cognitive development.

When does development cease? Is it when the animal is mature, as suggested by the analogy of a ball rolling down a hill and arriving at the ground? This is one possible definition. However, adult nervous systems are not static and some of the same kinds of reorganization of neural connections that occur during development are also seen in the adult (Purves, 1994). When a change occurs in an adult, e.g. damage to an axon, some compensatory reactions are seen (Whatson and Sterling, 1998). The analogy with building would suggest that, even after the house is complete, some repairs and extensions might occur, using similar principles to those used in its initial construction. Learning is an example of plasticity ('malleability') that is retained in adulthood. So, this section considers a continuity of principles that give plasticity to developing systems and, in a more limited way, to adult systems.

Neuron–neuron connections

General

When new demands are placed upon an adult, neural plasticity can sometimes be seen. For example, the female mammal is posed new problems when she suckles young for the first time. In rat mothers, neurons within regions of the somatosensory cortex are triggered via sensory input derived from tactile stimulation at the nipples. The cortical area concerned increases in size when suckling begins (Xerri *et al.*, 1994).

There can be competition between axons to innervate a target neuron. An example of this in a mature system is illustrated in Figure 6.7 (Purves, 1994). In (a), three axons (1, 2 and 3) innervate three target neurons (1', 2' and 3'). In (b), axon 2 is cut such that the innervation of neuron 2' is lost. In response (part (c)), sprouting occurs, triggered by chemical factors released from neuron 2'. That is to say, loss of innervation of neuron 2' (termed **denervation**) provokes the formation of new axon branches from neurons 1 and 3. The control of 2' by 1 and 3 is not necessarily permanent. If 2 re-grows, it can reinnervate 2' and displace the innervation by axons 1 and 3 (part (d)).

An example of competition for control of a target is provided by the developing visual system, discussed next.

The visual system

In the developing human visual system, the connections that form between neurons depend upon activity within the system, which is initially triggered by light (Blakemore, 1973; Hubel and Wiesel, 1965). So, what are the developmental processes that bring this system into being? Before answering this, let us digress briefly to consider the properties of the adult visual system, which we seek to explain.

Figure 6.8 should remind you of the neural connections from retinal ganglion cells (forming the optic nerve), to the lateral geniculate nucleus and then to the visual cortex. Note the cross-over of some axons of retinal ganglion cells at the optic chiasm. Thereby, each hemisphere derives inputs from each eye.

Electrical recordings can be made from cortical neurons while each eye is stimulated with light. The cortical neuron can then be categorized according to the strength of input to it. This ranges from evenly binocular, i.e. being driven with equal weighting by either the ipsilateral eye (that on same side as the brain region) or contralateral eye (that on opposite side to the brain region under consideration), to heavily monocular, i.e. being driven predominantly by input coming from either ipsilateral or contralateral eye.

Figure 6.9 shows the inputs to a large sample of neurons in the visual cortex and compares normal development (part (a)) with the situation in which a squint has been produced in one eye (part (b)). In part (a), most neurons are binocularly driven (groups 3 and 4), while some (group 1) are driven only by the contralateral eye and others (group 2) are mainly contralaterally driven. Some (group 7) are driven only by the ipsilateral eye. In part (b) relatively few neurons are driven equally by both eyes. A large number are influenced by only one eye.

It seems that in order for a cortical neuron to be captured by an input from both eyes, corresponding regions of the retina need to provide input to it. As you look at a detail within the present *word* in the text, its image falls on each retina. Neurons from this same region project to cortical neurons and activate them. Hence, firing of cortical neurons represents an integration of the detail of information within *word* in the two eyes. If the eyes are unable to perform this

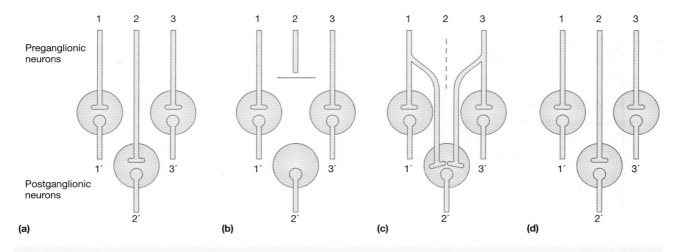

Figure 6.7 Growth of axon branches and synapses following denervation: (a) intact system, (b) denervation of neuron 2', (c) sprouting of axon terminals from 1 and 3, and (d) reinnervation from axon 2.

Source: after Purves (1994, p. 59).

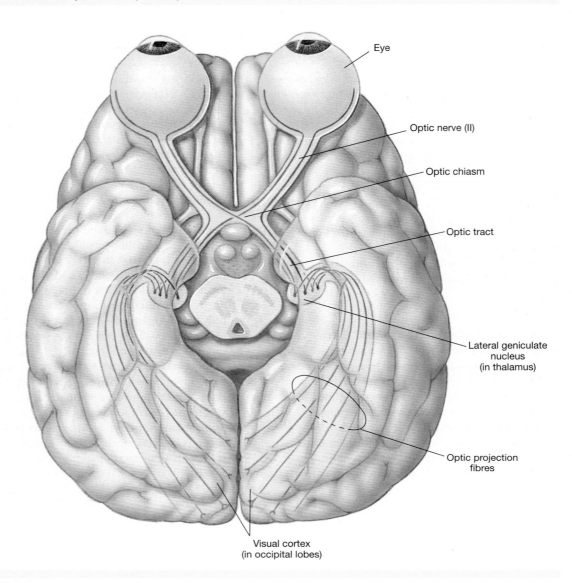

Figure 6.8 Visual pathways.

Source: Martini *et al.* (2000, Fig.15–23, p. 407).

integration because a squint disrupts eye movements, then one dominant connection will tend to capture all of the input to the cortical neuron.

Neuron–muscle connections

Introduction

There is plasticity in the developing neuron–muscle connections and also some plasticity remaining in these connections in adults. Adult muscles develop with exercise, whereby the size of existing muscle cells increases and new

cells are formed. Their innervation derives from sprouting of neighbouring axon branches (see Figure 6.10).

Spontaneous movement

A necessary condition for movement is the establishment of functional synapses between motor neurons and muscles. As evidence for the early appearance of such links, every mother knows that the foetus is not passive but shows considerable motor activity. During **gestation** (the period from fertilization to birth or hatching), the embryos of all species that have been studied exhibit movement at some stage

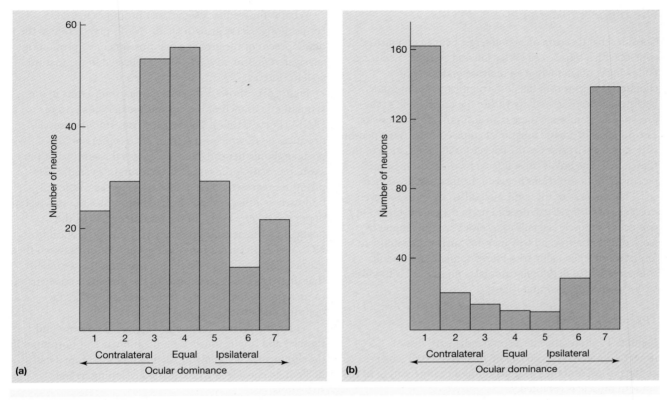

Figure 6.9 Histograms showing the responses of neurons in the visual cortex of adult cats: (a) normal and (b) after a squint has been produced. *Source*: Hubel and Wiesel (1965, Fig. 5, p. 1049).

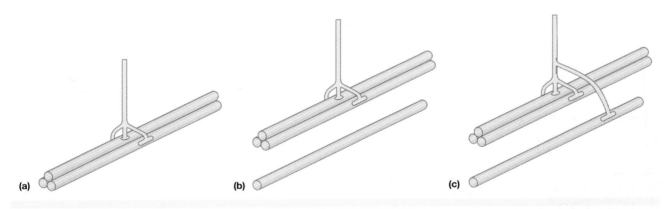

Figure 6.10 Sprouting of axon branches to innervate newly formed muscle fibres: (a) original system, (b) development of new muscle fibre and (c) extension of axon branch to innervate new fibre.

(Hamburger, 1963). For example, chicks show responsiveness to sensory stimulation prior to hatching. They also exhibit coordinated activity and some spontaneity (Provine, 1988).

Early spontaneous movements appear to be random but then coordination is imposed on this. Given the array of spontaneous movements, Robinson and Smotherman (1988) suggest a selection process by which certain are chosen, comparable to the developmental selection of neurons and synapses (discussed earlier).

The triggers to survival

Consider that the axon of a cholinergic neuron establishes contact with a muscle cell (Whatson and Sterling, 1998). Following contact, there is an increase in density of cholinergic receptors at the postsynaptic membrane and heightened electrical activity within the muscle cell. At the presynaptic membrane there is an accumulation of vesicles. The presence of a basic functional connection between neuron and muscle then serves as the trigger for differentiation of the muscle cell. The link is consolidated by chemical messages passing in both directions between the functionally joined cells. The chances of the continued differentiation and even existence of each cell can depend upon the establishment of contact. If a muscle cell fails to receive a synaptic input, it stops differentiating and will later die. Such vulnerability to loss of input is the hallmark of development. In an adult, compared with a developing animal, a muscle cell is less likely to die when synaptic input is lost.

The adult system

Figure 6.11 shows the effects on dendrites of loss of innervation to a target cell. Note their retraction when contact is lost and their regeneration once innervation of the smooth muscle is regained.

What is the feedback signal that promotes neural connections? Nerve growth factor (NGF) plays a role in the development of the growing nervous system by promoting survival of neurons. NGF is also implicated in the mature system (Purves, 1994).

Figure 6.12 shows a suggestion regarding axons in the sympathetic branch of the autonomic nervous system (ANS) (Purves, 1994). The target tissue, smooth muscle, produces NGF, which is taken up by receptors on the postganglionic neuron. NGF promotes the survival of the axon innervating the target. If the axon is severed, NGF promotes regrowth. NGF is also transported to the cell body, where it has several effects. It promotes the survival of dendrites (Figure 6.11). In the presence of NGF, the postganglionic neuron produces a different chemical from NGF, which, in turn, promotes the connection between the preganglionic and postganglionic neurons. It is assumed that there is a chain reaction with the preganglionic neuron in turn producing a trophic factor that influences the neurons that make synapses upon it.

So far, the present chapter has looked at neurons and muscles and briefly touched on the influence of hormones in development. The following section looks in more detail at hormones, considering links with developing neural structures.

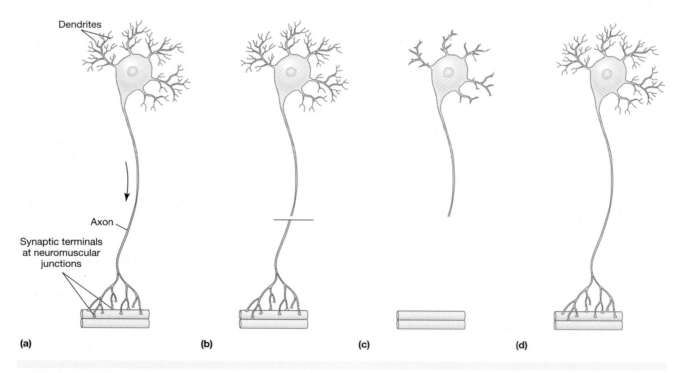

Figure 6.11 Effects on a neuron's dendrites of the loss of innervation of a target by a neuron's axon: (a) normal, (b) immediately after loss, (c) two weeks after loss and (d) after regeneration of the axon and restoration of innervation.

Source: after Purves (1994, p. 62).

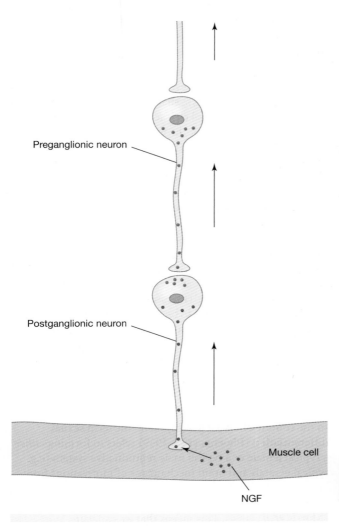

Preganglionic neuron

Postganglionic neuron

Muscle cell

NGF

Figure 6.12 Feedback effects triggered by a target.

Source: after Purves (1994, p. 66).

Section summary

1 Changes in neurons and their interconnections can be associated with changing properties of nervous systems and then to changes in cognition and behaviour.

2 Similar principles to those underlying early development also apply (in a more limited way) to plasticity in adults.

3 Stages of psychological development can sometimes be associated with identifiable changes in the nervous system.

4 In adults, as in developing systems, structural and functional connections tend to exert a self-reinforcing effect.

5 In the absence of such connections, links tend to get weakened.

6 There are regulatory processes such that, when an input is missing, other sources of input can increase their effects and tend to take over.

Test your knowledge

(Answers on page 176)

6.7 In Figure 6.8, the neurons represented by green in the half of the brain to the left of the figure receive which kind of input from the eye? (i) Ipsilateral, (ii) contralateral.

6.8 With reference to Figure 6.9, there is a different weight of contralateral, ipsilateral and equal control over cortical neuron activity comparing parts (a) and (b). What is the description of the neurons (which involves their anatomical location) that innervate such cortical neurons and thereby provide such a different weight of input comparing part (a) and (b)?

6.3

Hormones and development

Introduction

Chapters 2 and 3 introduced hormones: chemicals secreted into a blood vessel at one location and transported in the blood to another location, where they occupy receptors and produce action. However, there is a role to be considered now in addition to this so-called **activational effect**: the role of these same hormones in development.

Organizational and activational effects

Hormonal effects have traditionally been divided into **organizational effects** and activational effects (see Fitch and Denenberg, 1998). An organizational effect is a permanent, or semi-permanent, change in the *structure* of part of the nervous system that occurs (most often) during development as a result of hormones.

Figure 3.28 (p. 70) showed occupation of receptors by hormone at the surface of a cell. This is one mode of action, but another is for the hormone to penetrate the cell and affect the cell's nucleus. Occupation of receptors at the nucleus by hormone affects gene expression and thereby protein synthesis and the formation of new structures, e.g. sprouting of dendrites. Such structural changes (exemplifying organizational effects) were thought to be possible only during a **sensitive period** (sometimes termed a 'critical period') within early development. An example of an organizational effect is the role of sex hormones in the early development of the nervous system, exerting a bias towards one type of adult sexual behaviour or another.

By contrast, an activational effect of a hormone was traditionally thought not to involve structural changes (Fitch and Denenberg, 1998). It would commonly be seen in an adult animal and involve transient changes in the property of neurons. For example, by occupying receptors at a neuron, a hormone might make it easier to generate action potentials. Activational effects either occur for only so long as the hormone is present at the neuron or last for only a short time following removal of the hormone. The *structure* of neurons would be unaffected by whether their receptors are occupied by hormone, even though their functioning is changed.

To some extent, the original distinction still holds: some irreversible structural effects on the developing nervous system contrast with reversible effects in the adult. However, the distinction is not as clear-cut as it once appeared (Fitch and Denenberg, 1998). In some cases, hormones can induce structural changes also in adult nervous systems. For example, maintenance of the structure of the adult hippocampus relies upon the continued presence of hormones.

There is a plasticity of some neural systems throughout life and these are said to be 'permanently transient'. This depends upon the presence of hormones. For example, natural fluctuations in sex hormones in female rats are associated with changing *structures* within the hypothalamus and thereby changes in sexual behaviour (Fitch and Denenberg, 1998). In women, changes in some neural connections follow changes in hormone levels during the menstrual cycle (Stahl, 1997). Thus, a hormonal effect is described as lying somewhere on a continuum (that qualification seems to tell the story of psychology!) rather than being within one of two distinct categories of organizational or activational.

The development of the brain depends on the presence of circulating hormones (see Gould *et al.*, 1991). For example, the hippocampus contains receptors for hormones of gonadal origin (the **gonads** are the male testes and female ovaries) and hormones secreted from the adrenal gland among others. Changes in their levels can affect the development of the hippocampus and thereby affect later learning. For example, an animal deficient in hormone might have fewer dendritic spines and less chance for plasticity of connections.

Sexual development

Introduction

As a general term applicable across species, the term **sexual development** refers to the development of sex organs and neural systems underlying sexual attraction and behaviour, as well as secondary sexual characteristics such as, in the case of humans, the breaking of the male voice.

Our biological sex is determined by chromosomes (Chapter 2). As one combination of chromosomes, the cells of a normal male have an X and a Y chromosome. Those of the female have two X chromosomes. This is fixed at fertilization and remains the same throughout life. In the period shortly following fertilization, the structures that will later come to underlie the reproductive system (e.g. testes, ovaries, brain mechanisms) have the potential to develop into a male or female form. When investigators compare genetic males and females at a very early stage, termed the 'sexually indifferent stage' (Reinisch and Sanders, 1992), these structures are found to be identical. Initially, the term 'gonad' refers to an organ that can become either testis or ovary. The gonad, as with the rest of the reproductive structures, is initially described as *undifferentiated*. The structures later become differentiated.

Differentiation

In the context of sexual development, the term **sexual differentiation** (Phoenix *et al.*, 1959) refers to forming *either* a typical female *or* a typical male reproductive system (e.g. typical genitals and brain mechanisms of motivation) from an undifferentiated precursor structure. Sexual development has some striking similarities across species of mammal (Morris *et al.*, 2004). This means that we can gain considerable insight into the human process by studying rats. However, any extrapolation must be done with caution, since, of course, humans have a unique sexual self-identity and culture. What triggers differentiation?

As a general feature across species, in early development, a gene on the Y chromosome in males will normally induce the gonads to become testes. They release a class of hormone termed **androgen**, which (acting with other factors) causes the reproductive system to take the male form. Of the androgen class, testosterone is regarded as the principal one. In the absence of the Y chromosome and thereby the absence of secretions of androgens at the typically male levels, the gonads normally become ovaries and the reproductive system takes the female form (Reinisch and Sanders, 1992).

Before birth and shortly afterwards as part of differentiation, hormones play a role in establishing the structure of the CNS processes that later underlie sexual behaviour, as well as a variety of behaviours not directly related to reproduction (Fitch and Denenberg, 1998). With a focus on rats, researchers have established a principal site of the action of testosterone as being a nucleus of the preoptic area of the hypothalamus (POA) (Morris *et al.*, 2004). See Chapter 5, Figure 5.32, p. 128. (In this sense, the term 'nucleus' is used to refer to a collection of cell bodies forming a distinct structure within the CNS.) This nucleus is termed the **sexually dimorphic nucleus**, meaning that it has two ('di') different *morphologies* or structures when comparing male rats and females. So, the structure is abbreviated as SDN-POA. It is several times larger in males than females. Such differential development of the male nervous system is a feature of what is termed **masculinization** and is a result of the action of testosterone. In females, natural cell death occurs in this nucleus, a process that is inhibited by the local hormonal environment in the case of the male.

In some species, androgens pass across the cell membrane of neurons in regions such as the SDN-POA and attach to receptors in the cell's nucleus (sorry – but note the abrupt switch in meaning of the term 'nucleus'). These neurons later form part of the motivational processes underlying sexual behaviour. However, in other species (e.g. rats), androgens are converted chemically to oestradiol (yes – it is as if nature set out to confuse us), which then occupies receptors (Fitch and Denenberg, 1998). This conversion is termed **aromatization**. See Figure 6.13. Androgens or their aromatized product alter the expression of genes within the cell. As a developmental effect, this causes, for example, cells to grow or die, to survive when they would otherwise die, to extend dendrites or to form synapses. In females, oestrogen hormones play a role in differentiation.

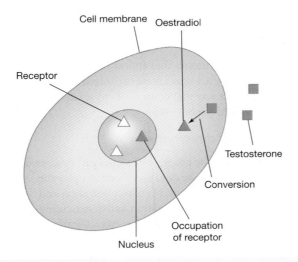

Figure 6.13 Entry of an androgen (testosterone) to the inside of a neuron of the male rat. In this case, it is then converted to oestradiol. Oestradiol occupies receptors at the nucleus, which then triggers the action of masculinization of the neuronal systems so affected.

As determinants of adult sexual preference and behaviour, the social context (e.g. maternal behaviour) plays a role in interaction with these early hormonal influences. For example, in humans, there can be different reactions towards the growing child depending upon whether it possesses male or female genitalia (Reinisch and Sanders, 1992).

Let us consider the kind of neural processes contained within the SDN-POA. In rats, the nervous systems of both males and females possess the basic processes (neural circuits) that underlie the later performance of both male sexual roles (e.g. mounting and thrusting) and female sexual roles (e.g. assuming an arched receptive posture). Depending upon the early hormonal environment, one or both of such behaviour types, masculine and feminine, can be observed later in either sex. That is, the neural circuits can be more or less strengthened or weakened and thereby more or less reactive to a given stimulus depending upon the early hormonal environment. This environment normally exerts a bias in one direction.

Presumably, the basis of such sexual differentiation is that certain synapses between neurons can be strengthened or weakened, hence making more or less effective connections within the circuit. See Figure 6.14. The neural circuit of which 1→1' forms a part might underlie mounting, whereas that involving 3→3' might underlie a receptive posture.

A nervous system that has a strong potential to trigger typical male behaviour is termed 'masculinized' and one with a strong potential to trigger female behaviour is said to be 'feminized', a process termed **feminization** (Reinisch and Sanders, 1992). In males, testosterone secreted by the testes has a masculinizing and defeminizing effect on such CNS structures. This is similar to its effect on the genitals, described earlier. In rats, brain structures are given a bias towards playing a role in typical male mating and away from the typical female pattern. See Figure 6.15(a).

A hormonal environment involving an absence of testosterone results in *demasculinization* and *feminization* and shapes the normal process that underlies female sexual behaviour. See Figure 6.15(b). Normal females (and males denied access at this early developmental stage to testicular hormones) show a bias towards female behaviour and away from male behaviour. Female rats and guinea pigs exposed early in life to androgens tend to show more male-typical behaviour and less female-typical behaviour when adult (Beach, 1975; Phoenix *et al.*, 1959).

How do investigators know that the effects can occur in either sex? They can observe the effects of, for example, artificially subjecting a female rat to male hormones, by injecting the mother during pregnancy with the hormones that exert a masculinizing effect in males. This increases the likelihood that female offspring will exhibit the male mating pattern when adult.

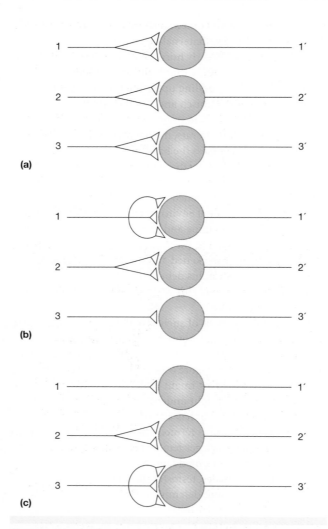

Figure 6.14 Some simple neuronal connections. (a) Initial, undifferentiated form, showing excitatory (neurons 1 → 1', 2 → 2' and 3 → 3') synapses. (b) Form changed by hormone exposure. Note strengthening of 1 → 1' and weakening of 3 → 3'. 2 → 2' remains unchanged. (c) Different change induced by a different hormonal environment. Note converse effect from (b): strengthening of 3 → 3' and weakening of 1 → 1'.

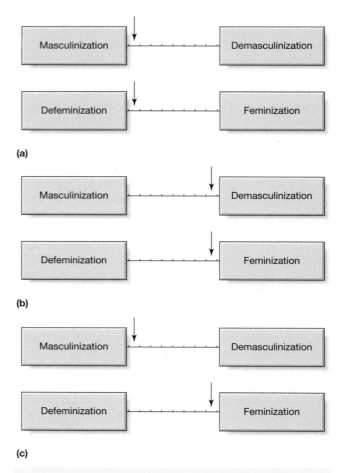

Figure 6.15 Sexual differentiation: (a) masculinization and defeminization, (b) demasculinization and feminization and (c) masculinization but no defeminization.

Although normally, masculinization and defeminization, or their converse, occur in parallel (Figures 6.15(a) and (b)), they can be independent. The hormonal environment can induce one process but not the other. For example, an animal might be masculinized but not defeminized, thus having a strong potential to exhibit both forms of behaviour, e.g. mounting and adopting the receptive position (Tobet and Fox, 1992) (Figure 6.15(c)).

These organizational effects of hormones can occur only at a particular stage of development (i.e. before and just after birth). Hence, psychologists would refer to there being a 'sensitive period' ('window of opportunity') during which they can occur. Hormones that appear following sexual maturity normally act upon these organized structures to activate them in a way that contributes to sexual behaviour (McCarthy and Albrecht, 1996).

Human sexual development

To what extent can the general principles just described also be applied to humans, or does social context play the dominant role? The actions, (1) masculinization and defeminization or (2) feminization and demasculinization, might occur somewhat as in other species. Clearly, there are normally two different sequences (genes) → (hormones) → (genitalia), which distinguish males and females. In the human brain, there is some difference between males and females, particularly in the preoptic area, analogous to sexual dimorphism in other species (Tobet and Fox, 1992).

However, it would be wrong to see genes and environment as two *independent* categories. Thus, the possession of different genitalia can then trigger different reactions, expectations and self-images. It is possible that some gender differences in sex role, etc. arise from assuming gender identities (Morris *et al.*, 2004). The question of just how much human sex differences reflect early hormone-dependent sexual differentiation of the brain remains to be answered unambiguously.

After having exerted developmental effects, sex hormones remain relatively inactive until puberty. At puberty there is a further input from gonadal hormone to sexual development. For example, in girls the breasts enlarge, whereas in boys, the voice breaks.

Reinisch and Sanders (1992) refer to a 'multiplier effect' in the determination of human sex differences. This term summarizes much of the material of the present section. At fertilization, the only difference between sexes is in their chromosomes. In males, there then occurs differentiation of the testes, with production of testosterone. Comparing males and females, this creates different hormonal environments for the developing foetus. These are associated with differences in development of sexual characteristics and CNS processes.

Following birth, the social context interacts with the developing child to produce sex differences. Boys will typically be treated differently from girls. One supposes that humans alone possess the notion of **gender identity**. Normally, at an age of between 2 and 4 years, a child acquires the concept 'I am a girl' or 'I am a boy' (Bancroft, 1989, p. 159). Events in the world, reactions and inner feelings are subsequently interpreted in terms of the concept. Hormonal and social influences play roles in forming this concept but psychologists imagine that, once acquired, it biases the interpretation that is placed upon experiences and knowledge related to sexuality. These different treatments and expectations will be encoded in the growing child's nervous system.

At puberty, the adult level of hormones is secreted and this promotes the development of sexual characteristics which serve to enlarge differences between the sexes. On the basis of their physique, muscle mass and secondary sexual characteristics, etc., boys will again typically be treated differently from girls (Mazur and Booth, 1998).

Unusual hormonal conditions

In some cases, there are unusual hormonal effects in humans ('natural experiments') and important clues regarding the role of hormones can be obtained by studying individuals who show these. For example, before birth some girls are exposed to high levels of testosterone produced by the adrenal gland, termed **congenital adrenal hyperplasia** (CAH) (Berenbaum, 1999). Girls with CAH show some masculinization of the genitals and a tendency to engage in male-typical play. On becoming adult, most girls with CAH are heterosexual but a larger percentage is homosexual as compared with controls. There is a shift towards male-typical occupations. Could this be because of parental treatment, the girls' own learned self-image or a hormonal masculinization

of the brain? We don't know, but Berenbaum argues for early masculinization of the brain.

Some genetic males (i.e. with XY chromosomes) produce normal levels of testosterone but have a dysfunction in the gene coding for the androgen receptor, termed a **complete androgen insensitivity syndrome** (CAIS) (Hines *et al.*, 2003). Hence, androgens cannot exert their effect. At birth, CAIS individuals appear to be girls and are unambiguously treated as this. As adults they have female bodily characteristics and assume a female gender identity, with a sexual orientation comparable to that of control women. Thus, as with rats, hormonal environment overrides what might otherwise be expected to occur based simply on chromosomal sex.

Section summary

1 Certain hormones have organizational and activational effects.

2 The distinction between early organizational and later activational roles is relative rather than absolute.

3 During the sensitive period, hormones exert an organizational effect on sexual organs and neural structures. In the adult, hormones exert an activational effect on these structures.

4 Androgens play a role in masculinization and defeminization.

5 Oestrogens secreted by the ovaries play a role in feminization.

6 There are some peculiarly human features of development that apply to sexuality, such as conscious awareness of gender identity.

Test your knowledge

(Answers on page 176)

6.9 Complete the following sentence: 'In order for a hormone to be able to target receptors at the cell nucleus, it must be able to cross the cell ____'.

6.10 Which of the following effects would be described as organizational and which activational? (i) A hormone induces the growth of new dendrites, (ii) for so long as the hormone is present at receptors on the neurons' surface, there is a facilitation of the generation of action potentials.

The brain: cognitive and social development

This section relates changes in brain processes to changes in cognition and behaviour. It also considers briefly social development. It starts with a focus on development of the cortex seen in the context of the development of other brain structures.

Cortical and subcortical structures and their interaction

The normal time-scale of development

In human newborns, a PET scan (Chapter 5) can be used to measure local glucose metabolism in brain regions (Chugani, 1994). The regions that are most active metabolically and, by implication most developed, are the primary sensory-motor cortex, thalamus, brain stem and cerebellum. These structures are commonly described as 'phylogenetically old', meaning that, relative to, say, the prefrontal cortex (Chapter 5) they emerged at an early stage of evolution. The limited behavioural repertoire of newborn humans is controlled predominantly by subcortical structures, including those underlying reflexes (e.g. the grasp response) organized at a brain stem level.

The pattern of metabolic activity across brain regions of newborns is sometimes seen in older children who have suffered brain damage. In the latter case, an abnormal persistence of so-called primitive reflexes is also observed. This points to a failure of cortical mechanisms to exert control over subcortical processes (Chugani, 1994).

In the first year, cortical development is indicated by the increasing formation of synaptic links, the appearance of more adult EEG patterns and an increase in cortical glucose metabolism (Schulte, 1974). Functional development, in terms of visuo-spatial integration with the motor system, corresponds to anatomical development as reflected in the level of local glucose metabolism. Chugani (p. 159) remarks that: 'the ontogeny of glucose metabolic patterns proceeds in phylogenetic order, with functional maturation of older anatomical structures preceding that of newer areas'. The last area to show maturation is the frontal cortex, corresponding to the acquisition of so-called higher cognitive abilities, discussed next. The cortex has greater plasticity than subcortical structures and is more strongly sensitive to experience (Elman et al., 1996).

The plasticity of cortical connections is central to ideas about development, e.g. the role of genes and environment (Elman et al., 1996). Distinct cortical regions normally emerge, each dedicated to processing only visual, auditory or somatosensory information (Chapter 5). Is this dedication specified genetically or the result of a combination of genetics and environmental stimulation during development?

Scientists investigate what happens when a sensory input is abnormal. Neurons can be taken over by other sensory inputs, so that boundaries between cortical areas show plasticity. For example, regions that process the spoken word in people with hearing can be 'captured' by the visual system, so as to process visuo-manual information associated with sign language in deaf children. In other words, cortical boundaries depend in part upon sensory inputs.

We now look at a specific example of cortical development in the context of the input from subcortical structures.

Vision: an example of cortical and subcortical interactions

Starting at a very early age, the human infant has a tendency to look at faces. The adaptive value is clear: faces signal vital information. What kind of process underlies this and how does it develop? In the beginning, the process appears to be organized at a subcortical level. Experiments have shown that features bearing even some crude resemblance to those of a face trigger attention (Elman et al., 1996). Of course, in the real world the initial trigger would be an actual human face. Using subcortical processes as a base, this focus of attention upon certain features possessed by a face leads to a build-up of more refined cortically based representations of the unique features of a human face.

There has been a tendency to explain this behaviour as either learnt or innate (see critique by Elman et al., 1996). Thus, it represents respectively the outcome of either a history of reinforcement from staring at an arbitrary object or the product of an innate face recognition process. The existence of the disorder **prosopagnosia**, a defect primarily in face recognition in brain-damaged adults, has been used as evidence for an innate face recognition module.

An alternative explanation takes a middle course between the extremes. Face recognition becomes 'modularized', i.e. brain circuits become specialized for this as the child gains experience with faces. As Elman et al. (p. 116) express it: 'Some minimal face-specific predispositions give development a kick start in this domain'.

This kind of analysis does more than simply assert the relatively uncontroversial point that both genes and environment are involved. Rather, it shows the nature of their interdependence.

We now turn to the development of one particular cortical region.

In the spirit of evolutionary psychology, it is sometimes argued that the localization of function, i.e. area x has responsibility for processing information X, is evidence for the innate genetic specification of brain structure. To use a favoured expression, 'innate systems have inherited their own dedicated neural architecture' (see Elman *et al.*, 1996, p. 378 for critique).

As Elman *et al.* somewhat ironically point out, with the advent of PET scans investigators are finding an ever-increasing number of such apparently dedicated systems. For instance, in chess-masters, specific regions of the brain are active at particular points in the game. Yet surely no one would suggest that dedicated chess-playing modules are genetically specified!

The role of representations

Introduction

An aspect of development consists in acquiring the ability to utilize *representations* of events (Piaget, 1954) (Chapter 5). Prior to this, the animal is dependent upon the stimuli themselves to trigger behaviour. For representations to control behaviour, they need to be held 'on-line' in the absence of the corresponding sensory stimulation. For example, when an object goes out of sight, continued pursuit of it depends upon a particular sort of memory, a representation, of the missing object.

There are several tasks which require (a) representations of events, (b) a focus of attention on a particular representation and (c) the suppression of any tendency to respond to other features. The fact that, in children, mature performance on these tasks appears at roughly the same age, suggests maturation of a common underlying process (Diamond *et al.*, 1994a, b). For example, in the **object permanence task**, a child observes an object being hidden behind a screen. Early in development the child acts as if such objects that have gone out of sight cease to exist. At a later stage, the child acts on the basis that they still exist (Piaget, 1954). If the object is to be retrieved, the child needs to act on the basis (a 'representation') of its existence and to inhibit any rival tendencies. This skill is acquired at a stage of development.

Brain regions

Development of the prefrontal cortex is closely implicated in the object permanence task (Fischer and Rose, 1994). EEG activity (Chapter 5) at the prefrontal cortex appears to be an index of the memory being utilized in behaviour; when children succeed in retrieving the object, activation is seen. Those who fail the task do not show activation. Also, on successful performance, an integration of activity between the prefrontal and occipital cortices is seen, suggestive that the solution involves simultaneous utilization of sensory information (e.g. the cover and the hand) and representations (of the hidden object). A rapid growth of synapses in the prefrontal cortex corresponds to acquisition of this capacity and the appearance of the associated EEG pattern.

The **A-not-B test** is a good measure of one feature of cognitive development and can be related to development of the brain (Diamond, 1996), as follows. A human infant is seated before a table which contains two identical wells. The experimenter places a favourite toy in one well, either to the left or the right, while the child observes this. The wells are then covered. A delay is imposed (e.g. 0–10 seconds) and then the child permitted to reach. If the child reaches to the correct target, the hidden toy is revealed. After the child has succeeded at the task a few times, the well in which the toy is hidden is reversed. Following reversal, children tend to make the mistake of persisting with the original choice rather than reversing. Increasing the length of the delay makes the task more difficult. With increasing age, children get more proficient: a longer delay is needed in order to induce them to make the error of repeating what they did on earlier trials.

A failure to perform this task correctly is seen by human infants of age 7.5–9 months, infant macaque monkeys of age 1.5–2.5 months and adult macaques who have suffered bilateral removal of the dorsolateral prefrontal cortex (Diamond *et al.*, 1994a, b). After suffering prefrontal brain damage, adult humans also experience difficulty. How do we explain this? Reaching to A earns a reward, and, with repeated experiences, there is a strengthening of this tendency. Following a move of the bait to well B, success requires inhibition of the tendency to reach to A. Diamond (1996, p. 1485) suggests that:

it is when we must act in a different way than our first inclination and when at least some of the information needed for action must be held in mind that dorsolateral prefrontal cortex is most clearly required.

The ability of adult monkeys to perform tasks that involve representations depends upon dopaminergic (DA) projections to the prefrontal cortex. Development of the ability corresponds to increases in levels of DA in the prefrontal cortex. In humans, it appears that this structure is not fully mature until the age of 10 years.

Adult cognition and brain plasticity

A much-publicized study concerned the spatial abilities and brains of London taxi-drivers (Maguire *et al.*, 2000). These men and women have to pass a formidable test on their knowledge of London streets and how best to get from A to B. From evidence on non-human species, the hippocampus has been implicated in spatial skills (Chapter 5). Could it be that London taxi-drivers have developed particular biologically identifiable changes in the hippocampus, corresponding to the functional demands of their task? Using an MRI study, Maguire *et al.* found enlargement of the posterior hippocampus in taxi-drivers, compared with controls.

It might be that this change does not represent adult plasticity but, rather, individuals with such enlargement and thereby good cognitive skills are attracted to taxi-driving. Maguire *et al.* suggest that this is not the case, since the magnitude of enlargement correlated with the length of time spent driving a taxi.

We now turn to consider development of a particular kind of representation of the world – a social representation.

Social development and autism

A key notion in social development is that children normally acquire what is termed a theory of mind (ToM) of the other (Baron-Cohen, 1999), i.e. the understanding that others have *intentions* in their behaviour (Chapter 5). Successful social interactions depend upon making decisions based upon this assumption, for example, *I think* that *Mary thinks* that the apple is in the box and therefore *I think* she will look there to find it. Some authors argue that there is a dedicated **theory of mind mechanism** (ToMM), which serves to extract information on the intentions and desires of others (Leslie, 1999).

The condition termed **autism** represents a different course of social development. There are deficiencies in the area of social communication and behaviour and failures in the use of the imagination in solving social problems. That is, it represents a deficiency in ToM. Children with autism have difficulty understanding that someone else might have a belief about the world that is different from their own. There is a deficiency specifically of a type of social cognition, in the absence of a more general cognitive deficit. It appears that the ToMM is compromised.

The evidence points to a strong genetic component in autism. So, which brain regions are involved? Based on evidence from brain imaging, a number of regions have been implicated, e.g. the right orbitofrontal cortex and the medial temporal lobe (Salmond *et al.*, 2005). Some evidence arises from posing ToM tasks to controls and seeing which parts of the brain are particularly active. Autistic individuals are then tested to see whether on being presented with the same challenges, the brain regions are differently activated. Evidence suggests differences from controls in terms of the developmental course of the formation of neurons and their interconnection. There could be a relatively low occurrence of programmed cell death in certain structures.

Children with autism are deficient on what might be termed 'folk psychology', i.e. the kind of everyday psychology that involves a theory of mind. However, there is also 'folk physics', the understanding of the movements of physical objects in space. Here children with autism appear to be superior to age-matched controls, as revealed in skills of mechanical manipulation.

Section summary

1. In human newborns, phylogenetically older brain regions tend to be the most active.

2. Phylogenetically older brain regions control more stimulus-driven behaviours.

3. With development, metabolic activity increases in phylogenetically newer regions that underlie cognitive aspects of behaviour.

4. Development involves acquiring both cognitive and social skills.

Test your knowledge

(Answer on page 176)

6.11 Which term accurately completes the following sentence: 'Concerning the dopaminergic projections, the _____ of dopaminergic neurons are located in the prefrontal cortex'. (i) Cell bodies, (ii) axon terminals.

6.4

Atypical development and health issues

This section considers some identifiable factors that can disrupt normal development and the role of biological psychology in understanding them. Studying atypical development provides useful insight into typical development (Munakata *et al.*, 2004).

Nutrition

The developing brain is more vulnerable to disruption from malnutrition than is the adult brain (Rosenzweig *et al.*, 1996). In humans, a positive relationship exists between (1) malnutrition during gestation and up to age 2 years and (2) a lowering of scores in measures of cognitive performance (Rizzo *et al.*, 1997). However, it is difficult to distinguish changes due specifically to malnutrition from other factors involved in social deprivation, such as stresses suffered by the parents and disrupted child-rearing practices. What would appear to distinguish some of these effects is the following observation. At the foetal stage and after birth, children of diabetic mothers, where there is a disturbance of nutrient regulation, exhibit delayed development compared with controls.

Occasionally the tragedy of war provides an 'experiment'. An example is the famine (*Hongerwinter*) suffered by the Dutch in 1944–1945 (Stein *et al.*, 1972). Birth cohorts that had been exposed to famine were compared with birth cohorts that were not exposed. Groups were selected based upon interview data obtained when men were drafted at age 18 into military service. Children in the famine group were born with relatively low weights. However, they did not show a higher frequency of mental retardation compared with the control group, indicating the resilience of the brain. Stein *et al.* point out that the study concerned mothers who had been adequately fed prior to the famine period. It also concerned a relatively short period of time. We should therefore not generalize to conditions of chronic famine. Also other tests might have detected effects. Subsequent research looking at the same population found an increased incidence of schizophrenia when adult (Brown *et al.*, 2000).

Environmental deprivation and enrichment effects

Does the physical environment in which a rat develops have effects on its brain (Bennett, 1976)? Rats were assigned randomly to one of three conditions, standard, impoverished and enriched, at weaning (about 25 days postnatal). Objects located in the enriched environment were changed daily.

Animals differed in a number of measures. Those raised in the enriched condition had higher levels of acetylcholinesterase (AChE) in their brains. This is an enzyme that breaks down ACh (Chapter 4). They also had higher weights of cerebral cortex, especially the occipital cortex (Bennett, 1976; Greenough, 1976). Other brain regions showed little difference between groups. Rearing in an enriched environment is associated with a greater extent of dendritic branching. However, exposure to enriched conditions does not inevitably lead to 'more' in every measure of brain structure. Under some conditions, an increase in dendritic branching is associated with a reduction in the density of dendritic spines (Kolb *et al.*, 1998), a reminder that development can be associated with pruning as well as growing.

Changes in the cerebral cortex are assumed to constitute the principal physical basis of changes in cognition. In general, rodents raised under enriched conditions do better in solving complex maze tasks than do other groups,

apparently by a better ability to utilize cues outside the maze (Greenough, 1976).

It is tempting to extrapolate from this to human educational and cultural practices but caution is in order (Bruer, 1998). Traditionally, the rodent experimental procedures involved extremes and we cannot, in any simple way, extrapolate to differences in, say, areas of a town and conclude that the poor are analogous to impoverished rats. It might be that a wide range of human environments provides adequate sensory stimulation.

One source of evidence on humans comes from studying the brains of children exposed to neglect, or to physical or sexual abuse. Using positron emission tomography, a study was made of socially deprived children raised in Romanian orphanages. It found decreased metabolic activity in frontal and temporal cortex, as well as cognitive deficits, e.g. attention and impulse control (Chugani *et al.*, 2001).

In another study and using magnetic resonance imaging, it was found that children exposed to neglect or abuse had a reduced size of corpus callosum, as compared with controls reared under healthy conditions (Teicher *et al.*, 2004). This structure is vulnerable since its maturation, as measured by the myelination of the axons that form it, is complete only in young adulthood. So, social context appears to play a role in the development of this pathway that links the two hemispheres. Of course, as the authors note, this observation on its own raises issues of lack of experimental control. Could a difference in the behaviour of such children present a cue to trigger abuse? Could there be an inherited tendency to a small brain region and this is also associated with abusive parents? Studies on rhesus monkeys under controlled conditions found a similar effect of an impoverished environment on the corpus callosum, thereby suggesting a causal influence from the environment in humans also.

Social and tactile stimuli

For social species, optimal development depends upon steering a course between the stressful situations of either sensory isolation or overcrowding (Greenough, 1976). Separation of an infant from its caregiver has a detrimental effect on development (Schanberg and Field, 1987). For non-human primates, Harlow and Harlow (1962) showed that deprivation of contact from a caregiver was associated with retarded growth and indices of stress, e.g. increased tendency to show stereotypies (Chapter 2).

In rats, an influence of maternal behaviour on pups was described in Chapter 2: strain differences in levels of aggression. A similar observation is that licking and grooming of rat pups by their mothers influences the development of the hormonal control system involving CRF and ACTH (Chapter 3) (Liu *et al.*, 1997; Meaney *et al.*, 1996).

Figure 6.16 shows an extension of the hormonal system introduced in Figure 3.27(b) (p. 69). CRF is synthesized within a nucleus of the hypothalamus (PVN) and is activated at times of stress. CRF triggers the release of ACTH, which in turn triggers the release of hormones of a class termed 'corticosteroids' from the adrenal gland. The hippocampus (among other structures) contains receptors for corticosteroids. Thereby, corticosteroids inhibit CRF release, a negative feedback effect.

There is developmental plasticity in this system. That is, the sensitivity of the pup's system is established early and depends upon maternal attention. Differences in mothers' behaviour are reflected in differences in the hormonal system of the pups. The biological basis of this is differences in the density of receptors to corticosteroids in the hippocampus. Corticosteroids are essential hormones but in excess are toxic to neural tissue, so possibly differences in their level have important life-long implications for human health (Sapolsky, 1997).

Rat pups subject to stroking tend to exhibit less anxiety when adult than controls. They also have a higher gain of weight and better performance on learning tasks (Schanberg and Field, 1987). Thus, it appears that the development of emotional circuitry in the brain can be influenced by early tactile stimulation. The therapy of tactile stimulation can compensate for some of the damaging effects of brain lesions,

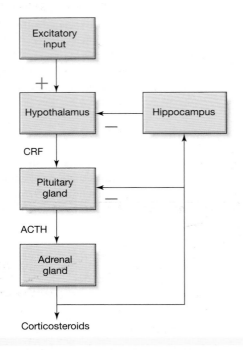

Figure 6.16 The hormonal control of corticosteroid secretion.

as indexed by the loss of cortical neurons (Kolb *et al.*, 1998). Some early studies pointed to enhanced development of human infants subject to supplementary tactile stimulation.

Play and its absence

In most species that exhibit play, there is a characteristic developmental time course, with the frequency of play increasing to a maximum in the juvenile phase and then declining (Panksepp, 1998a). In rats and some other species, deprivation of the opportunity for social play in the period following weaning and up to sexual maturity has detrimental effects on development (Vanderschuren *et al.*, 1997). The deprivation effect can be ameliorated by allowing brief periods of daily play.

Play consists of features of adult social, sexual and aggressive behaviour. Early deprivation does not affect the capacity to exhibit these behaviours when adult but disturbs their control by the normal contexts in which they occur. For instance, deprived animals take much longer than controls to assume a submissive posture when subject to attack by a dominant rat.

Seen in a developmental context, the function of social play appears to be one of facilitating adult social interactions and the formation of social hierarchies. It might also help to acquire the skills of interpreting social signals and facilitate links between species-typical actions (e.g. fighting, submitting) and the motivational control ('contextual') signals that time their expression.

Phenylketonuria revisited

Diamond (1996) investigated the ability of children who suffer from phenylketonuria (PKU) (Chapter 2) and are believed to have a deficit specific to dopamine (DA). PKU is a genetically determined enzymatic disorder, in which children are unable to convert one amino acid, phenylalanine (Phe), into another, tyrosine (Tyr). The blood level of Phe rises to a dangerous level and that of Tyr falls. Low levels of plasma Tyr result in low levels of Tyr in the CNS. DA neurons that project to the prefrontal cortex (discussed in the last section) are particularly sensitive to this.

Children for whom the condition has been diagnosed early and who have received continuous treatment are described as 'early continuous treatment-PKU' (ECT-PKU) individuals. Despite the treatment, they appear to have disruption of DA transmission. There is a range of cognitive impairments in these individuals. IQ is slightly lower than normal. They have difficulties with attention, persistence and problem-solving tasks that involve holding information in memory until a goal is reached and resisting the 'pull' of a familiar stimulus, such as the A-not-B task.

Diamond (1996) notes similarities with adults having damage to the dorsolateral prefrontal cortex, who also have difficulty in utilizing knowledge in controlling behaviour and overriding a prepotent response (Luria and Homskaya, 1964). An example of this is the **Wisconsin card-sorting test** (Figure 6.17). To solve it, participants need to sort cards according to a criterion of either colour or form. The criterion changes at the request of the experimenter. Participants are able to articulate verbally the correct criterion and have the intention to act according to it but get stuck in reacting according to the strongest stimulus–response link.

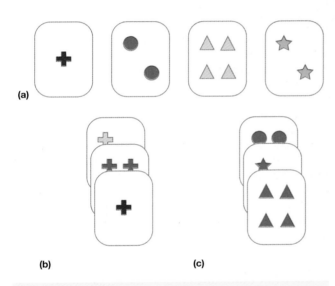

(a)

(b)   (c)

Figure 6.17 The Wisconsin card-sorting test: (a) cards, (b) sorted by shape criterion and (c) by colour criterion.

Section summary

1   Environmental complexity influences brain development of rats.

2   Social isolation can retard growth.

3   In rats, maternal behaviour influences the development of the infant's hormonal control system involving CRF and ACTH.

4   In humans, phenylketonuria (PKU) is associated with a disruption of the development of the prefrontal cortex.

(Answer on page 176)

6.12   Complete the missing brain structure: 'Disruption of the development of axons and associated myelin that make up the _____ disrupts the contralateral transmission of information'.

6.5

Ethology and a comparative perspective

Insights into development can be obtained by comparing species in terms of lifestyle and the problems that they have faced in evolution. Knowledge at this level can then be related to differences in development.

Brain development

Figure 6.18 compares brain development in some species (Dickerson, 1981; Dobbing, 1976). There is a phase of acceleration in growth, termed the 'brain growth spurt'. This occurs at different times relative to birth in different species. Note the contrast between the rat and the guinea pig, which correlates with differences in behaviour following birth. The

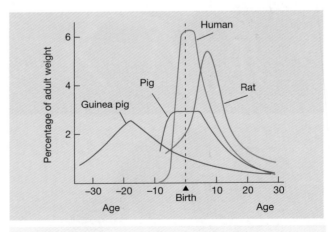

Figure 6.18 Comparison of species in brain development. The time-scale is in units of months for humans, days for the guinea pig and rat and weeks for the pig. Vertical axis is percentage increase in brain mass.

Source: Dobbing (1976, Fig. 2, p. 140).

guinea pig is a **precocial** species, being born relatively competent. The rat by contrast is an **altricial** species, being born dependent upon parental help. So, it can be misleading to compare animals of the same age but in different species. For example, a drug given to the mother just before birth might be harmless for the young guinea pig since brain development is already in an advanced stage. It could prove harmful for the developing human and disastrous for a rat.

The length of development

A striking feature of humans is the enormous time it takes them to reach maturity (on a slightly less serious note, you might like to nominate some personal favourites to illustrate this principle). This is interesting from a functional perspective, since as Elman *et al.* (1996) note, some species are literally up and running almost immediately after birth. In humans, for both offspring and parents, there are enormous costs attached to this length of development, in terms of vulnerability and effort expended in rearing. So what is its 'evolutionary logic'? Development depends upon interactions, both physical and social, and these take time. The period might be needed to permit sufficient opportunity for interactions between young and the environment.

Different species show different lengths of time before they can get up and move as well as achieve a level of independence. What kind of functional considerations underlie these differences?

Source: © Martin Harvey/CORBIS (top); © Ariel Skelley/CORBIS (bottom).

For example, complex social cognition would need to be assimilated before decisions on, say, mate choice are made (again, call on personal anecdotes to illustrate!). Time might be the price of building complexity from a limited store of genetic information.

Open and closed programmes

Introduction

The notion of a **closed programme** and an **open programme** closely relates to the present discussion. In some species, development results in an animal that reacts in a certain situation in a rather fixed species-typical way. Using a computer metaphor, Mayr (1974) argues that this is the result of a closed programme.

Cuckoos lay eggs in the nests of other species. The unwitting foster parents of a variety of different species raise the young adoptees. However, no matter who the foster parent is, the young cuckoo grows up to mate with other cuckoos. Again the specification is closed, i.e. it is open to little or no differential influence by the very different species that raise the young bird.

In some cases, a programme is closed by early experience. The environment can have a feature to which the programme becomes rigidly committed (Elman *et al.*, 1996). (This emphasizes the danger of any gene *versus* environment dichotomy.) Classical ethology made famous one example, **imprinting** (Lorenz, 1981). A newly hatched chick of some species, e.g. the greylag goose, follows the first moving object that it sees. The programme is left open, to be closed by whatever is the characteristic of this object.

The terms 'closed' and 'open' should perhaps be seen not to define two absolutely distinct categories but rather two ranges on a continuum of gene–animal–environment interdependence.

Functional considerations

From a functional perspective, what determines whether evolution will provide closed or open programmes? Animals having a short lifespan, especially invertebrates, have relatively little opportunity to learn by experience and tend to rely more heavily on closed programmes. In such animals, mating sometimes occurs only once and it is important to 'get the act together' on this occasion. In effect, instructions on what to do are inflexibly encoded on the basis of stimulus information.

An advantage of a closed programme is as an isolating mechanism, a way of eliminating mating with non-conspecifics. At best, such mating would waste time and, at worst, tie-up the reproductive process with a non-viable offspring. Mayr (1974, p. 657) summarizes it as: 'Selection should favour the evolution of a closed programme when there is a reliable relationship between a stimulus and only one correct response'.

Imprinting on Konrad Lorenz

Normally, the stimulus on which a bird imprints would be a parent but it can be another species or even Konrad Lorenz himself. The programme is closed by the first exposure, such that the chick will later seek the imprinted stimulus as parent, companion or mate. The programme cannot then be reversed. In one case, as a result of their early exposure to him, chicks persisted in following Lorenz as their object of choice. Popular images of Lorenz show him leading a flock of birds (Figure 6.19).

Figure 6.19 The Nobel Prize-winning Austrian zoologist Konrad Lorenz (1903–1989) being followed by a group of ducklings.
Source: Science Photo Library.

For animals of a longer lifespan, there is often more opportunity to learn and more reliance on open programmes. An open programme is used where crucial information can only be assimilated on the basis of individual experience. Consider, for example, where an animal lives in a colony but specific parent–offspring interaction is needed (e.g. feeding the young). The programme can only be closed by the experience of the individual with its parent (Mayr, 1974). However, mate selection is still often relatively closed.

Section summary

1 Species differ in the dimension of precocial–altricial.

2 We distinguish between closed and open programmes.

Test your knowledge

(Answer on page 176)

6.13 Which of the following would be described as the most precocial? (i) Pig, (ii) rat.

Bringing things together

The development of behaviour reflects developing neural processes but, in turn, development of neural processes depends on behaviour. The information that genes carry is insufficient to complete development. The additional information can only be derived from the internal environment (e.g. establishment of working connections between cells and the production of hormones) and the external environment. In turn, the environment is influenced by the behaviour of the developing organism.

Given the complexity of interactions that determine development, you might wonder whether the role of any factor can ever be understood. Rather than despair, complexity can be the stimulus for experimentation and theory. For example, a role of a hormone can be established but to do so can involve considering both the nervous system and the dynamics of interaction between two animals. Given such tortuously complex dynamic interactions underlying development, you might also have cause to wonder how a viable animal ever emerges. Even more so, how is sufficient consistency of form among conspecifics maintained that they are able to recognize each other as potential sexual partners and produce offspring to continue the consistency? Awe seems an appropriate reaction, as is, in more down-to-earth terms, a consideration of the stabilizing effects of environmental consistencies.

Moving on from development to consider adult systems, the kinds of change in the nervous system that underlie development (e.g. synaptic restructuring) can also be seen in some cases in adult nervous systems. These accompany different functional demands placed at different stages of life.

We asked, how do we distinguish between development and learning, or between maturation and learning? With newer findings, the distinction becomes even more blurred (Elman *et al.*, 1996). The plasticity of the adult nervous system contributes to the blur since we can no longer assume an absolute distinction between early (development) and later changes (learning). The old distinctions between experience-independent (development or maturation) and experience-dependent (learning) are now suspect. Elman *et al.* suggest that we might risk calling the early series of changes consisting of cell division, migration, etc., 'maturation' as distinct from learning. Life seemed simpler before but there is no going back now, so we have to live with complexity and try to better understand it.

Summary of Chapter 6

1   **Development depends upon several layers of interacting factors.**

2   **We have some understanding of how, in principle, genes and environment determine development.**

3   **Development of the nervous system consists of the net production of an increasing number of cells, accompanied by an increasing degree of complexity of these cells and their interconnections.**

4   **The changes in connections between cells associated with development have some similarities with more limited changes ('plasticity') in the adult system. In each case, changes depend upon what role the system of connected cells plays.**

5   **Hormones exert both organizational effects and activational effects on the nervous system and thereby behaviour. Sex hormones exemplify these roles.**

6   **The emergence of cognitive and social skills is associated with identifiable features of the development of the nervous system.**

7   **Atypical development can be contrasted with typical development and links made between developmental outcome, genes and environment.**

8   **Differences in functional demands posed on different species can be linked to differences in the development of their nervous systems.**

Further reading

A good general text is Michel and Moore (1995). For a recent review, see Munakata *et al.* (2004). For theoretical principles, see Elman *et al.* (1996). For the reciprocal relationship between biology and behaviour, see Gottlieb (1998) and Johnston (1987) and, for a fascinating historical and personal context, see Gottlieb (1997b). To link neural development and human brain size, see Deacon (1997). The social and ideological dimension and its link to brain development is discussed by Wexler (2006). Links between brain development and cognition are described by Munakata and Johnson (2006). Blakemore and Frith (2005) relate plasticity of the brain to education. For a good interactive perspective on sexual development, see Hines (2004). For the details of neuronal migration, see Liu and Rao (2004). For links between brain development and behavioural development, see Kagan and Baird (2004). Adult plasticity and neural development are described by Kempermann (2006). Normal brain development and how it can be disrupted by toxic substances is described by Miller (2006).

Signposts

You will meet development again many times in the chapters that follow and we will refer to the developmental/learning type of explanation. It will be useful to keep developmental issues in mind throughout the book. We now turn to look at sensory systems in the next three chapters.

Answers

Explanations for answers to 'test your knowledge' questions can be found on the website **www.pearsoned.co.uk/toates**

6.1   (ii) Phenotype
6.2   (ii) The bottom
6.3   Myelination
6.4   Zygote (or fertilized egg cell); genotypes; phenotypes
6.5   (i) An increase in the number of postsynaptic receptors; (iii) an increase in the number of presynaptic vesicles
6.6   (iii) Cholinergic
6.7   (ii) Contralateral
6.8   LGN cells (lateral geniculate nucleus cells)
6.9   Membrane
6.10 (i) Organizational; (ii) activational
6.11 (ii) Axon terminals
6.12 Corpus callosum
6.13 (i) Pig

CHAPTER 7

Sensory systems: general principles

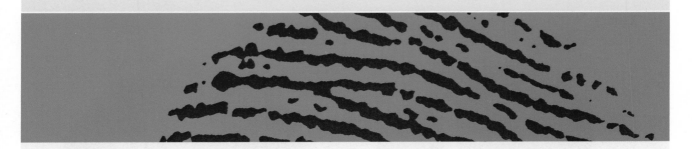

Learning outcomes for Chapter 7

After studying this chapter, you should be able to:

1. Appreciate how our perception of the world involves not just the detection of sensory events but also their interpretation.

2. Explain how both bottom-up and top-down processes are involved in our perception of the world. In so doing, explain what is meant by the homunculus fallacy.

3. Compare and contrast some sensory systems, thereby describing their common properties and also some differences between them.

Scene-setting questions

1 Why do we see flashes of light when we receive a blow to an eye?

2 Do we see what we expect to see?

3 Why does the idea of a 'little person in the head' generate controversy?

4 Why do swimming pools feel less cold after a while?

Objectively speaking, this is a hollow mask but it does not look hollow, no matter which perspective on it you take. What else determines our perception, apart from raw sensory input?

Source: courtesy of Richard Gregory and Priscilla Heard.

Introduction

How do we perceive the world so that we can behave in relation to it? Perception depends upon activity at various levels of the nervous system. At one level, a **sensory system**, which involves the eyes, ears, nose, skin or tongue, is responsible for (1) detecting the presence of physical events in the world, (2) conveying information about them to the brain and (3) doing some processing of information as it is conducted towards the brain. Information from the external environment contributes to the sensory qualities of visual, auditory, smell, tactile and taste sensations. These are termed the **exteroceptive** senses, since they provide information about *exterior* events, i.e. outside the body. A specialized tactile system for nociceptive stimuli was introduced (Chapter 3, 'The nervous and endocrine systems').

Survival and reproduction require the detection of events in the environment and, if appropriate, reacting to them. The ability to detect events depends upon the properties of sense organs, which can be better understood within a framework of functional explanation. Animals have evolved in specialized environmental ('ecological') niches in which particular information is vital to survival. For example, hawks rely on fine resolution of visual detail and detection of movement. They have evolved a different visual system from rats, which get by with a less sophisticated visual system and rely more on smell and touch. Humans are used to seeing the world through human eyes but it is useful to be reminded that different species vary widely in their sensory capacities.

In addition to sensory detection, *interpretation* of what is detected also occurs. Simply as a convenience, psychologists sometimes draw a distinction between 'sensory systems', which *detect* events, and 'perceptual systems', which *interpret* detected information (Eysenck, 1998). However, there is not always an entirely clear distinction between the roles of these systems.

Perception seems so natural and without effort that we have difficulty appreciating how subtle it is. It seems direct; there is a world out there and we perceive it with the help of eyes and ears, etc. In fact, the study of perception is full of traps and contradictions. The words that roll off our tongues effortlessly, such as 'event', 'stimulus' and 'information', seem unproblematic and are often the best that psychology can offer. However, problems arise when we consider them more closely, as will be described in the next section.

Section summary

1 Sensory systems, which involve eyes, ears, nose, skin and tongue, detect physical events in the world, convey information about them to the brain and do some processing of information *en route*.

Test your knowledge

(Answer on page 188)

7.1 Complete the following sentence: 'The sensory system involving nociceptive neurons detects ____'.

Sensory systems and perception

Linking the physical world and sensory detection

Let us look at what is involved in hearing. The physical stimulus that we perceive as sound consists of changes in the pressure of the air (Figure 7.1(a)). The tuning fork is hit and it starts to vibrate. The vibration produces waves of compression (relatively high pressure) and rarefaction (low pressure) in the air, which we perceive as sound. Figure 7.1(b) shows a graph of these changes in pressure, which takes a form described as a sinewave. The **wavelength** is the distance between any two corresponding points on the cycle, in the case illustrated, between two successive peaks. Suppose that the wave completes 50 cycles in one second (termed 50 hertz or 50 Hz for short). This is its frequency. Amplitude is the height of the waves of compression and rarefaction.

Figure 7.1(c) shows a different tuning fork, which vibrates at a different frequency, say, 100 Hz. See Figure 7.1(d). In this case, the amplitude is the same as in (b). Part (e) shows what happens if this tuning fork is struck harder; there is an increase in amplitude but the frequency remains the same. The ear converts such changes in pressure in the air to changes in the electrical activity of neurons.

If a listener is present, a sound is produced in the listener's auditory system by the arrival of pressure waves at the ear, a psychological phenomenon. However, 'sound' is also used to describe the pressure waves themselves, a physical phenomenon, as in to *detect a sound*. This is more convenient than the expression to 'detect pressure waves in a medium'.

Let us look at the term 'event'. Things happen in the outside world and there is our conscious perception of these events. Based upon consensus between observers and occasional objective measurement, the external events and our perception normally correlate. For example, a physical object (e.g. a tall person) is simultaneously associated with a conscious perception of tallness by more than one person. If necessary, perception can be confirmed with a tape measure.

Vision, as with other perceptual systems, works according to a principle described by Martin (1991, p. 330): 'Perception

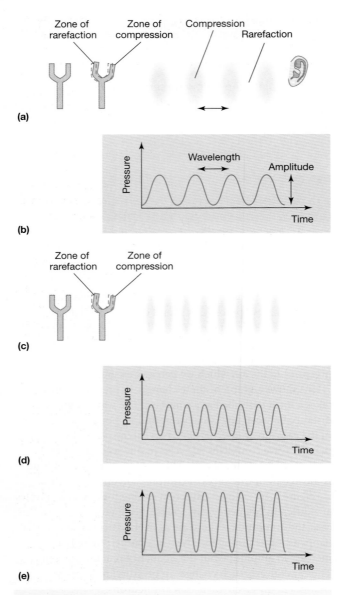

(a)

(b)

(c)

(d)

(e)

Figure 7.1 The production of sound: (a) tuning fork after being tapped (after Vander *et al.*, 1994), (b) changes in air pressure, (c) a different tuning fork, (d) changes in air pressure following tapping of fork shown in part (c) and (e) increased amplitude after a harder strike of the fork. *Source*: after Toates (1998c).

therefore can be shown to be an accurate *organization* of the essential properties of an object that allows us to *manipulate* the object successfully'.

The factors in perception

We sometimes use the expressions **data-driven** and **concept-driven** to refer to two aspects of perception. Clearly, perception depends upon the raw data available at the sense organs (e.g. the image at the retina), the data-driven aspect. This is sometimes termed the **bottom-up** aspect. Perception also depends upon concepts (e.g. memories, expectations), the concept-driven aspect, sometimes termed the **top-down** aspect (Berthoz, 1996). In such terms, perception depends upon an interaction between bottom-up (data-driven) and top-down (concept-driven) processes. Techniques such as PET and MRI scanning (Chapter 5, 'The brain') now enable insight into the brain mechanisms that underlie the top-down factor, though psychologists still know more about the bottom-up factor.

Psychology abounds with ambiguous figures, such as those that can be perceived as either two faces or a vase (Figure 7.2). Normally, perception alternates between the two. The data remain constant but different perceptions occur. We might logically speculate that the top-down processing changes and thereby the perception changes.

Figure 7.3 shows a series of black blobs against a white background. If you have not seen it before, it will probably look like meaningless blobs. If you turn to Figure 7.4 (on page 182) you will see the solution suggested. Now turn back to Figure 7.3 and a form should be apparent. Figure 7.3 has not changed between first and second viewing but the perception has. The same information is driving perception but the top-down contribution appears to have changed.

In some ways, the sensory systems of smell, taste and touch seem to have a simpler job to do than vision or hearing. Suppose that an animal tastes something that is intrinsically repulsive, such as a poisonous plant. It immediately expels the plant from its mouth. In a straightforward way, the taste is the stimulus for the reflex of expelling the substance. The information conveyed is a constant (or 'invariant') property of the world: the plant is repulsive, associated in functional terms with being dangerous.

Suppose that a **pheromone** (an airborne chemical that plays a role in communication between animals of the same

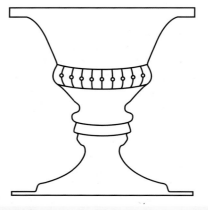

Figure 7.2 Face–vase illusion.

Source: Gregory (1998, Figure 1.4c, p. 11).

Figure 7.3 Black blobs against a white background.
Source: Carraher and Thurston (1966, Fig. 10, p. 18)

species) wafts from one animal to the nose of another. The pheromone has a certain chemical form and stimulates receptors in the nose. Whether the receiving animal responds or not can depend upon its own internal state, e.g. whether it is sexually receptive. However, the information that is conveyed can be understood simply in terms of the chemical that is detected. The information leaving the sender is intrinsically *invariant* and the receiver does not need an interpretation in order to extract **invariance**.

To appreciate fully the meaning of invariance, consider, by contrast, a sensory system which needs to *extract* what is invariant from a varying signal (Zeki, 1993). Vision illustrates this. To a prey animal, a hawk is still a hawk, whether it is near or far, viewed stationary, flying across the sky or towards the prey. Yet under these different circumstances the information detected by the eyes is very different. There is a small image when the hawk is far and a large image when it is near, and the image can be moving or stationary. What is invariant, the perception of the hawk, depends upon processing of the image by the eyes and brain. Invariance is extracted from the visual information. Even if the hawk suddenly disappears from view, e.g. when in a cloud, a prey animal needs to base behaviour on the 'perception' that the hawk is still in pursuit. An understanding of how such invariance is achieved requires that both sensory systems and perception are considered.

Try doing a drawing in only two dimensions of a three-dimensional object such as a cube. Even as bad an artist as I am can make such a two-dimensional representation look three-dimensional. Yet in reality it is only a collection of lines drawn in two dimensions. Our perception corresponds to an active process of interpretation based in part upon the drawing. Even if there really is a three-dimensional cube in the world, the image that it forms at our eyes is only two-dimensional and so the perceptual system still has to form a construction based upon the information provided by sense organs.

The perception that we term 'pain' depends upon actual or incipient tissue damage (data-driven) and sometimes reflects it rather directly. However, a person might experience pain 'in a limb' that does not exist any more or has never existed. In such cases, pain seems to be at least in part a top-down construct (which does not make it any less painful). Conversely, there can be tissue damage with little pain (Melzack and Wall, 1996). Thus the chapter will speak of a *nociceptive neuron* detecting *tissue damage* rather than, as do some authors, a *pain receptor* detecting *pain*. Pain is a psychological experience that normally, but not always, depends upon tissue damage. Pain is not a physical stimulus 'out there' to be detected.

So, a central message is that perception depends on sensory events but cannot be explained simply in terms of them. Rather, perception is an active construction that depends also on such things as emotion, knowledge stored in memory and expectations. In effect, we make sense of the world by constructing theories of what is happening. These theories are heavily influenced by sensory information but that information is put into context.

Biology and psychology

Knowing the properties of neurons and systems of neurons helps us to understand how events are detected and information conveyed to the brain. It is with the early stages of sensory detection that psychologists have the most detailed insight from biology. This doubtless has much to do with the fact that sensory systems are more accessible to investigation than the processes of interpretation that lie deeper in the brain.

As argued in Chapter 1 ('Introduction'), the flow of information between biology and psychology is a two-way street. A study of biology can suggest ways in which sensory and perceptual systems are constructed and operate. However, studying the psychology of perception can suggest what sort of processes to look for at a biological level (Zeki, 1993). If we can identify some characteristics of a sensory and perceptual process, i.e. what it is actually doing, this can help to identify underlying biological structures. For example, in Figure 7.5 most people see the bottom line as being longer than the top. This is an **illusion** since the lines are physically identical. So, given this property of the perceptual system, researchers know that, underlying perception, there is processing by the brain that involves distortion.

Feedback

Sensory detection and perception involve feedback, which highlights the impossibility of drawing neat boundaries between them. Top-down information can modulate bottom-up signals in the sensory pathways conveying information to the brain. For example, deciding what to do

Figure 7.4 Dalmatian in snow.

Source: Carraher and Thurston (1966, Fig. 10, p. 18)

(to flee or to fight) modulates the transmission of nociceptive information to the brain.

For another example, information arrives at the eyes, some processing is done on it and modified information is then conveyed to the cortex (Chapter 5, Figure 5.21, p. 120). Information regarding the outside world is interpreted. These later stages of visual processing feed back to modulate what is sent along the pathway from the eyes to the brain, a concept-driven, top-down aspect. Based upon the interpretation, the brain might command movements of the eyes and a scanning of the object. This brings additional information to the brain. Thus, eye movements change the flow of information. Similarly, a dog might detect a few molecules of an odour and the perception can trigger sniffing to maximize the flow of air to the receptors in its nose that are involved in smell.

The homunculus fallacy

It is difficult to explain what the brain does when we smell a rose or admire a painting. Therefore, we need all the help

that we can get and we tend, rightly, to devise analogies to help us. However, there is one mode of 'explanation' that is to be avoided and it is useful to give an early warning of its ubiquitous presence.

Skinner (1984) mocked this mode of explanation with the following example taken from an educational film. A person's finger is pricked and messages are sent along a nerve to the brain. Shortly afterwards, the person moves an arm so that the finger is taken away from the offending object. So much is uncontroversial. However, in the film the brain events were shown in terms of a little person lying asleep inside the real person's brain. The messages in the nerve wake up the little person who then proceeds to pull a lever, which activates muscles and the arm of the real person responds. Of course, if we want to pursue the 'explanation', we would presumably need to put a still smaller person in the head of the little person and yet another person inside this head, and so on indefinitely (Gregory, 1997). Clearly, this will not work. We need to stop thinking along these lines. This way of thinking is sometimes termed the **homunculus fallacy** (the fallacy of the little person in the head).

Although you might find this example amusing, there are more subtle variations on the same theme. Thus, some people imagine that the visual system recreates in the brain the image that falls on the retina. They imagine that in the brain there is some kind of inner screen onto which is projected, via the retina, an image. For example, a Rembrandt painting would appear there when we stand and admire one. There is no such inner screen; the Rembrandt is represented by a series of action potentials in neurons, none of which looks anything like the original painting.

What might make the homunculus fallacy tempting to some is that the representation of the body in the somatosensory and motor cortices does indeed preserve something of the form of the body, e.g. 'sensory homunculus' (Chapter 5). Also, the mapping of the retina onto the brain preserves the positional relationship at the retina but this lends no support to the idea of a homunculus of the form derided by Skinner. There is no reason to suppose that the chemicals of the brain turn yellow-gold when we view a Van Gogh sunflower!

A number of principles of sensory processing apply to each sensory system and the next section looks at these.

Figure 7.5 The Muller–Lyer illusion.

Section summary

1 Sensory systems are sensitive to physical events (e.g. changes in air pressure).

2 Perception depends upon the combined effect of data-driven (bottom-up) and concept-driven (top-down) factors.

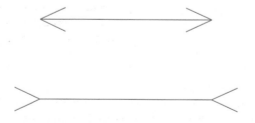

Figure 7.5 The Muller–Lyer illusion.

3 Some perceptual systems (e.g. vision) have the task of extracting what is invariant from a signal that is often varying greatly.

4 The term 'homunculus fallacy' refers to the idea of a little person in the head who interprets sensory events.

Test your knowledge

(Answers on page 188)

7.2 Two sounds, one of 50 Hz and another of 100 Hz, could be said with certainty to differ in which of the following? (i) Frequency, (ii) wavelength, (iii) amplitude.

7.3 Fill in the missing words in the following: 'Whereas a hormone is released into a _____ vessel and serves communication within one animal, a pheromone is released into _____ and serves as a communication _____ animals'.

7.1

General principles

Transduction

The neurons of our brain are not *directly* sensitive to the presence of such physical events as lights, odours and pressure waves in the air. Therefore, the first stage of processing is common to all sensory systems. It is a *translation* from physical events (e.g. a chemical on the tongue, damage at the skin) to an electrical signal, a change in membrane potential of specialized neurons at the periphery. This process is termed **transduction**. The book has described the transduction between a noxious stimulus and depolarization of a neuron. For other examples, there is transduction between (i) light at the retina and electrical signals and (ii) pressure waves in the air at the ear and action potentials. Of course, the sensory receptors of the eye and ear are not in immediate contact with the external environment but are within the organ.

Each sensory system is responsible for detecting a particular class of physical events. Within each system, the initial stage of detection, from physical stimulus to change in membrane potential, is done by **sensory receptors**. Figure 7.6 compares sensory receptors in nociception and vision. In part (a), the single nociceptive neuron spans the distance from periphery to CNS. This neuron can therefore be termed a

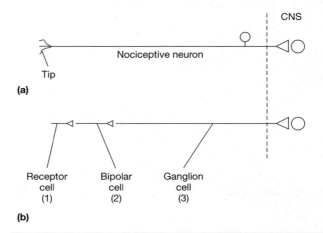

Figure 7.6 Sensory neurons involved in (a) nociception and (b) vision.

sensory receptor, though some would call just its tip the sensory receptor since it is here that the transduction occurs. In part (b), there are two further neurons between the sensory receptors that detect light at the retina and the CNS.

Afferent neurons convey information on sensory events to the CNS, either directly to the brain, as in the cranial nerves, or to the spinal cord and then to the brain (Chapter 3, 'The nervous and endocrine systems'). Each sensory system has general and specific features. As a general property, each translates physical events into an electrical signal that the nervous system can use. However, each receptor is specialized to detect only one type of physical event. A given sensory receptor usually responds only within a particular range of stimulation, e.g. in the olfactory system, to a few types of chemical.

In some sensory receptors, the change in membrane potential, if sufficient, gives rise immediately to an action potential (Chapter 4, 'The cells of the nervous system'). For example, a nociceptive neuron performs transduction between tissue damage and action potentials, which are transmitted along the axon to the CNS (Figure 7.6(a)). In other cases, a neuron serves as sensory detector (i.e. certain electrical changes occur in it) but action potentials appear only in neurons that are situated later in the sequence (Chapter 5). For example, in Figure 7.6(b), electrical changes are instigated in neuron 1 by light, which triggers changes in membrane potential in neuron 2 but it is only at neuron 3, the ganglion cell, where action potentials first appear. In each system, the language in which information is sent to the brain is that of the *frequency of action potentials in neurons*, termed 'neural encoding'.

The fundamental difference between sensory channels is in terms of (a) the particular neurons that carry the information and (b) the parts of the brain to which these neurons project. This is termed the **labelled-line principle**.

Consider some examples. Activity within particular neurons of the tactile system is interpreted as touch to a particular part of the body. Hearing and vision are based on the auditory nerve and optic nerve, respectively. The difference between hearing and vision is not based on the means by which information is carried, since it is by action potentials in each case. The retina is sensitive to light and not to sound. We see lights because neurons of the optic nerve are activated and hear sounds because neurons of the auditory nerve are active. However, if mechanical pressure is applied to the eye, owing to triggering action potentials we can sometimes see flashes that appear to be light. Objectively there is no light there but activity in this input channel is interpreted as light.

The information carried by action potentials

In a sensory system, specific physical events in the world trigger action potentials within particular neurons. Hence, the action potentials represent the triggering events. Such events can be characterized by, among other qualities, their duration and intensity. Pressure waves in the air are also associated with such qualities as pitch. How are these qualities encoded, given that the nervous system has only a series of action potentials available?

There are two means of conveying information about different qualities: (1) which neurons are active and (2) the pattern of action potentials within each of such neurons. As just noted, differences *between* sensory systems, say, auditory and visual, correspond to different nerves. Similarly *within* a given sensory system, differences are also conveyed by different neurons. Sugar tastes sweet and a lemon tastes bitter because different neurons tend to be triggered by those two chemical qualities. Different neurons within the auditory nerve are triggered by different frequencies of sounds.

Information can be carried by the *population* of neurons that is activated, termed **population coding**. For example, pressing a fine-pointed object gently on the skin triggers few sensory receptors with a low frequency of action potentials. As the same object is pressed more strongly, it triggers both increased frequency of action potentials in these neurons and triggers neurons that were previously inactive.

Within a given neuron, the *pattern* of action potentials generated by an event conveys information on that event. Normally information is carried by the frequency of action potentials, known as **frequency coding**. For example, the frequency of action potentials can code for intensity. (You might recall the example of temperature shown in Figure 3.4, p. 52.) See Figure 7.7(a) and (b). As the intensity of the physical stimulus increases, so does the frequency of action potentials, an example of frequency coding.

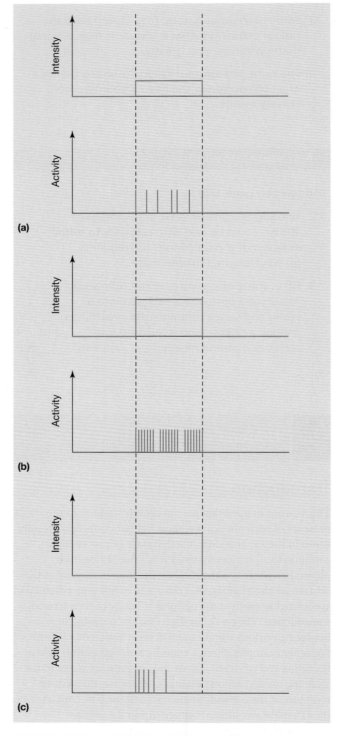

Figure 7.7 Frequency coding: (a) weak stimulus, (b) strong stimulus and (c) adaptation.
Source: Toates (1998c, Fig. 4.1, p. 102).

Figure 7.7(c) represents a type of receptor having the property of **adaptation**. The activity generated in the sensory neuron is high when the stimulus is first applied but decreases over the period of application. By contrast, the type of neuron that has the response represented in Figures 7.7(a) and (b) exhibits no adaptation: for as long as the stimulus is applied, the sensory neuron reacts in the same way.

Figure 7.8 shows the response of a neuron as a function of stimulus intensity. Suppose that this represents pressure applied to the skin. As action potential frequency goes up, so our conscious perception of pressure might increase in parallel. Note the threshold of intensity (A), which needs to be exceeded before there is any response by the neuron. Also the response does not increase indefinitely with increases in intensity. A saturation point is reached, at which the neuron produces action potentials at its maximum rate.

As just discussed, one code that can be employed in a sensory pathway is that increases in intensity of stimulation is encoded by increases in the frequency of action potentials. However, this is not the only code. In some cases, increasing intensity is associated with a decrease in action potential

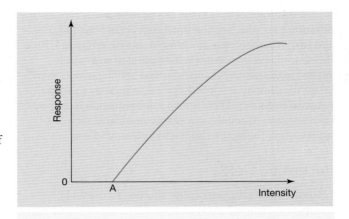

Figure 7.8 Relationship between intensity of a stimulus and response of a sensory neuron.

frequency. In the auditory system and for certain sound frequencies, the pattern of action potentials varies in synchrony with the pressure waves in the air (Rose *et al.*, 1971) (Figure 7.9).

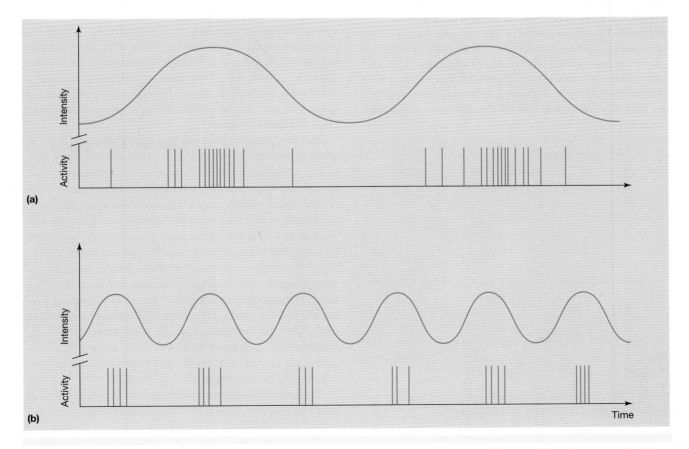

Figure 7.9 Encoding by means of pattern. Relatively low (a) and high (b) frequencies and the associated pattern of action potentials.

The duration of a stimulus can be encoded by the duration over which action potentials occur (Figure 7.7(a) and (b)). Another form of coding is shown in Figure 7.10: the neuron is active even when no physical stimulus is applied to the sensory channel, termed 'spontaneous activity'. When the stimulus is applied, there is an increase in action potential frequency. There is then some reduction in frequency, i.e. adaptation. When the stimulus is terminated there is a suppression of activity to below the background level.

Receptive fields

Let us reconsider the nociceptive neuron (Figure 7.11). Comparing Figures 7.11(a) and (b), the extent of branching of the tip is different. Correspondingly, the tip in part (a) reacts to tissue damage over a wider area than that in part (b). The area over which the neuron detects tissue damage is termed its **receptive field**. More generally, 'receptive field' of a neuron refers to the sensory area within which a stimulus is able to change the activity of the neuron (Hubel and Wiesel, 1959).

Sensory thresholds

For each sensory system, there is a minimum level of stimulation that can be detected, termed a **sensory threshold**. A very faint sound or light or a chemical in a very low concentration in the air might not be detected. Not only is there such an absolute threshold but also there exists in each sensory system a 'relative threshold'. You might be able to detect the change in illumination caused by one candle lit in a dark room but could you tell the difference in intensity

(a)

(b)

Figure 7.11 Nociceptive neurons: (a) large and (b) small receptive fields.

between 99 and 100 candles? Part of the limitation on what can be detected is set at the level of sensory transduction. For example, in Figure 7.8 no increase in action potentials occurs until point A has been reached. The stimulus needs to be larger than A to be detected.

Constancy and change

What conveys particularly important information about the world is change, in both space and time. Functional considerations can illuminate this. For example, imagine that a charging elephant is closing in on you. What matters most in avoiding the beast is the accurate detection of the contour between the dark skin of the elephant and the lightness of the sky. The exact shade of grey throughout the elephant is of less importance. Visual systems are especially tuned to detect contrast between regions.

Tactile systems are also tuned to detect contours, the edges of objects. For example, consider how we manage not to fall out of bed. Information on the bed's edge carries special importance to our tactile systems. In the time dimension, the importance of change is exemplified in the information carried by a sudden onset of sound as opposed to a steady background noise level. Change might be caused by the arrival of predator or prey. As a general feature, sensory systems are especially tuned to change, showing some adaptation at other times (though pain is an exception here). For example, when you first get into a swimming pool, it often feels very cold. After some exposure it feels much less cold. This is partly because neurons sensitive to low temperatures show adaptation over time. Figure 7.7(c) represents adaptation at the level of a sensory receptor, which is the basis of the psychological effect.

This completes our discussion of general principles; in the next two chapters we consider individual systems.

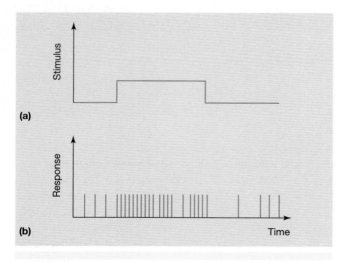

Figure 7.10 Coding set against a spontaneous background level of activity: (a) stimulus and (b) response.

Section summary

1 Detection is done by sensory receptors, which translate physical events in the world into an electrical signal in the nervous system, termed sensory transduction.

2 Information about different qualities is carried by (a) which neurons are active and (b) the pattern of action potentials over time within a given neuron.

3 The receptive field of a neuron is the area of sensory surface which when stimulated influences the activity of the neuron.

4 Sensory systems are particularly sensitive to *changes* in stimulation in the dimensions of space and time.

Test your knowledge

(Answer on page 188)

7.4 In Figure 7.6, which part of the CNS is represented in (i) part (a) and (ii) part (b)?

Bringing things together

The chapter was organized around the theme of generality (what sensory systems have in common) and specificity (what is the distinct feature of each system). Any sensory system faces the general problem of achieving transduction between physical events in the world and electrical changes in neurons. In some cases, e.g. nociception, a physical event translates into action potentials at the sensory receptor (Figure 7.6(a)). In vision, action potentials first appear two neurons removed from the sensory receptors (Figure 7.6(b)). Either way, each system 'speaks' to the brain in the language of action potentials in particular neurons. Specificity is apparent in that different sensory systems are sensitive to different features of the physical world involving different means of transduction.

Some sensory stimuli, such as a pheromone, intrinsically convey information about the world that can be used in the production of adaptive behaviour. In other cases, as in examples of vision, complex processes of

interpretation, top-down modulation and extraction of invariance from varying stimulus information are needed before adaptive behaviour is instigated.

Summary of Chapter 7

1 **Sensory systems detect information and project it to the brain, where it is interpreted.**

2 **Our perception of the world is sometimes direct but more generally it depends upon putting sensory information into a context of memories, emotions and expectations.**

3 **Neurons convey information to the brain, encoded in terms of which neurons are active and their level of activity.**

Further reading

For a good general account, see Hendry *et al.* (1999a); Martin (1991). For data-driven and concept-driven aspects, see Farah *et al.* (1999); Frith and Dolan (1997); Hendry *et al.* (1999a). For sensory coding, see Martin (1991). For receptive fields, see Reid (1999).

Signposts

The next two chapters will build on this one, using such notions as the receptive field of vision (Chapter 8, 'Vision') and that of the tactile sense (Chapter 9, 'The other sensory systems'). You might like to be alert to where specific instances illustrate the common features introduced in Chapter 7 and where they are peculiar to a system.

Adaptation to the environment (discussed in Chapter 2) requires that the brain is informed of events in both the external world and in its internal environment, so that appropriate action can be instigated. The chapter has looked at the external world (e.g. lights, sounds) and at the skin (e.g. nociception). There also exists sensory detection of such internal events as muscle stretch (to be discussed in Chapter 10, 'The control of movement') and body water level (Chapters 2, 3, 15, 'Motivation' and 16, 'Feeding and drinking'). Nociceptive neurons detecting tissue damage both at the skin and in the interior of the body are described in Chapter 14, 'Pain'.

Answers

Explanations for answers to 'test your knowledge' questions can be found on the website **www.pearsoned.co.uk/toates**

7.1 Tissue damage (or 'incipient' damage – getting near to damaging stimulation)

7.2 (i) Frequency and (ii) wavelength

7.3 Blood; the air; between

7.4 (i) The spinal cord if the tip is below the neck and the brain if the tip is above the neck; (ii) the brain.

CHAPTER 8

Vision

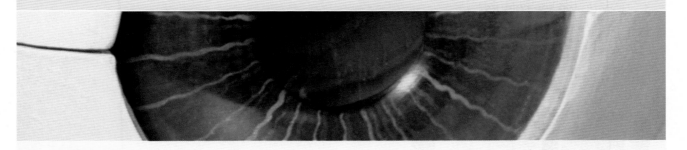

Learning outcomes for Chapter 8

After studying this chapter, you should be able to:

1. Justify the claim that visual perception depends upon both the bottom-up contribution from visual stimuli and a top-down contribution.

2. Explain how, in order to understand visual perception, we need knowledge of the properties of the cells of the retina and their interconnections.

3. Describe the route of information transmission in the visual system from eye to brain. While describing the receptive field properties of some of the cells encountered along the way, explain how these properties arise.

4. Explain what is meant by the terms 'stream' and 'parallel processing'. Link this to the structure of the visual system.

5. Explain what is meant by the expression 'functional specialization' within the system underlying visual perception.

6. Describe how the capacity to form images of the brain has increased our understanding of the top-down factor in visual perception and conscious processes.

Scene-setting questions

1 After looking at a photographic flash, you then look at a light wall. Why do you see a dark form of the flash floating in space? Why does it fade?

2 When you stare intently at a distant star it sometimes disappears. Why?

3 How do we see colours?

4 What underlies the attraction that human infants show towards faces?

5 Do we tend to see what we expect to see?

What determines how this ambiguous picture is perceived consciously?
Source: © Salvador Dali, Gala-Salvador Dali Foundation, DACS, London 2006

Introduction

Look around you and you will see a world of visual objects, such as a table, a chair and a book. You have a conscious **perception** of this world. When you close your eyes you can still conjure up images of such objects. Think of your action in the world. Sometimes your full conscious awareness is brought to bear on a problem involving vision, as in trying to thread a needle, decipher very small print or ride a bicycle along an icy road. At other times, through vision you can interact unconsciously with the world. For example, you negotiate your way along a crowded pavement, avoiding all collisions. You achieve accuracy even though your conscious mind is fully absorbed with thoughts of something else. How is all this integration between perception and action achieved?

Visual perception involves active processes, which depend upon both bottom-up factors (signals arising from light falling on the eye) and top-down factors (e.g. memories and

expectations) (Humphreys *et al.*, 1997). This chapter looks at both sets of processes and considers how visual perception depends upon their cooperation. A set of cells at the back of the eye converts light energy into electrical signals. This provides the bottom-up factor common to all visual perception and action. Cells in the eye also do some processing of information as well as transmitting it towards the brain.

Figure 8.1 can be used to demonstrate the processing that the CNS does on raw sensory input (von der Heydt, 1995). It allows us to distinguish between what is detected by the early stages of the visual system, and our perception of the world (Leopold *et al.*, 2003).

In the case of the Kanizsa triangle of Figure 8.1(a), people perceive a white triangle but it is illusory. If you examine the physical stimulus, you will see that there are no full sides to the triangle. Rather, any sides 'seen' are extrapolations by the brain. In part (b), is there a triangle of equal sides? The side to the right is clear. The base is not physically present but nonetheless it is perceived to be there. Conversely, the side to the left is physically present but is not generally perceived as part of a triangle. This illustrates that perception is much

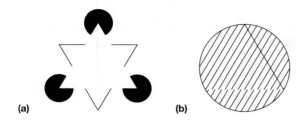

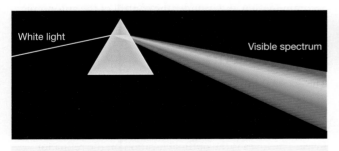

(a)   (b)

Figure 8.1 Reality and illusion: (a) Kanizsa triangle and (b) part real, part hidden and part illusory triangle.

Source: von der Heydt (1995, Fig. 23.1, p. 366).

more than seeing exactly what stimulates the eye. It is also dependent upon context and involves extrapolation beyond the physical image.

Considering the bottom-up aspect of perception, what is the nature of the stimulus, light? Light is difficult for most of us to understand. However, some familiarity with sound can help us since light has features in common with it. Chapter 7, 'Sensory systems', related pressure waves in the air to the perception of sound. Light and sound are characterized by wavelength and frequency. (However, whereas sound needs a medium through which to pass, e.g. air, light can pass through a vacuum.) Corresponding to variations in wavelength of light (physical stimulus) is the spectrum of colours that we perceive (the psychological dimension). For example, we usually describe light having a wavelength of 690 nanometres (nm) as red. Strictly speaking, red is a psychological quality, albeit one usually associated with a particular physical stimulus.

Figure 8.2 shows the visible spectrum, revealed by passing white light through a prism. You can see the component wavelengths of white light, corresponding to the colours of the spectrum.

The light emitted by, or reflected from, an object in part determines perception. By exploiting this input and stored information, the visual system extracts what is invariant about the world. For example, the hair of a blond person tends to look light under various conditions of illumination, from sunlight to moonlight. However, blondness is not intrinsic to the intensity of the light that is reflected from the hair and arrives in the eyes; blond people cannot be classified as sending off high levels of illumination in any absolute sense. More light is reflected from a person with black hair viewed in sunlight than a blond person in moonlight. What characterizes the blond person is that, *relative to a surround* (e.g. standing next to a dark-haired person), the blond hair tends to reflect more light. What is *invariant* is the hair's property of high 'reflectance' (i.e. it reflects a high percentage of light falling on it). Similarly, a robin's breast tends to look red because it reflects a large proportion of light of a particular wavelength, relative to other objects simultaneously present (e.g. its wings) (Zeki, 1993).

We turn first to consider processes within the eye, the bottom-up contribution.

Section summary

1 Visual perception depends on both bottom-up and top-down factors.

2 Light is characterized by wavelength, which is associated with the psychological phenomenon of colour.

3 The visual system extracts invariance by setting information in the image into context.

Test your knowledge

(Answer on page 217)

8.1 Complete the following: 'Expressed in *physical* terms, Figure 8.2 reveals a range of different visible _____ and corresponding _____'.

White light

Visible spectrum

Figure 8.2 The visible spectrum.

Within the eye

Detection of light in an image occurs at the layer of light-sensitive cells that form part of the **retina** of the eye (Figure 8.3). Also, some processing of information is performed by the cells of the retina. This section considers the properties of the eye as a whole and the cells that form the retina. It relates this to perception.

The eye's optics

Figure 8.3 should remind you of some features of the eye, introduced in Chapter 5, 'The brain'. The optics form an image of the outside world at the retina, i.e. the cornea and lens normally bring light to a focus there. The image on the retina is upside down and reversed left to right with respect to the external world (Gregory, 1997). The fact that the 'world' is upside down on the retina has no particular significance for vision, since the image has always been upside down. There is no homunculus looking at it. The important point is that there exists *consistency* between a particular pattern of image and the signals produced in particular neurons.

The eye is sometimes compared to a camera but, although this has some validity, it is wrong to pursue it too far. Like the camera, there is an apparatus for forming an image and photosensitive material (sensory receptors). However, the analogy breaks down if it is suggested that perception is like forming a photograph. Visual perception is an active construction based only in part upon information at the retina.

As shown in Figure 8.4, by means of contraction of the ciliary muscle, the lens adjusts its curvature in order for objects to remain in focus on the retina as their distance

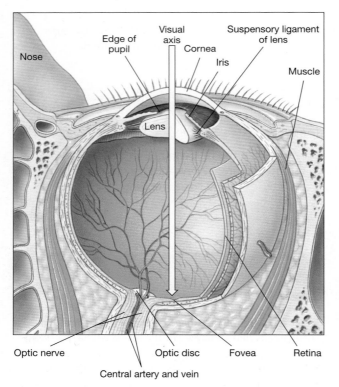

Figure 8.3 The eye.

Source: Martini *et al.* (2000, Fig.18-20e, p. 487).

George Stratton of the University of California wore an optical instrument to 'invert' the images on his retina (Stratton, 1897). For the first time in his life (probably in anyone's life), the image became objectively the 'right' way up relative to the external world. When Stratton was not wearing this apparatus, he was blindfolded. He was interested in how the visual system adapted, if at all, to the new conditions. He walked around for eight days wearing the apparatus. At first Stratton experienced a complete inversion of the external world. He reported (p. 344): 'Almost all movements performed under the direct guidance of sight were laborious and embarrassed'.

A role of memory and integration between sensory channels was evident, as well as some conflict between bottom-up and top-down contributions to perception (p. 345):

As regards the parts of the body, their pre-experimental representation often invaded the region directly in sight. Arms and legs in full view were given a double position. Beside the position and relation in which they were actually seen, there was always in the mental background, in intimate connection with muscular and tactual sensations, the older representation of these parts.

Towards the end of the period, Stratton experienced some adaptation to the new condition. Movements came to be made with respect to the new perceived position of objects and without a conscious readjustment. The nervous system can show some adaptation to even a complete inversion of the visual image.

from the eyes changes (Mellerio, 1966). This is known as **accommodation** and is under the control of the autonomic nervous system and smooth muscle (Chapter 3).

Eye movements

The external world is not static and objects of attention move relative to our eyes. Also, even when viewing detail in a static world, the object of attention can vary. In Figure 8.3, note a small depression at the centre of the retina, termed the **fovea**. The fovea is the optimal location on the retina for resolving fine details within the image. These fine details are the object of attention. When the image of the detail does not coincide with the fovea, movements are made to bring neurons that activate these muscles. Some eye movements are smooth, as when we track a smoothly moving target. Others are sudden and jerky, known as **saccadic eye movements**. Saccadic eye movements can be involuntary ('automatic'), to follow the sudden movement of the object of attention, corresponding to a move of the image from one retinal location to another. Saccadic movements can also be voluntary, as when we decide to move attention suddenly from one location to another.

Properties of receptors

Sensory detection

Figure 8.5 shows a simplified cross-section through a small segment of the retina. The eye's sensory receptors, **rods** and **cones**, form a layer within the retina. The chemicals contained within them (e.g. rhodopsin in rods) absorb light and, in doing so, the receptors change their electrical state (voltage). This is sensory detection. Note that, curiously, the eye is 'inside-out'. Light must pass through layers of other cells before reaching the sensory receptors.

The change in electrical activity that occurs at a sensory receptor when light is absorbed is not an action potential but a less abrupt change. On absorbing light, the rods and cones then pass on a message, via synapses, to other neurons, the bipolar cells (Figure 8.5). In turn, bipolars pass the information to ganglion cells, and so on.

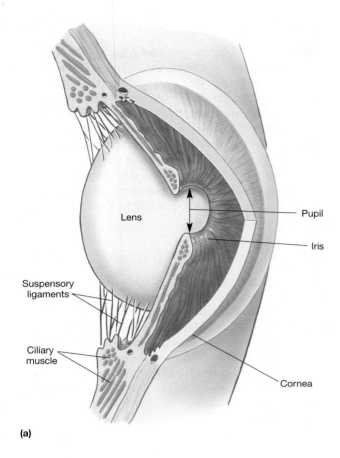

(a)

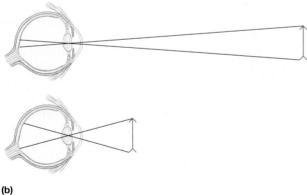

(b)

Figure 8.4 Accommodation: (a) lens and ciliary muscle and (b) accommodation for (above) far object and (below) near object.

Source: part (a) adapted from Martini *et al.* (2000, Fig. 18-21, p. 488).

fovea and object of attention into alignment. Such movement can be of the head or whole body or of the eyes relative to the head.

The eyes are rotated in their sockets by oculomotor muscles (examples of skeletal muscle) attached to the eyeballs. The oculomotor nerve (a cranial nerve) contains

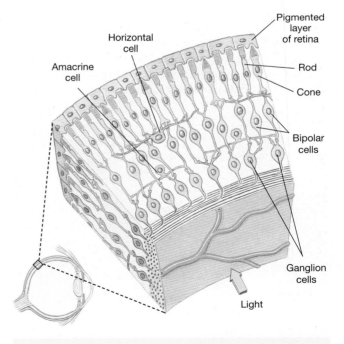

Figure 8.5 Cross-section through part of the retina.

Source: Martini *et al.* (2000, Fig. 18–22a, p. 490).

For the moment, let us focus on rods. Rods come in just one variety and Figure 8.6 shows an absorption curve of the chemical contained within them (Bowmaker and Dartnell, 1980). Rods exhibit maximum absorption ('sensitivity') to light of a wavelength of 498 nm, with the sensitivity to each side of this point being less. As far as the contribution to vision made by rods is concerned, our sensitivity to light of different wavelengths corresponds to the curve of absorption by the chemical contained within them.

Cones come in three forms corresponding to three different chemicals contained within them (Martin, 1998). The absorption characteristics of the three kinds of cone are shown in Figure 8.6, the significance of this for colour vision being explored later. The three types are termed 'long-wavelength' (L), 'medium-wavelength' (M) and 'short-wavelength' cones (S), indicating the wavelength of light to which they are most sensitive (Martin, 1998). These are abbreviated as L, M and S cones. Sensitivity to wavelength varies with each type of cone. Thus, the L cone is most sensitive to light of wavelength 564 nm, corresponding to yellow, but exhibits some sensitivity to wavelengths to each side of this. Light of wavelength corresponding to red is detected by L cones. A wavelength of 534 nm is perceived as green, the result of its absorption by both L and M cones. Light of short wavelength is perceived as blue.

Adaptation

When receptors absorb large amounts of light they show adaptation, i.e. their sensitivity is lowered (Gregory, 1997). The chemical within them is said to be 'bleached'. When the light is switched off, sensitivity slowly increases, termed 'dark adaptation'. You can demonstrate this by going from a light room into relative darkness. At first you will see rather little but then gradually you will perceive more of your surroundings. Some fraudulent Victorian spiritualists exploited this trick to make ghostly images appear after a while in the séance room.

If you look at a bright object briefly, you tend to see a bright **after-image** of it, a positive after-image. This is due to activity in the nerve carrying information to the brain outlasting the light stimulus. If you then divert your gaze to a light wall, a dark (negative) after-image of the object will appear on the wall. This is partly because the bright object has adapted the receptors in an area of retina; they are fatigued (Gregory, 1997). Neighbouring receptors are relatively non-fatigued and so yield a stronger signal. The fatigued area is interpreted as a dark object. In time, the after-image disappears, corresponding to when adaptation is equal across the receptors.

Between receptors and ganglion cells

In Figure 8.5, note the layers of cells (bipolar, amacrine and horizontal cells) that lie between receptors and ganglion cells. We shall focus on the sequence: receptor → bipolar cell → ganglion cell. The bipolar cells and other intermediate cells contribute to information processing by virtue of the connections that they form among themselves, with receptors and with ganglion cells. We shall consider the product of this processing in so far as it is reflected in the properties of ganglion cells.

Ganglion cells

Chapter 7 defined the receptive field of a given neuron in a sensory system in terms of the specific stimulus qualities that influence the neuron's activity. The present section introduces receptive fields in the visual system, defined in terms of the image at the retina. It asks, what features of the image falling on which part of the retina change the activity of the neuron under consideration? The connections within the retina are such that information on contours within the image is particularly emphasized.

Investigating the receptive field

To investigate the receptive fields of ganglion cells in the visual system, a cat was anaesthetized and its head held in a fixed position (Kuffler, 1953). Typically, ganglion cells exhibit some activity even when the animal is in complete darkness, an activity termed the 'spontaneous background activity'. See Figure 8.7. A small spot of white light was projected onto a screen in front of the cat. An electrode was inserted into the optic nerve to detect the electrical activity within the axon of a single ganglion cell.

The retina is explored with the spot of light and the activity of the ganglion cell observed. Note the electrical activity shown on the screen of the oscilloscope, the recording apparatus. Since the head is held in a fixed location, there is a

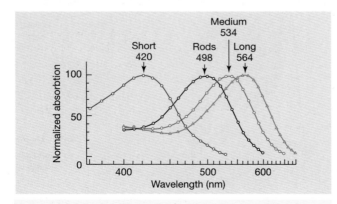

Figure 8.6 Absorption characteristics of rods and three types of cone.

Source: Bowmaker and Dartnall (1980, Fig. 2, p. 505).

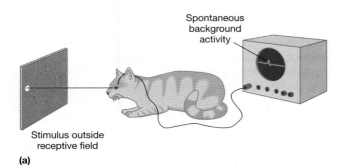

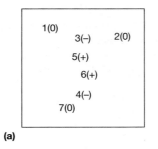

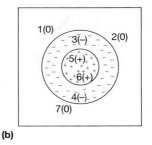

(a)   (b)

Figure 8.8 Results obtained from stimulating retina: (a) some points and (b) complete pattern of points joined together.

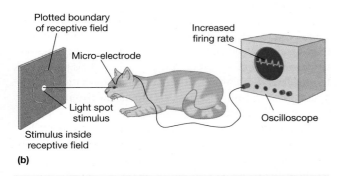

Figure 8.7 Investigating the receptive field. Spot (a) outside the receptive field of the cell and so activity is the same as the spontaneous background activity and (b) inside receptive field. (Note: in practice the size of receptive field is small compared with the size of screen.)

Source: Greene (1990, Fig. 10.5, p. 483).

one-to-one correspondence between the screen and the retina, so the investigator can map between them.

First, the spot is in location 1 on the screen (Figure 8.8(a)). Suppose that there is no change in frequency of firing from when the eye is in darkness. By definition, location 1 is outside the receptive field of the ganglion cell, i.e. stimulation at this site does not affect the neuron relative to its activity in darkness. Therefore, a zero (0) is indicated on the figure. Similarly, light falling at location 2 has no effect and a 0 is placed there. At location 3, the cell *reduces* its rate of firing relative to darkness. Light falling here is within the receptive field, since it influences firing. Since the cell fires less frequently, the light is within the *inhibitory* region of the receptive field and a minus sign is placed at 3. Similarly a minus sign is placed at 4. When light is projected to 5, the cell *increases* its rate of firing compared with darkness and a plus is placed at 5. The same is found at 6; 7 is outside the receptive field since light projected at 7 has no effect.

Suppose that we explore the entire retina, while recording from the same ganglion cell. Typically, we find the effect shown in Figure 8.8(b). If we join together all the pluses and then all the minuses, we obtain the shape shown. This

defines the receptive field of the ganglion cell, consisting of an excitatory centre (termed ON region) and an inhibitory surround (termed OFF region), an example of **centre–surround** organization (Hubel and Wiesel, 1959; Livingstone and Hubel, 1988).

The example illustrates that information can be conveyed by the inhibition of activity as well as by excitation. Inhibition to below the spontaneous rate conveys information on the presence of light in the OFF region. Thus, a single cell can signal two different events, which appears to be an economical way of operating.

ON centre cells

What is the optimal stimulus to trigger activity in the ganglion cell that has the receptive field shown in Figure 8.8? It is a spot of light that fills the excitatory centre but does not invade the inhibitory surround (Figure 8.9(a)). Note the excitation when the light is switched on.

What is the optimal stimulus to *inhibit* activity in the cell? Now it is an annulus of light that fills the surround region but does not invade the centre (Figure 8.9(b)). Typically, the cell shows a burst of activity when light in the surround region is turned *off* (Figure 8.9(b)).

Suppose a light stimulus covers the centre and surround. Light in one region has a cancelling effect relative to light in the other region. Its precise effect depends upon the relative contribution of the two regions of receptive field. Typically, they might be of equal weight and so there would be no response from the ganglion cell when light falls onto both regions (Figure 8.9(c)).

Let us make things really simple and consider just a single ganglion cell. What kind of light stimulus might correspond to Figure 8.9(a)? The light from a small star at night might just fill the ON region with no light falling in the OFF region. A bright sky would produce light falling on the entire receptive field and might not trigger any change in activity in the ganglion cell, as shown in part (c).

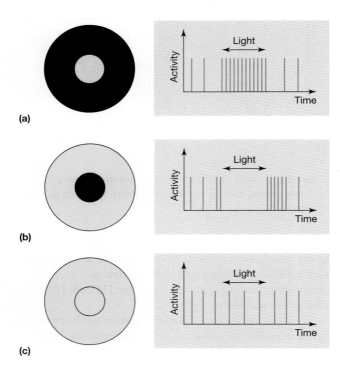

(a)

(b)

(c)

Figure 8.9 Responses of a ganglion cell: (a) light spot in centre region of receptive field, (b) light annulus in outer region and (c) illumination of the entire receptive field.

OFF centre cells

There are ganglion cells that have the opposite characteristic to Figure 8.9: light falling on the centre region inhibits the cell whereas light on the outer area excites it (Figure 8.10). What kind of stimulus triggers such activity? I am grateful to an Open University student of mine, Jackie, for suggesting a memorable example: a polar bear's black nose surrounded by pristine white fur. As it approaches, at some distance the black of the nose will just correspond to the centre region of the receptive field.

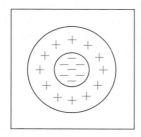

Figure 8.10 An OFF centre/ON surround characteristic of a ganglion cell's receptive field.

Lateral inhibition

The receptive field organization of the ganglion cells that has just been described is defined by *location* on the retina, irrespective of the wavelength of light. Different types of cone (L, M and S cones) within one area of receptive field excite the cell and a similar variety of cones in the other area exert an opposite effect (Livingstone and Hubel, 1988; Martin, 1998). In Figures 8.9 and 8.10, *any* visible wavelength of light falling within the ON area of the receptive field tends to excite the ganglion and light in the OFF area tends to inhibit it.

Let us look at this in terms of the neural input to the ganglion cell. One set of neural inputs to the ganglion cell tends to excite it, corresponding to the ON area. Another set tends to inhibit it, corresponding to the OFF. This property is termed **lateral inhibition**. It depends on information being communicated from receptors via bipolar, horizontal and amacrine cells (Figure 8.5).

Because of this type of organization, such ganglion cells are unable to signal information on wavelength. They simply signal light–dark contrast between the sub-regions of receptive field. Based upon this property, it is possible to speculate on the neural connections that other cells make with a ganglion cell (Figure 8.11(a)). For a ganglion cell with an excitatory centre and inhibitory surround receptive field, all receptors within the inner area (e.g. R_1 and R_2) make (through other cells) excitatory connections to the ganglion, whereas all those in the outer area (e.g. R_3 and R_4) make (through other cells) inhibitory connections. These other cells are the bipolar, amacrine and horizontal cells (Figure 8.5). However, not all ganglion cells are of this type and a type that signals differences in wavelength is discussed later.

There is overlap of receptive fields at the retina (Figure 8.11(b)). A given ganglion cell does not have exclusive territorial rights over a population of receptors. Rather, a receptor can contribute an input to many different ganglion

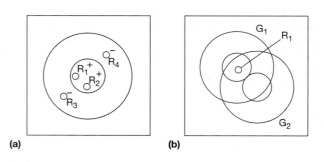

(a)   **(b)**

Figure 8.11 Receptive field properties. (a) Receptors within the centre region excite a ganglion cell. Receptors in the outer area inhibit it. (b) Overlapping receptive fields.

cells. Receptor R_1 is within the ON area of the receptive field of ganglion cell G_1 but in the OFF area of that of G_2.

Detecting detail

Sometimes an animal needs to resolve fine detail, e.g. a flying hawk distinguishing the movements of a mouse in a cornfield. At other times, less detailed and more global analysis is needed, e.g. a mouse detecting a slight change in overall intensity of illumination over a large area of the visual field that could be the shadow of a predator. Differences in these abilities vary across the retina, depending upon the region on which the image falls.

Cellular basis

There are many more receptors at the retina than there are ganglion cells. In humans, there are about 106 million receptors for 1 million ganglion cells. Hence, there is **convergence** of the outputs from receptors onto ganglion cells. A single ganglion cell derives its input from more than one receptor (Figure 8.5 shows some convergence). The extent of the convergence varies over the retina. At the fovea (Figure 8.3), there is a dense packing of cones and little convergence. By contrast, in the periphery, very many rods all feed their inputs into a single ganglion cell, i.e. a high convergence. See Figure 8.12.

The kind of visual processing that regions of the retina perform is a function of the variation in convergence. Where there is little convergence, i.e. at, or near, the fovea, the ability to resolve fine detail is high, described as high **acuity**. Receptive fields are very small.

Away from the fovea, there is a large convergence of inputs to ganglion cells and receptive fields are large. A large population of cells supplies excitatory inputs, corresponding to the ON region of receptive field, whereas another large population supplies inhibitory inputs, corresponding to the OFF region. In contrast to the fovea, the ability to resolve detail is less good since there is a pooling of output from receptors. However, as a result of pooling, the ability to detect the presence or absence of weak lights is relatively good, i.e. **sensitivity** is high.

An analogy

An analogy can help. Suppose that we need a profile of the rainfall at a series of streets of terraced houses. We inspect the flow of water down the drainpipes. Suppose that all the houses in a street have one single communal drainpipe. Monitoring flow within it would give a measure of even light rain falling anywhere in the street since the roofs are *pooling* what falls on all of them. However, we would not be able to resolve the detail of where in the street the rain was falling.

Suppose instead that each house has its own drainpipe. It might be difficult to detect the presence of a light rain since

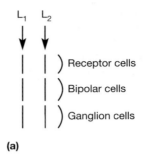

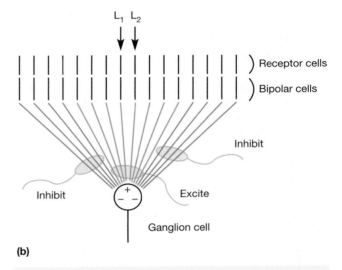

Figure 8.12 Different degrees of convergence. (a) Extreme foveal situation of no convergence, i.e. a one-to-one link between receptors and ganglions via bipolars. The eye can resolve the difference even between light L_1 and light L_2, since different one-to-one links are made. (b) Some convergence. Eight receptors all feed via bipolars to excite one ganglion cell and eight inhibit it. Contrast the surface area of excitation between (a) and (b).

rather little flow would be generated from what is caught by a single roof. If, however, it was pouring down at number 12 but dry at number 22 we would be aware of this from monitoring individual drainpipes. As you can see, two different sorts of information are derived from the communal and the individual drainpipes.

By analogy with the drainpipes, the eye has the benefit of both systems. When you resolve fine detail, as in threading a needle, by means of eye movements the image is brought to the fovea. When you want to detect the presence of a weak light stimulating a relatively large area of retina, the eyes move to bring the image away from the fovea. You can experiment with this. Find a faint distant star and stare in an attentive way at it. You might find that it then disappears. Staring corresponds to bringing its image to a focus at the fovea. The fovea is an area where the cells show little convergence of their outputs and therefore it is not associated with the capacity to integrate weak light over a relatively large area. This is the capacity needed to detect a weak light. Look to one side of the star, and it should reappear. This corresponds to the image falling on a rod-rich area, with considerable convergence of output and thereby a high capacity to detect weak lights.

Colour

Introduction

So far we have mainly considered the detection of images in terms of light–dark. How do we perceive colour? Imagine an eye that only has rods and is lacking cones. Could it extract information on the wavelength of light? You have seen that rods are *differentially* sensitive to wavelength (Figure 8.6), which might suggest that they are able to do this. However, it is not possible for rods to exploit this differential sensitivity to encode information on wavelength, for the following reason.

As shown in Figure 8.6, a light of 498 nm is the optimal to stimulate rods. See Figure 8.13. Suppose that a light of this wavelength (indicated as X) and intensity 100 units falls on the rods. It generates action potentials at a frequency of 100 per second in the associated ganglion cell. Now keeping light intensity at 100 units, suppose that the wavelength is changed to Y, to which the rods are less sensitive. The action potential frequency falls to, say, 50 per second. Can the frequency of action potentials in the ganglion cell thereby give a measure of wavelength? This might work provided that the light intensity always stays the same. But, of course, the world is not made up of lights having constant intensity. The rods and thereby the ganglion could not distinguish between a light of 100 units intensity at wavelength X and one of 200 units intensity at wavelength Y (Figure 8.13). Of course, we are able to make such distinctions. Blue looks blue whether it is an intense blue light or a faint one. So how is this achieved?

Role of cones

By employing more than one type of cone, the visual system *in effect* compares the responses of one cone with that of another (Figure 8.6). Suppose that a light of wavelength 420 nm falls on the retina. The S cone will always be more strongly stimulated than the M or L, irrespective of the intensity of light. Figure 8.14(a) demonstrates this. Contrast this with light of a wavelength of 534 nm (part (b)). The M cones are most activated, the L cones less so and the S cones the least. At 564 nm (part (c)), the L cones are most stimulated, the M cones less so and the S cones not at all. As shown, these ratios of responses will remain the same even if the intensity is halved to 50 units. That is to say, it is the *ratio* of responses between the component cones that determines colour.

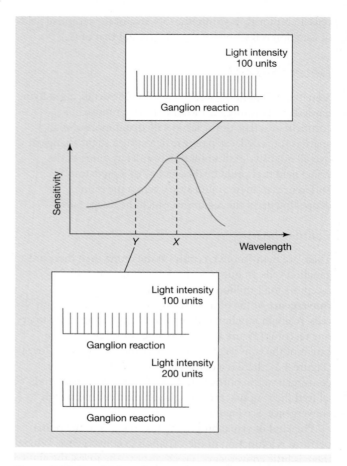

Figure 8.13 Sensitivity of a population of rods to different wavelengths and response of associated ganglion cell.

Source: after Toates (1998c, Fig. 4.21, p. 116).

You can demonstrate a colour illusion yourself (Figure 8.15) and understand it in terms of the properties of cones. Brightly illuminate the page, stare at the cross for 1–2 minutes and finally transfer your gaze to the white area. You should see colours appear for a while. They should be rather different from cross at which you stared. This is an illusion since the paper is white. How is it explained?

When light first falls on them, a population of cones tends to give a strong response. However, by exposure to light, they soon adapt or 'fatigue'. Other cones, which are relatively non-stimulated, will not fatigue. While you stare at the green area, this will fatigue M cones within an area of retina but L cones within this same area will be relatively non-fatigued, since they absorb little of the light at this wavelength. When you divert your gaze to the plain white area, the light that is stimulating the 'green-fatigued' area of retina is white. White light is made up of all the colours of the spectrum, including green and red (Figure 8.2). So the red component of the white light will stimulate preferentially a population of L cones, which are not fatigued, and therefore they give a

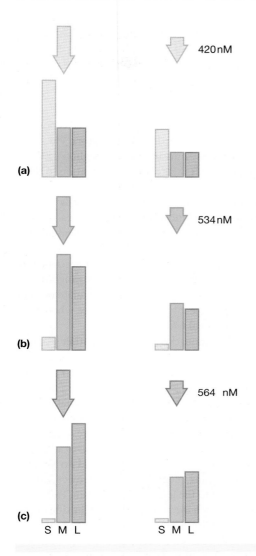

(a)

(b)

(c)

   S M L   S M L

Figure 8.14 Relative sensitivities of the three types of cones to three different wavelengths of light at two different intensities (left 100 units and right 50 units): (a) wavelength 420 nm, (b) 534 nm and (c) 564 nm.

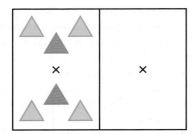

Figure 8.15 Coloured object for producing illusion.

strong response. The M component stimulates a fatigued population of M cones, which respond weakly. It is therefore as if the eye is being stimulated with red light and that is what you perceive. Within a short time, the red cones are as fatigued as the green and so the perception is of white.

One possible mode of connections to a ganglion cell is that the output from, say, M cones within an area excites the cell whereas the output from L cones inhibits it (an M^+L^- area) (Livingstone and Hubel, 1988). Thus, an increase in firing above the spontaneous level indicates medium-wavelength light and suppression to below this indicates long-wavelength light. This is termed **opponent-process coding** (Martin, 1998). A different receptive field property could consist of L cones exciting and M cones inhibiting, i.e. L^+M^- (Figure 8.16(a)). Still other ganglion cells have receptive fields based on area rather than wavelength (Figure 8.16(b)).

So much for processing by cells at the retina; we now consider the transmission of this information to the brain.

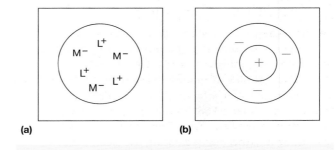

(a)   **(b)**

Figure 8.16 Opponent processing in inputs to a ganglion cell: (a) based on wavelength and (b) based on space at the retina.

Section summary

1 Oculomotor muscles rotate the eyes in their sockets to maintain the point of interest in the image in alignment with the fovea.

2 The retinal sensory receptors are rods and three types of cone. These absorb light and thereby change their electrical state.

3 Some retinal ganglion cells have a concentric (centre–surround) receptive field consisting of ON and OFF areas.

4 Light falling on the ON area excites the ganglion cell relative to its spontaneous firing rate whereas light falling in the OFF area inhibits it.

continued

Section summary *cont.*

5 The three types of cone have different sensitivities to the wavelength of light.

6 Acuity is high at and near the fovea.

7 On going away from the fovea, sensitivity to weak lights increases.

8 In opponent-process coding for colour, light that is absorbed by cones of one type excites a ganglion cell, whereas that absorbed by cones of a different kind inhibits it.

Test your knowledge

(Answers on page 217)

8.2 Which of the following types of cone have any sensitivity to light of a wavelength 580 nm? (i) Short, (ii) medium, (iii) long.

8.3 Consider the receptive field of a ganglion cell shown in Figure 8.9, the situation of part (a) and the light stimulus of duration marked 'light'. Which of the following would tend to increase the frequency of action potentials in the period marked 'light'? (i) Increasing the intensity of light, (ii) enlarging the size of the spot of light, (iii) decreasing the size of the spot of light.

8.4 In Figure 8.13, suppose that the rods are stimulated with light of wavelength Y and the response of the ganglion cell is 10 action potentials per second. What would be the expected response in action potentials per second for a shift of wavelength to X, while holding intensity constant? (i) 5, (ii) 20, (iii) 1.

8.5 Consider the receptive field shown in Figure 8.16(a). Suppose that just the central region of the receptive field (corresponding to the inner circle of part (b)) is illuminated with light of wavelength 620 nm. Which of the following would increase the activity of the ganglion cell? (i) Increasing the intensity of the light, (ii) keeping intensity constant but increasing the size of area within the receptive field stimulated, (iii) shifting the wavelength to 520 nm.

Basics of visual pathways

Introduction

The message from sensory receptors to bipolar cells conveys information about light absorbed by the receptors. Via synapses, bipolar cells relay information to ganglion cells (Figure 8.5). Ganglion cells then convey information to the brain as a pattern of action potentials in their axons. The first part of the bundle of axons of the ganglion cells constitutes the optic nerve, one of the cranial nerves. After entering the brain, the same bundle is termed the 'optic tract' (Figure 8.17).

As part of the 'classical' route (and that most described in psychology), Figure 8.17 shows a destination of ganglion cells: a nucleus of the thalamus, the lateral geniculate nucleus (LGN). LGN neurons project to the visual cortex, where they form synapses with cortical neurons.

As part of different ('non-classical') routes, other ganglion cells project to other destinations, e.g. the superior colliculus. This pathway, a **subcortical pathway**, also plays a role in perception.

The world viewed by the eyes is termed 'the visual field' (see top overlapping colours in Figure 8.17). Consider the visual field to the right of the midline of each eye. Light arising from the right half of the visual field arrives at the left half of each retina. Light from the left visual field arrives at the right half of each retina. Neural pathways project from the left half of each eye to the left half of the brain. Pathways from the right side of each eye project to the right side of the brain. Half the pathway from each eye crosses over to the other side, at the optic chiasm. Because of the cross-over of pathways, information arriving at each eye from a given object can be compared. The fact that the eyes have a slightly different perspective contributes to the perception of depth.

In stating that information is *conveyed* from the retina to the brain, an important qualification is needed. Information in the visual image is not converted one-to-one into an electrical signal that conveys exactly the same information. As just described, some information processing occurs. How this is done can be understood in terms of the connections between the neurons within the visual pathways. In the course of conveying information, some information potentially available in the image is *discarded* or given relatively little weight (e.g. on uniform illumination) and other information is *accentuated* (e.g. on changes in intensity or wavelength). The brain receives information already predigested as far as its importance is concerned.

Now for more details.

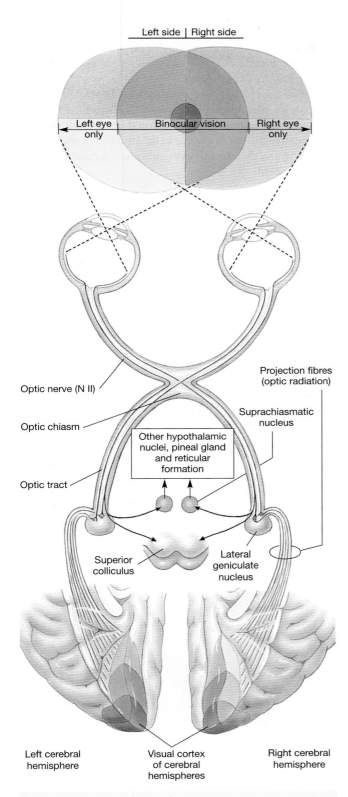

Left side | Right side

Left eye only | Binocular vision | Right eye only

Optic nerve (N II)

Optic chiasm

Optic tract

Other hypothalamic nuclei, pineal gland and reticular formation

Projection fibres (optic radiation)

Suprachiasmatic nucleus

Superior colliculus

Lateral geniculate nucleus

Left cerebral hemisphere

Visual cortex of cerebral hemispheres

Right cerebral hemisphere

Figure 8.17 The visual system.

Source: Martini *et al.* (2000, Fig. 18-25, p. 492).

Lateral geniculate nucleus

Ganglion cells have a concentric (centre–surround) receptive field. Ganglion cells synapse with LGN cells. Each LGN cell also has a concentric (centre–surround) receptive field property that is very similar to that of its associated ganglion cell. Suppose that a particular ganglion cell is a specialist at extracting information on colour. Because of its input, the associated LGN cell will also have this sensitivity and it will transmit information on colour to the cortex. Like ganglion cells, the receptive field of an LGN cell is in one or other eye but not both, i.e. LGN cells are monocular. LGN cells project their axons to the primary visual cortex.

The cortex

The role of different areas

The classical account (to which complications need to be added) is that LGN cells transmit visual information, which terminates at part of the visual cortex. This is termed the **primary visual cortex**, also known as the 'striate cortex', 'V1' and 'area 17' and occupies part of the occipital lobe. See Figure 8.17. Neighbouring areas that are also concerned with visual processing are termed 'prestriate cortex' (Zeki, 1993).

Neurons within the primary visual cortex process information to extract features of the visual world and also project information to the prestriate cortex. In some primate species, over 50% of the whole cortex is engaged in processing visual information.

Simple cortical cells

When the response properties of neurons in the visual cortex are examined, an orderly relationship between retina and cortex appears. Adjacent regions of retina are associated with adjacent neurons in the visual cortex, termed a **topographical map** (Zeki, 1993). Damage to a region of visual cortex is associated with loss of vision in a particular area of visual field, termed a 'scotoma'.

The receptive fields of cortical cells are typically different from those of ganglion and LGN cells. Remember – the receptive field of a cell anywhere in the visual system is defined by what stimulus of light *at the retina* alters the cell's activity. Rather than being concentric, a cortical cell typically has a slit-shaped receptive field and is termed a 'simple cortical cell' (Hubel and Wiesel, 1959) (Figure 8.18). It shows little or no response to a spot of light (though some cells with concentric receptive fields are also found here; von der Heydt, 1995). A given cortical cell can often be driven from light in the retina of either eye, i.e. they are binocular.

How do scientists explain the form of this receptive field? Part of the explanation is as follows (Hubel and Wiesel, 1959). Imagine a series of ganglion cells, G_1, G_2, ... Their receptive fields, made up from an ON centre and an OFF

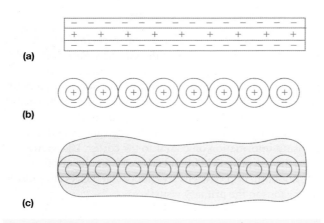

(a)

(b)

(c)

Figure 8.18 The properties of a simple cortical cell: (a) receptive field, made up of excitatory inner slit and inhibitory surround, (b) receptive fields of a series of ganglion cells that provide the excitatory input to the cortical cell and (c) optimal stimulus to trigger the cortical cell.

surround, form a straight line on the retina (Figure 8.18(b)). Each ganglion cell projects to a corresponding LGN cell, $G_1 \rightarrow LGN_1$, $G_2 \rightarrow LGN_2$, ... This *series* of LGN cells projects to excite a *single* cortical cell.

What is the optimal stimulus to trigger activity in this cortical cell? Activity in all the LGN cells that project to it. Such activity will derive from activity in all the ganglion cells that project to the LGN cells. What light stimulus will maximize the activity in these ganglion cells? A slit of light having a particular location and orientation (Figure 8.18(c)).

The sequence, receptor → bipolar → ganglion → LGN → simple cortical cell is an example of hierarchical processing.

For their contribution to neuroscience, in 1981, David Hubel, Roger Sperry and Torsten Wiesel were awarded the Nobel Prize. In his Nobel lecture, Hubel (1982) explained how he and Wiesel discovered simple cortical cells. In the tradition of Kuffler's study of ganglion cells, they had been presenting concentric stimuli to the retina but without much reaction from cortical cells. Then, by accident, the edge of the slide on which the test stimuli were presented cast a shadow in the form of a straight line on the screen. Hubel reported (p. 517) that 'the cell went off like a machine gun'. Never underestimate the role of luck and chance events in the process of scientific discovery.

Each stage extracts a new feature from the raw data at the retina and the sequence continues even beyond simple cells. However, hierarchical processing is only one mode of cortical processing: there is extensive ('top-down') feedback of information throughout the visual pathways and this also contributes to cortical processing (Ferster, 2004).

Some simple cortical cells respond to a bar of light at a particular orientation and location on the retina but are particularly sensitive to change in the stimulus. A slit of light appearing and then rapidly extinguishing is a powerful trigger to them.

Complex cortical cells

Suppose that a series of simple cells, all with receptive fields of the same orientation but different locations (L_1, L_2, ...) on the retina, excite another cortical cell, termed a complex cell (Figure 8.19). A slit of light at any of the locations is sufficient to excite the complex cell. Firing of this cell encodes the feature that there is a slit of light of a given orientation (in this case, vertical) somewhere within a region of retina. This appears to be the start of extracting a feature of invariance from the image. A zebra is still the same zebra even if it moves.

Concerning simple cells that are sensitive to a dynamic stimulus (rapid on–off), one could imagine a series of them all projecting to a complex cell. The optimal stimulus to trigger such a cell could be a line of light rapidly moving through the receptive field. In this way the basics of a movement detection system can be seen.

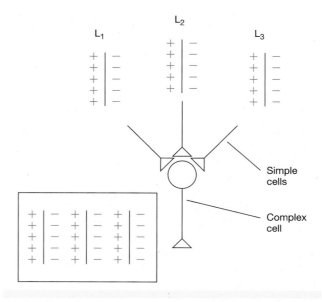

Figure 8.19 A complex cell with inputs from a series of simple cells.

Grandmother cells?

Such hierarchical information processing raises an interesting problem. Consider the sequence, retinal receptors, to bipolar cells, ganglion cells, then LGN cells, to cells in the primary visual area of the cortex and then to other regions of cortex. More and more features are 'extracted' from the information available at the image.

How we perceive, say, a yellow Volkswagen is still something of a mystery. Do we have a specific 'yellow Volkswagen' neuron at a late stage of processing in the cortex? The theory that we have a specific neuron for the perception of each object is summed up in the expression **grandmother cell**. Thus, following this line of theorizing, we would have a neuron specific to a particular grandmother (see Barlow, 1995).

It seems implausible that we have a single neuron (or even a dedicated number of neurons) for each perception. Remove this single neuron and we would fail to identify our grandmother! Only a slight accident or a lowered blood supply to the brain region might kill the neuron and then we would have a selective blindness for one grandmother (Zeki, 1993). In spite of the rejection of grandmother cells as being naive, scientists are at present unable to explain the later stages of perception.

Communication between the two hemispheres

General

Having established the route from eye to brain, this section considers some further routes of transmission of visual information.

Among other routes, the two hemispheres communicate visual information between themselves by means of the axons that form the corpus callosum. Thus, certain information processed in one hemisphere can be made available to the opposite hemisphere: in the later stages of processing, cells are found with receptive fields sensitive to information processed in either hemisphere (Bullier, 2004). The visual system provides a good means for investigating inter-hemispheric communication.

Figure 8.20 shows how some responsibilities are divided between hemispheres, e.g. language is mainly processed in the left. This hemisphere controls the activity of the right hand. The left hand is controlled from the right hemisphere.

In Figure 8.20, information from the right half of the visual field (indicated by the right hand with a pencil) is transformed from light to electrical activity in the left half of each retina (indicated blue) and then arrives in the left hemisphere (via pathways represented as blue). Information from the left visual field impinges on the right half of each retina (red), is transmitted via pathways (represented as red) and arrives at the right hemisphere.

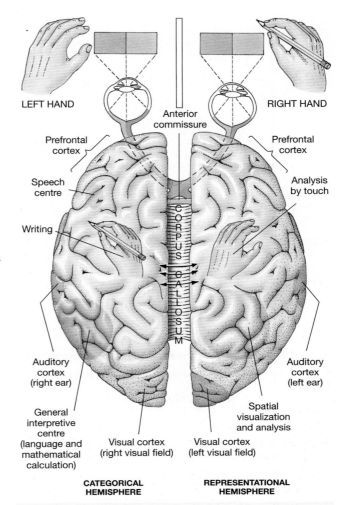

Figure 8.20 The brain emphasizing the corpus callosum.

Source: adapted from Martini *et al.* (2000, Fig. 16–8, p. 436).

Split brains

Sometimes the corpus callosum (Figure 8.20) is surgically cut to stop epilepsy that arises from abnormal electrical activity in one hemisphere influencing the other (Sperry, 1974). Patients receiving this operation are termed **split-brain** patients. Using such patients and tests in which images are very briefly flashed onto a screen, it is possible to send information to just one hemisphere, a 'divided visual-field presentation' (Figure 8.21). First, follow the sequence of Figure 8.20 shown as the 'red route'. Then you will appreciate that, when presented in the left visual field of Figure 8.21, the information 'nut' is available only to the right hemisphere. It is found that such patients can select the nut with the left hand but can neither select the correct object with the right hand nor verbalize 'nut'.

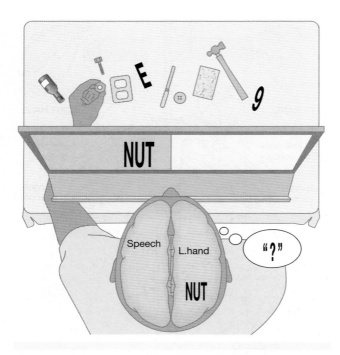

Figure 8.21 Projecting information to just one hemisphere.
Source: based on Sperry (1970), in Popper and Eccles (1977, Fig. E5-3).

If the right hand touches the objects or they are projected to the right visual field, the patient can verbally name them (follow the blue route of Figure 8.20). Each hemisphere can function on its own but the person cannot perform tasks that require inter-hemispheric communication.

Since the left hemisphere controls speech and therefore is responsible for reports of conscious experience, is it the case that only the left hemisphere is conscious? Although the right hemisphere can perform certain tasks, since these cannot be articulated verbally is the right hemisphere unconscious? Such questions pose enormous challenges for biological psychology.

We now look at some examples of processing that takes place beyond the primary visual cortex but in order to do so we need to look in a little more detail at the route from eye to brain.

Section summary

1 The classical sequence of information transfer is receptors → bipolar cells → ganglion cells → LGN cells → visual cortex.

2 Another route ('subcortical') is via the superior colliculus.

3 LGN cells have concentric receptive fields corresponding to the associated ganglion cells.

4 Simple cortical cells have slit-shaped receptive fields.

5 There is some hemispheric specialization.

6 The corpus callosum communicates visual information from one hemisphere to another.

Test your knowledge

(Answer on page 217)

8.6 Consider the simple cortical cell, the receptive field of which is shown in Figure 8.18 and the light stimulus shown. Which of the following would be expected to decrease the frequency of action potentials shown by the cell? (i) rotating the light stimulus to an orientation of 45° to that shown, (ii) Rotating the light stimulus to an orientation of 90° to that shown, (iii) keeping the position the same but increasing the intensity of light.

8.7 Figures 8.17 and 8.20 show cross-over of axons at the optic chiasm. These axons are part of which kind of cell?

8.8 Complete the following: 'When a person looks straight ahead, information from the left visual field arrives at the ____ half of each eye and is transmitted to the ____ hemisphere'.

Functional specialization: perception and action

Introduction

Anyone's first intuitive guess as to how the link between perception and action is organized might be rather as represented in Figure 8.22(a), i.e. a single 'general purpose' sensory-perceptual system (Goodale and Milner, 2004). Sensory systems detect events in the world. These events are then perceived by the brain, at which point they enter conscious awareness. On the basis of conscious perceptions, we then organize motor action.

In reality, perception and action are linked rather as in Figure 8.22(b). Within the visual system, there is **parallel processing**. That is to say, there exists a *division of labour* between our conscious perception of the world and our rapid action on the world, this being an example of **functional specialization** (Norman, 2002; Zeki, 1993).

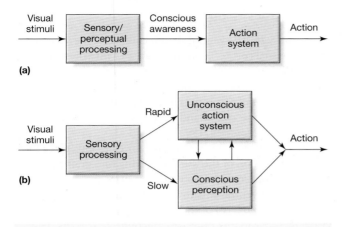

(a)

(b)

Figure 8.22 Perception and action: (a) intuitive view and (b) model of how perception and action really relate. There is a rapid unconscious route to action as well as a slow conscious route. There are interactions between these routes.

This distinction between perception and action can be better understood by first considering a related functional distinction, one that starts right at the retina, to which we now turn.

The initial stages of specialization

Qualities such as wavelength and movement are, to some extent, processed separately. This division of labour starts at the retina. Work on non-human primates reveals that different types of ganglion cell correspond to the start of separate systems ('channels') of processing (De Valois and De Valois, 1980; Merigan and Maunsell, 1993). We shall deal with the two best-known systems, though more exist (Kaplan, 2004). At the start of the two channels are two types of cell: magnocellular (abbreviated as magno or M) ganglion cells and parvocellular (parvo or P) ganglion cells.

The magno ganglion cells are especially sensitive to fast-moving stimuli and to differences in illumination in the image. They provide an input to the brain from which movement is calculated but are relatively insensitive to differences in wavelength. Their receptive fields are distributed over the retina.

The parvo ganglion cells are sensitive to stationary images and to colour, in that they tend to be strongly triggered by, say, contrast between red and green in the image (Zeki, 1993). Their receptive fields are found particularly at the fovea.

The functional segregation is emphasized at the LGN where the inputs from magno and parvo cells are anatomically segregated (Merigan and Maunsell, 1993) (Figure 8.23). Thus, a magno ganglion cell synapses onto an LGN cell, so the LGN cell has 'magno' properties similar to the magno ganglion cell.

A parvo ganglion cell synapses onto a different LGN cell, so that this LGN cell has similar properties to the parvo ganglion cell. Hence the information sent to the cortex remains functionally segregated, constituting what is termed a **magno system** and a **parvo system.**

The magno system is particularly tuned for changes in the image. Images that are visible with the help of only this system disappear within a few seconds if fixated (Livingstone and Hubel, 1988). Thus, it is tuned for the detection of moving objects. The parvo system is specialized for analysis of detail, which can take time and exploits differences in wavelength. The magno system appears to be evolutionarily older, with the parvo system being a more recent acquisition (Livingstone and Hubel, 1995).

In functional terms, the older system provides the trigger for a very rapid means of reacting to significant and dynamic, even life-threatening, events. The newer system provides the input to a slower but more fine-grained conscious resolution of detail in the visual world. These two somewhat distinct sources of information feed into two corresponding streams within the brain, as described next.

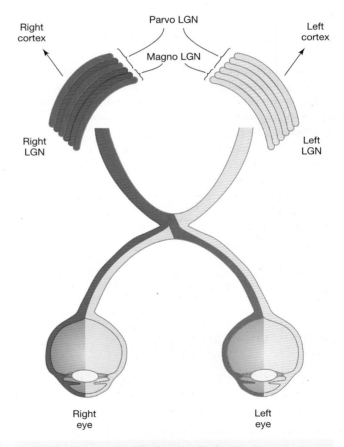

Figure 8.23 The LGN showing segregation of parvo and magno systems.

Source: after Bear *et al.* (1996).

Basics of the brain's streams

Figure 8.17 showed pathways of ganglion cells to the superior colliculus and we noted that some visual processing is carried out by such subcortical pathways. This is represented again in Figure 8.24. Note the subcortical route from the retina, via the superior colliculus and a region of the thalamus, termed the pulvinar, to the posterior parietal cortex. So, one division of processing is *between* cortical and subcortical processing. However, as Figure 8.24 shows, there also exists streaming *within* the cortex, and this is our primary concern here. These divisions exemplify parallel processing.

Basics of cortical streaming

Note that, beyond the visual cortex, further processing occurs at the prestriate area. Then visual information divides into the two streams for even more specialized processing (Figure 8.24). Of major importance in the psychology of vision was the recognition that there exists within the cortex a fundamental division of responsibility between two streams: the **ventral stream** and the **dorsal stream** (Norman, 2002; Ungerleider and Mishkin, 1982). There is still some controversy concerning exactly how the roles of these two streams should be characterized (Glover, 2004). However, with respect particularly to humans, a general consensus is as follows.

The ventral stream is involved in high-level visual cognition, the handling of *knowledge* about the world. The dorsal stream constitutes a rather direct link between certain visual stimuli and the control of *action* (Goodale and Humphrey, 1998).

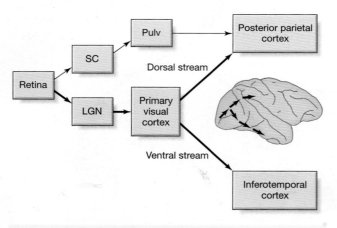

Figure 8.24 The streams of visual processing, showing subcortical route via the superior colliculus (SC) and cortical streams termed ventral and dorsal streams. LGN = lateral geniculate nucleus; pulv = pulvinar, a region of the thalamus.

Source: based on Goodale and Humphrey (1998, Fig. 1).

The ventral stream

See Figure 8.24. The ventral stream consists of the sequence, primary visual cortex → prestriate area → inferotemporal cortex. Within this stream, the inferior temporal cortex is the last stage in processing of purely visual information (Gross *et al.*, 1993). Parts of this route encode and process information on the size, shape, colour and texture of a visual object (Merigan and Maunsell, 1993).

The ventral stream is responsible for conscious perception and interpretation of the world involving fine-grained discrimination, comparison with memories and allocation of meaning. The ventral stream underlies our formation of perceptions ('models') of the world and our ability to use visual memory to link otherwise unconnected events. This stream is associated with our ability to articulate verbally the 'what is it' of the world, such as the shape and colour of something and the meaning attached to it.

The ventral stream is especially sensitive to events at the fovea, where resolution of detail is high (Baizer *et al.*, 1991). The ventral stream is dominated by the parvo system but with a considerable magno contribution (Kaplan, 2004; Merigan and Maunsell, 1993). It is somewhat slower than the dorsal stream (Boussaoud *et al.*, 1996). Under some conditions, the ventral stream can play a role in controlling action but its activity is not directly linked to action. There are no specified links between this stream and motor output. Rather the ventral stream has links to areas of brain underlying memory, semantics and planning (Goodale and Humphrey, 1998).

The dorsal stream

The dorsal stream consists of the sequence, primary visual cortex → prestriate area → parietal cortex (PC) (Reid, 1999) (Figure 8.24). It performs *visuomotor transformations* such as to allow adaptive interaction with the world, e.g. reaching to grasp an object. The dorsal stream is responsible for extracting information on the size and location of the object so that an appropriate motor response can be organized. The dorsal stream is dominated by information derived from the magno system (with a small parvo contribution) and has a relatively high sensitivity to information deriving from peripheral regions of the retina (Kaplan, 2004; Merigan and Maunsell, 1993).

Cooperation between streams and rationale for their existence

A 'perception' versus 'action' dichotomy captures part of the truth but a strict dichotomy would be over-simple. Our perception and action in the world have a seamless flow and coordination to them, so there seems to be a close interaction between streams, as indicated in Figure 8.22. Indeed, anatomical cross-connections and corresponding functional cross-referencing of information between streams are such that the streams are interdependent (Merigan and Maunsell, 1993).

Imagine that, through experience, objects become familiar and we acquire responses that are performed in association with them. The ventral stream acting together with the prefrontal cortex constructs plans and sets goals regarding these objects, e.g. pick a fruit (Goodale and Milner, 2004). Then, given the appropriate stimuli arising from these objects, the dorsal stream triggers the action in relation to them. For example, the ventral stream and its associated processing might compute that a fruit, with a certain colour, significance and nutritional value, is hanging on a branch and desirable, whereas the dorsal stream would compute and organize the hand movements for reaching and picking it.

Some division of labour between streams makes good sense from a perspective of 'design' and evolution. Consider the kind of processing involved in perception of an object, e.g. identification, attachment of meaning of exactly what it is, etc. This is very different from the calculations involved in direct interaction with the object, e.g. how to position the fingers in picking it up. If there were no such division of labour and everything went through a single channel, we might well be seriously slowed in our interactions with the world.

Evidence from illusions

If we have two visual streams, is it possible to dissociate them? A clever experiment permitted this. Take a look at Figure 8.25. In part (a), the inner circle, to the left, surrounded by small circles looks larger to most people than the circle to the right, surrounded by large circles. In fact, they are the same size. Conversely, in part (b) the two inner circles look the same size, even though that to the right is physically larger. Participants were asked to judge the size of such circles and the result was as just described. So, you can fool the perceptual part of the brain but can you fool the brain/hand?

To test this, a three-dimensional version of the illusion was constructed (Aglioti *et al.*, 1995). See Figure 8.26. Participants were asked to pick up the inner disc and the aperture of their grasp was recorded as the fingers prepared to take hold of it. It was found that the size of grasp was determined almost entirely by the actual size of the disc rather than its perceived size.

So, here is a functional dissociation between streams. Brain damage too can produce a dissociation, described next.

Lesions within the streams

As a general point, under some conditions, lesions to two different regions of the brain produce what is termed a **double dissociation**. That is, a lesion to a brain region y disrupts feature Y of behaviour but not feature X, whereas

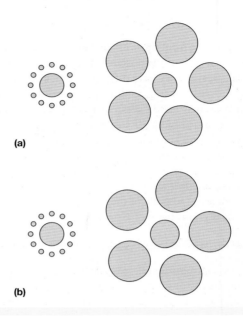

(a)

(b)

Figure 8.25 The Ebbinghaus illusion: (a) inner circles are the same size; (b) inner circles are of different sizes.

Source: Goodale and Humphrey (1998, Fig. 4, p. 198).

lesion to brain region x disrupts feature X but not Y. A double dissociation is a very valuable finding, since it reveals a specific behavioural deficit linked to restricted damage to a particular brain region. By contrast, if a lesion knocked out all processing this might tell us rather little.

To exemplify this principle, a double dissociation arises when the effect of a lesion to the dorsal stream is compared with that of one made to the ventral stream (Goodale and Humphrey, 1998; Mishkin *et al.*, 1983; Pohl, 1973). A lesion to the ventral stream disrupts perception but not action, whereas a lesion to the dorsal stream disrupts action but not perception.

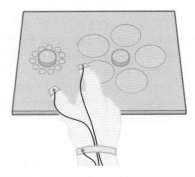

Figure 8.26 A three-dimensional version of the Ebbinghaus illusion, showing diodes emitting infrared light attached to thumb, finger and wrist. These allowed the trajectory of the response to be computed.

Source: Goodale and Humphrey (1998, Fig. 5, p. 199).

Damage to the dorsal stream

Patients suffering from **optic ataxia** have damage typically to the superior region of the posterior parietal cortex, part of the dorsal stream. They have difficulty in making directed reaching movements and in adjusting the orientation and magnitude of their hand's grasp in a way that would facilitate holding the target object (discussed by Goodale and Milner, 2004; Goodale and Humphrey, 1998). However, they are able to give a verbal description of its orientation. Their problem is not one of vision *per se*: patients can recognize people and can read. Neither is it a problem of motor control as such: patients can point to parts of their body with eyes closed. It is a specifically a problem of *visuomotor* translation.

Damage to the ventral stream

The term **visual agnosia** refers to an inability to recognize objects by the use of vision. It takes more than one form, a good example being the case of Dee Fletcher.

A personal angle
Dee Fletcher

In 1988 at the age of 34, Dee Fletcher, a Scottish woman living in Italy and working as a translator, suffered accidental carbon monoxide poisoning. This appears to have damaged regions of occipital cortex at the start of the ventral stream, while sparing the primary visual cortex and leaving the dorsal stream intact (Goodale and Humphrey, 1998; Goodale *et al.*, 1991). Dee cannot recognize relatives visually but has no trouble doing so based on their voices. She is deficient at identifying geometric shapes by vision but can do so by feel when placed in her hand. Dee has been studied extensively at the University of St. Andrews in Scotland.

Dee is impressive in her ability to perform action in the world directed to the same shapes that cause her trouble in their perception. For example, she is able to reach out and post a card through a slot in a way that is appropriate to the slot's orientation but without being able to verbally describe this orientation (see Figure 8.27). Whereas Dee can very accurately direct motor actions towards a target, she is unable to do the same towards an imaginary target displaced from the actual one. Dee is 'stimulus-bound', *acting* in relation to certain physically present stimuli in the visual world.

Dee can discriminate colours and indeed on the basis of this is able to recognize one of St. Andrews'

better-known psychology professors, who is famous for his multi-tinted hair.

Thus, comparing Dee and an optic ataxia patient (earlier) reveals a double dissociation between brain damage and deficit.

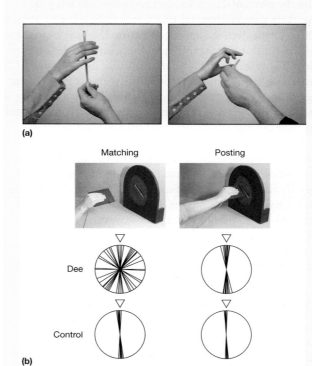

Figure 8.27 Visual abilities of Dee. (a) Grasping. Note that Dee can organize appropriate grasp of pencil, while being able only to guess whether it is horizontal or vertical. (b) (Left) matching and (right) posting tasks. Dee's results at matching and posting tasks, as compared to those of a control. White arrow head indicates orientation of slot for results shown.
Source: (a) Goodale and Milner (2004, Figure 2.1, p.17) (b) Goodale *et al.* (1991, Fig. 1).

Section summary

1 There is not just a single system underlying our perception and visually guided action.

2 Within the cortex there is parallel processing in the form of the ventral stream, involved mainly with perception, and the dorsal stream, involved mainly with action.

3 Certain visual illusions and brain damage can dissociate the streams.

Test your knowledge

(Answer on page 217)

8.9 Consider the 3-D version of the Ebbinghaus illusion shown in Figure 8.26 and relate this to Figure 8.25. (a) In part (a), reaching to the left disc, the size of grasp would be (i) smaller, (ii) bigger or (iii) the same as reaching to the right. (b) In part (b), reaching to the left disc, the size of grasp would be (i) smaller, (ii) bigger or (iii) the same as reaching to the right.

8.2

Functional specialization within perception

Introduction

So, there is functional specialization *between* perception and action. This section will show where functional specialization also occurs *within* the system of perception. Beyond the primary visual cortex and largely within the ventral stream, distinct cortical regions analyse particular qualities of the visual image, such as form, colour or motion. It represents a daunting achievement that, at some level, this all appears to be integrated to give a unified perception.

In spite of changing retinal information that a given object provides, the brain performs processing that yields a perception of its invariance, or, as it is often called, its **constancy**. For example, as a person walks towards you, the image of them on the retina increases in size but the person does not appear to get bigger. This is termed **size constancy**. Similarly, if an object is rotated, the image changes but the brain's processing yields the perception that shape has remained the same, termed 'shape constancy'.

How can particular parts of the visual system be identified with particular functional roles? A major source of understanding derives from brain-damaged patients who can exhibit quite selective deficits.

Analysis and identification of shapes

Filling in details

As an example of feature extraction, Figure 8.1 demonstrated illusory contours. In the ventral stream, cells have been identified in the prestriate area (but not V1) which encode illusory contours (Gross *et al.*, 1993) (Figure 8.28). In part (a) the cell responds to a real contour (light bar) when in an

orientation near to vertical but not when it is near to horizontal. Part (b) shows that the cell responds also to an *illusory* contour at the same orientation. The cell has extracted a feature from the information provided by the white stripes.

It appears that, at area TE (a region of the inferior temporal cortex), information comes together into an integrated representation of the object, involving comparison with memory (Gross *et al.*, 1993). Processing in this area encodes invariance, in that the object is interpreted as the same irrespective of where in the visual field it is located. As the sequence of processing along the ventral stream progresses, neurons become less sensitive to simple features (e.g. a straight line) at specific locations and more sensitive to complex features regardless of location. Neurons here are relatively insensitive to retinal image size and orientation on the retina.

The anterior regions of the temporal lobe encode 'prototypes' of visual objects, against which actual visual objects can be compared (Weiskrantz and Saunders, 1984). Memory storage is in a form that is independent of a number of features of the image such as its size at the retina. This means that it is not necessary to compute each new variation of an object, such as a new size or orientation, and assess it as a quite separate entity. It can be allocated to a category.

Size constancy

In estimating object size, the brain integrates information on distance and image size, termed 'size constancy'. If the image size doubles but its distance halves, the brain computes that the object has stayed the same size. Figure 8.4(b) shows how the image size gets bigger as the object gets nearer.

In each case of constancy, the brain's role is as a *categorizer* (Zeki, 1993). The brain does not remember the details of the varying information sent from an object as changes occur in its distance, orientation or wavelength of illumination. It perceives unchanging features attributed to the object.

Information processing at the level of the inferior temporal cortex involves calculating invariance, e.g. size constancy (Farah *et al.*, 1999). The processing performed there provides representations of objects *as they are in the world*, rather than as their image is on the retina. For example, a monkey with an intact inferior temporal cortex can learn to discriminate two objects based upon their absolute size even though they are at different distances. This involves not responding on the basis of image size at the retina alone. Monkeys with inferior temporal cortex lesions have difficulty with this task and are more strongly driven by retinal image size.

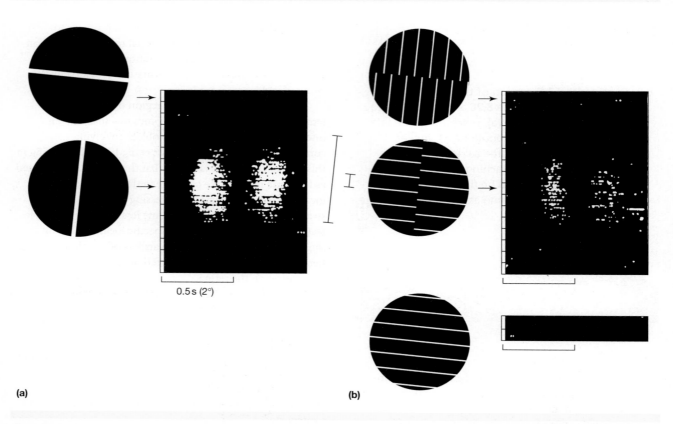

Figure 8.28 Response of a cell in prestriate area to (a) real and (b) illusory contours. Figure at bottom part of (b) shows that there is no response to control condition of stripes in the absence of illusory contour.

Source: von der Heydt and Peterhans (1989).

Face perception

Some information processed in the ventral stream at area TE projects to a neighbouring area of cortex termed the 'superior temporal polysensory area' (STP) (Farah *et al.*, 1999). Figure 8.29 shows the response of a neuron in the STP area. The preference for facial features is clear. Is this the much discussed grandmother cell (see earlier)? The neurons found so far are not specific for particular faces. They respond to monkey and human faces, as well as showing some sensitivity to other features (Gross *et al.*, 1993).

Types of agnosia

As noted earlier, a disruption of visual object recognition is termed visual agnosia. It is particularly seen when damage is to inferior temporal (IT) regions of cortex in both hemispheres or in just the right (Farah *et al.*, 1999; Pallis, 1955). It takes various forms.

In some cases, agnosia takes a specific form. In prosopagnosia, humans have difficulty in recognizing faces (Farah *et al.*, 1999; Rubens and Benson, 1971). They typically have suffered brain damage in the same areas of the temporal lobe that are activated during face recognition (as measured by electrical recording). Some can recognize faces in a general sense and might be able to identify their gender and expression but be unable to identify specific faces (Tranel *et al.*, 1988), even that of their partner. This suggests that attribution of specific identity is a further stage of processing beyond the identification of a general facial form.

Analysis of movement

Parts of the ventral stream that are driven mainly by the magno system extract information on movement. In rare cases, damage to a region of the stream leaves an individual with the inability to detect movement (Zihl *et al.*, 1983). Pouring tea appears as a series of frozen frames. An oncoming car would be perceived at a distance and then again when it is near, as if it is based on two frames cut from a film.

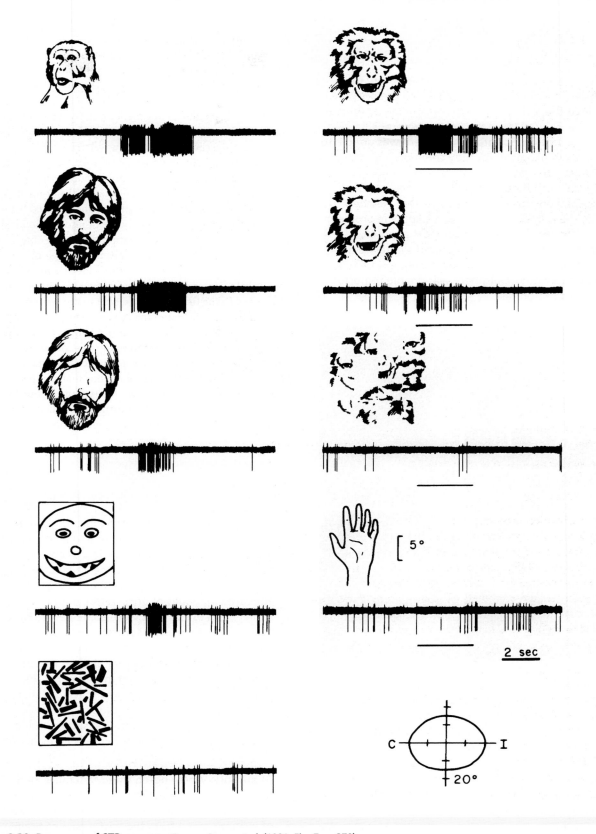

Figure 8.29 Response of STP neuron. *Source:* Bruce *et al.* (1981, Fig. 7, p. 379).

Seeing but not recognizing

A 47-year-old male physician with a history of heavy alcohol intake and damage to the occipital lobe of the left hemisphere was studied by Rubens and Benson (1971) at the Boston Veterans Administration Hospital. The patient was unable to recognize people or identify common objects. However, the problem was not perceptual processes as such. Even though unable to identify what objects were, he was able (unlike Dee Fletcher) to copy diagrams of them (Figure 8.30). The problem was described as 'associative visual agnosia', a failure to contextualize perceptions in terms of meaning. Rubens and Benson raise the issue of why the intact right hemisphere was unable to perform the recognition task.

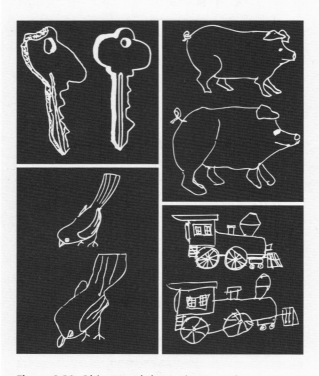

Figure 8.30 Objects and the patient's copies.

Source: Rubens and Benson (1971, p. 310).

Analysis of colour

A given object tends to look much the same colour in spite of differences in the balance of wavelengths of light that is projected at it and therefore differences in what is reflected, termed 'colour constancy' (Gregory, 1997; Zeki, 1993). For example, viewed under normal conditions, an orange looks basically of orange colour in a range of wavelengths of illumination. Some neurons in the ventral stream extract invariance in the form of colour constancy. What is invariant is the nature of the surface in terms of its physical properties, i.e. its tendency to absorb some wavelengths more than others.

The signal produced in ganglion cells corresponding to a coloured object is not sufficient to explain how the object looks the same colour in various wavelengths of illumination, i.e. colour constancy. Colour is not an intrinsic quality of an object that gets impressed upon the brain (Zeki, 1993). Rather, it is a quality computed in the brain, based upon information on wavelength of light reflected from an object placed in context. One source of information is to compare neighbouring areas. Suppose that two objects are placed side by side. In the long wavelength region, one reflects a relatively high intensity and another reflects a relatively low intensity. The brain appears to allocate the colour red to the first object and blue to the second.

That brain damage can make a person blind for just one quality is evidence for functional specialization. Blindness just for colour is termed 'achromatopsia'. Colour perception involves the primary visual cortex (which appears to analyze wavelengths) and other cortical regions that are specific for processing colour (which appear to attribute colour to an object, by placing wavelength information in context). Loss of either area means loss of colour perception.

Madame R

In 1888, Dr L. Verrey, an ophthalmic surgeon in Neuchâtel, Switzerland, described Madame R., 60 years of age, who experienced loss of colour sensation in the right part of the visual field (Verrey, 1888). Everything, including coloured objects, appeared in shades of grey. Verrey noted that earlier cases of such loss were accompanied by loss of other faculties such as reading. However, Madame R. seemed to represent a pure case of loss of colour sensation with other abilities remaining functional, albeit with slight impairment. This suggested that activity within a specific brain region is a necessary condition for colour analysis. Verrey noted that this was a notion that several authors had resisted. It continued to be resisted even after Verrey provided his evidence (Zeki, 1993).

At autopsy, Verrey noted that Madame R. had a discrete lesion in the left occipital lobe outside the primary visual cortex. Madame R. is a good example of insight gained from the misfortune of brain

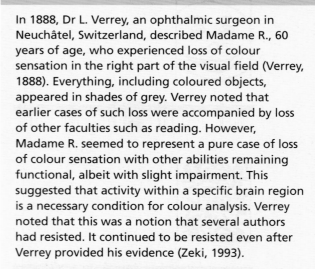

damage. Also, she exemplifies that evidence not fitting the current fashion still needs to be given serious consideration.

The next section considers in more detail the interactions of bottom-up and top-down contribution to perception.

Test your knowledge

(Answer on page 217)

8.10 Complete the following: 'As a person moves from 50 metres distance to 100 metres, the image of them on the retina _____ but they appear to remain _____ size'.

8.11 Consider the ganglion cell, the receptive field of which is shown in Figure 8.16(a). Suppose that it is located near to the fovea. Which system is this ganglion cell most likely a part of? (i) Magno, (ii) parvo.

Bottom-up and top-down factors in close-up

Introduction

The present section considers in more detail how bottom-up and top-down factors operate and their link with consciousness. Techniques of positron emission tomography (PET) and functional magnetic resonance imaging (fMRI) (Chapter 5, 'The brain') have provided valuable insight to this question (Frith and Dolan, 1997). This section describes their application to this issue.

Impoverished images

An example of the role of prior knowledge in perception was provided by the Dalmatian dog (Chapter 7, Figures 7.3 and 7.4). Figure 7.3 is an 'impoverished image', which at first is impossible to decipher. However, after the experience of Figure 7.4, it is difficult not to see a Dalmatian dog.

Similarly, when you first examine the images of Figure 8.31, they will probably look meaningless. However, try looking at Figure 8.32 (on the next page). When looking again at Figure 8.31 the images should make sense (Dolan *et al.*, 1997). It is possible to measure the activity of the brain when viewing each image of Figure 8.31, before and after exposure to Figure 8.32. The researchers suggest that parts of the brain that are concerned only with processing the visual input should be the same in both cases, since the image is the same (though top-down processing might affect even the input side). The assumption is that any changes in brain activity between first and second exposures represent the perception of the image, involving meaning and a top-down factor.

Comparing first and second exposures, those parts of the brain termed the 'primary visual areas' (primary visual cortex) showed no change in activity, suggesting that their activity is involved in extracting features of the image *per se.*

Increases in activity were noted in two areas when the image was viewed a second time. One of these is the medial parietal cortex (Figure 8.33). Other brain regions in which increases in activity between first and second viewing occurred depended upon what was viewed (Figure 8.34). When it was a human face, the right inferior temporal cortex increased in activity (part (a)). When it was an object, the left inferior temporal cortex increased in activity (part (b)).

Objects

Faces

Pre-learning

Figure 8.31 Impoverished stimuli to vision.
Source: Dolan *et al.* (1997, Fig. 1, p. 597).

Figure 8.32 A richer version of the image.

Source: Frith and Dolan (1997, Fig. 2).

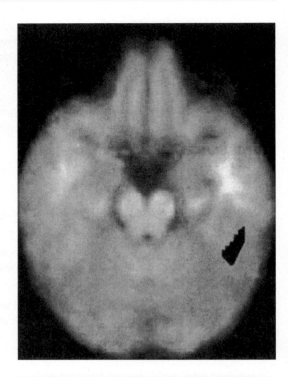

(a)

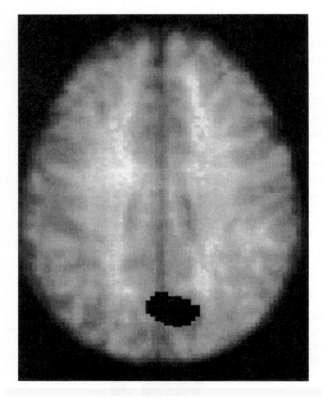

Figure 8.33 Averaged MRI scan of the brain of volunteers as seen in a horizontal slice when an impoverished image (face or object) was viewed for a second time. The black area represents activation in the medial parietal cortex (participant's front at top and left at left).

Source: Frith and Dolan (1997, Fig. 2, p. 1222).

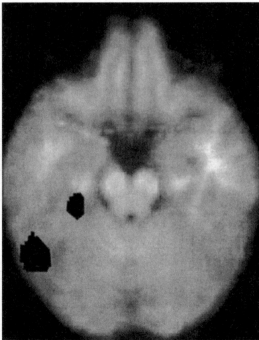

(b)

Figure 8.34 Activity of the inferior temporal cortex: (a) when a face is viewed and (b) when an object is viewed.

Source: Frith and Dolan (1997, Fig. 3, p. 1223).

So changes in brain activity mirror changes in perception. How can we explain what is happening? Frith and Dolan (1997) suggest that processing of the full figure could leave permanent traces, a representation, e.g. as modified synaptic connections. Thus, when the impoverished version is again presented, elements of this representation are triggered. Since the neural activity triggered now by the impoverished figure is similar to that triggered by the full figure, so too is the corresponding perception similar.

Global and local features

In Figure 8.35, what do you see? Presumably, a large letter S comprising a number of small letter Ls. Participants were given a number of different stimuli of the kind shown and asked to report the letter but instructed to respond either at a global level (group 1), i.e. S in Figure 8.35, or at a local level (group 2), i.e. L in the same figure (Fink *et al.*, 1996).

When participants were attending at a global level, increased activity at the right lingual gyrus (a region of prestriate cortex, the so-called visual association area) was observed. When they were responding at a local level, activity increased at the left inferior occipital lobe. In order to respond correctly according to instructions, presumably a brain region outside those concerned directly with visual processing must prime the areas responsible for interpretation of the image. The results of this experiment fit studies of patients with brain damage. Right-sided damage tends to disrupt global processing and left-sided damage tends to disrupt local processing.

Ambiguous figures

Figure 7.2 (p. 180) showed the famous face–vase picture, an ambiguous figure. It was produced by the Danish psychologist Edgar Rubin. In all probability, your perception of the figure will alternate between two possible solutions. For a while your perception will be as a vase and then it will switch to two faces. The raw sensory input ('bottom-up contribution') as detected on the retina is the same but it seems that the top-down contribution changes. The conscious mind cannot tolerate ambiguity and makes sense

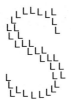

Figure 8.35 Visual stimulus.

Source: Frith and Dolan 1997, (Fig. 4, p. 1224).

of the world by fixing on one interpretation, only for that to be displaced by the alternative, and so on.

Different brain regions of the ventral stream are particularly active when viewing a face as compared with an inanimate object such as a vase (Andrews *et al.*, 2002). (If you would like the details, the fusiform face area (FFA) is activated when faces are perceived, while the lateral occipital area is activated by objects such as a vase.) Using fMRI, differential activation in the two regions was seen corresponding to the conscious perception, i.e. activation switched between regions in correlation with switches in conscious perception.

A way in which the question – 'what do you see?' – can be asked is to present different images to the two eyes and create **binocular rivalry**. The brain does not form a single perception that represents a compromise of the two possible perceptions. Rather, as in ambiguous figures, there is an alternation between images. It is also possible to ask non-human primates – what do you see (Blake and Logothetis, 2002)? In their case, researchers infer that something like conscious perception alternates between interpretations, much as in humans. For example, an upwards moving image could be presented to the left eye and a downwards moving image to the right eye. As an objective index, eye movements can be monitored and they exhibit a similar pattern to when humans are exposed to such stimuli. Corresponding movements in the two eyes indicate that a unified perception of movement upwards alternates with one of downwards.

Another index is, in effect, to ask the monkey what it sees *subjectively*. It is seated in front of a screen and presented with two levers. Suppose that an unambiguous single image of a cowboy on the screen is rewarded with fruit juice if the monkey moves the left lever. An unambiguous single image of the sun is rewarded with a movement of the right lever. When binocular rivalry is introduced by presenting both images together, the animal alternates between levers in a way assumed to reflect changing subjective perception.

It is now possible to monitor the changes that occur in the brain corresponding to the change in interpretation of the figure. Researchers can ask, which neurons change their activity in synchrony with changes in perception? In a region of the medial temporal cortex, a percentage of neurons changed their firing in synchrony with perception. The remainder changed with changes in visual stimulation but not with perception. As the probing went further into the stages of processing, i.e. further into the inferior temporal cortex (away from primary visual cortex), cell activity more strongly reflected perception. That is, a larger percentage of neurons changed activity with the perception.

How do you know that the monkey is 'telling the truth'? What is to stop it from just reacting randomly and thereby getting reward? Surely, only the monkey knows what it perceives, but does it? Researchers introduce 'catch trials' in between trials of exposure to binocular rivalry (Leopold *et al.*, 2003). In the catch trials, single images are presented and the monkey is checked to make sure that it is still responding appropriately in terms of image-lever association.

Section summary

1 Researchers can measure changes in activity of the brain when a person looks at an object, before and after the acquisition of a concept concerning its meaning.

2 It is possible to distinguish changes in brain activity that correspond to either local or global viewing.

3 In parts of the visual system, changes in neural activity correlate with changes in conscious perception.

Test your knowledge

(Answer on page 217)

8.12 Complete the following: 'Presenting different images to the two eyes creates a condition termed _____ rivalry'.

Bringing things together

Some key overall themes of the chapter are:

• visual perception is determined by interactions between bottom-up and top-down factors;

• the visual system extracts invariance ('constancy') from the varying image produced by a given object;

• there is functional specialization in the visual system including (a) parallel processing underlying perception and action and (b) separate brain regions are responsible for the components of visual perception, such as colour and shape.

The following chapter looks at touch, hearing, taste and smell and highlights some common features shared with vision as well as some differences.

Summary of Chapter 8

1 Visual perception is an active process. That is, information contained in light falling on the eye is placed into context, including that of expectations and meanings.

2 At the retina, light energy is converted to electrical signals, i.e. it is the site of detection. Cells in the retina also process information before transmitting it towards the brain.

3 The classical visual pathway projects information from the retina, via the lateral geniculate nucleus, to the visual cortex. Features are analyzed at each stage. Beyond the primary visual cortex, information is contextualized in terms of memory and meaning.

4 Brain structures that have a primary responsibility for action can be distinguished from those underlying perception.

5 There exists functional specialization in the system underlying visual perception. For example, a particular brain region might process only one quality, such as shape, movement or colour.

6 Imaging studies reveal the role of bottom-up and top-down factors in visual perception.

Further reading

For all of the neuroscience in this chapter, see Nolte (2002). For a very accessible and classic text on the physiology and psychology of vision (now in its 5th edition), see Gregory (1997) and, for something more advanced, Farah (2000). For a very readable account of the streams of visual processing, see Goodale and Milner (2004). For a more detailed general account from a neuroscience perspective, see both volumes of Chalupa and Werner (2004), Gazzaniga *et al.* (1998), Reid (1999). For eye movements, see Glimcher (1999).

Signposts

Excitation and inhibition are fundamental features of how nervous systems work and are seen throughout the nervous system. You met some examples in Chapter 3, 'The nervous and endocrine systems', where the basic principles were introduced. Considerable weight has been placed on these processes in the present chapter, where they underlie the antagonist properties of the sub-regions of the receptive field of some neurons. Further examples will be given of receptive fields for the sensory system of touch in the following chapter (Chapter 9, 'The other sensory systems'). Look out for a similar principle of organization. This chapter has briefly considered the phenomenon of consciousness, e.g. in contrasting the actions of the ventral stream and the dorsal stream. However, the complex philosophical issue raised by consciousness was taken for granted. This will be equally true of some other subsequent chapters. Chapter 21, 'Brains, minds and consciousness', confronts this issue. In so doing, examples from vision will be used.

Answers

Explanations for answers to 'test your knowledge' questions can be found on the website **www.pearsoned.co.uk/toates**

8.1   Frequencies; wavelengths (obviously in either order)
8.2   (ii) Medium, (iii) long
8.3   (i) Increasing the intensity of light
8.4   (ii) 20
8.5   (i) Increasing the intensity of the light, (ii) keeping intensity constant but increasing the size of area within the receptive field stimulated.
8.6   (i) Rotating the light stimulus to an orientation of 45° to that shown, (ii) rotating the light stimulus to an orientation of 90° to that shown
8.7   Retinal ganglion cells
8.8   Right; right
8.9   (a) (iii) The same as reaching to the right; (b) (i) smaller.
8.10 Halves; the same
8.11 (ii) Parvo
8.12 Binocular

 Interactions and animations relating to topics discussed in this chapter can be found on the website at **www.pearsoned.co.uk/toates**. These include

Animation: The eye and the retina

Interaction: The structure of the human eye

Interaction: The primary visual pathways from retina to visual cortex

Animation: The visual pathways from retina to visual cortex

Interaction: The dorsal and ventral visual pathways

CHAPTER 9

The other sensory systems

After studying this chapter, you should be able to:

1. Explain how transduction occurs between changes in air pressure and electrical signals in neurons. Do so in such a way that the term 'place code' can be applied to two different stages of auditory processing.

2. Explain how distortion of hair cells can inform the brain on the movement of the head.

3. Describe the sequence of neurons involved in the detection of tactile stimuli. Do so in a way that illustrates how particular weight is attached to contours and changes in stimuli.

4. Compare and contrast the neural processing underlying taste and smell.

1 Is the foetus sensitive to sounds?

2 How do we manage to stay upright?

3 Why does food 'lose its taste' when we have a cold?

4 Do smells affect mood?

5 Could pheromones affect us without us even detecting their presence?

Life requires an animal to detect information in various sensory channels, e.g. vision, hearing and touch. What are some similarities and differences between sensory systems?

Source: PhotoDisc, Inc.

Introduction

The last chapter looked at vision, whereas the remaining sensory systems are condensed into the present chapter. It is normal in treatments of sensory systems and perception that vision gets most space. This reflects the disproportionate amount of attention that researchers have traditionally paid to it.

Hearing

The ear converts changes in pressure in the air to changes in the electrical activity of neurons. Getting from air pressure to action potentials involves more than one stage of transduction, described shortly. The human ear (Figure 9.1), can detect sound frequencies between 30 and 20 000 Hz. Other animals have different ranges, sometimes extending further into the higher frequencies.

From air pressure to mechanical change

Air pressure changes are channelled by the external ear to the middle ear, where transduction into changes in mechanical oscillation of the tympanic membrane (ear-drum) occurs (Green and Wier, 1984; von Békésy, 1960). Movements of the ear-drum are the initial transduction; they *represent* changes in air pressure. When exposed to changes in pressure, such as those shown in Chapter 7, 'Sensory systems' (Figure 7.1, p. 180), the ear-drum vibrates in synchrony with air pressure changes, i.e. at the same frequency as the air. This representation in the form of ear-drum movements then causes other changes, described in a moment.

Outside the laboratory, most sounds do not consist of pure oscillations of the kind shown in Figure 7.1. They are more complex. However, it is a fundamental property of mathematics that complex waveforms can be reduced to a sum of simpler waves. Complex pressure changes can be represented by a sum of components (sine waves) of the kind in Figure 7.1. A complex sound is equivalent to a series of sine waves added together.

Imagine the infinite variety of pressure waves that we perceive, e.g. the various frequencies and amplitudes that are generated by an orchestra. The conductor, or even the audience, will not hear chaos. They identify individual instruments with characteristic frequencies and amplitudes. It is one thing to note that a complex wave is mathematically equivalent to a sum

of simpler waves but can the ear break them down and categorize a complex wave into its components? The ear does indeed *analyze* pressure waves in terms of components at different frequencies. How is this done?

From mechanical change to neural activity

The external and middle ears

As you saw, the first stage of transduction is from oscillations of pressure in the air to oscillations of the tympanic membrane. These changes of the membrane subsequently cause further changes deeper in the ear. See Figure 9.1. Within the middle ear, there is a sequence of three bones, the auditory ossicles. Oscillations of the tympanic membrane cause these bones to oscillate back and forth (von Békésy, 1960). At the oval window, the third ossicle of the sequence communicates oscillations to a fluid-filled coiled structure termed the cochlea. The membrane that forms the oval window vibrates back and forth in sympathy with the tympanic membrane and the ossicles. That is to say, it continues the process of encoding the frequency and amplitude of changes in air pressure.

This might seem to be cumbersome and it is not over yet! However, it is incredibly effective and there is a 'design consideration' underlying the complexity, discussed shortly. We

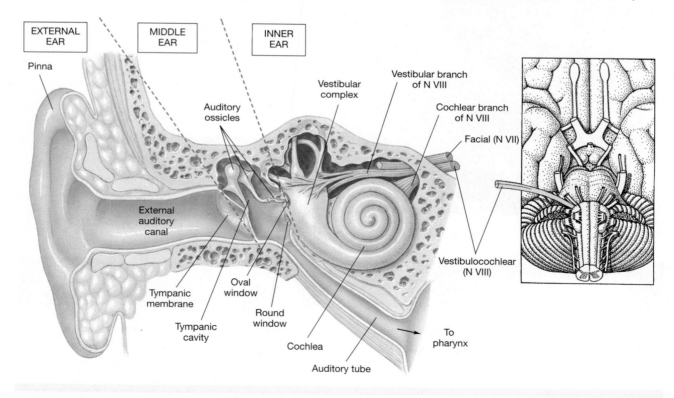

Figure 9.1 The ear. *Source:* Martini *et al.* (2000, Fig.18-9, p. 473).

now turn to the cochlea and investigate how changes in pressure within a fluid can cause changes in the activity of neurons.

The inner ear

Continuing the sequence of transmission, Figure 9.2 is a simplification of part of the auditory system. It shows transduction between oscillations of the tympanic membrane and vibrations of the basilar membrane, which is in the cochlea (von Békésy, 1960). Pressure waves at a particular *frequency* in the cochlea cause the basilar membrane to move back and forth at a *particular location*. The location depends on the frequency of the oscillations, a relationship termed a **place code**.

As Figure 9.3 shows, when the frequency of sound arriving at the ear is high, displacements in the basilar membrane occur near to the end at which it is secured, i.e. by the oval window (von Békésy, 1960). When the sound is of lower frequency, vibrations cause movements at points away from the oval window. In other words, there is transduction of the kind that frequencies of air pressure are represented by locations on the basilar membrane. The amplitude of changes in air pressure is represented by the amplitude of displacements of the basilar membrane. Suppose that there is more than one frequency of sound arriving at the ear. There are a corresponding number of sites of displacement on the basilar membrane. See Figure 9.4.

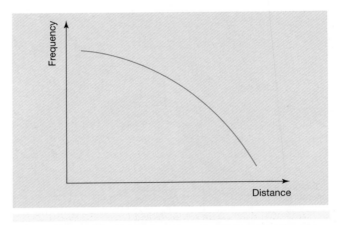

Figure 9.3 Frequency of sound as a function of the location on the basilar membrane that is most responsive to that frequency.

Associated with the basilar membrane are sensory receptors, fine cells termed **hair cells**. They form synaptic connections with neurons that project to the brain as part of the auditory nerve, a cranial nerve (Helfert *et al.*, 1991). See Figure 9.5. When hair cells are mechanically stimulated during displacement of the basilar membrane, electrical changes occur in them and thereby action potentials are triggered in the associated neurons. Action potentials are transmitted along the neurons forming the auditory nerve

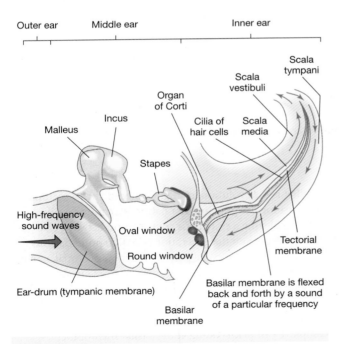

Figure 9.2 Transduction between oscillations of the tympanic membrane and displacement of the basilar membrane.

Source: Carlson (1994, Fig. 7.5, p. 186). Reprinted by permission of the publisher.

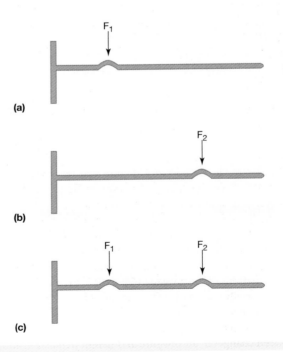

Figure 9.4 Points of displacement of the basilar membrane caused by tones of frequency (a) F_1, (b) F_2 and (c) F_1 and F_2 simultaneously.

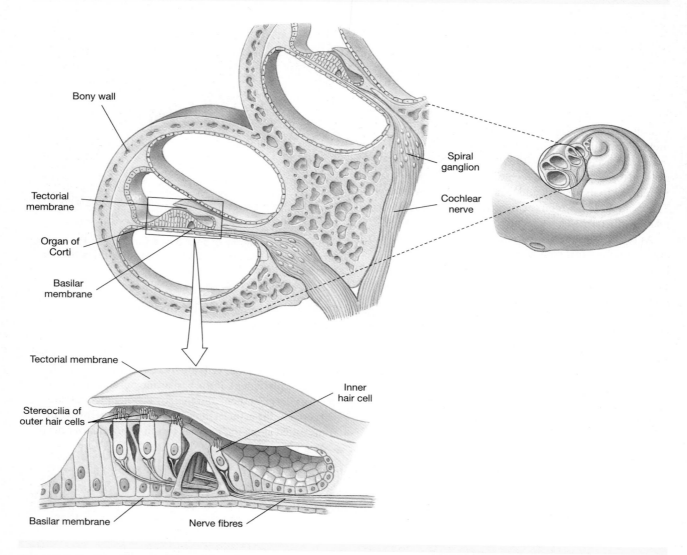

Figure 9.5 Section through the cochlea, showing the basilar membrane and surrounding structures.
Source: Martini *et al.* (2000, Fig. 18-16d, p. 481).

and arrive at the brain stem. Different neurons code for different sound frequencies. For example, frequency F_1 activates maximally one neuron and a lower frequency (F_2) maximally activates another neuron, the neurons corresponding to positions of membrane shown in Figure 9.4. As an additional means of coding, at very low frequencies, activity in certain neurons is in synchrony with the oscillations of air pressure (Chapter 7, Figure 7.9, p. 185).

Let's briefly summarize the sequence of transduction from air pressure to mechanical changes and then to electrical activity. Via membranes and bones, transduction, occurs between changes in air pressure at different *frequencies* and different *locations* of maximum vibration at the basilar membrane. There is then transduction between distortions of the membrane and activity within different *neurons*.

What is the evolutionary significance of such a seemingly cumbersome design? Couldn't nature have found a simpler way of achieving a systematic transduction between changes in air pressure and the generation of action potentials? At low frequencies, the cyclic pattern of action potential activity (i.e. burst–silence–burst …) in a number of neurons carrying information from the ear does indeed follow cyclic changes in air pressure (Chapter 7, Figure 7.9, p. 185). Why not code all frequencies in this way and hence cut out the complexity of place coding at the basilar membrane?

Playing designer can be a revealing exercise and it is interesting to see whether one can come up with better solutions. However, evolution can only act on what is already there. There is a limit to the rate at which neurons can produce action potentials, as set by the refractory period

(Chapter 4, 'The cells of the nervous system'). It is beyond the capacity of neurons to generate action potentials at a frequency of 20 000 per second in response to a 20 000 Hz frequency of sound. Even if evolution had 'invented' neurons with such a frequency range, there is still the problem of how to code for both frequency and amplitude of a given oscillation in the air. A second coding system would be necessary. Tinkering with one part of a system has knock-on consequences for other parts. Providing an efficient means of transduction between frequency and neural activity is the evolutionary rationale for place coding, which is perhaps not so cumbersome after all!

Neural mechanisms

The classical route of afferent projections

Figure 9.6 shows the classical sequence of neurally encoded information in the auditory system. Neurons convey information in the auditory nerve to the cochlear nucleus, where a synapse occurs (Helfert *et al.*, 1991). Information then ascends through various brain regions, e.g. inferior colliculus, medial geniculate nucleus of the thalamus, to the auditory cortex.

There is a series of neurons and synapses between the afferent input, the thalamus and then to the auditory cortex.

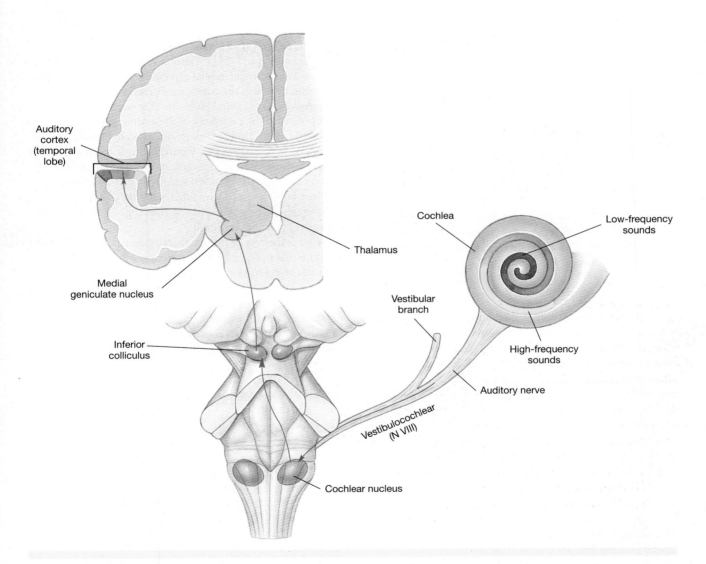

Figure 9.6 The auditory system. *Source*: Martini *et al.* (2000, Fig. 18-17, p. 483).

Some information remains on the same side and, as in Figure 9.6, other information crosses over. By means of partial cross-over, information derived from each ear can be compared and thereby information on the location of the sound source identified (described shortly). Neurons in the auditory system can be classified according to whether they are driven by the contralateral ear, ipsilateral ear or both (analogous to vision). Above the level of cochlear nucleus, neurons are often influenced by both, with a tendency for contralateral control to be stronger (Brown, 1999).

Tonotopic representation

It was noted that, at the basilar membrane, frequency is represented by location of disturbance on the membrane. A similar style of coding is preserved at the auditory cortex: particular neurons respond to particular sound frequencies, corresponding to particular basilar membrane locations. This is termed **tonotopic representation** (from the Greek '*tonos*', meaning tone and '*topos*', meaning place) or a 'place code' (Aitkin *et al.*, 1984). As with other sensory systems, there is some plasticity in cortical representation: frequencies that acquire particular relevance in the life of an animal can gain increased cortical representation (Weinberger, 1993).

Loudness

Intensity (amplitude) of pressure waves is coded in at least two ways (Green and Wier, 1984): the rate at which action potentials occur in a particular neuron and different thresholds of activation of neurons. Thus at a given region (x) of the basilar membrane there appears to be a population of sensory neurons all sensitive to frequency F_x but some are only triggered by high-intensity sounds corresponding to large displacements of the membrane.

Biaural processing

The auditory system is able to discriminate the location of the source of sounds, whether to left or right. This is, of course, vital to survival. How is it achieved? A source of sound that is to one side of the body will arrive at one ear slightly sooner than the other. Action potentials are initiated in the ear to this side slightly sooner than in the other ear (Hudspeth and Konishi, 2000; von Békésy, 1960). Neurons carrying information from each ear project to other neurons in a brain stem region (termed the superior olivary complex) that perform **feature detection** on incoming information (Tsuchitani and Johnson, 1991). For example, the brain exploits differences in the arrival times of action potentials to determine the direction of a sound's source.

The system can also exploit differences in intensity between the ears to extract a signal on location. If a source of sound is to the left, not only will the left ear receive stimulation slightly sooner than the right ear but stimulation will also be more intense. The right ear is said to be in a *sonic shadow* cast by the head. As an example of feature detection, certain neurons in the brain are sensitive to differences in intensity, being fed by information from each ear.

Different routes taken by auditory information

The route from the ears through the thalamus to the auditory cortex (Figure 9.6) is sometimes termed the 'classical route'. However, in addition, there is a route from the thalamus to the amygdala, introduced in Chapter 5, 'The brain' (Figure 9.7). The amygdala is an important site of emotional processing and, compared with the classical route, the auditory system has a 'short-cut' pathway for access to it (Le Doux, 1994).

Descending pathways

Through descending pathways, feedback ('top-down') control is exerted at all levels in the auditory system (Spangler and Warr, 1991). There is feedback from the auditory cortex to the medial geniculate nucleus and inferior colliculus, by which the cortex modulates ascending information. Also, neural pathways that start in the brain stem project to the periphery of the auditory system, modulating detection sensitivity and thereby the afferent signal (Warr *et al.*, 1986). In Figure 9.8, note the muscles that adjust the sensitivity of mechanical transduction. By the efferent signal to the muscles, sensitivity can be adjusted to ambient noise levels (decreasing sensitivity in a loud environment), thereby increasing the range of resolution of the system (von Békésy, 1960).

What is the role of this feedback? One role is as follows. Suppose that in Figure 9.9 the system normally (curve (a)) saturates at intensity X_1. It cannot resolve the difference between X_1 and X_2. However, with modulation to a decreased sensitivity (curve (b)), both intensities are represented on the ascending portion of the graph and so can be discriminated. (Look at the change in vertical axis as you move from X_1 to X_2.)

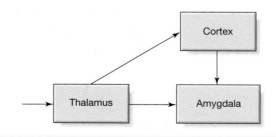

Figure 9.7 Routes of auditory information.

Source: based on Le Doux (1994).

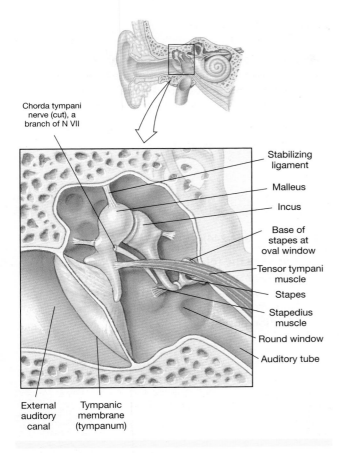

Chorda tympani
nerve (cut), a
branch of N VII

Stabilizing
ligament

Malleus

Incus

Base of
stapes at
oval window

Tensor tympani
muscle

Stapes

Stapedius
muscle

Round window

Auditory tube

External
auditory
canal

Tympanic
membrane
(tympanum)

Figure 9.8 Site of feedback control.

Source: based on Martini *et al.* (2000, Fig. 18-10b, p. 474).

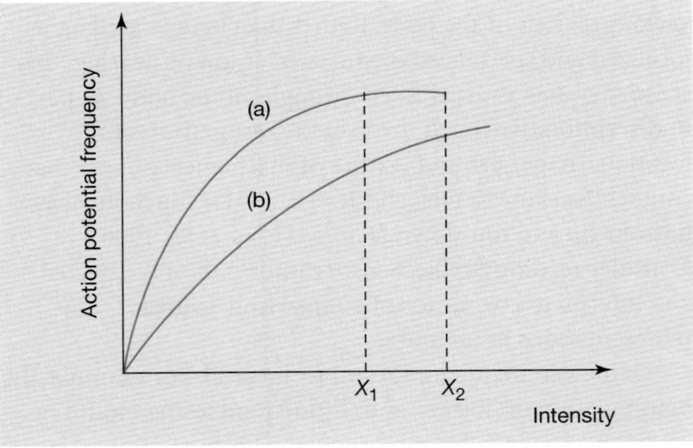

[Figure 9.9 graph: vertical axis "Action potential frequency", horizontal axis "Intensity", with curves labelled (a) and (b), and dashed vertical lines at X_1 and X_2.]

Figure 9.9 Relation between intensity and afferent signal (a) before and (b) after modulation.

Developmental factors

The developing foetus exists within a world that involves auditory stimulation (Fifer and Moon, 1988). In humans, the mother's voice reaches the foetus. After 24 weeks of

gestation, pure tones of external origin cause heart-rate changes. The foetus is also exposed to sounds of internal origin such as the maternal heartbeat and movements within the gastrointestinal tract. It is possible, if not probable, that the sounds impinging on the foetus play a role in the development of the auditory system.

Exposure to sounds within the uterus also appears to play an important role in emotional development. The infant is exposed to an association between particular voice features (frequency, intonation) and the chemical and somatosensory environment within the uterus. Newborn humans can discriminate their own mother's voice and show a preference for it (DeCasper and Fifer, 1980). Sounds experienced *in utero* have later emotional and motivational significance, e.g. playing a recording of the heartbeat has a calming effect (Fifer and Moon, 1988).

Section summary

1 The ear performs transduction between changes in pressure in the air and action potentials.

2 Different frequencies of sound cause different locations on the basilar membrane to vibrate, i.e. a place code. Different neurons, corresponding to the different locations, are activated.

3 Beyond the thalamus, auditory information takes different routes within the brain.

4 At the auditory cortex, neurons at different locations respond to different sound frequencies.

Test your knowledge

(Answers on page 244)

9.1 Suppose that a person has suffered damage to a particular narrow region of the basilar membrane. Which of the following might be expected to be the result? Loss of sensation for (i) a particular range of frequencies, (ii) a particular volume of sound.

9.2 In Figure 9.6, the area of auditory cortex coloured dark pink is responsible for encoding which frequency of sounds? (i) High, (ii) medium, (iii) low.

The vestibular system

The **vestibular system** provides information on the position of the head, which is used in coordinating action (Goldberg and Fernández, 1984). A negative feedback system detects disturbances to the body's equilibrium and triggers compensatory action. The **vestibular apparatus** of the inner ear detects changes in the position of the head and transmits information to the brain along a cranial nerve, the vestibulocochlear nerve (Chapter 3, 'The nervous and endocrine systems'). See Figure 9.10.

The vestibular apparatus comprises fluid-filled chambers: the semicircular canals (or 'ducts'), the utricle and the saccule, coloured blue in Figure 9.10(b). Because of the physical principle of inertia, when the head moves, the fluid tends to follow slightly behind the movement of the chambers themselves. Thus, there is a relative movement between the chambers and their fluid contents. This relative movement is detected by hair cells (similar to those in the auditory system) that are situated in the chambers. Electrical activity in neurons of the vestibulocochlear nerve is altered, which constitutes signals to the brain that encode the movement.

Suppose that the head moves in a particular direction. This movement causes a population of hair cells to bend in a given way, which excites action potentials (Figure 9.10(d)). When the head moves in the opposite direction, there is inhibition of action potentials in this population of neurons (Goldberg and Fernández, 1984).

Another population of hair cells has a different direction of sensitivity, for example, this might be the opposite of the first population or at right angles to it. By this means, the brain is informed of the movement of the head. The information is sent to the cerebellum, among other places, where it plays a role in maintaining stability. Via nuclei in the brain stem, signals are also sent to the sympathetic branch of the ANS such that heart-rate increases (Yates and Stocker, 1998). This might be understood in functional terms as a preparation for action at a time of disturbance.

In humans, evidence is also emerging to indicate a role for receptors of gravitational forces in such unlikely places as the kidney and veins of the limbs (Yates and Stocker, 1998). Such information is conveyed to the brain via the spinal cord and vagus nerve (Chapter 3).

Section summary

1 The vestibular apparatus of the inner ear detects changes in position of the head and transmits information to the brain along a cranial nerve, the vestibulocochlear nerve.

2 Following a disturbance to equilibrium, postural reflexes act to restore it.

Test your knowledge

(Answer on page 244)

9.3 Complete the following sentence: 'In the vestibular system, there is a transduction from a _____ distortion to an electrical signal in neurons. The latter takes the form of the _____ of action potentials'.

The somatosensory system

Introduction

The **somatosensory system** detects events arising from various regions of the body. Rather than being based on a localized and specialized organ, as in vision or hearing, this sensory system is distributed throughout the body. As part of it, **discriminative touch** involves the recognition of the location, shape, size and texture of mechanical objects that contact the skin (Kandel and Jessell, 1991). Touch involves bottom-up and top-down factors (Hsiao *et al.*, 1996). Consider reading Braille. Sensory information is detected and interpreted by means of comparison against representations in memory.

Tactile stimuli are important to survival. For example, the manipulation of objects, as in lifting food to the mouth or grasping a branch, depends upon an ability to resolve fine detail with paws or fingers. On a gross scale, a tactile stimulus might represent an event that requires defensive action. From a developmental perspective, the tactile sense is also of obvious importance; infants learn from self-generated movements, resultant contact with objects and the tactile

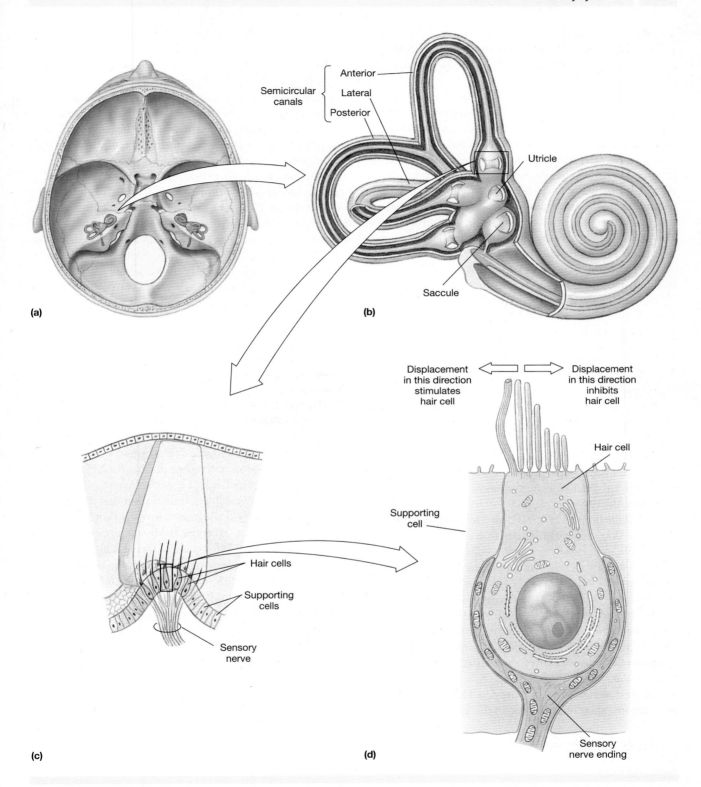

Figure 9.10 (a) The ear indicating the vestibular apparatus and (b)–(d) the vestibular apparatus in closer detail.

Source: Martini *et al*. (2000, Fig. 18–12, p. 476).

consequences of manipulation. In each case, the first stage of extracting tactile information consists in the activation of specialized receptors at the skin by objects. Each receptor has a receptive field at the skin.

In Chapter 3, you met neurons specialized for discriminative touch, tissue damage or temperature. Their cell bodies are in the dorsal root ganglia and such neurons are sometimes given the generic term 'dorsal root ganglion cells' or 'DRG cells'. (Other comparable neurons project information from above the neck as part of a cranial nerve.) Each class of DRG cell detects information, which is transmitted to distinct brain regions for further processing (e.g. via further projection cells to distinct regions of cortex). This provides **modality segregation**, e.g. between touch and temperature (Mountcastle, 1984).

The present section focuses upon just one of these qualities, discriminative touch involving harmless stimuli.

We tend to take the somatic sensory system for granted, perhaps since much of its work is done at an unconscious level. It is relatively easy for us to simulate blindness or deafness and thereby gain some understanding of what it is like to be without vision or hearing. To be defective in somatic sensory input is difficult for us to imagine. The very rare individual suffers this misfortune (Cole, 1991).

In Chapter 5, you met part of the system involved in processing tactile information, i.e. the somatosensory cortex and the mapping of the body, which constitutes the sensory homunculus (Figure 5.18, p. 118). Within the system of detecting innocuous touch, different regions of the body are represented in different regions of somatosensory cortex (Mountcastle, 1984).

How is the homunculus defined? Tactile stimulation of particular skin areas triggers activity in a cortical cell located at the point indicated by the homunculus. In humans, electrical stimulation of cortical neurons within the somatosensory area evokes the conscious sensation of tactile stimulation at the region of skin corresponding to the particular point of the homunculus (Penfield and Rasmussen, 1968). Damage to particular regions of somatosensory cortex disrupts somatosensation at particular points on the opposite side of the body as defined by the homunculus.

The next section looks in more detail at the neurons that form the first stage of processing in this system.

Sensory neurons

Neuron types

Around the body and just beneath the skin surface there are the tips of sensory neurons that detect different qualities of tactile stimulation, collectively termed **somatosensory neurons** (Darian-Smith, 1984). Some examples are shown in

Figure 9.11. Some tips consist simply of bare neuron endings (as in nociceptive neurons), whereas others are associated with either small capsules, termed 'Merkel's discs' or a single capsule, termed a 'Pacinian corpuscle'. The hair follicle receptor consists of a neuron ending wrapped around the root of a hair and it detects deflection of the hair. Figure 9.11(f) shows a small section of skin and the location of some receptors. Merkel's discs detect superficial touch whereas the Pacinian corpuscle detects deeper distortion of the skin.

Whether there is a bare neuron ending or an associated capsule, mechanical deformation, as in touch, causes depolarization (Chapter 4) at the tip. If this is strong enough, action potentials are instigated.

Action potentials travel from the tip along the axon to the CNS. For example, in Figure 9.11(c), displacements of the hair trigger action potentials in the associated neuron. You can test the presence of such neurons in your own body; try gently brushing the tips of hairs on, say, your arm and a sensation will be triggered.

Receptive fields

Figure 9.12 shows the receptive fields of some sensory neurons. You should recall that the receptive field is the area of sensory surface, which, when it is stimulated, affects the activity of the neuron. As a similarity with retinal ganglion cells, somatosensory neurons have receptive fields that vary in size between large and small (Greenspan and Bolanowski, 1996), as was shown in Chapter 7, Figure 7.11. The smaller receptive fields (e.g. at the fingertips) are associated with processing of information that shows greater tactile acuity, analogous to foveal vision. The arm is associated with larger receptive fields, analogous to vision away from the fovea. Differences in tactile acuity correspond to differences in the relative proportions of somatosensory cortex devoted to analyzing information from these body regions (Chapter 5, Figure 5.18). A small size of receptive field corresponds to a relatively large area of representation at the sensory homunculus.

The size of a receptive field of a somatosensory neuron is determined by the extent of the branching of its tip. See Figure 9.13.

Detection of information

Some somatosensory neurons show a rapid adaptation to tactile stimulation (Chapter 7, Figure 7.7(c)) and others show little adaptation (Darian-Smith, 1984). The former type signals only the onset of a stimulus, which often carries most information. They extract what is changing in the tactile stimulus. For example, in a manual skill of picking up an object, it is obviously important that the dynamics of any slip provide information to the nervous system.

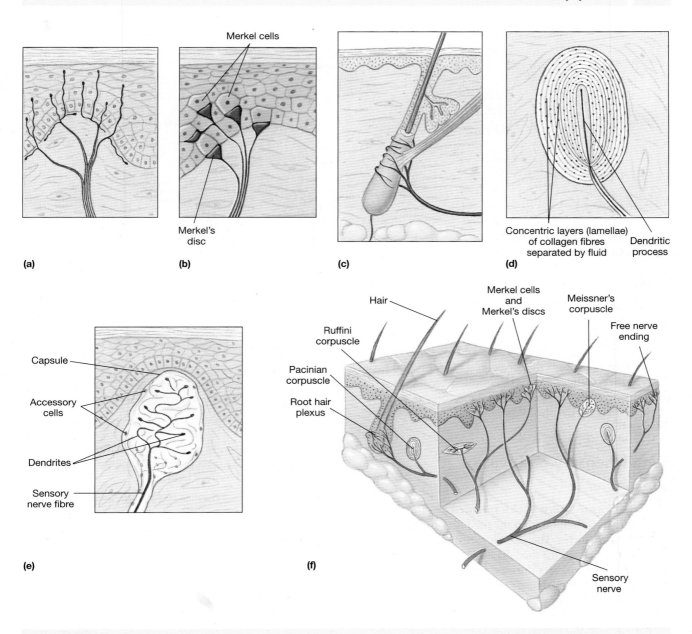

(a)

(b) Merkel cells / Merkel's disc

(c)

(d) Concentric layers (lamellae) of collagen fibres separated by fluid / Dendritic process

(e) Capsule / Accessory cells / Dendrites / Sensory nerve fibre

(f) Hair / Ruffini corpuscle / Pacinian corpuscle / Root hair plexus / Merkel cells and Merkel's discs / Meissner's corpuscle / Free nerve ending / Sensory nerve

Figure 9.11 Somatosensory neurons: (a) free nerve endings, (b) Merkel's disc, (c) free nerve ending associated with the root of a hair, (d) Pacinian corpuscle, (e) Meissner's corpuscle and (f) skin showing various receptors.

Source: after Martini *et al*. (2000, Fig. 18-3, p. 467).

Figure 9.12 Receptive fields of some sensory neurons.

Under constant conditions, we cease to be consciously aware of much of the tactile stimulation of the body, such as the pressure of the top of a sock or that of our 'rear portions' against the chair on which we are sitting. This is presumably due to both sensory processes and processes of attention. Usually, *changes* in stimulation are most important. From a functional perspective, the constant pressure of the substrate as, for example, you lie on the ground does not need to command attention but any changes, as in the ground

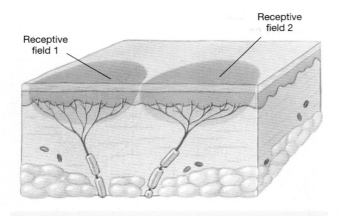

Figure 9.13 Receptive fields of two sensory neurons.

Source: Martini *et al.* (2000, Fig. 18-1b, p. 464).

shaking, are important. In general, tactile stimuli excite different types of sensory neuron simultaneously. Texture is a feature extracted by processing information provided by such patterns of stimulation (Martin and Jessell, 1991).

Nociceptive neurons that detect real or threatened tissue damage adapt rather little. In evolutionary terms, the information that they signal cannot be ignored. Alas, so often we must have wished that evolution had selected some other option.

Somatosensory pathways

Introduction

Chapter 5 (Figure 5.18, p. 118) introduced a route taken by harmless information from the periphery to the somatosensory cortex. The ascending neuron projects as part of a tract to nuclei of the medulla, where a synapse occurs. Other neurons then carry the message further by ascending to a nucleus of the thalamus (Kandel and Jessell, 1991). Note the cross-over of information from one side of the body to the opposite side of the brain.

The nucleus (the ventral posterolateral nucleus or VP nucleus) of the thalamus is comparable to that of the lateral geniculate nucleus in the visual pathway. The neurons with cell bodies in the thalamus, the third in the sequence, then project axons to the primary somatosensory cortex (Jones and Friedman, 1982).

Recording electrical activity

By placing the tips of fine electrodes within sensory neurons that convey information from the skin to the spinal cord, researchers monitor electrical activity (Vallbo, 1995). Through electrodes, the neuron can be stimulated electrically and the response recorded. Electrical activity of the neuron in response to mechanical stimuli at the skin can also be measured.

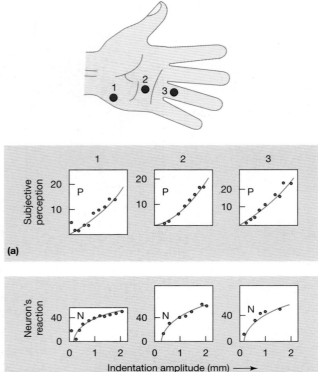

Figure 9.14 Responses to pressure (indentation) at three locations (1, 2 and 3): (a) subjective estimation of pressure and (b) response of sensory neuron.

Source: after Knibestol and Vallbo (1980, Fig. 9, p. 262).

Researchers investigate the relationship between: (a) the tactile stimulus at the skin, (b) action potentials in a sensory neuron and (c) people's verbal reports of what they feel. See Figure 9.14. (Also, neurons can be stimulated artificially by the electrode and subjective reports noted.) The activity of the neuron increases with pressure (indentation), though the rate of increase declines (i.e. the slope gets shallower). However, this declining rate of increase is not reflected in the psychological perception of intensity. Some neurons are sensitive only to *changes* in tactile stimulation. Others are active for as long as the deformation at the skin lasts.

There are neurons that, when electrically stimulated, trigger sensations of painless mechanical touch, rather than, say, pain or temperature. Alongside such neurons others convey information on temperature and tissue damage. If the intensity of applied stimulation is increased, people do sometimes report pain. This suggests that adjacent neurons that normally carry information on tissue damage are simultaneously excited.

Spatial acuity

We can also detect details in the stimulus, termed 'spatial acuity', analogous to visual acuity. Our ability varies with different regions of skin. One measure is the ability to discriminate between one and two points of pressure at the skin (Figure 9.15). Two points close together are applied to the skin and the person reports that there is only one point. They are gradually separated and there is a distance at which the person reports that there are two points. This defines the **two-point threshold** at that location, a measure of spatial acuity (Weinstein, 1968). The two-point threshold varies across the surface of the body; the back has low acuity (large threshold) and the fingers high acuity (low threshold) (Figure 9.15). With the assistance of a willing friend, you can try the experiment.

How does the difference in threshold arise? One factor is shown in Figure 9.16. In part (a), because of the physical segregation of their receptive fields, the profile of activity in the sensory neurons is different when comparing the effects of one and two stimuli. This is a region of high acuity, e.g. the fingertips. By contrast, in part (b), because of the overlap of their receptive fields, the profile in activity does not give a different signal comparing one and two points of stimulation. Although differences in receptive field size are a factor in determining differences in tactile acuity, there is not a one-to-one relationship (Greenspan and Bolanowski, 1996). Further processing is involved in the somatosensory pathway and this can mean some convergence of information and loss of acuity.

The connections that neurons make within the somatosensory pathway are an important factor in the information processing that occurs (Kandel and Jessell, 1991). Rather as with the visual system, as information ascends from the receptor level to the cortex, there are

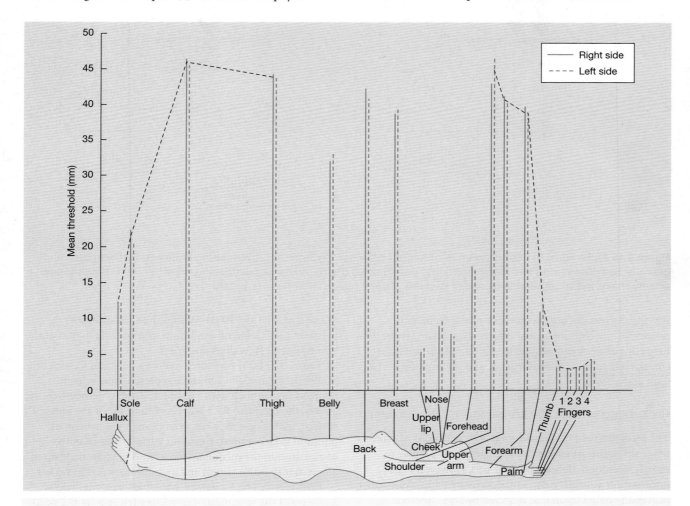

Figure 9.15 Variation in two-point threshold over the body surface. Increasing values represent increasing distances between points before two points can be discriminated.

Source: Weinstein (1968) in *The Skin Senses*, edited by D.R. Kenhalo, Fig. 10.5, p. 203. Courtesy of Charles C. Thomas Publisher, Ltd, Springfield, Illinois.

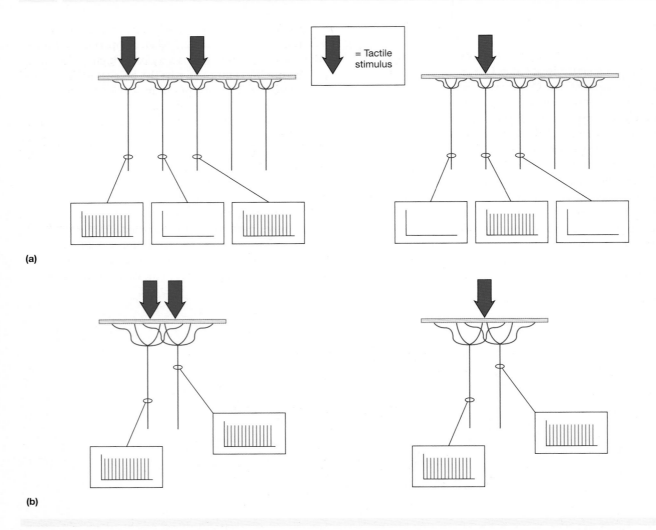

Figure 9.16 Differences in size and overlap of neuron branches. (a) Small non-overlapping branches. Distinct pattern of neural activity comparing two stimuli (left) and one stimulus (right). (b) Large overlapping branches. Two stimuli trigger activity that is indistinguishable from one stimulus. *Source*: Toates (1998c, Fig. 4.32, p. 128).

varying degrees of convergence. For example, there is relatively little convergence of information arising from the fingertips of a primate and hence high resolution. This is comparable to the low convergence and high resolution of light at the fovea.

Processing within the somatosensory pathway

The receptive field of dorsal root ganglion (DRG) neurons is made up simply of an excitatory region (comparable to retinal receptors), defined by their tips. However, as information ascends in the somatosensory pathways, further processing based upon that detected by DRG neurons occurs. The activity of neurons in the medulla depends upon activity in DRG neurons. Medulla neurons have receptive field properties that are more complex than DRG neurons, comparable to that of ganglion cells in the visual system

(Kandel and Jessell, 1991). Within the somatosensory pathway, there is lateral inhibition, comparable to that of the visual system. How does this arise?

Figure 9.17(a) shows three neurons, A, B and C, with cell bodies in the medulla and three representative sensory neurons (a, b and c), which excite A, B and C respectively. As always, the receptive field is defined in terms of the sensory surface, in this case the skin, even though the neuron in question is far removed from this surface. The receptive field of a neuron in the medulla, such as A, B or C, is made up of an excitatory (ON) region and an inhibitory (OFF) region.

Consider B. The excitatory area of its receptive field is made up of the terminals of neurons such as b (at the skin) and the inhibitory region is made up of the terminals of neurons such as a and c (at the skin). Activity in a and c inhibits B, acting via inhibitory connections (deriving from A and C) shown. Figure 9.17(b) shows the response to tactile

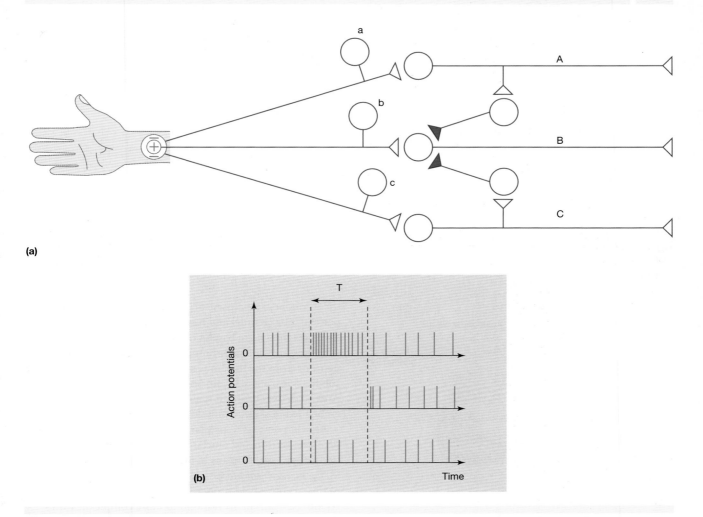

(a)

(b)

Figure 9.17 Receptive field properties: (a) neural connections and (b) response of neuron B. Upper trace: B is excited by activity in b (period T); middle trace: excitation of a and c; lower trace: a, b and c are simultaneously activated.

Source: after Kandel and Jessell (1991) *Principles of Neural Science*, 3rd Edition, p. 375. Reprinted with permission of The McGraw-Hill Companies, Inc.

stimulation in each region. Note the background 'spontaneous' level of activity of the medulla neuron (B) when there is no tactile stimulation. When a neuron such as b is active, B is excited. There are inhibitory connections from A to B and from C to B. Thus, excitation of a and/or c tends (via A and/or C) to inhibit B.

What is the optimal tactile stimulus to maximize activity in neuron B? A tactile stimulus that fills the centre region but does not invade the inhibitory surround. Figure 9.18 exhibits this. This is closely analogous to the ON centre/OFF surround ganglion cell shown in the visual system. Also by analogy with vision, at the skin there can be overlap of tactile receptive fields of medulla neurons, analogous to that of retinal ganglion cells.

Note that feature detection requires a process of inhibition. On their own, sensory neurons cannot discriminate between small and large tactile stimuli. Only

when they are connected together, as in Figure 9.17(a), is feature detection possible.

The axons of the medulla neurons project to the thalamus where further information processing occurs. Thalamic neurons then project this information to the cortex.

Cortical processing

At a gross level, you have met the sensory homunculus showing the relationship between the body surface and its representation at the somatosensory cortex. It is now time to look at a detailed part of this representation. The evidence derives mainly from studies on non-human primates.

Exactly how the somatosensory cortex should be classified varies to some extent with species (Kaas, 1996). Figure 9.19 shows a commonly used classification scheme, in which it has three divisions: the primary somatosensory cortex (SI),

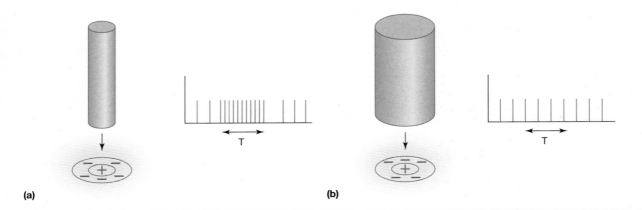

Figure 9.18 Two mechanical stimuli: (a) one that fills the excitatory region of receptive field and (b) one that covers both excitatory and inhibitory areas. Also shown is the excitation of a neuron such as B of Fig. 9.17 during application of the stimulus for time *T*.

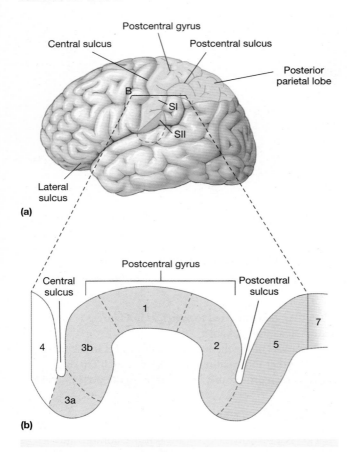

Figure 9.19 The somatosensory cortex: (a) the brain showing this region in relation to other parts and (b) enlargement of a section through it.

Source: Kandel and Jessell (1991) *Principles of Neural Science*, 3rd Edition, p. 368. Reprinted with permission of The McGraw-Hill Companies, Inc.

the secondary somatosensory cortex (SII) and the posterior parietal lobe (Kandel and Jessell, 1991). The numbered divisions shown are based on Brodmann's classification (Chapter 5). The major input from the thalamus is to area SI, neurons from the thalamus arriving mainly in two of its subdivisions: areas 3a and 3b (Randolph and Semmes, 1974). Area 3a derives its input mainly from sensory neurons embedded in skeletal muscles (Burton and Sinclair, 1996).

In what sense is SI primary and SII secondary (Hsiao *et al.*, 1996; Burton and Sinclair, 1996)? Clearly pointing to a 'secondary' role, neurons in SII derive a principal input from SI, i.e. *hierarchical processing*. Another criterion is the nature of the receptive field properties of neurons located in each region. Neurons in SII respond to more complex features than those in SI and are less specific to a given sensory region. They might be triggered by stimulation anywhere on an arm and its hand or even bilaterally driven by either hand. Some neurons respond only to particular shapes. Also, SII neurons are more sensitive to the factor of attention than are SI neurons, suggesting a top-down contribution. SII appears to be a site at which sensory information is compared with stored memories of the tactile features of objects.

Figure 9.20 shows in more detail the type of information processing associated with a part of region SI, in this case concerned with three fingers. In addition to the different properties of neurons within the different regions of Figure 9.19(b) (1, 2, 3a, etc.), neurons form distinct columns in the dimension running through successive layers from the surface inwards (i.e. layers i, ii, iii, etc.). In this dimension, neurons from the thalamus arrive at layer iv. Those in layers i and ii project to other cortical regions both within the somatosensory area (regions SI and SII) and outside. Projections from layers ii and iii to the posterior parietal

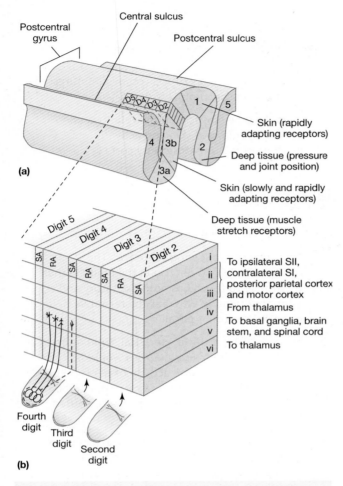

(a)

(b)

Figure 9.20 (a) and (b) Information processing in the primary somatosensory cortex.

Source: Kandel and Jessell (1991) *Principles of Neural Science*, 3rd Edition, p. 378 reprinted with permission of The McGraw-Hill Companies, Inc.

cortex take part in the integration of tactile information with other sensory modalities. Some projections remain on the same side of the brain ('ipsilateral') and others cross to the other side ('contralateral').

Note also in area 3b the distinction in location between neurons that process rapidly adapting (RA) and slowly adapting (SA) information. These derive inputs from receptors at the skin having rapid and slowly adapting characteristics respectively. One assumes that information computed on the basis of these inputs has different destinations beyond the somatosensory cortex. In terms of its role, one stream computes information on the dynamics of a situation in terms of action and the other more in terms of its static features.

Top-down modulation

So far we have spoken of the flow of information from periphery to CNS. However, there is also top-down modulation of information in these pathways. The activity in cortical areas SI and SII is a function of the focus of attention. When the task required tactile discrimination, there was higher activity recorded from neurons in these areas (Hsiao *et al.*, 1993). As a control, the task was set to require visual discrimination. Descending pathways modulate ('top-down') the activity of the sensory pathway, amplifying some signals and inhibiting others, e.g. by means of projections from cortical layer vi (Figure 9.20) to the thalamus (Deschenes *et al.*, 1998).

Development and plasticity

In mice, there is a topographic relationship between whiskers on the face ('vibrissae') and neurons in the somatosensory cortex (Van der Loos and Woolsey, 1973; Woolsey and Wann, 1976). That is to say, a map of which neurons are activated by tactile stimulation of which vibrissae shows topographic form (Figure 9.21). Each vibrissa is associated with a group of neurons in the cortex termed a 'whisker barrel'.

Damage to the sensory neuron associated with a given vibrissa (e.g. by removing the vibrissa) early in life disrupts the development of cortical neurons in the associated whisker barrel, in spite of there being three or more synapses between the primary sensory receptor and the cortical neuron (Figure 9.22). Thus, cortical development requires an intact input from the periphery.

In the absence of its normal input, neighbouring vibrissae can take over control of cortical cells, analogous to the take-over of cortical neurons by one eye (Chapter 6, 'Development and plasticity').

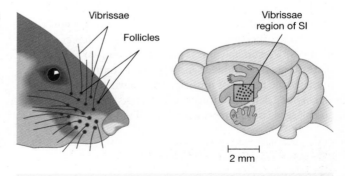

Figure 9.21 Relationship between vibrissae and neurons.
Source: Bear *et al.* (1996, p. 334).

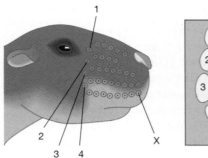
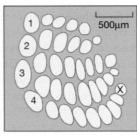

Figure 9.22 Damage to neurons (X) would result from damage to vibrissa X.

Source: after Whatson and Sterling (1998, Fig. 5.3, p. 146).

In rodents and primates, receptive fields vary as a function of peripheral damage (Merzenich *et al.*, 1983; Wall and Egger, 1971). Suppose that a skin region ('a') is associated with activation of a group of cortical cells (A). Furthermore, suppose that input from area 'a' ceases to arrive at the cortex as a result of localized damage in the sensory pathway. Neurons signalling information in neighbouring regions ('b and c') can take over control of cortical cells A. In other words, cortical receptive fields exhibit plasticity.

One factor that appears to contribute to this plasticity is that there exist all along connections from b and c, through intermediate neurons, to A. However, they are normally masked by the dominant a → A links and hence functionally ineffective. After the damage that prevents the expression of a → A links, (b,c) → A links become unmasked and hence functionally effective. This appears to trigger further changes in connectivity based upon such things as actual levels of cortical activity arising from tactile stimulation at b and c.

Even under natural (i.e. undamaged) conditions, the receptive fields of neurons in the somatosensory cortex are not always static. For example, as a monkey becomes proficient in using particular fingers to perform a novel motor skill, so the cortical receptive fields corresponding to these fingers increase in size and complexity (Merzenich *et al.*, 1996). Presumably this is part of the physical basis of increasingly fine-grained sensory-motor connections. In humans, the fingers of musicians that have the most skilled activity (e.g. left-hand fingers of violinists) appear to acquire an enlarged cortical representation (Elbert *et al.*, 1995).

Section summary

1 Somatosensory neurons detect tactile stimulation.

2 Differences in the size of the receptive fields of somatosensory neurons at different areas of the skin relate to differences in the ability to resolve fine detail.

3 Within the medulla, there are neurons with receptive field properties consisting of ON and OFF regions at the skin.

4 Cortical processing extracts complex features from the sensory input.

5 There is some plasticity in the relationship between regions of skin and activation of neurons in the somatosensory cortex.

Test your knowledge

(Answers on page 244)

9.4 Complete the following sentence: 'The receptive field of a neuron in the medulla that is sensitive to touch has both excitatory and inhibitory regions, whereas the receptive field of a DRG neuron is purely _____'.

9.5 In Figure 9.17, artificial electrical stimulation of which of the following neurons would be expected to reduce the activity of neuron B to below its spontaneous firing rate? (i) a, (ii) b, (iii) the two neurons with terminals coloured blue.

9.6 In Figure 9.18, the receptive field of a neuron in the medulla is shown. What kind of mechanical object would be the optimal stimulus to reduce the neuron's activity to below the spontaneous background rate and where would the object need to be applied?

 ## Chemical senses – taste and smell

Introduction

This section looks at two sensory systems that are sensitive to chemicals: taste and smell. In each, the detection of specific chemicals by **chemoreceptors** activates sensory neurons (McBurney, 1984). In evolutionary terms, the chemical senses are the oldest sensory systems, having a history of the order of 500 million years (Scott, 1990). Correspondingly, they mediate functions that are fundamental to existence, e.g. feeding and reproduction.

Taste and smell serve different, but related, functions. Both convey information to the CNS on chemicals present at the sensory detectors: the tongue and nose. However, its significance in terms of the animal's relation to the world is different between the two systems. Smell provides information on events and physical objects located some distance away, such as the pheromones (airborne chemicals used in communication between animals of the same species, as in mating) emitted by another animal. Of course, for taste to provide information, the object that is the source of it must already be in the mouth.

For most of us, attention is drawn to the failure of chemical senses only when we experience a cold.

We will deal first with taste and then with smell, noting similarities and differences.

Taste

Introduction

Taste signals information that is rarely neutral emotionally and motivationally (Scott, 1990). In addition to the prior analysis, done by touch, vision and smell to bring the substance to the mouth, taste analyses its appropriateness for ingestion or expulsion. An animal can be motivationally indifferent to much visual and auditory or even olfactory stimulation but this can hardly be so for taste.

Until recently, four primary ('basic') tastes were described: sweet, salty, sour and bitter (Coren *et al.*, 1994). Researchers now identify a fifth: *umami*, the word deriving from Japanese (Kurihara and Kashiwayanagi, 2000). It is particularly associated with Oriental cuisine. Primary tastes refer to *psychological* perceptions corresponding to different *physical* stimuli, i.e. broad classes of chemical molecules. This distinction is comparable to that in the visual and auditory systems between psychological dimensions (i.e. perception) and physical dimensions (i.e. light and pressure waves). Umami was included as a primary taste, since there are specific substances that preferentially trigger it and they are associated with activity in particular afferent neurons. Monosodium glutamate (a flavour-enhancing chemical used in Oriental cooking) is a powerful trigger, whereas other substances fail to trigger such neurons.

A sensation of sweetness is generally produced by sugars and signals the availability of nutrients that can be ingested and used as energy. Saltiness signals a substance such as sodium chloride, common table-salt. Salt is needed in the diet since its components, sodium and chloride, are essential for the functioning of the body. (You should recall the action potential at this point.) Sourness commonly indicates that a potential food has decayed and is to be avoided. In evolutionary history, a bitter taste is commonly indicative of poisonous plants and is, of course, to be avoided.

Sourness and bitterness are normally associated with rejection and avoidance, irrespective of circumstances and internal state of the body. However, in other cases, the reaction to a given substance depends upon physiological state. One distinguishes between the successive processes of (1) sensory detection of a chemical quality and (2) assessing its motivational significance. For example, the reaction to the perception of sweetness and saltiness depends to some extent upon the physiological state of the body.

Suppose we detect concentrated sodium chloride at the tongue. At a later stage of processing in the nervous system, this would normally trigger either acceptance or rejection as a function of the body's salt depletion or repletion. Even in sodium balance most mammals tend to ingest diets containing some sodium (Scott, 1990), a tendency amplified in salt deficiency. In our evolution, especially at times of salt deficiency, it would be adaptive to ingest salt. Sodium concentrations that are avoided in sodium balance are ingested in deficiency.

Sensory detection

On the surface of the tongue is a mosaic of small organs, known as 'taste buds', each made up of receptors for chemicals (Norgren, 1984) (Figure 9.23). Taste buds are also in regions of the mouth other than the tongue. The tips of sensory neurons make contact with these receptors. When specific chemicals are detected by the receptors of the taste buds, action potentials arise in the associated sensory neurons.

At one time it was believed that each specific taste cell and associated neuron would respond only to a specific chemical quality such as a sugar: a quality-specific private line to the brain. Indeed, depending upon the species, there are a number of neurons showing this property and hence providing **labelled-line coding** for such qualities as sweetness and salt (McCaughey and Scott, 1998).

However, it is probably more common that the taste receptors of each taste bud and the associated neuron respond to some extent to a range of chemical qualities. Different taste buds respond *differently* to them. Thus, the information carried in a given neuron cannot discriminate between a low concentration of a chemical to which it is highly sensitive and a high concentration of a chemical to which it is less sensitive. The fact that tastes can be resolved implies a comparison between signals carried by different neurons, so-called **across-fibre pattern coding** (Norgren, 1984). This comparison is done in the brain where there is an integration of information.

This is analogous to colour vision where a particular cone (e.g. an M cone) responds preferentially to one wavelength but is sensitive to some extent to other wavelengths (e.g. long wavelengths) (McCaughey and Scott, 1998). The further processing that is done to information from sensory neurons to extract taste information is something like opponent-process coding for colour.

It appears that, as a result of top-down modulation, there is some plasticity in terms of which neurons code for which sensory quality. In sodium deprivation, neurons in the

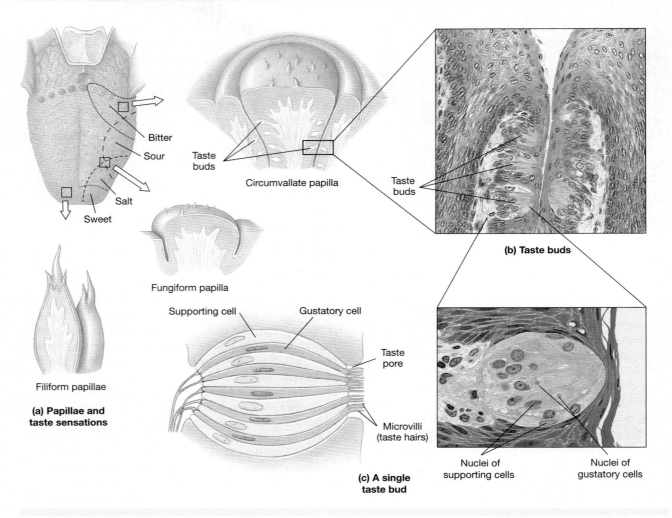

Figure 9.23 Taste buds: (a) papillae and taste sensations, (b) taste buds and (c) a single taste bud.

Source: Martini *et al.* (2000, Fig. 18-7, p. 471); (b) and (c) Copyright G.W. Willis/Visuals Unlimited.

sensory pathway that normally code for sugars (see next section) become responsive to sodium (Jacobs *et al.*, 1988). This appears to be a means by which the hedonic quality of sugars can be temporally borrowed by the sodium ingestion system and contribute to increased sodium intake.

From tongue to brain

Figure 9.24 was first introduced in Chapter 5 and it now points to some additional details: the receptors on the tongue in relation to the pathway of taste information carried by neurons to the gustatory cortex, in primates (Norgren, 1984). Sensory neurons travel as part of a cranial nerve (three of these are involved, facial, glossopharyngeal and vagus, as shown) to the nucleus of the solitary tract (NTS) in the medulla, where they terminate. Synaptic connection is made with further neurons that carry the information to a region of thalamus. These second-order neurons (with cell

bodies in the NTS) exhibit plasticity in terms of the chemical quality needed to trigger them. This involves top-down modulation based upon need states.

Neurons project from the thalamus to the gustatory cortex. In addition to the pathway shown, other routes project to other brain regions such as the amygdala and prefrontal cortex (de Araujo *et al.*, 2003). Throughout the routes of cortical processing, neurons can be identified that have 'preferred' tastes as trigger stimuli, such as umami.

Note a similarity with visual, auditory and somatosensory information, each of which also projects to its own region of thalamus. The similarity continues in that after the thalamus further neurons convey taste information to specific regions of cortex, which are specialized for processing it.

Much analysis of taste, in terms of appropriateness for ingestion, is performed at the brain stem (Grill and Kaplan, 1990). This process is sometimes termed a 'hedonic monitor'.

There are extensive feedback loops from cortex to lower structures in the taste pathway, by which ascending information can be modulated (Norgren, 1984). For example, the change in response of primary sensory neurons according to internal state (e.g. sodium balance) is due to a neural modulation mediated from higher levels of processing.

Smell

Introduction

The chemicals to which our noses are responsive in triggering smell (olfaction) are described as volatile. A principle applies to both olfaction and taste: there exists a distinction between the detection of chemical qualities and their motivational significance. Whereas certain odours will always evoke rejection and avoidance, others can evoke pleasantness/approach or unpleasantness/avoidance depending upon internal state. In a hungry person with a favourable history of associations, the smell of a favourite dish evokes approach but, following an association of the taste with a subsequent gastric upset, it might evoke avoidance. The difference lies in the context into which sensory detection is placed by further processing.

We are all familiar with daily discriminations on the basis of vision and sound. Olfaction can be more subtle and less accessible to conscious awareness. The capacity of mothers to detect the odours of their babies and for babies to prefer the maternal odour (Weller, 1998) might well exert a role in human communication and bonding.

Sensory detection

Sensory detection of volatile chemicals by the nose has some similarities to the detection of chemicals by the tongue. The nose contains specific receptors that are sensitive to particular chemicals. In humans there are some 50 million such olfactory receptors, located as shown in Figure 9.25.

By sniffing, we increase the flow of air into the nose and increase the contact of volatile chemicals with olfactory receptors. Olfactory receptors are parts of neurons that perform transduction of chemical information and also, in the form of action potentials, convey information away from the site of detection and towards the brain. However, whereas there are a few basic types of taste qualities and receptors, it appears that olfactory stimuli and receptors cannot be categorized into a few classes (Bartoshuk and Beauchamp, 1994). Rather, there seem to be hundreds of different types of receptor, each specialized for a particular olfactory quality.

According to the **lock and key principle**, a volatile chemical triggering a receptor is analogous to a neurotransmitter attaching to a receptor at a synapse

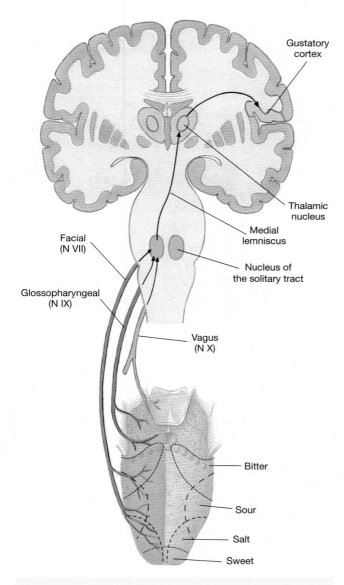

Figure 9.24 The taste system. Note the regions of concentration of the four ('classical') types of taste receptors. The diagram is drawn asymmetrically merely as a convenience for explanation.

Source: Martini *et al*. (2000, Fig. 18-18, p. 472).

Although the basic analysis of the chemical properties is done at this level, other brain regions also play a part in the decision to ingest or not, possibly by modulating the activity of the brain stem. Thus, tastes are put into a context of associations. For example, substances can increase in acceptance as a result of familiarity or become the targets of rejection as a result of nausea following their earlier ingestion. Much of this analysis appears to be performed at levels higher than the brain stem (Scott, 1990).

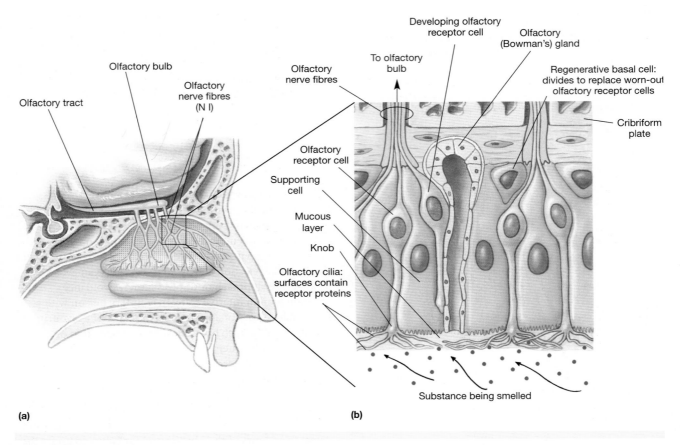

Figure 9.25 Olfactory system: (a) nasal cavity and (b) olfactory epithelium.

Source: Martini *et al*. (2000, Fig. 18-6, p. 470).

(Chapter 4). In each case, there is chemical specificity. Similarly, inserting the 'key' in the 'lock' (a) triggers further events within the cell and (b) is normally short-lived as there are processes that remove the 'key' shortly after its attachment (Coren *et al*., 1994).

There are many odours that we identify as belonging to specific objects in our environment (e.g. frying eggs, vegetable vindaloo, cigar smoke), each made up of many different chemicals. This implies that the outputs of numerous olfactory receptor types are combined to form our psychological perception of an odour. In other words, olfaction is a *synthetic* sense, one that puts together components of information to yield a combined perception (Carlson, 1994). In this sense, it is like vision. However, suppose three smells of familiar objects are present simultaneously, as in smoking a cigarette, while a curry is being served in the presence of someone wearing a strong perfume. We can still resolve the familiar components, so in this regard olfaction is *analytic*, something like hearing.

From nose to brain

The axons of olfactory receptors form synapses at the brain's olfactory bulb (Dodd and Castellucci, 1991). See Figure 9.25. Further neurons then convey olfactory information (as the olfactory tract) from the olfactory bulb to other brain regions, e.g. the olfactory cortex, amygdala and hypothalamus. Neurons are not organized in a topographic way at the olfactory bulb, so information on the site of the neuron originating the odour is lost.

Olfaction is the only system with a direct link to the cortex, bypassing the thalamus. Links to the amygdala provide rapid computation of the emotional significance of an odour and links to the hypothalamus have motivational significance, as in mating. Some information ultimately reaches the orbitofrontal cortex, where processing is thought to be associated with conscious awareness (Dodd and Castellucci, 1991). In the latter regard, olfaction is similar to other sensory systems. There are also fibres which carry information 'top-down' to make synapses in the olfactory bulb.

Pheromones

In a number of species, there is a distinct olfactory system, in addition to that just described: the **vomeronasal system** (Bartoshuk and Beauchamp, 1994). Its detectors are also in the nasal cavity. This system specializes in the detection of pheromones. As an example, in secreting pheromones certain species advertise their sexual arousal. By this means, a male can discriminate between potentially sexually receptive and unreceptive females. Distinct vomeronasal sensory neurons form synapses in the olfactory bulb. From the olfactory bulb, information is conveyed to brain regions concerned with, for example, reproduction, e.g. nuclei of the hypothalamus (Brennan and Keverne, 2004).

Evidence suggests that humans are sensitive to pheromones, a process that operates below conscious awareness (Monti-Bloch *et al.*, 1994). However, some doubt that it is the vomeronasal system that mediates this functional role in humans (Brennan and Keverne, 2004). Thus, the conventional olfactory system could be responsible for pheromone detection in humans. The attraction of perfumes suggests that these may simulate pheromones that play a part in human sexual attraction. A role for pheromones in humans was suggested by the observation that women living in close proximity to each other have a tendency to synchronize their menstrual cycles (Stern and McClintock, 1998). Similarly, group-living female rats tend to show a synchrony of oestrous cycles (McClintock, 1984), which is mediated by pheromones.

Stern and McClintock demonstrated experimentally that there are shifts of the menstrual cycle in response to pheromones produced by women. Secretions taken from under the arms of donors were applied just above the upper lip of recipient women and this shifted their cycle. The control condition was alcohol, the chemical base for the samples in the experimental conditions. This again suggests

that there might naturally be such a synchronization role. The direction of the shift, whether to bring the cycle forward or move it back, was such as to synchronize it with that of the emitter. This raises the possibility of two distinct pheromones having opposite effects. Women were not able to report the presence of the pheromone as distinct from the chemical base, indicating an unconscious effect.

It is interesting to speculate on the functional significance of such synchronization in group-living females, in terms of the advantage to the individual in timing mating. Could synchronized mating coordinate group activities such as hunting and caring for offspring? This has enormous implications for anthropological and feminist discourse and the opportunities for speculation are vast.

Weller (1998) speculates that there might be significant emotional reactions due to pheromonal communication between two people. This could play a role in differences in social reactivity or as one factor among others in the phenomenon of emotional contagion, by which one person's mood influences another (Hatfield *et al.*, 1993). It suggests that parapsychologists need to be vigilant about another possible route of communication of information in experiments on 'extra-sensory' perception.

Odour, emotion and mood

Odours are sometimes thought to have a more direct link to mood and emotion than do other sensory qualities. Compared with visual and auditory events, descriptions of odours have a more direct emotional label and thereby possibly a more personal 'meaning' (Ehrlichman and Bastone, 1992).

It might be that odours have more direct access to emotional processing, though cognitive factors (e.g. knowledge of what is the physical object giving rise to the odour) also play a role in labelling an odour. It is commonly said that odours have a peculiar ability to evoke emotion-laden memories from childhood. However, psychology lacks controlled studies showing that such odour-triggered memories are more potent than, say, visually cued memories. Since the trigger cues for any such odour → memory → emotion link would necessarily be personal and idiosyncratic, perhaps it is impossible to do formal research in this area.

In humans, anecdotal reports suggest that odour can influence mood, contributing to well-being (G.N. Martin, 1996) and some experimental evidence points in the same direction (Lehrner *et al.*, 2005). If psychological benefits derive from exposure to volatile chemicals, this is valuable no matter what the mechanism. However, it is not always certain that the route of such effects is via the olfactory system. Chemicals could be absorbed into the bloodstream via the lungs or through the skin in the case of massage oils and thereby influence the nervous system (Ehrlichman and Bastone, 1992).

A personal angle

A fortuitous observation

Martha McClintock, then an undergraduate at Wellesley College, Massachusetts, observed synchrony in menstrual cycles amongst her fellow students in her dormitory. At 20 years of age, she presented her insight to a conference on pheromones. Although the observation was met with some scepticism, she did the necessary formal observations and the study was published in the journal *Nature* shortly afterwards (McClintock, 1971). This was the trigger to a very fruitful research programme in the area of pheromones and behaviour.

From a functional perspective, it might make sense for unpleasant odours to trigger negative mood. Odours such as those deriving from rotting food are a sign of danger. Negative mood could motivate moving from the location.

Disorders of olfaction

With advancing years, humans become less sensitive to odours and elderly people commonly complain that foods lack taste (Smith and Duncan, 1992).

Analogous to other sensory systems, disorders of olfaction arise at various levels. There can be a failure of volatile chemicals to gain access to the olfactory receptors by a blockage of the passageway. Failures can arise in the transmission of information to the brain or in the processing of olfactory information by the brain. A significant percentage of patients with loss of smell ('anosmia') have suffered head injury. This can involve severing neurons within the olfactory nerve. Alzheimer's patients are commonly deficient in smell, which can probably be related to the degeneration of neural tissue in the brain that is the hallmark of this disease.

A phantosmia or olfactory hallucination (OH) consists of the perception of an odour that is not physically present at the nose (Greenberg, 1992). An OH can take the form of a familiar smell or something quite novel to the person's experience. Sometimes the OH assumes a specific form of the kind 'roses presented on a fortieth birthday'. Such hallucinations have hedonic properties of liking or disgust and a frame of reference in space, e.g. to the left or right. Sometimes hallucinations have an 'as if' quality to them: subjects feel that there are features in common with, say, the smell of cigar smoke but they know that no such odour is present. In other patients, the sensation has the vividness of a real odour.

OHs are associated with a number of conditions, one being epilepsy. This consists of sudden electrical activity, associated with such areas as the hippocampus and amygdala, with alteration of consciousness. This identifies very broadly some processing of smell information with these regions.

Following brain lesions, as in accidents, OHs are sometimes experienced. Greenberg suggests that some of these represent release phenomena, i.e. they are released under the conditions of reduced afferent input.

Interaction of taste and smell

Taste and smell usually act in cooperation in analyzing substances for ingestion. For example, the psychological perception described as the **flavour** of food depends on an interaction between them. In addition, information from tactile stimulation of the mouth plays a role (Scott, 1990).

When a cold impairs smell, food does not taste as it should. Some common foods, e.g. garlic, coffee and chocolate, are difficult to identify when smell is impaired (Coren *et al.*, 1994). Disorders of smell are commonly described in terms of failures of taste (Smith and Duncan, 1992).

So, having looked at taste and smell as distinct systems, it is insightful to consider their interaction. Evidence on this arises from human reports of specific interactions in the psychological experience of stimulation of taste and olfaction (Small and Prescott, 2005). For example, when a substance such as a solution of sucrose is being tasted, there is an enhancement of sweetness by the simultaneous olfactory stimulation by food odours such as vanilla.

An odour can enhance a taste or even trigger a taste sensation in the absence of a taste stimulus. This effect requires *congruency* of the components, that is to say, odours and tastes that have a history of being paired reinforce or substitute their effects. This suggests a process of learning by association, as briefly described in Chapter 3. Thus, you would not expect a strawberry odour to enhance or trigger the taste sensation of a fried egg.

What is the neural basis of this interaction? Neuroimaging studies reveal networks of brain regions, which are stimulated by either taste or odour. See Figure 9.26. From this, it seems reasonable to speculate that these regions are responsible for the integration of taste and olfactory information. Indeed, in some cases, activation is increased by simultaneous stimulation of both modalities. The orbitofrontal cortex (OFC) participates in such networks. In non-human primates, recordings from single neurons in the OFC reveal triggering by taste or smell stimuli, or both, pointing to a convergence of inputs.

Section summary

1 Taste and smell are initiated by the detection of specific chemicals by chemoreceptors.

2 Taste buds at the tongue detect the presence of chemicals.

3 Five primary tastes, sweet, salty, sour, bitter and umami, are psychological perceptions corresponding to broad classes of molecule at the tongue.

4 Olfactory receptors in the nose are sensitive to volatile chemicals.

5 The vomeronasal system is specialized for the detection of pheromones.

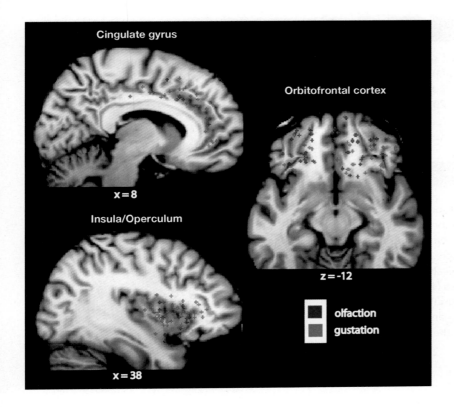

Figure 9.26 Diagram showing regions of activation of selected brain regions by either olfactory or gustatory (taste) stimuli.

Source: Small and Prescott (2005, Fig. 1, p. 347). Courtesy of Dana Small and John Prescott.

Test your knowledge

(Answers on page 244)

9.7 The glossopharyngeal and vagus are examples of what kind of nerves?

9.8 Complete the following: 'A pheromone is a substance that is _____ by one individual and that is _____ by another individual'.

Bringing things together

The chapter has spanned the sensory systems of hearing, the vestibular sense, touch, taste and smell. In each case, a specialized detector captures a range within a particular physical quality. It is possible to see some features in common between certain of the sensory systems and some differences. In each case, we can see that the sensory systems are particularly sensitive to information that plays a role in the survival and reproduction of the animal. In each case, an initial stage of detection of the physical event is followed by further

processing in which more complex features are extracted and the sensory event is placed in context.

The tactile sense, hearing and the vestibular sense involve cells that respond to mechanical distortion. There is some similarity in the type of cell that is found in the hearing system and the vestibular system. Taste and smell both respond to chemicals by a process of recognition of the form that the chemical takes.

Summary of Chapter 9

1 **The auditory system analyses sounds in terms of their frequency and intensity.**

2 **The vestibular system is sensitive to movements of the head and can trigger corrective action.**

3 **The somatosensory system detects tactile stimuli and involves specialized detectors at the skin that are sensitive to various kinds of mechanical distortion.**

4 **The senses of taste and smell are triggered by particular chemicals that attach to specific receptors.**

Further reading

For all of the neuroscience in this chapter, see Nolte (2002). For details of hearing, see Brown (1999). For the somatic sensory system, see Hendry *et al.* (1999b). For taste and olfaction, see Rouby *et al.* (2005).

Signposts

This completes the chapters devoted to sensory systems. However, we will need to use this information throughout the subsequent chapters. We considered chemoreceptors sensitive to events at nose and tongue. There are chemoreceptors that are sensitive to chemicals deep inside the body, discussed in various later chapters (13 'Stress and coping', 15 'Motivation', 16 'Feeding and drinking' and 17 'Sexual behaviour'). Chapter 20 ('Cognition and action') will return to the topic of sensory systems and their link with conscious experience.

Answers

Explanations for answers to 'test your knowledge' questions can be found on the website **www.pearsoned.co.uk/toates**

9.1 (i) A particular range of frequencies
9.2 (ii) Medium
9.3 Mechanical; frequency
9.4 Excitatory
9.5 (i) a; (iii) the two neurons coloured blue
9.6 A tube, the size and location of which coincides with the inhibitory surround
9.7 Cranial
9.8 Secreted (or released); detected (or sensed)

CHAPTER 10

The control of movement

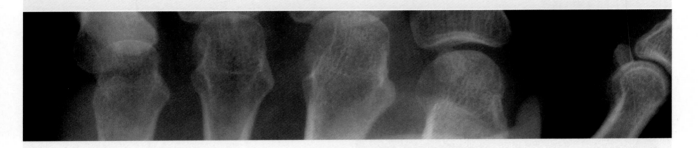

1 Describe the problems that the movement control system confronts and the basic 'design' principles that enable their solution.

2 Distinguish between feedback and feedforward, while explaining why both processes are needed. Distinguish between automatic and controlled processing.

3 Explain what is involved in detecting change while maintaining stability.

4 Describe the basic principles of neuromuscular control and relate these to the properties of motor neurons and skeletal muscles.

5 Describe what is meant by the term 'stretch reflex' and how it maintains stability in the face of a disturbance.

6 Identify some of the principal brain regions involved in motor control and outline their roles. Link this account to a consideration of when motor control goes wrong.

7 Distinguish the routes by which motor information descends from the brain to the periphery and compare their properties.

8 Understand the significance of performing mental simulations of actions and link this to the possible role of mirror neurons.

9 Outline what is meant by development of the nervous system, in the context of movement control.

Scene-setting questions

1 'That was a knee-jerk response!' is a term of mild abuse. What is this response and how is it produced?

2 'Sorry – I wasn't thinking – I went on autopilot.' Does this statement have any basis in biological psychology?

3 What goes wrong in Parkinson's disease?

4 Can you improve skills at, say, the piano or football by practicing in your imagination?

When do we need to pay full conscious attention to a single task and when can we trust the brain's automatic processes?

Source: Getty Images/Altrendo.

Introduction

First, imagine that you are simply standing still and waiting somewhere. You remain upright in spite of gusts of winds blowing against you and the occasional person bumping into you. Though we usually take such ability for granted, it represents an astonishing achievement on the part of the nervous and muscular systems; a shop-window dummy left balancing there would quickly fall to the ground. We manage the task without conscious attention being paid to it.

Now imagine that you start to move forward. Again, without thinking, you swing your legs back and forth, whilst moving the arms in synchrony. The control of movement is a crucial role of the nervous system but, in moving, you also need to maintain the body's stability, in this case, in an upright position. So, to trigger *change* against a background of *stability* is a task that evolution has solved.

Look at the effortless way in which you can negotiate and manipulate your environment, lifting objects and placing them in different locations, swinging a tennis racket, pressing doorbells or doing fine-grained and attention-demanding tasks such as sewing a novel stitch. In each case, there is coordination of muscles by the nervous system in order to achieve a goal, sometimes termed a **set-point**. So much of behaviour appears to be spontaneous, as in the tasks just described or when you decide to get out of bed for no obvious external trigger. These exemplify what is termed an **action** (Jahanshahi *et al.*, 1995), as introduced in Chapter 2, 'Genes, environment and evolution'.

Now contrast this with the automatic response of moving the foot quickly from a hot object. Some behaviour is triggered by external events and this, by contrast, is described as a 'reaction'.

Figure 10.1 summarizes the essence of the chapter. First note the 'Stimulus' that acts on the 'Neuromuscular system' to trigger 'Behaviour'. This is the part described by the term 'reaction' and is exemplified by that shown to a noxious stimulus.

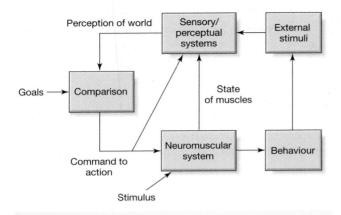

Figure 10.1 Neuromuscular control.

Now let's turn to the 'action' part of behaviour, where a role is played by the internal factor of a decision to act. In deciding, we establish goals; hence the arrow marked 'Goals'. The goal set can be as simple as standing upright without falling over or as complex as hitting a winning tennis stroke. Whatever the goal, the problem that it sets for the control of movement is to try to align the actual state of affairs with the goal. In other words, the system has the task of minimizing any disparity between the way things are and the way that the goal, in effect, says that they should be. In the case of standing upright, we simply need to maintain the goal of the *status quo* whereas movement is called for in other cases.

In Figure 10.1, 'Sensory/perceptual systems' detect 'External stimuli', which gives the 'Perception of world'. 'Sensory/perceptual systems' utilize information such as vision, and a comparison is made with the goal. The task of movement control is to try to minimize any difference that this 'Comparison' detects between the goal and how the world actually is. Exactly how this is achieved forms the theme of the present chapter. 'Behaviour' changes the 'External stimuli', as in hitting the ball with the racket.

Our 'Sensory/perceptual systems' are informed not only of the external world but also of events within the body. Quite unconsciously, we monitor the activity of our skeletal muscles. The CNS is constantly informed of their contraction, represented as 'State of muscles'. The term **proprioception** refers to the special sensory system that monitors muscles and feeds information on this to the CNS. Try closing your eyes and touching the tip of your nose with your finger. Although you do not have vision as a guide, you can still do it. Proprioception informs you of the state of the muscles and can be exploited as a guide.

Performing tasks, even of standing upright, requires signals from sensors of the state of your body, such as those of proprioception and those making up the vestibular apparatus (Chapter 9, 'The other sensory systems'). If you

accidentally tilt from the vertical, these sensors detect this and instigate corrective action. Such tasks involve coordination over the activity of numerous skeletal muscles.

Imagine yourself performing some skilled action for the first time, such as tennis. Your behaviour is controlled consciously by the disparity between the way that things are and how you would like them to be. Wimbledon tennis champions all started out this way but the acquisition of skill has given them some additional processes to exploit. These will be discussed shortly.

Note one other feature of Figure 10.1. The 'Command to action' is also shown going to our 'Sensory/perceptual systems'. The brain compares what has been commanded with the effect this has on the world, through 'External stimuli'. Future modification can be made to this command, based on outcomes.

The next section looks at the issue of how we adjust behaviour so that the actual state is as closely aligned as possible to the goals that we set.

Section summary

1 The brain sets goals and, by means of its control of behaviour, attempts to match these.

2 Maintaining stability is a goal set by the nervous system.

3 Actions are organized against a background of maintaining some stability.

4 A system of proprioception detects the activity of skeletal muscles.

5 Proprioception as well as vestibular signals are involved in maintaining stability in the face of disturbances.

6 Particular stimuli trigger some behaviour, as a reaction rather than an action.

Test your knowledge

(Answers on page 273)

10.1 Complete the following: 'Neural signals within the _____ system, involving hair cells, detect unintended movement of the head and trigger corrective action'.

10.2 Complete the following: 'A system of proprioception detects the state of _____ muscles and feeds this information to the _____'.

Basics of control

This section looks at some of the principles that underlie the control of movement. Later sections consider the details of how the nervous system achieves these tasks.

Types of control

Negative feedback

Negative feedback was introduced in Chapter 2. It was noted that deviations of a body parameter from its normal ('optimal') level triggers action so as to restore normality. For example, when body temperature falls, shivering is triggered and this generates heat, which tends to raise body temperature back to normal. This same principle is employed in the control of movement. In terms of Figure 10.1, when the sense organs indicate that something is not aligned with a goal, action is taken to restore alignment.

In order to raise money for charities, village fetes sometimes offer various games that challenge contestants' visual and motor skills. One consists of having to pass a loop of metal wire along a bending metal wire but without the loop touching the inner wire. If contact is made, an electric bell rings and this is scored as a miss. Skill comes in not letting the loop come too close to the inner wire. If you find the loop getting near the wire, you take corrective action to move it away. Any deviation from the desired position is the trigger for action, i.e. negative feedback. To the novice, such a task is done with conscious awareness focused on it. You could verbally articulate what you were trying to achieve. However, the body also exploits negative feedback in quite unconscious ways, as follows.

It was noted that, when there is a disturbance to the body, triggered by a gust of wind, corrective action occurs, such that you do not fall over. Sensors in the skeletal muscles and vestibular apparatus detect the disturbance and trigger a change to the signal sent to the skeletal muscles. This then restores stability and it is all done without there necessarily being conscious intervention. You just consciously set the goal to stand upright and the rest is done unconsciously.

When we try to perform a new action, we tend to be clumsy and make mistakes. Regular practice usually improves performance, termed 'motor learning' (Willingham, 1998). The system learns by mistakes; what is achieved is compared with the goal. Error tends to cause (i) immediate action such as to eliminate error and (ii) learning to adjust future action.

Feedforward

Negative feedback is central to the control of movement: disturbance of values from the goals that are set tend to evoke a corrective reaction. However, this is not the only process involved and an additional process that is exploited by movement control is termed **feedforward**. In order to understand this, we need to consider some of the problems with relying only upon negative feedback, especially where speed is important.

For error to be able to drive action, by definition an error must first occur and be detected, information on it must be fed back and then action triggered. It takes time for information to be fed back to the CNS and action to be triggered. When things change rapidly, negative feedback might not be able to trigger action quickly enough. The solution that evolution has found is to employ feedforward, which operates within a framework of negative feedback and makes up for the latter's shortcomings.

In a simple unlearned form, feedforward is illustrated when we raise an arm out to one side of the body. At *the same time*, we automatically tilt the body slightly in the opposite direction to counter the disturbance to equilibrium that would *otherwise* occur. Tilt is not a response to a disturbance to equilibrium but is caused by putting into effect the intention to raise the arm. By reacting even before a disturbance to equilibrium occurs, it is said to avoid ('preempt') any disturbance.

Feedforward controls can also be learned based upon past experiences of acting by means of negative feedback. In such cases, feedforward control is something like a calculated guess as to what action is needed. To clarify this with a simple example, let us return to body temperature. Suppose that your body temperature drops as a result of an unexpected exposure to a cold environment. In response to cooling, the body triggers heating action such as shivering. This brings temperature back to normal – a biologically vital process. However, with the use of intelligence, you can do even better than this. Suppose that you hear from the weather forecast that the temperature has dropped sharply. You might wrap up warmly on leaving home. This is not in response to body cooling but a calculated guess that you will be cold unless you take this action. It thereby prevents chilling, a form of feedforward.

To return to movement control, suppose movements have been repeatedly performed under the guidance of negative feedback to bring something into alignment. The brain acquires memories of the movements and the circumstances under which they were triggered. It can then instigate action slightly sooner than would be triggered on the basis of negative feedback. Action is based on a calculation of the *possibility* of future error, i.e. feedforward (Ito, 1984). Feedforward is also illustrated in the following example.

Consider an interaction between two animals, e.g. a predator chasing a prey. The predator exploits information on the distance between itself and the prey in order to try to close the gap. If the prey changes direction suddenly, the

What kind of control system underlies a task of this kind?

Source: © Winfried Wisniewski/zefa/Corbis.

predator recognizes this and takes corrective action. This exemplifies negative feedback. However, on close examination, the predator also exploits feedforward. When the moves of the prey can be predicted, the predator's behaviour is directed to where the prey will most likely be in future (Rosenblueth *et al.*, 1968). See Figure 10.2. This is, of course, why prey such as antelope suddenly change direction when they are being chased by a lion – they reduce the opportunity for the predator to predict their position.

The difference between the novice tennis player and the Wimbledon champion is that the former is relying very heavily

on negative feedback, whereas the latter has an array of feedforward possibilities available. Hence, the champion anticipates the moves of the ball and acts so fast that the behaviour could not be guided moment-by-moment simply by negative feedback. If, however, an error appears because of a failing by the feedforward processes, then this is registered and future behaviour adjusted accordingly. Actions and feedback on their consequences are memorized and used to adjust behaviour in the future, so goals can be achieved more effectively.

Controlled and automatic processing

Basics

Imagine you are walking across an icy and sloping bridge. You pick your steps very carefully and slowly, consciously focusing attention on the single task of moving but without slipping. You do not converse with anyone, since this would divert your attention from the task at hand. You feel the way forward, holding onto a railing and you monitor the effects of your feet, alert to any slight slippage. You are relying on moment-by-moment feedback, since this is your first experience of ice.

Now imagine yourself in summer, walking over the same bridge. You are in conversation with a friend and give hardly a thought to the action of walking. In the first case, you brought full conscious awareness to the problem and this illustrates **controlled processing** (Schneider and Shiffrin, 1977). In the second case, the task was done without bringing conscious awareness to it and it would be said to involve **automatic processing**. Your conscious awareness was engaged elsewhere, with the conversation.

New tasks start out generally in the mode of controlled processing and with a weight on negative feedback. When you first start to learn to ride a bicycle, you are conscious of every move you make. When you become skilled at it, control shifts to a more automatic mode. If, however, the bicycle starts to skid on ice, you quickly bring full conscious awareness to the task. Our learning of a new skill and devoting conscious effort to it often involves silent speech-based instructions to ourselves (Seitz and Roland, 1992).

Although controlled and automatic represent two distinct modes, in practice most, if not all, tasks will be done by exploiting a combination of both. Even doing something in the conscious controlled mode will make considerable use of some automatic processes.

Behaviour that requires conscious decision-making is described as **voluntary action**. It is said to have a purpose, intention, goal or end-point, which we can consciously reflect upon and articulate. By contrast, other aspects of behaviour are described as 'automatic reactions' or **involuntary reactions**, also termed reflexes, e.g. withdrawal of a hand from a noxious object.

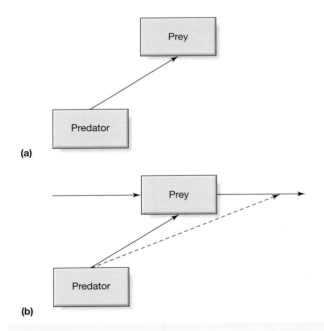

Figure 10.2 Trajectory of a predator based upon (a) a stationary prey and negative feedback and (b) moving prey and negative feedback alone (solid) compared with system that has, in addition, feedforward (dotted).

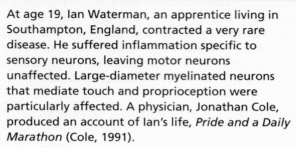

At age 19, Ian Waterman, an apprentice living in Southampton, England, contracted a very rare disease. He suffered inflammation specific to sensory neurons, leaving motor neurons unaffected. Large-diameter myelinated neurons that mediate touch and proprioception were particularly affected. A physician, Jonathan Cole, produced an account of Ian's life, *Pride and a Daily Marathon* (Cole, 1991).

Ian's movements and life were devastated by the disorder, indicating the importance of feedback from the body. He was in limbo. Since feedback from the mouth as from elsewhere was lacking, speech was very difficult. Ian could feel pain since the small-diameter axons that convey information on tissue damage were unaffected. When not looking at them, Ian's limbs would sometimes move on their own, indicative of the importance of feedback in maintaining stability. Amazingly, Ian learned to exploit visual feedback in regaining mobility. Recalibration of motor commands was a difficult trial-and-error process, involving full conscious control in place of unconscious proprioceptive feedback. Even a moment's loss of vision was disruptive and there was no spare cognitive capacity to permit daydreaming during walking. Ian could exploit his intact sense of temperature even without the use of vision, e.g. when in bed he knew that he had moved a leg on detecting a cooler place.

With extensive repetition, voluntary ('controlled') behaviour moves to become automatic, and takes on certain new properties (Thach, 1998). Suppose that, over repeated experiences, controlled behaviour is performed by repetition of a given sequence of component acts A_1, A_2, A_3..., etc. With the move to automatic control, triggering of A_1 tends to trigger A_2, which then triggers A_3 and so on. Once such learned (feedforward) sequences are able to be run off automatically, they offer speed but also allow a sparing of conscious brain processes for engaging in other tasks.

Role of the CNS

The nervous system is organized at different levels of control. Some reflexes have a degree of autonomy from the brain and are organized at the spinal cord (Chapter 3, 'The nervous and endocrine systems'), though even here the brain does not remove its connection to the local control. The brain still exerts some influence over reflexes, adjusting their parameters according to circumstances and making them stronger or weaker. At the other end of the scale, some tasks require full conscious awareness to give moment-by-moment guidance. In all cases, a response is the product of one integrated system involving brain, spinal cord, peripheral neurons and muscles.

To function optimally, speed is often essential. Conscious reactions based upon feedback are relatively slow and processing can become overloaded with information. The solution is to delegate some limited control to other levels, such as reflexes and brain processes that operate on automatic ('autopilot') control. However, conscious processes still monitor their success or failure. How the parts of the system and levels interact in producing adaptive behaviour is the central problem to be addressed in this chapter.

Skill learning

There is a distinction between learning skills (e.g. to ride a bicycle) and learning knowledge (e.g. that Chisinau is the capital of Moldova). Different brain regions are activated during learning of these different tasks. By positron emission tomography (PET) (Chapter 5, 'The brain'), Seitz and Roland (1992) measured blood flow in the brain during skill learning, involving finger movements of the right hand similar to typing. There was activation in motor regions of the left motor cortex and the right cerebellum. Areas involved in acquiring a memory for facts and locations, e.g. the hippocampus, were not activated.

Differences in brain processes correspond to the dimension controlled–automatic (Jenkins *et al.*, 1994; Raichle *et al.*, 1994). When a task becomes automatic, there appears to be some short-circuiting of the higher-level goal-directed and cognitive processes. Jenkins *et al.* measured regional cerebral blood flow (rCBF) (Chapter 5) by PET scanning as people became skilled at a motor task. The cerebellum (Chapter 5) was strongly activated during learning of a new task but less so when skill was acquired. As a person becomes skilled at a finger movement (e.g. 'touch the thumb twice with index finger'), activation of speech areas of the cortex declines (Seitz and Roland, 1992). This corresponds to a reduction in the use of silent 'inner speech' by people to solve the problem. The nervous system stores programmes for well-practised responses that can sometimes be executed even if feedback from the muscles is disrupted due to disease (Marsden *et al.*, 1984).

Resisting the performance of a response

When a task ('response') becomes automatic, its trigger stimulus creates a strong tendency to produce the response (Reason, 1979). Suppose that you consciously try to perform behaviour incompatible with what the stimulus tends to evoke. Behaviour requires resistance to the automatic tendency and is performed *in spite of* the powerful but inappropriate external cue. A classic example is the **Stroop test** (Figure 10.3), where a person is asked to name the colour of ink in which words are written, the words being incompatible colour names (Stroop, 1935). Thus, the word GREEN might be written in red ink and the task requires the person to respond 'red', ignoring the stimulus 'green'. This task is difficult since it requires controlled processing to override the automaticity of a lifetime's experience of responding 'green' to the word GREEN. Have a go at it and you will soon see. If your fellow students appear to be doing very well, check that they are not cheating by squinting!

This section has emphasized joint control by negative feedback and feedforward. The following section gives some instances of how stability is maintained in a changing world with the help of such control.

(a)	(b)
RED	GREEN
GREEN	RED
YELLOW	BLUE
BLUE	YELLOW
RED	BLUE
YELLOW	GREEN
BLUE	RED
GREEN	YELLOW

Figure 10.3 The Stroop test: (a) incompatible and (b) compatible lists.

Section summary

1 Negative feedback control, based upon disparity, is at the core of movement control.

2 Action depends upon negative feedback, e.g. via the eyes and from within the muscles.

3 Feedforward control involves taking action in anticipation of events likely to occur.

4 Negative feedback control acts in combination with feedforward control, the latter bringing the advantage of speed.

5 Behaviour can be classified into categories such as voluntary movements and reflexes.

6 Most behaviour is a compound of voluntary and involuntary/reflex components.

7 Voluntary behaviour is directed towards a goal of which we are consciously aware.

8 A distinction is between the controlled mode (i.e. conscious and with focused attention) and the automatic mode (unconscious and without focused attention).

9 A criterion of skill acquisition is when a task is performed automatically.

10 In association with highly trained tasks, it requires resistance not to respond to a stimulus.

Test your knowledge

(Answers on page 273)

10.3 Complete the missing words in the following: 'Acting in response to a deviation from a goal is described as _____ control, whereas ('anticipatory') acting so as to prevent a deviation is termed _____ control'.

10.4 Complete the missing words in the following: 'In the Stroop test, on being asked to respond according to ink colour, giving the response 'green' to the word RED written in green ink requires _____ processing associated with full _____ awareness'.

How stability is maintained

Introduction

Not only do stimuli fall on our sense organs but we are *active* in the world and this changes our relation to the external world. Thus, the brain confronts a fundamental design problem. Suppose that the eyes detect an image moving across the retina. This could be because something has moved in the external world relative to our eyes. Alternatively, it could be that the world has stayed still but the eyes have moved. A move of the body or just the eyes relative to a stationary world can cause a similar change in input to the exteroceptive ('arising in the outside world') senses as when the world changes (Gregory, 1997). In either case, there will be a movement of the image across the retina. Clearly, distinguishing the two is vital, so how is it achieved?

Similarly, a problem arises from interpreting a changing signal from the vestibular apparatus. This indicates that the vestibular apparatus (and presumably the whole head!) has moved somewhere in space, but what caused this? Did something in the world move us, as in an earthquake, or did the head move as a result of our voluntary action in a stable world?

This section gives some examples to illustrate how such problems are solved by the nervous system.

Eye movements

Consider the difference between Figures 10.4(a) and (b). In (a), the eye remains stationary and the object moves, whereas in (b) the external world is stationary and the eye moves (image of a stable world moves across the retina). We perceive correctly in (a) movement of the object and in (b) a stationary world, in spite of the fact that the image moves across the retina in both cases. In (b) information on the image movement and the eye movement cancel each other out, so that no movement is perceived. This indicates that perception is based upon both exteroceptive information and eye movements.

How do eye movements provide information for perception? Figure 10.5 shows two possibilities: the **inflow** theory and **outflow theory** (von Holst and Mittlestaedt, 1950). In each case, exteroceptive and intrinsic information is compared. Also, there is the same source of exteroceptive information, derived from image movement at the retina, conveyed via the optic nerve. However, the intrinsic source is different between (a) and (b). According to the inflow theory (a), the brain bases its calculation on *feedback* from the muscles. There are receptors located within eye muscles and these are said to provide the intrinsic information. By contrast, the outflow theory (b) suggests that information is based on the command to move (see also Figure 10.1). The latter is a variety of feedforward. In effect, the nervous system indicates that it has made a command to move the eyes and it anticipates that this will cause the muscles to move the eye.

An experiment can tease the theories apart. An after-image (Chapter 8, 'Vision') is fixed on the retina of the person in a dark room. The eye is then gently poked. The 'object' that the after-image represents does not appear to move. This favours outflow theory, since there is no command to the eye muscles and no change in exteroceptive input. Presumably there is an inflow from the muscles as a result of a poke-induced 'passive' change, which, if inflow theory were correct, should trigger perception of movement (Gregory, 1997).

Eye muscles can be paralyzed by curare, which blocks the junction between the motor neurons and the muscle, so commands cannot trigger contraction by the muscle. When the person attempts to move the eyes (i.e. makes commands), the world appears to spin around (Gallistel, 1980), which again supports outflow theory.

So, something to do with the command to action is involved in the perception of stability and movement

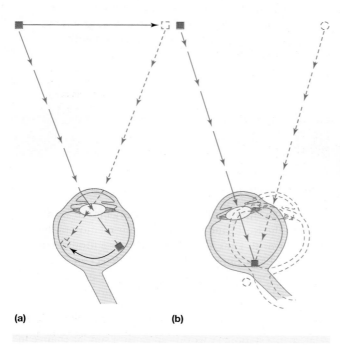

(a)   **(b)**

Figure 10.4 Movement: (a) stationary eye and changing world (object moves from left to right) and (b) stable external world but changing eye position (eye moves direction of pointing from square to round object).

Source: adapted from Gregory (1997, Fig. 6.1, p. 100).

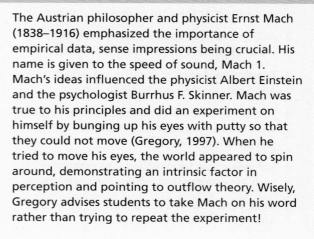

A personal angle

The importance of getting data

The Austrian philosopher and physicist Ernst Mach (1838–1916) emphasized the importance of empirical data, sense impressions being crucial. His name is given to the speed of sound, Mach 1. Mach's ideas influenced the physicist Albert Einstein and the psychologist Burrhus F. Skinner. Mach was true to his principles and did an experiment on himself by bunging up his eyes with putty so that they could not move (Gregory, 1997). When he tried to move his eyes, the world appeared to spin around, demonstrating an intrinsic factor in perception and pointing to outflow theory. Wisely, Gregory advises students to take Mach on his word rather than trying to repeat the experiment!

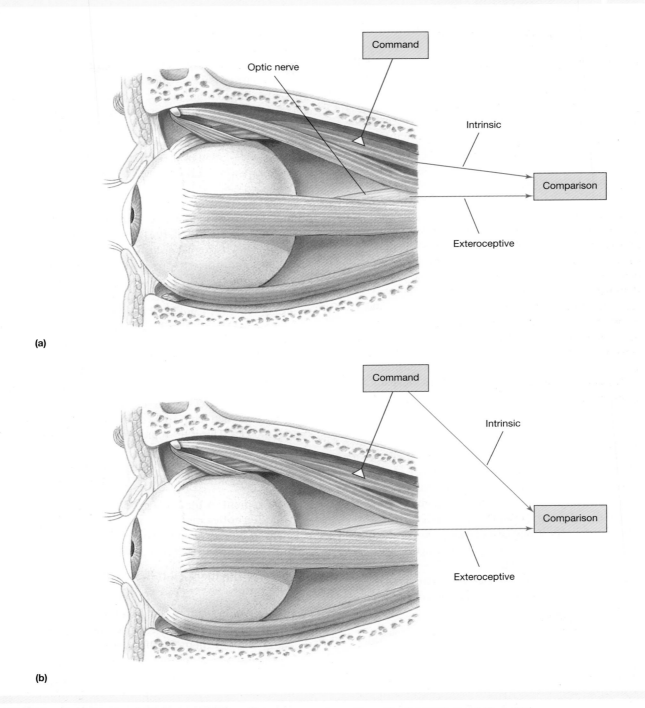

Figure 10.5 Two theories: (a) inflow and (b) outflow. *Source*: adapted from Martini (2000, Fig.10-5b, p. 268).

(MacKay, 1966). Possible sources of information range from the initiation of the command to move the eyes to the activity of motor neurons. Such ideas are summed up in terms of a so-called 'efference copy' or **corollary discharge** (von Holst and Mittelstaedt, 1950), i.e. a copy of the ('efferent') signal to the muscles is exploited for perception. In fact, information at an early stage in the production of movement appears to be used. Neurons within the parietal cortex encode locations of objects in visual space (Duhamel *et al.*, 1992). Prior to an eye movement, the anticipated new location of existing stimuli is calculated, i.e. an 'expectation' (Gallistel, 1980), and compared with their actual location after the movement. If the new situation corresponds to that calculated, perception is of a stable world.

The vestibulo-ocular reflex

Suppose that we are focused on something but voluntarily move our heads. Without any compensatory eye movements, the image would tend to move across the retina. This situation has the potential to spoil any effort to focus on a particular object. Nodding your head in agreement with someone would take your attention away from their eyes – not an adaptive strategy in a close romantic encounter. However, in reality, the head movement triggers compensatory movement of the eyes, so that the image tends to be stabilized on the retina, the **vestibulo-ocular reflex** (Ito, 1984). See Figure 10.6.

Movement of the head is detected by means of sensory input from the vestibular apparatus and its semicircular canals (Chapter 9). This triggers motor output to the eye muscles, so as to maintain stability of the eyes' direction of pointing. The parameters of this reflex can change over time, e.g. muscles become less effective with age. Unless checked, this would diminish the efficacy of the reflex. In fact, if the image fails to stabilize, other parameters are modified to compensate, i.e. motor learning. The neural link from semicircular canals to eye muscles through the brain stem is modified, by the action of what is termed a 'sidepath'. See Figure 10.6.

Maintaining postural stability

In order to stand upright without falling, the body's centre of gravity needs to be within the area of the base of support at the feet. Outside this, we are doomed to crash. Two types of disturbance might cause the centre of gravity to move beyond the safe zone: (1) an unexpected disturbance from outside, e.g. a very strong gust of wind, and (2) an expected change from inside, self-generated movements, e.g. voluntarily extending a limb.

Unexpected disturbances elicit corrective action by negative feedback, whereas, as we just noted, predicted

changes by deliberate action instigate compensation as feedforward. If you are standing in a train that starts unexpectedly to move forward, this tends to cause you to sway backwards. However, this deviation initiates postural reflexes tending to bring the body's centre of gravity forward and restore the vertical posture. Postural reflexes are automatic, have a quick reaction time and are organized subcortically. There are several processes involved in detection of deviation from upright, including vision, information from muscles in the legs and signals from the vestibular system.

Factors termed 'cognitive' or 'higher' can influence postural reflexes by modulating neural signals at brain stem and spinal levels (Rothwell, 1994). For example, an expectation of an external disturbance can influence the magnitude of the corrective response. Learning is reflected in a modification of these reflexes with experience. Negative feedback and feedforward collaborate in achieving (1) control of movement and (2) stability of both body and perception. Negative feedback triggers corrective action in response to unexpected externally imposed disturbances. The disturbance to the body is the cue to action. Where movement is voluntarily triggered, rapid feedforward is recruited in parallel.

Whether by reflexes or voluntary behaviour, by feedback or feedforward, action is produced by motor neurons and skeletal muscles. This is the topic of the next section.

Section summary

1 Movement of the body produces changes in exteroceptive input. The perception of a stable world derives from comparing commands to movement and exteroceptive consequences.

2 The vestibulo-ocular reflex helps to stabilize the image on the retina.

3 Potential unwanted disturbances associated with voluntary movements can be anticipated. To pre-empt them, feedforward systems make postural adjustments.

Test your knowledge

(Answer on page 273)

10.5 A boxer (i) 'throws' a 'long punch' and (ii) later receives an unexpected heavy punch to the upper body. What is the type of process responsible for stabilizing the body in these two conditions?

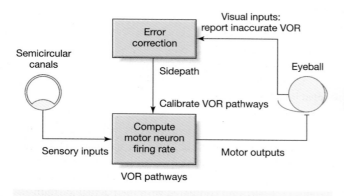

Figure 10.6 The vestibulo-ocular reflex (VOR).

Source: Reprinted with permission, from Lisberger (1988, Fig. 1, p. 729).

Muscles and motor neurons

Introduction

Movement occurs by adjusting the degree of shortening of skeletal muscles (Chapter 3). Increased activity of the motor neurons that innervate the muscle cause shortening, termed 'contraction', which increases the force that the muscle exerts. In vertebrates, motor neurons only excite skeletal muscles, there being no inhibitory motor neurons. However, motor neurons are subject to both excitation and inhibition.

Skeletal muscle

A muscle attaches to the skeleton by tendons. Figure 10.7 shows a simplified section through a muscle. The muscle is composed of **muscle fibres** (the constituent cells) and blood vessels. In some cases, the muscle is a distance from the part of the body that it moves and the tendon is long, e.g. muscles that move the fingers are in the forearm.

Action potentials in motor neurons trigger action potentials in muscle fibres. As more muscle fibres are triggered into activity, the force generated by contraction increases. We look next at neurons within the spinal cord that determine the activity of motor neurons.

Spinal cord organization

Figure 10.8 shows slices of spinal cord at three levels and some typical neural connections found there. Consider two motor neurons, A and B, and the location of their cell bodies in the ventral horn of the spinal cord (grey matter of the cord towards the front of the body) at slice 2. These two motor neurons, along with many others in parallel, innervate skeletal muscles.

As represented in Figure 10.8, there are various inputs that activate motor neurons: (a) sensory neurons also at level 2 in the spinal cord, (b) other levels in the cord, above (e.g. neuron D, the cell body of which is at level 1) and below (e.g. neuron C, the cell body of which is at level 3) and (c) the brain (via neurons that descend in the cord, indicated here as 'From brain'). The sensory input to motor neuron A arrives first at a short interneuron, which, in turn, makes contact with A. Typically, such interneurons are controlled both locally as part of a reflex and from the brain. A sensory neuron to motor neuron B synapses directly with it. A collateral of this neuron projects upwards, carrying sensory information to the brain. The input from the brain makes direct synaptic contact with motor neuron A but influences B through the short interneuron.

Neurons descending from the brain perform various functions. Some release classical neurotransmitter and excite motor neurons. Others release a different neurotransmitter and inhibit the same motor neurons. Through such neurons,

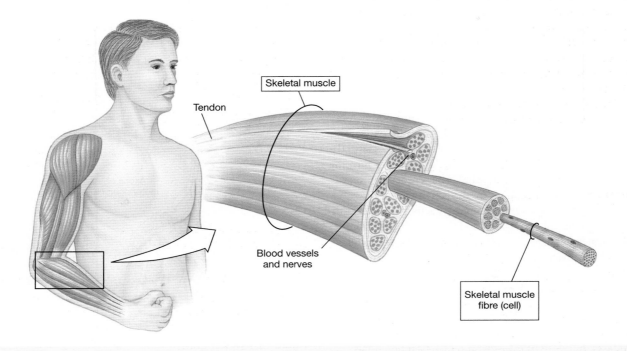

Figure 10.7 Skeletal muscle. *Source*: Martini *et al.* (2000, Fig. 9-1, p. 242).

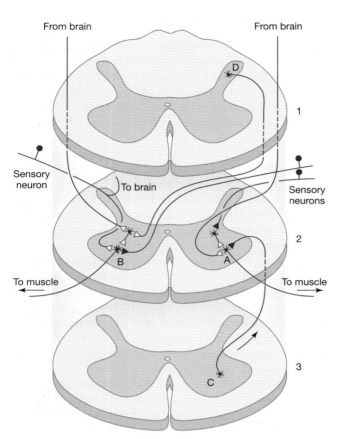

Figure 10.8 Sections of spinal cord at three levels. (Left–right asymmetry is for convenience of explanation only.)

Source: modified from Toates (1997b, Fig. 4.1, p. 113).

commands to action by the brain are put into effect. Imagine that the neuron 'From brain' that synapses on the interneuron is of this kind.

Other neurons from the brain release neuromodulators (Chapter 4, 'The cells of the nervous system') that affect the reactivity of the stimulus–response connections organized at a spinal level. Imagine that the neuron 'From brain' forming a link with neuron A is of this kind. The sensory neuron's effect on the muscle depends on the activity in this descending pathway. A motor neuron's activity is determined by the net effect of excitatory and inhibitory inputs from brain, other spinal levels and sensory neurons. Thus, the control of movement depends upon inhibition of motor neurons as much as their excitation.

Motor neurons and myelin

Axons of motor neurons are myelinated (Chapter 4), which increases the speed of transmission of action potentials. High speed is important since it permits information to

be conveyed rapidly from CNS to muscle. If a disease destroys myelin, speed is slowed and hence there is disruption of movement.

Motor units

The synapse between a motor neuron and a muscle fibre is termed a 'neuromuscular junction' (Chapter 4). At a muscle, typically the axon of a motor neuron branches (Figure 10.9). Each axon branch forms a synapse with a single muscle fibre and a given fibre is innervated by only one motor neuron. A motor neuron and the muscle fibres that it innervates make up a **motor unit**. Activity in a given motor neuron triggers activity in all the muscle fibres that make up the motor unit.

Motor units vary in size, with one motor neuron innervating few or many muscle fibres. Where high resolution is present, e.g. at the fingers, a given motor neuron innervates relatively few fibres. Coarse-grained control is associated with larger motor units.

Strength of contraction can be increased in two ways or by a combination of both: (a) increasing the frequency of action potentials in those motor neurons that are already active or (b) increasing the number of motor neurons and thereby motor units that are simultaneously activated, termed 'recruitment'. Increased excitation of motor neurons implies increased input to them, e.g. from a pathway arising in the brain.

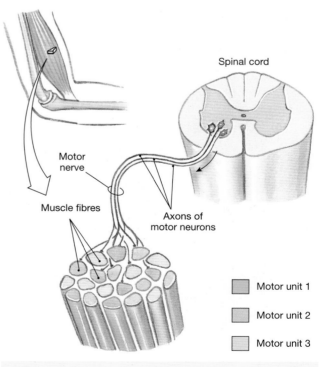

Figure 10.9 Motor units.

Source: Martini *et al.* (2000, Fig. 9-13, p. 252).

The neuromuscular junction

The neurotransmitter employed at the neuromuscular junction of skeletal muscle is acetylcholine (ACh). Neuromuscular function requires that neurotransmitter is eliminated from the synaptic gap immediately after it attaches to receptors (Chapter 4). Acetylcholine is broken down rapidly by an enzyme, acetylcholinesterase (AChE), manufactured by the cholinergic (motor) neuron. Thereby, rapid changes in motor neuron activity can trigger correspondingly rapid changes in muscular contraction. If there is disruption of the breakdown of ACh, as in some pathological conditions, muscular control is correspondingly disrupted.

So far we have looked at how signals in motor neurons trigger contraction in muscle fibres. We now consider how whole muscles (composed of such fibres) act in moving a limb.

The arrangement of muscles

Figure 10.10 shows the muscles that control the position of the forearm and represents a general principle. The forearm's position depends upon equilibrium between the contraction of two opposing muscles: the biceps and triceps (part (a)). If the contraction of a muscle changes, the bone, and thereby the limb with which it is linked through a tendon, moves to a new equilibrium.

Figure 10.10(b) shows the result of increased contraction of the biceps muscle: raising the forearm. A movement in which the angle is decreased (in this case, from θ_1 to θ_2) is termed **flexion**. The term **extension** refers to a movement that increases the angle. Contraction of the triceps causes extension of the forearm, an increase in angle to θ_3 (Figure 10.10(c)).

A pair of muscles that produces opposite mechanical effects, as in Figure 10.10, constitutes a pair of **antagonist muscles**. Antagonistic control represents a general feature of how skeletal muscles produce action. It compares with antagonistically acting chemicals in the case of smooth muscle (Powley, 1999; Chapter 3).

This section has described the flow of information in one direction: the activation of muscles by motor neurons. The next section looks at this in connection with information transmission in the opposite direction, from muscles to the CNS.

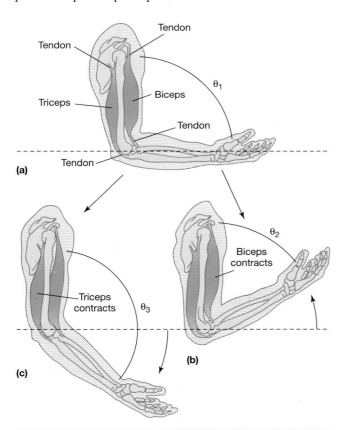

Figure 10.10 Muscles that control the forearm: (a) start, (b) flexion and (c) extension.

Source: adapted from Vander *et al*. (1994) *Human Physiology*, Fig. 1-33, p. 332, reprinted by permission of The McGraw-Hill Companies, Inc..

Section summary

1 Activity of motor neurons in the spinal cord is determined by local sensory inputs, inputs from other levels of the cord and from the brain.

2 Various inputs either excite or inhibit motor neurons.

3 Skeletal muscle is made up of muscle fibres.

4 Activity in motor neurons triggers activity in muscle fibres.

5 Action potentials within muscle fibres triggers contraction of the muscle.

6 A motor unit consists of a motor neuron and the muscle fibres that it innervates.

Test your knowledge

(Answers on page 273)

10.6 In vertebrates, motor neurons have which of the following effects on skeletal muscle? (i) Excitation, (ii) inhibition, (iii) either excitation or inhibition.

10.7 In Figure 10.8, how would you characterize neuron C? (i) Sensory, (ii) motor, (iii) interneuron.
continued

10.8 Suppose that contraction of a skeletal muscle is artificially induced by a pulse of activity in its associated motor neurons. Injection of which of the following would be expected to increase the degree of contraction? (i) An acetylcholine antagonist, (ii) a chemical that destroys acetylcholinesterase.

10.1

The control of skeletal muscle

Introduction

This section looks at the nervous system control of the activity of skeletal muscles, involving feedback from muscles to the CNS. Action potentials in sensory neurons detect the state of the muscle and this constitutes one factor that determines the activity of motor neurons, i.e. proprioception (Gordon and Ghez, 1991). To understand how this information is extracted, it is necessary to look more closely at the construction of muscle.

Types of muscle fibre

Most muscle fibres exert force and are termed **extrafusal muscle fibres**. Their activity is controlled by what are termed **alpha motor neurons**.

There is also another type of muscle fibre, known as **intrafusal muscle fibres** (Figure 10.11). These intermingle with extrafusal fibres and, in a similar way, are innervated by motor neurons. These motor neurons are classed as 'gamma motor neurons'. However, intrafusal muscle fibres serve a different function from the extrafusal muscle fibres. Rather than exerting force in moving limbs, they detect overall muscle stretch. Activity by gamma motor neurons simply adjusts their contraction to match that of their associated extrafusal muscle fibres.

The terminal of the axon of a sensory neuron is wrapped around an intrafusal muscle fibre and it signals the degree of stretch of the fibre (see Figures 10.11 and 10.12). The combination of muscle fibre, motor neuron and sensory neuron is termed a **muscle spindle** and the ending of the sensory neuron is a **stretch receptor**. As part of a feedback system, such sensory neurons form synapses upon the motor neurons that innervate the muscles with which they are associated (Figure 10.12). You will see shortly how a negative feedback loop involving proprioceptive information maintains the stability of the system.

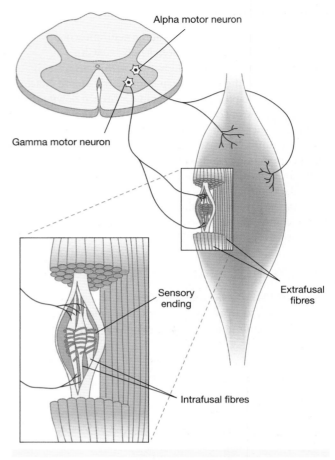

Figure 10.11 Muscle showing different types of fibre.
Source: Bear *et al.* (1996, Fig. 3.18, p. 367).

Stability in the face of disturbance

Reflexes can compensate for disturbances. Whether disturbances are to equilibrium or to the integrity of tissue by damaging stimuli, there are similar principles of organization, as this section will show.

Disturbances to equilibrium

Negative feedback systems compensate for an unexpected disturbance to equilibrium. Consider a stable situation, e.g. carrying a weight or just standing upright. Forces exerted by muscles overcome external forces that would otherwise make us collapse. Contraction of the muscles is set by the activity of motor neurons. Suppose that the muscles are disturbed by an unexpected external force, termed a 'passive change'. This distinguishes it from an active change, caused by a change in activity of motor neurons.

Figure 10.12 shows the neural system underlying the **stretch reflex**. For example, imagine that this shows your arm and you are carrying a weight, e.g. a shopping bag that is half

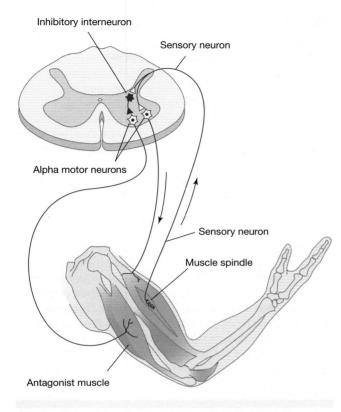

Figure 10.12 Feedback control of skeletal muscle.

Source: Bear *et al*. (1996, Fig. 13.22, p. 370).

position. It occurs rapidly, without conscious intervention (Gordon, 1991).

The speed of the local reflex is an important contribution to maintaining stability. However, the afferent information is also projected to the brain and correction of the remaining error depends upon recognition of the disturbance and increased centrally organized motor response (Evarts, 1984).

The knee-jerk response also demonstrates the negative feedback that maintains stability. See Figure 10.13. The muscle is stretched by the doctor tapping the knee with a hammer. The stretch triggers a compensatory increase in contraction of the extensor muscle, which causes the leg to jerk into the air. Although this is an artificial situation, it illustrates that a disturbance is resisted. By maintaining different values of contraction in the flexor and extensor muscles, the leg can be held in different positions, each defended against disturbances.

full. Then the weight of the bag is suddenly and unexpectedly increased. Without your knowing, someone might have slipped a very heavy weight into the bag, which disturbs the muscles controlling the position of the arm. They will no longer be contracted appropriately for the half-empty bag, as set by motor neuron activity.

The increased weight causes a slight lowering of the arm, which stretches the flexor muscle (biceps muscle). Information on the new level of stretch is instantly detected by sensory neurons with endings embedded in the muscle and is fed to the spinal cord. With increased stretch, the frequency of action potentials in the sensory neurons increases. This triggers increased activity in the alpha motor neurons innervating the biceps muscle. It causes increased contraction which, to a considerable extent, counters the disturbance. This is the stretch reflex (Ito, 1984).

Because of the inhibitory interneuron, the sensory signal causes reduced activity in the alpha motor neurons innervating the triceps (antagonist) muscle. This exerts an effect in the same direction as increased contraction of the flexor muscle (Gordon and Ghez, 1991), i.e. the principle of **reciprocal inhibition** (Floeter, 1999b). As a result of changes in neural activity to both muscles, a corrective response occurs. This partly returns the arm to its previous

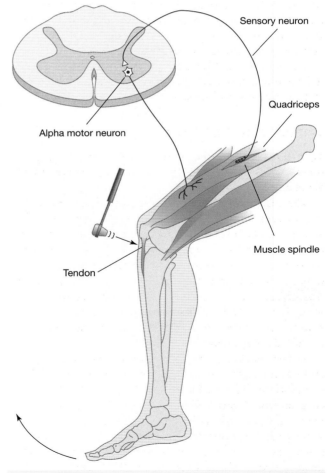

Figure 10.13 The knee-jerk response.

Source: Bear *et al*. (1996, Fig. 13.7, p. 366).

The reaction to a noxious stimulus

A spinal reflex protects against sudden local tissue damage at a limb caused by an external stimulus (Chapter 3). In Figure 10.14, the position of the arm is the net result of contraction of flexor and extensor muscles. Suppose that a noxious stimulus, e.g. a pin, touches the bottom of the hand. In nociceptive neurons, this instigates action potentials, which are transmitted to the spinal cord, to excitatory synapses with interneurons. In turn, interneurons form excitatory synapses on alpha motor neurons that activate the extrafusal fibres of the flexor (biceps) muscle. The flexor muscle contracts and thereby the arm is raised. In parallel, inhibition is exerted on the motor neuron that controls the extensor muscle (Gordon, 1991).

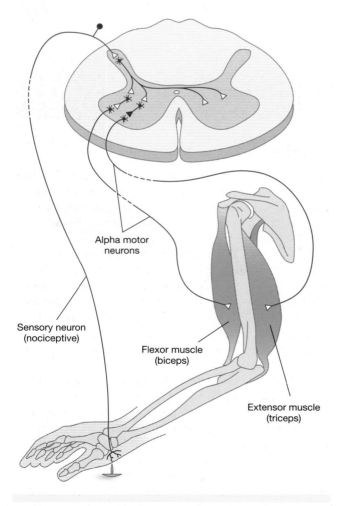

Figure 10.14 The nociceptive reflex.
Source: Guyton (1991, Fig. 54-8, p. 597).

Alpha motor neurons

Sensory neuron (nociceptive)

Flexor muscle (biceps)

Extensor muscle (triceps)

Interactions within the spinal cord

Events at one level of spinal cord are influenced by events at other levels. For example, treading on a noxious object and quickly withdrawing the foot could potentially disturb bodily equilibrium. In practice, we usually maintain equilibrium. How? Performance of the reflex triggers postural adjustments to maintain stability. Apart from synaptic contact within a layer of spinal cord, branches of the sensory neuron that detects the noxious stimulus extend to other spinal levels to influence other muscles (Figure 10.8). Their reaction causes the distribution of weight to change, to compensate for the defensive reaction.

Local autonomy

Figures 10.12–10.14 illustrate how reflexes are organized locally at a section of spinal cord (e.g. slice 2 in Figure 10.8). The sensory-motor sequence does not involve information transmitted via the brain. The time delay observed between external stimulus and muscular response is so short that the reaction cannot be caused by a message travelling up to the brain and back down the spinal cord. In resisting disturbances, speed can be crucially important. If all information had to travel up to the brain and down again before correction could be instigated, extra time would be involved. Fast reaction times can allow a stable position to be maintained, and make the difference between superficial and serious damage.

Local organization can achieve much. However, it does not have complete autonomy from controls at other levels. Other regions of the spinal cord as well as the brain are able to exert some control over the kinds of reflex just described (Figure 10.8).

Modulation by the brain

The strength of reflexes is modulated by the brain as a function of experience, e.g. learning when it is optimal to exhibit a reflex in full or inhibit it (Everts *et al.*, 1984). Also, emotion can modulate the magnitude of reflexes. This is exemplified by the knee-jerk reflex and the startle reflex, which is triggered by an unexpected stimulus (Lang *et al.*, 1990).

As effective as local negative feedback is, we do not remain like statues in a fixed position all day, responding only to disturbances. Rather we are the agents of change. Goals can be altered and we can consciously instigate movement, as discussed now.

Voluntary behaviour

Voluntary behaviour takes many forms, such as walking or combing your hair. This section considers just one form of voluntary behaviour, to illustrate how the brain, spinal cord and motor neurons cooperate.

In the form of rhythms

Imagine you are walking or jogging. Behaviour is characterized by rhythms of muscular activity in the legs and arms, rhythms that seem to run their course automatically. How does the CNS organize this? A type of motor programme, termed a **central pattern generator** (CPG), which generates oscillations, is organized at the brain stem and spinal cord (Gallistel, 1980).

We consciously initiate and terminate commands that recruit control by CPGs but, once switched in, CPGs operate automatically. Automaticity spares our brain for activities such as conversation. When we are in, say, a 'walking mode', a frequency of local oscillation is selected top-down by the brain acting on spinal circuits (Lacquaniti *et al.*, 1999). Synchronized oscillations of activity are produced in motor neurons that innervate the muscles of the legs, arms and shoulders, etc. Excitation of some motor neurons is accompanied by inhibition of others. The CPG that produces alternating excitation and inhibition is intrinsic to the spinal cord. However, the pattern of motor activity can be influenced by feedback from the muscles. Adjustments can be made through local reflexes, for example, in response to changes in the muscle's operating characteristics or a sudden change in the texture of the ground under the feet.

It is now time to investigate how and where commands to action arise and thereby to look at a range of voluntary behaviours.

Section summary

1 Proprioceptive information on contraction is fed back to the CNS.

2 Muscle is composed of extrafusal fibre (by which force is exerted) and intrafusal fibre (by which proprioceptive feedback is generated).

3 Feedback on the stretch of intrafusal muscle fibres influences activity in associated motor neurons.

4 External disturbances cause a change in tension in intrafusal muscle fibres and trigger a counter reaction.

5 By organizing reflexes locally, delays are minimized.

6 Oscillations that control limbs are programmed automatically (e.g. in the spinal cord) but switched on and off voluntarily by the brain.

Test your knowledge

(Answers on page 273)

10.9 This question relates to Figure 10.12. Complete the following: 'Artificial stretch of the biceps muscle triggers _____ activity in the sensory neuron, _____ activity in the alpha motor neuron innervating the biceps and _____ activity in that innervating the triceps muscle'.

10.10 This question relates to Figure 10.14. Complete the following: 'The effect of increased activity in the sensory neuron is one of _____ activity in the inhibitory interneuron and thereby _____ activity in the motor neuron that innervates the extensor muscle'.

10.2

The control of movement by the brain

Introduction

The control of movement depends upon interaction between various regions of the brain. Output signals are produced and are either conducted in cranial nerves (Chapter 3) or descend in the spinal cord. These output signals finally activate skeletal muscles. See Figure 10.15.

Figure 10.16 summarizes some brain regions and pathways involved in movement that is executed via the spinal cord. Note direct pathways from the motor cortex to spinal cord neurons involved in motor action and also the pathways that descend to the spinal cord via synapses in the brain stem (not shown in Figure 10.15). The cerebellum receives sensory information and information on motor commands.

The higher areas represent decision-making and strategy, etc. At the bottom of the hierarchy is the process of *execution*, embodied within motor neurons with cell bodies in the spinal cord. At each lower level, the options become less open-ended and more constrained, based upon locally available information (Redgrave *et al.*, 1999).

In a hierarchy, commands are issued at a high level without specifying exactly how they are to be implemented by lower levels (Gallistel, 1980; Toates, 1998a). By analogy, military decisions can be made by the UN Security Council

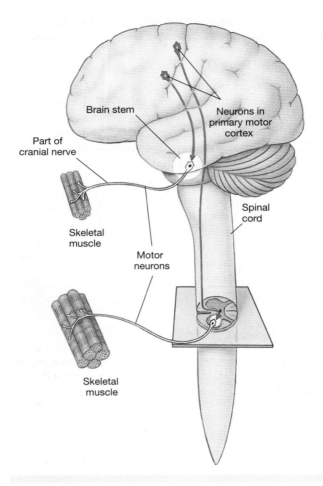

Figure 10.15 Motor control.

Source: adapted from Martini *et al.* (2000, Fig. 16-3(a) p. 428).

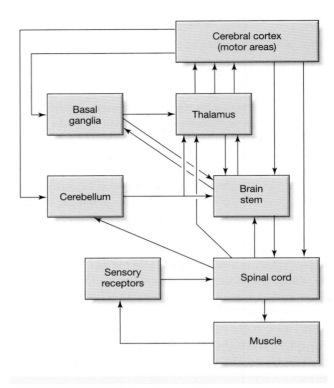

Figure 10.16 Motor control. Breaking a link at a box indicates a synaptic link within the box.

(e.g. initiate peace-keeping operation) without reference to the specifics of how each foot-soldier will execute them (e.g. protect a particular village). Although the flow of commands is from top to bottom, there is also a flow of information in the opposite direction (Prescott *et al.*, 1999). Feedback is sent on the state of each level, i.e. what has actually been achieved. The lower spinal cord level is informed of the state of muscles, detailed information that is not normally available to the higher levels of conscious decision-making (von Holst and Mittelstaedt, 1950). It would be inefficient for attention to be drawn to information that can be best utilized simply at a low level (by analogy, the Security Council does not need precise details of events at each street in each village).

The cortex

Introduction

In Figure 10.16, the box marked 'Cerebral cortex (motor areas)' can be divided into several areas. The highest level of control (in the 'hierarchy') is one of deciding *strategy* and is embodied within regions of the cerebral cortex outside the primary motor cortex. The next layer down is concerned with *tactics* and is embodied within the primary motor cortex, subcortical brain regions and cerebellum.

Figure 10.17 reminds you of the location of the primary motor cortex (M1) on the precentral gyrus (Chapter 5). Other cortical areas, the premotor area (PMA) and the supplementary motor area (SMA), are also involved in movement control and project to the primary motor cortex (Tanji and Kurata, 1985). The SMA also projects to the brain stem.

As a first approximation, the premotor area is associated with strategy: *planning* of movement and selection of possible programmes for action, which is then translated into tactics, or *implemented*, by the primary motor cortex (Wise, 1984). The premotor area derives inputs from other regions of

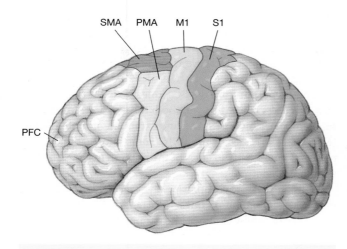

Figure 10.17 Some cortical regions involved in movement control. M1 = primary motor cortex, PFC = prefrontal cortex, PMA = premotor area, S1 = somatosensory cortex, SMA = supplementary motor area.

cortex, concerned with extracting perceptual information, e.g. occipital, temporal and parietal (Willingham, 1998). Thus, the planning is based in part upon current information on the body and the external world, i.e. sensory-motor integration. The posterior parietal cortex computes features of objects that serve as the targets for action (Chapter 8).

We will look in more detail at the role of some cortical regions.

Primary motor cortex

The motor homunculus (Chapter 5, Figure 5.22, p. 121) indicates the responsibility that parts of primary motor cortex (M1) have for control over regions of the body. The expression 'control over regions of the body' does not mean that a region of M1 has *exclusive* control, since other brain regions are also implicated. However, investigators are able to associate specific bits of the body with specific cortical areas.

Consider, for example, that neurons in an area of M1 labelled 'finger' are active. This is associated with activity in pathways that descend to those motor neurons in the spinal cord that control the finger (Evarts *et al.*, 1984). When this region of cortex is stimulated by an electrode, there is a response by a finger on the opposite side of the body to the side stimulated. Tumours, at a particular location on the homunculus, affect motor control at the part of the body indicated. A stroke (Chapter 5) affecting the motor cortex results in loss of motor function in a region defined by the homunculus. The relationship between cortical motor areas and muscles has some plasticity, reflecting experience of using muscles (Schieber, 1999).

The primary motor cortex encodes a movement in space by a part of the body, as indicated by the motor homunculus (Carpenter *et al.*, 1999).

Prefrontal cortex (PFC)

Planning action and then producing it can depend upon memories of stimuli no longer present and exploiting imagined scenarios (Goldman-Rakic, 1995). The prefrontal cortex (PFC) has a responsibility for self-instigated voluntary ('willed') actions that are not triggered by stimuli.

In some tasks, the PFC is strongly activated during learning but not once the task has become automatic (Raichle *et al.*, 1994). The PFC plays a role where there is a need to overcome habitual behaviours. This involves, in parallel, a suppression of the tendency to react to the triggers to habitual behaviour and a favouring of the strength of any 'non-habitual' stimuli. This is exemplified by the Stroop task in which reacting to the ink colour can only be achieved by suppressing the tendency to react to the word meaning (Cohen and Servan-Schreiber, 1992).

Following damage to the PFC, a person is more 'stimulus-bound', i.e. vulnerable to stimuli capturing behaviour. For example, in a doctor's consulting room, a PFC patient might reach out to a familiar object and grab it even though this would otherwise have been considered 'inappropriate behaviour', termed **utilization behaviour** (Lhermitte, 1983).

Supplementary motor area (SMA)

Similarly, activation of the SMA is at its maximum at the start of training and decreases with skill acquisition (Jenkins *et al.*, 1994; Seitz and Roland, 1992). Associated with a voluntary movement there is a wave of electrical activity recorded at the motor cortex, termed a 'motor potential'. This is observed at about 55 ms before the muscular activity starts. At about 800 ms before the muscular activity starts, a change in electrical activity is seen at the SMA. This is termed a **readiness potential** and appears to be a physiological correlate of preparing for action.

Somatosensory cortex

Just across the central sulcus from the primary motor cortex is the somatosensory cortex, concerned with processing tactile information (Figure 10.17). In an evolutionary context, the proximity of these regions would appear to be no coincidence. Feedback via the tactile sense is crucial for the production of movement. There are specific projections from regions of somatosensory cortex to the corresponding regions of primary motor cortex (e.g. from that concerned with processing tactile information from the thumb to the region controlling the thumb).

The cortex collaborates with the basal ganglia and cerebellum, to which the discussion now turns.

The basal ganglia

Structure and connections

A group of subcortical nuclei, termed the **basal ganglia**, are involved in the control of movement (Holmes, 1939; Marsden, 1987). They are situated to each side of the brain's midline and include, among others, the caudate nucleus, putamen and globus pallidus (Figure 10.18). A collective term for the caudate nucleus and putamen is the striatum. Researchers know of the basal ganglia's (BG's) involvement in movement:

1 through the thalamus, the BG outputs convey information to areas of cortex concerned with motor control;

2 neurons of the BG are active at times correlated with movement;

3 damage to the BG is associated with disturbances to movement (Mink, 1999).

Major sources of input to the BG are the cortex and brain stem (Figure 10.16) (Prescott *et al.*, 1999). Looking more closely at BG components, inputs from the cortex project specifically to the striatum (Graybiel *et al.*, 1994). Neural activity in the striatum is modulated by dopaminergic (DA) projections that arise from a midbrain region termed the substantia nigra, meaning 'black substance' (Figure 10.19).

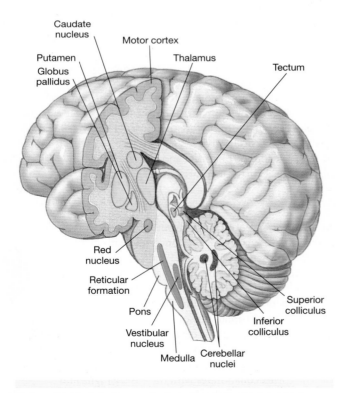

Figure 10.18 A focus on the basal ganglia and cerebellum.
Source: Martini *et al.* (2000, Fig. 16-5, p. 430).

The rich input to the BG from the prefrontal cortex suggests an important role for this link in planning action, and possibly also cognition unrelated to movement (Berns and Sejnowski, 1998). The BG appear to have access to information on wishes, goals and feelings, etc. (Marsden, 1984).

A major output from the BG projects, via the thalamus, to areas of cortex concerned with both the preparation, e.g. the supplementary motor (SMA), and execution of motor action (Marsden, 1987). See Figure 10.16. Some information projects from the BG to areas of the brain stem concerned with motor control.

Within the BG, there are pathways exerting both excitatory and inhibitory links. If there is disease within excitatory or inhibitory links, the parameters are distorted and movement control is disrupted.

The role of the basal ganglia

What do the BG do? There are several theories (Prescott *et al.*, 1999) and what follows tries to capture a common feature of them.

Based on prediction of the next move, the BG appear to be able to select motor programmes and hold them slightly 'off-line' in the SMA in readiness for the appropriate signal to place them 'on-line' at the primary motor cortex and trigger action (Robbins and Everitt, 1992). The BG compute 'get-ready' information based upon scene-setting cues that are not themselves direct triggers to action but which specify conditions under which direct stimuli can trigger 'now go' (Schultz *et al.*, 1995). A runner awaiting the starting pistol might epitomize this situation. Some BG neurons are under the control of motivational signals, e.g. hunger, which signal the appropriateness of 'go' towards food-related stimuli.

Evidence suggests a role for the BG in producing automatic sequences of actions, where one component can be reliably selected on the basis of the preceding component (Jeannerod, 1997; Marsden, 1984). Once a sequence has been initiated, the BG could be responsible for triggering the remainder. Sequences arise from learning, e.g. a well-practised skill.

Parkinson's disease

Disruption of dopamine (DA) in the BG can profoundly disturb movement (Berns and Sejnowski, 1998). The basis of Parkinson's disease (PD) is degeneration of DA neurons with cell bodies in the substantia nigra (Figure 10.19). In turn, there is a disturbance to the signals that the BG transmits to the supplementary motor area (SMA), such that the SMA is unduly inhibited (Jahanshahi and Frith, 1998). In PD, there is either an inability to initiate movement ('akinesia') or slowness in initiation ('hypokinesia') (Marsden, 1987). There is also 'bradykinesia', slowness in performing movement. Jahanshahi and Frith (1998, p. 502) characterize PD as

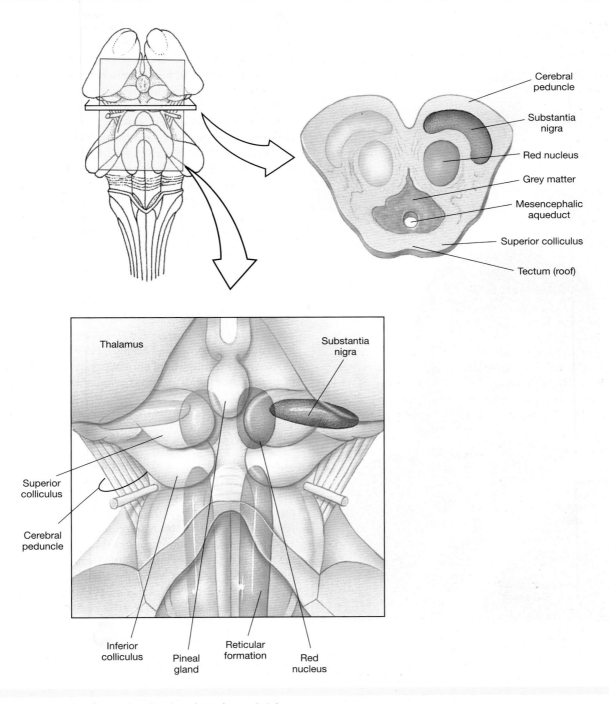

Figure 10.19 The brain stem, indicating the substantia nigra.

Source: Martini *et al.* (2000, Fig. 15-7a, p. 401).

difficulty in translating the 'will to action' into 'action': PD patients 'know what they want to do but cannot do it'.

For voluntary behaviour, the PD patient needs a large amount of concentration and will-power in overcoming muscular rigidity. Thus, patients have a disability in instigating action, e.g. putting into action an internally and spontaneously generated wish to get up (Jahanshahi *et al.*, 1995).

The difficulty in 'self-instigating' behaviour contrasts with greater ease in responding to strong external cues (Jahanshahi and Frith, 1998); PD patients 'react better than they act'. For example, an otherwise immobile patient might

What happens to the control system for movement in Parkinson's disease?

Source: Empics.

be able to get up and leave if the word 'fire' is shouted. Auditory cues in the form of a rhythm can also help. Similarly, PD patients can sometimes walk more easily if visual cues with which they can pace their steps are given, e.g. stripes on the ground (Rothwell, 1994, p. 493).

Disorders of balance appear to be due to deficiencies in BG projections to brain stem nuclei that control posture (Marsden, 1987). This could explain difficulties in the coordination of anticipatory postural corrections that accompany voluntary movement (Sanes and Evarts, 1985).

The PD patient has difficulty in executing the sequence of movements that normally constitute a motor plan. This is particularly so when the task requires coordination and combining component movements, either simultaneously or sequentially, into compound movements (Marsden, 1987).

It is not possible to treat PD with DA as such (Coté and Crutcher, 1991). DA cannot cross the blood–brain barrier (Chapter 5) and enter the nervous system. However, DA agonists can be used (Stocchi, 1998). Certain treatments depend on the fact that neurotransmitters are synthesized within neurons from 'precursor substances'. *L*-Dopa, a precursor to DA in the synthetic pathway, is able to cross the blood–brain barrier (Sacks, 1982). It boosts the production of transmitter in the DA neurons that still remain, which has some therapeutic effect.

Huntington's disease

Another disorder of the basal ganglia, Huntington's disease (Chapter 2), consists of excessive movements. It is caused by degeneration of cholinergic and GABA-ergic neurons within the striatum (Kropotov and Etlinger, 1999; Reiner *et al.*, 1998). Such neurons would normally exert inhibition on inappropriate candidates for behavioural expression.

The cerebellum

Connections to the cerebellum

The cerebellum is informed of intended actions and feedback from behaviour. It is provided with information from the motor cortex and information on posture and movement (Ghez, 1991a,b), e.g. proprioceptive, visual and vestibular information (only some of this is shown in Figure 10.16). Cerebellum outputs project (a) via the thalamus to the cortex (e.g. primary motor cortex) and (b) to the spinal cord, superior colliculus, vestibular nucleus and the red nucleus (Holmes, 1939; Thach *et al.*, 1992). See Figure 10.16 for some of these links. In (i) receiving information on action from the cortex, (ii) computing information and (iii) projecting information back to the cortex, the cerebellum and basal ganglia have common features as modulators of motor action (Figure 10.16).

Defining the role of the cerebellum

The cerebellum (Figures 10.16 and 10.18) appears not to have an executive role, sometimes being termed a 'silent area'. Its electrical stimulation causes neither sensation nor, usually, a motor response. The control exerted by the cerebellum is unlike that of the cortex in that one side of the motor cortex controls the body on the opposite side, whereas one side of the cerebellum has a role in the control of muscles on the same side.

The role of the cerebellum in handling feedback is seen over long periods of time, e.g. modifications as skills are acquired, and also on a moment-by-moment basis in the control of ongoing behaviour. In the course of movement, the cerebellum can revise the programme in the light of feedback.

The cerebellum is involved in the smooth performance of behaviour, i.e. controlling the *form* of movement, once started (Ito, 1984). Its role is to coordinate movements to form coherent patterns, such that goals are met optimally (Bastian *et al.*, 1999). It compares the actual state of the body and muscles with the goals set and progress towards meeting them. We noted earlier the vestibulo-ocular reflex, which is an example of this role.

The cerebellum acts at an unconscious level in predicting outcomes and adjusting internal conditions to be appropriate (Chapter 5; Courchesne and Allen, 1997). It appears to be an intermediate step between the goals set by the cortex and their implementation in motor output (Marr, 1969). Its outputs, to motor regions of cortex and brain stem nuclei, indicate its function in coordinating component responses of parts of the body into coherent strategies of whole-body action (Thach *et al.*, 1992). Postural corrective reflexes appear to be modulated so that they occur in a way that is appropriate to the goal. Thus, reflexes that maintain standing can be switched in when the goal is to stand but not at other times.

Participants were set a pursuit task, to maintain alignment between the tip of a stylus held in their hand and a moving target (Grafton *et al.*, 1994). Success consisted of learning to predict the trajectory of the moving target and to maintain the hand in the right position. With a PET scan, Grafton looked at regional cerebral blood flow and found an increase in the cerebellum. Rate of improvement correlated positively with increases in local blood flow.

A move to automaticity

The cerebellum appears to link negative feedback and feedforward (Ito, 1984). With experience of a task, it allows the weight of control to shift from negative feedback to feedforward. At the start of learning, it monitors performance in negative feedback mode, guided moment-by-moment by consequences. As a task becomes skilled, a store of possible solutions is acquired. Given an intention to act in a situation, the links (motor cortex) → (cerebellum) → (motor cortex) are activated and appropriate motor reactions instigated. If the consequences reveal a failure to meet the goal, the content of the memory store can be modified. Where a sequence of responses (R_1, R_2, R_3...) is involved, the cerebellum has a role in learning it, so that each component is produced automatically in response to the previous component (e.g. R_3 triggered by the production of R_2) (Thach, 1998). This is a role also attributed to the basal ganglia, suggesting close cooperation between these structures.

Some reactions are extremely rapid, e.g. a Wimbledon tennis champion making a move. The speed is formidable, with little opportunity for moment-by-moment revision. Such 'ballistic' moves need to be computed in advance and triggered automatically as feedforward but within a context of feedback-guidance (Bastian *et al.*, 1999).

Damage to the cerebellum

Patients with damage to the cerebellum have difficulty in modifying behaviour with experience and executing smooth and accurate actions, known as 'ataxia' (Holmes, 1939). They often show an awkward walk. Unlike Parkinson's patients, they are not deficient in initiating movement.

In an experiment investigating the role of the cerebellum in motor learning, participants wore prism spectacles, which shifted their visual world through an angle of 15 degrees to the right. See Figure 10.20. The task was to hit a dartboard with a dart. To do this, the participant had to aim the dart not at the location where the dartboard appeared to be but slightly to the side, to compensate for the shift. As shown in Figure 10.20(b), controls with an intact cerebellum showed an initial error, which was corrected over trials until normal performance was attained. Removal of the spectacles was followed by an error in the opposite direction. As shown in (c), participants with a damaged cerebellum had no such correction (Thach *et al.*, 1992).

The brain stem

Some organization of posture and movement occurs in the brain stem. In certain cases, the same nuclei have a role in activation within the sympathetic branch of the ANS (Chapter 3; Yates and Stocker, 1998). Thus, a sudden movement, as in energetically getting up, can trigger increased sympathetic activity. Exercise is associated with parallel activation of somatic and autonomic nervous systems.

Some species-typical motor patterns, e.g. licking and swallowing, are organized in nuclei of the brain stem (Berntson and Micco, 1976). Influences outside the brain stem, e.g. the hypothalamus, modulate these systems making them more or less likely to gain expression in behaviour. Different combinations of species-typical motor patterns can be assembled according to central motivation (Spruijt *et al.*, 1992). For example, an aggressive motivation will play a role in assembling attack-related patterns.

(a)

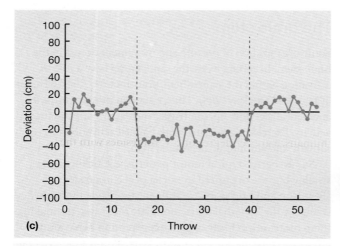

(b)

(c)

Figure 10.20 Dart-throwing task: (a) participant wearing spectacles (b) result for control and (c) result for patient with damage to cerebellum. Dotted lines indicate start and end of period of wearing spectacles.

Source: Thach *et al.* (1992), Figs 5a, 5b and 5c, pp. 428, 429 and 431.

The next section considers the transmission of information from brain to motor neurons.

Section summary

1 Different regions of primary motor cortex are associated with control of different body regions.

2 The prefrontal cortex has a role in the instigation of voluntary action and in resisting inappropriate tendencies to respond triggered by physically present stimuli.

3 The basal ganglia play a role in coordination of movement.

4 Degeneration of DA neurons in the substantia nigra leads to Parkinson's disease.

5 The cerebellum adjusts movement in the light of experience, both moment-by-moment and over repeated experiences.

6 The cerebellum links negative feedback and feedforward.

Test your knowledge

(Answers on page 273)

10.11 Complete the missing words in the following, which relates to Figure 10.17: 'The primary motor cortex lies just _____ to the central sulcus, whereas the somatosensory cortex lies just _____ to it'.

10.12 Complete the following: 'Parkinson's disease is associated with disruption to _____ ergic neurotransmission'.

From brain to motor neurons

Introduction

You have seen how the brain organizes the control of movement and how motor neurons and skeletal muscles work. This section fills in the gap: how information is communicated from the brain to motor neurons.

Motor neurons have cell bodies in the brain stem or spinal cord (Figure 10.15). The axons of motor neurons with cell bodies in the brain stem form part of the cranial nerves. They innervate the muscles of the head. Motor neurons with cell bodies in the ventral horn of the spinal cord innervate the muscles of the remainder of the body (see also Figure 10.8). In Figure 10.15, note also the neurons in primary motor cortex, which innervate the motor neurons.

This section concerns the routes of information transmission (from brain to motor neuron) that occur via the spinal cord. One of these is shown in Figure 10.15 and the section also considers another route by which motor neurons in the spinal cord are activated. It looks at how voluntary behaviour is produced via these routes.

Neurons descend from the brain and make synaptic contact either with motor neurons (Figure 10.15) or with short interneurons, which, in turn, synapse on motor neurons (Figure 10.8). In addition, tendencies to respond that arise as a result of local factors can be inhibited by activity in descending pathways.

The corticospinal tract

One route is termed the **corticospinal tract** (or pathway), which you first met in Chapter 5. This was the pathway that was shown in Figure 5.22 (p. 121) and is shown again as the spinal pathway of Figure 10.15. The cell bodies of the neurons that form this tract are located mostly in the primary motor cortex and the axons cover the distance to specific locations in the spinal cord (motor neurons or local interneurons that contact motor neurons). This system of neurons is sometimes termed the **pyramidal system** and the pathway of axons is called the **pyramidal tract**. Within the medulla, the corticospinal tract can appear to be pyramid shaped, from which the name derives (by coincidence the cell bodies of these neurons are also somewhat pyramid-shaped). As you can see in Figure 5.22, there is a cross-over of axons from one side of the CNS to the other, just below the medulla ('decussation'). Thus, the motor cortex of one half of the brain is responsible for the control of muscles on the other side of the body.

The corticospinal tract brings the advantage of manual dexterity. It is mainly associated with the control of fine-grained processes, e.g. movement of the fingers in manipulating objects. A number of factors contribute to this ability. The pathway from brain to muscle is relatively direct and the cortex mediates a 'high-magnification' resolution of motor information in the following way. Regions of motor cortex at the start of this route have relatively large areas of motor homunculus (Figure 5.22) associated with them. The axons are myelinated and some have a relatively large diameter, which contributes to a high speed of transmission of action potentials (Chapter 4). Each axon innervates relatively few muscle fibres.

Very high resolution of motor movements is obtained, particularly within certain parts of this system, e.g. some finger controls in primates can have a one-to-one exclusive relationship between an individual neuron of the tract and an individual motor neuron.

A non-corticospinal tract

Other descending tracts, sometimes collectively termed **non-corticospinal tracts**, start in the brain stem. They do not occupy the pyramid-shaped region of the medulla and hence are sometimes termed **extrapyramidal pathways**. Exemplifying this is the rubrospinal tract. It starts in the red nucleus of the midbrain (Figure 10.19) and terminates on interneurons in the spinal cord, which then make synaptic contact with motor neurons. This tract exerts more coarse-grained control than the corticospinal tract, e.g. over whole limbs. Inputs to the red nucleus are derived from the motor cortex and the cerebellum. Maintenance of posture and balance, as well as movement, is the responsibility of the non-corticospinal pathways.

A given neuron of this pathway can have axon branches that link to motor neurons at different sites in the body and these broad patterns of neural connections form a basis for motor coordination. Thus, different parts of the body (e.g. arms and legs) innervated in this way act in a coordinated fashion in maintaining stability and controlling movement.

Herein, there lies a contrast between the corticospinal and non-corticospinal pathways. The corticospinal pathway controls individual muscles that produce action in relative isolation, e.g. fine control over a finger. Non-corticospinal pathways are responsible for coordination of action involving several groups of muscles, e.g. in maintaining balance of the whole body. However, there is not an absolute distinction between the roles of the two pathways. Rather, the contrast represents two points on a continuum. Smooth and accurate movement can depend upon interactions between the pathways. There is some ability for compensation: if one pathway is damaged, the other can assume additional responsibility.

From an evolutionary perspective, it is interesting to consider a difference in weight attributed to the tracts. In humans, a greater degree of control resides with the corticospinal tract than with the rubrospinal tract.

Section summary

1 Information is transmitted from the brain down the spinal cord in corticospinal and non-corticospinal tracts.

2 The corticospinal tract starts at the cortex and is responsible for fine-grained motor actions, e.g. by the fingers.   *continued*

Test your knowledge

(Answers on page 273)

10.13 Complete the following: 'Neurons of the corticospinal tract mediating _____-grained control by the fingers are associated with relatively _____ areas of the motor cortex, as indicated by the motor homunculus'.

10.14 Complete the following: 'Motor units associated with postural control by the non-corticospinal tracts are relatively _____, whereas those of the corticospinal tract associated with control of the fingers are relatively _____'.

Motor imagery

Introduction

Cognition and motor action are interdependent (Jeannerod, 1997), e.g. in humans, motor systems have a close connection to the imagination. We can perform **motor imagery** even in the absence of physical movement. Even those of us lacking any creative musical talent can enjoy the imagery of conducting Beethoven's 5th, in the role of an actor rather than a spectator.

Musical or sporting skill can sometimes be improved by observing the moves of an accomplished person and imagining yourself to be performing them (Jeannerod, 1997). Evidence suggests that such simulations can sometimes be beneficial and reorganization of the neural circuits underlying the planning of motor action takes place. You might then do some fine-tuning of the skill even in a crowded bus or in bed! Musicians and sportspeople often practise in this way (Feltz and Landers, 1983; Stephan *et al.*, 1995).

The time needed to simulate an action in imagination (e.g. to write a signature) is similar to the time that the action would take in reality (Decety and Michel, 1989; Decety *et al.*, 1989). The length of a mental simulation reflects such factors as the size of any weight carried in performing the task and the task's complexity. For example, in reality, walking on very narrow beams takes longer than

on wide beams, as is also true for its mental simulation. In people with Parkinson's disease, as the actual motor reaction is slowed, so is the simulated action. Where the disease affects only one side of the body there is also a slowing of imagined movements involving that side.

Biological bases

Imagination

Does the conscious simulation of action exploit similar processes to those employed in performing the behaviour? Some computation of the exact motor response is performed by brain stem and spinal cord mechanisms, to which it appears we have no conscious access. Therefore, it would seem that, in our imagination, we 'target' the high-level commands to the motor system (Jeannerod, 1997).

When a person simulates action mentally, increased electrical activity can be detected in the skeletal muscles that would be involved if the action were really being executed (Jacobsen, 1931; Shaw, 1940). In some cases, this reflects the magnitude of the imagined task, e.g. increasing muscular activity accompanying increased imagined exertion of force. Such results suggest that imagining an action involves excitation of a motor programme, which is then not executed because of inhibition (Decety *et al.*, 1990). The inhibition sometimes fails to oppose the excitation completely and some increase in motor neuron activity occurs.

Cerebral blood flow shows that performance of a skilled movement is accompanied by activation of the primary motor cortex, supplementary motor area and basal ganglia. Mental simulation of movement also involves the activation of a similar population of regions (Dominey *et al.*, 1995). The cerebellum is especially activated in an imagined motor task, e.g. tennis (Decety *et al.*, 1990).

Mental imagery can give insight into the determinants of ANS activation (Chapter 3). Performing physical exercise increases heart-rate and respiration, as does imagining it (Decety *et al.*, 1991, 1993), but the latter is probably not sufficient to provide an excuse for staying in bed and avoiding the gym. People whose limbs are paralyzed also show an increase in autonomic measures when they attempt a motor response (Gandevia *et al.*, 1993).

Instruction, imitation and mirror neurons

Certain neurons in a region of the premotor cortex and the parietal cortex of monkeys are active when the monkey performs a particular motor action or watches another animal (monkey or human) doing the same (Di Pellegrino *et al.*, 1992). Such neurons are termed **mirror neurons**, since their activity 'reflects' the performance of the other individual (Rizzolatti and Craighero, 2004). So, one trigger for mirror neuron activity is the visual presentation of an interaction between an object and another individual's effector, e.g. hand or mouth. For example, observing the grasping of a piece of food is a trigger to certain mirror neurons. The sight of either the object alone or another individual miming the action is insufficient to trigger them. Suppose that the monkey observes a noisy action such as tearing and mirror neuron activity is monitored (Kohler *et al.*, 2002). Subsequently, presenting the sound alone triggers a number of the same mirror neurons.

What could be the functional value of mirror neurons? They could have evolved to serve imitation. They could facilitate motor learning. Establishing representations of actions based on observation, and doing so in a motor region of the brain, could facilitate the performance of the action when later initiated spontaneously. For a social species, they could facilitate coordination of activity.

Do mirror neurons exist in humans? Although investigators lack single-cell recordings, evidence suggests that they do. For example, passively observing the action of another is associated with a desynchronization of electrical activity in the motor cortex, as is active performance of the behaviour (Rizzolatti and Craighero, 2004). This points to further possible links between biological and social psychologies. If you find yourself mirroring the gestures of another, you might like to reflect on the possible contribution of mirror neurons.

Jeannerod (1997) speculates about interaction between teacher and pupil, in which a manual skill is demonstrated. He suggests that, in the pupil, there is activation of motor regions involved in planning which has similarities to the pattern that occurs prior to performance (Stephan *et al.*, 1995). Reciprocally, when the teacher watches the pupil, there is a similar pattern of activation as that shown by the teacher performing the action.

Section summary

1 Mental simulation (imagination) of an action has features in common with performance, e.g. there is a correlation in the length of time taken to perform them.

2 The term 'mirror neuron' refers to a type of neuron that is active in performing behaviour or observing another performing it.

Test your knowledge

(Answer on page 273)

10.15 A mirror neuron is a member of which of the following classes of neuron? (i) Sensory, (ii) motor, (iii) interneuron.

Development of motor systems

The newborn or 'new-hatched' are not simply a bundle of uncoordinated reflexes, since even the embryo shows a degree of coordination, which increases after birth or hatching (Gottlieb, 1973; Prechtl, 1981). During development, the acquisition of increasing sensory-motor ability opens up new possibilities for exploiting the environment (Benson, 1990). Increasing skill is related to developmental changes in the nervous system. For example, development of descending mechanisms of control gives an increasing capacity for coordination over reflex responses in serving high-level goals.

The age of appearance of motor controls indicates the development of the neural control systems underlying them (Chapter 6, 'Development and plasticity'; Michel and Moore, 1995). For example, the capacity of human infants to show precision grasping is indicative of the maturation of neurons that link the motor cortex to spinal interneurons and motor neurons controlling the hand. Maturation of glial cells and the associated myelination of motor pathways is another factor that contributes to development of motor abilities.

Traditionally, researchers suggested that development consists of increasing cortical inhibition exerted on reflexes, associated with the portrait of the newborn as being essentially subcortically controlled (see Michel and Moore, 1995, for discussion). This is indeed part of the story. Primitive automatic reflexes are brought under increasing degrees of control by the later maturing cortical structures characterized as 'higher-order' and 'voluntary'. Thus, the disappearance of reflexes indicates maturation of the cortical regions that exert top-down inhibition. For example, the disappearance of the palmar grasp reflex is associated with the maturation of the supplementary motor area of the cortex (Michel and Moore, 1995). Later brain pathology is associated with the reappearance of previously suppressed reflexes.

A more general principle is that reflexes become incorporated into higher levels of control, i.e. goal-directed behaviour is constructed in part from reflexes (Michel and Moore, 1995). That is to say, with development, reflexes come under increasing degrees of high-level control. High-level inhibition exerted on reflexes clearly plays a role. However, with development, as well as some inhibition there is also some increase in top-down excitatory control of reflexes (Chapter 6; Schulte, 1974) or their replacement by the top-down control (McDonnell and Corkum, 1991). There is a changing *balance* between factors giving rise to new patterns of control (Teitelbaum, 1977).

Section summary

1 Development consists, in part, of the acquisition of top-down control over reflexes.

Test your knowledge

(Answer on page 273)

10.16 In addition to neurons, maturation of what other type of cell contributes to the development of motor skills?

10.4

conscious control of action involving negative feedback is dedicated to the task. Even under these conditions, behaviour still relies upon some automatic implementation of sequences organized at lower levels in the hierarchy.

A consideration of the limited capacity of conscious processes and the need for speed explain why there is a delegation of some responsibility for predictable movements to brain stem and spinal mechanisms. In the cases of (a) defence against tissue damage, (b) control of posture and (c) production of oscillatory movements underlying locomotion considerable organization is at the spinal cord but with modulatory input from the brain.

Bringing things together

Throughout the chapter you have seen how the brain exploits different means to control movement. Negative feedback is central to understanding this; the brain exploits differences between the way that the world is and the way that it should be according to our goals. Any difference is used to produce behaviour that tends to correct the difference. Although this is fundamental to control, it is supplemented by another process: feedforward. In this way, you have the benefits of negative feedback but can avoid its disadvantage of slowness. Thus, feedforward control provides a facility for anticipating potential disparity with what is intended and triggering action so as to pre-empt this disparity. Feedforward brings increased speed of responding.

Some control of behaviour requires full conscious awareness, e.g. learning new skills or in resisting habitual behaviour. However, when behaviour becomes predictable, it can be performed at a more automatic level. The shift from full conscious control of a task to an automatic mode can be identified with a changing responsibility of different brain regions.

The nervous system sometimes places weight upon physically present stimuli and preceding responses. Thereby, it produces sequences of behaviour in an automatic mode. This is appropriate in situations of high predictability where circumstances are invariant across trials. Where circumstances are novel or changing, automatic processes cannot perform the task and

Summary of Chapter 10

1 **The nervous system sets goals and produces movements to meet them, against a background of maintaining stability.**

2 **Both negative feedback and feedforward are used in movement control.**

3 **In perceiving the world, the nervous system uses information on external events and movement of the body.**

4 **Neural influences at different levels of the CNS affect the activity of motor neurons, which, in turn, triggers contraction in skeletal muscles.**

5 **The state of skeletal muscles is monitored by specialized detectors and this information is used in maintaining stability as well as in controlling movement.**

6 **Movement control depends upon an interaction between regions of cortex, basal ganglia, cerebellum and brain stem.**

7 **Different tracts convey information between the brain and motor neurons.**

8 **Even in the absence of overt behaviour, potential movements can be represented ('imagined') by the activity of specialized groups of neurons in the brain.**

9 **Development is associated with the acquisition of increasingly refined possibilities for motor control.**

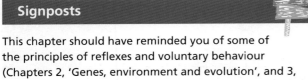

Further reading

For a text with links to learning, see Schmidt and Lee (2005). For all the neuroscience in this chapter, see Nolte (2002) and Chapters 30–38 of Gazzaniga (2004). For skeletal muscle control, see Bear *et al.* (1996). The role of the spinal cord in movement control is described by Pierrot-Deseilligny and Burke (2005). Parkinson's disease is described in Lozano and Kalia (2005) and Hanin *et al.* (2005).

Signposts

This chapter should have reminded you of some of the principles of reflexes and voluntary behaviour (Chapters 2, 'Genes, environment and evolution', and 3, 'The nervous and endocrine systems') and how vision guides action, introduced in Chapter 8, 'Vision'. You will meet again the principles of negative feedback and feedforward that were developed in this chapter. They will be discussed in Chapter 15, 'Motivation', and in Chapter 20, 'Cognition and action'.

Answers

Explanations for answers to 'test your knowledge' questions can be found on the website
www.pearsoned.co.uk/toates

10.1   Vestibular
10.2   Skeletal muscles; central nervous system
10.3   Negative feedback; feedforward

10.4   Controlled; conscious
10.5   (i) Feedforward; (ii) negative feedback
10.6   (i) Excitation
10.7   (iii) Interneuron
10.8   (ii) A chemical that destroys acetylcholinesterase
10.9   Increased; increased; decreased
10.10 Increased; decreased
10.11 Anterior; posterior
10.12 Dopamin
10.13 Fine; large
10.14 Large; small
10.15 (iii) Interneuron
10.16 Glial cells

Interactions and animations relating to topics discussed in this chapter can be found on the website **www.pearsoned.co.uk/toates.** These include

Animation: The role of the muscle spindles in muscle function

Interaction: The monosynaptic stretch reflex

Interaction: The motor areas of the cerebral cortex

CHAPTER 11

Learning and memory

Learning outcomes for Chapter 11

After studying this chapter, you should be able to:

1. Describe the link between the terms 'learning' and 'memory', while noting different forms of learning and memory.

2. Distinguish between non-associative and associative forms of learning. Then distinguish between two types of associative learning, while explaining the meaning of the term 'associative'.

3. Describe the ways in which memory can be categorized. Justify the criteria for such classification.

4. Identify some of the biological bases of learning and memory in terms of brain processes and structures. Outline the kinds of evidence that lead to an association between learning/memory and a brain region and how this suggests the existence of more than one form of learning/memory.

5. Justify the claim that functional and evolutionary considerations help to explain the existence of different types of learning and memory.

6. Explain how we can link the properties of neurons and their interactions to an understanding of the biological basis of learning and memory.

1 Why is conditioning so-called?

2 How can some memories be so durable?

3 How does trauma (e.g. in a traffic accident) often disrupt memory?

4 Why are memories not always a faithful reproduction of actual experienced events but sometimes involve distortions and creative elements?

5 How can I improve my memory?

Which different forms of memory are being revealed simultaneously in this situation?

Source: © Digital Vision.

Introduction

Look back over your life and try to think of when you have used the terms 'learning', 'remember', 'forget' and 'memory' to describe everyday events. In so doing, consider three things:

1 What do all the examples have in common that makes the general expression 'learning and memory' applicable?

2 What is the relationship between **learning** and **memory**?

3 How are learning and memory revealed?

Of course, each person will have different experiences but the following is probably representative.

If I am told a telephone number, I say it out loud to myself repeatedly while dialling it. In this way, it stays in my memory long enough to make the call but then it is forgotten.

When I would meet a new student group each year, I would hear their names and then forget them. This was before I acquired the technique of forming an immediate association. So, when someone introduces himself as Nelson, form the first association to come into your head. Suppose that it is with Nelson Mandela. So, now form an image of your Nelson as he speaks to a group of African students at a political rally.

I can remember a wealth of facts, such as my wife's birthday (yes, really) and that Bonn was the German capital. I can *consciously declare* such knowledge. I learnt French in school and, having used it since, it has stayed in my memory.

I can remember what I ate for breakfast today but not that for the Thursday of last week. I have a good memory of exactly where I was when I learned of US President John Kennedy's assassination in 1963. It was at home near Cambridge, with my father, watching the BBC evening news. I vividly recall our shock. The question 'Can you remember where you were when you learned of President Kennedy's assassination?' became something of a hallmark of the strength of emotionally significant memories. Times move on and academics age, whereas students stay the same age. Sadly, new tragedies appear and they illustrate the same point. These days the question is more likely to relate to the attack on the twin towers in New York on September 11th 2001. For my memory of 9/11, I can check the accuracy of recall with three other people.

I can remember how to ride a bicycle and tie shoelaces but I cannot *consciously declare* this memory to anyone in words. I can only *demonstrate* it. The memory relates directly to a particular behaviour.

I spent last weekend with an old friend, who is now sadly suffering a loss of memory. He could not remember from one period of two minutes to the next what I had said to him but he recognized me and could tell me in detail of his army experiences 60 years ago. This involved the recall of the joy of the war ending. He could remember how to use English grammar in constructing articulate sentences. He was still adept at employing chopsticks when we ate a Chinese meal.

So what do these experiences exemplify about learning and memory?

1 Learning refers to exposure to a situation and to the act of *acquiring* information or skill that is triggered. Corresponding to this learning, the term 'memory' describes the process of storage and recall. Some types of learning involve information about events in the world, such as those of Kennedy's assassination. Other types of memory involve not events but skills, such as how to use chopsticks.

2 Some memories are very transient and fragile unless active steps are taken to counter the tendency to forget. They can be rehearsed or made into unique associations so that they stand out. Other memories exhibit incredible durability even though you do nothing to try to remember the events.

3 Some memories can be consciously ('explicitly') declared as in 'Bonn was the German capital'. Other memories, such as those of how to ride a bicycle, cannot be consciously articulated. Rather they involve ('implicit') procedures of what to do. The memories might not exactly be '*in* the muscles' but seem to be closely connected with their control.

4 Certain memories have a personal reference in terms of episodes of individual experience, such as recalling what I had for breakfast yesterday. A single episode needs to stand out against the background of numerous breakfasts eaten over the years. Memory permits a form of 'time-travel': by recalling events, we can recreate something of the situation in which the memory was acquired. We can relive the emotion associated with the event, surely a part of the essence of possessing consciousness. Other memories relate to more publicly available information such as the name of a capital city.

5 When memories are of emotionally potent events, they tend to be particularly durable and well recalled.

6 With disease, different memories are not equally vulnerable to disruption. There can be a failure to update memories in the light of new episodes of experience, while long-established memories are intact. The memory for words, grammar and skills can sometimes be retained in the face of severe loss elsewhere.

This chapter concerns the biological foundations of learning and memory. These foundations embody change as a result of experience and are a type of plasticity. Learning refers to the behavioural act through which an animal either (a) later changes behaviour or (b) at least, acquires the *potential* for future change. Learning is the means by which certain *changes* in the brain (memories) are produced.

Memory refers to (1) the internal change that underlies learning (i.e. what is stored) and (2) the process of recall of learning and its expression in behaviour. The internal change in the brain outlasts the remembered event to which it relates, sometimes for decades.

Learning and memory exploit adaptive processes. Therefore, psychologists would not cite just any change in behaviour (e.g. one arising from brain damage) as an instance of learning and memory.

The task of a biological psychology of learning and memory is to try to link three different levels of their description:

1 The psychology of these phenomena.

2 The brain regions that are involved.

3 Their cellular basis in terms of neurons and the connections between them.

The following sections give some pointers to the nature of the links. The chapter starts with a look at the psychology of learning and memory. There then follows an account of the brain mechanisms and then the cellular basis.

Section summary

1 Learning refers to a behavioural experience, which is associated with change and which exploits adaptive processes.

2 Memory is the process that encodes the learning experience.

3 Different types of learning and memory exhibit different properties.

4 There are differences in the vulnerability of different types of memory to disruption.

5 The physical basis of memory is a change in the brain.

Basics of learning

This section looks at some of the better-known types of learning. It represents those most easily able to be studied in the laboratory and linked to their biological roots.

Habituation

A basic kind of learning can be demonstrated, as follows (Groves and Thompson, 1970; Sharpless and Jasper, 1956). An experimenter repeatedly presents a stimulus (e.g. a tone) that triggers a response but does not pair this stimulus with anything. If the stimulus has no significant consequence, a decrease in the magnitude of the response commonly occurs. If this behavioural change can be attributed to *central* changes among neurons, it is termed **habituation**. (You doubtless have shown habituation to a ticking clock.)

An example is provided by the marine snail *Aplysia* (Chapter 5, 'The brain'). When the gill and siphon are stimulated by a jet of water, the animal withdraws its gill (Kandel, 1991). If the stimulus is repeatedly applied, a reduction in the magnitude of the reflex occurs. See Figure 11.1. For another example, in dogs, at first a tone might evoke the response of orientation towards its source. Habituation would be evidenced by a decline in the magnitude of this response.

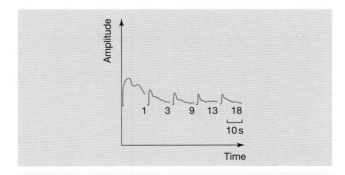

Figure 11.1 Habituation in *Aplysia*.

Source: Kandel (1976, Fig. 12-1, B-2, p. 543).

In principle, such decreases could be due to sensory adaptation (Chapter 7, 'Sensory systems') or muscle fatigue. However, suppose that they can be shown to be due to changes at neither sensory nor motor ends but that arise from ('central') changes at the intervening neurons. In this case, the phenomenon constitutes habituation. So, habituation refers to the combination of behaviour and the underlying neural mechanism.

Habituation is a relatively simple example of learning. The animal is exposed to a situation and changes behaviour as a result. The underlying changes in the nervous system constitute a basic form of plasticity: memory.

From a functional perspective, how do psychologists explain habituation? If a stimulus is presented repeatedly with no significant consequence, it appears *on average* to be adaptive to respond less strongly to it. For example, by withdrawing the gill, *Aplysia* uses energy. Not responding is an economy. However, life is a trade-off and, on a given occasion, it might prove beneficial to respond. The ripple that normally signals 'nothing of significance' might, on one occasion, be caused by a predator with a taste for biting off gills. The nervous system can only generate behaviour that has *on average* been adaptive in the animal's evolutionary history.

Habituation is shown where the experimenter simply presents a stimulus repeatedly and does not explicitly associate events. Hence, it is termed 'non-associative'. By contrast, conditioning exemplifies **associative learning**, which involves the experimenter arranging a relationship (termed a **contingency**) between two events. This is discussed in the next two sections.

Classical conditioning

One form of associative learning is **classical conditioning** ('Pavlovian conditioning') (Pavlov, 1935/1955). Its explanatory foundation is that Pavlov observed that dropping meat-juice into the mouth of a hungry dog elicits the secretion of saliva in the mouth and digestive juices in the stomach.

Some terms

Consider Figure 11.2. The process linking meat in the mouth and salivation is an **unconditional reflex**, common to all dogs. Salivation is termed an **unconditional response** (UCR) and food an **unconditional stimulus** (UCS). The significance of the term 'unconditional' will become apparent in a moment (the expression 'conditioned' is sometimes seen where 'conditional' is used here).

Pavlov presented a **neutral stimulus**, such as a bell, just before food. At the start, the bell is 'neutral' in that it has no prior connection with food and no capacity to elicit salivation. After a few pairings of bell and food, even the bell on its own triggers salivation. The bell has become a

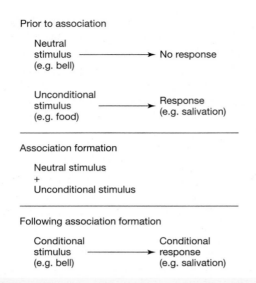

Figure 11.2 The phases of classical conditioning

conditional stimulus (CS) and salivation in response to it is the **conditional response** (CR). The term 'conditional' means that the capacity of the bell to trigger salivation is *conditional upon* pairing with food. It has no unconditional capacity to elicit salivation. By contrast, the food has an unconditional capacity. (The term 'conditional stimulus' is sometimes used to refer to the neutral stimulus prior to conditioning, as well as after it.)

This is a relatively simple case but it illustrates well the notion of *change* as the basis of learning. The amount of saliva triggered by the bell increases with the number of times the bell is presented together with food. This change in saliva secretion is a measure of learning. Corresponding to this, a memory is formed within the brain.

Function

Classical conditioning confers an adaptive advantage: by reacting to the CS, the animal is ready for the arrival of the UCS. For example, by salivating to cues predictive of food, the dog's body is prepared for the arrival of food. For another example, male fish of the species blue gouramis (*Trichogaster trichopterus*) were exposed to a rival male, the appearance of which was either signalled by a red light (CS) or unsignalled (Hollis, 1997). Those males that had a warning of the arrival of the other fish were in a position of attack readiness and at an advantage in competition for territory.

What is learned?

What *exactly* is learned when an animal is exposed to a pairing of a neutral stimulus and an unconditional stimulus? Given that the food triggers salivation as an automatic reflex,

does the bell come simply to trigger a reflex of salivation? Alternatively, or in addition, the animal might learn something about the world, which it can exploit in different ways. For instance, suppose that, following conditioning, the dog is in another room. Would it come running at the sound of the bell? Anyone who has kept a dog will doubtless opt for the second possibility since the sound of a can-opener can be a highly effective CS for locomotion. In this case, psychologists say that the animal has formed an association between two events: stimulus$_1$ predicts stimulus$_2$. This is termed a **stimulus–stimulus association**, and it can be used flexibly in behaviour. However, under some circumstances, animals simply form a straightforward and automatic link ('reflex-substitution') like that shown in Figure 11.3, i.e. between a stimulus and a response (O'Keefe and Nadel, 1978; White, 1989). This is described as a **stimulus–response association** (S–R learning).

Instrumental conditioning

The other class of associative learning is **instrumental conditioning** (Mackintosh, 1974). The animal is 'instrumental' in what happens, e.g. in correctly negotiating a maze. The experimenter arranges a contingency between behaviour and a consequence, e.g. getting food. Sometimes the type of instrumental conditioning that is studied in the Skinner box is termed **operant conditioning** (Skinner, 1966).

The essence of instrumental conditioning is **reinforcement**, introduced in Chapter 2, 'Genes, environment and evolution' (Skinner, 1966). Suppose that, on a number of occasions, a hungry rat is placed in the start-

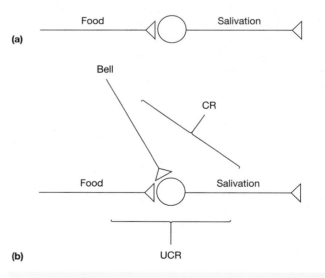

Figure 11.3 Reflex substitution: (a) unconditional reflex and (b) following conditioning, in which the bell acquires some of the capacity of the food.

box of a T-maze (Figure 11.4) and has a choice of turning left or right. To the left, it finds food (reward) but to the right there is an empty food-well. At first, the rat takes the right and left turns roughly 50:50. With experience, it takes only the left. Food acts as a reinforcer for the left turn and 'reinforcement' refers to a *procedure* by which behaviour is changed (Skinner, 1966).

In the laboratory, a situation is arranged such that getting food is *conditional upon* performing a particular behaviour, a left turn. A contingency between behaviour and an outcome is arranged. Such contingencies also arise naturally in nature.

Reinforcement is of two kinds. **Positive reinforcement** is the procedure of *gaining* something contingent upon behaviour, where the behaviour is observed to increase in frequency. For example, food positively reinforces the lever-pressing behaviour of a hungry animal. **Negative reinforcement** refers to a procedure whereby behaviour is strengthened by the *termination* of something. For example, learning to press a lever to terminate a loud noise constitutes negative reinforcement (Wise, 1988).

The term **punishment** refers to a procedure whereby the frequency of showing behaviour is lowered as a result of the consequence of doing so. For example, suppose an animal learned to press a lever in a Skinner box. If then lever-pressing is followed by shock and thereby its frequency is reduced, this would constitute punishment.

A special form of associative learning is described next.

Taste-consequence learning

Learning relates not only to events in the external world. We can also learn links between external events and consequences inside the body. Suppose an animal ingests a novel food and later experiences gastrointestinal upset. Typically, it is reluctant in future to ingest food with this flavour, termed 'taste-aversion learning' or the 'Garcia effect', introduced in Chapter 1, 'Introduction' (Garcia, 1989). Normally events that are associated by conditioning cannot

be very far apart. For example, for salivary conditioning, the food must arrive within a second or so of the bell for a link to be formed. By contrast, taste-aversion learning is characterized by a delay of several hours that can elapse between tasting and gastrointestinal upset. For some species, e.g. rats, it is an effect largely specific to taste; it is more difficult to associate a visual or auditory stimulus with gastrointestinal upset.

In humans, taste-aversion learning shows where an evolutionarily old process can be more powerful than rationality (Garcia, 1989). Suppose that a person develops a taste-aversion to a food. However, they get to know that there was no connection between the food and illness. They often still avoid this food.

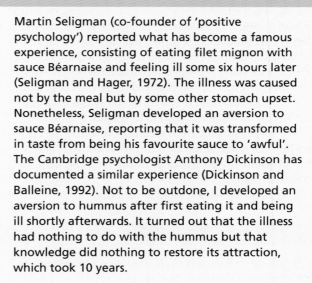

A personal angle

For psychologists, where does the blame lie?

Martin Seligman (co-founder of 'positive psychology') reported what has become a famous experience, consisting of eating filet mignon with sauce Béarnaise and feeling ill some six hours later (Seligman and Hager, 1972). The illness was caused not by the meal but by some other stomach upset. Nonetheless, Seligman developed an aversion to sauce Béarnaise, reporting that it was transformed in taste from being his favourite sauce to 'awful'. The Cambridge psychologist Anthony Dickinson has documented a similar experience (Dickinson and Balleine, 1992). Not to be outdone, I developed an aversion to hummus after first eating it and being ill shortly afterwards. It turned out that the illness had nothing to do with the hummus but that knowledge did nothing to restore its attraction, which took 10 years.

In addition to learning about aversive effects, preferences can be acquired by learning. These are based upon favourable consequences of ingestion of a particular taste, e.g. to favour a food associated with correction of vitamin deficiency (Rozin and Schulkin, 1990).

Forming cognitive maps

In their brains, animals construct cognitive representations of the environment, termed **cognitive maps** (Tolman, 1932). Consider the apparatus shown in Figure 11.5 (Morris, 1981). A tank is filled with water and a submerged platform placed in it. Though rats have poor vision, milk is added to make sure that they cannot see the platform. A rat is then placed

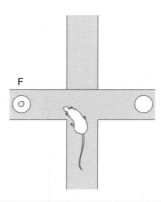

Figure 11.4 T-maze.

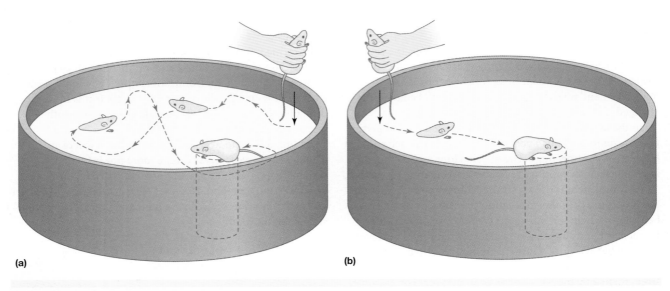

(a)   (b)

Figure 11.5 The Morris water maze apparatus: (a) first trial and (b) later trial.

into the water and the trajectory of its swimming recorded (Figure 11.5(a)). Ultimately, it reaches the platform and climbs out of the water. It is then put back in at a different location and the trajectory observed. After a number of trials, the rat starts to swim directly towards the platform, regardless of where the rat is placed (Figures 11.5(b) and 11.6). If the platform is removed, the rat swims back and forth in the area where it used to be (Figure 11.6(b)).

The response is different according to where the rat is put into the water. It seems to involve knowledge about the environment, which can be utilized flexibly, i.e. a 'cognitive map'.

The following section looks at memory.

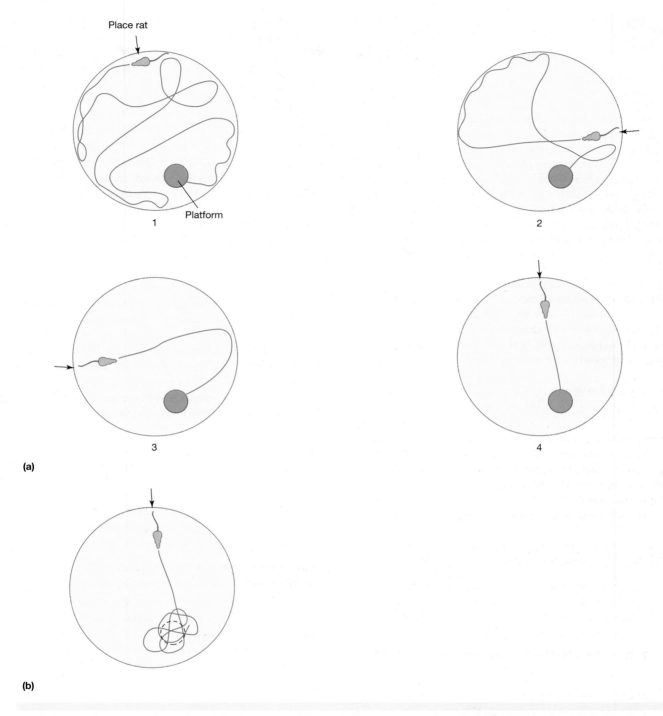

Figure 11.6 Behaviour in the Morris maze: trajectory followed (a) over repeated trials (1–4) and (b) when platform is removed.

Basics of memory

Introduction

Whenever learning occurs, by definition a memory is formed. Traditionally, researchers into learning paid most attention to rats learning tasks in mazes and Skinner boxes. By contrast, memory researchers more often employed humans memorizing such things as lists of words (Baddeley, 1997). Therefore, there has not been as much integration as might be desired.

Researchers try to categorize memory into different classes (Squire, 1994). Different systems of memory mean that we cannot simply state, for example, that 'memory is impaired'. Rather, we need to specify which class of memory is impaired (Tulving, 1995). Also a claim might need qualification of the kind that either acquisition or retrieval of information is impaired but not both.

In classifying memory, there is not absolute agreement on the criteria and various classifications exist side-by-side (Foster and Jelicic, 1999). What follows must therefore be a crude and broad-brushstroke approach.

Types of memory

Declarative/explicit – non-declarative/implicit

With reference particularly to humans, a way of dividing memory is into **declarative memory** and **non-declarative memory** (Squire, 1994). See Figure 11.7. A declarative memory is for a fact or an event in the world, e.g. Paris is the capital of France. We have conscious access to it, and having retrieved it into consciousness, can choose whether to express it in behaviour (Schacter and Tulving, 1994b). The term 'declarative' derives from the fact that humans can verbally declare the content of such memory. Declarative memory corresponds to the most common lay use of 'memory' and 'to remember' (Squire, 1994). Declarative memories can be acquired rapidly, e.g. in a single exposure (Moscovitch, 1994) and used in an indefinite series of different and novel situations (Eichenbaum, 1994).

Another term that means much the same as declarative memory is **explicit memory**. We can be verbally explicit about the content. Since the ability to verbalize recall is the criterion for 'explicit', strictly speaking, it is applicable only to humans (Eichenbaum, 1994).

In contrast to declarative/explicit memory is non-declarative memory or **implicit memory** (Claparède, 1911; Squire, 1994). It cannot be expressed or 'declared' verbally. Being able to ride a bicycle exemplifies non-declarative memory. The distinction is between knowing 'what' (e.g. the explicit memory that Paris is the French capital) and knowing 'how' (e.g. the implicit memory of how to use chopsticks).

A major class of non-declarative memory is that underlying skills and habits. It is covered by the term **procedural memory** and is automatic and unconscious (Eichenbaum, 1994; Schacter and Tulving, 1994b). Conscious awareness has, at best, a vague and fuzzy insight into such memory. Its contents cannot be described as true or false but only as more or less adaptive in a given situation. Procedural memories are usually acquired slowly and incrementally (see O'Keefe and Nadel, 1978).

It is doubtful whether there are tasks that involve purely either explicit/declarative or implicit/procedural memory (Eichenbaum, 1994). All tasks probably require something of each. The question is perhaps best framed as some tasks being more or less dependent upon one or other system.

Semantic and episodic memories

For humans, a distinction within declarative memory is between **semantic memory** and **episodic memory** (Tulving, 1972). Semantic memory refers to that for facts. Episodic memory refers to a particular episode of *personal experience*. Griffiths *et al.* (1999, p.74) offer a memorable example:

Remembering getting soaked in the London rain last Tuesday is an example of episodic memory, but knowing that it often rains in England is an example of semantic memory because it need not be acquired as a result of a personal experience of getting wet.

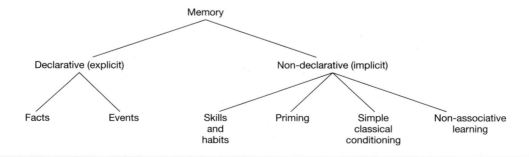

Figure 11.7 Classification of memory. *Source*: Reprinted with permission, from Squire and Zola-Morgan (1991, Fig. 3).

Occasionally, brain damage can disrupt episodic memory, while leaving semantic memory intact (Nielsen, 1958; Tulving, 1999).

A personal angle

N.N.

A male patient, N.N., studied by Endel Tulving in Toronto had suffered head injury in a traffic accident (Tulving, 1985b). N.N.'s linguistic skills and general knowledge were intact. N.N. could draw a picture of the Statue of Liberty and could even define rather well the meaning of 'consciousness'. He had knowledge about his past, e.g. names of his schools, but the memory was devoid of personal events ('episodes') of experience. As Tulving describes it, N.N.'s life has an 'impersonal experiential quality'.

Episodic memory has a tag of 'what', 'where' and 'when' for single instances. There is evidence that the bird species the scrub jay (*Aphelocoma coerulescens*) can exploit such memory in utilizing what it has cached (Chapter 1; Clayton and Dickinson, 1998). The bird seems to know about each item of food and where it has been hidden.

Memory as a function of time

Memory classification presented so far is based on what is learned and how it is learned. Another classification is based on time, the *temporal* dimension, though it broadens to a wider consideration than this. With reference to declarative memory and based mainly upon humans, different temporal stages of memory are identified, varying from only about 0.5 s to a lifetime (Baddeley, 1997).

Figure 11.8 shows a classical representation of the temporal stages involved in learning visual or auditory information. The first stage is termed 'sensory registration' and is specific to a sensory system. It has been studied in the visual system (termed 'iconic memory') and auditory system (termed 'echoic memory'). There is a process of recoding that translates between sensory registration and the next stage, termed **short-term memory (STM)**. STM has a limited capacity and information tends to decay from it unless it is actively rehearsed, e.g. reciting a telephone number. The traditional view is that, following a brief holding in STM, information is normally either lost or is transferred to **long-term memory (LTM)**. The capacity of LTM seems virtually limitless and its durability potentially a lifetime.

Information is said to be either lost from STM or subject to **consolidation**. Memories that are consolidated are stored in the relatively durable form of LTM, as opposed to the more fragile STM. The durable physical embodiment of memory is termed an **engram**. Memory consolidation is surrounded by controversy and there could well be several different processes contributing to it (Meeter and Murre, 2004). An attempt at a broad consensus is presented here.

The short-term versus long-term distinction is relative rather than absolute. At a given point in time, a memory might be in part in each location. Some memories linger for much longer than a few seconds before being lost, e.g. what you ate for breakfast this morning. However, some kind of distinction, albeit ill-defined, between a more fragile 'provisional' memory and a more durable one still holds.

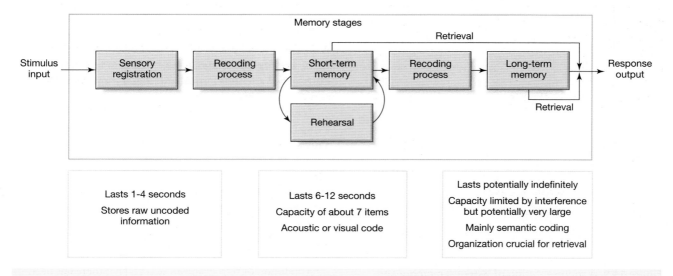

Figure 11.8 A classical representation of the temporal stages of memory. *Source*: Cohen (1990, Fig. 12.10, p. 596).

Working memory

The classification shown in Figure 11.8 has proven its value. However, limitations became apparent and a new model emerged, based on the concept of **working memory** (Baddeley and Hitch, 1974). See Figure 11.9. This borrowed important features of the STM/LTM distinction but incorporated additional features. A memory is said to be 'working' when it is active and involved in information processing. Working memory underpins cognition and conscious thought. In the spirit of the STM part of the old model, subsets of working memory hold information while it is transferred into LTM. Indeed, to capture this feature of memory and for historical continuity, the expression 'STM' is still used in the literature, alongside working memory.

Working memory does more than just hold memories while they are transferred into a more permanent form. Another of its roles can be illustrated as follows. Can you recall an image of former US President Bill Clinton? On the occasion(s) when you first saw him, his image was held in STM/working memory and was then assimilated into a durable form. Imagine now his features and even try to draw a sketch of him. You were probably not thinking of him prior to reaching this paragraph. If so, his memory was secure in your brain but was inactive. Now it is active and is *working* as in being used to draw a sketch. It has re-entered working memory and presumably will exit from it in a paragraph or two (or maybe not!).

So, as a part of working memory, this temporary store of active information can perform additional tasks, such as reasoning and comprehension. Rather than being simply a passive store, information is held in working memory while it is *actively* manipulated (see Petrides, 1994). Baddeley (1994, p. 351) defines working memory as: 'the system for the temporary maintenance and manipulation of information, necessary for the performance of such complex cognitive activities as comprehension, learning and reasoning'.

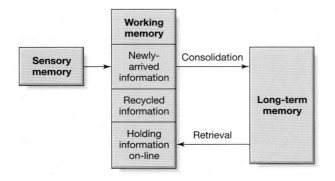

Figure 11.9 A representation of working memory and its links.

A **central executive** is said to supervise the subsystems of working memory and is associated with holding information in conscious awareness. Within working memory, an articulatory control process recycles speech-based information as inner speech. Visual information can enter working memory either directly via visual perception of the external world or by the internal production of a visual image. Such an image can be manipulated, e.g. rotated. Try it now with Bill Clinton. Skills such as negotiating an environment involve manipulating a visual image (Baddeley, 1997).

An important factor in understanding memory is to consider its loss, the topic of the next section.

Amnesia

The term **amnesia** means 'the pathological inability to learn new information or to retrieve information that has already been acquired' (Purves *et al.*, 1997, p. 549). Amnesia is sometimes due to trauma, as in brain injury (Milner, 1966). A failure to recall events experienced before the trauma is termed **retrograde amnesia** and a failure to remember those experienced after it is termed **anterograde amnesia** (Butters and Cermak, 1986).

Traditionally, it has been assumed that memory is held in a fragile and transient form as activity (expressed as STM or a division of working memory) until it is consolidated into a durable form, LTM (Lewis, 1979). If consolidation is disrupted, then memory is lost. In these terms, retrograde amnesia might be explained as trauma disrupting consolidation of memories formed prior to the trauma.

Retrograde amnesia often displays a temporal gradient: the memory for events nearest the time of trauma is most disrupted, with that for earlier events less so. The traditional interpretation of retrograde amnesia is that there has been insufficient time for events just prior to the trauma to become consolidated. However, there are problems with this (Lewis, 1979):

1 Some patients show retrograde amnesia for events extending over years. Can consolidation really take that long?

2 Amnesia often displays shrinkage. Memories that were apparently lost immediately after trauma appear later, indicating that they were present all along. This suggests a failure of **retrieval** rather than consolidation.

3 Within the zone of retrograde amnesia there are often islands of retained memory.

A personal angle
Princess Diana's bodyguard

Traumatic events are sometimes of legal and political significance, apart from their medical importance. In the car accident in Paris that killed Princess Diana in 1997, there was only one survivor, her bodyguard Trevor Rees-Jones. After his recovery, police were keen to interview him, to establish the circumstances of the accident, e.g. was a second car involved? However, he was unable to recollect the events immediately before the accident. Some memory returned slowly in the subsequent months.

It is now time to look at the nervous system and the physical basis of learning and memory.

Section summary

1 Memory is classified into (a) declarative ('explicit') memory (associated with conscious recollection) and (b) non-declarative ('implicit') memory (which cannot be consciously recalled).

2 A category of non-declarative memory is that underlying habits and skills, termed procedural memory.

3 Within declarative memory, a distinction is between semantic memory (for facts) and episodic memory (for episodes of personal experience).

4 Working memory is a multi-aspect store of information in which information is held while it is actively manipulated.

5 Amnesia refers to a pathological failure of memory.

Test your knowledge

(Answers on page 300)

11.4 Which type of memory is revealed in the following? (i) How to balance on a rocking boat, (ii) that the biggest city in Holland is Amsterdam, (iii) what you had for breakfast on a visit to Amsterdam.

11.5 Which type of amnesia is revealed in the following lapses of memory associated with injury in a traffic accident? (i) A failure to recall whether the lights at the junction were red or green, (ii) a failure to remember the first questioning by police after the accident.

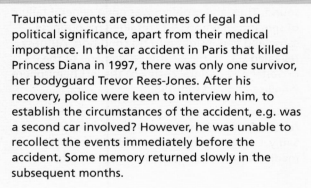

Studying the brain

Introduction

Detailed investigation of the brain gives insight into the nature of learning and memory. For example, PET scans reveal which brain regions are most active under particular conditions of learning and posing a recall task to memory. Measuring the effects of experimental lesions in non-humans and accidental brain damage in humans also provides understanding.

A source of insight into *systems* of memory has been when damage to the brain disrupts one kind of memory, while leaving another intact (Schacter and Tulving, 1994a,b). Damage sometimes impairs declarative memory but not procedural memory. Damage to a different region disrupts procedural memory but not declarative memory. This is termed a double dissociation (Chapter 8, 'Vision').

Both cortical and subcortical structures are involved in learning and memory. As shown in Figure 11.10, regions of temporal and parietal cortex are assumed to be the cortical sites at which memories are stored. The role of the hippocampus appears to be a dual one: to act as (i) a temporary store of information held immediately after the learning experience and (ii) a site from which consolidation of the memory by the cortex is controlled (Meeter and Murre, 2004). The hippocampus is thought to be a fast-learning system whereas the cortex is slower. Hippocampal damage disrupts more recently acquired memories, while leaving older ones intact. This suggests that, with time, the cortex is able to consolidate memories but, until this is achieved, the hippocampus is needed either to store them or to gain access to them.

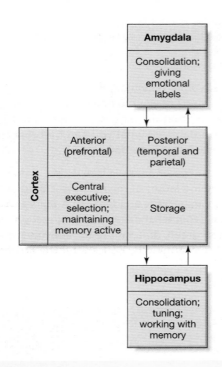

Figure 11.10 Role of some brain regions.

In 1888, the case of an 80-year-old German salesman, Gottlieb L. (G.L.), was reported (article reprinted as Lissauer, 1988). During a trip to Krotoschin, G.L. had been blown against a fence in a wind and banged his head. He reported difficulties seeing but had normal visual acuity. He was able to draw objects by copying them.

G.L.'s problem was specific to associating the meaning of objects with their visual stimulus. For example, he described an apple as a portrait of a woman. Whereas G.L. could not recognize a whistle by sight, he was able to name it by its sound. Thus, the problem was not a general failure of semantic memory. G.L. retained his business sense and had insight into his condition. Autopsy revealed G.L. to have suffered damage to the occipital and parietal cortex of the left hemisphere (Shallice and Jackson, 1988).

When he was only 27 years old, Heinrich Lissauer reported the case of G.L. at a conference in Breslau. Sadly, Lissauer, who was also noted for other medical achievements, died three years later.

The role of the prefrontal cortex is thought to be that of controlling memory, i.e. retrieving memory and holding it in a 'working' state so it can be used. The amygdala plays a role in enhancing consolidation, described in the next chapter.

This section looks at types of memory from the perspective of these brain regions and the different kinds of learning and memory tasks that researchers have presented.

Memory storage – cortical regions

In human patients undergoing brain surgery, local electrical stimulation of a part of the temporal cortex tends to evoke a particular memory, suggestive of localization (Penfield and Rasmussen, 1968). Experiments on non-human primates show that regions of cortex concerned with modality-specific processing (e.g. vision) and other regions concerned with multimodal processing (e.g. vision and tactile) are involved in memory (Petrides, 1994). For example, inferotemporal cortex is involved in later stages of visual processing (Chapter 8) and visual memory. Its damage can disrupt visually based memory, leaving memories based on other modalities intact.

As an aspect of working memory, Baddeley and Hitch's (1974) model involves the retrieval of visual memories. By this means, mental images can be manipulated. When humans are asked to *visualize* themselves negotiating an environment, there is an increase in blood flow to the occipital cortex

(Roland and Friberg, 1985). Of course, this region is otherwise activated by visual stimulation from the external world (Chapter 8). Patients who have lost colour vision through damage to the occipital lobes also lose the capacity to think with coloured images (see Baddeley, 1997). They can sometimes draw a picture of an object from memory but be unable to say what colour the object should be.

In other cases, brain-damaged patients are unable to access semantic memory by touch but can do so by vision.

Executive functions

Basics

As part of the executive function of working memory, the prefrontal cortex (PFC) has a role in the utilization of memory to control cognition and action. To do so, it draws on ('reinstates') memories that are stored in more posterior cortical regions. This involves maintaining the activity of a memory, i.e. holding it 'on-line' so that its content can be utilized in controlling behaviour (Fuster, 1997). In humans, based on intentions, the PFC helps to guide memory searches, direct thought processes, plan action and select and implement encoding, processes that are open to conscious introspection (Moscovitch, 1994).

Take what is involved when you are asked a question – where were you on Christmas day ten years ago and what did you do? In so far as you have any answer, it is unlikely to 'jump out at you' automatically. Rather, a lengthy retrieval process involving various strategies is likely. The role of the PFC is, in Moscovitch's terms, one of 'working-with-memory', corresponding to the role of the central executive.

Damage to the brain

Although humans with damage to PFC can assimilate new information, they are deficient in organizing its recall (Milner, 1964, 1971). They have conscious insight into their deficiency, scoring low on measures of their confidence that they can recall information. The PFC has a role in discriminating true from false memories and its damage can result in 'confabulation' ('false memory', claiming as true experience something that did not occur) (Schacter, 1997).

Humans with damage to PFC experience difficulty in inhibiting inappropriate information, termed 'utilization behaviour' (Chapters 5 and 10; Lhermitte, 1983). They show interference from previously activated memories. In the laboratory, this consists of intrusions from a memory test conducted a few minutes earlier. At a biological level, this appears to reflect a failure of what would normally be a PFC inhibition on processing carried out by more posterior cortical regions. For example, to remember where and when a memory was acquired might require extensive inhibition of 'false leads'.

Non-human primates with damage to the PFC are impaired in tasks that require observation of an event, its holding in working memory and its use in action slightly later (Petrides, 1994). Damage to other cortical areas does not have this effect.

Dopamine has a role in such tasks. Disruption of dopaminergic neurotransmission at the PFC has a disruptive effect on their performance (Chapter 6, 'Development and plasticity').

Interacting aspects of memory

Figure 11.11 illustrates the interaction between the PFC and more posterior cortical regions (parietal and temporal) in performing tasks involving working memory (Petrides, 1994). However, a number of tasks that require working memory (e.g. recognition of an object, understanding speech) remain relatively unimpaired following damage to the PFC. Memory can be triggered in an automatic way, driven by stimuli that match the memory. This suggests that PFC damage does not disrupt the store of memory (e.g. the sensory attributes of a memory) and points to this region's involvement in management of memory, i.e. activating a memory even in the absence of appropriate sensory input and holding it 'on-line'.

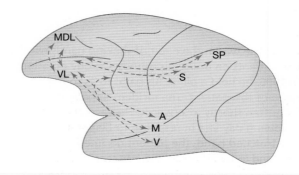

Figure 11.11 Interaction between prefrontal and posterior cortical regions and between prefrontal regions. S, somatosensory; SP, visuo-spatial; A, auditory; M, multimodal; V, object vision; VL, ventrolateral PFC, MDL, mid-dorsal lateral PFC.

Source: Petrides (1994, Fig. 16, p. 73).

The human amnesic syndrome

The phenomenon

In humans, damage specifically to the medial temporal lobe involving the hippocampus leads to the **amnesic syndrome**, consisting of an apparent failure to assimilate new episodic and semantic information (Milner, 1966). It might be more accurate to consider several amnesic syndromes subsumed under this heading. However, there is difficulty deciding how to formalize such classification. It could be in terms of (i) cause, e.g. from an infection that damages neural tissue, (ii) the site of brain damage (e.g. specific region of temporal lobes) or (iii) the nature of the memory loss.

A personal angle

The hidden pin

In 1911, the Swiss psychologist Edouard Claparède reported an observation on an amnesic patient, in what might now be considered an unethical procedure. Claparède's patient was a 47-year-old woman in the refuge at Bel-Air. She had been ill since 1900 and appeared unable to update her memory. She didn't know where she was or how old she was. She asked the nurse who had cared for her for 6 months, '*à qui ai-je l'honneur de parler?*' (to whom do I have the honour to speak?). However, she could name without error the capital cities of Europe and could negotiate her way around the refuge.

continued

Claparède was in the habit of shaking hands with the patients on doing his rounds. On one occasion, in 1906, he held a pin in his hand so as to prick the hand of this patient. The incident appeared to be forgotten shortly afterwards. However, the following day and in response to Claparède's outstretched hand, the patient declined to advance hers and jerked it away. She had learned an association between the psychologist and trauma. In terms of memory, she had formed an implicit memory of the traumatic event. The result of Claparède might be put down to a single uncontrolled observation, but subsequent research has confirmed its broad applicability.

Usually, beyond this anecdote, little acknowledgement is given in the English-speaking world to Claparède's early profound insights into memory and its classification.

Claparède (1911) demonstrated a dissociation: by the index of behaviour, the patient appeared to remember but was unable to recall consciously the episode that triggered the change in behaviour. The emotional intensity of the experience might be implicated in its retention (Markowitsch, 1995), suggesting involvement of an intact amygdala (Chapter 12, 'Emotion').

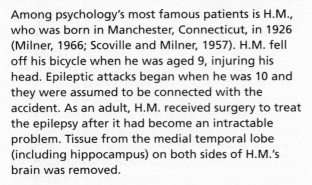

Among psychology's most famous patients is H.M., who was born in Manchester, Connecticut, in 1926 (Milner, 1966; Scoville and Milner, 1957). H.M. fell off his bicycle when he was aged 9, injuring his head. Epileptic attacks began when he was 10 and they were assumed to be connected with the accident. As an adult, H.M. received surgery to treat the epilepsy after it had become an intractable problem. Tissue from the medial temporal lobe (including hippocampus) on both sides of H.M.'s brain was removed.

Following the operation, H.M. was able to recall vividly information acquired in early life, e.g. a holiday in Florida. His personality appeared largely unchanged and there was no general intellectual impairment. However, he could recall little of the 12 years prior to the operation. For example, he did not remember the death of a favourite uncle three years before.

H.M. experiences an unchanging anterograde amnesia for episodic and semantic information (Corkin, 2002). For example, he is unable to remember the faces of people he meets after the operation. A psychologist might spend the morning testing him but in the afternoon H.M. would act as if the psychologist were a stranger. People who have come to H.M.'s house regularly for 6 years are not recognized. Reading and rereading the same magazine creates no impression of familiarity. The failure to update such memories is a hallmark of the amnesic syndrome (Baddeley, 1997).

H.M. has a capacity for working memory, since he is able to carry on a normal conversation and can understand jokes. This requires some minimal level of retention of what has just been heard and said. On being asked to recall the number 584, H.M. was able to do so even 15 minutes later, apparently by means of constant verbal rehearsal. However, after the task was over, the number and H.M.'s strategy in remembering it were lost to his memory.

Motor skills (procedural memories) are well maintained, e.g. how to mow a lawn. He shows improvement on the performance of learning new skills such as reverse mirror-drawing in which he has to acquire new eye–hand coordination (Corkin, 1968; Milner, 1966). H.M.'s ability to learn new skills is typical of the amnesic syndrome. However, such patients have no consciously accessible memory of acquiring the skill. H.M. has insight into his problem and, in response to a question he cannot answer, is inclined to respond that he has 'trouble with his memory'. An MRI scan of H.M.'s brain was performed in 1992 and 1993 and details of the extent of the damage analyzed (Corkin *et al.*, 1997).

Patients such as H.M. ('amnesic patients') exemplify the amnesic syndrome. Baddeley (1997) cites H.M. as possibly providing the strongest evidence for a distinction between STM and LTM. Each seems to be functioning but there is a failure either of *certain* contents of STM to enter LTM or of *certain* contents of LTM to become accessible to conscious recall (Lewis, 1979).

Retained memories

A form of memory that is retained in the amnesic syndrome is revealed in the 'word-completion test' (Warrington and Weiskrantz, 1970). A person is presented with a word, e.g.

ASSASSIN, and asked to recall it. Typically, amnesics cannot consciously recall it. However, suppose that they are asked to complete a word cued by A--A--IN. They show a higher probability of responding ASSASSIN as a result of prior presentation of ASSASSIN. Behaviour has been influenced by the prior presentation even though they cannot consciously recall the earlier event. The prior experience produces **priming** at later recall, a form of non-declarative memory (Figure 11.7). Amnesic patients can acquire motor skills (procedural learning) though they are not conscious of doing so and cannot articulate the learning experience (Weiskrantz and Warrington, 1979). H.M. exemplifies this.

Common features of what is spared

Are there common features of the tasks at which amnesic humans are unimpaired (Weiskrantz, 1982)? In each task, the appropriate response, the index of memory, can be produced without placing the explicit question 'Do you remember this?' They can be solved by a straightforward mapping from sensory input to recalled memory and triggering by a cue, e.g. A--A--IN tends to trigger the memory ASSASSIN as a result of earlier presentation of ASSASSIN. Similarly, amnesics reveal intact memory in, say, reverse-mirror drawing, cued by the sight of the apparatus.

Amnesics can show good recall of some episodic and semantic information that was encoded before the onset of the disorder. Information assimilated prior to the disorder might have benefited from repeated reactivation and forms part of a more automatic retrieval (Johnson and Chalfonte, 1994).

Korsakoff's syndrome

Patients suffering from **Korsakoff's syndrome** exhibit profound deficiencies of memory. It is a form of amnesia that is similar to, but distinct from, the classical form just described and has a distinct cause. This syndrome is normally due to a thiamine (vitamin B1) deficiency, as a consequence of excessive alcohol intake. There are global signs of loss of brain tissue, this particularly being the case for the frontal lobe (Oscar-Berman *et al.*, 2004) and hippocampus (Sullivan and Marsh, 2003). Deficits of executive function are evident, i.e. working with memory, as in the Wisconsin card-sorting task (Chapter 6).

Having focused on primate, particularly human, studies, we now turn to a study of learning and memory in rats. A somewhat similar pattern of memory types emerges from this study.

A foraging task

Insight into different types of learning and memory and their biological bases has been obtained from studying foraging tasks in various species. Some general principles emerge, and can be illuminated by tasks set to laboratory rats.

Taking food at a particular site can deplete it. What factors determine when to leave the site and when to come back?

Source: PhotoDisc, Inc.

The win–shift task

Is there a non-human model of declarative memory? Of course, as noted earlier, rats cannot literally declare anything but they can be set tasks that require forms of memory that appear similar to human equivalents. One such tests the ability to learn and recall a particular instance of experience and to use it in the control of behaviour.

Figure 11.12 shows an Olton eight-arm maze (Olton *et al.*, 1979). Each arm contains a hidden morsel of food. The rat is placed in the centre and, when all eight doors are lifted, it has a choice of arm. Having depleted an arm of food, the optimal strategy is not to revisit that arm but to visit the others (see Figure 11.13). This involves recalling the arms already visited. The rat needs to visit each of the eight arms once only, to obtain a small reward at each goal, termed **win–shift**. Win–shift means that, having 'won' one reward, the animal has to shift to a different arm to win another. Rats become very good at performing this task.

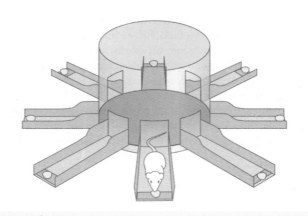

Figure 11.12 The radial maze.

Source: Bear *et al.* (1996, Fig. 19.12, p. 537).

The task requires the brain to *inhibit* the tendency arising from learning based on reinforcement. Reinforcement would *strengthen* a tendency to repeat the response to a particular arm at which reward had just been found. Having

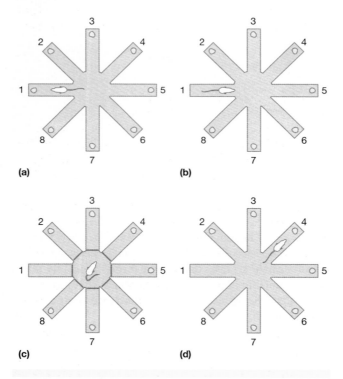

(a)   **(b)**   **(c)**   **(d)**

Figure 11.13 Radial maze: (a) rat about to deplete arm 1 of food, (b) return to centre, (c) doors descend so rat is held in centre for a few seconds, to put a load on memory, and (d) an unvisited arm (e.g. 4) forms the goal.

been reinforced at arm 1, the rat has to enter a different arm next time. The reinforcement of visiting arm 1 can only impede a solution and its effect must be resisted. Success seems to require representations of events, i.e. depleted sites and prospective sites of food, and avoiding sites that have been depleted.

Success seems to involve a combined capacity to use (1) spatial cues in a cognitive map and (2) a representation of the current state of each arm (i.e. as 'food' or 'depleted'). Weight appears to be given to each *particular instance* of recent experience, an 'episode' in resisting the reinforcement process (though a simpler process might also be involved; see Griffiths *et al.*, 1999). In these terms, the memory of the event that just happened, the rat's removal of a pellet, needs to be used in deciding whether to revisit an arm. Neither current sensory stimuli nor a weighted average of experience can solve the task. Rats with damage to the hippocampus (termed 'hippocampals') tend to repeat visits to arms that they have just depleted. They seem to be deficient at exploiting spatial cues outside the maze to establish where they are in space and, within this framework, to represent the state of the arm as 'food' or 'depleted' (Jarrard, 1993).

The win–stay task

The same radial maze can also be used to study procedural learning and reveal the role of a subcortical site of a procedural memory. Figure 11.14 shows a different schedule of reward, termed **win–stay**. In getting reward at one arm and when the experimenter signals that it has been re-loaded with food, the rat needs to return immediately to this same arm. The arm in which reward is located (in this case, arm 1) is always indicated by a light and the task is solved by 'staying with the light'.

Solution of the win–stay task seems to be based upon food strengthening a habit ('reinforcement'), i.e. a simple S–R learned association between a light at an arm and an approach response (Petri and Mishkin, 1994). Any win–shift tendency would disrupt this task since the light is 'telling' the rat to repeat what it has just done. Normally rats find it easier to learn a win–shift task than a win–stay (Packard *et al.*, 1989). It could be relevant that, in the rat's natural environment, having depleted one location, it would appear to be natural to switch to elsewhere.

A double dissociation

By selective lesions, Packard *et al.* (1989) performed a double dissociation of these two foraging tasks. When animals were trained on a win–shift task, fornix lesions disrupted behaviour (the fornix is a brain region linking the hippocampus to the

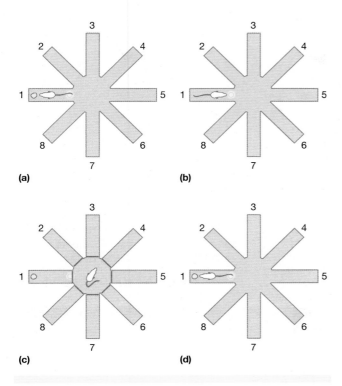

Figure 11.14 Win–stay task.

control of behaviour). Lesions to the fornix disrupt utilization of the hippocampus. The hippocampus is thought to mediate the use of a cognitive map. Lesions of the caudate nucleus, a region of the basal ganglia (Chapter 10, 'The control of movement'), had no effect.

For the win–stay task, animals with lesions to the caudate nucleus were disrupted. This structure exerts an influence near to the motor output side and appears to be involved in S–R learning. By contrast to win–shift, the performance of animals with lesions to the fornix was *improved* relative to controls. By disrupting the expression of the hippocampus in behaviour, the tendency of the animal to show win–shift is disrupted and thereby the win–stay response is favoured.

Eye-blink conditioning

Introduction

We have looked at evidence from humans and rats using tasks particularly adapted to each species. In this final section, we look at a 'model system' in which human and certain non-human species can be set the same task.

Closure of the eyelid is a defensive reaction triggered by such unconditional stimuli as a puff of air to the eye and is termed the **eye-blink reflex**. If a neutral stimulus is paired with the unconditional stimulus, the neutral stimulus becomes transformed into a conditional stimulus that has the capacity to trigger eyelid closure. That is, as a result of classical conditioning, there emerges the 'conditional eye-blink reflex'. The eye-blink reflex has been well studied and it serves to identify some of the biological bases of learning and memory (Woodruff-Pak, 1999). When comparing mammalian species, the brain structures underlying the conditional eye-blink reflex exhibit close similarities and the neural circuit has been clearly identified.

In rabbits

In studying eyelid closure in rabbits, a tone (CS) is paired with an air-puff (UCS), while brain events are observed (Krupa *et al.*, 1993; Thompson, 1990). Neurons were found in the cerebellum, which, prior to conditioning, responded to neither tone nor puff. Following conditioning, they responded to the tone. In regions of the cortex (outer layer) of the cerebellum, electrical activity followed the CS, came just before the CR and mirrored the magnitude of the CR. Lesions of these areas abolished the CR but left the UCR intact. Such conditioning does not require an intact hippocampus and would seem to be simple stimulus–response learning with a procedural memory as its basis.

In humans

For humans, eye-blink conditioning is relatively easy to perform and can serve as a useful diagnostic tool for detecting abnormalities. For example, amnesic humans can learn a conditional eyelid response but cannot remember the learning experience (Thompson, 1990). Patients suffering from damage to the cerebellum are impaired in their ability to be conditioned to produce an eyelid response. For unilateral damage, the impairment is specific to the eye that is ipsilateral to ('same side as') the damaged cerebellum (Woodruff-Pak *et al.*, 2001).

In humans, there is some loss of the neural tissue of the cerebellum with age. The loss appears to be suffered by one particular class of neuron, termed the 'Purkinje cell', which is vulnerable to toxins such as alcohol. In one study, a positive correlation was found between the size of the cerebellum and strength of conditioning attained after 90 pairings of tone and air-puff (Woodruff-Pak *et al.*, 2001). Strength of conditioning was measured in terms of the percentage of times a CR was exhibited following presentation of the CS. See Figure 11.15.

The next section considers these types of memory and the underlying brain mechanisms in the context of the evolutionary and functional types of explanation (Chapter 2).

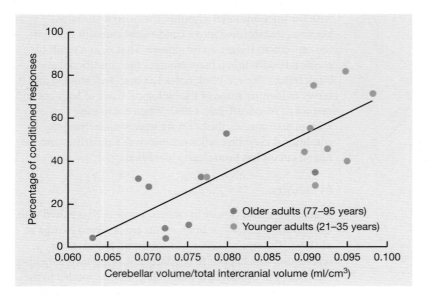

Figure 11.15 The strength of the conditional response of eye-blink as a function of the volume of the cerebellum for adults of various ages. Volume of cerebellum was measured by MRI.

Source: Woodruff-Pak *et al.* (2001, Fig. 4, p. 353).

Section summary

1 Regions of temporal and parietal cortex are involved in memory storage.

2 Prefrontal cortex appears to be part of the physical embodiment of the central executive, which is involved in 'working with memory', as in directing searches.

3 In the human amnesic syndrome, there is damage to the medial temporal lobe. People (e.g. H.M.) fail to update their memory with declarative information. Their procedural memory is intact.

4 Hippocampal rats are deficient at a win–shift task set in an Olton maze.

5 Specific learning tasks can be set so as to reveal a role of the basal ganglia and cerebellum in procedural learning and memory.

Test your knowledge

(Answers on page 300)

11.6 In a win–stay task in the radial maze, what is the optimal solution to maximize food intake?

11.7 In a win–shift task in the radial maze, what is the optimal solution to maximize food intake?

Linking brains to evolution and function

Introduction

So far, we have briefly considered the functional role of learning and memory. This section returns to the topic in the context of different types of memory and the role of brain processes.

In both evolution and development, different systems of learning and memory appear to emerge at different stages. When a new system emerges, it increases the behavioural possibilities. Tulving (1985a, p. 387) suggests an analogy: 'we can think of an airplane with an autopilot as a more advanced or higher system than one without it, but we would not think of the autopilot alone as a higher system than the airplane'.

Tulving argues that the earliest system of learning and memory to appear in evolution and development is the procedural. Semantic memory emerges from this and brings the novel feature of being able to represent events that are not physically present. In turn, episodic memory emerges from semantic memory and allows representation of unique instances of individual experience. Tulving suggests that (p. 387): 'each higher system depends on, and is supported by, the lower system or systems, but it possesses unique capabilities not possessed by the lower systems'. In this interpretation, the lowest system, procedural, can exist without the other two and semantic memory can exist without episodic memory.

It is a general rule that, in evolutionary terms, new processes are relatively vulnerable to disruption, as compared with old processes (Ribot, 1885). Memory in general follows this principle. However, there can be disruption to implicit memory, leaving explicit intact. We have seen instances of this in the present chapter and Chapter 8 described such a case.

Evolutionary psychology
Different specialized adaptations

From a functional perspective, different forms of memory would be expected to reflect the different demands of the environments in which they evolved (Sherry and Schacter, 1987). In the terms of evolutionary psychology (Chapter 2), different systems of learning and memory appear to have evolved to serve different specialized functions and to reflect different 'design criteria' (Klein *et al.*, 2002a). According to this perspective, understanding can best be gained not by considering the tasks that learning and memory can perform but what they were 'designed' to perform.

Sherry and Schacter suggest that memory systems reveal 'functional incompatibility'. This means that 'an adaptation that serves one function cannot, because of its specialized nature, effectively serve other functions' (p. 439). A single general 'all-purpose' system could not meet these demands.

The distinction does not necessarily mean that different systems are located in entirely different anatomical sites. Sherry and Schacter give taste-aversion learning as an example of a specialized learning and memory system. They also illustrate the argument with some other examples, such as song learning and food caching.

Song learning

Sherry and Schacter identify song learning in birds as a special class of learning and memory. Its features include (a) neural systems that are dedicated to the task (identifiable brain nuclei), (b) a time-frame in early life during which learning can occur, (c) a considerable time between when a song is learned by the young bird and its performance when adult and (d) specificity in exactly what is learned. Birds learn songs specific to their species, often with a local dialect. This suggests a template for song recognition, with a capacity for fine-tuning by local experience. Such specificity serves to attract conspecific mates and warn potential rivals.

In canaries, two brain nuclei control singing. There is a positive correlation between their size and the size of the song repertoire. Both nuclei show variation in size over the year, correlated with the time when songs are performed. Increases in volume are due to a proliferation of neurons and glial cells (Chapter 4, 'The cells of the nervous system').

Food caching

Some species of bird cache food, described earlier in this chapter and in Chapters 1 and 5 'The brain' (Sherry and Schacter, 1987). The bird has a specialized memory system that enables it to remember the locations. Food is typically retrieved several days after caching. Following this, the bird does not revisit the site. This seems to involve a variety of episodic memory, similar to that of rats solving the radial maze task. The memory involved in caching food (a transient memory) is fundamentally different from that in song learning (a durable memory). Lesions to the hippocampus disrupt the ability to locate cached food.

Declarative and non-declarative learning and memory in primates

As functional specialization of learning and memory by primates, including humans, Sherry and Schacter contrast forms of declarative memory and non-declarative memory. They consider the evolution of, on the one hand, a declarative system that enables one-trial learning of specific episodes and, on the other, a non-declarative incremental learning system underlying habits and skills. Think about how the skill of riding a bicycle is achieved. The memory underlying it is not acquired on a single trial. Rather, sensory-motor links that were successful in maintaining stability tended to be strengthened and assimilated into a bank of solutions, i.e. by feedback some links are encouraged and others discouraged.

In contrast to skill learning, Sherry and Schacter suggest that episodic memory has evolved to assimilate unique information peculiar to an instance, i.e. to emphasize *variance* between episodes.

Sherry and Schacter propose a functional criterion for deciding how many different memory systems there are, which can be used alongside other criteria, such as susceptibility to brain damage. What they term a conservative perspective is that (p. 449): 'distinct memory systems evolve only when there is functional incompatibility between the properties of an existing system and the demands posed by a novel environmental problem'.

Having looked at the more gross brain structures and functional considerations, the next section looks at the cellular basis of learning in memory in terms of changes at the level of individual neurons, which encodes memory.

Section summary

1 Functional incompatibility is assumed to have led to the evolution of distinct memory systems.

2 In evolution, procedural memory appears to be the oldest type of memory.

3 Semantic memory seems to be evolutionarily more recent than procedural memory. In turn, episodic memory appears to emerge from semantic memory.

4 Functionally, there seems to be incompatibility between the properties of procedural and semantic memories in terms of what they are 'designed' to perform.

Test your knowledge

(Answer on page 300)

11.8   In terms of both evolution and development, which is thought to be the earliest memory system to appear?

Cellular mechanisms

The basic idea

There is more than one starting point for investigating the cellular (neuronal) basis of learning and memory. As one possibility, consider again brain regions. Different regions play roles in different types of learning and memory and we described connections between brain regions, such as those linking prefrontal cortex and more posterior regions of cortex. If we are able to associate memory with particular brain regions, in principle it is possible to associate it with the properties of some of the connections between neurons that are located in these regions.

Another starting point is with the psychology of learning and memory. Recall that some memories, such as those underlying motor skills, are formed gradually. Others are formed in a single exposure, such as those relating to a traumatic incident. Consider also the staggering differences in the rate of apparent loss of memory. Some memories are very fragile, being lost in seconds if they are not rehearsed. Others are durable over a lifetime. As physical bases, what kind of internal changes might give rise to these different properties of memory?

The extremes of fragility and durability of memory have led researchers to suggest that memories are encoded in at least two different forms, which provides the organizing theme of this section:

1 Patterns of activity in networks of neurons.

2 The strength of connections between neurons.

These are not necessarily entirely distinct forms of storage; the same networks that are active as a temporary store might have their connections strengthened as the more permanent store.

Consider first a procedural memory. Learning of a skill appears to correspond directly to a gradual change in the strength of connection between particular neurons. For example, learning to use chopsticks corresponds to a strengthening of certain successful connections, i.e. those directing the bean-curd to the mouth, and a weakening of those connections that lead it to falling into your lap. However, there are also instances of where memory seems first to be encoded in a form other than as a change in strength of connections between neurons, as follows.

Consider a declarative memory, for example, that formed by hearing a person's name for the first time. This is encoded immediately in short-term memory and in a form that can easily be lost. With repetition of exposure to the name or rehearsal, it comes to be relatively stable in long-term memory. An assumption underlying the study of memory is that such short-term and fragile memories are first encoded as patterns of activity within populations of neurons, most likely in the hippocampus or cortex. The hippocampus appears to be involved in maintaining the activity of such a temporary store and consolidating it in the cortex (Meeter and Murre, 2004). Consolidation of memory with time and repetition is believed to correspond to a transfer of memory from this fragile form to a more durable form. Durable long-term memories are thought to be encoded in changes in the *structure* of connections between neurons in the cortex.

We will now look in more detail at these ways of holding information.

Changes in activity

By means of a change in frequency of action potentials, how might a circuit of neurons encode a memory? See Figure 11.16. A stimulus (A) sets up a cycle ('reverberation') of activity in a circuit of neurons 1–3 (pattern A). Stimulus B sets up a reverberation in a different circuit (B) and stimulus C activates circuit C. There is consistent mapping between different stimuli and different patterns of neural activity. This is a necessary condition in order to consider neural activity to embody memory. Another necessary condition is that activity can be triggered, even in the absence of the stimulus that is encoded by, for example, associated stimuli or an attempt to recall a specific memory.

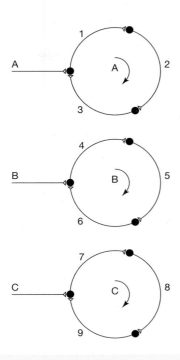

Figure 11.16 Neurons forming the physical basis of memory.

It is generally assumed that particular sets of neurons are active at the time a memory is formed and the same set is activated when the memory is later revived (Mishkin, 1982). For example, neural systems within the inferior temporal cortex are known to be activated by visual patterns (Chapter 8) and are believed to play a role in encoding visual memories of the same patterns (Mishkin, 1982).

Memories are of varying duration. It is possible that when a stimulus sets up a pattern of activity, this lasts only a few seconds or minutes. When memories are held for longer (e.g. for a lifetime), a translation process would have to occur. The assumption is that memory is translated from the more transient and fragile form of patterns of activity to the more durable form of structural changes in connections between neurons, the topic of the next section.

Structural changes

Structural changes might either directly encode a memory, as in certain forms of procedural learning of a skill, or occur only as a result of activity in patterns of neurons that form a temporary store. The latter is termed consolidation.

The Hebb synapse

In an influential theory, Hebb (1949) proposed that memory consolidation consists of structural change at one or more synapses (described in Chapter 3, 'The nervous and

endocrine systems'). A synapse exhibiting such a change in efficacy is therefore termed a **Hebb synapse**. Differences of opinion concern whether changes at synapses encoding a memory are local to a part of the brain or distributed widely.

What happens at the synapse as it changes strength with learning? In terms of the classical conditioning of salivation, Figure 3.15 (p. 60) suggested that, accompanying the exposure to the paired bell and food, there is an increased efficacy at certain synapses. Transformation of the neutral stimulus into the conditional stimulus is based on such a change.

Presumably, there are chemical changes such as growth of new receptors at the postsynaptic membrane or increased synthesis of neurotransmitter at the terminal of the presynaptic neuron, or both. At this scale, researchers perform detailed biochemical analysis of the events that accompany learning and memory formation.

Changes at synapses, such as growth of dendritic spines (Chapter 4), accompany learning (Hosokawa *et al.*, 1995). See Figure 11.17. These changes might be the same as occur during early development (Chapter 6). What would distinguish one set of such changes as a possible basis of memory is a correlation of physical change with the learning experience and meeting a number of other conditions, described shortly.

Consider the case where memory is first encoded by patterns of activity. This is a fragile and transient form of storage. How might such a transient pattern become consolidated into durable structural changes? One proposal is that those synaptic links that are activated in the dynamic phase become strengthened by use. As a function of activity, neurotransmitter synthesis could increase and there could be a growth in the number of receptors at the postsynaptic membrane.

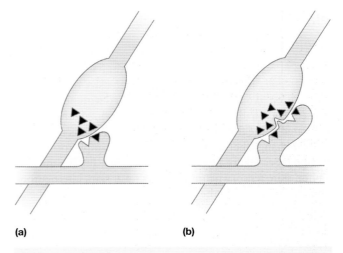

(a)   **(b)**

Figure 11.17 Suggested changes at a synapse involving a dendritic spine and which accompany learning: (a) prior to and (b) after learning.

Source: based on Hosokawa *et al.* (1995, Fig. 10, p. 5570).

Consolidation – static or dynamic?

Traditionally, it was believed that, after consolidation has taken place, the memory is fixed more-or-less permanently in the form of new connections between neurons. However, this view is at odds with the observation that memory can exhibit a reconstructive and dynamic feature (Nader, 2003). For example, people distort ('confabulate') memory and recalling a story is known to introduce creative shifts of the narrative.

Biologically orientated research has found a possible basis for this effect (Lewis, 1979). Evidence suggests that even apparently well-consolidated memories can be disrupted at a time when they are reactivated. Electric shock to the brain can disrupt an old memory if given when this memory is in an active state. Of course, we do not normally go around getting electric shocks to our brain corresponding to distortions of memory. However, more subtle triggers to disruption might normally be present. Indeed, there might even be a lifelong process of reconsolidation of memory; memory is reconsolidated after each activation (Nader, 2003). So, in this view, what was considered to be a stable lifelong feature of our cognition is really a constantly dynamic process.

You might wonder whether this could be exploited to get rid of those memories that people would prefer to be without, such as intrusive obsessive thoughts. Just reactivate the unwanted memory and then try to trigger the biological equivalent of pressing a computer's delete button, such as giving an electric shock to the brain. Theorists are working on such ideas (Nader, 2003).

The next section gives two examples of the kind of structural change that underlies memory.

Plasticity in *Aplysia*

Habituation

Kandel (1991) chose a relatively simple animal, the marine snail *Aplysia californica*, and studied a defensive reflex and its habituation. If a tactile stimulus is repeated with no harmful consequence, habituation occurs, as shown in Figure 11.1 (repeated as the first part of Figure 11.18). What is the cellular change that forms the basis of this simple form of learning? See Figure 11.19. Note the pathway linking the siphon skin, sensory neuron with its tip at skin, interneuron and motor neuron to the gill. A tactile stimulus excites the sensory neuron at skin, which in turn excites the interneuron, and so on.

Action potentials arise at the sensory neuron with its tip at the siphon skin. They travel the length of this neuron and release transmitter from the terminal. As habituation proceeds, so there is a decline in the amount of transmitter that is released. This draws attention to changes at the

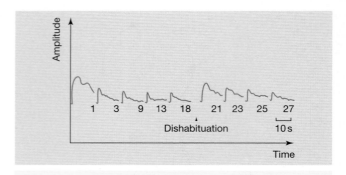

Figure 11.18 Habituation and dishabituation in *Aplysia*. On one occasion, between the 18th and 21st presentation of the harmless test stimulus, another stimulus (a strong tactile stimulus to the neck) was given.

Source: Kandel (1976, Fig. 12-1, B-2, p. 543).

terminal. The basis of the change in transmitter release appears to be a change in properties of calcium channels in the membrane. When an action potential arrives at the terminal, it causes calcium to enter the neuron and trigger the release of transmitter (Chapter 4). If the calcium channels partly close, this lowers the amount of transmitter that is released. So, the durable embodiment of this memory lies in the closure of calcium channels.

Such changes can last for minutes, a form of STM, or even several weeks, a type of LTM. They underlie habituation in a number of species. The changes concern synapses involved in a motor response; they are not dedicated only to memory storage.

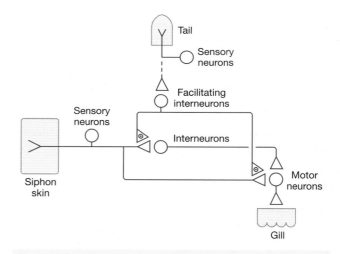

Figure 11.19 Suggested neural system underlying habituation and sensitization, showing representative neurons.

Source: Kandel and Jessell (1991) *Principles of Neuroscience*, 3rd Edition, Fig. 65.3, p. 1013, reprinted by permission of The McGraw-Hill Companies, Inc.

Sensitization

Another behavioural phenomenon illustrating plasticity is **sensitization** (Kandel, 1976). Suppose that a noxious stimulus is applied to *Aplysia*. After this, the animal tends to respond more strongly even to harmless stimuli. Sensitization makes adaptive sense; a context of noxious stimulation is probably a dangerous one, in which it could be of value to be prepared to react strongly in a defensive mode. A particular manifestation of sensitization is **dishabituation**: an increase in strength of a response that had previously been habituated (Figure 11.18).

Figure 11.19 shows the neural connections that appear to underlie both habituation and sensitization. The latter involves 'facilitating interneurons'. Note the axo-axonal synapses (Chapter 4) that the facilitating interneuron makes on the terminals of the sensory neuron that is part of the link from siphon skin to motor neuron. Suppose that a single noxious stimulus is applied to, say, the tail of *Aplysia*. This triggers action potentials in the sensory neuron with its tip at the tail, which triggers activity in the facilitating interneuron. Action potentials arriving at the terminals of the facilitating interneuron sensitize the synapses that the sensory neuron from the siphon skin forms with the motor neuron and interneuron. At some synapses, the chemical released by the facilitatory interneuron is serotonin. It facilitates the entry of calcium into the neuron terminal at the arrival of an action potential and makes synapses more sensitive. These are the opposite effects to those that form the basis of habituation. (These links do not permit a stimulus at the tail to trigger a motor response by the gill.) Following sensitization, when the sensory neuron at the siphon skin is triggered, more neurotransmitter is released from its terminals. This is the basis of the increased response indicative of sensitization.

The work of Kandel and associates raised the prospect of a reductionist approach gradually building up cumulative knowledge. After documenting neural connections in *Aplysia*, they might be able to extend the approach to vertebrates. However, caution is in order. *Aplysia* has a relatively simple nervous system with some large and clearly identified neurons. There is controversy as to whether principles developed from *Aplysia* can be generalized to vertebrates, the topic of the next section.

Protein synthesis

Introduction

Even using a vertebrate, it is possible to investigate whether changes in structure occur at the time a memory is formed. First, a brief digression sets the research into its theoretical context, for which an analogy helps (Rose, 1992).

Imagine that the structure of the body is like a house designed by a highly eccentric architect. Every few minutes the builder takes out a brick from the house and breaks it up. The builder then puts in a new brick in place of the old one. The house retains its original shape, even though the actual ingredients are constantly changing. Over time, the rate at which bricks are removed and added is equal, so there is no net brick addition. The architect then decides to add a porch. During its construction, there is a net addition of bricks to the house.

By analogy, the body is constructed of proteins, which are constantly being broken down and replaced. However, a given body still looks like the same you or me of last week. The overall form remains the same but the precise components change. The general assumption is that memory involves the formation of some new synapses or reinforcement of existing ones. Since these are constructed from proteins, it might be possible to detect increased **protein synthesis** in brain regions following learning.

Bricks are made of component substances and so are proteins. Synthesis of proteins requires a supply of simpler substances normally obtained in the diet. If one of these is labelled radioactively and injected, it will also tend to be incorporated into proteins. If a brain region is showing a high rate of protein synthesis, it should later show a relatively high content of radioactively labelled material. This seemingly needle-in-haystack search is the theoretical rationale behind the studies.

Passive avoidance learning

To study changes in the brain, it would be good to find a memory that is formed in a short time, ideally, in a single experience. There are examples of such memories. One is imprinting (Chapter 6). A better example for establishing the cellular basis of memory is one-trial **passive avoidance** learning in chicks (young domestic chickens). Passive avoidance involves learning *not* to do something that is followed by noxious consequences. Exposure to the situation is very rapid and the formation of memory can be studied in the period immediately following the experience. Passive avoidance will be employed here to illustrate more general principles (Rose, 1992).

Chicks tend to peck at small objects but, if the experience of pecking is a noxious one, they tend to avoid the object in the future. Chicks are offered a small white bead that is attached to the end of a wire. For one group ('experimentals'), the bead is coated with a noxious (bitter) tasting substance, methylanthranilate. For the controls, it is simply coated with water. On tasting the substance, the experimentals shake their heads and wipe their bills. The bead appears to taste disgusting. The controls show no such reaction.

The index of learning is that experimentals tend to avoid the bead in the future, whereas controls have no hesitation in pecking it. Where is the change in physical structure, the memory, corresponding to such learning? Just after the training trial, chicks can be injected with a radioactive substance, e.g. fucose, a sugar, that is used in the synthesis of the structure of neurons. Suppose that memory is stored as a change in this structure. More radioactive sugar would be incorporated into the brain of the chick that learns than into that of the control. Later, the quantity of radioactive substance in the brains of the two groups is compared. Experimentals have a higher level than controls.

How can one be sure that the change following learning is the physical embodiment of memory? The chick learns and the change occurs, but this might just be correlation. What are the criteria of memory?

Criteria of memory

Rose (1992) proposed criteria that need to be met for a change to qualify as the embodiment of memory; five of these are as follows:

1 There must be a physical change at a location in the brain. This will probably be an increase in synaptic structure but in principle it might be a loss of some synapses.

2 Other factors that accompany learning (e.g. arousal or stress) must be ruled out as causes of the change in structure.

3 If structural changes are prevented from happening, memory should not be formed. Injection of chemicals that inhibit protein synthesis should prevent learning.

4 A lesion to the site of memory should disrupt its expression in behaviour. (This raises the issue of whether a particular memory is localized to one site or distributed over many regions.)

5 The neurons at the site of proposed memory formation should show altered electrical characteristics.

Criteria (1)–(5) above were met in the case of the learning of passive avoidance. Thus, the proposal that changes forming the physical base of memory occur in particular brain areas was supported. More specifically, there is a growth in the number of dendritic spines (Chapter 4) in certain areas, suggesting the formation of new synaptic connections.

Long-term potentiation

Bliss and Lømo (1973) discovered a phenomenon termed **long-term potentiation** (LTP), exhibited at excitatory synapses in mammals. Suppose that a *presynaptic* neuron is active at a high frequency but for only a short time. For certain neurons, Bliss and Lømo found that this exposure caused a change in the reactivity of the *postsynaptic* neuron that lasted for hours or even days. In other words, presynaptic activity caused a 'long-term potentiation' of the ability of the postsynaptic neuron to be excited. Use of a synapse strengthened its efficacy, something anticipated by Hebb (see earlier). Could this be the long-sought-after basis of plasticity in the mammalian nervous system? What was responsible for the change at the synapse underlying this effect?

The neurotransmitter glutamate acts at several receptor types on postsynaptic membranes. Two of these are particularly important in LTP: the AMPA and the NMDA receptors (Martin *et al.*, 2000) (Figure 11.20). Exactly what is going on in LTP is, at the time of writing, a topic of debate. One theory is that AMPA receptors 'hide' inside the neuron (Figure 11.20(a)). Occupation of NMDA receptors triggers the movement of AMPA receptors to the surface (Figure 11.20(b)). When they are at the surface, the receptivity of the postsynaptic membrane to glutamate is increased and this is the basis of LTP. There is evidence for the presence of AMPA receptors below the surface of the postsynaptic membrane.

At one level of analysis, LTP might be the biological basis of long-term memory (Collingridge, 1997). This would suggest that in some cases LTP can remain for a lifetime. A given memory would probably be encoded by LTP at a number of synapses distributed throughout the brain. Forgetting might consist of a loss of such potentiation.

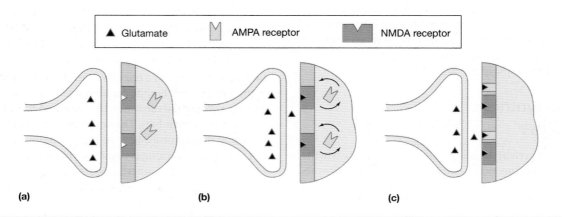

Figure 11.20 Long-term potentiation: (a) before activity in presynaptic neuron, (b) activity in presynaptic neuron and (c) after LTP. *Source:* after Collingridge (1997, Fig. 2).

Section summary

1 Memory appears to be encoded by changes in activity and structure of neurons.

2 Hebb proposed that the durable physical basis of memory is a change in structure at certain synapses.

3 Corresponding to habituation in *Aplysia*, calcium channels at the presynaptic membrane close and the amount of transmitter released from the sensory neuron decreases. Sensitization corresponds to opening calcium channels at the presynaptic membrane.

4 During passive avoidance learning in chicks, increased levels of protein synthesis occur.

5 Activity in a presynaptic neuron can cause long-term potentiation in the postsynaptic neuron.

The adaptive value of non-associative and associative learning is clear. Thus, habituation is a means of conserving energy and Pavlovian conditioning gives the advantage of anticipation. Instrumental conditioning permits an animal to exploit the environment to gain food, water and a mate etc.

The chapter illustrated the value of considering brain mechanisms and evolutionary/functional types of explanation in parallel. In terms of evolutionary psychology, some distinct systems of learning and memory emerge in evolution since they serve different functional considerations. The problem that procedural memory solves (e.g. gradual accumulation of a motor skill over repeated exposure) is very different from that solved with the help of an episodic memory (e.g. where a particular item of food was stored on a particular occasion). A memory system serving the one could not serve also the other.

Test your knowledge

(Answers on page 300)

11.9 With reference to Figure 11.19, suppose that sensitization is caused by a noxious stimulus to the tail. A given tactile stimulus is applied to the siphon skin before and after the noxious stimulus. In response to the tactile stimulus, in which of the following neurons would increased activity be seen after the noxious stimulus had been applied? (i) The sensory neuron with tip at the siphon skin, (ii) the interneuron, (iii) the motor neuron.

11.10 With regard to Figure 11.20, long-term potentiation could be blocked by injection of which of the following at the time of activity in the presynaptic neuron? (i) A glutamate antagonist, (ii) a specific AMPA antagonist, (iii) a specific NMDA antagonist.

11.5

Bringing things together

The chapter has described the type of plasticity of the nervous system and behaviour that is termed 'learning and memory'. There exist several distinct systems of learning and memory that serve different roles and reflect different evolutionary pressures.

Summary of Chapter 11

1 **Learning refers to a behavioural experience and memory refers to a type of change that occurs as a result of the experience and that encodes information about it.**

2 **Some simple forms of learning (e.g. habituation) are non-associative, whereas associative learning is exemplified by classical and instrumental conditioning.**

3 **Different types of memory are characterized by differences in the type of information that is encoded and differences in their durability and vulnerability to disruption.**

4 **Various brain regions are involved in learning and memory. Different regions are associated with different types of memory and different roles in processing memory, e.g. site of short-term or long-term storage.**

5 **Seen in evolutionary terms, some differences in types of memory can be linked to the incompatibility in what is required to solve different problems that confront an animal.**

6 **At a cellular level, it is believed that memory is stored as patterns of activity within sets of neurons and as changes in strength of synaptic connection between neurons.**

Further reading

For a more detailed account and one which takes an integrated perspective on learning and memory, see Anderson (2000). For memory as a whole, including biological aspects, see Dudai (2002). For the neuroscience of memory, see Chapters 47–52 of Gazzaniga (2004). On biology and the classification of memory, see Foster and Jelicic (1999). For different levels of instrumental learning, see Balleine and Dickinson (1998). For working memory, linking the psychology and biology, see Andrade (2002). For episodic memory, see Griffiths *et al.* (1999). For a good review with some emphasis on the role of the hippocampus, see Eichenbaum and Cohen (2001).

Signposts

Subsequent chapters will call on information introduced here. Chapter 12, 'Emotion', will describe the process by which traumatic experiences are particularly well remembered. It will also describe the role of conditioning in emotion, e.g. learning fears by classical conditioning. Chapter 15, 'Motivation', will look again at the issue of reinforcement. Instrumental conditioning is central to the expression of motivation. The role of both this and classical conditioning in feeding, sex and drug-taking is discussed in Chapters 15–18.

Answers

Explanations for answers to 'test your knowledge' questions can be found on the website **www.pearsoned.co.uk/toates**

11.1   Plasticity
11.2   (i) Habituation
11.3   Prior to conditioning, neutral stimulus; after conditioning, conditional stimulus
11.4   (i) Procedural, (ii) semantic, (iii) episodic
11.5   (i) Retrograde, (ii) anterograde
11.6   Repeat visits to the arm cued by light
11.7   Visit each arm only once
11.8   Procedural
11.9   (ii) The interneuron, (iii) the motor neuron
11.10 (i) A glutamate antagonist, (iii) a specific NMDA antagonist

>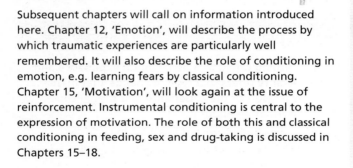
>
> **Interactions and animations** relating to topics discussed in this chapter can be found on the website at **www.pearsoned.co.uk/toates**. These include
>
> **Interaction:** Terminology used in classical conditioning
>
> **Interaction:** The main components of the synaptic junction

CHAPTER 12

Emotion

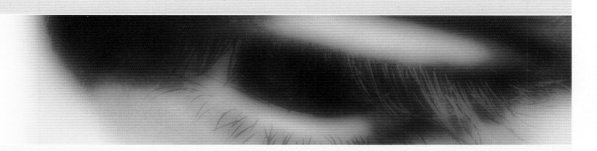

Learning outcomes for Chapter 12

After studying this chapter, you should be able to:

1. State what is meant by the term 'emotion' and describe the coordinated role that emotions play in behaviour, physiology, cognition and subjective affective experience.

2. Explain how emotions arise, describe their properties and link this to functional and evolutionary types of explanations. Outline the basic principles of affective neuroscience.

3. Give a detailed account of some representative emotions, highlighting how they meet the criteria for using the term 'emotion'.

4. Present a balanced and critical account of the theory that emotions are triggered by peripheral feedback.

5. Describe some of the principal brain regions that form the biological basis of emotions, while identifying the kinds of evidence on which this description is based.

6. Give an account of some of the neurochemicals involved in emotion and link this to the understanding of chemical interventions to alter emotion.

7. Describe the effects of some specific emotions on cognition, memory and reflexes.

Scene-setting questions

1 In coping with life, do emotions help or hinder?

2 Is there conflict between emotions and rationality?

3 What is the relationship between 'gut-feelings', physiology and behaviour?

4 Why do we blush?

5 Why is it difficult to conquer 'irrational' fears?

6 How well can introspection give insight into the causes of emotion?

7 Why are emotionally coloured memories sometimes particularly durable?

The facial expression suggests a positive emotion. How does the brain produce emotion? How can we interpret signs of it in others?

Source: PhotoDisc, Inc.

Introduction

Try to reflect on some experiences in your life that you would describe as 'emotional', such as those of joy, fear, anger or frustration. What characterizes such experiences as emotions? See if you can find any common features. For example, think of the frustration of turning up on a promising date, only to find that the prospective partner has pulled out. What did it *feel* like? Think of a fearful situation, when your heart pounded especially strongly and your gut was disturbed and compare that with the experience of anger. Now think of an embarrassing situation when blood rushed to the skin of your face. On a more positive note, can you recall shivers and goose-bumps on hearing a favourite piece of music or the joy at seeing a loved one?

When did someone last identify your emotion by the expression on your face? Can you guess that someone has a problem from their facial expression?

There might be emotionally powerful events that are well etched into your memory – 'I will always remember where I was and how I felt then'. Were you ever in an emotion of fear and thereby interpreted a harmless situation as one of threat? On an automatic level, you might have 'jumped out of your skin' in response to a sudden harmless touch by someone. You have doubtless heard of unfortunate people caught up in a conflict and traumatized for long periods afterwards, with flashbacks to the traumatic events.

Such reflection can identify some features of emotion that are also confirmed by a more scientific study and which form the organizing theme of Chapter 12, as follows.

1 An emotion plays a role in controlling behaviour. For example, the behaviour associated with fear is different from that associated with anger or joy. Fear can lead us to try to escape from a situation, anger to assert our rights. Emotions favour some actions (e.g. fear favours escape or freezing immobile), and counter others (e.g. fear inhibits feeding) (Oatley and Jenkins, 1996). In joy, we are likely to reach out to others. You have some freedom in what you do in response to an emotion. In a state of strong fear, you might run, hide or call the police but you are not likely to start cooking. From an evolutionary perspective, we can see emotions' advantage to fitness – for example, by fleeing in response to danger, we tend to survive.

2 The strength of reflexes can be altered by an emotion. The obvious example is being in a state of fear and 'jumping out of your skin' in response to even a harmless sudden stimulus.

3 By means of the autonomic nervous system, emotions play a role in controlling the activity of the body's physiology. The body's reactions, e.g. those of the circulation and gut, are different in fear as compared to joy. Emotions *coordinate* behaviour and physiology (e.g. in fear, running is associated with heart rate acceleration) (Hess, 1981).

4 Each emotion involves a subjective conscious experience ('experiential factor'). There is a characteristic feeling of being afraid and this is very different from the experience of joy or embarrassment. Emotions are characterized by pleasure and pain, termed 'affect' (Chapter 2, 'Genes, environment and evolution'). We want to repeat those situations associated with positive affect, whereas we try to avoid those of negative affect.

5 Emotions influence the brain's information processing (Windmann and Krüger, 1998), e.g. how the brain interprets information and its focus of attention. They play a role in memory. Events associated with strong emotions are likely to be stored well in memory and often surface regularly.

6 An emotion can trigger a few stereotyped patterns of muscular activity, for example, those controlling the

human face muscles. Thereby, human facial expressions reveal emotion (Ekman, 1992).

Figure 12.1 summarizes the role of emotion. A number of different stimuli, S_1, S_2, S_3..., trigger a particular emotion. In turn, the emotion organizes a number of functionally coherent effects: on behaviour, physiology ('Autonomic'), on sensory processing, on enhancing memory for the events, on reflexes and on affective states ('Subjective').

Not just for humans but looking more broadly across species, when in a particular emotional state, animals have a *tendency* to behave in certain ways, e.g. in fear, to freeze or flee. According to the emotion, there is a set of highly probable outputs of somatic and autonomic nervous systems (Hess, 1981).

Anger or fear (e.g. running from a charging bull) activates the sympathetic branch of the autonomic nervous system (ANS) (Chapter 3, 'The nervous and endocrine systems'). The terms 'emotion' and 'emotional arousal' are used synonymously with 'sympathetic activation' (Lang, 1988). However, there can be situations termed 'emotional' in which the parasympathetic branch is activated (Vingerhoets, 1985). The latter occur where the animal remains immobile, e.g. faced by a predator or in submitting to a dominant animal. In a rather different state, relaxation is associated with reduced sympathetic and increased parasympathetic activity. The heart beats less energetically and blood is conveyed to the gut to facilitate digestion and absorption.

The effects of emotion on cognition are manifest in changes in perception and memory. The subjective aspect of emotions cannot be measured directly, though facial reactions are strongly indicative of it. By definition, only the person experiencing emotion can give a verbal report of a subjective state. However, we make guesses of subjective state based upon empathy with fellow humans and might extrapolate that the cry of an animal in pain is an effective communication of subjective state.

The sections that follow will describe and link the four aspects to emotion: (1) behavioural, (2) physiological, (3) cognitive and (4) subjective/affective.

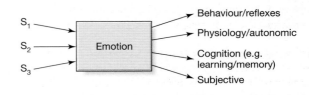

Figure 12.1 Any of a number of stimuli, S_1, S_2,..., trigger an emotion, which has the coordinated effects shown.

Section summary

1 Emotion has functionally coherent effects on behaviour, physiology, cognition and subjective affect.

2 Emotions play a role in favouring certain courses of action.

3 Particular emotions trigger some rather stereotyped reactions, e.g. human facial reactions.

4 Emotion and emotional arousal usually mean activation of the sympathetic system.

Test your knowledge

(Answer on page 328)

12.1 Complete the following: 'Embarrassment is associated with the _____ of blood vessels just under the skin. The smooth muscles that line the walls of the blood vessels are under the control of the _____ nervous system'.

The nature and function of emotion

This section considers what emotions are and the nature of their triggers. It shows how a parallel consideration of causation, development/learning, evolution and function can increase our understanding of emotion.

Linking causation, function and evolution

Emotions have an influence on a range of processes, from voluntary behaviour to reflexes. This section considers some points on this range and the associated functional significance.

A limited flexibility under pressure

Imagine you confront the same bear in the forest, as in Chapter 3. From the perspective of your survival, the bear needs to command your undivided attention and to be at the 'spotlight of conscious awareness' (Baars, 1997). Other potential demands that are less urgent (e.g. seeking food) can be put off until later. You have never seen a bear before. So what do you do? Do you search your memory for a rational solution to the problem, trying to remember earlier encounters with large objects and carefully weighing up the possibilities for action? Most probably not, since time is too pressing.

The emotion of fear automatically gives priority to certain options and acts against others (Tooby and Cosmides, 1990). For example, you might instantly flee or freeze. The nervous system appears to be programmed to react with fear to any large moving object (cf. Damasio, 1996). Our ancestors in evolution were confronted by large menacing animals and this suggests an evolutionary history for the reaction.

Suppose that you decide to run to a tree. Skeletal muscles need energy and oxygen. Fear triggers sympathetic activation, which increases the muscles' blood supply. Note the functional significance of the emotion: it exerts compatible influences over behaviour and physiology. Given the luxury of time and a safe distance, declarative memories of past fear-related situations might be revived and brought to conscious awareness, with possible solutions suggested.

There are two cautions that need to be made here. (1) Our evolutionary heritage cannot tell us exactly what to do in a situation. It can only favour some options over others. (2) A particular favoured option might turn out to be a mistake – after all, bears can run fast and climb trees! Emotions create tendencies to do what, on average, succeeded in our evolutionary past.

Tightly organized muscular reactions

An emotion creates a strong tendency to behave in a limited range of ways but with some flexibility with what is actually done. However, it also triggers some relatively fixed and inflexible reactions. The underlying principle has application to a few specialized cases in numerous species: emotions exert control over rather stereotyped patterns of neuromuscular activity. Psychologists assume that, where showing specific reactions has been successful in evolution, the underlying controls will be hard-wired in the CNS. This is an economic way of solving a problem.

We noted earlier the case of the human facial muscles and their control by emotion. For another example, Darwin (1872/1934) observed the principle of 'antithesis': a dog's posture in one emotion (e.g. anger) can be the opposite of that in an opposed emotion (e.g. joy). See Figure 12.2. This is an effective and unambiguous means of communication between dogs – and incidentally from dog to human! A similar principle of hard-wiring is illustrated by the calls made by a number of species. These are stereotyped and enable emotional states to be discriminated, e.g. for social species, the distress call at separation is distinct from the call of comfort at reunion with a parent (Panksepp *et al.*, 1978; Kalin *et al.*, 1995).

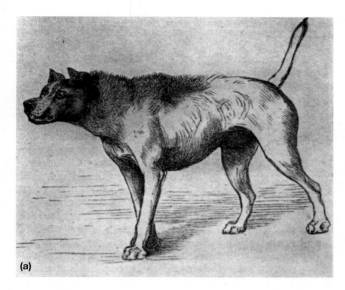

Figure 12.2 Two opposite emotions and associated reactions: (a) hostility and (b) as Darwin described it, 'a humble and affectionate frame of mind'.

Source: Darwin (1872/1934, Figs. 1 and 2, pp. 1 and 15).

Learning, memory and individual experience

Although emotions create some tendencies that are universals, we should not ignore the role of *individual* learning in the production of emotions and their expression. There are universal emotions but learning adjusts both what triggers them and their precise form of expression. For example, being in a place associated with trauma in the past (e.g. the earlier experience of seeing a bear in the forest) can trigger fear (Gray, 1987a). Emotions enhance the formation of memories for the emotion-producing event (Bower, 1992; Herz, 1997). If the representation is tagged as emotional in this way, merely seeing, or thinking about, the forest can affect future decision-making. In future, it would be advantageous to show caution in the forest or stay away. We might develop a fear of forests, even though we loved them prior to this. Unfortunately, such a process can lead to irrational fears.

Affective neuroscience

Introduction

The expression **affective neuroscience** refers to a school of neuroscience that now forms a principal focus for the study of emotion. It is associated with Panksepp (1998a), who claims that there are systems of emotion and affect that have crucially important common characteristics across different mammalian species. Some of these are shared with non-mammals, e.g. birds. Affective neuroscience has also become a banner and rallying call to psychologists (a) to put emotions at 'centre-stage', (b) to see an evolutionary continuity of affect and emotion and (c) to give the study of subjective events its rightful place in psychology. It is a call for *affective* neuroscience to take its place alongside *cognitive* neuroscience (Davidson *et al.*, 2002).

Of course, it is obvious that human and non-human species alike exhibit such outward manifestations of emotion as attack and escape, accompanied by autonomic changes. However, Panksepp goes further than this and urges a leap across species boundaries in making the assumption that non-human animals have emotional and affective *experiences* similar to our own. Panksepp (1994, p. 37) suggests that emotions shared by all mammals are: 'anger–rage, anxiety–fear, joy–play–happiness, sorrow–distress, and curiosity'. Anger–rage is suggested by attacking and biting, whereas fear is suggested by freezing and fleeing. Alarm calls of an isolated animal are indicative of sorrow–distress.

Panksepp writes (p. 29):

> From the moment of birth, brain emotional systems allow humans to begin operating in the world as spontaneously active organisms with a variety of ingrained values and goals that mould and become moulded by experience.

Neural bases

Panksepp postulates that the basic neural systems that underlie emotions have the following characteristics:

1. They are very similar in structure and function across vertebrate species. They were laid down in subcortical structures early in mammalian evolution and have changed relatively little.

2. They are largely specified by genetic information and are therefore very similar among members of a given species.

3. When different species are compared, it is evident that a given emotion is associated with similar, if not identical, physiological (e.g. hormonal) changes.

4. Different species possess some very different brain structures outside the regions specifically concerned with emotion (e.g. newly evolved cortical structures). There are

also vastly different bodies and ecological niches. This means different triggers to emotion and different modes of emotional expression.

5 The potential for affective experience is established by basic brain regions, though how that potential is channelled depends on individual experience.

Some evidence within affective neuroscience derives from electrical stimulation of subcortical regions of non-humans. Interpretations are reinforced by the effects of chemical manipulations, which excite or inhibit emotional expression. Homologous structures exist in humans and it seems reasonable that they serve a similar function. Damage to some brain regions leaves the capacity to perceive a stimulus intact but disrupts the capacity to attach emotional significance to it (Le Doux, 1998), hence producing an (albeit tentative and grey) line of fracture between emotion and cognition. Conversely, emotion appears to survive lesions to other regions (e.g. newly evolved regions of cortex), which disrupts cognition (Le Doux, 1998).

Panksepp (1994, p. 45) suggests the following criteria for defining neural systems of emotion:

1 The underlying circuits respond unconditionally to stimuli arising from major life-challenging circumstances. That is, we do not need to learn to fear certain events. The system is formed so as to react to life-threatening triggers.

2 The circuits organize those forms of behaviour (and concurrent autonomic-hormonal changes) that have proved adaptive in the face of such life-challenging circumstances during the evolutionary history of the species.

3 Emotive circuits change the sensitivities of sensory systems relevant for the behaviour sequences that have been aroused.

4 Neural activity of emotive systems outlasts the triggering circumstances. Suppose that a trigger to fear (e.g. predator) appears and then goes out of sight. The fear does not fall immediately but persists.

5 Emotive circuits can come under the conditional control of emotionally neutral environmental stimuli. Neutral stimuli paired with unconditional triggers become conditional triggers to emotion.

6 Emotive circuits have reciprocal interactions with brain mechanisms that elaborate higher decision-making processes and consciousness.

Panksepp suggests that raw affective experience is critically dependent on the activity of a collection of distributed brain systems. Of course, the cognitive side of emotion can be very different comparing, say, humans and mice. Language presumably gives us a much wider

experience of emotion, e.g. based upon mental reflection. However, at base when comparing mammalian species, Panksepp suggests that we can identify common features of brain mechanisms and their expression. Although there are differences among species in emotional expression, there are also some striking similarities in function, which also encourages a search for similar underlying processes (Le Doux, 1998). For example, although a deer might run, a fish swim and a bird fly from danger, at a level of function each different motor response serves the same end of distancing from danger (Plutchik, 1980). Similarly, the adaptive advantage of freezing with fear would seem to pose similar design considerations across species.

Subjective experience

Identifying the properties of conscious states can help the search for underlying neural systems (Panksepp, 1994). For example, emotions, as subjectively felt, commonly linger for a long time after the triggering event has terminated and, presumably, there is neural activity that lasts the same time.

In treating and studying schizophrenic and cancer patients, Heath (1986) obtained correlations between stimulated electrical activity in brain regions (septum and regions of the amygdala) and the patient's report of pleasure. Correlated changes in electrical activity and subjective report followed a manipulation such as the administration of drugs. The pain of cancer was reduced by stimulating the so-called pleasure regions of the brain (Chapter 15, 'Motivation'). Other brain regions, including parts of the amygdala, are associated with negative affect when stimulated.

A subjectively described emotion that causes distress in modern society is anxiety, an ill-defined free-floating fear of events that might happen (Ramos and Mormède, 1998). Sometimes it takes the form of existential angst (fear of existence and a perceived meaningless life) and we only have insight from verbal reports of sufferers. However, by adopting a comparative perspective, there are a number of animal models that might represent features of human anxiety. For example, an anxiety-evoking situation for rats is the elevated maze (a maze located some distance off the ground). A rat is placed on an elevated plus-maze, having two open and two closed arms, and its reluctance to go out onto the open arms is a measure of anxiety.

Biological determination or cultural relativity?

Evolution and Darwin

Darwin (1872/1934) emphasized the role that emotions play in evolution. He believed that emotions continue to be useful in humans (p. 171): 'Expression in itself, or the language of the emotions, is certainly of importance for the welfare of mankind'. However, Darwin's reader is left to speculate whether some human emotion is still adaptive, or is adaptive in a different way from the advantage it served in earlier evolution. Adaptive value might change in the course of evolution, a form of 'inertia'. An example is that of baring the teeth by angry humans (see Griffiths, 1997). Darwin speculated that originally this was a preliminary to attack, for which the teeth were employed. Now it forms part of the facial signal of anger but could still be adaptive.

Public display of emotion is sometimes said to be irrational and people are urged not to be emotional. This assumes conflict between emotions and rational cognition. On occasion we react in response to *gut*-feelings (note the expression) and later regret it. However, the fact that we sometimes get it wrong does not argue against an adaptive value of emotions, any more than our diet not always being optimal shows that it is maladaptive to feed. Emotion and cognition normally operate as an integrated whole, with emotion exerting an influence on decision-making. In this way, some appropriate consideration is usually made of the likely affective consequences of an action (Damasio, 1996).

Darwin classified the expressions of emotion in various species including humans. He also made cross-cultural comparisons to explore whether emotions are universal or culturally relative, finding that widely different cultures show much the same emotions. For example, the triggers to, say, disgust cause similar facial reactions across cultures. These are also observed in blind people, who have not had the opportunity to learn by imitation.

Social constructivism

Are human emotions biologically determined universals, as Darwin believed, or culturally relative constructions? Focusing on the diversity of emotional expression in different cultures, rather than its consistency, **social constructivism** suggests that emotions are culturally relative. For example, they might be reactions that are imitations of culture-specific role models. Particular emotions might be reinforced by a particular society. This is sometimes couched as being in opposition to biological determination. In a given situation, some cultures would find emotional reactivity appropriate whereas others would discourage it. For example, within Europe, continentals commonly find amusement at the apparent coolness of the English (Darwin, 1872/1934, p. 134). Is it then unrealistic to seek universal biological underpinnings?

In confronting what is often presented as a neat dichotomy between biology and culture, caution is needed. Inevitably, biology and culture each have a role to play in emotional development (Chapter 6, 'Development and plasticity'). So, any dichotomy of biology *versus* culture is surely false. A further complication is that similarities in behaviour within a species can owe as much to universal features of environments as to similar genetic contributions (Chapter 2).

A point concerns the aspect of emotion that is being compared. Is it emotional expression or the cognitive triggers of emotion? There appear to be just a few emotions that are common across cultures and even species but, within certain limits, different culture-specific stimuli trigger them (Panksepp, 1998a). Griffiths (1997, p. 55) noted that studies by Ekman: 'show that people in all cultures respond in a similar way to things that frighten them. They do not show that people in all cultures respond in a similar way to the same things'.

On a spectrum of universality versus relativity, the safest location is doubtless somewhere between the extremes. Let's assume a few universal brain structures that organize a small number of basic emotions located under the broad headings of positive /approach and negative/withdrawal (Panksepp, 1994). These structures show evolutionary continuities across species and similarities between individuals. There appear to be some universal triggers of emotion (e.g. fear to large moving animals or falling), panic and depression to the loss of a loved one. They are manifest in behaviour early in development, such as anger at frustration at being thwarted in reaching for an object (see Griffiths, 1997).

There are also culture-specific aspects to triggers. The way in which emotions are triggered and expressed can differ to some extent between cultures and individuals, as a function of imitation and reinforcement, etc. (Cacioppo *et al.*, 1992). Humans learn the cultural norms of emotional expression. Presumably, there is a two-way flow of information, from the brain mechanism underlying emotion to its culturally coloured expression and also from the culture-specific environment to the basic emotion.

Cultural relativity can be applied to the public expression of universal emotions, something Ekman (1984) terms **display rules**. Thus, people from Japan exhibit similar reactions to Americans when they are alone but suppress emotional expression in the presence of an experimenter. Voluntary controls that enable expression to be suppressed would seem a likely candidate for cultural relativity and individual differences (Cacioppo *et al.*, 1992).

The development of emotion in non-human animals is also dependent to some extent on the environment (Griffiths, 1997). Monkeys that have been socially deprived exhibit fear but the reaction is less easily interpreted by other monkeys than is the fear reaction of an animal that experienced a normal social development (Miller *et al.*, 1967). In dogs, normal development of the experience of pain and avoidance of damaging stimuli depends upon social factors (Melzack and Scott, 1957).

Stimuli and their appraisal

You might recall events that have in the past triggered your emotions, such as hearing a loud explosion. Such triggers to emotion can be understood in terms of their intrinsic physical properties. Contrast this with the fear that you would feel if you calculated your income and outgoings, finding that your accounts did not balance. Such emotion is triggered not by an external event as such but only after sophisticated cognitive processing of external events.

Scientific evidence conforms to common-sense experience: emotions are triggered by both raw sensory features and the interpretation placed upon sensory events (Lazarus, 1984). Some emotions are primitive, rapid responses to situations and can bypass cognition (Zajonc, 1980). For example, by their intrinsic quality, certain odours elicit positive and negative emotions (Alaoui-Ismaïli *et al.*, 1997). In many species, only basic processing is needed for the fear that is triggered by snakes (Le Doux, 1989).

The term 'cognition' can be used to refer to the 'high-level', longer and slower route by which emotion is produced. There is an interpretation (which might, or might not, correspond to reality) before emotion is experienced. An important aspect of therapy for such disorders as anxiety (Salkovskis, 1985) and coronary heart disease (Allan and Scheidt, 1996a) is getting patients to *interpret* emotionally sensitive events in less negative and threatening ways (Chapter 13, 'Stress and coping').

In humans, the triggers for emotion appear to vary on a continuum from (i) stimuli as such that act directly and automatically to (ii) cognitive interpretations of stimuli, involving goals and the perception of the intentions of others, etc. (Johnson and Multhaup, 1992; Stein and Jewett, 1986). Evolutionary considerations suggest the retention of a quick and effective emotional system.

Unconscious determinants

Reflecting a rapid route to emotion, there can be triggers that do not reach conscious awareness. See Figure 12.3 (Winkielman *et al.*, 2005). Participants were set the task of deciding the gender of a person presented in an image for 400 ms ('gender identification'). They were then asked to pour, consume and assess a drink. Prior to the gender identification task, they were presented with subliminal images (i.e. images that failed to reach conscious awareness). The images ('subliminal emotion') were of happy, neutral or angry faces and were presented for 16 ms. As is shown in Figure 12.4, the subliminal images affected the amount of drink poured and consumed.

Claparède's patient, Madame X (Chapter 11, 'Learning and memory'), illustrated a similar point. She showed fear in her behaviour but could not consciously recall the episode that triggered the fear (the hidden pin in the hand).

Consciousness seems so immediate and pressing and indeed we often have conscious insight into the determinants of our emotion. However, we sometimes assume that it provides a privileged and infallible route but this may not always be so (Bauer and Verfaellie, 1992).

Social interaction

Emotion plays a central role in social interactions between animals both during development and when adult.

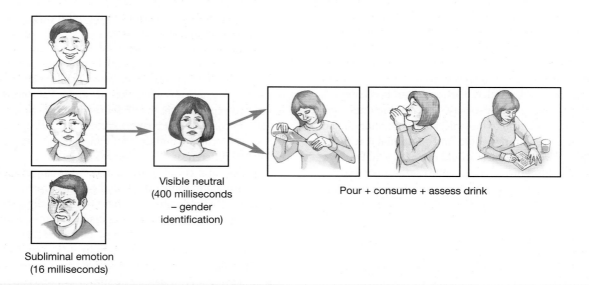

Subliminal emotion
(16 milliseconds)

Visible neutral
(400 milliseconds
– gender
identification)

Pour + consume + assess drink

Figure 12.3 Experimental design employed by Winkielman *et al.* (2005).
Source: Toates (2004, Fig. 1.2, page 5).

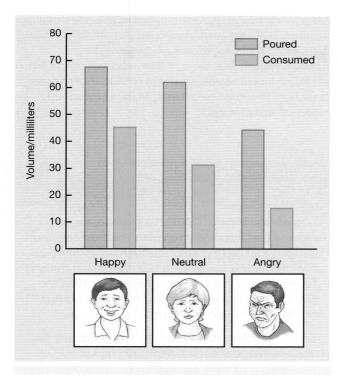

Figure 12.4 Results obtained by Winkielman *et al.* (2005).

Source: Toates (2004, Fig. 1.3, page 5).

Emotions play a role in interactions between adult social animals, as in triggering vocal signals and in interpreting them. In some species, e.g. squirrel monkeys (Ploog, 1986), vocalizations are specific to different emotions. In humans, vocalization has, of course, obtained some autonomy from emotions, though it can still sometimes be a good index of them.

In humans, emotions are associated with characteristic facial reactions as part of a 'package'. Meeting a new person (or even a new dog!), whom we perceive to be of good intention, is accompanied by positive emotion, involving approach, eye contact and smiling. The same solution can be employed on numerous occasions. We decipher signals emitted by others. Seeing that another has an expression of disapproval does not tell us exactly what to expect but it reduces the possibilities.

Emotions have a privileged route to the motor control programmes that underlie facial expression and are central to social interaction (Ekman *et al.*, 1983). They are not the only route: we have some voluntary conscious control over our expressions. However, this is limited. It is difficult to fake facial expressions by will-power, something politicians and bad actors learn to their embarrassment (Damasio, 1996).

We now look at a few examples of particular emotions, illustrating in more detail some of the points made so far.

Consider an infant rat that gets isolated. Its vocalizations seem to indicate negative emotion (Panksepp, 1994). They alert the mother to the pup's state and location and they facilitate retrieval.

The sound and facial expression of a human baby crying seem also to indicate negative emotion. The baby persists until a caregiver takes corrective action, e.g. feeding or bringing a source of warmth. For the very young baby, one does not need to postulate awareness of intentions or goals; emotions seem to organize reactions automatically. In mothers, the recorded sound of a baby's cry triggers activation in brain regions concerned with emotional processing (Lorberbaum *et al.*, 2002). This is associated with subjective emotions of sadness, anxiety and an urge to help. On the more positive side, an infant's smile can evoke emotions of approach from the caregiver.

In their social interaction, there appear to be mutual reward and positive reinforcement between child and caregiver (Tronick, 1989). Emotional expression forms an important part of the behavioural interaction. From this beginning, the child's capacity to exert social control emerges (Chorpita and Barlow, 1998). Such infant emotions, together with the action they help to trigger and their consequences, develop into voluntary and goal-directed action. As Tronick notes, emotions guide and motivate emerging social interaction rather than disrupt it.

Section summary

1 An emotion favours a limited range of behavioural options.

2 Emotions trigger certain specific responses, exemplified by the reactions of the human facial muscles.

3 Affective neuroscience suggests that there are a few universal brain structures that organize a small number of basic emotions, under the broad headings of positive/approach or negative/withdrawal. These structures are similar across mammalian species.

4 Although there are some biological universals to human emotion, the stimuli that trigger emotion and the form of its expression are sensitive to cultural differences.

5 There are certain determinants of emotion that do not reach conscious awareness.

6 Emotions and affect play a fundamental role in the dynamics of social interaction.

Test your knowledge

(Answer on page 328)

12.2 Complete the following, which relates to conditioning: 'Emotion and affect are triggered by certain _____ stimuli and also by _____ stimuli. The latter class owe their efficacy to pairing with _____ stimuli'.

Some emotions and their triggers

This section looks at some representative emotions and their triggers: fear, the anger associated with frustration, embarrassment, trust and social attachment.

Fear

A range of events trigger fear, some of them evident on first exposure and others reflecting learned experience. This section considers a part of this range of triggers.

A special adaptation

Certain stimuli trigger intense fear in humans, a notable example being snakes (Öhman and Mineka, 2003). A number of species, including other primates, also show such fear of snakes and it appears to reflect an ancient evolutionary adaptation. Not only do most humans show strong fear, but we form aversive conditional associations with snakes more rapidly than with control stimuli.

Le Doux (1989) considers the reaction to the image of a snake at the eyes. An immediate automatic response is withdrawal of one's body from a snake on the path just under the feet. In a quite different context, your cognitions (p. 272): 'determine that a snake is a vertebrate, that it is biologically closer to an alligator than to a cow . . .'. The reasoning is done at a safe distance, say in a zoo. It involves semantic associations and consciousness and does not necessarily lead to any emotion or behaviour.

Consider the two following claims:

- If the fear of snakes is evolutionarily old, it might not require conscious awareness for its expression.
- Unconscious emotional organization is usually assumed to be mediated by subcortical mechanisms (Öhman and Mineka, 2003).

To illuminate these claims, the technique of backward masking was employed. A brief visual 'test' stimulus of a snake image (duration 30 ms) was presented, followed immediately by a masking stimulus. The masking stimulus is known to disrupt cortical processing of the test stimulus. Participants could not consciously perceive the test stimulus. Nonetheless, those of them who expressed a fear of snakes showed an enhanced skin conductance response (a measure of autonomic activity) to the unconsciously processed snake images.

Evolutionary psychology
A fear module

Öhman and Mineka (2001, 2003) propose a fear module that is specially tuned to the most common dangers that were present throughout mammalian evolution. Thus, we tend to fear snakes and spiders far more than guns and cars. This is in spite of the fact that the latter present a vastly greater threat to those of us living in industrialized societies.

Öhman and Mineka suggest that the module is fast and automatic and it has dedicated neural processes as its basis, centred on the amygdala. The module is encapsulated ('self-contained') in that it is influenced little, if at all, by advanced human conscious cognition. For example, people suffering from phobias usually acknowledge that their fears are irrational and excessive but such conscious insight does little or nothing to calm them (Mineka and Öhman, 2002). (Of course, certain TV naturalists make their living by handling deadly snakes. Such people are either fear-deficient or able to exert considerable inhibition on any fear module.) It is not merely snakes that are able to trigger the module. In primates including humans, threatening faces also have easy access to it.

Unconditional and conditional stimuli

A number of stimuli elicit fear on first presentation. For example, a rat does not have to learn how to freeze based upon trauma (Bolles, 1970). On first confrontation with a predator (e.g. a cat) and where escape is impossible, rats freeze, a species-specific defence reaction (SSDR).

Neutral stimuli paired with unconditional emotional stimuli acquire a conditional capacity to evoke emotion. For example, exposure of rats to the hair from a cat immediately reduces play, as they assume a fearful posture (Panksepp, 1998a). Subsequently, rats show fear in the cage (a conditional fear) even though all signs of cat have been eliminated. This biases behaviour towards vigilance and caution, and away from play.

For another example, pairing a bell with a shock (UCS) gives the bell a fear-evoking property as a CS. Such fear conditioning is possible across various animal groups, including fruit-flies, snails, birds, lizards, fish, rabbits, rats, monkeys and humans (Le Doux, 1994). This strongly points to its adaptive advantage. In rats, a cue paired with shock disrupts the appetitive behaviour of lever-pressing for food reward, termed a **conditioned emotional response** procedure.

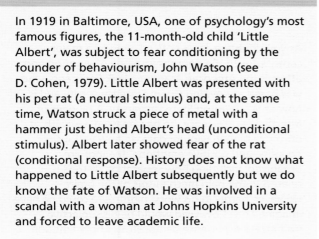

A personal angle

Little Albert

In 1919 in Baltimore, USA, one of psychology's most famous figures, the 11-month-old child 'Little Albert', was subject to fear conditioning by the founder of behaviourism, John Watson (see D. Cohen, 1979). Little Albert was presented with his pet rat (a neutral stimulus) and, at the same time, Watson struck a piece of metal with a hammer just behind Albert's head (unconditional stimulus). Albert later showed fear of the rat (conditional response). History does not know what happened to Little Albert subsequently but we do know the fate of Watson. He was involved in a scandal with a woman at Johns Hopkins University and forced to leave academic life.

Subsequent research has shown that classical conditioning of fear is not quite the simple process envisaged by Watson. Some 'neutral stimuli' are easier to turn into CSs than are others (Öhman, 1986). Little Albert's rat could well have already been a candidate that is strongly biased towards fear-triggering. It is easier to condition elevated levels of anxiety to snake-related 'neutral stimuli', such as pictures of snakes, than to flower-related neutral stimuli (Öhman and Mineka, 2003).

Frustration

Frustration describes the particular quality of the emotion of anger that is triggered when an actual state of the world is less good than an expected and desired state. This is an example of where an emotion can only be understood in terms of a sensory event in context, i.e. reality compared against the expectation. The anger associated with frustration might seem like a peculiarly human emotion but this appears not to be the case. Rats show a negative emotion of this kind. One way to induce it is to train a rat to earn pellets in a Skinner box and then put it on extinction conditions (omit the pellets). The emotion causes the release of stress hormones (Chapter 13) and an increased tendency to escape or aggression, depending upon the environment (Gray, 1987a).

Lewis et al. (1990) examined human infants, age 2–8 months, who were presented with the reward of an audiovisual stimulus. Presentation either was made following an arm movement ('contingent condition') or was made irrespective of any arm movement ('non-contingent condition'). Facial expressions were observed. Infants in the contingent condition showed a higher index of interest and joy during the acquisition phase and greater anger in extinction. Lewis et al., concluded that extinction causes frustration as a result of loss of control. The positive emotion at acquisition and frustration at extinction indicate sensitivity and flexibility of the infant's interaction with the environment. The fact that such emotions were not seen in the non-contingent group points to the role of the active participation of the child in emotion. Anger under extinction conditions was associated with an *intensification* of the arm movement that had been instrumental.

Embarrassment

So-called 'violations of social conventions', e.g. belching, trigger an emotion of embarrassment that is distinct from shame, fear and guilt (Keltner and Buswell, 1997). People perceive that they have little control over such a situation, which arises by accident rather than intention, are uncertain how to act and report feeling (p. 254) 'funny, awkward, foolish, nervous, surprised, and self-conscious'. Embarrassment is accompanied by smiles, laughter, disturbances to speech, shifting eye positions, a 'rigid slouched posture', aversion and a so-called 'silly smile'. Blushing consists of a reddening of the face, neck, ears and the upper regions of the chest. It is caused by enlargement of surface capillaries.

Is the autonomic adjustment that is associated with embarrassment characteristic of just this emotion? Blood flow to the cheek increased more when people were placed in an embarrassing situation than one associated with fear. Embarrassment is associated with a reduction in heart-rate, suggestive of a move towards parasympathetic and away from sympathetic activation.

Darwin (1872/1934) referred to blushing as (p. 153) 'the most human of all expressions', suggesting something uniquely human. However, Keltner and Buswell (1997) see human embarrassment as part of an evolutionary continuity, which is related to social appeasement in non-humans. An embarrassed human, e.g. assuming a hunched posture, has similarities to other species in appeasement. A dominant conspecific showing threat is the trigger for a subordinate's appeasement and a threat to social identity triggers embarrassment. In group-living species, appeasement sends signals to a conspecific that might serve to restore social stability. The evolutionary roots could lie in embarrassment being a gesture of submission that restores social stability by evoking sympathy in others or at least deflects hostility.

Trust

An emotion of trust is one that is central to successful human social relations. It involves tilting the approach/avoidance reactions to another human in the direction of approach (Kosfeld *et al.*, 2005). Kosfeld *et al.*, found that the application of the neurohormone oxytocin via a nasal spray to people during a business negotiation increased the amount of trust that they showed. In a number of species, oxytocin is a neurohormone involved in forming bonds. The effect obtained by Kosfeld *et al.*, was specifically a social one; oxytocin neither increased a general tendency to risk-taking nor did it enhance mood. Within bounds, trust is, of course, a good thing but you might prefer to be a little cautious of someone who tries to waft synthetic oxytocin in your direction.

Attachment and social distress

An index of a negative emotion, 'distress', is given by **distress vocalization** (DV): the crying that the young of all mammalian species (and some non-mammalian) exhibit following enforced separation from a caregiver (Herman and Panksepp, 1978). Figure 12.5 shows the distress vocalizations of guinea pigs as a function of age and different contexts. The close proximity of a caregiver suppresses DVs. This is usually most effectively the mother but in some species the father is particularly good in this role.

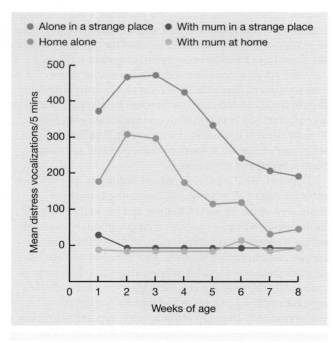

Figure 12.5 Distress vocalizations of guinea pigs.

Source: Panksepp (1998a, Figure 14.3, p.266).

The term **opioid** refers to a particular natural neurochemical employed by the CNS. On the basis of their chemical form and function, opioids are part of a group of neurochemicals termed **neuropeptides**. Opioids play a role in reducing social distress and social contact triggers their release. The related term **opiate** refers to the drug class represented by heroin, which has opioid agonist properties.

In humans, breaking bonds, as in separation, divorce and bereavement, might have features in common with separation distress in non-humans (Panksepp, 1986).

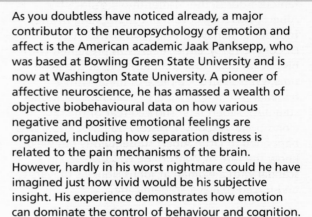

A personal angle

A psychobiologist's awful insight

As you doubtless have noticed already, a major contributor to the neuropsychology of emotion and affect is the American academic Jaak Panksepp, who was based at Bowling Green State University and is now at Washington State University. A pioneer of affective neuroscience, he has amassed a wealth of objective biobehavioural data on how various negative and positive emotional feelings are organized, including how separation distress is related to the pain mechanisms of the brain. However, hardly in his worst nightmare could he have imagined just how vivid would be his subjective insight. His experience demonstrates how emotion can dominate the control of behaviour and cognition.

Let me quote Jaak's own words, which describe the efforts of his friends to persuade him to continue writing his classic text, *Affective Neuroscience* (Panksepp, 1998a, p.x):

' . . . during the middle of the present efforts, I underwent the most painful time of my life: My precious daughter, Tiina Alexandra, died along with three friends, on a dismal Good Friday evening in 1991 when a drunken driver, evading arrest, careened into their car. After that event, my spirit was demoralized, and I could not face the labours of this book for several years. Through the magic of friends and modern psychiatric drugs, my spirits were partially restored'.

In the sphere of emotions, life and science can meet in a most poignant way. Jaak's experience demonstrates vividly that brain systems that serve adaptive functions can be the source of sustained emotional distress. However, even out of the extremes of tragedy can come good: human empathy is such that Jaak was led to establish a Memorial Foundation for Lost Children. This demonstrates the motivational role of emotion.

Studying non-humans offers possible insight into such human conditions as the depression that can follow separation (Panksepp *et al.*, 1988).

So far, we have focused on triggers to emotion from outside the body. The following section looks at internal factors – the role of feedback from the periphery in central emotion.

Section summary

1 There are some particularly potent triggers to fear, e.g. snakes in the case of humans. Such observations lead to the notion of an adapted 'fear-module'.

2 Frustration is induced when a desired and expected state of the world fails to occur.

3 Violations of social conventions trigger embarrassment. It is associated with parasympathetic activation.

4 Oxytocin enhances trust.

5 Breaking a social bond triggers distress. This is evident across a range of mammalian species and has an identifiable neurochemical basis.

Test your knowledge

(Answers on page 328)

12.3 In terms of classical conditioning and Little Albert, how would the rat be described (i) prior to Albert meeting Watson, (ii) after the experience with Watson?

12.4 With regard to Figure 12.5, what would be the expected effect on DVs of injecting an opiate drug, for the groups (i) alone in a strange place and (ii) with mum at home?

Feedback from the periphery

Introduction

People wear particular expressions characteristic of their moods. Was it ever suggested to you to try to 'wear a happy smile'? The implication is that 'putting on' an emotional expression might actually influence the central emotion. We need to consider the role of feedback from the periphery in influencing emotion, as in the case of wearing a smile.

During the history of psychology, argument has raged over the importance of the role of peripheral sensations. Some notable investigators proposed that emotion, as an activity of the CNS, depends upon feedback from the periphery (Damasio, 1996; James, 1890/1950; Schachter and Singer, 1962). This section gives something of the flavour of the discussion. The American philosopher, William James, is regarded as *the* pre-eminent pioneer of psychology. Therefore, his theory is worth discussing, even though few now believe it in quite such a strong form as was advanced by him.

The James–Lange theory

William James and the Danish physician Carl Lange separately suggested that emotion arises as indicated by Figure 12.6(a). James noted that common sense suggests that we see a bear, feel fear and then run. By contrast, he suggested the time sequence that (1) we see the bear, (2) react with the somatic and autonomic nervous systems and (3) feedback from these peripheral reactions determines the emotion as felt subjectively.

Cannon (1927) argued that emotion cannot be as simple as this. For example, the visceral (meaning 'of the organs of the body') changes are too slow to form the basis of emotional experience. If the James–Lange theory were right, subjective emotion would be eliminated by cutting the connection between the periphery and the CNS, yet signs of emotion are not lost (Cannon, 1927).

Suppose that, in response to an emotional event, a person does not react with the somatic nervous system. Only the ANS is strongly activated. Is there sufficient differentiation of autonomic reactions to account for the rich diversity of emotions? There is some differentiation (Ekman *et al.*, 1983). Anger tends to be associated with a stronger reaction by noradrenalin (norepinephrine) and fear by adrenalin (epinephrine) (Henry, 1986). In actors, there is a greater increase in blood pressure and heart-rate in inducing anger than fear. However, peripheral differentiation is probably inadequate to account for the rich variety of emotions.

Cognitive–physiological theory

Basics of the theory

Figure 12.6(b) shows a development of the James–Lange theory. Feedback from the periphery acts in combination with cognition in determining emotion. One prominent theory along these lines places an emphasis on visceral input, as follows.

Although Schachter and Singer (1962) gave an important role to feedback from the viscera, in their theory, feedback

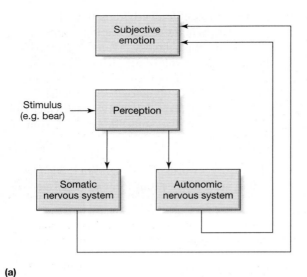

(a)

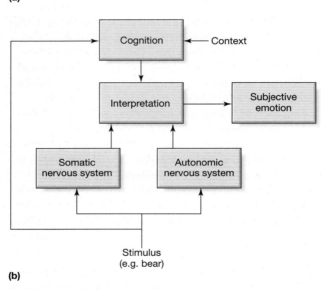

(b)

Figure 12.6 Theories of emotion involving feedback: (a) James–Lange theory and (b) Schachter–Singer theory.

does not determine the *type* of emotion. The type, whether it is joy, fear or anger, is determined by a cognitive interpretation. See Figure 12.6(b). According to this theory, cognition on its own is not able to determine emotion. Rather, the combination of cognition and visceral response determines it. Without cognition, visceral arousal is diffuse and undifferentiated but, given cognition, we can interpret it. The brain searches for meaning and labels visceral arousal in terms of cognitions.

Schachter (1975, p. 531) gives the example:

Imagine a man walking alone down a dark alley when a figure with a gun suddenly appears. The

perception–cognition 'figure with a gun' in some fashion initiates a state of physiological arousal, this state of arousal is interpreted in terms of knowledge about dark alleys and guns, and the state of arousal is labelled 'fear'.

If experienced as part of sexual arousal, the same visceral arousal might be labelled 'joy', 'lust' or 'love'.

Evidence

Is visceral arousal sufficient to produce emotion or is cognition also needed (Schachter, 1975)? Researchers injected people with adrenalin and then asked them to introspect. In most cases, the reply was not indicative of emotion. People tended to respond with 'I feel *as if* I were afraid' or 'I feel *as if* I were happy'. Schachter suggests that they are responding 'cold', on the basis of memories of emotion, but are not experiencing full emotion. In one version of the experiment, participants were given a cognition, e.g. before the injection they were spoken to about deceased relatives. In this condition, in some cases a 'hot' emotional reaction was obtained.

In another study, three groups of people were used: (a) adrenalin injected, (b) control injected and (c) injected with a blocker of sympathetic nervous system activity (Schachter, 1975). In a situation of humour, differences were in the predicted direction: the adrenalin-injected people laughed the most and those injected with the sympathetic blocking agent laughed the least (though criticism can be levelled at such studies; Reisenzein, 1983).

For humans and non-humans, emotional reactivity can survive breaking links from the sympathetic nervous system to the CNS. However, Schachter (1975) suggests that, in such cases, the emotion and its expression were well established, i.e. acquired before breaking the links. He appeals to a study made on patients with breaks to the spinal cord at different levels (paraplegic and quadriplegic patients). Patients were divided into five groups defined by the site of the lesion. The higher the lesion, the less the flow of neurally carried information to and from the viscera, though if the vagus nerve (Chapter 3, 'The nervous and endocrine systems') is intact, some information can still be transmitted via it. Feedback from facial expression and from crying is also intact. In addition, there are chemical means (e.g. hormonal) by which peripheral events might influence the CNS.

Schachter argues that if his formulation is correct, one should see decreasing emotionality as the height of the lesion increases. Emotional reactivity was rated, based upon asking patients about the intensity of emotional experience after injury compared to before. Schachter plotted the data and the prediction was confirmed: the higher the lesion, the lower the emotional reactivity. Reports of the patient's internal state suggest that they feel 'as if' emotionally aroused but their reaction is 'cold'.

Reisenzein (1983) urged caution; patients with spinal cord injuries undergo a variety of changes. They have various sources of information available to the CNS, including factual knowledge of the damage, apart from that mediated via feedback from the periphery. Memory is deceptive and the passage of time necessarily complicates reports from patients made before (intact state) and after (injured state). In patients with injuries to the spinal cord, Chwalisz et al. (1988) reported intense emotional arousal even where there was little feedback from the periphery.

A problem with the formulations of James–Lange and Schachter–Singer is that, before the peripheral emotional reaction can occur, there must be central processing of the significance of the stimulus as a trigger for behaviour and autonomic effects (Le Doux, 1998). At some level, the brain must calculate that a bear is threatening in order to instigate running. It is hard to see that this could be done in an 'emotionless' way.

Contemporary perspectives

General

Contemporary evidence suggests that peripheral signals do play a role in emotion. Feedback from the periphery can amplify central emotion (Chwalisz et al., 1988; Haller et al., 1998; Reisenzein, 1983). Discoveries suggest a range of possibilities for feedback from the periphery to the CNS but still CNS processing is necessary to trigger the peripheral reactions.

Various hormones are released by stress-evoking situations (Chapter 3), some peculiar to the nature of the situation (Panksepp, 1998a). Some influence the CNS, though their time course of action suggests emotional biasing over hours rather than a reaction in a fraction of a second. The arousal of physical exercise can enhance emotions, the quality depending upon context and expectation, etc. (Steptoe, 1993). As will be discussed in Chapter 13, events in the immune system can influence emotion. The reaction to an infection can lead to a depressed mood. This suggests that negatively coloured cognitions are sensitized.

Recent research has located regions of the brain that are specifically activated by feedback signals from the body via the spinal cord and the vagus nerve (Craig, 2004; Critchley et al., 2004). Regions of the insula cortex (termed 'interoceptive cortex' in Figure 14.6, p. 362) among others exhibit sensitivity to interoceptive signals. This information could mediate the influence of the body on day-by-day affective changes. There are indications that people of high emotional sensitivity are particularly tuned to such feedback and have relatively large areas of cortex devoted to interoceptive processing.

Beta-blockers

A reduction in peripheral autonomic activity can be induced with, presumably, a reduction in feedback, by adrenergic blockers (the sympathetic branch employs adrenalin (epinephrine) between neurons and smooth muscles) (Reisenzein, 1983). **Beta-blockers**, employed by actors and musicians to reduce excessive cardiac activity, are in this class. Their action is primarily at cardiac muscle. They reduce peripheral activity but there are mixed reactions as far as anxiety is concerned. Where the principal problem is peripheral arousal (e.g. a perceived heart-rate that is a cause of concern), they are of value but this does not show that the effect is mediated via feedback within the ANS. Where central anxiety without specific reference to peripheral indices is the problem, there is little evidence of efficacy.

Somatic nervous system

What applies to the ANS seems also to apply to the somatic nervous system. For example, motor outflow to, or feedback from, the muscles that determine the expression of the face has some influence on experienced emotion (Chwalisz et al., 1988) and autonomic reactions (Ekman et al., 1983). This is indicated in Figure 12.6(b) by the link 'somatic nervous system' → 'interpretation'. Suppose people are asked to put on particular reactions by the facial muscles, which correspond to particular emotional expressions. However, no emotion is suggested in the request. This has emotion-specific effects on the ANS. Under normal conditions, the facial expression itself would depend upon central emotion, so there appears to be a reciprocal interaction. However, the moral appears to be that it is worth 'putting on' a happy face.

Somatic markers

Damasio (1996) proposes an interactionist view of emotion. Feedback from autonomic and somatic nervous systems and hormonal feedback form an intrinsic part of our emotional profile. The brain cannot usefully be viewed in isolation from the remainder of the body. Emotion and emotional memory have a reference in terms of associated bodily sensations, termed the **somatic-marker hypothesis**. Thus, a memory of fear has a reference in gut feelings. This can literally derive from the viscera, the activation of which would form a loop with the memory currently activated. However, with experience, it might derive from what is termed an **as if loop** of information. This is activity that is intrinsic to the CNS and is based upon a memory of how 'gut feelings feel' (it is 'as if' the body is reacting).

An example of an 'as if' effect was described by Valins (1970). He showed pictures of naked females to males and deceived them by presenting recordings of heartbeats, which the males were told were their own. Valins had control over the recorded heartbeat. Men tended to rate slides as more attractive if they were accompanied by higher heart-rates. One interpretation is that participants had a lifetime of experiencing their own heartbeat mediated over conventional neural channels. The augmented feedback was interpreted in this context. In Damasio's (1996) terms, it would seem that Valins tapped into an 'as if loop', a CNS emotional circuit, that can operate with some independence from normal triggers and simulate peripheral arousal.

The following section looks at brain regions involved in emotion.

Section summary

1 Feedback from autonomic and somatic nervous systems plays a role in emotion.

2 The somatic-marker hypothesis suggests that feedback plays a role in emotion and that memories of feedback can form 'as if' versions of emotional arousal.

Test your knowledge

(Answer on page 328)

12.5 What is the significance of the blood–brain barrier (Chapter 5, 'The brain') for feedback theories of emotion?

Role of brain regions

Introduction

This section looks at the brain regions that form the basis of emotion, in terms of its production (our primary focus) and the interpretation of emotion shown by others. The section assumes that emotion depends upon a number of brain regions acting in interaction. Within this interacting network, different brain regions have rather different roles in emotional processing. Figure 12.7 summarizes a view of the place of emotion as an intermediate factor linking, as inputs, cognition and raw stimuli and, as outputs, behavioural and autonomic reactions. Note the role of feedback from the periphery in emotion. We shall start with the box labelled 'emotional processing'.

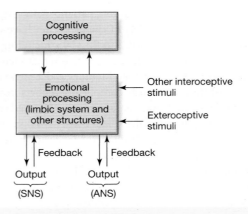

Figure 12.7 Summary of the control of emotion and its role.

The limbic system

Introduction

Traditionally, an important focus for investigating emotion has been the so-called **limbic system** (MacLean, 1958), made up of a number of brain structures, with extensive connections to brain regions outside the system. See Figure 12.7. Information on exteroceptive events (e.g. visual and auditory), as well as interoceptive events (e.g. certain hormone levels), forms inputs to the limbic system. Also, highly processed information ('cognition') is conveyed there. In turn, the limbic system influences cognition, behaviour and the general physiology of the body.

The 'limbic system theory of emotion' proposed that the neural basis of emotion is the interaction between the brain structures that form this system. What has counted as a part of the limbic system has changed somewhat over the years (Oatley and Jenkins, 1996) but has included the septum, cingulate gyrus ('cingulate cortex'), hippocampus and amygdala. Indeed, so flexible has the limbic system proven to be that a number of researchers want the term banned from psychology but it refuses to go. See Figure 12.8. These days, parts of the prefrontal cortex are included in the limbic system, because of their intimate connections with the other limbic regions and their role in emotion.

Experimental evidence

Klüver and Bucy (1939) removed large parts of the temporal lobes, including the amygdala, in monkeys. The subjects became calm and ceased to show normally aggressive and fearful reactions. What became known as the **Klüver–Bucy syndrome** consists of a separation between the sensory processing of stimuli and the attribution of

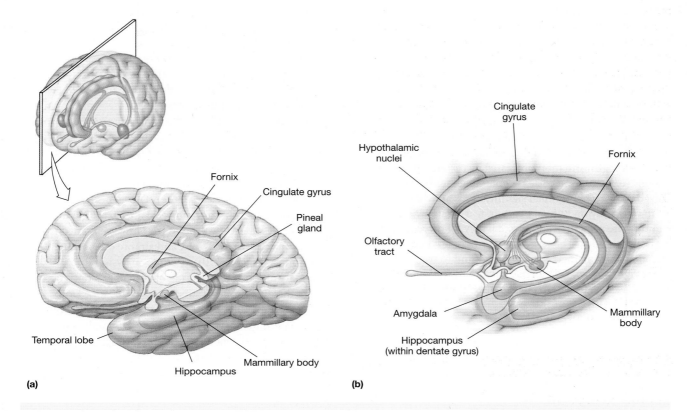

Figure 12.8 Traditional notion of the limbic system. *Source*: Martini *et al.* (2000, Fig. 15–12, p. 394).

emotional and affective value to them (Le Doux, 1992). Sensory processing remains intact but such attribution is disrupted. Similar (but milder) changes occur when a lesion of just the amygdala is made.

Applied to humans, the role of these structures in the production of emotion can be contrasted with that of the cortex in cognitive processing. Electrical stimulation of the limbic system of conscious patients triggers emotion (Ervin and Martin, 1986), whereas stimulation of most of the cortex does not trigger reports of emotion or signs of autonomic activation (Le Doux, 1991).

Ploog (1986) stimulated different parts of the limbic system of squirrel monkeys and obtained different vocal reactions (e.g. growling, shrieking). These correspond, Ploog argued, to the elicitation of different emotions rather than simply the tapping of different motor outputs. Autonomic and somatic responses were elicited at the same time.

A contemporary perspective

The limbic system theory has value in drawing attention to the physical basis for emotions. However, of course, it needs refinement. Trying to define limbic, as opposed to non-

limbic, structures is problematic (Le Doux, 1991). Some authors included newly evolved cortical structures, though they play a role in more than just emotional processing. A clear distinction between limbic (emotional) and cortical (cognitive) processing now appears an over-simplification (Le Doux, 1991). Emotional expression survives cortical removal. However, under more normal conditions the cortex appears to be involved in the fine-tuning of emotional experience and labelling, as implied by the input from cognitive processing in Figure 12.7.

The hippocampus is an area originally assigned to the limbic system, though its role in emotion remains controversial (Gray, 1987a; Le Doux, 1991).

A safe statement regarding the limbic system theory would be along the following lines (cf. Le Doux, 1991). The structures of the system play a role in emotion. However, they do so in interaction with structures outside the system. Furthermore, some structures of the system play roles in processing other than emotional. The safety of the statement needs to be seen in context – a similar claim might be made for almost any link between brain and mind/behaviour!

A part of the limbic system, the amygdala, forms the topic of the next section.

The amygdala

Introduction – linking psychology and structure

Electrical stimulation of the amygdala (see Figure 12.9) in humans is associated with subjective reports of negative or positive emotion, depending upon which nuclei are stimulated (Aggleton and Mishkin, 1986). Aggleton and Mishkin (p. 281) described the amygdala as 'the sensory gateway to the emotions', noting that emotions commonly depend upon a compound of different sources of sensory information. Information processed by certain other brain regions (e.g. temporal cortex) comes together in the amygdala, where emotional significance is attached to it.

In one study on humans, certain fear-related visual stimuli were presented and immediately followed by a masking stimulus. The target stimuli were not perceived consciously. Nonetheless, they were found to trigger activity in the right amygdala (Morris *et al.*, 1998). This pointed to an unconscious trigger to emotion at the amygdala.

Inputs to the amygdala

Inputs to the amygdala arise from various cortical and subcortical sources. Olfactory information has a more direct input to the amygdala than do other sensory channels (Aggleton and Mishkin, 1986) (Chapter 9, 'The other sensory systems'). Note the input from the olfactory bulb in Figure 12.9. Olfactory input (e.g. a pheromone) carries information by virtue of its raw sensory properties as such, whereas the emotional significance of a visual stimulus might only be established after elaborate processing.

There are alternative routes by which some sensory systems project information to the amygdala. Different pathways are concerned with (1) extracting crude features of sensory input rapidly and triggering action (the so-called 'quick and dirty' route) and (2) slower and more refined analysis (the 'slow and clean' route). Thus, sensory information (e.g. from ears and eyes) after reaching the thalamus takes one of two routes (or both simultaneously): the classical route to the cortex and a more direct route to the amygdala (Figure 12.10). A crude analysis, rapid emotional arousal and triggering of certain reactions occur through the direct route (Carlsson *et al.*, 2004; Le Doux, 1989) (Figure 12.10(a)). The speed advantage of the route from thalamus to amygdala is partly because only one synapse is involved, whereas the route through the cortex (Figure 12.10(b)) has several.

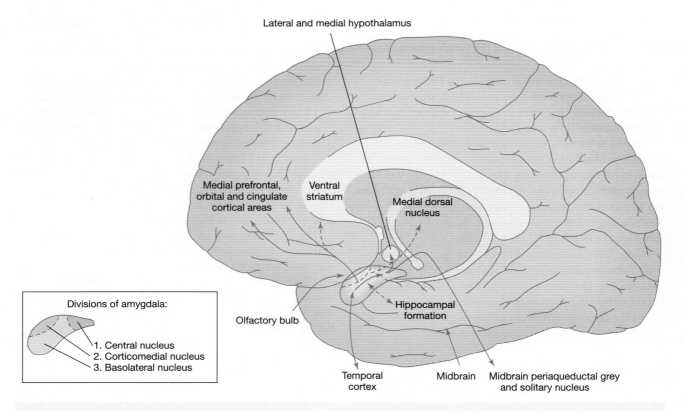

Figure 12.9 The amygdala in relation to other brain regions. Inset: the nuclei of the amygdala.

Source: Figure 15.6 (1996) Martin, JH. Neuroanatomy: Text and Atlas, 2nd Edition, p.458. Reprinted with permission of The McGraw-Hill Companies, Inc.

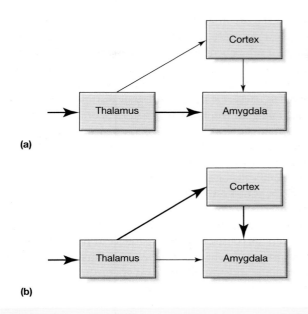

(a)

(b)

Figure 12.10 Routes by which information gets to amygdala: (a) with emphasis upon a direct route from the thalamus and (b) with emphasis upon a route via thalamus and cortex.

Some inputs derive from modality-specific cortical regions (e.g. visual and auditory) (Aggleton and Mishkin, 1986). This input to the amygdala gives an emotional aspect to particular sensory-related events. In addition, there are inputs from regions of cortex that are not modality-specific, e.g. prefrontal cortex. This link is believed to mediate the relationship between advanced stages of cognitive processing and emotion, either to amplify or inhibit emotion according to the nature of the cognition (Carlsson *et al.*, 2004; Drevets, 2001).

The amygdala also receives inputs from the hippocampus, which is involved in cognitive processing. Context is important in emotion and, via signals from the hippocampus, the amygdala is able to take this into account (Rosen and Schulkin, 1998). Thus, the roar of a lion might be emotionally neutral or pleasant when it is heard from the safety of a safari park bus. However, the same sound would most likely assume a different colouring when walking alone through a forest.

Thus, emotions can be triggered by different simultaneous levels of input to the amygdala. A rapid arousal of emotion might set the scene for interpreting the input via the cortex, which arrives slightly later. There is scope for conflict. Owing to the direct link to the amygdala, some basic stimulus features (e.g. a phobic object) might tend to trigger negative emotion, whereas more refined processing of the same object (e.g. based upon knowledge gained in therapy) would tend to inhibit it. A possible interpretation of, say,

cognitive therapy is that this corresponds to strengthening the contribution of the indirect route (Le Doux, 1998).

The amygdala also receives information on internal physiology, e.g. via the brain stem, which, in turn is informed by hormones, and the vagus nerve (Chapter 3) concerning the viscera of the body. Artificial electrical stimulation of the vagus nerve affects the firing of neurons in the amygdala. Under natural conditions, this route could mediate a role of emotional arousal generated by feedback from the viscera.

Integration of information involves not only extensive input to the amygdala but also connections between these sources of information. Anatomical evidence reveals networks of intrinsic connections within the amygdala. Links from the basolateral nucleus to the central nucleus are shown in Figure 12.9.

Outputs from the amygdala

The amygdala has a role in attributing *emotional significance* to events and, in so doing, interacts with other brain regions involved with emotional processing, e.g. cortex, hypothalamus and brain stem (Aggleton and Mishkin, 1986). Figure 12.11 shows a summary of some outputs of the amygdala, these being involved in behavioural, autonomic and conscious ('experiential') aspects of emotion. Emotion has a role in cognition, and pathways from amygdala to the cortex and hippocampus suggest that this role is mediated in part by the amygdala (Le Doux, 1989). For example, memories are better consolidated if they are of emotionally coloured information (described shortly).

Some outputs from the amygdala project to subcortical sites, e.g. hypothalamus, midbrain, periaqueductal grey and solitary nucleus, which are also concerned with producing emotion and the behavioural and bodily reactions to it, e.g. elevated heart-rate (Aggleton and Mishkin, 1986).

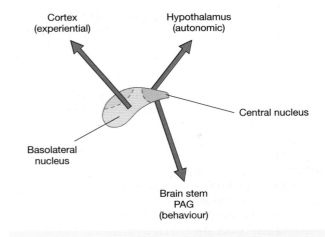

Figure 12.11 Some major outputs of the amygdala.

Effects of damage to the amygdala and connected regions

In monkeys, bilateral amygdalectomy (removal of amygdala on both sides) leaves the animal emotionally relatively unresponsive to stimuli that would normally be arousing (Aggleton and Mishkin, 1986). For example, there is loss of the fear normally shown to loud sounds, snakes and capture by humans.

Suppose that connections are broken between a modality-specific region of cortex (e.g. visual cortex) and the amygdala. We might expect that emotional reactivity to information specific to the modality would be impaired, relative to that shown to information derived from other modalities.

A personal angle

A drab visual world

In Florida, Bauer (1982) describes a man who could no longer be emotionally aroused by visual stimuli. In 1979, the patient, a former city-planner aged 39, suffered a head injury in a motorcycle accident. His visual world became drab and dull. He stopped hiking since nature appeared 'all the same' and he was no longer attracted by the sight of the opposite sex. However, the disruption was modality-specific; he could experience normal emotional arousal to stimulation via other sensory modalities. Music gave him an uplift. Bauer tested the patient's autonomic reactivity to visual images. A diminished reactivity to visual stimuli was seen, compared with intact controls. The disturbance appeared to be caused by bilateral lesions to the pathway linking visual processing areas of the cortex to the limbic system, e.g. the amygdala. It could not be explained by a disturbance to vision as such.

In humans, extensive damage to both amygdala (e.g. as a result of viral encephalitis) can result in general emotional flatness. H.M. (Chapter 11) received bilateral amygdalectomy (among large amounts of other tissue being removed). Investigators reported emotional flatness. On the rare occasions that he exhibited anger or irritability, it was short-lived.

There are reports that patients with amygdala damage on both sides are particularly disrupted in their ability to generate negative emotion (Damasio, 1999), e.g. emotion based on the facial expression of negative emotion in others (Adolphs and Tranel, 2003). This is compatible with the notion of an adapted fear module (described earlier), which is tuned for the detection of threats common in our evolutionary history.

We need to consider closely the cause of amygdala damage. Damage caused by sudden trauma might give less scope for subsequent adaptation and relearning than that caused by a slow degenerative disease (Siebert *et al.*, 2003). For patients with degenerative disease affecting the amygdala, Siebert *et al.* reported some disruption in interpreting the emotional expressions of other people but not a dramatic loss of the ability. The patients might have acquired alternative strategies and pathways not involving the amygdala.

A double dissociation was reported by Bechara *et al.* (1995). A patient, suffering from bilateral damage to the amygdala, failed to show a conditional fear response to a stimulus paired with a loud sound. However, the patient was able to recall consciously the experience of conditioning. Conversely, a patient with damage to the hippocampus failed to recall the same conditioning experience but exhibited a conditional autonomic response (a skin conductance change) to the cue paired with the loud sound. Although failing to form a conditional association, the patient with amygdala damage showed an autonomic response to the loud sound itself. This points to the role of regions outside the amygdala.

A personal angle

The hidden pin revisited

Chapter 11 described Claparède holding a pin in his hand as he shook a patient's hand. The patient formed an implicit memory (revealed by a reluctance to approach Claparède) but not an explicit memory of the incident. Investigators do not know what neural damage the patient had suffered but, based on her behaviour, Le Doux (1998) speculated that although the temporal lobe was damaged, her amygdala functioned normally. Thus, she clearly processed emotional information (suggesting an intact amygdala) but her processing of episodic memory (Chapter 11) was disrupted, suggesting damage to the hippocampus.

The cortex

Some regions of prefrontal cortex are labelled 'limbic' because of their role in emotion. With particular reference to the cortex, some researchers suggest that one hemisphere is more emotional than the other. However, we might need to distinguish between the production/experience of emotion and the interpretation of emotion in others (Heller, 1990).

The role of emotion in behaviour

The social behaviour of monkeys, rats and cats is disrupted by lesions of right or left frontal cortex (Kolb and Taylor, 1990). This is not surprising, given the role of the frontal lobes in memory, planning and inhibition of inappropriate behaviour (Chapter 11). The effect illustrates the impossibility of drawing neat divisions between cognition and emotion. In lesioned non-human primates, social interaction is at a low frequency and abnormal, e.g. an increased tendency to submission or fighting rather than coming together of equals. Animals become solitary and rarely groom socially. Kolb and Taylor conclude that (p. 139): 'damage to the frontal and temporal regions of all mammalian species seems to lead to unambiguous changes in social/affective behaviour that are strikingly similar across species'. More specifically, it appears that, following *pre*frontal lobe damage, emotion and behaviour are more strongly determined by physically present stimuli as such, rather than processing based upon predictions of social responses in others.

Humans with frontal damage tend to show less social interaction than controls, e.g. they stand more physically distant from others (Kolb and Taylor, 1990). Tranel *et al.* (1994, p. 143) suggest that the disruption caused by frontal damage: 'stems not from defective presence or absence of basic social knowledge, but rather from an inability to select and implement a reasonable option in real-world behaviour'. The prefrontal cortex appears to integrate information on (1) the current situation, (2) emotionally coloured memories of past instances and (3) anticipated emotional consequences of current actions. It is involved in somatic-marker signalling (or 'biasing'; see earlier) and holding the contributory bits of information in (conscious) working memory while decisions on behaviour are made (Damasio, 1996).

You met the case of Phineas Gage in Chapter 1, 'Introduction'. He was the unfortunate man who suffered damage to the prefrontal region of his brain, as a result of an explosion causing an iron bar to pass through it. Gage became irresponsible and subject to emotional outbursts. The prefrontal cortex has a role in planning, and Damasio (1986) speculates that Gage was defective in the ability to utilize emotional information concerning the consequences of his actions, e.g. an offence at swearing. In so far as Gage retained a theory of mind, it was deficient in the contribution of emotion to the self or others. Gage appeared to be left stuck in the 'here-and-now'.

Hemispheric differences

There is some hemispheric asymmetry in human emotion. Activity of the left prefrontal cortex (PFC) underlies positive moods and approach behaviour. Its under-activity is associated with depression and withdrawal (Davidson,

2003). A process of anticipation that goal-directed action will bring reward is organized within the left PFC. Depression is associated with a failure of such anticipation to control cognition and behaviour (Davidson *et al.*, 2002). The right PFC is more active in negative moods and withdrawal (Heller, 1990).

Asymmetry is seen in the effect of brain damage (Heilman and Bowers, 1990). Patients with right hemispheric lesions appear to be either indifferent to misfortune or euphoric in mood (Davidson, 1984; Tucker *et al.*, 1990). The reaction of their sympathetic nervous system to painful stimuli is less than that of controls. Patients with damage to the right frontal lobe show a high frequency of spontaneous speech (Kolb and Taylor, 1990). By contrast, patients with damage to the left frontal lobe commonly exhibit depression (Davidson, 1984) and show little spontaneous speech (Kolb and Taylor, 1990). Their sympathetic reactivity tends to be higher than that of controls (Heilman and Bowers, 1990).

Perception of emotion in others

In humans, for the perception of emotion (e.g. emotional reactions of others), the right hemisphere seems to have an advantage over the left (Tucker and Frederick, 1989). Emotional tone is more easily detected when sounds arrive at the left ear, which projects mainly to the right hemisphere (Chapter 9). Similarly, the right hemisphere has an advantage for visual emotional information. Information from the left side of the visual field is projected to the right hemisphere (Chapter 8, 'Vision'). Look at the nose in Figure 12.12 and describe the emotion shown. To most right-handed people (b) appears happier than (a), though they are mirror images.

Judgements of emotional value tend to be more positive when information is projected to the left hemisphere than to the right (Heller, 1990). Patients with right hemispheric damage (e.g. temporal and parietal lobes) have difficulty

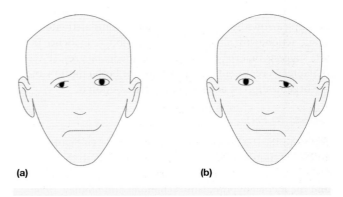

(a)   (b)

Figure 12.12 Two faces.

Source: Oatley and Jenkins (1996, Fig. 5.5, p. 146).

understanding emotional expression in others, e.g. facial reactions and speech intonation (Heilman and Bowers, 1990).

The hypothalamus

The hypothalamus is involved in the production of a range of different emotions, such as anger and fear. Some evidence on its role comes from electrical stimulation of the different nuclei from which it is composed.

Hess (1981) implanted electrodes in cats and stimulated regions of the hypothalamus. In certain areas, stimulation had two functionally related effects: (1) triggering defence and attack and (2) apparent excitation of the sympathetic system in the form of an accelerated heart-rate. By contrast, stimulation of a different hypothalamic region triggered behavioural calming and slowing of the heart. Electrical stimulation of distinct hypothalamic regions of the cat suggests two distinct types of aggression: affective ('rage') aggression, involving the medial hypothalamus, and ('non-emotional') predatory aggression, involving the lateral hypothalamus (A. Siegel, 2005). Based on studies involving electrical stimulation of the hypothalamus, rage appears to be an aversive state that the animal strives to reduce. By contrast, activity in the 'predatory region' is not aversive (Chapter 15).

Some evidence from human patients lends support to the involvement of the hypothalamus in emotion. In one patient, a tumour of the hypothalamus was associated with rage (Reeves and Plum, 1969) (if you want the specific region, it was the ventromedial part). Surgical lesions of parts of the hypothalamus have been reported to have a calming effect (Sano et al., 1970).

The midbrain periaqueductal grey

Emotions were described earlier as exerting a 'tendency towards a class of behaviour'. This is a first stage of emotional processing. However, ultimately behaviour needs to be decisive, e.g. to flee or freeze, but not to be jammed in some middle position. Therefore, contributions to behaviour and ANS activity (summarized by the lower downwards-pointing arrows in Figure 12.7) must be translated into a single action, with all other options inhibited. Evidence in rats suggests that the midbrain 'periaqueductal grey' (PAG) (Chapter 5) represents a neural basis for both emotion and the organization of decisive action based upon it.

Inputs to PAG

Inputs to the PAG derive from various levels. In Figures 12.9 and 12.11, note the signals from the amygdala to the PAG. Other projections to the PAG arise from the prefrontal cortex and the medial hypothalamus (Bandler and Shipley, 1994; A. Siegel, 2005). Discrete inputs from the cortex appear to target discrete PAG columns and thereby affect particular sets of functionally related actions. Speculatively, this might be the site at which two sets of information come together: (i) initial processing of emotional significance and (ii) the sensory features of the situation in terms of the selection of action (Dampney, 1994). Another source of input to the PAG is the superior colliculus (Chapter 5; Redgrave and Dean, 1991). This structure performs primitive feature analysis of visual stimuli (e.g. a large moving object overhead) and sends a signal to PAG for triggering rapid action. More refined analysis depends upon other sources of input.

Action controlled by the PAG

Electrical stimulation of particular neurons in the PAG triggers specific courses of action (Bandler and Shipley, 1994). Neurons of the PAG are organized into functionally specific columns, e.g. one plays a role in the organization of freezing and another in active defence. Neurons within a specific column play roles in several functionally related outputs (Dampney, 1994).

Stimulation within certain columns of the PAG elicits passivity and lowered heart-rate. This reaction characterizes the defeat pattern of rats, a *passive strategy*. Neurons within other columns exert effects on the functionally related outputs of active defence (fighting) and acceleration of heart-rate through outputs to the ANS (Dampney, 1994). There is increased blood flow to the limbs and decreased flow to the viscera. Confrontation and flight represent *active strategies* for dealing with threat.

Vocalization depends on PAG neurons. In cats (de Lanerolle and Lang, 1988) and primates (Larson et al., 1988), specific PAG sites are associated with specific calls indicative of emotion and intention. For example, there are calls of defeat, submission or attack and calls indicating friendly intention.

Certain PAG neurons project to the medulla where they synapse on neurons that form projections to the preganglionic neurons controlling the activity of the heart (Chapter 3; Dampney, 1994). This is the route by which emotions mediate their effects on heart-rate.

This completes the introduction to brain regions and emotion. The next section considers some of the neurochemistry associated with the activity of these regions.

> ### Section summary
>
> 1 The limbic system is made up from a number of brain regions involved in emotion, e.g. cingulate cortex (cingulate gyrus) and amygdala. The evidence suggests that emotion arises from a network of interacting brain regions including those of the limbic system.
>
> 2 The amygdala attributes some emotional significance to stimuli.

3 There is hemispheric asymmetry in emotional processing.

4 Depression of, or damage to, the left hemisphere is associated with negative mood.

5 Stimulation of regions of the hypothalamus elicits emotional expression in behaviour and autonomic reactions.

6 At the midbrain periaqueductal grey, in addition to a contribution to emotion, a *particular* course of behaviour is computed.

Test your knowledge

(Answer on page 328)

12.6 Of the two routes shown in bold in Figure 12.10, which, part (a) or part (b), corresponds to that described as 'quick and dirty'?

12.3

Neurochemicals

We considered very briefly the role of opioids in emotion. This section looks at the role of some further neurochemicals. Space precludes a detailed discussion of this vast subject and so we shall be selective. A further look at this topic is given in the next chapter where the role of neurochemicals in stress is discussed. Neurochemicals have both general and specific effects in emotion and its expression. For example, the neurochemical acetylcholine appears to have a specific role in the hypothalamic region involved in rage (A. Siegel, 2005).

Neurochemicals involved in ascending pathways

Ascending pathways employing dopamine, noradrenalin and serotonin innervate structures of the limbic system (A. Siegel, 2005). Evidence on their role is derived from detailed study of neuroanatomy and the effects of therapeutic drugs. For example, one ascending system of dopaminergic neurons is termed the meso*limbic* dopamine system on account of its targeting of limbic structures. That dopaminergic neurons project to the amygdala, suggested a possible dopaminergic involvement in depression (Drevets, 2001). In treating depression, drugs that target serotonin are often effective and this points to a role of serotonin in emotion. Boosting serotonin transmission tends to lower aggression, possibly acting on sites in the amygdala (A. Siegel, 2005), which could implicate a role for serotonin in rage.

Amino acids

Excitatory and inhibitory amino acids act as neurotransmitters in certain brain regions concerned with emotion (Glue *et al.*, 1993). For some negative emotions, glutamate appears to be an excitatory neurotransmitter, and gamma-aminobutyric acid (GABA) an inhibitory neurotransmitter. These substances mediate, respectively, anxiety and its inhibition. A reduced sensitivity of GABA receptors appears to be part of the basis of what Glue *et al.* (p. 60) term 'overarousal, vigilance and fearful anticipation'. The clinical state of depression is associated with a lower than normal level of GABA in the cerebrospinal fluid (Chapter 5) and plasma (Sutanto and de Kloet, 1993).

Some drugs that are used to improve mood block excitatory amino acid transmission (Glue *et al.*, 1993). However, glutamate has receptors throughout the brain in regions having various cognitive and motor functions (Panksepp, 1998a). Only if a receptor subtype specifically involved in fear could be identified, is there hope for developing a therapy.

So-called 'benzodiazepine receptors' are found throughout the brain's fear circuits (Panksepp, 1998a). Unusually, a receptor type is named after the drug that targets the receptor and is used in treatment of a disorder. The drug classes termed benzodiazepines and barbiturates bind to sites at the subtype $GABA_A$ receptor, enhance GABA function and thereby tend to reduce anxiety (Glue *et al.*, 1993). Prolonged stress can reduce the number of benzodiazepine receptors within the CNS, an effect mediated via corticosteroids. Ethanol also has effects on enhancing GABAergic transmission, revealed in a temporary lowering of anxiety. Highly anxious people have reduced sensitivity to barbiturates.

Anti-anxiety drugs, **anxiolytics**, such as the types of benzodiazepine termed chlordiazepoxide and diazepam ('Valium'), have an established role in human psychopharmacology. Animal models of their action are available. For example, they help rats to overcome their fear of moving along the open arms of an elevated maze, whereas **anxiogenics** (drugs that increase anxiety) increase their reluctance to do so (Ramos and Mormède, 1998). Antidepressants are without effect on this task. Another test of drugs thought to target anxiety is the social interaction test. Anxiety counters a rat's tendency to interact socially with conspecifics, and alcohol, an anxiolytic, inhibits the effect of anxiety and increases social interaction.

Distress, as measured by distress vocalizations (DVs), is increased by glutamate agonists, which suggests a role for glutamate in the distress system (Panksepp, 1998a). Diazepam decreases DVs in rat pups and anxiety in humans

(Insel *et al.*, 1988). Insel *et al.*, suggest that a receptor system has evolved to serve a function of distress-calling early in development. They raise the possibility that the action of such anti-anxiety agents as diazepam in adults is mediated by 'a residue of these developmental effects'.

Section summary

1 Various neurochemicals have specific or general effects on emotion.

2 Excitatory and inhibitory amino acids are involved in brain regions underlying anxiety.

Test your knowledge

(Answer on page 328)

12.7 Complete the following: 'An ascending neural system involved in emotion is termed the mesol___c dopamine system'.

Some other effects of emotions

So far, we have focused on the role of emotion in behaviour, internal physiology and subjective affect. However, as Figure 12.1 showed, emotion does more than this and the present section considers three further roles. Two of these have been introduced already: effects on cognition and on learning and memory. The third effect is on certain reflexes that are not actually triggered by emotion as such but their strength is altered by emotion.

Effects on cognition

On experiencing an emotion, thoughts and memories that are functionally related to that emotion can sometimes be more easily retrieved and accessed than incompatible ones (Bargh and Tota, 1988). In an emotional state, ready access to memories congruent with that state might prove relevant for adaptive action and thinking out new strategies of coping (Tooby and Cosmides, 1990). Attention can be selectively drawn to compatible features of the environment. For example, anxiety biases attention processes towards the perception of threat (Rosen and Schulkin, 1998).

Stimulating brain regions such as the amygdala in chronically ill patients (see earlier) triggers (1) mood

changes, (2) a tendency to mood-specific behaviour and (3) memories congruent with the mood (Heath, 1986).

What appears to be a normally adaptive process can also play a role in serious pathology. Depressed individuals have ready access to depressive thoughts (Bargh and Tota, 1988; Tucker *et al.*, 1990). The rumination (mental 'chewing-over') of negative and often guilt-related thoughts by depressed patients appears to be facilitated by over-activity of the amygdala (Drevets, 2001). The perceptual systems of people with phobias 'favour' detection of the object of their fear (Öhman, 2005).

Effects on forming memory

Introduction

Emotionally coloured experiences are often particularly well remembered. Emotion can strengthen memory consolidation (Chapter 11) (Herz, 1997). The persistent arousal following emotional experience and associated hormonal changes appear to be involved (Bower, 1992). Emotional arousal allocates priority to processing the emotion-evoking event and triggers its recycling in working memory.

Mechanisms

Cahill *et al.* (1996) employed positron emission tomography (PET; Chapter 5) to investigate the role of the amygdala in emotionally coloured memory. Participants (right-handed, males) were given two PET scans, while watching (1) neutral material and (2) material that was emotionally negative. It was predicted that (a) emotionally loaded material would be better recalled and (b) there would be increased activity of the amygdala associated with this.

Participants were injected with *F*-fluoro-2-deoxy-glucose (FDG) to determine metabolic rate. The highest concentration of FDG gathers in regions that are the most

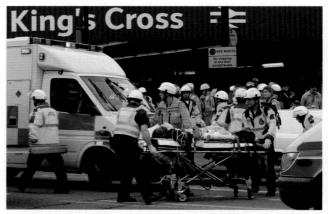

We usually form rather durable memories of traumatic incidents that we experience or learn about, such as the London bombings in 2005. What is the mechanism underlying this?

Source: © David Parry/epa/Corbis.

The neuroscientist Joseph Le Doux has featured large in the present chapter. He relays an anecdote from his childhood in Eunice, Louisiana, when he was on a fishing trip (Le Doux, 1992, p. 269):

Suddenly, I noticed that the bank of the stream below was covered with more snakes than I ever care to see again. Had I not seen those snakes, my memory of that experience would surely be much less vivid than it is. I am unable to recall the more mundane events occurring before or after encountering the snakes, but I remember the image of the snakes slithering in the mud and the appearance of the surrounding countryside as if this experience had just happened yesterday. The arousal of emotion, fear in this case, presumably made me remember for more than 30 years the details of this excursion with such clarity.

Dr Le Doux describes his 'immense fear of snakes' (Le Doux, 1998, p. 179) and this reaction forms an important part of his scientific argument on emotion.

active metabolically. Figure 12.13 shows scatter plots for the number of films recalled and the glucose metabolism of the right amygdala for (a) emotional and (b) neutral material. There is a significant positive correlation between the metabolic activity and the conscious recall of emotional material, but no correlation for neutral material.

Specifically the basolateral amygdala is involved in this aspect of memory (McGaugh, 2004). It appears that, by means of its neural projections to other brain regions (e.g. cortex), the amygdala enhances consolidation there.

Consider Figure 12.14. In emotion, the hormones adrenalin and corticosteroids are secreted in increased amounts and they are the initial trigger to a series of events that affect the establishment of memory (McGaugh, 1992). For example, there is improved retention of memory when injections of these hormones are made following training. Adrenalin seems to act via a circuitous route in activating peripheral adrenergic receptors on the vagus nerve (Chapter 3, Figure 3.30, p. 74). Acting via the nucleus of the solitary tract (NTS) (Chapter 5, Figure 5.31, p. 127), activation of the vagus nerve then influences the amygdala. This triggers the release of noradrenalin in the brain, which activates the projections involved in enhancing memory formation.

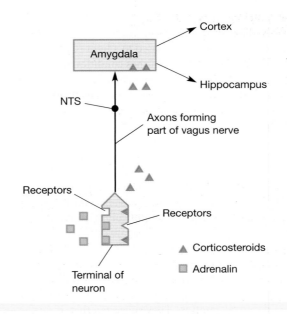

Figure 12.14 Effects on memory consolidation

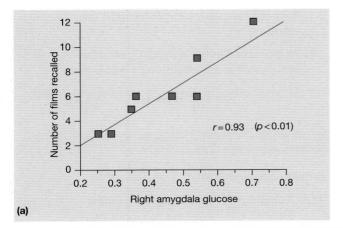

(a)

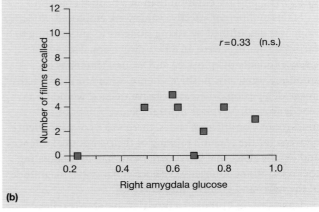

(b)

Figure 12.13 Scatter plot for number of films recalled and metabolic activity of the right amygdala: (a) emotional film session and (b) neutral film session. *Source:* Cahill *et al.* (1996, Fig. 3).

In addition, corticosteroids readily enter the brain and are thought to attach to receptors at the basolateral amygdala, where they exert the effect of enhancing memory (McGaugh, 2004).

The human startle reflex

It is almost certain that you have felt the **startle reflex** in action, a response to a sudden unexpected stimulus. Suppose that you are watching a horror movie and someone touches your back as they walk past. You are likely to flinch or jump. Fear accentuates your reaction, compared to when, say, watching a comedy. In humans, the startle reflex consists, in addition, in a blink of the eyes (Ehrlichman *et al.*, 1997; Lang *et al.*, 1990).

A conditional stimulus (CS) that has earlier been paired with an aversive unconditional stimulus (UCS) can affect the startle reflex. Rats are first exposed to a light (CS) paired with shock (UCS), which establishes conditional fear to the light (Davis, 1992). They are then subjected to a tone. The tone triggers the startle reflex. Startle can be measured in the presence or absence of the light. In spite of its pairing with shock, they do not react with startle to the light itself, showing that the light is not able to trigger this reflex. However, if light and tone are presented together, the light *amplifies* the reaction to the tone. This shows the influence of fear conditioned to the light.

Emotion triggered in various ways affects the strength of the startle reflex. In humans, amplification of the startle reflex can be used as an index of negative affect, e.g. during withdrawal from addictive drugs (Mutschler and Miczek, 1998). For another example, unpleasant odours increase it and pleasant odours decrease it (Ehrlichman *et al.*, 1997). Lang *et al.* (1990) investigated the relationship between this reflex and central emotion. They suggested that, if a reflex is incompatible with an emotion, the magnitude of the reflex would be reduced. For example, the startle reflex would be weaker in a positive emotion than in a neutral emotion.

Slides of different affective value were employed. Affective value was determined by asking students to give a rating to each slide. Ratings were on a two-dimensional scale of valence (quality of emotion) and arousal (intensity of emotion). Typically, 'positive valence' would be an attractive image of a person, whereas 'negative valence' would be a bloody wound. A typical 'neutral valence' might be a mushroom. For different slides, there was a correspondence between (a) the person's ranking of their emotional valence and (b) the effect that viewing the slide had in modulating the reflex. Slides of negative valence enhance the magnitude of the reflex and positive ones lower it.

Davis (1992) proposed a model of the startle reflex (Figure 12.15). There is a direct stimulus–response (sound–muscles) link that is mediated via the brain stem. The strength of this link is modulated top-down by

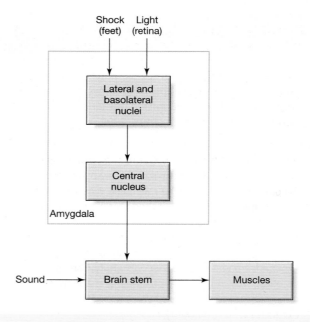

Figure 12.15 A representation of the role of conditioned fear in potentiating the startle reflex.

Source: adapted from Davis (1992, Fig. 41.3, p. 474).

emotion. Within the lateral and basolateral nuclei of the amygdala, an association is formed between light and shock. This gives information on the light access to the central nucleus of the amygdala from which neurons extend to the brain stem structures that underlie the startle reflex (cf. Adamec, 1997). The signal from the amygdala modulates the strength of the reflex.

Section summary

1 Emotion tends to trigger access to those memories that are compatible with the emotion.

2 As embodied in the amygdala, emotion enhances the consolidation of memories.

3 Emotion alters the strength of the startle reflex.

Test your knowledge

(Answer on page 328)

12.8 Complete the following with respect to Figure 12.15: 'Whereas the input marked "Sound" t_____ the startle reflex, that derived from the amygdala m_____ its strength'.

Bringing things together

If you take another look at Figure 12.1, you will see that it summarizes much of the evidence presented in the chapter. Various inputs have the common property of triggering a particular emotion. This emotion then has functionally coherent effects on behaviour, physiology, cognition (e.g. learning/memory), as well as subjective feelings. Its effects on behaviour consist of giving priority to certain actions (e.g. fear prioritizes escape), causing fixed patterns of reaction (e.g. alarm calls, characteristic facial expressions) and influencing the startle reaction.

In the spirit of affective neuroscience, the chapter proposes that a rapport between neuroscience and the investigation of subjective states is not only possible but indeed necessary.

It was suggested that some brain regions have more to do with cognition (e.g. posterior regions of cortex) and others (e.g. hypothalamus) more to do with emotion. However, anything but basic stereotyped emotional expression depends on both. Psychologists cannot draw a neat boundary between cognition and emotion. The amygdala has a role in attributing emotional significance to stimuli and thoughts. Some stimuli both of internal and external origin target the amygdala directly whereas others first involve complex processing. Thoughts presumably arise in the cortex and are attributed with emotional value by the amygdala. Clearly, for this to happen there has to be a thought and there has to be a cortex. So, in this sense, the cortex is involved in emotional processing.

Summary of Chapter 12

1 **Emotions exert a coordinated influence on behaviour, physiology, cognition and subjective experience.**

2 **There are some basic emotions that are common across mammalian species. The triggers to these emotions and the form of their expression vary between species and between human cultures.**

3 **The biological psychology of emotion can be exemplified by the study of fear, frustration, embarrassment, trust and social attachment. In each case, comparing species can give valuable insights.**

4 **Feedback from the periphery, e.g. skeletal muscle and autonomic effects, plays some role in the production of emotion by the CNS.**

5 **Various interacting brain regions form the neural basis of emotion. These include the amygdala, hypothalamus and periacqueductal grey.**

6 **Different neurochemicals play general or specific roles in the production of emotions.**

7 **Emotion exerts a role in cognition, learning and memory, as well as in modifying the strength of certain reflexes.**

Further reading

For general accounts by eminent researchers in the area, see Le Doux (1998) and Panksepp (1998a). For a handbook of affective science, see Davidson *et al.* (2003). For the perspective of a leading researcher in which links are made with motivation, see Rolls (2005). The link between emotion, evolution and rationality is made by Evans and Cruse (2004). For a good account of the rationale of a biological psychology of emotion, see Scherer (1993). For a classical and accessible paper on behavioural effects of infection, see Hart (1988). For the neuroscience of emotion, see Chapters 70–78 of Gazzaniga (2004).

Signposts

This chapter has revisited some of the material of Chapter 11, 'Learning and memory'. It considered the roles of (i) classical conditioning in the production of emotion, (ii) the hippocampus in declarative memory and (iii) emotion in enhancing memory consolidation. Chapter 14 'Stress and coping' is based on the assumption that stress corresponds to processes of negative emotion being stretched to beyond their adaptive limits. The emotions provide an input to motivation (Öhman and Mineka, 2001). Fear and anger motivate escape and aggression. The emotions associated with bonding and breaking bonds act as powerful motivators of behaviour. Breaking social bonds motivates attempts to restore them. Hence, we shall revisit emotion in Chapter 15, 'Motivation'.

Answers

Explanations for answers to 'test your knowledge' questions can be found on the website **www.pearsoned.co.uk/toates**

12.1 Dilation; autonomic
12.2 Unconditional; conditional; unconditional
12.3 Neutral stimulus; conditional stimulus
12.4 (i) It would reduce the level; (ii) no effect.
12.5 To influence emotional processing by the brain, the substance must either be able to cross the blood–brain barrier in some way or be able to trigger peripheral neurons that project to the brain (e.g. as part of the vagus nerve).
12.6 (a)
12.7 Limbic
12.8 Triggers; modulates

 Interactions and animations relating to topics discussed in this chapter can be found on the website at **www.pearsoned.co.uk/toates.** These include

Animation: The James Lange theory

Interaction: Some of the main brain areas involved in emotion

Interaction: The low and high roads to the amygdala

Animation: The effects of benzodiazepines on punished responding

CHAPTER 13

Stress and coping

Learning outcomes for Chapter 13

After studying this chapter, you should be able to:

1. State what is meant by the term 'stress', while linking this to physiology, psychology and the principle of homeostasis.

2. Identify the criteria that point to the existence of stress. Relate these to the measures of stress that are normally employed.

3. Describe features of the two principal neurohormonal systems that are stretched excessively under conditions of stress. Explain why these two systems assume such a defining role in stress.

4. Explain why stress cannot simply be defined in terms of the potential stressors present in a situation. Outline the role of contextual factors such as coping.

5. Describe some of the basic features of the immune system and how the system can be affected by stress. In so doing, suggest how stress might have a part in exacerbating certain disorders that involve suppression of the immune system.

6. Identify some of the principal brain regions that are implicated in the condition termed 'stress'. Relate the role that they serve under stress-free conditions to their performance in the condition of stress.

7. Show where an understanding of the general principles of stress can help to explain the bases of a number of disorders: depression, coronary heart disease, post-traumatic stress disorder, irritable bowel syndrome and ulcers.

8. Outline how an understanding of the psychobiology of stress can give useful pointers as to how to reduce stress and thereby make a positive contribution to health.

Scene-setting questions

1 Can someone actually enjoy stress?

2 Is stress invariably harmful to health?

3 Are stress-related diseases 'psychosomatic'?

4 How can the gut be sensitive to stress?

5 Can you die from a 'broken heart'?

6 Can science show how to live with stress or how to beat it?

Stress in such an extreme situation is triggered by the failure to resolve a pressing problem over a period of time. How good is this as a general criterion of stress?

Source: Getty Images/Workbook Stock.

Introduction

Many of us know **stress** only too well through personal experience. Think of some situations that you have experienced, which you would describe as stressful. (At this moment, I am experiencing the latest in a long series of mishaps – an unidentified water leak somewhere in our house. It feels that I am eminently qualified to write this chapter.) People report such things as isolation, being under siege, long-term anticipation of final exams, chronic ill-health, loss or breakdown of a close relationship and unemployment as being stressful. Is there a common feature that characterizes these situations?

They all engage our attention, pose demands for action and change, are largely uncontrollable and, in most cases, arrive against our wishes. They all tend to leave us feeling helpless and a failure and they occur over periods of weeks or months. We cannot cope, sometimes expressed as not having a **coping strategy** or 'coping resources'. Similarly, in non-humans, stimuli that cause stress, termed **stressors**, are often such things as prolonged exposure to noise or social conflict.

Stressors tend to add their effects. You hear comments like, 'I might just have coped with the divorce *on its own* but not with that and the unemployment together'. So, we are looking for neuropsychological processes that tend to cumulate negative effects.

In everyday use, stress mostly refers to psychologically disturbing events or events with psychological associations and it involves long-term overload (Ursin and Olff, 1993). A challenge is to try to define the common biological and psychological features of situations described as stressful.

Most would argue that stress is always negative and predisposes to illness but some suggest that mild stress can be exhilarating and only severe stress is bad. We all know of the workaholic entrepreneur driven by the 'adrenalin rush' of stress. Such people may indeed be stimulating their adrenalin secretion but it is likely that they have considerable control over the situations in which they *willingly* engage. They are not stressed in the sense of being helpless and chronically beset by circumstances not of their choosing. Hormonal reactions do not always tell the whole story: as will be described shortly, they need to be seen in context.

To understand stress, let us recall the account of homeostasis given in earlier chapters. The body is constructed so as to keep its important parameters within close limits. When they shift from these, action is taken to bring them back. If something such as body temperature or water level were to shift far from its norm, death would follow. A somewhat similar notion can be applied to stress. We try to protect our 'psychological homeostasis' by taking various actions, such as avoiding psychological overload, seeking comfort from others, finding prediction and control in our lives and avoiding conflict, etc. Stress represents a chronic disturbance to such *psychological* homeostasis. Characteristic disturbances to the physiology of the body, such as high blood pressure and adrenalin levels, are associated with this.

Although we normally think of stressors as being psychological, two things need to be emphasized: (1) through the CNS, psychological stressors exert wide-ranging effects on the physiology of the body and (2) some of these same effects on the body can be triggered by physiological stressors, i.e. deviations from physiological homeostasis as in loss of blood (Selye, 1973). See Figure 13.1.

The term 'stress' can be used to cover the response to both psychological and physiological triggers (Ursin and Olff, 1993) and it thereby points to common reactions in the body. Physiological and behavioural mechanisms that are adaptive within a range (Chapter 12, 'Emotion') can be stretched beyond this. Over a prolonged period, such stretching is associated with psychological and physiological disruption described as 'stress' (Archer, 1979).

Of course, evolution did not produce systems that are intrinsically geared to produce pathology. Rather, stress is the pathological stretching of adaptive behavioural system to beyond their adaptive range. For example, an elevated heart-rate and blood pressure can be adaptive in the short term in facing natural threats, such as bears. These same changes can become seriously maladaptive if they are chronically activated day-after-day with little or no escape from the triggers to stress.

Awareness of stress is an important health issue. Stress can sometimes be better managed. We can direct attention to psychological states that are opposite to stress, as aspects of physical and psychological health.

Section summary

1 A long-term disturbance to psychological homeostasis is described as 'stress'.

2 Stress is associated with wide-ranging changes in the physiology of the body.

3 Physiological stressors, such as loss of blood, trigger some of these same changes.

Test your knowledge

(Answer on page 352)

13.1 Complete the following: 'In its most usual sense, stress can be described as a chronic _____ to psychological homeostasis'.

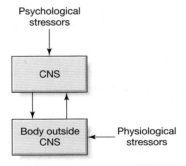

Figure 13.1 Stress, as determined by physiological and psychological stressors.

Characterizing stress

This section considers a number of starting points for arriving at an understanding of stress.

Signs of stress: arousal

Confronted with a stressor, an animal shows a pattern of EEG **arousal**, also termed 'activation' (Chapter 5, 'The brain'; Ursin and Olff, 1993). Protracted arousal gives a possible indication of stress.

In this situation, animals take both behavioural and physiological (e.g. autonomic) action. The sympathetic nervous system is usually excited and thereby adrenalin (epinephrine) and noradrenalin (norepinephrine) are released into the blood stream in increased amounts. Hormones of the class termed corticosteroids (Chapter 6, 'Development and plasticity') are usually secreted at a high rate and they mobilize metabolic resources in the body. The set of reactions is termed the 'emergency reaction'. Long-term excitation of these hormonal systems gives an indication of stress.

Types of stressor

External stimuli

Consider an animal that is exposed to 'potential stressors', e.g. (a) confrontation with predators, (b) dealing with dominants of the group or (c) competing for food and reacting to rivals in overcrowded conditions. As a reaction, heart-rate accelerates. The animal might have an action available that reliably corrects the situation. In other words, it has a coping strategy, such as to avoid, make an appeasement gesture or flee. Suppose it suffers no ill effects; after each contact, heart-rate rapidly returns to normal. Lengthy confrontation is avoided and the notion of stress would seem inappropriate. This is coping, by the criteria of the success of behaviour and the relatively light demands on the corticosteroid system and the autonomic nervous system (ANS).

The chapter concerns where a coping strategy is unavailable, the challenge cannot be countered and the animal is stressed. For example, it might take evasive action with autonomic activation but repeatedly fails to get away from a dominant animal.

Typically, secretion of corticosteroids (Chapter 6) and sympathetic activation with heart-rate acceleration would occur over long periods (von Holst, 1986). The persistence of arousal and failure to resolve the situation are associated with a range of characteristic pathology, such as ulcers and blocking of arteries. The coexistence of behavioural and physiological indices encourages use of the term 'stress'.

Cognitive processes

Some potential stressors, e.g. loud sounds, can be defined in terms of their physical properties. However, many situations that cause stress are not so easily defined (Ursin and Olff, 1993). Rather, what evokes stress is an event placed in the *context of earlier experiences.*

Corticosteroid secretion is sensitive to situations placed in context. For example, novelty of a situation can trigger it. Novelty is not some intrinsic property of an environment. Rather, it is the feature that the environment is unfamiliar in the context of previously experienced environments.

Similarly, loss of control in a previously instrumental situation (i.e. extinction in a Skinner box) triggers release of corticosteroids. Earning a reward smaller than expectation is another trigger that can only be understood in terms of what was expected (Chorpita and Barlow, 1998), i.e. frustration is a trigger. This implies comparison of expected and actual events and a triggering by the difference.

In humans, loss of something such as a job is a stressor but this is not a physical stimulus comparable to a loud noise. We might stress ourselves through endless problem-solving, as in trying to balance dubious financial accounts, or by engaging in 'inner dialogues' on personal failure (Burell, 1996). In this case, stressors are characterized by such features as 'informational discrepancy', e.g. reality differs from expectations (Ursin and Olff, 1993), or there is an inability to solve a problem. Attempts to cope with cognitive challenges are associated with sympathetic activation (Steptoe, 1993). In trying to define stress, a measure in such a case might be a verbal report, e.g. 'I feel that I cannot cope any longer'.

In social species, isolation from conspecifics causes stress, the 'isolation syndrome' (Chapter 12, 'Emotion'; Greenough, 1976). Evidence of stress is provided by a comparison with the unstressed behaviour and the hormonal profile of a stable socially housed animal.

Physiological stimuli

Physiological disturbances, e.g. blood loss and stretch of the bladder (Selye, 1973), trigger activation and corticosteroid release. The mobilization of resources in this 'general emergency reaction' supports any specific action also triggered. For example, a physiological challenge such as loss of blood triggers specific behavioural homeostatic actions such as seeking water and salt to correct the disturbance (Chapter 16, 'Feeding and drinking').

Behavioural indices

Confronted with a stressor we might flee or fight, and activate the sympathetic system, and these actions might or might not be successful. Another strategy is passivity, with parasympathetic activation and inhibition of the sympathetic system (Fowles, 1982). Confronted with a dominant animal, a subordinate sometimes reacts in this way. Typically, when an active strategy fails, an animal switches to the passive mode. According to the definition suggested here, a failure of strategy over long periods constitutes stress. This can be either an active strategy with sympathetic dominance or passivity with parasympathetic dominance.

To summarize what has just been said and to complete the picture, psychologists can give four criteria of stress.

Four criteria of stress

Research on stress identifies four criteria that point to its existence and can be applied across species, as follows (Toates, 1995):

1 Over time, action occurs in response to a situation but it fails to correct this situation.

2 There is excessive and protracted activity in neurohormonal systems. Typically, this would be the sympathetic branch and the system that secretes corticosteroids from the adrenal gland (Selye, 1973; von Holst, 1986) or both. Instead of sympathetic activation, there can be excessive activity within the parasympathetic branch.

3 There is vulnerability to certain pathology (e.g. gastric ulceration, hypertension, depression and disorders associated with suppression of the immune system) (Moberg, 1985).

4 There is a tendency to show apparently pointless behaviours such as stereotypies or inflicting self-harm (Mason, 1991; Chapter 2, 'Genes, environment and evolution').

In our case, to lower stress we might target voluntary behaviour. There could be some choice, e.g. we might readjust priorities and work less. We might be able to change how we interpret and react to events. Interventions might target the physiology of the body, e.g. drugs to lower the vigour of the heart's pumping.

The following section looks in more detail at the two neurohormonal systems that are most obviously involved in stress.

Section summary

1 External stimuli, defined as stressors, trigger behavioural and physiological activation.

2 The stress-evoking capacity of external events can often only be understood by taking account of their context and interpretation.

3 Humans can stress themselves by cognitive triggers such as protracted and unsuccessful problem-solving.

4 A capacity for coping reduces the impact of potential stressors.

5 An animal can be defined as stressed when coping resources are inadequate for the task.

6 Other criteria of stress are increases in (a) activity by neurohormonal systems, (b) the tendency to certain pathology and (c) the tendency to perform stereotypies.

7 Stress can be associated with (a) active strategies and sympathetic domination or (b) passive strategies with a bias towards parasympathetic activity.

Test your knowledge

(Answer on page 352)

13.2 Apart from catecholamines, increased release of what other class of substance is triggered by stress?

Two neurohormonal systems

Introduction

The perspective introduced here corresponds to the 'classical stress story'. The focus is on two neurohormonal systems, introduced earlier (Chapters 3, 'The nervous and endocrine systems' and 6): the sympathetic branch of the ANS and the system that releases corticosteroids. The latter was introduced in terms of the sequence corticotropin releasing factor (CRF) → ACTH (Figure 3.27, p. 69) and developed in Chapter 6 as the full sequence CRF → ACTH → corticosteroids. Prolonged activation of these two systems can be used as one index of stress and it plays a role in disorders characterized as 'stress-related'.

The autonomic nervous system

Stress is associated with altered activity throughout the ANS, affecting its various outputs, such as the stomach and intestine. A principal concern is with parts that affect the circulatory system. We address this first.

Sympathetic branch

Emergencies activate the sympathetic branch of the ANS (SNS), especially when there is a perception of action being possible. SNS activation triggers changes in the body, e.g. increased heart-rate. Also, a number of blood vessels are constricted but those in active skeletal muscles are dilated, facilitating blood flow.

SNS activation releases catecholamines: (a) noradrenalin from sympathetic neurons and (b) adrenalin (A) and noradrenalin (NA) from the adrenal gland. See Chapter 3 (Figure 3.29, p. 73) and Figure 13.2. In humans, most

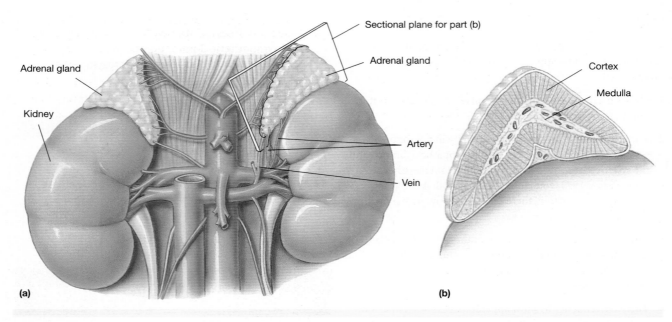

Figure 13.2 The adrenal gland and its division into medulla and cortex: (a) anterior view and (b) sectional view.
Source: Martini *et al*. (2000, Fig. 19-10, p. 510).

noradrenalin in the blood originates from the terminals of neurons of the SNS, some at the inner region of the adrenal gland, the **adrenal medulla**. Plasma adrenalin originates in the adrenal medulla (Musselman *et al*., 1998).

Within the circulatory system, adrenalin and noradrenalin occupy two types of receptor: alpha adrenergic and beta adrenergic. For example, when these catecholamines occupy beta receptors at cardiac muscle, the frequency of the heartbeat is increased. The therapeutic drug class termed 'beta blockers' acts at this site (Scheidt, 1996). Cardiac muscle is excited by (1) direct sympathetic input via neurons and (2) noradrenalin and adrenalin, which arrive via the bloodstream (Dampney, 1994). In response to sympathetic activation, blood flow through the heart can increase by a factor of 5. Occupation of catecholamine receptors on the smooth muscles that govern the diameter of blood vessels adjusts blood flow such that working skeletal muscle receives adequate blood (Vander *et al*., 1994).

Parasympathetic branch

Parasympathetic activity is seen in day-to-day maintenance, e.g. promoting digestion, involving restraint on the heart. However, increased activation can occur in emergencies when no active strategy is perceived as possible (Bohus and Koolhaas, 1993).

The hypothalamic pituitary adrenocortical system

Introduction

Corticosteroids are secreted from the outer layer of the adrenal gland, the **adrenal cortex** (Figure 13.2). There are different corticosteroids having similar properties. In rats, the principal one is corticosterone (Bohus and de Kloet, 1981). In humans, it is cortisol (Baxter and Rousseau, 1979). Corticosteroids act throughout the body, e.g. at times of threat to mobilize energy and, at the brain, to alter arousal and cognitive and emotional processing (Erikson *et al*., 2003). In primates, receptors for corticosteroids are found in the hippocampus, amygdala and regions of prefrontal cortex.

Consider Figure 13.3. At the first stage of the system, neurons with cell bodies at the paraventricular nucleus of the hypothalamus (PVN) (Chapter 5, Figure 5.32, p. 128) secrete corticotropin releasing factor (CRF), sometimes termed 'corticotropin releasing hormone' (Dunn and Berridge, 1990). At the pituitary, occupation of receptors by CRF releases adrenocorticotrophic hormone (ACTH). The sequence of hormones, CRF → ACTH → corticosteroids, is called the **pituitary adrenocortical system** (or pituitary adrenocortical axis). Since activity in the hypothalamus is the trigger for CRF secretion, this sometimes gives the axis the title 'hypothalamic pituitary adrenocortical system'. Mercifully, this is commonly abbreviated to 'HPA system' or 'HPA axis'.

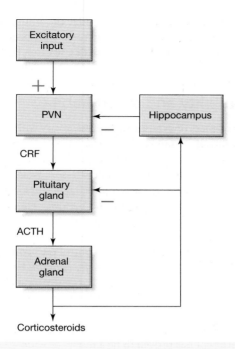

Figure 13.3 The system involved in the release of corticosteroids and their feedback effect

In Figure 13.3, note the inhibition that corticosteroids exert on the pathway that leads to their own secretion. If such negative feedback is functioning optimally, when a stressor is terminated there is a prompt shut-down of the HPA axis and corticosteroid level quickly falls (Cullinan *et al.*, 1995). Malfunction can arise from inadequate negative feedback, in which case hormonal activation can long outlive the stressor. For example, excessive levels of corticosteroids can be toxic to neural tissue, e.g. in the hippocampus (Bremner, 1999). This can have negative effects on memory (Kim and Diamond, 2002).

Triggers

Acting via CNS processing, what triggers the set of hypothalamic neurons to release CRF? The HPA system is sensitive to (1) events in the internal environment (e.g. blood loss) and (2) analysis by other parts of the brain that a challenge is arising in the external environment (e.g. a threat) (Chorpita and Barlow, 1998). Psychological stimuli to stress are characterized by the common property of *uncertainty, challenge or threat and the possible need to take action.*

A long-term elevation of corticosteroid levels points to stress, since (a) this occurs at times of threat or the impossibility of resolving a challenge, (b) it is associated with failure to resolve the problem and (c) it has pathological consequences. However, brief activation of the HPA system cannot in itself indicate a stressor (Willner, 1993). Brief activation is a response to uncertainty (e.g. novelty, aversive stimulus) or arousal, whereas chronic activation reflects an inability to resolve uncertainty. From a functional perspective, triggering of corticosteroids by novelty makes adaptive sense since this represents a situation in which an animal might be called upon to fight, flee or freeze.

Where a clear and well-tried strategy is available, there is little excitation of the HPA axis, even though a potential stressor is present. For example, if a tone is presented just before shock, the tone comes to evoke HPA activation. However, consider when the animal successfully learns to perform an avoidance response by reacting quickly to the tone. Over the period of learning, there is a gradual diminution in HPA activation until it returns to near baseline (Coover *et al.*, 1973).

Activation of the two systems

Successful action

To return to our favourite example (well, my favourite, at least), suppose that we meet a bear and run. The threat triggers SNS activation, which, among other things increases heart-rate. It also triggers HPA activation, which increases the supply of glucose to the blood. Both effects aid survival. Increased secretion of adrenalin and corticosteroid makes fuels such as glucose available from reserves. Fats are mobilized and their concentration in the blood increases (Guyton, 1991). Fats are metabolized (i.e. chemically converted to provide the fuel for action) as part of the physical exertion in running.

Assuming that one escapes, activity in the two neurohormonal systems might normally return to near baseline. If this happens the system is working optimally, i.e. the challenge promotes behavioural and neurohormonal actions that serve to resolve the challenge.

Stress and some consequences

Stress occurs when neurohormonal systems are excited in a way that is unjustified by the associated behaviour. A classic example consists of exciting these systems while in a sedentary situation, e.g. internal turmoil caused by anger directed at the boss but where neither fighting nor fleeing is advised.

Why is stress damaging to health? Among other reasons, fatty substances termed lipids that are brought into the bloodstream in large amounts are a problem. If they are not metabolized, they tend to gather on the walls of arteries. This is a process termed **atherosclerosis** (or arteriosclerosis) (Scheidt, 1996). A long-term elevation of lipid levels, associated with them not being metabolized (e.g. during stressful inactivity), risks the health of the circulation.

A similar argument can be applied to the HPA system. Activation of the HPA system followed by a quick return to a basal level characterizes an efficient response (Dienstbier, 1989). Excessive levels of corticosteroids over a protracted period are damaging, e.g. to the immune and nervous systems (Seeman and Robbins, 1994). If corticosteroid level declines only slowly, this indicates a continued excitation of the HPA system, an inefficient function. Ageing can be associated with excessive boosting of the HPA system with an associated weakening of negative feedback.

We now look at some of the situations that trigger stress.

Section summary

1 Stress is associated with an identifiable pattern of physiological changes.

2 Stressors commonly cause activation of the sympathetic system and a lowering of activity within the parasympathetic system.

3 Stress is sometimes associated with activation of the parasympathetic system.

4 Stressors trigger the hypothalamic pituitary adrenocortical system.

5 A healthy profile consists of a rapid activation of sympathetic and HPA systems and then a quick return to baseline.

6 One risk associated with stress is the deposition of lipids on the walls of the arteries.

Test your knowledge

(Answer on page 352)

13.3 With respect to Figure 13.3, what would be the effect of injecting (i) a CRF antagonist, (ii) corticosteroids?

Stressors, contexts and reactions

Introduction

Whether a potential stressor becomes an actual stressor can depend on context, e.g. (1) the capacity to predict when the stressor will occur, (2) opportunities for action and (3) what the animal does in response to the potential stressor and the outcome of this. Other factors include the history of the animal. Exposure to a stressor can change the animal, so that the future reaction to stressors is different. This section also considers the idea that, confronted with a stressor, there can be more than one strategy.

Predictability and controllability

The consequences of exposure to a stressor vary with **controllability**. If an animal can exert control to terminate a stressor, indices of stress are lower, as compared with a passive ('yoked') control exposed to the same stressor (Weiss, 1972). Chronic lack of control is a developmental precursor of adult anxiety and depression (Chorpita and Barlow, 1998).

Weiss (1971) subjected yoked pairs of rats to electric shock to the tail. Both received identical shocks but, whereas one could exert control, the other ('control rat') could not. The active rat could terminate shock *for both rats* by turning a wheel, a coping strategy. The passive (control) rat also had access to a wheel but its actions were ineffective as far as the shock was concerned. Active rats showed greater weight gains and less gastric ulceration than did yoked controls. This experiment has proved to be a model of wide application, pointing to the importance of control. In humans, the impact of potential stressors is ameliorated by gaining control (Allan and Scheidt, 1996b). For example, a high pressure of work becomes less stressful if the person has capacity to make decisions on how the work is done.

Even in the absence of control, an animal that has some **predictability** of potential stressors shows fewer signs of stress compared with one without predictability, as indexed by gastric ulceration (Weiss, 1971). For example, predictability can be obtained where a warning sound occurs before shock.

Exposure to inescapable shock can lead to **learned helplessness**: an animal appears to learn that it has no agency, thereby gives up and is 'resigned' to the situation. Following this condition, if a contingency of escape or avoidance is introduced, the animal fails to take appropriate action (Seligman, 1975). Learned helplessness is not 'non-behaving'. Rather, it exemplifies emotional-biasing of behaviour towards passivity, mediated via active inhibition of skeletal muscles. Experience with inescapable shock increases a rat's tendency to freeze in other situations, e.g. after shock in a novel environment. Passivity in the face of uncertain threat has some of the hallmarks of anxiety. This offers possible links with theorists who see anxiety as a precursor to depression (Chorpita and Barlow, 1998).

Sensitization

The reaction to a potential stressor depends also on past history. Exposure to a stressor can sensitize the nervous system such that the future behavioural and hormonal reaction to a stressor is increased (Sorg and Kalivas, 1995).

Sensitization can be very long-lasting, even for a lifetime. In rats, exposure to an inescapable stressor can trigger a long-term increase in the tendency to immobility and a reduction in social interaction, as well as increased HPA response to novelty (van Dijken *et al.*, 1993).

Developmental and age factors

Suppose that infant rats are briefly handled by the experimenter, involving separation from the mother. This intervention has a protective ('inoculating') effect regarding the impact of subsequent stressors. As an adult, the rat has a more healthy profile of HPA activity and an increased tendency to explore a novel environment (Castanon and Mormède, 1994). A capacity for control in the face of stressors when young gives rise to adult resilience, 'toughening-up' (Dienstbier, 1989), indexed by a greater density of corticosteroid receptors and lower levels of corticosteroids. Conversely, extended periods of separation from the mother have a detrimental effect upon later functioning of the HPA system.

Ageing is normally associated with some loss of corticosteroid receptors in the brain, reduced negative feedback and increasing levels of corticosteroids (Anisman *et al.*, 1998).

Active and passive strategies

Introduction

The strategy that an animal adopts on confrontation with a stressor depends upon various circumstances. Related to the strategy, Henry (1982) described two types of stress, which differ in the hormonal axis that is most activated:

1 The sympathetic system is associated with the behaviour of fight and flight and is activated when the power to gain access to such things as food or a mate is challenged: '. . . and the subject perceives that an adequate response is feasible'.

2 The HPA axis is strongly activated by: 'adverse conditions, such as immobilization, in which the animal is helpless'.

For various species (e.g. mice, rats and possibly humans), individuals have a bias towards either an active or a passive reaction (Castanon and Mormède, 1994), each with its characteristic hormonal profile. Genetic differences are associated with different biases. However, the two behavioural options are not entirely distinct hormonally. Thus, a strategy of fight or flight with sympathetic activation also involves activation of the HPA axis. This difference in strategy suggests the application of the term 'personality' also to non-humans. Henry suggests that there is an adaptive advantage in having the facility to inhibit behavioural tendencies to fight or flee. If an animal is confronted by

regular challenges for which neither option is viable, there could be advantages in staying still.

An animal can be biased towards one strategy but have the facility for showing the other, albeit at a higher threshold. For instance, it might learn that one strategy has failed and then switch to the other. However, in stress either strategy can 'get stuck' outside its adaptive range. This leads to the notion of different kinds of stress, arising from a failure of one strategy or the other.

The next two sections review some classical studies of reaction to stressors in different species, looking for general principles.

Tree shrews

Von Holst (1986) placed a tree shrew (*Tupaia belangeri*; Figure 13.4) into a cage where a resident conspecific was already housed. A fight followed, the outcome of which established a victor (i.e. dominant) and a defeated animal ('vanquished'). According to their behaviour, the 'vanquished' group could be further divided into 'subdominants' and 'submissives'. Subdominants took active steps to avoid dominants. Submissives, by contrast, were passive and unresponsive, sitting in the corner in a way characterized as 'apathetic' or 'depressive'. In response to the threats of the dominant, they neither fled nor attempted to defend themselves.

Subdominants and submissives gradually lost weight. After 10 days of the encounter, testosterone concentration fell by 30% in subdominants and 60% in submissives. After 20 days, blood testosterone level doubled in dominants.

Corticosteroid concentration was elevated for the first three days in all animals, though more so in submissives than in dominants or subdominants. Following the establishment of a dominance relationship, this fell to its initial value in both dominants and subdominants. In the submissives, by contrast, corticosteroid levels were elevated dramatically (by 300%) and remained so throughout.

Figure 13.4 Tree shrew.
Source: © Rod Williams/naturepl.com

Von Holst looked at the level of tyrosine hydroxylase, a chemical in the synthetic pathway for catecholamines, in the adrenal glands. Following the encounter, this was not significantly changed in dominants and decreased by about 30% in submissives. It increased by more than 100% in subdominants, suggestive of sympathetic activation. The fact that their adrenal noradrenalin content increases by about 30% also points to this.

Figure 13.5 compares heart-rates for representative dominants and subdominants. In both cases, there is a sharp elevation on first meeting. In dominants, this soon returns to normal, whereas that of the subdominants remains elevated throughout. Note the near disappearance of the normal day–night rhythm in the magnitude of heart-rate in subdominants.

Dominants seemed to suffer no ill effects from the confrontation. Weight and testosterone levels were well maintained. Their heart-rate was restrained, in spite of the fact that they were required to exert authority in the occasional fight. According to the criteria proposed here, dominants were not stressed. They had a coping strategy. By

contrast, both subgroups of vanquished animals were stressed. They lost weight and showed lowered reproductive capacity. Neither strategy, active or passive, seemed to work. The elevated heart-rate of subdominants would have been appropriate for a short-term fight or flight strategy with a high energy requirement. However, over long periods such elevation indicates that the underlying problem has not been solved. The physiological profile is inappropriate to behaviour. By the criterion of chronic elevated corticosteroids, submissives were also stressed. Such elevation is appropriate for increased activity. However, their behaviour was that of passivity, a situation in which elevated HPA activity would seem inappropriate.

Primates

Sapolsky (1990a,b) studied wild olive baboons (*Papio anubis*) living in social troops of 50–200 animals, in East Africa (Figure 13.6). Sapolsky (1990a, p. 863) notes that olive baboons have little threat from predators which 'leaves them hours each day to devote to generating social stressors for

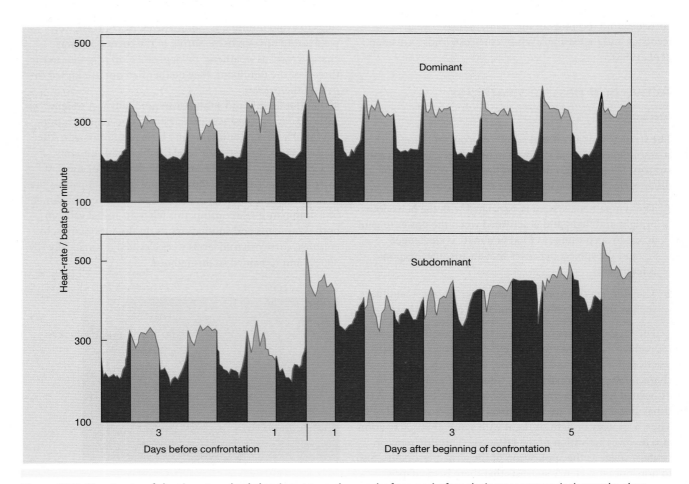

Figure 13.5 Heart-rate of dominant and subdominant tree shrews, before and after their encounter: dark purple, day; light purple, night. *Source*: von Holst (1986, Fig. 3, p. 665).

Figure 13.6 Olive baboons.

Source: GerryEllis/Minden/FLPA

each other'. Thus, they might provide a model of some stresses of humans in affluent societies. Baboon society is hierarchical with dominants gaining most desirable resources, e.g. food and resting sites. Fights over dominance are frequent and often with serious injury. Riddled with cunning and deception, the worst aspects of baboon society appear to be as Machiavellian as those of humans.

In a stable hierarchy, low-ranking baboon males have a higher basal level of cortisol than do high-ranking males. However, in response to a challenge, dominant males show a sharper rise in cortisol secretion than do lower ranks. Sapolsky associates the high basal levels of cortisol of low-ranking baboons with events in their lives that trigger the HPA axis, e.g. disruption of on-going activities, lack of predictability and control, frustration and being the innocent victim of displaced aggression. When there is instability in a hierarchy, e.g. a baboon equivalent of an impending *coup d'etat*, dominant males exhibit chronic elevated cortisol.

In 1984, East Africa experienced a drought and the time that needed to be spent in foraging increased considerably. This was associated with less aggression: as Sapolsky terms it (p. 865) the drought was 'a hidden blessing for subordinate individuals'.

Sapolsky (1990a, p. 874) speculates: 'If one were giving stress management courses to baboons . . .', and his advice is little different from that applicable to humans. Emphasis would be on acquiring predictability and control, forming reliable alliances, gaining skill at assessing social situations and finding suitable outlets for frustration. Success involves picking few fights and winning these.

The chapter now turns to the role of the immune system in stress.

Section summary

1 The impact of a stressor can be reduced by predictability and control.

2 In a situation of inescapable shock, learned helplessness can develop.

3 Exposure to a stressor can sensitize subsequent reactions to stressors.

4 There can be a bias towards either active or passive coping strategies.

5 Failure of either active or passive strategies corresponds to stress.

Test your knowledge

(Answer on page 352)

13.4 Which neurohormonal system is particularly triggered at times when a threat is presented and *active* steps are taken to counter it?

Stress and the immune system

Introduction

The *immune system* deals with threats to the body, of the kind that are within its boundaries (Evans *et al.*, 1997). This type of threat is described by the term **pathogen**. These are harmful bacteria and viruses, which can enter the body through, for example, cuts to the skin or the food that is eaten or during sexual contact. The immune system is our defence against these invaders from outside and also against cancerous cells.

Stress has effects upon the immune system. Furthermore, events within the immune system affect the brain processes associated with stress. This section considers these interacting factors.

The interaction between psychological states, as embodied in the nervous system, and the endocrine and immune systems is summarized in such terms as 'psychoneuroimmunology' or 'psychoendoimmunology' (Ader and Cohen, 1985). If this book had been written in the

1970s or 1980s, it is very unlikely to have had even a mention of the immune system. It is relatively recently that the interactions between, on the one hand, the nervous and endocrine systems and, on the other, the immune system have been formally recognized. The existence of links from psychological states to immune activity provides a framework for understanding how stress can increase proneness to infectious disease (Cohen, 1996).

Some details of the immune system

Consider the cells (Chapter 1, 'Introduction') that make up the immune system: many millions of them, termed white cells or **leucocytes**. They are stored at certain 'depots' in the body, such as the spleen, from which, they are supplied to the body fluids. Leucocytes are carried in the body fluids (e.g. blood) to all parts of the body. They patrol, being, metaphorically speaking, on the look-out for invasion. Detection of pathogens activates the immune system. Immune cells launch an attack, which, if successful, destroys the invader. Our principal concern is with one class of leucocyte, known as the **lymphocyte**. When the body is invaded by bacteria or viruses, lymphocytes multiply ('proliferate') and go on the offensive (Evans et al., 1997). In launching an attack, chemicals termed **cytokines**, are released from cells of the immune system.

Interactions between immune and nervous systems

The immune system influences the brain and the endocrine system and also it is influenced by them. This section looks at each of these directions of influence in turn.

The effects of the immune system

The immune activation in response to infection has consequences for nervous and endocrine systems. For example, cells of the immune system release hormones that affect the CNS. Cytokines, released as part of the immune response, influence the activity of the nervous system (Dunn, 1989). Thereby, the CNS is informed of the activity of the immune system. The cytokine interleukin-1 (IL-1), which is released from activated immune cells, plays an important role here. Cytokines injected into the cerebrospinal fluid (Chapter 5) have a potent effect on behaviour, which leads to the suggestion that, under natural conditions, central cytokines influence behaviour (Chapter 12). Injection of IL-1 produces a 'sickness reaction' of fever, withdrawal from social contact and reduction of exploration, etc. (Larson, 2002).

Information on immune cell activity from the periphery to the brain is conveyed in part by means of neural links (Yirmiya, 1997). A major part of the effect of IL-1 on the brain is mediated via the vagus nerve (Figure 3.30, p. 74). Neurons within this nerve are triggered by IL-1 detected at their tips and they convey this information to the brain.

Interleukin-1 (IL-1) causes the release of CRF from the hypothalamus (Sapolsky et al., 1987), suggesting the appropriateness of the term 'stressor'. In turn, the CRF excites ACTH and corticosteroid release.

In response to infection by a virus, the body is not in the best condition to be active and typically the animal curls up in a lethargic ball until recovery (Hart, 1988). This exemplifies coordination between behaviour and physiology. However, in humans, in what appears to be an exaggeration of an adaptive reaction, activation of the immune system can contribute towards a depressed mood (Yirmiya, 1997).

That the brain is sensitive to these signals has led to the notion that the immune system can be considered to be an internal sensory organ, i.e. one responsible for detecting bacteria and viruses, etc. Maier and Watkins (1998) suggest that we underestimate the importance of the immune system for psychological state. Day-to-day fluctuations in mood might depend at least in part upon changes within the immune system.

Effects on the immune system

The nervous system affects the activity of the immune system, this being both mediated directly and through the endocrine system. At times the nervous system excites the immune system and at other times inhibition is exerted (O'Leary, 1990). Cells of the immune system have receptors for substances on their walls, which, in the nervous and endocrine systems, constitute neurotransmitters and hormones. In this way, the nervous and endocrine systems can influence the activity of the immune system.

Sympathetic neurons innervate the organs that constitute part of the immune system (Ballieux and Heijnen, 1987), organs that would normally be packed with leucocytes. The leukocytes contain receptors for the transmitter released by these neurons, suggesting that nervous system activity can excite or inhibit the release of leucocytes into the body fluids. Activation of the immune system appears to be specifically by the sympathetic branch.

Stress can inhibit, or 'down-regulate', the activity of the immune system (Evans et al., 1997). For example, the human immune response is down-regulated by such chronic stressors as divorce, bereavement, sleep deprivation and war (Maier et al., 1994). Down-regulation means a less effective defence against challenges.

Rats that have been exposed to stressors have a decreased activity of immune cells. Placing a rat in a situation of helplessness has a detrimental effect upon the immune system and the ability to reject a tumour (Laudenslager *et al.*, 1983). To have some coping capacity, e.g. the capacity to terminate shock by lever-pressing, is of benefit. It is not easy to generalize from this to humans.

Cohen (1996) asked volunteers to fill in stress- and life-events questionnaires and then exposed them to the common cold virus by nasal drops. They were then quarantined. Blood samples were taken to assess infection. Would stress increase the risk of an upper respiratory illness? There was a significant effect in this direction. Even where people did not subjectively feel that they were stressed, life-events normally termed 'stressful' were associated with increased susceptibility to illness.

Some cells of the immune system, a type of lymphocyte termed 'natural killer' (NK) cells, target cancerous cells and destroy them. However, the relationship between stress and the onset and development of cancer in humans is, at the time of writing, still controversial. The link between depression and health as mediated by the immune system is also not entirely clear (Stein *et al.*, 1991). There are indications that cervical cancer is more likely in women who report hopelessness and that cancer patients with social support are better able to survive (Edelman and Kidman, 1997). Optimism appears to speed wound-healing after surgery, an effect that is mediated, it would appear, in part via an enhanced immune activity (Kiecolt-Glaser *et al.*, 1998).

The *acute* application of some stressors, i.e. a change over minutes rather than hours or days (e.g. a public speaking task), can trigger *up*-regulation (Evans *et al.*, 1997). The acute phase of up-regulation might be due to sympathetic activity.

Stressors can exert effects through routes other than those nervous and endocrine system processes described so far. For example, divorce or bereavement might mean less sleep and exercise and an increase in alcohol and cigarette consumption, with independent effects on disease. Also by changes in physiology (e.g. blood flow), stressors might influence disease through routes other than the immune system (Maier *et al.*, 1994). Some stressors lower the production of saliva, probably with a reduction in protection of the oral cavity (Evans *et al.*, 1997). In stress, people might be more inclined to seek the company of others, with increased risk of such things as the common cold and influenza.

Function

Consider first that events in the immune system affect the nervous system. Suppose that an animal is suffering an infection. It could be in its interests to rest and sleep, to allow recovery to occur (Hart, 1988). Therefore, it could be advantageous for chemical messengers that are secreted by activated cells of the immune system to steer behaviour in this direction.

Why should the nervous and endocrine systems influence the immune system? For example, why does stress tend to lower the activity of the system? It might prove crucial to distinguish two phases of stress: (1) an acute phase, during which the immune system seems to be excited, and (2) a chronic phase, during which it seems to be inhibited (Maier and Watkins, 1998). A time of sympathetic activation might well correspond to fight or flight, when presumably there is a risk of injury and infection (O'Leary, 1990). To boost immune activity at this time could make good adaptive sense. On the other hand, the suppression of immune function during chronic stress might be a means of restraining the activity of the (already excited) system at a time when infection might be less likely.

At first sight, it might seem logical to play safe; surely the bigger the immune response, the better. However, nothing in life comes free and there are costs attached to immune activity. In terms of resources, there is an energy cost (Sapolsky, 1992). Also, an activated immune system can launch an attack not just upon disease agents such as bacteria but also against parts of the 'self' (Råberg *et al.*, 1998), the so-called autoimmune disorders. So, under some conditions, there could be an adaptive advantage in restraining the immune system.

A caution

Psychoneuroimmunology (PNI) gives a scientific basis to some folk wisdom on the capacity of the 'mind to affect the body' (Evans *et al.*, 1997). PNI evokes reactions ranging from scepticism to unqualified acceptance. To sceptics, the effects seem fragile and offer little clinical hope. To some of those into alternative holistic approaches, it is attractive to attribute ills to a psychological construct, stress. However, we must avoid exaggerated claims of the kind that psychological factors are all-important and the causation of, say, cancer lies 'all in the mind'.

A critical approach recognizes interacting factors in disease onset and development. The psychological effect is only one (albeit important) factor among many that influence the immune system and might thereby influence disease. We need more cautious claims of the kind that, under some conditions, certain stressors can affect parts of the immune system and probably disease onset and development.

Having looked at the more peripheral parts of the picture we now look at the brain mechanisms that underlie the stress reaction.

1 The immune system protects the body against 'invaders' that have penetrated its boundary, e.g. viruses and bacteria, as well as cancer.

2 There are reciprocal links between nervous, endocrine and immune systems.

3 The immune system affects the nervous system and thereby influences behaviour.

4 The nervous system can both excite and inhibit the activity of the immune system.

5 Chronic stress, a state of the CNS, can inhibit the activity of the immune system.

6 Some effects of stress on the immune system appear to be mediated by corticosteroids.

Test your knowledge

(Answer on page 352)

13.5 By what criterion could we class a cytokine as a hormone?

Brain mechanisms

Introduction

So far, our focus has been mainly on the more peripheral features of stress, in terms of hormones, the circulation and immune system, etc. We turn now to the brain and consider those processes that are the neuropsychological embodiment of stress. There are some closely related leads in this investigation, as can be appreciated from Figure 13.7:

1 In stress, the neural mechanisms underlying such emotions as fear or anger (Chapter 12) are activated over long periods of time. A reconsideration of the basics of these mechanisms and their prolonged activation is therefore a lead (Rosen and Schulkin, 1998).

2 The two hormonal systems described earlier (the sympathetic and HPA systems) are triggered by activity in particular parts of the brain. Therefore, psychologists can look at release of these hormones and trace the causal links back into the brain.

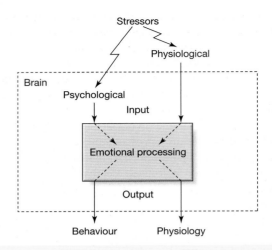

Figure 13.7 The brain is put into states of stress by means of stressors and their interpretation (the 'input'). In turn, the brain provides signals to the neurohormonal systems of stress (the 'output').

3 In the brain, there are links between (1) and (2) and investigators can try to trace them.

We shall now examine these sources of insight.

Initial triggers to emotion and stress

A principal focus of emotion research is the amygdala, as a site where some emotional significance is attached to events. Chapter 12 noted that some stimuli, such as loud sounds, evoke emotion simply by virtue of their sensory properties. This draws attention to neurons within sensory pathways having collaterals that project to brain regions (e.g. amygdala) underlying stress. By contrast, other triggers such as frustration cannot be defined by sensory events *per se* but only by the comparison of sensory events with memories. Such 'cognitive input' suggests the involvement of the hippocampus and cortical processing (Glue *et al.*, 1993). Certain products of the immune system affect regions of brain underlying stress, as represented by 'physiological' in Figure 13.7.

Corticotropin releasing factor

Introduction

A neurochemical of the brain that plays a central role in emotional processing is corticotropin releasing factor (CRF) (Dunn and Berridge, 1990). So, in the study of stress, we need to consider the activity of this neurochemical. CRF was described earlier as a hormone, part of the HPA axis (Figure 13.3). At the pituitary gland, it plays this *peripheral* role (peripheral, that is, relative to regions deep in the brain). However, CRF also acts as a neurotransmitter or neuromodulator deep in the CNS, a *central* role. Stressors trigger coordinated CRF activity in both central and peripheral roles. First, we look at the controls of CRF secretion when it acts as a hormone and we then consider its role as a neurotransmitter.

Hormonal role

CRF-containing neurons with cell bodies in the hypothalamus form the start of the HPA axis (Figure 13.3). These neurons receive inputs from various regions, e.g. other hypothalamic regions, brain stem, hippocampus and the central nucleus of the amygdala (Chapter 12; Amaral and Sinnamon, 1977). These neurons therefore form a common focus for various sources of information, conveying, in functional terms, 'challenge and the need to take action'.

Neurotransmitter roles

Now we need to change hats, or, to be precise, roles of CRF and switch attention to a different role of the same substance.

CRF-containing neurons convey emotion-related information between various parts of the brain. Cell bodies of CRF-containing neurons are found in the amygdala (Bohus and Koolhaas, 1993). CRF's wide representation throughout the limbic system and in structures concerned with autonomic control suggests a coordinated role in autonomic and behavioural outputs, which is stretched excessively in stress.

Intracerebral CRF injection leads to EEG signs of arousal and to an increase in the acoustic startle response (Chapter 12), an index of stress and anxiety (Dunn and Berridge, 1990). In exciting the locus coeruleus, CRF activates noradrenergic transmission over large areas of brain, discussed next.

Noradrenergic systems and the locus coeruleus

In reaction to stressors, noradrenalin (NA) acts peripherally as both neurotransmitter and hormone (Chapters 3 and 12). It is broadcast widely, attaches to a broad distribution of receptors and thereby influences diverse organs (e.g. cardiac muscle and smooth muscle in blood vessel walls). The same chemical is used in the CNS, where it is also widely distributed and serves a neuromodulatory role at diverse targets (Zigmond *et al.*, 1995). The functional coherence of noradrenalin's dual role in periphery and CNS, points to interesting evolutionary roots. That is to say, in both cases, stressors trigger its release.

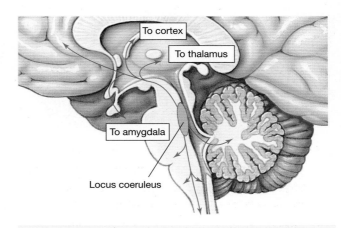

Figure 13.8 The human locus coeruleus and projections. Descending projections influence the ANS.

Source: Figure 3.17 (1996) Matin, JH. Neuroanatomy: Text and Atlas, 2nd Edition, p. 87. Reprinted with permission of The McGraw-Hill Companies, Inc.

Activity within noradrenergic neurons that project from the locus coeruleus appears to be an important feature of stress, associated with both behavioural and sympathetic activity (Dampney, 1994). See Figure 13.8.

Triggers to the sympathetic system

Moving to the output side of the brain, a nucleus that integrates information ('integrative nucleus') and controls sympathetic activity is located in the medulla (Figure 13.9; Dampney, 1994). Neurons project from here to sympathetic preganglionic neurons with cell bodies in the spinal cord and controlling the circulatory system (in Figure 13.8, note the link to the spinal cord). Figure 13.9 shows inputs to the 'integrative nucleus' from the lateral hypothalamus, nucleus of the solitary tract, paraventricular nucleus of the hypothalamus and the periaqueductal grey (Chapter 5). These brain regions are involved in recruiting defensive behaviours in response to threats. Considering adaptive functioning, the link with the sympathetic system points to coherence between behaviour (fight and flight) and physiology. In stress, these systems show elevated activity over long periods of time.

Following sections look at disorders associated with stress and, in so doing, further insight into the brain mechanisms that have been discussed in this section can be gained.

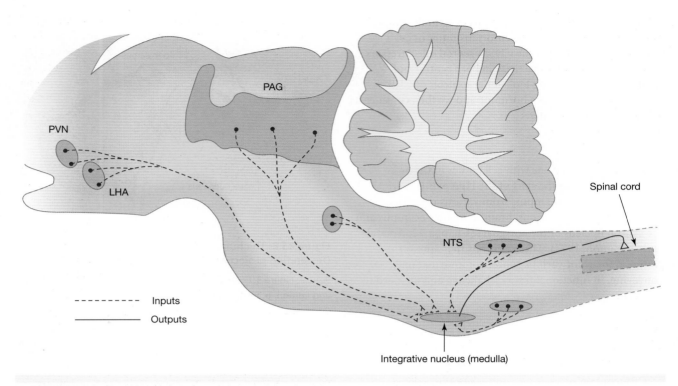

Figure 13.9 Some connections with an integrative nucleus in the medulla. LHA, lateral hypothalamic area; NTS, nucleus of the solitary tract; PAG, periaqueductal grey; PVN, paraventricular nucleus of hypothalamus.

Source: adapted from Dampney (1990, Fig. 3, p. 65).

Section summary

1 Looking at the basic brain mechanisms of emotion and their protracted activation gives a lead to understanding stress.

2 In actions within the CNS and in triggering the HPA axis, corticotropin releasing factor (CRF) appears to play functionally coherent roles in its behavioural, autonomic and hormonal effects.

3 In stress, noradrenalin activation occurs in the periphery and CNS, indicating functional coherence.

4 Central noradrenergic systems trigger behavioural and autonomic activation.

5 The locus coeruleus and NA neurons that project from it have a pivotal role in activation at times of stress.

Test your knowledge

(Answer on page 352)

13.6 CRF acts as a hormone or a neurotransmitter or both. Justify your answer.

Depression

Chapter 3 briefly considered depression and we now extend this account. Stress and depression can usefully be studied together, since stress is a risk factor for depression (Bremner, 1999). This section looks at some areas of overlap in the two conditions.

The HPA axis

Depression is associated with enlargement of the adrenal gland, increased activity of the HPA axis and elevated levels of cortisol in the blood (Holsboer and Barden, 1996). What triggers this activation? The drive from CRF-containing neurons at the start of the HPA axis is increased. Increased drive might arise from the increased activity of noradrenergic neurons of the locus coeruleus that is observed in depression (Ur *et al.*, 1992).

An important factor in depression appears to be weakened negative feedback of corticosteroids in the brain. By reducing this inhibitory effect, the excitatory link is less opposed and thereby this contributes to HPA excitation (Holsboer and Barden, 1996). See Figure 13.3. Major depression is associated with some loss of tissue at the hippocampus, which could be the product of the toxicity of excessive corticosteroid levels (Bremner, 1999). A range of antidepressants tend to lower activity in the HPA axis (Mitchell, 1998) and an interesting idea is that antidepressants exert some effect by increasing corticosteroid feedback on the HPA axis (Barden *et al.*, 1995). Increasing age appears to lower the efficacy of corticosteroid feedback at the hippocampus (Seeman and Robbins, 1994) and might be a contributory factor to depression. Cushing's disease, which involves excessive secretion of corticosteroids, is commonly followed by depression (Holsboer and Barden, 1996).

The CNS affects the HPA axis and, reciprocally, the HPA axis (e.g. elevated corticosteroids) affects the CNS. Disturbances within these interactions appear to be fundamental to depression. By their actions at the brain, corticosteroids appear to bias towards negative emotion (Schulkin, 1994), vigilance and avoidance of conflict (van Honk *et al.*, 1998). Of course, in small doses and over a limited time period such changes could be adaptive.

Breier *et al.* (1988) found a tendency for people who had experienced separation from a parent in childhood to be predisposed to develop psychopathology when adult. Their cortisol levels were higher than controls.

In depression, there is increased blood flow to the amygdala and medial orbitofrontal cortex, both regions having a high density of corticosteroid receptors (Erikson *et al.*, 2003). Thereby, elevated levels of corticosteroids appear to contribute to the negative bias to cognition in depression.

Role of CRF as a neurotransmitter

The activity of CRF in the brains of people suffering depression is elevated (Mitchell, 1998), i.e. there is a higher release level. This plays a role in increased activity in brain areas concerned with processing negative emotion, e.g. regions of the amygdala. In depression, increased activity of the locus coeruleus and the associated NA systems appears to be due to increased CRF-mediated input to the locus coeruleus. It might constitute an important biological basis of depression (Curtis and Valentino, 1994; Ur *et al.*, 1992). A number of effective treatments for depression lower CRF levels (Markou *et al.*, 1998), e.g. some antidepressant drugs

oppose the excitatory effects of CRF in the locus coeruleus (Curtis and Valentino, 1994). Increased CRF activity in the brain is observed during withdrawal from drugs, pointing to common features between this state and depression (Markou *et al.*, 1998). Suicide victims show down-regulation (Chapter 4, 'The cells of the nervous system') of CRF receptors in their frontal cortex, suggestive of hypersecretion of CRF (Markou *et al.*, 1998).

Section summary

1 In depression there is activation of the HPA axis.

2 Elevated corticosteroids appear to give a negative bias to mood.

3 Injection of CRF into the brain triggers features of depression and there is evidence of CRF activation in depression.

4 On balance, evidence suggests noradrenergic activation in depression.

Test your knowledge

(Answers on page 352)

13.7 Complete the following: 'A decrease in corticosteroid feedback action in the brain causes _____ activity in the HPA system'.

13.8 In what way could the material in this section make any sense in terms of the functional type of explanation?

13.3

Stress and the cardiovascular system

Background

Associations between mental state and the heart have been observed for some 4500 years (Williams, 1989) and stress is central to the relationship.

What is termed **coronary heart disease (CHD)** is a disorder of the vessels that supply blood to the heart, in almost all cases consisting of atherosclerosis within the coronary arteries (Scheidt, 1996). CHD is the biggest killer in Western countries. This section explores the link between stress, personality and the health of the circulatory system.

Type A and Type B personalities

Early research identified **Type A behaviour**, particularly associated with CHD, the person who exhibits it being termed a 'Type A' (Friedman and Rosenman, 1959). Type A behaviour consists of being under excessive time-pressure, aggressively competitive, over-ambitious and easily aroused to hostility by situations judged as trivial by non-Type As. Billings *et al.* (1996) observe that CHD patients appear to be (p. 244): 'especially prone to the cultural emphasis on individualism and accomplishment, characteristics that promote isolation rather than interpersonal connection'.

The SNS is hyper-reactive in Type As, with the parasympathetic under-active (Friedman, 1996). There is high secretion of corticosteroids and (usually, though not always) a high blood level of cholesterol and a tendency to heart attacks (Williams, 1989). The cause of the problem appears to lie in a chronic tilting of the sympathetic– parasympathetic balance towards the sympathetic (Roberts, 1996). So what tilts the balance? Friedman (1996) incriminates covert features of the Type A personality, consisting of insecurity and a low value of self-esteem. The perfectionist goals of self-esteem through achievement are never reached.

A personal angle
The role of hostility

A patient, B.G., a successful businessman, aged 44, enjoyed getting his own way (Williams, 1989). B.G.'s mode of operation was to threaten others into surrender. (You might well know a 'B.G.' or two!) One day, B.G. was driving his car, as always in a hurry, when another motorist had the audacity to overtake. B.G.'s reaction would invariably be to find a means to 'pay the bastard back', by accelerating and emitting a warning blast on the horn. However, this time things were different. Just as B.G. was getting into attack mode, he had an experience as 'though a red-hot poker was being driven into the centre of his chest'. B.G. had his first heart attack.

A record of the electrical activity of the heart, an electrocardiogram, was made, and was normal. B.G.'s pain went away and he was free of symptoms for several days. Alas, on the day scheduled for discharge from hospital, disaster struck as a blood sample was being taken. B.G. switched into the anger mode, whereupon 'the red-hot poker hit his chest again'. The electrocardiogram indicated that the blood supply to B.G.'s heart was inadequate. Arteriosclerosis had almost completely blocked one of the arteries. Surgeons removed a vein from B.G.'s leg and transplanted it to the heart.

Williams employed therapy to target B.G.'s hostility and lack of trust. B.G. lived in a world populated by people whose incompetence demanded eternal vigilance. Williams prescribed behaviour modification in the hope that B.G. could alter his behaviour and cognitions. B.G. is not an isolated case. A positive correlation is found between hostility score and magnitude of arteriosclerosis of the coronary arteries.

Type B behaviour is the opposite of the Type A, i.e. relaxed and without hostility and competitiveness (Friedman, 1996). The 'Type B' has a relatively high level of self-esteem and feelings of security and can tolerate the mistakes of others. Type Bs do not exhibit the neurohormonal abnormalities of Type As. Blood cholesterol is relatively low.

Although we are all probably familiar with some 'textbook' Type As and Type Bs, it is wrong to think in terms of an absolute bimodal distinction. Rather, a person might lie somewhere between the two or show a mixture of the two according to context.

Rather than personality, could some other factor correlate with Type A behaviour and contribute to the effects on the coronary condition (Steptoe, 1993)? For example, Type As probably smoke or drink more alcohol than Type Bs. However, personality is an independent factor that contributes in interaction with other factors such as smoking (Williams, 1989). There is disagreement as to whether all the characteristics of the Type A are equally toxic, with some theorists placing a particular blame on hostility.

B.G. illustrates two aspects of coronary heart disease: (1) the chronic background state of hostility and atherosclerosis that sets the scene and (2) that in some cases, but not all, an emotional incident is the immediate trigger to a heart attack (Allan and Scheidt, 1996b).

There is a clear link between low socio-economic status (SES) and poor health (Gallo and Matthews, 2003). Numerous factors mediate this link but one is central to the present chapter: low SES is associated with a high frequency of negative cognitive and emotional reactions and low coping resources. The link appears to be mediated in part by the SNS and HPA systems.

Negative emotion does not necessarily have to be expressed in overt behaviour to influence the ANS. By the use of the imagination and sub-vocal speech, people mentally re-run, and ruminate on, perceived injustices and personal insults (Allan and Scheidt, 1996b). Therapy for cardiac health counters covert 'behaviour': it monitors the 'inner dialogue' for the appearance of hostile thoughts and challenges them (Burell, 1996).

Section summary

1 Among the factors that determine coronary health is personality.

2 A distinction can be drawn between Type A and Type B behaviours, corresponding to Type A and Type B people.

3 Early studies found Type As to be more prone to coronary disease.

4 In Type As, there is excessive reactivity by the SNS.

Test your knowledge

(Answer on page 352)

13.9 You are trying to devise a drug to assist Type As with lowering the effects of their over-reactivity on the circulatory system but not setting out to target the CNS. Your first thought would probably be antagonists to which kind of neurochemical?

Post-traumatic stress disorder

The phenomenon

The condition termed **post-traumatic stress disorder (PTSD)** seriously disrupts many lives. It follows trauma in which there is actual or threatened death or serious injury to the sufferer or another person (Friedman *et al.*, 1995). Some core symptoms of PTSD are regular activation of memories relating to the incident, nightmares and high SNS arousal (Davis *et al.*, 1997). In addition to core symptoms, depression, aggression, irritability and impulsiveness are common. PTSD is associated with a heightened magnitude of the startle response (Orr *et al.*, 1995) and increased heart-rate acceleration to sounds (Pallmeyer *et al.*, 1986).

Only a fraction of people exposed to trauma develop the disorder, which raises issues concerning the characteristics of sufferers (Yehuda *et al.*, 1995). Over one-third of the US soldiers who served in Vietnam have experienced PTSD (Davis *et al.*, 1997).

Biological bases

Pitman *et al.* (1993) refer to 'emotive biasing' in PTSD and suggest that its embodiment could be sensitization of links from the basal amygdala to the ventromedial hypothalamus, a

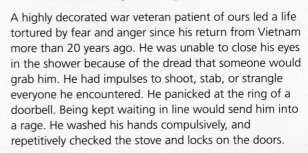

A personal angle
The tragedy of war

Pitman *et al.* (1993, p. 145) report:

A highly decorated war veteran patient of ours led a life tortured by fear and anger since his return from Vietnam more than 20 years ago. He was unable to close his eyes in the shower because of the dread that someone would grab him. He had impulses to shoot, stab, or strangle everyone he encountered. He panicked at the ring of a doorbell. Being kept waiting in line would send him into a rage. He washed his hands compulsively, and repetitively checked the stove and locks on the doors.

The patient illustrates three features of PTSD: (1) the coexistence of heightened fear and anger, (2) a range of situations in which over-reactivity is shown and (3) an association with other disorders, e.g. obsessive–compulsive disorder.

form of long-term potentiation (Chapter 11, 'Learning and memory'; Adamec, 1997). Artificial stimulation of the amygdala is associated with 'memory flashback', suggesting that it triggers a search for emotionally tagged material that is brought into conscious awareness (Charney *et al.*, 1995). A range of stimuli might come to activate the amygdala and thereby retrieve traumatic memories (Le Doux, 1998). There is evidence suggesting damage to hippocampal tissue, in the cases of combat-related and childhood-abuse related PTSD. This is manifest as some loss of volume of this structure (Bremner, 1999). Given the role of the hippocampus in memory, early harm to this structure could have enormous implications for the recall of childhood memories (or a failure to do so).

One's intuitive guess would be that the HPA axis would also be chronically activated in this condition. Since the hippocampus is damaged and excessive corticosteroid levels are toxic to this structure, elevated levels of corticosteroids would be expected to accompany PTSD. However, there is some controversy on whether this is the case (Bremner, 1999; Yehuda *et al.*, 1995).

Section summary

1 Trauma, where there is actual or threatened death or serious injury, can trigger post-traumatic stress disorder (PTSD).

2 The hallmarks of PTSD are regular activation of traumatic memories, nightmares and SNS activation. Depression, aggressivity, irritability and impulsivity are often also shown.

Test your knowledge

(Answer on page 352)

13.10 In PTSD, there is evidence pointing to a toxic effect of corticosteroids on the hippocampus. Not everyone subject to trauma suffers from PTSD, so is there any other possible explanation for why sufferers from PTSD might have a lower than normal volume of hippocampus?

Influence of stress on the gut

Introduction

Common sayings point to a belief that there exist causal links between mental states and gastrointestinal function. A link between stress and gastrointestinal disorders is indicated by (a) 'nervous irritation' and (b) peptic ulceration, in the stomach and part of the small intestine, the duodenum (Levenstein, 1998). This section looks at these two examples of brain → gut links.

Irritable bowel syndrome

A disorder of the gut that arises in part through stress is the **irritable bowel syndrome** (IBS) (Stam *et al.*, 1997). The diagnostic criteria of IBS involve abdominal distension and pain, associated with abnormal patterns of defecation. Stressful events commonly precede the onset of an episode of IBS. IBS is especially prevalent in patients with psychiatric illnesses, e.g. anxiety, depression and PTSD. People commonly attribute the symptoms of IBS to stress, while targeting depression or anxiety is often an effective way of alleviating it (Meyer and Gebhart, 1994).

The enteric nervous system (ENS) stimulates coordinated patterns of gastrointestinal activity (termed 'motility') involving waves of contraction (Chapter 3). The ANS modulates activity within the ENS. In IBS, it appears that activity is abnormal as a result of increased sensitivity somewhere within these networks of neurons (Stam *et al.*, 1997). Transit of material through the small intestine is slowed but large intestine transit is accelerated (Williams *et al.*, 1988). IBS patients show a higher than normal sensitivity to gut distension. There could be abnormal modulation of the link between the sensory detection of material in the gut and motor action by the smooth muscles. The modulatory signal would be sensitive to stress.

Figure 13.10 summarizes some flows of signals involved in gut motility and sensation. Disturbances within any of these could underlie IBS. Note the route from the external world to the CNS, then through the ANS to the enteric nervous system (ENS) and hence to smooth muscles of the gut wall. Abnormal activity in this pathway is assumed to underlie the stress-mediated contribution to IBS. However, a contribution might also arise from sensory neurons in the gut wall feeding back through the pathway ENS → ANS → CNS. Abnormal sensitivity of this route or abnormal gut contents could set up disturbances in the feedback pathway, which might in turn influence motor outflow to the gut (Meyer and Gebhart, 1994).

Although there is a psychosomatic aspect of IBS, it should not be seen simply as a brain-driven ('psychological') disorder. Local factors, such as a gut infection, can also trigger it (Stam *et al.*, 1997). It is most accurately characterized as an interaction of local and central factors. Thus, an infection is more likely to trigger IBS in patients having prior stressful experiences.

Ulcers

Animal models show that **ulcers** can be triggered by several stressors. In baboons, gastric ulceration is highest in subordinates, who are subject to most social stress (Uno *et al.*, 1989). Increased risk of ulceration in people under stress (e.g. economic collapse) has argued for the existence of psychosomatic disorders (Levenstein, 1998). As noted earlier, animals exposed to an uncontrollable aversive situation tend to develop gastric ulcers (also termed 'peptic ulcers'). Amelioration of the impact of stressors can be obtained by allowing the animal some facility for control (Weiss *et al.*, 1976).

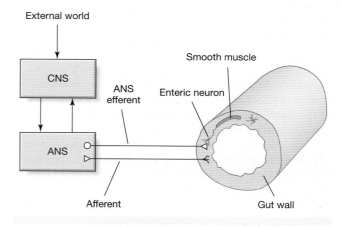

Figure 13.10 Some flows of information underlying gut motility.

Source: based on McKee and Quigley (1993).

There are neural and hormonal links between CNS and stomach (e.g. the vagus nerve). This provides a basis for expecting there to be causal links between psychological states and stomach pathology. However, a sensational discovery was reported by the Australian doctor, B.J. Marshall, and it moved attention away from psychological factors: a microorganism, the bacterium *Helicobacter pylori*, is involved in peptic ulcers (Marshall, 1995). Targeting this with antibiotics led to a cure in many cases, which caused some to dismiss psychosomatic causes. In 1998, Levenstein wrote (p. 538):

When *H. pylori* burst on the scene a few years ago, it revolutionised views on the aetiology and treatment of peptic ulcer. Psychosocial factors were quietly but firmly escorted off the stage, and gastroenterologists in particular banished psychological considerations with something approaching relief.

This was misguided science; the world does not always divide into neat physical *versus* psychological categories. Most people have the microorganism in their stomachs but most do not develop peptic ulcers (Weiner, 1996). Some are not infected but still develop them. Antibiotic medication is not effective for all patients. Recognition of the role of a microorganism does not lower the importance of a contribution from stress. There is the possibility of interaction between them. For example, stress can probably increase the vulnerability of the stomach wall to bacterial infection (Overmier and Murison, 1997). The immune system normally mounts an attack against bacteria but might be compromised in stress.

Section summary

1 The enteric nervous system organizes contractions of the gut. The irritable bowel syndrome (IBS) is a disturbance to this.

2 Stress, the effects of which are mediated via the CNS and ANS, is a causal factor implicated in IBS.

3 Peptic ulcers can be caused jointly by psychological factors and bacterial infection.

Test your knowledge

(Answer on page 352)

13.11 What type of muscle is involved in the irritable bowel syndrome? It is innervated by neurons of which system?

Positive action for health

A better understanding of stress can not only alert us to avoid stressful situations but also to try to maximize situations that are low on stress or can counter stress. It is unfortunate that, in the history of psychology, most emphasis has been on negative emotions. However, there is a growing recognition of the role of positive emotions (Burgdorf and Panksepp, 2006), as reflected in the term 'positive psychology'. Taking a rather more optimistic position, we can learn to promote good health and happiness rather than simply the reduction of negative indices. Optimism can be good for health, with the possibility that part of the effect is mediated via the immune system (Taylor *et al.*, 2000).

With regard principally to effects on the heart and circulatory system, this section looks at some contexts within which the body appears to react favourably.

Social contact

Introduction

Concerning the role of maladaptive social reactions in coronary disease, action can be taken to undermine toxic Type A effects (Williams, 1989). Since learning seems to be involved in the acquisition of a hostile way of reacting, relearning might help to change behaviour and cognitions. Psychologists emphasize that, for healthy development, it is important for a child to be able to trust another human.

For several disorders, people who are socially isolated run a greater risk than those who are happily socially integrated (Allan and Scheidt, 1996b). A caring social relationship seems to offer defence against stress. The presence of a friendly other person can moderate the effect of a stressor, as indexed by heart-rate or the rise in fatty acid levels in the blood (Bovard, 1985; Steptoe, 1993) or length of recovery following surgery (Kiecolt-Glaser *et al.*, 1998).

Support groups for patients with coronary heart disease attempt to create conditions that counter isolation and alienation and thereby boost self-esteem (Billings *et al.*, 1996). The term **belonging** refers to a particular lifestyle, social context and way of reacting. The individual forms part of a harmonious network, with meaning and purpose in life, and has a capacity for prediction, control and coping. Goals are acceptable and attainable within a social network and the person values friendship above the acquisition of material resources (Allan and Scheidt, 1996b).

Comparing cultures

Japanese culture emphasizes good interpersonal skills, social interaction and trusting interdependence, stability, cohesion and achievement by the common group more than do Western cultures. Japanese show lower hostility scores than Americans. By contrast, Marmot and Syme (1976, p. 246) suggest that people in American and Northern European cultures:

display almost opposite characteristics to the protective features described, i.e. lack of stability, accent on the individual rather than the group, and a high likelihood of an individual finding himself in a situation for which his world-view has left him unprepared.

Are these social differences manifest as differences in health? The United States has one of the highest rates of heart attacks in the developed world (Marmot and Syme, 1976). By contrast, the Japanese have one of the lowest. Comparing Japanese living in Japan and California, the Californians have a much higher rate than those in Japan. Again, diet and smoking apparently can account for only part of the effect. Thus, comparing Japanese males eating a similar diet in Japan or California, the Californians had higher levels of blood cholesterol.

Explaining the effects

What could be the link between social factors and the circulatory system? At one stage in the chain, the effect appears to be mediated by what are termed 'lipoproteins'. Lipids (fats) such as cholesterol are found in the blood-stream in two forms, high-density lipoproteins (HDL) and low-density lipoproteins (LDL) (Scheidt, 1996). The ratio LDL/HDL gives an index of the risk of atherosclerosis, a high ratio being associated with a high risk (Roberts, 1996). As this ratio decreases, there is a decrease in the frequency of heart attacks. Could psychological factors be one determinant of this ratio? Looking at a group of 17-year-old Israeli people, the ratio was higher in the non-religious than in the religious people (Friedlander *et al.*, 1987). This could reflect differences in belonging and social cohesion.

What influences differences in circulatory systems between individuals? How can positive social bonds with other humans influence the system? Psychobiological theories (Bovard, 1985) relate to the idea that humans have evolved as part of a social matrix. Presumably, underlying such social interaction, there are brain processes of motivation and emotion (Panksepp, 1982) that play a role in seeking and maintaining social bonds. Trusting social contact moderates SNS activity (Bovard, 1985).

In early childhood, the Type B, in contrast to the Type A, was typically exposed to affection and admiration (Friedman, 1996). There might also be a role for genetic differences.

Meditation

Meditation, when a person sits relaxed, with closed eyes, and performs a repeated simple mental activity, triggers the 'relaxation response' that counters trends towards SNS domination and hyperarousal (Bracke and Thoresen, 1996). Simultaneously, the parasympathetic contribution is strengthened (Sakakibara *et al.*, 1994). Group meetings for coronary heart disease patients involve meditation on feeling states and use of self-control in such forms as guided imagery (Billings *et al.*, 1996).

Section summary

1 Belonging (e.g. having a social bond) seems to benefit coronary health.

2 The effect of social contact seems to be mediated via the CNS restraining the SNS.

Test your knowledge

(Answer on page 352)

13.12 Therapeutic interventions such as meditation tend to lower activity in which branch of the nervous system?

13.4

Bringing things together

A protracted disturbance to our psychological homeostasis causes stress, associated with unsuccessful attempts to counter the disturbance. Neurohormonal systems that are triggered by particular stressors serve a useful function when activated *under appropriate conditions*. For example, confronted with a bear and having a capacity to run, accelerated heart-rate and a high rate of secretion of cortisol are adaptive. It seems to follow that such reactions are not to our advantage when we are stuck for hours in a traffic-jam or endlessly chewing-over our rejection for promotion. These days, at least among readers of the present text, stress hormones are more likely to be triggered by traffic jams than bears.

Stress exemplifies the need to take an integrative perspective. Thus, psychological states such as depression and anxiety have a basis in the brain, which has effects outside the CNS, e.g. in the accumulation of deposits on blood vessels or forming lesions in the walls of the stomach. Such phenomena illustrate the shortcomings of logic based upon 'either/or', e.g. a disorder is either somatic or psychological. For example, gastric ulceration appears to reflect interaction between bacterial infection and CNS-mediated events. Similarly, cardiovascular disease is the result of interactions between (1) such things as diet and smoking and (2) psychological states, not to forget the possible role of genetic differences underlying nervous system differences.

Figure 13.11 develops a diagram shown in Chapter 3 (Figure 3.36, p. 79) and will help to consolidate your understanding. Included now is the immune system. Note the ANS links to endocrine and immune systems and the influence of the immune system on the brain.

Summary of Chapter 13

1 The term 'stress' normally describes a long-term disturbance to psychological homeostasis.

2 Stress is associated with unsuccessful attempts to cope, excessive activity within certain neurohormonal systems and a proneness to a particular range of disorders.

3 Two neurohormonal systems, the sympathetic branch of the autonomic nervous system and the pituitary adrenocortical system, involving corticosteroids, form a principal focus for understanding stress.

4 The level of stress depends on context, e.g. (i) the capacity to predict when a stressor will occur, (ii) opportunities for action and (iii) what is done in response to the potential stressor and the outcome of this action.

5 Stress reactions within the nervous system have effects on the immune system. Reciprocally, activity in the immune system has effects on the nervous system and thereby stress-related behaviour.

6 Identifiable brain regions form the neural basis of stress and convey information to the neurohormonal systems that are activated under stress.

7 Stress increases the tendency to suffer from depression.

8 Stress has important implications for the health of the circulatory system.

9 Post-traumatic stress disorder (PTSD) follows trauma in which there is actual or threatened death or serious injury to the sufferer or another person

10 Stress can manifest as pathology of the stomach and intestine.

11 Interventions designed to lower the harmful effects of stress are based on lowering negative emotion and excessive sympathetic activity.

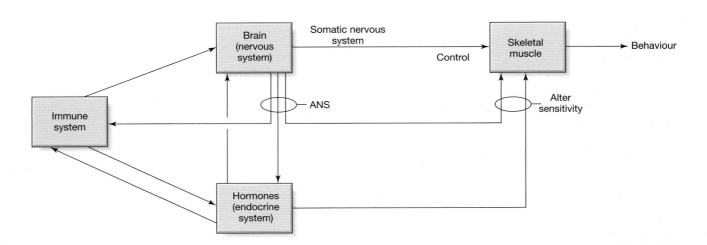

Figure 13.11 Nervous, endocrine and immune systems.

Further reading

For classical writing on stress, see Selye (1973). Sapolsky (2004) is also something of a classic, now in its 3rd edition. An account written by an eminent researcher in the area is McEwen (2004). For a good account, including theoretical and historical aspects, see Cooper and Dewe (2004). The link between stress and poverty is explored by Sapolsky (2005). For a (somewhat heavy-going) account of stress, see Toates (1995). For applied ethology and stress, see Moberg and Mench (2000). For stress and the immune system, see Evans *et al.* (2000) and Clow and Hucklebridge (2002).

Signposts

This chapter has built upon Chapter 12 'Emotion'. Emotional processes were described as being stretched beyond their adaptive range in stress. Stress is clearly involved in pain, the topic of the next chapter. It will also be discussed in terms of its contribution to schizophrenia in Chapter 22, 'When things go wrong'.

Answers

Explanations for answers to 'test your knowledge' questions can be found on the website **www.pearsoned.co.uk/toates**

13.1   Disturbance (or, say, 'challenge')
13.2   Corticosteroids
13.3   Lowered levels of ACTH and corticosteroids, increased levels of CRF; lowered levels of CRF and ACTH and a lowered rate of release of corticosteroids
13.4   That involving the sympathetic nervous system
13.5   It conveys information in the blood stream to a location where it influences neural processing
13.6   Both. As a hormone in the link to ACTH secretion; as a neurotransmitter in communication within the CNS
13.7   Increased
13.8   That prolonged depression could reflect an exaggeration of a strategy that is adaptive in the short-term, e.g. increased vigilance and temporary withdrawal from confrontation
13.9   Adrenalin and noradrenalin
13.10 There could be a genetic/developmental influence leading to (1) lower than normal hippocampal volume and (2) increased tendency to PTSD
13.11 Smooth, enteric nervous system
13.12 Sympathetic nervous system

CHAPTER 14

Pain

Learning outcomes for Chapter 14

After studying this chapter, you should be able to:

1. Describe what is meant by nociception and anti-nociception, while linking this to the subjective feeling of pain.

2. Apply the functional type of explanation to pain, while also considering the functional value of a system of anti-nociception. Give examples of pain that cannot be explained in any simple adaptive terms and speculate as to why not.

3. Describe the route that nociceptive information takes from periphery to brain, while relating this to the observation that there is not a simple one-to-one link between the magnitude of the noxious stimulus and the intensity of pain.

4. Outline the basic principles of the gate theory of pain and describe the phenomena of pain that it is able to explain.

5. Identify some of the principal brain regions involved in pain and describe the link between these regions and the associated ascending and descending neural pathways.

6. Describe the best-known forms of analgesia and the sites in the nociceptive system with which they are associated. Link analgesia to an understanding of the bases of pain.

7. State what is meant by the terms 'referred pain' and 'phantom pain' and explain how knowledge of the basics of pain allows us to understand them better.

8. Justify the claim that cognitive factors, such as expectations, play a part in pain. Link the role of cognitive factors to the biological bases of pain.

Scene-setting questions

1 How can something so debilitating as pain be said to be adaptive?

2 Why do we rub sore eyes?

3 Can you really suffer the *pain* of a broken heart?

4 What is it like to experience a phantom limb?

5 What is a placebo? Does it suggest 'mind over matter'?

6 Can you 'feel' the pain being suffered by another person?

Under which circumstances can a person suffer injury but feel little pain?

Source: Topham Picturepoint/TopFoto.co.uk

Introduction

What is pain? In all probability you can remember well such an experience. It must be the exceedingly rare individual who cannot recall some experience of pain. Subjectively, pain is an unpleasant feeling that is usually caused by damage to the body and from which we try to escape. Pain, as from a toothache or a gut infection, takes command of attention (Eccleston and Crombez, 1999). We might be indifferent to certain sounds, tactile stimuli or smells but pain is different: it poses overwhelming demands and moves us into action. People also speak of the pain of a rejection in love, something that also will not let go, and the pain of seeing someone else in distress. In understanding pain, we need to ask, are these just examples of the use of a colourful metaphor, or can we feel real pain from a broken heart or empathy?

People behave in ways characterized as pain-related and can offer verbal reports on their inner experience. They describe their pain in terms of intensity, say, mild or excruciating, and can usually locate the pain's source. Sometimes it is also possible to describe the pain's quality, e.g. gnawing, grinding, sharp, dull or stabbing. This suggests different stimuli that would be identified as the cause of the problem.

Most strikingly, pain has a quality of intense *negative affect*, meaning that it feels bad. It is said to be 'affective'. Do non-human animals suffer a similar affective experience? Of course, we do not know what subjective states they experience, if any. However, most of us would probably suggest that they can suffer in this way. Their behaviour (e.g. writhing, squealing or jumping) suggests it. It forms a clear pattern associated with tissue damage and threat of such damage.

Biological psychology uses the term **nociception** to refer to the detection of tissue damage or threatened damage. It also describes a **nociceptive system**, i.e. one that responds to tissue damage or potential damage (Melzack and Wall, 1996). The nociceptive system triggers action in an attempt to minimize the offending stimulation. Looking at the nervous system, we see close similarities in the nociceptive systems of humans and such non-humans as rats. Therefore, the present chapter assumes that we and non-humans (or, at least, the more complex ones such as rats and dogs) share similar aversive experiences.

As well as a nociceptive system, there is a system of **anti-nociception**. Activity within this system reduces nociceptive sensory input to brain regions that underlie pain. For example, suppose that someone is engaged in competitive sport (as in the famous case of the American boxing champion Sonny Liston) or escape from a battlefield.

Activity of the anti-nociceptive system means that they are less likely to even notice wounds that they suffered (Melzack and Wall, 1996).

The medical community and sections of the lay public try to alleviate pain, a process termed **analgesia**. Substances that alleviate pain are known as **analgesics**. Analgesia can either correspond to a direct reduction of activity in the nociceptive system or an increase in activity of the anti-nociceptive system, which in turn decreases nociceptive activity.

The next section takes a functional perspective on nociception and anti-nociception.

Section summary

1   In response to tissue damage, a nociceptive system produces pain and triggers action of a kind that tends to minimize this pain.

2   There exists also an anti-nociceptive system, which counters pain and the tendency to show pain-related behaviour.

Test your knowledge

(Answer on page 370)

14.1   Which of the following would be suggested as analgesics? (i) an agonist to the nociceptive system, (ii) an antagonist to the nociceptive system, (iii) an agonist to the anti-nociceptive system, (iv) an antagonist to the anti-nociceptive system.

Adaptive value of pain

Introduction

The adaptive value of a nociceptive system and pain is that this permits flexible solutions to the problem of tissue damage and the threat of it. For example, we can move our bodies around until we happen upon a position that minimizes our pain or we can remove a thorn from the foot. We can recruit social help: caregivers can help to remove thorns, empathize with us and bring comfort. Suppose that an animal injures a limb. If pain then triggers rest, this increases the recovery chances. Surely, most of us have taken to bed in pain, e.g. a severe headache or general bodily discomfort caused by influenza. Rest improves our chances of recovery.

Pain-related behaviour has a layer of cultural relativity in its expression. Different cultures show different pain-related strategies of reacting, e.g. stoicism or expression of distress (Craig, 1995). In some cultures, rituals that seem to be excruciatingly painful to us are engaged in voluntarily in religious causes.

There are some very rare humans who are born with an inability to experience pain in response to tissue damage. Studying them can give useful insight into the adaptive value of pain.

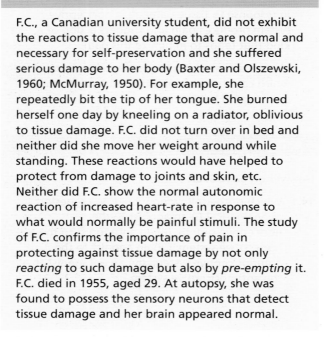

A personal angle

F.C.

F.C., a Canadian university student, did not exhibit the reactions to tissue damage that are normal and necessary for self-preservation and she suffered serious damage to her body (Baxter and Olszewski, 1960; McMurray, 1950). For example, she repeatedly bit the tip of her tongue. She burned herself one day by kneeling on a radiator, oblivious to tissue damage. F.C. did not turn over in bed and neither did she move her weight around while standing. These reactions would have helped to protect from damage to joints and skin, etc. Neither did F.C. show the normal autonomic reaction of increased heart-rate in response to what would normally be painful stimuli. The study of F.C. confirms the importance of pain in protecting against tissue damage by not only *reacting* to such damage but also by *pre-empting* it. F.C. died in 1955, aged 29. At autopsy, she was found to possess the sensory neurons that detect tissue damage and her brain appeared normal.

Why has an anti-nociceptive system evolved? A possibility is as follows (Bolles and Fanselow, 1980). Pain triggers adaptive behaviour such as licking wounds and resting until recovery. However, this has a net adaptive value only under certain conditions, i.e. when there is no greater immediate threat. At times, fighting or fleeing might have to take precedence and would require resisting the tendency to engage in pain-related behaviour. Thus, it might have proven useful to inhibit the activity of the nociceptive system, e.g. when fleeing injured from a predator. In humans, anecdotal evidence suggests that even serious injury incurred, for instance, on a battlefield is sometimes only associated with pain when the victim is away from danger (Bromm, 1995).

Why so intense and pervasive?

Clearly, an attention-grabbing system is called for, so that cognitive and behavioural resources are directed to minimizing the most important event, the input from tissue damage. Why though, from a functional viewpoint, does pain create *so strong* a negative emotion, which has consequences that are often debilitating? It might seem maladaptive for the body to experience something so powerful. It is perhaps possible to see an adaptive significance of the intensity of pain, as follows.

Pain commands our attention but also *forces* us to take particular adaptive actions, like staying still or favouring a damaged ankle by not putting too much pressure on it. From the viewpoint of evolution, it could even be argued, 'no pain, then no pleasure'. Pleasure encourages us to engage in activities such as eating, pursuing a mate or exploring a new environment. However, to follow the guide of pleasure would not always be to our benefit. Pain counters the lure of pleasure, as in getting up too soon from the sick bed.

We humans, the most intellectual of creatures, have the benefits of sophisticated reasoning abilities. However, the use of 'cold cognition' or even 'slightly warm cognition' would be unable to present a counter to engaging in pleasurable activities. Without persuasion by pain, we might not be able to make sufficiently rational choices to guarantee the health of our own bodies (cf. Ainslie, 1975). Even when we could understand the source of our pain, cold reasoning might have little effect on our behaviour. It would be no match for the temptations to 'get up and go' in the present. For some people, the pain of a headache from the occasional hangover is even *too little* to deter over-drinking except for a short period. It would surely be to our detriment to take a 'morning-after super-drug' to eliminate such headaches since the pain is 'telling us something and moving us not to do something'.

You might feel that some pains have adaptive value and need to be intense, e.g. those of a sprained ankle or a hangover headache. By keeping weight off the ankle, we speed its recovery. However, you might wonder how, say, the pain of childbirth or the severe and chronic pain of cancer could possibly be the products of an adaptive process. It is possible to suggest an explanation and this has two parts, as described next.

For pain to be an overall adaptive feature does not require every instance to be precisely appropriate in intensity. Indeed, evolution could only possibly have provided solutions that *on average* worked to our ancestors' advantage (Sufka and Turner, 2005). As a general solution, we are equipped to feel pain in response to damage in most parts of our body. Given this basic 'design', inevitably there will be situations in which pains arise that are not obviously to our advantage. Chronic pain appears to represent a stretching of otherwise adaptive systems to outside their adaptive range.

Evolutionary psychology
The age at which pain is experienced

The second aspect of the argument is that many of the chronic pains, such as those associated with cancer, appear most commonly in later years. At this stage, humans are past the age at which reproduction could normally have taken place in our early evolution. Hence, in evolutionary history, such pains would not necessarily have been experienced sufficiently often to be a disadvantage in terms of passing on genes.

Although of general adaptive value, of course, we normally attempt to minimize pain. In so doing, we often pay lip-service to its value; the next-day hangover can be treated with aspirin and the good resolution not to drink to excess again.

We now turn to considering the nervous system processes that embody the nociceptive and anti-nociceptive systems.

Section summary

1 Pain has adaptive value in allowing flexible solutions to protect against tissue damage.

2 At times it could be adaptive not to react to tissue damage and this provides the likely reason for the evolution of an anti-nociceptive system.

3 Chronic pain appears to be an exaggerated activation of otherwise adaptive processes.

Test your knowledge

(Answer on page 370)

14.2 Rats exhibit the response of freezing in certain situations of fear. What could be the relevance of the anti-nociception system to such freezing and its functional significance?

14.1

The role of tissue damage and the sensory input side

Introduction

This section looks at the role of tissue damage and the sensory side of pain. It describes the specialized neurons that detect tissue damage and convey information on this to the CNS. It considers the properties of these neurons and asks how the signal that they produce contributes to pain. A later section describes what happens to this information when it reaches the brain. Whilst acknowledging the role of tissue damage, the chapter will discuss the limitations of trying to understand pain simply in terms of the input side.

Initial stage of a nociceptive pathway

Neurons that are activated by tissue damage are termed nociceptive neurons (Chapter 3, 'The nervous and endocrine systems'). In Figure 14.1, note the representative nociceptive neuron, by which information is transmitted from the periphery to the dorsal horn of the spinal cord. Tissue damage has a particular ability to trigger activity in these neurons, though some other stimuli have a limited capacity to do so.

At the tip of the axon of the nociceptive neuron, there is a free nerve ending sensitive to tissue damage. The tips of nociceptive neurons are termed **nociceptors** (detectors of 'noxious' stimulation). The branching of the tip defines the neuron's receptive field. Nociceptive neurons come in different forms corresponding to different types of stimuli that best activate them, e.g. described as 'sharp' or 'burning'. Nociceptive neurons have a high threshold: only strong stimulation will significantly excite them. In Figure 14.1, note also the other type of neuron, the large-diameter neuron. This type of neuron is sensitive to harmless touch but it also plays a role in pain, as will be discussed later.

The neurons in the spinal cord with which nociceptive neurons form synapses are termed **T cells** (Figure 14.1), meaning transmission cells (as distinct from immunological T cells). Nociceptive neurons release neurotransmitter that activates T cells. There appears to be more than one type of neurotransmitter released, the evidence suggests that the principal ones are glutamate and substance P (Jessell and Kelly, 1991). T cells convey nociceptive information to the brain, e.g. in the **spinothalamic tract** (STT) (Figure 14.1).

The STT is not the only ascending pathway involved in pain but it can be used to exemplify the principles. Electrical stimulation of the STT results in the conscious sensation of pain. Surgical lesions of the tract can reduce pain but this is not always so.

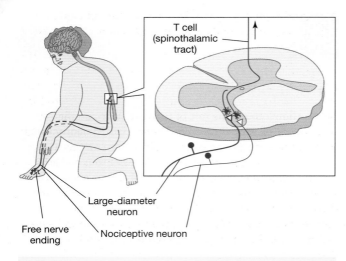

Figure 14.1 Sketch of body and part of the nervous system showing section of spinal cord. Also shown are a nociceptive neuron and a large-diameter neuron, sensitive to harmless touch.

Source: Toates (1997c, Fig. 4.2, p. 70).

Tissue damage, either to the tip itself or in its immediate vicinity, is normally the necessary stimulus to excite nociceptive neurons. When a neighbouring cell is damaged, chemicals are released and come into contact with nociceptors. This increases the chances that action potentials will arise. The high threshold of nociceptive neurons is due to the fact that their axons are of small diameter and are often termed 'small-diameter fibres'.

Since nociceptive neurons are particularly sensitive to noxious information, they are often termed 'pain receptors'. However, to be precise, they detect tissue damage rather than pain. Pain is not like light or sound, a physical quality able to be detected. It is a complex sensation and emotion organized by the brain, and tissue damage does not invariably trigger pain. So the terms 'nociceptor' and 'nociceptive neuron' are preferred.

In Figure 14.1, imagine a region of body surface and the tips of nociceptive neurons located there. Typically, as shown, there are also other neurons with tips in the same area and with axons projecting to the spinal cord in parallel with those of nociceptive neurons. These axons are of larger diameter, have a lower threshold of activation and are often termed 'large-diameter neurons'. They can be triggered by nociceptive stimulation but even harmless stimuli, such as gentle touch, are sufficient. Both types of neuron make synapses in the dorsal horn of the spinal cord, though at slightly different locations (Figure 14.1). Thereby, they trigger activity in other neurons which then convey messages up the spinal cord to the brain. However, information derived from both types of neuron is also processed locally at the spinal cord location shown and this forms a focus in trying to understand pain.

No simple through-line

At one time it was thought that a simple one-to-one 'through-line' links activity in nociceptive neurons and the intensity of pain. Thus, patients who reported pain where no tissue damage ('organic disorder') could be identified were highly problematic. They might be referred to psychiatrists and/or labelled as malingerers (Melzack, 1993). Their pain, if it existed at all, was thought to have a quality different from 'real pain' and to be the business of the social, rather than biological, sciences.

We now know that there is no *simple* through-line; the magnitude of pain sometimes does not reflect tissue damage. This provides one rationale for the study of the *psychology* of pain.

Suppose, for the sake of argument, that there were a direct link. Presumably, a surgical lesion at some point in the pathway would cure pain. By comparison, a lesion anywhere in the optic nerve would destroy vision. Indeed, surgery for chronic pain was once guided by making lesions in the so-called pain pathway. Again pointing to the true complexity, in many cases pain unfortunately returned after surgery (Melzack, 1993).

Today theorists and clinicians appreciate the complexity of pain. There can be intense pain with little evidence of tissue damage. Even after removing the initial trigger to pain, e.g. a tumour, the pain sometimes persists (Keefe *et al.*, 2005). There can be a relief of pain as a result simply of taking medicine of completely arbitrary content provided that the patient has a belief in its efficacy. So, we have a complex system with interacting factors, only one of which is the nociceptive sensory input.

The next section looks at an influential theory of pain, which attempts to account for a range of phenomena partly in terms of events at the input side.

Section summary

1 Nociceptive neurons have small-diameter axons and a relatively high threshold of stimulation. They detect tissue damage by means of free-nerve endings at their tips.

2 Neurons with larger diameter axons are sensitive to non-noxious stimuli, i.e. have a lower threshold.

3 Both types of neuron form synapses in the dorsal horn of the spinal cord, where information processing occurs.

4 Pain commonly, but *not always*, corresponds to tissue damage and activity in nociceptive neurons.

The gate theory

Basics of theory

In 1965, a new theory of pain, termed the **gate theory** appeared (Melzack and Wall, 1965). Its authors were the first to admit that the details might well be wrong but they were convinced that the important principles would stand the test of time. Gate theory offered explanations for a number of phenomena, such as (1) why pain does not bear a simple relationship to tissue damage and (2) how the CNS could produce an anti-nociceptive effect. The theory proposed two processes of anti-nociception, both of which involve the site in the spinal cord where nociceptive neurons form synapses. First, there is the activity of large-diameter neurons of the kind shown in Figure 14.1. Second, there are pathways of neurons that descend from the brain. The ideas are summarized in Figure 14.2 and the assumptions of gate theory are as follows:

1 The capacity of nociceptive neurons to excite T cells (Figure 14.1) is not constant. There is, metaphorically speaking, a gate which determines this capacity (Figure 14.2(a) and (b)). When the gate is open, action potentials in small-diameter neurons trigger action potentials in T cells. When it is closed, activity in small-diameter neurons fails to instigate as much activity in T cells.

2 The ratio of activity in large-diameter neurons to that in small-diameter neurons, arising in the same region of the body (Figure 14.1) is one factor that determines opening and closing of the gate. Active large-diameter neurons are good news for the sufferer since this tends to close the gate.

3 Activity in a descending neural pathway from the midbrain also tends to close the gate. See the more realistic representation of Figure 14.2(c). Note the inhibitory synapse from neuron (1) onto the nociceptive neuron and the inhibitory link through what is termed a 'small neuron' (S).

4 Cognitive processes organized in the brain influence gating, by means of their input to descending pathways described in (3).

Consider the local region of spinal cord where nociceptive and other neurons from a particular small region of the body make synapses (Figures 14.1 and 14.2(c)). Small neurons (S) within this local region exert an influence in controlling the opening and closing of the gate (Figure 14.2(c)). Activity in S inhibits the nociceptive pathway ('closes the gate'). So, the more the activity in S, the greater is the inhibition on the nociceptive pathway. What determines activity of neuron S? It is excited by activity in either large-diameter neurons or descending pathways from the brain, or both. This is represented by the two open triangles adjacent to S in Figure 14.2(c). Note also neuron 1 which represents another route of descending inhibition on the nociceptive pathway.

Concerning the neurochemistry of anti-nociception, a principal focus in gate theory is opioids (Chapter 12, 'Emotion'). Opioids are a class of natural anti-nociceptive (analgesic) substances, e.g. the natural enkephalins.

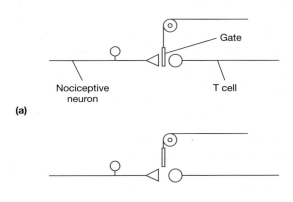

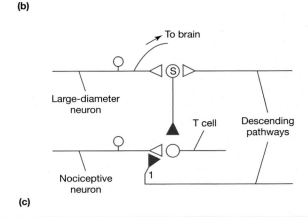

Figure 14.2 Gate theory expressed (a–b) by the analogy of a real gate: (a) closed, (b) open and (c) a more realistic representation, showing neurons involved. Open triangles, excitation; closed triangles, inhibition.

Figure 14.3 shows in close-up some of the synaptic processes that appear to be implicated in gating. An opioid termed enkephalin appears to be the chemical released by neurons of type S. The precise form of inhibition exerted by such neurons is uncertain. However, there are opioid receptors at the terminals of nociceptive neurons and at the T cells (Benedetti and Amanzio, 1997). By occupying receptors at the terminal of nociceptive neurons, enkephalin seems to reduce the amount of excitatory neurochemical that is released. By occupying sites at the T cell, enkephalin opposes the excitation of this cell. Figure 14.3 also shows an inhibitory link from the brain synapsing directly onto the nociceptive neuron. Elsewhere, there are also opioid receptors in the brain at regions where descending inhibitory pathways arise (Harris, 1996). Acting on neurons in the brain, opioids excite these descending pathways.

Functional significance

From a functional perspective, what advantage is there for the nervous system to be constructed in the manner suggested by gate theory? Why do large-diameter neurons inhibit the effect of activity in nociceptive neurons and thereby give anti-nociception? A possibility is as follows. The reduction of pain would encourage animals to lick their

wounds (a reinforcement process), which would cleanse the wounds. Why is there descending inhibition? The possible logic was advanced earlier, i.e. an anti-nociceptive system is activated when the animal is engaging in such defensive behaviour as fighting or fleeing.

Opening the gate

As well as processes that close the gate, other processes appear to open it (Benedetti and Amanzio, 1997). The neurochemical cholecystokinin (CCK) 'opens the gate'. CCK is found at spinal sites (Figure 14.4) and in various brain regions. Like opioid receptors, CCK receptors are both pre- and postsynaptic. In causing an increase in pain, termed **hyperalgesia**, the sites of action of CCK might act in a functionally related way and be symmetrical with the role of opioids in analgesia. Analgesia induced by opioids is inhibited by CCK and enhanced by CCK antagonists. Opening the gate would appear to be a means of accentuating the role of the nociceptive system, e.g. when attention to wounds is especially important.

The value of the gate theory

Gate theory is now an established part of teaching on pain. A gate that is influenced in part by psychological ('cognitive') factors is of great significance for an integrative biological psychology. The theory provided a broad framework for considering how interventions to control pain might work. For example, it might help to understand the traditional Chinese technique of acupuncture. Translated into the terms of gate theory, we can investigate the possibility that pain-relieving effects of acupuncture correspond to closing the gate (Filshie and Morrison, 1988). In this way, there might be some synthesis between Eastern and Western traditions. In Western terms, acupuncture might be a means of tapping into an endogenous (meaning from a source within the body) opioid system.

Later sections will show how some phenomena of pain can be illuminated by the gate theory. Next we need to look at some details of the brain processes involved in pain and thereby give some further embodiment to the theory.

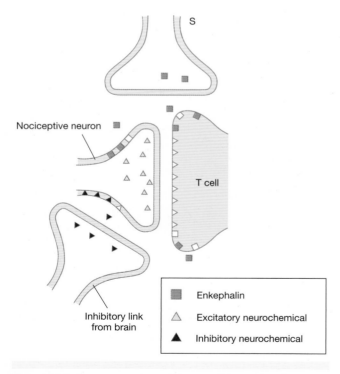

Figure 14.3 Representation of the possible mode of action of enkephalin released from neuron S and that of another (unspecific) inhibitory neurochemical, labelled simply as 'inhibitory neurochemical'.

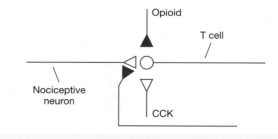

Figure 14.4 Gate showing inhibition and excitation.

1 Gate theory suggests that the relationship between activity in nociceptive neurons and T cells, depends, metaphorically, upon a gate.

2 Activity in (a) large-diameter afferent neurons and (b) descending pathways closes the gate.

3 In neural terms, the gate is provided in part by the activity of short interneurons at the spinal cord.

4 Evidence points to opioids playing the crucial role in closing the gate.

5 There are neural processes (employing CCK) that open the gate.

(Answers on page 370)

14.4 In Figure 14.2(c), activity in which of the ascending and descending neurons shown would minimize activity in the T cell?

14.5 In Figure 14.3, injection of an antagonist to which of the following would tend to increase activity in the T cell? (i) The inhibitory neurochemical, (ii) enkephalin, (iii) the excitatory neurochemical.

Brain processes

Introduction

Figure 14.5 summarizes both what has been described so far and the contents of the present section. In the spinal cord, sensory information ('Nociceptive input') ascends to the brain, conveying information on tissue damage. Information also descends in the spinal cord and plays a role by influencing the ascending information. At the brain, pain arises from the activity in circuits of interacting brain regions, which are triggered by, among other things, the sensory input. This central 'computation' of pain then plays a role in pain-related behaviours such as yelling or resting. It also plays a role in autonomic nervous system reactions such as sweating and heart-rate acceleration. This section looks at the brain processes underlying pain.

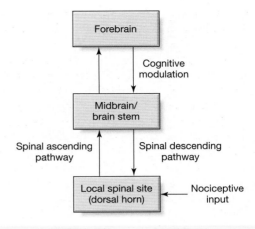

Figure 14.5 Different levels of the nervous system involved in pain.

Terminations of ascending pathways

Figure 14.6 shows ascending nociceptive information arriving at various sites in the brain, via the spinothalamic tract. Synapses are formed in the midbrain, including the periacqueductal grey (labelled 'Homeostatic regions'), as well as with nuclei in the thalamus (MDvc and VMpo). This ascending information will have been already modulated at sites in the spinal cord, as described by gate theory.

The pain matrix

Processing in the brain underlies (1) the affective quality of pain, i.e. its negative emotional value, and (2) the discriminative quality, e.g. where in the body the pain appears to be located. Where in the brain is such processing done?

Figure 14.6 showed some of the pathways and brain regions involved in pain. Ascending information arrives at various identifiable brain regions that are involved in the computation of pain, e.g. the two nuclei of the thalamus. Further neurons then convey information from these thalamic nuclei to other regions, such as the anterior cingulate cortex (ACC). The collection of interacting brain regions that forms the biological basis of pain is termed the **pain matrix**.

In humans, some neurons of the somatosensory cortex, among other cortical regions, respond specifically to nociceptive stimuli, primarily on the contralateral side of the body (Area 3a in Figure 14.6). There is some topographic organization of neurons sensitive to nociceptive stimuli, comparable to that of neurons responsive to harmless somatosensory stimuli. This suggests that such neurons extract sensory and discriminative aspects of nociceptive stimuli (Kenshalo and Douglass, 1995; Rainville *et al.*, 1997).

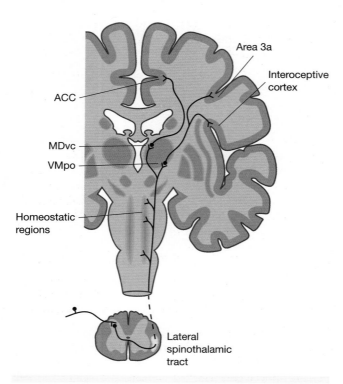

Figure 14.6 Neural processes involved in pain. MDvc and VMpo are two nuclei of the thalamus.

Source: Craig (2003, Figure 2, page 11).

The anterior cingulate cortex (ACC) appears to be closely involved in the affective aspect of pain. In humans, positron emission tomography (PET) reveals an increase in regional cerebral blood flow in the ACC produced by nociceptive (but not harmless) stimuli. Nociceptive input to the ACC on one side of the brain tends to activate the ACC on both sides. This points to the role of the ACC in affective rather than sensory discriminative processing.

For patients suffering from chronic pain, surgical lesions of the ACC reduce the emotional ('affective') but not sensory aspects of pain. Patients having such lesions sometimes report that, although they still feel pain, it bothers them less (Rainville *et al.*, 1997).

A study investigated the effect of hypnosis on pain and blood flow to selected brain regions. Hypnotic suggestion was given that the patient would experience either increased or decreased strength of pain, while the actual nociceptive stimulus was held constant. Such suggestion changed pain's actual affective rating and blood flow to the ACC but not to the somatosensory cortex. A positive correlation emerged between the unpleasantness rating and activation of the ACC, as indexed by blood flow. Only the ACC showed changes consistent with different affective values, which Rainville *et al.* interpreted to mean that it is involved in affective rating. Anatomical connections between ACC and somatosensory cortex suggest that there is integration of these regions in determining the normal experience of pain.

The pain of social rejection is also associated with activation of the ACC (Chapter 1, 'Introduction'; Eisenberger *et al.*, 2003). This cause is termed a 'psychogenic trigger', meaning that it lies in psychological processing as distinct from the noxious stimulus of tissue damage. Yet this result gives psychogenically triggered pain a sound biological basis in the brain that is very similar to the basis of that triggered by a noxious stimulus.

Descending pathways

Electrical and chemical stimulation of descending pathways from brain to spinal cord can reduce pain. Areas of the midbrain, e.g. the PAG (Fields and Basbaum, 1994), are a source of the descending signals. There is a cortical input to the PAG, e.g. from the ACC, by which cognitive information appears to modulate the activity of the PAG (Figure 14.5). The PAG projects to other axons in the midbrain, which in turn project downwards to the spinal cord and to the region of the terminals of nociceptive neurons in the dorsal horn (Mason, 1999).

We now consider mechanisms of analgesia. These can be understood in the context of what has been described so far, including gate theory and the brain matrix of pain.

Section summary

1 Nociceptive information arrives in the brain stem and thalamus. Information arriving at the thalamus is projected to cortical sites.

2 Neurons in regions of the somatosensory cortex encode the sensory properties of pain. Those in the anterior cingulate cortex encode the affective properties of pain.

3 Information descends from the brain and influences activity in ascending pathways.

Test your knowledge

Answer on page 370)

14.6 A message from a nociceptor (free-nerve ending) to the anterior cingulate cortex crosses how many synapses?

Techniques of analgesia

A principal concern of the healing professions is analgesia: the reduction of pain. This section gives a few examples of where an understanding of biological processes is relevant to explaining the action of some analgesic procedures.

The role of large-diameter neurons

According to gate theory, gentle stimulation of low-threshold large-diameter neurons tends to close the gate. This suggests the use of therapy that exploits their excitation. Humans doubtless discovered long ago a relationship between such stimulation and analgesia. Most know that rubbing a painful site tends to reduce pain (e.g. the sore eyes of hay fever sufferers), at least in the short term. Rubbing stimulates the large-diameter neurons, the tips of which are at the site of irritation alongside the nociceptors. Various therapeutic techniques, e.g. electrical stimulation, involve, in effect, massaging the skin. There is the therapeutic technique termed **transcutaneous electrical nerve stimulation** (TENS). TENS involves applying weak electrical stimulation at the skin corresponding to an affected area. This is of sufficient intensity to generate activity in large-diameter neurons but not sufficient to trigger (high-threshold) nociceptive neurons.

Analgesic chemicals

Introduction

Analgesics can act either peripherally or centrally and they can be swallowed, injected or applied locally to the skin. Antagonists to neurotransmitters involved in pain might seem an obvious candidate for analgesia. If there were a neurotransmitter employed only in the nociceptive system, then we might have optimism for the development of a safe and targeted antagonist (Jessell and Kelly, 1991). Alas, nature is not usually so favourable to our endeavours. Neurotransmitters tend to be multi-purpose, acting at different sites in the CNS and serving different roles. Any neurotransmitter involved in pain will probably also form part of non-pain-related systems. Targeting this transmitter in sufficient strength to reduce pain might create new problems at other parts of the CNS. For example, glutamate is employed in the nociceptive system but also more widely in the CNS.

Aspirin

Prostaglandins and other substances are released from damaged cells. They sensitize any nociceptors that are in the vicinity of the damage. This increases the chances that tissue damage will initiate action potentials. Aspirin is a peripherally acting analgesic that blocks the synthesis of prostaglandins. Thereby, aspirin lowers the frequency with which action potentials are generated (compare Figures 14.7(a) and (b)).

Lignocaine

The passage of action potentials depends on the movement of sodium into the neuron. Lignocaine blocks sodium channels in the membrane of neurons of all kinds. In Figure 14.7(c), suppose that an injection of lignocaine is given at a location between 2 and 3. If, within a length of axon, sodium channels are blocked, the action potential is unable to pass the affected region and comes to an end on reaching it. Lignocaine does not discriminate in favour of neurons carrying nociceptive information. If you have been injected with it at the dentist, you tend to feel numb in the mouth as a result of blocking sensory information. You have difficulty initiating movements at the mouth as a result of blocking motor neurons.

Centrally acting drugs

A class of analgesics, termed opiates, e.g. heroin and morphine, is well established for its action upon the CNS (Figure 14.7(d)). Years before the role of natural endogenous opioids (e.g. enkephalin) was established, it was of course known that opiate drugs have analgesic qualities. There are opioid receptors at the terminal of nociceptive neurons and at T cells (Figures 14.3 and 14.4). These are occupied by, say, morphine. This lowers the chances that action potentials arriving at the terminal are able to release sufficient neurotransmitter to stimulate activity in T cells. In addition, opioid receptors in the brain are occupied and this activates descending inhibitory pathways. Both sites of action have a mutually reinforcing action in triggering analgesic effects, 'closing the gate'.

Melzack (1988) reported that many people are denied narcotic (opiate) treatment for pain, since it is feared that they might become addicted. He argues that the risk is minimal and the reason for misunderstanding is simple: an unwarranted generalization from addicts to the person suffering from pain. Melzack suggests that morphine could alleviate the pain of cancer in between 80% and 90% of patients.

Comparing addicts and people in pain, the motivation of why people seek narcotics is quite different. Psychologically healthy people without a history of drug abuse do not usually become addicts on exposure to narcotics. One study looked at 11 882 patients, without a history of drug abuse. Of these, only four later showed abuse and for only one was abuse described as 'major' (Melzack, 1988). The Yom Kippur war resulted in

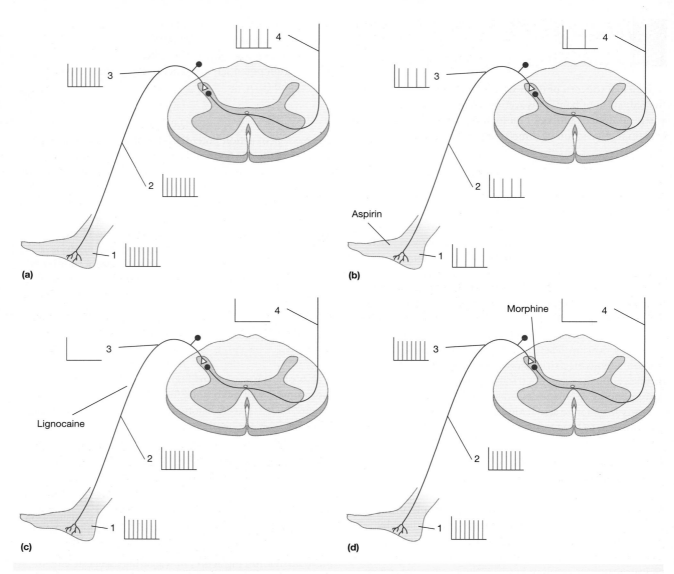

Figure 14.7 Action potentials arising at the tip of a nociceptive neuron (1) and monitored at two points along the axon (2 and 3) and in the T cell (4): (a) control, (b) with aspirin, (c) with lignocaine, injected between locations 2 and 3, and (d) with opiates. *Source*: after Toates (1997c, Fig. 4.6, p. 77).

thousands of Israeli casualties and these were treated with morphine but not one case of addiction was reported.

Rather as was the case with opiates and opioids, for some time anecdotal reports have suggested a role for cannabis in pain relief. Only later was it realized that the body produces its own cannabis-like substances ('cannabinoids'), which have a role in anti-nociception. There are receptors for cannabinoids at various sites within the CNS (Pertwee, 2001). Evidence points to a combined action of opioids and cannabinoids in anti-nociception. More recently, synthetic versions of cannabis have been tested and shown to have potent analgesic effects. The potential for pain therapy, for example, combined opiate-cannabinoid treatment, is under investigation.

Section summary

1 Aspirin lowers the frequency with which action potentials arise in nociceptive neurons and thereby has an analgesic effect.

2 Lignocaine blocks sodium channels in neurons including those in nociceptive neurons.

3 Opiates act on the CNS. They (a) block the capacity of nociceptive-neurons to trigger T cell activity and (b) activate a descending inhibitory pathway.

14.7 Complete the following sentence: 'The threshold of activation of nociceptive neurons is relatively _____, whereas that of large-diameter neurons is relatively _____ '.

14.8 Which of the following has a relatively broad effect on neurons, whether involved in nociception or not? (i) aspirin, (ii) lignocaine, or (iii) opiates.

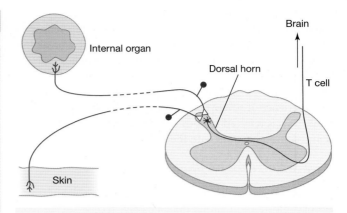

Figure 14.8 A possible neural basis of referred pain.

Source: after Toates (1997c, Fig. 4.5, p. 75).

Anomalous phenomena

This section considers two examples of phenomena that might be termed anomalous by the criterion of not fitting common-sense understanding. They start to make sense in light of understanding the neural systems that form the biological basis of pain.

Referred pain

Suppose that there is tissue damage at a localized site. At times, pain is felt to be associated not with this site but with (i.e. 'referred to') some other site (Vahle-Hinz *et al.*, 1995). There exist some striking examples of such **referred pain**. Pain arising from tissue damage at the heart can be experienced at the left shoulder and arm. A kidney stone can trigger pain that is referred to the genitals. The pattern of referral is not haphazard but can be understood in terms of the developmental origin of the neurons involved (Chapter 6, 'Development and plasticity'). For example, nociceptive neurons with their tips at an internal organ (e.g. the heart) can trigger the same T cells as those with their tips at the skin (e.g. left shoulder and arm) (Figure 14.8) (Pomeranz *et al.*, 1968). Note that neurons from both an internal organ and a region of skin make synaptic contact on the T cell in the spinal cord.

In terms of neural signals and pain, why should tissue damage at, say, the heart, be perceived as arising at the skin? Why are pains having their origin at the skin not referred to the heart? The answer might lie in our relative familiarity with experiencing pain. Presumably, most of us know pain arising from tissue damage or threatened damage at our skin (e.g. banging a toe against a door) and such pain usually makes sense. For tactile stimulation, there is a relationship between the body region stimulated and the area of

somatosensory cortex activated, i.e. the sensory homunculus (Chapter 5, 'The brain'). Possibly, when nociceptive messages from the heart arrive at such brain regions, we interpret them in terms of the more familiar stimuli.

Phantom pain

Introduction

People with a part of the body (e.g. a limb) amputated often still feel pain, apparently 'in' the missing part, termed **phantom pain** (Melzack, 1993). Melzack (1989, p. 2) describes reports from amputees, for example: 'I continue to feel my leg as vividly as I felt my real leg and I often feel a burning pain in my foot'. It is not just limbs that are felt as phantoms; following their surgical removal, the rectum, breasts, bladder and penis can all be experienced much as before. Even after seven years following amputation, some 60% of people suffer phantom pain related to a lost limb. Phantom pains can be similar to pains that were felt much earlier, i.e. when the missing part was still present. This suggests that specific memories play a role. However, such memories are not always essential. For example, people born without a limb can still suffer phantom sensations 'in' the missing limb.

Amputees use such expressions as sweaty, cold or itchy to describe the phantom limb. The feeling of the presence of a missing limb can be so real that amputees have difficulty, for example, in not getting out of bed 'onto' the missing limb. Points of reference that helped to define the limb when it was intact, e.g. the tightness of a ring on a finger or the pain of a sore on the foot, can persist in vivid detail.

There are three situations in which the phantom pain can be experienced apparently 'in' the absence of corresponding sensory input to the brain (Melzack, 1989): (1) after amputation, (2) when a body region remains but its sensory input to the spinal cord has been lost or (3) where a break in the spinal cord occurs. In (3), the feeling corresponds to a body region below the break. For paraplegics, where a total section of the spinal cord has been suffered, there can still be the experience of severe pain relating to a location below the break. This is referred to body sites for which, it appears, no neural communication with the brain is possible.

How do we explain phantom pain?

Theorists now view the brain as an active processor of sensory information, rather than a passive receiver. It seems that the brain has the intrinsic capacity to generate pain even in the absence of nociceptive stimulation. In trying to understand this, Melzack (1989) made the following points:

1 Patterns of activity in neural networks in the brain encode both nociceptive and harmless events in the world. Such patterns would normally be triggered by sensory inputs but do not always depend on them.

2 The sensation of a phantom body part feels like a real part. This suggests that brain processes activated are those that would, under normal circumstances, be triggered by afferent information arising from the lost part.

3 During the phantom experience, certain brain processes are active autonomously and 'revive' experiences associated with the part before there was a break in its connection with the brain.

Melzack (1989) denies that 'sensations are produced only by stimuli and that perceptions in the absence of stimuli are psychologically abnormal'. The evidence from pain is that sensory input adds to the sensations that are intrinsically produced by the brain. In such terms, it might be more accurate to view the phantom limb as a normal experience of the body rather than a psychological aberration.

There is another factor that appears to be implicated in phantom pain and also increases in intensity of chronic pains associated with actual tissue damage. This is the phenomenon of **wind-up**: increased sensitivity of synapses in the nociceptive pathway, something like long-term potentiation (Sufka and Turner, 2005). Thereby, activity in the nociceptive pathway could be self-reinforcing, resulting in increased activity in the pain matrix. There is also reorganization ('plasticity') within the sensory areas of the brain, which could also contribute to the effect (Flor *et al.*, 1995).

The following section looks at other effects that also challenge any simple view of pain.

Test your knowledge

(Answer on page 370)

14.9 With regard to Figure 14.8 suppose that there is tissue damage at the internal organ and that this is felt as coming from the skin. What would be the expected effect of, in addition to this, activity in the nociceptive neuron that projects from the skin?

Cognitive and social factors: theory and therapy

This section considers a cognitive approach to pain and links it to social factors. In these terms, therapies that address such things as goals, expectancies, attitudes and attention are given a rationale.

Cognitive targeting

Distraction of a person by a demanding task or improving the person's emotional state can lower pain. Conversely, 'catastrophizing' pain, by focusing intense negative evaluation on it, is likely to make the pain worse (Craig, 1994). It would seem that general mood and emotional factors lock themselves into the processing of pain.

Cognitive interventions for pain tend to focus upon how patients interpret their pain in terms of its implications (Weisenberg, 1994). Therapeutic techniques used include relaxation, trying to divert attention and the forming of

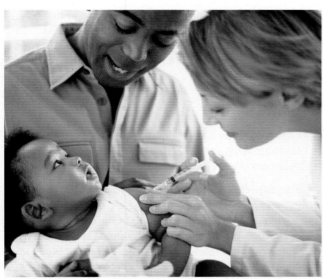

What might be going on in such situations apart from the arrival of a chemical in the body?

Source: Ian Hooton/Science Photo Library

positive images. Therapists attempt to teach patients to see themselves as active agents who have some control, i.e. self-efficacy, rather than being hopeless and helpless victims.

One theoretical rationale for the efficacy of such interventions is the gate theory, where cognitive factors influence the descending pathway. Indeed, the perception of self-efficacy in the face of pain is associated with triggering both opioid and non-opioid analgesia (Bandura *et al.*, 1987).

Placebo effects

Introduction

The term **placebo effect** applies to a number of areas of experience, including pain (Beecher, 1955). In the case of pain, a placebo is an intervention (by substance or other procedure) that appears to have no obvious *intrinsic* capacity to lower pain but which in fact reveals an analgesic capacity. For example, an injection *procedure* itself (even in the absence of the known analgesic substance) might acquire some capacity to exert an analgesic ('placebo') effect. This capacity is demonstrated when injection of a chemically inert substance subsequently lowers pain.

How do we explain this effect? In part, it can be the outcome of classical conditioning. This is because, in the past, the injection (e.g. from morphine) has caused pain relief. Hence, by association, the syringe and the context of the injection can acquire some pain-relieving capacity, i.e. a history of associations between the procedure (conditional stimulus), the drug (unconditional stimulus) and the pain relief (unconditional response). However, conditioning is not

the whole explanation for all instances of the placebo effect (Stewart-Williams and Podd, 2004). It does not always require a history of associations. Thus, if a person is simply told that pain-relief is to be expected, there can be some tendency for it to be experienced.

Less well known than the placebo effect, is the effect symmetrical to it, the **nocebo effect**: an aversive state induced by the expectation of something aversive (Benedetti and Amanzio, 1997). An *increase* in pain can result from a contextual factor that has been associated with an increase in pain.

Examples of the placebo effect

Perhaps the best-known examples of the placebo effect concern inert chemicals. In order of increasing placebo efficacy, there is (1) a tablet, (2) intramuscular injection (e.g. mild saline) and (3) intravenous injection of the same substance (Wall, 1993).

There exists a surgical placebo, which can be powerful (Cobb *et al.*, 1959). For instance, an inadequate supply of blood to the cardiac muscle causes the pain of patients suffering from angina pectorisis. Of the patients in one study, the majority were seriously disabled by their condition and unable to work. An operation for the condition consisted of tying arteries that do not supply the heart but that run nearby. The rationale and hope behind this was that the disturbance of blood flow would stimulate sprouting of some new blood vessels through the heart muscle. A large number of patients received this operation and many were happy with its outcome. However, in spite of the success, investigators were unable to find any evidence of sprouting of new vessels. This prompted a **double-blind study** (i.e. one in which neither patient nor therapist knows into which group a patient has been allocated) into the possibility that the benefit reflected a placebo effect.

For a control group, basic surgery was done but only to the extent that the arteries were temporarily exposed. This gave the patient the impression that the full operation had been performed, whereas, in fact, no tying of arteries was made. A serious ethical problem arises here: in the interests of scientific research, some patients had to be told lies. This would probably mean that a similar study could not be performed these days. For both experimental and control groups there was a significant reduction in pain.

Placebo effects and the brain

What could be the biological basis of the placebo? If we subscribe to an integrative biological psychology, then we would argue that such a basis must exist. Otherwise, we are in the area of inescapable mystery. Indeed, in fMRI studies, brain areas associated with pain, the pain matrix (see Figure 14.6),

The personal experience of the placebo effect by the eminent London pain researcher, Patrick Wall (one of the authors of 'gate theory'), is revealing. Wall (1993, p. 192) writes:

When doctors who are not involved in a therapy under trial learn that it turns out to be a placebo, they howl with laughter. When you are the subject in a trial and discover that you have reacted to a placebo, as I have, you feel a fool. When you are the proponent or inventor of a therapy, whether based on contemporary rationale or old-fashioned faith, you are resentful of the need for placebo testing. If the test reveals a substantial placebo component in the response, diversions are created to eliminate consideration of the placebo effect.

such as the anterior cingulate cortex (ACC) and thalamus, exhibit lower activity following a placebo treatment effect (Petrovic *et al.*, 2002; Wager *et al.*, 2004).

Since opioids are known to be involved in endogenous pain relief (anti-nociception), could it be that they are triggered as part of the placebo response? Evidence for this is that the placebo effect is reduced by an injection of the opioid antagonist naloxone.

Close examination of the ACC reveals that it has subdivisions that exhibit different properties. Thus, activity of the caudal region of the ACC is associated with pain as such, whereas the rostral region is excited by opioids. This suggests that the rostral region could be a site of anti-nociception that antagonizes the caudal region. The placebo condition is associated with activation of the rostral region, as is the case with hypnotic suggestion.

People differ in the extent to which they show a placebo effect. Some are termed 'high placebo responders'. Interestingly, such high responders also exhibit a relatively high sensitivity of the rostral region to opioids. This raises the possibility that a biological basis of high placebo responding can be identified in terms of a relatively high sensitivity of such brain regions to opioids.

What determines the input to the ACC that is associated with the placebo response? Since the ACC is a cortical region and there are rich connections across the cortex, cognitive processing concerning anticipation of pain relief computed elsewhere in the cortex could converge on this region. Indeed, increased activity in regions of the orbitofrontal cortex (OFC) is observed during analgesia triggered by a placebo. In humans, the OFC is a region associated with the formation of goals and expectations. The placebo would seem to be an example of just such cognitive processing. The OFC has connections with the ACC and with the brain stem and it appears to be associated with pain reduction based on

cognitive processing. Increased activity is seen in the periaqueductal grey region (PAG) following a placebo treatment and this could depend upon a cortical influence. As noted earlier, the PAG is a source of descending neurons implicated in analgesia.

A pain shared?

- 'I feel your suffering.'
- 'My heart aches for you.'
- 'Your pain is shared with us all.'

These are expressions not just of sympathy but of **empathy**, which refers to a capacity for a person to put themselves in another's place and to experience something of what it is like. At first, this might all sound far removed from the objective and somewhat impersonal world of biological psychology. However, biological psychology might not always be quite what it at first seems. It has some interesting things to say about human empathy.

Theorists suggest that, when empathy occurs, the observation of the emotional state of another (e.g. pain) triggers features of this same state in the brain of the observer. Brain imaging techniques permit us to put this to the test. They give a glimpse of what regions of the brain are doing when someone professes empathy for the pain of another (Singer *et al.*, 2004). Using an fMRI technique, women's brains were examined while their male partners were subject to painful stimulation to the hand.

Observing the partner in pain triggered parts of the brain of the observer that are normally triggered by painful stimuli, the pain matrix. However, the whole range of the brain's pain matrix was not triggered. Rather, only those parts associated with the quality of *affect* were excited. For example, the observer's anterior cingulate cortex was activated. Regions of somatosensory cortex triggered by nociceptive stimulation of the self were not activated in empathy. In accordance with other research, this suggests a role of this region in sensory and discriminative aspects of nociception, rather than affective aspects. Interestingly, as Figure 14.9 shows, there is a positive correlation between the score on an empathy scale and the degree of excitation of the ACC in response to the pain of the partner. (We can only imagine the breakfast table conversation that this study later triggered among the participants and the degree of marital empathy that was produced!)

What could be the possible functional significance of such an empathy system? One argument is as follows. We are a social species and we have adapted to a life of bonding with others. To share the emotion of someone close to us would tend to move us into action in response to their pain. For this, we only need to trigger the affective parts of the pain matrix rather than the sensory-discriminative parts. Indeed, we need to be able to discriminate pain in another person from pain that is endogenous to us (i.e. based on our own

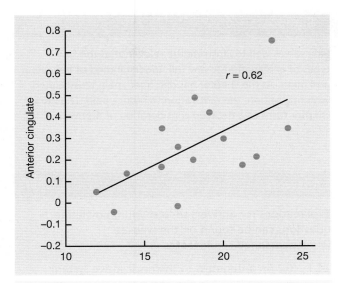

Figure 14.9 Relationship between empathy rating of individuals and the associated activation of the ACC.

Source: reprinted with permission, from Singer *et al.* (2004).

tissue damage). If too much of the pain matrix were activated, we might mistake the source of pain. The sensory side of another's suffering is detected through our eyes and ears, etc., which labels it as primarily theirs in its origin.

Section summary

1 A placebo is an intervention (e.g. substance or procedure) that shows a capacity to lower pain simply as a result of conditioning or a belief as to its efficacy.

2 We explain the placebo effect in terms of conditioning but also as a result of an expectation of pain relief from verbal information.

3 The placebo effect has a biological basis in inhibiting parts of the brain's pain matrix.

4 A biological basis of empathy consists of the activation of regions of the observer's pain matrix.

Test your knowledge

(Answer on page 370)

14.10 With regard to Figure 14.6, which of the CNS regions labelled appear to be active during the experience of empathy for a pain sufferer?

Bringing things together

Pain is enigmatic and its study reveals anomalies. Pain is often overwhelming in its attention-grabbing capacity and the potency with which it can take control of consciousness and behaviour. Yet, it can sometimes be reduced by diverted and focused attention, as in competitive sport, or even by nothing more than taking a sugar pill in expectation of relief. We now understand pain much better in terms of the contribution of specific types of neurons, routes of information transmission to and from the brain and brain mechanisms. Some factors can be defined at the neural level, e.g. (1) the properties of peripheral neurons, i.e. small- and large-diameter neurons and (2) connections that neurons make within the spinal cord.

A pain matrix of interacting brain regions that forms the biological basis of pain is now identified. This matrix does not respond in a one-to-one fashion to nociceptive input. Rather, such input is only one contributory factor. Such things as motivation, attention, mood, expectations and memories also play a part in determining pain. A broader approach involves (1) a gate mechanism at the spinal level and (2) some active participation of the brain in pain and anti-nociception. Knowledge of the involvement of regions of prefrontal cortex in pain can be interpreted in terms of their general role in the control of motivation, emotion, expectation and decision-making. This gives some biological basis to the known influence of such factors in pain.

The placebo effect can be better understood now in terms of its biological roots. Insights into the processes underlying the effect (e.g. expectation) reinforce our basic understanding of pain. For example, we know that recognized parts of the pain matrix are affected by placebo treatments. Taking a biological psychology perspective, such observations offer the possibility of explaining a range of phenomena within a single integrative framework.

Viewing pain from a functional perspective also gives useful insights that can be linked to the neural processes. The evolution of an anti-nociceptive system in addition to the nociceptive systems raises issues on the adaptive value of such joint control. The observation that the anti-nociceptive system is recruited at times when it would be maladaptive to react to tissue damage, as in focused fight or flight, gives an indicator of function. Such considerations could provide a functional context in which to view the clinical role of distraction and positive expectation in bringing pain relief.

Summary of Chapter 14

1   A nociceptive system underlies the production of pain, whereas activity within an anti-nociceptive system lowers pain.

2   Pain has adaptive value in protecting us from tissue damage and keeping us out of harm until we recover. At times it could be adaptive to inhibit pain and this seems to be the reason for the evolutionary appearance of an anti-nociceptive system.

3   Nociceptive neurons detect tissue damage and this leads normally to the sensation of pain. However, pain is not simply a one-to-one reflection of their activity.

4   As a metaphor, the spinal cord is the location of a 'gate'. As the gate opens, so nociceptive information passes, on its way to the brain. When the gate is closed information does not pass further.

5   It is possible to identify brain regions that have distinct roles in the discriminative and affective aspects of pain.

6   The role of different analgesics (pain-reducing substances) can be understood in terms of their actions at various sites in the nociceptive system.

7   Referred pain and phantom-limb pain are two phenomena that challenge any simple interpretation of pain.

8   The placebo effect and pain triggered by witnessing another person in pain point to the complex cognitive processing that also forms part of the causation of pain.

Signposts

Pain serves well to illustrate the relevance of the four types of explanation to any full understanding of behaviour and mind. As the chapter has described, pain is associated with motivation: the motivation to reduce pain. The next chapter turns to a detailed consideration of motivation.

Answers

Explanations for answers to 'test your knowledge' questions can be found on the website **www.pearsoned.co.uk/toates**

14.1   (ii) An antagonist to the nociceptive system; (iii) an agonist to the anti-nociceptive system.

14.2   Freezing is adaptive, since by remaining motionless an animal tends to avoid detection. If it were to respond to tissue damage by, for example, licking a wound this would act counter to the effect

14.3   An increase in pain

14.4   The large-diameter neuron and the two neurons labelled 'Descending pathways'

14.5   (i) The inhibitory neurochemical and (ii) enkephalin

14.6   2

14.7   High; low

14.8   (ii) Lignocaine

14.9   Increased pain felt as coming from the skin

14.10 Anterior cingulate cortex

Further reading

Pain is viewed in a psychological and philosophical context in Aydede (2006). Pain in the broad context of cognition and treatment is described by Horn and Munafo (1997). For the work of the pioneers of gate theory, see Melzack and Wall (1996) and Wall (2002). For hypnosis and its relation to gate theory, see Chaves and Dworkin (1997). Cognitive therapy and pain is described by Thorn (2004). For the placebo effect, see Evans (2004), Engel *et al.* (2002) and Moerman (2002). For an integrative perspective on depression and pain, see Meana (1998).

CHAPTER 15

Motivation

Learning outcomes for Chapter 15

After studying this chapter, you should be able to:

1. Explain the reasons why psychologists employ the term 'motivation' and describe the role it is thought to play in the control of behaviour. Compare and contrast some types of motivation.

2. Describe the properties associated with motivation and its link to behaviour. In so doing, demonstrate an understanding of the terms 'appetitive', 'consummatory', 'reward' and 'incentive'.

3. Identify the neural processes underlying motivation, while linking these to specific and general factors that are involved in the translation between motivation and action.

4. Describe how both behavioural and intrinsic physiological processes contribute to the regulation of body temperature and thereby exemplify a link between homeostasis, motivation and behaviour. In this context, distinguish between negative feedback and feedforward.

5. Identify the neurohormonal processes underlying parental and affiliative behaviours. Link their operation to the functional type of explanation.

6. Describe the contribution of biological, learning, cognitive and social factors to aggressive motivation and behaviour, so as to demonstrate their interaction. In this context, apply the term 'dynamic interaction' to the links between biological factors and the social environment.

7. Describe what we mean by the expression 'exploratory behaviour'. Link this to its underlying neural bases and functional significance.

Scene-setting questions

1 Do we always like the most that which we want the most? If not, why not?

2 Is human violence inevitable? Is fighting an instinct that we can't 'bottle-up'? Is aggression reinforcing?

3 Is love an addiction?

4 Why are curiosity and novelty-seeking such powerful factors in human behaviour? What makes some people sensation-seekers?

What motivation underlies such behaviour? How can we best describe it?

Source: © Digital Vision.

Introduction

Consider what motivates your circle of friends. Typically, Parminder might be nursing a broken heart after having been abandoned by Tony and she tries to contact him several times every day. She normally has a workaholic devotion to the study of psychology, directed to the goal of becoming a clinical psychologist, but she is now seriously disrupted in her studies. Parminder is *motivated* to regain the bond of affection – this is her dominant goal. The student group is sympathetic to Parminder but urges her to let go: 'He was no good for you. You were never happy'.

Tom is simply motivated to seek women for what he can get out of them, not having an emotional commitment in the world. Tom is always described by the student group as their 'textbook extravert and sensation-seeker'.

Svetlana can't go for long without a cigarette, whereas Nigel likes to gamble. Friends nag Svetlana about the dangers of her smoking and she tries to quit but without success. Nigel never wins at gambling and his friends can't see why he keeps at it. By contrast, Margaret has found God and spends time in meditation and Bible reading. Tom, forever the cynic, suggests that this is her 'opium', just like Svetlana's cigarettes. Margaret counters with the argument that every rewarding activity is bound to have a biological basis in the activity of the brain. However, this in no way undermines her beliefs or reduces their value to her life.

Harry, something of a connoisseur of exotic foods, is feeling sorry for himself, after having eaten what was then a delicious meal but being taken ill afterwards. The mere thought of the exotic food is painful – his motivation towards it has been lost – and now, at best, he can consider only 'regular' Western food. Normally, another of his favourite pursuits is exploring the countryside but that has had to be put on hold for a day or two. Sean complains endlessly about university food and is told that, if he were hungry enough, he would be happy to eat it. Ho can never make up his mind about things. He is constantly torn between different activities.

The author's brief venture into popular fiction might be far from reflecting your social circle but should serve to illustrate a few points:

1   Motivation is a process that gives direction, intensity and goals to behaviour and is associated with a focus of attention. Parminder cannot ignore Tony in order to focus on psychology.

2   There can be conflict between motivations. Svetlana wants to quit smoking but finds cigarettes irresistible. Parminder accepts what her friends say but cannot let go of Tony. Ho's indecision implies competition between motivations for the control of his behaviour.

3   Motivation has something to do with the search for pleasure, more or less obvious in different people. Tom appears to be motivated by a simple hedonism. Harry's motivation towards food is very much guided by the pleasurable or aversive consequences of tasting it.

4   Parminder illustrates that some motivation is based on powerful social attachments and trying to restore them once lost. However, the strength of her motivation is not a reflection of the level of pleasure that Tony brought to her. There appears then to be no simple equation between motivation and pleasure.

5   Some motivations relate rather clearly to basic biological processes, none more so than in Tom's case. However, Parminder's behaviour also makes sense biologically. Maintaining social bonds and resisting their break-up is of obvious importance to both sexes in survival and rearing children. Harry's exploration of the countryside provides stimulation to the senses. In our evolutionary roots, it would seem advantageous to know our environment. Other motivations reflect processes that were not involved in our early evolution. Cigarettes and casinos were not around then, but they are able to hijack basic processes of motivation and reward.

6   Motivation depends upon external and internal events. Foods vary in their attractiveness but if Sean were hungry enough, he might feel better about university food.

7   Motivation depends in part upon the consequences of our past actions. We expect to find understandable consequences of actions that serve either to sustain or to deter them. Harry's aversion to exotic cuisine makes sense. We can't understand why Nigel carries on gambling. We might expect to be able to identify something that Margaret 'gets out' of her spiritual devotion, such as inner tranquility as based in opioid activation.

8   Some motivations relate to immediate rewarding consequences. Svetlana's cigarette will deliver nicotine to her brain within a few seconds of puffing it. She is being asked to counter this pull with thoughts of possible aversive consequences that could be years into the future. Similarly, Parminder's goal of becoming a clinical psychologist will take years to realize.

Clearly, in what motivates people, there can be enormous variation among individuals. The richness and variety of human motivation are unique. Sometimes motivations blend in subtle ways, as in taking a meal for its nutrient value and for social contact. However, for some basic insight, we will need to focus on just a few motivations that are common across species – to regulate body temperature, seek social contact, feed, drink, mate and explore, etc. Building on these foundations, we can start to gain understanding of the special features of human motivation.

So, let us turn to some principles of motivation that are more applicable across species. There are several aspects to the term 'motivation' (Toates, 1986). It refers to the *variability* of behaviour: people tend to be motivated to seek food when they need nutrients but food becomes less attractive after ingesting a large amount. When we are hot, a cold temperature motivates approach but, when we are cold, it motivates our avoidance. Similarly, people's reaction to a sexual stimulus varies as a function of their level of sexual motivation, as embodied in regions of the brain that are sensitized by sex hormones.

Some forms of motivation help to maintain the homeostasis of the body in a rather obvious way. The motivations associated with temperature, food and water fall into this class. As was discussed in Chapter 1, 'Introduction', the principle of homeostasis has several closely related aspects:

- Survival is possible only if certain parameters of the body such as its water level and temperature are maintained within limits.

- Behavioural and intrinsic physiological action is taken that serves to maintain the parameters within these limits.

- Deviation of a parameter from its normal value tends to cause physiological and behavioural corrective action, the latter being associated with motivation.

The motivation for social attachment is about maintaining contact with a 'special other': partner, parent or child. Loss of contact promotes the motivation to regain contact, a kind of 'social homeostasis'. Sexual motivation appears not to be directly concerned with homeostasis. Exploration is about information, i.e. motivation is directed to gaining particular types of sensory stimulation.

In terms of passing on genes, consider an animal in the wild. It needs to avoid harm, e.g. being eaten or suffering tissue injury. It needs to obtain food, water and shelter, to sleep, to explore, to defend against extremes of temperature, to mate and in some cases invest effort in raising young. Some species migrate or hibernate. To do these things, the animal needs to (a) detect information in the environment (presence of food, mate, etc.) and (b) monitor internal conditions (levels of nutrients, hormones, etc.). Regions of the brain involved with motivation produce action on the basis of a *combination* of these sources of information. Some behaviour is of the *approach* kind (termed 'appetitive'), in which increasing stimulation is of adaptive value, e.g. getting to food or a mate. Other behaviour is of the *avoidance* or *escape* kind, to prevent or minimize contact with aversive events (Glickman and Schiff, 1967).

In the wild, time is often at a premium and behaviour involves benefits and costs (Chapter 2, 'Genes, environment and evolution'). Given conflicting requirements, motivations compete for expression, e.g. to mate or eat. Animals appear to perform computations and arrive at decisions. For example, an animal might be dehydrated, a cost in terms of the risk to body fluids. There is the motivation to search for water, the finding of which could be very beneficial. However, the water hole might be distant and, at the time in question, be a location of predators, so it could pay to wait.

Some tasks demand urgent action, whereas others can be delayed, which implies inhibition on lower-priority activities. In rats, hunger suppresses social play (Vanderschuren *et al.*, 1997). Fear inhibits a range of motivations such as that underlying play (Panksepp, 1998a). From functional considerations, a time of danger is not a time for play. Chapter 2 discussed the jungle fowl, whose weight falls while she incubates eggs. Prioritization is given to incubation; the motivation to incubate inhibits the tendency to feed.

In the next two sections, we look at some common features of motivation, its expression in behaviour and some

processes associated with this. Then, subsequent sections will look at some examples of particular motivations, considering common features and differences between them. Subsequently, Chapters 16–18 look in more detail at feeding, drinking, sexual behaviour and drug-taking.

Section summary

1 Motivation refers to brain processes that take internal and external factors into consideration. These processes give direction and intensity to behaviour and underlie its variability.

2 There can be competition between motivations for expression in behaviour.

3 Some motivations are linked closely to maintaining the homeostasis of the body.

Test your knowledge

(Answer on page 396)

15.1 Which of the following behaviours is tied closely to maintaining an optimal condition within the tissues of the body ('homeostasis')? Feeding, drinking, temperature regulation, sex, exploration.

Properties of motivation

Introduction

In the context of neuroscience, the term 'motivation' refers to the activity within specific regions of the brain that gives direction and intensity to behaviour. Motivation is associated with *flexibility* of behaviour, in that a given motivation can be expressed in a variety of different ways. For example, feeding motivation is revealed in the behaviour of a rat that opens a sack, learns to press a lever in a Skinner box or negotiates a maze to get food. The consequence of gaining food changes its future behaviour, e.g. to make lever-pressing more likely in the future. This is an example of the developmental/learning type of explanation introduced in Chapter 1.

In humans, there seems an endless variety of different ways in which a given motivation can gain expression in behaviour – just think what Parminder might try next to achieve the goal of winning back the affections of Tony. In the expression of motivation in behaviour, learning plays a crucial role. We learn how to act to achieve our goals. So, among other things, this section will introduce the role of learning in the link between motivation and behaviour.

Appetitive and consummatory phases

For such things as feeding and sex, two phases of the control of behaviour are identified: 'appetitive' and 'consummatory' (McDougall, 1923). The **appetitive phase** refers to the means necessary to get to an 'end-situation', e.g. running a maze to get to food or a sexual partner. The term **consummatory phase** refers to what the animal actually does in the end-situation, e.g. eating or mating. In non-humans, the flexibility of the appetitive phase generally contrasts with the species-typical inflexible pattern of the consummatory phase (e.g. lordosis in female rats, described in Chapter 3, 'The nervous and endocrine systems') (Epstein, 1982). Similarly, wide individual differences are evident in the appetitive phase of gaining food but the consummatory phase is usually more stereotyped.

Reward and incentive

Chapter 11, 'Learning and memory', described the term 'reinforcement'. This section introduces some more on the psychology of learning: terms that link learning, motivation and behaviour.

Reward

The term **reward** is used to describe something with which the animal acts to maintain contact, e.g. a cool drink when thirsty (White, 1989). It relates to the consummatory phase and it describes a CNS consequence of sensory contact with something that is ranked as positive. The reward value of a stimulus can be assessed by, for example, the length of time

an animal spends in contact with it. In human subjective terms, reward describes the degree of liking for something. As the opposite of reward, 'aversion' refers to something from which the animal withdraws and subsequently avoids. In humans, it is reflected in such terms as displeasure, pain and disgust.

Suppose that a hungry animal is first held in the white arm of a T-maze that contains food (Figure 15.1(a)). In future when given the choice, the animal typically prefers spending time in the white arm even if it is empty (parts (b) and (c)), as measured by the relative length of time that it spends there. A **conditioned place preference (CPP)** has been established and the food is said to be rewarding (White, 1989). By observing an animal's preference, a CPP test shows a common property shared by different rewards, e.g. food, drugs, a sexually attractive conspecific (Everitt, 1990; Harris *et al.*, 2005) and the opportunity to engage in social play with a conspecific (Vanderschuren *et al.*, 1997).

Incentive

The term **incentive** is used to describe an animal's attraction towards rewards. If you wonder why we need two terms, reward and incentive, please be patient. Incentive relates to the appetitive phase and conveys the sense of an animal being 'pulled' to the reward. Rewarding things such as food, water, drugs and sexual contact come to form incentives.

Classical conditioning between external stimuli and incentives plays a vital role in motivation. By their pairing with primary incentives, neutral stimuli become **conditional incentives** and they then exert an influence on behaviour. For example, by its pairing with food, the white arm in Figure 15.1 has become a conditional incentive. For another example, feeding can be aroused in 'satiated' animals by a cue that has been paired with food delivery when the animal was hungry (Weingarten, 1984). The cue becomes a conditional incentive. Sexual arousal can be increased by cues that were

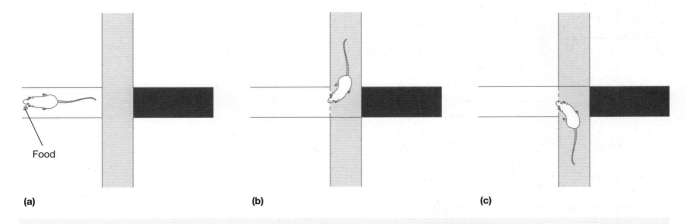

(a)   (b)   (c)

Figure 15.1 Conditioned place preference: (a) conditioning phase, (b) and (c) testing phase.

earlier associated with mating (Domjan, 1994). A cue paired with injection of an intravenous drug in a Skinner box can revive lever-pressing for the drug following extinction (Stewart *et al.*, 1984). Conditional cues associated with shock can trigger aggression in the presence of a conspecific (Berkowitz, 1993).

Under some conditions, a given object might lose reward value but still maintain incentive value. Thus, animals occasionally are attracted to food that they do not eat (Dickinson and Balleine, 1992). Conversely, following certain brain lesions, food can trigger ingestion when it is placed in the mouth, i.e. it is rewarding, but an animal fails to be attracted towards it even following deprivation (Berridge and Valenstein, 1991), i.e. it has lost incentive value.

Hedonic ('affective') states

Introduction

In humans, associated with each positive ('appetitive') motivation there is a factor of positive affect ('pleasure'). To what extent a common system underlies the pleasures of the consummatory phase, e.g. eating and sex, is unclear (Panksepp, 1998a). There might be a common neural process (e.g. in the septal area or the amygdala) and distinctions between types of reward might arise from differences in sensory channels activated.

Human experience

To humans, ingestion of food is hedonically good, bad or indifferent (Cabanac, 1971). A combination of external and internal factors, e.g. the intrinsic properties of the food and the body's level of nutrients, determines hedonic reactivity. Figure 15.2 shows a result for temperature that makes a similar point (Cabanac, 1998). For low ('hypothermic') core body temperatures, warmth at the skin is pleasant, whereas cold is pleasant when the core of the body is high ('hyperthermic'). That the pleasure or displeasure of a local skin temperature is a function of internal temperature (e.g. cold is pleasurable in hyperthermia) is termed **alliesthesia** (Cabanac, 1998). This all makes sense in terms of homeostasis and biological adaptation: e.g. when the body is hypothermic, it is advantageous to approach warm environments.

Whether we should extrapolate affect to non-humans is a matter of scientific taste but the lay public has no hesitation in doing so. An experiment relevant to this issue is described next.

Taste reactivity test

Do non-human species experience affect? We can speculate based on behaviour, an example being shown in the **taste reactivity test** (Berridge *et al.*, 1981). See Figure 15.3. A

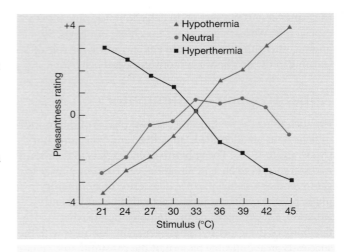

Figure 15.2 Pleasantness ratings of a temperature stimulus as a function of three different body temperatures.

Source: Cabanac (1979).

cannula is implanted so that small quantities of liquid nutrient are applied to the rat's tongue. Behaviour is observed from below in a mirror and recorded by a video camera. A lexicon of reactions, positive and negative, is constructed (Figure 15.4).

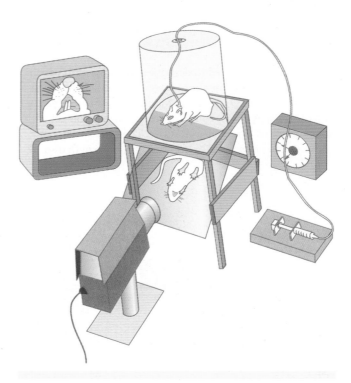

Figure 15.3 The taste reactivity test.

Source: Grill and Berridge (1985, Fig. 3, p. 13).

Ingestion sequence

Aversion sequence

Figure 15.4 Sample reactions. Top row: acceptance, i.e. ingestive reactions – rhythmic mouth movements, protrusions of the tongue, etc; bottom row: rejection, i.e. aversive reactions – chin rubs, paw wipes, etc.

Source: Berridge *et al.* (1981, Fig. 1, p. 366).

The test provides a measure of motivation as related to consummatory behaviour. Some substances (e.g. saccharine) trigger acceptance whereas others (e.g. quinine) trigger rejection. Concentrated sodium chloride solution triggers rejection when the animal is in sodium balance but, following sodium depletion, it is accepted. This indicates the influence of physiological state on motivation and clearly relates to homeostasis. After an otherwise desirable substance has been paired with gastrointestinal illness (Chapter 11), the same substance triggers rejection. A memory of the past contact modulates the reactivity to the incentive.

Very young children, even newborns, also exhibit characteristic facial reactions when coming into contact with substances, indicative of affect (Steiner, 1979), as illustrated in Figure 15.5.

Figure 15.5 Human baby feeding.

Source: © Michael Keller/CORBIS.

We now turn to consider some of the neural bases of the processes described in this section.

Section summary

1 Such things as food, water and sexual contact serve as rewards, i.e. an animal acts to maintain contact with them.

2 Motivation is revealed in behaviour in the appetitive and consummatory phases.

3 The term 'incentive' refers to the capacity of rewards to attract.

4 Cues paired with incentives acquire motivational value by classical conditioning. They become 'conditional incentives'.

5 Motivation arises from a combination of external ('incentives') and internal (e.g. nutrient level) signals.

6 Affective ('hedonic') experiences depend upon internal physiology in a way that makes adaptive sense.

Test your knowledge

(Answers on page 396)

15.2 Complete the following: 'Pressing a lever in a Skinner box, is an example of the _____ phase of behaviour whereas eating the food is an example of the _____ phase'.

15.3 A tone is paired with the presentation of a drug a number of times. Subsequently, a rat presses a lever in a Skinner box to earn the tone on its own. In the terminology of conditioning, what adjective before 'incentive' qualifies the description of the tone?

15.4 A particular nutrient solution triggers positive ingestive reactions in rats. Other than over-eating, what would shift the reactions in a negative direction?

15.1

The neuroscience of motivation

Introduction

Having described a few general principles, we now look at some brain mechanisms that underlie motivation, with an emphasis on those that link motivation to action. We ask two closely related questions – are there general *principles* of neural organization underlying motivation that can be applied across different motivations? Can we go further and find any common neural processes that serve different motivations?

From a 'design' point of view, we might argue along the following lines. Parameters of the body such as temperature and water level require specialized and dedicated neural processes. These monitor just one such quality and, when it departs from optimum, they play a role in a specific corresponding motivation. However, in the appetitive phase, no matter what the incentive is, the problem posed seems to be rather similar when comparing different motivations. The most potent incentive needs to form the focus of attention, engage behaviour by linking to motor control and offer competition over any other candidates for control.

Similarly, in the consummatory phase, there could be at least some common processes underlying rewarding effects, e.g. the reward of the taste of food and that of sexual contact. Any reward needs to serve to keep the animal going at a task for so long as the task is still rewarding.

We might expect to find less in the way of common processes underlying the motor side of the consummatory phase – after all, mating is rather different from feeding!

So, let us see what the evidence shows, considering first the role of incentives in the appetitive phase.

Dopamine, incentives and approach behaviour

The mesolimbic dopaminergic pathway

Central to contemporary thinking about motivation is a *general* 'incentive system' or 'seeking system'. This serves any *specific* motivation that can gain access to it (Blackburn *et al.*, 1992). The biological basis of the 'incentive system' involves a dopaminergic pathway, the **mesolimbic dopamine pathway**, part of which starts in the ventral tegmental area (VTA) and terminates in the nucleus accumbens (N.acc.), a region of the ventral striatum (Everitt and Robbins, 1992). See Figure 15.6. When this pathway is activated by a particular incentive, the animal tends to approach the incentive. So, DA

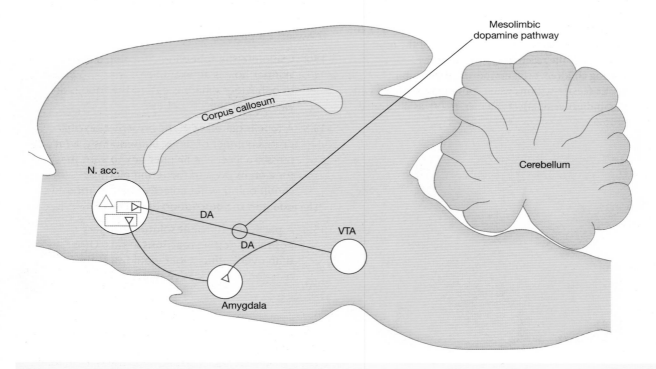

Figure 15.6 The mesolimbic dopamine (DA) pathway in the rat brain.

Source: after Bardo (1998, Fig. 1, p. 57).

activation increases the power of incentives to engage behaviour. An 'all-purpose' appetitive system makes adaptive sense rather than each motivation having its own dedicated approach system.

By employing PET, the dopaminergic activity of the ventral striatum (which includes the nucleus accumbens) was studied in a group of patients suffering from Parkinson's disease (de la Fuente-Fernández *et al.*, 2002). In their case, the reward was considered to be the clinical benefit following a placebo treatment. The *expectation* of receiving this reward was associated with dopaminergic activation in the region of the N.acc.

Consider Figure 15.7. The N.acc. appears to serve as interface, in which information on motivational significance is (1) computed and (2) transmitted towards processes ('Motor control') at or near the basal ganglia, which organize behaviour (Chapter 10, 'The control of movement'; Mogenson, 1984).

Different motivations exert an influence on behaviour via the nucleus accumbens. So how do these specific factors exert a role over the approach to incentives? As shown in Figure 15.7, the N.acc. receives information from a number of other brain regions, e.g. the cortex, amygdala and hippocampus. We focus now on the amygdala.

The amygdala and incentive learning

The amygdala is involved in learning about the conditional significance of positive events such as those related to food and sexual partners (Everitt, 1990; Wang *et al.*, 2005) as well as negative events (Chapter 12, 'Emotion'). That is, the amygdala has a role in attributing motivational value to otherwise neutral stimuli following their pairing with rewarding or aversive events. Acting via the amygdala, these (now 'conditional') stimuli are able to engage behaviour. The lateral and basal nuclei of the amygdala are involved in attributing conditional incentive value to such things as the

lever in the Skinner box associated with food reward (Wang *et al.*, 2005). This contributes to making lever-pressing the goal of behaviour. As shown in Figure 15.7, the amygdala projects to the nucleus accumbens, which is the next link in the chain leading to the motor output that underlies approach behaviour.

Drug addicts show an exaggerated response of the amygdala to drug-related cues (Bechara, 2005). This includes the reward of money, a capacity which might well depend upon an association with the purchase of drugs.

For another example, in the conditioned place preference task, a rat associates one arm of a T-maze (e.g. the white arm) with reward (e.g. mate or a drug infusion) and prefers spending time there. Following lesions to the lateral amygdala, rats show motivational indifference towards the arms (McDonald and White, 1993; White and McDonald, 1993).

Focusing specifically on the basolateral amygdala (Chapter 12, Figure 12.9, p. 318,), projections from here go to the nucleus accumbens (Figure 15.7; Everitt and Robbins, 1992). This link mediates the effect of conditional stimuli and damage to it disrupts their capacity to engage behaviour. However, it does not disrupt consummatory behaviour. Rats with lesions to the basolateral amygdala exhibit normal copulation and normal drinking following deprivation.

The functional significance of a process by which conditional stimuli gain control of behaviour is clear: based upon past experience, it leads the animal to incentives and keeps an animal going at a goal-directed task even in the absence of the primary reward.

Wanting versus liking

Basics of the distinction

Dopamine (DA) is implicated in the motivational role of incentives and in forming conditional incentives. Is dopamine also involved in the reward process, e.g. the hedonics of taste? Dopamine depletion reduces food intake but is this just because food fails to form an incentive to attract the rat? It might be that the taste of food loses its rewarding impact.

The taste reactivity test (see earlier) allows researchers to separate possible effects of DA depletion. Suppose that DA mediates the reward of something, in human terms it underlies the experience of pleasure. It would follow that when DA is depleted, food loses its hedonic impact. Berridge and Valenstein (1991) performed the taste reactivity test, expecting that the reaction to food in the mouth would be shifted in a negative direction. This was not the case; dopamine-depleted rats reacted to food in the same way as did controls.

This research suggested that the *incentive value* of food (its 'incentive salience') depends upon DA, i.e. its capacity to attract attention and 'pull' the animal towards it. When DA is

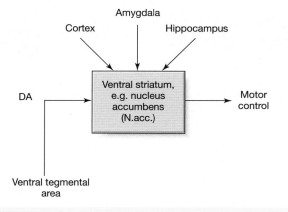

Figure 15.7 Role of the nucleus accumbens.

depleted, the appetitive ('wanting') phase is disrupted. However, if the animal receives food in the mouth, the food's hedonic impact ('liking') is not diminished. The role of DA has been described as focusing: the strength of one particular incentive is amplified in the face of competing possibilities for action which are inhibited (Mogenson *et al.*, 1993).

Of course, if not DA, then another neurochemical underlies the reward value, e.g. that of food in the mouth or sexual contact (Robinson and Berridge, 1993). Evidence suggests that activity by the brain's opioid systems is the biological basis of several, if not all, types of reward (Ågmo and Berenfeld, 1990; Panksepp *et al.*, 2002). In a taste reactivity test, injecting opioid agonists makes the reaction to food more positive (Rideout and Parker, 1996). The injection of opiate drugs acts as a very potent reward. Loss of opioid systems lowers the reward of social contact (Moles *et al.* 2004).

The incentive system employing dopamine and the reward system employing opioids show close interaction (Depue and Morrone-Strupinsky, 2005). On a psychological level, we tend to want what we like but there is not a perfect correlation between wanting and liking (Robinson and Berridge, 1993).

A genetic modification

Suppose that we create a hyper-dopaminergic state. What would Berridge and associates predict? That animals would show a heightened attraction to incentives ('wanting') but that the taste reactivity ('liking') would not alter. So how do we create this state? You may recall from Chapter 4, 'The cells of the nervous system' that, after its release from presynaptic terminals and occupation of receptors, dopamine is taken back into the cell from which it is released, a process termed 'reuptake'. Peciña *et al.* (2003) created a strain of mutant mice using the technique of 'gene knock-down'. Specifically, the dopamine transporter gene was knocked-down, so that very little dopamine was transported back into the cell from which it was released. Hence, there is an elevation of dopamine at the receptors on the postsynaptic membrane.

For food reward, the mutant mice showed quicker learning, a decreased length of time to run a maze and fewer distractions, compared with controls. This pointed to increased wanting. However, there was no difference in reaction to the taste of the reward, pointing to liking's insensitivity to dopamine levels.

Individual differences in human personality

Humans differ of course in how they are influenced by rewards, e.g. by the relative weight of immediate reward ('instant gratification') versus delayed reward. Do differences in the activity of reward regions of the brain link to differences in personality?

Using the technique of fMRI, Cohen *et al.* (2005) investigated the possible link between differences in activation of regions of the brain associated with the reward of money and differences in extraversion. Figure 15.8(a) shows the activation of three such regions by money reward: the orbitofrontal cortex (Figure 5.33, p. 129), the nucleus accumbens (Figure 5.31, p. 127) and the amygdala. Figure 15.8(b) shows differences in activation of two of these structures and the participants' scores on extraversion. A positive correlation is evident. This could give leads that enable links to be established between brain structures and individual differences in sensitivity to reward. Note also that the structures most sensitive to reward are influenced by dopamine, pointing to further challenges in terms of the relationship between this neurochemical and the dimension of liking and wanting. Yet further challenges come in trying to associate the individual differences revealed in Figure 15.8(b) to differences in alleles coding for dopamine receptors.

The next section turns to the 'mechanics' of the consummatory phase.

The mechanics of consummatory behaviour

The consummatory phase of rat behaviour is somewhat stereotyped. Rats eat and mate in a rather standard way. This implies tightly organized controls of the motor output. Much of the organization of consummatory behaviour such as feeding, mating and attack is done at brain stem sites (Chapter 10; Berntson and Micco, 1976). The neural processes that underlie organized patterns of neuromuscular control ('prescriptions') are located in these regions.

So, what is the link between motivation and consummatory behaviour? The hypothalamus contains

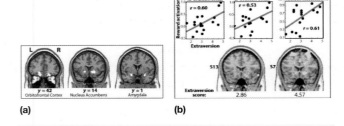

Figure 15.8 Linking activation of reward regions of the brain and personality differences: (a) three regions affected by reward and (b) link between activation (vertical axis) and extraversion score (horizontal axis). Increasing score on horizontal axis = increasing extraversion. Lower part activations for two participants, whose extraversion scores are indicated.

Source: Cohen *et al.* (2005, Fig. 2, p. 854 and Fig. 3, p. 856). Figures by courtesy of Dr Michael Cohen.

distinct nuclei (Chapter 5, 'The brain'), sensitive to particular chemicals in the fluid that bathes them, e.g. glucose (Chapter 16, 'Feeding and drinking') or testosterone (Chapter 17, 'Sexual behaviour'). These nuclei exert a tendency towards a particular consummatory behaviour by favouring activation of the lower-level neural circuits that organize it. For example, in functional terms, feeding reflexes are potentiated at times of nutrient need (Berntson and Micco, 1976). Neural systems in, among other regions, the striatum integrate individual acts such as licking, chewing and swallowing to form functionally coherent sequences (Aldridge and Berridge, 1998).

A consideration of the appetitive and consummatory phases is central to the topic described next.

Electrical stimulation of the brain

Introduction

Psychologists observe the behaviour of animals with electrodes implanted in their brains, through which electric current is delivered. This procedure is known as 'electrical stimulation of the brain' (ESB). There are two variations on this theme: the animal or the experimenter triggers the delivery of electric current. This section looks at each.

Intracranial self-stimulation

One of the best-known results in psychology is that of Olds and Milner (1954). Electrodes are implanted into the brain of rats with the tip in one of a number of different regions, e.g. the lateral hypothalamus (LH). They are taught to press a lever to deliver electric shocks to the particular region. This is termed electrical self-stimulation of the brain or **intracranial self-stimulation** (ICSS). The vigour with which rats engage in ICSS suggests that they are tapping into a 'pleasure centre' and this term rapidly acquired popularity. It seemed as if they were simulating some of the conditions of, say, feeding or sexual orgasm but bypassing the sensory processes that would normally mediate it.

Dopaminergic systems are involved in ICSS. Loss of dopamine is followed by a fall in ICSS. Thus, dopamine came to be described as a pleasure neurotransmitter and a loss of dopamine as 'anhedonia' (Wise, 1982). However, as just noted, we now have reason to believe that dopamine is not mediating pleasure but rather is involved in incentive approach ('wanting'). So, maybe rats are not triggering pleasure centres but 'incentive centres'.

For ICSS in the lateral hypothalamus, Panksepp (1998a, p. 145) notes:

The outward behaviour of the animal commonly appears as if it is trying to get something behind the lever. In other words, an invigorated exploratory attitude is sustained throughout. This is not the type of behaviour one sees when animals are either pressing levers to obtain conventional rewards or when they are actually engaged in *consuming* them.

Electrically induced behaviour

If the experimenter (rather than the rat) controls the current, a rat can be induced to engage in behaviour such as going over to food and eating. This is termed **electrically induced behaviour** (EIB). Typically, if the same electrode that supports ICSS (e.g. in the lateral hypothalamus) is stimulated under the experimenter's control, the animal engages in behaviour such as sniffing and exploration. If food is present, it will eat (Valenstein, 1969).

Stimulation elicits various behaviours, according to the location of the electrode and other factors such as availability of incentives (Robbins and Everitt, 1999).

The next four sections look at some specific behaviours associated with motivation: temperature regulation, social attachment, aggression and exploration. These will illustrate the general principles described so far in this chapter, such as homeostasis, the role of incentives and conditioning, etc. In each case, the focus will be on how motivation arises and how it relates to behaviour. The next section looks at a homeostatic system and the neural systems dedicated to detecting the state of a physiological parameter and linking this to motivation and action.

Section summary

1 There is an incentive system, a principal biological basis of which is the mesolimbic dopamine pathway.

2 The mesolimbic dopamine pathway starts in the ventral tegmental area (VTA) and projects to the nucleus accumbens (N.acc.).

3 Loss of dopamine from the mesolimbic dopamine pathway causes a loss of appetitive ('incentive') motivation.

4 There are specific motivational inputs to the mesolimbic dopamine pathway from other brain regions, such as the amygdala and hippocampus.

5 There is a distinction between wanting and liking and manipulations can affect one and not the other. Wanting is mediated by dopamine whereas liking appears not to be.

6 Some consummatory behaviour is organized at the brain stem and coordinated by higher brain regions, e.g. cortex and striatum.

Temperature regulation

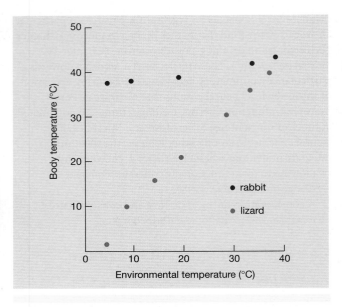

Figure 15.9 Body temperature and environmental temperature for a rabbit (blue dots) and a lizard (red dots).

Introduction

According to their body temperature, animals are motivated to seek warmth or cold, a clear example of homeostasis. Correspondingly, sources of either warmth or cold act as rewards, as shown in Figure 15.2 for humans. Life is possible only if body temperature remains within a range, the magnitude of which depends upon the species. For mammals and birds, the range is narrow.

Body temperature is said to be regulated by means of comparison with a set-point (Chapter 10) of temperature (Cabanac, 1998). The term 'set-point' describes the temperature set ('defended') by the system. Deviations from the set-point trigger actions that bring the regulated variable back to the set-point (Cabanac and Russek, 1982). The set-point can vary slightly. It is elevated at times of fever and shows some fluctuation over the 24 hours of day–night. However, at any time, the set-point value is defended against disturbances.

The body temperature of humans exemplifies well that deviations from the normal (set-point) level can exert a powerful influence on internal physiology, motivation and behaviour. For fish, reptiles and amphibians, although the range of tolerance is wider, there are still optimal temperatures for maximizing efficiency (Blumberg and Sokoloff, 1998).

In lay terms, animals are warm-blooded (birds and mammals) or cold-blooded (amphibians, reptiles and fish). However, body temperature of a so-called cold-blooded animal can sometimes be as warm as that of a warm-blooded one, e.g. a snake basking in the sun. The distinction refers not so much to actual body temperature but to (a) the range of temperatures compatible with life and (b) the extent to which an animal is at the mercy of the environment. A reptile can survive a wider range of body temperatures than can a mammal. The reptile's body temperature depends upon the environment to a greater extent than that of a warm-blooded animal. The body temperature of a mammal

or bird tends to remain near to constant. Figure 15.9 compares body temperatures of a rabbit and a lizard when exposed to different environmental temperatures.

Regulation and control

Introduction

Actively holding body temperature near constant exemplifies regulatory behaviour and homeostasis (Chapter 2). Actions that serve regulatory behaviour are termed *control* actions (Cabanac and Russek, 1982). For example, sweating and panting are controlled, whereas body temperature is regulated. Similarly, drinking and urination are said to be controlled, whereas body-fluid level is regulated.

For survival, it is biologically imperative that body temperature is defended, whereas it is adaptive for sweating and panting to fluctuate *in the service of* body temperature.

Two means of control

Two kinds of control are exerted to regulate body temperature: intrinsic physiological and behavioural (Blumberg and Sokoloff, 1998). Intrinsic control involves effectors of the ANS (Chapter 3) such as sweating and changing the diameter of blood vessels near the skin to facilitate heat exchange. Shivering is an intrinsic control similar to autonomic actions but involves skeletal muscle. Behavioural and autonomic controls serve the same end, are complementary and there can be a trade-off between them. When temperature regulation cannot be achieved by behaviour, more of the burden is carried by autonomic processes (Cabanac, 1998). Autonomic processes are costly and there is an adaptive value in behavioural control relieving them of long-term exertion.

Examples of behavioural control

Behavioural control consists of certain species-typical reflexes and performing whole-body motivated actions. Whole-body actions involve (a) changing body position relative to the present environment, (b) moving to a new environment or (c) remaining in the same location and producing action to change it, e.g. building a nest, huddling with other animals or pressing a lever in a Skinner box for heat (Carlisle, 1966). In humans, such behaviour is associated with reports of affect (Figure 15.2).

Among different species, behavioural control is more widely found than is intrinsic control. All species so far tested show selection of a temperature environment. Fish select an appropriate water temperature and can be trained in an operant task to gain access to it (Satinoff, 1983). There is a richness of means by which humans regulate body temperature, e.g. to light fires or seek shelter. We can also anticipate future needs by taking pre-emptive action ('feedforward'), e.g. putting on extra clothes on hearing the weather forecast. All these criteria point to the existence of motivation.

Neural processes

Neural characteristics

There are neurons the activity of which depends strongly upon body temperature. They are found in the hypothalamus and other sites in the CNS, including the spinal cord, and in the periphery (Bligh, 1972). (However, not all such neurons are necessarily involved in temperature regulation.) There are so-called 'warm neurons', where frequency of producing action potentials increases with temperature. What are termed 'cold neurons' have the opposite characteristic: as temperature falls, their frequency of generation of action potentials increases (Figure 15.10).

Temperature-sensitive neurons at the core and periphery play a role in temperature regulation. If core temperature shifts from its optimal value, autonomic and behavioural control is triggered. However, threats to body temperature usually arise first from outside the body, e.g. sudden cold winds, rather than from within it. Outside disturbances do not immediately affect core temperature (and the neurons there) since the core is shielded. However, if action is not taken, core temperature will subsequently be affected, so it is crucial that temperature detected at the periphery can trigger action.

The role of peripheral temperature-sensitive neurons in behavioural and autonomic control represents feedforward (Chapter 10). By reacting immediately to peripheral temperature, the animal can often avoid ('pre-empt') central shifts of temperature.

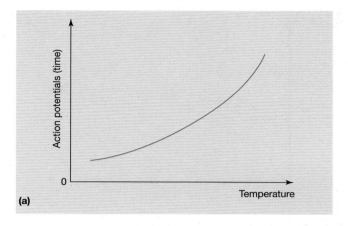

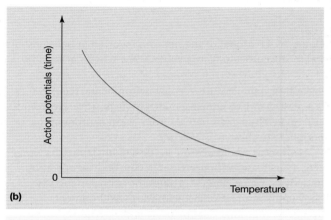

Figure 15.10 Response characteristics of (a) warm and (b) cold neurons in terms of action potentials per unit of time.

Various locations in the brain and spinal cord play roles in computing signals that are employed in temperature control (Satinoff, 1983). The preoptic area of the hypothalamus (Figure 5.32, p. 128) has attracted most attention, as the brain region where the motivational basis of temperature is computed (Gordon and Heath, 1986). Local heating or cooling at this site is an effective trigger for a thermoregulatory response. It is here that injections of neurotransmitters are particularly effective in altering temperature regulation.

A simple model

The truth is that we do not know exactly how signals involved in temperature regulation are computed. However, this need not deter intelligent speculation. Figure 15.11 suggests how temperature-sensitive neurons at the core and periphery *might well* interact in the control of behaviour and in changing the reward value of external temperatures. Neuron$_1$ is a 'warm neuron' in the brain (e.g. preoptic area of the hypothalamus), i.e. its activity increases with core body temperature. When it is active, it excites neuron$_3$, which motivates the animal to seek a cold environment and thereby

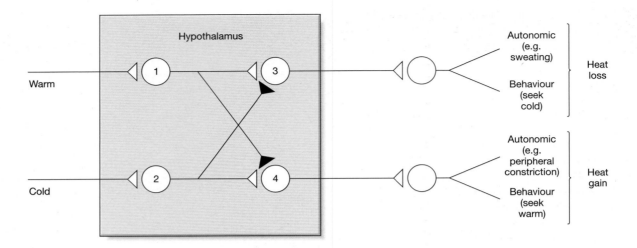

Figure 15.11 Model of the neurons involved in behavioural temperature regulation. △, excitation; ▲, inhibition.
Source: after an illustration by Albert Miller in Heller *et al.* (1978).

lower body temperature. A cold environmental temperature is a reward and, to humans, is affectively positive. Neuron$_1$ is also excited by signals derived from warm neurons at the periphery (indicated as 'Warm').

Neuron$_2$ is a 'cold neuron' in the hypothalamus. Its activity increases with decreases in core body temperature. Its activity, via neuron$_4$, motivates the animal to increase body temperature. Contact with warm environments becomes rewarding. Cold neurons in the periphery excite neuron$_2$ (indicated as 'Cold'). Note inhibitory links between the 'warm control pathway' and the 'cold control pathway'.

Figure 15.12 illustrates the zones of control to each side of a thermo-neutral range and the corresponding neural bases of control. Within the thermo-neutral range, the animal is not motivated to perform temperature-related activities.

This section has looked at an example of the link between homeostasis, motivation and behaviour, which serves the inner environment. The following considers an example of social behaviour.

Section summary

1 Body temperature is regulated by control of autonomic processes and the influence of motivation on behaviour.

2 When set-point and actual body temperature get out of alignment by a significant amount, physiological and behavioural control is triggered to restore normality.

3 Temperature-sensitive neurons at the CNS and periphery play a role in temperature regulation.

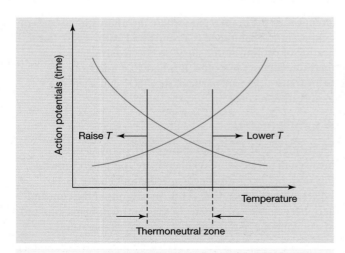

Figure 15.12 Activity of temperature-dependent neurons and the associated behavioural actions.

Test your knowledge

(Answers on page 396)

15.6 In Figure 15.11, suppose that the animal is in a thermoneutral environment. What would be the behavioural effect of injecting an agonist to the neurotransmitter employed in the link from the neuron marked 'Warm' to neuron$_1$?

15.7 In Figure 15.11, detection of extreme cold at the periphery has what effect on the activity of neuron$_3$?

15.2

Social behaviour

Introduction

This section looks at two motivations and the behaviour that is associated with each: **nurturant behaviour** (parental behaviour) and **social attachment**, i.e. bonding (introduced briefly in Chapter 12). In some species, such as humans, the two motivations overlap. That is to say, a social attachment, between an infant and mother, develops at the same time as the mother performs nurturant behaviour, e.g. suckling (Panksepp, 1998a).

Nurturant behaviour and social attachment reveal several features of motivation:

1 Behaviour leads to reward and this supports learning that leads to further social contact (Panksepp, 1998a).

2 Distress is exhibited when contact is broken and this motivates restoration of contact.

3 Mammals perform various tasks for the reward of regaining broken contact, e.g. rat mothers learn to lever-press for the reward of reunion with pups (Lee *et al.*, 2000).

4 The reaction towards an infant depends upon the *combination* of the properties of the infant, e.g. its odour, and the internal neurohormonal condition of the mother.

5 Specific brain regions are involved in the control of maternal behaviour and attachment. These regions show properties similar to those underlying certain other emotions and motivations, such as pain and sex.

We consider first nurturant (mainly maternal) behaviour and then attachment, bearing in mind that there can be considerable overlap between them.

Nurturance

The term 'nurturant behaviour' is employed to describe the care given by a parent to its offspring (Panksepp, 1998a).

Motivational basis

The mother's reaction to infants varies with her physiological condition, a pointer towards a motivational variable. The young are attractive to a nursing mother rat. For example, she attempts to regain contact with them if they get lost. Such attraction to an appropriate incentive is a property in common with other motivations (Ferris *et al.*, 2005).

In mammals, events prior to the birth of her young put the mother's body into a condition that increases the chances of nurturant behaviour following birth. The stimulus of pups normally triggers avoidance or attack in female rats. However, if the female is in the appropriate neurohormonal state, she shows attraction, approach and nurturance. Prior to birth and influenced by the neurohormonal condition, rat mothers build a nest. Following birth, pups that are displaced from the nest are returned by the mother. In this neurohormonal state, environmental cues that are associated with pups form conditional incentives and these then attract the mother. In a place preference test shortly after giving birth, rat mothers show a preference for a location that had been associated earlier with pups. This is even when tested against a location associated with cocaine injection (Mattson *et al.*, 2003). By 16 days after giving birth, preference switches to the cocaine-associated side. Such a change in response exemplifies a central motivational change (Lee *et al.*, 2000).

Neurobiology

A nursing mother rat's approach behaviour to her pups involves the mesolimbic dopamine system (Ferris *et al.*, 2005). If the system is disrupted, so is maternal behaviour. Human mothers show activation in this area when confronted by the challenge of an infant cry (Lorberbaum *et al.*, 2002). The amygdala exerts a role in the attraction of a nurturant female rat to a location associated with pups.

The mother's motivational change in reaction to pups involves a cocktail of neurohormonal changes, most prominent being changes in activity of estrogens, oxytocin, prolactin and opioids (Rosenblatt, 1992). For example, injections of oxytocin into the brain increases the tendency that she will exhibit nurturant behaviour.

Figure 15.13 shows some of the brain circuitry underlying maternal behaviour in the rat. Neuronal circuits that are based in the preoptic area of the hypothalamus (POA) and the ventral bed nucleus of the stria terminalis (VBN) constitute what Panksepp (1998a) terms a 'central integrator'. Information on pups and related cues ('sensory inputs') is conveyed to the central integrator, where sensory information is attributed motivational value. The neurons in these sites are a location of a high density of receptors to the neurochemicals involved in maternal behaviour. Changes in neural activity that occur comparing occupation of these receptors and loss of occupation form the basis of motivational changes. Lesions to these areas are particularly disruptive of maternal behaviour (Lee *et al.*, 2000). Outputs from the integrator are projected to various brain regions concerned with organizing maternal behaviour ('behavioural output').

Towards the end of pregnancy and in the first few days following giving birth, there is an increase in oxytocin activity in the brain, involving an increase in density of oxytocin receptors at the central integrator. The periacqueductal grey (PAG) is also a region rich in receptors for oxytocin. Oestrogen acts on neurons in the region corresponding to the central integrator. These effects

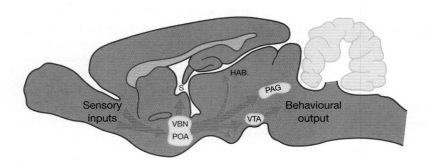

Figure 15.13 Neural processes underlying maternal behaviour in the rat. VTA = ventral tegmental area, a brain region closely connected with the attraction of incentives. PAG = periacqueductal grey, a region involved in emotional processing. S = septal area, a reward-related area. POA = preoptic area. VBN = ventral bed nucleus of the stria terminalis.

Source: Panksepp (1998a, Figure 13.4, p. 254).

increase the tendency to exhibit nurturant behaviour. After the young appear, the rewarding effects of social contact are closely associated with the activity of opioids and oxytocin (Nelson and Panksepp, 1996).

Social attachment and isolation

Introduction

Following the early experience of nurturance (e.g. suckling), dedicated systems of emotion and motivation within the brains of certain species of mammals and birds maintain social attachment with selected conspecifics (Panksepp, 1994). These are exemplified by those between a caretaker (usually a parent) and the growing young, between siblings or between monogamous sexual partners. The term 'social attachment' refers to the tendency of individuals of certain species to keep proximity to another and to show distress when it is lost. Lorenz (1981) studied this process in birds, i.e. the tendency for the newly hatched to follow the mother (Chapter 6, 'Development and plasticity'). To what extent the circuitry shown in Figure 15.13 can be generalized to cover attachment remains to be seen.

Motivational basis

It appears that a dedicated motivational process with its own form of reward underlies the formation and expression of social attachment (Bowlby, 1973; Panksepp, 1998a). Babies deprived of social contact fail to thrive normally, even though their needs for warmth and nutrition, etc. might well be accommodated.

Disruption of attachment

An index of a negative emotion, 'distress', is given by distress vocalization (DV): the crying that the young of all mammalian species (and some non-mammalian) exhibit on enforced separation from a caregiver (Herman and Panksepp, 1978). Consider an infant rat that gets isolated. Its vocalizations alert the mother to the pup's state and location and they facilitate retrieval and return to the nest.

The neurobiology of attachment and its breaking

The trajectory of the neural system underlying distress starts at the brain stem in structures common to all mammals and birds (Panksepp, 1994). It appears that this system overlaps with pain. In humans, the subjective feeling of social distress is commonly described in terms of pain (Eisenberger and Lieberman, 2004). In guinea pigs, electrical stimulation of the preoptic area, periacqueductal grey area and amygdala elicit DVs (Panksepp *et al.*, 1988).

A number of endogenous neurochemicals are implicated in the emotional processing underlying attachment and distress at its breaking. These include opioids, prolactin and endorphins. Panksepp *et al.* (1988) suggest that DVs are an index of the activity of an emotion circuit that involves opioids. Opioids and oxytocin inhibit the emotion associated with breaking social attachment (Panksepp *et al.*, 1988). Figure 15.14 shows the role of opiates in suppressing distress vocalization in 6–8-week-old puppies and Figure 15.15 shows the effect of oxytocin and prolactin in chicks.

For a range of social species, injections of opiates reduce social contact (less 'gregariousness'). Opioid antagonists increase gregariousness (Panksepp, 1998a). Injection of the opioid agonist morphine to either mother or infant rhesus monkeys causes a decrease in the amount of clinging between mother and infant. Conversely, the opioid antagonist naltrexone increases it (Kalin *et al.*, 1995). When a monkey is groomed by another there is an increase in levels of ß-endorphin (Keverne *et al.*, 1989).

Mutant mice that lack the gene coding for μ-opioid receptors do not exhibit attachment behaviour (Moles *et al.*, 2004). They are able to discriminate, for example, odours associated with the mother, so they are not deficient in sensory discrimination. Rather, they do not show a *preference* for such odour. The deficiency is therefore one related to motivation and reward. This suggests that opioids are employed in the neural systems that mediate social reward. Neither do such mice exhibit distress on removal from the mother. Again, this suggests that separation distress is based upon opioids.

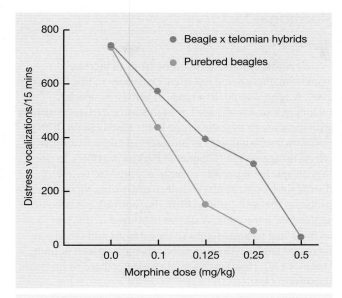

Figure 15.14 The effect of morphine (an opiate having opioid agonist properties) injections on the distress vocalizations produced by puppies following separation.

Source: adapted from Panksepp *et al.* (1978, Fig. 2, p. 612).

There is a role of oxytocin in the formation of the attachment that an infant rat shows to its mother. Nelson and Panksepp (1996) speculate that physical contact with the mother triggers oxytocin release, which forms part of the

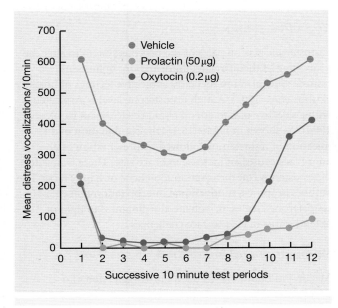

Figure 15.15 The effect of prolactin and oxytocin on distress vocalizations in 5–6-day-old chicks isolated from the flock.

Source: adapted from Panksepp (1996, Fig. 1, p.50).

basis of the social reward. Olfactory stimuli associated with the mother acquire conditional incentive value for pups in that they are preferentially approached. This preference formation is abolished by oxytocin antagonists.

We now turn to a rather different example of motivation, that underlying aggression.

Section summary

1 Mammals exhibit nurturant behaviour to offspring. Maternal behaviour represents the most obvious and widely represented example of this.

2 Attachments ('bonds') are formed between parents and offspring and between reproductive partners. Animals are motivated to maintain these bonds.

3 Young animals exhibit distress vocalizations when separated from caregivers.

4 Identifiable biochemicals such as opioids and oxytocin play a role in parental and attachment behaviour and the distress of separation.

Test your knowledge

(Answer on page 396)

15.8 How would you relate the terms 'opioid' and 'opiate'? In so doing, demonstrate the use of the term 'agonist'.

Aggression

Introduction

For certain species, we can classify aggression into types. In the case of predators, such as cats, one possible division is between that associated with rage (e.g. against an attacking animal) and that directed towards a prey, termed **predatory aggression** (A. Siegel, 2005). By this criterion, our prime concern is with rage-related aggression, and the term 'aggression' will mean this unless otherwise stated.

Aggression is a form of threatening and destructive behaviour, having a particular emotional and motivational basis. The trigger most usually arises from events in the external world and their interpretation, taking the form of challenges. Aggressive behaviour acts to eliminate the challenge and restore the *status quo*. Berkowitz (1993, p. 11) defines aggression in humans as: 'some kind of *behaviour*, either physical or symbolic, *that is carried out with the intention to harm someone*'. Such a definition is problematic when considering non-human species where behaviour itself has to be used as the index.

Aggression depends upon a combination of external and internal events: environmental, hormonal and learning factors (Panksepp, 1998a). In humans, the underlying emotion is often described as anger.

A distinction can be drawn between human aggression of a kind that is premeditated and that which is impulsive (Best *et al.*, 2002). In premeditated aggression, there is planning and reflection involving conscious intentions. By contrast, impulsive aggression appears to be triggered immediately by an environmental event, with little or no prior conscious reflection. However, it is probably wrong to see a neat dichotomy here. Presumably, a history of having minor expressions of premeditated aggression will increase the chances of impulsive aggression.

The various causes of aggression

Expectations that are violated are a primary trigger for aggression, e.g. withholding expected reward (Ulrich and Favell, 1970). However, certain trigger stimuli appear to cause aggression by their intrinsic properties. In rats, electric shock triggers attack of a nearby inanimate object (Pear *et al.*, 1972).

Learning

Learning influences aggression. For example, a history of winning fights increases the tendency to future aggression. In humans (Leyens and Fraczek, 1986) and rats (Ulrich and Favell, 1970), a cue paired with shock acquires a conditional capacity to stimulate aggression.

Is there a consequence of aggression that increases the tendency to repeat the behaviour in the longer term? Squirrel monkeys can be taught an operant task for the reward of an inanimate object that is attacked (Azrin *et al.*, 1965). Termination of shock after onset of aggression strengthened the tendency to aggression. A question to be pursued shortly is, if aggression is reinforcing, is it positively or negatively reinforcing?

The psychological state in which aggression is reinforcing appears to be one of aversion (cf. Ulrich and Favell, 1970). An environment associated with such aggression might even acquire some conditional incentive value for the animal. From PET studies in humans, there is evidence that revenge for a perceived injustice can take on certain appetitive and positive affective qualities (de Quervain *et al.*, 2004; Knutson, 2004). The desire for punishment and the opportunity to inflict it caused activation within the caudate nucleus.

Hormonal factors
Basics

Widely across species, testosterone tends to increase aggression, there being just a few exceptions to this (Dabbs, 2000; A. Siegel, 2005). In a range of vertebrate species, including humans, the level of aggression correlates positively with the amount of testosterone in the blood (Brain, 1979).

Testosterone has both organizational and activational effects on aggression (Chapter 6; Berkowitz, 1993). In non-human species, especially rodents, exposure to testosterone during development plays a role in organizing those neural processes that will come to form the motivational basis of aggression in the adult. A system organized in this way shows an increased responsiveness to testosterone and thereby an increased tendency to aggression when the animal is adult (Brain, 1979). How far this might be generalized to humans remains unclear.

In most species, males tend to be more aggressive than females. This is usually attributed to males' relatively high level of testosterone (Berkowitz, 1993).

In men, there is a positive relationship between (1) aggression and anti-social behaviour and (2) levels of testosterone (Bernhardt, 1997). Testosterone level correlates with the tendency to gain dominance, and aggression is one way of achieving this. Competitive sport is another (Campbell *et al.*, 1997). However, socioeconomic status is an important variable. The correlation between testosterone level and antisocial behaviour holds for males of low rather than high socioeconomic status (Bernhardt, 1997).

Cognitive changes

Testosterone acts on parts of the nervous system to alter the processing of threat-related information. In humans, testosterone injection increases subjective feelings of hostility (Dabbs *et al.*, 2002). A high testosterone level is associated with a selective bias to attend to angry faces (van Honk *et al.*, 1999). As shown in Figure 15.16, the combination of an injection of testosterone followed by presentation of an angry face causes an increase in heart-rate. There is no effect of testosterone on the reaction to neutral or happy faces. The authors propose a motivational interpretation that (p. 241) testosterone creates an 'enhanced willingness to fight or defend status in face-to-face challenges'.

Dominance and aggression

Mazur and Booth (1998) distinguish aggression and dominance. They regard *antisocial behaviour* (e.g. rebelliousness) in humans as an attempt by individuals in subordinate roles to assert dominance. This does not need to be by violence, though it can be. Mazur and Booth suggest that, in men, testosterone is associated with the tendency to exert dominance, through a variety of means.

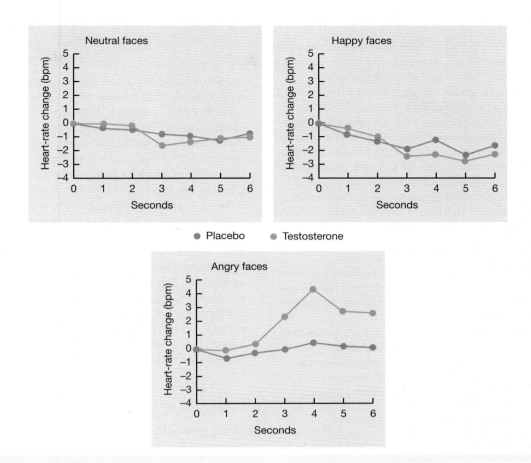

Figure 15.16 Heart-rate changes triggered by faces in testosterone or placebo-injected participants.

Source: van Honk *et al.* (2001, Figure 1, page 240).

Young American males forming part of an urban street 'honour culture' of maintaining status and respect, while showing hyper-responsivity to insults, tend to exhibit high testosterone levels. This suggests that the hormone biases towards holding status. Within the USA, southerners display more of an honour culture and a higher testosterone response to a challenge than do northerners (Cohen, 1998).

Dynamic interaction

The relationship between testosterone and behaviour is a 'two-way street' (Mazur and Booth, 1998). Testosterone increases aggression. Typically, winning fights or competitions can trigger an increased level of testosterone, whereas defeat is followed by a lowering (Campbell *et al.*, 1997; Rose *et al.*, 1975). Explicit aggression, as defined earlier, is not necessarily shown.

In humans, a dynamic process can lead to long-term behavioural 'stability', in which cause and effect become indistinguishable (Archer, 1994). Early experiences and modelling can bias a male towards a competitive and aggressive style. An initially high testosterone level would strengthen this. Winning fights, whether physical or verbal, and exposure to violent role models could elevate testosterone level, to reinforce and maintain the strategy. (Discussions tend to be dominated by consideration of the male but females also produce testosterone and can behave aggressively; Snowdon, 1998.)

There is some malleability in hormone–environment interaction. High-testosterone men can get into a vicious circle, characterized by a downward social spiral. However, with slightly changed circumstances, and more skilled exploitation of dominance, they might ascend socially. Cohen (1998, p. 368) suggests: 'testosterone may facilitate successful boardroom maneuvering as much as successful barroom brawling'.

Neural mechanisms

Aggression is determined by interactions between particular brain regions. Manipulations of some regions with drugs and lesioning have more effect than others.

Non-humans

Lesioning and stimulation of the brain have been employed to study the neural bases of fear and aggression in non-humans (Kling, 1986; Moyer, 1986). There are particular neural circuits, which elicit a tendency to aggression when stimulated in the presence of a suitable target (A. Siegel, 2005). Neurons involved in controlling aggression project from the amygdala to the *medial* hypothalamus and then to the PAG. Descending signals activate the motor acts of aggressive behaviour, which are organized in part at brain stem sites. In cats, by contrast to the role of the medial hypothalamus in controlling rage-related aggression, the *lateral* hypothalamus has a prime role in predatory aggression. This insight has emerged from fine-grained targeted studies involving lesions, electrical and chemical stimulation.

Neurons involved in the motivation underlying aggression are the targets of testosterone. Evidence points to the involvement of neurons of the medial hypothalamus and regions of the limbic system, such as the amygdala (Albert *et al.*, 1987; A. Siegel, 2005).

Animals of various species learn to terminate stimulation of regions of hypothalamus associated with affective aggression ('rage'), suggesting negative reinforcement (A. Siegel, 2005). This is quite unlike the result found for neighbouring regions associated with predatory attack.

Neural bases of human aggression

Humans with implanted electrodes in their brains (e.g. in the amygdala) sometimes report feeling anger when the current is turned on but are able to inhibit aggression (Moyer, 1986).

Aggression can sometimes be provoked by tumours of the brain (Moyer, 1986), e.g. in the anterior hypothalamus, amygdala or septum. In some cases, removal of the tumour corrects the aggression. Aggression is not expressed as simply a particular response, suggesting a motivational interpretation. For example, a motorist might drive his car aggressively as well as commit acts of direct violence.

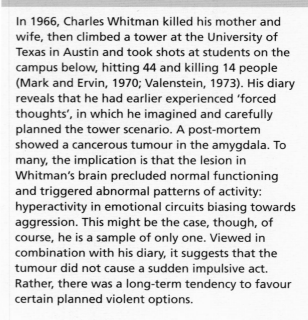

A personal angle

Ms X.

King (1961), in Pittsburgh, PA, studied a patient with an electrode tip implanted in her amygdala. When a current of 4 mA stimulated the brain, no effect was observed. On increasing this to 5 mA, she verbalized signs of anger and her fear of attacking the experimenter. She did not report pain. The fact that Ms X. reported anger and made aggressive remarks suggests that the electrode targeted an emotional/motivational neural system, rather than a motor system.

A personal angle

Charles Whitman

In 1966, Charles Whitman killed his mother and wife, then climbed a tower at the University of Texas in Austin and took shots at students on the campus below, hitting 44 and killing 14 people (Mark and Ervin, 1970; Valenstein, 1973). His diary reveals that he had earlier experienced 'forced thoughts', in which he imagined and carefully planned the tower scenario. A post-mortem showed a cancerous tumour in the amygdala. To many, the implication is that the lesion in Whitman's brain precluded normal functioning and triggered abnormal patterns of activity: hyperactivity in emotional circuits biasing towards aggression. This might be the case, though, of course, he is a sample of only one. Viewed in combination with his diary, it suggests that the tumour did not cause a sudden impulsive act. Rather, there was a long-term tendency to favour certain planned violent options.

Mechanisms of restraint

There are personal costs and social sanctions associated with aggression, so it is likely that society is spared much violence because of restraint (inhibition) processes. There could be an inhibition of aggressive motivation *per se* or of its expression (Spoont, 1992).

Raine *et al.* (1997) performed a positron emission tomography (PET) study (Chapter 5) on a sample of murderers who had pleaded 'not guilty by reason of insanity'. Lower glucose metabolism in several brain regions was found in murderers, compared with controls. We can speculate that these regions would normally be involved in restraining aggression. The regions included those that underlie control based upon working memory (e.g. prefrontal cortex) and the coming together of different sources of information (e.g. the corpus callosum). It would be expected that working memory would normally play a role in exerting restraint based upon anticipated (e.g. punishing) outcomes.

Following damage to the orbital/medial prefrontal cortex, there is an increased tendency to impulsive violence (Best *et al.*, 2002). From this, Best *et al.*, were led to study patients suffering from 'intermittent explosive disorder', who exhibit a chronic tendency to violence that is out of proportion to the triggers. In the sample studied, there was no evidence of prior brain damage but nonetheless patients performed relatively badly on tests designed specifically to reveal prefrontal processing (Chapter 20, 'Cognition and action').

Best *et al.* speculate that there is a deficiency in inhibitory projections that run from the prefrontal cortex to the amygdala. In addition, patients revealed a cognitive bias towards interpreting anger and disgust in human faces, as compared to controls.

Neurotransmitters

Acetylcholine

Acetylcholine tends to facilitate aggression (A. Siegel, 2005). Regions of hypothalamus can be identified, which, when electrically stimulated, trigger aggression. Microinjections of cholinergic agonists there also tend to trigger aggression. Application of cholinergic antagonists tends to inhibit aggression.

Catecholamines

Some evidence points to increased activity in noradrenergic and dopaminergic pathways being implicated in aggression (Haller *et al.*, 1998; A. Siegel, 2005). For humans, dopaminergic and NA activity in the brain tend to correlate positively with impulsive aggression (Coccaro, 1989; Eichelman, 1988). Drugs used in the control of impulsive aggression in humans include those having DA or NA antagonist effects, sometimes combined with a serotonin agonist effect (Coccaro, 1989).

There are reports that stimulating CNS noradrenalin (NA) release in rats leads to heightened aggression and chemically lesioning of NA reduces aggression. However, the picture is less clear than for acetylcholine. This could be because different NA receptor subtypes have different effects on aggression (A. Siegel, 2005). It is also unclear as to the extent that any effects of catecholamines are specific to aggression or are general effects common across motivations and behaviours.

Serotonin

As a rather reliable effect found across species, a negative correlation exists between (a) brain serotonin (5-HT) level and (b) the tendency to aggression (Pihl and LeMarquand, 1998; A. Siegel, 2005).

For humans, abnormally low levels of serotonin are associated with impulsive ('irritable') aggression, rather than premeditated violence (Coccaro, 1989). Aggression appears to be only one form of impulsive behaviour among others that are influenced by low levels of serotonin (Coscina, 1997). This suggests under-reactivity of a serotonin-mediated **behavioural inhibition system** (Depue and Spoont, 1986). Activity within this system acts to restrain aggression, among other impulsive behaviours. Serotonin serves a role in the inhibition of behaviour by cues that

herald threat and so its reduction would remove a source of inhibition on aggression (Pihl and LeMarquand, 1998).

Bernhardt suggests that a low serotonin level can accentuate negative affect, which biases to aggression (Berkowitz, 1993).

At what locations in the nervous system does serotonin exert its effects? There are ascending serotonergic pathways that terminate in regions known to be involved in aggression, such as the amygdala (Spoont, 1992). Presumably, normal levels of serotonergic transmission at such regions restrain aggression.

Alcohol and aggression

The consumption of alcohol in large amounts by humans is associated with aggression (Pihl and LeMarquand, 1998). There are various sites of action of alcohol in the CNS at which it increases the risk of aggression. Alcohol (a) increases dopaminergic activity, which promotes forward engagement with a range of incentives, (b) encourages the breaking of boundaries, e.g. interpersonal, (c) directly sensitizes aggression and (d) lowers restraint.

If anxiety inhibits aggression, the lifting of this by alcohol will weaken a natural brake. Alcohol disrupts cognitive functioning, with a particular targeting of working memory (Chapter 11). Working memory allows the representation of anticipated future scenarios and their utilization in the control of current behaviour. Impairment of working memory might bias the weight of control, to favour physically present stimuli and weaken cognitive representations of future negative consequences of aggression.

Genes and environment

Suppose two individuals in a species differ in the tendency to aggression. Is this because of genetic or environmental differences, or both (Fuller, 1986)? We argued that the triggers to aggression are in the environment. However, in humans and other species, there is evidence that genetically determined differences exist between individuals in their tendency to aggression (Berkowitz, 1993; Bowman, 1997). Such genetic differences would mediate their effects via differences in such things as brain structures and levels of hormones and neurotransmitters.

As Fuller (1986, p. 206) notes: 'The most extensive selection for differences in animal emotionality was carried out by individuals who had never taken a course in genetics nor heard of Darwin . . .'. For hundreds of years, humans have developed animals' behavioural traits (e.g. aggression in dogs) by selective breeding.

The next section, exploration, completes the discussion of the four examples of motivations.

Test your knowledge

(Answers on page 396

15.9 Complete the following sentence: 'Testosterone has both _____ and activational effects on aggression'.

15.10 This question relates to Figure 15.16. The combination of angry face and testosterone triggers increased activity in which branch of the autonomic nervous system?

15.11 A region of the hypothalamus that is associated with aggression has been identified and an electrode implanted there. Suppose that a rat learns to press a lever in a Skinner box to terminate electrical stimulation of this region. What term would be used to qualify the description 'reinforcing'?

Exploration

Introduction

Exploration of their environment is widely seen in different species (Welker, 1961). By this means, animals acquire information, e.g. that object X is situated at location Y (Menzel, 1978). Similarly, play enables the animal to learn and test possibilities for future action.

In a natural environment, could curiosity serve a useful function? *Source*: Getty Images/Photographer's Choice.

The acquisition of information that involves investigation by whole-body approach to objects is termed **exploratory behaviour**.

From a functional perspective, exploration allows an updated representation of the environment that can be exploited for such things as locating food and escape routes. Regular exploration of even a familiar environment presumably confirms the *status quo* ('checking').

Species differences

Which sense organs are employed for exploration depends on the relative refinement of the species' sensory channels (Welker, 1961). The sensory channel favoured tends to correspond to an enlarged cortical representation of sensory processing in that channel (Chapter 5). In rats, exploration involves whiskering and sniffing (O'Keefe and Nadel, 1978). In the grey squirrel, visual features are the strongest trigger, whereas in the mole the tactile sense provides the principal input. The notion of 'advanced species' is somewhat suspect in these egalitarian times. However, it is difficult to find an acceptable alternative. Exploration tends to be higher in 'advanced species', with more cerebral cortex (Glickman and Sroges, 1966; Figure 15.17).

Rats and monkeys raised in an enriched environment show a greater attraction to novelty and more manipulation of objects than those raised in a dull environment (Renner and Rosenzweig, 1986). This might have something to do with differences in dopamine levels.

The bases of exploration

Motivational basis

Exploration is especially triggered when the actual environment differs from stored representations in memory ('expectations') of this same environment (Bardo *et al.*, 1996). Although moderate disparities elicit approach and exploration, large disparities can trigger fear and avoidance. The reward of a novel object can reinforce lever-pressing in a Skinner box. In a place preference test, rats develop a preference for the arm of a T-maze that is associated with the opportunity to explore a novel object contained therein (Bevins and Bardo, 1999). Hence, novelty has incentive and reward properties similar to such rewards as food and sex.

In anxiety, exploration is reduced and rats favour contact with familiar regions of an environment. Hence, exploration is a measure of the efficacy of drugs designed to counteract anxiety (Chapter 12). For example, in an elevated maze, anxiolytics (anti-anxiety drugs) increase exploratory tendencies (Ramos and Mormède, 1998).

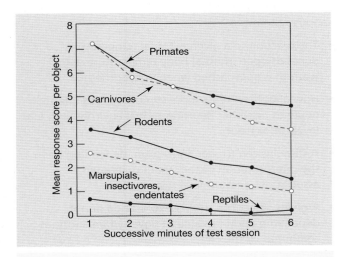

Figure 15.17 Comparison of different animals in terms of exploration.

Source: Glickman and Sroges (1966, Fig. 1, p. 161).

Cognitive mapping

O'Keefe and Nadel (1978) proposed that exploration helps to form a 'cognitive map' in the animal's brain – a representation of the environment (Chapter 11). Changes in the environment then revise this map. Exploration is not triggered by particular stimuli *per se* but by a comparison between stimuli and this internal representation. Novelty is not something 'out there' to be detected but the outcome of this comparison. A new object introduced into a familiar space prompts attention and exploration until it is represented in a revised cognitive map. Objects removed are erased from the representation. Exploration of an initially novel object is intense at first but then declines with exposure, presumably corresponding to the object becoming represented in the cognitive map.

Given a choice between arms leading to a goal, rats show **spontaneous alternation**: they tend to choose a different arm from that chosen last time (Montgomery, 1952). They tend to alternate the choice of arm (e.g. black versus white, irrespective of side) rather than the mechanical act involved in negotiating the maze. This implies (1) a memory of the choice and (2) selection based upon relative novelty. Alternation seems to be a variety of exploration.

The neuroscience of exploration

The neural embodiment of the motivation underlying exploration doubtless consists of numerous interacting brain regions. This section focuses on the two regions about which we have most insight. Information on novelty is extracted in such brain regions as the hippocampus, and links are then made with the mesolimbic dopamine pathway, where approach to particular objects is organized.

The mesolimbic dopaminergic pathway

The mesolimbic dopamine system and the notion of a seeking system form a focus of research in exploration and novelty-seeking (Bardo *et al.*, 1996; Besheer *et al.*, 1999). Activation of this system is associated with exploration: it appears that, under its influence, external objects become attractive as the incentives for exploration. When moving from a familiar compartment to a novel compartment there is activation of dopamine observed at the nucleus accumbens (N.acc.). The activity of single neurons of the N.acc. correlates with exploratory behaviour (Henriksen and Giacchino, 1993). Differences in exploration between strains of rat can be linked to intrinsic differences in the reactivity of this dopaminergic system (Depue and Collins, 1999).

In rats, microinjections of a DA antagonist into the N.acc. block increased activation in a novel environment, though there is no reduction in the normal activity in a familiar environment (Hooks and Kalivas, 1995). A dopamine D1 receptor antagonist blocks the attribution of incentive value to an arm associated with a novel object (Besheer *et al.*, 1999).

Role of the hippocampus

O'Keefe and Nadel (1978) attribute a role to the hippocampus in forming a cognitive map. Spontaneous alternation is a useful measure of exploration and gives an understanding of the role of this structure. Hippocampally lesioned rats tend not to show spontaneous alternation. Spontaneous alternation is only shown after 28 days of age in rats, whereas in the more precocial guinea pig it is seen in the first week of life (Altman *et al.*, 1973). This suggests that, in the infant rat, either there is an inability to hold the relevant information or, if the information is held, it is not utilized in exploration. In the rat, the hippocampus is relatively immature at birth and develops in the postnatal period, which might account for the delayed appearance of spontaneous alternation.

It appears that the hippocampus modulates other brain regions that organize exploration. It is assumed that it exerts an influence on the nucleus accumbens such that novel objects trigger approach associated with exploration (Mogenson, 1984). Hippocampal damage does not abolish exploration (Clark, *et al.*, 2005). However, the normal reduction ('habituation') of exploration as objects lose their novelty is less evident. This suggests that the loss of the hippocampus is associated with a failure of the objects to become familiar.

Sensation seeking and personality differences

A certain level of novelty seeking, especially in younger adults, could be adaptive in encouraging the seeking of new environments with the possibility of encountering new sources of food and mates (Douglas *et al.*, 2003). The observation that dopamine is involved in exploration led to the suggestion that human sensation-seeking might be understood in terms of dopamine activity (Bardo *et al.*, 1996).

Could differences in sensation-seeking between individuals be explicable by differences in the reactivity of their dopaminergic neurotransmission? There exists a known genetic contribution to differences in the dimension extravert–introvert. There is some suggestion that this is mediated in part through differences in dopaminergic neural systems, though the data are controversial (Rammsayer, 2004).

Section summary

1 Exploratory behaviour establishes and updates representations of the environment.

2 Novelty triggers exploration.

Test your knowledge

(Answer on page 396)

15.12 A rat is observed to show a high frequency of alternation of arms in a T-maze, between the left white arm and the right black arm. After having turned left on a trial, the rat is returned to the maze. However, between trials, the colour of the arms is quickly reversed so that black is now to the left and white to the right. What effect would this be expected to have on the tendency to take the right arm?

15.4

Bringing things together

The central theme of this chapter has been the search for underlying general principles of motivation as well as features specific to each motivation. Processes and principles that are applicable across motivations include incentive, reward, affect and conditioning, as well as the interactive role of external and internal factors. Particular brain regions are involved in attributing motivational value to appropriate stimuli, e.g. food, water and social stimuli. Stimuli are compared with memories and motivation depends upon the outcome of the comparison. A role of dopamine and opioids in various motivations was noted.

Motivational processes were described as those involving a changing responsiveness to external stimuli as a function of internal events. This was exemplified in various systems:

- The reaction to a given external temperature depends upon internal body temperature, e.g. warmth is approached when in hypothermia.

- How a mother treats social stimuli, such as infants, depends upon her neurohormonal environment, e.g. levels of oxytocin.

- A stimulus can trigger aggression, depending upon the interpretation of the stimulus, learned associations and levels of testosterone.

- A given object can trigger exploration or not depending upon its value of novelty/familiarity, as computed by the CNS.

Figure 15.18(a) represents general features of motivation and appetitive behaviour, determined by external and internal factors. The incentive contributes to motivation and, in turn, motivation directs behaviour to maximize contact with the incentive (Bindra, 1978). Conditional stimuli (CSs) also play a role. For example, stimuli paired with presentation of food acquire a conditional strength to trigger feeding motivation. Sexual motivation is increased by stimuli that were paired in the past with sexual activity. Figure 15.18(a) shows incentives compared with memories of past contact and motivation influenced by the outcome. For example, in taste-aversion learning the animal tends to avoid the particular food in future (Chapter 11; Garcia, 1989). Factors such as fear can inhibit a motivation such as feeding, as represented by the arrow 'Inhibit'.

In some cases, motivation can be understood in terms of homeostasis. Temperature regulation is an obvious example. Both behaviour and intrinsic physiology defend the body against disturbances. Aggression might also be understood in terms of the defence against threats to the integrity of the body or to resources that the animal is holding. Figure 15.18(b) shows motivation to be involved in both flexible and more species-typical behaviour.

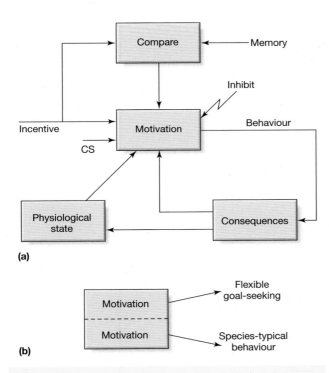

(a)

(b)

Figure 15.18 (a) Some general features of a motivational system and (b) dual role of motivation.

Summary of Chapter 15

1 The term 'motivation' refers to a type of process that underlies the control of behaviour. Motivation gives direction, goals and varying responsiveness to behaviour. The control of behaviour involves selection among motivations that compete for expression.

2 Certain stimuli such as food, water and sexual contact are described as 'rewards' and, in humans, contact with them is associated with pleasure. The expression 'incentive' defines the capacity of rewards to attract us.

3 There are brain regions that are specific to particular motivations and also some general processes that serve a range of different motivations.

4 Body temperature is regulated by the control exerted over both behaviour and internal physiology. Deviations from an optimal body temperature motivate behaviour that tends to return temperature to its optimal value.

5 In mammals, basic and dedicated processes of motivation and reward underlie nurturant (e.g. maternal) behaviour and attachment (bonding).

6 Aggression is behaviour that inflicts damage on another and is usually a response to challenges. Testosterone increases the tendency to show aggression.

7 Exploration is a type of behaviour that maintains variety in the flow of sensory input and assimilates information on the environment.

Further reading

For general introductions, which set the biology of motivation and emotion into a broader context of psychology, see Beck (2004) and Reeve (2004). For links with the remainder of ethology, see McFarland (1999). For an extensive review of the neuroscience of motivation, see Berridge (2004). For behavioural temperature regulation, see Hart (1988). For parental behaviour, see Numan and Insel (2003) and Kinsley and Lambert (2006). For aggression, see A. Siegel (2005). For the role of testosterone, see Dabbs (2000).

Signposts

The next three chapters will look in more detail at some examples of particular motivational systems that have been introduced in this section. General principles of motivation will be to the fore.

Answers

Explanations for answers to 'test your knowledge' questions can be found on the website **www.pearsoned.co.uk/toates**

15.1   Feeding, drinking, temperature regulation
15.2   Appetitive; consummatory
15.3   Conditional

15.4   Taste-aversion conditioning
15.5   The white arm
15.6   A tendency to seek a cold environment
15.7   It reduces the activity of $neuron_3$
15.8   An opioid is a natural neurochemical. An opiate is something taken from outside that has similar properties to its endogenous equivalent. Opiates such as morphine are agonists at opioid receptors in the body
15.9   Organizational
15.10   Sympathetic
15.11   Negatively
15.12   It would lower it

CHAPTER 16

Feeding and drinking

Learning outcomes for Chapter 16

After studying this chapter, you should be able to:

1 Demonstrate where the principles of homeostasis, regulation and negative feedback can be applied to understanding feeding and drinking. However, show also how behaviour can sometimes depart from the simple predictions arising from such processes.

2 Describe what happens to nutrients after they enter the body, in terms of their conversion, storage and utilization.

3 Identify some of the nutrient forms and sites in the body that are involved in the control of feeding. Describe the kind of process that links nutrients to signals that are exploited in the control of feeding.

4 Describe the contribution of sensory and learning factors to the control of feeding. In so doing, explain how their contribution can only be fully understood in the context of internal events and the consequences of ingestion.

5 Describe what is meant by the term 'satiety' and what we believe are the factors that contribute to it.

6 Identify some of the principal brain regions involved in the control of feeding and present the evidence that leads us to implicate them.

7 Describe some instances of when the control of feeding 'goes wrong'. Discuss the extent to which our understanding of basic principles of feeding control can illuminate how things go wrong and the role of therapeutic interventions.

8 Describe the physiology of body fluids and sodium and link these to the controls of water and sodium intake.

Scene-setting questions

1 What makes us hungry and what terminates this sensation?

2 If feeding evolved to serve regulation, how can it be associated with such problems as anorexia nervosa and obesity? Why do we often eat in the absence of any 'need'?

3 Could pregnancy sickness serve an adaptive function connected with food intake?

4 Why does salt make us thirsty?

Several factors play a role in wanting and liking foods. What are they and how do they interact?

Source: Topfoto/Rachel Epstein/Image Works.

Introduction

Cast your mind back over your own experience of feeding and drinking and reflect on what determines this behaviour. The following is a possible range of observations:

- Perhaps you have experienced the problem of putting on excess weight – if not, doubtless a friend has. Because of attractive foods rich in sugar and fat that are on offer, delicatessens and supermarkets are places to be wary of at such times.

- Some likes and dislikes might have arisen from the *associations* that you have formed with particular foods. If you ate something only under pressure, you might not now be able to face it. If a food was associated with illness, you might not have been able to eat it again.

- You might have craved particular foods at particular times in your life.

- It is probably the case that you have declined more food on the grounds of feeling full, only to recover your appetite with the next course.

- If you ate a particular food for lunch, you might want to eat something different for your evening meal, even though you like very much the lunchtime food.

- Perhaps you have skipped a meal and yet not felt particularly hungry as a result. You might even have been surprised to be reminded that you were so occupied that you missed a regular meal.

- Particular foods have links to particular times of eating. You might love a curry for lunch but not be attracted to it for breakfast.

- At times of stress, you might find yourself seeking foods such as chocolate as a form of comfort.

Such examples illustrate a number of features of the control of feeding:

1 Although feeding motivation is sensitive to the level of nutrients in the body, there is not a tight one-to-one dependence. Excess body fat is sometimes associated with only a limited capacity to inhibit further intake. In stimulating feeding, there is a powerful role played by attractive foods, in spite of taking in excessive amounts. Conversely, missing a meal is not necessarily associated with a greatly increased hunger.

2 A history of recent food intake influences current intake. For example, variety plays a role in food intake. Appetite can be revived by a new food.

3 A range of cultural factors play a role in determining what attracts us and when. For some of us, curry does not go with breakfast.

4 Cravings are directed to particular foods pointing to a high degree of specificity.

5 Associations that we have with a particular food can play an important role in how attractive it is.

6 Foods are eaten for various reasons, such as to relieve distress. Such intake is not tied to a general deficit of nutrients.

In this chapter, we consider how the *combination* of internal factors (e.g. nutrient levels) and external factors (e.g. the incentive of food and associated conditional stimuli) determine feeding and drinking. Each meal or drink will inevitably arise from such a combination. We will discuss first the internal and then the external factor, considering how they interact in determining behaviour.

From a functional perspective, survival requires that tissues throughout the body are supplied with nutrients and water. With respect to Figure 16.1 and 'Physiological regulation', deficits tend to trigger 'Behavioural control', i.e. feeding or drinking. Reciprocally, ingested substances affect 'Physiological regulation'.

In the 'basic design', feeding maintains nutrient status at an optimal level and 'regulation' describes this. There is *some* regulation associated with feeding. For example, food deprivation is a trigger to hunger and food intake is said to induce **satiety**. The term satiety describes the loss, or reduction, of appetite as a result of ingestion. After a period of deprivation and weight loss, body weight recovers when feeding is restored. Conversely, force-feeding an animal causes weight gain but normal weight is regained when feeding returns to normal. However, it is clear that any such homeostatic aspect is only one feature of the control of food intake, as evidenced by the current epidemic of obesity.

Sometimes feeding is not in response to a current energy deficit, for example, eating at a particular optimum time of day when food is most readily available. However, much of this can still be understood in terms of regulation and optimizing survival chances (Strubbe and Woods, 2004). Under abnormal conditions (such as living in London or Chicago!), not all feeding and drinking contribute to optimal regulation.

Among a number of controls of drinking, one is unambiguous: body-fluids are regulated. Survival depends upon their near constancy and loss triggers drinking. Regulation is generally much tighter than is the case for body nutrients. However, an animal sometimes drinks even though there is not a deficit of body-fluids (A.N. Epstein, 1990). For example, if small pellets of food are presented intermittently to a hungry rat, it drinks enormous amounts, so-called 'schedule-induced polydipsia' (Falk, 1971). Such drinking occurs *in spite of*, rather than because of, the state of body-fluids, which is one of over-hydration. The frustration of getting only small pellets might be the trigger to drinking.

Although there are exceptions pointing to where physiological regulation is not an all-encompassing explanation of feeding and drinking, much insight has come from considering the regulatory aspect. Regulation of nutrient and fluid environments is achieved by coordination between (1) behavioural control of ingestive behaviour and (2) physiological control over events in the interior of the body (Figure 16.1). Only by looking at 1 and 2 simultaneously, can we fully understand what is happening. Regulation of nutrient levels involves (1) feeding and (2) changes in such internal factors as insulin secretion (Chapter 3, 'The nervous and endocrine systems'). Regulation of body-fluids involves control over (1) drinking and (2) blood vessel diameter and urine production by means of secretion of arginine vasopressin (Chapter 3). Again, this points to similarities with regulation of body temperature, where there are also internal (e.g. shivering, sweating) and external (e.g. moving location) controls.

Closely related to notions of incentive (Chapter 15, 'Motivation'), we speak of an **appetite** directed towards a substance (Bolles, 1980). A food is coded by the CNS in terms of its basic sensory properties and its **palatability**: the tendency to ingest that the substance triggers as a result of its 'liking properties'. Palatability depends upon taste, nutrient levels in the body and any earlier associations with the substance, e.g. taste-aversion learning can change palatability from positive to negative. Palatability mediates between substances and their intake: energy and nutrient states gain expression in behaviour by their influence on palatability. However, highly palatable foods can be taken even in spite of no 'need'.

The next section considers the physiology of nutrients, energy and water.

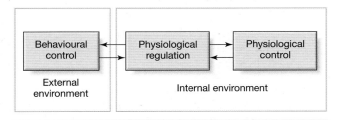

Figure 16.1 Regulation and control. Physiological regulation occurs as a result of behavioural control (feeding, drinking) and physiological control (e.g. over rate of production of urine, insulin secretion).

Test your knowledge

(Answers on page 422)

16.1 Does the drinking that occurs on restoration of water following dehydration reveal negative feedback?

16.2 The role of arginine vasopressin described here is as (a) a hormone or (b) a neurotransmitter?

Some physiology

This section gives some background to understand the regulatory bases of feeding and drinking. Further details of body-fluids will be given later when the chapter focuses on drinking.

Cells, fuel and metabolism

As was noted (Chapter 1, 'Introduction'), various cells (e.g. neurons, skin cells), which serve different roles, have features in common. Each cell is surrounded by a membrane, which shows various degrees of resistance in allowing substances to cross. The inside of the cell consists largely of fluid and the membrane is bathed on the outside by fluids. Cells require energy, vitamins and amino acids for the synthesis of proteins. Ions are needed for the cell's electrical properties. These are all obtained by ingestion. They move through the stomach and intestine and are transported to the cells via the body-fluids.

Digestion

Food and water enter the mouth, pass down the oesophagus and then appear in the stomach. After the stomach, substances appear in the first stage of the intestine, the duodenum. In the stomach and intestine, food is broken down and chemically changed. This is termed **digestion** and it involves the 'digestive system'. The anatomical pathway from mouth to anus is the 'alimentary tract'.

The cells

Cells need, among other things, fuel that yields energy by metabolism (Chapter 5, 'The brain'). Figure 16.2 represents a cell. Fuel and water are transported from the fluid that bathes it, extracellular fluid, to the cell's interior. Fuel is used as a source of energy to perform the functions of the cell, e.g. synthesis of proteins and transport of ions across the membrane (Chapter 4, 'The cells of the nervous system'). Heat, water and carbon dioxide are produced (as products of metabolism of fuel) and released from the cell. The rate at which fuel is used by the body is termed the **metabolic rate**, which corresponds to the rate of heat production.

The conversion of ingested chemicals is complex and only a simplified explanation is given here. Consider a species such as rat or human, taking meals of carbohydrate. During digestion, foods in the form of carbohydrates are converted to glucose. Glucose is a fuel that cells use. The problem faced by a feeding system might appear to consist simply of obtaining sufficient carbohydrate to guarantee a continuous supply of glucose to each cell. Alas, life is not so simple. Although carbohydrates can meet energy needs, other dietary constituents, i.e. ions, vitamins and amino acids, are also needed. For an animal such as a rat or human, the diet needs to consist of carbohydrates, proteins and fats.

Also there are problems of supply and storage. Animals are not equally active throughout the 24 hours. Rats are active at night and humans tend to be active during the day. As Figure 16.3 shows, during the night the rat eats in excess of metabolic rate (i.e. in excess of immediate need for fuel). During the day, when the rat does most sleeping, it eats less than metabolic rate. For metabolic needs in the inactive phase, it relies upon energy stored in the body earlier. Such

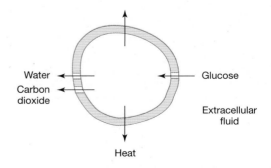

Figure 16.2 A cell.

Source: Toates (1980).

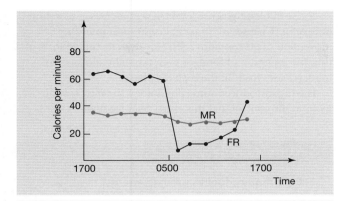

Figure 16.3 Metabolic rate (MR) and feeding rate (FR) in calories per minute (1 calorie = 4.2 joules) for a group of rats. Lights out 17.00–05.00; lights on 05.00–17.00.

Source: Le Magnen *et al*. (1973, Fig. 1).

storage is in a different chemical form from glucose, e.g. as fat, which is a more economical form than carbohydrate.

Absorption and the conversion of fuels

Species such as rats and humans take distinct meals with intervals between. A short time after eating, absorption of food from the alimentary tract starts: the **absorptive state** (Vander *et al*., 1975). Nutrients are absorbed into capillaries that line the wall of the intestine and they then travel in the hepatic portal vein to the liver (Figure 16.4). At the liver, they

can be dispatched immediately for use by tissues or can be chemically converted and stored. Whether stores are built up or depleted depends upon hormones (e.g. insulin) that are sensitive to energy availability.

Although not forgetting the complications, we can still focus on carbohydrates. Figure 16.5 shows the fate of glucose during the absorptive state, in the case where glucose is arriving at a rate higher than it is needed for current use as a fuel by cells. Some incoming glucose is used immediately in metabolism by cells. The remainder is chemically converted and put into storage. Storage consists of some glucose being converted to fat at the liver and then transported to deposits throughout the body, known as 'adipose tissue'. Some glucose is converted to fat at the adipose tissue. A final fraction of incoming glucose is converted to glycogen and held at the liver and muscles. Insulin is released in the absorptive state and thereby facilitates the uptake of glucose by cells.

Figure 16.6 considers where absorption of a meal is complete: the **post-absorptive state**. The fuel required by cells is now derived from intrinsic sources, i.e. the stores that were built up during earlier absorptive states.

To understand metabolic events in the post-absorptive state, physiologists distinguish between neurons and other cells. Neurons can use mainly only one substrate of energy: glucose. Non-neural cells, by contrast, can use glucose and other substrates, e.g. those termed 'fatty acids'. In the post-absorptive state, glucose is obtained by chemical conversion of stores at adipose tissue as well as at lean tissue (i.e. muscle).

In the post-absorptive state, there is potentially a problem of availability of sufficient glucose for the nervous system. Suppose that the vast number of non-neural cells throughout the body were able to grab available glucose and thereby starve the nervous system of its one viable fuel. The brain would be in very serious trouble. What stops this from happening? Under these conditions, non-neural cells have a

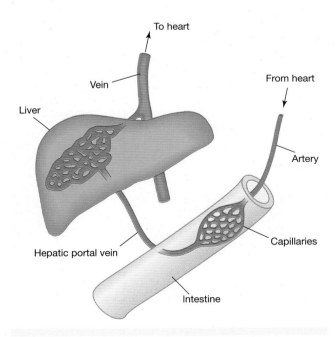

Figure 16.4 Nutrient absorption from the gut.

Source: adapted from Carlson (1977).

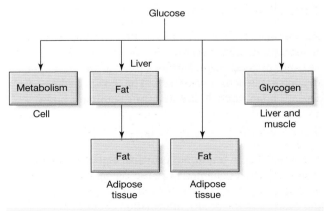

Figure 16.5 The absorptive state in the case of glucose.

Source: adapted from Vander *et al.* (1975) *Human Physiology*, Fig. 18.1, p. 603, reproduced with permission of The McGraw-Hill Companies, Inc.

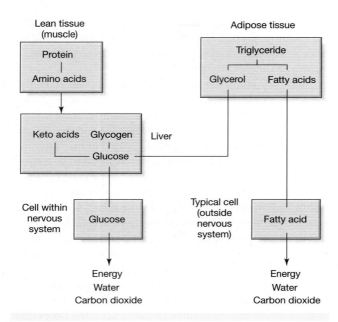

Figure 16.6 The post-absorptive state.

Source: adapted from Vander, *et al*. (1975) *Human Physiology*, Fig. 19.1, p. 649, reproduced with permission of The McGraw-Hill Companies, Inc.

bias towards utilizing fatty acids and away from utilizing glucose. That is to say, there is a suppression of insulin secretion, which prevents non-neural cells from acquiring glucose. Available glucose is exploited by the nervous system. In this state, glucose is derived from other substrates (e.g. fat laid down in adipose tissue at times of abundance) (Figure 16.6). The suppression of insulin gives a bias to the breakdown of stores. This yields not only glucose but also fatty acids that are used as the energy substrate by non-neural cells.

Figures 16.5 and 16.6 provide an important lesson for the study of feeding. A term such as 'body energy store' is a convenient summary. However, there is not a single homogeneous regulated variable to which behavioural control could, even in principle, be attached. Energy is stored in various chemical substrates throughout the body and exchange between them depends upon hormones and food arriving in the body. Indeed, as will be shown, feeding depends upon multiple signals arising within the body.

Internal and external information

Anticipation is an important principle in digestion and insulin secretion (Chapter 3). In the 'cephalic phase' of digestion (that triggered via the sensory organs such as sight and sound and the brain), information about available food in the environment can influence the secretion of juices in the stomach. The advantage of such anticipation (by means of classical conditioning) is that the stomach can quickly start digestion.

A rise in blood glucose level triggers increased secretion of insulin (Chapter 3). In turn, insulin promotes the movement of glucose into cells. However, in anticipation of this, the ingestion of food, or even the sight and smell of food, releases insulin: the cephalic phase.

Having introduced some physiology, the next section looks at the control that this exerts over feeding.

Section summary

1 Cells require fuel to provide energy.

2 Fuel can be derived from carbohydrates.

3 In the absorptive state, nutrients are absorbed from the gut.

4 In the post-absorptive state, no nutrients are absorbed and fuel is derived from intrinsic sources.

5 Insulin controls glucose availability to cells.

6 Non-neural cells require insulin for glucose uptake whereas neurons do not.

7 Some control actions anticipate the physiological changes to which they relate.

Test your knowledge

(Answers on page 422)

16.3 The events labelled in Figure 16.5 would be most likely to be seen in which time period of Figure 16.3? (i) 17.00–18.00, (ii) 06.00–07.00.

16.4 In Figure 16.3, at what time is metabolic need exactly matched to nutrient gain by feeding? (i) 17.00, (ii) 05.00, (ii) 06.00.

 The internal cue for feeding

Introduction

Feeding clearly involves negative feedback and this principle is the first focus for the present section, complications being discussed later. What is detected in the body, where does detection occur and how does it contribute to feeding? Investigators look for the sites of the neural transducers that link nutrient level to a neural signal underlying feeding. This section considers some possibilities.

Investigators believe that a signal derives from the level of a nutrient or something to do with its metabolism by specific cells. There now appear to be multiple systems, each sensitive to different nutrients (Berthoud, 2002). What follows is a simplified picture concentrating on the role of glucose and fats.

A glucose-based signal

Introduction

Evidence points to the brain and liver as being the sites of cells that detect glucose level or are sensitive to its metabolism (Booth, 1993a). In rats fed *ad libitum* (meaning food is freely available all the time), a small decline in blood glucose level tends to occur just prior to meals (Le Magnen, 1981). Similarly, a fall in blood glucose tends to come just before requests for meals in laboratory-based humans (Campfield, 1997). This suggests that feeding is sensitive to blood glucose level, though in itself does not prove a causal connection. A type of neuron might be sensitive to the concentration of glucose in the fluid that bathes it. In Figure 16.7, such a neuron would respond to changes in concentration with changes in frequency of action potentials.

The nature of the signal

An early idea was that, when blood glucose level fell, this was the cue to feed: the 'glucostatic theory'. In this context, **glucoreceptors** were postulated, i.e. neurons in the brain that signal the local availability of glucose or its metabolism. Figure 16.7 shows glucose receptors on the membrane. In part (a), glucose concentration is low, relatively few sites are occupied and the frequency of action potentials is low, so hunger is triggered. In part (b), glucose concentration is high, associated with a high frequency of action potentials and no hunger.

Some of the time, people with diabetes have a relatively high level of blood glucose and, if the glucostatic theory were true, they would not experience hunger. In fact, even when blood glucose is abnormally high, they still experience hunger (Smith and Epstein, 1969). Glucostatic theory cannot explain this, so a modification to it was needed.

To take up glucose, neurons in general do not require insulin. However, it was suggested that a very small atypical sample of neurons that are insulin-dependent is used in feeding control. Such neurons exist and there is a concentration of insulin receptors in the regions of the hypothalamus concerned with the control of feeding (Kaiyala *et al.*, 1995; Langhans and Scharrer, 1992). Figure 16.8 represents the possibility that feeding control is based on a set of neurons that are sensitive to their ability to *utilize* glucose as a fuel and that insulin is involved. Part (a)

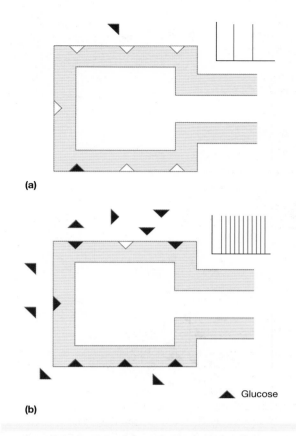

(a)

(b)

▲▲ Glucose

Figure 16.7 Neuron sensitive to glucose: (a) low concentration and (b) high concentration. White triangles = unoccupied glucose receptors.

represents a lack of insulin and little glucose can be transported across the membrane. A low frequency of action potentials is generated. This would be a cue to hunger. Part (b) represents a high level of insulin and the associated transport of glucose across the membrane. There is a high rate of glucose metabolism and a high frequency of action potentials. This would be the cue not to feed.

What would this theory predict regarding people with diabetes? If glucose is unable to be transported across the membrane and to be utilized, this would trigger hunger. The fact that people with diabetes experience hunger might be explained in this way.

The substance 2-deoxy-D-glucose (2-DG) has similarities with glucose (Chapter 5) and competes with it for passage across the cell membrane (Booth, 1979). However, it is not metabolized within the cell and it prevents the metabolism of glucose. Figure 16.9 represents the injection of 2-DG (Smith and Epstein, 1969). 2-DG blocks the sites at which glucose is normally transported across the membrane. Also, the metabolism of glucose is blocked, which is represented by the locked combination of 2-DG and glucose. Since little glucose is taken into cells, its concentration in the blood is

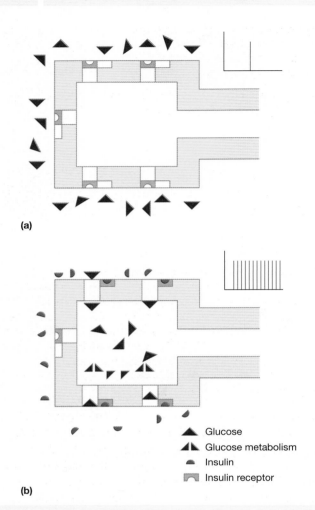

(a)

(b)

▲ Glucose
▲▲ Glucose metabolism
◣ Insulin
⌂ Insulin receptor

Figure 16.8 Neuron sensitive to the ability to utilize glucose for metabolism (represented by the breaking apart of glucose molecules): (a) no insulin; glucose transport across membrane blocked and (b) insulin present; receptors occupied and glucose transport facilitated.

relatively high. Injection of 2-DG triggers feeding. This favours the model of Figure 16.8 rather than that of 16.7, since feeding is triggered in spite of high levels of glucose in the blood and the fluid bathing neural tissue.

Location of receptors

Nutrients are absorbed across the wall of the intestine into capillaries and then into the hepatic portal vein, and so to the liver (Figure 16.4), and then distributed throughout the body. At the liver and hypothalamus, there exist glucoreceptors: neurons sensitive to local glucose metabolism (Langhans and Scharrer, 1992). They appear to provide signals used in triggering feeding. Energy exchanges at the liver are monitored and a control signal extracted (Friedman and Stricker, 1976). Nutrients are converted from

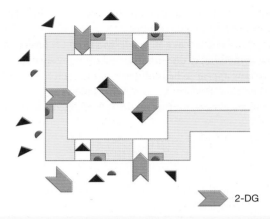

⇨ 2-DG

Figure 16.9 Following the injection of 2-DG. Symbols as in Figure 16.8.

one form to another at the liver (Figures 16.5 and 16.6). The liver can derive nutrients from sources other than the alimentary tract and is in an ideal place to monitor what is leaving the gut.

When nutrient availability at the liver reaches a low level, feeding tends to be triggered (Booth, 1978). Injections of 2-DG into the hepatic portal vein are especially effective in triggering feeding (Langhans, 1996). An injection of glucose into the hepatic portal vein induces satiety, whereas the same injection made elsewhere in the circulation is less effective. Signals are carried from liver to brain as part of the vagus nerve (Chapter 3; Novin, 1993). If neural transmission along the nerve is blocked, the satiating effect of hepatic portal vein infusion is eliminated. At the brain, these neurons form synapses at the nucleus of the solitary tract, also termed 'nucleus of the tractus solitarius' (see Figure 5.31, p. 127) and from there further projections convey signals to the lateral hypothalamus (Langhans and Scharrer, 1992). This information is then involved in the determination of feeding. Various nuclei of the hypothalamus integrate such incoming sources of information to determine a feeding signal (described shortly).

Giving the liver a role in the control of feeding has an important implication (Booth and Toates, 1974; Stricker, 1990). Feeding is triggered not by an absolute deficit of energy, since there are normally large energy reserves, but by a transition in the source of energy currently being utilized. That is, in the post-absorptive state, metabolic fuel is derived from intrinsic stores rather than from the gut. It appears that, depending partly upon the phase within the light–dark rhythm of activity, when the reliance upon intrinsic sources of fuel reaches a threshold, feeding is aroused.

The liver is in a strategic location to 'know' of intrinsic energy transactions. See Figures 16.4–16.6. From a perspective of 'evolutionary design', it makes sense for the liver to be implicated in feeding. Although energy deficiency at the brain appears to be a cue to feed, energy availability there is normally well maintained even after an extensive fast. By contrast, the liver is affected within a few hours of fasting; it goes from being a net receiver of glucose to a net supplier. As Novin (1993, p. 20) expresses it: 'The brain is the beneficiary of this regulation, not the primary initiator'.

In principle, signals derived from the liver can convey information on general metabolic state, taking into account nutrients arriving from the gut and those converted within the liver. At times (e.g. in the inactive period of the light–dark rhythm) nutrients converted in the liver are sufficient to inhibit feeding even though no nutrients are arriving from the gut (Booth, 1978).

To summarize, the assumption is that the decision to feed is made at the brain. Therefore, neural connections that convey information from the liver to the brain, i.e. within the vagus nerve, are implicated (Langhans, 1996).

A fat-based signal

Evidence suggests that the feeding system is also sensitive to the level of fat deposits. As these increase, so feeding tendency tends to be reduced. How could the nervous system monitor these since fat deposits are located throughout the body? Specific hormones are released from fat cells and convey information to the brain. One of these is termed leptin and, as the size of fat deposits increases, so does **leptin** level (Ahima, 2005). Insulin levels also rise in proportion to the size of fat deposits.

At the brain, integration of information on nutrient state at different sites and such things as the sensory properties of food is made. The outcome is the decision to feed or not (Berthoud, 2002). A later section will look at the neural signals that arise from glucose and leptin levels.

Having considered the internal factor that triggers feeding, we now look at the role of sensory factors.

The role of sensory factors, learning and cognition

Introduction

This section looks at the role of sensory, learning and cognitive factors in feeding. These include food and food-related stimuli, i.e. incentives, and such things as social context and time of day (Levitsky, 2005). Taste and smell are our principal concern but food-related stimuli include visual and somatosensory cues. These provide initial positive feedback such as to maintain ingestion but then an inhibitory effect sets in (Smith, 1996). The role of taste was summarized by Scott (1990, p. 260):

I propose that the sense of taste is like a Janus head placed at the gateway to the city. One face is turned outward to its environment, to warn of and resist the incursion of chemical perils while recognizing and encouraging the receipt of required goods. The other looks inward to monitor the effects of admitted wares on the city's activity and to remain current with its needs.

Flavour preference

Humans and rats exhibit a preference for sweet tastes. The hedonic reaction to sweet is opioid-mediated (Rogers, 1995). From a functional perspective, why does the tongue contain receptors sensitive to sweet? In mammals, one obvious candidate is to reinforce suckling since milk tastes sweet. It is possible that in evolution there was a scarcity of sweet nutrients, so we retain a strong tendency to take them when available. Ripe fruits taste sweet and thereby signal the availability of nutrients. Fruits also contain vitamins and minerals; ingestion would be positively reinforced by taste. Hedonic rating depends on a food's intrinsic properties in interaction with the physiological state of hunger/satiety (Chapter 15). Foods tend to lose their attraction after they have been ingested in large amounts (Cabanac, 1971).

Some substances are rejected as a result of a sour or bitter taste. A memory of an experience with them is formed and they can be avoided in the future (Chapter 11, 'Learning and memory'). Human newborns exhibit a facial expression of rejection on tasting a sour or bitter substance (Steiner, 1979). Since a bitter sensation commonly signals poisons, we imagine that in evolutionary terms this has protected humans.

In the long term, exposure to a particular food tends to increase the liking for it. Conversely, in the short term, ingestion tends to decrease the liking (described shortly). As Logue (1991, p. 100) expresses it: 'For food preferences, familiarity does appear to breed (some) contempt, while absence makes the heart grow (somewhat) fonder.'

The role of learning

Learning plays an important role in assessing substances suitable for ingestion and determining how much to eat (Booth, 1980).

Sensory–sensory effects

Suppose that a novel taste is paired with an established, preferred taste. Following pairing, the novel taste tends to acquire properties of the established taste (Rogers, 1995). This could partly explain the following effect. Tea and coffee are intrinsically bitter and someone who tastes them for the first time tends to add sugar. However, after a number of tastings of the combination of sugar and beverage, the beverage can be perceived as tasty even without sugar. There is the problem of why the effect does not extinguish with repeated tasting of sugar-free drink.

Exteroceptive conditional stimuli

In humans and rats (Weingarten, 1984), stimuli paired with the presentation of food acquire incentive value; they can trigger intake of a food even though rats have been 'satiated' on the same food by having it *ad libitum*. Preschool children were given items of food to eat in a particular location and exposed to visual and auditory cues ('context') (Birch *et al.*, 1989). Subsequently, even after having recently eaten, children were likely to be triggered to eat in a feeding-associated context compared with a non-feeding-associated context.

Sensory post-ingestive effects

Preferences and aversions are adjusted according to the consequences of ingestion, an example of learning (Booth, 1993b). The flexible parameters of the programme are determined on the basis of learning about the post-ingestive consequences of ingesting a food. However, if these consequences alter, there remains the possibility of readjustment. For example, given a choice between arbitrary flavours added to foods, rats tend to develop a preference for

the flavour associated with nutrient gain (Sclafani, 1997). Post-ingestive consequences might also involve mood-altering effects mediated by, for example, the availability of substrates used in the synthesis of different neurotransmitters (Rogers, 1995).

A substance that yields beneficial effects following ingestion, e.g. an amino acid when in a state of deficiency, tends to be positively ranked (Booth, 1993b). Preferences can be associated with taste, odour, texture or visual characteristics. The best-known relationship between ingestion and its consequences is taste-aversion learning, the Garcia effect (Chapter 11). At a neural level in studies on rats, plasticity can be identified: the palatability of a substance devalued by taste-aversion learning becomes encoded within the brain as if it were intrinsically aversive (Berridge, 1995; Scott and Giza, 1993). In rejecting the previously acceptable food, the rat acts as if it tastes bad.

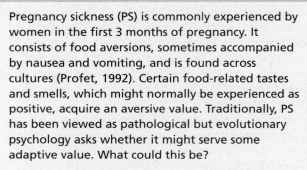

Evolutionary psychology
Pregnancy sickness

Pregnancy sickness (PS) is commonly experienced by women in the first 3 months of pregnancy. It consists of food aversions, sometimes accompanied by nausea and vomiting, and is found across cultures (Profet, 1992). Certain food-related tastes and smells, which might normally be experienced as positive, acquire an aversive value. Traditionally, PS has been viewed as pathological but evolutionary psychology asks whether it might serve some adaptive value. What could this be?

Substances that are harmless to adults can prove lethal to the early developing embryo. In our early evolution as hunter-gatherers, humans probably sampled from a rich variety of plant items. Could PS prevent intake of certain substances that are potentially harmful to the vulnerable foetus? The observation that women who experience PS suffer a lower frequency of spontaneous abortions suggests that this might be so. PS appears to lower the threshold of rejection of foods that could prove toxic to the foetus.

The foods associated with PS are often ones with a pungent smell or a bitter or highly spicy taste, which would be likely to signal possible toxins. Bland vegetables are usually well tolerated. The trigger stimuli are also ones that would probably have been present in our early evolutionary environment much the same as now. Modern industrial toxins appear not to induce PS.

Considering PS as a possible adaptation can inform the investigation of the brain mechanisms underlying it. Analysis points to the involvement of a brain stem mechanism similar, if not identical, to that involved in taste-aversion learning (Profet, 1992). Logically, in early evolution such an existing mechanism might have been co-opted by PS. It would be sensitized during early pregnancy, probably by features of the mother's hormonal environment.

Social factors and habits

In humans, the timing of the onset of meals depends on habit and social cues, such as the time of day and other people offering a meal (Langhans and Scharrer, 1992). After skipping lunch, we sometimes do not feel hungry mid-afternoon. Being with other people who are eating tends to increase the size of a meal taken. Another social factor facilitating intake might be imitation. Conversely, children sometimes acquire an aversion for a food by observing other children not enjoying it (Logue, 1991).

Section summary

1 Taste is a determinant of food intake.

2 Within limits, the sweetness of a food increases its reward/incentive value.

3 Animals form associations between tastes and the consequences that follow ingestion.

4 Social and time factors play a role in food intake.

Test your knowledge

(Answer on page 422)

16.6 A rat comes to develop a preference for an arbitrary odour paired with a nutrient-bearing food. How would the odour be described? (i) Unconditional stimulus, (ii) conditional stimulus, (iii) innate stimulus.

16.1

Satiety

Introduction

Satiety is the absence of hunger, induced specifically by ingestion. It accounts for only one possible cause of why feeding is terminated. Other reasons include inhibition due to a competing demand, as in escaping from a predator, and loss of appetite from nausea.

In satiety, is feeding terminated by a reversal of those same events that triggered feeding? This would seem to be impossible: when a meal ends, most of what was ingested can still be in the stomach. Depending upon the size of meal and speed of taking it, relatively little might have been absorbed. Such considerations suggest that a distinct process of satiety plays a role in terminating a meal. In rats, a characteristic pattern, termed the **behavioural satiety sequence**, consists of the end of feeding and then a switch to grooming (Antin *et al.*, 1975). Its appearance in response to, say, a drug is significant for the researcher, since it suggests that the drug mimics natural satiety rather than inducing distraction or nausea.

Determinants of satiety

Several factors acting in combination determine satiety (Powley and Phillips, 2004). These are (a) pre-absorptive, e.g. oral stimulation by taste, the mechanics of chewing and swallowing, stomach stretching ('distension'), particular peptides released from the upper intestine by nutrients, and (b) post-absorptive, e.g. detection of nutrients at the liver (Mei, 1994).

The alimentary tract contains receptors for mechanical stretch and chemical contents, e.g. sugars and amino acids. Detection of nutrients in combination with detection of mass plays a role in satiety. The contribution to satiety from the stomach is conveyed neurally to the brain in the vagus nerve (Powley and Phillips, 2004). The signal from gastric factors involves some plasticity; in the light of post-ingestive consequences, the animal calibrates the gastric contribution according to the properties of the food just ingested (Deutsch, 1983).

Insulin reaching the brain plays a role in satiety (Hoebel, 1997). Since plasma insulin concentration increases as a function of body fat deposits, this would seem to provide a negative feedback effect, restraining feeding and thereby the size of the fat deposits.

Cholecystokinin (CCK)

Food in the upper gut triggers the release of 'satiety peptides', one of which is cholecystokinin (CCK) (Smith and Gibbs, 1994). CCK is also released as a neurotransmitter in the brain. In rodents, CCK that is released in the brain acts at sites involved in the control of feeding, e.g. hypothalamus, and helps to induce the behavioural satiety sequence (Antin *et al.*, 1975; Hoebel, 1997). Hence, there appears to be functional coherence in its roles as gut peptide and neurotransmitter. In the brain, CCK appears to act in combination with insulin and leptin. There is still speculation about the generality of the rodent data to primates.

Injected CCK inhibits feeding, whereas CCK antagonists increase it to above the control level (Corp *et al.*, 1997). Without further evidence, the fact that injected CCK inhibits feeding might be attributed to, say, nausea. However, the increase in food intake caused by CCK antagonists suggests a **physiological effect** of CCK on feeding (as opposed to an abnormal or pathological effect). This expression implies that the exogenous source mimics the normal role of the natural neurochemical. If a substance has one effect and its antagonist the opposite, this tends to be taken as evidence suggesting a physiological effect.

How does CCK inhibit feeding? There are receptors to CCK located at the afferent terminals of gut neurons that form part of the vagus nerve. Hence, food in the gut causes the release of CCK, which activates such neurons. CCK appears to sensitize stretch receptors in the gut (Read, 1992) and to slow gastric emptying (Blackshaw and Grundy, 1993). All such factors increase the strength of the inhibitory link from gut to brain that is triggered by food in the gut (Moran, 2000). Cutting the vagus nerve, which carries information from gut to brain, reduces or eliminates the satiety-inducing effect of CCK injections.

Sensory-specific satiety

To some extent, satiety is specific to the taste of food recently ingested, termed **sensory-specific satiety (SSS)** (Clifton *et al.*, 1987; Le Magnen, 1967). Thus, satiety depends on a memory of sensory properties along with other information (e.g. metabolic activity). External factors can only be understood in the context of the animal's history.

Figure 16.10 shows the result of an experiment on rats. To investigate the effect of variety, the amount eaten under conditions of choice is compared with when only a single diet is available. The foods A–D were of identical chemical composition, except for the addition of a different taste label to each, e.g. lemon or almond. On test day 1, rats were allowed 30 minutes with diet D, followed by 30 minutes with diet B, and so on. As you can see, variety stimulates intake, compared with when the same diet is available throughout.

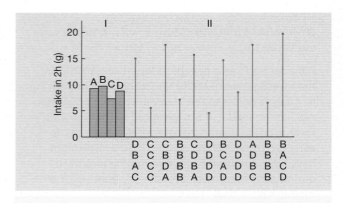

Figure 16.10 The quantity of food eaten by rats in 2 h. In phase I, they are fed four different diets, A, B, C and D, on four successive days. In phase II, either variety or no variety is allowed on alternate days.

Source: Le Magnen (1967, Fig. 13, p. 25). Used with permission.

Sensory-specific satiety makes sense as a process for encouraging variety in the diet. Sources of food signalled by different flavours might provide different minerals, vitamins and amino acids. Also, by avoiding any one food, there is a reduced risk of accumulating particular toxins that might be associated with that food (Profet, 1992).

In our early evolutionary environment, this would have served regulation. However, in sugar-rich and variety-rich Western societies, there is the disadvantage of its contribution to obesity.

Having discussed the factors that contribute to feeding, we now turn to consider the brain mechanisms underlying feeding motivation and the behaviour of feeding.

Section summary

1 Satiety depends upon an interaction of different factors (e.g. taste, mechanics of chewing, stomach filling and CCK).

2 To some extent, satiety is specific to a recently ingested food.

Test your knowledge

(Answer on page 422)

16.7 The role of CCK involving the vagus nerve and described in this section is (i) pre-absorptive or (ii) post-absorptive?

16.2

Brain mechanisms and eating

Introduction

This section looks at the neural embodiment of some of the processes underlying feeding. Considering the behavioural phenomena and physiological studies described so far, we come to an investigation of the brain alerted for particular processes showing the following properties:

- At certain locations in the brain, nutrient levels are translated into motivational signals underlying food seeking and ingestion.

- In determining feeding motivation, the brain integrates various signals (e.g. on glucose levels and fat deposits) from different parts of the body.

- A satiety signal arises from food in the gut.

- Palatability is based on intrinsic properties of tasted foods and nutrient levels, amongst other things.

- Learned aversions are formed and these transform the palatability of a given substance from positive to negative.

Feeding is controlled by a *network of interacting brain regions*, including regions of the hypothalamus, cortex and brain stem (Grill and Kaplan, 1990). This idea was introduced in simplified form in Figure 5.31 (p. 127). For example, detectors of nutrient state (e.g. glucose receptors) appear to be distributed in various brain regions. The fact that detectors exist in more than one place might contribute fail-safe ('redundancy') to the system.

Psychologists distinguish those brain processes that are engaged in, on the one hand, the appetitive phase of approaching food ('wanting') from, on the other, those engaged in liking and consuming food, such as calculating palatability (Chapter 15). Certain experimental interventions can isolate one such process rather than another. For example, manipulations of the mesolimbic dopamine pathway reveal that it has a crucial role in the wanting phase. However, we also need to acknowledge that we are dealing with a whole interacting system of brain regions and, under

natural conditions, an effect on one process will have implications for all. For example, in liking something we tend to increase our wanting for it.

Interacting brain regions

In rats, a link between the sensory input of food in the mouth and the motor output that controls feeding is organized at the brain stem (Berridge, 1995; Grill and Kaplan, 1990). The mechanics of rejection based upon taste (e.g. of concentrated quinine) is also organized at this level. However, the brain stem is not a fixed pathway between oral stimulus and motor response; the relationship is modulated. Signals on energy state and satiety computed at a higher level (e.g. hypothalamus) act at the brain stem level to modulate the reaction to taste stimuli (Figure 16.11).

Brain stem controls are sufficient for the basics of the link between taste and consummatory behaviour (Grill and Kaplan, 1990). A rat with the brain stem surgically isolated from the rest of the brain, a so-called **decerebrate**, can still ingest food placed in the mouth. However, the rat will die unless it is maintained by oral or gastric infusion. The brain stem is unable to organize appetitive behaviour. Also the decerebrate cannot learn taste-aversion associations.

A focus for investigating the neural bases of feeding has been the hypothalamus, the topic of the next section.

The hypothalamus

Introduction

Particular nuclei of the hypothalamus contain neurons (described earlier) that are sensitive to events at their own local environment, e.g. glucose level. These nuclei are also in receipt of information on nutrient-related events occurring elsewhere, such as the liver (Blackshaw and Grundy, 1993). Such hypothalamic neurons are also sensitive to inputs from the gustatory and olfactory systems (Chapter 9, 'The other sensory systems'). This points to their role in the integration of internal and external information (Gervais, 1993). In non-human primates, taste information is transmitted to the cortex, e.g. to the orbitofrontal cortex (Rolls, 2004). This

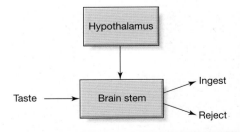

Figure 16.11 Modulation of brain stem circuitry by higher brain regions.

could be a means by which motivational signals are translated into appetitive motor action, e.g. approach food.

Role of nuclei and chemical factors

Several neurochemicals and nuclei within the hypothalamus have been implicated in the control of feeding. For example, glutamatergic neurotransmission, particularly in the lateral hypothalamus, is involved. Local application of glutamate or its agonists triggers feeding in satiated rats (Lee and Stanley, 2005).

The **arcuate nucleus** is a principal focus for integrating nutrient-related information. Neurons that synthesize a substance termed neuropeptide Y (NPY) are located there. They project to the lateral hypothalamus and paraventricular nucleus, where they are usually thought to exert a role in triggering feeding (Kaiyala *et al.*, 1995), though exactly what NPY is doing is still unclear (Södersten *et al.*, 2003). Food deprivation increases the release of NPY. It appears that, within this nucleus among others, serotonin has a role in producing satiety (Halford *et al.*, 2005).

There is a concentration of insulin receptors in the arcuate nucleus. Insulin can cross the blood–brain barrier (Chapter 5). Insulin injected into the hypothalamus *inhibits* feeding and appears to exert its effect at least in part by inhibiting the production of NPY. Caution is needed in interpreting the effects of insulin. By its action in the hypothalamus, insulin inhibits food intake and thereby indirectly limits fat storage. However, its effect in peripheral tissue is to lower blood glucose and convert such fuels into fat. The latter factor might well indirectly *stimulate* feeding by denying the brain access to glucose (Woods *et al.*, 1996).

Leptin receptors are found at a high concentration in the arcuate nucleus (Geary, 2004). Leptin, secreted from fat cells, is able to cross the blood–brain barrier and occupy receptors, thereby signalling the size of fat deposits and inhibiting feeding. The arcuate nucleus also contains ghrelin receptors (Geary, 2004). Ghrelin is a hormone released by the stomach when empty, which has the effect of stimulating appetite.

Lesion studies

Lesions of the lateral hypothalamus (LH) (Chapter 5) cause a cessation or reduction in feeding, termed **aphagia**. Caution is in order in interpreting lesions to the LH (Winn, 1995). In earlier studies, some reduction in feeding was due to damage to nearby neural pathways, causing a general disruption of coordinated action (Stellar, 1990). Later studies targeted more specifically just the LH and revealed its role in feeding.

By contrast to the LH, damage to the ventromedial hypothalamus (VMH) causes increased food intake, termed **hyperphagia**, and obesity (Stellar, 1990). Following lesions to the VMH, it appears that disruption of the motivational process underlying satiety is only one among several factors involved in increased feeding.

Integration of sensory and internal information

In the macaque monkey, the role of neurons of the lateral hypothalamus (LH) in integrating external and internal nutrient-related information has been studied (Rolls, 1994). These neurons respond to either the taste or sight of food or, in some cases, to both. LH neurons normally respond to food only when the animal has been deprived: their response appears to be an index of motivation. Concerning taste, they are activated specifically by nutritive solutions (e.g. glucose) on the tongue. Action potential frequency relates to nutrient concentration.

Some hypothalamic neurons appear to be part of the physical basis of sensory-specific satiety. If a monkey has been fed to satiety on a particular food, this is reflected in a lowering and then cessation of activity of certain neurons. However, if the available food is changed, corresponding to the renewed triggering of ingestion, the neurons increase in activity.

Figure 16.12 shows a simple representation of a hypothalamic 'motivation neuron', based on these considerations. This term is a summary for the role of neurons that determine motivation. A plus sign indicates an increase in motivation and a minus sign a decrease. Taste neurons detect substances in the mouth and other neurons detect food-related items via the visual pathways. This information triggers 'Memory' of past encounters with the food in question. Such memory processing of information on the food is performed at cortical and other sites and then projected to the hypothalamus. The activity of neurons conveying sensory information is independent of internal states such as energy depletion. By contrast, nutrient level and memories of previous associations with the food modulate the activity of 'motivation neurons'. For example, the phenomenon of sensory-specific satiety illustrates this role of memory; activity recovers with a change of nutrient.

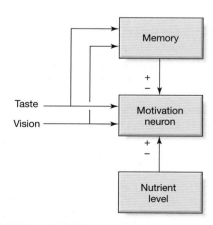

Figure 16.12 Suggested neural representation. Sensory information triggers 'Memory', which then acts to modulate activity in 'Motivation neuron'.

Some hypothalamic neurons respond to formerly neutral stimuli that have been paired with food, e.g. the syringe delivering glucose. In the language of conditioning (Chapter 11), the taste of food is the unconditional stimulus and the response of the neuron to taste is the unconditional response. The object paired with food is the conditional stimulus and the response of the neuron to the object's presentation is the conditional response. When the object is no longer paired with food, the neurons cease firing in response to its presentation: extinction (Rolls, 1993). This embodies the process of learning about incentive cues associated with foods.

Palatability and its experimental manipulation

The computation of palatability gives the signal 'ingest' or 'reject'. As represented in Figure 16.13, information is computed on the food's sensory quality and palatability.

Various manipulations allow experimenters to target the palatability computation done by the brain and thereby to estimate the role of palatability in ingestion under natural

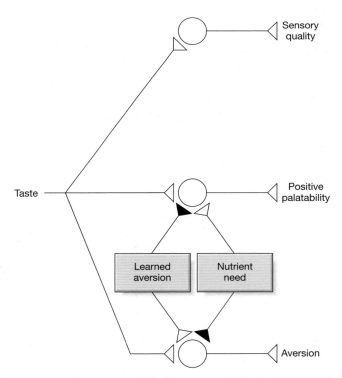

Figure 16.13 Computation of palatability. Note the excitatory contribution of nutrient need to positive palatability and the inhibitory contribution to aversion. Conversely, a learned aversion contributes an inhibitory effect on positive palatability. △, excitation; ▲, inhibition.

conditions. We can identify some of the brain regions involved in the palatability computation. Some manipulations allow us to assess the changes in palatability that occur within a meal. Others allow us to examine long-term changes in the neural circuitry underlying changing palatability. This section looks at examples of each.

The role of opioids

Endogenous opioids play a role in feeding, enhancing the palatability of food (Mercer and Holder, 1997). Reciprocally, the taste of palatable foods increases endogenous opioid activity. This amounts to positive feedback that prolongs a meal (Hoebel, 1997). It seems then that endogenous opioids form part of a 'go' signal that ensures the animal keeps feeding until satiety sets in and the positive palatability rating is lost.

Injected opioid agonists increase feeding whereas antagonists decrease it. Opioid antagonists lower palatability, their impact being greater the higher the palatability. For example, naloxone decreases the intake of a 10% sucrose solution (highly palatable to rats) but not that of chow food, the standard diet of laboratory rats. Morphine injections increase palatability as indexed by facial reactions to taste (Chapter 15; Doyle *et al.*, 1993).

The injection of the opioid antagonist naltrexone affects the amount of food eaten by humans (Yeomans and Gray, 1997). See Figure 16.14. Note that the injection did not affect the hunger rating at the outset but it reduced the level of intake needed to correct hunger. This suggests that opioids do not alter the level of hunger as such but affect the palatability of the food.

In the taste reactivity test, substances are placed on the rat's tongue and palatability assessed (Chapter 15). It is a means of observing the effects of chemical manipulations. Evidence suggests that opioids naturally act on receptors at the nucleus accumbens (N.acc.) and thereby increase the liking of food (Peciña and Berridge, 2000). Taste information from the tongue is projected, via the nucleus of the solitary tract, to the N.acc. In rats, microinjections of morphine into the N.acc. shift the taste reactivity to food in a positive direction. It appears that a distinct region of the N.acc. mediates such liking and a different region (acting by means of dopamine) mediates wanting.

A role for GABA

There is a role of GABA in feeding. Benzodiazepine agonists potentiate $GABA_A$ neurotransmission and also potentiate food intake. They increase the positive rating of sweet tastes, pointing to an action via palatability (Richardson *et al.*, 2005) rather than through anxiety reduction. The neurons implicated in the effect appear to be located at various sites such as the brain stem and nucleus accumbens.

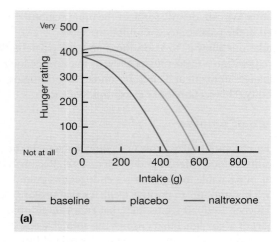

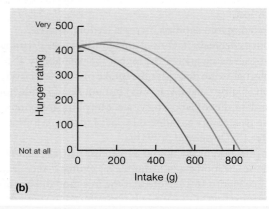

Figure 16.14 Ratings of hunger plotted against amount ingested: (a) a not highly rated pasta with cheese sauce and (b) a higher rated pasta with tomato sauce.

Source: Yeomans and Gray (1997, Figure 1, p.18).

Taste-aversion learning

Taste-aversion learning (Chapter 11) is an example of a long-term changed reactivity to a given substance (Figure 16.13). That is to say, the previously acceptable substance becomes unacceptable as a result of the nausea following ingestion. The biological basis of this is *plasticity* within the neural circuits that underlie feeding (Spray and Bernstein, 2004). In terms of Figure 16.13, we look for a biological embodiment of changes in the links from the box marked 'Learned aversion', i.e. increasing the strength of both the inhibitory and excitatory synapses.

As the neural embodiment of the acquired aversion, neural changes occur at various levels: the amygdala, hypothalamus and nucleus of the solitary tract (NTS). Taste-aversion learning transforms the activity elicited at certain regions of the NTS by the normally palatable substance saccharin to one characteristic of the bitter substance quinine. Links from the hypothalamus to the brain stem need to be intact for a rat to react to a substance as devalued

following a taste-aversion experience (Berridge, 1995). This reflects hierarchical control over the brain stem.

Having looked at the bases of normal food intake, we now consider some examples of disturbances to this.

Section summary

1 Brain stem circuits assess palatability, to trigger ingestion or rejection.

2 Certain regions outside the brain stem (e.g. hypothalamus) modulate its reactivity and thereby mediate controls such as that by taste-aversion learning.

3 At the hypothalamus, information on food-related objects is integrated with signals on body nutrient state.

4 Lesions to the LH lower food intake whereas those to the VMH increase it.

5 Opioids appear to be implicated in giving foods their palatability.

Test your knowledge

(Answer on page 422)

16.8 In the control of food intake, brain stem neurons are modulated by neurons projecting from which of the following? (i) Cerebellum, (ii) hypothalamus, (iii) lateral geniculate nucleus.

Abnormalities of feeding

Introduction

Serious problems are caused by over- and under-eating, which can call for therapeutic intervention, e.g. cognitive-behavioural techniques or even drugs to reduce or increase appetite. There is potential commercial value of antagonists and agonists to neurotransmitters underlying appetite and satiety (Cooper and Higgs, 1994). A drug needs to be specific and have minimal undesirable side effects. Simply to know that it reduces appetite is not enough; it might do so by inducing sickness. To have a physiological effect of operation, it needs to exert an effect such as mimicking natural satiety.

Is behaviour always based on a realistic measure of the body or a distorted one?

Source: © Ariel Skelley/CORBIS.

Anorexia

Anorexia nervosa

The expression **anorexia** describes loss of appetite, which can arise from various causes, e.g. cancer, or specifically constitute 'anorexia nervosa' (AN). AN can be defined as 'the relentless pursuit of thinness through self-starvation, even unto death' (Bruch, 1974, p. 4). The patient commonly has a fear of obesity and consciously pursues its avoidance (McHugh, 1990). An obsessive and perfectionist need for control appears to be universal and this gets channelled into avoidance of feeding. People with anorexia have a distorted perception of their body and tend to judge themselves as larger than they are objectively.

Anorexia is sometimes accompanied by bulimia nervosa: binges of eating followed by self-induced vomiting or taking laxatives. The nature of the typical AN patient might give some insight into its causation (McHugh, 1990), these being young women from their teenage years to their 30s.

Starvation stimulates production of endorphins, as does strenuous physical exercise and this often accompanies eating disorders (Davis and Claridge, 1998). The body might develop an 'auto-addiction' to opioids.

There are problems of disentangling cause and effect. People with anorexia tend to be abnormal in their interpretation of sensations arising from the stomach (Robinson, 1989). At times of severe starvation, the rate of gastric emptying is slowed. This could induce abnormally high satiety and thereby contribute to the condition.

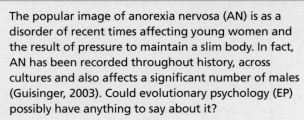

Evolutionary psychology

Anorexia nervosa

The popular image of anorexia nervosa (AN) is as a disorder of recent times affecting young women and the result of pressure to maintain a slim body. In fact, AN has been recorded throughout history, across cultures and also affects a significant number of males (Guisinger, 2003). Could evolutionary psychology (EP) possibly have anything to say about it?

Given that AN disrupts life and is often fatal, how could it reveal an adaptation? EP encourages lateral thinking and often suggests counter-intuitive answers. Remember the point made elsewhere that something could have been adaptive in an early evolutionary environment but is pathological in contemporary society.

Guisinger suggests that AN might be the outcome of a motivational process that is triggered by weight loss and that encouraged individuals to stop food-searching in a given location and move elsewhere. In our evolutionary past, the environment associated with weight loss would not have been a good one – elsewhere there might be more food available. Note that in AN, associated with refusal of food, excessive exercise is very common. A number of non-human species also show the combination of refusing food and excessive physical activity when weight falls. Consider also the natural phenomenon of 'migratory restlessness' that some species show prior to migration.

But why, in contemporary Western society, do certain humans initially let their weight fall? This could be due to social pressures. These are interesting ideas that are well worth investigating.

Cancer-associated anorexia

Cancer is commonly associated with anorexia (McHugh, 1990). A number of factors appear to be implicated. The disease affects taste thresholds and distorts preferences (Grunberg, 1985) but in some cases the treatment is a factor. Cytokines, e.g. interleukin-1 and 'tumour necrosis factor', are secreted as part of the defensive response to the tumour (Chapter 13, 'Stress and coping') and these have anorexic effects (Bernstein, 1996).

Taste-aversion learning plays a role in cancer-associated anorexia (Bernstein, 1996); a taste can be devalued as a result of its association with the ongoing disturbance to the body. Based upon rat models, part of the internal state that devalues the rating of food is the presence of tumour necrosis factor. In rats, the anorexic effect of a tumour, as mediated via taste-aversion learning, is reduced by cutting the vagus nerve or making lesions within the nucleus of the solitary tract. This reinforces the assumption of a role for cytokines since they mediate effects through this route (Chapter 13).

Chemotherapy can play a role in food aversion. For example, patients who eat a novel-flavoured ice-cream prior to therapy can develop an aversion to its taste (Bernstein and Webster, 1985). Cancer patients commonly experience nausea and sometimes even vomiting in anticipation of receiving chemotherapy. Such nausea might then form a link with food ingested hours earlier.

Obesity

In humans, **obesity** consists in having a body weight that is more than 20% higher than the ideal for the person's height (L.H. Epstein, 1990). The 'ideal' is defined by life insurance criteria.

Determinants

The stability of body-fat levels appears to reflect equilibrium between contributory factors. One of these is that body-fat stores have some inhibitory effect on feeding (e.g. via leptin). Also, in humans, body weight is perceived in a mirror or on scales and compared against an ideal (Booth, 1980). Activity plays a crucial role in burning metabolic fuels. Alas, increased weight is often associated with lowered activity, giving rise to a vicious circle.

Given that motivation is the result of a balance of orosensory and satiety factors, it seems that in the obese this balance is only achieved at a higher level of intake. Obesity illustrates the point that feeding depends upon various factors. For example, stress and anxiety might be associated with general activation that causes salience to be attached to food-related cues (Robbins and Fray, 1980a,b). Because of its effects on peripheral tissue, excessive secretion of insulin could contribute to obesity, even though in the brain insulin tends to inhibit feeding. Another factor might be the cultural determinant of meal-time. In non-humans, a large meal tends to be followed by a large post-meal interval, whereas with humans meal-times tend to be relatively fixed. A meal may be of a size that is unjustified metabolically by the time since the last.

When obese people are compared with controls, few reliable differences are observed in feeding (Logue, 1991). However, the obese tend to be particularly externally triggered, i.e. strongly attracted by highly palatable foods (Rodin, 1980). A factor that might also play a role is the anticipatory rise in insulin secretion triggered by sweet substances appearing in the mouth or even the sight of attractive food.

Social facilitation, which is known to be a factor in increasing intake, could be a contributory factor to current high levels of obesity (Levitsky, 2005). It is possible that we are eating more frequently outside the home and in larger social groups, e.g. the business lunch or conference dinner.

Obese parents tend to have obese children. Surveys that compare identical and fraternal twins suggest a role for both genetic (Foch and McClearn, 1980) and environmental (Rodin, 1980) factors. Differences in metabolic rate might in part mediate the genetic effect. Pima Indians living in Arizona are especially prone to obesity, whereas those living in Mexico are not (Ravussin *et al.*, 1994). Thus, there might be genetic bias factors towards obesity that are revealed only in certain environments, in this case the 'fast-food' culture of the United States.

Evolutionary psychology

Obesity

Current obesity makes sense in terms of an early evolved process that triggers eating when food is available, i.e. incentives play a primary role. Of course, our evolution did not take place in a world of supermarkets and abundance. In an environment of uncertain food supply, there is value in triggering feeding when food is available and storing fuels within the body at times of abundance (VanItallie and Kissileff, 1990). Alas, in continuous abundance, this process can prove maladaptive.

Therapeutic intervention

Understanding normal intake can point to therapeutic interventions, albeit types that are somewhat shocking. For example, surgeons can try to augment negative feedback, e.g. by inserting an intragastric balloon (Blackshaw and Grundy,

1993). Removing part of the stomach surgically is another intervention (Halmi, 1980). Reduced food intake appears to arise from a relatively strong signal from distension of the smaller stomach that remains, e.g. via increased secretion of peptides that mediate satiety (Strader and Woods, 2005).

Another technique is surgery for bypassing part of the intestine (Bray, 1980). This works by reducing food intake and by lowering absorption.

Drug therapy should ideally tilt the natural balance of appetite–satiety in favour of satiety. Certain serotonin agonists appear to reduce intake by enhancing natural satiety, as indexed by the behavioural satiety sequence. Since the serotonin 5-HT$_{1B}$ and 5-HT$_{2C}$ receptors seem to be most closely implicated in satiety, agonists that specifically target these offer promise as agents in weight control (Halford *et al.*, 2005). Rimonabant, an antagonist to the cannabinoid receptor CB$_1$, lowers food intake in rodents and offers hope for treating human obesity (Carai *et al.*, 2005). It particularly lowers intake of highly palatable foods and also increases metabolism. (Anecdotally, people who take cannabis report increased appetite.)

As behaviour therapy (L.H. Epstein, 1990), patients are taught to lower the rate of intake. This could allow more time for the secretion of satiety hormones and hence obtain stronger satiety. By restricting the availability of foods, sensory-specific satiety might be exploited.

Food cravings

Food **craving** sits uncomfortably in a section on eating disorders; who has not craved a certain food? The discussion should not be taken to mean that occasional craving is abnormal. However, excessive craving might be considered abnormal and can be associated with binge eating, guilt and depression (Tiggemann and Kemps, 2005). The object of craving tends to be such things as chocolate and ice-cream. One feature of such craving is the element of conflict, ambivalence and tension involved, especially when binging (Rogers and Smit, 2000). This indicates the complex cognitive and social factors that lock into the basic biology of feeding.

Cravings are more likely in certain psychological and physiological states, e.g. stress, a phase of the menstrual cycle, dieting and pregnancy. Patients suffering from depression commonly experience cravings, especially for sweets and chocolate. Those patients specifically experiencing Seasonal Affective Disorder (SAD) report that their negative mood is decreased by giving in to the craving.

Cravings might owe their existence to a memory of the combination of the intrinsic properties of the substance sought and mood-altering effects following its ingestion, such as a lowering of anxiety.

Craving could be characterized as 'excessive wanting'. Indeed, researchers are drawn to study the role of dopamine-based incentive motivational processes in trying to understand its bases (Sobik *et al.*, 2005).

Mercer and Holder (1997) propose that changes in the level of activity of endogenous opioids (EOs) are part of the basis of the subjective feeling of craving. Stress induces craving for certain foods and is often associated with increases in EO levels, as well as activation of dopaminergic systems. Mercer and Holder suggest that stress might be a mediating factor in a number of EO-associated conditions of craving, e.g. obesity, bulimia nervosa and pregnancy. Opioid addicts denied access to their drug report intense cravings for sweet foods.

The discussion now turns to drinking, where it is shown that a number of principles similar to those underlying feeding apply.

Section summary

1 Certain drugs target the nervous system and change appetite.

2 In anorexia nervosa, food is rejected in the interests of thinness. It might in part be explained by an auto-addiction to endogenous opioids.

3 Obesity is a reflection of an abnormal balance between food intake, metabolism and lifestyle. An abundance of palatable and energy-rich foods is a contributory factor.

4 Excessive craving for food is usually directed to particular foods.

Test your knowledge

(Answer on page 422)

16.9 Based on our current insight, which of the following might be worth pursuing as a treatment for obesity? (i) a CCK antagonist, (ii) a leptin antagonist, (iii) a leptin agonist.

Drinking and sodium ingestion

Introduction

This section looks at drinking and the intake of sodium ('sodium' is employed as short-hand for sodium chloride: chloride ions are assumed to accompany sodium). Since sodium chloride is often located within foodstuffs, sodium appetite and ingestion would be equally at home in the feeding section. However, sodium levels are tied inextricably to body-fluid levels and there are interactions between the appetites for water and sodium.

Water and sodium ingestion are normally linked closely to regulation. Our understanding has been advanced considerably by focusing on one aspect of behaviour: the role of body fluids in controlling ingestion and thereby the role of ingestion in serving regulation. This focus is reflected in the present chapter. However, to remind you of the general message, ingestion is not tied one-to-one to correcting deficits.

The body fluids

Introduction

The body of an animal such as a rat or human is about 68% water by weight. The composition of the fluid compartments, in terms of ions (e.g. sodium) and water, is closely regulated (Ramsay and Thrasher, 1990). The behaviour involved in regulation consists in part in control over the intake of water and sodium. Water is gained by drinking, by the water content of food and from the metabolism of food. Depending on the species, there are a number of ways in which water is lost, e.g. sweat, urine, evaporation from the skin (as in rats spreading saliva) and respiration.

Gradients and equilibrium

To understand movement of water in the body, we need to reconsider concentration gradients and equilibrium

(Chapter 4). Do you recall the example of smoke in a room? Smoke tends to find its equilibrium, i.e. an even distribution.

Figure 16.15 shows a U-tube, with a membrane dividing it. The membrane is semipermeable, meaning that some substances can pass easily across it, whereas others encounter difficulty. On each side of the membrane, a salt solution of equal concentration is placed (part (a)). Let us relate this to body fluids and the semipermeable membrane that surrounds cells. Suppose that water can freely pass from one side of the U-tube to the other but sodium has difficulty in crossing. The system is in equilibrium.

Suppose now that some extra sodium chloride is introduced to the left side (part (b)). This disturbs the equilibrium of concentration across the membrane. Therefore, water migrates from the region of low to high sodium concentration until a new equilibrium is attained (part (c)).

From this you can now understand one reason why drinking sea-water makes you thirsty. The concentrated sodium chloride in the gut pulls water from the blood, dehydrating the body fluids.

Distribution of water in the body

Consider the water of the body to be divided into compartments (Figure 16.16). The largest is the cellular compartment (or 'intracellular compartment'): the total of the water in the cells. Water not in the cells is defined as the extracellular compartment, which can be subdivided into the plasma (the fluid part of the blood) and interstitial compartment. The term 'vascular' refers to the plasma and

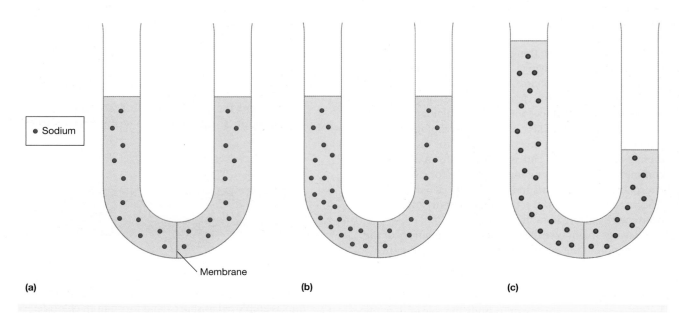

(a)   (b)   (c)

Figure 16.15 U-tube and semipermeable membrane: (a) equilibrium, (b) addition of sodium chloride and (c) new equilibrium.

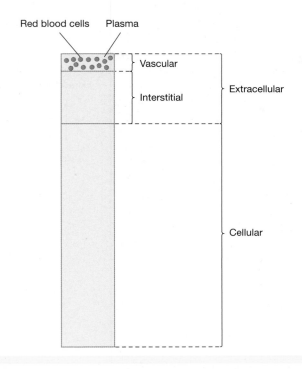

Red blood cells   Plasma

Vascular

Interstitial

Extracellular

Cellular

Figure 16.16 Distribution of water in the body.

the cells of the blood, e.g. red blood cells. If disturbances to equilibrium arise between extracellular and cellular compartments, water will move across the membrane. We now turn to consider how the fluid compartments of Figure 16.16 relate to motivation and behaviour.

Extracting a motivational signal from the body fluids

Introduction

Loss of body fluids tends to trigger motivation and drinking. Ingested water corrects the loss (Fitzsimons, 1990), exemplifying negative feedback. Motivation increases with deficit. There is collaboration between internal physiological and behavioural controls (Figure 16.1), i.e. the kidney is also part of a similar negative feedback system (Chapter 3). For instance, injection with sodium chloride more concentrated than the blood ('hypertonic'), triggers the kidney to excrete urine concentrated in sodium chloride. This partly eliminates the disturbance. The injection also stimulates drinking, which acts in parallel to restore normality. Such control by disturbances, i.e. negative feedback, is vital but it is only part of the story.

Drinking can partly reflect habit or can be in association with meals and, in effect, anticipate loss of water (Fitzsimons, 1990). This aspect is feedforward (Chapter 10), rather than negative feedback. However, to establish a basis of analysis we will focus on the negative feedback aspect by considering how deviations of body fluids from normal stimulate drinking.

The cellular compartment

Figure 16.17 shows what happens when some hypertonic sodium chloride solution is injected into the blood. The concentration of sodium chloride in the plasma increases, which amounts to the same thing as decreasing the concentration of water. Water moves from cellular to extracellular compartments. Cellular dehydration triggers thirst motivation and drinking. As can be seen in Figure 16.17(c), loss is only from the cellular compartment. There is expansion of extracellular volume but still drinking is triggered. This indicates that extracellular swelling does not inhibit the excitatory effect of cellular shrinkage.

The stimulus to motivation is not the overall loss of water from the cellular compartment *per se*. Indeed, it is difficult to see how this could be measured. Rather, *a sample* of the compartment is taken and drinking is based on this. What does this mean? When you sample food you take just a spoonful of it and taste it. You assume that the sample is representative of the whole dish, i.e. same saltiness and spice flavour throughout. Similarly, heat-sensitive neurons in the brain are said to sample body temperature.

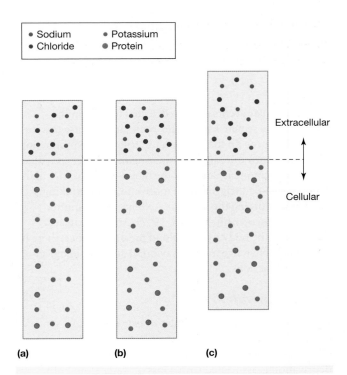

- Sodium
- Chloride
- Potassium
- Protein

Extracellular

Cellular

(a)   (b)   (c)

Figure 16.17 Injection of hypertonic saline into the blood: (a) prior to injection, (b) immediately following injection and (c) slightly later.

What sample of neurons triggers drinking? A group of neurons in the brain, which constitute an **osmoreceptor**, is involved (Ramsay and Thrasher, 1990).

The extracellular stimulus

There is also an extracellular stimulus to thirst (Ramsey and Booth, 1991), revealed even in the absence of cellular dehydration. The means of inducing extracellular depletion include loss of blood, termed **haemorrhage**, and sweating. A loss of isotonic extracellular fluid (isotonic means of the same concentration as the blood) triggers an appetite for both water and sodium (Fitzsimons, 1990).

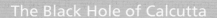

A personal angle

The Black Hole of Calcutta

We can take into account human subjective reports in understanding thirst (Fitzsimons, 1990). There is the experience of prisoners held in 'The Black Hole of Calcutta'. This expression is synonymous with being captive under hot, airless conditions and it dates from a very tragic incident in Calcutta in 1758. 'Raging thirst' was described. Prisoners obtained some relief by licking their own sweat, immense pleasure being gained in capturing drops that fell from the head. This suggests that sweat was able to produce some satiety of the appetites for both water and sodium. It highlights reward obtained by oral stimulation.

Extracellular events are also detected by cells in the kidney. These secrete a hormone, renin, in response to a loss of blood volume. In the blood, renin triggers the production of another hormone, angiotensin. Angiotensin serves a dual role: as a hormone it can cross the blood–brain barrier and act in the CNS to trigger thirst motivation and drinking, thereby reinforcing the intrinsic CNS neurotransmitter actions of angiotensin (Hoebel, 1997). Angiotensin acts throughout the body to raise blood pressure. Hence, there is functional coherence in its behavioural and physiological ('intrinsic') actions.

Water deprivation

Loss of water from either cellular or extracellular compartments triggers drinking. If both are depleted, their effects add together (Fitzsimons and Oatley, 1968). Water deprivation is associated with a loss of water from both compartments (Figure 16.18). Water is lost first from the extracellular compartment (e.g. urine, sweat) and the cells

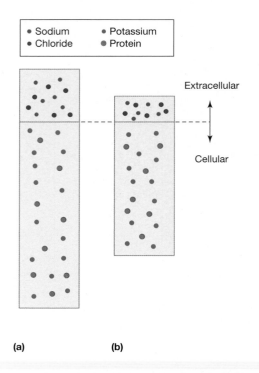

Figure 16.18 Water deprivation: (a) normal state and (b) deprived state.

then compensate this compartment to some extent, inducing cellular dehydration.

Thirst satiety

From a 'design perspective', straightforward negative feedback would encounter a problem comparable to that in the feeding system. Loss of water from cellular or extra-cellular compartments triggers drinking. However, water that is ingested takes time to get through the stomach, intestine and into the blood. Cellular replenishment takes still longer. Yet animals drink quickly an amount that reflects the size of deficit (Ramsay and Thrasher, 1990).

By the time an animal has drunk enough to correct its deficit and terminate drinking, much of the water is still in the stomach and intestine. This implies satiety, which inhibits the excitatory tendency arising from fluid loss. In other words, there is short-term negative feedback, which, in effect, gives advance warning of the water about to arrive in the fluid compartments. Satiety derives from sites such as the mouth, stomach and liver, as well as performance of the swallowing reflex (Stricker and Sved, 2000) (Figure 16.19).

In humans, on allowing drinking following water deprivation, thirst, as indexed by subjective reports, is reduced within 2.5–5 minutes (Verbalis, 1991). Significant correction of the loss in the cellular compartment takes about 20 minutes. Following the start of drinking, Figure

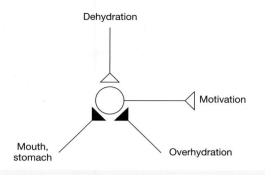

Figure 16.19 Drinking tendency as the difference between excitatory and inhibitory factors.

16.20 shows the time-course of the factors that contribute to satiety. Note the rise and fall in strength of (1) the oropharyangeal (mouth) factor, corresponding to detection of water by the mouth, and (2) gastrointestinal factors, corresponding to stomach filling and emptying. There is a rise in strength of the post-absorptive factor, corresponding to the absorption of water from the alimentary tract.

Normal drinking

Much of the drinking by humans and rats appears to occur for reasons other than deficits. Indeed, given an adequate supply of available fluids and a mild climate, deficits might seldom arise (Kraly, 1991). In humans, much drinking appears to be due to habit and social factors, e.g. to drink tea at break times (Rogers, 1995). This can pre-empt deficits. The quantity of fluid taken each day can vary greatly, depending on how tasty it is and its availability without exerting effort (Engell and Hirsch, 1991). Nonetheless, our

focus is on drinking triggered by fluid loss, the neuroscience of which is the topic of the next section.

The neuroscience of drinking

As with feeding, the neural substrates underlying drinking appear to be distributed over brain regions (A.N. Epstein, 1990). Circuits in the brain stem organize the motor pattern of licking to gain water: these circuits are modulated by motivational influences from the forebrain. The lateral hypothalamus appears to be a site at which neural signals of body-fluid state are integrated and from which information is transmitted to the brain stem (Winn, 1995).

The cellular stimulus

Osmoreceptors are located in a region alongside the hypothalamus and the blood–brain barrier is relaxed at this site (Stricker and Sved, 2000). This permits ready interaction between the blood and these cells. Microinjections of hypertonic saline into the region, but not elsewhere, trigger drinking, which suggests that cellular dehydration at this location is the stimulus (Figure 16.21). Similarly, a control of secretion of arginine vasopressin (Chapter 3) arises from such osmoreceptors. Thereby, there is coordination between behavioural and physiological controls. In water-deprived

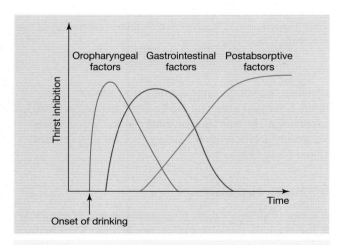

Figure 16.20 Time-course of some of the factors that contribute towards the satiety of drinking.

Source: Verbalis (1991, Fig. 19.5, p. 323).

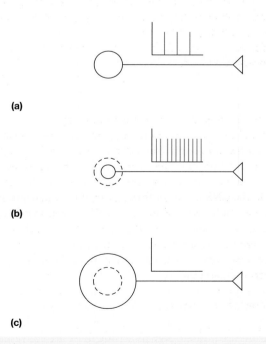

Figure 16.21 Proposed osmoreceptor: (a) equilibrium, (b) dehydration of the osmoreceptor and increased action potential frequency and (c) over-hydration and inhibition of activity.

Source: adapted from Verbalis (1990, Fig. 8, p. 444).

dogs, infusion of pure water into the region where the receptors are located inhibits drinking (Thrasher, 1991). Such small infusions do not correct dehydration in the remainder of the body's cells.

In addition to cellular detectors alongside the hypothalamus, there could be cellular detectors at other sites in the CNS or outside it, such as the alimentary tract and liver (Johnson and Thunhorst, 1997; Meï, 1993). Of course, motivation is believed to be a brain process and so a signal from peripheral detectors would be transmitted to the brain, where it would be integrated with signals from CNS detectors. The liver is located just beyond the gastrointestinal tract. Therefore, in so far as receiving ingested material, the liver could be well suited for a receptor that detects the presence of water (Haberich, 1968). A receptor could provide a short-term satiety signal, as part of an early-warning system (Novin, 1993).

The extracellular stimulus

Figure 16.22 shows a proposal for the role of detectors of extracellular fluid level. At one or more locations in the circulation, a signal on blood volume is detected, i.e. a sample is taken (labelled 'Extracellular'). This could arise from the stretch of a particular blood vessel. Humans appear to be less sensitive to such a signal than are other species, except under extreme conditions (Rolls, 1991). It seems that, under conditions of fluid balance, a signal arising from the filling of a blood vessel inhibits thirst motivation (Fitzsimons, 1991). Following loss of extracellular volume, the signal detecting such filling diminishes in strength. This lowers the inhibition and thereby arouses thirst. Excitation is provided by a neuron that either constitutes an osmoreceptor or is triggered by one. Loss of cellular fluid ('Cellular') increases action potential frequency.

Under normal conditions, angiotensin arising from the blood and triggered by loss of body fluids is able to cross the blood–brain barrier. The barrier is relaxed at those sites where neurons sensitive to angiotensin are located (Fitzsimons, 1998). In the brain, angiotensin triggers thirst, more strongly in rats than in humans (Rolls, 1991). Angiotensin appears to act as an amplifier of the neural signal of loss of blood volume (Fitzsimons, 1990). Angiotensin also triggers sodium appetite, sodium being needed to maintain extracellular volume.

The sites where angiotensin can influence neurons are examples of circumventricular organs (Chapter 5). The subfornical organ is such a site, where angiotensin-sensitive neurons are located. Signals arising there are conveyed to the hypothalamus, where they are involved in motivational processing.

Angiotensin injected into certain regions of the brain (e.g. anterior hypothalamus and preoptic area) is a potent trigger to drinking. Indeed, the efficacy of injected angiotensin

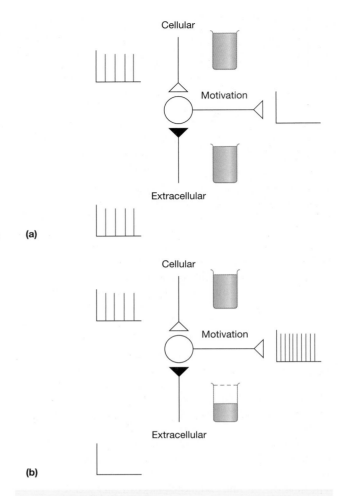

Figure 16.22 Simplified model of the basis of a thirst signal. (a) Fluid balance. A 'background' level of activity arises from the osmoreceptor and the detector of stretch in a blood vessel. (b) Loss of blood (extracellular loss). The inhibitory neuron is inactive, which allows excitation of the motivation neuron.

represents one of the most dramatic and reliable brain–behaviour links that can be demonstrated in biological psychology. The effect is a motivational one; injected rats vigorously press a lever in a Skinner box for water reward (Fitzsimons, 1998).

Sodium appetite

It is easy to show a sodium appetite in rats and to relate it to homeostasis. In humans, within normal limits a link between sodium need and sodium appetite is less reliably revealed (Verbalis, 1990). However, a very effective control of sodium levels is exerted by the kidney, the ion being retained at times of deficiency and excreted at times of excess.

A personal angle

D.W. – The boy who craved salt

In 1940, from Baltimore, USA, a report appeared on a boy, D.W., with an excessive craving for salt (Wilkins and Richter, 1940). Owing to an abnormality with control by the kidney, he lost large amounts of salt in the urine. This created a deficit of sodium chloride in the blood, which triggered craving. At one year of age, he compulsively licked and chewed salt off various items of food. He showed pleasure when tasting pure salt. Later, the boy came to associate salt with the container in which it was kept and was agitated until he could gain access to it. The craving made sense; it fitted homeostasis and kept him alive. When D.W. was admitted to hospital, he was given only the standard hospital diet and, sadly, died at age $3\frac{1}{2}$ years.

In rats, loss of extracellular fluid, e.g. haemorrhage, is a stimulus to sodium appetite. Angiotensin, a mediator of thirst in response to loss of extracellular fluid, also triggers sodium appetite (Hoebel, 1997).

In humans, very early experience of sodium deficiency is associated with a high appetite for salt in later years (Leshem, 1998). This suggests that early activation of the renin–angiotensin system sensitizes sodium appetite.

Section summary

1 Loss of fluid from cellular or extracellular compartments or both triggers drinking.

2 Loss from the cellular compartment is measured by osmoreceptors in the brain.

3 Loss from the extracellular compartment is measured by detectors of blood volume.

4 Angiotensin is a powerful trigger to thirst motivation.

5 Satiety is determined by a combination of factors including stomach fullness and the oral detection of water passing the mouth.

6 In humans, much drinking reflects habit and social factors.

Test your knowledge

(Answer on page 422)

16.10 In Figure 16.22 what effect would cellular loss of fluid have on the activity of the neuron marked 'cellular'? (i) Increase it, (ii) decrease it.

16.3

Bringing things together

For feeding and drinking, the strength of motivation depends on the detection of physiological variables at several sites, as well as external factors such as the presence of food or water. Receptors in the brain and sites outside the CNS (e.g. liver) detect physiological variables and translate them into signals used in motivation. Multiple controls (e.g. time of day, cultural norms) are involved in triggering feeding and drinking. Negative feedback based on deficits is only one such control. Ingestive behaviour is switched off by an interaction of factors, pre-absorptive (oral and gastric) and post-absorptive, somewhat different from those that switch it on.

Insight into feeding and drinking can be gained by comparing their biological bases. Further comparisons are between these two and the bases of behavioural controls over body temperature. In each case, there is defense of a body variable and homeostasis applies. However, there are important differences between systems in this regard. Body temperature is tightly defended. Although the set-point varies over the course of 24 hours, at any point in time temperature normally departs little if at all from it. Body water content is also usually tightly regulated, certainly relative to nutrient levels. Just look around and see the variation in human weights and contrast this with the minute variation in body temperature between individuals.

Like heat, water cannot be stored, so excess is lost as urine. By contrast, excess calories cannot easily be lost. If nutrients are taken in excess of immediate needs, some is normally transformed and stored, e.g. as fat. The stored chemical is available for later utilization as fuel. Although there is negative feedback, food intake and consequently weight are the result of a variable balance between excitatory and inhibitory factors. It appears to be part of our evolutionary design to take foods when they are available and to be triggered by sensory hedonism and variety. Alas, in present-day society with an inactive lifestyle, such a control can deliver pathological outcomes.

The proteins that form the structure of our bodies and vitamins and minerals essential for life are derived from nutrients. However, much of what we eat is simply employed as fuel and an important factor is the availability of fuels for metabolism. If intake is insufficient to maintain metabolism, the body literally burns itself. Probably a crucial factor in the evolution of controls of feeding is the ability to maintain blood glucose level so that sufficient glucose is available for the needs of the nervous system.

The body must obtain sufficient water to compensate for loss. However, constancy reflects more than simply acquiring enough water to replace losses. Maintenance of the fluid environment is crucial for optimal functioning of the body's organs. Cellular events proceed within a fluid matrix. Exchanges of ions across the cell membrane, e.g. the action potential, take place within a fluid environment. From functional considerations, it might be expected that drinking would arise unambiguously from a reduction in body fluids. This is indeed so.

16.4

Summary of Chapter 16

1 **Control exerted on (a) behaviour (feeding and drinking) and (b) physiology regulates the internal nutrient and fluid environments of the body.**

2 **Feeding provides the cells throughout the body with energy as well as chemicals serving particular specialized roles.**

3 **Feeding motivation is sensitive to levels of body glucose and fats.**

4 **The power of foods to trigger ingestion depends upon both their intrinsic properties and learning about the foods and the consequences of ingestion.**

5 **Ingested food causes satiety, which inhibits further food intake.**

6 **Identifiable and interacting brain regions underlie the control of feeding.**

7 **Although there is a range of food intake levels compatible with good health, nonetheless serious deviations to each side of this are found.**

8 **Body-fluids are distributed into distinct compartments. The tight regulation of these by means of the control of drinking is crucial to survival.**

Further reading

It is worth looking at the journal *Appetite*. For feeding, see Woods and Stricker (1999). For drinking, see Stricker and Verbalis (1999). For the neuroscience of feeding, see Berthoud and Seeley (1999). For biological factors viewed within a broader context of psychology, see Ogden (2002). For eating disorders, see Fairburn and Brownell (2005) and Hofbauer (2004). For sodium appetite, see Schulkin (2005).

Signposts

This chapter should have consolidated the link between homeostasis, motivation and behaviour (Chapter 15). Bear in mind that, although homeostasis is applicable to feeding and drinking, it is very much a qualified version that applies in the case of feeding. We now consider another example of motivation, that of sex. In this case, the principle of homeostasis appears not to be applicable. However, of course, sexual motivation and behaviour depend upon a combination of internal and external factors. As you will see, a role is suggested for a dopamine-based wanting system. Chapter 18 looks at drugs, where the notion of craving, introduced here, will reappear.

Answers

Explanations for answers to 'test your knowledge' questions can be found on the website **www.pearsoned.co.uk/toates**

16.1   Yes. It exemplifies negative feedback
16.2   (i) A hormone
16.3   (i) 17.00–18.00
16.4   (ii) 05.00
16.5   (ii) Leptin and (iii) insulin
16.6   (ii) Conditional stimulus
16.7   (i) Preabsorptive
16.8   (ii) Hypothalamus
16.9   (iii) A leptin agonist
16.10   (i) Increase it

CHAPTER 17

Sexual behaviour

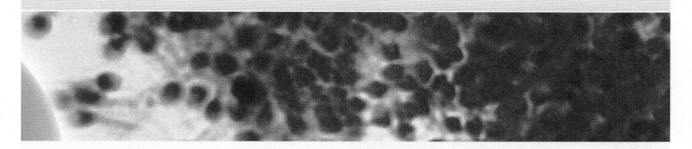

Learning outcomes for Chapter 17

After studying this chapter, you should be able to:

1. Describe some of the general and specific features of sexual motivation and behaviour. In this context, compare and contrast sexual motivation/behaviour with some other forms of motivation/behaviour.

2. Describe the interacting factors that underlie sexual motivation and behaviour. Summarize the role of (a) external and internal factors and (b) central and peripheral factors.

3. Describe what is meant by the term 'sex hormones' and the factors that determine their secretion.

4. Describe the insights derived from a comparative approach to the study of sexual motivation and behaviour. Give instances of similarities and differences across species and link this to their biological bases.

5. Outline what are the particular features of human sexual desire. Link this to the assumptions of evolutionary psychology.

6. Describe the basic principles underlying the response of genital arousal, in terms of descending pathways, local neurons and smooth muscle. Link this to the dynamic interaction of central and peripheral factors and to how this process can fail to function optimally.

7. Describe the role of some endogenous and artificial substances, in terms of our basic understanding of sexual desire and arousal.

8. Present a brief but critical account of the possible role of biological psychology in explaining human sexual orientation.

Scene-setting questions

1   Is there something very special about human sexual behaviour?

2   Are people aware consciously of what arouses them sexually?

3   Are there animal models of human sexual promiscuity and fidelity?

4   Why does novelty arouse for some? Why do other people insist on only one-to-one intimacy?

5   Is love 'blind'?

6   Is the term 'gay gene' meaningless?

How do central and peripheral factors interact in human sexual desire?

Source: Image courtesy of The Advertising Archives.

Introduction

Consider the following headlines:

- 'Top politician risked everything for one night of illicit passion – loyal wife heartbroken'.

- 'It's official now! Sex is good for your health. Over-sixties urged to keep on in there'.

- 'Emergence of a new urban group – young and happy asexual men and women – a growing phenomenon'.

- 'Judge urges castration for repeat sex offenders. One chance and then you're out'.

- 'Viagra for women – the answer to loss of desire. Feminist activist protests – the pipe-work is not the problem'.

- 'Boffins discover the gene for adultery – bishop condemns research as giving a licence to sin'.

- 'Sobbing Hollywood star tells biographer – "When the trust went, the love went and when that happened all desire went"'.

- 'Far-right politician slams expensive "psycho" treatment for paedophiles – they are beyond hope'.

The following represent some of the issues for biological psychology that are raised by these headlines.

1   Sex can be an especially strong motivation that causes people to ignore obvious dangers in answering its pull. Novelty can play a potent role for some individuals. Restraint mechanisms are often ineffective.

2   Sexual activity is said to be good for us, which points to such things as possible endorphin release by sexual behaviour and its long-term calming effect. However, total abstinence from sexual behaviour appears to be perfectly possible for some people. Therefore, sex is rather different from feeding and drinking.

3   The remark about castration is surely based on the assumption that sexual motivation is powerfully influenced by sex hormones.

4   The claim that Viagra can solve the problem of lack of female desire and fulfilment is based on the assumption that a peripherally acting drug can correct what many see

as a central problem. The feminist critique is that lack of appropriate and considerate sexual stimulation, poor self-image and low desire need to be addressed directly, rather than the answer being sought in the reaction of peripheral blood vessels. However, we should not ignore the role of peripheral factors.

5 The sobbing actor illustrates that complex emotions can be associated with sexual motivation and desire. To some, sexuality is intimately tied to romantic love and trust, whereas to others, such as the disgraced politician, it might be quite removed from such considerations. The claim regarding a gene for adultery points towards the role of variety in sexual motivation. It also suggests biological determinism, in the sense that a particular gene could be associated directly with a particular feature of behaviour. Biological psychology might wish to qualify such claim of a one-to-one link.

6 The remark that treatment for paedophiles is a waste of money suggests that there is inflexibility in the triggers to sexual desire. Once set, attempts to shift the target to more acceptable outlets would be fruitless. Scientific insight into the development of sexual desire is obviously relevant to assessing such claims.

This chapter discusses how events inside the body and outside interact to determine sexual motivation and behaviour.

Section summary

1 We need to distinguish the high motivation associated with sex and the lack of a life-threatening disturbance to the bodily tissues associated with sexual abstinence.

2 Variety of the partner can play a role in sexual motivation.

3 In interpreting human sexuality and its problems, we need to take care not to focus too narrowly on peripheral reactions.

Test your knowledge

(Answer on page 444)

17.1 In what ways is sexual motivation (i) similar to and (ii) different from the motivations associated with feeding and drinking?

An organizing framework

Introduction

To organize the chapter, Figure 17.1 summarizes some general principles of sexual motivation, physiology and behaviour. The figure could appear daunting or cold but don't be put off – it really is all rather obvious when you look more closely. You might wonder whether human sexuality can really be captured by a series of such boxes and arrows. The intention is not to reduce something complex to simply a sequence of mechanical actions. Of course, the diagram cannot capture all the factors underlying human sexuality but it shows how, in part, sexuality 'works'. It can be taken apart, as follows.

Motivation and the sexual incentive

Consider first the 'object of one's desire', or, for something less romantic but more broadly applicable: the 'Incentive' for sexual motivation. Sexual motivation is excited by the 'Incentive', represented by arrow 1 from 'Incentive' to 'Sexual motivation'. For example, in humans 'Incentive' might be weighted towards visual stimuli. Also, there is some (though not overwhelming) evidence that both men and women exude pheromones, which affect their incentive value (Cutler, 1999; Grammer *et al.*, 2005). Of course, the incentive can also take the form of images as in erotic movies (Both *et al.*, 2005). According to the species, animals vary in the

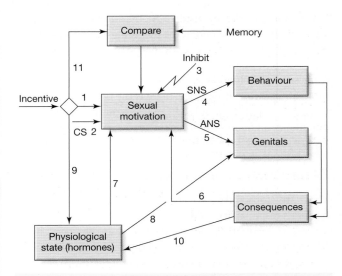

Figure 17.1 Model of sexual motivation and behaviour.

extent to which they are sexually motivated by one individual or another. Dogs show idiosyncratic choices (Beach and LeBoeuf, 1967) as do humans (as doubtless you have already observed!).

Sexual motivation is also excited by conditional stimuli (CS) that in the past have been associated with incentives (Domjan, 1994). In rats, the CS can be a light or sound that has, under the control of an experimenter, been presented with the incentive. In humans there are countless natural possibilities for such associations. Arrow 2, from CS to 'Sexual motivation', represents the link between CS and its effect in exciting motivation.

Various factors inhibit sexual motivation (Ågmo et al., 2004), so arrow 3 represents inhibition ('Inhibit'). For example, in social animals, motivation depends upon the individual's place in a hierarchy (Herbert, 1995). The presence of an aggressive dominant can counteract sexual motivation.

Sexual incentives are placed into the context ('Compare') of memories of past encounters (arrow 11). In some species, mating is preferentially triggered when the potential incentive is an established mate. In other species or individuals, motivation is particularly stimulated by a change of partner.

Linking to behaviour and physiological responses

Arrow 4 represents the link between sexual motivation and sexual behaviour ('Behaviour'). The initials SNS stand for 'somatic nervous system' (SNS), the system that mediates this link. You will hardly need reminding that sexual behaviour has something to do with the use of skeletal muscles, controlled by the SNS. Making this point is not trivial though, since, by distinction, the autonomic nervous system is also represented in the diagram. The ANS mediates internal changes at the 'Genitals', hence the initials alongside arrow 5. In humans, motivation influences vaginal congestion with blood or penile erection. However, if motivation is low or negative, there is the possibility of CNS inhibition of genital arousal. Even when motivation is potentially high, inhibition (again, arrow 3) might prevent or reduce the genital reaction.

Behavioural consequences

There are 'Consequences' of behaviour (e.g. orgasm, partner's responsivity) and events at the genitals (e.g. erectile success or failure, triggering of pain) that are perceived by the individual. That is, these consequences feed back to further excite or inhibit sexual motivation (arrow 6). The capacity of a conspecific to trigger motivation depends upon the history of past sexual contacts: a 'reinforcement' effect. This factor is, of course, particularly well known in humans. Over the longer term, in male rats, a failure to achieve penile insertion (intromission) leads to loss of interest, extinction

(Everitt, 1995). In female Syrian hamsters, sexual experience sensitizes dopamine responsivity in the nucleus accumbens (Kohlert and Meisel, 1999), which might exemplify a general effect across species.

Role of hormones

Consider now the box marked 'Physiological state (hormones)'. So-called sex hormones, produced at the testes, ovaries and adrenal gland, exert central (CNS) (arrow 7) and peripheral (arrow 8) effects (Bancroft, 1989). For example, testosterone sensitizes motivational processes, so that sexual stimuli are effective in triggering motivation, i.e. arrow 7 (Beach, 1947). Conversely, defeat and stress can inhibit such hormone secretion and thereby cause a reduction of interest in sexual behaviour (Rose et al., 1975). Sex hormones can influence the sensitivity of the genitals, i.e. arrow 8. A sexually arousing stimulus can increase secretion of sex hormones (arrow 9), possibly contributing to positive feedback (Stewart, 1995). Women's menstrual cycles show some dependence upon sexual activity (arrow 10) (Cutler and Genovese-Stone, 1998).

Special human features

Of course, human sexuality has features not shared by rat sexuality: complex and peculiarly human cognition and emotion. For example, autonomic effects, e.g. elevated heart-rate, can be *interpreted* as sexual arousal and thereby contribute to arousal (Valins, 1970). Even giving false feedback to people on an 'elevated' heart-rate can increase the attraction of a potential partner. Guilt, self-image and fantasy are involved in human sexuality. By use of a limitless imagination, humans can be sexually motivated even in the absence of external cues. However, the chapter assumes that human and non-human sexuality share some features.

Human males occupy more space in the chapter than do females. This does not reflect a male chauvinist bias by the author but represents the fact that male sexuality has been more extensively researched (Bartlik et al., 1999a).

Development

Figure 17.1 represents the adult. How did this system come into being? There is a sequence of interacting developmental effects (Chapter 6, 'Development and plasticity'). In this context, hormones play a different role from that shown in the adult system of Figure 17.1. There is an early exposure of the brain to hormones released in the body and this plays a role in the *formation* of 'developing motivational processes' (Figure 17.2). For a social species, early interactions with conspecifics, such as playing, also influence the development of motivational processes (Beach, 1947). The direction of later sexual attraction and behaviour is influenced by various

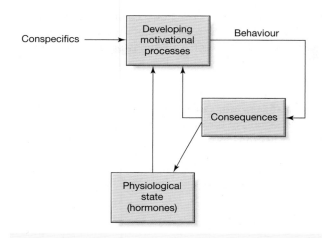

Figure 17.2 Influences on the development of sexual motivational processes.

early effects including hormonal. In humans, depending upon the culture, there might also be different 'role models' in the form of peers, films, advertising and books, etc.

The following sections will look at various aspects of Figure 17.1, such as the role of incentives, hormones, conditional stimuli and the genitals. However, the central theme is that as well as looking at the parts, we need to consider their interdependence in the whole system. We consider first hormones.

Section summary

1 Sexual motivation arises from interaction between internal factors (e.g. hormones) and external factors (e.g. a partner and conditional stimuli).

2 There are interactions between (1) sexual motivation, a CNS process, and (2) arousal of the genitals.

3 There are some common features in the sexual behaviour of humans and non-humans. However, there are also peculiarly human factors such as guilt and self-image.

Test your knowledge

(Answer on page 444)

17.2 In Figure 17.1, loss of motivation as a result of erectile failure would be associated with which combination of arrows? (i) 5, 6, (ii) 4, 6?

Control of the secretion of sex hormones

General

As represented in Figure 17.1, hormones play a role in both central motivation and peripheral (genital) processes. There are some general principles of hormonal control applicable to both sexes (Vander *et al.*, 1994) and we first consider these. We then look at what is specific to males or females.

The term 'androgen' is a generic one used to refer to a class of hormone (Chapter 6). Androgens play a role in both male and female reproduction. The best-known androgen is testosterone. The term **oestrogen** is similarly a generic one used to refer to a class of hormones, found in females. Various oestrogens have some similar effects. Oestradiol, an oestrogen, is secreted by the female ovaries. Androgens and oestrogens are examples of a class of hormone termed **steroids**.

Figure 17.3 represents a sequence of actions in the control of hormone secretion (a *hormonal axis*) that is equally applicable to males and females (Frohman *et al.*, 1999). This involves the hypothalamus, pituitary gland and the gonads (female ovaries and male testes). A logical starting point is the hypothalamus and the axis is termed the **hypothalamic pituitary gonadal axis**. Sexually related external stimuli are able to excite hormone secretion in this axis. They act via pathways from, for example, olfactory detection to the hypothalamus (Larriva-Sahd *et al.*, 1993). Note the secretion of gonadotropin-releasing hormone (GnRH) from neurons in the hypothalamus.

GnRH travels only a short distance in a special blood vessel before reaching the anterior pituitary gland. Here, GnRH triggers the release of follicle-stimulating hormone (FSH) and luteinizing hormone (LH) into the general bloodstream (similar to the action of CRF, in Chapter 6).

FSH and LH circulate in the bloodstream and exert their effects at the gonads, to cause secretion of sex hormones. Because of their effects on the gonads, FSH and LH are sometimes given the generic name **gonadotropins**. As a result of the action of FSH and LH at the gonads, androgens in the male and oestrogens in the female are secreted into the general bloodstream. They then exert various effects throughout the body. Figure 17.3 indicates effects exerted by these hormones at the anterior pituitary, the hypothalamus and the reproductive tract ('produce gametes', i.e. sperm and egg cells).

During foetal life and shortly afterwards, secretion of GnRH, FSH, LH and the sex hormones is high. This corresponds to the period of sexual differentiation (Chapter 6). It is followed by a period of inactivity on the part of GnRH and the subsequent hormones. At puberty, there is a

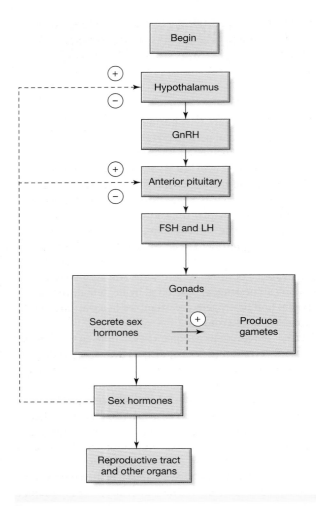

Figure 17.3 Hormonal axis.

Source: adapted from Vander *et al.* (1994) *Human Physiology*, Fig. 19-1, p. 649, reproduced with permission of The McGraw-Hill Companies, Inc.

sharp rise in activity in this axis. This reaches a stable level in human males but in females there is oscillation in the axis corresponding to the menstrual cycle. In later years, there is a reduction in activity in the axis (Sternbach, 1998). In men and women, loss of sexual desire is a common symptom of pituitary tumours, associated in males with loss of testosterone production (Lundberg, 1992).

We now consider the features of the axis shown in Figure 17.3 that are specific to, first, the male and then the female.

The male

In men, testosterone is the androgen most in evidence and is often taken as representative of this group. Normally, in an adult, the neurons that secrete GnRH show bursts of action

potentials at about every two hours (Bancroft, 1989). GnRH then triggers the remainder of the hormonal axis. Note both the plus and minus signs associated with the feedback effects of hormones. Represented by a minus sign, within part of the hypothalamus, testosterone restrains activation of the axis. It exerts inhibition on the hypothalamic neurons that secrete GnRH. However, acting on other regions of the hypothalamus, testosterone sensitizes neurons, as represented by the plus sign. This increases sexual motivation. In the male, there is only negative feedback at the anterior pituitary, so ignore the + sign there for the moment.

The female

The female reproductive system is characterized by its cycle of activity, the **oestrous cycle**, which, in humans, is termed the menstrual cycle (Beach, 1947). The rate of secretion of GnRH varies over the 28-day (approximately) menstrual period. There are also changes in responsiveness of the anterior pituitary to GnRH and of the ovaries to FSH and LH over the period.

At a certain time within this cycle the chances of pregnancy are greatest. These cycles are the result of interactions between the ovaries, anterior pituitary and hypothalamus. The ovaries secrete the hormones, oestrogen and progesterone. As with the male, the sequence starts with the secretion of GnRH from neurons within the hypothalamus. The feedback effect of oestrogen at the anterior pituitary and possibly also the hypothalamus is associated with minus and plus signs. This means that, at times during the monthly cycle, oestrogen excites activity and at other times it inhibits activity (Bancroft, 1989). Considering the phase represented by the + sign, such positive feedback is seen as a surge in LH preceding ovulation.

The discussion now turns to a comparative perspective on sexual behaviour and the role of hormones is described throughout.

Section summary

1 Androgens are a class of hormone that includes testosterone, whereas oestrogens are a class that includes oestradiol.

2 The hypothalamic pituitary gonadal axis starts in the hypothalamus and triggers hormonal release from the pituitary gland. Pituitary hormones then trigger release of hormones (androgens or oestrogens) at the gonads.

Test your knowledge

(Answer on page 444)

17.3 Which hormone travels the shortest distance between release and site of action? (i) GnRH, (ii) FSH, (iii) LH.

A comparative perspective

Introduction

This section looks at general principles of sexual motivation and behaviour. The subsequent two sections concern primarily humans. Whether discussing males or females, rats or humans, some general features of Figure 17.1 will be central. For example, 'motivation' both influences, and is influenced by, peripheral events.

Stimulus factors

The stimulus of a conspecific plays a role in sexual motivation. However, the power is not something that is simply intrinsic to the features of the conspecific. Rather, stimuli are put into context and compared against memories of previous encounters (Figure 17.1). In this aspect, familiarity or novelty can play a role.

Pheromones

In rodents, olfaction strongly influences sexual behaviour (McCarthy and Albrecht, 1996). Pheromones are detected by an olfactory organ, the vomeronasal organ (VNO) (Chapter 9, 'The other sensory systems'), which exists in humans (Cutler *et al.*, 1998). For most rodent species, removal of the olfactory bulbs eliminates both the motivation for, and the performance of, sexual behaviour. The evidence on pheromones is based upon observations of a change in behaviour on being exposed to them. In humans, their efficacy is not necessarily associated with conscious awareness of their presence (Grammer *et al*, 2005).

Conditioning

Figure 17.1 includes a role for conditioning. Various species, e.g. the fish species the three-spine stickleback (*Gasterosteus aculeatus*), learn to associate a neutral stimulus with the presentation of an opposite-sex conspecific (Jenkins, 1997). The tendency for the male Japanese quail (*Coturnix japonica*), a bird species, to approach a female and the effectiveness of copulation are increased (e.g. a lowering of latency to copulate) by presenting a CS that has been paired with a sexually receptive female (Domjan *et al.*, 1998). Pavlovian conditioning appears to give an increase in fitness (Chapter 2, 'Genes, environment and evolution'), since exposure to the CS increased the amount of sperm ejaculated.

The role of novelty

Do animals prefer to mate exclusively with one partner or to be attracted to others? That is to ask, how is familiarity/novelty a factor in sexual motivation? Depending upon the species, an animal, human or otherwise, that is apparently sexually satiated can sometimes be rearoused sexually by changing the partner (Beach, 1947). This is an example of stimuli being placed in context and a role of memory of past partner(s). The phenomenon is termed the **Coolidge effect**, named after US President Calvin Coolidge (1872–1933). Presidential reputations in this area are not a new phenomenon.

The term 'Coolidge effect' can be used in the narrow sense of revival from satiety by a partner change or more widely to refer to a preference for novelty. In male rats, presentation of a novel female is associated with activation of brain dopamine at the nucleus accumbens (Fiorino *et al.*, 1997). Species vary in the extent to which they exhibit the Coolidge effect (Dewsbury, 1981), e.g. old-field mice, a monogamous species, do not show it (old is part of the species title not a reference to age!).

On functional grounds, the Coolidge effect relates to strategies for maximizing genetic perpetuation by increasing genetic diversity.

A personal angle
The Coolidge effect

The story, which might be apocryphal, is as follows (Dewsbury, 1981). President Coolidge (who was of Puritan background) and Mrs Coolidge were on a visit to a farm. They were taken on separate tours. On passing the chickens, Mrs Coolidge asked whether the rooster (i.e. male) copulates more than once per day. The answer was 'Dozens of times', to which Mrs Coolidge responded, 'Please tell that to the President'. When the President got to the pens and was told of the motivation of the rooster, he asked, 'Same hen every time?' and got the reply, 'Oh no, Mr President, a different one each time'. The President then made the remark that destined him for a place in psychology, 'Tell that to Mrs Coolidge!'

A focus on the male rat

This section is primarily about rats but with a cautious eye to extrapolation to other species. It looks at some factors that determine sexual motivation and behaviour, first in males and then in females.

Appetitive and consummatory phases

There are two phases of sexual behaviour: (1) an appetitive ('preparatory') phase that brings male and female into contact and (2) a consummatory phase, consisting of mounting and intromissions (penile thrusts) culminating in **ejaculation** (Beach and Whalen, 1959). Ejaculation is triggered by contractions of smooth muscle. Processes (1) and (2) depend upon testosterone acting at the brain (Everitt, 1995).

The appetitive phase is associated with various measures: (1) the vigour of pursuit to establish contact with a female, (2) the preference for a location where a sexually receptive female is situated, (3) the tendency to approach an environment where subjects have been exposed to a female, i.e. a conditioned place preference (Chapter 15, 'Motivation') and (4) the intensity of operant behaviour rewarded with a conditional stimulus, a light (CS), that has been paired with presentation of a receptive female. Each measures the motivation towards a female but in the absence of copulatory behaviour. This *flexible phase* of sexual behaviour might have more inter-species generality, e.g. to humans, as opposed to the consummatory phase, which is reflex-like in rodents but obviously more flexible in humans.

In an operant task, responding for the light CS declines after castration (Everitt, 1995) and there is a loss of the preference for a place associated with a receptive female. Following replacement of testosterone, behaviour returns slowly to pre-castration levels. **Anti-androgens** are artificial substances that compete with androgens at the target sites but do not have the excitatory effects of androgens (Sitsen, 1988). Therefore, they constitute antagonists to androgen. In rats, the effect of anti-androgens depends upon earlier experience. Sexual motivation is suppressed more in sexually naive than in sexually experienced animals.

Chapter 15 described a fracture line between appetitive and consummatory aspects and raised the possibility that lesions can disrupt one aspect but not the other. The following section looks at evidence for this.

Brain structures

A number of brain structures, such as the amygdala, are implicated in sexual motivation and behaviour. Neurons within these structures contain receptors for sex hormones, which are thought to sensitize the neurons.

Lesions of the basolateral region of the amygdala (Chapter 12, 'Emotion') disrupt the capacity of a sexual stimulus to become a CS for which rats perform an operant task. However, these lesions do not disrupt consummatory behaviour (Everitt *et al.*, 1989). The amygdala is involved with attaching emotional or reward value to CSs and its output is directed to the ventral striatum, for example, the nucleus accumbens (N.acc.). In the appetitive phase, dopamine is closely involved in the activity of the N.acc. Disruption of dopamine transmission in this region disrupts the appetitive but not consummatory aspect of behaviour (Everitt, 1990).

A region of hypothalamus (Chapter 5, 'The brain', Figure 5.32, p. 128), the medial preoptic area (mPOA), plays a crucial role in sexual behaviour. Sensory channels project information to the mPOA, so it is informed, for example, of tactile and olfactory events that are relevant to mating. The mPOA is rich in receptors for testosterone and their occupation changes the characteristics of its neurons, e.g. so that they are more likely to be excited by sexual stimuli (Pfaff and Pfaffmann, 1969).

Lesions to the mPOA disrupt the consummatory phase. There is a loss of the initial components of mating, i.e. clasping and mounting (Everitt, 1995). The hypothalamus appears to coordinate spinal mechanisms underlying the reflexive consummatory sequence. Nuclei in the brain stem control the reflex-like acts of mounting and thrusting. By projections to the brain stem, the mPOA modulates their expression into a functionally coherent sequence.

A summary of some component systems underlying mating is shown in Figure 17.4: (a) the mesolimbic system arouses appetitive sexual behaviour (Chapter 15), (b) the medial preoptic area of the hypothalamus (mPOA) controls the expression of genital reflexes, and (c) the nigrostriatal system (Chapter 10, 'The control of movement') controls somatomotor patterns, i.e. the motor pattern involved in pursuit of a female, and the flexible organization of mounting.

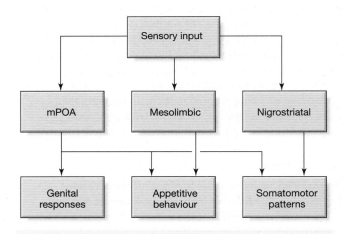

Figure 17.4 Components of male rat sexual behaviour.

Source: Hull (1995, Fig. 10.1, p. 235).

Testosterone exerts a long-term sensitization of the processes underlying male sexual behaviour and it is believed to do so in part by maintaining brain dopamine (DA) activity (Hull, 1995). DA appears to modulate mating moment-by-moment and to play a functionally coherent role in facilitating appetitive and consummatory aspects. Copulation increases DA release in the mPOA. The microinjection of a DA agonist into the mPOA tends to promote sexual activity.

A focus on the female rat

Appetitive and consummatory phases

A female rat having sexual motivation exhibits appetitive behaviours towards a male, similar to those of the male, just described. The term **proceptivity** describes this appetitive phase, i.e. the female's active approach and solicitation behaviour (e.g. running, hopping).

As the consummatory phase, she tends to exhibit 'lordosis' (raising the rump and deflecting the tail, which facilitates intromission) in response to his tactile contact (Beach, 1947). The term **receptivity** is employed to describe the tendency to exhibit lordosis to the appropriate tactile stimulus. Motivational controls influence each of these behavioural outputs. In the wild, female rats play a role in the timing, pacing and termination of sexual contact.

Hypothalamic modulation of lordosis

Although lordosis is a response absent in most primates, it has proven its worth as a 'model system' to study sexual behaviour. Lordosis depends upon (1) a trigger stimulus, tactile stimulation, and (2) the action of oestrogen on the brain during a period of at least 24 hours prior to the tactile stimulus (i.e. sensitization). Full receptivity depends upon a combination of exposure to oestrogen for two days followed by a few hours of exposure to progesterone (Flanagan and McEwen, 1995). Loss of ovarian hormones is followed by an immediate loss of sexual behaviour, unlike in male rats where the comparable loss of hormones does not lead to an abrupt termination of sexual behaviour (Beach, 1947).

The neurons that are sensitized by oestrogen are located in the hypothalamus, specifically in the ventromedial nucleus and some other nuclei (Flanagan and McEwen, 1995) and their activity has an excitatory effect on lordosis. Although, comparing across species, the exact role of the hypothalamic neurons differs, there is a general principle that neurons in the hypothalamus that are sensitive to sex hormones play a pivotal role in mating (Pfaff, 1989).

Figure 17.5 is a simplified version of the neural circuitry underlying lordosis. Tactile stimulation by the male excites somatosensory neurons (4), which transmit the information to the spinal cord. Through interneurons (5), this information is transmitted to motor neurons with cell bodies in the spinal cord (6), which activate the muscles that perform the response.

Information on the tactile stimulus ascends in the spinal cord to the brain, conveying information to neurons in the lower brain stem (7) and midbrain (8). Information descends from neurons in the hypothalamus (1), to the midbrain (2) and then to the lower brain stem (3). From here, the message is conveyed down the spinal cord, where it has an effect on motor neurons, modulating the strength of the reflex.

When the neurons within the hypothalamus have been sensitized by oestrogen, this increases the probability that the female will show lordosis in response to the tactile stimulus. In effect, the hypothalamus allows the tactile stimulus to trigger the reflex at a time when the female is motivated and fertilization is possible.

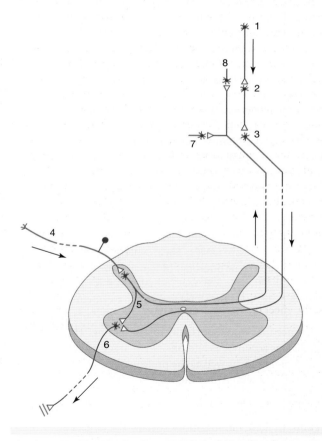

Figure 17.5 Neural circuitry underlying lordosis. (Afferent and efferent information is bilateral but for simplification only one side is shown. For convenience the spinal cord is shown as vertical, though the female would be in the horizontal position.)

Source: adapted from Pfaff (1989).

Pair bonding

By contrast to the rat, a number of species form long-term **pair bonds**, which involve sharing some form of 'nest' (e.g. a burrow in the ground or a bed-sitter in Copenhagen) and responsibility for bringing up offspring. In such species, there is a tendency towards monogamy, though this is not always an absolute. So-called 'extra-pair' mating is sometimes seen. Other species do not form pair bonds and show a more 'promiscuous' mating strategy.

Looking at the natural lifestyle of different species has helped us to understand the neural mechanisms underlying sexual motivation (Young and Wang, 2004). The study of certain species of vole has provided valuable insight into different mating strategies (Young and Wang, 2004). The prairie vole (*Microtus ochrogaster*) forms pair bonds, exhibits monogamy and shares responsibility for care of offspring. Rather touchingly, fidelity is usually shown even 'beyond the grave': most who lose their mate do not acquire a new partner. By contrast, the montane vole (*Microtus montanus*) shows neither monogamy nor shared responsibility.

A way of interpreting differences between species is in terms of variations on the 'basic design' exemplified by the rat. A focus of investigation into vole mating is the motivation pathway projecting from the ventral tegmental area to the nucleus accumbens and prefrontal cortex (Chapter 15). In Figure 17.4, this is the link sensory input → mesolimbic → appetitive behaviour. In monogamous species, e.g. the prairie vole, this link is selectively triggered by a *particular partner* (Young and Wang, 2004).

So how did the partner acquire this capacity and what sustains monogamy? In the prairie vole, mating establishes the exclusive bond but sometimes just cohabitation is sufficient. Two neuropeptides are implicated: oxytocin and arginine vasopressin (AVP). Their experimental infusion promotes rapid pair bonding. In females, oxytocin is particularly effective, whereas in males AVP is most effective. In the female, infusion of antagonists to oxytocin into certain brain regions blocks the acquisition of the partner preference that would normally follow mating. This is true of the nucleus accumbens and one of its target regions, the ventral pallidum, as well as the prefrontal cortex.

Compared with a non-monogamous species, the monogamous species, the prairie vole, has a higher density of oxytocin receptors at the nucleus accumbens and some other regions. In these monogamous species, the targets of oxytocin correspond to brain regions involved more generally in reward. This suggests that, in evolutionary terms, these 'general' reward circuits as represented in the rat ('basic design') have been specifically tuned by the pair-bonding process.

The activation of dopaminergic neural systems is critical for pair-bond formation. Oxytocin modulates the ability of an opposite-sex conspecific to trigger activity in these regions and thereby to trigger appetitive sexual behaviour. In the female, activation of *both* dopamine and oxytocin receptors in the N.acc. is necessary for pair-bond formation. See Figure 17.6. Part (a) shows the 'basic design' of a non-monogamous species such as the rat. There is a straightforward link between a DA neuron with cell body in

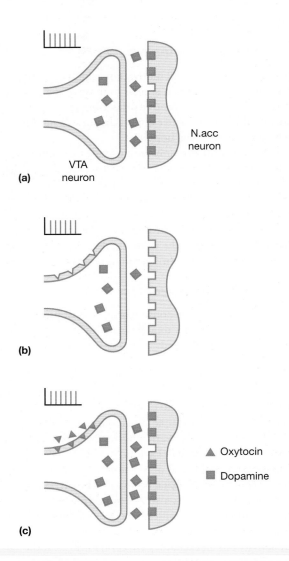

Figure 17.6 Sequence of neurons showing possible role of oxytocin. (a) Non-monogamous species with a relatively uncomplicated link from VTA neuron to N.acc. neuron. (b) and (c) Monogamous species, showing modulation of dopaminergic link by oxytocin. In (b) dopaminergic neuron active but little DA release and (c) as for (b) but occupation of oxytocin receptors permits DA release.

the VTA and a neuron of the N.acc. Parts (b) and (c) show a monogamous species. In part (b), oxytocin has not yet exerted its effect. In part (c) oxytocin occupies receptors and thereby modulates activity in the pathway.

By means of gene transfer, researchers converted individuals of a promiscuous species, the meadow vole, into animals showing pair bonding (Lim *et al.*, 2004). To do this, the genes that code for receptors to arginine vasopressin taken from prairie voles were injected into the brains of meadow voles.

So what triggers the release of oxytocin? The presence of an opposite-sex conspecific does, as in cohabitation or in the first mating. That is, oxytocin mediates social recognition. So, the incentive motivation properties of dopamine activation become coupled with a particular partner signature.

Satiety

So far we have mainly considered factors that increase sexual motivation. How does sexual satiety arise? Following orgasm(s)/ejaculation, satiety occurs. This reflects a feedback effect on motivation (Figure 17.1).

What lowers motivation is not a reversal of hormonal sensitization. Satiety is not caused by a fall in testosterone level. Nor in males is it caused by loss of seminal fluids as such. Rats with seminal vesicles removed still show normal motivation (Beach and Wilson, 1963).

Extrapolating from evidence in rats, and depending upon species and sex, orgasm/ejaculation can be quickly followed by active inhibition on sexual motivation (Rodriguez-Manzo and Fernandez-Guasti, 1994). This involves changes in serotonergic and noradrenergic neurotransmission.

Yohimbine increases the release of noradrenalin. It appears to act centrally and, if it is injected into male rats, a revival of sexual motivation and capacity to copulate follows (reviewed by Mann *et al.*, 1996). Yohimbine has often been taken by men to increase sexual desire, i.e. as an **aphrodisiac** (chemical aid to sexual desire), but I don't know of a controlled study demonstrating its efficacy.

GABA prolongs satiety shown post-ejaculation and might be a natural inhibitory neurotransmitter (Andersson and Wagner, 1995). The levels of the neurohormone oxytocin increase sharply at the time of ejaculation in human males (Murphy *et al.*, 1987) and might play some role in the inhibitory process. Oxytocinergic neurons appear to modulate ascending signals from the genitals (Murphy, 1993a). High prolactin levels inhibit sexual behaviour and prolactin is released following ejaculation.

This section has outlined general principles of the organization of sexual motivation and behaviour. The following two sections focus on human sexuality.

Human sexual desire

Introduction

With the help of Figure 17.1, the present section looks at human sexual desire and response. It considers such things as the role of hormones in desire (link 7). Clearly, there is interdependence between desire and response: the genital response both depends upon desire and, in turn, influences desire. The section after this one focuses on the sexual response.

Triggers to desire

What are the particular features of a partner that trigger human sexual motivation/ desire? Why do certain individuals attract us more than others? It is sometimes said that 'beauty is in the eye of the beholder', implying an idiosyncratic and culturally dependent process. The saying suggests an individual history of learning to be attracted to certain individuals.

There are, of course, cultural variations in what is found attractive such as, in some African cultures, the insertion of objects to swell the lips. There are also countless idiosyncratic tastes, such as being turned on by someone wearing spectacles. This has nothing to do with evolutionary design: wearing glasses, a recent development in evolutionary time, surely signals no more than relatively bad eyesight! But evolutionary psychology has some interesting things to say on the subject of desire.

Evolutionary psychology
Desire

Evolutionary psychology (EP) acknowledges cultural factors but argues that beauty is only partly 'in the eye of the beholder'. Rather, people tend to find attractive that which is most likely to help their genes to perpetuate (Little *et al.*, 2002). Thus, at the time in the menstrual cycle when there is the highest chance of becoming pregnant, women's faces and body odours are judged as most attractive to men (Roberts *et al.*, 2004; Singh and Bronstad, 2001).

There are universal standards of attraction that cut across social and cultural divides (Rhodes and Zebrowitz, 2002). For example, Hollywood stars are not just the product of media persuasion. Can EP identify reasons why there should be universal standards, such as favouring symmetry of the face? In principle, it could just be an arbitrary convention to which we all subscribe. By favouring certain characteristics, offspring will tend to be produced that will inherit the desirable characteristics and so will be relatively attractive to potential partners. Could there be more to it than this?

Males tend to favour youthfulness and clear skin in a woman's face. EP argues that youthfulness correlates with fertility and a clear skin correlates with health and lack of parasites. These represent unconscious influences. According to EP, women interpret information from a man's face in assessing such things as his reliability as a partner in terms of care for offspring. What is perceived as attractive in a man varies as a function of the menstrual cycle and the nature of the most likely interaction with him – as long-term partner or short-term 'fling' (Scheib, 2001).

Could it be that those characteristics that we find attractive, such as a reasonable symmetry in the face, are correlated with health and reproductive potential? Some theorists argue that symmetry is indicative of 'good genes' and a healthy development (an 'honest signal'), whereas facial asymmetry or abnormality is a signal of deviation from optimal development.

Of course, those having the money can resort to plastic surgery and thereby cheat the system: their enhanced outward phenotype is not an 'honest' signal of their genotype or internal phenotype. Critics of EP suggest that there is little evidence indicating a correlation between looks and health (see Rhodes and Zebrowitz, 2002). Even if there were, it might mean only that attractive people attract better social support.

Neural processes

In humans, features of a sexual partner are most likely computed cortically, synthesized at the temporal cortex and come together to acquire emotional significance at the amygdala (Gloor, 1986; Gorman, 1994). This would fit with a broad interpretation of the role of the amygdala across species. At the amygdala there are receptors for sex steroids which might exert a developmental bias on neural processing to favour certain features of the incentive (Adkins-Regan *et al.*, 1997).

Patients with epilepsy focused on the temporal lobe can experience a range of emotions triggered by epileptic discharge (Gloor, 1986). These include sexual feelings having a quality associated with real sexual contact, related to a particular situation and in some cases resulting in orgasm. A relatively high frequency of sexual deviation is found among male temporal lobe epilepsy patients (Kolársky *et al.*, 1967). Brain lesions present early in life might disrupt expression of normal programmes of sexual emotional labelling and produce abnormal links between perception and motivation. Changes in sexual orientation have been reported following lesions of the temporal lobe (Miller *et al.*, 1986).

The right hemisphere appears to be more tuned to extract the emotional significance of stimuli than is the left (Chapter 12) and to be dominant for triggering desire. For patients suffering a unilateral stroke, loss of sexual desire is greater if the lesion is in the right as opposed to the left hemisphere (Lundberg, 1992). In principle, this might be due, say, to depression subsequent to the stroke. However, depression is more frequently seen in damage to the left hemisphere (Chapter 12). The cortical–amygdala links of the right brain might have more involvement in mediating information on sexuality.

As a general feature, the prefrontal cortex appears to restrain emotional expression (Chapter 12). There are reports of a lifting of sexual inhibition and increased sexual expression in patients suffering from frontal damage (Miller *et al.*, 1986), including those given frontal lobotomy for intractable emotional distress (Freeman, 1973).

Hormones

Men

Extrapolating from non-humans, androgens sensitize regions of the brain that underlie sexual motivation (Everitt and Bancroft, 1991). In men, androgens appear to focus interest on erotic targets and to trigger desire. Loss of androgens leads to a decline in sexual interest (Skakkebaek *et al.*, 1981). However, an adequate level of androgens cannot compensate for deficiencies in other factors. With increasing age, most men show a slowly decreasing sexual capacity, which parallels a decrease in testosterone secretion (Bancroft, 1988). However, differences among individuals are large.

After removal of the testes (e.g. because of cancer), androgen level falls rapidly, within hours. However, the level probably does not reach zero since some androgens are produced by the adrenal gland (Bancroft, 1989). There is usually a reduction in, and then loss of, sexual motivation. This is as measured by subjective reports of the frequency with which sexual thoughts occur and the arousal associated with them. If androgens are replaced, there is a restoration of normal erotic thoughts, in frequency, content and quality (Bancroft, 1989). However, individual differences are great, with previous experience, cognitions and expectations being important factors (Beach, 1947).

Women

Both oestrogens and androgens are involved in women's sexual behaviour (Mazenod *et al.*, 1988). Androgens are secreted from the adrenal gland (Bancroft, 1989). Boosting androgen level can increase sexual motivation (Money *et al.*, 1988), whereas anti-androgens, given to women to counter acne, reduce it. As with men, testosterone appears to exert its primary effect at cognitive and motivational processes of desire and fantasy.

If androgens play a major role, it might explain how sexual motivation can continue after menopause when oestrogen levels drop sharply. Supplementary androgen given at this time improves sexuality (Mazenod *et al.*, 1988).

What is the role of oestrogen? Receptors for oestrogen are located in various brain regions that are involved in emotion and sexual motivation (e.g. hypothalamus, amygdala). Oestrogen can change the activity of neurons (Sherwin, 1991). Also, the brain contains enzymes that convert androgens to oestrogens.

Over the menstrual cycle, the level of oestrogen in the blood varies, as does that of testosterone (Dabbs, 2000). Does sexual motivation vary in phase with hormones? Some find little variation (Myers and Morokoff, 1986), whereas others find a relationship to general well-being and sexual activity (Bancroft, 1989). Both variables were lowest in the week prior to menstruation and highest in the week following. Of course, humans have unique insight into their biological condition. Women know about their current biological state and the possibility of pregnancy, which might contribute to fluctuations in sexual interest.

Compared with younger women, postmenopausal women have a lower level of androgens. However, in about half of postmenopausal women, the ovaries continue to secrete testosterone. Both the ovaries and the adrenals synthesize and secrete androgens and they seem to have a crucial role in female sexual motivation before and after menopause (Leiblum *et al.*, 1983).

Hormone replacement therapy offers the hope of compensating for the loss of hormones at menopause or following the removal of the ovaries from premenopausal women but is not without complications (Cutler and Genovese-Stone, 1998). Some studies have shown increased sexual enjoyment following this procedure, e.g. a heightened libido (Mazenod *et al.*, 1988).

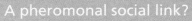

Evolutionary psychology

A pheromonal social link?

In a controlled study, women's sexual desire and fantasy were found to be increased by exposure to the odours of other women who happen to be breastfeeding (Spencer *et al.*, 2004). Under natural conditions, would we expect to see such an effect? What might EP say about it? It might be argued that, in a social species, the presence of a breastfeeding woman is indicative of an availability of nutrients and therefore a good time for mating.

Sexual desire and love

Of course, people vary in the extent to which sexual desire is associated with romantic love for one particular individual. So how does romantic love interact with sexual desire? Romantic attachment appears to have a different biological basis from that of sexual desire, the former sharing more in common with caregiver–infant attachment (Bartels and Zeki, 2004). People sometimes show romantic 'crushes' in the absence of sexual desire, so it seems that two somewhat distinct systems merge in the case of romance with sexual desire (Diamond, 2004). In evolutionary terms, it could be that a system underlying bonding between infant and caregiver was adapted ('co-opted') to serve monogamy.

The prairie and montane voles might each serve as a suitable role model for a different section of the human population! Could the prairie vole be a model for human pair bond formation? Young and Wang (2004) acknowledge that it would be premature to claim this as yet. However, plasma oxytocin levels are elevated at the time of orgasm in women, whereas sexual arousal elevates plasma AVP levels in men.

Bartels and Zeki (2000) studied participants who described themselves as 'truly, deeply and madly in love'. Their brains were scanned by fMRI while they viewed pictures of their loved ones and this was compared against control stimuli of pictures of friends. The anterior cingulate cortex and insula, brain regions known to be involved in emotional processing, were strongly activated by the romantic partner.

Deactivation was noted in the amygdala and prefrontal cortex. Since the amygdala is associated with attaching negative emotion to threatening stimuli, this could provide a biological basis for why love 'makes us blind' (Bartels and Zeki, 2004). So, be warned.

Section summary

1. There is some cultural and individual variation on what is judged as sexually attractive.

2. There are also some universal standards of what is attractive.

3. Evolutionary psychology suggests that people find most attractive those qualities which best signal a fitness advantage.

4. Temporal lobe structures such as the temporal cortex and amygdala have a role in the computation of sexual attraction.

5. Androgens sensitize sexual desire.

Test your knowledge

(Answer on page 444)

17.5 In women, androgens are secreted from: (i) the pituitary gland, (ii) the adrenal gland, (iii) the pancreas.

17.1

The human sexual response

Introduction

There are common features of the male and female sexual response. Both the penis and the vagina are vascularized (full of blood vessels). In the unaroused state, these vessels are relatively constricted and therefore have a low blood volume. Their filling with blood underlies erection of the penis and clitoris.

That human sexuality depends upon a combination of voluntary and involuntary aspects (Mazenod *et al.*, 1988) is the basis of some of the inherent problems such as erectile failure. Sexuality provides a vivid illustration of the limits to which there is autonomy within the ANS. Performance or even desire can be inhibited by fear, pain or ill-health. The ANS processes responsible for the genital reaction of filling with blood ('engorgement') depend upon an input from the CNS indicating sexual motivation. However, even if desire is present, this input can be overridden by inhibitory factors at times of stress and performance failure.

Physiology of the male response

Genital arousal

The penis is normally not erect (it is 'flaccid') because the small arteries that supply it with blood are relatively constricted (Murphy, 1993a,b). Whether they are dilated or constricted is determined by the contraction of small smooth muscles embedded in their walls (Chapter 3, 'The nervous and endocrine systems'). In arousal, relaxation of smooth muscle dilates the vessels and causes engorgement of the penis with blood, i.e. erection. The state of the muscles is determined by the activity of the ANS neurons that innervate the area (in Figure 17.1, link 5).

Which brain regions control the autonomic signals to the penis in humans? As in rats, an integrating centre for organizing (or 'modulating') erection is the medial preoptic area of the hypothalamus (Garcia-Reboll *et al.*, 1997). It is a region sensitive to testosterone. There are projections from the hypothalamus to the preganglionic neurons involved in the erectile process.

In the unaroused state, the flaccid condition of the penis is maintained mainly by background activity in sympathetic neurons that innervate smooth muscle (Murphy, 1993b). Erection results from (a) inhibition of sympathetic neurons and thereby a reduced adrenergic effect and (b) increased parasympathetic activity and thereby increased cholinergically-induced relaxation of smooth muscle. By various means, these neural influences affect the muscle.

Some neurotransmitters exert a facilitatory local effect and others an inhibitory effect. Nitric oxide facilitates erection (Garcia-Reboll *et al.*, 1997). It appears to be either released from cholinergic neurons or by their action on other tissue (de Groat and Booth, 1993). Other factors include peptides, such as vasoactive intestinal polypeptide (VIP): VIP is released at times of sexual arousal and relaxes smooth muscle, contributing to erection (Ottesen *et al.*, 1988). It appears to be coreleased from the same neurons that release ACh.

Local ('reflex') and central factors determine the activity of sympathetic and parasympathetic neurons (Money, 1960; Figure 17.7). As the reflexive component, tactile stimulation of the penis excites afferent neurons, i.e. sensitive mechano-receptors (e.g. neuron 1). Their tips are located across the surface of the penis, especially its head. Activity in afferent neurons excites interneurons in the spinal cord, represented by neurons 2 and 3. Neuron 3 forms synaptic contact with a parasympathetic preganglionic neuron (4), which synapses on postganglionic neuron 5. Relaxation of smooth muscle in the wall of a small artery is determined by the activity of neurons such as 5. As the muscle relaxes, so blood volume and erection increase. The activity of neuron 4 is determined by a combination of local and central factors, which act via neuron 3. Neuron 3 is excited by signals from the brain via

the spinal cord (6) and (via 3, 4 and 5) activity in neuron 6 can excite erection.

Note the link between genital and brain events: neuron 1, acting via neuron 2, sends a signal to the brain, which can increase motivation. Inhibition is exerted upon neuron 3 by neuron 7, which descends from the brain. Thereby, genital arousal is inhibited.

There appear to be androgen-dependent and androgen-independent processes underlying erection (Bancroft, 1995). How are androgens involved in the erectile process? Androgens play a role in motivation and by this route can influence erectile function (Everitt and Bancroft, 1991).

Orgasm/ejaculation

The neural basis of the control of ejaculation has certain similarities to that of erection. The reflex is triggered by a combination of afferent information from local tactile stimulation and descending excitation from the brain. However, whereas parasympathetic activation underlies erection, activity in sympathetic neurons triggers ejaculation (Sitsen, 1988).

Ejaculation/orgasm is followed by a refractory period, involving descending inhibition upon the erectile process (Figure 17.7; Murphy, 1993a,b). Ejaculation/orgasm tends to restore neural input to the small smooth muscles of the penis to normal. As a result, blood vessels in the penis return to their state prior to stimulation.

Holstege *et al.* (2003) employed a PET study to examine changes in regional cerebral blood flow (rCBF) during ejaculation. Areas of most intense activation included a region around the ventral tegmental area (VTA). The VTA area is activated in the 'rush' associated with heroin and cocaine injection, pointing to a similar biological basis to sexual reward. Indeed, people taking these drugs often use sexual descriptions to capture the 'rush' of drugs. Activation of the cortex was primarily on the right side, pointing again to the asymmetry in this regard. Although the participants had their eyes closed, activation was seen in the visual cortex, presumably reflecting use of the visual imagination. There was a deactivation of the amygdala, possibly pointing to a suppression of negative emotional processing that accompanies euphoria.

Physiology of the female response

Genital arousal

It appears that much of Figure 17.7 is equally applicable to women. The clitoris contains erectile tissue similar to the penis and sexual arousal can be indexed objectively by erection of the nipples and clitoris (Bancroft, 1989). As in men, local sexual arousal is determined by activity in the autonomic neurons that innervate the region. It appears that parasympathetic activation causes (1) local dilation of small

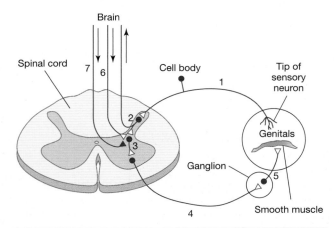

Figure 17.7 Simplified model of the neural basis of erection, showing the parasympathetic contribution.

Source: after Toates (1997c, Fig. 3.6, p. 53).

arteries in the clitoris and vaginal wall and (2) secretion of vaginal lubricating fluid. As in males, in addition to cholinergic and adrenergic effects, a role is served by neurons employing vasoactive intestinal polypeptide (VIP) fibres, which are found at the female genitalia (Ottesen *et al.*, 1988). Changes in neural activity and release of neurochemicals lead to smooth muscle relaxation and increased blood flow. Such measures correlate positively with women's own report of their sexual arousal (Hoon *et al.*, 1976).

Oestrogen affects the sensitivity of the tissues of the reproductive system (Wagner and Sjöstrand, 1988), a peripheral hormonal effect (Figure 17.1). One of the local effects of oestrogen is vasodilation and increased blood flow to vaginal tissue. At menopause, as the level of oestrogen falls, there is a decrease in this blood flow and a decrease in vaginal lubrication.

In addition to the feedback route via neuron 2 in Figure 17.7, recent evidence points to a route of communication via the vagus nerve (Komisaruk and Whipple, 2005). Hence, some genital sensations can survive even a break of the spinal cord at a site that would preclude sensation via the spinal route. Being unaware of the vagus nerve link, some doctors have dismissed as fantasy such sensations in their women patients with a spinal break.

Orgasm

An objective index of orgasm is a series of rhythmic contractions of the vagina and uterus (Whipple and Komisaruk, 1999). This is similar to the process that triggers ejaculation in males. Features of Figure 17.7 apply to women as to men, e.g. a combination of local afferent information arising from the genital region and reciprocal influences with the brain determine orgasm.

In women, orgasm, or a series of them, is usually followed by satiety. This corresponds to a loss of the various physiological signs of arousal, e.g. heart-rate comes down to a normal level as does genital vasocongestion. In general, a woman's capacity for multiple orgasms is larger than that of a man (Darling *et al.*, 1991). This suggests that inhibition takes effect more slowly in women though, of course, any loss of the genital reaction of arousal has a less obvious impact. It appears that neural circuits in the brain organize orgasm with associated outflows to the genitals and to hedonic circuitry. Vivid orgasmic imagery can occur even in the absence of a spinally mediated reaction, as in the dreams of paraplegic patents. How much the link via the vagus nerve is involved is an interesting question.

Holstege and Georgiadis (2004) found a similar pattern of changes in rCBF in women's orgasm compared with men's. The ventral tegmental area appeared to be activated in both cases. In addition, there is activation of the paraventricular nucleus of hypothalamus at orgasm (Komisaruk and Whipple, 2005). PVN activity could be the trigger for the release of oxytocin.

Not altogether surprisingly, real and faked orgasms showed rather different patterns of brain activity (*When Harry met Sally* not withstanding)! The faked orgasm was accompanied by activation only of regions of the brain involved with voluntary motor responses such as motor cortex and cerebellum.

What is the function of female orgasm? First, the muscular reaction might assist the movement of sperm and thereby increase the chances of fertilization. Second, the emotional aspect, coloured by intense pleasure, encourages further sexual behaviour.

A personal angle
Orgasmic dreams

M.M., a 32-year-old woman from Baltimore, fell down stairs and broke her spine (Money, 1960). She was paralyzed from the waist down. M.M. exhibited immense perseverance and was able to care for a 6-year-old son from her wheelchair. M.M. had erotic dreams and reported (p. 378): 'in my dreams I have always reached a climax and that's more than has actually happened to me since I've been like this'.

Avoiding dichotomies

It is apparent from Figure 17.7 that a dichotomy of whether genital arousal is *either* reflexive *or* psychogenic is misleading (Sachs, 1995). The process has reflex-like and psychogenic aspects, which interact.

Activity in neurons 6 and 7 depend in large part upon cognitive factors. On the excitatory side (6), these would be such things as the attractiveness of the partner, feedback on behaviour and use of the imagination. On the descending inhibitory side (7), there might be anxiety aroused by guilt or the perception of failure. For example, if the male perceives erectile failure, this can trigger a vicious circle that removes the necessary parasympathetic activity and triggers sympathetic activity.

Problems with the sexual response

Erectile dysfunction

The term **erectile dysfunction** (ED) refers to a failure to maintain an erection. Among sexual disorders in males, ED is the most common (Bancroft, 1989). There is a somewhat comparable condition in women, a failure of engorgement of the vaginal area.

ED can reflect a lack of interest in the partner. It can follow damage to the neurons underlying the erectile process, in the brain, spinal cord or peripheral nerves. Another cause is the side effects of certain antidepressants, which have an anti-cholinergic effect that opposes vasodilation (Ellison, 1998).

Suppose that there is an inadequate excitatory activity in the descending pathway, represented by neuron 6 of Figure 17.7. This might be due to neural damage. However, the neurons might be intact but there could be a problem in producing the appropriate excitation in the brain. This is often referred to as a 'psychological' or 'psychogenic' cause. There might be excessive sympathetic activity associated with, say, anxiety, which exerts a descending inhibition on the erectile process (Krane *et al.*, 1989).

The cause of ED can be associated with the hydraulics of the circulation. Anything which impairs the blood supply to the penis will be dysfunctional. For example, there can be local blocking of blood vessels, caused by fatty deposits (Bancroft, 1989).

In explaining ED, we sometimes see a dichotomy. ED is said to reflect *either* an **organic cause**, that is to say, a recognized physiological problem (e.g. blocked arteries), *or* a **psychogenic cause**, i.e. defined, by exclusion, as something that does not have such an identifiable basis (e.g. depression or marital conflict). However, this dichotomy can be misleading (Sachs, 1995). In some cases, we might attribute the *initial* cause to either source but, once the problem has appeared, it is likely that several interacting factors will be involved.

Spinal cord damage

Damage to the spinal cord can interrupt ascending and descending messages between brain and genitals and thereby disrupt sexual function. There is a loss of sensation from the body corresponding to that part below the level of the break, as well as loss of top-down ('psychological') influence on erection. However, some erectile capacity might remain as a result of intact reflex pathways, e.g. $1 \rightarrow 2 \rightarrow 3 \rightarrow 4 \rightarrow 5$ in Figure 17.7. Indeed, some men with a total break of the spinal cord can exhibit erection (Money, 1960).

A personal angle

A paraplegic patient

In Baltimore, A.S, a 23-year-old male, had suffered a spinal break (Money, 1960). A.S. had been mistakenly shot by a policeman, was paralyzed and lacking sensation from below the waist. He remained stoic, without resentment and was uninhibited in discussing sexual matters. Asked about changes in erectile patterns, A.S. replied (p. 375):

Well the biggest thing, you don't control it, no more. It controls itself. At times you may be sitting down and

playing cards or something and you won't have women or sex or nothing on your mind, and all of a sudden it rises on you. And then at times you can be – at times that you want it, it won't harden up on you for nothing.

On the occasions that A.S. was able to secure an erection it was by tactile stimulation of the penis. A.S. was able to have intercourse, noting that during this (p. 375):

All the time it's going on up in your head you're figuring on what you could do if you could still have the movements of your hips and discharge and all like that, instead of feeling nothing happens.

Section summary

1 Swelling of local blood vessels causes penile and clitoral erection and vaginal arousal.

2 Small arteries that supply blood to the genitals are normally constricted. Sexual excitement is associated with relaxation of smooth muscle in the walls of vessels and thereby their dilation.

3 A combination of local (i.e. genital) and central events determines the activity of the neurons that innervate the smooth muscles of the genitals.

4 The activity of the sympathetic and parasympathetic nervous systems determines the contraction and relaxation of the smooth muscle at the genitals.

5 Erectile dysfunction can be caused by local and central factors in interaction.

6 A condition in females that is analogous to erectile dysfunction is a failure of the genitals to attain engorgement.

Test your knowledge

(Answers on page 444)

17.6 In Figure 17.7, which of the following is an autonomic preganglionic neuron? (i) 7, (ii) 6, (iii) 4, (iv) 5.

17.7 With respect to Figure 17.7, consider an effect described in the text in the section 'Physiology of the female response – Genital arousal'. Oestrogen would be expected to affect activity of which neuron? (i) 1, (ii) 4, (iii) 5.

Effects of chemicals on sexual behaviour

Introduction

This section explores the role of some natural neurochemicals and the effect of some drugs on human sexual function. Use of aphrodisiacs, substances that target sexual desire, can be dated to as far back as 3000 BC in China and to 2500 BC in Egypt (Taberner, 1996). Alternatively, drugs can target sexual performance by improving the levels of engorgement at the genitals. Although this is a valid distinction in terms of target, for reasons evident in Figure 17.1 targeting either desire or performance could have consequences at both.

Dopamine

A broad assumption in the literature is that dopamine (DA) has a central role in sexual incentive motivation but there is not agreement on this (Paredes and Ågmo, 2004). For men suffering from erectile dysfunction, DA agonists, such as apomorphine, appear to improve sexual functioning but, alas, side effects often preclude their use (Murphy, 1993b). Their action is central rather than peripheral. There are reports of increased libido following use of L-dopa (a precursor of DA) (see Sitsen, 1988). However, they have been treated uncritically and have led even to the production of an 'adult' movie extolling L-dopa's virtues. Some DA reuptake blockers increase sexual desire in women (Bartlik *et al.*, 1999a).

Serotonin

In men and women, a side effect of certain selective serotonin reuptake inhibitors (SSRIs), e.g. clomipramine used as a treatment for obsessional neurosis and depression, is sometimes that of blocking ejaculation/orgasm (Sitsen, 1988) and a reduction in desire. However, by the same token, such drugs can also alleviate premature ejaculation. Enhancing serotonergic activity in rats reduces measures of sexual motivation (Ågmo *et al.*, 2004). Such evidence suggests an inhibitory role of serotonin in the control of sexual behaviour.

Alcohol

Men and women report that alcohol increases sexual desire and pleasure (Van Thiel *et al.*, 1988). Investigators gave participants various doses of alcohol and their reactions to an erotic film were measured. For males, reactions were penile engorgement, increased heart-rate and arousal, the latter indexed by self-report (Rosen, 1991). At low doses of alcohol, a slight increase in penile swelling was observed but, conforming to the popular image, larger doses had an inhibitory effect. Males sometimes exhibited a lower engorgement but still reported that they believed alcohol to be increasing engorgement. Parallels with the effect of alcohol on actual and imagined driving skills come to mind.

Women were asked for subjective reports of arousal and their vaginal state was measured objectively. Blood flow to the genitals decreased as a function of increasing quantities of alcohol. However, as levels of alcohol increased, there was an increase in reported subjective arousal.

A personal angle
Shakespeare's insight

If ever there were a good observer of human behaviour, it was surely Shakespeare, insight into the sexual response being no exception. In *Macbeth* (Act Two, Scene Three), we find the effect of alcohol described:

Lechery, sir, it provokes, and unprovokes; it provokes the desire, but it takes away the performance. Therefore much drink may be said to be an equivocator with lechery; it makes him, and it mars him . . .

Short-term and long-term effects of drugs

Drugs can have short- and long-term effects, which might act in the same direction or be rather different. There are two detrimental effects of alcohol (ethanol) on erectile capacity. First, as just noted, a short-term negative (but reversible) effect is seen. In alcoholics, there is a more serious long-term deterioration, which is seen even during abstinent periods. This loss might be attributed in part to reduced levels of testosterone, the production of which is inhibited by alcohol (Van Thiel *et al.*, 1988). Also, alcohol can damage the central and peripheral neurons involved in erection.

Ethanol exerts inhibitory effects at several locations on the hypothalamic pituitary gonadal axis (Figure 17.3), e.g. hypothalamus and pituitary. It also decreases the density of gonadotropin (i.e. LH and FSH) receptors at the testes.

The immediate effect of drugs such as cannabis and opiates can be to heighten desire, arousal and enjoyment. A significant percentage of those using cannabis and cocaine do so for this purpose (Buffum *et al.*, 1988). However, these drugs and nicotine lower the production of testosterone. Hence, the long-term effect of taking them in large amounts can be to lower erectile capacity. Given the tendency to observe immediate rather than delayed effects, users might well emphasize sexually stimulating effects.

Viagra

Viagra and some similar drugs are an important treatment for erectile dysfunction. Viagra acts by enhancing the action of nitric oxide (NO) at the penis. In Figure 17.7, imagine stimuli acting through neurons 2 and/or 6 and then 3, 4 and 5 to trigger the release of NO, which, via a further chemical process, induces smooth muscle relaxation (Goldstein *et al.*, 1998). Viagra does not trigger muscle relaxation in the absence of sexual excitation and so spontaneous erection is not seen.

Viagra is also effective in heightening sexual feelings in women (Bartlik *et al.*, 1999b).

Section summary

1   The chemical content of alcohol and beliefs on its efficacy influence the sexual response.

2   Large amounts of alcohol can have a detrimental effect on erection. It lowers testosterone secretion and can damage neurons.

3   Various drugs are associated with a short-term positive effect on sexual arousal and enjoyment but might have a long-term detrimental effect on performance.

4   Viagra enhances the effects of nitric oxide on smooth muscle relaxation.

Test your knowledge

(Answer on page 444)

17.8   With regard to Figure 17.7, an agonist acting at which of the following neural junctions would serve as a possible treatment for erectile dysfunction? (i) 1 and 2, (ii) 2 and 3 and (iii) 7 and 3.

Sexual orientation

Introduction

This section looks at sexual orientation, i.e. whether heterosexual or homosexual. Non-human animals sometimes show homosexual mating attempts (Beach, 1947). However, exclusive homosexuality is seen only in humans.

Could a biological approach be useful for gaining insight into such orientation?

In general, comparing homosexual and heterosexual males, no significant differences in testosterone levels have been established. Evidence is mixed on hormonal differences between homosexual and heterosexual women, some studies reporting higher levels of testosterone in homosexual women (Gladue, 1988). Even if hormonal differences were to appear, from this alone we could not necessarily conclude a direction of causality (hormone) → (orientation), since lifestyle differences might cause the hormonal change. There might be differences in sensitivity of neural tissue to circulating hormone or there might be early developmental differences in organization of neural structures.

Neural structure

Evidence on differences in certain brain regions has been obtained from brains at autopsy. See Figure 17.8. Homosexual and heterosexual males appear to differ in the structure of the third interstitial nucleus of the anterior hypothalamus (LeVay, 1991). This area is smaller in women than in men and is smaller in homosexual males than in heterosexuals. Differences that correlate with brain structure have emerged in studying lesbian and heterosexual women, though they have been less well researched (Gladue, 1994).

According to one study, the suprachiasmatic nucleus of the hypothalamus (SCN) (Chapter 5) is 1.7 times larger in homosexual men compared with heterosexuals (Swaab and Hofman, 1990). No difference in SCN is found between males and females. Swaab and Hofman suggest that it is very unlikely that homosexual behaviour could cause such an increase in cell number. Rather, early development is more likely to be implicated.

Differences between homosexual and heterosexual males in the midsagittal area of the anterior commissure (AC), which conveys information between the two hemispheres, have been reported (Allen and Gorski, 1992). The AC is not directly involved in sexual behaviour. Homosexual men were found to have an AC area 18% larger than heterosexual women and 34% larger than heterosexual men. Most of the homosexual sample had died of AIDS, so might this explain the effect? As Allen and Gorski note, AIDS-associated neuropathology normally manifests as atrophy of the nervous system.

Taken in the context of reports concerning differences in nuclei of the hypothalamus between homosexual and heterosexual males, Allen and Gorski suggest that their results are evidence against a single brain structure underlying sexual orientation. Rather, a number of different structures and global differences in information processing are more likely to be implicated.

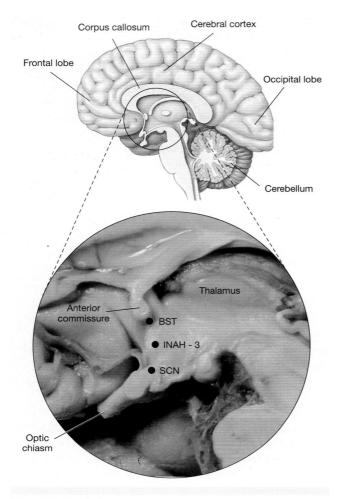

Figure 17.8 Brain differences between homosexual and heterosexual males. SCN, suprachiasmatic nucleus; INAH-3, third interstitial nucleus of the anterior hypothalamus.

Source: Martini et al. (2000, Fig. 15-13a, p. 395) (top); Baum (1999, Fig. 47.11) (bottom).

A proposal for a gene

Introduction

In the early 1990s, the expression 'gay gene' appeared. What could be meant by this? We should not ask, 'which is the most important: genes or environment?' (Chapter 2). Whether an individual is homosexual, heterosexual, bisexual or totally uninterested in sex inevitably depends upon genes and environment acting in complex ways (Pillard and Weinrich, 1986). Also, we should not dichotomize into neat categories of homosexual or heterosexual and we need to recognize overlap. The orientation shown in the domain of fantasy needs to be considered as well as that of overt behaviour (Gladue, 1988). The genetic contribution could involve multiple genes (Hyde, 2005a).

So how could we frame the question to fit with a scientific understanding? We might ask whether differences between individuals in terms of sexual orientation are determined in part by genetic differences. In other words, could a gene interacting with the environment give a bias towards homosexuality?

Some studies look at the correlation in sexual orientation between twins, comparing identical and fraternal twins. The correlation in orientation towards either homosexuality or heterosexuality is higher in identical than fraternal twins (Gladue, 1994; Hyde, 2005a). However, since the correlation is not perfect in identical twins, such studies suggest a role for environmental factors.

The route of influence

The existence of a genetic factor does not in itself tell us how it is translated into behaviour (Chapter 6). In principle, it might act by, say, physical appearance, with certain looks being more attractive to potential homosexual, rather than heterosexual, mates. However, we should not reject the idea that genetically mediated differences act at the level of motivation. There could be differences in sexual differentiation of the brain comparing homosexuals and heterosexuals (Gladue, 1994). Genetic differences might act at the level of the biological process or bias the way that the developing child is treated.

LeVay (1991) concludes that the evidence points to there being a genetic bias towards sexual orientation. If it acts at a motivational level, what might this gene be coding for? The consistent distinction between homosexual and heterosexual males is one of the *object of desire* rather than a specific behaviour pattern (Gorman, 1994).

Function

It might appear that a 'gay gene' would be at a strong disadvantage in terms of genetic perpetuation since by definition it would tend to bias towards sex that is genetically unproductive (Chapter 2).

Evolutionary psychology

How could the gene be favoured?

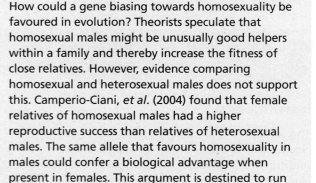

How could a gene biasing towards homosexuality be favoured in evolution? Theorists speculate that homosexual males might be unusually good helpers within a family and thereby increase the fitness of close relatives. However, evidence comparing homosexual and heterosexual males does not support this. Camperio-Ciani, *et al*. (2004) found that female relatives of homosexual males had a higher reproductive success than relatives of heterosexual males. The same allele that favours homosexuality in males could confer a biological advantage when present in females. This argument is destined to run and run!

Section summary

1 Comparing homosexual and heterosexual males, differences have been found in hypothalamic nuclei and in the area of the anterior commissure.

2 Some evidence is compatible with there being genetically determined differences underlying sexual orientation mediated via brain structure but other interpretations cannot be ruled out.

Test your knowledge

(Answer on page 444)

17.9 Is the statement that 'different hormones are found in homosexuals as compared with heterosexuals' (i) true or (ii) false?

Bringing things together

The chapter has emphasized a dual approach: looking for features of sexual behaviour that can, with caution, be generalized across species and seeing these in the context of specifically human aspects. Features of Figure 17.1 have a broad application but there are special human aspects such as knowledge about pregnancy and contraception, guilt and imagination.

The importance of a *circle of causes* emerges in human sexuality (Bancroft, 1989; Figures 17.1 and 17.7). Desire and arousal can be understood in these terms. Sexual dysfunction might be understood as breaking the circle at a point between the central factors and the genital response. It might be possible to localize the initial dysfunction to a particular point in the circle. However, there can be subsequent effects at various points on the circle. A local abnormality might be corrected locally but leave lasting effects throughout the circle. For example, vaginal discomfort might be corrected by hormonal treatment. However, it might leave a lasting negative memory that cannot so easily be reversed. Similarly, the occasional erectile dysfunction might trigger anxiety that introduces positive feedback.

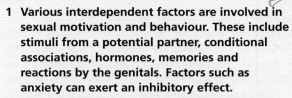

Summary of Chapter 17

1 Various interdependent factors are involved in sexual motivation and behaviour. These include stimuli from a potential partner, conditional associations, hormones, memories and reactions by the genitals. Factors such as anxiety can exert an inhibitory effect.

2 Under the initial control of events in the brain, sex hormones are released into the blood stream and exert various effects throughout the body, including the brain.

3 A study of non-human species reveals some basic principles, which can (but only with due caution) be generalized across species.

4 Understanding human sexual desire requires knowledge of species-specific biological and cultural determinants.

5 The blood flow to the genitals is determined by both central and local factors. In turn, there is feedback arising at the genitals and projecting to the brain.

6 An array of different neurochemicals is involved in sexual motivation and the sexual response.

7 The study of sexual orientation requires extreme subtlety and points to caution in any assertion of a 'gene for' a particular characteristic.

Further reading

For the aspects of sexual behaviour described here, see LeVay and Valentine (2006). Many details of the material of the present chapter are found in Hyde (2005b). For a comparative perspective, see Zuk (2003). Sexual orientation is discussed by Wilson and Rahman (2004). For an incentive perspective, see Ågmo et al. (2004). For the so-called gay-gene debate, see LeVay (1993).

Signposts

The present chapter should have reminded you of Chapter 6, 'Development', as well as exemplifying material from Chapter 15, 'Motivation'. The next chapter considers psychoactive drugs and addiction and, after reading it, you should be able to appreciate links to the present chapter. As noted, some people are motivated to take drugs to enhance sexual desire or performance. Also, we shall briefly mention the phenomenon of sexual addiction. Drugs tap into biologically conventional processes, such as those underlying sexual desire and pleasure.

Answers

Explanations for answers to 'test your knowledge' questions can be found on the website **www.pearsoned.co.uk/toates**

17.1 (i) sex is similar to feeding and drinking in the sense that it is highly motivating and depends upon a combination of external and internal factors. The strength of motivation rises and falls with internal and external factors; (ii) sex is different in that there is no life-threatening physiological disturbance associated with its abstinence.

17.2 (i) 5, 6.

17.3 (i) GnRH

17.4 (ii) 5 and (iv) 3

17.5 (ii) The adrenal gland

17.6 (iii) 4

17.7 (i) 1

17.8 (i) 1 and 2, (ii) 2 and 3

17.9 (ii) False

CHAPTER 18

Drugs and addiction

After studying this chapter, you should be able to:

1. Discuss some of the problems that arise in trying to define the terms 'drug' and 'addiction', while relating the discussion to an understanding of the brain and the social context.

2. Explain some of the processes that are thought to underlie the craving, seeking and taking of drugs in humans, while discussing the viability of animal models of these phenomena.

3. Describe the effects of some addictive and non-addictive drugs on the CNS and explain what this tells us about the biological bases of addiction. Discuss the notion of addiction to non-chemical activities, noting similarities and differences with drug-based addictions.

4. Critically discuss some of the best-known models that have been advanced to explain addiction.

Scene-setting questions

1 Why do people keep on taking drugs – to escape from reality or because the body comes to need them?

2 Does the effect of a drug depend on social context and expectations?

3 Is love like being addicted to a drug? Can sex be addictive?

4 Can you get addicted to the Internet?

5 Which is more addictive, heroin or nicotine?

6 What effect does ecstasy have? What is an LSD trip like?

7 Why can't people 'just say no' to drugs?

WARNING

WHERE THERE'S SMOKE THERE'S HYDROGEN CYANIDE

Tobacco smoke contains hydrogen cyanide. It can cause headaches, dizziness, weakness, nausea, vertigo and stomach aches in smokers and non-smokers.

Health Canada

Qualité classique, au g-bi énique
Smooth Flavour, Classic Quality

1-800-311-2000

Why are warnings so often ineffective in countering drug-taking?

Source: Image courtesy of The Advertising Archives.

Introduction

When have you noticed 'drugs and addiction' discussed in the media? What was the context and what did these terms mean? The following is a fair reflection of some typical items of the national news.

- 'Agony of pop-star on entering top rehabilitation clinic – one more drink could be the last'.

- 'Police find drugs in football star's penthouse love-nest'.

- 'Yuppie weekend cocaine users are warned by London police that they are not above the law'.

- 'Popular family vicar's life ruined by secret Internet sex addiction'.

By contrast, here are two imaginary headlines that you probably have never encountered but which reveal as much as those above.

- 'One-man drug-crazed crime-wave fuelled by need for mushrooms'.
- 'Housing estate ruled by fear of ecstasy gangs'.

These examples illustrate a number of points:

1 The criteria used to define the term 'drug' are as much legal, social and moral as they are psychological or biological. When you read about the footballer's 'drugs', you surely thought of heroin, cocaine or cannabis rather than tobacco or alcohol. The common expression 'drugs and alcohol' suggests that alcohol is not a drug. Yet it shows clear features in common with 'drugs', such as powerful mind-altering effects and a potential for addiction.

2   Some substances that are taken for their psychological effects are addictive whereas others are not. Some are normally discussed in the context of the social problems that they produce, associated with addiction. Are all drugs addictive? Certainly some, such as heroin, can be and they make the headlines. Nicotine is addictive but is perfectly legal and only rarely associated with crime, except smuggling.

3   Can you be addicted to something that is not a chemical? Since gambling and Internet sex can take control of a person's life and lead to ruin, we might include them under this heading. The challenge is to find features of addiction that are common across chemically related and non-chemically related activities.

4   Lots of people take ecstasy and magic mushrooms for their strong mind-altering effects. In the swinging 1960s, LSD was popular. Reports of addiction are extremely rare. So, there can be mind-altering drugs that have little or no potential to induce compulsive behaviour.

5   Some addictive substances are associated with serious crime and social disruption, whereas others are not. For some individuals, casual 'social use' of drugs is possible, whereas, for others, this switches to compulsive use. However, addiction is not intrinsic to the substance but is a complex property of the chemical and social context. Most of us drink socially but rather few become alcoholic. Some people manage to use 'hard drugs' only occasionally, e.g. the weekend (yuppie) cocaine user. What conditions tip only some individuals into a pattern of compulsive use?

6   One feature that seems to cover all addiction is the notion of *conflict*. The pop-singer highlights the conflict involved with the compulsive use of alcohol. A person can have clear conscious intentions to resist but finds him/herself pulled in the opposite direction. Someone engages in an activity to excess even though it brings serious problems, such as loss of job, home, family and health. The person might acknowledge this and wish to resist but the behaviour has become compulsive.

7   Certain drugs are associated with an aversive effect when they are no longer taken, termed **withdrawal**, the symptoms being **withdrawal symptoms**. The pop-singer was suffering from the pain of withdrawal.

The word 'drug' covers many substances taken, on the one hand, to counter and avoid disease, depressed mood or pain and, on the other, for a 'euphoric high' or spiritual enlightenment. This chapter is concerned with a particular group of **psychoactive drugs** taken to alter mood and cognition. It looks at their effects on the CNS and behaviour and the reasons people take them. Mood-altering drugs are not a heterogeneous class. They have different effects and people differ in their motivation to take them. However, there are some common features in the effects of a number of drugs (e.g. heroin, alcohol, caffeine, nicotine).

In each case, the drug can come to exert a strong motivational pull on the user, even though he or she acknowledges harmful effects. Drugs such as heroin, cocaine, alcohol and nicotine are taken for their rapid mood-altering properties. The enormous strength of motivation associated with taking some, e.g. heroin, is shown by the fact that people pay large sums and risk disease, loss of family, violence and death to obtain them.

Insight into drug-taking comes from at least three sources:

1   Behaviour of various species.

2   Subjective reports by humans.

3   Looking at the brains of humans and non-humans.

Biologically orientated research is directed to the neural basis of drug action, i.e. linking neurobiology to behavioural and experiential evidence. This involves trying to identify brain systems that have the following properties:

1   Their activity reflects motivation, is affected by conditional stimuli and is changed by the arrival of a drug.

2   The brain systems change with the development of drug-taking, e.g. a switch to compulsive use.

3   Links between these regions and both sensory input and motor output can be identified.

4   They can be related to conventional motivation, such as feeding and sex.

Although, to understand drug effects, the drug's chemical properties are crucial, these properties cannot alone explain drug-taking behaviour (Peele, 1985). Environmental and personality factors are also involved. So, biological insight needs to interface with an understanding of social determinants. Explanations should be compatible with the vastly different levels of drug-taking that appear when comparing individuals or cultures or a given individual over the 'ups-and-downs' of life (Peele and Alexander, 1985).

Humans provide subjective insight into the affective and cognitive events associated with seeking and taking drugs and withdrawal. Investigators relate these to psychological theory, but urge caution in the interpretation of subjective evidence. Verbal reports give unique insight into mood and the thoughts that occupy consciousness but, as discussed later, they might not always provide an infallible guide to the causes of behaviour (Robinson and Berridge, 1993).

Of course, evolution did not produce special processes dedicated to drug-taking. Drug-taking is best understood in a context of conventional adaptive behaviour with which it shares properties, such as sex, feeding and exploration. Drugs motivate in a way that has similarities with conventional rewards, e.g. pressing levers to obtain the reward of either food or injections of heroin intravenously (Chapter 15, 'Motivation'). Drugs exploit ('hijack') conventional motivational processes (e.g. mesolimbic dopamine system).

The following section looks at some characteristics of drug taking.

Section summary

1 A number of psychoactive substances strongly attract people, associated with the risk of addiction.

2 Other psychoactive substances have a low addiction potential.

3 Some activities that are not associated with taking chemicals into the body also have the potential to develop addiction.

4 Addiction is characterized by compulsion even in the face of serious harm done by the activity.

Test your knowledge

(Answer on page 465)

18.1 Which of the following has a low addiction potential? (i) Nicotine, (ii) heroin, (iii) LSD.

Characteristics of drug-taking

This section looks at some of the properties of human drug-taking and the use of animal models to explain it. The motivation to take drugs is a complex function of the chemical properties of the drug as well as environmental factors, such as the location, the presence of other individuals and cues associated with drug-taking. Motivation depends also upon a range of cognitive and emotional factors such as self-image and mood. Non-humans can provide models of some features of drug-taking but these features need to be considered in terms of some peculiarly human brain and behaviour.

The link to natural neurochemicals

By interacting with receptors on neurons, psychoactive drugs have psychological effects. Some drugs, such as the opiates, are chemically very similar to substances that the body produces naturally ('opioids'). These natural substances play a role in emotions, as in social bonding and distress calls (Chapter 12, 'Emotion', and Chapter 15) and in the inhibition of pain (Chapter 14, 'Pain'). The body also contains its own source of cannabis-like chemicals (Chapter 14). This suggests that externally obtained chemicals influence those motivational and emotional processes that employ the natural equivalent. An understanding of the role of the natural chemicals (e.g. in social bonding) could provide valuable insight into why people are motivated to supplement them from outside, e.g. to reduce loneliness or alienation. The natural chemicals are evolutionarily old and this encourages the search for general principles applicable across species.

Withdrawal effects

Observable symptoms

In both humans and rats, if taking a drug such as heroin or alcohol is discontinued, observable withdrawal symptoms can occur (Wise, 1988). In humans, for opiates, these include aversive bodily signs, such as cramps, convulsions, sweating and a 'flu-like' condition (Koob, 1999). Rats shake their bodies (termed 'wet-dog shakes'), similar to a dog after it has got wet. Such withdrawal symptoms become paired with environmental cues and there can be 'conditional withdrawal symptoms', triggered by conditional stimuli paired with earlier withdrawal (Wikler, 1965). Withdrawal symptoms can also be triggered under normal conditions by injecting an opiate antagonist such as naloxone. Presumably this is due to blocking an endogenous opioid system and hence tilting the affect process in a negative direction.

An animal model of withdrawal from cocaine exists (Mutschler and Miczek, 1998): rats in withdrawal have elevated startle reflexes and a higher rate of ultrasonic vocalizations, both indices of negative affect (Chapter 12). In a **discrimination test** one can, in effect, ask the rat what the state feels like. For example, it can be rewarded with food for turning to the left when in drug withdrawal but to the right when not in withdrawal. Other states can be induced to see whether they are perceived as similar to withdrawal. Rats generalize between cocaine withdrawal and the state induced by the anxiogenic (anxiety-inducing) drug pentylenetetrazol (PTZ), i.e. they are perceived as similar.

Withdrawal symptoms are different according to the drug in question but what they all share is a state of negative affect (Baker *et al.*, 2004).

Unobserved signs

Psychologists cannot decide whether positive or negative affect is the most important for explaining the compulsive feature of drug-taking. It might well be naive to try to divide causes too neatly. However, negative affect is not necessarily

What is the role of context in drug-seeking and the effects of drugs? *Source*: Janine Wiedel Photolibrary/Alamy.

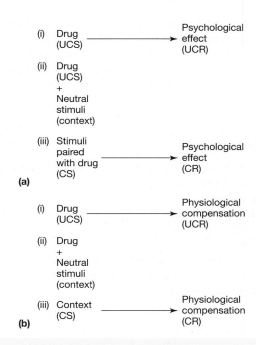

Figure 18.1 Conditioning of drug effects: (a) the motivational role, (b) role in compensation. (i) The unconditional role of a UCS triggering a UCR, (ii) pairing of drug-taking (UCS) with neutral stimuli and (iii) neutral stimuli become conditional stimuli (CS) having a capacity of their own (CR).

always associated with observable signs of withdrawal (Baker *et al.*, 2004). On being without a drug, e.g. cocaine, there can be an aversive state reported without any external signs of withdrawal (Koob, 1999). Agony can be a private thing. In rats and humans, withdrawal signs are partly dependent upon social context (Alexander *et al.*, 1985). Withdrawal will be discussed again shortly in the context of addiction.

In any actions that are motivated to obtain drugs, the principles of conditioning are central, as described in the next two sections.

Classical conditioning

Classical conditioning plays an important role in various stages of drug-taking. See Figure 18.1.

Motivational effects

One effect of classical conditioning is to increase the motivation associated with drug-seeking and taking (Stewart *et al.*, 1984). See Figure 18.1(a). Let us assume that drugs are unconditional stimuli that elicit unconditional effects on the body. If neutral stimuli in the environment are repeatedly paired with drug-taking, they become conditional stimuli (CSs). For example, a syringe is a neutral stimulus prior to it being used to inject drugs. After this, it takes on new motivational properties: the sight of a syringe can come to evoke wanting a drug. Similarly, an open packet of cigarettes and lighter are CSs associated with nicotine (Thewissen *et al.*, 2005). The term 'needle freak' refers to the ability of heroin addicts to experience something similar to the effect of a drug simply by going through the rituals of injection of a neutral substance.

By classical conditioning, a location associated with a drug can acquire incentive motivational properties (Chapter 15). For example, a rat prefers the side of a T-maze in which it received an injection of drug, a conditioned place

preference (Bozarth, 1987). Given that classical conditioning underlies drug seeking and craving, it is logical to suppose that extinction procedures ('exposure') should be a therapeutic tool in combating drug-taking. Alas, exposure to drug-related cues in the absence of the drug has disappointing results (Marissen *et al.*, 2005).

Homeostatic reactions

Apart from psychoactive effects, drugs have other effects on the body. For example, heroin has effects on respiration. These are a disturbance to homeostasis and they trigger physiological counter-measures by the body. In this context, the drug is the unconditional stimulus (UCS) that triggers physiological compensation (UCR). Such counter-measures also occur within the addict's normal environment, which contains cues that can be conditioned, e.g. a particular room, friends and the sight of the syringe. Such conditional cues in the environment (CS) come to trigger some compensation (CR). See Figure 18.1(b).

Suppose that a user has a history of taking a drug in a particular context. Then, on one occasion, the drug is taken in a novel environment, not containing the familiar CSs. In the absence of the CR component of compensation, the counter-reaction would be expected to be weaker. Addicts suffering or dying from an overdose commonly do so when injecting in an unfamiliar environment (Siegel, 1984). In fact, in purely chemical terms, the size of their dose might not appear excessive. However, in the absence of conditional counter-measures, the dose is, in effect, larger.

Instrumental conditioning

Introduction

In terms of instrumental conditioning, questions on drug-taking are framed around principles of reward and aversion, positive and negative reinforcement. Placed in an operant situation, animals can be persuaded to take drugs such as heroin by infusion through a cannula (Stewart *et al.*, 1984). It appears that different brain regions mediate the positive reinforcement (e.g. gain of pleasure) and negative reinforcement (e.g. loss of pain) aspects of drug-taking (Bechara *et al.*, 1998; Wise, 1988).

Negative reinforcement

Animals can be motivated to seek drugs because of a reduction that they cause in an aversive condition. Even though explicit physiological signs of withdrawal might not be evident, there can still be a CNS state of negative affect, the reduction of which by taking the drug constitutes negative reinforcement (Baker *et al.*, 2004). One might be able to infer an aversive state only from an animal's avoidance of external stimuli associated with being in the state. Soon after exposure to opiates, rats show avoidance of cues associated with their absence even though there are no observable physiological signs of withdrawal. Cocaine and amphetamine are not associated with aversive signs outside the nervous system but can be negatively reinforcing in alleviating a 'psychological distress syndrome' (see Robinson and Berridge, 1993).

The periaqueductal grey (Chapter 5, 'The brain') appears to be the site of negative reinforcement (Wise, 1988). Drugs that target receptors in this region seem to lower an aversive effect.

Animals seem to behave so as to maintain the level of natural opioids within limits. Isolated rats take more drugs than socially housed rats (Alexander *et al.*, 1985; Wolffgramm and Heyne, 1991). In laboratory rats, there may be something equivalent to a permanent withdrawal effect as a result of chronic low levels of endogenous opioids. This offers parallels with the suggestion that humans take drugs as self-medication for social alienation or other forms of psychological distress (Markou *et al.*, 1998). A negative mental state can be associated with cognitions about self-image and worthlessness (Peele, 1985). Cocaine use in humans tends to increase at times of perceived negative self-image (Singer, 1993).

Positive reinforcement

The *positive effect* of drugs refers to reward that can be induced even in the absence of a negative state. Its physical base is associated with the dopamine (DA) pathways ascending from the ventral tegmental area (Chapter 15) (Wise, 1988). In these terms, drugs form positive incentives to be pursued like sex or the taste of food (Robinson and Berridge, 1993; Stewart *et al.*, 1984). Activity at certain nuclei would tend to be rewarding in that it would move the animal to seek and 'consume' drugs. Rats can learn an operant task for drug reward, e.g. for microinjections into selected brain regions, even in the absence of any indices of withdrawal (Stewart *et al.*, 1984). Similarly, it seems that removal of withdrawal symptoms cannot explain how humans first move in a direction of addiction. Heroin addicts commonly crave drugs when in the presence of drug-related cues.

In both humans and rats, a trigger for drug-seeking is presentation of small amounts of drug or cues associated with it (Shaham and Stewart, 1995). For example, suppose a rat has learned an operant for intravenous drug reward but this has been extinguished by omission of drug. A small portion of drug is then injected 'free'. This is a cue to trigger re-arousal of the operant task. An arbitrary cue that had been paired with drug-delivery can maintain drug-seeking even in the absence of drug (Falk, 1994).

The factors of (1) reward and positive reinforcement and (2) aversion and negative reinforcement cannot always be distinguished absolutely. A consensus view appears to be that, in a given individual, both types of processes can play a part in drug-taking with the relative weight shifting with circumstances (Bechara *et al.*, 1998; Koob, 1999; Wise, 1988).

Craving

As an example of subjective evidence, the term 'craving' (Chapter 16, 'Feeding and drinking') describes an urge to take a drug and mental occupation with obtaining it (Franken, 2003; Markou *et al.*, 1993). Craving is associated with limbic system activation (Chapter 12; Childress *et al.*, 1999). Similarly, humans also report cravings for particular foods (Kassel and Shiffman, 1992). As a subjective state made available by verbal report, craving is a peculiarly human phenomenon. However, features of human craving can be modelled by non-humans (Chapter 15), e.g. lever-pressing by rats on extinction conditions in a task previously reinforced with drug. In humans, a lowering of the intensity of cocaine craving is caused by the agent desmethylimipramine. In rats, this also lowers responding in extinction, i.e. they tend to stop lever-pressing sooner (Fuchs *et al.*, 1998).

Defining addiction

Addiction refers to a person's abandonment to a pursuit, involving the neglect of other things and compromising the quality of life. After discontinuation of the addictive activity for short or long periods, there is a tendency to return to it ('relapse') (Peele and Degrandpre, 1998). There are a number of criteria that are employed to justify the term 'addiction' but not universal agreement on how many of these need to be present.

Link with withdrawal

To some experts, withdrawal symptoms offer a possible objective index of addiction (discussed by Wise, 1987). Their *presence* is certainly a useful pointer. However, some people described as addicted do not show physiological signs of withdrawal. It was once argued that cocaine is not addictive since there is not a pattern of associated ('extraneural') physiological withdrawal symptoms. However, this now seems an irrational criterion given the craving associated with the drug and its social and crime-related implications (Stolerman and Jarvis, 1995; Volkow *et al.*, 1997).

Curing withdrawal symptoms often has only a minimal effect in treating addiction (Wise, 1988). Subjective withdrawal symptoms do not correlate well with physiological signs of withdrawal (Henningfield *et al.*, 1987; Peele, 1985).

Other indices and criteria

Addiction is associated with craving (see earlier). It is also associated with **tolerance**, meaning that increasing amounts of drug need to be taken to obtain a given effect.

These days, 'addiction' is often used in non-chemical contexts, e.g. 'love addiction'. The broad usage points to important common features between drug and non-drug objects (Koob, 1999). However, it also raises a dilemma. If everything from praying and watching football to intravenous heroin use has the potential to be 'addictive', the word might appear to be devalued. Alternatively, are there qualitatively different types of addiction? One way round this is to employ 'addiction' only where there are elements of danger, conflict and disruption to life involved.

A view that conforms to neuroscience and psychology is that all addictions have physical aspects and psychological aspects, as two sides of the same coin. That is to say, the psychological aspects are rooted in the brain. Thus, drugs and non-drug-related addictive behaviour would represent two different routes to tap a similar or identical underlying process. The motivation to take drugs might, like love, be based upon positive incentive motivational properties with the possibility of aversive effects of loss and abstinence.

Contextual factors

Contextual factors are important in drug-taking. For example, in humans, substances such as nicotine and caffeine

Rats housed in a rich physical and social context. Why are researchers interested in the effect of environmental enrichment on the tendency to drug-taking?

Source: courtesy of Bruce Alexander.

presumably owe their high intake as much to their legality, relatively low cost, ready availability and compatibility with performing other tasks as to any intrinsic chemical properties.

This section looks at two examples of contextual factors.

The social dimension

A rat or non-human primate pressing a lever in a Skinner box might seem to exemplify the pure addictive potential of a drug, uncomplicated by cognition, social interaction and culture. However, experiments in which animals have worked for a drug at a very high rate (a) make the drug readily available by intravenous infusion for minimal effort, (b) have not allowed alternative sources of reward and (c) involve a highly restrained physical context (Peele and Degrandpre, 1998). If availability is made more difficult, intake is lower.

Alexander *et al.* (1985) measured the oral intake of morphine solution by rats in a large social environment. Intake was only one-eighth that of isolated rats. Alexander and Hadaway (1982, p. 371) remark: 'The restrictive, isolated conditions of standard laboratory housing may be inherently stressful to mobile, social animals like rats and monkeys, and their self-administration of heroin could simply provide relief'. The presence of alternative sources of reward (e.g. social) offers effective competition to drug-taking in rats and humans (Peele, 1985).

In humans and non-humans, Peele and Degrandpre (1998) see a consistent pattern: cocaine has an addictive potential that is a function of both the chemical itself and the social context. Many humans can be described as 'occasional users', showing controlled use, e.g. monthly. Considerations of family and professional life are taken into account and restrain intake. Most American servicemen who employed opiates in Vietnam did not take their problem back to the United States with them at the end of the war (Robins *et al.*, 1975). Patients who self-administer narcotics for pain relief do not normally crave drugs when outside the clinical context (Chapter 14).

The dimension of control

The effects of a drug depend in part upon the nature of the *control* that the user is able to exert, which seems to be important for the addictive potential.

A rat pressing a lever in a Skinner box for drug reward is performing a particular behaviour, within a particular environment, under its own control. Effects of drugs taken under the animal's own control and their withdrawal effects are stronger than those experienced by a passive paired ('yoked') control receiving the same drug (MacRae and Siegel, 1997).

In humans, taking a drug involves performance of a procedure, a mechanical act or 'ritual', in a context of environmental and social cues. Changing the ability to control a situation can change the effect of the drug. If drugs are administered outside the control of the individual, they are perceived as being not so hedonically potent (Alexander and Hadaway, 1982). The particular route of administration can be important to some users (Peele, 1985). Control is qualified by history, context and goal.

The importance of control was emphasized in Chapter 13, 'Stress and coping', and it may be that drugs tap into this fundamental process (cf. Peele, 1985).

Section summary

1 Some psychoactive drugs such as the opiates are very similar to natural neurochemicals.

2 Classical conditioning plays a role in drug-seeking and the effects of drugs.

3 Cessation of drug-taking can be associated with objective measures of withdrawal. Negative affect is a less obvious effect.

4 The reinforcement for drug-taking appears to be both positive and negative.

5 Human craving can be modelled by animals placed on extinction conditions.

6 Context plays a crucial role in drug-seeking.

Test your knowledge

(Answer on page 465)

18.2 Consider the phenomenon termed 'needle freak' and suppose that an addict is given a neutral substance, thinking that it is heroin. Using the terminology of classical conditioning, how would you describe (i) the act of injection and (ii) the effect of the injection?

Drugs and drug-taking

This section looks at some of the activities that are related to drugs and addiction. It considers addictive drugs and also some drugs with little addictive potential.

Amphetamine and cocaine

The motivational potency of amphetamine and cocaine appears to depend mainly upon their ability to increase levels of dopamine (DA) at dopaminergic synapses (Pierce and Kalivas, 1997; Wang and McGinty, 1999). Cocaine blocks DA reuptake (Chapter 4, 'The cells of the nervous system'). Amphetamine both blocks reuptake and triggers the release of DA into the synapse (Grace, 2001; Wise, 1988).

Amphetamine

In rats, microinjections of amphetamine into the nucleus accumbens (N.acc.) are rewarding in designs employing place preference and self-infusion by lever-pressing (Bardo, 1998). See Figure 18.2.

On the positive side, human amphetamine users report increased attention and energy and changes in cognition (Ellinwood, 1967, 1968; Klee and Morris, 1997). An improvement in self-image is one of the first effects. Ordinary events take a heightened significance and the universe appears to 'make sense'. The drug gives novelty to an otherwise dull world, suggesting that it taps into an exploration process. Objects can (Ellinwood, 1968, p. 48): 'stimulate curiosity and a search for new categories and significance, or attempts to expand, change and distort the categories or unknown object for mutual reconciliation'. Users sometimes engage in mechanical manipulation of objects, e.g. repeated assembly and taking apart (Ellinwood and Kilbey, 1975). In distorting cognition, amphetamine has features in common with the hallucinogens (see later). On the negative side, humans can experience paranoia-inducing cognitive changes in their interpretation of the world.

Cocaine

See Figure 18.3. The N.acc. might be involved in cocaine reward (Maldonado *et al.*, 1993). However, evidence suggests that the primary site of action is outside the N.acc. For example, a conditioned place preference test is relatively insensitive to manipulation of the level of dopamine in the N.acc. (Baker *et al.*, 1996). Based on microinjection studies and conditioned place preference tests, a site of cocaine's action appears to be the DA projections to the prefrontal cortex (Bardo, 1998). However, its effect on behaviour seems to depend on connections from this region to the N.acc. (a glutamate-mediated link is shown). Why there is a difference in target neurons between amphetamine and cocaine is not clear.

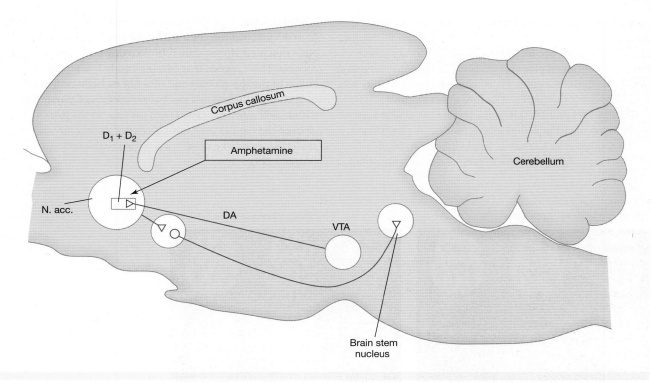

Figure 18.2 Suggested reward site of amphetamine in the rat brain. D_1 and D_2 are dopamine receptor subtypes.
Source: adapted from Bardo (1998, Fig. 1, p. 57).

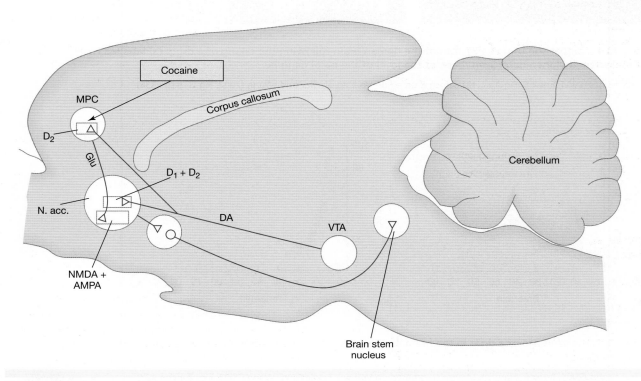

Figure 18.3 Suggested reward pathways of cocaine in the rat brain. Glu, glutamate; MPC, medial prefrontal cortex; NMDA, glutamate *N*-methyl-D-aspartate receptors.   *Source*: Bardo (1998, Fig. 2, p. 58).

In intravenous self-administration, DA antagonists sometimes increase the intake of cocaine and amphetamine, i.e. compensation occurs (Bardo, 1998). DA antagonists block a conditioned place preference. For humans, the power of cocaine to induce euphoria is reduced when DA receptors are blocked (Gunne *et al.*, 1972; Jönsson *et al.*, 1971).

Figures 18.4 and 18.5 show the level of cocaine in the brain following its injection intravenously. By comparison, the level of another substance, methylphenidate, is also shown. Like cocaine, this blocks reuptake of dopamine but it is less addictive. The subjective feeling of 'high' is also shown. In each case, you can see a sharp rise and fall of the 'high'. Note that methylphenidate is broken down more slowly than cocaine. This suggests that cocaine's addictive potency is linked to the sharp onset and offset of its biological effect.

Although there is not an obvious pattern of physiological withdrawal signs associated with cocaine, in the drug's absence the regular user can experience depression and anxiety (termed 'the crash'), associated with craving (Koob, 1999).

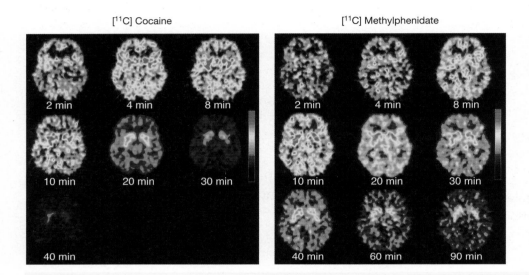

Figure 18.4 Comparison using a PET scan of the human brain following the taking of a drug: (a) labelled cocaine and (b) labelled methylphenidate. Scan taken at the level of the basal ganglia.

Source: Toates (2004, Book 6, Figure 1.13), which is based on Volkow, Fowler and Wang (2002, Fig. 1, page 356).

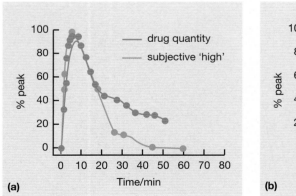
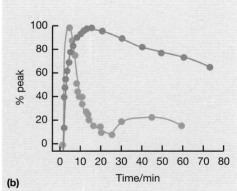

Figure 18.5 The presence of a drug in the brain and the subjective 'high' experienced by the user: (a) cocaine, (b) methylphenidate.

Source: Toates (2004, Book 6, Figure 1.14), which is based on Volkow, Fowler and Wang (2002, Fig. 2, page 357).

A personal angle

Sigmund Freud

Early in his career, Freud's interest was attracted to cocaine (Clark, 1980). Dr Theodor Aschenbrandt had experimented on cocaine's effects on weary Bavarian soldiers, whose motivation and attention were revived. Freud tried the drug and reported: 'A few minutes after taking the cocaine one suddenly feels light and exhilarated' and he wrote to his wife in 1884: 'In my last severe depression I took coca again and a small dose lifted me to the heights in a wonderful fashion. I am just now busy collecting the literature for a song of praise to this magical substance' (Clark, 1980, p. 59).

Freud was criticized for his liberal attitudes but responded that he had never advocated injection, merely ingestion. That Freud did not develop an addiction to cocaine in spite of taking it for 10 years (Sulloway, 1979) exemplifies that addiction depends on the interaction of the drug with the whole person and environment. However, Freud was wrong to assume that he could harmlessly wean an addicted friend off morphine with the help of cocaine. One might expect cross-sensitization and indeed the friend became a cocaine addict (Gay, 1988).

Opiates

Heroin is a member of the class of drug termed opiates, which includes morphine, and which target opioid receptors. Heroin addicts are commonly characterized by isolation, a negative self-image and feelings of depression and the futility of life (Tokar *et al.*, 1975). To addicts, opiates give happiness, an increased sense of detachment and a reduced sense of awareness. One addict reported that 'heroin does something for a sick ego'. The reports of opiate addicts suggest that drugs create a euphoria that is tied to altered perceptions of self and the world.

Opiates have both rewarding and aversion-removing effects. Figure 18.6 shows some brain sites of opiate reward.

Among other sites of action, it appears that opiates either excite neurons that form excitatory synapses upon DA neurons in the ventral tegmental area (VTA) or they inhibit neurons that inhibit DA neurons (Wise, 1988). In rats, minute local injections of opiates into the VTA are rewarding, an effect that is reduced or eliminated when the DA system is blocked (Wise and Bozarth, 1987). Also, microinjections of opiates in the N.acc. are rewarding (Bardo, 1998).

Evidence points to the rewarding effect of opiates, i.e. incentive motivational processes, being sufficient to motivate opiate intake (Wise, 1988). In rats, the first injection has some rewarding effect, when by definition there can be no withdrawal effect, at least as defined in terms of exogenous drug. Thus, if a naive rat is exposed to a particular environment during which it experiences a single morphine

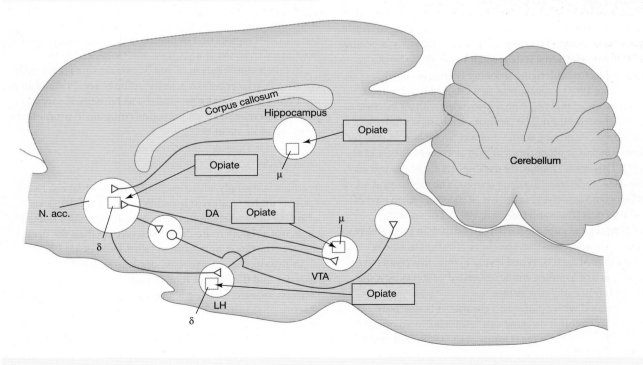

Figure 18.6 Opiate sites of reward action in the rat brain. LH, lateral hypothalamus; δ, delta opiate receptor; μ, mu opiate receptor. *Source*: Bardo (1998, Fig. 3, p. 59).

injection, it will subsequently show a preference for being in that environment (Wise and Bozarth, 1987). However, we cannot ignore the suggestion that laboratory rats are permanently in a state similar to mild drug-withdrawal.

The periaqueductal grey (PAG) (Chapter 12) appears to be a principal CNS site of aversion alleviation by opiates (Wise, 1988). Dependent rats, but not non-dependent ones, learn to press for infusion into the PAG (Wise and Bozarth, 1987). If specifically this region is first targeted with opiates and then an opiate antagonist is given, withdrawal symptoms are seen.

There are various bodily manifestations of opiate withdrawal, e.g. rats exhibit 'wet-dog shakes'. Also opiates might exert an aversion-alleviation effect outside the CNS, by, for example, removing gastrointestinal cramps (Wise, 1988). However, as noted earlier, there do not need to be obvious physical signs of withdrawal for us to suppose that an opiate-sensitive negative affective state exists.

Nicotine

Of all addictive substances, nicotine would probably rank worldwide as that causing the most harm to its users (Pomerleau and Pomerleau, 1984). However, it was only in the mid-1990s, with lawsuits against tobacco companies, that its addictive potential was fully recognized. By comparison with opiates and cocaine, the subjective effects of cigarettes are more subtle, diffuse and hard to define.

Motivational mechanisms

There are nicotine withdrawal symptoms, including irritability and depressed mood (Gilbert et al., 1997). However, a positive incentive-motivational state is often suggested to be the principal factor underlying smoking (Pomerleau and Pomerleau, 1984), especially in first establishing the habit. Smokers report that nicotine is associated with an increase in mental concentration. The motivational basis underlying a given smoker can vary, sometimes a cigarette being taken for relaxation and at other times to gain alertness (Gilbert et al., 1997). This again emphasizes the importance of context and control in understanding drug actions. The mechanical act of smoking and associated taste (e.g. of nicotine) form part of the attraction (Rose and Corrigal, 1997). For smokers, smoking-related cues are particularly strong in their ability to capture attention and increase the motivation to smoke (Hogarth et al., 2003). When trying to quit, this points to the importance of avoiding smoking-related contexts, as is the case with other addictive drugs.

Compared with opiates and cocaine, it is relatively difficult to establish nicotine as a reinforcer in an operant situation in non-humans (Donny et al., 1998; Stolerman and Jarvis, 1995). Place preference conditioning is similarly more difficult (Rose and Corrigal, 1997). The potent reinforcement potential in humans might, in addition to cross-species processes, depend upon the mechanical act of smoking (e.g. holding and puffing) and species-specific effects on cognitive processing. In rats, it is easier to obtain operant behaviour for nicotine (as for a variety of drugs) if the reward is associated with arbitrary extrinsic (i.e. 'contextual') cues such as a light or sound. Once established, omission of such a cue can lower responding.

Neurochemistry

The motivational effects of nicotine are not surprising when we consider its profile of absorption. After inhaling, nicotine is taken into the blood and appears in the brain very rapidly. Within as little as seven seconds of puffing, 25% of inhaled nicotine has already crossed the blood–brain barrier (Pomerleau and Pomerleau, 1984). Nicotine leaves the brain rapidly after the cigarette has been smoked. These dynamics provide optimal conditions to associate the neurochemical changes with the sight of the cigarette, the action of smoking and the environmental context (i.e. classical conditioning). To make matters worse, nicotine is a special drug in combining universal availability and legality with a capacity to facilitate work performance!

Nicotine's motivational effects seem to depend upon actions on a variety of neurochemical systems, e.g. cholinergic, serotonergic and opioidergic, and hormonal systems (Dani and Heinemann, 1996; Koob, 1999). These various neurochemical systems come together in influencing the mesolimbic dopaminergic pathway (Chiamulera, 2005). Nicotine shares the property of dopaminergic (DA) activation with other addictive drugs. Nicotine activates cholinergic (nicotinic) receptors on DA neurons, e.g. those that project from the VTA to the N.acc. (Rose and Corrigal, 1997).

In rats, a combination of stress and nicotine is especially effective in triggering DA activity in the N.acc. (Takahashi et al., 1998). If this can be generalized to humans, it suggests a process whereby stress and nicotine combine to promote the intake of more nicotine.

Addictive potential

Nicotine is strongly addictive (Stolerman and Jarvis, 1995). Patients under treatment for addiction to hard drugs and who also smoked cigarettes were questioned. They ranked cigarettes as being more difficult to give up than the drug that was the target of treatment (Kozlowski et al., 1989).

In Britain, the average male smoker smokes 17 cigarettes each day and the average female smoker 14 per day. Light smokers are rare. Craving is a common phenomenon in the absence of a cigarette and smokers generally rate their chances of giving up as low. About 40% of smokers who have suffered a heart attack resume smoking while still in hospital and most do so within 48 h of leaving intensive care. Even surgery for lung cancer fails to deter some 50% of the smokers who undergo the operation.

Alcohol

Acting on various neurotransmitters, alcohol has effects such as to lower anxiety, by which it can mediate negative reinforcement, and to induce mild euphoria (Chick and Erickson, 1996; Koob, 1999). Alcohol triggers activity in the body's natural opioid system, which might, in turn, promote craving for more (Mercer and Holder, 1997). Craving can be particularly exacerbated within certain external contexts (e.g. being in a bar) or internal contexts (e.g. stress or depression). The alcohol withdrawal effect has similarities with that of opioids and might also involve the PAG (Wise, 1988). Opiate agonists tend to increase alcohol consumption and antagonists tend to decrease it (Davidson and Amit, 1997). Wand *et al.* (1998) suggest that differences between individuals in tendency to alcoholism are mediated via different levels of endogenous opioid activity. Those prone to alcoholism appear to have an intrinsically low level of opioid activity.

Alcohol normally has relatively little reinforcement value to rats. However, strains of alcohol-preferring rats can be selectively bred (McBride and Li, 1998).

Marijuana

Marijuana has been used for more than 4000 years for therapeutic (Chapter 14) and recreational reasons (Stahl, 1998). The psychoactive ingredient of marijuana is delta-9-tetrahydrocannabinol (THC). The brain manufactures its own supply of a marijuana-like substance, termed anandamide, and contains cannabinoid (CB) receptors. A subtype, the CB1 receptor, is believed to mediate the rewarding effects of cannabinoid substances. Marijuana appears to act by boosting mesolimbic DA transmission and altering serotonergic neurotransmission (Gessa *et al.*, 1998).

There is a relatively slight withdrawal effect after discontinuation of marijuana. This may be explicable by the fact that there is not such a sharp onset–offset profile of effect as with other drugs; after appearing in the blood, cannabinoids are stored in body fats and then slowly released (Stahl, 1998) (which explains why some people, who are afraid of being tested, take harder drugs, since their time-frame of detection is shorter). If there is receptor adaptation during the acute phase, the 'endogenous' source of drug from body fat might cushion the system against withdrawal effects for the time that it takes the receptor state to recover. Marijuana illustrates the earlier point about context-dependency of drug effects. People high in anxiety can find that this is increased by the drug (Szuster *et al.*, 1988).

Caffeine

Regular users of relatively large amounts of caffeine (in the form of tea or coffee) report a withdrawal effect (e.g. headaches, sleepiness, irritability) when intake ceases (Griffiths and Woodson, 1988). A double-blind placebo-controlled study demonstrated that the effects are due to loss of the caffeine content of the beverage *per se* (Phillips-Bute and Lane, 1998). Caffeine does not reliably cause hedonic feelings in humans. Rather, it often induces anxiety. The fact that it is the world's most widely used psychoactive drug points to the inadequacy of hedonic explanations of drug-taking and suggests that wanting relates in no simple way to liking (Chapter 15).

How does caffeine act? There are receptors in the CNS to the natural substance adenosine. When these are occupied by adenosine, this inhibits the activity of the neurons bearing these receptors. Dopaminergic neurons are among those having this type of receptor on their surface. Caffeine is similar to adenosine but, by occupying its receptors, caffeine prevents the action of adenosine. Hence, a source of inhibition on neurons involved in wanting and reward is lowered.

Hallucinogens

The term **hallucinogen** refers to a class of drug for which the primary action is to change sensory perception (Aghajanian, 1994; Delgado and Moreno, 1998). It includes lysergic acid diethylamide (LSD), mescaline (from a type of cactus) and psilocybin (from a type of mushroom) and their effect in altering cognition is termed 'psychedelic' (Stahl, 1996). The person taking such a 'trip' might feel a sense of union with the universe or with God. Disorientation and panic are termed a 'bad trip', a state that can be characterized by paranoia and delusions.

It is difficult if not impossible to teach animals an operant task for hallucinogens and they have a low addictive potential in humans (Griffiths *et al.*, 1979). One special case is that monkeys in sensory isolation sometimes learn an operant task for them (Siegel and Jarvick, 1980). Monkeys exhibit orientation, tracking and startle responses, as if the drug is simulating external sensory stimulation. This might have features in common with animals kept in monotonous conditions working for a change in sensory stimulation (Chapter 15).

A common property of the substances just named is that their hallucinogenic potency is proportional to their ability to inhibit serotonergic neurons by acting at serotonin (5-HT$_2$) receptors (Aghajanian, 1994). In turn, the serotonin effect mediates changes at the locus coeruleus, which has broad noradrenergic projections throughout the brain.

Activity within the locus coeruleus appears to alter processing such that target neurons have a lower level of spontaneous activity and higher response to sensory stimulation. This seems to be the basis of distorted (e.g. heightened) perception and cognition induced by psychedelic drugs.

The doors of perception

In *The Doors of Perception*, the English writer and philosopher Aldous Huxley gives a vivid account of his experiments with mescaline. On the perception of an ordinary shelf of books, he writes (Huxley, 1972, p. 13): 'Like the flowers, they glowed, when I looked at them, with brighter colours, a profounder significance. Red books, like rubies; emerald books; books bound in white jade . . .'.

Not just perception but also priorities change, in that the mescaline user (p. 18): 'finds most of the causes for which, at ordinary times, he was prepared to act and suffer, profoundly uninteresting' and mescaline took Huxley from (p. 27): 'the world of selves, of time, of moral judgements and utilitarian considerations . . .'.

Huxley suggested that the mescaline experience was similar to one small aspect of the cognition of schizophrenics (Chapter 22, 'When things go wrong'). Huxley died on 22 November 1963 (the same day as John F. Kennedy), from cancer; his last moments being spent under the influence of LSD injected by his wife (Huxley, 1969).

Ecstasy

Ecstasy, chemical name 3,4-methylenedioxymethamphetamine (MDMA), became a popular recreational drug only in the late 1980s (Steele *et al.*, 1994). It promotes the release and blocks reuptake of serotonin and dopamine, which mediates psychedelic effects. It is often taken at large social gatherings termed 'raves'. Ecstasy's effects include elevated mood, sensual awareness and attention and a sense of 'awareness with others' (Stahl, 1996). On the negative side, there are reports of increased anxiety, panic attacks and psychosis (Steele *et al.*, 1994), as well as possible damage to the nervous system (McCann *et al.*, 1998).

Similarities and differences among drug-related activities

In spite of diverse effects, a subgroup of psychoactive drugs activate some common neural systems. Activation of dopamine, especially at the N.acc., appears to be a common factor in those that are addictive, e.g. amphetamine, cocaine, nicotine, morphine and alcohol (Everitt *et al.*, 2001). Those that are non-addictive, e.g. hallucinogens, have a primary site of action elsewhere in the CNS.

In humans, there are similarities in the subjective effects of opiates, amphetamines and cocaine. A former cocaine addict can be at risk from relapse by an occasional use of heroin and the heroin addict is at risk from cocaine. In rats, an extinguished heroin habit can be reinstated by a 'free' priming delivery of cocaine and vice versa. This provides some rationale for the demand for total abstention from all drugs that is commonly made on rehabilitation programmes. Wise (1988, p. 125) notes that nicotine and alcohol can activate DA neurons in the VTA:

The possibility that nicotine, alcohol, and even caffeine may activate the same neural circuitry suggests other drug stimuli that may put an ex-addict at risk. Of these, smoking represents a potential stimulant to relapse that may be widely underestimated.

In people with a history of cocaine-taking, nicotine accentuates craving in the presence of cocaine-related cues (Reid *et al.*, 1998).

Even caffeine might not be harmless in this regard. Evidence suggests that it can increase the tendency to take nicotine (Bernstein *et al.*, 2002). There is a possible rat model of this. Figure 18.7 shows the number of responses for intravenous nicotine by rats having available either plain water or water with caffeine added.

1. Amphetamine and cocaine increase levels of synaptic dopamine.

2. Opiates target opioid receptors and interact with dopaminergic neurotransmission. They have reward and aversion-alleviation effects.

3. Nicotine is rapidly absorbed into the bloodstream, enters the brain and affects a number of neurochemical activities, e.g. dopamine.

4. If operant behaviour for self-infusion of nicotine is associated with an arbitrary external cue, it is easier to produce.

5. Alcohol interacts with endogenous opioids.

6. Drugs such as LSD, termed hallucinogens, target serotonin.

(Answer on page 465)

18.3 In the experiment shown in Figure 18.7, what is the point of having two holes and recording nose-pokes in both (one connected to nicotine delivery and the other having no consequence)?

18.1

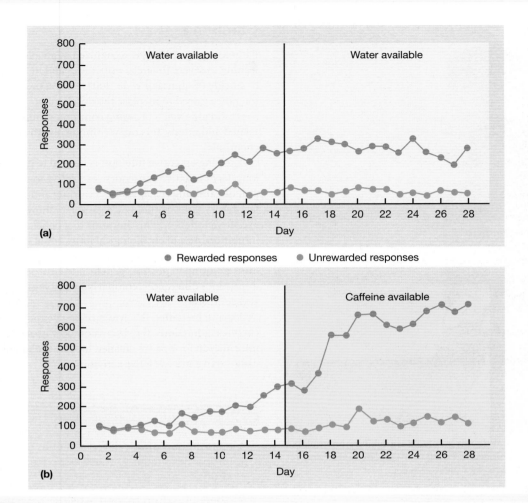

Figure 18.7 Responses rewarded with intravenous nicotine when (a) plain water is available and (b) when caffeine solution is available at day 14. The response was poking the nose into a hole (active). As a control, another hole was present into which a response did not trigger nicotine infusion (passive).

Source: Toates (2004, Figure 1.17) based on Shoaib *et al.* (1999, Fig. 3).

So much for this subgroup of drugs, which have the potential for addiction; let us now consider some non-drug-related activities that have similar properties.

Non-drug-related activities

Introduction

Popular language refers to a number of non-drug-related activities as being similar to drug-taking, including having the potential to become addictive. Does biological psychology offer any insights that would give a basis to such a description? As an example, playing video games can be highly engaging for some individuals. This activity is

associated with activation of brain dopamine in the striatum (Koepp *et al.*, 1998).

Internet addiction

Adapting addiction to the 21st century, Griffiths (1999) identified Internet addiction, according to the core components of addiction. These are (1) salience, domination of thought processes by the target activity, (2) a modification of mood when engaged in the activity, (3) tolerance, increasing amounts of activity are required to achieve the same effect, (4) withdrawal symptoms (mood lowering), (5) conflict, e.g. within the individual and with others over time and money spent, as well as disruption to life, and (6) relapse.

All of the criteria listed can apply to any kind of Internet activity. However, specifically using the Internet to obtain sexual excitement can combine all of these

Some activities that do not involve drug-taking nonetheless show addictive properties. Could there be any underlying similarities? *Source:* Luca DiCecco/Alamy.

features with social disapproval or in some cases strong legal sanctions against the activity (in the case of searching for under-age images). This use of the Internet is a well recognized problem.

Sexual addiction

Use of the term 'sexual addiction' refers to the element of conflict, in addition to excessive sexual activity. The activity can be very costly in money and time and is socially disapproved. Often sexual addiction arises at times of particular stress (Schneider and Weiss, 2001) – stress is known to exacerbate chemical addictions too. Addictive sexual behaviour could then be reinforced by the anxiety reduction associated with engaging in the activity (Leiblum and Rosen, 2000, p. 471). Sometimes addictions coexist. For example, the sex addict often has simultaneously an addiction to alcohol or illicit drugs. Cross-sensitization between activities might be expected.

A favoured treatment for sex addiction is the use of selective serotonin reuptake inhibitors (SSRIs) (Coleman, 2005), suggesting the need for an integrative psychobiological approach to its understanding.

Gambling

Pathological gambling is recognized as an addictive activity, leading to severe financial difficulties and in the worst cases to suicide (Goudriaan *et al.*, 2004). It is associated with tolerance ('need to increase the dose') and craving, suggesting the value of seeing common ground with drug-related addictions. It is often combined with addictions to chemicals.

Exerting executive function is needed to give weight to long-term negative consequences relative to the immediate pull of gambling (Chapter 11, 'Learning and memory'). In laboratory tasks, pathological gamblers show deficits in executive function. This amounts to a deficiency in response inhibition. As a likely biological basis, some evidence points to deficits in functioning of the prefrontal cortex. There are leads pointing to possible genetic and neurochemical (e.g. dopamine) differences, comparing pathological gamblers and controls.

Having presented the evidence on chemical and non-chemical addictions, the discussion now uses this information for a more detailed look at explanations of drug-taking and addictive activities.

Section summary

1 Certain non-drug-related activities exhibit properties similar to those associated with drugs.

2 Some non-drug-related activities have the potential to become addictive.

Test your knowledge

(Answer on page 465)

18.4 If compulsive sexual behaviour is reinforced by anxiety reduction, what adjective qualifies such reinforcement? (i) Positive, (ii) negative.

Trying to explain addiction

After having described the phenomena and some explanatory terms, this section looks in more detail at some theories that attempt to give a broad explanation of drug-taking and addiction. Although the explanations sometimes seem to be in competition, the section will point to where their features can be reconciled.

Two orientations

In the context of opiate drugs, Alexander and Hadaway (1982) proposed a distinction between two explanatory frameworks: the **exposure orientation** and the **adaptive orientation**. According to the exposure orientation, addiction arises simply from exposure to drugs. Drugs irreversibly change the body so that, beyond a threshold, the individual wants and 'needs' more. However, according to the adaptive orientation, drugs are a support, chemotherapy for the mind, which allows the individual to function better at times of psychological need. Some people need such support ('a crutch'). The newly recognized non-chemical addictions such as to sex or the Internet appear also to provide a similar and temporary emotional support.

You may feel that each perspective contains elements of the truth. Also, one could suggest reasons why only some individuals become addicted, such as an intrinsically high sensitivity of incentive motivational processes (Chapter 15).

Affective states

Introduction

Taking drugs such as alcohol, heroin and cocaine has affective ('hedonic') consequences. It is therefore tempting to assume that the strength of motivation to take a drug correlates closely with the subjective euphoria obtained by taking it. Although a positive correlation exists, there is no simple equivalence (Robinson and Berridge, 1993). With repeated drug use, subjectively reported hedonism can decline, whereas craving increases. In some cases, the first encounters with drugs (opiates, alcohol and nicotine) are unpleasant rather than euphoric and yet people are still moved to repeat the experience (Wise and Bozarth, 1987). Paranoia can result from amphetamine use but the habit persists (Ellinwood, 1967).

So, although affect plays an important role, it cannot fully explain the phenomena. Let us turn first to what might be explained by its role.

A model

Figure 18.8 represents positive and negative affective states with mutual inhibition, indicated by negative signs (Solomon and Corbit, 1974). A neutral affective state is the result of a balance between the two. These states depend in part upon stimuli, cognitions and goals, etc. Affect is closely related to cognition, e.g. negative affect exerts a bias towards experiencing negative thoughts and interpretations and triggering memories of negative events (Baker *et al.*, 2004). Negative cognition (e.g. from personal failure) tends to excite negative affect.

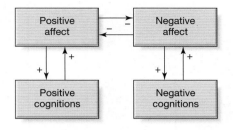

Figure 18.8 Model of affective states.

Given an appropriate social context, after entering the body drugs appear to tilt the balance temporarily in a positive direction. Thus, over a middle range, the distinction between gaining a positive effect and reducing a negative one becomes somewhat academic.

It appears that the normal balance giving life a slightly positive affect (if you are lucky!) is maintained by, among other things, a background level of endogenous opioid activity within the CNS (Skoubis *et al.*, 2005). See Figure 18.9(a). Opioid antagonists block the positive effect of natural opioids and thereby move the balance in a negative direction. This triggers or amplifies signs of social distress (Chapter 12). See Figure 18.9(b). Excessive stimulation in a positive direction by, say, opiate drugs (Figure 18.9(c)) would be followed by some neural adaptation of the system (Christie *et al.*, 1997). Adaptation would tend to tilt net affect in a negative direction by such means as loss of opioid receptors (Figure 18.9(d)). Injection of an opioid antagonist would then shift it still further in a negative direction (Wise, 1988). It appears that an aversive state can arise either as a withdrawal reaction to the absence of the drug or from stress, depression, anxiety and, in addition in humans, personal life crises (Baker *et al.*, 2004; Singer, 1993). Drugs (and possibly some non-drug-based activities) then bring temporary relief.

Negative affect can be (but is not necessarily) associated with physiological signs of withdrawal outside the nervous system (Christie *et al.*, 1997; Koob, 1999). If drugs are readily available, their intake can be motivated by positive incentive processes. After they become unavailable, accompanied in some cases by explicit withdrawal, the control might shift to avoidance of negative affect (Baker *et al.*, 2004).

Automatic and controlled intake

As with other types of behaviour, that associated with drugs reflects processes organized at different levels of the CNS. These range from the controlled conscious choice to seek a drug for its anticipated beneficial effects to automatic responding to drug-related cues (Tiffany, 1990). Presumably, any instance of drug-seeking reflects a balance between these factors. It appears that drug-seeking starts in a conscious

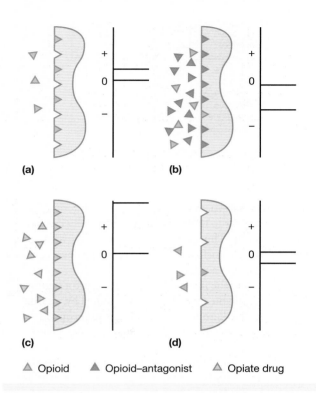

(a) **(b)**

(c) **(d)**

△ Opioid ▲ Opioid–antagonist △ Opiate drug

Figure 18.9 Suggested role of opioids, opioid antagonists and opiates and the associated level of affect. Neural events (left) and level of contribution to affect (graph to right). (a) Basal level in drug-free condition, (b) immediately after injection of opioid antagonist, (c) immediately after injection of opiate drug and (d) period after opiate drug has left the body.

('intentional') mode and then switches to a more automatic mode with experience. The addict becomes increasingly at the mercy of the pull of drug-related stimuli in the environment (Everitt *et al.*, 2001).

There is a rat model of this shift of weight (Vanderschuren and Everitt, 2004). Normally, activities such as feeding are inhibited by cues that signal aversive events. Lever-pressing in a Skinner box drops when such a cue is presented. Rats working for cocaine also exhibit such inhibition *early in their experience*. However, after extensive exposure, they cease to react to such cues and go on lever-pressing regardless. This might model the human addict's indifference to warning signs. Even after extensive exposure, not all rats switch to a compulsive pattern of use in which they are indifferent to such aversive cues (Deroche-Gamonet *et al.*, 2004). This points to individual differences, presumably in the sensitivity of dopaminergic pathways. We can speculate that such differences might also be present comparing individual humans.

An addicted human is commonly in a dilemma: a part of the mind seems to be offering restraint but another part,

which mediates the compulsive pull, seems stronger. Which parts of the brain underlie these different tendencies? As noted, subcortical processes such as the nucleus accumbens and periaqueductal grey appear to be the primary bases of drug-seeking. It is especially the ventromedial prefrontal cortex (VMPFC) that mediates restraint and opposes the pull of lower brain regions. Activity in the VMPFC acts as the neural embodiment of processes termed 'self-directed' and 'willpower' (Bechara, 2005). With the help of this region, representations of harmful future consequences are retrieved as part of working memory and exploited in restraint. Individual differences in susceptibility to addiction could be embodied in different balances between mechanisms underlying impulsive reactivity (e.g. to drug-related cues) and restraint.

Once in the body, a drug itself might change weight between such levels. Consider what happens when, for example, alcohol enters the body. This would tend to lift the restraint that is normally offered on certain alcohol-related behaviour (e.g. seeking yet another drink) by higher-level cognitive controls (Chapter 15). Also drugs such as cocaine can damage the prefrontal cortex. This could thereby chronically weaken the role of restraint on drug-taking (or possibly any associated non-drug-based addictive activity).

Incentive sensitization theory

Introduction

A highly influential theory of drug-addiction with broad application across addictive substances is the **incentive sensitization theory** (Robinson and Berridge, 1993). It is based on three features of addiction: (1) craving, (2) that craving and drug-taking can be reinstated long after drug use has ceased and (3) 'as drugs come to be "wanted" more-and-more, they often come to be liked less-and-less' (p. 249). A rationale for the theory is summed up in a question posed by Ellinwood and Escalante (1970, p. 189): 'A puzzling, yet central, question in the study of the amphetamine psychosis is why individuals who are experiencing acute terror and other unpleasant effects continue to use amphetamines in large doses'.

Wanting and liking

Consider the paradox that drugs such as heroin can be liked less and less as they are sought more and more. This is not to say that they invariably are liked less and less with time. It is just that this can occur. Subsequent research that was triggered by the paper of Robinson and Berridge, has found examples of where liking and wanting appear to increase in parallel (Willner *et al.*, 2005). Let us assume that there can be (but there is not always) such a dissociation between liking and wanting.

Some might explain the dissociation by means of a switch from positive to negative reinforcement. Robinson and Berridge do not deny that this may capture part of the truth but suggest it is not the defining feature of the paradox. Rather they argue that, with repeated use of drugs, there is sensitization of the neural system of wanting, which becomes uncoupled from liking. Only the wanting mechanism is sensitized. This causes a pathological focus of perceptual, attention and motivational processes upon drug-related stimuli and thoughts. The change in neural sensitivity is long-lasting and can be permanent, which renders addicts vulnerable to relapse even after years of abstinence. According to the theory, the mesolimbic DA system is the neural system that underlies the attribution of incentive value, termed **incentive salience**, and that is sensitized by drugs (Chapter 15).

Further evidence includes the following. Withdrawal effects, unconditional or conditional, appear not to be able to explain relapse. Addicts commonly do not attribute relapse to withdrawal. Craving is often highest immediately after taking the drug, when presumably any aversive state has been partly if not wholly eliminated. This provides a rationale for the advice of maintaining total abstinence. In rats, drug infusion into the brain can prime and reinstate drug-taking. Robinson and Berridge do not deny that increasing hedonism can result from drug use but merely that it alone cannot explain addiction (cf. Peele and Alexander, 1985). Nicotine is highly addictive and yet one imagines that few smokers would associate its use with unrestrained euphoria (see also earlier account of caffeine).

According to the theory, incentive salience and pleasure are not entirely separate processes. Indeed, applied to conventional motivational systems, it would be a maladaptive design feature if they were. Incentive salience is normally maintained in part by the pleasure that follows engagement with the incentive (Figure 18.10). For example, foods that evoke a positive affective rating are normally sought. However, drug-taking does not represent adaptive behaviour and some dissociation between wanting and liking is introduced. Increased sensitization is experienced subjectively as craving for drugs.

Stress

The theory suggests a link between stress and drug-taking: stress contributes to taking drugs and, by implication, the process is one of negative reinforcement. The drug takes away the sharp edge of stress. Such a process surely plays a role but, in addition, stress appears to increase the incentive salience attributed to drug-related stimuli. Both addictive drugs and stress sensitize DA activity (Robinson and Berridge, 1993).

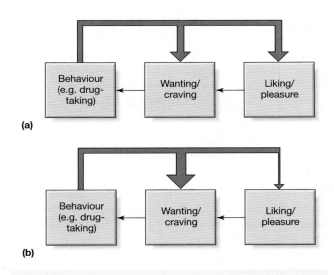

Figure 18.10 Situation (a) before and (b) after sensitization. States of positive affect ('hedonism') increase incentive salience. However, with experience, wanting/craving increases but liking/pleasure sometimes decreases.

Source: Toates (1998b, Fig. 2.25, p. 55).

Therapy

As therapy, the theory gives a rationale for extinction procedures, i.e. repeated exposure to drug-related cues under guidance. However, clinically based extinction programmes might not generalize to the multitude of drug-related stimuli of the street. As noted earlier, results have been disappointing. Perhaps the only effective treatment would be a chemical to undo sensitization but there is no immediate prospect of that (Robinson and Berridge, 1993).

Integration

A qualification needs to be made to the incentive sensitization theory and can easily be accommodated: drugs do not unconditionally sensitize a craving process divorced from the context in which the drug was taken. As noted, patients taking narcotics to counter pain do not usually crave drugs outside the clinical context (Chapter 14). Thus, particular cognitions, goals and strategies are part of the sensitization process.

Bechara *et al.* (1998) and Wise (1988) present models in which opiate addiction is explained by two distinct processes. First, there is an incentive motivational process. However, according to this model, once addiction develops, the weighting can change such that motivation is based largely on a second and distinct process: avoidance of aversive effects of withdrawal. Fewer 'highs' are reported and larger and larger doses are required to sustain avoidance of aversion. Craving can be based upon either process. According to this model, the role of positive incentive motivation becomes masked when control shifts to the aversion avoidance system. Suppose that withdrawal effects are alleviated, e.g. by prescription of the substitute drug methadone. The positive incentive motivational system then dominates intake.

Evolutionary considerations

So far, we have looked at the causal processes underlying drug-taking but it is useful to reconsider evolutionary aspects (Chapter 2, 'Genes, environment and evolution'). Drugs have psychoactive effects by directly acting on the CNS. This is in contrast to, say, food or sex. In such conventional systems, rewarding effects are first mediated via sensory systems and subsequently activate the CNS. Thus, drugs appear to short-circuit part of the system that underlies interaction with conventional incentives and to tap directly into reward systems.

Evolutionary psychology
A false signal

From an evolutionary perspective, the propensity to take drugs can be understood by their ability to stimulate and overwhelm processes of natural biological reward that underlie conventional interactions, e.g. to approach food or a sexual partner (Nesse and Berridge, 1997). As Nesse and Berridge note (p. 64): 'Drugs of abuse create a signal in the brain that indicates, falsely, the arrival of a huge fitness benefit'. (They use fitness here in the ethological sense of Chapter 2: an increase in reproductive potential, rather than a measure of good health.)

Section summary

1 The exposure and adaptive orientations can each explain some features of drug-taking.

2 The incentive sensitization theory distinguishes between wanting and liking.

Test your knowledge

(Answer on page 465)

18.5 With reference to Figure 18.9, suppose that the same quantity of opiate drug as represented in part (c) were to be injected under the conditions of part (d). Which of the following would be the expected outcome in terms of affect? (i) A level the same as part (c), (ii) the same as before, i.e. as shown in part (d), (iii) somewhere between the situations shown in parts (c) and (d).

18.2

Bringing things together

To return to the contrast between the exposure orientation and the adaptive orientation, much evidence favours the latter. As a general principle, people seem to take drugs as part of a problem-solving exercise in order to improve their cognitive and affective states. This may be in desperation, in a state of existential angst or as part of spiritual enlightenment. Both chemical and non-chemical based activities can be recruited to such ends.

Rat models tend to support the adaptive orientation. The amount of drug that a rat takes is heavily dependent upon social context and other available rewards. The fact that nicotine is such a potent reinforcer for humans and relatively weak for rats might be explained in terms of the kinds of peculiarly human problems that it helps to solve, e.g. vigilance and promoting social interaction.

However, somewhat in favour of the exposure orientation, it seems that the drug-related solution to a problem is more probable as a result of exposure, as suggested by the incentive sensitization theory. Also the move from controlled to automatic processes underlying intake highlights that exposure and repetition increase the tendency to take a drug.

Drug-taking appears to be motivated by positive and negative affect. A number of features are common with conventional motivations (e.g. craving and the role of classical conditioning) and non-chemical-related behaviours can take on addictive features. Drugs such as nicotine and heroin tap into conventional incentive motivational processes involving dopamine and opioids and appear to sensitize them. Such processes are clearly of adaptive value in a conventional context. For example, fitness maximization requires us to be pulled towards mates and sources of food at times of energy deficiency. Pavlovian conditioning between neutral cues and biological incentives is clearly adaptive and our conscious mind might usefully be occupied by such thoughts. However, this adaptive principle can break down when encountering a drug that taps into such a pathway, grossly sensitizes it and yet creates little in the way of negative feedback. Drugs that have a primary action not on dopaminergic and opioidergic systems, such as ecstasy and LSD, do not have this addictive potential (but that, of course, does not make them safe).

On reflection, how realistic are 'animal models' of drug-taking? Of course, we cannot ask rats whether they experience mood-altering effects such as euphoria. We only have nervous system activity and behaviour as suggestions. Aspects of the behaviour of rats and non-human primates suggest commonality with the actions of drugs in humans.

Although animal models might capture features of human behaviour, we need to consider the more complex cognitive and cultural context of human drug-taking. Humans start to take drugs for various reasons that seem peculiarly human, such as peer pressure. A contribution to, say, alcohol or heroin consumption may arise from a combination of chemical effects experienced within a context of a peer-group and social approval (Peele, 1985). We are reminded of the cognitive interpretation that can be attached to various bodily sensations (Chapter 12). Drug-takers sometimes need to be instructed by peers in how to interpret drug-induced changes in sensation. Once initiated, it might be that features of human drug-taking can be captured by animal models.

4 **Other activities, not drug-related, can become addictive in ways similar to drugs, probably based on dopamine activation.**

5 **Various theories attempt to explain addiction. It is possible to see some compatible features between them.**

Further reading

For a general introduction to drug effects, see Snyder (1996) or Gossop (2000). For a detailed look at the range of addictive substances and the underlying neurobiology, by two well-known researchers in the area, see Koob and Le Moal (2006). Goldstein (2001) links biology and social policy on drugs. For a classical text that takes a broad integrative overview of addictions, chemical-based and non-chemical based, see Orford (2001).

Signposts

The discussion of drugs and addiction concludes the four chapters that are grouped under the heading of 'motivation', though the next chapter 'Sleep and waking' includes a mention of motivation. You will return briefly to the issue of drug-taking in Chapter 20, 'Cognition and action', where the issue of emotions and decision-making is discussed.

Answers

Explanations for answers to 'test your knowledge' questions can be found on the website **www.pearsoned.co.uk/toates**

18.1 (iii) LSD

18.2 (i) Conditional stimulus (CS); (ii) conditional response (CR)

18.3 This demonstrates selectivity of choice and that the behaviour is controlled by its consequences (gaining nicotine). Otherwise, if there were only one hole, any such increase in responding over time might simply reflect heightened activity

18.4 (ii) Negative

18.5 (iii) Somewhere between the situations shown in parts (c) and (d)

Summary of Chapter 18

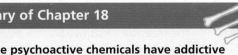

1 **Some psychoactive chemicals have addictive properties, as do certain activities not related to obtaining chemicals.**

2 **The motivation to take a drug and the effect of the drug depend not only upon the drug's chemical properties but also upon a range of contextual factors such as control, conditional stimuli and social factors.**

3 **Drugs that can become addictive have the common property of targeting the brain's mesolimbic dopamine system.**

CHAPTER 19

Sleep and waking

Learning outcomes for Chapter 19

After studying this chapter, you should be able to:

1 Present the evidence that sleep is an active state of the brain, rather than one of passivity.

2 Define what is meant by a 'circadian rhythm' and describe how sleep is influenced by such a rhythm. Thereby, describe what is meant by the terms 'biological clock', 'period', 'phase' and '*Zeitgeber*'.

3 Show where causal, developmental, evolutionary and functional types of explanation are relevant to understanding sleep and how most insight can derive from their parallel consideration.

4 Explain the relevance of the concept of motivation to understanding sleep.

5 Describe why investigators believe that there is more than one type of sleep.

6 Identify some of the principal brain regions that are involved in the control of sleep and distinguish the roles that they serve. Link this to some of the principal neurochemicals.

7 Show where a comparison of the development of sleep in different species can contribute to our broad understanding of the principles underlying sleep.

8 Describe how the phenomena associated with dreaming can be better understood by taking a biological perspective. Link this to the question of whether dreaming serves a function.

9 Explain how an understanding of the basics of sleep can illuminate sleep disorders.

1 Why do we sleep?

2 Why does coffee keep us awake?

3 Do all animals sleep?

4 Why do we dream?

5 Dreams have curious twists of story-line. Do dreams make any sense?

6 Can behavioural science help us to sleep better?

Does sleep serve to keep us out of danger (as here for shelter during the London blitz) or to maintain homeostasis, or both?

Source: Topham Picturepoint/TopFoto.co.uk

Introduction

- Heidi: 'How did you sleep?

- Carlos: 'Please don't ask me – it was awful – I had a series of bizarre and frightening dreams – about snakes and dragons – and then me being chased by people in funny hats. One of them turned into you.'

- Heidi: 'Freud would have had a great time with you!'

- Carlos: 'To be honest, I don't believe a word of all that stuff about interpreting dreams. It's not scientific. But I have had a lot of stress lately.'

- Heidi: 'I can't remember my dreams from last night but I am sure that I had one. I just couldn't get to sleep – I had something worrying on my mind.'

Does this sound familiar? Dreams reflect an altered state of consciousness, which is rather different from any waking state and which is often emotionally charged. This chapter will investigate sleep, waking and dreaming, considering how they are produced by the brain.

The complex organization of brain activity in sleep and the cognitive richness of dreaming make sleep a prime candidate for investigation by psychologists (Hobson, 1986). Indeed, one of psychology's famous controversies concerns what interpretation, if any, should be placed on dreaming and thereby what is one possible function of sleep (Eysenck, 1985; Freud, 1967; Jung, 1963).

During sleep, modulation is exerted on sensory processing such that the threshold of detection of stimuli is raised (Coenen, 1995). The transition from waking to sleep is from where thought is strongly influenced by external sources to a mainly 'endogenous' (meaning 'driven from within') generation of mental activity in dreaming (Hobson,

1990). However, anecdotally, parents are said to be woken by a baby crying, as opposed to insignificant stimuli of similar intensity. Experimental evidence supports such an effect, showing processing of information from the outside world (Oswald *et al.*, 1960).

There is also limited behaviour shown in sleep, e.g. the periodic reorganization of the position of the body. This prevents damage to the skin and the circulation from confinement and pressure.

Different species spend a small or very large proportion of time in sleep and yet there exists no convincing theory of *why* animals sleep (Rechtschaffen, 1998). Sleep is not a unitary state. As indexed by the brain's changing electrical activity, there are different types of sleep, which might serve different functions (Benington and Heller, 1995). In some phases of sleep, the nervous system can exhibit as much activity as during waking. So, sleep is not a passive process (a 'default state'), corresponding to fatigue of neurons (Dement, 1994). Sleep is an active process, based on particular patterns of activity in specific pathways of neurons (Hobson, 1986). Since we spend about one-third of our lives in sleep, it is perhaps the activity with which we invest the largest amount of time. This makes our lack of understanding of its function(s) surprising.

A fundamental feature of sleep is its rhythmic nature. So, to understand sleep, we next turn to consider the bases of rhythms.

Section summary

1 Sleep is an active state, in which the brain shows patterns of high activity.

2 In sleep, information processing is based mainly upon intrinsic sources of information rather than extrinsic sources.

3 There is more than one type of sleep.

4 The function of sleep is still unclear but, by taking a broad perspective of biological psychology, investigators can make informed suggestions.

Test your knowledge

(Answer on page 487)

19.1 Suppose someone argues that we sleep in order to avoid being active and thereby minimize the risk of accidents and predation. Into which of the four types of explanation (Chapter 1, 'Introduction') does this fall?

Rhythms of sleep–waking

Rhythms of sleep–waking reflect the 24 hour light–dark cycle of the environment. Other rhythms match the Earth's rotation around the sun, e.g. winter hibernation and seasonal mating cycles. This section will look at some general points about biological rhythms and then relate them to sleep.

Terminology of rhythms

The length of time taken for a rhythm to complete one cycle is its **period**, illustrated by the pendulum of Figure 19.1(a). The period is measured as the time from any point on the cycle to when the same point is reached again (part (b)), e.g. the period of waking–sleep is normally 24 hours. The period of a woman's menstrual cycle is approximately 28 days. The term 'phase' refers to a particular point on the cycle. As Figures 19.1(c)–(e) show, two rhythms having the same period can either be in phase (part (c)) or out of phase by various amounts ((d) and (e)).

Circadian rhythms

Introduction

A predictable feature of the environment is that, for as long as there has been life (and much more!), our planet has rotated on its axis once every 24 hours. Even for an animal exposed to the British weather, 24 hour cycles of light and dark follow each other regularly.

In its evolutionary origins, the body's own rhythm doubtless arose as a reflection of the 24 hour light–dark cycle. So, is our cycle of sleep–waking simply dependent upon this light–dark cycle? No: the body contains its own **biological clock**. This is a type of oscillator ('rhythm generator') that has an endogenous ('from within') and inflexible tendency to cycle with a period of approximately 24 hours (Mistlberger and Rusak, 2005). Information corresponding to the 24 hour rhythm of light–dark is encoded in the endogenous rhythm generator. This underlies the rhythms of activity and sleep that animals, including humans, exhibit. The rhythm produces alternating tendencies (1) to search for a sleep site and sleep and (2) to wake and be active. We do not need to learn that the light–dark cycle has a period of 24 hours, since our endogenous rhythm produces changes in our behaviour that correspond to it. We cannot properly adjust to cycles of light–dark that differ widely from 24 hours (Moore-Ede *et al.*, 1982), demonstrating the endogenous nature of the rhythm.

Apart from the inflexible nature of the 24 hour *period* of the rhythm, there is a flexible aspect concerning its *phase*. When an animal moves from one time zone to another, rhythms shift into alignment with the new

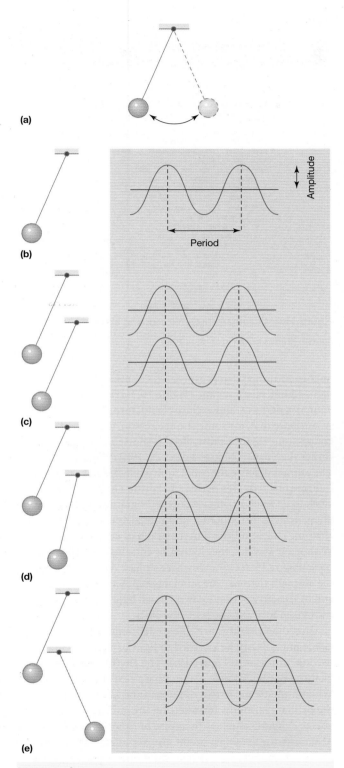

Figure 19.1 Oscillations: (a) pendulum, (b) the meaning of 'period'. Two pendulums: (c) in phase, (d) out of phase and (e) further out of phase.

Source: adapted from Toates (1992).

rhythm of the environment (Mistlberger and Rusak, 1994). This offers flexibility to behaviour, allowing the animal to take local circumstances into account (e.g. migration over large distances).

Definition of terms

Variables such as body temperature, hormone secretions and sleep–waking exhibit a **circadian rhythm** (Moore, 1999). For a rhythm to meet the criteria of being *circadian*, it must show the following two characteristics (Moore-Ede *et al.*, 1982): (1) a cycle lasts approximately 24 hours and (2) the rhythm is generated internally. It is not enough to observe that a physiological or behavioural variable shows a rhythm with a period of 24 hours, since, in principle, the rhythm might not be internally driven. It might depend entirely on the external 24 hour cycle of light–dark. Social factors, such as the convention of getting up for work and the sound of breakfast television from a neighbour's flat, may be generating the rhythm. However, as we just noted, an intrinsically generated rhythm does underlie such things as cycles of sleep and activity (Mistlberger and Rusak, 2005; Moore, 1999). To establish the existence of circadian rhythms, subjects are observed in a special environment in which, as far as is possible, external timing signals are eliminated.

A personal angle

A clever experiment

In 1729, the French astronomer Jean Jacques d'Ortous de Marian performed an elegantly simple experiment (Moore-Ede *et al.*, 1982). He noticed a 24 hour rhythm in the opening of the leaves of a plant. Was this dependent upon the rhythm in light level? He put the plant in darkness and observed a similar rhythm, thereby strongly suggesting endogenous generation of the rhythm.

In humans, to establish the endogenous generation of a circadian rhythm, a participant needs to be housed somewhere such as in a deep mine under constant illumination.

Although the rhythm is endogenous, external factors normally play a role in its timing, as when an individual shifts from one time-zone to another. An extrinsic factor that sets the timing of a circadian rhythm is called a ***Zeitgeber*** (Moore-Ede *et al.*, 1982). The term derives from the German words *Zeit* (time) and *geber* (giver). In coming into phase with the *Zeitgeber*, the circadian rhythm is said to show *entrainment* to it.

In 1962 and in a cave 114 m under the Alps at Marguareis, on the French–Italian border, the French cave researcher Michel Siffre set up camp in a tent (Siffre, 1965). Ambient temperature was at or below 0 °C and he was cut off from the outside world. A battery provided power for a weak light that was kept on all the time. There was no indication of the light–dark cycle of the outside world. Siffre was without a radio or a watch. His only lifeline with the outside world was by telephone to a research station. He informed them of times of retiring and waking, eating, etc. Siffre still exhibited a rhythm of sleep–waking, albeit with a period slightly longer than 24 hours. Such evidence points strongly to a circadian rhythm underlying sleep–waking (Moore, 1999).

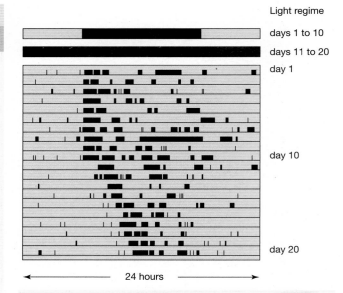

Figure 19.2 Circadian rhythm: record of activity.

Source: Brady (1979, Fig. 2–5, p. 10).

Consider an animal, rat or human, sleeping deep in a cave or burrow so that no light reaches it. It would not be informed on the light-level of the world in order to become active. By exploiting a circadian rhythm, the animal can be woken up or persuaded to retire as appropriate. It can also migrate to different time-zones without difficulty since a circadian rhythm can 're-entrain' with the external *Zeitgeber*.

Activity in the cockroach

Cockroaches tend to be active at night and, if placed in a running wheel, run then. In Figure 19.2, this is shown for the period 1–10 days, when the animal was subject to a cycle of 12 hours light–12 hours dark. The dark half of the period is associated with an immediate increase in activity.

At day 11, the cockroach was subject to continuous darkness. A rhythm of activity continued under these conditions, even though it shifted in phase. Each successive bout of activity occurred a little later. The cockroach has an endogenous rhythm generator, which produces cycles of activity of slightly more than 24 hours. The behaviour when there is a light *Zeitgeber* present (i.e. days 1–10) is the combined effect of the animal's endogenous rhythm and the *Zeitgeber* of light–dark.

Mechanism of entrainment

If you have travelled to a different continent, you might have experienced jet-lag. However, within a few days you were probably in synchrony with your new environment, in terms of rhythms of body temperature and when you felt like going to sleep. For a gross simplification, consider a hypothetical

nocturnal animal that is exposed to an unusual 12 hour light–12 hour dark regime (Figure 19.3(a)). At first, the animal is perfectly and exclusively nocturnally active.

Suppose that, for some strange reason, the animal's endogenous rhythm shifts. Sleep is shortened and it surfaces earlier than usual (Moore-Ede *et al.*, 1982) (Figure 19.3(b)). The animal is active for some time while it is light ('dusk'), indicated by red. This period of exposure to light causes the clock to be reset. In other words reprogramming occurs; a phase delay is introduced to the animal's endogenous rhythm. This is indicated in the graph of later activity. Within a few cycles, the rhythm re-entrains to the light–dark cycle. Figure 19.3(c) shows where a phase delay creeps into the animal's rhythm. The animal is exposed to light at the end of its active period ('dawn'). Such light exposure shifts its rhythm forward, i.e. resets the clock.

Circadian rhythms are able to drift out of phase and hence animals can be exposed to light or darkness at the 'wrong' times, as in Figure 19.3. The rhythm needs a facility to be 'kicked back' into phase as it starts to drift. When humans move to a different time zone, daylight is the primary stimulus for resetting the circadian clock. Social *Zeitgebers* such as the noise of other guests in a hotel or the call for breakfast might also act to re-entrain much as light does. There are species differences in the relative roles of light, social factors, food intake and exercise in setting the phase of the circadian rhythm (Mistlberger and Skene, 2004).

The following section considers the function of sleep.

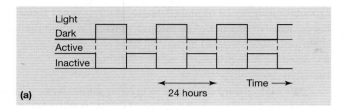

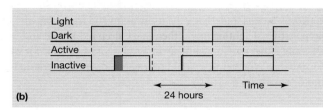

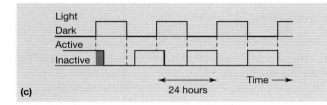

Figure 19.3 Light–dark cycle and activity rhythm: (a) normal, (b) re-entrainment following a phase advance and (c) re-entrainment following a phase delay.

Section summary

1 The rotation of the Earth is highly predictable and is reflected in the activity of the nervous system.

2 A rhythm of period approximately 24 hours, which is endogenously programmed, is termed a circadian rhythm.

3 Waking–sleep exhibits a circadian rhythm.

4 The phase of circadian rhythms is set by environmental stimuli.

5 An external stimulus that sets the phase of a circadian rhythm is known as a *Zeitgeber*.

Test your knowledge

(Answers on page 487)

19.2 Complete the following: 'Comparing the sleep patterns of people living in Dublin and Moscow would reveal a difference in _____ but the same _____'.

19.3 Complete the following: 'In Figure 19.3, light is serving as a _____, which shifts the phase of the _____ rhythm underlying sleep-activity'.

The function of sleep and its link to causation

What is the functional value of sleep? The answer might involve a combination of various theories on why we sleep, especially since sleep is not a uniform state but is composed of different types (Roffwarg *et al.*, 1966). Broadly speaking, theories on function can be grouped into three categories, as below.

Homeostasis: a restorative function

Introduction

Homeostatic theory is closest to common-sense understanding. It is supported by the observation that sleep deprivation increases the pressure to sleep, lowers the latency of sleep onset and increases the length of subsequent sleep (Benington, 2000). The fact that animals (e.g. rats) die from extended sleep deprivation (Rechtschaffen, 1998) suggests a homeostatic function.

Candidate processes

Sleep could serve the homeostatic function of restoration following 'the "wear and tear" of wakefulness' (Horne, 1988, p. 25). More specifically, it might 'restore the natural balance among the neural centres' (Guyton, 1991, p. 661) or serve a restorative function within the immune system (Hobson, 1999). Sleep loss impairs information processing by the CNS. Reimund (1994, p. 231) suggests that sleep: 'maintains the integrity of neural tissue – a consequence of the energetically sensitive and demanding nature of neural tissue'.

Suppose that, during waking, a biochemical (e.g. a product of metabolism) increases in concentration in the body. Sleep might reduce or eliminate this chemical (Cravatt *et al.*, 1995). Alternatively, a biochemical might be depleted during waking. According to Horne (1988), with the exception of the nervous system, the body does not require sleep for repair. General bodily repair can occur during relaxed wakefulness. For example, sleep appears to serve no better than sleepless rest to correct muscular fatigue. The brain is the organ that shows the most marked change between sleep and relaxed wakefulness and that benefits most from sleep (Hobson, 1986).

Although evidence suggests a restorative function, its exact nature remains elusive (Horne, 1988). There is a list of possible substances that *might* constitute a substance regulated by sleep (Rechtschaffen, (1998). Function could relate to several candidate substances.

Linking function and causation

If the functional explanation is that sleep serves to restore a substance ('X') to an optimal level, there might be a straightforward translation from this to causation (Figure 19.4). That is to say, deviation of X from its optimal level might be detected and this motivates sleep (Cravatt *et al.*, 1995). Restoration of equilibrium would trigger waking, i.e. homeostasis by negative feedback.

Inactivity/safety

Sleep might have evolved to keep animals inactive at particular times (Meddis, 1977). Depending upon their habitat, properties of sensory systems and presence of predators and prey, etc., a given species is best equipped to be active in either the light or dark. For example, humans have relatively poor vision at night. Therefore, they are programmed to be inactive then, relatively safe from predators and accidents (Jouvet, 1975). By contrast, rats exploit smell and touch, not having good vision. According to this theory, they are active at night when they are least visible to predators. In terms of fitness (Chapter 2, 'Genes, environment and evolution'), animals sleep at those times when, in their evolution, there was relatively little *benefit* to be gained and a high *cost* of being active. Inactivity might also allow conservation of resources, e.g. energy (reviewed by D.B. Cohen, 1979).

No matter what the functional explanation, on a causal level sleep involves a rhythmically varying internal signal of cycle length 24 hours. Thus, the difference between

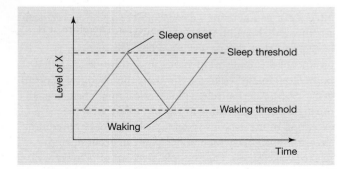

Figure 19.4 Model of sleep based on the regulation of substance X (in principle the waking and sleeping thresholds might be reversed).

explanations in terms of homeostasis and safety is not about the presence or absence of an internal signal. It is about the significance of this signal in the evolution of sleep, i.e. as regulated variable (homeostasis) or as timing cue (inactivity/safety hypothesis).

In principle, if sleep evolved to serve safety rather than homeostasis, it might prove possible to resist it. An anti-sleep tablet might be invented, e.g. an antagonist to neurotransmitters in neural circuits underlying the motivation and triggering of sleep. Artificial lighting might then make sleep redundant and we could either party or indulge the Protestant work ethic for 24 hours a day. Whether this would represent a desirable scenario is another matter.

Maintaining the brain and its plasticity

Introduction

A function of sleep might be to help to maintain the functional stability and plasticity of the neural systems of the brain (Benington and Frank, 2003; Moruzzi, 1966). Such plasticity could take the form of the production of new neurons or changes in the connections between existing neurons. The effects of use and disuse in development of neural systems were discussed in Chapter 6, 'Development and plasticity'. Seen in such terms, sleep might provide a process for selectively strengthening certain synapses and eliminating others, depending upon whether they are part of a functioning circuit (Jouvet, 1975). This could apply to early development or to the adult, or both. Development is a time of change in the nervous system and young animals exhibit much sleep (see later).

Some brain regions show little change in activity during sleep and waking (Horne, 1988). Their role is largely preprogrammed and routine. So, if the function of sleep is to facilitate plasticity, it seems as if these regions have, putting it metaphorically, no need to sleep. For example, the part of the brain stem concerned with respiration might be expected to be of this kind. Its activity is consistent over time and, of course, respiration can hardly be switched off to allow maintenance. By contrast, the cerebral cortex is commonly exposed to novel unpredictable situations and it seems to 'need to switch off-line and sleep'.

Stability of serotonergic systems

In rats, sleep deprivation disrupts serotonergic neurotransmission. More specifically, the disruption is to that mediated by one subtype of serotonin receptor: the 5-HT_{1A} subtype (Roman *et al.*, 2005). Roman *et al.* note the damaging effects of sleep deprivation on mental health, such as increasing the risk of depression. Disruption to serotonergic neurotransmission by loss of sleep could, at least in part, mediate such effects.

Generation of new neurons

Some regions of the brain preserve the ability to generate new cells even in the adult. The hippocampus is the most studied region in this regard. Experiments have shown that sleep deprivation impairs seriously the capacity of the CNS to generate new neurons in such regions (Guzman-Marin *et al.*, 2005). This suggests that a function of sleep is to permit the plasticity associated with the production of new neurons. By now, you might be feeling that you should decline your next late-night party invitation.

Learning and memory

A form of plasticity that has attracted much attention in sleep research is that associated with learning and memory (Chapter 11, 'Learning and memory'). In principle, those changes between neurons that are the embodiment of learning and memory might be influenced by sleep.

Memory consolidation is generally thought to occur by means of strengthening synaptic connections in the brain with use. Sleep could allow refreshment of established, but seldom used, memories by simulating their activation (Kavanau, 1998). New experiences might be best assimilated into memory during sleep, when the organism is not actively producing behaviour (D.B. Cohen, 1979). This could be described by analogy with a library: presumably, cataloguing could be best done at times when the library is shut ('sleeping') and books are being neither returned nor borrowed.

Some argue that consolidation of memory is harmed by sleep deprivation (Benington and Frank, 2003). Animal experiments reveal that a period of learning or exposure to environmental enrichment is followed by increased sleep. Some patterns of neural activation seen in sleep correspond to the patterns observed during an immediately prior learning experience (Hobson and Pace-Schott, 2002). However, the data on the importance of sleep for learning and memory are very controversial and open to various alternative interpretations (J.M. Siegel, 2001, 2005).

A combined function

An explanation of the function of sleep might involve a combination of the three factors introduced above, as follows (cf. Rechtschaffen, 1998). Sleep tends to be programmed at times when, in evolutionary history, it was to our net benefit to be inactive. Irrespective of whether pressure for sleep to evolve also came from homeostatic imbalance, benefits for the body might be earned by sleep. Inactivity would allow bodily resources to be conserved. During sleep, fine-tuning of neurons might occur, involving synthesis of components. The brain might be 're-programmed', i.e. exhibit plasticity.

The notion of core sleep and optional sleep

Horne (1988) proposed that neuronal repair normally occurs in the first few hours of sleep and he terms the sleep necessary for such repair **core sleep**. So, repair seems to require less time than that which we normally spend in sleep. The remainder of sleep might simply be a means of keeping us inactive, termed 'optional sleep'. Such a dual-process function might be mapped onto a dual process model of causal mechanisms. Optional sleep would be programmed by a motivational process that has an intrinsic 24 hour rhythm at its base. By contrast, the pressure for core sleep would come not from time within the intrinsic 24 hour rhythm but from the length of time since the last sleep.

Such a dual-factor theory is represented in simplified form in Figure 19.5. The homeostatic ('core') factor is shown in part (a). As the time since the last sleep increases, so the tendency to sleep increases. Part (b) shows the cyclic factor. The figure is a simplification in that the small peak in sleep tendency in the mid-afternoon is not shown. This coincides with the time of siesta of some cultures. Mid-afternoon can be problematic for drivers trying to stay awake at the wheel (Horne, 1995). Figure 19.5(c) indicates that the tendency to sleep depends upon a combination of factors shown in parts (a) and (b). The tendency does not increase monotonically as a function of deprivation (Figure 19.5(c)). For example, someone would feel less sleepy at time B than at time A even though they have been deprived for longer at B.

We shall return to the homeostatic factor in sleep, considering the possibility that its regulation not only explains part of the function of sleep but also one of the causal factors.

Comparing species

Animals live in different habitats with different evolutionary pressures. Sleep occurs in most species, including all mammals (Horne, 1988). That sleep is seen so widely might point to a homeostatic function. However, the relative importance of the three possible functions that we have attributed to sleep might vary with species. Therefore, it is useful to compare species' sleeping patterns, as well as looking at developmental effects within a species. As discussed later, brain development, involving the formation of new neural structures, might pose its demands for sleep.

The natural habitat of some species of dolphin is such that sleep would appear to put their *immediate* safety at great risk (Mukhametov, 1984). Yet they show brief periods of sleep, suggesting that these are necessary for homeostasis or re-programming or both. The Indus dolphin lives in muddy waters, which are liable to serious turbulence. It is blind and, in order to navigate, it relies upon a very effective sonar system. Permanent alertness might seem to be imperative

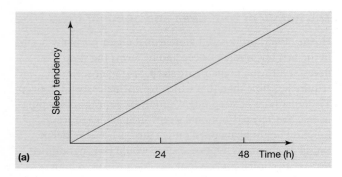

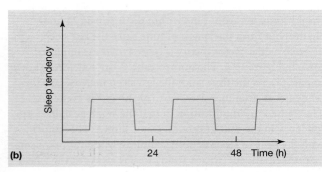

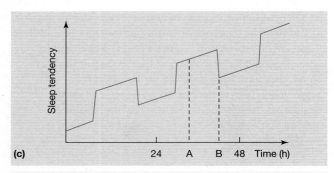

Figure 19.5 Simplified representation of the strength of tendency to sleep: (a) a function of time since the last sleep, (b) a function of the intrinsic 24 hour rhythm and (c) a combination of (a) and (b). (Note that in reality the factors combine in a more complex way than indicated in part (c).)

Source: based on Dijk (1997, pp. 10–13).

but, amazingly, even under these conditions, the Indus dolphin sleeps. This consists of naps, each of a few seconds' duration, taken many times a day. Presumably, they constitute core sleep.

Researchers studied the electrical activity of the brains of two species of dolphin, the bottlenose dolphin and porpoise (Mukhametov, 1984). Each half-brain takes it in turns to sleep, hemispheres being shifted every two hours! The total time spent in sleep is about 12 hours. The shift between hemispheres enables vigilance to be maintained at all times, albeit that offered by only an awake half-brain. This suggests

that a role (e.g. neuronal repair) is performed in each hemisphere as it sleeps.

Effects of sleep deprivation

Insight into the function of sleep is obtained from studying its deprivation. Enforced sleep deprivation is a controversial procedure but, as long ago as 1894, it was carried out on animals (Bentivoglio and Grassi-Zucconi, 1997). Brain damage appears to be the result. In humans, there are reports of death by sleep deprivation as punishment and torture. More benignly, people occasionally volunteer to deprive themselves of sleep.

A personal angle

Randy Gardner

There are a few heroes of sleep research, one being a 17-year-old boy from California, Randy Gardner. He lasted 264 hours without sleep, i.e. almost 11 days (Gulevich *et al.*, 1966). Randy's 'voluntary' deprivation was 'enforced' by a team who worked in shifts to keep him awake. His attempt was done under medical supervision and researchers thereby found a person to study. Neither during nor after deprivation, could doctors find reason for serious concern about Randy's health. Starting at day 4, Randy experienced lapses of memory. Visual perception was altered in the form of the world taking on illusory properties, 'waking dreams'. At 262 hours of wakefulness, he was given a psychiatric interview. He was coherent and no loss of contact with reality was found. In spite of these disturbances, Randy held on to reality throughout and did not show seriously disturbed ('psychotic') behaviour. Randy went to bed at the end of 11 days but slept for only 14–15 hours.

What are we to conclude regarding Randy Gardner? With a population of only one, caution is needed. However, the tentative conclusions correspond to those for other sleep-deprived people: that psychological function is disrupted but it is hard to find obvious disruption outside the CNS (Horne, 1988). Horne suggests that a number of factors were crucial to Randy's success: (1) his motivation, (2) the support of his friends and (3) having an activity, as an alternative to sleep. Though finding disruption is difficult, a common assumption is that physiological homeostasis is impaired by prolonged deprivation, such that death can be hastened (Hobson, 1999).

Section summary

1 There are three principal explanations of the function of sleep: it (a) serves a restorative (homeostatic) function, (b) keeps us inactive and (c) allows plasticity and repair of the brain.

2 Sleep appears to facilitate plasticity in the form of (re)structuring parts of the brain. The theory that it is involved in learning and memory is controversial.

3 Developing nervous systems involve much structuring, which might explain large amounts of sleep early in life.

4 Sleep might serve a combination of the functions described.

5 One theory postulates a dual function: core sleep is needed for effective neural, and thereby psychological, functioning. Optional sleep might serve simply to keep us immobile.

6 The wide presence of sleep in different species suggests a homeostatic and/or restructuring function.

Test your knowledge

(Answers on page 487)

19.4 Complete the following: 'The universal presence of sleep across species and individuals strongly suggests that, in functional terms (Chapter 2), any _____ of sleep are outweighed by its _____'.

19.5 Change in which type of component cellular structure in the nervous system is most usually associated with plasticity?

19.2

The motivation to sleep

So far, the chapter has described sleep as a brain state; the animal is either asleep or awake. Of course, animals do not simply pass instantly from the brain state of waking to that of sleep. Rather, sleep–waking has motivational characteristics. Depending upon the species, an animal might need to find a suitable sleeping location and be persuaded to retire there by the onset of sleepiness. A number of species invest time and effort in finding, building and defending sleeping sites (Hobson, 1986).

Chapter 15, 'Motivation', noted that a given motivation varies in strength and there is usually competition among motivations for expression in behaviour. Being sleepy can powerfully motivate us to seek a suitable shelter. In so doing, sleep can compete very effectively with other candidates for expression in behaviour. Pain competes with sleep, as many know to their cost. Also, strong competition arises from simply having something 'on your mind'.

At times, prolonged sleep seems to be an adaptive behavioural strategy. For example, animals recovering from a bacterial or viral infection often show long periods of sleep and this makes adaptive sense in aiding recovery (Chapter 13, 'Stress and coping'; Hart, 1988). Under these conditions, we can envisage a tendency to sleep being dominant in any competition with, say, a tendency to get up to feed.

At other times, we might have a suitable sleeping site and a strong motivation but custom can force us to try, with limited success, to inhibit sleep tendencies. (If you doubt this, try looking behind you during the lectures at an academic conference, immediately after lunch.). The amount of time that we spend sleeping also seems to increase at times when there is little else to do. This appears to apply equally to some non-humans. For example, when restricted to the house and fed adequately, domestic cats and dogs pass large amounts of time in sleep.

The period of sleep shows some flexibility in that its duration can be extended or shortened according to prevailing circumstances. In terms of the dichotomy between core sleep and optional sleep (discussed earlier), it would seem logical that the optional phase offers such flexibility. Anecdotal evidence suggests that, if a task is made particularly demanding or interesting, this can increase its competitive strength relative to sleep. For example, soldiers in war have been forced to show extended periods of vigilance and hence suffer sleep deprivation. However, the notion of core sleep would be expected to offer serious limits to flexibility. Apparently, during the Second World War, a number of British pilots were killed after falling asleep in flight (Horne, 1988).

Section summary

1 Sleep is associated with motivation that directs behaviour towards a sleeping site.

2 Sleep shows competition for expression with other activities.

Characterizing sleep

Up to this point in the chapter, as a simplification, sleep has been described as if it is a unitary state. This might be true of simple animals but it is not true of birds and mammals (Rechtschaffen, 1998). Rather, there are distinct types of sleep. This section looks at these and considers a principal investigative tool: electroencephalography (EEG), i.e. recording the brain's electrical activity by electrodes attached to the scalp (Chapter 5, 'The brain').

Types of sleep

Sleep and waking vary in their quality and depth. Apart from electroencephalography, another indicator that allows characterization of different types of sleep is that of the movements of the eyes (Hobson, 1999). By this characteristic, in combination with EEG differences, a distinction in types of sleep is evident.

At stages during sleep, the eyes rotate in their sockets, known as 'rapid eye movements'. By this measure, sleep can be divided into two types: **rapid eye movement sleep** (**REM sleep**), when such movements occur, and **non-rapid eye movement sleep** ('non-REM sleep' or 'NREM sleep'), when they do not (Aserinsky and Kleitman, 1955). A night's sleep is characterized by alternation between REM and NREM phases, a typical night for an adult volunteer being shown in Figure 19.6.

Bouts of REM sleep, normally lasting 5–30 minutes, occur during the night at about every 60–90 minutes. The first bout is usually at some 80–100 minutes after the start of sleep. In the case of Randy Gardner, the REM periods observed during the first night of sleep following deprivation were over three times the amount normally shown. This suggests a compensation process. Apart from the presence or absence of eye movements and the EEG, sleep can be classified by reports from the sleeper after being woken, e.g. whether he or she was dreaming.

Figure 19.7 shows an electroencephalogram of a human brain during various stages of waking and sleep. Figure 19.8 helps you to interpret it. In Figure 19.7, stages of alertness, relaxation and sleep are represented by a sequence of recordings from top to bottom. At the top is the electrical activity termed **beta activity**, associated with alert waking. It is of a relatively low amplitude and high frequency. Drowsiness is associated with a decrease in frequency and an increase in amplitude of the signal, characterized as **alpha activity** (an alpha wave). In Figures 19.6 and 19.7, note the stages of non-REM sleep (1–4) through which the person

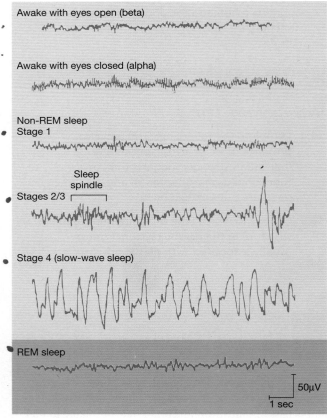

Figure 19.7 Stages of waking and sleep as characterized by an electroencephalogram.

Source: Purves *et al.* (1997, Fig. 26.1, p. 498).

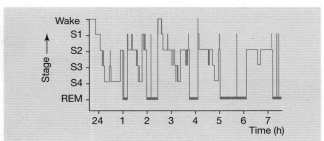

Figure 19.6 Stages of waking and sleep. S1–S4 indicate stages of non-REM sleep.

Source: Carskadon and Dement (1994, Fig. 2-7, p. 20).

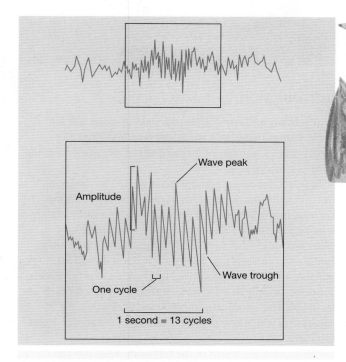

Figure 19.8 A closer look at part of an EEG recording.

Source: Hobson (1988, p. 14). Copyright © 1986 by J. Allan Hobson, MD.

passes first; there are a number of irregularities but, as a general trend, amplitude of the waves increases and their frequency decreases. As the person passes through stages 1 to 4, the threshold for waking becomes higher (Carskadon and Dement, 1994).

In evolutionary terms, non-REM sleep appears to be the precursor of REM sleep (Kavanau, 1994); REM sleep relates to the evolution of the cortex. Reptiles appear not to exhibit REM sleep and in birds it is a relatively small percentage of total sleep time. With a sophisticated cortex, mammals show a relatively large percentage of REM sleep. However, there is no simple relationship between the extent of REM sleep and a species' cognitive capacities (D.B. Cohen, 1979). Thus, the opossum shows more REM sleep than a human (Jouvet, 1975). We now look more closely at these two categories of sleep.

Non-REM sleep

During non-REM sleep, there is a lowering of metabolism. The sympathetic nervous system is slightly less active than in quiet waking and the parasympathetic system is activated (Hobson, 1986, 1999), thereby biasing towards conservation of resources. Arterial pressure, respiratory rate, heart-rate and metabolic rate are reduced.

In non-REM sleep, there is some inhibition of sensory information at the level of the thalamus (Coenen, 1995). For example, even if the optic nerve is active, this can fail to excite the corresponding LGN neurons in the thalamus

(Chapter 8, 'Vision'). Cognitive/mental activity appears to be minimal in this phase (Carskadon and Dement, 1994), which is sometimes termed 'dreamless sleep'. However, dreams do occasionally occur during non-REM sleep.

Because of the low frequency of the waveform, stage 4 of non-REM sleep is termed **slow-wave sleep** ('synchronized sleep') (Figure 19.7). The activity of a large number of neurons is synchronized, thereby giving a relatively large electrical signal. The oxygen consumption by the brain falls by up to 45%. Core sleep, as defined by Horne (1988), corresponds to periods of both slow-wave sleep and REM sleep.

REM sleep

Characteristics

REM sleep is characterized by a relatively low amplitude of EEG signal, in distinction to the large amplitude of the preceding slow-wave sleep. This phase of sleep is also described as 'desynchronized', i.e. the activity of large populations of neurons tends not to be in synchrony. Individual neurons fire independently rather than being driven collectively by a rhythmic input. However, some synchrony presumably occurs even in this phase for low-amplitude rhythms to be detectable. A relatively large amount of information processing appears to take place across the population of neurons that is freed from the rhythmic input (Antrobus, 1991).

Yet another name for REM sleep is 'paradoxical sleep'. The paradox is that, even though the sleeper is deep in sleep, the total activity of the brain is as great as, or even greater than, in attentive waking (Figure 19.7) (Jouvet, 1975). Thus, at a neural level there are similarities between REM sleep and waking, both states of 'activation' (Steriade, 1994). This suggests similarities in information processing in the two states (Llinás and Paré, 1991). The level of metabolism of the brain during REM sleep is similar to the waking state. If people are woken during REM sleep, they commonly report that they were dreaming (Hobson, 1999). Such observations led to the suggestion that, whereas non-REM sleep is concerned with physiological homeostasis, REM sleep serves a psychological function (D.B. Cohen, 1979).

During REM sleep, in contrast to the cortex, the hippocampus shows synchronized waves of activity termed **theta waves** (Siegel, 1994). These are similar to those shown during exploration (Chapter 15).

Motor systems

During REM sleep, motor regions of cortex are excited (Jouvet, 1975). Why then do we normally not aimlessly move, with arms and legs flying around the bedroom? Simultaneously with the excitation of the motor cortex, inhibition is exerted on motor neurons. Such inhibition opposes excitatory effects and prevents movement.

Although most muscles are inhibited, those that determine the rotation of the eyes function normally, as revealed in rapid eye movements.

Broader implications

During REM sleep, people can process information on salient stimuli, which can become incorporated into the story-line of a dream (Rechtschaffen *et al.*, 1966). What could appear to be a paradox is that, during this state, the evoked potential (Chapter 5) in response to sensory stimulation can be as high as during waking even though the person is not woken by the stimulus (Llinás and Paré, 1991). The thalamic–cortical projections that convey sensory information are working much as in waking (Steriade, 1994). So why isn't sleep interrupted?

We need to shake off a deeply seated way of thinking about the brain. If we feel that the brain should be quiet during sleep and any abnormal signal will wake it up, we are thinking of a passive brain which merely reacts to events. The evidence of sleep is that the brain is normally highly active. Sensory input *modulates* rather than *instigates* brain activity (Llinás and Paré, 1991).

Having defined some properties of sleep, we now consider the brain mechanisms that control sleep.

Section summary

1 Sleep can be divided into phases, according to the pattern of the EEG and other criteria.

2 The rapid eye movement phase of sleep (REM sleep) is associated with desynchronized electrical activity of the brain.

3 By exclusion, the other phase of sleep is defined as non-rapid eye movement sleep (non-REM sleep).

4 One type of non-REM sleep, termed 'slow-wave sleep' (synchronized sleep), is characterized by synchronization of the activity of relatively many neurons.

Test your knowledge

(Answers on page 487)

19.7 The motor neurons controlling which skeletal muscles are not inhibited during REM sleep?

19.8 Complete the following: 'Stage 4 of non-REM sleep is characterized by a relatively _____ frequency and _____ amplitude of signal'.

Brain mechanisms

Introduction

Which brain processes determine waking–sleep and are there regions that have a particular responsibility? Not surprisingly, a number of interacting brain regions form the basis of sleep waking.

A search for sleep mechanisms is guided by theory, an understanding of the patterns of neural activity and the corresponding behavioural phenomena. For example, sleep is not a passive state that occurs when neurons fatigue (Aserinsky and Kleitman, 1955). Animals are motivated to find a suitable sleep site. They do not normally fall into inactivity and unconsciousness, like losing the picture when the power supply to a TV set is drastically reduced. Sleep can be induced by electrical stimulation at brain sites (e.g. midbrain), which is compatible with its being an active state (Hobson, 1986).

We can ask questions of the following kind. Are there particular neurotransmitters or hormones associated with particular brain regions, the level of which shows an association with times of sleep? Can investigators identify brain regions where the circadian rhythm that underlies sleep is generated?

Transitions between states of waking–sleep, as seen in the thalamus and cortex and other linked structures such as the amygdala, appear to be determined in large part by projections from the brain stem (Llinás and Paré, 1991). These projections spread extensively and appear to modulate brain states. They form the topic of the next section.

Brain stem mechanisms

The ascending reticular activating system

A system organized in the reticular formation of the brain stem is termed the ascending reticular activating system (ARAS) (Moruzzi and Magoun, 1949). See Chapter 5, Figures 5.15 and 5.16 p. 116.

Sensory information is transmitted to the brain along the spinal cord and in the cranial nerves. These are sometimes termed the classical sensory pathways, e.g. visual, tactile and nociceptive pathways. Collaterals of the axons in the classical pathways project to the ARAS. By this means, sensory information in the classical pathways increases the activity of the ARAS (Jouvet, 1975; see Figure 5.16). In turn, by its projections throughout the brain (e.g. to the thalamus) the ARAS triggers waking. For example, electrical stimulation of the ARAS triggers waking and EEG signs of arousal (Jouvet, 1975). Lesions to the ARAS can disrupt the cycle of sleep–waking.

The ARAS is non-specific in that sensory information in a number of channels all project to it. Researchers have been able to specify details of brain stem nuclei that have an activational role and, in addition, other nuclei, which, by their activity oppose waking and promote sleep. This forms one of the biological bases of the assertion that sleep is an active process.

Identifying nuclei

Looking in detail at the ARAS and other regions, researchers have identified specific parts of the brain stem containing distinct groups of neurons that play *integrative* roles in waking and sleep (Hobson, 1999). Ascending projections of these neurons broadcast information widely to other brain regions (e.g. cortex, thalamus and hypothalamus). Activity in ascending pathways sets higher brain regions into states along the dimension of sleep–waking (Steriade, 1994). The integrative nature of certain regions of brain stem in sleep–waking is indicated by the fact that their excitation has several functionally related effects at different sites in the CNS.

Apart from inducing the characteristic sleep–waking pattern by means of ascending projections, descending pathways from the brain stem inhibit skeletal muscles, hence preventing motor activity (Hobson, 1999). Thus, there can be activation of motor regions of the brain without behaviour. Hobson suggests that this might play a role in the widespread appearance of imagined movement in dreams.

Sleep is not determined by brain stem nuclei acting in isolation. Having something important 'on our mind' can prevent us from falling asleep. What is the neural embodiment of these processes? This effect would seem to be mediated by connections from the cortex to lower brain regions (Hobson, 1986).

A number of different groups of brain stem neurons have different roles in sleep, as follows.

Noradrenergic systems

Noradrenergic (NA) neurons from the locus coeruleus project widely, e.g. to the cortex (Chapter 5; Chapman, 1995). See Figure 13.8, p. 343. Wakefulness is in part determined by increased activity of these neurons, and REM sleep by their decreased activity (Hobson and Stickgold, 1994). They are almost silent during REM sleep. Neurons carrying information from the body on threatening stimuli (e.g. tissue damage) make projections to the locus coeruleus. These serve to trigger waking and alertness (Chapman, 1995).

Serotonergic systems

Serotonergic neurons with cell bodies in brain stem nuclei termed the raphe nuclei also play a role in waking–sleep (Jouvet, 1975). Their activity appears to act like the NA

neurons to promote waking (Sutton *et al.*, 1992). Blocking serotonin synthesis leads to insomnia. Waking corresponds to a dominance of the NA and serotonergic neurons. Corresponding to the shift from waking to non-REM sleep, there is a decline in activity of NA and serotonergic neurons, accompanied by increased activity of cholinergic neurons (Hobson, 1999).

Cholinergic systems

Cholinergic neurons with cell bodies in the pons region of the brain stem and elsewhere are involved in sleep–waking (Figure 19.9) (Hobson, 1996). Some exhibit a high activity at times of REM sleep (Hobson and Stickgold, 1994), which suggests that normally they play a role in programming REM sleep by their activity. When electrically stimulated, they trigger a change in the EEG pattern from synchronized to desynchronized. Injecting a cholinergic agonist into the pons triggers signs of REM sleep (Hobson, 1999).

During REM sleep, there is activation of the lateral geniculate nucleus (LGN) by cholinergic signals (Jouvet, 1975). A neural circuit from the pons (P) to the LGN (G) and then to the occipital cortex (O) is usually abbreviated as the **PGO system** (see Figure 5.21, p. 120, for the latter part of this system). This same neural system is responsible for the eye movements that designate the REM state.

In parallel with triggering activity in the PGO system, there is modulation of sensory inputs. The combination of this and inhibition upon motor output during REM sleep means that the brain is 'off-line', i.e. relatively functionally isolated and under intrinsic control (Hobson, 1999). PGO signals also form an input to the amygdala (Chapter 12, 'Emotion'), which could account for the emotional tone of dreams (Hobson, 1999).

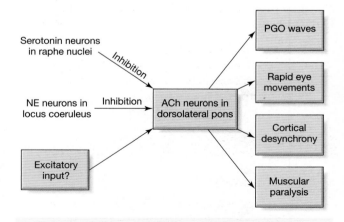

Figure 19.9 Role of ACh neurons in pons.

Source: adapted from Carlson (1994, p. 289). Reprinted by permission of the publisher.

A reciprocal interaction model

Based upon the brain stem nuclei just described, Hobson and McCarley (see Hobson, 1986) proposed a **reciprocal interaction model** of sleep. It was designed to show how transitions between REM and non-REM sleep occur. The model was based on mutual inhibition between, on the one hand, cholinergic neurons (ACh) and, on the other, serotonergic and noradrenergic (NA) (Figure 19.10). When the cholinergic system dominates, REM sleep is programmed, whereas domination of noradrenergic and serotonergic systems inhibits REM sleep. Reciprocal inhibition enables decisive swings between REM and non-REM sleep (Pace-Schott and Hobson, 2002).

This model is relevant to the issue of whether REM sleep is necessary for memory consolidation (discussed earlier). People taking the class of antidepressant termed MAO inhibitors give a bias towards noradrenergic/serotonergic control and hence have reduced REM sleep. However, there is no evidence that they have impaired capacity for learning and memory (J.M. Siegel, 2005).

The hypothalamus

Basics

Various interacting nuclei of the hypothalamus have a role in producing sleep and waking (Mistlberger, 2005). For example, activity by the anterior hypothalamus promotes sleep, whereas activity of the posterior hypothalamus promotes waking. There appears to be a kind of 'push-pull', or 'flip-flop', reciprocal antagonism between the neural systems within these regions. Hence, transitions between waking and sleeping tend to be decisive, with the brain being in either one state or the other.

Rhythm generation

A characteristic of sleep–waking is its 24 hour rhythm. Certain hypothalamic and brain stem nuclei (just described)

exert rhythmic effects upon a broad expanse of other brain regions as the basis of sleep–waking. But what determines the rhythm of these controls? A nucleus of the hypothalamus, the suprachiasmatic nucleus (SCN) (see Chapter 5, Figure 5.32, p. 128), plays a principal role, as 'master clock', in generating the circadian rhythm (Pace-Schott and Hobson, 2002). There are links from this master clock to brain regions that underlie sleep and arousal: other hypothalamic and brain stem nuclei (Mistlberger, 2005).

Although the SCN rhythm is endogenous, its phase is influenced by *Zeitgebers*. How do *Zeitgebers* influence the rhythm? One route is as follows. Pathways lead from the retina to the SCN (Chapter 8, Figure 8.17, p. 201) and they convey information on the light–dark cycle of the external world (Harrington *et al.*, 1994). By means of this information, the SCN entrains the internal rhythm to the light–dark cycles of the external world. A lesion of the SCN disrupts the circadian rhythm of sleep (Mistlberger, 2005).

Figure 19.5 suggested two factors underlying sleep, a cyclical and a non-cyclical one. Lesions to the SCN leave the non-cyclical contribution somewhat undisturbed. A tendency to sleep still arises as a function of time since the last sleep and roughly the same amounts of REM and non-REM sleep occur as in intact animals (Mistlberger, 2005). The lesion disrupts the circadian factor and sleep phases occur at random throughout the 24 hours.

Even isolated individual neurons of the SCN show a strong circadian rhythm in their activity and metabolism, indicating that 'rhythmicity' is an intrinsic property of them (Moore, 1999). In early development, such neurons show rhythms even before they form synapses with other neurons. Presumably, the rhythmicity of the individual neurons contributes to rhythmicity of the collection of neurons within the SCN.

The SCN pacemaker triggers a circadian cycle of release of the hormone melatonin from the pineal gland (Figure 5.11, p. 114; Arendt, 1997). Some evidence suggests that this hormone plays a role in the coordination of the effects of pacemaker neurons of the SCN.

A sleep factor?

To return to an earlier discussion, is it possible to identify a natural **sleep factor** ('Factor S'), e.g. in the CNS? That is, can scientists find a substance that increases in level during sleep deprivation and that, if injected into the body, induces sleep? Cerebrospinal fluid taken from the brain of a sleepy animal tends to induce sleep in a recipient (Pappenheimer, 1983). Using goats, researchers extracted a substance ('Factor S') from the fluid in the ventricles of the brain (Chapter 5, Figure 5.27, p. 125). Injection of Factor S into other animals triggered sleep. It is also possible to extract Factor S from human urine. Human Factor S causes increases in sleep when injected into rabbits.

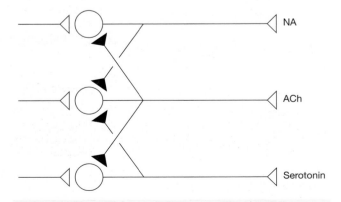

Figure 19.10 Reciprocal interaction model of sleep.

Source: adapted from Sutton *et al.* (1992, Fig. 4, p. 141).

The halves of a dolphin's brain show independence in their times of sleep, as do estimated REM cycles of human mother and foetus (D.B. Cohen, 1979). This suggests that any principal sleep factor is intrinsic to the CNS, rather than being a general circulatory factor.

A personal angle

Siamese twins

Lenard and Schulte (1972), in Göttingen, Germany, observed the sleep–waking patterns of a pair of female Siamese twins (with common circulation), joined at the head. Independent EEG records are evidence for the existence of independent brains. The authors reported: 'From their behaviour and their reactions towards the environment they appeared to be completely different personalities'.

In comparing the twins by EEG recording, they exhibited sleep and waking, as well as REM and non-REM phases of sleep, at completely separate times. The authors suggest that this case and others, in which there is extensive connections between the circulations, argue against a factor in the blood as being a trigger for sleep–waking. Unfortunately, at age 21 days, the twins died under anaesthesia before they were able to receive an operation designed to separate them.

Adenosine is a favoured candidate to serve as a sleep factor (Basheer *et al.*, 2004). Adenosine serves as a neuromodulator and also acts to protect cells. Its levels in extracellular fluid rise following injury to cells. Caffeine, found in coffee and tea, acts as an antagonist to adenosine and is known to counter sleep.

During extensive waking, adenosine accumulates in the brain. Adenosine attaches to receptors and thereby changes patterns of neural activity. The assumption is that the affected neurons form part of the neural basis of sleep. Microinjection of adenosine into the preoptic nucleus of the hypothalamus, as well as certain brain stem regions known to be implicated in sleep, has the effect of triggering sleep. As implied by Figure 19.5, there must be a site of integration between any such homeostatic sleep factor and the circadian influence. Specific nuclei in the hypothalamus are thought to play this role.

There are also other candidates that appear to contribute to sleep. Oscillations in the cerebrospinal fluid level of the cytokine interleukin-1 (IL-1) (Chapter 13), are synchronized with sleep–waking cycles, peak values being at the start of sleep or during sleep (Krueger *et al.*, 1998). Apart from any possible intrinsic role within the brain as a neurochemical, IL-1 is produced in the body following infections and a response by the immune system. Activated IL-1 appears to promote sleep at times when it is adaptive for the animal to remain immobile, e.g. following infection. Cytokines generated throughout the body by immune activation appear to promote sleep by means of a neural link to the brain, the vagus nerve.

So much for the adult system of sleep–waking; we now turn to development.

Section summary

1 The axons of cholinergic, noradrenergic and serotonergic neurons with cell bodies in the brain stem project to the cortex and other regions and modulate activity corresponding to the basis of sleep–waking.

2 The suprachiasmatic nucleus is the site of a circadian rhythm generator.

3 The tendency to sleep can be influenced by outside factors, such as the level of light serving as a *Zeitgeber*. The suprachiasmatic nucleus mediates the influence of such outside factors.

4 Research is directed to identifying a so-called 'sleep factor', adenosine being a prime candidate.

Test your knowledge

(Answers on page 487)

19.9 Acting via the retina, *Zeitgebers* influence activity at the suprachiasmatic nucleus, so as to bring the circadian rhythm into phase with the external light–dark cycle. What is the term used to describe this process?

19.10 How is the relationship of caffeine to adenosine described?

Development

For a given species of animal, sleep occupies a varying fraction of the 24 hour period at different ages. A study of the development of sleep might give some important insights into its general function and underlying mechanisms.

Humans

A circadian rhythm appears to be functioning at birth but does not make connection with the control of sleep until the child is about 6–12 weeks of age (Ferber, 1994). At age 6, the average human spends about 600 minutes a night in sleep (Horne, 1988). By age 30, they are spending about 420 minutes. The longer sleep in children correlates with periods of brain development, and could perhaps be explained in terms of it.

Changes with age are seen not only in the total amount of sleep but also in its components. The maximum amount of REM sleep (15 or more hours per 24 hours) is observed in the foetus at 6 months of age (Hobson, 1986). There is a high rate of brain development at this age (Chapter 6). These observations would be compatible with the theory that sleep is necessary for structuring (or restructuring) CNS circuits (Chokroverty, 1994).

Foetuses exhibit considerable muscular activity in REM sleep. This could be a practice effect as connections within the motor regions of the brain are structured. The existence of activity in the PGO system in REM sleep suggests a form of surrogate 'visual' stimulation that could be used for neural structuring within the visual system (Roffwarg *et al.*, 1966). In such terms, sleep would be a time of endogenous stimulation in the absence of exogenous stimulation.

Comparing individuals and species

The newborn of various species, including most mammals and chicks, show a high percentage of REM sleep at around birth or hatching (Kavanau, 1994). In the newborn human, about one half of sleep is REM sleep. For a baby born 2 months prematurely it is 80%.

Not all species exhibit a high percentage of REM sleep immediately following birth. So-called 'precocial' species (e.g. the goat, guinea pig and antelope) do not (Jouvet-Mounier *et al.*, 1969). This term refers to species that get up and go soon after birth or hatching, as opposed to a relatively helpless ('altricial') species such as humans. Precocial species emerge into the world already equipped with relatively advanced brains and physical abilities for movement. For REM sleep, a precocial species (guinea pig) is compared with two altricial species (cat and rat) in Figure 19.11. For the altricial species, a sharp decline in percentage of REM sleep as a function of age can be seen.

The ontogenetic hypothesis

The observation of a large percentage of REM sleep in the newborn of certain species led to the **ontogenetic hypothesis** of REM sleep (Horne, 1988), which suggests that its function is to do with development of the brain. As age increases, neural development declines in parallel with the decline in REM sleep. According to this hypothesis, REM sleep is a

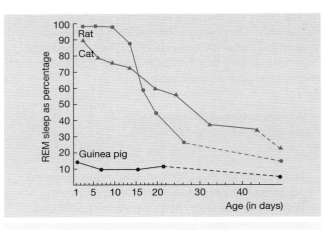

Figure 19.11 REM sleep as a percentage of total sleep for rat, cat and guinea pig.

Source: Jouvet–Mounier *et al.* (1969, Fig. 21, p. 236).

means of providing the brain with the stimulation that is needed for development.

The hypothesis might also explain why the percentage decline in REM sleep following birth is much less in precocial species. Presumably, development largely takes place before birth, when REM sleep would provide 'surrogate stimulation' of the brain. Following birth, stimulation necessary for any remaining neural development might occur as a result of sensory input from the world. In adulthood, REM sleep might provide a minimal stimulation to maintain the working efficiency of the brain.

Section summary

1 The newborn or newly hatched of many (altricial) species show a high percentage of REM sleep relative to adults.

2 The newborn of precocial species do not show this high percentage of REM sleep.

3 According to the ontogenetic hypothesis, REM sleep is connected with brain development.

Test your knowledge

(Answer on page 487)

19.11 Consider again the reciprocal interaction model, described in the last section. An examination of the type of sleep shown by the rat immediately following birth suggests that it is controlled by a domination of which neurochemical system?

Dreaming

Basic principles

A person woken during non-REM sleep will occasionally report dreaming. However, REM sleep is the phase that is primarily associated with dreaming (McCarley, 1995). It has been suggested that the function of REM sleep might be that important information processing related to the meaningful dream content can take place. However, there are good arguments against this position. For example, dream content typically bears little resemblance to the kind of cognitive tasks that engaged the dreamer in the days prior to the dream (J.M. Siegel, 2005). It is difficult to see that the foetus could have much to dream about during its 15 hours of REM sleep per 24 hours. REM sleep in early development might represent a 'test-run' of the information processing circuits that will be used later.

Dreams normally appear to arise from activity within the visual system (McCarley, 1995), with some individuals dreaming in colour. The material of dreams is primarily visual and it involves movement (Hobson, 1986). In REM sleep, blood flow is relatively high in cortical areas associated with visual processing, whereas it is relatively low in frontal regions concerned with planning and organization in time (Madsen *et al.*, 1991). Long-term goals, rational planning and coherence seem to be absent in dreams with their often chaotic organization, as one is 'carried along through time by circumstances that crop up in an unpredictable way' (Melges, 1982, p. 4; Carlson, 1994). In dreams 'the temporal structure of past, present, and future is often condensed and interchanged' (Madsen *et al.*, p. 506).

Over certain episodes, there is at least some coherence between, on the one hand, dream content and, on the other, emotional and autonomic processing (Roffwarg *et al.*, 1966). An exciting content is associated with bodily signs of activation. Erotic dreams are associated with bodily sexual arousal (Hobson, 1986).

During the dreaming phase, the brain has relatively little noradrenalin (norepinephrine) available. This might explain why we are so bad at recalling dreams, since increasing NA availability increases recall.

Who dreams?

It seems that dreaming in those born blind or who lost sight when they were very young does not correspond to 'seeing' (Hobson, 1989). They appear to tap into auditory or tactile processing when they dream. People born blind do not perform rapid eye movements during sleep periods that would be classified as REM sleep by the criterion of EEG recording. However, people who, later in life, suffer blindness do show rapid eye movements. The content of dreams

commonly involves the theme of movement and the motor cortex is activated during REM sleep (McCarley, 1995).

Do only humans dream? This raises philosophical issues since we do not know that non-humans have subjective awareness. One can always question humans but, of course, no other species can be asked for verbal reports. The essence of dreaming is its subjective nature. As far as objective indices are concerned, rapid eye movements, among other bodily responses, are shown during sleep by most species of mammal (Hobson, 1986). Dog owners sometimes report signs of agitation in their animals during sleep.

Function

What is the function of dreams, if any? A library analogy might help: dreaming could represent 're-cataloguing' the events acquired during the day, involving removal of some information. Indeed, some argue that there is meaningful cognition corresponding to dreams. Times of trauma might correspond to when emotionally significant material needs to be processed (Davis, 1985) and this could produce the material of nightmares. Chapter 13 noted that nightmares are prevalent in post-traumatic stress disorder.

Some authors see here a creative aspect to dreams (D.B. Cohen, 1979). Noting that their frequency increases at times of stress, Panksepp (1998a, p. 128) suggests that dreams provide: 'an endless variety of ideas, especially when life is stressful and we need to entertain new alternatives'. However, it could be that dreaming has no such function and might simply be an inevitable by-product of brain activity. In this case, dreaming would be termed an 'epiphenomenon'. The bizarre nature of dreams with their sudden and irrational changes of story-line might equally suggest that they represent the product of a process that has little meaning in

Do dreams relate to real-life problems in need of a solution?

Source: John Anster Fitzgerald/Private Collection/Bridgeman Art Library.

terms of content. A model that might be able to account for this aspect of dreams is described next.

Towards a neuropsychological model

R. McCarley and J.A. Hobson proposed an **activation–synthesis model** of dreaming (see Hobson, 1986). This suggests that dreams are the subjective awareness of neural events in, for example, the visual system triggered by influences from the brain stem. The dream is, in a sense, the best guess or hypothesis of a story-line that can be imposed on neural events, i.e. a synthesis based upon activation. According to this model, the fact that primarily the visual and motor systems are stimulated from the brain stem explains the visual and movement content of dreams. Presumably, if the olfactory system were stimulated, the dream content would have a strong representation from smell.

A personal angle
Heresy in sleep research

In response to the reciprocal interaction model, Hobson (1996, p. 471) writes:

By challenging the reigning Freudian theory of psychoanalysis, these heretical articles elicited more letters to the editor than the *American Journal of Psychiatry* had ever received before. Naturally and understandably, most of the letters attacked us as insensitive materialists and unenlightened Philistines. We proposed, for example, that dream amnesia could be ascribed to aminergic [refers to the ascending pathways of catecholamines] demodulation of the forebrain (rather than Freudian repression) . . .

Unlike the psychoanalytic model, the activation–synthesis model does not involve disguises or codes. The psychoanalytic interpretation has difficulty with the explicitly sexual, terrifying and disgusting content of dreams (Hobson, 1986). If these represent merely a censored version, the mind boggles in trying to imagine what the unconscious content might be like! However, Hobson does not dismiss all psychoanalytic interpretation and retains (p. 166):

the emphasis of psychoanalysis upon the power of dreams to reveal deep aspects of ourselves, but without recourse to the concept of disguise and censorship or to the now famous Freudian symbols. My tendency, then, is to ascribe the nonsense to brain–mind dysfunction and the sense to its compensatory effort to create order out of chaos. That

order is a function of our own personal view of the world, our current preoccupations, our remote memories, our feelings, and our beliefs.

The dreams that occur in REM sleep are considered by some to be similar to certain psychopathological states or LSD-induced states (Panksepp, 1998a). Specifically, this is suggested by their qualities of hallucination and delusion, confabulation and irrational transitions of logic and creative novel combinations of ideas. Investigating brain mechanisms underlying dreams might illuminate psychopathology. On a personal level, the phenomenology of dreaming (e.g. the frustration, impotence and fear) might give insights into the existential state of some sufferers from mental disorder.

Section summary

1 During REM sleep, dreams frequently occur.

2 A possible analogy is that dreams are like recataloguing a library.

3 A model of dreams is based on neuromodulation of areas of the brain by neurons with cell bodies at the brain stem.

Test your knowledge

(Answer on page 487)

19.12 The brain state associated with dreaming is normally dominated by control from which neurochemical system?

Issues of health

Introduction

Estimates suggest that up to 40 million Americans have chronic problems of disturbed sleep (Edelman, 1994). Disturbances can be discussed relative to both a norm and a possible optimal level. In terms of a need for sleep, some experts quote the figure of 7 to 8 hours per 24. People who sleep less than 4 hours or more than 9 hours per night have an increased mortality from stroke, coronary artery disease and cancer (Chokroverty, 1994).

A circadian pattern, consisting of two distinct periods of sleep and waking, tends to be the norm for young people. By old age, the two-state circadian pattern is less evident. It is often replaced by frequent night-time waking and daytime naps.

There are a number of sleep disorders (e.g. excessive daytime sleepiness, insomnia, night terrors and sleep walking) that either can be treated or which one would like to treat. Insomnia is an example of where an understanding of sleep can help the treatment of its disorder.

Insomnia and managing sleep

The phenomenon

The term **insomnia** describes a subjective feeling of inadequate sleep (Zorick, 1994). Insomniacs seem to overrate the extent to which they lose sleep. There is disparity between subjective report and an EEG measure (Mendelson, 1990). Insomniacs are poor at estimating how much time it takes them to fall asleep; they tend to overestimate by a factor of 3 (Walsh *et al.*, 1994). Similarly, the effects of sleeping pills, although often only modest, are perceived to be much greater in terms of increased length of sleep.

Insomniacs commonly attribute poor work performance, irritability and fatigue, as well as mood disturbances, to the disorder. They suffer from a relatively high frequency of other medical (e.g. heart attacks) and psychological problems (Walsh *et al.*, 1994), though, of course, separating cause and effect poses great difficulty. Insomniacs also have a relatively high frequency of traffic accidents.

Causes

Insomnia appears to be due to over-activity of NA projections arising in the brain stem (Hobson, 1999). There are various causes of insomnia, including stress, disruption of a social bond, excess alcohol, pain, disturbance to the circadian rhythm with shift-working, as well as psychiatric disorders (Zorick, 1994). Insomnia can be a cause of insomnia, e.g. worry about the consequences of insomnia can promote it (Watts *et al.*, 1995).

Treatment

Light should be kept out of the bedroom. Coffee, alcohol and nicotine should be avoided, particularly near to sleep time (Zarcone, 1994). Sleep appears to be subject to Pavlovian conditioning (Hobson, 1986). Animals sleep best in a place where they have slept in the past. Associations between the bedroom and activities that are connected with being awake should be minimized (Stepanski, 1994). Reading or watching television in bed might be a bad idea.

Some daytime napping is often inevitable in elderly people. However, too much napping can impair night-time sleep (Horne, 1992). The elimination of the ingredients of sleeping pills from the body is relatively slow in the elderly. This can

increase daytime sleepiness. Not surprisingly, insomniacs tend to take daytime naps more frequently than controls. Horne recommends that, for young and middle-aged insomniacs, such naps should be avoided. Naps tend to reduce tiredness and thereby reduce the capacity to fall asleep at night. They lower the strength of control that the circadian rhythm exerts over sleep (Zorick, 1994). For drivers, the afternoon period is one of a relatively high risk of accidents and sleepiness might contribute to this (Horne and Reyner, 1995). Journeys might usefully be broken for a nap at such times.

Behavioural disturbances during sleep

In some disorders of non-REM sleep, such as sleep walking, sleep talking and night terrors, inhibition is inadequate. There are unopposed motor commands to certain sets of muscles and behaviour is thereby triggered (Keefauver and Guilleminault, 1994). During REM sleep, some people act out their dreams with overt behaviour such as hitting. This can have obvious dangers for the sufferer and for their sleep partner.

A personal angle

A nightmare scenario

Schenck *et al.* (1986) working in Minneapolis, reported the case of a 72-year-old retired farmer, without any history of aggression or psychiatric disturbance. His wife witnessed his 'wild dreams' in which he would shout, hit out and kick not only his wife but also the walls and furniture. The following day his hands were sore. A CT brain scan suggested neural degeneration in the pons and cerebellum. Another patient, a 70-year-old retired farmer tried to strangle his wife as he enacted a struggle with a bear. Behaviour indicates a failure of the inhibition of skeletal muscles, manifest in acting out the dream. In some cases, damage to the pons caused by a tumour can be identified, pointing to a deficiency in this region in the organization of descending inhibition on skeletal muscles.

Narcolepsy

The term **narcolepsy** refers to bouts of sudden sleepiness experienced during the day, associated with weakness of skeletal muscles (Siegel, 2004). The phenomenon draws attention to the natural role of a peptide, known as hypocretin (sometimes termed orexin). The cell bodies of neurons that employ this transmitter are found in the hypothalamus and their axons project to the nuclei in the brain stem that play a major role in sleep, described earlier. Narcolepsy is associated with abnormally low levels of hypocretin. Targeting this neural system by drugs is an active research area in trying to find a cure for narcolepsy.

Section summary

1 Insomnia is a subjective feeling of inadequate sleep.

2 It is possible to bring sleep under better control, e.g. to avoid substances that promote waking and to resist naps and 'sleep-ins'.

3 Narcolepsy involves sudden intense sleepiness during the day.

Test your knowledge

(Answer on page 487)

19.13 Suppose that the room in which someone sleeps regularly acquires a capacity to trigger sleep. What term might be used to describe such a stimulus to sleep?

19.4

Bringing things together

Sleep is a good example of the value (if not imperative) of considering causal, developmental, evolutionary and functional types of explanations together (Chapter 2). However, we do not know the function served by this behaviour, with which we spend a third of our lives. Evidence suggests a combination of functions: homeostatic (restorative), keeping immobile and reorganization of the brain.

We have a reasonably good understanding of how neural processes contribute to sleep and waking, e.g. the role of projections from nuclei in the brain stem. The fact that periods of the most brain development are also periods of the most sleep suggests that the facilitation of reorganization of the brain ('plasticity') provides a functional reason for sleep. This fits with the observation that sleep deprivation disrupts the generation of new neurons in the hippocampus.

There is still much room for informed speculation.

Summary of Chapter 19

1 **Sleep represents an altered state of consciousness. It is accompanied by a limited range of behaviour and characteristic patterns of brain activity.**

2 **Sleep is controlled in part by an internally driven rhythm, termed a circadian rhythm.**

3 **There are likely to be several different functions served by sleep. Although we cannot identify these with certainty, it is insightful to study causation and function in parallel.**

4 **The parameter of sleep-waking is associated with motivation, which directs an animal towards finding a sleeping site.**

5 **The electrical activity of the brain points to there being more than one type of sleep.**

6 **Identifiable neural processes adjust the activity of brain processes in a cyclical fashion, corresponding to sleeping and waking, as well as to different types of sleep.**

7 **Development is associated with fundamental changes in sleep patterns.**

8 **Dreaming represents a subjective experience associated with identifiable patterns of activity in the brain.**

9 **Disorders of sleep can help us to understand the basics of sleep.**

Further reading

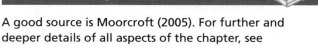

A good source is Moorcroft (2005). For further and deeper details of all aspects of the chapter, see Kryger *et al*. (2005). For the thoughts of a leading researcher in the area, see Hobson (2003, 2004). For a multiple perspective on sleep, see Pace-Schott *et al*. (2003). For the role of cholinergic systems, see Perry *et al*. (1999). For the link with health, written by a distinguished sleep researcher, see Dement (2001).

Signposts

You have seen how the principles of homeostasis, introduced in Chapters 1 and 2 and revisited in Chapter 15, are of central importance to understanding sleep. You also have seen how each of the four types of explanation (Chapters 1 and 2) – causal, developmental, evolutionary and functional – has a role in understanding sleep. In trying to define sleep, the issue arises of the exact meaning of the term 'consciousness'. Hence, much of the material in this chapter is relevant to Chapter 21, 'Brains, minds and consciousness'.

Answers

Explanations for answers to 'test your knowledge' questions can be found on the website **www.pearsoned.co.uk/toates**

19.1   Functional
19.2   Phase; period
19.3   *Zeitgeber*; circadian
19.4   Costs; benefits
19.5   Synapses
19.6   Deprivation
19.7   Those responsible for eye movements
19.8   Low; high
19.9   Entrainment
19.10   Antagonist
19.11   Cholinergic
19.12   Cholinergic
19.13   Conditional stimulus

Interactions and animations relating to topics discussed in this chapter can be found on the website at **www.pearsoned.co.uk/toates.** These include

Animation: The brain stem and sleep

Animation: The suprachiasmatic nucleus and sleep

Interaction: The main brain areas involved in circadian rhythms

CHAPTER 20

Cognition and action

Learning outcomes for Chapter 20

After studying this chapter, you should be able to:

1. Describe the links between cognition and action and thereby state what is meant by the term 'goal'.

2. Present a balanced and critical account of the notion of modularity. Link this to understanding how real brains work.

3. Explain why cognition and action require the existence of a process of attention. Relate this to the biological bases of attention.

4. Describe what is meant by the term 'hemispheric asymmetry' and the types of experimental evidence that lead us to this notion.

5. Describe the link between the performance of goal-directed action and the role of the prefrontal cortex.

6. Show where an understanding of language can be enriched by a parallel application of the four types of explanation: causal, developmental, evolutionary and functional. Link this to the brain mechanisms underlying human language and a consideration of what is special about language in humans.

Scene-setting questions

1   Why can't we do more different things all at the same time?

2   Is the mind organized as modules?

3   'You need to pay attention to what you are supposed to be doing!' What happens when you pay attention?

4   Is using a mobile phone whilst driving really hazardous?

5   A popular 'new-age' image is that the left hemisphere is reductionist, 'Western', logical and mathematical, whereas the right is holistic, 'Eastern', creative, intuitive and artistic. Is this true?

6   In the brain, what is involved when we resist temptation? Why are some people not so good at it?

How do we manage to do more than one thing at a time?

Source: Getty Images/The Image Bank.

Introduction

The term **cognition** refers to knowledge about the world and this chapter concerns how cognition is exploited in action. Cognition can only be used in action if it can link to motor control, which is inevitably a further consideration of the chapter. Our various motivations are associated with goals (Norman and Shallice, 1986). We are hungry, so we set the goal of preparing a meal. We need social company, so we invite friends around for a meal, thereby combining social and food-related goals.

Imagine you are preparing a meal, having set the overall ('high-level') goal of presenting the finished meal to guests. Moving towards this goal requires sub-goals to be met, e.g. to boil potatoes and clean lettuce. Each goal and sub-goal has associated with it memories of actions that are expected to lead to its achievement. Each sub-goal requires yet further sub-goals to be met, e.g. remove the lettuce from the refrigerator, turn on the tap and finally put the lettuce in a salad dryer. Within each such level, there can be competition for control, as in interrupting the drying of the lettuce to switch off the boiling potatoes. So, successful behaviour involves goals, plans for achieving them, allocation of time and calling up memories of appropriate actions.

In the middle of making the meal, the telephone rings and a friend asks for instructions on how to get to your home. So, your attention becomes occupied by the auditory channel, as you focus on the conversation. You balance the portable phone under your chin, listening, as always, with the right ear (or for some people, the left). You talk and continue the cooking. At one point, quite unintentionally, you stop cooking in order to make arm gestures to accompany giving the directions.

In your lifetime's experience of cooking, the behaviour of picking up an egg has a strong association with the mechanics of breaking it against the edge of a dish. However, this time the goal requires the unbroken egg to be placed in a saucepan and boiled. While your attention is diverted by the conversation, the stimulus of the sight of the egg and a dish triggers the breaking reaction. This is against the interests of the goal and, as your attention returns briefly to the sub-goal of boiling an egg, you realize what you have done and utter 'concentrate, you fool!' or something stronger.

At times you are strongly tempted to taste what you are making. You find this hard to resist even though you know that it will show on your waist-line some time later. After taking a number of generous samples, finally you manage to resist.

A number of features of cognition and the link to action are illustrated by this example:

1. Behaviour has a goal (or 'purpose'): a state that does not at present exist is represented by the brain/mind and action is taken to bring an actual state into alignment with it.

2. Attention is involved in allocating priority among the possible controls of behaviour. Attention shifts the focus between them, according to changing circumstances. It underlies the allocation of cognitive resources. Success at a task requires attention to be allocated appropriately.

3. Behaviour can be captured by strong stimulus–response links (e.g. egg → break), especially when attention is directed elsewhere.

4. There could be a difference in sensory channels between the sides of the head when it concerns their ability to process information. Is this indicative of a hemispheric difference in the brain?

5. It comes so naturally to use hands to give directions even though, in the absence of a video-link, it clearly cannot be of much help to your distant friend. Speech seems to be linked naturally with motor acts. This suggests that speech is not a self-contained cognitive system.

6. There can be conflict between the temptation of immediate rewards (taste of food) and delayed punishments (thoughts of increased weight).

The chapter will look at goal direction, decision-making, attention, hemispheric differences and language. It starts by considering the issue of modularity: whether the brain is made up of a number of specialized processors.

Section summary

1. Actions are associated with goals.

2. Goals are associated with sub-goals.

3. Attention is allocated to different stimuli and tasks.

4. Behaviour can be captured by certain stimuli, particularly if attention wanders from the task set.

Test your knowledge

(Answer on page 515)

20.1 Complete the following sentence: 'The process of _____ favours processing of some stimuli at the expense of others'.

20.1

Modularity

Introduction

A question that has been much discussed in psychology goes along the following lines. To what extent is information processing in the brain done by specialized modules that act in parallel, with each being dedicated to solving only a *single* type of problem? By contrast, to what extent is it done by flexible all-purpose *central processes*? Figure 20.1 shows the nature of this distinction. Each module is dedicated to just one task. Damage to a module would be expected to disrupt just one sort of information processing, leaving the rest intact. By contrast, disruption to central processing would be expected to produce gross global deficits revealed in many domains.

Of course, as you have seen, ears and the auditory channel do a very different job from eyes and the visual channel, and, if this were all the argument is saying, it would be banal. Rather, it is claiming that processing within the brain itself is specialized to a degree that we might never have guessed.

There is the notion that the brain contains a number of *modules*, each having a special way of operating such that it is dedicated to only a particular task. This is known as **modularity** (Fodor, 1985). Modules are described as 'encapsulated', meaning that they can act with autonomy from processing elsewhere in the CNS. According to the modularity view, both types of process, encapsulated modules and general-purpose central processing, exist and serve complementary roles in adaptive cognition and behaviour.

To what extent does human information processing exhibit modularity? There is clearly some dedication of brain structures to particular tasks. For example, the brain mechanisms underlying the processing of colour seem to be dedicated to only one such task, as do those for face recognition (Chapter 8, 'Vision'). Some human disorders suggest modularity since just one feature of cognition appears to be impaired, among otherwise apparently normal functioning (Karmiloff-Smith *et al.*, 1995). In autism, social cognition is

deficient in the context of some normal non-social cognition. In the rare disorder termed 'Williams syndrome' (also known as Beuren's syndrome), speech and social interaction are typically normal, in the face of severe disruption of other functions such as problem-solving, visuospatial integration and planning (Karmiloff-Smith *et al.*, 1995). Face recognition is normal or even better than that of controls.

Properties and function of modules

The term 'information encapsulation' refers to the property of modular processes to operate with independence from influences outside the module, e.g. central processes. Fodor (1985) argues that modular systems are hard-wired, autonomous, domain specific and innately specified. They are typified by perceptual processes, which are driven automatically by sensory input ('bottom-up') and are very fast. As another example, it was noted in Chapter 12 ('Emotion') that with the help of a rapidly reacting 'fear module', you tend to survive to see another day.

Also pointing to modularity, visual illusions appear even in the face of accurate knowledge about the object. For example, the Muller–Lyer illusion (Figure 7.5, p. 182) occurs even though we know rationally that the lines are of equal length. The illusion is said to be the product of a particular module and thereby immune from the central processing that knows that the lengths are equal. We are consciously aware of only the output of modules, in this example the conscious perception that the lines are unequal. We have no insight into how we arrived at that conscious perception. By contrast, we can be aware of some intermediate steps and processing operations of central processes (Moscovitch and Umiltà, 1990). What Fodor calls 'higher' cognitive processes, e.g. thinking, are said not to show modularity and encapsulation.

On the functional significance of modules, Moscovitch and Umiltà (1990, p. 13) suggest that modules supply central processing with information about the world '. . . quickly, efficiently, and without distortion from the beliefs, motivations, and expectations of the organism'. Such modules must be 'immune to higher-order influences'.

According to Fodor, the development of modular systems follows a fixed course as does their malfunction. By contrast, there exist 'true higher cognitive faculties' (Fodor, 1985, p. 4), central processes that are 'slow, deep, global rather than local, largely under voluntary (or, as one says, "executive") control'. They are exemplified by thought and problem-solving. Fodor (p. 4) suggests:

The surface plausibility of the *Modularity* picture thus lies in the idea that Nature has contrived to have it both ways, to get the best out of fast dumb systems *and* slow contemplative ones, by simply refusing to choose between them.

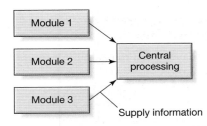

Figure 20.1 Modules and central processes.

In some cases, with experience, component modules are assembled and the assembly takes on features of a bigger module. Reading is a possible example of this. Presumably, modules devoted to speech and vision are integrated in reading (Jusczyk and Cohen, 1985). With experience, reading can take on automatic properties, as in the Stroop task (Chapter 10, 'The control of movement').

Links to biology

In principle, the domain of a module could be identified by brain damage. This might selectively disrupt just one component process, or one process might be spared in the face of disruption to others (Morris, 1996a,b). By this criterion, examples of modular processing include that for colours, location of sounds and faces. It appears that each of these can be impaired in isolation and each can survive even severe **dementia** (gross and general cognitive impairment) (Chapter 22, 'When things go wrong').

Another feature of modules is said to be their 'shallow output'. For example, patients with dementia can sometimes reproduce, say, speech but without insight into its semantic content. Some Alzheimer's patients are able to read and even correct grammatical mistakes without understanding the material.

Double dissociations (Chapter 8) are one possible feature of modules. That is, brain damage x would disrupt behaviour X, while leaving Y intact. Conversely, damage y would disrupt behaviour Y whilst leaving X intact. Such evidence is suggestive of modular organization, though there might also be a double dissociation within what might appear to be the so-called central all-purpose system (Moscovitch and Umiltà, 1990). For example, following damage, one form of memory can be disrupted while others remain essentially intact (Chapter 11, 'Learning and memory'; Gross, 1985). Double dissociations can occur between episodic and semantic memory (Temple and Richardson, 2004).

Critiques of modularity

There are a number of critiques of classical modularity and these can serve as a stimulus to sharpen our thinking on the subject. For example, is modularity genetically specified? Traditionally, the notions of modularity and genetic specification have been linked. However, in terms of a contemporary understanding of development (Chapter 6, 'Development and plasticity'), modularity appears to arise in part from interaction with the environment. Thus, a module might be 'the *emergent product* of development, not its starting point' (Karmiloff-Smith *et al.*, 1995).

Rather than strict encapsulation, there can be interactions between so-called modules, such as visual and auditory processing (see later) (Glucksberg, 1985).

There are some problems with Fodor's criteria for distinguishing modular and central systems (Moscovitch and Umiltà, 1990). For example, attention is a central process and yet a switch of it can be both rapid and mandatory, e.g. in response to one's own name said loudly.

There is good reason to blur Fodor's distinction between modules and a central system, so that a dichotomy gets replaced by a continuum (that must surely give you a strong feeling of déjà vu!) (Gardner, 1985). Even central systems can exhibit features of modularity and can break down in ways that suggests modularity (as in the case of memory). Conversely, processing within modules can be subject to central top-down controls, which reduces their encapsulation (Caplan, 1985). For example, Chapter 8 described top-down factors in perception, e.g. expectancy.

The message to take with us

We can gain insight into brain, cognition and behaviour by looking at fracture lines: brain damage can sometimes disrupt one information processing system, leaving another apparently intact. There can sometimes be parallel ways of solving a problem, only one of which might be disrupted by a lesion (Coltheart, 1985). We should be on guard not to make dogmatic assumptions about unitary global processes that in reality might be composed of a number of divisible subsystems (cf. Rizzolatti and Berti, 1993). In a clinical context, it might prove vital not to assume a broad disruption of all processing and thereby to miss islands of intact functioning. We can be vigilant for ways in which features of modularity can manifest. For example, comparing *between* memories, either semantic or episodic memory can be disrupted (showing some properties of modules), with no global impairment (Temple and Richardson, 2004). However, there can also be disruption *within* each of these, e.g. semantic memory for numbers can remain intact in the face of disruption to memory for non-number information.

Given several 'ifs' and 'buts', the issue of modularity is a useful one to hold in mind in discussing cognition and action.

Section summary

1 Fodor divided processes into modules and central cognition.

2 Modules were said to exhibit information encapsulation.

3 The distinction is useful to hold in mind but is not a clear-cut one.

4 Evidence suggests that modularity emerges from the process of development.

Test your knowledge

(Answer on page 515)

20.2 Complete the missing words in the following:
'In a double dissociation, a lesion to brain
region x disrupts behaviour X but leaves
_____ Y _____, whereas lesion y disrupts
_____ Y but leaves X _____'

Attention

Introduction

The term **attention** relates to the common experience that a given stimulus can be perceived with different amounts of subjective clarity at different times (Rizzolatti, 1983). That is, the power of a stimulus to engage awareness depends upon the amount of attention allocated to its processing. At times we show high attention in a general sense ('vigilance'), whereas at other times we are lacking in vigilance, if not unconscious (Chapter 19, 'Sleep and waking'). The present section is concerned primarily with the role of attention in directing processing to particular stimuli and away from others, at a given point in time. Such attention is needed for the efficient focus on only certain stimuli, the generation of *coordinated* behaviour based on a limited sub-set of the total sensory input and, thereby, the avoidance of chaos.

Stimuli compete for access to awareness and attention biases their competitive value (Posner, 1993). Broadly speaking, the competition is not just for awareness but also for the control of action based on this. Bringing sensory events to awareness involves a high degree of selection (Desimone, 1992). For example, on looking at a crowd, in spite of many faces simultaneously forming an image on the retina, we can usually only recognize one or two at a time.

Attention is most commonly studied in the context of vision and hearing (Driver and Spence, 1994) but the notion applies also to other senses, e.g. the tactile (Lloyd *et al.*, 1999). Attention is also involved in the focus on internal events. For example, we might be able to concentrate on mental arithmetic or, conversely, be unable to resist the intrusion into awareness of pain or unwanted thoughts (Eccleston and Crombez, 1999; Tallis, 1995).

Attention processes are distinct from sensory and motor processes but clearly interact with them.

Types of attention

We can classify attention in the way described below (Perry and Hodges, 1999). However, these are not mutually exclusive classes. Accounting for a given instance of cognitive processing might well need to involve two or three such types.

Sustained attention

Sustained attention refers to the ability to hold attention over considerable periods of time ('vigilance'). It underlies the capacity to detect a signal over long periods (Broadbent, 1958), e.g. to inspect a radar screen and report when a signal appears. Sleepiness represents a state of the brain that can be contrasted with the ability to show high sustained attention.

Selective attention

Selective attention and its shifting refer to the capacity to focus on a limited range of information while reducing the strength of distraction. For example, an instruction 'find the red socks in the drawer' calls on this capacity. We orientate attention such that one particular stimulus is processed rather than another. For example, even with the eyes stationary, we can be cued to expect an object at one location in space. Cueing means that preferential processing is allocated to information corresponding to this area (Aston-Jones *et al.*, 1999). Selective attention is the principal form of attention to be considered here.

Divided attention

Divided attention is the ability to share attention processes and perform more than one task simultaneously (Perry and Hodges, 1999). Typically, the participants perform tasks A and B separately, their performance is measured, and then they are asked to perform A and B simultaneously. The detriment in performance as compared to the scores for A and B separately is a measure of the difficulty of simultaneous performance.

Determinants of attention

A distinction can be made between two factors that determine attention (Posner, 1980). There is a 'bottom-up factor' (also termed 'involuntary' and 'passive'), as when a *stimulus* captures attention by its strength, novelty or sudden appearance. There is a 'top-down factor' (also termed 'voluntary' and 'active'). This describes the role of such things as knowledge of the situation, motivation, instructions given by an experimenter, or goals set in a search task. Though a convenient descriptive distinction, of course, active and passive factors interact in each example of attention.

The nature of selective attention

This section introduces some of the processes that underlie the control of selective attention.

Overt and covert orientating

Selective attention is served by two possible means of action, described in this section. Consider when the eyes move to bring the image of a selected part of the world to the fovea (Chapter 8) or when the body turns to maximize the impact of a particular event. Such realignment of the body or part of it to alter sensory inflow is termed **overt orientating**. The term **covert orientating** refers to the act of focusing on a particular object, location or stimulus feature without making any movement of eyes or other body region (Posner, 1980). For example, even with the image stationary at the centre of the retina, there are features of the image to which we can direct attention and subject to more detailed processing.

Figure 20.2 shows a demonstration of selective attention involving covert orientating. The person was required to fixate the eyes on a central point on a screen ('Fixation point'). A cue was presented consisting of either a plus sign or an arrow pointing right or left. The cue directed the focus of attention. If the cue, in the form of the plus sign, appeared in the centre, this indicated an equal chance of the target being to left or right. To see whether attention could be directed to right or left, the cue took the form of the arrow. A target, a circle, was then flashed very briefly onto the screen. The task

was to detect whether this target appeared to the left, to the right, or at the fixation point. Thus, if people are able to exert selective attention towards one side, they would be expected to do better when cued correctly by the arrow.

Only trials on which no eye movements occurred were used, hence revealing the effect of purely covert shifts of attention. When the arrow pointed to the appropriate direction ('honest signal'), reaction time of detection was faster than for no cue. For the opposite direction of pointing ('dishonest signal'), it was slower. This demonstrates increased efficiency arising from exploiting the cue to focus on an appropriate area of visual space. This area was allocated priority in terms of processing information arising there.

There are similarities between overt and covert orientating (Desimone, 1992). For example, the eyes can only point at one part of the whole visual world and decisions are made as to the priority target. Overt and covert orientating work as an integrated system (Rizzolatti *et al.*, 1987). A change of covert orientation (from A to B) is usually associated with a corresponding eye movement shortly afterwards, to bring B into alignment with the fovea (Wurtz *et al.*, 1982).

Selective attention applies also to auditory information: for example, in the 'cocktail party phenomenon' (Cherry, 1966), one voice or word engages attention.

Cross-modal interaction

To what extent does selective attention within one sensory system interact with that of another? Can a person focus

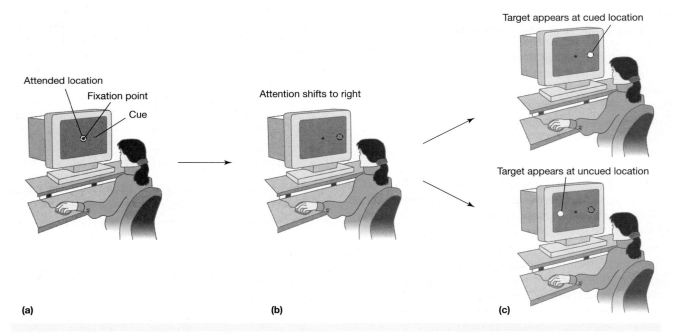

(a) **(b)** **(c)**

Figure 20.2 Experiment demonstrates covert orientating: (a) cue presented, (b) attention shifts and (c) target appears.
Source: Bear *et al.* (1996, Fig. 21.15, p. 603).

attention to the left as far as visual stimuli are concerned but simultaneously to the right as far as auditory stimuli are concerned? A focus of one modality tends to give a selective advantage to the compatible field in the other modality also (Driver and Spence, 1994). This makes functional sense in that attention mechanisms have presumably been selected to serve action. Salient information detected in one modality and from one side (e.g. the sound of a potential predator) might usefully cause a focus of attention on other sensory information to that side (e.g. visual stimuli of movement).

The action of attention signals

Attention alters the sensitivity of neural pathways, thereby making some stimuli more likely to capture processing resources than others.

Nature of influence

Two questions immediately arise concerning how attention influences the pathways that link stimuli with awareness: at what point in the pathway does this influence exert its effect? What is the nature of the influence called 'attention', which acts on neural pathways? The evidence points to attention acting at various locations in the sensory pathway. For example, in vision, these range from the primary visual cortex to later stages of processing in the ventral stream (Chapter 8) (Shomstein and Yantis, 2004). The nature of the influence is usually assumed to be one of 'modulation', alas a confusing term given the use of 'module' just described. It suggests that, in attended channels, there is amplification of the activity that would otherwise occur and, in unattended channels, there is reduced activity (Kanwisher and Wojciulik, 2000).

Attention signals can modulate *within* a sensory system (e.g. in vision, to emphasize colour rather than shape) or *between* sensory systems (e.g. to favour auditory stimuli relative to visual (Shomstein and Yantis, 2004)). The latter can explain partly why even hands-free mobile phones can be a hazard when driving (Strayer *et al.*, 2003).

A personal angle

S.B.

In Germany, S.B., a former student of engineering, suffered strokes at age 22 years (in 1990) and again one year later (Engelien *et al.* 2000). These severely damaged his auditory cortex on both sides, such that S.B. was not usually aware consciously of sounds. PET studies revealed that S.B.'s auditory cortex was normally only very slightly triggered by sounds. The remainder of the auditory system appeared to function normally. Researchers found that S.B. was consciously aware of sounds only when his selective and undivided attention was paid to the auditory channel. For example, he could voluntarily focus on this channel, as in trying to hear the sound of the door-bell at a time when visitors were expected. S.B. exemplifies the role of the top-down factor in attention.

Covert selective attention within the visual system

Moran and Desimone (1985) and Luck *et al.* (1997) projected images onto the retina of monkeys and measured the responses of neurons at various locations in the visual system. They examined the ventral stream, i.e. primary visual cortex → prestriate area → inferior temporal cortex (Chapter 8). Monkeys were trained to fixate their eyes upon a spot on a screen throughout the test and the receptive field of a particular neuron in the inferior temporal (IT) cortex was mapped in terms of area on the screen. IT neurons have large receptive fields and are triggered by complex patterns. With eyes still fixed, the animal was trained to shift covert orientation to one of two locations within the receptive field as directed by a cue. See Figure 20.3.

In the first part of the experiment, single stimuli were employed. An IT neuron that was sensitive to a red stimulus but insensitive to a green stimulus within its receptive field was found. (Other IT neurons would be sensitive to green and insensitive to red.) Compare parts (a) and (b), where single stimuli are used. In the second part of the experiment, red and green stimuli were presented together and attention was cued to the location of each stimulus in turn. Compare parts (c) and (d), where the identical two stimuli are present but the site of cueing changes. When attention was drawn to the location of the red stimulus, activity in the IT neuron was high. When it was drawn to the location of the green stimulus, activity in the neuron was low. This was in spite of the fact that the otherwise effective red stimulus was still present (compare (d) with (a) and (c)).

Comparing (c) and (d), since the eyes did not move and the same red and green stimuli were present in both cases, stimulation at the retina was the same. However, the effect of the red stimulus depended upon the target of covert orientation. In other words, attention modulated the activity of neurons according to its locus.

Brain regions and controls of attention

Introduction

We have considered the role of attention but where in the brain does it arise? We have already considered the brain stem controls of sleeping and waking (Chapter 19). These clearly set the overall tone of the brain so that it exhibits

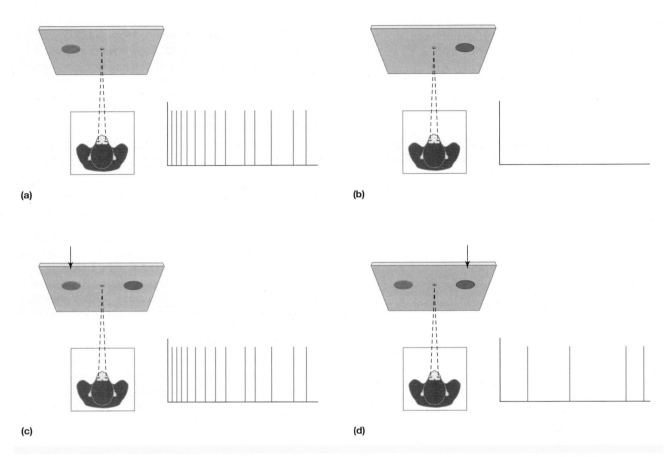

Figure 20.3 Selective attention and the response of an IT neuron with animal's eyes fixated at the central spot. Responses to (a) red stimulus alone (note activity), (b) green stimulus alone (note absence of activity), (c) and (d) to both stimuli with attention cued to (c) red and (d) green.

varying degrees of alertness. Studies point to activation in the prefrontal and parietal regions of the right hemisphere as indicative of sustained attention in any sensory channel (Sarter *et al.*, 2001). The vigilance decrement over time is mirrored in reduced levels of activation there.

What is happening in the brain when we focus attention?

Source: Ethno Images, Inc./Alamy.

We are now concerned with attention directed to particular features of sensory input. Evidence suggests a network of brain regions dedicated to the control of such attention, which are distinct from, though they interact with, sensory and motor systems (Desimone, 1992; Karnath *et al.*, 2002; Posner and Petersen, 1990).

We will look next in more detail at the role of some of the brain regions involved in attention.

Prefrontal cortex

Forming the so-called 'anterior attention system', the prefrontal cortex (PFC) plays a top-down role in each of the three forms of attention (D'Esposito *et al.*, 1995; Sarter *et al.*, 2001). Regarding divided attention, the investigators looked at performance on two separate tasks that each predominantly activated posterior brain regions. Performing either task on its own was not associated with PFC activation. When people performed both tasks simultaneously, the dorsolateral PFC was activated. D'Esposito *et al.* suggest that a role of the dorsolateral PFC is to allocate and coordinate the limited resource of attention.

The fronto-parietal system

The fronto-parietal system is embodied in interacting neural circuits that involve parts of the frontal and parietal lobes (Kanwisher and Wojciulik, 2000). It is the source of modulatory attention signals that are transmitted to other regions.

There is a 'posterior attention system' (PAS), located within the posterior parietal lobe of each hemisphere (Posner and Petersen, 1990). The PAS modulates the sensitivity of certain neural systems that perform cognitive processing. When a person switches attention from one location to another (a top-down influence), there is activation of the posterior parietal lobe (Posner, 1993). It appears that the PAS is involved in covert switches of attention from one location to another.

Disruption of attention

Certain sites of brain damage are followed by a **neglect syndrome** (also termed 'sensory neglect' or 'spatial neglect'), and this provides a major source of insight into brain mechanisms of attention (Posner, 1993). Stimuli that would normally undergo processing in the hemisphere contralateral to the lesion are processed abnormally. For example, they are associated with an unusually long reaction time or there is no awareness of them. In severe cases, half the visual world including half the patient's own body appears not to exist to them (Halligan and Marshall, 1993). The neglect syndrome highlights a normal capacity to divide attention along a spatial dimension (Farah *et al.*, 1993). Neglect is more common with damage to the right hemisphere than the left (Posner, 1993). This suggests that the basis of the control of attention in both hemispheres is located within the right hemisphere.

Traditionally, in humans damage to the posterior parietal cortex is thought to be the cause of the cortical contribution to neglect, though some associate it more closely with regions of temporal cortex (Karnath *et al.*, 2001). Damage to regions of basal ganglia and thalamus is also followed by sensory neglect (Karnath *et al.*, 2002).

So far we have briefly mentioned a hemispheric difference. We now look in more detail at the specialization of the two hemispheres.

3 Overt orienting serves selective attention by a realignment of the body (or part of it) to alter sensory inflow.

4 Covert orientating refers to an intrinsic change in the focus of attention without moving the body or part of it.

5 A passive switch of attention is in response to external events whereas an active change is due to a top-down factor.

6 The activity of neurons in sensory processing pathways reflects the role of attentional factors.

7 A neglect syndrome refers to a failure of part of the sensory space to enter awareness.

Test your knowledge

(Answer on page 515)

20.3 Complete the following statement, which relates to Figure 20.3(c) and (d): 'Cueing of attention to the _____ corresponding to the green light lowers activity in the cell indicated'.

Hemispheric asymmetry

Introduction

The term **lateralization** (Kosslyn *et al.*, 1999) refers to an asymmetry, whereby one side of the brain takes a disproportionate role in a particular type of information processing. It appears to be especially evident in humans (Trevarthen, 1984). We normally show little evidence of asymmetry in everyday life (except the preferential use of one hand), since the brain works as an integrated whole. Special tests are needed to reveal it.

In right-handed people, the basis of language tends to be lateralized in the left hemisphere (discussed later). The right hemisphere typically is specialized for perception of visual patterns, e.g. faces, and global or holistic organization, including emotionally loaded information. The left hemisphere is better at analytic cognition (Tucker and Williamson, 1984).

Some evidence for functional asymmetry derives from deficits shown by patients suffering disease or brain damage.

However, apart from general difficulties of interpretation of brain damage (Chapter 5), the inherent plasticity of the brain means that compensation can sometimes mask the failure of a damaged region.

Anatomical differences

In humans, differences in the anatomy of the cerebral hemispheres appear to be related to differences in function (Kosslyn *et al.*, 1999). A focus of interest is a region termed the planum temporale (PT), which is generally larger in the left hemisphere than in the right (Figure 20.4) (Geschwind and Levitsky, 1968) and for most people speech is based in regions of the left hemisphere that include the PT. In right-handed people, the angle that the Sylvian fissure forms with the horizontal is generally larger in the right hemisphere than in the left (Figure 20.5). In most right-handed people, but only a minority of left-handed or ambidextrous people, the left Sylvian fissure is longer than the right.

The normal asymmetry in PT, favouring the left side of the brain is a stimulus for theorizing about the role of the PT (Shapleske *et al.*, 1999). For example, the PT performs speech processing in the left hemisphere. However, the extent of the bias that normally favours the left in fact varies across people and in a minority of cases it is either non-existent or there is even a bias in favour of the right hemisphere. Such individual differences are the trigger to try to correlate the extent of hemispheric differences in brain anatomy with behavioural differences. For example, the asymmetry in size tends to be less in left-handed people.

In humans, asymmetries in the planum temporale and Sylvian fissure are evident even before birth (Chi *et al.*, 1977). Yeni-Komshian and Benson (1976) looked at the length of the Sylvian fissure in a sample of brains of humans, chimpanzees and rhesus monkeys. For each individual, they plotted the length of fissure for the left brain against that of the right brain. See Figure 20.6. The left fissure was longer in 84% of the humans, 80% of the chimpanzees and 44% of the rhesus monkeys. A particularly strong deviation from equality in humans is evident.

Evidence on asymmetry extends even to prehistory. Neanderthals lived during a period of some 30 000 to 230 000 years ago (Stringer and Gamble, 1993). Evidence suggests that they showed hemispheric asymmetry (LeMay, 1976).

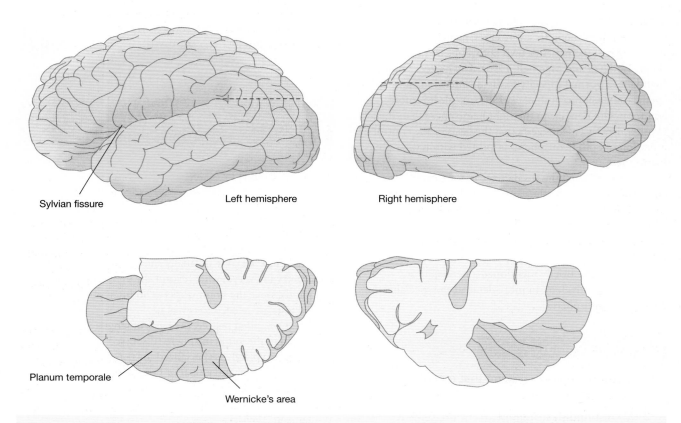

Sylvian fissure · Left hemisphere · Right hemisphere · Planum temporale · Wernicke's area

Figure 20.4 Comparison of left and right hemispheres, showing larger planum temporale of left.

Source: Geschwind (1979, p. 165). Courtesy of Carol Donner.

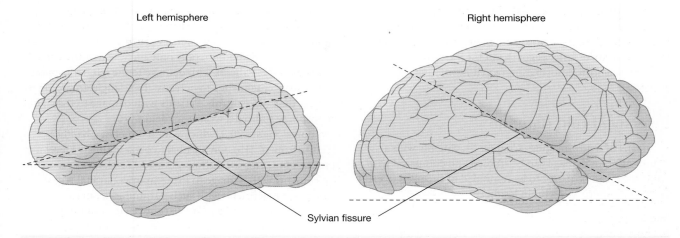

Left hemisphere

Right hemisphere

Sylvian fissure

Figure 20.5 The angle that the Sylvian fissure forms with the horizontal.

Source: Kosslyn *et al.* (1999, Fig. 58.4, p. 1526).

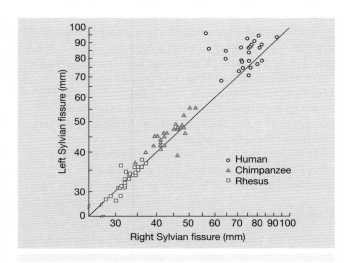

Figure 20.6 The length of the Sylvian fissure of the left half of the brain against that of the right for each individual. Sloping line represents equality.

Source: Reprinted with permission from Yeni-Komshian and Benson (1976, Fig. 1, p. 388).

Differential targeting

Differences between hemispheres can be revealed by presenting information to the left or the right. For example, presenting information to only one ear means that the contralateral hemisphere tends to be at an advantage since there is a stronger contralateral than ipsilateral projection of auditory information (Chapter 9, 'The other sensory systems'). In the visual system, information can be targeted to one or other hemisphere (Chapter 8), though with an intact corpus callosum it becomes available to both.

A personal angle

An asymmetrical 'French' Neanderthal

The remains of a Neanderthal male were found in 1908 in a cave at La Chapelle-aux-Saints in the south-west of France (Boule and Anthony, 1911). From mouldings made of the skull of this male, the form of the underlying brain tissue could be estimated. It appeared that the left hemisphere was slightly different from the right in a way similar to modern humans.

Visual tasks

Even for people with intact inter-hemispheric communication, information can be directed to one hemisphere (Kosslyn *et al.*, 1999). Suppose that such information is of a kind normally processed predominantly in one hemisphere. If it is directed to the hemisphere not normally employed, it must either be processed by different means from normal or cross inter-hemispheric connections to be processed in the usual way. Crossing the hemispheres takes some 15 ms. Either way, slowing of reaction and degradation of processing might appear.

Consider the three word forms, GOAT, *goat* and goat. Are they the same or different? In meaning, they are of course the same, but in specific form they are different. People were asked whether such words are the same or different, being asked to respond by a criterion of either semantics or specific form. In applying different criteria, different input–output processors are, by definition, involved. By projecting sensory information to one or other hemisphere, e.g. by a 'divided visual field presentation' (Chapter 8), it is possible to detect differences in the way in which the hemispheres process information. There is evidence for parallel processing with a superiority of the left hemisphere in identifying meaning (e.g. GOAT is the same as goat) and for the right hemisphere in extracting form information (e.g. it is different) (Geffen *et al.*, 1972).

Selective brain damage

By means of neuroimaging (Chapter 5), patients with a region of brain damage can be studied and compared with controls. It can be useful to be reminded of the need to exert caution in interpreting brain lesions.

Global and local processing

There appears to be a distribution of responsibility between hemispheres for the analysis of a visual scene based upon its content (Robertson *et al.*, 1988). There are various ways of trying to capture the basis of the distinction, e.g. in terms of global and local levels.

Which way is the triangle of Figure 20.7(a) pointing? Most people see it pointing to the left (i.e. 270° from the vertical in a clockwise direction) but, in principle, it might equally point either at 30° or 150° from the vertical. Consider the same triangle embedded in the pattern of part (b); people now tend to see it pointing at 30° from the vertical. The solution depends upon whether local or global processing is employed. Responding at a local level is faster when an image is briefly projected in the right visual field (left hemisphere) and it is faster at a global level when projected to the left visual field (right hemisphere) (Robertson and Delis, 1986).

Robertson and Delis studied patients who had suffered unilateral brain damage through a stroke (Chapter 5, 'The brain') or had had a tumour removed. Patients had intact visual fields and normal visual acuity. They were briefly presented with an image of a triangle and asked to state the direction in which it was pointing. The triangle was embedded within a configuration of other stimuli forming a straight line, similar to Figure 20.7(b). Patients could respond either according to the orientation of the line

('aligned' condition) or according to one of the other two possible orientations of the triangle, i.e. when taken out of context ('single' condition). They were told that there was no right answer and should report only the way that the triangle appeared to be. Patients with damage to the left hemisphere had a stronger tendency to perceive the triangle according to context than did controls. Patients with damage to the right hemisphere showed a weaker tendency.

Look at Figure 20.8, which you first met in Chapter 8 (Figure 8.35, p. 215). On a global ('coarse-grained') level it is a letter S but, on a local ('fine-grained') level, it is a series of Ls. Humans with damage to the temporal–parietal region were presented briefly with such a stimulus. Damage to the right hemisphere had a more disruptive effect upon global processing whereas damage to the left hemisphere tended to disrupt local processing (Robertson *et al.*, 1988). Robertson and Delis (1986) suggest that their results support the proposal that local and global processing are performed by parallel processes. These are, at least during early stages, independent.

Such results are important to a long-standing discussion in psychology – is local processing done first and then the global picture extracted from this or is there a coarse analysis of the whole picture and then fine-grained analysis performed (Robertson *et al.*, 1988)? Rather than either of these modes of processing, there appears to be parallel processing of global and local features. This could offer an advantage in speed of processing.

The emergence of this hemispheric difference might relate to the development of reading skills and the specialization of the left hemisphere for this (Kosslyn, 1988).

Split-brain patients

Patients with a cut in the axons linking the two hemispheres, so-called split-brain patients (Chapter 8), provide valuable evidence on hemispheric differences (Sperry, 1974). A surgical cut of the corpus callosum and anterior commissure to control epileptic seizures prevents communication between hemispheres. Thus, split-brain patients offer the advantage that information can be targeted to one hemisphere, in the absence of communication with the other

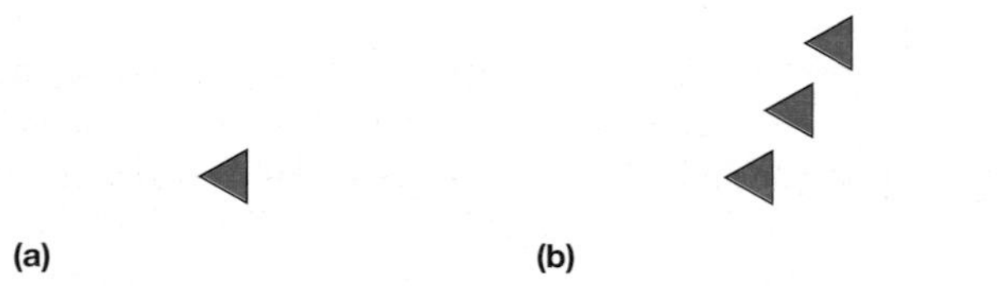

(a)　　　　　**(b)**

Figure 20.7 Triangle (a) alone and (b) embedded into larger pattern.

Source: Robertson and Delis (1986, Fig. 1).

Figure 20.8 Visual stimulus.

Source: Frith and Dolan (1997, Figure 4, p.1224).

through the corpus callosum. Patients reveal the possibilities for information processing by the isolated system. By projecting sensory information to one or other hemisphere, the mode of processing by this hemisphere can be studied in what is as near to controlled within-subject conditions as might be hoped for. The patient's history and temperament, etc., are 'controlled' in this within-subject design.

The damage is under surgical control and targets 'only' a defined and observable population of axons (Kosslyn *et al.*, 1999). Cell bodies of nuclei are not the target of the lesion, with the complications of interpretation and spread of effect that this might entail. However, conclusions need to be considered in the context of some qualifications:

1 Behaviour is normally the product of interaction between hemispheres (Sperry, 1974). The performance of a hemisphere in isolation might be deceptive regarding its role prior to surgery, when in interaction with the opposite hemisphere. There might be reorganization of processing systems following surgery (particularly if the patient is young), so that the performance of a hemisphere is changed.

2 The operation is a last resort after years of suffering and failed medication (Kosslyn *et al.*, 1999). These patients cannot be assumed to be like controls in all other regards.

3 Split-brain patients would not normally act in such a way that information is projected solely to one hemisphere.

Split-brain patients have provided evidence for symmetry (Sperry, 1974). In general, the left hemisphere is superior in the perception of words presented visually and the right hemisphere is superior in non-language-related visuospatial tasks (Trevarthen, 1984).

In split-brain patients, Sperry (1974, p. 11) reports: 'The mute, minor hemisphere, by contrast seems to be carried along much as a passive, silent passenger who leaves the driving of behaviour mainly to the left hemisphere'. Sperry reports that the right hemisphere shows a specialization for holistic ('*Gestalt*') cognition, e.g. perceiving spatial relationships.

Creativity

Evidence suggests that the left hemisphere is specialized for fine-grained and reductionist processing whereas the right's role is global, holistic and large scale. Does this lend support to the notion that the right hemisphere is the more creative? This would fit with a popular assumption that the left is rational, logical and scientific, whereas the right is intuitive and creative. Similarly, the Eastern world is seen to be holistic and the Western rational and logical.

Hines (1991) criticizes such dichotomies on several grounds. It is simplistic to argue that science is not creative while art is not rational. If the dichotomy were true, it suggests a double dissociation: left hemisphere damage

should disrupt rational processes but not artistic, whereas right hemisphere damage should have the opposite effect. In general, there is no evidence to suggest such a neat dichotomy (Alajouanine, 1948). Visual creative skills are indeed often undisturbed after left hemisphere damage. However, creative writing is typically disrupted by left hemisphere damage (Gardner, 1982).

Creativity appears to depend upon a number of component skills, e.g. high motivation and a capacity for extensive prior organizing of information, the ensemble presumably having a wide distribution throughout the brain. Creativity appears to be a complex amalgam of detail and holistic form. The left hemisphere might well have more responsibility for the former and the right for the latter but is detail any less creative than overall form? Only through cooperation between these component processes does creativity emerge.

Test your knowledge

(Answer on page 515)

20.4 Complete the following sentence, which relates to the study of hemispheric differences: 'To link most readily visual and language-based cognition, visual stimuli need to be presented in the _____ visual field'.

20.4

 Goal-directed behaviour

Introduction

This section concerns how goals are involved in the control of behaviour. Goals relate both to the external environment (e.g. move the red book to the left) and to internal representations of the environment (e.g. I want my books to be symmetrical on the shelf). Goals relate to inner motivational conditions, e.g. I am sleepy and so I seek a bed for the night.

For something to become the goal of action, it needs to attract resources of attention and thereby dominate processing capacity (Duncan, 1993). Irrelevant external stimuli need to be ignored or resisted in the pursuit of goals. The goal of behaviour can suddenly change, implying a switch of attention from one feature of the environment to another. Thus, the material here meshes naturally with that on attention (earlier).

Goals, sub-goals and action

As noted in the introduction to this chapter, there is a hierarchy of control, consisting of high-level goals (e.g. make a meal) and sub-goals that serve the high-level goal (e.g. boil eggs). There is competition for expression at different levels, e.g. to wash lettuce or interrupt this to switch off boiling potatoes. Behaviour can be 'ambushed' by stimuli that have strong associations, even though the behaviour that they trigger is at odds with the overall goal (Reason, 1984).

Another point that can be made from the example is that humans have the capacity to think things out 'off-line'. We could plan a meal while we sit on the train going home. We can run simulations and test outcomes. This has features in common with the logical ordering and sequencing involved in really making the meal.

A psychological model

The tasks just described are said to be under the control of a central executive system (CES) or a 'supervisory attentional system' (SAS) (Norman and Shallice, 1986). The CES selects memories and brings them 'on-line' (Chapter 11). The CES can hold the memory on-line, in the face of competing goals. On a moment-by-moment basis, behaviour adjusts to changing circumstances in the interests of meeting the goal. If a particular action is assessed to be failing, it can be replaced by a different action directed to the same goal.

Where is the CES? Is it in a particular location of the brain? There is reason to associate it with the prefrontal cortex, a principal focus of this section.

The prefrontal cortex

This section links the goal-directed aspect of behaviour to one of its principal bases in the brain: the prefrontal cortex (PFC). Figure 5.33, p. 129 showed the prefrontal cortex and some of its divisions.

Introduction to role of the PFC

In hierarchical terms, Fuster (1999) describes the PFC as: '... "motor" cortex of the highest order in that it supports the cognitive functions that co-ordinate the execution of the most elaborate and novel actions of the organism'.

The PFC plays a role in holding a memory in an *active* state (Chapter 11) so that it can be utilized in purposive behaviour and in inhibition of competing tendencies (Dehaene and Changeux, 1989; Fuster, 1997). However, the process of control that utilizes the active memory is vulnerable to interference, e.g. capture by salient stimuli. The PFC serves to guide memory searches, direct thought processes, plan action and resist capture. Patients with PFC damage are often deficient in these regards. Thus, the PFC forms a biological basis for the control of the sequencing of complex and often creative behaviour, e.g. speech, as well as 'pure cognition', such as reasoning that can ultimately lead to action (Waltz *et al.*, 1999).

Goal-directed action is based on the temporal integration of a number of component behaviours. For example, speech depends in part on the responses of another person. The PFC is required to formulate plans of the kind 'if event y occurs and situation M prevails, then do A, but if event z occurs then do B'. This involves information on the memory of recent events, computation based upon this, holding representations of motor action and inhibiting incompatible behaviour (Fuster, 1999). In some cases, the logic represented is of the kind 'if event (x) then wait time T and perform X'.

In ontogeny and phylogeny, PFC is among the last brain regions to develop (Fuster, 1999). In ontogeny, it is one of the last regions to undergo myelination (Chapter 6), associated with the emergence of more complex goal-directed behaviour.

Rolls (2004) and colleagues investigated the role of the orbitofrontal region of the PFC (Figure 5.33, p. 129) in goal-directed activity in non-human primates. As an integral part of adaptive goal-directed action, certain neurons in the PFC encode the value of rewards. For example, a high activity of a particular neuron encodes the high reward value of the taste of a palatable food when in need of nutrients.

Prefrontal lobe connections

Of all neocortical regions, the PFC shows the richest interconnection with other brain areas (Fuster, 1997, 1999). These links and the information they transmit highlight its role as a coordinator of action. There are reciprocal links with other regions of cortex, the brain stem, hypothalamus, amygdala, hippocampus and thalamus. Signals from the brain stem and hypothalamus convey information to the PFC on the internal environment of the body. This can be used in decision making, e.g. to seek food. Information exchanged with other cortical regions appears to be used in high-level sensory-motor integration (Chapter 10), e.g. messages to primary motor cortex reflect goals that need to trigger movement. There are projections from PFC to the nucleus accumbens (Deutch *et al.*, 1993), forming a link to motivated activities. Connections from the PFC to the basal ganglia also implicate a role of the PFC in motor control.

Damage to the PFC

Monkeys with PFC lesions have difficulty in performing tasks that involve bridging a delay between presentation of the stimulus cue and the associated reaction (Jacobsen, 1936). This points to a failure to retain information on-line over the delay. Bianchi (1922, p. 186) found that lesioned animals lack coherence and focus.

Humans with PFC damage exhibit failures in holding an appropriate memory in an active state (working memory) and resisting interference in the course of goal-directed behaviour (Fuster, 1997). Patients with PFC damage, especially of the orbitofrontal region, tend to exhibit one or more of the following: (a) an abnormally high distractibility, (b) hyperactivity and (c) problems with the inhibition of impulsivity. Irrelevant factors intrude, as in the capture of behaviour by extraneous stimuli and the failure to recruit task-relevant information in the completion of a task (Duncan, 1986). Patients have difficulty resisting reaching out and grasping objects brought near to them (Lhermitte, 1983). Patients are deficient on tasks that involve changing behaviour in the light of changing outcomes of action. For example, they do badly at the Wisconsin card sorting task (Chapter 6).

Studying patients, Luria *et al.* (1964) noted the failure of feedback to correct errors. Stimuli irrelevant to the task capture behaviour. For example, a patient on being asked to draw a square was 'captured' by a conversation going on nearby and incorporated features of it into the drawing (Luria, 1966). Behaviour appears to lose its active nature, being more a passive reaction to stimuli.

The disruption following PFC damage represents a: 'defect in the way behaviour is controlled by the match between what is to be, and what has been achieved' (Duncan, 1986, p. 281). Patients typically disengage from a task before it is completed but without the failure at completion motivating completion. Human frontal patients can often articulate verbally what is the nature of the task and acknowledge their failure to achieve the goal but be unable to utilize this information in correcting future behaviour. Humans with damage to the dorsolateral PFC exhibit a lack of motivation and spontaneity (Fuster, 1999). Behaviour is described as being routine and in the here-and-now, lacking planning and perspective.

Monitoring brain events

Suppose that a task requires a subject to wait time T between stimulus presentation and performing a response. In monkeys, increases in electrical activity over time T can be recorded from neurons in the dorsolateral region of the PFC and appear to encode the plan for motor action

A personal angle
Wilder Penfield and his sister

In the early 1930s, tragic circumstances provided the pioneering Canadian neurosurgeon, Wilder Penfield, with a unique opportunity to study the effects of frontal lobe disruption on behaviour. His sister suffered from a tumour of the prefrontal region, which he operated to remove when she was aged 43. During the six hour operation in Montreal, she talked to her brother and others of the surgical team. Tissue to within a centimetre of the prefrontal gyrus (Chapter 5) was removed. Following the operation, Penfield observed a disruption in her capacity to plan, a 'loss of power of initiative' (Penfield and Evans, 1935).

('preparatory set') to be put on-line after T elapses (Fuster, 1999). Apart from such 'set-cells', other neurons, located in the dorsolateral PFC, play a role in encoding events ('memory cells') used in the formulation of plans. Such neurons play a role in encoding working memory (Chapter 11). They are activated for so long as the task requires the utilization of the memory. In such terms, the CES would be responsible for activation of such memories.

Social behaviour and decision-making

The PFC patient often has problems with social behaviour, as exemplified by Phineas Gage (Chapter 12). Baddeley *et al.* (1997, p. 192) speculate: 'it is possible that skilful social behaviour inherently involves a dual-task component requiring the simultaneous maintenance of one's own interests and concerns at the same time as paying due attention to the concerns of those around'.

The failure of PFC patients to inhibit inappropriate behaviour (e.g. temper tantrums) is particularly associated with damage to the orbitomedial region (Fuster, 1997). This sometimes drives patients into conflict with the law. The patient has problems utilizing memories that could provide information on scripts of possible future social interaction and thereby lacks social skills (Grafman, 1989). Undue weight is given to current situations and powerful physically present stimuli. How could this be explained?

According to the 'somatic marker hypothesis', decision making is normally guided by a kind of rerun of basic emotions (Chapter 12). For example, a clear fear-evoking stimulus ('primary inducer') triggers a basic emotion. Memories of such events or simply imagining them ('secondary inducers') triggers something of a copy of the basic emotion, mediated via the ventromedial region of the prefrontal cortex (corresponding approximately to what others term orbitofrontal cortex). In this way, triggering negative emotion by the prospect of a future negative outcome tends to deter an unwise action and contribute to rational decision-making.

Patients who have suffered damage to the ventromedial region of the prefrontal cortex (VM PFC) exhibit serious deficits in decision-making even though they have no general loss of intelligence (Bechara, 2004). They have problems with planning and in social relationships.

The **Iowa gambling task** is employed to assess decision-making (it is named after the university location of Damasio, Bechara and colleagues, and sometimes termed the 'Bechara gambling task' but, with modesty, not by Bechara himself!). Participants are asked to gamble and, to do so, to make a series of choices from any one of four decks of cards. Two of these decks (A and B) deliver a high immediate gain early in the game but a particularly high loss later, and are characterized as 'disadvantageous decks'. The two other decks (C and D) yield a small immediate gain but also only a very small future loss, an 'advantageous deck'. The relative gain and loss of each deck is known to the experimenter but not to the participant.

Figure 20.9 shows the result for patients with damage to the VM PFC, as compared to controls with no brain damage ('normal controls') and controls with damage to the occipital or temporal cortex ('brain-damaged controls'). As can be seen, controls learn by experience. They give due weight to the long-term negative outcome of choice A or B. VM patients do not show this. Rather they exhibit what is called 'myopia for the future'.

It was suggested that this failure to take long-term negative consequences into account models the patients' failure in their social lives. Bechara *et al.* made a physiological measure, an index of autonomic arousal,

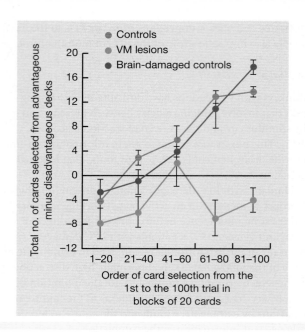

Figure 20.9 Relative choice of advantageous and disadvantageous cards over the sessions of trials.

Source: Bechara (2004, Fig. 2, p. 32).

during the task: the skin conductance response (SCR). As can be seen in Figure 20.10, both VM patients and controls showed a SCR response on picking a card and being told the outcome: good or bad. However, a striking difference came in the moment just prior to selection, particularly from the risky piles A and B. This suggests that decision-making is normally guided by an emotional signal and this is deficient in VM patients.

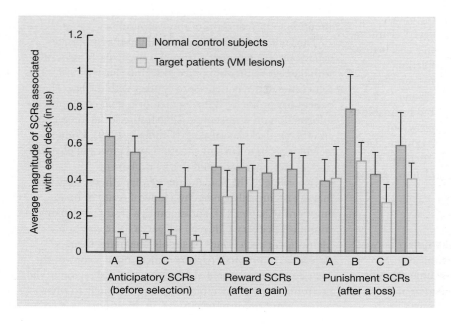

Figure 20.10 Results of skin-conductance response for normal controls and VM PFC patients, under conditions of reward and punishment, as well as anticipation.

Source: Bechara (2004, Fig. 3, p. 32).

Bechara *et al.* compared unilateral VM PFC damage with bilateral damage. As can be seen in Figure 20.11, damage to the right brain has a particularly disruptive effect. This suggests that the right PFC is usually more strongly involved in such decision-making based on anticipation of negative outcomes.

It could be that normal populations vary naturally in the extent to which somatic markers mediated via the VM PFC exert an influence. Imagine yourself wondering whether to take that second portion of pizza. The prospect of immediate reward is pulling you in the here-and-now. With luck, the prospect of future weight gain will evoke a negative emotion, a 'somatic marker', which will deter you. The point of this balance appears to vary between people such that, for example, obese people and drug-addicts are less sensitive than controls to future negative consequences. They tend to do badly at the Iowa gambling task (Davis *et al.*, 2004).

The frontal lobes and the central executive system

Having looked at the role of the PFC, we can ask, is the PFC the anatomical location of the central executive system? Evidence implicates this area. However, we need to avoid the simple assumption of identity between a role and an anatomical location, as in referring to any patient having problems with executive control as a 'frontal' (Baddeley, 1996). The PFC constitutes a large structure, which probably plays multiple roles. Are we to rule out other roles by designating it as 'executive'? Conversely, a premature assumption of identity might rule out other regions having an executive role. Damage is often not confined to the frontal lobes but involves other structures as well.

Section summary

1 The notion of behaviour being goal-directed involves:

   (a) a hierarchy of goals and sub-goals;
   (b) a tendency for behaviour to persist until the goal is met;
   (c) competition between goals;
   (d) inhibition of inappropriate behaviour.

2 Goal-directed behaviour can be 'ambushed' by strong stimuli.

3 Psychologists converge on a notion described by such terms as 'central executive system' and 'supervisory attentional system'.

4 The prefrontal cortex is involved in planning and executing sequences of goal-directed action.

5 Damage to the prefrontal cortex disrupts the capacity to exert coherent action.

6 Somatic markers play a role in decision-making.

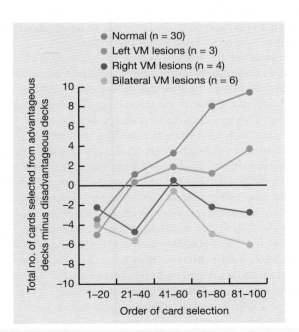

Figure 20.11 Results of the net advantageous choices over trials for normal controls, unilateral left VM PFC damage, unilateral right PFC damage and bilateral damage.

Source: Bechara (2004, Fig. 4, p. 33).

Test your knowledge

(Answers on page 515)

20.5 Complete the following: 'During development, the emergence of control by the prefrontal cortex is associated with _____ of the axons that convey information between this structure and other brain regions'.

20.6 Complete the following: 'Patients with damage to the VM PFC exhibit normal sensitivity to _____ consequences of their actions but reduced sensitivity to the _____ of consequences'.

20.5

Language

Introduction

This section describes language and considers speaking, listening, reading and writing. It discusses brain structures that underlie language and the evolution of language. Looking across species, something corresponding to a language has the common feature of being a vehicle for the transmission of information. In humans, the content of language can take an apparently infinite variety of forms and is unique in its abstractness. Component sources of information (words) can be combined in unique ways to convey information on any aspect of experience or imagination. Spoken language is composed of individual sounds termed **phonemes**.

The listener's understanding of spoken language involves processes similar to those described for vision (Chapter 8). Invariance is involved: a word needs to be interpreted to mean the same in spite of diverse pronunciations. Conversely, the same pronunciation might need to be interpreted differently according to context, e.g. 'pen' as a writing instrument or something to restrain cattle.

Evolutionary and functional perspectives

Introduction

Language is universal in human societies, which suggests an evolutionary advantage (Liberman, 1995). It is not difficult to appreciate the evolutionary advantage of language to hunting and gathering, in terms of conveying intentions and contributing to coordinated action (Pinker and Bloom, 1990). Also, information can be transmitted from generation to generation, circumventing the need to learn by direct

'How do we explain the association between speech and manual gestures?'

Source: Empics.

experience of hazardous things, such as dangerous animals and floods.

One view is that language evolved from gestures made with the hands and face (see Richards, 1987). It can hardly be coincidence that we tend to accompany words with hand gestures. There are functional advantages of spoken as opposed to gestural language, e.g. that it frees the hands for other uses and can still be used for communication when the listener is out of sight (Lieberman, 1991).

Psychologists describe reading and writing as 'culturally engineered' types of language (Caplan *et al.*, 1999); genetics and development do not produce an organism with a natural tendency to acquire them. Explicit education is needed for their acquisition. These skills have appeared rather late in evolution and it seems that we do not have the comparable dedicated sensory-motor pathways in the same way as we have for speaking and understanding the spoken word. However, we use ('co-opt') brain regions dedicated to vision and spoken language, pointing to an example of something like modularity emerging with development in a particular culture.

Comparative issues

Non-humans also communicate information, e.g. warning signals on sighting a predator, and of course communal hunting (as in wolves) requires coordination. Some non-human languages even involve symbolic representations. For example, by means of dances, bees communicate information on the location of food sites (Caplan *et al.*, 1999). Non-human primates convey signals on intentions and thereby can even sometimes employ deceit ('telling lies').

The essence of human language, defined by Bear *et al.* (1996, p. 579) is: 'a remarkably complex, flexible, and powerful *system* for communication that involves the creative use of words according to the rules of a systematic grammar'.

Opinion differs on whether human language is best considered qualitatively different from the communication of other species or different only in degree (Caplan *et al.*, 1999). Are there evolutionary precursors evident in non-linguistic skills of non-humans, or is it an evolutionary 'shot-in-the-dark' peculiar to humans (Pinker and Bloom, 1990)? To consider this topic requires integration between evolutionary theory and understanding of neural mechanisms (Greenfield, 1991), discussed shortly.

One is reluctant to assert dogmatically that no non-human equivalent of human language exists but this seems likely to be the case. Whether non-humans can be taught a symbolic language system is a topic of controversy. For example, chimpanzees use stereotyped vocal expressions in a limited range of situations and these can be mapped in stimulus–response terms. There are instances of combinations of symbols being employed but the evidence of an abstract skill of creative symbol manipulation and expression is not compelling. That is not to deny the richness of problem solving in non-humans. However, nothing compares with the seemingly infinite variety of messages that humans can construct and understand.

Brain mechanisms – classical studies

Introduction

The comprehension and production of speech involves a neural system that extends from the inner ear to the motor mechanisms underlying control of the muscles involved in speech. Some extraction of speech sounds and their accentuation occurs at the cochlea and subsequent levels within the auditory pathway (Chapter 9; Honjo, 1999). As with other motor skills, language appears to exhibit some capacity for automatization, implying parallel pathways triggered under different circumstances (Whitaker, 1983).

Patients with brain damage, resulting from trauma, as in accidents, or stroke, or a result of brain surgery, provide insight into the neural bases of language (Lenneberg, 1967). Disruption, or loss, of language ability is termed **aphasia**. Patients appear not to have literally 'lost' language, as in being returned to a prelinguistic state; rather, they have problems with language use. Aphasia is commonly associated with some disruption of writing, termed **agraphia** and reading, termed **alexia**.

Broca and Wernicke

Perhaps the most significant contribution to understanding the brain mechanisms of language was the observation that selective disruption to speech is caused by damage to a region of the frontal lobe of the left hemisphere (Broca, 1861). Comparable damage to the right hemisphere is not associated with aphasia in most cases (Geschwind, 1972; Marie and Foix, 1917). Subsequently, this region of the left frontal lobe came to be known as **Broca's area** (pronounced roughly as in the English 'broker's'). See Figure 20.12. Exactly what constitutes the boundaries of Broca's area is open to discussion (Greenfield, 1991) and there are sub-areas within it. However, as a first approximation for relating structure and function, Broca's area serves as a landmark.

Wernicke (1874) found another region of the left hemisphere where accidental damage also disrupted speech, and this became known as **Wernicke's area** (pronounced roughly as Vehr-knee-ker's). The planum temporale, discussed earlier in this chapter, corresponds to a large part of Wernicke's area. Figure 20.12 shows Wernicke's area in the context of Broca's area, the auditory cortex and the angular gyrus. Exactly what constitutes Wernicke's area is also open to discussion; there are individual differences in the exact site of the processing attributed to it (Honjo, 1999).

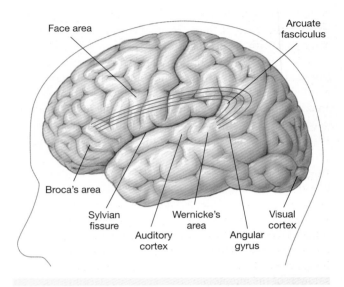

Figure 20.12 The left hemisphere showing areas concerned with language.

Source: Geschwind (1972, p. 78). Courtesy of Donald Garber.

A personal angle

Paul Broca and Tan

A patient of Paul Broca, in the hospital at Bicêtre, France, had lost his speech, except for single syllables (Broca, 1861). He responded simply with 'tan, tan' to each question and made gestures. Thereby, he acquired the name Tan. Tan was aware of his situation and showed normal intelligence. As the extent of the lesion spread, Tan came to lose the use of his right arm and could gesticulate only with his left arm and hand. Tan died on 17 April 1861, aged 51 years. Autopsy revealed damage to the left frontal lobe. From this observation, the affected area controlling speech acquired the name 'Broca's area'. Tan reminds us that a lesion in motor regions of the left brain affects motor control on the right of the body.

Characterizing aphasias

Although damage to either Broca's or Wernicke's area disrupts speech, there tends to be a difference in the nature of the disruption in the two cases (Lenneberg, 1967). What follows is an account of the 'textbook' distinction, though individual differences are large and there is often an overlap of symptoms. Usually any lesion that disturbs language affects both production and comprehension to some extent.

In **Broca's aphasia** (sometimes called 'motor aphasia', 'expressive aphasia' or 'non-fluent aphasia'), the problem is principally with the organization of speech *production* (Damasio and Geschwind, 1984). Speech becomes slow, laboured, without its usual rhythms and with the endings of words omitted (Geschwind, 1972). Patients with Broca's aphasia sometimes have difficulty finding the right word and in constructing grammatically correct sentences (Geschwind, 1979). They often have particular difficulty with 'function words', those for which the role is defined by context, e.g. 'if' and 'but'. Patients with Broca's aphasia are not completely free of problems with comprehension, which appear particularly in more difficult sentences.

Broca's area has links with the region of motor cortex that controls motor aspects of speech, e.g. muscles of the face ('face area'), which points to a role towards the motor output side. However, Broca's aphasia is not synonymous with paralysis of the muscles involved in speech (Geschwind, 1972) and the term 'motor' in describing aphasia needs qualification. A patient might be able to sing a melody using such muscles. Patients can utter certain words, e.g. familiar nouns such as chair, relatively easily.

Broca's area should not be viewed in isolation. Rather, disruption of speech appears to depend on breaking subcortical neural connections between Broca's area and anterior regions of the frontal cortex (Lieberman, 1991). Liberman (1995, p. 568) describes the prefrontal cortex as 'at once our "think tank" and fine motor control sequencer'. Language appears to exemplify the role of this structure in terms of the control of action.

As a first approximation, in **Wernicke's aphasia** (sometimes termed 'receptive aphasia' or 'fluent aphasia'),

understanding written and spoken language is disrupted but speech is relatively fluent (Damasio and Geschwind, 1984). Function words can be expressed as well as words denoting content. Speech can sound normal. Only on analysis of content is abnormality detected (Geschwind, 1972). Speech often fails to convey a rational meaning. The location of Wernicke's area next to the auditory cortex (Figure 20.12) suggests that it is where word meanings are associated with word sounds. It appears to represent the site of a higher order of analysis comparable to later stages of the ventral stream in visual processing (Chapter 8, and earlier in the present chapter). Wernicke's area is linked to Broca's area by a bundle of neurons termed the 'arcuate fasciculus', a route of information transfer. See Figure 20.12.

The Wernicke–Geschwind model

Geschwind (1972, 1979) developed a model of language processing based upon the ideas of Wernicke, and it became known as the **Wernicke–Geschwind model**. It has the status of a 'classical model' (or 'iconic model') and represents connections between brain regions involved in language (Figure 20.13). The model is sometimes described as a 'disconnection theory' of language impairment since it draws attention to disruption that can arise from disconnecting different components of the system. Although now seen as an over-simplification, it summarizes important features of how language works and has served well to stimulate research, organize thinking and give a framework for clinical practice.

In the model, the role of Broca's and Wernicke's areas is much as just described. Note the link from Broca's area to the area of the motor cortex that controls the face. Figure 20.13(a) represents repeating aloud words spoken by another

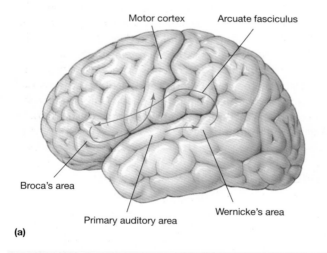
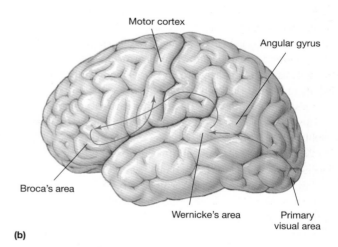

Figure 20.13 The Wernicke–Geschwind model in representing the tasks of repeating in speech (a) a spoken word and (b) a written word.

Source: Geschwind (1979, p. 163). Courtesy of Carol Donner.

person. Information is processed at the auditory cortex ('Primary auditory area'), which passes information to Wernicke's area. This information is linked to a word representation at Wernicke's area, which then transmits information on the word representation to Broca's area. At Broca's area, information on the word calls up an articulation programme for uttering it, which is then transmitted to the motor cortex where the muscular response of speech is instigated. In Wernicke's aphasia, Broca's area is not sent appropriate information to generate rational speech.

Part (b) represents the sequence involved in repeating aloud a word presented visually. Information on words, extracted by visual processing areas ('primary visual area'), is conveyed to Wernicke's area and enters the same pathway as that involved in auditory processing. One might imagine that the visual information taps into the same representations of words as are triggered by sounds. The model can account for aphasia of the Broca and Wernicke kinds and can also account for some additional phenomena.

Damage to tissue lying between Broca's and Wernicke's areas causes what is termed 'conduction aphasia' (Damasio and Geschwind, 1984). As predicted by the model, a problem arises in repeating words, since this involves transferring auditory information to the motor system of speech.

Brain mechanisms – later insights

Beyond the Wernicke–Geschwind model

The Wernicke-Geschwind model has served as a valuable organizing framework within which subsequent findings can be interpreted. However, later insights have shown levels of complexity that are not captured by this model.

There is not simply the one-way flow of information as suggested by the model. Impairment of Broca's area can disturb language perception as well as production (Honjo, 1999). Broca's area is activated even in trying to think of a word without pronouncing it (Hinke *et al.*, 1993). This points to there being similarities in the organization of thought and overt action.

Broca's and Wernicke's areas are no longer understood as playing homogeneous or monolithic roles in language (Poeppel and Hickok, 2004). Rather there are subdivisions of each, serving different roles.

The Wernicke–Geschwind model assumes a channelling of information in auditory and visual codes into a common auditory processing system. In the case of reading, it suggests an obligatory translation of visual information into an auditory code. Under some conditions, such a flow of information between visual and auditory processing occurs but it appears not to be the only route of information transfer involved in reading (Coltheart, 1985; Henderson, 1986). In some cases, reading can survive intact from damage

to Wernicke's area that severely disrupts speech, which suggests a route that bypasses speech mechanisms.

The Wernicke–Geschwind model was a stimulus to Petersen *et al.* (1988), who used a PET study to investigate changes in cerebral blood flow accompanying processing of words. People were presented with words and, over trials, processing demands were changed. Different levels of complexity were required of the participants. The logic was that, as the level of complexity increased, additional brain regions would be activated. Activation at one level was subtracted from the immediately higher level. In this way, an estimate was made of additional processing needed at each increasing task demand. Words were either presented visually or by sound.

At the first level, the word was simply presented, either visually or spoken. This enabled just the lowest level of pure sensory processing to be measured (well, in principle, at least!). To calculate this in the case of visual presentation, visual fixation upon a target word was compared with fixation without word presentation. This comparison gave a measure of visual processing demands triggered by a word (termed 'sensory' condition).

At the second level of task demand, people were asked to speak aloud the word presented. This was to enable regions concerned with output coding and motor control to be identified ('output' condition). At the third level, people were asked to find a use for the word, e.g. if 'cake' were the word, a person might find 'eat'. This level allowed brain regions associated with semantics to be identified ('association' condition).

Figure 20.14 shows regions of *additional* activation seen with each new level of task demand. Note the distinct non-overlapping regions of sensory cortical activation for visual (e.g. areas 1 and 2) and auditory (e.g. areas 7 and 8) stimuli. Responses of the visual cortex to words (1 and 2) are similar to responses to non-word visual cues. Activation of areas of occipital cortex outside primary visual cortex (3, 4 and 5) is peculiar to words and could represent areas concerned with processing visual word forms. Damage to such areas can lead to alexia, a disruption to reading words not associated with other language disruption (Damasio and Damasio, 1983). Areas of motor cortex involved in producing output overlap between visual (e.g. 12) and auditory (e.g. 18) presentations. Note the prefrontal areas involved in the association task for visual and auditory presentations (e.g. 26 and 29).

These results are not in accordance with the serial processing of the Wernicke–Geschwind model, where access to semantic information whether visually or auditorily triggered is via a phonological code (a sound-based code). No activation near to Wernicke's area or the angular gyrus was seen in response to visual stimuli (Figure 20.14). Visual and auditory information appeared to take parallel routes to the output side.

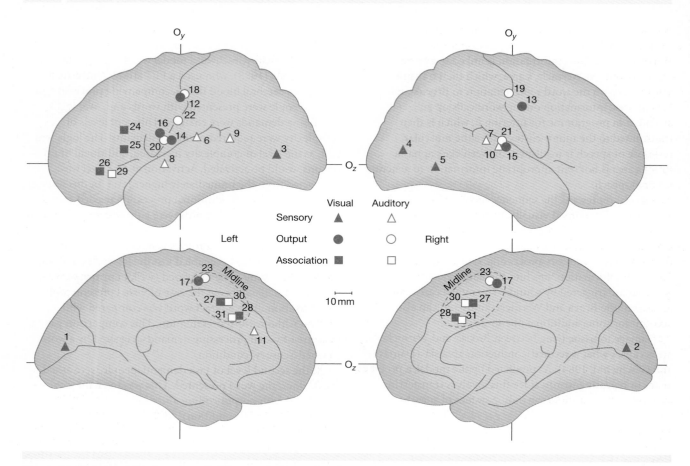

Figure 20.14 Lateral (top) and medial (bottom) views of regions of activation under different conditions for each hemisphere.

Source: Petersen *et al.* (1988, Fig. 1, p. 586).

A more comprehensive explanatory model would need also to accommodate the following observation. According to the site of lesion, patients can be selectively disrupted in understanding *either* spoken *or* written words. (Under some conditions, visual information on words is encoded phonologically.) Still further features that would need to be incorporated into an explanatory account would include a reference to the importance of subcortical pathways, e.g. thalamus and basal ganglia (Chapter 10), involved in language.

Split-brain patients

Evidence from split-brain patients (Chapter 8) reinforces the conclusion that the left hemisphere is normally dominant for speech (Sperry, 1969). When information on an object is presented visually in a way that triggers processing by the left hemisphere, the person is normally able to identify verbally what it is. When visual information arrives at the right hemisphere, verbal identification is often not possible since the cut corpus callosum means that visual information cannot connect with the language apparatus. Similarly, if the

right hand feels an object out of sight, the patient can name it but not if the left hand feels it. However, the right hemisphere has some language abilities. Split-brain patients can react on the basis of some simple visual language cues such as the written word of a common noun projected to the right hemisphere.

Disrupting normal processing

There are various techniques for producing what is termed a **functional lesion** and these have brought considerable insight into the bases of language (Boatman, 2004; Penfield and Rasmussen, 1968). Unlike conventional lesions, which involve permanent damage (e.g. cutting pathways), functional lesions involve only a temporary inactivation of part of the brain. The techniques are used for patients about to undergo brain surgery.

In the technique of **electrocortical mapping**, an electrical current is generated for a period of some 5–10 s. The current passes between two electrodes located at the surface of the cortex. In this way, just a local portion of the grey matter of the cortex is targeted. This disrupts processing by the targeted region, thereby producing a functional lesion merely for the duration of stimulation. The deficits in language processing can be correlated with the site of the associated functional lesion. For example, disruption of a very circumscribed region of temporal lobe of the left hemisphere (specifically within the superior temporal gyrus) disrupted the discrimination of syllables (Figure 20.15). This region was adjacent to the primary auditory cortex (Boatman, 2004).

At certain sites in the left hemisphere, stimulation disrupts the capacity to name objects (Ojemann, 1990). See Figure 20.16. For bilingual people, the site of disruption of naming a given object can be different for the two languages. Wide individual differences were found in the sites at which naming was disrupted.

Electrocortical mapping is a means of creating functional lesions at local sites *within* a hemisphere. The next technique to be described enables comparison *between* hemispheres.

In the **Wada technique**, a fast-acting anaesthetic is injected into the carotid artery supplying blood to one hemisphere (Milner, 1974). The duration of action of the anaesthetic is some 5–10 minutes (Boatman, 2004). On the side contralateral to the injection, the limbs quickly become immobile and there is a loss of sensation. When the injection is made to the side dominant for speech, there is disruption of speech. The technique confirms that the left hemisphere is normally dominant for speech. Where there is early damage to the left hemisphere, speech tends to be more often controlled by the right hemisphere. The technique reveals right hemispheric dominance in only a very small percentage of the population (Boatman, 2004).

Streaming

Evidence suggests a basic distinction between streams of processing of auditory information that is comparable to the

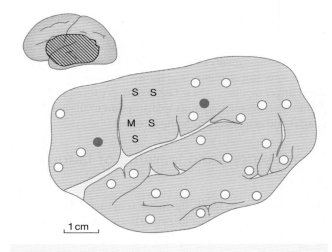

Figure 20.16 Sites of stimulation ○ and locations at which naming was significantly disrupted ● for a 24-year-old female patient. Shaded area in small figure is shown enlarged in larger figure.

Source: Ojemann (1990, Fig. 1).

distinction between ventral stream and dorsal stream, described for vision in Chapter 8 (Hickok and Poeppel, 2004). There appears to be a common route until the superior temporal gyrus is reached at which point there is a streaming. Rather as with vision, a dorsal stream is involved in action (in this case, speech production), whereas a ventral stream is concerned with speech perception and attribution of meaning to it.

The dorsal stream is strongly lateralized to the left hemisphere, whereas the ventral stream appears to be less strongly lateralized. Thus, damage to the left temporal cortex does not invariably disrupt speech comprehension. Results in split-brain patients, as well as those undergoing the Wada test with anaesthetic targeted to the left hemisphere, also point to the retention of speech comprehension ability by the right hemisphere.

A comparative approach to the brain mechanisms

Could there be some common features between brain regions underlying language and those underlying other forms of information processing (Ullman, 2004)? Given that evolution is a tinkerer building upon pre-existing structures, we might expect some common principles of organization. For example, in vision, there is an interaction between cortical regions and subcortical structures (Chapter 8). So, we might expect that any features unique to language and humans will coexist with processes and brain regions common to other forms of cognition and other species. There is a rich source of comparative data to be tapped.

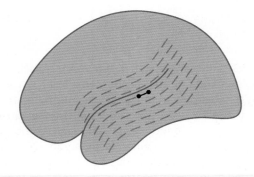

Figure 20.15 Location of brain region that is associated with a deficit in auditory discrimination (black line). Grey lines are regions stimulated without effect on auditory discrimination.

Source: Boatman (2004, Figure 1, p. 51).

It appears that the production of language, as with other motor skills, depends upon interactions between cortical structures, the basal ganglia and cerebellum. Developmental language impairments can occasionally be associated with other motor impairments (e.g. shown on a task that calls for rapid finger tapping). These tasks relate to procedural memory and evidence points to disruption to the basal ganglia and cerebellum as being involved.

Development and learning of language

Basics

On first learning to speak, the infant is influenced primarily by the spoken sounds that he or she hears. This implies the formation of links between a brain system underlying sensory speech codes and that underlying the motor system responsible for speech production (Hickok and Poeppel, 2004). There is evidence that the auditory–speech link arising in early development remains intact in the adult.

A famous dispute

The acquisition of language forms the focus of one of psychology's best-known controversies, that between Skinner (1957) and Chomsky (1959). Biological insight is central to this debate. Skinner suggested that learning a language is much like learning anything else, i.e. based on a very general process of reinforcement and entirely dependent upon exposure to an appropriate environment of reinforcers.

By contrast, Chomsky suggested that a dedicated, specialist and genetically determined brain structure serves to organize language, i.e. a module. This is an adaptation that is peculiar to the human species. Metaphorically, this structure is 'just waiting' for even a minimal exposure to a language and it springs into action. From the start, there is implicit ('advance') knowledge of a grammar common to all languages. In this view, modularity is such that language requires little influence from other cognitive processing systems for its inevitable development (see Abbeduto and Boudreau, 2004). Modularity is also suggested by cases of spared language ability in the presence of retarded development in other cognitive domains.

How does the skill of language develop? Is it, as Skinner suggested, just like learning any other skill? Alternatively, is it, as Chomsky argued, based upon a dedicated genetically determined speech module? You might well be experiencing echoes from an earlier dichotomy on genes versus environment, which has been largely laid to rest with the understanding of contemporary biological psychology.

A compromise position

Subsequent insights point to a compromise position, with both a genetic tendency and environmental stimulation playing roles. That is, there exists some tendency towards language acquisition particularly based in the left hemisphere, given a normal exposure to a spoken language. Humans are said to be *prepared* to learn a language, expressed in speech (Caplan *et al.*, 1999). Given the structure of the nervous system and vocal apparatus and the presence of a linguistic culture, sensory-motor pathways develop in such a way that the emergence of spoken language is a near certainty (Liberman, 1995).

There is a normal and distinct developmental time-course of language acquisition up to the age of 7 years (Trout, 2001). If access to a language is denied during this period, subsequent acquisition is more laboured and production is not so effortless. Johnson (1997, p. 142) suggests that: 'small variations on the basic architecture of the cortex may be sufficient to "attract" language processing to some regions during normal functional brain development'.

Evidence on early damage to brain regions is crucial to the issue of dedicated regions. Although Broca associated speech with the left hemisphere, he was aware that in some cases of early damage to the left, the right can take over responsibility (Smith and Sugar, 1975). For the young brain, there is some evidence for 'equipotentiality', i.e. that early damage to the left hemisphere has little effect on subsequent language acquisition, which is equally well handled by the right. Adults suffering comparable damage experience serious disruption. However, even in children, there appear to be subtle disorders of language following left hemisphere damage (Vargha-Khadem *et al.*, 1994). This suggests some initial bias towards language acquisition by the left hemisphere but again points to the need to qualify the notion of dedicated modules. Beyond the phase of early neural development and plasticity, structures become more fixed and committed (Lenneberg, 1967).

A personal angle

A successful executive

In 1953, Smith and Sugar, based at Ann Arbor, Michigan and Chicago, performed a left hemispherectomy (removal of a hemisphere) on a boy of age 5$\frac{1}{2}$ years to counter epileptic seizures. The patient exhibited normal language, verbal and non-verbal reasoning when tested at age 26 years. He was a successful executive and simultaneously pursued a university degree in sociology. As the authors note, since the entire cortex on the left side of the brain was removed, it is to the right hemisphere that we need to look for the site of the function. Both parents were right-handed.

Are brain areas that are normally used for sound and language understanding triggered by, say, visual input in deaf people? In the absence of normal input, they might be captured by other channels. Looking at temporal lobe areas normally associated with auditory/speech processing, Neville (1991) found event-related potentials (Chapter 5) to visual stimuli to be greater in deaf people than in those with hearing.

Sign language

To what extent is the organization of language specific to vocal expression? Insight can be gained by studying those who employ a visual system of gestures, termed sign language, e.g. in the absence of a speech facility and/or to speak to deaf people (Poizner *et al.*, 1990). Information conveyed by hands and face can be as grammatically structured, semantically rich and subtle as the spoken word. In deaf people, sign language activates some cortical areas normally triggered by the spoken word in controls with hearing (Nishimura *et al.*, 1999).

Poizner *et al.* studied sign language in patients with damage to the right hemisphere. Sign language showed minimal disruption. Conversely, in patients with left hemispheric damage, disruption was serious for sign language but minimal for non-language-based visuospatial cognition (though this point is controversial, as discussed by Greenfield, 1991).

Evidence from the Wada test and PET scans also points to a left hemispheric specialization for sign language, leading to the conclusion that this hemisphere specializes for language irrespective of its mode of perception and expression (Poizner *et al.*, 1990). That is to say, sound is not a necessary input to obtain such left hemisphere specialization.

Patients with disrupted sign language typically retain the ability of non-language-based manual mime, e.g. the gesture of smelling a flower. This suggests different neural bases for language and non-language-based gesture and that the left hemisphere is specialized for symbolic expression (Nishimura *et al.*, 1999).

Language and object manipulation

Both language and assembling objects with the hands involve hierarchical control of sequential action (Greenfield, 1991). For example, children as young as 20 months spear food objects with a fork, dip the combination of food-on-fork into sauce and then bring it to the mouth. Similarly, language has a hierarchical structure: phonemes combine to form words, words form sentences and sentences are subordinate to the goal of conveying meaning. Greenfield suggests that the skills of language and object combination involve parallel development in terms of ontogeny and phylogeny. Figure 20.17 shows an example of hierarchical development of language with age. The words 'more' and 'grapejuice' form a sub-assembly.

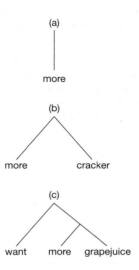

Figure 20.17 Development of language: (a) one word utterance, (b) combination of words and (c) hierarchical organization in which 'more' and 'grapejuice' are combined at a lower level than the combination with 'want'.

Source: Greenfield (1991, p. 533).

Do the skills of language and object combination represent distinct cognitive modules with distinct neural bases? If so, in adapting the language of evolution (Chapter 5), we would speak of an 'analogy' between them. Alternatively, both might be based on the same neural system, and we would speak of 'homology'. It is surely no coincidence that the favoured hand for fine-grained object manipulation is the right, with control primarily in the left-hemisphere along with speech (Lieberman, 1991). Both involve hierarchical control of sequencing.

Brain damage could give us some pointers. For example, are Broca's aphasics also disrupted in other hierarchical tasks? Grossman (1980) found a subgroup of Broca's aphasics who were unable to produce hierarchically organized speech. Rather, they emitted a series of agrammatical single word utterances. They also had difficulty in forming a hierarchical structure in a visuo-mechanical copying task.

Greenfield suggests that Broca's area consists of two subregions, which derive from common precursor tissue (Figure 20.18). Broca's area might start life as tissue that is undifferentiated (Chapter 6) with regard to the potential modality. Modality-specific development then occurs. Region 1 develops a speciality for manual object manipulation and region 2 becomes specialized as a grammar circuit for speech. In Figure 20.18, note the input from anterior regions of frontal cortex. These develop with maturation of prefrontal cortex and mediate planning and sequencing.

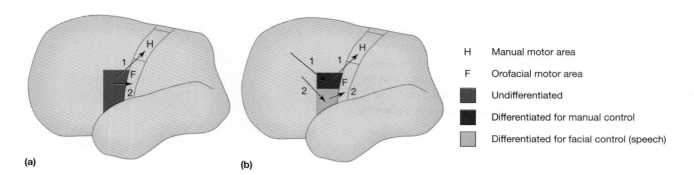

(a)   (b)

H	Manual motor area
F	Orofacial motor area
■	Undifferentiated
■	Differentiated for manual control
■	Differentiated for facial control (speech)

Figure 20.18 Suggested subdivisions of Broca's area (marked blue). (a) Early in development, the system is relatively undifferentiated. However, there is a bias towards links between Broca's area and motor cortex responsible for manual control (H) (link 1) and orofacial motor control, involved in speech (F) (link 2). (b) Later in development. Boundary lines associated with Broca's area are now shown, indicating delineation of the area and a clear division of responsibility within the area. Also shown to appear at this stage (arrows coming from the left) are inputs from prefrontal cortex.

Source: Greenfield (1991, Fig. 11, p. 543).

Section summary

1 Spoken language is universal. This suggests the possibility that there is a genetically based tendency towards its acquisition.

2 Reading and writing are clearly not universal and usually involve extensive education.

3 Among others, Broca's and Wernicke's areas are two brain regions involved in processing of language.

4 The nature of aphasia depends upon the brain region damaged.

5 In the absence of a spoken language, brain regions that would normally underlie this ability can be taken over by other processing, e.g. that mediating sign language.

6 Neural mechanisms underlying speech might differentiate from precursor neural tissue having a potential to be involved in other hierarchically organized action.

Test your knowledge

(Answers on p. 515)

20.7 In which of the brain's lobes are (i) Broca's area and (ii) Wernicke's area located?

20.8 Complete the following: 'The arcuate fasciculus consists of the _____ of neurons, linking Wernicke's and Broca's areas'.

Bringing things together

The aspects of behaviour and cognition that are described in this chapter can be related, as illustrated by language. Language provides a good example of a function that shows some degree of modularity, e.g. in its survival in Williams syndrome. However, it does not depend on a unique encapsulated predetermined brain module. Rather, certain cortical architecture lends itself to capture by learning as a result of exposure to a language culture. Thereby, certain properties of modularity develop with experience. Comprehension and production of language involve the focusing of attention on particular aspects of incoming information. Language illustrates principles of goal-direction and hierarchy, involving inhibition on inappropriate associations. Hemispheric differences underlying the control of language are well established.

Summary of Chapter 20

1 **Our actions are associated with goals and, in order to achieve these, various amounts of attention are allocated to associated stimuli and tasks.**

2 **The notion of modularity in cognition has proven to be a valuable stimulus to our thinking but needs careful qualification.**

3 **The capacity of a stimulus or cognition to occupy awareness is not constant. Rather it is modulated by a process called attention.**

4 There is difference between the hemispheres in terms of the information processing that they carry out.

5 The prefrontal cortex has a principal role in setting goals and adjusting behaviour to meet them.

6 Certain brain structures give a bias towards the acquisition of language but there is developmental plasticity and environmental stimulation is crucial.

Further reading

It is worth keeping an eye on the journals *Trends in Neurosciences* and *Trends in Cognitive Science*. Fuster (2005) presents a unifying approach to cognition and action. Language is discussed by Pulvermuller (2003) and its evolutionary aspects by Corballis (2003). Willingham (2004) is a major contributor to cognition and action. The social dimension of action is described by Frith and Wolpert (2004). For hemispheric differences, see Zaidel and Iacoboni (2003). For the neuroscience of attention, see Chapters 39–46 of Gazzaniga (2004), for language, see Chapters 54–60 and for higher cognition, see Chapters 61–69.

Signposts

At various points in the book, 'cognitive' was employed, in terms of information processing. These uses of the term can now be fitted into a broader context. You met briefly hemispheric differences in the context of language (Chapter 8, 'Vision') and emotion (Chapter 12, 'Emotion'). Animals were said to exploit cognitive maps (Chapter 11, 'Learning and memory'). For Phineas Gage (Chapter 12), we spoke of a failure of cognitive control mediated via the frontal lobes to resist tendencies organized at a lower level. We spoke of the hippocampus mediating cognitive control as in overcoming a win–stay strategy and showing win–shift. All of these involve knowledge of the world, its use in the control of behaviour and inhibition of competitive tendencies. Chapter 13, 'Stress and coping', discussed expectations about the world and a comparison of sensory input against these. Chapter 14, 'Pain', discussed cognitions such as expectancy effects and placebos.

Answers

Explanations for answers to 'test your knowledge' questions can be found on the website **www.pearsoned.co.uk/toates**

20.1 Attention

20.2 Behaviour; intact; behaviour; intact (instead of behaviour, cognition is another possibility)

20.3 Area (or, of course, location or region)

20.4 Right

20.5 Myelination

20.6 Immediate; anticipation

20.7 (i) Frontal; (ii) temporal

20.8 Axons

 Interactions and animations relating to topics discussed in this chapter can be found on the website at **www.pearsoned.co.uk/toates.** These include

Animation: The function of the two cerebral hemispheres

Interaction: The hemispheric localization of language function in right and left handers

Animation: Wernicke–Geschwind model

Interaction: The location of the main areas involved in language comprehension and production

Interaction: Can you spot the difference between Broca's and Wernicke's aphasia?

CHAPTER 21

Brains, minds and consciousness

Learning outcomes for Chapter 21

After studying this chapter, you should be able to:

1. Convince even a non-psychologist or sceptical hard-nosed scientist that the phenomenon of consciousness is a topic worthy of study. Present an argument that calls on conscious and behavioural experiences and thereby link subjective and objective perspectives. Relate this discussion to an understanding of how brains work.

2. Compare and contrast information processing that is done with full conscious awareness and that done unconsciously. Thereby, define the special features of conscious processing.

3. Explain what is meant by the term 'neural correlates of consciousness'. Identify some neural correlates and describe the evidence that implicates the brain regions in conscious processing. Discuss whether we can go beyond the term 'correlate' and infer a causal brain–consciousness link.

4. Describe the evidence and informed speculation that is involved in taking a comparative approach to consciousness. Apply evolutionary and functional types of explanation to it.

5. Discuss the philosophical issue of how consciousness links to the physical brain. Show where biological psychology is relevant to this.

1 What is the relationship between mind and brain? Why is it sometimes termed the mind–brain *problem*? Would it be more correctly described as the consciousness–brain problem?

2 Do reports of conscious insight give a good account of the causes of behaviour?

3 Do non-human animals experience consciousness?

4 Is there a 'ghost in the machine' – something immaterial in addition to neurons? Is there a soul?

5 Is the conscious mind united or is it divisible?

6 Can a computer be conscious?

What is it like to be a bat?

Source: PhotoDisc, Inc.

Introduction

What is stimulating your sensory systems right now? The smell of coffee or the sound of a CD playing, or both? Take a glance around the room. What is happening in your visual world as you look up from *Biological Psychology?* These questions relate to the present and you probably answered in terms of conscious awareness. However, on reflection, it is clear that there are stimuli impinging of which you normally have little conscious awareness. Such things as the tightness of a shoe or the pressure of your weight on the chair can be brought into conscious awareness, even though it is unlikely that they were there just before starting this chapter. However, they were providing information to the CNS.

You probably thought only about the external environment but your internal organs are also providing the CNS with much information, such as that concerning the contraction of your stomach. If you are lucky, most of this does not reach conscious awareness.

Now try reflecting on your past, on episodes of special personal experience. These will also occupy your conscious mind even though they are of events no longer present, and some will be tinged with emotion. Now speculate on your plans for the future. Conscious thought clearly opens up possibilities that take us beyond the present.

Suppose that you hear a recorded message containing a telephone number and you search for a pen to write it down. As you do so, you will doubtless repeat the number to yourself out loud or silently. The number engages your conscious processing and continues to do so for as long as you repeat it.

So, the content of **consciousness** can have something to do with the maintenance of sensory activity over time.

My consciousness appears to capture a phenomenon with certain characteristics: a capacity to self-reflect upon my existence, to recall experiences from the past ('episodic memories'), to hold information in my mind's eye and to manipulate it, to run mental simulations of future possible scenarios and to feel the hot quality of emotion. My consciousness would appear to be closely associated with the feeling of being a free agent, able to act voluntarily or to refrain from acting. I am also conscious of being conscious.

As individuals, we employ a theory of mind of other people (Chapter 6, 'Development and plasticity'), which often means a theory of their conscious awareness. We tend to associate consciousness with their free-will, personal agency and responsibility. We judge others by what we suppose to be the content of their conscious awareness, involving their intentionality. Such considerations are important to how we view ourselves as humans, with social, political, ethical and religious connotations.

Consciousness has been mentioned at several points in the book and the present chapter will return to discuss these topics, as well as introduce some new and related material. The focus now is consciousness as a topic in its own right and we will view it in the context of brains and minds. For example, Chapter 1, 'Introduction', described identity theory, which attempts to link brain and mind, and we will be able to illuminate this using biological evidence.

Consciousness will be described as one feature of the **mind**, a feature having certain peculiar properties not possessed by all aspects of 'mind'. Much of the mind functions unconsciously. By general consensus, consciousness means (Searle, 1993, p. 61): 'subjective states of sentience or awareness'. There is a 'raw feel' of experience associated with consciousness and this aspect is sometimes termed **phenomenal consciousness**. It is difficult to capture the term 'phenomenal consciousness' in words, and the best I can do is 'what it feels like to be conscious'.

Of course, consciousness cannot be observed objectively and publicly. However, to each individual conscious being, their own phenomenal consciousness surely seems to be especially vivid and obvious. It is perhaps the feature of our existence about which we are most familiar and expert. Yet philosophers and psychologists agonize over even how to construct the right questions to gain deep insight (Nagel, 1974).

Biological psychology has a role at the interface between the objective and the subjective. In other words, this is between, on the one hand, an account of the brain in terms of neurons, synapses and neurotransmitters, etc., and, on the other, our reports of our own conscious awareness. Such terms as 'seeing', 'believing', 'feeling' and 'fearing' normally all imply phenomenal conscious states. Biological psychology tries to identify which particular patterns of neural activity

and which brain regions are consistently associated with each such conscious state (Dehaene and Naccache, 2001). It asks further – is there something that characterizes such brain states systematically, as distinct from those not associated with conscious awareness?

This issue was discussed in Chapter 1 in terms of a patient reporting depression. The core symptom of depression, as experienced by patients, is a particular negative subjective conscious state. However, this state can equally be characterized in terms of the activity of neurons and hormones, etc. The issue is also brought out clearly, in the case of pain (Chapter 14, 'Pain'), where the conscious report of negative affect is, of course, central to any diagnosis. The conscious report of craving for drugs (Chapter 18, 'Drugs and addiction') tells a similar story.

The 1990s saw a mushrooming of articles and books on consciousness, in which authors argued that its study should be at the heart of psychology (e.g. Baars, 1997). Some proclaimed it as the last and most important scientific challenge. In several cases, pioneering authors on consciousness have come from biological psychology (Gray, 1995; Panksepp, 1998a; Pribram, 1986; Rozin, 1976; Weiskrantz, 1997). In theorizing about consciousness, psychological concepts, such as the 'self', appear alongside definable biological events such as blood flows to different brain regions and dopamine levels. This makes the study of consciousness a rather unconventional and hybrid science.

Questions raised in the present chapter will include the following.

In terms of brain processes:

- What is the relationship between activity of the brain and conscious experience?

- What kind of information processing, involving which brain regions, is associated with consciousness, as opposed to unconscious processes?

- Can a study of consciousness be reduced to a study of the physical brain?

- What is the effect of brain damage on conscious experience?

- Can a study of the brains of different species illuminate consciousness?

In terms of function:

- Do conscious processes confer an advantage in terms of fitness (Chapter 2, 'Genes, environment and evolution')?

- Do they come at a cost?

- Does the lifestyle of certain species suggest the existence of, and functional advantage of, consciousness?

First we will look at consciousness in the context of information processing.

1 Consciousness is a subjective feature of our existence with which we are well aquainted.

2 Within biological psychology, an aspect of the study of consciousness consists of trying to relate phenomenal consciousness to activity of systems of neurons in the brain.

Test your knowledge

(Answer on page 532)

21.1 Complete the missing word in the following: 'A task of biological psychology is to link the objective study of brains to the _____ evidence of conscious report'.

Conscious and unconscious information processing

Introduction

Cognition and behaviour are mediated by a combination of conscious and unconscious processes (Bargh and Chartrand, 1999). Only a very limited subset of the information processing performed by the nervous system is available to conscious inspection (Gray, 1995). For example, we have no conscious insight into the stages of sensory processing, such as those involved with size constancy. We simply have access to the *products* of processing in the form of a conscious perception of the world (Chapters 7–9). Similarly, we normally have little or no insight into motor programming underlying our behaviour, e.g. a choice of which muscle is activated. Chapter 10, 'The control of movement', considered controlled processing, performed with conscious awareness, versus automatic processing, performed unconsciously. Even with controlled processing, we have conscious insight into only (i) intended actions, which then automatically recruit the appropriate motor apparatus and (ii) the consequences of our actions.

This present section looks at the distinction between conscious and unconscious processes in cognition and the control of behaviour and asks, what are the characteristics of these processes?

The basics of conscious processing and experience

At a given point in time, the contents of consciousness are described by the term **qualia** (Searle, 1993). For example, 'qualia' describes the conscious perception of the colour red or, a moment later, the smell of coffee. Of course, qualia depend upon such things as activity by sensory receptors and neurons of the brain. However, the term 'qualia' conveys the subjective conscious aspect that requires a description over and above such objective data.

Conscious experiences are structured; although they are influenced by sensory data, patterns are constructed based upon this data and categories are imposed. For example, Chapter 8 'Vision' noted the intolerance that conscious processing shows towards ambiguity. The face-vase (Chapter 7, Figure 7.2, p. 180) is seen as *either* two faces *or* a vase but not as both at once. For another example, Figure 21.1 is usually seen as a face, even though no actual face looks much like this (Searle, 1993). Such information processing breaks down in Capgras's syndrome, where a patient cannot perceive 'familiar' people as familiar.

Conscious states are associated with moods, e.g. elation, depression or joy.

Conscious contents ('qualia') that are generated in the absence of the corresponding external stimuli and reactions appear to have features in common with what is generated by actual external events (Kosslyn, 1988). Objective evidence gives a biological basis for this. For example, the fusiform face area (Chapter 8) is triggered by an image of a face and by simply imagining a face (O'Craven and Kanwisher, 2000). Inner 'speech' contains mistakes ('slips') rather like external

Figure 21.1 Face.

Source: Searle (1993, Fig. 1, p. 66).

speech (Baars, 1993). As was noted in Chapter 10, simulation of action in the imagination has similarities to real action. Simulation of a cautious and careful movement is slow, corresponding to the speed of the real movement.

The cognitive unconscious

Paradoxically, placing scientific attention on consciousness reveals how much of the control of cognition and behaviour is performed by processes to which we do *not* have conscious access (Bargh and Chartrand, 1999). The processing of stimulus information can proceed to a surprising extent without engaging conscious awareness. Not only raw stimulus features but also semantic associations can be triggered at a preconscious level (Velmans, 1991).

The so-called 'cognitive unconscious', involves the simultaneous parallel processing of several streams of information. Belief in its existence is based on various observations, some within biological psychology (Kihlstrom, 1993). For example, consider activity in the amygdala, a brain region associated with emotion (Chapter 12, 'Emotion'). Activity can be triggered by the very brief presentation of an image of a face that wears an expression of fear, even though this image does not reach conscious awareness (Morris *et al.*, 1999). Similarly, researchers have looked at the priming of word completion in amnesic patients with temporal lobe damage (Chapter 11, 'Learning and memory'). Such patients cannot consciously recall the word but provide evidence of its processing at an unconscious level. For example, even presenting a word, e.g. ELASTIC, in a way that it is not consciously registered means that subsequently the cue ELA..... is more likely to be completed as ELASTIC than as, say, ELATED.

The link between conscious and unconscious processing

Introduction

Various features of cognition and behaviour point to the special role that conscious processing plays, as distinct from unconscious processing. Figure 21.2 shows the link between these types of processing. A range of unconscious processes provide information to conscious processing and in turn are influenced by conscious processing. Conscious processing selects from the information provided and exploits unconscious processing in the production of behaviour.

Perception

Conscious processing interprets the actions of specialized unconscious processing systems (Gazzaniga, 1993). For example, consider the ambiguous face-vase figure (Chapter 7, 'Sensory systems', and Chapter 8). Processors of the visual system present both possible interpretations to conscious

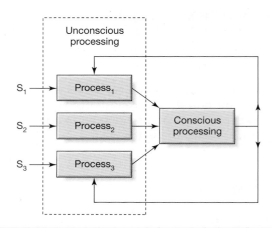

Figure 21.2 Unconscious and conscious processes.

processing, which selects alternately *either* two faces *or* a vase as the content of awareness.

Whether one uses the language of modules and central processors (Chapter 20, 'Cognition and action') or automatic versus controlled processing (Chapter 10), the point is much the same. An array of unconscious parallel operations extract information and process it, while only a fraction of this gains access to conscious awareness (Kihlstrom, 1993). So, the contents of conscious awareness are focused and limited (Baars, 1993).

Conscious processing is specialized to handle information at times of uncertainty, i.e. when things do not run according to plan. For example, at times of anxiety ('something on the mind') there is repeated intrusion of anxiety-related cognition into other sequences of conscious thought (Gray, 1995). Such prioritizing can be just awful – e.g. when you can't get an unwanted thought out of your mind – but it is not difficult to see that in its roots it has served an adaptive role.

Goal-setting

Our spontaneous setting of goals ('having intentions') (Dehaene and Naccache, 2001) and pursuit of them by various routes are processes that are accessible to consciousness (Chapters 10 and 20). Such conscious goals are implemented by processes lower in the hierarchy, to which we do not have conscious access. We consciously monitor progress towards the goal. Goal-setting is associated with a central executive system (Chapters 11 and 20), which is involved in allocating processing resources to task demands (Block, 1991).

Conscious processing instigates action where routines ('habits') are not available or helps to resist routines and temptation (Norman and Shallice, 1986; Schrödinger, 1958). For example, consider the Stroop test (Chapter 10). We set the conscious goal of reporting ink colour, though there is interference from word meaning. Conscious processing is involved in the attempt to override the response of reporting word meaning, in the interests of ink colour.

If consciousness is engaged when things do not go according to plan, this implies feedback on the state of the world, which is compared with intentions (Baars, 1997). When these coincide we 'tick over' on automatic control. However, the moment that significant disparity is detected, it is brought to conscious awareness for specialized processing. This can result in novel action to solve the present problem and formation of new memories for future reference.

Creativity

Conscious processing has a role in intuitive, insightful and creative operations of a character that cannot (at least, as yet!) be modelled by digital computers (Penrose, 1990). Within consciousness we are able to associate weird ideas and images, and thereby arrive at novel creative combinations. However, even creative inspiration sometimes appears to pop into consciousness from nowhere, presumably after extensive unconscious processing (Baars, 1997; Velmans, 1991). This suggests a time sequence of information processing: conscious → unconscious → conscious, pointing to downwards and upwards flows of information in Figure 21.2.

A personal angle

A neuroscientist's unconscious processing

The pioneering neuroscientist, Nobel prize-winner and theorist of brain-mind relations, Sir John Eccles, described the role of his unconscious processing in yielding creative solutions (Eccles, 1989, p. 233). You might like to take inspiration from him:

When I am searching for a good new idea, I fill up my mind with the knowledge of the problem and my critical evaluation of the attempted solutions of that problem. Then I await the outcome of the mental tension so created. Maybe I take a walk, as Einstein often did, or I listen to music . . . I don't struggle with my mind under tension, but hope that a good creative idea will burst forth, and often it does.

The self and theories of mind

For humans, consciousness is involved in predicting the moves of other people. This involves exploiting information on the conscious intentions of others (Klein, 1991).Whether we are psychologists, preachers, traffic wardens, tax inspectors, conmen or whatever, we tend to explain the behaviour of

others in terms of their preceding behaviour and (inferred) mental states, a theory of mind (Chapter 5, 'The brain'). That is, we form representations ('models') of the mental states of others, involving their affective states and intentions, and we extrapolate to their most likely behaviour.

Barlow (1990) notes that neuroscience's insights play little role in how we treat other people but our 'folk theories' of the minds of others play a profound role. Even though they might sometimes fail us, our models of the mind appear to have a certain utility in predicting behaviour.

Section summary

1 Conscious processing imposes order on cognition and behaviour and is associated with moods.

2 Consciousness provides a means for simulating conditions in the absence of sensory input.

3 The cognitive unconscious, a system of rapid parallel processing, provides information to consciousness.

4 A variety of roles are attributed to consciousness in generating adaptive and coherent sequences of cognition and behaviour.

5 Modelling the self and the mind of others is a specialized role attributed to advanced (e.g. human) conscious cognition.

Test your knowledge

(Answer on page 532)

21.2 Complete the missing words in the following: 'In the case of the ambiguous face-vase figure, sensory systems provide _____ possible interpretations and conscious perception _____ between these interpretations'.

Basis in the brain

Introduction

What kind of neural activity is necessary and sufficient for conscious experience? Which brain regions and neurochemicals are implicated? We shall discuss the **neural correlates of consciousness** (Dehaene and Naccache, 2001).

By this is meant those patterns of neural activity that are associated particularly with conscious processing. The link here between biology and psychology is a two-way street. Psychological data and theory can provide clues in the search for neural processes (Crick, 1994). For example, a privileged route to reaching conscious awareness is given to novel information. So, Gray (1995) asked, where is novelty detected by the brain?

Linking psychology and biology

This section looks at a range of phenomena related to consciousness that arise within psychology. It considers what they show about the conscious–unconscious distinction and what they suggest regarding the link to neural processes.

Representing information

Evidence suggests that conscious processing is required in order to maintain stimulus information in an active state following termination of the stimulus (Dehaene and Naccache, 2001). In the absence of engaging conscious processing, much stimulus information will normally be lost. By an 'active state' is meant that patterns of activity in particular circuits of neurons are triggered by the stimulus and encode its presence after the stimulus is no longer present. Working memory and its anatomical basis in regions such as the prefrontal cortex are an important part of this capacity.

The notion that conscious processes are involved in representing events even in their physical absence obtains support from observation of patients with Charles Bonnet syndrome, named after the French-Swiss philosopher. They experience spontaneous hallucinations, the occurrence of which is accompanied by increased activity in the ventral stream of visual processing (ffytche *et al.*, 1998). Activity is somewhat specific to the nature of the hallucination, being marked in regions processing colour when the hallucination is in colour and in the fusiform face area when the hallucination is of faces.

The controlled-automatic dimension

There is a change of activity in brain regions as a task moves from controlled ('conscious') processing to unconscious ('automatic') control (Chapter 10). Hence, certain regions are identified as having a special role in conscious processing. For example, with automaticity, a lowering of activation is seen in the prefrontal cortex and anterior cingulate cortex but reactivation occurs there if the routine fails.

Attention

Conscious awareness is linked to attention (Chapter 20), which points to the role of the modulation of sensory information by such structures as the prefrontal cortex, brain stem, parietal cortex and thalamus. Indeed, selective attention needs to be paid to an event as a prior condition for it to engage conscious processing (Dehaene and Naccache, 2001). Using Crick's (1994) metaphor, there is a 'spotlight of attention' that brings into conscious awareness only a fraction of the available information, e.g. a small subset of the information extracted by our sense organs. In the neglect syndrome (Chapter 20), a stimulus might be undetectable at one location in sensory space as a result of the presence of a stimulus at another. However, the neglected stimulus can be detected if presented on its own. A stimulus needs to gain attention in order to appear within conscious processing and there is competition between stimuli for this resource (Dehaene and Naccache, 2001).

Speed of switches within conscious processing

The contents of consciousness can change very quickly as in the switches of the face-vase figure. This directs the search to the comparable dynamics of switches in the underlying neural activity. Such switches in patterns of neural activity have been identified (Chapter 8).

Complexity is not enough

In a sense, you are a highly sophisticated mathematician. You might well not have realized this before and find my insight into your ability bizarre, but I am confident that it is true. The reason that you might not know this is that the sophistication to which I refer does not reach conscious awareness. It resides in parts of the brain associated with unconscious processing. Just consider the formidable unconscious computation that is involved in the motor skills of walking upright, jogging or even having an amateurish shot at playing tennis. So, complexity of processing on its own is insufficient for an association with consciousness. Thus, highly complex parallel processing that proceeds in an automatic fashion does not trigger awareness, e.g. the computations predicting the limbs' optimal location in tennis.

The cerebellum is specialized for the kind of parallel computation involved in automatic and unconscious features of cognition and behavioural control (Figure 21.2). The cerebellum is usually involved little, if at all, in discussions of consciousness (Penrose, 1990), in spite of having more neurons than any other brain region. The tasks that it performs would probably defy any but the most sophisticated university mathematician if they were to be made explicit in numbers. We simply could not perform them consciously. Yet, consider being asked to solve a relatively trivial but normally rare problem, such as 'What is 13 times 3 minus 4?' Most of us need to bring our conscious awareness to solving it since we lack automatic routines for doing so (Dehaene and Naccache, 2001).

Sleep-waking

The brain alternates between states of consciousness in sleep–waking (Chapter 19, 'Sleep and waking'). Changes in level of awareness are programmed by the ascending neural processes and these structures are important in understanding the phenomena of consciousness (Coenen, 1998). REM sleep, involving dreaming, has features in common with conscious awareness and might be considered a special 'altered state of consciousness'. Ascending cholinergic projections to the thalamus and cortex appear to play a crucial role in consciousness, including that of the REM phase of sleep. Their disruption can profoundly change conscious experience (Perry *et al.*, 1999). Changes of conscious awareness with anaesthetics are associated with changes of cholinergic transmission.

Having looked at the psychological phenomena and what they suggest about consciousness, we now look more closely at the brain structures.

Brain structures

General points

Activity in the brain stem and thalamus seems to be necessary for consciousness (Penfield, 1966). Damage to these brain regions can destroy the capacity for most behaviour, whether consciously or unconsciously mediated (Gray, 1995). Parts of the brain stem that control respiration are clearly vital to conscious experience but they are probably no more vital to it than they are to unconscious cognition or to spinal reflexes. By comparison, activity of the heart is also necessary. The quest is to locate brain regions that have a special contribution to *conscious* processes (Libet, 1993b).

Evolutionarily old structures

In spite of many investigators' emphasis on sophisticated cortical structures, Panksepp (1998a) argues persuasively that subcortical emotional systems provide a fundamental ingredient to consciousness (Chapter 12). These systems set the emotional tone of the brain and are reflected in moods.

Cortical–thalamic interaction

Some believe that an important basis of conscious experience lies in the neural activity associated with interactions between the cortex and thalamus (Crick, 1994). There appear to be both direct and indirect links, involving patterns of reverberation in neuronal activity throughout the circuits. See Figure 21.3.

As shown, the thalamus is a gateway for access of sensory input to the cortex (Baars, 1993). For example, there are reciprocal circuits linking the lateral geniculate nucleus (LGN) and the visual cortex. Particular activity within a

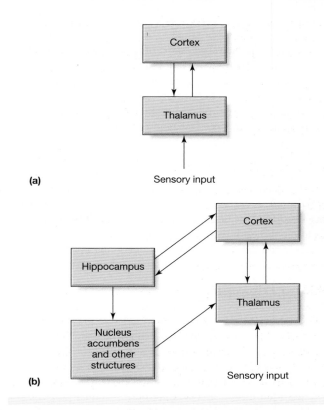

Figure 21.3 Reverberatory circuits between the thalamus and cortex: (a) direct, described by Crick (1994) and (b) involving the hippocampus, described by Gray (1995).

subset of thalamic neurons, as in the LGN, might be able to sustain awareness on a visual input. Activity of such a circuit is believed to underlie the 'conscious-like' cognition of dreaming in REM sleep (Chapter 19).

Figure 21.3(b) shows a suggested role of the hippocampus and some other structures in forming a loop involving the cortex. In this model, the hippocampus detects disparity between actual states of the world and expected states. When disparity is detected, there is a biasing of the content of consciousness so as to process the associated sensory information. Conscious awareness corresponds to the information that gains access to such loops. Novel input readily gains access. However, we should not simply see the hippocampus as the seat of conscious awareness; its damage does not destroy consciousness (Chapter 11), though it distorts its contents (see commentaries to Gray, 1995).

As a general point, loops of neural connections must have special features for consciousness to emerge from them. There are plenty of neural loops in the CNS that are associated with processing that is inaccessible to conscious awareness, e.g. motor control via the cerebellum and basal ganglia (Gray, 1995).

Manipulation of brain activity

We speak of the neural *correlates* of consciousness, as in the face-vase illusion, but correlation does not prove causation. Do particular changes in neural activity actually cause changes in conscious perception? To investigate this, we need to manipulate the neural events and observe what happens to conscious awareness (Dehaene and Naccache, 2001). In some cases, the manipulation is done for us, as in specific brain damage, where aspects of conscious perception are predictably lost (described shortly).

Ideally, *reversible* changes in brain activity would be created and the effects observed. An example of this is the temporary inactivation of the brain regions that process visual motion, which abolishes the conscious perception of movement (Beckers and Zeki, 1995). Patients undergoing brain surgery have received electrical stimulation, described next.

Penfield's study

Artificial electrical stimulation of the visual cortex evokes subjective visual sensations, which suggests that electrical activity of the cortex is a basis of consciousness (Newsome and Salzman, 1993). In a classical study, Penfield (1966) found that specific episodic sensations were triggered by stimulation through cortical electrodes (Chapter 11). The pattern of temporal lobe activation preceding an epileptic attack is accompanied by complex visual sensations (Penfield and Rasmussen, 1968).

Libet's study

During surgery, the brain can be electrically stimulated for various lengths of time and the effects observed. Libet *et al.* (1991) found that a low intensity of stimulation had to last a minimum time *T* before a signal reached conscious awareness. At the same intensity, if stimulation lasted for less than *T*, it would trigger only non-conscious processing. The experiment was carried out on patients being treated for intractable pain. Electrodes had been implanted in the ventrobasal thalamus, whereby researchers were able to stimulate the system normally involved in tactile detection and involving the somatosensory cortex (Chapter 9, 'The other sensory systems').

Effects of brain damage

General

A way of gaining insight is to look at (a) how the action of particular neural processes relates to the nature and content of consciousness and (b) how abnormality of such processes relates to abnormal consciousness (an example is schizophrenia, discussed in the next chapter) (Gray, 1995). For example, profound changes to consciousness are associated with loss of dopamine (DA) (Sacks, 1982). These include loss of will, emptiness of consciousness, distortion of time and hallucinations. For another example, the neglect syndrome (Chapter 20) can be associated with damage to the parietal cortex (Umiltà and Zorzi, 1995).

Although studies point to a crucial role of the cortex in consciousness (just described), somewhat paradoxically, based upon surgical experience, Penfield (1966, p. 234) reported that 'Consciousness continues, regardless of what area of cerebral cortex is removed'. It appears that specific areas of cortex are involved with triggering specific aspects of conscious awareness related to particular sensory events.

Disrupted memory

Chapter 11 described dissociations between explicit and implicit memories. Can you remember Claparède's pin experiment? There was dissociation between implicit and explicit memory. We assume that with a failure of episodic memory, H.M. (Chapter 11) suffered from a seriously disordered consciousness in terms of its potential for information processing.

Disrupted visual processing

Damage to the ventral stream of cortical processing disrupts conscious visual perception but leaves intact the patient's ability to perform rapid unconscious visually guided action (Chapter 8). This was exemplified by Dee Fletcher. A dissociation in vision that tells a similar story, is as follows.

It used to be believed that in humans a lesion in the visual cortex caused total blindness in the corresponding region of the visual field. The effect would be comparable to that of a lesion in the retina, i.e. total blindness in an affected region. However, we now know that patients can retain a certain visual capacity corresponding to the affected area, termed 'blindsight' (Weiskrantz, 1976), a subject introduced in Chapter 1.

Where is the unconscious processing taking place in blindsight? Neurons that pass from the lateral geniculate nucleus to cortical regions other than the primary visual cortex (Fries, 1981) could play a role. The route involving the superior colliculus (subcortical system) (Figures 8.17, p. 201 and 8.24, p. 206), and projecting to the dorsal stream, is another possibility.

Humans are not necessarily aware consciously of all the determinants of their behaviour. To generalize from D.B., intact humans might be expected under some conditions to detect events and behave on the basis of them without having conscious awareness of doing so. Traditionally, human sensory and perceptual systems have been studied on the basis of people's reports of what they perceive, this being fundamental to clinical assessment. However, D.B. serves as a warning that such reports might need careful qualification. As Weiskrantz (1976, p. 118) notes: 'an "unexpected" revelation of a capacity may occur when one uses an unusual method of testing for it'.

D.B. was born in 1940 in a small market town in England (Weiskrantz, 1976). Life was normal until he reached 14, when D.B. reported headaches on the right side of his head. These were usually preceded by the appearance of a phantom flashing light. In his 20s, D.B. noticed a blank region in the left visual field. A tumour in the tissue of the primary visual cortex (V1) was identified. In 1973, D.B. received brain surgery to remove the diseased tissue and this greatly improved his well-being. He was largely free of headaches and phantom flashes of light. However, most of D.B.'s left visual field was blind.

D.B.'s ophthalmic surgeon observed that D.B. retained a capacity to locate objects more accurately than at chance level, in what was apparently a blind left visual field. For example, by his own account, D.B. was not able to see an outstretched hand but nonetheless would reach for it with some accuracy. D.B. was able to point to objects, while denying that he could see them. He could even discriminate a pattern of stripes from a uniform grey. There was a separation between D.B.'s ability and his conscious awareness of it.

So, based on a comparison with the performance of blindsight patients, what does conscious perception bring to us that is distinct from unconscious processing? For visual stimulation in the 'blind' region, these patients can *react to* particular triggers in an automatic fashion. For example, at better than chance, they can respond to the question, 'Was that vertical or horizontal?' They can *react* by shaking the experimenter's outstretched hand, a highly probable stimulus-response connection. However, they cannot *act* – they are unable to instigate novel actions based on the visual information extracted in the 'blind' region (Weiskrantz, 1997). So, here is a feature of normal conscious processing that is highlighted by its absence. Furthermore, we can report on our conscious mental states based on visual stimulation whereas, by definition, blindsight patients have nothing to report regarding visual stimulation of the blind part of the field (Dehaene and Naccache, 2001).

Inter-hemispheric communication

Surprising to any view on consciousness is the observation that if one hemisphere is anaesthetized, as in the Wada technique (Chapter 20), patients retain consciousness (discussed by Kinsbourne, 1993).

What is the result of splitting the cerebral hemispheres by cutting the corpus callosum (Sperry, 1974)? Is consciousness split in two, as if there are two conscious minds associated with one brain?

William McDougall, one of the founders of British psychology, believed in the unitary nature of consciousness, unconditional upon a unified brain. Sir Cyril Burt (a co-founder) remembers McDougall:

saying more than once that he had tried to bargain with Sherrington . . . that if ever he should be smitten with an incurable disease, Sherrington should cut through his corpus callosum. 'If the physiologists are right' – and by physiologists I suppose he meant Sherrington himself – 'the result should be a split personality'. 'If I am right', he said, 'my consciousness will remain a unitary consciousness'. And he seemed to regard that as the most convincing proof of the existence of something like a soul.   (Quoted from Zangwill, 1974, p. 265.)

If information is targeted to each hemisphere in turn, separate cognitive processing can be triggered in each hemisphere (Sperry, 1974). These cognitions can be in conflict with each other as far as the potential for coherent behaviour is concerned. This strongly suggests that the necessary cognition underlying consciousness can be truly split. Whether phenomenal consciousness itself is split remains a tricky philosophical question. Lacking access to the dominant left hemispheric speech system, the right hemisphere of split-brain patients is often described as 'minor' or 'silent' (Sperry, 1974). Does the right hemisphere have, in any sense, a conscious mental life of its own? Is it simply acting on 'autopilot' control in the absence of awareness? Without having the operation, we do not know 'what it is like to be a split-brain patient'.

Differential targeting of information to different hemispheres is, of course, an artificial procedure. In a situation of 'normal' processing, it would possibly have been of some comfort to McDougall to know that cutting the corpus callosum can have little effect on processing, e.g. verbal IQ remains intact (Gazzaniga, 1993). In split-brain patients, it sometimes appears that the unified conscious experience arises from the dominant left hemisphere imposing an interpretation upon behaviour that is elicited from either disconnected hemisphere.

Could two conscious entities associated with one brain enter into a dialogue with each other, commenting upon their consciousnesses? In split-brain patients, MacKay (1987) found independence in terms of simultaneous and different sensory evaluations. There were also distinct modes of motor control between the two hemispheres. However, he found no evidence to suggest two distinct forms of consciousness. Indeed, in response to some subtle probing, one patient responded, 'Are you guys trying to make two people out of me?'

The binding problem

The unity of conscious experience involves the integration of components of information. The problem of how this is achieved is sometimes termed the **binding problem** (Searle, 1993). For example, there is integration of the smell and sight of a rose to give a unified perception. So, are different patterns of neuronal activity, representing the colour and smell, *in some way* bound together? Does everything come together at one point, sometimes described as a 'theatre' of consciousness? This locus, associated with conscious awareness, is supposed to lie somewhere deep in the brain.

Some argue that, in reality, there is no convergence of neural inputs to one site (Dennett, 1993). They suggest that no brain area derives input from every sensory source. Information processing remains parallel, e.g. as in the visual streams (Chapter 8).

This debate will doubtless run and run, as will the topic of the next section!

Functional and comparative issues

This section applies the evolutionary and functional types of explanation (Chapter 1) to the phenomenon of consciousness. It will describe the close links between speculation on function and that on evolutionary appearance. It is also an example of insights to be gained from taking a comparative approach, i.e. comparing different species.

Function

Consciousness appears to be an evolutionary development that builds on unconscious cognitive processing (Rozin, 1976). In such terms, its function seems to be one of exerting control over unconscious processes. This may be necessary once brains reach a certain complexity, so that there can be coordination and coherence in behaviour and cognition. Thereby flexibility can be achieved and processing that was originally encapsulated within a range of single parallel processes can be integrated and exploited as part of a coherent strategy.

Consciousness must presumably serve some adaptive function for it to have emerged in evolution. Suppose that consciousness requires specific brain mechanisms for its support, or, at least, it requires development of existing structures. Their appearance in evolution might well have come at a considerable cost. Human brains are large and energy-demanding, and the size of head needed to contain them creates problems for mother and child at the time of birth.

The severe disability of amnesic patients points to an advantage of conscious processing (Weiskrantz, 1997). Similarly, as noted earlier, a blindsight patient will not normally *instigate* action based upon the blind visual field.

Dennett (1993) suggests a possible evolutionary scenario. Having evolved language for social communication, our immediate ancestors found an advantage in talking out loud to themselves. This could trigger memories and serve as a 'holding device' for keeping a memory active, necessitating working memory (Chapter 11). An evolutionary refinement of this was sub-vocal speech, one feature of consciousness.

Comparative issues

Introduction

At what stage in evolution consciousness appears is a matter of debate (Reber, 1992). The roles that consciousness is thought to serve, e.g. goal-setting and coordinated action, seem to be needed widely across species. Therefore, consciousness might not be a recent arrival (MacKay, 1991). We need to distinguish between necessary background conditions and specific conditions for consciousness to exist. For example, consciousness presumably builds on processes involved in wakefulness, since these provide a necessary condition for the experience and, of course, exist very widely across species (Coenen, 1998; Chapter 19).

What is it like ...?

It is often asked whether dogs, or fish or even amoeba are conscious. One way of expressing this is: what is it *like to be* a certain species? Nagel (1974) achieved fame with his article entitled 'What is it like to be a bat?' He speculated on the basis of the bat's sensory apparatus, e.g. possession of sonar guidance and nociceptive neurons, but concluded that it is impossible to know what it is like, without being a bat! Lacking language, a bat most likely has a limited range of conscious content compared with us. Presumably, it cannot entertain the conscious cognition of, for example, fear of old age, since this requires a symbolic language. However, a bat might experience affective conscious states, such as those associated with tissue damage or mating. The neural mechanisms that support these show broad generality across mammalian species (Chapter 12; Panksepp, 1998a).

Why was the bat chosen, when the subject might equally have been, say, the spider or chimpanzee? Dennett (1993) speculates that few would want to attribute consciousness to the former and few would deny it to the latter, so the bat is a more challenging choice for speculation.

Despite the impressive cognitive skills of a number of non-human species, especially among the primates, their behaviour suggests a limited range of conscious processing, confined largely to present events (Donald, 1991).

Brain structure

Gray (1993) poses the question, 'Does a species have the brain structure assumed to underlie conscious experience?' His argument is based strongly on abnormal consciousness of schizophrenia (see the next chapter) and is attributed to abnormal interactions between structures such as the cortex and hippocampus. On this basis, rats clearly are candidates, in terms of meeting a necessary condition, and amoebas clearly are not. However, consciousness might also emerge in evolution by some other mechanism. By analogy, vision in insects and vertebrates is based on rather different processes (Gray, 1995).

There is evidence for blindsight in monkeys with damage to the visual cortex. By means of an operant task, monkeys are, in effect, asked the question, did you see that light? When information is projected to the affected region, they report that they did not see any stimulus but nonetheless react appropriately on the basis of its presence (Cowey and Stoerig, 1995; Weiskrantz, 1997).

Memory

The capacity to recall episodes of personal experience would seem to be a crucial feature of human conscious experience. Do other species show evidence of episodic memory? Some bird species do (Chapters 1, 5 and 11), which might reflect a necessary component for the experience (Griffiths *et al.*, 1999).

A self-concept

It might be useful to distinguish between consciousness in the sense of (a) some form of sentience and a possession of goal-setting processes and (b) *self*-consciousness involving complex representations of the mental state of self and others. The latter might be an evolutionary development of the former, apparent only in species with a sophisticated social cognition, such as us.

Possession of a self-concept would seem relevant to possession of conscious awareness, though whether we can equate these is open to discussion. Do different species have a 'self-concept'? To investigate this, Gallup (1977) observed the behaviour of monkeys and apes in front of mirrors. Under anaesthetic, Gallup placed red marks on some animals at a location out of sight by their direct vision, e.g. on the forehead. On recovery and after inspection in the mirror, in some cases, the animals repeatedly touched the area marked. This suggested that they identified it as part of their own body (a 'theory of self'). In both human infants and those non-human primate species that exhibit the effect, it appears at a certain developmental stage (de Veer and van den Bos, 1999).

The issue of animal consciousness is more than one of intellectual curiosity for psychologists. An important input to the animal welfare debate and thereby agricultural policy derives from such theorizing (Wiepkema, 1987).

Test your knowledge

(Answer on page 532)

21.4 Complete the following sentence: 'From a functional perspective, it is assumed that, for consciousness to have emerged in evolution, the _____ associated with it exceeded the _____.'

Some philosophical considerations

Introduction

Having got through most of the book, you are now in a position to consider again some of the philosophical material (Chapter 1). For example, we should not take the existence of consciousness for granted, since a large amount of processing takes place perfectly well in the absence of conscious awareness. This section briefly considers what biological psychology can learn from such discussion and how it might contribute insight.

Consciousness and the mind–body problem

Basics

It is interesting why philosophers use the expression mind–body *problem*. Presumably, it is because the aim of science is to reduce the diversity of nature to a few fundamental principles (Nagel, 1993). The problem comes in the basic conceptual difficulty of fitting the mind–brain relation to such principles.

It is not that we lack data; we have a rich source of information from first-hand experience. For example, a person can report when an ambiguous figure changes in its conscious interpretation, as in the face-vase figure, etc. (Chapters 7 and 8). This can be correlated with changes in brain activation. Rather, we lack a conceptual framework in which to interpret why such stimulation and brain activity is associated with *phenomenal* consciousness. This is described as the **hard problem** of consciousness (Chalmers, 1996).

So, instead of the 'mind–body problem', we might more accurately describe the philosophical hurdle as the 'brain–consciousness problem' (Gray, 1993). This is because in principle there is no problem in explaining how the aspect of mind that consists of unconscious cognition can arise from the brain. A computer analogy gives good insight. As Nagel writes (p. 2): 'The facts of consciousness are facts about how things are *for* some conscious subject, whereas physical facts are facts about how things are, full stop'.

Consciousness is essentially a 'first-person' phenomenon and cannot be understood in such terms from another's perspective (Searle, 1993). Thus, Searle suggests it is not meaningful to ask whether a computer is conscious.

Nagel sees the task of psychology as to be relating such 'how things are *to*' (italics added) to 'how things are', the latter being defined by brain processes. Although the presence of particular neural mechanisms is a prior condition for certain conscious experiences, we cannot infer the existence of the experiences based on those mechanisms. For example, certain minimal conditions need to be met at the retinal level for the experience of colour but these mechanisms only predict a capacity to discriminate wavelength (Chapter 8), not the phenomenal consciousness ('raw feel' or 'qualia') of colour.

Chapter 1 noted that identity theory is accepted by most biological psychologists. However, this is not the only theory on mind–brain. Another is as follows.

Dualism

Some philosophers, most notably the eminent French philosopher René Descartes, have argued that the domains of mind and brain are fundamentally different, such that one could exist without the other. In this view, the conscious mind might even take leave of the physical brain and wander off on its own or it might survive the death of the physical body. Such a view is termed **dualism**, since it involves a fundamental duality between a physical and a mental domain. This is a good example of where biological psychology impinges upon theology (Crick, 1994; Eccles, 1989).

Even if one believes in such a duality then, at the least, it is necessary to postulate that an interaction normally exists between the mental and physical domains. Ideas arising in the mental domain can only be translated into action with the help of muscles, so a mind → body link is needed. Conversely, it is clear that events in the physical body influence mental life (i.e. body → mind). For example, a rotting tooth is very much in the world of the physical and yet its manifestations can become all too evident to your conscious mind.

These days, dualism is not favoured in biological psychology.

Emergent properties

A popular expression for understanding consciousness is 'emergent property' (Chapter 1). Implying just such a property, Searle (1993) argues (p. 64): 'just as one cannot reach into a glass of water and pick out a molecule and say "this one is wet", so one cannot point to a single synapse or neuron in the brain and say "this one is thinking about my grandmother" '. However, Gray (1987b) points out a weakness in this analogy: based upon the properties of the constituent molecules, the liquidity of water can be predicted by a chemist. There is nothing about neurons or their assemblies that predicts subjective awareness.

When we consider the qualities of consciousness such as intentionality and goal-setting, to most of us it becomes no clearer. Thus, we can build goal-seeking into a room temperature control system employing a thermostat (e.g. hold temperature at 18 °C) but most of us would not suppose that we have thereby built consciousness into it. The experiment with the face-vase illusion can give us confidence in the generality of similar conscious experiences across individuals but does not help to explain how it arises. All we might be able to do is, given that we know of the existence of conscious experience, to predict qualities of its content, as in the frequency of switches in conscious perception (Libet, 1993a).

The astonishing hypothesis

Francis Crick's outspoken work entitled *The Astonishing Hypothesis: The Scientific Search for the Soul* is a neuroscience perspective on consciousness and an assault on dualism (Crick, 1994). In words much cited, Crick defines the astonishing hypothesis as (p. 3):

that 'You', your joys and your sorrows, your memories and your ambitions, your sense of personal identity and free will, are in fact no more than the behaviour of a vast assembly of nerve cells and their associated molecules.

The term 'no more than' is, as elsewhere, open to some ambiguity and controversy. Clearly, complex properties emerge from such an assembly of pure physical matter and Crick does not deny this. He denies that there is a consciousness or soul that can have an existence *distinct from the physical body and can survive its disintegration.*

Free-will

Introduction

Personal attitudes to the issue of mind–brain tend to be associated with corresponding attitudes to that of free-will and determinism (Zohar, 1990). For example, a denial of the special significance of consciousness tends to be associated with a parallel dismissal of that of free-will (e.g. Skinner, 1971, 1984), whereas consciousness tends to be emphasized by those putting their faith in free-will (Rogers, 1959). Traditionally, the approach of biological psychology holds to a belief that, at least in principle, events are determined in ways that are open to public observation and prediction (Chapter 1). For example, the behaviour of both saints and sinners is often rather predictable (Sutherland, 1975) but need that imply that they act without free-will?

An elusive problem

On examination, the notion of free-will is somewhat elusive, even though most of us have the feeling that we possess it. One soon gets into great difficulty in trying to state clearly

The law treats the guilty as free agents responsible for their own behaviour. Is there anything biological psychology could contribute to this issue?

Source: james andrew/Alamy.

what we mean by the term. We risk falling for the homunculus fallacy, of inventing a little ('free') person and putting him/her in the head (Chapter 7; see Bargh and Chartrand, 1999). Although few could doubt that our behaviour is largely determined by genes and environment, the notion of free-will seems to suggest (a) an element of indeterminacy that stands outside such deterministic processes and (b) the process is open to scrutiny only to the person concerned. That is, a person could always have acted otherwise.

The issue is commonly framed in terms of a dichotomy between free-will and determinism. However, it might be more fruitful to see genes and environment setting a framework for, and limits on, the exercise of free-will (Stevens, 1990; cf. Bargh and Chartrand, 1999). For example, if deterministic genetic and environmental factors exert a bias towards, say, drug addiction, it might take greater exertion of this mysterious inner factor of free-will to stay off drugs (Zohar, 1990).

An input from neuroscience

Even having to live with dilemmas ('conundrums'), can biological psychology give some help? It probably cannot give any definitive answers that would allow you to win your case, for or against free-will, in the student bar or debating society. However, it can give a framework for approaching the debate – bits of circumstantial evidence that might tentatively be brought out for one or other viewpoint. These bits of evidence might later fit a more persuasive theory.

The capacity to represent the self and the consequences of one's actions and to utilize these in the control of behaviour would seem to be a necessary condition for free-will (Frith, 1996). Such representations appear to involve the prefrontal cortex, in actions based upon anticipated future costs and benefits. Phineas Gage (Chapter 1) is usually mentioned here to exemplify a person who lost some social and moral responsibility following damage to his prefrontal cortex. Brain damage tends to be a mitigating factor in moral responsibility (Chapter 1), especially if it disrupts the capacity to link decision-making and action (MacKay, 1974). PET and fMRI scans might permit a refinement of this notion, which seems analogous to a computer hardware fault. One might perform PET scans of people's brains and correlate activity with their reports of the conscious feeling of making free decisions, as opposed to acting in response to external triggers. In the absence of any such fault, abnormal behaviour might be analogous to a computer software abnormality.

Reacting on the basis of conscious goals, rather than by automatic processing based upon stimulus input, might seem to be one criterion of being free. Resisting temptation by means of a conscious goal would be a good example. These seem to move us near to the notion of 'will' but the 'free' remains problematic. Consider the capacity to generate future scenarios in conscious awareness but not to put them into action. This might be sufficient to give us the perception of free-will (Crick, 1994).

Much of the activity of the ANS (Chapter 3, 'The nervous and endocrine systems') appears to be 'involuntary', whereas much of the control of the skeletal muscles appears to be 'voluntary' (Baars, 1997). Whether any of this provides an escape route from hard determinism is something you might like to consider.

An experimental approach

Can we bring the issue of free-will into the laboratory? One experimenter, Benjamin Libet, famously did just this. Libet worked on the basis that a self-paced voluntary act is normally accompanied by a readiness potential (Chapter 10) (Libet, 1993b). This potential, which is recorded from the scalp, is observed some 800 ms or so before the movement (Chapter 5).

Libet found that the readiness potential appears to begin some 350 ms before a conscious intention to act arises. In other words, following the logic of this paradigm, one is consciously aware of the 'decision' to act only after the programming of the act has already been instigated unconsciously. The somewhat counterintuitive conclusion is that we know what we have 'chosen' to do only after we have already decided unconsciously to do it! This alarms many people since it seems to reduce us to mere automatons, slaves to the environment and unconscious forces. So what is the role of consciousness in voluntary acts?

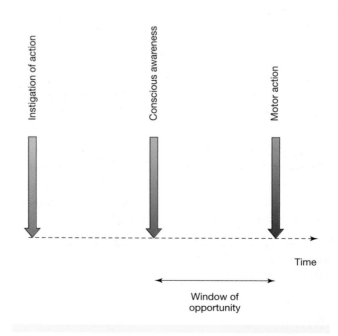

Figure 21.4 Components of action.

Normally we have a feeling of free-will surrounding much of our day-to-day integrated long-term planning and execution of action. However, Libet suggests that conscious processes do not play a role in the *instigation* of a voluntary motor act. As shown in Figure 21.4, there is a 'window of opportunity' between the conscious awareness of a decision to act and the execution of the act. Within this time, consciousness can veto the decision and block it. Thus, a somewhat constrained role for consciously mediated free-will might be suggested – it has been expressed as we don't have 'free-will' but we have 'free-won't'. How good this experimental paradigm is as a representation of conscious choice in real life is a matter of some debate. However, based on evidence such as Libet's, some argue that such a feeling of free-will is an illusion (Wegner, 2003).

Frankly, what we mean by 'free' remains a philosophical problem that biological psychology can do little to illuminate. Sorry!

Section summary

1 The 'mind–body' problem is one of how mind and body relate, i.e. how does phenomenal consciousness relate to the physical matter of the brain?

2 Consciousness is often described as an emergent property of the brain.

3 It is as yet unclear how phenomenal consciousness emerges from matter.

4 Crick's 'astonishing hypothesis' suggested that we are nothing but an assembly of such biological components as neurons.

5 Circumstantial evidence can be gathered to illuminate the issue of free-will and determinism but no conclusive case yet made.

Test your knowledge

(Answer on page 532)

21.5 Complete the following: 'The property of consciousness is said to _____ from the properties of the combination of neurons that make up the brain.'

Bringing things together

The chapter has shown where we can approach the topic of consciousness from the perspective of biological psychology. Causal, evolutionary and functional explanations each have a role to play. The study of consciousness is based upon (i) objective evidence from studying the brain, (ii) subjective reports of phenomenal consciousness and (iii) trying to form links between (i) and (ii) by the use of metaphor and analogy (e.g. 'binding', 'searchlight', 'theatre' and 'executive').

Consciousness has a curious Janus-head nature. Pointing one way, and relatively non-controversially, the term 'consciousness' describes a class of information processing. This distinguishes it from instances of information processing to which we do not have conscious access. In principle, there is relatively little difficulty in describing the nature of at least some of the information processing that is associated with consciousness (Oatley, 1988). Although there are problems here, they are relatively 'easy problems'. Sophisticated computer models related to neural structures might seem to be the way to gain insight here.

As shown at various points in the present book, biological psychology is making considerable progress in identifying the neural correlates of consciousness and also showing evidence of causal links from neural activity to conscious events. At this level, there is equally little difficulty in answering the question, what is consciousness for?

It appears that there are not special brain regions that are exclusively associated with conscious processing, though some appear to be exclusively associated with unconscious processing. Certain processes might operate at either unconscious or conscious levels, depending upon the activity within them. For example, it was noted that stimulation for a time period below T might not reach awareness, whereas that of duration above T becomes conscious. The same processes that are involved in visual perception in response to a stimulus are activated when the person simply imagines the same stimulus.

With the head pointing in the other direction, the personal and phenomenological aspects of consciousness remain elusive, the 'hard problem'. It has a holistic and idiosyncratic feel that seems to defy scientific analysis. The nature of the hard problem of consciousness can be summed up as, why does some processing have this peculiar state of existential awareness and subjective affect associated with it?

Summary of Chapter 21

1 Within biological psychology, the study of consciousness involves trying to relate objective data (brain events and behaviour) and subjective data (conscious experience).

2 Much information processing occurs outside conscious awareness. Processing that is accompanied by conscious awareness gives overall coherence and coordination to cognition and behaviour.

3 Psychologists identify certain types of information processing and particular brain regions as having a role in consciousness.

4 Speculations on the function of consciousness and its emergence in evolution are closely linked.

5 Biological psychology is central to the issue of how the conscious mind relates to the physical brain.

Further reading

For excellent and relatively accessible articles, see the *Journal of Consciousness Studies*. It is well worth looking at the journal *Consciousness and Cognition*. It is also worth scanning the journal *Trends in Cognitive Sciences*. Jeffrey Gray, one of the world's most distinguished biological psychologists, tackled consciousness. Sadly, he died at around the time of publication of his book (Gray, 2004). Blackmore (2005) presents the perspectives of various eminent researchers and theorists. Wegner (2003) gives a controversial perspective on free will, which he links to the brain. For 'personal angle' accounts of links with emotion, see Panksepp (1998a) and Damasio (1999). Libet (2005)

presents an account of his life's work in this area. Personally, I like Velmans (2000) for clear statements of the problem of consciousness. For links with vision, see Logothetis (1999). For links with memory, see Griffiths *et al.* (1999). For the neuroscience of consciousness, see Chapters 30–38 of Gazzaniga (2004).

Signposts

This chapter should have reinforced messages on consciousness that appeared throughout the preceding chapters. It has looked in more depth at theories of brain–mind introduced in Chapter 1. Chapter 8, 'Vision', looked at the distinction between unconscious (dorsal) and conscious (ventral) streams of processing. Chapter 10, 'The control of movement', considered actions performed with or without full conscious awareness. Chapter 11, 'Learning and memory' related conscious awareness to types of memory, i.e. declarative and non-declarative. Chapter 12, 'Emotion', considered unconscious and conscious determinants of emotion. Chapter 15, 'Pain', described an unwanted content of consciousness. Consciousness will be at centre-stage in Chapter 22, 'When things go wrong', where we look at disturbances to it, especially manifest in schizophrenia and obsessive compulsive disorder.

Answers

Explanations for answers to 'test your knowledge' questions can be found on the website **www.pearsoned.co.uk/toates**

21.1 Subjective
21.2 Two; alternates
21.3 Visual cortex; superior colliculus
21.4 Benefits; costs
21.5 Emerge

CHAPTER 22

When things go wrong

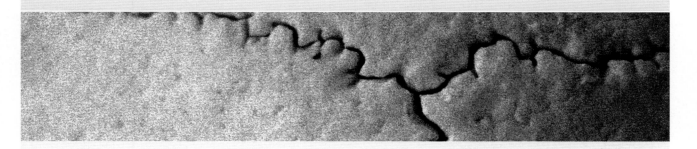

After studying this chapter, you should be able to:

1. Discuss critically the controversial issues raised by a consideration of things 'going wrong' in brain, mind and behaviour. Relate the evidence from biological psychology to the sufferer's own conscious awareness.

2. Defend the position that a comprehensive understanding of Alzheimer's disease requires investigation at cellular, whole-brain and psychological levels.

3. Appreciate why it is imperative to consider both causal and developmental types of explanation in trying to understanding schizophrenia. Link the evidence on disordered cognition and conscious awareness to disordered brain processing.

4. Describe, in the context of obsessive-compulsive disorder, how people can have insight into the irrationality of their thoughts and yet not be able to resist the persuasion of these thoughts. Present the case for an integrated perspective of biological psychology on obsessive-compulsive disorder.

5. Present the evidence that points to attention deficit hyperactivity disorder as being the outcome of a conflict between controls of behaviour. Discuss some of the theoretical and social issues that arise from describing this condition as a 'disorder'.

Scene-setting questions

1 Does a psychological disturbance imply a brain disturbance?

2 How can disease disturb the contents of conscious awareness?

3 What is it like to experience schizophrenia?

4 What is the scientific meaning of 'obsession'? How can obsessive-compulsive disorder drive us to act against our rational insight?

5 Is attention deficit disorder a biological abnormality or social labelling? Is this a logical dichotomy?

Howard Hughes was a talented, fearless and creative test pilot, engineer and film producer. How could he have fallen ill with a condition in which the rational mind is dominated by irrational fear?

Source: © Bettmann/CORBIS.

Introduction

How do psychologists decide when things have gone wrong in brain, behaviour and conscious experience? Classifications and explanations here can be controversial, with dichotomies of the form 'biological *versus* social'. The continuing theme of the present book is that such dichotomies are fundamentally misleading. Thus, social causes of psychological distress are mediated via the brain. Reciprocally, biological causes of distress affect our social cognitions and interactions.

The notion of 'going wrong' might be defined in terms of a *deviation from normal*, as in contrast to what occurs in most of the population. However, this is problematic. The brains/minds of Einstein and Mozart doubtless differed greatly from normal but we would not thereby attribute mental illness to them. Conversely, if most of the population became depressed, such a criterion would suggest that the problem has somehow solved itself!

Another possible, but far from perfect, criterion is in terms of function: things have gone wrong when the person has a greatly reduced reproductive capacity, as in clinical depression. This state is one associated with neurohormonal imbalances that can harm the structure of the nervous system and cause withdrawal from social contact.

Perhaps least controversially, things can go wrong by the criterion of a sufferer's own mental distress. They can also go wrong for society, in that a person might be a danger or nuisance to others. No single criterion of things going wrong offers a gold standard, and in practice psychologists usually adopt a composite of all three. By each such criterion, biological psychology has assumed a key role in understanding abnormality and in devising its treatment.

It is possible that you have had some experience of things becoming seriously upset in your psychological life or you have observed this in people close to you. Try to reflect on this, in terms of disturbances from what is desired in both conscious mental life and behaviour. For example, you might have experienced intense negative emotions as in fear, grief or the breaking of a romantic relationship. These are not abnormal in terms of how frequently they occur, since very many people have had at least one such event to bear. However, they are deviations from what is desired. Your conscious mind would have been inescapably focused on the negative event, and you might have noted deviations from normal in behaviour and activities controlled by your autonomic nervous system. Your functioning might well have been disrupted. Possibly you have felt strong anxiety over a situation, in some cases acknowledging that the reaction was out of proportion to the true danger or risk.

Have you been troubled by intrusive thoughts that enter your head and refuse to go away? For example, it could be that you have been unduly worried as to whether you locked the front door or switched off the gas. This might have led you to check more than usual.

Did you ever feel apathy, lack of volition, e.g. in response to psychological overload or after exposure to an infectious illness? Can you recall how it felt?

In such cases, a deviation of mental processing from what is desired can come to dominate mental life and behaviour, with any luck for only a temporary period. Reflecting on these experiences can give you at least some insight into serious and chronic psychological distress.

Have you ever woken from a nightmare in intense relief to have gained your voluntary, rational and sequential pattern of conscious thought processing and your contact with reality? Reflecting on such an experience, can you recall what it felt like to be the victim of seemingly random thought processes, with only the most tenuous and irrational associations between them? This might give some limited glimpse into the kind of mental disturbance where contact with reality is lost.

You have surely reacted impulsively in a situation in order to gain immediate benefit, when, on reflection, restraint would have served better your long-term interests. For example, you might have rubbed eyes made sore by hay fever in the certain knowledge that this will bring immediate relief but be followed by greater discomfort. This might give some insight into conditions in which impulsivity comes to dominate behaviour.

Taking some examples of when things go wrong, this chapter will consider the links between cognition (including that evident in conscious awareness), behaviour and the underlying biology. Patients' reports are usually in terms of distressing conscious experiences, beliefs, persuasions and emotions but treatments are often pharmacological. The chapter reflects a crucially important question: how does psychology bridge the gap between these areas of description, so that integrative explanations can be provided (Kapur, 2003)?

We will look at four examples of things going wrong: dementia that takes the form of Alzheimer's disease, schizophrenia, obsessional compulsive disorder and attention deficit hyperactivity disorder.

Section summary

1 A task of biological psychology is to attempt to link abnormality of underlying biology to when things go wrong in cognition, conscious experience and behaviour.

2 An important criterion of things going wrong is human suffering. Others include reduction in functional ability and, more problematically, deviation from the most common experience.

Test your knowledge

(Answer on page 557)

22.1 What is a problem inherent in using abnormality as a criterion of things going wrong?

22.1

Alzheimer's disease

Introduction

The term 'dementia' (Chapter 20, 'Cognition and action') can be defined as a 'cognitive impairment in multiple spheres' (Brandt and Rich, 1995, p. 243). An impairment of memory is necessary for the diagnosis of dementia, though in some cases there might be more a failure of attention than memory as such (Richards, 1996). Broadly, dementia can arise from various causes, e.g. stroke or hardening of the arteries of the brain. This section describes dementia arising from degenerative brain disease, the most common being **Alzheimer's disease (AD)**.

A personal angle
Alois Alzheimer and Auguste D.

Alois Alzheimer was born in Marktbreit, Germany, in 1864. In 1906, he described a form of dementia, termed Alzheimer's disease by his colleague, Kraepelin (Maurer *et al.*, 1997). Alzheimer's observations were of a 51-year-old woman, Auguste D., who showed impaired memory and comprehension. In 1995, Alzheimer's file on Auguste D. was discovered. It contains an entry for 26 November 1901:

She sits on the bed with a helpless expression. What is your name? *Auguste*. Last name? *Auguste*. What is your husband's name? *Auguste, I think*. Your husband? *Ah, my husband*. She looks as if she didn't understand the question.

Auguste D. died in 1906. From the autopsy, Alzheimer identified abnormalities in the cellular structure of her cerebral cortex, consisting of the loss of intact cells and the accumulation of pathological material. Alzheimer's observations represent an important identification of a biological basis of cognitive change.

The AD patient normally deteriorates slowly (Morris, 1996a), starting with slight impairments in episodic memory (personal autobiographic events) and the ability to find words. Names that were previously familiar are often forgotten and objects misplaced. As disease advances, there can be deficits in attention, language, reasoning and spatial memory (Brandt and Rich, 1995), as well as disturbances to emotion and

What might the creative work of the famous novelist Iris Murdoch tell us about Alzheimer's disease?
Source: © Julian Calder/CORBIS.

perception (including hallucinations). On a more optimistic note, education, an active mind and rich experience seem to help prevention of dementia (Ott *et al.*, 1995).

A personal angle
Iris Murdoch

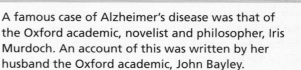

A famous case of Alzheimer's disease was that of the Oxford academic, novelist and philosopher, Iris Murdoch. An account of this was written by her husband the Oxford academic, John Bayley.

Iris Murdoch provided researchers with an ideal opportunity for a natural ('ecologically viable') within-subject observation. By objective analysis, they compared her early writing style with the writing done when there was reason to believe that early signs of AD were present (Garrard *et al.*, 2005). A reduction in the complexity of the language used in the final novel was noted. Reviews labelled it as disappointing in comparison to earlier works.

The researchers suggest that Iris Murdoch exemplifies a subtle cognitive decline that can be present years before overt symptoms appear.

AD is characterized by patterns of specific cognitive decline rather than a 'global impairment' and cognitive changes are linked to malfunction of particular biological structures (Morris and Becker, 2004). Brain regions can be linked to their normal contribution to cognition and, in AD, to disruption of this contribution. Researchers can relate cognitive decline to changes in cerebral blood flow and EEG patterns. Fine-grained changes in the cellular structure of the nervous system can be linked to gross structural changes in brain regions and cognition.

Defining the cognitive deficit

Memory

An early failure of episodic memory is a feature of AD. After this, there tends to be dysfunction of semantic memory. For example, the AD patient might respond 'hippopotamus' or more broadly 'animal' on being shown a picture of a rhinoceros.

In some respects, AD resembles the amnesic syndrome. In both cases, performance can be normal in tasks that involve procedural memory, such as sensory-motor skills (Brandt and Rich, 1995). However, AD patients can show certain selective deficits of memory (e.g. spatial memory) not shown in the amnesic syndrome.

Knowledge of the self (e.g. what kind of person am I?) can be preserved in AD, in the face of the broader loss of episodic and semantic memories (Klein et al., 2002).

Attention and executive control

AD patients show deficits in attention (Francis et al., 1999). Some researchers characterize the disorder as a lack of awareness (Perry et al., 1999), including lack of awareness of the impairment itself. Patients often have difficulty shifting attention, e.g. between local and global processing (Perry and Hodges, 1999). Problems with divided attention are seen when AD patients are exposed to a conversation between two or more people and are asked to identify 'who said what?'

The central executive often shows signs of malfunction, since AD patients have difficulty in allocating processing capacity within working memory, holding a given cognition in focus and inhibiting inappropriate responses (Baddeley et al., 1991).

Psychiatric symptoms

AD patients sometimes exhibit 'psychiatric symptoms' (Lopez and Becker, 2004). These include psychotic symptoms, such as hallucinations and delusions, as well as disruptive behaviour, e.g. aggression. Apathy is commonly seen in AD patients (Morris and Hannesdottir, 2004).

Fracture lines

Access to the meaning of words can be impaired, while their correct grammatical use is retained (Chertkow and Bub, 1990). A group of AD patients were able to distinguish objects from non-objects as well as were controls. However, they were impaired in the ability to attach a name to the objects.

For some AD patients, perception of individual items and appreciation of their semantic significance are intact only if the items appear in a simple context. Other items disrupt perception of target items (Saffran et al., 1990). This is demonstrated by the 'tablecloth experiment'. People are asked to close their eyes, an item is placed on the table and they are then asked to open their eyes and 'pick up the thing on the table'. Patterns on the tablecloth make the task more difficult.

Changes in gross brain structure and activity

Introduction

AD is somewhat selective to regions of brain and types of cell within regions (Damasio et al., 1990). Gross changes in various structures are noted. The gyri become thin whereas the ventricles and sulci (Chapter 5, 'The brain') are enlarged. See Figure 22.1. Most atrophy is in temporal lobe structures, e.g. hippocampus and entorhinal cortex (a region of cortex in contact with the hippocampus). There is a particularly

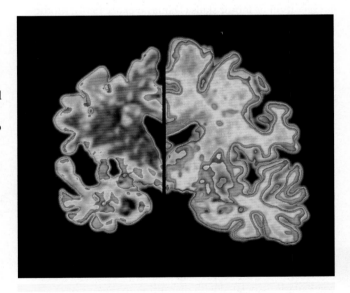

Figure 22.1 Sections through human brains. Left: Alzheimer's patient; right: control brain

Source: Alfred Pasieka/Science Photo Library

marked reduction in cerebral blood flow and glucose metabolism in the temporal lobe, indicative of loss of neurons or lower activity in remaining neurons or both (Morris, 1996c). A spread of pathology from the temporal lobes to parietal and frontal lobes can be associated with a disruption of attention, in addition to an initial impairment of memory (Perry and Hodges, 1999).

Linking structure and function

There is a correspondence between brain regions that exhibit hypo-metabolism (as revealed during PET scans) and the loss of faculties normally associated with these structures (Morris, 1996a). Degeneration of pathways linking particular structures can be linked to the normal interdependence between these structures as the basis of features of cognition.

The entorhinal cortex is a channel of communication between other cortical structures and the hippocampus. Degeneration of the hippocampus and the closely associated cortex occurs early in the disorder and underlies the early disruption of episodic memory (Morris and Becker, 2004). Reductions in hippocampal volume and deficits in episodic memory can serve as a warning ('preclinical') sign of a risk of AD before the full symptoms appear (Small *et al.*, 2004).

Degeneration of the temporal and parietal cortex is associated with disruption of language and semantic memory. Low levels of metabolism ('hypo-metabolism') of the parietal lobe correspond to a disruption of the capacity to shift attention (Parasuraman, 2004). Conversely, sparing of the motor cortex from pathology is correlated with a preservation of motor skills (Damasio *et al.*, 1990). Motor skills are also associated with the basal ganglia and cerebellum among other regions (Chapter 10, 'The control of movement') and these areas are preserved in AD.

A gradient of pathology can sometimes be seen, extending from the so-called higher-order cortical areas, where more abstract computation is performed (Chapter 8, 'Vision'), to primary sensory areas, e.g. visual cortex, where little pathology is seen.

Connections between cortical regions, assumed to be essential for executive function, are disrupted (Perry and Hodges, 1999). Although loss of executive function points to frontal damage, some reports suggest that frontal regions are affected later and often less severely than other areas (Morris, 1996c). To serve executive function requires the capacities to call upon memory systems located in the temporal cortex. So, loss of executive function might be caused by affected regions outside the frontal region. Psychotic symptoms are particularly associated with disruption to regions of prefrontal cortex and anterior regions of temporal cortex (Lopez and Becker, 2004).

In some cases, cerebral asymmetry (Chapter 20) in reduced metabolism can be linked to aspects of cognitive decline. For example, visuospatial decline is associated with right hemispheric hypo-metabolism, whereas verbal deficits are associated with left hemisphere hypo-metabolism (Morris, 1996b,c).

Occasionally, on performing a cognitive task, AD patients show a more widespread activation of cortical structures than controls. This suggests that failures can sometimes trigger recruitment of processing capacity elsewhere. Disruption of the corpus callosum interferes with inter-hemispheric communication (Morris, 2004).

A genetic factor

AD is not directly and obviously genetically determined in a way comparable to Huntington's disease (Chapter 2). However, as one factor in a complex picture, particular genes appear to exert a tendency towards its appearance. Specifically, an allele of the *ApoE* gene, termed the ε4 allele, increases the probability of AD appearing (Parasuraman, 2004). A useful strategy is to observe changes in cognition in individuals with this genotype even in the absence of dementia (possible 'preclinical signs'). Individuals aged 50–65 years and with the allele but not showing dementia tend to have reduced metabolism in various cortical regions (Reiman *et al.*, 1996) and some mild failures of episodic memory (Bondi *et al.*, 1999). These indicate possible warning signs for AD.

How is the influence of the *ApoE* gene mediated? Evidence suggests its role in a particular cholinergic neurochemical system that projects from a subcortical region to the cortex, described shortly.

Cellular changes

At a cellular level, the first stage of AD can be characterized as the 'cell sickness stage' (Small, 2005). Neurons start to show malfunction in terms of reduced activity. In the second phase, the 'histological stage', an accumulation of pathological material is observed (described shortly). The final stage, the 'cell death stage', consists of the loss of neurons, seen as gross changes in brain volume (Figure 22.1). Detection of the cell sickness stage, associated with mild cognitive impairment, could perhaps offer most hope for therapeutic intervention. PET and fMRI imaging can detect the lowered metabolic activity characterizing this stage.

A feature of AD is the presence in the brain of abnormal tissue, termed 'neurofibrillary tangles' and 'senile plaques' ('neuritic plaques') (Damasio *et al.*, 1990). A neurofibrillary tangle is initially found within neurons, where it disrupts neural communication. It later comes to represent the remains of a once-functioning neuron that has degenerated. Senile plaques are extracellular pathological material that arises from the degeneration of cells. Postmortem staining of brain tissue reveals the presence of such material.

Senile plaques contain ß-amyloid protein (Morris, 1996c). This accumulates during the illness (McDonald and Overmier, 1998). The fact that injections of ß-amyloid protein into rats cause neuronal degeneration and impairment of memory suggests a causal role in AD, though there are some doubts on this (Neve and Robakis, 1998).

A diagnosis based on behavioural and cognitive tests is provisional until autopsy, when biological changes can be investigated.

Neurotransmitter changes

Abnormalities in various neurotransmitters are seen in AD (Curran and Kopelman, 1996). The disorder probably reflects disturbed interactions between these neurochemicals. However, the principal focus of investigation is a deficiency in cholinergic transmission.

Cholinergic transmission

Acetylcholine (ACh) has a role in attention, learning and memory (Francis *et al.*, 1999). Most ACh derives from the terminals of neurons which project to the cortex from subcortical sites.

Alzheimer's patients show deficits of the enzyme choline acetyltransferase (ChAT), which is responsible for the synthesis of ACh. Hence, depletion of ACh and failures of cholinergic transmission occur in the cerebral cortex and are thought to form an important basis of AD (Parasuraman, 2004). This is termed the **cholinergic hypothesis** of AD. Disruption of cholinergic transmission is seen early in the disease and its magnitude correlates with the degree of cognitive impairment.

A suggestion of a causal link from ACh disruption to cognitive impairment is that, in controls, temporary blocking of cholinergic transmission (e.g. with antagonists) produces certain symptoms of memory impairment characteristic of AD (Curran and Kopelman, 1996). A possible animal model of such features consists of making lesions that damage the ascending cholinergic pathways (Robbins *et al.*, 1997). Some of the resultant cognitive deficits appear to reflect disrupted attention.

Therapy consists of trying to increase cholinergic transmission. This can occur by administration of substances that boost ACh synthesis, block the breakdown of ACh at the synapse, act as agonists to ACh or boost its release (Francis *et al.*, 1999). See Figure 22.2. Such drugs can offer some limited hope of delaying the advance of AD.

Suppose that an intervention boosts cholinergic transmission. Unless this is targeted, the effect will be a general one. Cholinergic systems other than the target neurons are likely to exhibit exaggerated function. For instance, brain regions unaffected by AD, e.g. brain stem and thalamus (Richards, 1996) and the ANS, employ ACh.

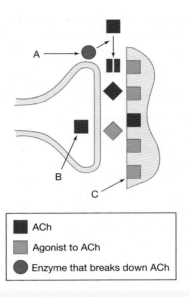

Figure 22.2 Some targets for ACh-related drugs in treating AD. A, inhibit enzyme that breaks down ACh; B, boost synthesis of ACh; C, inject agonist to ACh.

Gastrointestinal tract discomfort is a common side-effect of drugs that target ACh (Francis *et al.*, 1999). Sceptics suggest that in some cases chemical therapy is analogous to trying to solve the problems of a country with a petrol shortage by flying over it in helicopters and pouring petrol over it (Baddeley, 1997).

Not all evidence suggests that the deficit in cholinergic transmission is primary (Damasio *et al.*, 1990). Although patients tend to show cholinergic deficiencies, some have normal levels of cholinergic activity, indexed by, for example, ChAT levels. Conversely, other disorders that do not involve dementia are associated with an ACh deficiency.

Glutamatergic transmission

A theory proposed as an addition to the cholinergic hypothesis is the glutamatergic hypothesis. Glutamate is an excitatory amino acid (EAA) neurotransmitter and a major target of cholinergic neurons appears to be EAA neurons (Francis *et al.*, 1999). Loss of EAA neurotransmission might be exacerbated by loss of ACh input. Glutamatergic neurons convey information between cortical regions and from the cortex to other regions, e.g. to the thalamus and basal ganglia (Francis *et al.*, 1993). There is extensive use of glutamatergic neurons in the input and output pathways of the hippocampus. Evidence suggests that such pathways degenerate at an early stage of AD.

AD remains a very distressing condition for many families and it is an imperative to find a cure for it. The discussion now turns to schizophrenia.

Schizophrenia

Introduction

Consider the following accounts made by patients:

- '. . . I avoided going out because people on the street could read my thoughts. My mind was transparent . . . I complained of hearing voices telling me to do different things, which I felt compelled to do . . . I felt everyone was against me, even the nurses and doctors . . . ' (22-year-old man, Joe, cited by Birchwood and Jackson, 2001).

- 'Just prior to my acute admission, I announced to my aged father, who was in bed, Satan in the form of the Loch Ness Monster was going to land on the lawn and do it for us if we both remained together in the house. By this time, I heard the voice pretty constantly . . . the voice continued for four months.' (26-year-old man, Errol, cited by Birchwood and Jackson, 2001).

The condition termed **schizophrenia** covers a range of sub-conditions, having features in common. In the popular imagination, schizophrenia is taken to mean 'two people in one head'. This is not a correct interpretation since there is the one unitary individual, albeit a seriously disturbed one.

In 1911, Bleuler described schizophrenia as 'the "splitting" of the differing psychic functions' within the one individual (Bleuler, 1950, p. 8). This was characterized by 'a specific type of alteration of thinking, feeling, and relation to the external world' (p. 9). The split is typically between cognition and emotion, e.g. inappropriate emotional reactions to events.

Core symptoms include (a) hallucinations, most usually of an auditory kind (e.g. 'hearing' absent voices that make utterances of a personal nature), (b) **delusions** and (c) thought disorder, e.g. as manifest in incomprehensible speech (Frith, 1987). Delusions can be defined as beliefs of a kind that are at odds with cultural norms, e.g. (i) that actions are controlled by an outside agency, (ii) that messages for the sufferer are being inserted into TV broadcasts or (iii) that the sufferer is in fact Napoleon.

The patient's ability to 'recognize reality' is impaired to the extent that functioning in society can be very problematic (Birchwood and Jackson, 2001). Of course, there are many people who hold unusual views that are at odds with cultural norms but we would not wish to say such eccentrics have serious mental illness. For people with schizophrenia, abnormal consciousness and behaviour are experienced as distress and they can be a danger to themselves or others. Typically, there can be 'emotional blunting', loss of volition (apathy) and a withdrawal from contact with the outside world.

The age of onset of the illness is most usually in the mid to late 20s. For some individuals, there is just one episode of schizophrenia but for most there are repeated episodes or the condition becomes chronic (Birchwood and Jackson, 2001).

How do we describe accurately general features in these psychological phenomena, so as to understand the biology of the abnormal processes? That is, how do we summarize what has gone wrong? The next section addresses this.

Describing and classifying schizophrenic behaviour

Schizophrenia is classified as a **psychosis**, in that there is a break with reality. Signs and symptoms of schizophrenia are classified into positive and negative and most patients exhibit both (Frith, 1992). The positive group is defined by what is *present* relative to controls, e.g. delusions, thought disorder, hallucinations and repetitive stereotyped behaviour. The negative group is defined by *absence*, e.g. deficiencies of motivation, social interaction, energy, fluency of speech and normal signs of affect. However, this distinction is not entirely clear-cut (Frith, 1987). For example, does thought disorder exemplify the presence of abnormal cognition or the absence of normal cognition? Another classification is into experiential ('inner world') symptoms and observable signs. Experiential symptoms include delusions and hallucinations. Observable signs include social withdrawal and abnormalities of speech.

Kraepelin (1919, p. 21) observed: 'We almost always meet in the train of thought of the patients indications of stereotypy, of the persistence of single ideas'. It seems there is a deficiency in the ability to perform temporal ordering and balancing of cognition and stimulus information. He wrote (p. 25):

the patients are not in a position to accomplish that mental grouping of ideas which is requisite for their survey and comparison, their subordination among one another and for the discovery of contradictions. In this respect they resemble dreamers . . . .

Bleuler (1950, p. 16) described the guidance of normal thought and behaviour by a goal, involving exclusion of irrelevant thoughts. By contrast, he gave (p. 26) the example of a schizophrenic patient who, on being asked to name members of her family, responded with 'father, son' followed by 'and the Holy Ghost'. This is not an arbitrary association (Chapman and Chapman, 1973); indeed, it might be quite appropriate in a theological context. However, *in the actual context* of the utterance, it was an intrusion into the rational sequence of thoughts/words.

This example illustrates that overcoming the tendency to react to strong stimuli, defined by well-established associations, presents a particular difficulty for people with schizophrenia. Sensory strength ('salience') tends to dominate over meaning ('semantic relevance'). For example, in being asked to generate lists of bird names and producing 'swan', the patient is then likely to give 'lake' rather than, say, 'duck' (Frith, 1992). The patient's cognitive processing is captured by the strength of the association 'swan-lake'.

Another problem is with deficiencies in using a theory of mind (intention) of the other. Hence, metaphor is missed in the interests of literal meaning. Kalat (2004) offers the memorable example that, on being told 'When the cat is away the mice will play', the person with schizophrenia tends to take this as a literal account of animal behaviour, rather than a metaphor for human action.

Whereas people with schizophrenia can perform normally on relatively straightforward motor tasks, difficulties emerge with increasing task complexity (Schmolling, 1983). This points to a disturbance to central integrative control rather than to peripheral systems. For negative signs, Frith (1992) suggests that deficiencies of action, social interaction and speech are all examples of a defect of *self-instigated* behaviour. Typically, a patient responds to questions but will not enlarge upon the straightforward answer.

Having characterized some features of the abnormality, how do we *explain* its appearance? At a psychological (i.e. cognitive) level, how do we explain what has gone wrong? The next section addresses this.

Psychological explanatory frameworks

This section looks at several psychological explanations for what goes wrong in schizophrenia. Each captures a different feature and so they are not in competition. Later sections

endeavour to link the psychological phenomena to their biological bases.

Immediacy hypothesis

Salzinger (1971) proposed the **immediacy hypothesis**: schizophrenic behaviour is (p. 601) 'more often controlled by stimuli which are immediate in their spatial and temporal environment . . .'. For example, in speaking, people with schizophrenia come under the control of words that they have just uttered rather than being able to suppress their influence on the basis of having just uttered them. Hence they tend to repeat these same words.

Goal-directed action, whether in external behaviour or thinking, requires central executive control (Chapters 10 and 20). This accentuates some intrinsically weak but contextually salient ideas and associations to bring them into expression. It inhibits those that are physically salient but semantically inappropriate to current intentions. This is impaired in schizophrenia.

Regularity and novelty

Hemsley (1996, p. 143) notes that stored information:

normally interacts with the encoding, comprehension, and/or retrieval of new information by guiding attention, expectancies, interpretation, and memory search. Schizophrenia, therefore, is viewed as a disturbance in the moment by moment integration of stored material with current sensory input.

Schizophrenic patients tend to treat as novel the same stimuli as are experienced as familiar by controls. That is to say, patients have a deficiency in exploiting 'redundancy' in repeated sensory information. A move from controlled to automatic processing (Chapter 10) exemplifies the normal exploitation of stored regularity, by which information processing demands are minimized and this is deficient in schizophrenia (Serper *et al.*, 1990).

Metarepresentation

Frith (1992) suggests that schizophrenia involves a failure of a **metarepresentation** of the self.

According to Frith, such a metarepresentation underlies normal self-awareness. Not only do we have goals and intentions but *we are aware* that *we* are having them. We form mental representations of ourselves in relation to our intentions and their achievement or otherwise. Such a theory is needed to assess the intentions of others, for example, in distinguishing pretence from serious intent. The intentions of others are likely to be misinterpreted since people with schizophrenia show deficiencies in interpreting the emotions of others (Wong and Van Tol, 2003). This appears relevant to delusions of persecution.

An author's own metarepresentation

In describing the notion of metarepresentation, Frith (1992, p. 116) writes:

While thinking what to write at this point, I have been staring straight out of the window. In front of me are many trees. When I become conscious of this activity, what I become conscious of is 'me looking at trees'. This is the critical feature of conscious awareness. It is not representing 'a tree' because I was looking at the tree for some time without being aware of it. It is representing 'me looking at a tree'. This is a representation of a representation and, hence, a metarepresentation.

Action control

Closely connected to the notion of a disrupted metarepresentation, Frith (1992) argued that schizophrenia is a disturbance to the instigation of action; people with schizophrenia feel that they do not control their own actions. Rather, an external agent 'pulls the strings'.

External agency

Mellor (1970, p. 18), working in Manchester, England, reports a conversation with a female schizophrenic patient, a 29-year-old shorthand typist:

When I reach my hand for the comb it is my hand and arm which move, and my fingers pick up the pen, but I don't control them . . . . I sit there watching them move, and they are quite independent, what they do is nothing to do with me . . . . I am just a puppet who is manipulated by cosmic strings. When the strings are pulled my body moves and I cannot prevent it.

As positive symptoms, thoughts are perceived as being inserted into the head from outside. In auditory hallucinations, the voice might be recognized as being the sufferer's own but is nonetheless felt as alien. Whether it is behaviour or a private thought, the sufferer perceives something *unwilled* to be happening.

Comparing theories

This section has described several psychological theories. They have a common feature: schizophrenic behaviour reveals a breakdown of cognition as used in rational thought processing, the control of behaviour and social interaction. There is a move away from sequential control by appropriate internal representations and towards determination by external stimuli and irrelevant internally produced cognition. There is a fault in the processing of 'what leads to what' and 'what causes what'.

Having considered psychological aspects of schizophrenia, we can now link these to biology.

Disrupted brain regions
Introduction

Insight can be obtained from examining the brains of people with schizophrenia and comparing with individuals not suffering from schizophrenia but who exhibit some of the same symptoms, e.g. as in brain damage (Weinberger, 1987). Consider first the positive symptoms and where they also occur in other disorders. Trauma and tumours can be associated with similar symptoms in non-schizophrenic patients. This occurs most frequently when damage affects subcortical brain regions such as those of the limbic system. In non-schizophrenic patients, unusual electrical activity particularly in the temporal cortex, amygdala and hippocampus is associated with hallucinations and perceptual distortions.

Concerning the negative symptoms, such as social withdrawal and loss of motivation, these are most commonly associated with lesions of the frontal lobe, especially the dorsolateral prefrontal cortex (Weinberger, 1987).

This section first considers overall brain structure and then looks at particular brain regions. From the study of the brains of patients with schizophrenia, a number of researchers report lower than normal sizes both of the overall brain and of various brain regions, as well as under-activity in such regions. However, there are also counter-examples of normal overall volumes of whole brains and regions, so these are trends rather than absolutely reliable indicators (Wong and Van Tol, 2003).

Overall brain structure

Some earlier accounts had denied any biological basis to schizophrenia but such thinking now appears to be seriously wrong. Such evidence as enlarged ventricle size in schizophrenic patients was important in directing researchers and psychiatrists to the biological bases of the disorder (Bullmore and Fletcher, 2003). However, enlarged ventricles are rather a non-specific biological index, not peculiar to schizophrenia. Indeed, there appears to be no unique index (by analogy with crime fiction, no 'smoking gun') of this condition.

The hippocampus

Patients with schizophrenia typically show a reduction in the size of the hippocampus that cannot be accounted for by overall shrinkage of the brain (Nelson *et al.*, 1998). Schmajuk and Tyberg (1991) suggest that animals with hippocampal lesions exhibit features in common with schizophrenic patients. They argue for a similarity of inducing conditions, observing a relationship between schizophrenia and pregnancy or birth complications (PBC). A combination of PBC and a genetic predisposition to hippocampal vulnerability might bias towards the condition. Hippocampal damage could result from anoxia (lack of oxygen) or a viral infection.

The hippocampus has connections to the mesolimbic dopamine system. Damage to the hippocampus appears to lower restraint on this dopaminergic pathway and thereby boosts dopamine activity (Wong and Van Tol, 2003). See Figure 22.3.

In rats, hippocampal damage disrupts the capacity to utilize contextual information. As we have noted already, people with schizophrenia also have difficulty with utilizing context.

The cortex

Imaging studies permit insights into structural and functional differences between control brains and those of people with schizophrenia. Occasionally schizophrenia appears in childhood. With the help of MRI scanning, such cases offer an opportunity to study brain development and compare this with development in unaffected individuals (Thompson *et al.*, 2001). Figure 22.4 compares the loss of grey matter observed in two such populations over a five-year period. The accelerated loss in affected individuals is evident in a range of cortical regions: frontal, temporal and parietal.

Another imaging study asked, what is the biological basis of hallucinations ('hearing voices')? McGuire and Shah (1993) performed a PET scan on the brains of schizophrenic patients at the time when they were experiencing auditory hallucinations. As a control, the same patients were examined when they had recovered from hallucinations. Increased blood flow was seen particularly in Broca's area (which underlies the production of speech), when auditory hallucinations were experienced.

Figure 22.5 shows a result of a PET scan of a patient with schizophrenia, who experienced both auditory and visual

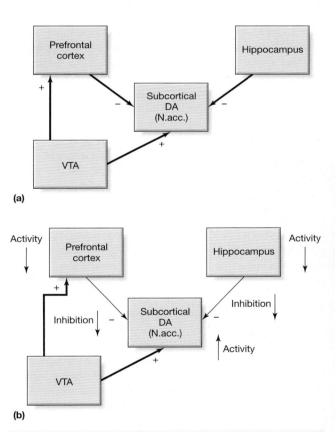

Figure 22.3 Suggested model of schizophrenia: (a) control condition showing excitatory influences (+) and inhibitory influences (–) on subcortical dopamine and (b) schizophrenic condition, in which there is a reduction in activity at the prefrontal cortex and hippocampus and a correspondingly reduced inhibitory activity. Thereby, there is an increased level of subcortical dopamine activity.

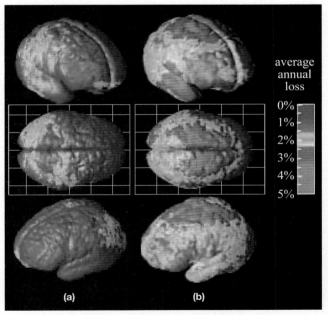

Figure 22.4 Average rate of grey matter loss over a 5-year period in (a) controls and (b) adolescents suffering from schizophrenia.

Source: Thompson *et al.* (2001, Fig. 1a, p. 11651).

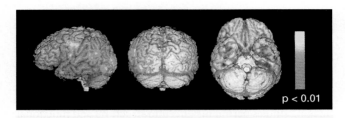

p < 0.01

Figure 22.5 Brain activity during the experience of hallucinations as studied by PET.

Source: Silbersweig *et al.* (1995, Fig. 2a, p. 178).

hallucinations (Silbersweig *et al.*, 1995). He was requested to relax, with eyes closed and to press a button when the hallucination occurred. Although the primary visual and auditory cortices were not activated, later stages of processing that normally derive information from these channels were activated. The result points to common features between hallucinations and actual sensory experience in terms of their biological bases. Note the lack of activation in the prefrontal cortex, which might also be significant in terms of the lack of volition concerning the experiences. Unlike in the study by McGuire and Shah, Broca's area was not activated.

Deficiencies in working memory, planning and sequencing suggest abnormality of the prefrontal cortex (PFC) (Wong and Van Tol, 2003). As just noted, there is overlap in the symptoms of schizophrenia and frontal lobe damage, specifically damage to the dorsolateral PFC, e.g. low motivation, social withdrawal, unchanging facial expressions and impaired judgment (Frith, 1992). In both disorders, there are problems with the use of working memory.

People with schizophrenia often show a 'hypofrontal' pattern, e.g. low frontal blood flow (measured by rCBF) during the course of performing certain cognitive tasks (Berman and Weinberger, 1991; Wong and Van Tol, 2003). An example is the Wisconsin card sorting test (Chapter 6, 'Development and plasticity'). This task exemplifies the use of context: participants need to sort cards according to a rule that they extract from observing their earlier choices and from the experimenter's feedback.

Although patients with PFC damage exhibit some similarities with schizophrenic patients, there are also differences and so this could only be a part of the problem with schizophrenia (Fuster, 1999). Theorists speculate that, in schizophrenia, abnormalities arise in cortical–subcortical pathways of which the PFC forms a part. See Figure 22.3.

The medial prefrontal cortex (MPFC) shows abnormalities in schizophrenia (Wong and Van Tol, 2003). Projections from this region play a role in modulating subcortical dopamine levels. The MPFC and hippocampus are implicated in schizophrenia and they not only both influence subcortical dopamine levels but are

interconnected. Projections run from the hippocampus to the MPFC and release glutamate.

Having considered particular structures, we now turn to a principal neurochemical pathway that appears to be implicated in schizophrenia. In this way, we can link the structures just described with the neurochemistry of the neurons that pass between them.

The dopamine hypothesis

The **dopamine hypothesis** of schizophrenia proposes that an important biological basis of the disorder consists of an abnormality within dopamine (DA) neurotransmission (Carlsson, 1998; Carlsson and Carlsson, 1991). Evidence favours this. First, there is the efficacy of **neuroleptic drugs** in treating schizophrenia (Lipska *et al.*, 1999). Neuroleptic drugs, such as chlorpromazine, reduce DA transmission. Conversely, 'abused' drugs that enhance DA transmission, e.g. amphetamine and L-dopa, can make the condition worse.

Second, the prefrontal cortex is a prime target of DA neurons projecting from subcortical sites and evidence (already discussed) implicates this structure in schizophrenia.

Third, recent years have seen the emergence of a better understanding of the normal role of dopamine in the control of behaviour. This suggests that its role is that of attributing salience to events (Chapter 15, 'Motivation'). Hence, theorists can speculate on what happens when this goes wrong. Schizophrenia can be characterized in part as excessive salience ('importance') being attached to what would be described as neutral events by controls (Kapur, 2003).

The dopamine hypothesis has served a useful role in highlighting abnormality in a specific neurochemical and it has subsequently been refined several times. Thus, postmortem studies of schizophrenic brains do not suggest an overall increase in DA activity (Davis *et al.*, 1991). Rather, subcortical dopamine *over-activity* could result from prefrontal cortical *under-activity* and thereby low inhibition exerted on subcortical structures (Weinberger, 1987). See Figure 22.3. Of the types of DA receptor (Chapter 4, 'The cells of the nervous system'), patients with schizophrenia have a higher concentration of the D_2 type than do controls, though this might sometimes be a consequence of their medication.

Initial refinements of the dopamine hypothesis suggested that neuroleptics specifically exert their effects at subcortical dopamine receptors. However, researchers have recently suggested that it is neuroleptic action at dopamine D_2 receptors in the prefrontal cortex that brings therapeutic value (Winterer and Weinberger, 2004). It could reduce D_2 activity and, in effect, increase the relative activity at D_1 receptors.

Giving a primary role to dopamine should not mean that we ignore other neurotransmitters. Dopamine forms a part of complex neural circuits involving numerous neurochemicals.

Having established some of the fundamentals of the biology of schizophrenia, we can now go on to consider some so-called 'animal models' of features of the condition. These models also point to abnormalities of DA transmission in particular brain regions.

Animal models of features of the disorder

As a disturbance to thinking and the will, it might appear that schizophrenia is a peculiarly human disorder. Doubtless there are features that cannot be captured by animal models. However, a number of experimental procedures used on non-humans produce results resembling features of schizophrenia (Ellenbroek and Cools, 1990). This section looks at three of these animal models.

Amphetamine-induced effects

In humans, the drug amphetamine (which stimulates DA transmission) can exacerbate the symptoms of schizophrenia and induce symptoms in people without schizophrenia (Kokkinidis and Anisman, 1980). Users report the effect of the drug being to produce 'an acute sense of novelty and curiosity' (Ellinwood, 1967, p. 278) and they experience auditory and visual hallucinations.

In non-humans, behaviour that resembles schizophrenia is triggered by amphetamine (Chapter 18, 'Drugs and addiction'). This includes stereotyped repetitive behaviour, the idiosyncratic focus of attention on a seemingly arbitrary object ('abnormal salience') and self-grooming of particular body parts (Ellenbroek and Cools, 1990).

Amphetamine-injected monkeys exhibit persistence, cognitive inflexibility and reduced social interaction. The frantic grooming of a particular bit of skin (analogous to skin-picking actions of human users) suggests triggering by hallucinatory bugs (Nielsen et al., 1983). Such monkeys show eye-tracking, grabbing into the air and attacking, as if targeted to non-existent objects, which might capture features of psychotic hallucinations (Nielsen et al., 1983; Schlemmer and Davis, 1983).

People with schizophrenia tend to persist with directing behaviour to a stimulus even though it is no longer associated with reward (Ridley and Baker, 1983). Similarly, amphetamine appears to amplify the capacity of particular stimuli to trigger behaviour in situations where controls can inhibit such tendencies (Frith, 1992). This behaviour might have features in common with the maintenance of psychotic delusional beliefs and persistence of cognitive set (cf. Shakow, 1963).

Prepulse inhibition

Schizophrenic patients exhibit a particular problem of overload when stimuli appear in rapid succession (Geyer et

al., 1990). They suffer fragmentation of cognition and action in a situation that would, to controls, represent a coherent and manageable sequence of events. A possible animal model of abnormality in handling sequences is as follows.

On presentation of a loud sound or air-puff, animals, including humans, exhibit a 'startle response' (Chapter 12, 'Emotion'). Let us use 'S2' to refer to a stimulus that triggers this response. By contrast, the term 'S1' is used to describe a weaker stimulus that does not trigger startle. Insight can be gained by comparing the response to S2 alone and to S2 presented in association with S1. If a stimulus (S2) that normally triggers startle is preceded by a weak stimulus (S1) given 60–120 ms before S2, controls show inhibition of the startle response (Geyer et al., 1990). Since S1 is of inadequate strength to trigger the startle response itself, the effect of S2 can be clearly compared under the two conditions. See Figure 22.6. The influence of S1 on the response to S2 is termed **prepulse inhibition** (**PPI**) and is deficient in people with schizophrenia, i.e. they show a relatively large response to S2. Figure 22.7 shows the deficiency, as measured by eyelid movements.

Rats injected with the DA agonist apomorphine show a reduction in the strength of prepulse inhibition (Geyer et al., 1990), so the neural circuitry that mediates prepulse inhibition appears to be sensitive to DA. Micro-injections of apomorphine into the nucleus accumbens (Chapter 15) but not other brain regions disrupt prepulse inhibition. Geyer et al. relate this to the observation of mesolimbic DA (Chapter 15) over-activity in schizophrenia and suggest that the disruption of prepulse inhibition might capture features of the human condition. Rats with damage to the hippocampus have impaired PPI (Wong and Van Tol, 2003).

Latent inhibition

Normally, after exposure to repetitive stimuli that signal nothing of significance, the stimuli fail to engage our conscious processing. The information is filtered out by the processes that control access to consciousness. As noted, schizophrenic patients tend to pay attention to stimuli that are ignored by controls. For example, a repeated anonymous car horn heard from a distance could be interpreted as a personal message. There could be an animal model of this tendency to attend to redundant stimuli, as follows.

The term **latent inhibition** refers to the effect of pre-exposure to a stimulus on retarding the subsequent capacity of the stimulus to form predictive associations (Solomon and Staton, 1982; Young et al., 1993). Suppose a group of rats are given pairings of tone and shock and then the capacity of the tone to elicit fear is tested. See Figure 22.8. Group 1 rats are subject to such conditioning and exhibit fear to the tone. Group 2 rats are treated in the same way, except that a prior phase of exposure to the tone alone is given. Such prior exposure reduces the subsequent capacity of the tone to

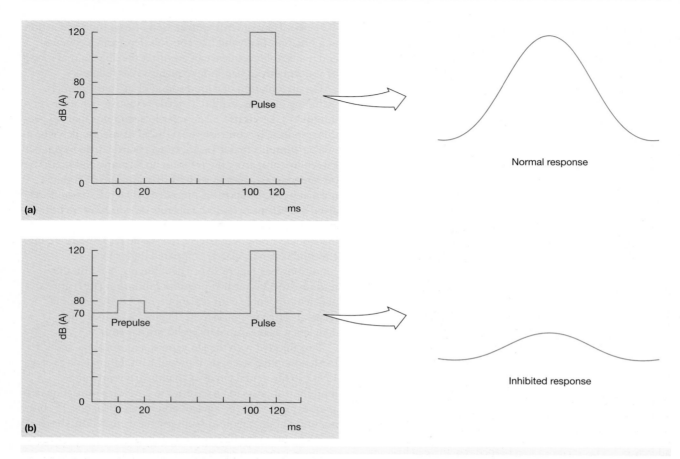

Figure 22.6 Prepulse inhibition: (a) response to a pulse alone (S2) and (b) response to the same pulse (S2) when a 'prepulse' (S1) is given. *Source*: Geyer *et al.* (1990, p. 486).

trigger fear. It seems that, in the phase of prior exposure, the rats learn that the tone signals nothing of importance; it is 'redundant'. This experience makes it more difficult to learn later that the tone predicts shock. Group 3 rats are treated like group 2 but in the phase of prior exposure to the tone they are injected with amphetamine. Note that this disrupts the effect of the prior exposure, moving group 3 in the direction of group 1, an effect obtained also in humans (Solomon *et al.*, 1981).

Gray *et al.* (1991) describe this as 'over-attention' to what is classified as a redundant stimulus by controls. In rats, the effect of microinjections of amphetamine on latent inhibition is specific to an injection that targets the nucleus accumbens (Solomon and Staton, 1982). Excess DA in the prior-exposure phase is subsequently associated with attending to the tone. Schizophrenic patients tested in the acute phase of the illness fail to show latent inhibition, i.e. they exhibit over-attention to redundant stimuli. They act something like amphetamine-injected subjects (Group 3).

Common features

Are there common features in the models described in this section? Amphetamine boosts levels of DA, suggesting the involvement of a hyper-dopaminergic state in schizophrenia. The disruption of prepulse inhibition and latent inhibition by amphetamine appear to involve an over-reactivity to stimuli, a shift in the weighting of control away from cognitions (e.g. memories of past events) and to current sensory information processed out of context. These phenomena appear to fit Hemsley's argument on schizophrenia being a failure to contextualize sensory information (see earlier).

The prospect of psychobiological integration has emerged from this section. That is, abnormalities of neurotransmission in certain brain regions seem to give an abnormal weight to information that would be treated as redundant by controls.

Having described the biology of the brain and the disorder, we need to ask when and how the disorder appears.

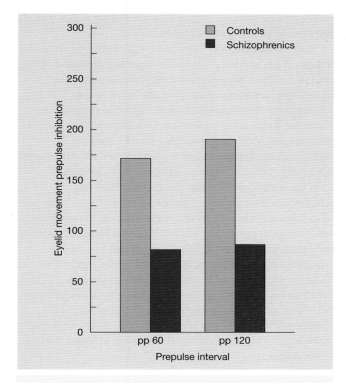

Figure 22.7 The magnitude of prepulse inhibition in controls and patients with schizophrenia. The graph shows not the response as such but the *difference* between the response to pulse alone and the response to pulse when accompanied by the prepulse. pp = prepulse interval in ms.

Source: Geyer *et al.* (1990, Fig. 2, p. 487).

So, we now look at the genetic, evolutionary and developmental factors.

Development, evolution, genes and environment

Evidence is converging on the view that multiple genetic and environmental factors exert a bias towards an abnormality in neural development that underlies the disorder (Andreasen, 1999). According to current ideas about the nervous system, any theory of interactive genetic–environmental–developmental determination must mesh with the assumption that disturbed behaviour and mental processes reflect abnormality in the nervous system.

The role of genes

Twin studies suggest the role of a genetic factor in schizophrenia (Gottesman and Moldin, 1998; Lenzenweger and Dworkin, 1998). Thus, studies show a higher concordance (Chapter 6) of schizophrenia when comparing monozygotic ('identical') twins, i.e. genetically identical, than dizygotic ('fraternal' or 'non-identical') twins. This means that if one half of the pair of monozygotic twins is affected, so too is it likely that the other half is affected. However, the concordance of monozygotic twins is not perfect. The fact that there is some discordance between monozygotic twins points to the role of environmental factors.

Valuable evidence has been obtained from looking at the close relatives of people with schizophrenia, relatives who as yet show no signs of the disorder and consider themselves to

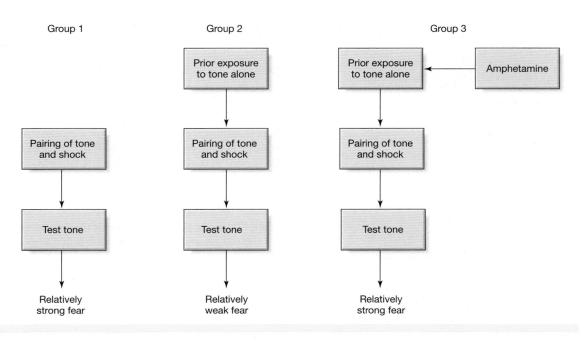

Figure 22.8 Latent inhibition.

be well (Fletcher, 2004). These relatives tend to show certain mild cognitive abnormalities as well as abnormal patterns of brain activity in those regions most closely associated with schizophrenia. This again suggests a genetic contribution to the disorder.

Understanding the role of genes in schizophrenia is probably something like that of understanding their role in height or IQ (Chapter 2, 'Genes, environment and evolution'). Rather than a single gene, several genes appear to act jointly in their contribution to schizophrenia. Current thinking suggests that the genetic influence is not all-or-none but lies on a continuum throughout the whole population, and presents varying degrees of **liability** to the disorder. With a strong liability, environmental factors would then be more likely to trigger the condition (Claridge, 1990). The environmental factor could be complications during the birth of the affected individual or later stress. How might these interacting genetic and environmental factors be manifest? One possibility is in the disruption of dopamine neurotransmission, just discussed.

Developmental abnormalities

The age at which schizophrenia appears is most commonly in the 20s and 30s (Frith, 1992). Prior to this, careful observation reveals that certain relatively mild cognitive, emotional and motor abnormalities are commonly evident in those going on to manifest the disorder. They exhibit some lack of a sense of 'agency'. Such indicators point to a long-term developmental course to what is later revealed more explicitly and unambiguously (Birchwood and Jackson, 2001). What could be the biological basis of the developmental disorder?

Weinberger (1987) suggests that an abnormality in the development of the nervous system starting at the foetal stage is manifest in relatively mild abnormalities of cognition and behaviour in childhood. Later, with further brain development, the trajectory of this same abnormality underlies the full expression of the disorder. There appears to be a relatively high incidence of trauma during pregnancy in those babies who subsequently develop schizophrenia. For example, after epidemics of influenza, there is an increased frequency of births of infants who go on to develop schizophrenia (Sham *et al.*, 1992). Another factor suggesting a developmental trajectory leading to the full-blown disorder is that the maturation of the dorsolateral prefrontal cortex only occurs in early adulthood. This structure is closely associated with schizophrenia (Weinberger, 1987).

Evolutionary explanations

Schizophrenia exerts a terrible cost on sufferers and inflicts disruption on families. In functional terms, the fitness value of the sufferer is relatively low (Avila *et al.*, 2001). Given that the evidence points to a genetic involvement, you might wonder why evolution has not selected out the alleles that are responsible for the genetic contribution.

Evolutionary considerations can trigger lateral thinking, as follows. Try to suppose that, under some conditions, the alleles tend to confer an *advantage* on their possessors. However, under other conditions these same alleles can lead to schizophrenia. For example, it could be that possessing the alleles but without the experience of stressors in early development is advantageous, whereas with stressors it becomes disadvantageous. Life is invariably a trade-off between costs and benefits, and this could be one more example.

Is there any evidence that the alleles underlying schizophrenia might under some conditions be advantageous? There is no direct evidence of this but there are some tantalizing suggestions. There are some similarities between artistically creative individuals and people with schizophrenia (Andreasen, 2005; Nettle and Clegg, 2006). These two groups tend to occur together in families. Finding novel creative solutions to problems of survival could surely have been an advantage in evolution. Furthermore, such individuals tend to be attractive to the opposite sex (Nettle and Clegg, 2006), the functional advantage of which hardly needs restating.

Role of stress

What could trigger the initial signs of schizophrenia? Why should symptoms of schizophrenia return after years of someone being free of them? There are probably many factors but one that has been identified is psychosocial stress. In individuals with a tendency to schizophrenia, stressors such as those of disturbed family dynamics might be sufficient to trigger the symptoms or their reappearance. This is termed the **vulnerability model** (Zubin and Spring, 1977). It suggests that, the stronger the tendency, the milder the stress that is sufficient to reach the threshold of triggering the disorder. Of course, the experience of schizophrenia itself would be expected to constitute a stressor, with the risk of a vicious circle.

There is empirical evidence to support a role of stress. Commonly stressful events ('life events') occur in the lives of people prior to the onset of the disorder (Bebbington *et al.*, 1993).

What could be the biological basis of the effect of stress? Stress causes the release of DA (Gray *et al.*, 1991). Also, corticosteroids are triggered by stressors; they accentuate DA activity and are commonly at elevated levels in schizophrenia (Walker *et al.*, 1998).

Biological or social? A false dichotomy

Consideration of the role of genes and development has social and political implications. Schizophrenia used to be a target for radical critiques of the so-called medical model (Barney, 1994), especially with the anti-psychiatry approaches popular in the 1960s and 1970s (Laing, 1960; Szasz, 1971). Some suggested that there is no biological basis to schizophrenia; rather it is simply a way of reacting to an impossible social context. Few would take that view today. Simplistic social–biological dichotomies have been shown to be seriously inadequate. However, we need to recognize (a) the role of stress in exacerbating the symptoms (Wright and Woodruff, 1995) and (b) that genes are only suggested as bias factors. Recognizing a genetic factor does not undermine the importance of environmental determinants in the womb and later.

For an analogy, consider that high blood pressure lies on a continuum of values of blood pressure from low through normal to high. High blood pressure increases the chances of stroke and heart failure, etc. but it does not mean that they will inevitably follow. It would be foolish to deny that high blood pressure is a biological condition, even though it is continuous with normal pressure (Claridge, 1990).

The sociopolitical dimension comes into focus with the observation that the incidence of schizophrenia is much higher in relatively disadvantaged social groups, such as low-income immigrant families (Cooper, 2005). Part of this can be accounted for by 'social drift', i.e. that a history of schizophrenia tends to cause social decline. However, not all of it can be explained in this way. Being brought up in a decaying inner-city area is a risk factor for schizophrenia. Exactly why socioeconomic disadvantage gives a bias to this condition is as yet unknown and is a topic of investigation. Stress would seem a probable candidate. Recognition of the socioeconomic factor and sharing the political motivation to improve people's lives in no way undermines the importance of considering biological (e.g. genetic) factors.

Section summary

1 Signs and symptoms of schizophrenia can be divided into positive and negative.

2 Positive signs include delusions, thought disorder, hallucinations and a tendency to stereotyped behaviour. Negative signs include deficiences of motivation and social interaction.

3 Schizophrenic behaviour exhibits a tendency towards control by physically present stimuli and away from control by representations and context.

4 Injection of amphetamine mimics some symptoms of the disorder.

5 Disruption of inhibition of the startle reflex and latent inhibition are features of the condition and can be demonstrated in 'animal models'.

6 A disturbance to dopaminergic neurotransmission appears to be a fundamental feature of the disorder.

7 Abnormality in the interactions between the prefrontal cortex, hippocampus and nucleus accumbens appear to be a central basis of the disorder.

8 The neural abnormality underlying schizophrenia appears to emerge during the course of development.

9 Accounts in terms of biology versus social context are inherently misleading.

Test your knowledge

(Answers on page 557)

22.3 What is it about the processing of a neutral stimulus that is disrupted by amphetamine injections?

22.4 For schizophrenia, what can be said about the concordance of identical twins, both in absolute terms and relative to fraternal twins?

22.2

Obsessive-compulsive disorder

Introduction

Consider the following accounts by sufferers from **obsessive-compulsive disorder** (OCD).

- '. . . an irresistible intrusion of a disagreeable image, which you always wished away, but could not dismiss, an incessant persecution of a troublesome thought . . . Such has of late been the state of my own mind'. *Samuel Johnson, 18th century English writer and philosopher.*

- '. . . I found myself touching particular objects that were near me, and to which my fingers seemed to be attracted by an irresistible impulse . . . Now I need not tell you that what impelled me to these actions was the desire to prevent my mother's death . . .' *George Borrow, 19th century English author and explorer.*

- '. . . I was sitting in the beauty parlour, and I heard the woman who sat next to me telling this other woman that she had just come back from the children's hospital where she had visited her grandson who had leukaemia. I immediately left; I registered in a hotel and washed for three days'. *Judy, an American OCD patient, reported by Dr Edna Foa.*

- 'I'm still thinking about the bad impression I must have made on the former colleague I met in the supermarket' *Herr Z., a German patient, in response to his psychiatrist's question, 'What are you thinking now?', posed 4 hours into a 9 hour session of brain surgery to treat OCD.*

What do these accounts have in common? Each problem consists of the repetitive intrusion into conscious awareness of a thought that the person would rather not have (Toates and Coschug-Toates, 2002). The thought usually frightens, shames or disgusts, and always engages processing resources that would, from the sufferer's perspective, be better spent with some other cognition. The intrusion sounds an alarm and the nervous system is brought into a defensive ('security') mode (Szechtman and Woody, 2004).

The thought is associated with a compulsion, i.e. a tendency to take action that represents an attempt to solve the problem. This can take the form of washing the hands in response to the obsession of contamination or endless checking rituals in response to the fear that a door is not locked. Sometimes the action is associated with the prevention of an unwanted event, e.g. touching something to prevent a death. In some cases, the obsession triggers a 'cognitive compulsion' rather than overt behaviour. This takes the form of a counter thought or extensive thinking ('rumination') that has the goal of trying to solve the underlying problem.

The most common contents of obsessions are found across cultures and relate to adaptive considerations of security and stability. However, in OCD, they are an irrational distortion or exaggeration of what is adaptive. For example, within limits, washing is an adaptive and universal act. By contrast, washing hands for hours in detergent until they are bleeding is unambiguously pathological. Similarly, within limits, protecting the family and checking are sensible actions, surely of considerable evolutionary significance. At times of scarcity, some limited hoarding makes sense.

Defining and trying to explain OCD

Although the thought patterns might appear bizarre, they are unlike psychosis in that OCD sufferers have insight into their problem. They realize that the intrusions arise within their own minds rather than from an outside agency. Thus, sufferers usually acknowledge the irrationality and excessiveness of their condition but can do little or nothing to alter it. Often the person knows rationally that, say, the door is locked but this knowledge is inadequate to resist the 'habit-like' pressure to keep checking. In other words, there is

A personal angle
OCD and Hollywood

Probably the best-known case of OCD is that of the Hollywood film producer and aviation pioneer Howard Hughes, who was obsessed with fear of contamination. He was depicted by Leonardo DiCaprio in the film *The Aviator*. DiCaprio was so keen to give an accurate portrayal of OCD that he was coached by the OCD expert and University of California academic Jeffrey Schwartz, author of *Brain Lock*. In learning his role, the actor also observed an OCD patient going about his rituals. DiCaprio himself had experienced mild 'obsessional quirks' when a child, such as not stepping on the cracks of the pavement, and these reappeared during shooting. As a result of the film, he developed a keen interest in the disorder and gave his highly valued support to OCD charity work in the United States and the United Kingdom.

competition between distinct systems of processing within the nervous system (Szechtman and Woody, 2004).

What causes OCD? There is no universal agreement on this. In some cases, it appears to be associated with a traumatic incident. In some sufferers, there are clear signs of obsessional and perfectionist features of personality prior to the disorder. These might set the context for the disorder.

Brain processes

Introduction

Although OCD is not associated with neural degeneration, there are clear indications of malfunction in the brain of sufferers. A focus of research is on abnormal activity within the reciprocal links between the prefrontal cortex and the basal ganglia. Among other sources of information, there is functional imaging using PET scans. This reveals abnormalities of regional cerebral blood flow (rCBF) and glucose metabolism in the caudate nucleus of the basal ganglia and the orbitofrontal cortex (OFC) during baseline conditions (Chamberlain *et al.*, 2005). Figure 22.9 shows a PET scan of the brain of an OCD sufferer and a control. High levels of activity in the OFC of the OCD sufferer are evident. We can surmise that this reflects conscious efforts to resolve the problem posed by the obsessions.

It is possible to provoke the symptoms of OCD by presentation of individually specific trigger stimuli and observe brain activity. The caudate nucleus and OFC exhibit particular increases relative to baseline. When therapeutic techniques are successful, levels of activity in the caudate nucleus become more normal.

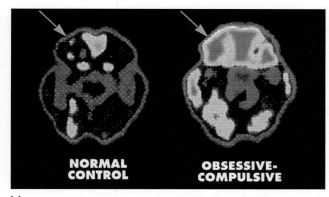

(a)

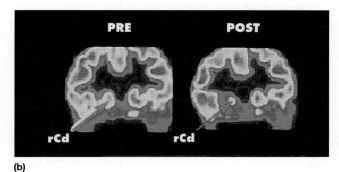

(b)

Figure 22.9 PET scans of control and OCD brain, indicating high activity level of OFC in OCD patient. (a) horizontal 'slice' of the brain and (b) coronal slice at location of caudate nucleus. rCd = right caudate nucleus.

Source: courtesy of Jeffrey Schwartz.

Habit formation

Graybiel (1997) gave a theoretical perspective on OCD. To understand her argument, consider that habit formation is an integral and adaptive feature of our behaviour (Chapter 10). Routine activities go onto a kind of 'autopilot control', mediated by the basal ganglia. Thereby, we do not normally need to devote conscious processing resources to them. Graybiel and associates suggest that, in OCD, such a process takes a maladaptive form. Conscious awareness is alerted as the habit becomes excessive in its execution, yet, cruelly, the resources normally made available by conscious processing are inadequate to resist the habit. Since considerable evidence implicates failures of inhibition in OCD (Chamberlain *et al.*, 2005), it is reasonable to suppose that there is a failure of the orbitofrontal cortex to make appropriate inhibitory modulation of basal ganglia activity underlying the excessive habits.

Traditionally, the basal ganglia were seen as being involved only in the control of movement but more recently they have been implicated in cognition too (Graybiel, 1997).

Indeed, the most extensive projection from the basal ganglia is directed to the frontal lobes. Reciprocally, there is massive input to the basal ganglia from the frontal lobes. This suggests an involvement in cognition. The significance for OCD appears to be along the following lines. Just as the basal ganglia have a role in producing motor patterns, so they generate 'cognitive habits', adaptive routines of processing information. In OCD, this process gets out of control, with the triggered cognition being repeatedly and pathologically brought into conscious awareness.

Treatments

Psychological treatments

Psychological treatment most often consists of encouraging the patient to confront the content of the obsession under the therapist's support. For example, someone with a fear of contaminated hands would be encouraged to reduce slowly the amount of time spent hand-washing and to experience living with the consequences. The rationale is that the OCD will be undermined by learning that nothing bad happens.

The technique of **brain lock** is based on the patient's understanding that there are abnormal patterns of brain activity at the time of the experience of obsession, as in Figure 22.9 (Schwartz, 1996). The patient is encouraged to entertain a healing 'counter thought' of the kind 'it is not me – rather, it is simply my brain that has got stuck'.

Pharmacological treatment

The favoured pharmacological treatment for OCD is selective serotonin reuptake inhibitors (SSRIs) (Chamberlain *et al.*, 2005). These boost levels of serotonin at the synapse. There are reports that successful SSRI therapy is associated with normalization of activity in the orbitofrontal cortex (i.e. decreased activity), probably mediated via changes in ascending serotonergic neural pathways. However, a percentage of sufferers fail to respond positively to SSRIs.

Electrical stimulation

For the most serious cases where other treatments have failed, **deep brain stimulation (DBS)** has been used as a treatment (Gabriëls *et al.*, 2003). An electrode is implanted surgically and then electric current is passed through the electrode's tip. The target chosen for the tip is a brain region termed the internal capsule. The rationale is that this region is part of a pathway between cortical and subcortical structures. Hence, stimulating it electrically is likely to alter the flow of information in the circuits implicated in the cycling of unwanted information in OCD. What exactly does the current do? It might cause, in effect, a lesion by blocking the normal traffic of action potentials. It might trigger inhibitory circuits. It is very early days yet in this technique.

Surgical lesions

OCD can become so debilitating that, as a last resort, some patients have been subjected to the controversial procedure of selective surgical lesioning to a part of the brain in an attempt to reduce the intensity of the disorder (Mashour *et al.*, 2005). A possible rationale for surgical intervention is the over-activity exhibited in certain links between the prefrontal cortex and basal ganglia. These appear to correspond to endless loops of unwanted information cycling therein. One target of lesions has been the anterior cingulate cortex and these techniques have shown considerable success in OCD. The awful and impossible dilemma posed is whether the risk of the occasional serious negative consequences of the operation, such as a tendency to anti-social behaviour, outweighs the benefits (Bejerot, 2003).

Link with other disorders

Sufferers from OCD have a relatively high probability of suffering also from other disorders such as Tourette's syndrome, which consists of unwanted repetitive movements such as tics and inappropriate vocal utterances (Chamberlain *et al.*, 2005).

This joint occurrence, termed **comorbidity**, suggests a common genetic tendency to OCD and such disorders. A research effort on several fronts could reveal common candidate genes. It also focuses attention on a possible common basis of each abnormality in the basal ganglia, which might give rise to repetitive automatic reactions of different kinds. In OCD, there is also a very high risk of depression. Antidepressants are the favoured medication for OCD, which suggests a possible common feature in the causation of depression and OCD.

The implication for biological psychology

This account of OCD has made a general and broad point about biological psychology. The primary and core distress of OCD usually arises in the domain of conscious experience, though of course the behavioural manifestations can bring external problems. Some treatments are of a psychological kind, e.g. cognitive therapy. Others are of a biological kind, e.g. drugs. Whichever is used, the evidence suggests that successful therapy corresponds to parallel corrections of abnormalities of brain events and mental events.

The following section considers another disorder that has some overlap with OCD (Chamberlain *et al.*, 2005) and also exhibits pointers to a failure of inhibitory processes.

Section summary

1   Obsessive compulsive disorder consists of the repetitive intrusion into consciousness of unwanted thoughts.

2   Obsessions trigger behavioural or cognitive compulsions, which represent a fruitless attempt to counter the obsession.

3   OCD is associated with abnormal activity of the orbitofrontal cortex and caudate nucleus.

Test your knowledge

(Answer on page 557)

22.5   What is the immediate biological effect of drugs termed SSRIs?

Attention deficit hyperactivity disorder

Introduction

What is termed **attention deficit hyperactivity disorder (ADHD)** consists of three primary symptoms: (a) poor sustained attention, (b) hyperactivity and (c) impulsiveness (Barkley, 1997). Some individuals show a predominance of inattention, while others show a predominance of hyperactivity/impulsiveness. A third group exhibit a combination of these factors, both in strong measure (Levy and Hay, 2001). Inattention is characterized by the problem of relatively high distractibility and a difficulty with sustaining attention. Children with the predominant inattentive characteristic can be inert and dreamy rather than exhibiting hyperactivity (Sagvolden *et al.*, 2005). That there can be rather different subtypes of ADHD raises the issue of whether it can usefully be classified as a single disorder.

Children with ADHD often show clumsiness, indicative of problems with motor control (Sagvolden *et al.*, 2005). Disorders of language and speech are commonly found (Levy and Hay, 2001). This correlation raises interesting questions – does ADHD impair speech or do speech problems play a role in ADHD? Or, do these problems develop in parallel, with each problem contributing to the other? Do they reflect a common underlying brain process?

The latter seems the most likely, with there being a common basis in problems with motor control (Ullman, 2004).

Children with ADHD talk more than children without ADHD, directed to others or to themselves. They have greater difficulty in resisting temptation and deferring gratification. Symptoms usually appear before the age of 7 and the ratio of boys to girls diagnosed with ADHD is about 3:1. ADHD is associated with poor school performance and later employment and social problems. At the start of the 20th century, there were reports of a condition termed 'failure of moral control' (Still, 1902), which appears to be very similar to what would today be termed ADHD.

Should ADHD be seen as a distinct condition, an identifiable instance of pathology with observable biological roots? Current researchers are inclined to view it as representing an extreme location on a continuum that encompasses the entire population, rather like height (Levy and Hay, 2001). Thus, to some degree, we all exhibit attention/inattention. Of course, just like height, ADHD has its biology!

Characterizing the underlying dysfunction

Psychological description and explanation

At a psychological level of description, ADHD can be characterized in part as an abnormality in the closely interdependent processes of (i) attention and working memory (Denney and Rapport, 2001), (ii) forming associations between events (Sagvolden *et al.*, 2005) and (iii) response inhibition (Barkley, 1997). Much of behaviour is normally controlled by cognitive *representations* of events, goals and anticipated consequences of behaviour. Cognitive processes give us the capacity to act even in the absence of the events that are represented. ADHD can be characterized by a weakening of the power of such representations held in working memory to control behaviour and an increased power of physically present stimuli to do so. Extraneous stimuli are less able to be resisted.

An example of association formation, which shows abnormality in ADHD, is described by the term 'reinforcement' (Chapter 11, 'Learning and memory'). We all form associations and we are all subject to a process of reinforcement. The argument goes that children with ADHD are at one end of a continuum of these processes: they form certain associations less well.

Consider the very young infant first engaging in interaction with his or her environment. Certain actions will be positively reinforced, i.e. the environment has effects that increase the future frequency of these actions. For example, a parent might smile at the child and thereby increase the frequency with which the child looks at the parent. Other behaviour will not be reinforced or may even trigger aversive consequences such that it tends to drop out of the child's behavioural repertoire. Normally, some of these consequences would be immediate and others would be delayed.

As a general principle for all of us, delayed reinforcers are less effective than immediate reinforcers, i.e. there exists a 'delay of reinforcement gradient'. In ADHD, there appears to be a steeper than normal gradient: ADHD involves an abnormality in the capacity of delayed consequences to control behaviour. Therapeutic interventions emphasize the importance of immediate reinforcement by the caregiver (Sagvolden *et al.*, 2005). If there is a high density of immediate and potent reinforcement, as in playing video games, children with ADHD can sustain attention.

Under experimental conditions, children with ADHD also show impaired extinction compared with controls. That is to say, when the reinforcer is omitted, they continue to respond for longer. Under natural conditions, this could be manifest in the child's failure to prune maladaptive responses from his or her behavioural repertoire.

The behaviour of the child with ADHD is more strongly determined by physically present stimuli and immediate reinforcement, relative to such internally represented determinants as hindsight and forethought (Barkley, 1997). This would fit with the suggestion that ADHD represents a deficiency in the top-down exertion of a processing resource such as attention (Borchgrevink, 1989).

Consider an action that has both immediate and longer-term consequences. Whether to perform it or not sets up a conflict and to inhibit behaviour requires an executive function. Restraint can mean forgoing immediate positive consequences but obtaining delayed consequences. This points to a deficit of executive functioning in ADHD, implicating the prefrontal cortex (Hagemann *et al.*, 2002).

Language and action

There are some unique features of human language (Barkley, 1997). Any language is a means of communication but human language is also a means of reflection. In reflection, the person formulates plans and runs mental simulations of them. There is a delay between the receipt of information and a response (if any) made on the basis of it. The exploitation of language can also involve 'separation of affect', as in feeling anger but not expressing it. During a delay, speech can be used as an internal means of communication; hypothetical messages can be generated and tested before a commitment is made to utter one. Self-directed speech is thought to underlie the developing child's capacity to anticipate consequences of actions and to bridge gaps between events with, for example, restraint (Sagvolden *et al.*, 2005). This capacity appears to be deficient in children with ADHD, who are said to be poor at self-monitoring and self-regulation.

Biological description and explanation

In linking the psychology of ADHD to its biology, we seek neural mechanisms that are involved in (a) representations of events distant in space and time and (b) others that are involved in stimulus-driven reactions. In ADHD, the power of neural mechanisms underlying (a) appears to be relatively weak compared to those underlying (b).

Investigators are converging on the idea that a primary biological basis of ADHD consists of abnormalities in the reciprocal neural pathways that link the striatum (a region of the basal ganglia) and the prefrontal cortex (Sullivan and Brake, 2003). Brain imaging studies reveal such abnormality. The abnormality gives rise to a deficiency in behavioural inhibition, which is manifest as failures of self-control and goal-direction (Barkley, 1997). Evidence points also to an involvement of abnormality in regions of the cerebellum (Castellanos and Swanson, 2002).

As far as neurochemistry is concerned, the focus is on dopaminergic (DA) and noradrenergic (norepinephrinergic) (NA) neurotransmission (Arnsten, 2001). Abnormalities of interaction between PFC and striatum are associated with abnormalities of DA neurotransmission in the neural circuits. For example, dopaminergic neurons project from subcortical sites to the prefrontal cortex. In ADHD, under-activity in one dopaminergic target, the prefrontal cortex, appears to co-exist with over-activity in another, the striatum (Castellanos and Swanson, 2002).

The prefrontal cortex (PFC) appears to form part of the biological basis of the use of working memory and language in the control of action. This capacity is sensitive to the activity of catecholamines at the PFC (Taylor and Jentsch, 2001). The PFC can represent temporal sequences of events and utilize past events and projections to future events in the goal-directed control of current behaviour. The PFC is required for complex novel behaviour, e.g. involving delays between instigating events and response performance. This delay needs to be protected from interference by extraneous events. Barkley suggests that deficits in inhibitory control would be manifest in impulsivity, distractibility and hyper-reactivity, the core symptoms of ADHD.

Employing functional magnetic resonance imaging (fMRI) of the brain and a task requiring inhibition of responding, Vaidya et al. (1998) found abnormalities of function in the frontal cortex and striatum of ADHD children. Rubia et al. (1999) observed lower activity in the frontal lobes in people with ADHD aged 12–18 years. They suggested that this fits with the notions of delayed maturation of the frontal lobes in children with ADHD and impaired inhibitory control.

There are at least two main reasons to suspect that there is abnormality in DA and NA neurotransmission in ADHD. First, the drugs used to treat ADHD (described shortly) increase synaptic levels of DA and NA (Sullivan and Brake, 2003). Second, activity by DA neurons is known to underlie the process of reinforcement. Where a high density of potent reinforcers is able to sustain attention in ADHD, this appears to depend upon the ability to trigger sufficient release of dopamine (Sagvolden et al., 2005).

Drug treatment

According to theoretical rationale, therapeutically effective drugs might be expected to normalize the balance of the controls of behaviour. Favoured treatments for ADHD consist of employing a psychomotor **stimulant** such as d-amphetamine or methylphenidate ('Ritalin') (Sahakian, 1978). Such drugs boost catecholaminergic (DA and NA) action by blocking neurotransmitter reuptake (Taylor and Jentsch, 2001) and tend to improve attention (Chapter 20; Gittelman-Klein and Abikoff, 1989). The drugs appear to increase responsiveness to context. For example, in a school class, there would be increased directed focus of attention, associated with decreased activity, whereas increased activity would be shown in physical education (Shaywitz and Shaywitz, 1989).

It seems to be a paradox that effective drugs for ADHD, a *hyperactivity* syndrome, are psychomotor *stimulants* (Robbins et al., 1989). However, by improving attention, such drugs appear to increase the power of internal signals ('cognitions') to control behaviour, while not increasing the power of external distracting stimuli. There are several possible modes of action of stimulants that could contribute to their treatment efficacy. They may well all be simultaneously present.

One effect appears to be at the prefrontal cortex (Sullivan and Brake, 2003). By boosting catecholamine action, they increase the efficiency with which working memory can be utilized in the control of behaviour. Noradrenalin plays roles in attention and by boosting its level at the PFC, the role of distracting information could be reduced in favour of a goal-related signal (Berridge, 2001).

Another effect appears to be subcortical and is indeed at first sight paradoxical (Grace, 2001). Suppose that, in ADHD, there is an unusually low level of background release of catecholamines. Any stimulus that triggers their release, e.g. a novel sound or sight in the environment, could cause a relatively large percentage increase in their level. If stimulants boost the level of background release of catecholamines, this could mean a smaller rise in DA in response to trigger stimuli. This might be the biological embodiment of a lower reactivity to stimuli that stimulants produce.

An animal model

There are two possible animal models of ADHD: (i) non-human species treated in such a way as to trigger features in common with ADHD and (ii) the 'natural' behaviour of particular inbred strains of animal. With reference to the first category, children with ADHD show an unusually high preference for immediate rewards, even though they might be less intrinsically desirable, as opposed to more desirable but delayed rewards. A possible animal model of this is the rat with dopamine depletion at the nucleus accumbens. It chooses to take freely available but relatively undesirable food rather than to perform instrumental responding for a more desirable food (see Sagvolden *et al.*, 2005).

With regard to the second category, there is the rat strain termed the 'spontaneously hypertensive rat' (SHR). This strain shows a number of features of behaviour similar to children with ADHD. For example, when trained in an instrumental situation but with reward no longer available ('extinction conditions'), such animals have difficulty in inhibiting responding (Sagvolden, 2000).

The term 'cognitive impulsiveness' is used to describe a feature of ADHD and it means deficits in planning ahead. Consider the following possible animal model. A rat is exposed to two levers. In order to earn reward, it is required to press lever 1 a number of times and then press lever 2. In other words, lever 2 is more closely associated in time with reward than is lever 1. Compared with control rats, it is very difficult to train SHR rats to perform more than six or seven presses of lever 1 before switching to lever 2.

It is not just the behaviour that shows similarities: dopamine deficiencies have been found in the SHR strain, modelling a feature of the biology of ADHD.

Genetic and environmental factors

Heredity

ADHD tends to run in families (Faraone and Biederman, 1998). Parents of ADHD children have a relatively high probability of exhibiting it. As is also the case for schizophrenia (see earlier), twin studies point to a genetic heritability. ADHD appears to be a so-called 'multi-factorial disorder', meaning that multiple genes and environmental factors play a role in causation (Rutter, 2001). ADHD could be mediated by several interacting genes, each contributing only a small effect. To be precise, it appears that certain genes have *alleles* (Chapter 2) that exert a bias towards ADHD.

Candidate genes involved in dopaminergic (DA) function have been identified, pointing to an abnormality in this neurochemical system. Exactly which aspect of dopaminergic function is affected is a matter of research investigation. One candidate is the genes that code for the structures (the 'transporter') involved in the reuptake of dopamine from the synaptic cleft into the presynaptic neuron (Waldman and Rhee, 2002). Abnormality here seems to be reflected in a higher than normal clearance of dopamine from the synaptic cleft (Castellanos and Swanson, 2002).

As one factor, it is possible that genes exert a bias towards seeking particular environments, which in themselves help to trigger ADHD. For example, they could, from generation to generation, lead their possessors to environments that encourage sensation-seeking.

Environmental factors

There is a tendency for ADHD in children to be associated with their mother suffering pregnancy and delivery complications (PDCs) (Sprich-Buckminster *et al.*, 1993). PDCs are frequently associated with hypoxia (low availability of oxygen) at birth which could have a damaging effect upon neural tissue. The prefrontal cortex could be particularly vulnerable (Sullivan and Brake, 2003). Children with ADHD typically have low birth weights (Sagvolden *et al.*, 2005). ADHD families tend to be troubled by psychosocial adversity, conflict and negative communication (Faraone and Biederman, 1998). There are difficulties here in disentangling what is cause and effect, and in distinguishing causation and correlation. In principle, there might be the same genetic predisposition to both ADHD and social conflict.

Social implications of ADHD

An increasingly high prevalence of ADHD raises social, philosophical and ethical issues (Panksepp, 1998b). What are the implications of a chemical cure for a condition that some regard as not being primarily a biological dysfunction? Indeed, what does it mean to describe a condition as 'not biological'? This point was addressed in connection with schizophrenia, earlier in the chapter. Even if ADHD corresponds to one end of a continuum, this does not make it 'non-biological' any more than being tall or having high blood pressure is 'non-biological'. What does ADHD show regarding the dynamics of gene–environment effects, introduced earlier (Chapter 2)?

Identification of biological factors in ADHD in no way undermines the importance of social context. ADHD tends to be more strongly represented in families that have a history of social deprivation and that are likely to experience particular difficulties in coping with the special needs of a child with ADHD (Sagvolden *et al.*, 2005). An excess of negative emotion in a family context makes the situation worse. A failure to offer immediate positive reinforcement for adaptive behaviours could play a fundamental role in development of ADHD.

ADHD is not purely a Western disease, a product of a particular technological lifestyle, but is represented in various cultures throughout the world (Sagvolden *et al.*, 2005). However, cultural differences, as in different styles of parenting, might well contribute to its frequency of occurrence. Our culture places a high premium upon education and remaining focused on abstract problems. This could create a context in which impulsivity is problematic. One can imagine other contexts such as hunting, where different demands are posed.

1 Attention deficit hyperactivity disorder consists of three primary symptoms: (a) poor sustained attention, (b) hyperactivity and (c) impulsiveness.

2 ADHD is associated with a failure of response inhibition, which implicates a deficiency in control by the frontal lobes.

3 The process of reinforcement is abnormal in ADHD.

4 A suggestion is that ADHD sufferers have difficulty in exploiting silent language as a means of reflection.

Test your knowledge

(Answer on page 557)

22.6 What is it about the performance of the spontaneously hypertensive rat under extinction conditions that suggests that it is a suitable animal model of ADHD?

22.3

Bringing things together

This chapter has looked at four representatives of a wider range of disorders, which illustrate different aspects of a biological perspective. For each, an understanding of behavioural and cognitive disorder can be gained by considering events within the brain. We also looked briefly at the relevance of the developmental/learning type of explanation to how things go wrong.

Alzheimer's disease illustrates a disorder for which there is an abnormality at a cellular level: looked at under a microscope, the brain tissue of sufferers shows differences from controls. Schizophrenic patients show certain biological markers such as enlarged ventricular size, though there is not an unambiguous cellular index as in AD. OCD was used to illustrate a condition in which sufferers can have great insight as to its causation. ADHD illustrated a disorder of behavioural control. In each case, distinct biological bases were described.

There are some similarities between schizophrenia and ADHD. Schizophrenic patients and children with ADHD

(Barkley, 1997) have great difficulty with the Stroop task and there is the suggestion that in both cases there are problems with the prefrontal lobes in exerting control.

Schizophrenia and ADHD have been the target of arguments on the role of biology *versus* the environment. If the logic developed in this book is to be believed, the term '*versus*' is singularly inappropriate, since only by considering the dynamic interaction can we understand the disorder.

Summary of Chapter 22

1 A task of biological psychology is to link (i) abnormal cognition and behaviour to (ii) abnormality of underlying biological processes.

2 Alzheimer's disease is a type of breakdown of cognitive processes, which is associated with identifiable pathology at the levels of both fine cellular structure and gross brain anatomy.

3 Schizophrenia is an example of a psychosis, a class of disorder in which contact with reality is lost. The underlying neural abnormalities appear to arise during development.

4 In obsessive-compulsive disorder, contact with reality is preserved. Evidence reveals links between the cognitive abnormality of obsessive thoughts and biological abnormality.

5 Attention deficit hyperactivity disorder can be characterized by abnormalities of attention, reinforcement and response inhibition. Animal models capture some of its features.

Further reading

Alzheimer's disease is discussed by Hanin *et al.* (2005) and a carers' perspective is given by Burns (2005). A detailed account of cognitive aspects is found in Morris and Becker (2004). For schizophrenia, see Williamson (2005) and for a developmental perspective on it, see Harrop and Trower (2003) and Sharma and Harvey (2006). For OCD, see Schwartz (1996) and Toates and Coschug-Toates (2002). ADHD is discussed by Selikowitz (2004). Barkley (2000, 2005) is a major contributor to our understanding of ADHD. For details of the role of stimulant drugs, see Solanto *et al.* (2001).

Signposts

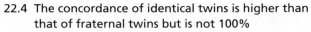

That's it! You are now at the end. I hope that Chapter 22 showed that the investment of the earlier 21 chapters was worth it.

Answers

Explanations for answers to 'test your knowledge' questions can be found on the website **www.pearsoned.co.uk/toates**

22.1 You would tend to include deviations in such desirable features as creativity but would exclude such things as depression once a majority of a population suffered from them

22.2 Episodic memory

22.3 Amphetamine injections tend to disrupt the learning that a neutral stimulus signals nothing of significance, i.e. it is redundant

22.4 The concordance of identical twins is higher than that of fraternal twins but is not 100%

22.5 To block the reuptake of serotonin and hence to increase synaptic levels of this neurotransmitter.

22.6 It persists with responding for a relatively long time in extinction

 Interactions and animations relating to topics discussed in this chapter can be found on the website at **www.pearsoned.co.uk/toates.** These include

Animation: The time lag of antidepressant drug therapy

Animation: How traditional antipsychotic drugs work

Interaction: The Carlsson–Lindqvist model of how chlorpromazine works

Glossary

A

ablation Surgical removal of part of the brain, a form of lesioning (Chapter 5).

absorptive state The state after eating, during which absorption of food from the alimentary tract occurs (Chapter 16).

accommodation The changes in curvature of the lens as the distance of an object changes. These serve to keep the object in focus (Chapter 8).

across-fibre pattern coding The language in which taste information is encoded, involving a comparison between signals carried by different neurons (Chapter 9).

action Behaviour that is not obviously triggered as a reaction, in the case of humans, 'voluntarily' (Chapter 2). Movement defined in relation to what is achieved rather than its precise form, e.g. hitting a nail with a hammer (Chapter 10).

action potential A sudden spike of electrical activity in a neuron. Action potentials form the language of the nervous system (Chapter 3).

activational effect A reversible change in sensitivity or activity as a result of hormone (Chapter 6).

activation-synthesis model A model of dreaming, which suggests that dreams are the subjective awareness of neural events in, for example, the visual system triggered by influences from the brain stem (Chapter 19).

acuity The ability of a sensory system to resolve fine detail (Chapter 8).

adaptation (a) A characteristic that has been selected because it fits an animal to its environment (Chapter 2). (b) Decrease in activity in a sensory neuron over the period of application of a stimulus (Chapter 7).

adaptive Something that evolved because it served a function that helped to promote the survival of the genes of the animal showing that specific characteristic (Chapter 1).

adaptive orientation The view that drugs are a support that allows the individual to function better at times of psychological need (Chapter 18).

adrenal cortex The outer layer of the adrenal gland, the source of corticosteroids (Chapter 13).

adrenal medulla The inner region of the adrenal gland. The source of catecholamines secreted as hormones (Chapter 13).

affect A quality along a dimension of pleasure–displeasure associated with conscious awareness. One might extrapolate that some non-human species have a similar experience (Chapter 2).

affective neuroscience A school of thought which suggests that there are systems of emotion and affect that have crucially important common characteristics across different mammalian species (Chapter 12).

afferent neuron A neuron that conveys information towards a given site (Chapter 3).

after-image The effect of a visual stimulus, still perceived after it has been extinguished (Chapter 8).

agonist A substance that occupies receptors and has a similar effect to the natural chemical that would normally occupy them (Chapter 4).

agraphia Disruption of writing ability (Chapter 20).

alexia Disruption of reading ability (Chapter 20).

allele A variant of a gene (Chapter 2).

alliesthesia The change in hedonic reaction to a given stimulus as a function of changing internal state (Chapter 15).

alpha activity (an alpha wave) A phase of EEG activity associated with drowsiness (Chapter 19).

alpha motor neuron Type of motor neuron that innervates extrafusal muscle fibres (Chapter 10).

altricial An animal born dependent upon parental help (Chapter 6).

Alzheimer's disease (AD) A type of dementia with characteristic biological indices in terms of brain cellular structure (Chapter 22).

amnesia An inability to learn new declarative information or to retrieve such information that has been acquired. Associated with pathology (Chapter 11).

amnesic syndrome An apparent failure to assimilate new episodic and semantic information following damage to the medial temporal lobe involving the hippocampus (Chapter 11).

analgesia The process of reducing pain (Chapter 14).

analgesic A substance, the effect of which is to reduce pain, e.g. morphine (Chapter 14).

analogy (a) A system that can be compared with another and exhibits some common features (Chapter 1) and (b) a term that refers to the independent emergence of a characteristic in evolution. Common evolutionary pressures gave rise to the same characteristic (Chapter 5).

androgen A class of hormone that induces the reproductive system to take the male form. Testosterone is one of this class (Chapter 6).

animal model The use of an animal example to capture features of a human system (Chapter 1).

anorexia Literally, loss of appetite. More objectively, a reduction in food intake (Chapter 16).

A-not-B test A test in which a participant must select a target (A) under which an object has been seen to be recently placed, even though there has been extensive prior experience of selecting target B (Chapter 6).

antagonist A substance that occupies receptors but does not exert any effect on the second cell, thereby blocking the natural neurotransmitter action (Chapter 4).

antagonist muscles Skeletal muscles that exert contraction acting in opposite directions (Chapter 10).

anterograde amnesia A failure to remember events experienced after trauma (Chapter 11).

anti-androgen An artificial substance that competes with androgens at their target sites but does not have the excitatory effects of androgens (Chapter 17).

anti-nociception An intrinsic process that is triggered under certain conditions and that blocks the transmission of nociceptive information (Chapter 14).

anxiogenics A class of drug that increases anxiety (Chapter 12).

anxiolytics A class of drug that lowers anxiety, e.g. benzodiazepine (Chapter 12).

aphagia Cessation or reduction in feeding observed over a considerable period of time, e.g. as a result of a brain lesion (Chapter 16).

aphasia Disruption or loss of language ability (Chapter 20).

aphrodisiac Chemical that increases sexual desire (Chapter 17).

appetite A measure of the tendency to gain access to a substance and ingest it, by virtue of its taste properties (Chapter 16).

appetitive phase A phase of behaviour leading up to contact with biologically appropriate objects such as a mate (Chapter 15).

arcuate nucleus A nucleus of the hypothalamus, which forms a principal focus for integrating nutrient-related information (Chapter 16).

aromatization The process of converting androgens to oestradiol (Chapter 6).

arousal A state recorded from the brain indicating concentration and focus (Chapter 13).

as if loop Activity that is intrinsic to the CNS and is based upon a memory of how 'gut feelings feel' (Chapter 12).

ascending reticular activating system (or just 'reticular activating system', abb. ARAS) A system of ascending projections from the brain stem that modulate the brain's responsivity to external stimuli. Adjusts dimension of sleep–arousal (Chapter 5).

associative learning Learning in which the experimenter arranges a contingency between two events (or nature presents a similar contingency). Classical and instrumental learning are two types of associative learning (Chapter 11).

atherosclerosis (or arteriosclerosis) Gathering of fatty substances on the walls of arteries (Chapter 13).

attention A process that gives weight to some sensory input relative to other inputs (Chapter 20).

attention deficit hyperactivity disorder (ADHD) A disorder characterized by poor sustained attention, hyperactivity and impulsiveness (Chapter 22).

auditory cortex The region of cortex at which auditory information arrives and where the cortical processing of it first occurs (Chapter 5).

autism A condition in which there are deficiencies in the area of social communication and behaviour and failures in the use of the imagination in solving social problems (Chapter 6).

automatic processing That which is unconscious and effortless (Chapter 10).

autonomic ganglion (pl: autonomic ganglia) A structure that houses the cell bodies of neurons of the autonomic nervous system, lying between CNS and effectors (Chapter 3).

autonomic nervous system (ANS) That part of the nervous system that exerts action on the internal environment (Chapter 3).

axon The long process that forms part of a neuron and along which action potentials are transmitted in serving the neuron's role in communication (Chapter 3).

B

basal ganglia A group of subcortical nuclei that are involved in the control of movement amongst other things (Chapter 10).

behavioural inhibition system A system that serves to restrain impulsive reactions (Chapter 15).

behavioural satiety sequence A characteristic sequence observed in rats following the termination of feeding as a result of having ingested sufficient food. Grooming forms part of the sequence (Chapter 16).

belonging Being part of a stable community and having a harmonious lifestyle, social context and way of reacting (Chapter 13).

benefit A positive contribution to fitness associated with a particular behaviour (Chapter 2).

beta activity A phase of EEG activity associated with alert waking (Chapter 19).

beta-blocker A type of drug that blocks sympathetic neurotransmission at the cardiac muscle and hence restrains heart-rate (Chapter 12).

binding problem The problem of how distinct streams of information come together to form a unified conscious perception (Chapter 21).

binocular rivalry A situation of competition in perception that arises from the presentation of different images to the two eyes (Chapter 8).

biological clock An intrinsic timing process having features in common with a manufactured clock. It underlies the circadian rhythm (Chapter 19).

blindsight The capacity to react appropriately to visual stimuli about which the person has no conscious awareness (Chapter 1).

blood–brain barrier A barrier between the brain's neurons and blood vessels (Chapter 5).

bottom-up (or 'data-driven') The contribution to perception or behaviour deriving from stimuli physically present (Chapter 7).

brain Rostral part of the central nervous system (Chapter 1).

brain lock A technique used in the treatment of obsessive compulsive disorder, which involves the patient's attribution of the problem to dysfunction of their brain (Chapter 22).

Broca's aphasia Aphasia that arises from damage to Broca's area. It is particularly associated with difficulty in expressing language (Chapter 20).

Broca's area An area of the human left frontal cortex concerned with speech production (Chapter 20).

C

catecholamine A subgroup of monoamines, consisting of dopamine, adrenalin and noradrenalin (Chapter 3).

causal explanation Explanation in terms of one event causing something to happen a moment later (sometimes called 'proximate causation') (Chapter 1).

cell The very small building blocks of the body (e.g. neurons). The body contains many billions of cells (Chapter 1).

cell body The part of the cell that houses the genetic material of the cell (Chapter 3).

central executive A suggested process which supervises the subsystems of working memory (Chapter 11).

central nervous system (CNS) The brain and spinal cord (Chapter 3).

central pattern generator (CPG) A motor programme that generates oscillations and is organized at the brain stem and spinal cord (Chapter 10).

centre–surround A form of organization of receptive field (e.g. at the retina) in which stimulation of a centre region exerts an opposite effect to that of the surround (Chapter 8).

cephalic phase In the case described in this book, the release of a hormone triggered by external sensory information arriving at the brain (Chapter 3).

cerebral cortex A telencephalic structure, the outer layer of the brain, made up of folds and ridges (Chapter 5).

cerebrospinal fluid (CSF) Fluid derived as a filtration from the fluid component of the blood. It fills the brain's ventricles and the central canal that runs throughout the spinal cord (Chapter 5).

chemoattraction Attraction of part of a growing cell towards chemical cues in its environment (Chapter 6).

chemoreceptor A type of receptor that is sensitive to the presence of chemicals. Chemoreceptors are the first stage of the taste and smell systems (Chapter 9).

cholinergic hypothesis An hypothesis to account for Alzheimer's disease, in terms of the loss of cholinergic function (Chapter 22).

chromosome Structure at which genes are located. With the exception of gametes, the human nucleus contains 46 chromosomes (Chapter 2).

circadian rhythm A rhythm that (a) has a period of approximately 24 hours and (b) is generated internally (Chapter 19).

circumventricular organs Specialized collections of neurons not protected by the blood–brain barrier and which serve to detect chemicals within the blood (Chapter 5).

classical conditioning A type of conditioning in which a neutral stimulus is paired with an unconditional stimulus. Also termed 'Pavlovian conditioning' (Chapter 11).

closed programme Programme underlying development which results in an animal that reacts in a certain situation in a rather fixed species-typical way (Chapter 6).

cognition Knowledge about the world (Chapter 20).

cognitive map A cognitive representation of the environment (Chapter 11).

command neuron For certain systems, a neuron in the brain that plays a high-level role in coordinated hierarchical control (Chapter 3).

comorbidity The occurrence of a number of conditions simultaneously in the same patient (Chapter 22).

comparative approach An approach to explanation that is based on the comparison of the behaviour of different species, often with the aim of explaining human behaviour (Chapter 1).

complete androgen insensitivity syndrome (CAIS) A condition in which genetic males produce normal levels of testosterone but have a dysfunction in the gene coding for the androgen receptor (Chapter 6).

computerized tomography (CT) A technique of structural imaging for forming 3-dimensional images (Chapter 5).

concentration gradient A gradient for a specific chemical arising from an uneven distribution. The gradient tends to break down the uneven division (Chapter 4).

concept-driven The contribution to perception from concepts, e.g. memories, expectations (Chapter 7).

concordance The extent to which twins correlate in something, such as height or IQ score (Chapter 6).

conditional incentive Something (e.g. a sound) that owes its incentive value to a process of pairing with an incentive such as food (Chapter 15).

conditional response (CR) The response produced by a conditional stimulus (Chapter 11).

conditional stimulus (CS) A stimulus that owes its capacity to a history of association with an unconditional stimulus, e.g. the bell in a salivary conditioning experiment (Chapter 11).

conditioned emotional response An emotional reaction to a conditional stimulus that has been paired with a traumatic event (Chapter 12).

conditioned place preference (CPP) A preference for a location based upon an earlier experience there, such as drug infusion (Chapter 15).

cone A type of sensory receptor, located at the retina (Chapter 8).

congenital adrenal hyperplasia (CAH) The condition in which some girls are exposed to high levels of testosterone prior to birth and show some masculinization of the genitals and a tendency to engage in male-typical play (Chapter 6).

consciousness A phenomenon associated with a sub-set of cognitive processing skills and with awareness and feelings (Chapter 21).

consolidation The process of strengthening a memory after its acquisition (Chapter 11).

constancy The perception of constant features of a given object, in spite of differences in the image that it forms at the retina, e.g. perception of a constant size even as distance varies (Chapter 8).

consummatory phase The phase of behaviour involving direct interaction with a biologically relevant object, e.g. the act of eating food (Chapter 15).

contingency The relationship that exists between two events, i.e. given one the other will occur (Chapter 11).

contralateral The opposite side of the brain to the region under consideration (Chapter 5).

controllability The capacity to exert control over a stressor, e.g. to terminate a loud sound by pressing a lever (Chapter 13).

controlled processing That which is conscious, effortful and planned (Chapter 10).

convergence The pooling of the output of a number of light receptors, so as to feed, via bipolar cells, onto a single ganglion cell (Chapter 8).

Coolidge effect Revival of sexual motivation by means of novelty of the partner (Chapter 17).

coping strategy A strategy to put into effect when exposed to a stressor that helps to make the situation less aversive (Chapter 13).

core sleep The amount of sleep that is needed to serve restorative functions, e.g. neuronal repair (Chapter 19).

corollary discharge A signal equal and parallel to that sent to the muscles and which is used in the computation of perception. Also termed 'efference copy' (Chapter 10).

coronary heart disease (CHD) A disorder of the vessels that supply blood to the heart, mainly atherosclerosis within the coronary arteries (Chapter 13).

corticospinal tract (or pathway) A tract running from the motor cortex to local levels of spinal cord. Neurons of the tract synapse either at or near to motor neurons. Sometimes termed pyramidal system (Chapter 10).

cost A negative contribution to fitness associated with a particular behaviour (Chapter 2).

covert orientating Intrinsic focusing of processing on part of the sensory information without bodily movement (Chapter 20).

cranial nerve Nerve linking the brain and periphery not by the spinal cord (Chapter 3).

craving An urge for something, e.g. drug, such that conscious awareness is occupied by thoughts of the missing thing (Chapter 16).

cytokine Chemical released from activated cell of the immune system (Chapter 13).

D

Dale's principle The principle that any given neuron synthesizes and releases only one type of neurotransmitter. It is now known to be only partly true (Chapter 4).

data-driven (or 'bottom-up') The contribution to perception or behaviour deriving from stimuli that are physically present (Chapter 7).

decerebrate A subject with the brain stem surgically isolated from the rest of the brain (Chapter 16).

declarative memory A form of memory involved in knowing something, e.g. a fact about the world. It can be articulated verbally (Chapter 11).

deep brain stimulation (DBS) A form of treatment in which an electrode is implanted surgically and then electric current is passed through the electrode's tip. A treatment for OCD. (Chapter 22).

delusion A belief of a kind that is at odds with cultural norms (Chapter 22).

dementia A cognitive impairment involving memory and attention (Chapter 20).

denervation Loss of a neural input to a structure (Chapter 6).

depolarization A move of membrane potential towards zero, away from the polarized value (Chapter 4).

dermatome A region of body associated with the innervation of a particular spinal nerve (Chapter 3).

design A metaphor employed to understand the principles of evolution, suggesting that it is as if living beings were designed for life in their environment (Chapter 2).

determinism The notion that for every event there can in principle be identified a cause (Chapter 1).

determinist One who believes in a lawfulness of behaviour (Chapter 1).

developmental/learning explanation A type of explanation of behaviour that is based upon events over substantial portions of time, such as hours or days. It embraces both development and learning (Chapter 1).

differentiation The formation of different cells from more similar precursor cells (Chapter 6).

digestion The chemical breakdown of food in the alimentary tract (Chapter 16).

discrimination test A test in which, in order to earn a reward, a rat must discriminate its bodily state as being one of, e.g., hunger or withdrawal from cocaine. Choice in the test and earning of reward is based on such discrimination (Chapter 18).

discriminative touch A system with receptors covering the skin surface, which performs fine-grained resolution of tactile stimuli at the skin. It is involved in the recognition of the location, shape, size and texture of mechanical objects that contact the skin (Chapter 9).

dishabituation A particular example of sensitization as an increase in strength of a response that had previously been habituated (Chapter 11).

display rules The social rules and conventions that govern the expression of behaviour (e.g. emotional reactions) in public (Chapter 12).

distress vocalization (DV) The crying that the young exhibit on enforced separation from a caregiver (Chapter 12).

dizygotic twins (or 'fraternal twins', abb. DZ) Each member of a pair of DZs derives from a separate zygote and so they are not genetically identical (Chapter 6).

dopamine hypothesis A hypothesis to account for schizophrenia, in terms of disrupted dopamine function (Chapter 22).

dorsal root ganglion Structure that contains the cell bodies of sensory neurons (Chapter 3).

dorsal Towards the back or top of the head (Chapter 3).

dorsal stream A stream of visual information leading to the parietal cortex, and which organizes action (Chapter 8).

double-blind study A study in which neither the participant nor the person with whom they are in contact (normally scientist or therapist) knows to which group (experimental or control) each participant has been allocated (Chapter 14).

double dissociation Damage at a brain region (x) impairs an aspect of behaviour (X) but leaves Y intact, whereas damage to another brain region (y) disrupts another behaviour (Y) but leaves X intact (Chapter 8).

down-regulation The process by which there is a loss of receptors at a postsynaptic membrane as a result of high levels of stimulation by neurotransmitter (Chapter 4).

dualism The philosophical suggestion that there exists a distinction between two separate domains: physical and mental (Chapter 21).

E

effector Muscle or gland (Chapter 3).

efferent neuron Neuron that carries information away from a given structure (Chapter 3).

ejaculation Expulsion of seminal fluids from penis (Chapter 17).

electrical synapse A synapse where there is direct electrical contact between the presynaptic neuron and the postsynaptic neuron (Chapter 4).

electrically induced behaviour (EIB) Behaviour triggered by electrical current applied through an implanted electrode, where the timing of the application of current is controlled by the experimenter (Chapter 15).

electrocortical mapping A technique that involves generating an electrical current for a period of some 5–10 seconds. The current passes between two electrodes located at the surface of the cortex and disruptions to behaviour are noted (Chapter 20).

electroencephalography (EEG) The study of the brain's activity by electrodes that are attached to the surface of the head. The record is termed an electroencephalogram (also abbreviated EEG) (Chapter 5).

electron microscopy A technique for obtaining a very high magnification of a sample of tissue so that its details can be resolved (Chapter 5).

embryo (at times also termed 'foetus') The animal at the start of life, e.g. in the uterus (Chapter 6).

emergent property The notion that, at each level of increasing complexity, new properties emerge. These are not evident at the lower level (Chapter 1).

empathy A capacity for a person to put themselves in another's place and to experience something of what it is like (Chapter 14).

encephalization The degree to which brain size exceeds what might be expected on the basis of body weight (Chapter 5).

endocrine system The system consisting of the hormones of the body and their receptors at target organs (Chapter 3).

engram The durable physical embodiment of memory (Chapter 11).

enteric nervous system (ENS) Network of neurons in the wall of the gut (Chapter 3).

enzyme A chemical that alters the speed of a chemical reaction (Chapter 2).

episodic memory A memory of a particular episode of personal experience (Chapter 11).

erectile dysfunction (ED) Failure to maintain an erection (Chapter 17).

ethology A branch of zoology concerned with the study of behaviour (Chapter 1).

evoked potential (or 'event-related potential', abb. ERP) The change in electrical activity in the brain triggered by a stimulus, as recorded at the surface (Chapter 5).

evolution The theory that animals emerge from a simpler form of life by a gradual series of changes over long periods of time (Chapter 1).

evolutionary explanation A type of explanation which is in terms of events in the evolutionary history of the animal under consideration (Chapter 1).

evolutionary psychology A school of psychology concerned to explain behaviour in functional terms appropriate to the early evolutionary environment (Chapter 2).

explicit memory A term that means much the same as declarative memory. We can be verbally explicit about the content (Chapter 11).

exploratory behaviour Behaviour that serves to increase the information available to an animal by means of investigation and orientation of sense organs (Chapter 15).

exposure orientation The view that addiction arises simply from a certain level of exposure to drugs (Chapter 18).

extension Movement of a limb in which the angle is increased (Chapter 10).

exteroceptive A term to describe those senses, such as vision, that convey information to the brain concerning the external environment (Chapter 7).

extracellular fluid The fluid that is not in the cells and is made up of the interstitial fluid and the plasma (Chapter 4).

extrafusal muscle fibre Fibres of skeletal muscle the function of which is the exertion of force (Chapter 10).

extrapyramidal pathways Pathways of motor control that start in the brain stem (hence contrast to the pyramidal tract that starts in the cortex) (Chapter 10).

eye-blink reflex Reflex reaction of the eyelid to noxious stimulus such as an air-puff (Chapter 11).

F

feature detection The extraction of information on particular features of sensory events such as their location in space (Chapter 9).

feedforward Action taken, not in response to a departure of a regulated variable from a set-point, but in anticipation of a deviation that might arise (Chapter 10).

feminization The process of forming the typical female structures (Chapter 6)

fitness The potential of an animal to pass on its genes (Chapter 2).

flavour The sensation triggered by food that is a product of the combination of taste and olfactory stimulation (Chapter 9).

flexion Movement of a limb in which the angle is decreased (Chapter 10).

fovea A small depression at the centre of the retina specialized to resolve fine detail (Chapter 8).

frequency coding Information carried by the frequency of action potentials (Chapter 7).

functional explanation Explanation in terms of how something has contributed to reproductive success during evolutionary history (Chapter 2).

functional imaging A technique for looking at the brain in action, i.e. which parts of the brain are relatively active or inactive at given times (Chapter 5).

functional lesion Local disruption to a site of neural tissue in a way that is reversible (Chapter 20).

functional specialization Beyond the primary visual cortex, distinct cortical regions analyze particular qualities of the visual image, such as form, colour or motion (Chapter 8).

G

gamete Collective term for sperm and egg cells (Chapter 2).

ganglion (pl: 'ganglia') A group of the cell bodies of neurons in the peripheral nervous system (Chapter 3).

gate theory The theory of Melzack and Wall, which suggests that nociceptive information is gated at sites within the spinal cord (Chapter 14).

gender identity Acquisition of the concept 'I am a girl' or 'I am a boy' (Chapter 6).

gene The unit of inheritance of information from one generation to another by means of reproduction (Chapter 1).

gene expression The switching on of genes, triggering the manufacture of proteins (Chapter 6).

genotype The collection of all the genes within an individual. Each cell contains an identical set of genes, constituting the genotype (Chapter 2).

gestation The period from fertilization to birth or hatching (Chapter 6).

gland Site at which hormones are secreted (Chapter 3).

glial cell A type of cell found in the nervous system but distinct from neurons. It serves a supportive role (Chapter 4).

glucoreceptor A neuron the activity of which depends upon its availability of glucose or the metabolism of glucose (Chapter 16).

Golgi stain The result of a technique of staining (Golgi staining), which reveals whole cells (Chapter 5).

gonadotropin A generic term for FSH and LH (Chapter 17).

gonads The male testes and female ovaries. Adjective is gonadal (Chapter 6).

grandmother cell A hypothetical cell at the core of the theory that we have a specific neuron for the perception of each object, e.g. we would have a neuron specific to a particular grandmother (Chapter 8).

growth cone The swollen ending of an extending axon or dendrite, with fine extensions termed 'filopodia' (Chapter 6).

H

habituation A form of non-associative learning in which there is a decline in the response to a stimulus that is presented repeatedly but with no significant consequence (Chapter 11).

haemorrhage Loss of blood (Chapter 16).

hair cell A type of cell in which deformation causes electrical changes that are the start of the process of detection. They are found in the ear (Chapter 9).

hallucinogen A class of drug the primary action of which is to change sensory perception (Chapter 18).

hard problem The problem of how physical matter can give rise to phenomenal consciousness (Chapter 21).

hard-wired A description for synaptic connections and neuronal systems that exhibit little flexibility and often show consistency from one animal to another within a species (Chapter 2).

Hebb synapse When memory consolidation occurs, structural changes are assumed to take place at one or more synapses. Such modified synapses are termed 'Hebb synapses' (Chapter 11).

hedonic Having a quality of positive affect or pleasure (Chapter 2).

heritability The degree to which differences in a characteristic are due to genetic differences (Chapter 2).

hierarchical control Control in which higher levels of the CNS (more rostral) control lower (more caudal) levels (Chapter 3).

homeostasis The principle that physiological events are maintained nearly constant and that action is taken to defend this (Chapter 1).

homology Comparing two species, a term that refers to a common evolutionary origin of something (i.e. a common precursor at an earlier stage of evolution) (Chapter 5).

homunculus fallacy The fallacy of explaining perception or behaviour by explicitly or implicitly involving a person in the head doing the controlling (Chapter 7).

hormone Chemical messenger secreted into the blood at one location and carried in the blood to another location(s) where it exerts effects (Chapter 1).

Huntington's disease (or 'Huntington's chorea') Disorder characterized by involuntary movements of the body, personality changes and forgetfulness (Chapter 2).

hyperalgesia An increase in pain (e.g. caused by the injection of a chemical) (Chapter 14).

hyperphagia Excessive intake of food over a considerable period of time, e.g. as a result of a brain lesion (Chapter 16).

hyperpolarization A move of membrane potential to a more negative value than the resting potential (Chapter 4).

hypothalamic pituitary gonadal axis A causal sequence of events running from (1) activity in the hypothalamus (secretion of gonadotropin-releasing hormone) to (2) the secretion of pituitary hormones and (3) their effect at the gonads in triggering hormonal release (Chapter 17).

I

identity theory A theory that suggests that for every mental event there is a corresponding brain event (Chapter 1).

illusion A distortion of perception relative to an objective measure of sensory information (Chapter 7).

imaging A technique of viewing a structure or structure/activity of the brain by means of forming images of it, such as PET or MRI (Chapter 5).

immediacy hypothesis A hypothesis to account for schizophrenia, in terms of a heightened sensitivity to physically present stimuli as opposed to representations (Chapter 22).

immune system A system involving specialist cells that serves to defend the body against invasion (e.g. from viruses and bacteria) and against cancerous cells (Chapter 1).

implicit memory Another term for non-declarative memory (Chapter 11).

imprinting The process whereby the behaviour of newly hatched chicks of some species is fixed by a single early experience. For example, the chick follows the first moving object that it sees (Chapter 6).

incentive A stimulus, e.g. food or a mate, which plays a role in producing motivation and attraction (Chapter 15).

incentive salience The value of an incentive as measured by its capacity to attract (in terms of attention and movement) (Chapter 18).

incentive sensitization theory A theory that drugs such as opiates increase the salience of stimuli related to drug-taking, e.g. the sight of the needle. This leads to craving (Chapter 18).

induction The influence of a group of cells on the development of a neighbouring cell (Chapter 6).

inflow theory The theory that the perception of movement is based in part upon feedback from the muscles (Chapter 10).

inhibitory neuron A neuron, the activity of which has the effect of lowering the activity in a postsynaptic neuron (Chapter 3).

insomnia A subjective feeling of inadequate sleep (Chapter 19).

instrumental conditioning A form of associative learning in which an outcome (e.g. getting food) depends upon behaviour (e.g. turning left in a maze) (Chapter 11).

interneuron A neuron that is neither sensory nor motor (Chapter 3).

intracellular fluid The fluid that is inside cells (Chapter 4).

intracranial self-stimulation (ICSS) Electrical stimulation of the brain through an implanted electrode that is contingent on a response (e.g. lever-pressing) by the subject (Chapter 15).

intrafusal muscle fibres Fibres that intermingle with extrafusal fibres and serve the function of detecting muscle stretch (Chapter 10).

invariance That which is unchanging about sensory information with regard to its source. Perceptual systems can extract this, based upon changing sensory input from the source (Chapter 7).

invertebrate Those species of animal that do not have a backbone (Chapter 5).

involuntary reaction Something triggered by external stimulus and avoiding conscious decision-making (Chapter 10).

ion Electrically active particle (Chapter 4).

Iowa gambling task A task in which the relative weights of gains and losses associated with choices can be adjusted to test participants' choices. Also known as the Bechara gambling task (Chapter 20).

ipsilateral The same side of the brain as the region under consideration (Chapter 5).

irritable bowel syndrome (IBS) A disorder of the gut consisting of inappropriate contraction, triggered by both local events at the gut and central stress-related factors (Chapter 13).

K

Klüver–Bucy syndrome A syndrome that follows ablation of parts of the limbic system in monkeys (Chapter 12).

Korsakoff's syndrome A subgroup of the amnesic syndrome, normally due to vitamin deficiency associated with excessive alcohol intake (Chapter 11).

L

labelled-line coding A system of coding in which a particular neuron would be sensitive to, and transmit information on, a particular quality such as sweetness or salt (Chapter 9).

labelled-line principle Differences in encoding information can be in terms of the particular nerves that carry the information (Chapter 7).

latent inhibition The effect of pre-exposure to a stimulus on retarding the subsequent capacity of the stimulus to form predictive associations. In the pre-exposure phase, it appears that the stimulus is labelled as redundant (Chapter 22).

lateral inhibition Inhibition across the sensory surface from one location to another (e.g. light at one retinal location inhibits the effect of light at another) (Chapter 8).

lateralization Asymmetry in which one side of the brain takes a disproportionate role in a particular aspect of processing, e.g. language tends to be handled mainly by the left hemisphere (Chapter 20).

learned helplessness Based on exposure to unavoidable trauma, the acquisition of a cognition of powerlessness and inability to influence events (Chapter 13).

learning A process or procedure by which, in the light of experience, an animal either (a) changes behaviour or (b) acquires the potential for future change (Chapter 11).

leptin A hormone released from fat stores and which plays a role in satiety (Chapter 16).

lesion Disruption of part of the brain, either deliberate or accidental. The procedure is called lesioning (Chapter 5).

leucocyte Mobile cell that forms part of the immune system (Chapter 13).

liability The notion that there exists a tendency to suffer from a disorder such as schizophrenia that could reflect a genetic influence (Chapter 22).

limbic system A collection of brain structures, e.g. amygdala, the activity of which is assumed to underlie emotion (Chapter 12).

lock and key principle The principle that (1) the neurotransmitter is like a key that fits only one lock: the receptor (Chapter 4) and (2) that a particular odour attaches to a particular receptor (Chapter 9).

long-term memory (LTM) A memory held over long periods of time. The potential storage capacity is unlimited (Chapter 11).

long-term potentiation (LTP) A change in the reactivity of a postsynaptic neuron that lasts for hours or even days, following brief activity in a presynaptic neuron (Chapter 11).

lordosis In female rats, a stereotyped reflexive body arching organized largely at a spinal and midbrain level and shown when she is sexually receptive (Chapter 3).

lymphocyte One class of leucocyte (Chapter 13).

M

magnetic resonance imaging (MRI) A technique for revealing structural details of the brain. A version termed 'functional magnetic resonance imaging' (fMRI) detects changes in oxygen consumption (Chapter 5).

magno system A system of communication in which a magno ganglion cell communicates with a magno LGN cell and thereby segregated information is projected to the cortex (Chapter 8).

malleability The property of certain neural processes that they are able to compensate for disturbances (Chapter 6).

masculinization The formation of typical male structures under the influence of androgen (Chapter 6).

maturation Changes that occur in the nervous system corresponding to development, e.g. formation of myelin (Chapter 6).

membrane potential Electrical voltage across a cell (magnitude normally −60 to −70 mV) (Chapter 4).

memory A change in the nervous system that underlies learning and its recall (Chapter 11).

mesolimbic dopamine pathway A pathway of dopaminergic neurons, which starts in the ventral tegmental area (VTA) and terminates in, amongst other places, the nucleus accumbens (N.acc.) (Chapter 15).

metabolic rate The rate at which fuel is used by the body, which corresponds to the rate of heat production (Chapter 16).

metabolism Chemical conversion of a substance within the body. For example, the term is used with reference to the obtaining of energy from chemicals (Chapter 3).

metabolite The breakdown product of the metabolism of a chemical (Chapter 4).

metarepresentation A representation of a representation (Chapter 22).

microelectrode An electrode with a very fine tip, capable of recording from single neurons. The technique of making recordings from a single neuron is termed 'single-unit recording' (Chapter 5).

mind As used here, it refers to the information processing systems of the human brain, some of which are open to conscious introspection but most of which are unconscious (Chapter 21).

mirror neuron A type of neuron that is active when an animal performs a particular motor action or watches another animal do so (Chapter 10).

modality segregation A segregation of information arising from different types of sensory receptor, e.g. between touch and temperature, as this information is projected to the brain and processed therein (Chapter 9).

modularity The notion that the brain is composed of a number of modules each dedicated to a particular task (Chapter 20).

module Largely self-contained unit of processing which is able to handle only one type of information. Evolutionary psychology postulates their existence. An influential theory of Fodor is based on the suggestion that the brain contains a number of such units (Chapter 2).

monoamine Class of neurochemical including dopamine, adrenalin, noradrenalin (known, respectively, as 'epinephrine' and 'norepinephrine' in the American literature), and serotonin (also termed 5-HT) (Chapter 3).

monozygotic twins (or 'identical twins', abb. MZ) MZs derive from a single zygote and are genetically identical (Chapter 6).

motivation A process underlying the control of behaviour and giving it strength and direction (Chapter 2).

motor homunculus A bizarre figure drawn alongside the motor cortex, defined by the areas of the body over which control is exerted by neurons in corresponding regions of motor cortex (Chapter 5).

motor imagery The simulation of movement in the imagination, in the absence of actually moving (Chapter 10).

motor neuron A neuron that carries information to a muscle causing contraction (Chapter 3).

motor unit A motor neuron and the muscle fibres that it innervates (Chapter 10).

muscle fibre The constituent cells of muscle (Chapter 10).

muscle spindle Combination of muscle fibre, motor neuron and sensory neuron (Chapter 10).

mutation A change in the genes contributed to reproduction by one partner, with respect to the precursor genes. The altered phenotype that results from this change in genotype is termed a 'mutant' (Chapter 2).

myelin Part of specialized glial cell forming an insulating coating around an axon. Such an axon is said to be myelinated (Chapter 4).

N

narcolepsy Bouts of sudden sleepiness experienced during the day, associated with weakness of skeletal muscles (Chapter 19).

natural selection The selection of characteristics on the basis of their viability in the environment. A means by which evolution occurs (Chapter 2).

nature The contribution to behaviour that arises from what is given, normally a reference to the genetic contribution at fertilization (Chapter 1).

negative feedback A system in which deviations from an optimal state tend to cause action that returns the state to its optimal value (Chapter 1).

negative reinforcement Something (e.g. loud noise) that is removed contingent on a particular behaviour, where this increases the future frequency of showing this behaviour (Chapter 11).

neglect syndrome A consequence of damage to the posterior parietal lobe involving neglect of part of the sensory input, e.g. denying that a part of the sensory world of touch or vision exists (Chapter 20).

nerve A bundle of axons in the peripheral nervous system, physically located alongside each other and extending over the same distance (Chapter 3).

nerve growth factor (NGF) A specific neurotrophic factor (Chapter 6).

nervous system The brain, spinal cord and peripheral nerves (Chapter 1).

neural correlates of consciousness Those patterns of neural activity that are associated particularly with conscious processing (Chapter 21).

neurohormone A chemical having features of both a hormone and a neurotransmitter. They are released from neurons and travel in the blood (Chapter 3).

neuroleptic drug A type of drug used in the treatment of schizophrenia, which acts by blocking dopamine receptors (Chapter 22).

neuromodulation The action of modulating the activity of neurons by means of a neuromodulator (Chapter 3).

neuromodulator A chemical messenger having a relatively diffuse modulatory effect. Compared with neurotransmission, there can be a relatively large distance within the CNS from the site of release to that of action (Chapter 3).

neuromuscular junction Special type of synapse that links a neuron and a muscle cell (Chapter 4).

neuron A type of cell within the nervous system, which is specialized at transmitting and processing information (Chapter 1).

neuropeptides A group of chemical messengers, which includes natural opioids. Also known simply as 'transmitter' (Chapter 12).

neurotransmitter A substance that communicates one-to-one between a neuron and either another neuron or a muscle cell. It acts at a synapse. Also known simply as 'transmitter' (Chapter 3).

neurotrophic factor (or 'chemotrophic factor') A life-giving chemical secreted by target cells and taken into cells with which they make contact (Chapter 6).

neutral stimulus (NS) A stimulus having no particular effect, other than orientation of sense organs (Chapter 11).

Nissl stain The result of a technique of staining (Nissl staining), which reveals cell bodies (Chapter 5).

nocebo effect An aversive state induced by the expectation of something aversive (Chapter 14).

nociception The detection of tissue damage (Chapter 14).

nociceptive neuron A neuron the tip of which is sensitive to tissue damage, thereby instigating action potentials (Chapter 3).

nociceptive system The system involved with detecting tissue damage and taking action to minimize this (Chapter 14).

nociceptor The tip of specialized neurons, nociceptive neurons, which detect noxious stimulation (Chapter 14).

node of Ranvier The exposed portion of an axon between myelin sheaths (Chapter 4).

non-corticospinal tracts Tracts of descending motor control that start in the brain stem (in contrast to corticospinal tracts) (Chapter 10).

non-declarative memory A form of memory that the person cannot articulate by conscious recall, e.g. how to ride a bicycle (Chapter 11).

non-rapid eye movement sleep ('non-REM sleep' or 'NREM sleep') Generic term for those phases of sleep during which rapid eye movements are not observed (Chapter 19).

nuclei Plural of nucleus (Chapter 3).

nucleus (a) The structure that contains the genetic material of the cell (Chapter 2). (b) A group of cell bodies of neurons in the brain (Chapter 3).

nurturant behaviour Behaviour that describes the care given by a parent to its offspring (Chapter 15).

nurture The contribution to behaviour that arises from the environment (Chapter 1).

O

obesity Excessive weight. In humans, it consists in having a body weight that is more than 20% higher than the ideal for the person's height (Chapter 16).

object permanence task A task in which a child observes an object being hidden behind a screen. At a stage of development, the child acts on the basis that the object still exists (Chapter 6).

obsessive-compulsive disorder (OCD) A condition characterized by intrusive thoughts and often associated compulsive rituals (Chapter 22).

oestrogens A generic term for a class of hormones produced by the female ovaries and involved in sexual behaviour (Chapter 3).

oestrous cycle A cycle of hormonal secretion in females, which underlies reproduction and sexual motivation (Chapter 17).

ontogenetic hypothesis A hypothesis to explain the amount of REM sleep shown by the newborn of different species. It proposes that REM sleep serves a developmental function in the brain (Chapter 19).

ontogeny The history of the development and growth of the individual. Sometimes compared and contrasted with phylogeny (Chapter 1).

open programme A programme underlying development which involves flexibility as a function of different environmental events (Chapter 6).

operant conditioning The type of instrumental learning in which the animal paces itself, normally demonstrated with a Skinner box (Chapter 11).

opiate An artificial form of chemical that has very similar properties to the opioids that the body produces naturally (Chapter 12).

opioid A class of natural chemical that has similar properties to morphine and heroin, and which modulates behaviour, e.g. to reduce reactions to tissue damage (Chapter 12).

opponent-process coding Coding in which one sensory quality, e.g. green light, excites a neuron, whereas another, e.g. red light, inhibits it (Chapter 8).

optic ataxia The result of damage typically to the superior region of the posterior parietal cortex, part of the dorsal stream. Patients have difficulty with visually guided actions (Chapter 8).

organic cause Something for which a disturbance in the physiology of the body can be identified (Chapter 17).

organizational effect A change in the structure that occurs during development as a result of hormones (Chapter 6).

osmoreceptor A neuron or group of neurons the activity of which is sensitive to their swelling as a result of their fluid content. They are assumed to provide a signal for thirst and its satiety (Chapter 16).

outflow theory The theory that the perception of movement is based in part on the command to move the muscles (Chapter 10).

overt orientating A change in position of the body or part of it to alter sensory inflow (Chapter 20).

P

pain matrix The collection of interacting brain regions that forms the biological basis of pain (Chapter 14).

pair bond A bond formed between monogamous sexual partners (Chapter 17).

palatability The reaction to a substance, which depends upon taste, deficit and any earlier associations with the substance (Chapter 16).

parallel processing The situation where information arising from a given source is processed by two or more streams acting in parallel, e.g. in the visual system (Chapter 8).

parasympathetic branch ('system' or 'division') A branch of the autonomic nervous system. It is generally excited at times of passivity (e.g. relaxation) (Chapter 3).

parvo system A system of communication in which a parvo ganglion cell communicates with a parvo LGN cell and thereby segregated information is projected to the cortex (Chapter 8).

passive avoidance A contingency arranged such that an animal can avoid an aversive outcome by refraining from performing a behaviour, such as stepping down from a platform (Chapter 11).

pathogen Threat to the body that is within its boundary, e.g. bacteria (Chapter 13).

perception The conscious awareness of events in the world associated with sensation through sensory systems (Chapter 8).

period The time that it takes a rhythm to complete one cycle (Chapter 19).

peripheral nervous system That part of the nervous system that is not in the brain or spinal cord (Chapter 3).

PGO system A neural circuit that projects from the pons (P) to the LGN (G) and then to the occipital cortex (O) and which plays a role in sleep (Chapter 19).

phantom pain The perception of pain in a bodily location that no longer exists (Chapter 14).

phenomenal consciousness Impossible to capture the term in words but something like 'what it feels like to be conscious' (Chapter 21).

phenotype The biological form or behaviour which exists at any point in time: the form that appears as a result of the genotype exerting an effect within the environment (in distinction to genotype, which is simply the genetic contribution) (Chapter 2).

phenylketonuria A mental disorder associated with a metabolic imbalance and caused by a mutation in a single gene (Chapter 2).

pheromone An airborne chemical that plays a role in communication between animals of the same species (with reference to mating) (Chapter 7).

phoneme The individual sounds that make up a language (Chapter 20).

phylogeny The history of development of species. Sometimes compared and contrasted with ontogeny (Chapter 1).

physiological effect The effect of a chemical intervention that seems to mimic a natural effect (Chapter 16).

physiology The science involved in the study of how the body works, involving such things as the circulation and nervous system, etc. (Chapter 1).

pituitary adrenocortical system (or pituitary adrenocortical axis) The sequence of hormone actions: CRF → ACTH → corticosteroids (Chapter 13).

place code A code in which different frequencies of sound are represented in terms of different locations in the nervous system, e.g. at the basilar membrane (Chapter 9).

placebo effect An otherwise neutral process that has a pain reduction effect based on belief as to its efficacy and/or learning (Chapter 14).

plasticity The capacity of nervous systems and behaviour to exhibit change, e.g. in the light of experience (Chapter 3).

population coding Information encoded by means of which of a population of neurons is activated (Chapter 7).

positive reinforcement A strengthening procedure by which a behaviour is more likely to be repeated in the future as a result of its consequences on past occasions (Chapter 11).

positron emission tomography (PET) A measure of metabolism and blood flow in different regions of the brain (Chapter 5).

post-absorptive state The state when absorption of food is complete and the body relies on intrinsic sources of energy (Chapter 16).

postsynaptic neuron A neuron that is influenced by activity in a presynaptic neuron. At a chemical synapse, it has receptors for the neurochemical released (Chapter 3).

postsynaptic potential The change in membrane potential at a site in a postsynaptic neuron caused by the arrival of an action potential at the terminal of a presynaptic neuron (Chapter 4).

post-traumatic stress disorder (PTSD) A type of stress reaction triggered by traumatic experience and involving regular activation of memories relating to the incident, nightmares and high sympathetic arousal (Chapter 13).

precocial An animal born in a condition relatively competent for independent existence (Chapter 6).

predatory aggression Aggression that a predator directs towards its prey (Chapter 15).

predictability The capacity to predict events, e.g. the arrival of a stressor such as shock based on prior cues such as a light (Chapter 13).

prefrontal cortex The anterior part of the cortex of the frontal lobes (i.e. excluding regions directly concerned with motor control such as the motor cortex) (Chapter 5).

prepulse inhibition (PPI) The inhibition of the response to a stimulus S2 by presenting a weak stimulus S1 just prior to S2 (Chapter 22).

presynaptic neuron A neuron that instigates activity in a postsynaptic neuron. At a chemical synapse, it releases neurotransmitter (Chapter 3).

primary visual cortex The region of occipital lobe at which visual information arrives. It is known as the 'striate cortex', 'V1' and 'area 17' (Chapter 8).

primate The group of species made up of monkeys, chimpanzees, gorillas and humans, amongst others (Chapter 1).

priming A beneficial effect of prior exposure on subsequent recall (Chapter 11).

principle of localization Discrete parts of the nervous system are concerned with discrete roles (Chapter 5).

procedural memory A memory that takes the form of a procedure, i.e. how to do something (Chapter 11).

proceptivity Active approach and solicitation behaviour by a female (Chapter 17).

programmed cell death (PCD) Systematic death of large numbers of cells, in a way that has functional significance for the establishment of an effective nervous system (Chapter 6).

proprioception The system that involves detection of the contraction of skeletal muscles and transmission of this information to the CNS (Chapter 10).

prosopagnosia A defect in face recognition (following brain damage) (Chapter 6).

protein Large chemical structures that are constituents of our bodies (Chapter 1).

protein synthesis The building of proteins, fundamental constituents of the body (Chapter 11).

psychoactive drug A type of drug that exerts a psychological effect (Chapter 18).

psychogenic cause Something not having an identifiable initial trigger in the body's physiology and assumed to represent a psychological cause (normally with reference to a disturbance) (Chapter 17).

psychopharmacology The science involved with the effects of drugs on the nervous system and thereby behaviour (Chapter 3).

psychosis A kind of disruption to mental activity in which there is a break with reality (Chapter 22).

punishment A procedure whereby the frequency of showing behaviour is lowered as a result of the consequence of doing so, e.g. shock (Chapter 11).

pyramidal system See pyramidal tract and corticospinal tract (Chapter 10).

pyramidal tract Pathway of axons that make up the corticospinal tract (Chapter 10).

Q

qualia States of conscious awareness expressed in terms of content (Chapter 21).

R

rapid eye movement sleep (REM sleep) A phase of sleep characterized by the appearance of rapid jerks of the eyes in their sockets and a signature EEG pattern (Chapter 19).

reaction Behaviour triggered by an external event, as in the case of a reflex (Chapter 2).

readiness potential A change in electrical activity seen at the SMA, some 800 ms before the muscular activity starts (Chapter 10).

receptive field The area of sensory surface stimulation of which changes the activity of the neuron in question (with regard to location and size at the sensory surface) (Chapter 7).

receptivity The willingness of a female animal to accept the male's sexual approach, involving the performance of a mating posture (Chapter 17).

receptor (a) Structures at a cell that are occupied by natural chemicals, which then affect the functioning of the cell. (b) The tip of a sensory neuron that is sensitive to a physical event (not to be confused with a receptor molecule) (Chapter 3).

receptor cells (or 'receptors') Cells that are sensitive to physical events, e.g. light receptors in the eye (Chapter 5).

reciprocal inhibition A control process in which an increase of excitation of a flexor muscle is accompanied by a decreased excitation of the antagonist extensor and vice versa (Chapter 10).

reciprocal interaction model A model of the neural basis of sleep in which there is mutual inhibition between (1) cholinergic neurons and (2) serotonergic and noradrenergic neurons (Chapter 19).

reductionism A process of trying to explain events at one level (e.g. behaviour) by looking at a lower level (e.g. the interactions between neurons and hormones) (Chapter 1).

referred pain Pain felt to be associated not with a site of actual tissue damage but 'referred to' another site (Chapter 14).

reflex A relatively stereotyped response to a given stimulus (Chapter 2).

refractory period Period of time that must elapse following an action potential before a given section of axon can be stimulated again to produce another (Chapter 4).

regulatory behaviour Behaviour that regulates the internal environment, e.g. drinking in response to dehydration (Chapter 2).

reinforcement (a) Defined as a procedure that changes behaviour, e.g. if a hungry rat turns left at a choice point in a maze and receives food, the food is said to reinforce the left turn (Chapter 2). (b) At a theoretical level, a process of strengthening S–R links (Chapter 11).

replication The process of producing new cells from the division of precursor cells. The process is intrinsic to a given individual (Chapter 2).

reproduction The process of forming a fertilized egg cell from a sperm cell joining with an egg cell (Chapter 2).

resting potential The membrane potential of a neuron when it is not conducting an action potential (normally about –60 to –70 mV) (Chapter 4).

retina A layer at the back of the eye where light-sensitive cells are situated (Chapter 8).

retrieval Gaining access to stored information, activating a memory (Chapter 11).

retrograde amnesia A failure to recall events experienced before the trauma (Chapter 11).

reuptake The process by which neurotransmitter is taken back into the neuron from which it was released (Chapter 4).

reuptake inhibitor A drug that blocks the reuptake of neurotransmitter from the neuron that released it (Chapter 4).

reward An outcome of behaviour, the experience of which motivates further contact with the given object and to which animals are motivated to regain contact (Chapter 15).

rod A type of sensory receptor, located at the retina (Chapter 8).

S

saccadic eye movement Rapid movements of the eyes in their sockets that serve to keep the fovea in alignment with the object of attention (Chapter 8).

satiety The loss, or inhibition, of appetite following ingestion as a result of a sufficiency of intake (Chapter 16).

schizophrenia A form of psychosis having a developmental origin and characterized by symptoms such as hallucinations (Chapter 22).

second messenger A chemical that is released within a neuron as a result of the occupation of receptors by neurotransmitter and which serves a communication role (Chapter 4).

selfish gene The notion that the actions of a gene are such as to code for its own success, even at a cost to others, hence the metaphor 'selfish' (Chapter 2).

semantic memory A memory for facts, e.g. 'Paris is in France' (Chapter 11).

sensitive period (sometimes termed a 'critical period') A period (usually with regard to development) during which a process is sensitive to a change, e.g. as triggered by a hormone (Chapter 6).

sensitivity A measure of the ability to detect the presence or absence of even weak stimuli (Chapter 8).

sensitization A term to describe a system that responds more strongly even to innocuous stimuli, after a noxious stimulus has been applied (Chapter 11).

sensory homunculus A bizarre-looking person located alongside the somatosensory cortex, defined by regions of cortex associated with corresponding regions of the sensory surface of the body (Chapter 5).

sensory neuron A neuron that detects information on events in the external world or inside the body (Chapter 3).

sensory receptor Cell or part of cell that detects physical events and links this to a change in membrane potential (Chapter 7).

sensory-specific satiety (SSS) Satiety that is specific to a particular, recently ingested, food (Chapter 16).

sensory system A system that detects physical events, conveys information about them to the brain and does some processing of information (Chapter 7).

sensory threshold Minimum level of stimulation that can be detected (Chapter 7).

set-point The value at which a negative feedback system tends to bring a regulated variable. Deviations of the variable from the set-point tend to be self-eliminating (Chapter 10).

sex chromosomes The 23rd pair of chromosomes, which differ between males and females. Females have an XX combination and males an XY combination (Chapter 2).

sexual development Development of sex organs and neural systems underlying sexual behaviour, as well as secondary sexual characteristics such as the male voice breaking (Chapter 6).

sexual differentiation Formation of either a typical female or typical male reproductive system (e.g. genitals, breasts, brain mechanisms of motivation) from an undifferentiated precursor structure (Chapter 6).

sexually dimorphic nucleus (SDN) A nucleus of the preoptic area of the hypothalamus, which is the target of androgens and larger in males than females (Chapter 6).

short-term memory (STM) A memory of limited capacity and concerning recently acquired information (sometimes termed 'primary memory') (Chapter 11).

side effect Effect of a drug that is unintended in its prescription (Chapter 4).

size constancy A phenomenon in which a given object tends to trigger a constant perception, in spite of variation in the image that it produces at the retina as a function of change in distance (Chapter 8).

skeletal muscles Muscles through which action is exerted on the external world (Chapter 3).

Skinner box An apparatus in which an animal effects change, such as pressing a lever or pecking a key and thereby earns a reward, such as a pellet of food (Chapter 1).

sleep factor A suggested natural chemical that arises in the body and which triggers sleep (Chapter 19).

slow-wave sleep ('synchronized sleep') A stage of non-REM sleep characterized by a low-frequency signal measured by EEG (Chapter 19).

smooth muscle Muscle through which the autonomic nervous system exerts action on the internal environment, e.g. changing the diameter of blood vessels (Chapter 3).

social attachment The attachment that exists between a parent and offspring or between monogamous sexual partners (Chapter 15).

social constructivism (or 'social constructionism') A school of thought within psychology that suggests that much of our mental life and behaviour is to be understood in terms of the constructs that a society places upon these events (Chapter 12).

sodium–potassium pump Pump that expels Na$^+$ from cells and pulls in K$^+$ (Chapter 4).

soft-wired A description for neuronal systems and connections that exhibit plasticity, e.g. as a result of experience (Chapter 3).

somatic nervous system That part of the nervous system that effects action on the external world (Chapter 3).

somatic-marker hypothesis The hypothesis that emotions are labelled in the CNS in terms of their physiological associations outside the CNS. Thus, a frame of reference for fear might be, among other things, an accelerated heart-rate. The brain then models these effects and can create something of them even in the absence of the peripheral effect (Chapter 12).

somatosensory cortex The region of cortex at which tactile information arrives and where the cortical processing of it first occurs (Chapter 5).

somatosensory neuron A type of neuron the tip of which is sensitive to tactile stimuli. The tips are located across the surface of the skin (Chapter 9).

somatosensory system The system involving the detection and processing of information on touch (Chapter 9).

spatial summation The addition of the effects at a postsynaptic neuron that arise from inputs to this neuron occurring at different locations (Chapter 4).

species-typical behaviour (STB) A type of behaviour exhibited by most, if not all, members of a particular species (Chapter 2).

spinal cord Column of neurons within the backbone (Chapter 1).

spinal nerve A nerve formed by the convergence of neurons transmitting afferent and efferent information between the CNS and the periphery (Chapter 3).

spinal reflex A reflex organized at the level of the spinal cord (Chapter 3).

spinothalamic tract A pathway in the spinal cord, which carries, among other things, ascending nociceptive information (Chapter 14).

split-brain A brain in which communication between hemispheres is restricted, or eliminated, by cutting the corpus callosum (Chapter 8).

spontaneous alternation The tendency of a rat to alternate its choices of arm taken in a T-maze (Chapter 15).

staining A histological technique whereby neurons are labelled chemically to aid their identification (Chapter 5).

startle reflex A reaction of, among other things, flinching and defensive adjustment when exposed to particular, e.g. intense, stimuli (Chapter 12).

stereotypy A repetitive behaviour with no obvious goal or end-point, such as head-shaking (Chapter 2).

steroid A class of hormone that includes androgens and oestrogens (Chapter 17).

stimulant A class of drug that boosts noradrenergic and dopaminergic neurotransmission and is used in the treatment of ADHD (Chapter 22).

stimulus–response association (S–R) Learning that involves forming an association between a particular stimulus and a particular response (Chapter 11).

stimulus–stimulus association An association that an animal learns of the form that one stimulus leads to another stimulus (Chapter 11).

strain A subdivision within a species (Chapter 2).

stress A state of lengthy disturbance to homeostasis, deriving from physiological or cognitive triggers. A protracted inability to resolve an underlying problem (Chapter 13).

stressor Something that triggers stress, such as infection, noise or social conflict (Chapter 13).

stretch receptor Tip of a sensory neuron that is sensitive to stretch in associated muscle (Chapter 10).

stretch reflex A reflex that counters disturbances to the set position of a limb (Chapter 10).

stroke Disruption of brain function caused by blocking an artery in the brain or rupture of a blood vessel (Chapter 5).

Stroop test A test in which a person is asked to name the colour of ink in which words are written, the words being incompatible colour names (Chapter 10).

structural imaging A technique for looking at the structure ('anatomy') of the brain in terms of sizes and locations of different regions, etc. (Chapter 5).

subcortical pathway A pathway by which sensory information is transmitted other than via the cortex (Chapter 8).

sympathetic branch ('system' or 'division') A branch of the autonomic nervous system. It is generally excited at times of activity (Chapter 3).

synapse The region where one neuron communicates with another cell, normally by chemical means (Chapter 3).

synaptic cleft The gap between the membrane of the presynaptic and postsynaptic cells (Chapter 4).

synaptic delay The time taken for information to pass across a synapse, i.e. between arrival of an action potential and the start of electrical events in the postsynaptic cell (Chapter 3).

T

T cell Neuron that transmits nociceptive information from local regions of spinal cord to the brain. They are excited by nociceptive neurons which form synapses on them within the spinal cord (Chapter 14).

taste reactivity test A test in which samples of solutions are placed on the tongue of rats and the rat's affective reactions monitored by video (Chapter 15).

taste-aversion learning (or the 'Garcia effect') Devaluation of a particular taste as a result of it being followed by gastrointestinal upset (Chapter 1).

temporal summation The addition of postsynaptic potentials that arise as a result of a sequence of events in a presynaptic neuron (Chapter 4).

testosterone A hormone secreted in males and females and involved in sexual motivation and aggression (Chapter 3).

theory of mind The cognitive representation within one animal of the state of mind of another, e.g. regarding the other's emotion and intention (Chapter 5).

theory of mind mechanism A proposed mechanism, which is thought to serve to extract information on the intentions and desires of others (Chapter 6)

theta wave Synchronized waves of activity shown by the hippocampus during REM sleep and at other times (Chapter 19).

threshold The level of depolarization at which an action potential is triggered (Chapter 4). The point at which a sensory event starts to influence detection (Chapter 7).

tolerance A situation of drug use, where increasing amounts of drug need to be taken to obtain a given effect. Can also be applied to some non-drug-related activities such as gambling (Chapter 18).

tonotopic representation A representation in which different locations at the basilar membrane are represented by different locations at the auditory cortex. Thus, different frequencies of sound correspond to different cortical locations (Chapter 9).

top-down A mode of influence from higher levels of the nervous system to lower, e.g. from perception to sensory analysis (Chapter 7).

topographical map A representation in which adjacent regions of sensory surface (e.g. retina) are associated with adjacent neurons in the brain (e.g. visual cortex) (Chapter 8).

tract (or 'pathway') A number of axons within the CNS transmitting information along the same route (Chapter 3).

transcutaneous electrical nerve stimulation (TENS) A technique that involves applying weak electrical stimulation at the skin and thereby reducing pain (Chapter 14).

transduction Translation from physical events (e.g. a chemical on the tongue) to an electrical signal, a change in membrane potential of neurons (Chapter 7).

two-point threshold The distance between two points used as tactile stimuli at the skin at which the person can discriminate that there are two points rather than one point present. The smaller the distance, the higher is the tactile acuity at that point (Chapter 9).

Type A behaviour Behaviour consisting of being under excessive time-pressure, aggressively competitive, over-ambitious and easily aroused to hostility (Chapter 13).

Type B behaviour Relaxed behaviour, without undue hostility and competitiveness (Chapter 13).

U

ulcer A type of damage (lesion), in this case to the gut, caused by both local factors, e.g. bacterial infection, and central stress-related factors (Chapter 13).

unconditional reflex A reflex the formation of which does not require conditioning, e.g. in dogs, the reflex underlying the production of salivation to food in the mouth (Chapter 11).

unconditional response (UCR) A response that does not depend upon a history of conditioning, e.g. salivation to food in the mouth (Chapter 11).

unconditional stimulus (UCS) A stimulus that has a capacity to elicit a response without a prior history of conditioning, e.g. food can unconditionally elicit salivation in hungry dogs (Chapter 11).

up-regulation The process by which there is an increased density of receptors at a postsynaptic membrane as a result of abnormally low levels of stimulation by neurotransmitter (Chapter 4).

utilization behaviour Behaviour shown by patients with damage to the prefrontal cortex, in which they reach out to a familiar object and grab it even though this would otherwise have been considered 'inappropriate behaviour' (Chapter 10).

V

ventral Towards the belly or lower part of the brain (Chapter 3).

ventral stream A stream of visual information leading to the temporal cortex and associated with conscious perception (Chapter 8).

ventricles Large spaces in the brain that are filled with cerebrospinal fluid (Chapter 5).

vertebrate Those species of animal that have a backbone (Chapter 5).

vestibular apparatus A mechanism in the inner ear, which provides the sensory input to the vestibular system. The apparatus detects changes in the position of the head and transmits information on this to the brain along a cranial nerve (Chapter 9).

vestibular system The system that underlies balance based upon information arising in the vestibular apparatus (Chapter 9).

vestibulo-ocular reflex Compensatory movement of the eyes, accompanying head movement, so that the image tends to be stabilized on the retina (Chapter 10).

viscera The internal organs of the body, e.g. stomach and intestine. The associated adjective is 'visceral' (Chapter 3).

visual agnosia A condition in which there is an inability to recognize objects by the use of vision (Chapter 8).

visual cortex The region of cortex at which visual information arrives and where the cortical processing of it first occurs (Chapter 5).

voluntary action Behaviour that requires conscious decision-making and is said to have a purpose, which we can consciously reflect upon and articulate (Chapter 10).

voluntary behaviour Human behaviour that is associated with a conscious goal or intention (Chapter 2).

vomeronasal system A distinct olfactory system, with receptors in the nose, and which is responsible for the detection of pheromones (Chapter 9).

vulnerability model A model which suggests that stress contributes to the vulnerability of a person to suffer from schizophrenia (Chapter 22).

W

Wada technique A technique in which a fast-acting anaesthetic is injected into the carotid artery supplying blood to one hemisphere. Changes in cognition and behaviour are then observed (Chapter 20).

wavelength The distance between any two corresponding points on a cycle (Chapter 7).

Wernicke's aphasia Aphasia that is associated with damage to Wernicke's area. It is particularly associated with understanding language (Chapter 20).

Wernicke's area An area of the human temporal cortex concerned with the interpretation of language (Chapter 20).

Wernicke–Geschwind model A model of language involving interactions between a number of brain regions (Chapter 20).

wind-up The phenomenon of increased sensitivity of synapses in the nociceptive pathway (Chapter 14).

win–shift A situation where, having obtained reward at one location, an animal needs to move elsewhere to obtain another reward (Chapter 11).

win–stay A situation in which, having obtained reward at one location, an animal needs to revisit that location to obtain further reward (Chapter 11).

Wisconsin card-sorting test A task in which people need to sort cards according to a criterion of either their colour or form. The criterion changes at the request of the experimenter (Chapter 6).

withdrawal An aversive state triggered by the termination of drug intake (Chapter 18).

withdrawal symptoms Aversive bodily and psychological events triggered by the absence of a drug in dependent individuals (Chapter 18).

working memory A broad and multi-aspect memory class. In addition to a temporary store of information, it also performs manipulation of stored information (Chapter 11).

Z

Zeitgeber An extrinsic factor that sets the timing of a circadian rhythm (Chapter 19)

References

Abbeduto, L. and Boudreau, D. (2004) Theoretical influences on research on language development and intervention in individuals with mental retardation. *Mental Retardation and Developmental Disabilities Research Reviews*, **10**, 184–192.

Adamec, R. (1997) Transmitter systems involved in neural plasticity underlying increased anxiety and defense – implications for understanding anxiety following traumatic stress. *Neuroscience and Biobehavioral Reviews*, **21**, 755–765.

Ader, R. and Cohen, N. (1985) CNS–immune system interactions: conditioning phenomena. *Behavioral and Brain Sciences*, **8**, 379–394.

Adkins-Regan, E. (2004) *Hormones and Animal Social Behavior*, Princeton University Press, Princeton.

Adkins-Regan, E., Mansukhani,V., Thompson, R. and Yang, S. (1997) Organizational actions of sex hormones on sexual partner preference. *Brain Research Bulletin*, **44**, 497–502.

Adolphs, R. and Tranel, D. (2003) Amygdala damage impairs emotion recognition from scenes only when they contain facial expressions. *Neuropsychologia*, **41**, 1281–1289.

Aggleton, J.P. and Mishkin, M. (1986) The amygdala: sensory gateway to the emotions. In *Emotion – Theory, Research and Experience*. Volume 3: *Biological Foundations of Emotion* (eds R. Plutchik and H. Kellerman), Academic Press, Orlando, pp. 281–299.

Aghajanian, G.K. (1994) Serotonin and the action of LSD in the brain. *Psychiatric Annals*, **24**, 137–141.

Aglioti, S., DeSouza, J.F.X. and Goodale, M.A. (1995) Size-contrast illusions deceive the eye but not the hand. *Current Biology*, **5**, 679–685.

Ågmo, A. and Berenfeld, R. (1990) Reinforcing properties of ejaculation in the male rat: role of opioids and dopamine. *Behavioral Neuroscience*, **104**, 177–182.

Ågmo, A., Turi, A.L., Ellingsen, E. and Kaspersen, H. (2004) Preclinical models of sexual desire: conceptual and behavioural analyses. *Pharmacology, Biochemistry and Behavior*, **78**, 379–404.

Ahima, R.S. (2005) Central actions of adipocyte hormones. *Trends in Endocrinology and Metabolism*, **16**, 307–313.

Aiello, L.C. and Wheeler, P. (1995) The expensive-tissue hypothesis. *Current Anthropology*, **36**, 199–221.

Ainslie, G. (1975) Specious reward: a behavioral theory of impulsiveness and impulse control. *Psychological Bulletin*, **82**, 463–496.

Aitkin, L.M., Irvine, D.R.F. and Webster, W.R. (1984) Central neural mechanisms of hearing. In *Handbook of Physiology*. Section 1: *The Nervous System*, Vol. III, Part 2 (ed. I. Darian-Smith), American Physiological Society, Bethesda, pp. 675–738.

Akil, H., Campeau, S., Cullinan, W.E., Lechan, R.M., Toni, R., Watson, S.J. and Moore, R.Y. (1999) Neuroendocrine systems 1: overview – thyroid and adrenal axes. In *Fundamental Neuroscience* (eds M.J. Zigmond, F.E. Bloom, J.L. Roberts and L.A Squire), Academic Press, San Diego, pp. 1127–1150.

Alajouanine, T. (1948) Aphasia and artistic realization. *Brain*, **71**, 17–241.

Alaoui-Ismaïli, O., Robin, O., Rada, H., Dittmar, A. and Vernet-Maury, E. (1997) Basic emotions evoked by odorants: comparison between autonomic responses and self evaluation. *Physiology and Behavior*, **62**, 713–720.

Albert, D.J., Dyson, E.M. and Walsh, M.L. (1987) Intermale social aggression: reinstatement in castrated rats by implants of testosterone propionate in the medial hypothalamus. *Physiology and Behavior*, **39**, 555–560.

Aldridge, J.W. and Berridge, K.C. (1998) Coding of serial order by neostriatal neurons: a 'natural action' approach to movement sequence. *Journal of Neuroscience*, **18**, 2777–2787.

Alexander, B.K. and Hadaway, P.F. (1982) Opiate addiction: the case for an adaptive orientation. *Psychological Bulletin*, **92**, 367–381.

Alexander, B.K., Peele, S., Hadaway, P.F., Morse, S.J., Brodsky, A. and Beyerstein, B.L. (1985) Adult, infant, and animal addiction. In *The Meaning of Addiction* (ed. S. Peele), Lexington Books, Lexington, pp. 73–96.

Allan, R. and Scheidt, S. (1996a) *Heart and Mind. The Practice of Cardiac Psychology*, American Psychological Association, Washington.

Allan, R. and Scheidt, S. (1996b) Empirical basis for cardiac psychology. In *Heart and Mind. The Practice of Cardiac Psychology* (eds R. Allan and S. Scheidt), American Psychological Association, Washington, pp. 63–123.

Allen, L.S. and Gorski, R.A. (1992) Sexual orientation and the size of the anterior commissure in the human brain. *Proceedings of the National Academy of Sciences*, USA, **89**, 7199–7202.

Altman, J., Brunner, R.L. and Bayer, S.A. (1973) The hippocampus and behavioural maturation. *Behavioural Biology*, **8**, 557–596.

Amaral, D.G. and Sinnamon, H.M. (1977) The locus coeruleus: neurobiology of a central noradrenergic nucleus. *Progress in Neurobiology*, **9**, 147–196.

Anderson, J.R. (2000) *Learning and Memory: An Integrated Approach* (2nd ed.), Wiley, New York.

Andersson, K-E. and Wagner, G. (1995) Physiology of penile erection. *Physiological Reviews*, **75**, 191–236.

Andrade, J. (2002) *Working Memory in Perspective*, Psychology Press, Hove.

Andreasen, N.C. (1999) A unitary model of schizophrenia. *Archives of General Psychiatry*, **56**, 781–787.

Andreasen, N.C. (2005) *The Creating Brain: The Neuroscience of Genius*, Dana Press, New York.

Andrews, T.J., Schluppeck, D., Homfray, D., Matthews, P. and Blakemore, C. (2002) Activity in the fusiform gyrus predicts conscious perception of Rubin's vase-face illusion. *NeuroImage*, **17**, 890–901.

Anisman, H., Zaharia, M.D., Meaney, M.J. and Merali, Z. (1998) Do early-life events permanently alter behavioral and hormonal responses to stressors? *International Journal of Developmental Neuroscience*, **16**, 149–164.

Antin, J., Gibbs, J., Holt, J., Young, R.C. and Smith, G.P. (1975) Cholecystokinin elicits the complete behavioral sequence of satiety in rats. *Journal of Comparative and Physiological Psychology*, **89**, 784–790.

Antrobus, J. (1991) Dreaming: cognitive processes during cortical activation and high afferent thresholds. *Psychological Review*, **98**, 96–121.

Archer, J. (1979) *Animals under Stress*, Edward Arnold, London.

Archer, J. (1994) Testosterone and aggression. *Journal of Offender Rehabilitation*, **21**, 3–25.

Archer, J. (1996) Sex differences in social behavior. *American Psychologist*, **51**, 909–917.

Arendt, J. (1997) Melatonin. In *Sleep Science: Integrating Basic Research and Clinical Practice. Monographs in Clinical Neuroscience*, Vol. 15 (ed. W.J. Schwartz), Karger, Basle, pp. 196–228.

Arnsten, A.F.T. (2001) Basic neuroscience: introduction. In *Stimulant Drugs and ADHD: Basic and Clinical Neuroscience* (eds M.V. Solanto, A.F.T. Arnsten and F.X. Castellanos), Oxford University Press, Oxford, pp. 73–75.

Aserinsky, E. and Kleitman, N. (1955) Two types of ocular motility occurring in sleep. *Journal of Applied Physiology*, **8**, 1–10.

Aston-Jones, G.S., Desimone, R., Driver, J., Luck, S.J. and Posner, M.I. (1999) Attention. In *Fundamental Neuroscience* (eds M.J. Zigmond, F.E. Bloom, S.C. Landis, J.L. Roberts and L.R. Squire), Academic Press, San Diego, pp. 1385–1409.

Avila, M., Thaker, G., and Adami, H. (2001) Genetic epidemiology and schizophrenia: a study of reproductive fitness. *Schizophrenia Research*, **47**, 233–241.

Aydede, M. (2006) *Pain: New Essays on its Nature and the Methodology of its Study*. MIT Press, Cambridge.

Azrin, N.H., Hutchinson, R.R. and McLaughlin, R. (1965) The opportunity for aggression as an operant reinforcer during aversive stimulation. *Journal of the Experimental Analysis of Behavior*, **8**, 171–180.

Baars, B.J. (1993) How does a serial, integrated and very limited stream of consciousness emerge from a nervous system that is mostly unconscious, distributed, parallel and of enormous capacity? In *Experimental and Theoretical Studies of Consciousness* (eds G.R. Bock and J. Marsh), Wiley, Chichester, pp. 282–303.

Baars, B.J. (1997) *In the Theatre of Consciousness*, Oxford University Press, New York.

Baddeley, A. (1994) Working memory: the interface between memory and cognition. In *Memory Systems 1994* (eds D.L. Schacter and E. Tulving), MIT Press, Cambridge, pp. 351–637.

Baddeley, A. (1996) Exploring the central executive. *Quarterly Journal of Experimental Psychology*, **49A**, 5–28.

Baddeley, A. (1997) *Human Memory – Theory and Practice*, Psychology Press, Hove.

Baddeley, A.D. and Hitch, G. (1974) Working memory. In *The Psychology of Learning and Motivation*, Vol. 8 (ed. G.H. Bower), Academic Press, New York, pp. 47–89.

Baddeley, A.D., Bressi, S., Della Sala, S., Logie, R. and Spinnler, H. (1991) The decline of working memory in Alzheimer's disease. *Brain*, **114**, 2521–2542.

Baddeley, A., Della Sala, S., Papagno, C. and Spinnler, H. (1997) Dual-task performance in dysexecutive and nondysexecutive patients with a frontal lesion. *Neuropsychology*, **11**, 187–194.

Baizer, J.S., Ungerleider, L.G. and Desimone, R. (1991) Organization of visual inputs to the inferior temporal and posterior parietal cortex in Macaques. *Journal of Neuroscience*, **11**, 168–190.

Baker, D.A., Khroyan, T.V., O'Dell, L.E., Fuchs, R.A. and Neisewander, J.L. (1996) Differential effects of intra-accumbens sulpiride on cocaine-induced locomotion and conditioned place preference. *Journal of Pharmacology and Experimental Therapeutics*, **279**, 392–401.

Baker, T.B., Piper, M.E., McCarthy, D.E., Majeskie, M.R. and Fiore, M.C. (2004) Addiction motivation reformulated: an affective processing model of negative reinforcement. *Psychological Review*, **111**, 33–51.

Balleine, B.W. and Dickinson, A. (1998) Goal-directed instrumental action: contingency and incentive learning and their cortical substrates. *Neuropharmacology*, **37**, 407–419.

Ballieux, R.E. and Heijnen, C.J. (1987) Brain and immune system: a one-way conversation or a genuine dialogue? In *Progress in Brain Research*, Vol. 72 (eds E.R. de Kloet, V.M. Wiegant and D. de Wied), Elsevier Science, Amsterdam, pp. 71–77.

Bancroft, J. (1988) Reproductive hormones and male sexual function. In *Handbook of Sexology. Vol. 6: The Pharmacology and Endocrinology of Sexual Function* (ed. J.M.A. Sitsen), Elsevier Science Publishers, Amsterdam, pp. 297–315.

Bancroft, J. (1989) *Human Sexuality and its Problems*, Churchill Livingstone, Edinburgh.

Bancroft, J. (1995) Effects of alpha 2 antagonist on male erectile response. In *Pharmacology of Sexual Function and Dysfunction* (ed. J. Bancroft), Excerpta Medica, Amsterdam, pp. 215–224.

Bandler, R. and Shipley, M.T. (1994) Columnar organization in the midbrain periaqueductal gray: modules for emotional expression? *Trends in Neurosciences*, **17**, 379–389.

Bandura, A., O'Leary, A., Taylor, C.B., Gauthier, J. and Gossard, D. (1987) Perceived self-efficacy and pain control: opioid and nonopioid mechanisms. *Journal of Personality and Social Psychology*, **53**, 563–571.

Barden, N., Reul, J.M.H.M. and Holsboer, F. (1995) Do anti-depressants stabilize mood through actions on the hypothalamic–pituitary–adrenocortical system? *Trends in Neurosciences*, **18**, 6–11.

Bardo, M.T. (1998) Neuropharmacological mechanisms of drug reward: beyond dopamine in the nucleus accumbens. *Critical Reviews in Neurobiology*, **12**, 37–67.

Bardo, M.T., Donohew, R.L. and Harrington, N.G. (1996) Psychobiology of novelty seeking and drug seeking behavior. *Behavioural Brain Research*, **77**, 23–43.

Bargh, J.A. and Chartrand, T.L. (1999) The unbearable automaticity of being. *American Psychologist*, **54**, 462–479.

Bargh, J.A. and Tota, M.E. (1988) Context-dependent automatic processing in depression: accessibility of negative constructs with regard to self but not others. *Journal of Personality and Social Psychology*, **54**, 925–939.

Barkley, R.A. (1997) Behavioural inhibition, sustained attention, and executive functions: constructing a unified theory of ADHD. *Psychological Bulletin*, **121**, 65–94.

Barkley, R.A. (2000) *A New Look at ADHD: Inhibition, Time, and Self-control*, Guilford Press, New York.

Barkley, R.A. (2005) *ADHD and the Nature of Self-control*, Guilford Press, New York.

Barkow, J.H., Cosmides, L. and Tooby, J. (1992) *The Adapted Mind: Evolutionary Psychology and the Generation of Culture*, Oxford University Press, New York.

Barlow, H. (1990) The mechanical mind. *Annual Review of Neurosciences*, **13**, 15–24.

Barlow, H. (1995) The neuron doctrine in perception. In *The Cognitive Neurosciences* (ed. M.S. Gazzaniga), MIT Press, Cambridge, pp. 415–435.

Barney, K. (1994) Limitations of the critique of the medical model. *Journal of Mind and Behavior*, **15**, 19–34.

Baron-Cohen, S. (1999) The cognitive neuroscience of autism: evolutionary approaches. In *The New Cognitive Neurosciences* (ed. M.S. Gazzaniga), MIT Press, Cambridge, pp. 1249–1257.

Bartels, A. and Zeki, S. (2000) The neural basis of romantic love. *NeuroReport*, **11**, 3829–3834.

Bartels, A. and Zeki, S. (2004) The neural correlates of maternal and romantic love. *NeuroImage*, **21**, 1155–1166.

Bartlik, B., Kaplan, P., Kaminetsky, J., Roentsch, G. and Goldberg, J. (1999a) Medications with the potential to enhance sexual responsivity in women. *Psychiatric Annals*, **29**, 46–52.

Bartlik, B., Legere, R. and Andersson, L. (1999b) The combined use of sex therapy and testosterone replacement therapy for women. *Psychiatric Annals*, **29**, 27–33.

Bartoshuk, L.M. and Beauchamp, G.K. (1994) Chemical senses. In *Annual Review of Psychology*, Vol. 45 (eds L.W. Porter and M.R. Rosenzweig), Annual Reviews Inc., Palo Alto, pp. 419–449.

Basheer, R., Strecker, R.E., Thakkar, M.M. and McCarley, R.W. (2004) Adenosine and sleep-wake regulation. *Progress in Neurobiology*, **73**, 379–396.

Bastian, A.J., Mugnaini, E. and Thach, W.T. (1999) Cerebellum. In *Fundamental Neuroscience* (eds M.J. Zigmond, F.E. Bloom, S.C. Landis, J.L. Roberts and L.R. Squire), Academic Press, San Diego, pp. 973–992.

Bateson, P. (1979) How do sensitive periods arise and what are they for? *Animal Behaviour*, **27**, 470–486.

Bauer, R.M. (1982) Visual hypoemotionality as a symptom of visual-limbic disconnection in man. *Archives of Neurology*, **39**, 702–708.

Bauer, R.M. and Verfaellie, M. (1992) Memory dissociations: a cognitive psychophysiology perspective. In *Neuropsychology of Memory* (eds L.R. Squire and N. Butters), Guilford Press, New York, pp. 58–71.

Baum, M.J. (1995) Reassessing the role of medial preoptic area/anterior hypothalamic neurons in appetitive aspects of masculine sexual behaviour. In *The Pharmacology of Sexual Function and Dysfunction* (ed. J. Bancroft), Excerpta Medica, Amsterdam, pp. 133–142.

Baum, M.J. (1999) Psychosexual development. In *Fundamental Neuroscience* (eds M.J. Zigmond, F.E. Bloom, S.C. Landis and L.R. Squire), Academic Press, San Diego, pp. 1229–1244.

Baxter, D.W. and Olszewski, J. (1960) Congenital universal insensitivity to pain. *Brain*, **83**, 381–393.

Baxter, J.D. and Rousseau, G.G. (1979) Glucocorticoid hormone action: an overview. In *Glucocorticoid Hormone Action* (eds J.D. Baxter and G.G. Rousseau), Springer-Verlag, Berlin, pp. 1–24.

Beach, F.A. (1947) A review of physiological and psychological studies of sexual behavior in mammals. *Physiological Reviews*, **27**, 240–307.

Beach, F.A. (1975) Behavioral endocrinology: an emerging discipline. *American Scientist*, **63**, 178–187.

Beach, F.A. and LeBoeuf, B.J. (1967) Coital behaviour in dogs. I. Preferential mating in the bitch. *Animal Behaviour*, **15**, 546–558.

Beach, F.A. and Whalen, R.E. (1959) Effects of ejaculation on sexual behavior in the male rat. *Journal of Comparative and Physiological Psychology*, **52**, 249–254.

Beach, F.A. and Wilson, J.R. (1963) Mating behavior in male rats after removal of the seminal vesicles. *Proceedings of the National Academy of Sciences USA*, **49**, 624–626.

Bear, M.F., Connors, B.W. and Paradiso, M.A. (1996) *Neuroscience: Exploring the Brain*, Williams and Wilkins, Baltimore.

Bebbington, P., Wilkins, S., Jones, P., Foerster, A., Murray, R., Toone, B. and Lewis, S. (1993) Life events and psychosis: initial results from the Camberwell Collaborative Psychosis Study. *British Journal of Psychiatry*, **162**, 72–79.

Bechara, A. (2004) The role of emotion in decision-making: evidence from neurological patients with orbitofrontal damage. *Brain and Cognition*, **55**, 30–40.

Bechara, A. (2005) Decision making, impulse control and loss of willpower to resist drugs: a neurocognitive perspective. *Nature Neuroscience*, **8**, 1458–1463.

Bechara, A., Nader, K. and van der Kooy, D. (1998) A two-separate-motivational-systems hypothesis of opioid addiction. *Pharmacology, Biochemistry and Behavior*, **59**, 1–17.

Bechara, A., Tranel, D., Damasio, H., Adolphs, R., Rockland, C. and Damasio, A.R. (1995) Double dissociation of conditioning and declarative knowledge relative to the amygdala and hippocampus in humans. *Science*, **269**, 1115–1118.

Beck, A.T. (1967) *Depression – Clinical, Experimental, and Theoretical Aspects*, Staples Press, London.

Beck, R.C. (2004) *Motivation: Theories and Principles*, Pearson Education, Upper Saddle River.

Becker, J.B., Breedlove, S.M. and Crews, D. (1992) *Behavioral Endocrinology*, MIT Press, Cambridge.

Beckers, G. and Zeki, S. (1995) The consequences of inactivating areas V1 and V5 on visual motion perception. *Brain*, **118**, 49–60.

Beecher, H.K. (1955) The powerful placebo. *Journal of the American Medical Association*, **159**, 1602–1606.

Bejerot, S. (2003) Psychosurgery for obsessive-compulsive disorder – concerns remain. *Acta Psychiatrica Scandinavica*, **107**, 241–243.

Benedetti, F. and Amanzio, M. (1997) The neurobiology of placebo analgesia: from endogenous opioids to cholecystokinin. *Progress in Neurobiology*, **51**, 109–125.

Benington, J.H. (2000) Sleep homeostasis and the function of sleep. *Sleep*, **23**, 959–966.

Benington, J.H. and Frank, M.G. (2003) Cellular and molecular connections between sleep and synaptic plasticity. *Progress in Neurobiology*, **69**, 71–101.

Benington, J.H. and Heller, H.C. (1995) Restoration of brain energy metabolism as the function of sleep. *Progress in Neurobiology*, **45**, 347–360.

Bennett, E.L. (1976) Cerebral effects of differential experience and training. In *Neural Mechanisms of Learning and Memory* (eds M.R. Rosenzweig and E.L. Bennett), MIT Press, Cambridge, pp. 279–287.

Benson, J.B (1990) The significance and development of crawling in human infancy. In *Advances in Motor Development Research*, Vol. 3 (eds J.E. Clark and J.H. Humphrey), AMS Press, New York, pp. 91–142.

Bentivoglio, M. and Grassi-Zucconi, G. (1997) The pioneering experimental studies on sleep deprivation. *Sleep*, **20**, 570–576.

Berenbaum, S.A. (1999) Effects of early androgens on sex-typed activities and interests in adolescents with congenital adrenal hyperplasia. *Hormones and Behavior*, **35**, 102–110.

Berkowitz, L. (1993) *Aggression – Its Causes, Consequences and Control*, McGraw-Hill, New York.

Berman, K.F. and Weinberger, D.R. (1991) Functional localization in the brain in schizophrenia. In *Review of Psychiatry*, Vol. 10 (eds A. Tasman and S.M. Goldfinger), American Psychiatric Press, Washington, pp. 24–59.

Bernhardt, P.C. (1997) Influences of serotonin and testosterone in aggression and dominance: convergence with social psychology. *Current Directions in Psychological Science*, **6**, 44–48.

Berns, G.S. and Sejnowski, T.J. (1998) A computational model of how the basal ganglia produce sequences. *Journal of Cognitive Neuroscience*, **10**, 108–121.

Bernstein, G.A., Carroll, M.E., Thuras, P.D., Cosgrove, K.P. and Roth, M.E. (2002) Caffeine dependence in teenagers. *Drug and Alcohol Dependence*, **66**, 1–6.

Bernstein, I.L. (1996) Neural mediation of food aversions and anorexia induced by tumour necrosis factor and tumours. *Neuroscience and Biobehavioral Reviews*, **20**, 177–181.

Bernstein, I.L. and Webster, M.M. (1985) Learned food aversions: a consequence of cancer chemotherapy. In *Cancer, Nutrition, and Eating Behavior: A Biobehavioral Perspective* (eds T.G. Burish, S.M. Levy and B.E. Meyerowitz), Lawrence Erlbaum, Hillsdale, pp. 103–116.

Berntson, G.G. and Micco, D.J. (1976) Organization of brainstem behavioral systems. *Brain Research Bulletin*, **1**, 471–483.

Berridge, C.W. (2001) Arousal- and attention-related actions of the locus coeruleus-noradrenergic system: potential target in the therapeutic actions of amphetamine-like stimulants. In *Stimulant Drugs and ADHD: Basic and Clinical Neuroscience* (eds M.V. Solanto, A.F.T. Arnsten and F.X. Castellanos), Oxford University Press, Oxford, pp. 158–184.

Berridge, K.C. (1995) Food reward: brain substrates of wanting and liking. *Neuroscience and Biobehavioral Reviews*, **20**, 1–25.

Berridge, K.C. (2004) Motivation concepts in behavioral neuroscience. *Physiology and Behavior*, **81**, 179–209.

Berridge, K.C. and Valenstein, E.S. (1991) What psychological process mediates feeding evoked by electrical stimulation of the lateral hypothalamus? *Behavioral Neuroscience*, **105**, 3–14.

Berridge, K.C., Grill, H.J. and Norgren, R. (1981) Relation of consummatory responses and preabsorptive insulin release to palatability and learned taste aversions. *Journal of Comparative and Physiological Psychology*, **95**, 363–382.

Berthoud, H-R. (2002) Multiple neural systems controlling food intake and body weight. *Neuroscience and Biobehavioral Reviews*, **26**, 393–428.

Berthoud, H-R. and Seeley, R.J. (1999) *Neural and Metabolic Control of Macronutrient Intake*, CRC Press, Boca Raton.

Berthoz, A. (1996) Neural basis of decision in perception and in the control of movement. In *Neurobiology of Decision-Making* (eds A.R. Damasio, H. Damasio and Y. Christen), Springer, Berlin, pp. 83–100.

Besheer, J., Jensen, H.C. and Bevins, R.A. (1999) Dopamine antagonism in a novel-object recognition and a novel-object place conditioning preparation with rats. *Behavioural Brain Research*, **103**, 35–44.

Best, M., Williams, J.M. and Coccaro, E.F. (2002) Evidence for a dysfunctional prefrontal circuit in patients with an impulsive aggressive disorder. *Proceedings of the National Academy of Sciences USA*, **99**, 8448–8453.

Bevins, R.A. and Bardo, M.T. (1999) Conditioned increase in place preference by access to novel objects: antagonism by MK-801. *Behavioural Brain Research*, **99**, 53–60.

Bianchi, L. (1922) *The Mechanism of the Brain and the Function of the Frontal Lobes*, Livingstone, Edinburgh.

Billings, J.H., Scherwitz, L.W., Sullivan, R., Sparler, S. and Ornish, D.M. (1996) The lifestyle heart trial: comprehensive treatment and group support therapy. In *Heart and Mind. The Practice of Cardiac Psychology* (eds R. Allan and S. Scheidt), American Psychological Association, Washington, pp. 233–253.

Bindra, D. (1978) How adaptive behaviour is produced: a perceptual–motivational alternative to response-reinforcement. *Behavioral and Brain Sciences*, **1**, 41–91.

Birch, L.L., McPhee, L., Sullivan, S. and Johnson, S. (1989) Conditioned meal initiation in young children. *Appetite*, **13**, 105–113.

Birchwood, M. and Jackson, C. (2001) *Schizophrenia*. Psychology Press, Hove.

Blackburn, J.R. and Pfaus, J.G. (1988) Is motivation really modulation? A comment on Wise. *Psychobiology*, **16**, 303–304.

Blackburn, J.R., Pfaus, J.G. and Phillips, A.G. (1992) Dopamine functions in appetitive and defensive behaviours. *Progress in Neurobiology*, **39**, 247–279.

Blackmore, S. (2005) *Conversations on Consciousness: Interviews with Twenty Minds*, Oxford University Press, Oxford.

Blackshaw, L.A. and Grundy, D. (1993) Gastrointestinal mechanoreception in the control of ingestion. In *Neurophysiology of Ingestion* (ed. D.A. Booth), Pergamon Press, Oxford, pp. 57–77.

Blake, R. and Logothetis, N.K. (2002) Visual competition. *Nature Reviews Neuroscience*, **3**, 13–23.

Blakemore, C. (1973) Environmental constraints on development in the visual system. In *Constraints on Learning* (eds R.A. Hinde and J. Stevenson-Hinde), Academic Press, London, pp. 51–73.

Blakemore, S-J. and Frith, U. (2005) *The Learning Brain: Lessons for Education*. Blackwell Publishing, Oxford.

Bleuler, E. (1950) *Dementia Praecox or the Group of Schizophrenias*, International Universities Press, New York.

Bligh, J. (1972) Neuronal models of mammalian temperature regulation. In *Essays on Temperature Regulation* (eds J. Bligh and R. Moore), North-Holland, Amsterdam, pp. 105–120.

Bliss, T.V.P. and Lømo, T. (1973) Long-lasting potentiation of synaptic transmission in the dendate area of the anaesthetized rabbit following stimulation of the perforent path. *Journal of Physiology*, **232**, 331–356.

Block, N. (1991) Evidence against epiphenomenonalism. *Behavioral and Brain Sciences*, **14**, 670–672.

Blumberg, M.S. and Sokoloff, G. (1998) Thermoregulatory competence and behavioral expression in the young of altricial species – revisited. *Developmental Psychobiology*, **33**, 107–123.

Boatman, D. (2004) Cortical bases of speech perception: evidence from functional lesion studies. *Cognition*, **92**, 47–65.

Bohus, B. and de Kloet, E.R. (1981) Adrenal steroids and extinction behaviour: antagonism by progesterone, deoxycorticosterone and dexamethesone of a specific effect of corticosterone. *Life Sciences*, **28**, 433–440.

Bohus, B. and Koolhaas, J.M. (1993) Stress and the cardiovascular system: central and peripheral physiological mechanisms. In *Stress – From Synapse to Syndrome* (eds S.C. Stanford and P. Salmon), Academic Press, London, pp. 75–117.

Bolles, R.C. (1970) Species-specific defense reactions and avoidance learning. *Psychological Review*, **77**, 32–48.

Bolles, R.C. (1980) Historical note on the term 'appetite'. *Appetite*, **1**, 3–6.

Bolles, R.C. and Fanselow, M.S. (1980) A perceptual–defensive–recuperative model of fear and pain. *Behavioral and Brain Sciences*, **3**, 291–323.

Bolton, D. and Hill, J. (1996) *Mind, Meaning, and Mental Disorder – The Nature of Causal Explanation in Psychology and Psychiatry*, Oxford University Press, Oxford.

Bondi, M.W., Salmon, D.P., Galasko, D., Thomas, R.G. and Thal, L.J. (1999) Neuropsychological function and apolipoprotein E genotype in the preclinical detection of Alzheimer's disease. *Psychology and Aging*, **14**, 295–303.

Bonner, J.T. (1958) *The Evolution of Development*, Cambridge University Press, Cambridge.

Booth, D.A. (1978) *Hunger Models: Computable Theory of Feeding Control*, Academic Press, London.

Booth, D.A. (1979) Metabolism and the control of feeding in man and animals. In *Chemical Influences on Behaviour* (eds K. Brown and S.J. Cooper), Academic Press, London, pp. 79–134.

Booth, D.A. (1980) Acquired behaviour controlling energy intake and output. In *Obesity* (ed. A.J. Stunkard), W.B. Saunders, Philadelphia, pp. 101–143.

Booth, D.A. (1993a) *Neurophysiology of Ingestion*, Pergamon Press, Oxford.

Booth, D.A. (1993b) A framework for neurophysiological studies of ingestion. In *Neurophysiology of Ingestion* (ed. D.A. Booth), Pergamon Press, Oxford, pp. 1–17.

Booth, D.A. and Toates, F.M. (1974) A physiological control theory of food intake in the rat. *Bulletin of the Psychonomic Society*, **3**, 442–444.

Borchgrevink, H.M. (1989) Cerebral processes underlying neuropsychological and neuromotor impairment in children with ADD/MBD. In *Attention Deficit Disorder: Clinical and Basic Research* (eds T. Sagvolden and T. Archer), Lawrence Erlbaum, Hillsdale, pp. 105–130.

Both, S., van Boxtel, G., Stekelenburg, J., Everaerd, W. and Laan, E. (2005) Modulation of spinal reflexes by sexual films of increasing intensity. *Psychophysiology*, **42**, 726–731.

Boule, M. and Anthony, R. (1911) L'encéphale de l'homme fossile de la Chapelle-aux-Saints. *L'Anthropologie*, **22**, 129–196.

Boussaoud, D., di Pellegrino, G. and Wise, S.P. (1996) Frontal lobe mechanisms subserving vision-for-action versus vision-for-perception. *Behavioural Brain Research*, **72**, 1–15.

Bovard, E.W. (1985) Brain mechanisms in effects of social support on viability. In *Perspectives in Behavioral Medicine*, Vol. 2 (ed. R.B.Williams), Academic Press, Orlando, pp. 103–129.

Bower, G.H. (1992) How might emotions affect learning? In *The Handbook of Emotion and Memory – Research and Theory* (ed. S-A. Christianson), Lawrence Erlbaum, Hillsdale, pp. 3–31.

Bowlby, J. (1973) *Attachment and Loss*, Vol. II, *Separation*, Hogarth Press, London.

Bowmaker, J.K. and Dartnall, H.J.A. (1980) Visual pigments or rods and cones in a human retina. *Journal of Physiology*, **298**, 501–511.

Bowman, M.L. (1997) Brain impairment in impulsive violence. In *Impulsivity – Theory, Assessment, and Treatment* (eds C.D. Webster and M.A. Jackson), Guilford Press, New York, pp. 116–141.

Bozarth, M.A. (1987) *Methods of Assessing the Reinforcing Properties of Abused Drugs*, Springer-Verlag, New York.

Bracke, P.E. and Thoresen, C.E. (1996) Reducing Type A behavior patterns: a structured-group approach. In *Heart and Mind. The Practice of Cardiac Psychology* (eds R. Allan, and S. Scheidt), American Psychological Association, Washington, pp. 255–290.

Brady, J. (1979) *Biological Clocks*, Edward Arnold, London.

Brain, P.F. (1979) Effects of the hormones of the pituitary–gonadal axis on behaviour. In *Chemical Influences on Behaviour* (eds K. Brown and S.J. Cooper), Academic Press, London, pp. 255–329.

Brandt, J. and Rich, J.B. (1995) Memory disorders in the dementias. In *Handbook of Memory Disorders* (eds A.D. Baddeley, B.A.Wilson and F.N.Watts), Wiley, Chichester, pp. 243–270.

Bray, G.A. (1980) Jejunoileal bypass, jaw wiring, and vagotomy for massive obesity. In *Obesity* (ed. A.J. Stunkard), W.B. Saunders, Philadelphia, pp. 369–387.

Breier, A., Kelsoe, J.R., Kirwin, P.D., Beller, S.A., Wolkowitz, O.M. and Pickar, D. (1988) Early parental loss and development of adult psychopathology. *Archives of General Psychiatry*, **45**, 987–993.

Bremner, J.D. (1999) Does stress damage the brain? *Biological Psychiatry*, **45**, 797–805.

Brennan, P.A. and Keverne, E.B. (2004) Something in the air? New insights into mammalian pheromones. *Current Biology*, **14**, R81-R89.

Broadbent, D.E. (1958) *Perception and Communication*, Pergamon Press, Oxford.

Broca, M. (1861) Perte de la parole, ramollissement chronique et destruction partielle du lobe antérieur gauche du cerveau. *Bulletin de la Société Anthropologie*, **2**, 235–238.

Bromm, B. (1995) Consciousness, pain and cortical activity. In *Pain and the Brain: From Nociception to Cognition* (Advances in Pain Research and Therapy, Vol. 22) (eds B. Bromm and J.E. Desmedt), Raven Press, New York, pp. 35–59.

Bronson, G.W. (1982) Structure, status, and characteristics of the nervous system at birth. In *Psychobiology of the Human Newborn* (ed. P. Stratton), Wiley, Chichester, pp. 99–118.

Brown, A.S., van Os, J., Driessens, C., Hoek, H.W. and Susser, E.S. (2000) Further evidence of relation between prenatal famine and major affective disorder. *American Journal of Psychiatry*, **157**, 190–195.

Brown, M., Keynes, R. and Lumsden, A. (2001) *The Developing Brain*. Oxford University Press, Oxford.

Brown, M.C. (1999) Audition. In *Fundamental Neuroscience* (eds M.J. Zigmond, F.E. Bloom, S.C. Landis, J.L. Roberts and L.R. Squire), Academic Press, San Diego, pp. 791–820.

Bruce, C., Desimone, R. and Gross, C.G. (1981) Visual properties of neurons in a polysensory area in superior temporal sulcus in the macaque. *Journal of Neurophysiology*, **46**, 369–384.

Bruch, H. (1974) *Eating Disorders*, Routledge and Kegan Paul, London.

Bruer, J.T. (1998) Brain and child development: time for some critical thinking. *Public Health Reports*, **113**, 388–397.

Buffum, J., Moser, C. and Smith, D. (1988) Street drugs and sexual function. In *Handbook of Sexology*. Vol. 6: *The Pharmacology and Endocrinology of Sexual Function* (ed. J.M.A. Sitsen), Elsevier Science Publishers, Amsterdam, pp. 462–477.

Buller, D.J. (2005) *Adapting Minds: Evolutionary Psychology and the Persistent Quest for Human Nature*, MIT Press, Cambridge.

Bullier, J. (2004) Communications between cortical areas of the visual system. In *The Visual Neurosciences* (Vol. 1) (eds L.M. Chalupa and J.S. Werner), MIT Press, Cambridge, pp. 522–540.

Bullmore, E. and Fletcher, P. (2003) The eye's mind: brain mapping and psychiatry. *British Journal of Psychiatry*, **182**, 381–384.

Burell, G. (1996) Group psychotherapy in project new life: treatment of coronary-prone behaviors for patients who have had coronary artery bypass graft surgery. In *Heart and Mind. The Practice of Cardiac Psychology* (eds R. Allan and S. Scheidt), American Psychological Association, Washington, pp. 291–310.

Burgdorf, J. and Panksepp, J. (2006) The neurobiology of positive emotions. *Neuroscience and Biobehavioral Reviews*, **30**, 173–187.

Burns, A. (2005) *A Guide to Alzheimer's Disease*, Hodder Arnold, London.

Burton, H. and Sinclair, R. (1996) Somatosensory cortex and tactile perceptions. In *Pain and Touch* (ed. L. Kruger), Academic Press, San Diego, pp. 105–177.

Buss, D.M. (1999) *Evolutionary Psychology: The New Science of the Mind*, Allyn & Bacon, Boston.

Buss, D.M. (2005) *The Handbook of Evolutionary Psychology*, Wiley, New York.

Buss, D.M., Larsen, R.J., Westen, D. and Semmelroth, J. (1992) Sex differences in jealousy: evolution, physiology and psychology. *Psychological Science*, **3**, 251–255.

Buss, D.M., Larsen, R.J. and Westen, D. (1996) Sex differences in jealousy: not gone, not forgotten, and not explained by alternative hypotheses. *Psychological Science*, **7**, 373–375.

Buss, D.M., Haselton, M.G., Shackelford, T.K., Bleske, A.L. and Wakefield, J.C. (1998) Adaptations, exaptations, and spandrels. *American Psychologist*, **53**, 533–548.

Butler, A.B. and Hodos, W. (1996) *Comparative Vertebrate Neuroanatomy: Evolution and Adaptation*, Wiley, New York.

Butters, N. and Cermak, L.S. (1986) A case study of the forgetting of autobiographical knowledge: implications for the study of retrograde amnesia. In *Autobiographical Memory* (ed. D.C. Rubin), Cambridge University Press, Cambridge, pp. 253–272.

Cabanac, M. (1971) Physiological role of pleasure. *Science*, **173**, 1103–1107.

Cabanac, M. (1979) Sensory pleasure. *Quarterly Review of Biology*, **54**, 1–29.

Cabanac, M. (1992) Pleasure: the common currency. *Journal of Theoretical Biology*, **155**, 173–200.

Cabanac, M. (1998), Thermiatrics and behavior. In *Physiology and Pathophysiology of Temperature Regulation* (ed. C.M. Blatteis), World Scientific Publications, Singapore, pp. 107–125.

Cabanac, M. and Russek, M. (1982) *Régulation et Controle en Biologie*, Les Presses de l'Université Laval, Quebec.

Cacioppo, J.T. and Berntson, G.G. (1992) Social psychological contributions to the decade of the brain. *American Psychologist*, **47**, 1019–1028.

Cacioppo, J.T., Uchino, B.N., Crites, S.L., Snydersmith, M.A., Smith, G., Berntson, G.G. and Lang, P.J. (1992) Relationship between facial expressiveness and sympathetic activation in emotion: a critical review, with emphasis on modeling underlying mechanisms and individual differences. *Journal of Personality and Social Psychology*, **62**, 110–128.

Cahill, L., Haier, R.J., Fallon, J., Alkire, M.T., Tang, C., Keator, D., Wu, J. and McGaugh, J.L. (1996) Amygdala activity at encoding correlated with long-term, free recall of emotional information. *Proceedings of the National Academy of Sciences USA*, **93**, 8016–8021.

Cairns, R.B. (1979) *Social Development*, W.H. Freeman, San Francisco.

Campbell, A., Muncer, S. and Odber, J. (1997) Aggression and testosterone: testing a bio-social model. *Aggressive Behavior*, **23**, 229–238.

Camperio-Ciani, A., Corna, F. and Capiluppi, C. (2004) Evidence for maternally inherited factors favouring male homosexuality and promoting female fecundity. *Proceedings of the Royal Society of London B* **271**, 2217–2221.

Campfield, L.A. (1997) Metabolic and hormonal controls of food intake: highlights of the last 25 years – 1972–1997. *Appetite*, **29**, 135–152.

Cannon, W.B. (1927) The James–Lange theory of emotions: a critical examination and an alternative theory. *American Journal of Psychology*, **39**, 106–124.

Caplan, D. (1985) A neo-Cartesian alternative. *Behavioral and Brain Sciences*, **8**, 6–7.

Caplan, D., Carr, T., Gould, J. and Martin, R. (1999) Language and communication. In *Fundamental Neuroscience* (eds M.J. Zigmond, F.E. Bloom, S.C. Landis, J.L. Roberts and L.R. Squire), Academic Press, San Diego, pp. 1487–1519.

Carai, M.A.M., Colombo, G. and Gessa, G.L. (2005) Rimonabant: the first therapeutically relevant cannabinoid antagonist. *Life Sciences*, 77, 2339–2350.

Carlisle, H.J. (1966) Heat intake and hypothalamic temperature during behavioral temperature regulation. *Journal of Comparative and Physiological Psychology*, 61, 388–397.

Carlson, N.R. (1977) *Physiology of Behavior*, 1st edn, Allyn and Bacon, Boston.

Carlson, N.R. (1994) *Physiology of Behavior*, 5th edn, Allyn and Bacon, Boston.

Carlson, N.R. (1998) *Physiology of Behavior*, 6th edn, Allyn and Bacon, Boston.

Carlson, N.R. (2003) *Physiology of Behavior*, 8th edn, Allyn and Bacon, Boston.

Carlsson, A. (1988) The current status of the dopamine hypothesis of schizophrenia. *Neuropsychopharmacology*, 1, 179–203.

Carlsson, A. and Carlsson, M. (1991) A faulty negative feedback control underlies the schizophrenic syndrome? *Behavioral and Brain Sciences*, 14, 20–21.

Carlsson, K., Petersson, K.M., Lundqvist, D., Karlsson, A., Ingvar, M. and Öhman, A. (2004) Fear and the amygdala: manipulation of awareness generates differential cerebral responses to phobic and fear-relevant (but nonfeared) stimuli. *Emotion*, 4, 340–353.

Carpenter, A.F., Georgopoulos, A.P. and Pellizzer, G. (1999) Motor control encoding of serial order in a context-recall task. *Science*, 283, 1752–1757.

Carraher, R.G. and Thurston, J.B. (1996) *Optical Illusions and the Visual Arts*. Reinhold Publishing Corporation, New York

Carskadon, M.A. and Dement, W.C. (1994) Normal human sleep: an overview. In *Principles and Practice of Sleep Medicine* (eds M.H. Kryger, T. Roth and W.C. Dement), Saunders, Philadelphia, pp. 16–25.

Castanon, N. and Mormède, P. (1994) Psychobiogenetics: adapted tools for the study of the coupling between behavioral and neuroendocrine traits of emotional reactivity. *Psychoneuroendocrinology*, 19, 257–282.

Castellanos, F.X. and Swanson, J. (2002) Biological underpinnings of ADHD. In *Hyperactivity and Attention Disorders of Childhood* (2nd edition) (ed. S. Sandberg), Cambridge University Press, Cambridge, pp. 336–366.

Chalmers, D.J. (1996) *The Conscious Mind: In Search of a Fundamental Theory*, Oxford University Press, New York.

Chalupa, L.M. and Werner, J.S. (2004) *The Visual Neurosciences* (Vol. 1 and 2), MIT Press, Cambridge.

Chamberlain, S.R., Blackwell, A.D., Fineberg, N.A., Robbins, T.W. and Sahakian, B.J. (2005) The neuropsychology of obsessive compulsive disorder: the importance of failures in cognitive and behavioral inhibition as candidate endophenotypic markers. *Neuroscience and Biobehavioral Reviews*, 29, 399–419.

Chapman, C.R. (1995) The affective dimension of pain: a model. In *Pain and the Brain: From Nociception to Cognition* (Advances in Pain Research and Therapy, Vol. 22) (eds B. Bromm and J.E. Desmedt), Raven Press, New York, pp. 283–301.

Chapman, L.J. and Chapman, J.P. (1973) *Disordered Thought in Schizophrenia*, Appleton-Century-Croft, New York.

Charney, D.S., Deutch, A.Y., Southwick, S.M. and Krystal, J.H. (1995) Neural circuits and mechanisms of post-traumatic stress disorder. In *Neurobiological and Clinical Consequences of Stress. From Normal Adaptation to Post-traumatic Stress Disorder* (eds M.J. Friedman, D.S. Charney and A.Y. Deutch), Lippincott-Raven, Philadelphia, pp. 271–287.

Chaves, J.F. and Dworkin, S.F. (1997) Hypnotic control of pain: historical perspectives and future prospects. *International Journal of Clinical and Experimental Hypnosis*, XLV, 356–376.

Cherry, C. (1966) *On Human Communication: A Review, a Survey and a Criticism*, MIT Press, Cambridge.

Chertkow, H. and Bub, D. (1990) Semantic memory loss in Alzheimer-type dementia. In *Modular Deficits in Alzheimer-type Dementia* (ed. M.F. Schwartz), MIT Press, Cambridge, pp. 207–244.

Chi, J.G., Dooling, E.C. and Gilles, F.H. (1977) Left–right asymmetries of the temporal speech areas of the human fetus. *Archives of Neurology*, 34, 346–348.

Chiamulera, C. (2005) Cue reactivity in nicotine and tobacco dependence: a 'multiple-action' model of nicotine as a primary reinforcement and as an enhancer of the effects of smoking-associated stimuli. *Brain Research Reviews*, 48, 74–97.

Chick, J. and Erickson, C.K. (1996) Conference summary: consensus conference on alcohol dependence and the role of pharmacotherapy in its treatment. *Alcoholism: Clinical and Experimental Research*, 20, 391–402.

Childress, A.R., Mozley, P.D., McElgin, W., Fitzgerald, J., Reivich, M. and O'Brien, C.P. (1999) Limbic activation during cue-induced cocaine craving. *American Journal of Psychiatry*, 156, 11–18.

Chokroverty, S. (1994) *Sleep Disorders Medicine: Basic Science, Technical Considerations and Clinical Aspects*, Butterworth-Heinemann, Boston.

Chomsky, N. (1959) Review of 'Verbal Behaviour' by B.F. Skinner. *Language*, 35, 26–58.

Chorpita, B.F. and Barlow, D.H. (1998) The development of anxiety: the role of control in the early environment. *Psychological Bulletin*, 124, 3–21.

Christie, M.J., Williams, J.T., Osborne, P.G. and Bellchambers, C.E. (1997) Where is the locus in opioid withdrawal? *Trends in Pharmacological Sciences*, 18, 134–140.

Chugani, H.T. (1994) Development of regional brain metabolism in relation to behaviour and plasticity. In *Human Behavior and the Developing Brain* (eds G. Dawson and K.W. Fischer), Guilford Press, New York, pp. 153–175.

Chugani, H.T., Behen, M.E., Muzik, O., Juhász, C., Nagy, F. and Chugani, D.C. (2001) Local brain functional activity following early deprivation: a study of post institutionalized Romanian orphans. *Neuroimage*, 14, 1290–1301.

Chwalisz, K., Diener, E. and Gallagher, D. (1988) Autonomic arousal feedback and emotional experience: evidence from the spinal cord injured. *Journal of Personality and Social Psychology*, 54, 820–828.

Claparède, M.E. (1911) Récognition et Moïté. *Archives de Psychologie*, 11, 79–80.

Claridge, G. (1990) Can a disease model of schizophrenia survive? In *Reconstructing Schizophrenia* (ed. R.P. Bentall), Routledge, London, pp. 157–183.

Clark, B.J., Hines, D.J., Hamilton, D.A. and Whishaw, I.Q. (2005) Movements of exploration intact in rats with hippocampal lesions. *Behavioural Brain Research*, **163**, 91–99.

Clark, R.W. (1980) *Freud – The Man and the Cause*, Random House, New York.

Clayton, N.S. and Dickinson, A. (1998) Episodic-like memory during cache recovery by scrub jays. *Nature*, **395**, 272–274.

Clifton, P.G., Burton, M.J. and Sharp, C. (1987) Rapid loss of stimulus-specific satiety after consumption of a second food. *Appetite*, **9**, 149–156.

Clow, A. and Hucklebridge, F. (2002) *International Review of Neurobiology*. 52. *The Neurobiology of the Immune System*. Academic Press, New York.

Cobb, L.A., Thomas, G.I., Dillard, D.H., Merendino, K.A. and Bruce, R.A. (1959) An evaluation of internal-mammary-artery ligation by a double-blind technique. *New England Journal of Medicine*, **260**, 1115–1118.

Coccaro, E.F. (1989) Central serotonin and impulsive aggression. *British Journal of Psychiatry*, **155** (suppl. 8), 52–62.

Coenen, A.M.L. (1995) Neuronal activities underlying the electroencephalogram and evoked potentials of sleeping and waking: implications for information processing. *Neuroscience and Biobehavioral Reviews*, **19**, 447–463

Coenen, A.M.L. (1998) Neuronal phenomena associated with vigilance and consciousness: from cellular mechanisms to electroencephalographic patterns. *Consciousness and Cognition*, **7**, 42–53.

Cohen, D. (1979) *J.B. Watson – The Founder of Behaviourism*, Routledge and Kegan Paul, London.

Cohen, D. (1998) Shaping, channeling, and distributing testosterone in social systems. *Behavioral and Brain Sciences*, **21**, 367–368.

Cohen, D.B. (1979) *Sleep and Dreaming: Origins, Nature and Functions*, Pergamon Press, Oxford.

Cohen, G. (1990) Memory. In *Introduction to Psychology*, Vol. 2 (ed. I. Roth), Lawrence Erlbaum, Hove, pp. 570–621.

Cohen, J.D. and Servan-Schreiber, D. (1992) Context, cortex, and dopamine: a connectionist approach to behaviour and biology in schizophrenia. *Psychological Review*, **99**, 45–75.

Cohen, M.X., Young, J., Baek, J-M., Kessler, C. and Ranganath, C. (2005) Individual differences in extraversion and dopamine genetics predict neural reward responses. *Cognitive Brain Research*, **25**, 851–861.

Cohen, S. (1996) Psychological stress, immunity, and upper respiratory infections. *Current Directions in Psychological Science*, **5**, 86–90.

Cole, J. (1991) *Pride and a Daily Marathon*, Duckworth, London.

Coleman, E. (2005) Neuroanatomical and neurotransmitter dysfunction and compulsive sexual behavior. In *Biological Substrates of Human Sexuality* (ed. J.S. Hyde), American Psychological Association, Washington, pp. 147–169

Collingridge, G. (1997) Mind the gap. *Medical Research Council News*, No. 74, pp. 24–27.

Coltheart, M. (1985) Cognitive neuropsychology and the study of reading. In *Attention and Performance XI* (eds M.I. Posner and O.S.M. Marin), Lawrence Erlbaum, Hillsdale, pp. 3–37.

Cooper, B. (2005) Immigration and schizophrenia: the social causation hypothesis revisited. *British Journal of Psychiatry*, **186**, 361–363.

Cooper, C.L. and Dewe, P. (2004) *Stress: A Brief History*, Blackwell Publishing, Oxford.

Cooper, S.J. and Higgs, S. (1994) Neural processing related to feeding in primates. In *Appetite – Neural and Behavioural Bases* (eds C.R. Legg and D. Booth), Oxford University Press, Oxford, pp. 212–242.

Coover, G.D., Ursin, H. and Levine, S. (1973) Plasma-corticosterone levels during active-avoidance learning in rats. *Journal of Comparative and Physiological Psychology*, **82**, 170–174.

Corballis, M.C. (2003) *From Hand to Mouth: The Origins of Language*, Princeton University Press, Princeton.

Coren, S., Ward, L.M. and Enns, J.T. (1994) *Sensation and Perception*, Harcourt Brace, Fort Worth.

Corkin, S. (1968) Acquisition of motor skill after bilateral temporal-lobe excision. *Neuropsychologia*, **6**, 255–265.

Corkin, S. (2002) What's new with the amnesic patient H.M.? *Nature Reviews Neuroscience*, **3**, 153–160.

Corkin, S., Amaral, D.G., González, R.G., Johnson, K.A. and Hyman, B.T. (1997) H.M.'s medial temporal lobe lesion: findings from magnetic resonance imaging. *Journal of Neuroscience*, **17**, 3964–3979.

Corp, E.S., Curcio, M., Gibbs, J. and Smith, G.P. (1997) The effect of centrally administered CCK-receptor antagonists on food intake in rats. *Physiology and Behavior*, **61**, 823–827.

Coscina, D.V. (1997) The biopsychology of impulsivity: focus on brain serotonin. In *Impulsivity – Theory, Assessment, and Treatment* (eds C.D. Webster and M.A. Jackson), Guilford Press, New York, pp. 95–115.

Coté, L. and Crutcher, M.D. (1991) The basal ganglia. In *Principles of Neural Science* (eds E.R. Kandel, J.H. Schwartz and T.M. Jessell), Appleton and Lange, Norwalk, pp. 647–659.

Courchesne, E. and Allen, G. (1997) Prediction and preparation, fundamental functions of the cerebellum. *Learning and Memory*, **4**, 1–35.

Cowey, A. and Stoerig, P. (1995) Blindsight in monkeys. *Nature*, 373, 247–249.

Craig, A.D. (2003) Pain mechanisms: labelled lines versus convergence in central processing. *Annual Review of Neuroscience*, **26**, 1–30.

Craig, A.D. (2004) Human feelings: why are some more aware than others? *Trends in Cognitive Sciences*, **8**, 239–241.

Craig, K.D. (1994) Emotional aspects of pain. In *Textbook of Pain* (eds P.D. Wall and R. Melzack), Churchill Livingstone, Edinburgh, pp. 261–274.

Craig, K.D. (1995) From nociception to pain: the role of emotion. In *Pain and the Brain: From Nociception to Cognition* (Advances in Pain Research and Therapy, Vol. 22) (eds B. Bromm and J.E. Desmedt), Raven Press, New York, pp. 303–317.

Cravatt, B.F., Prospero-Garcia, O., Siuzdak, G., Gilula, N.B., Henriksen, S.J., Boger, D.L. and Lerner, R.A. (1995) Chemical characterization of a family of brain lipids that induce sleep. *Science*, **268**, 1506–1509.

Crick, F. (1994) *The Astonishing Hypothesis: The Scientific Search for the Soul*, Simon and Schuster, London.

Critchley, H.D., Wiens, S., Rotshtein, P., Öhman, A. and Dolan, R.J. (2004) Neural systems supporting interoceptive awareness. *Nature Neuroscience*, 7, 189–195.

Cullinan, W.E., Herman, J.P., Helmreich, D.L. and Watson, S.J. (1995) A neuroanatomy of stress. In *Neurobiological and Clinical Consequences of Stress. From Normal Adaptation to Post-traumatic Stress Disorder* (eds M.J. Friedman, D.S. Charney and A.Y. Deutch), Lippincott-Raven, Philadelphia, pp. 3–26.

Curran, H.V. and Kopelman, M.D. (1996) The cognitive psychopharmacology of Alzheimer's disease. In *The Cognitive Neuropsychology of Alzheimer-type Dementia* (ed R.G. Morris), Oxford University Press, Oxford, pp. 255–277.

Curtis, A.L. and Valentino, R.J. (1994) Corticotropin-releasing factor neurotransmission in locus coeruleus: a possible site of anti-depressant action. *Brain Research Bulletin*, 35, 581–587.

Cutler, W.B. (1999) Human sex-attractant pheromones: discovery, research, development, and application in sex therapy. *Psychiatric Annals*, 29, 54–59.

Cutler, W.B. and Genovese-Stone, E. (1998) Wellness in women after 40 years of age: the role of sex hormones and pheromones. *Disease-a-Month*, 44, 423–546.

Cutler, W.B., Freidman, E. and McCoy, N.L. (1998) Pheromonal influences on sociosexual behavior in men. *Archives of Sexual Behaviour*, 27, 1–13.

Dabbs, J.M. (2000) *Heroes, Rogues and Lovers*, McGraw-Hill, New York.

Dabbs, J.M., Karpas, A.E., Dyomina, N., Juechter, J. and Roberts, A. (2002) Experimental raising or lowering of testosterone level affects mood in normal men and women. *Social Behavior and Personality*, 30, 795–806.

Damasio, A.R. (1996) *Descartes' Error*, Papermac, London.

Damasio, A.R. (1999) *The Feeling of What Happens: Body and Emotion in the Making of Consciousness*, Harcourt Brace, New York.

Damasio, A.R. and Damasio, H. (1983) The anatomic basis of pure alexia. *Neurology*, 33, 1573–1583.

Damasio, A.R. and Geschwind, N. (1984) The neural basis of language. *Annual Review of Neuroscience* (eds W.M. Cowan, E.M. Shooter, C.F. Stevens and R.F. Thompson), Annual Reviews Inc., Palo Alto, pp. 127–147.

Damasio, A.R., Van Hoesen, G.W. and Hyman, B.T. (1990) Reflections on the selectivity of neuropathological changes in Alzheimer's disease. In *Modular Deficits in Alzheimer-type Dementia* (ed. M.F. Schwartz), MIT Press, Cambridge, pp. 83–100.

Damasio, H., Grabowski, T., Frank, R., Galaburda, A.M. and Damasio, A.R. (1994) The return of Phineas Gage: clues about the brain from the skull of a famous patient. *Science*, 264, 5162, 1102–1105.

Dampney, R. (1990) The subretrofacial nucleus: its pivotal role in cardiovascular regulation. *News in Physiological Sciences*, 5, 63–67.

Dampney, R.A.L. (1994) Functional organization of central pathways regulating the cardiovascular system. *Physiological Reviews*, 74, 323–364.

Dani, J.A. and Heinemann, S. (1996) Molecular and cellular aspects of nicotine abuse. *Neuron*, 16, 905–908.

Dantzer, R. (1986) Behavioural, physiological and functional aspects of stereotyped behaviour: a review and a reinterpretation. *Journal of Animal Science*, 62, 1776–1786.

Darian-Smith, I. (1984) The sense of touch: performance and peripheral neural processes. In *Handbook of Physiology*. Section 1: *The Nervous System*, Vol. III, Part 2 (ed. I. Darian-Smith), American Physiological Society, Bethesda, pp. 739–788.

Darling, C.A., Davidson, J.K. and Jennings, D.A. (1991) The female sexual response revisited: understanding the multiorgasmic experience in women. *Archives of Sexual Behavior*, 20, 527–540.

Darwin, C. (1872/1934) *The Expression of the Emotions in Man and Animals*, Watts and Co., London.

Darwin, C. (1874/1974) *The Descent of Man and Selection in Relation to Sex*, Rand, McNally and Co., Chicago.

Davidson, D. and Amit, Z. (1997) Effect of ethanol drinking and naltrexone on subsequent drinking in rats. *Alcohol*, 14, 581–584.

Davidson, R.J. (1984) Hemispheric asymmetry and emotion. In *Approaches to Emotion* (eds K.R. Scherer and P. Ekman), Lawrence Erlbaum, Hillsdale, pp. 39–57.

Davidson, R.J. (2003) Affective neuroscience and psychophysiology: toward a synthesis. *Psychophysiology*, 40, 655–665.

Davidson, R.J., Pizzagalli, D., Nitschke J.B. and Putnam, K. (2002) Depression: perspectives from affective neuroscience. *Annual Review of Psychology*, 53, 545–574.

Davidson, R.J., Scherer, K.R. and Goldsmith, H.H. (2003) *Handbook of Affective Sciences*, Oxford University Press, New York.

Davis, B.D. (1985) Sleep and the maintenance of memory. *Perspectives in Biology and Medicine*, 28, 457–464.

Davis, C. and Claridge, G. (1998) The eating disorders as addiction: a psychobiological perspective. *Addictive Behaviors*, 23, 463–475.

Davis, C., Levitan, R.D., Muglia, P., Bewell, C. and Kennedy, J.L. (2004) Decision-making deficits and overeating: a risk model for obesity. *Obesity Research*, 12, 929–935.

Davis, K.L., Kahn, R.S., Ko, G. and Davidson, M. (1991) Dopamine in schizophrenia: a review and reconceptualization. *American Journal of Psychiatry*, 148, 1474–1486.

Davis, L.L., Suris, A., Lambert, M.T., Heimberg, C. and Petty, F. (1997) Post-traumatic stress disorder and serotonin: new directions for research and treatment. *Journal of Psychiatry and Neuroscience*, 22, 318–326.

Davis, M. (1992) Analysis of aversive memories using the fear-potentiated startle paradigm. In *Neuropsychology of Memory* (eds L.R. Squire and N. Butters), Guilford Press, New York, pp. 470–484.

Dawkins, R. (1976) *The Selfish Gene*, Oxford University Press, Oxford.

Dawson, G. (1994) Development of emotional expression and emotion regulation in infancy – contributions of the frontal lobe. In *Human Behavior and the Developing Brain* (eds G. Dawson and K.W. Fischer), Guilford Press, New York, pp. 346–379.

Deacon, T.W. (1997) What makes the human brain different? *Annual Review of Anthropology*, 26, 337–357.

de Araujo, I.E.T., Kringelbach, M.L., Rolls, E.T. and Hobden, P. (2003) Representation of umami taste in the human brain. *Journal of Neurophysiology*, **90**, 313–319.

DeCasper, A.J. and Fifer, W.P. (1980) Of human bonding: newborns prefer their mothers' voices. *Science*, **208**, 1174–1176.

Decety, J. and Michel, F. (1989) Comparative analysis of actual and mental movement times in two graphic tasks. *Brain and Cognition*, **11**, 87–97.

Decety, J., Jeannerod, M. and Prablanc, C. (1989) The timing of mentally represented actions. *Behavioural Brain Research*, **34**, 35–42.

Decety, J., Sjöholm, H., Ryding, E., Stenberg, G. and Ingvar, D.H. (1990) The cerebellum participates in mental activity: tomographic measurements of regional cerebral blood flow. *Brain Research*, **535**, 313–317.

Decety, J., Jeannerod, M., Germain, M. and Pastene, J. (1991) Vegetative response during imagined movement is proportional to mental effort. *Behavioural Brain Research*, **42**, 1–5.

Decety, J., Jeannerod, M., Durozard, D. and Baverel, G. (1993) Central activation of autonomic effectors during mental simulation of motor actions. *Journal of Physiology*, **461**, 549–563.

de Groat, W.C. and Booth, A.M. (1993) Neural control of penile erection. In *Nervous Control of the Urogenital System* (ed. C.A. Maggi), Harwood Academic, Chur, pp. 467–524.

Dehaene, S. and Changeux, J-P. (1989) A simple model of prefrontal cortex function in delayed-response tasks. *Journal of Cognitive Neuroscience*, **1**, 244–261.

Dehaene, S. and Naccache, L. (2001) Towards a cognitive neuroscience of consciousness: basic evidence and a workspace framework. *Cognition*, **79**, 1–37.

de la Fuente-Fernández, R., Phillips, A.G., Zamburlini, M., Sossi, V., Calne, D.B., Ruth, T.J. and Stoessl, A.J. (2002) Dopamine release in human ventral striatum and expectation of reward. *Behavioural Brain Research*, **136**, 359–363.

de Lanerolle, N.C. and Lang, F.F. (1988) Functional neural pathways for vocalization in the domestic cat. In *The Physiological Control of Mammalian Vocalization* (ed. J.P. Newman), Plenum Press, New York, pp. 21–41.

Delgado, P.L. and Moreno, F.A. (1998) Hallucinogens, serotonin and obsessive-compulsive disorder. *Journal of Psychoactive Drugs*, **30**, 359–366.

Dement, W. (2001) *The Promise of Sleep: The Scientific Connection between Health, Happiness and a Good Night's Sleep*, Pan Macmillan, London.

Dement, W.C. (1994) History of sleep physiology and medicine. In *Principles and Practice of Sleep Medicine* (eds M.H. Kryger, T. Roth and W.C. Dement), Saunders, Philadelphia, pp. 3–15.

Dennett, D.C. (1993) *Consciousness Explained*, Penguin, Harmondsworth.

Denney, C.B. and Rapport, M.D. (2001) Cognitive pharmacology of stimulants in children with ADHD. In *Stimulant Drugs and ADHD: Basic and Clinical Neuroscience* (eds M.V. Solanto, A.F.T. Arnsten and F.X. Castellanos), Oxford University Press, Oxford, pp. 283–302.

Depue, R.A. and Collins, P.F. (1999) Neurobiology of the structure of personality: dopamine, facilitation of incentive motivation, and extraversion. *Behavioral and Brain Sciences*, **22**, 491–569.

Depue, R.A. and Morrone-Strupinsky, J.V. (2005) A neurobehavioral model of affiliative bonding: implications for conceptualizing a human trait of affiliation. *Behavioral and Brain Sciences*, **28**, 313–395.

Depue, R.A. and Spoont, M.R. (1986) Conceptualizing a serotonin trait – a basic dimension of constraint. *Annals of the New York Academy of Sciences*, **487**, 47–62.

de Quervain, D.J-F., Fischbacher, U., Treyer, V., Schellhammer, M., Schnyder, U., Buck, A. and Fehr, E. (2004) The neural basis of altruistic punishment. *Science*, **305**, 1254–1258.

Deroche-Gamonet, V., Belin, D. and Piazza, P.V. (2004) Evidence for addiction-like behavior in the rat. *Science*, **305**, 1014–1017.

Deschenes, M., Veinante, P. and Zhang, Z-W. (1998) The organization of corticothalamic projections: reciprocity versus parity. *Brain Research Reviews*, **28**, 286–308.

Desimone, R. (1992) Neural circuits for visual attention in the primate brain. In *Neural Networks for Vision and Image Processing* (eds G.A. Carpenter and S. Grossberg), MIT Press, Cambridge, pp. 343–364.

D'Esposito, M., Detre, J.A., Alsop, D.C., Shin, R.K., Atlas, S. and Grossman, M. (1995) The neural basis of the central executive system of working memory. *Nature*, **378**, 279–281.

DeSteno, D.A. and Salovey, P. (1996) Evolutionary origins of sex differences in jealousy? Questioning the 'fitness' of the model. *Psychological Science*, **7**, 367–372.

Deutch, A.Y. and Roth, R.H. (1999) Neurotransmitters. In *Fundamental Neuroscience* (eds M.J. Zigmond, F.E. Bloom, S.C. Landis, J.L. Roberts and L.R. Squire), Academic Press, San Diego, pp. 193–234.

Deutch, A.Y., Bourdelais, A.J. and Zahm, D.S. (1993) The nucleus accumbens core and shell: accumbal compartments and their functional attributes. In *Limbic Motor Circuits and Neuropsychiatry* (eds P.W. Kalivas and C.D. Barnes), CRC Press, Boca Raton, pp. 45–88.

Deutsch, J.A. (1983) Dietary control and the stomach. *Progress in Neurobiology*, **20**, 313–332.

De Valois, R.L. and De Valois, K.K. (1980) Spatial vision. *Annual Review of Psychology*, **31**, 309–341.

de Veer, M.W. and van den Bos, R. (1999) A critical review of methodology and interpretation of mirror self-recognition research in nonhuman primates. *Animal Behaviour*, **58**, 459–468.

Dewsbury, D.A. (1981) Effects of novelty on copulatory behavior: the Coolidge effect and related phenomena. *Psychological Bulletin*, **89**, 464–482.

Diamond, A. (1996) Evidence for the importance of dopamine for prefrontal cortex functions early in life. *Philosophical Transactions of the Royal Society of London B*, **351**, 1483–1494.

Diamond, A., Ciaramitaro, V., Donner, E., Kjali, S. and Robinson, M.B. (1994a) An animal model of early-treated PKU. *Journal of Neuroscience*, **14**, 3072–3082.

Diamond, A., Werker, J.F. and Lalonde, C. (1994b) Toward understanding commonalities in the development of object search, detour navigation, categorization, and speech perception. In *Human Behavior and the Developing Brain* (eds G. Dawson and K.W. Fischer), Guilford Press, New York, pp. 380–426.

Diamond, L.M. (2004) Emerging perspectives on distinctions between romantic love and sexual desire. *Current Directions in Psychological Science*, **13**, 116–119.

Dickerson, J.W.T. (1981) Nutrition, brain growth and development. In *Maturation and Development: Biological and Psychological Perspectives* (eds K.J. Connolly and H.F.R. Prechtl), William Heinemann Medical Books, London, pp. 110–130.

Dickinson, A. and Balleine, B. (1992) Actions and responses: the dual psychology of behaviour. In *Problems in the Philosophy and Psychology of Spatial Representation* (eds N. Eilan, R.A. McCarthy and M.W. Brewer), Blackwell, Oxford, pp. 277–293.

Dienstbier, R.A. (1989) Arousal and physiological toughness: implications for mental and physical health. *Psychological Review*, **96**, 84–100.

Dijk, D-J. (1997) Physiology of sleep homeostasis and its circadian regulation. In *Sleep Science: Integrating Basic Research and Clinical Practice. Monographs in Clinical Neuroscience*, Vol. 15 (ed. W.J. Schwartz), Karger, Basle, pp. 10–33.

Di Pellegrino, G., Fadiga, L., Fogassi, L., Gallese, V. and Rizzolatti, G. (1992) Understanding motor events: a neurophysiological study. *Experimental Brain Research*, **91**, 176–180.

Dismukes, R.K. (1979) New concepts of molecular communication among neurons. *Behavioral and Brain Sciences*, **2**, 409–448.

Dobbing, J. (1976) Vulnerable periods in brain growth and somatic growth. In *The Biology of Human Fetal Growth* (eds D.F. Roberts and A.M. Thomson), Taylor and Francis, London, pp. 137–147.

Dodd, J. and Castellucci, V.F. (1991) Smell and taste: the chemical senses. In *Principles of Neural Science* (eds E.R. Kandel, J.H. Schwartz and T.M. Jessell), Appleton and Lange, Norwalk, pp. 512–529.

Dolan, R.J., Fink, G.R., Rolls, E., Booth, M., Holmes, A., Frackowiak, R.S.J. and Friston, K.J. (1997) How the brain learns to see objects and faces in an impoverished context. *Nature*, **389**, 596–599.

Dominey, P., Decety, J., Broussolle, E., Chazot, G. and Jeannerod, M. (1995) Motor imagery of a lateralized sequential task is asymmetrically slowed in hemi-Parkinson's patients. *Neuropsychologia*, **33**, 727–741.

Domjan, M. (1994) Formulation of a behavior system for sexual conditioning. *Psychonomic Bulletin and Review*, **1**, 421–428.

Domjan, M., Blesbois, E. and Williams, J. (1998) The adaptive significance of sexual conditioning: Pavlovian control of sperm release. *Psychological Science*, **9**, 411–415.

Donald, M. (1991) *Origins of the Modern Mind: Three Stages in the Evolution of Culture and Cognition*, Harvard University Press, Cambridge.

Donny, E.C., Caggiula, A.R., Mielke, M.M., Jacobs, K.S., Rose, C. and Sved, A.F. (1998) Acquisition of nicotine self-administration in rats: the effects of dose, feeding schedule and drug contingency. *Psychopharmacology*, **136**, 83–90.

Doran, M. and Gadian, D.G. (1992) Magnetic resonance imaging and spectroscopy of the brain. In *Quantitative Methods in Neuroanatomy* (ed. M. Stewart), Wiley, Chichester, pp. 163–179.

Douglas, L.A., Varlinskaya, E.I. and Spear, L.P. (2003) Novel-object place conditioning in adolescent and adult male and female rats: effects of social isolation. *Physiology and Behavior*, **80**, 317–325.

Doyle, T.G., Berridge, K.C. and Gosnell, B.A. (1993) Morphine enhances hedonic taste palatability in rats. *Pharmacology Biochemistry and Behavior*, **46**, 745–749.

Drevets, W.C. (2001) Neuroimaging and neuropathological studies of depression: implications for the cognitive-emotional features of mood disorders. *Current Opinion in Neurobiology*, **11**, 240–249.

Drevets, W.C., Price, J.L., Simpson, J.R., Todd, R.D., Reich, T., Vannier, M. and Raiche, M.E. (1997) Subgenual prefrontal cortex abnormalities in mood disorders. *Nature*, **386**, 824–827.

Driver, J. and Spence, C.J. (1994) Spatial synergies between auditory and visual attention. In *Attention and Performance XV* (eds C. Umiltà and M. Moscovitch), MIT Press, Cambridge, pp. 311–332.

Dudai, Y. (2002) *Memory from A to Z: Keywords, Concepts and Beyond*, Oxford University Press, Oxford.

Duhamel, J-R., Colby, C.L. and Goldberg, M.E. (1992) The updating of the representation of visual space in parietal cortex by intended eye movements. *Science*, **255**, 90–92.

Duncan, J. (1986) Disorganization of behaviour after frontal lobe damage. *Cognitive Neuropsychology*, **3**, 271–290.

Duncan, J. (1993) Selection of input and goal in the control of behaviour. In *Attention: Selection, Awareness, and Control – A Tribute to Donald Broadbent* (eds A. Baddeley and L. Weiskrantz), Clarendon Press, Oxford, pp. 53–71.

Dunn, A.J. (1989) Psychoneuroimmunology for the psychoneuroendocrinologist: a review of animal studies of nervous system–immune system interactions. *Psychoneuroendocrinology*, **14**, 251–274.

Dunn, A.J. and Berridge, C.W. (1990) Physiological and behavioral responses to corticotropin-releasing factor administration: is CRF a mediator of anxiety or stress responses? *Brain Research Reviews*, **15**, 71–100.

Eccles, J.C. (1989) *Evolution of the Brain: Creation of the Self*, Routledge, London.

Eccleston, C. and Crombez, G. (1999) Pain demands attention: a cognitive–affective model of the interruptive function of pain. *Psychological Bulletin*, **125**, 356–366.

Edelman, G.M. (1987) *Neural Darwinism*, Oxford University Press, Oxford.

Edelman, N.H. (1994) Foreword. In *Sleep Disorders Medicine: Basic Science, Technical Considerations and Clinical Aspects* (ed. S. Chokroverty), Butterworth-Heinemann, Boston, pp. 219–239.

Edelman, S. and Kidman, A.D. (1997) Mind and cancer: is there a relationship? – A review of evidence. *Australian Psychologist*, **32**, 1–7.

Ehrlichman, H. and Bastone, L. (1992) Olfaction and emotion. In *Science of Olfaction* (eds M.J. Serby and K.L. Chobar), Springer-Verlag, New York, pp. 410–438.

Ehrlichman, H., Kuhl, S.B., Zhu, J. and Warrenburg, S. (1997) Startle reflex modulation by pleasant and unpleasant odors in a between-subjects design. *Psychophysiology*, **34**, 726–729.

Eichelman, B. (1988) Toward a rational pharmacotherapy for aggressive and violent behavior. *Hospital and Community Psychiatry*, **39**, 31–39.

Eichenbaum, H. (1994) The hippocampal system and declarative memory in humans and animals: experimental analysis and historical origins. In *Memory Systems 1994* (eds D.L. Schacter and E. Tulving), MIT Press, Cambridge, pp.147–201.

Eichenbaum, H. and Cohen, N.J. (2001) *From Conditioning to Conscious Recollection*. Oxford University Press, New York.

Eisenberger, N.I. and Lieberman, M.D. (2004) Why rejection hurts: a common neural alarm system for physical and social pain. *Trends in Cognitive Sciences*, **8**, 294–300.

Eisenberger, N.I., Lieberman, M.D. and Williams, K.D. (2003) Does rejection hurt? An fMRI study of social exclusion. *Science*, **302**, 290–292.

Ekman, P. (1984) Expression and the nature of emotion. In *Approaches to Emotion* (eds K.R. Scherer and P. Ekman), Lawrence Erlbaum, Hillsdale, pp. 319–343.

Ekman, P. (1992) Facial expressions of emotion: new findings, new questions. *Psychological Science*, **3**, 34–38.

Ekman, P., Levenson, R.W. and Friesen, W.V. (1983) Autonomic nervous system activity distinguishes among emotions. *Science*, **221**, 1208–1210.

Elbert, T., Pantev, C., Wienbruch, C., Rockstroh, B. and Taub, E. (1995) Increased cortical representation of the fingers of the left hand in string players. *Science*, **270**, 305–307.

Ellenbroek, B.A. and Cools, A.R. (1990) Animal models with construct validity for schizophrenia. *Behavioural Pharmacology*, **1**, 469–490.

Ellinwood, E.H. (1967) Amphetamine psychosis: I. Description of the individuals and process. *Journal of Nervous and Mental Disease*, **144**, 273–283.

Ellinwood, E.H. (1968) Amphetamine psychosis: II. Theoretical implications. *International Journal of Neuropsychiatry*, **4**, 45–54.

Ellinwood, E.H. and Escalante, O. (1970) Chronic amphetamine effect on the olfactory forebrain. *Biological Psychiatry*, **2**, 189–203.

Ellinwood, E.H. and Kilbey, M.M. (1975) Amphetamine stereotypy: the influence of environmental factors and prepotent behavioral patterns on its topography and development. *Biological Psychiatry*, **10**, 3–16.

Ellison, J.M. (1998) Antidepressant-induced sexual dysfunction: review, classification, and suggestions for treatment. *Harvard Review of Psychiatry*, **6**, 177–189.

Elman, J.L., Bates, E.A., Johnson, M.H., Karmiloff-Smith, A., Parisi, D. and Plunkett, K. (1996) *Rethinking Innateness. A Connectionist Perspective on Development*, MIT Press, Cambridge.

Emerson, E. and Howard, D. (1992) Schedule-induced stereotypy. *Research in Developmental Disabilities*, **13**, 335–361.

Engel, L.W., Guess, H.A., Kleinman, A. and Kusek, J.W. (2002) *The Science of the Placebo: Toward an Interdisciplinary Research Agenda*, BMJ Books, London.

Engelien, A., Huber, W., Silbersweig, D., Stern, E., Frith, C.D., Döring, W., Thron, A. and Frackowiak, R.S.J. (2000) The neural correlates of 'deaf-hearing' in man. *Brain*, **123**, 532–545.

Engell, D. and Hirsch, E. (1991) Environmental and sensory modulation of fluid intake in humans. In *Thirst: Physiological and Psychological Aspects* (eds D.J. Ramsey and D. Booth), Springer-Verlag, London, pp. 382–390.

Epstein, A.N. (1982) Instinct and motivation as explanations for complex behavior. In *The Physiological Mechanisms of Motivation* (ed. D.W. Pfaff), Springer, New York, pp. 25–58.

Epstein, A.N. (1990) Prospectus: thirst and salt appetite. In *Handbook of Behavioral Neurobiology*, Vol. 10, *Neurobiology of Food and Fluid Intake* (ed. E.M. Stricker), Plenum Press, New York, pp. 489–512.

Epstein, L.H. (1990) Behavioural treatment of obesity. In *Handbook of Behavioral Neurobiology*, Vol. 10, *Neurobiology of Food and Fluid Intake* (ed. E.M. Stricker), Plenum Press, New York, pp. 61–73.

Erikson, K., Drevets, W. and Schulkin, J. (2003) Glucocorticoid regulation of diverse cognitive functions in normal and pathological emotional states. *Neuroscience and Biobehavioral Reviews*, **27**, 233–246.

Ervin, F.R. and Martin, J. (1986) Neurophysiological bases of the primary emotions. In *Emotion – Theory, Research and Experience*. Vol. 3, *Biological Foundations of Emotion* (eds R. Plutchik and H. Kellerman), Academic Press, Orlando, pp. 145–170.

Evans, D. (2004) *Placebo: Mind over Matter in Modern Medicine*, Harper-Collins, London.

Evans, D. and Cruse, P. (2004) *Emotion, Evolution and Rationality*, Oxford University Press, Oxford.

Evans, P., Clow, A. and Hucklebridge, F. (1997) Stress and the immune system. *The Psychologist*, **10**, 303–307.

Evans, P., Hucklebridge, F. and Clow, A. (2000) *Mind, Immunity and Health: The Science of Psychoneuroimmunology*, Free Association Books, London.

Evarts, E.V. (1984) Hierarchies and emergent features in motor control. In *Dynamic Aspects of Neocortical Function* (eds G.M. Edelman, W.E. Gall and W.M. Cowan), Wiley, New York, pp. 557–579.

Evarts, E.V., Shinoda, Y. and Wise, S.P. (1984) *Neurophysiological Approaches to Higher Brain Functions*, Wiley, New York.

Everitt, B.J. (1990) Sexual motivation: a neural and behavioural analysis of the mechanisms underlying appetitive and copulatory responses of male rats. *Neuroscience and Biobehavioral Reviews*, **14**, 217–232.

Everitt, B.J. (1995) Neuroendocrine mechanisms underlying appetitive and consummatory elements of masculine sexual behaviour. In *The Pharmacology of Sexual Function and Dysfunction* (ed. J. Bancroft), Excerpta Medica, Amsterdam, pp. 15–35.

Everitt, B.J. and Bancroft, J. (1991) Of rats and men: the comparative approach to male sexuality. In *Annual Review of Sex Research*, 2 (ed. J. Bancroft), Society for the Scientific Study of Sex, Allentown, pp. 77–117.

Everitt, B.J. and Robbins, T.W. (1992) Amygdala–ventral striatal interactions and reward-related processes. In *The Amygdala: Neurobiological Aspects of Emotion, Memory, and Mental Dysfunction* (ed. J.P. Aggleton), Wiley, New York, pp. 401–429.

Everitt, B.J., Cador, M. and Robbins, T.W. (1989) Interactions between the amygdala and ventral striatum in stimulus–reward associations: studies using a second-order schedule of sexual reinforcement. *Neuroscience*, **30**, 63–75.

Everitt, B.J., Dickinson, A. and Robbins, T.W. (2001) The neuropsychological basis of addictive behaviour. *Brain Research Reviews*, **36**, 129–138.

Eysenck, H.J. (1985) *Decline and Fall of the Freudian Empire*, Penguin, Harmondsworth.

Eysenck, M. (1998) Perception and attention. In *Psychology: An Integrated Approach* (ed. M. Eysenck), Addison Wesley Longman, Harlow, pp. 138–166.

Fairburn, C.G. and Brownell, K.D. (2005) *Eating Disorders and Obesity: A Comprehensive Handbook*, Taylor and Francis, London.

Falk, J.L. (1971) The nature and determinants of adjunctive behavior. *Physiology and Behavior*, **6**, 577–588.

Falk, J.L. (1994) The discriminative stimulus and its reputation: role in the instigation of drug abuse. *Experimental and Clinical Psychopharmacology*, **2**, 43–52.

Farah, M., Humphreys, G.W. and Rodman, H.R. (1999) Object and face recognition. In *Fundamental Neuroscience* (eds M.J. Zigmond, F.E. Bloom, S.C. Landis, J.L. Roberts and L.R. Squire), Academic Press, San Diego, pp. 1339–1361.

Farah, M.J. (2000) *The Cognitive Neuroscience of Vision*, Blackwell, Oxford.

Farah, M.J., Wallace, M.A. and Vecera, S.P. (1993) 'What' and 'where' in visual attention: evidence from the neglect syndrome. In *Unilateral Neglect: Clinical and Experimental Studies* (eds I.H. Robertson and J.C. Marshall), Lawrence Erlbaum, Hove, pp. 123–137.

Faraone, S.V. and Biederman, J. (1998) Neurobiology of attention-deficit hyperactivity disorder. *Biological Psychiatry*, **44**, 951–958.

Feltz, D.L. and Landers, D.M. (1983) The effects of mental practice on motor skill learning and performance: a meta-analysis. *Journal of Sport Psychology*, **5**, 25–57.

Fenwick, P. (1993) Discussion. In *Experimental and Theoretical Studies of Consciousness* (eds G.R. Bock and J. Marsh), Wiley, Chichester, pp. 118–119.

Ferber, R. (1994) Sleep disorders of childhood. In *Sleep Disorders Medicine: Basic Science, Technical Considerations and Clinical Aspects* (ed. S. Chokroverty), Butterworth-Heinemann, Boston, pp. 417–428.

Ferris, C.F., Kulkarni, P., Sullivan, J.M., Harder, J.A., Messenger, T.L. and Febo, M. (2005) Pup suckling is more rewarding than cocaine: evidence from functional magnetic resonance imaging and three-dimensional computational analysis. *Journal of Neuroscience*, **25**, 149–156.

Ferster, D. (2004) Assembly of receptive fields in primary visual cortex. In *The Visual Neurosciences* (Vol. 1) (eds L.M. Chalupa and J.S. Werner), MIT Press, Cambridge, pp. 695–703.

ffytche, D.H., Howard, R.J., Brammer, M.J., David, A., Woodruff, P. and Williams, S. (1998) The anatomy of conscious vision: an fMRI study of visual hallucinations. *Nature Neuroscience*, **1**, 738–742.

Fields, H.L. and Basbaum, A.I. (1994) Central nervous system mechanisms of pain modulation. In *Textbook of Pain* (eds P.D. Wall and R. Melzack), Churchill Livingstone, Edinburgh, pp. 243–275.

Fields, R.D. (2004) The other half of the brain. *Scientific American*, **290**(4), 54–61.

Fifer, W.P. and Moon, C. (1988) Auditory experience in the fetus. In *Behavior of the Fetus* (eds W.P. Smotherman and S.R. Robinson), Telford Press, Caldwell, pp. 175–188.

Filshie, J. and Morrison, P.J. (1988) Acupuncture for chronic pain: a review. *Palliative Care*, **2**, 1–14.

Fink, G.R., Halligan, P.W., Marshall, J.C., Frith, C.D., Frackowiak, R.S.J. and Dolan, R.J. (1996) Where in the brain does visual attention select the forest and the trees? *Nature*, **382**, 626–628.

Finlay, B.L. and Darlington, R.B. (1995) Linked regularities in the development and evolution of mammalian brains. *Science*, **268**, 1578–1584.

Fiorino, D.F., Coury, A. and Phillips, A.G. (1997) Dynamic changes in nucleus accumbens dopamine efflux during the Coolidge effect in male rats. *Journal of Neuroscience*, **17**, 4849–4855.

Fischer, K.W. and Rose, S.P. (1994) Dynamic development of coordination of components in brain and behaviour – a framework for theory and research. In *Human Behavior and the Developing Brain* (eds G. Dawson and K.W. Fischer), Guilford Press, New York, pp. 3–66.

Fitch, R.H. and Denenberg, V.H. (1998) A role for ovarian hormones in sexual differentiation of the brain. *Behavioral and Brain Sciences*, **21**, 311–352.

Fitzsimons, J.T. (1990) Thirst and sodium appetite. In *Handbook of Behavioral Neurobiology*, Vol. 10, *Neurobiology of Food and Fluid Intake* (ed. E.M. Stricker), Plenum Press, New York, pp. 23–44.

Fitzsimons, J.T. (1991) Evolution of physiological and behavioural mechanisms in vertebrate body fluid homeostasis. In *Thirst: Physiological and Psychological Aspects* (eds D.J. Ramsey and D. Booth), Springer-Verlag, London, pp. 3–22.

Fitzsimons, J.T. (1998) Angiotensin, thirst, and sodium appetite. *Physiological Reviews*, **78**, 583–686.

Fitzsimons, J.T. and Oatley, K. (1968) Additivity of stimuli for drinking in rats. *Journal of Comparative and Physiological Psychology*, **66**, 450–455.

Flanagan, L.M. and McEwen, B.S. (1995) Ovarian steroid interactions with hypothalamic oxytocin circuits involved in reproductive behaviour. In *Neurobiological Effects of Sex Steroid Hormones* (eds P.E. Micevych and R.P. Hammer), Cambridge University Press, Cambridge, pp. 117–142.

Fletcher, P.C. (2004) Functional neuroimaging of schizophrenia: from a genetic predisposition to the emergence of symptoms. *Brain*, **127**, 457–459.

Floeter, M.K. (1999a) Muscle, motor neurons, and motor neuron pools. In *Fundamental Neuroscience* (eds M.J. Zigmond, F.E. Bloom, S.C. Landis, J.L. Roberts and L.R. Squire), Academic Press, San Diego, pp. 863–887.

Floeter, M.K. (1999b) Spinal motor control, reflexes, and locomotion. In *Fundamental Neuroscience* (eds M.J. Zigmond, F.E. Bloom, S.C. Landis, J.L. Roberts and L.R. Squire), Academic Press, San Diego, pp. 889–912.

Flor, H., Elbert, T., Knecht, S., Wienbruch, C., Pantev, C., Birbaumer, N., Larbig, W. and Taub, E. (1995) Phantom-limb pain as a perceptual correlate of cortical reorganization following arm amputation. *Nature*, **375**, 482–484.

Foch, T.T. and McClearn, G.E. (1980) Genetics, body weight, and obesity. In *Obesity* (ed. A.J. Stunkard), W.B. Saunders, Philadelphia, pp. 48–71.

Fodor, J.A. (1985) Precis of *The Modularity of Mind*. *Behavioral and Brain Sciences*, **8**, 1–42.

Foster, J.K. and Jelicic, M. (1999) *Memory: Systems, Process, or Function*, Oxford University Press, Oxford.

Fowles, D.C. (1982) Heart rate as an index of anxiety: failure of a hypothesis. In *Perspectives in Cardiovascular Psychophysiology* (eds J.T. Cacioppo and R.E. Petty), Guilford Press, New York, pp. 93–123.

Francis, P.T., Sims, N.R., Procter, A.W. and Bowen, D.M. (1993) Cortical pyramidal neurone loss may cause glutamatergic hypoactivity and cognitive impairment in Alzheimer's disease: investigative and therapeutic perspectives. *Journal of Neurochemistry*, **60**, 1589–1604.

Francis, P.T., Palmer, A.M., Snape, M. and Wilcock, G.K. (1999) The cholinergic hypothesis of Alzheimer's disease: a review of progress. *Journal of Neurology, Neurosurgery, and Psychiatry*, **66**, 137–147.

Franken, I.H.A. (2003) Drug craving and addiction: integrating psychological and neuropsychopharmacological approaches. *Progress in Neuro-Psychopharmacology and Biological Psychiatry*, **27**, 563–579.

Freeman, W. (1973) Sexual behaviour and fertility after frontal lobotomy. *Biological Psychiatry*, **6**, 97–104.

Freud, S. (1967) *New Introductory Lectures on Psychoanalysis*, Hogarth Press, London.

Friedlander, Y., Kark, J.D. and Stein, Y. (1987) Religious observance and plasma lipids and lipoproteins among 17-year-old Jewish residents of Jerusalem. *Preventive Medicine*, **16**, 70–79.

Friedman, M. (1996) *Type A Behavior: Its Diagnosis and Treatment*, Plenum Press, New York.

Friedman, M. and Rosenman, R.H. (1959) Association of specific overt behavior pattern with blood and cardiovascular findings. *Journal of American Medical Association*, **169**, 1286–1296.

Friedman, M.I. and Stricker, E.M. (1976) The physiological psychology of hunger: a physiological perspective. *Psychological Review*, **83**, 409–431.

Friedman, M.J., Charney, D.S. and Deutch, A.Y. (1995) *Neurobiological and Clinical Consequences of Stress. From Normal Adaptation to Post-traumatic Stress Disorder*, Lippincott-Raven, Philadelphia.

Fries, W. (1981) The projection from the lateral geniculate nucleus to the prestriate cortex of the macaque monkey. *Proceedings of the Royal Society of London B*, **213**, 73–80.

Frith, C. (1987) The positive and negative symptoms of schizophrenia reflect impairments in the perception and initiation of action. *Psychological Medicine*, **17**, 631–648.

Frith, C. (1996) Brain mechanisms for 'having a theory of mind'. *Journal of Psychopharmacology*, **10**, 9–15.

Frith, C. and Dolan, R.J. (1997) Brain mechanisms associated with top-down processes in perception. *Philosophical Transactions of the Royal Society of London B*, **352**, 1221–1230.

Frith, C. and Wolpert, D. (2004) *The Neuroscience of Social Interaction: Decoding, Influencing and Imitating the Actions of Others*, Oxford University Press, Oxford.

Frith, C.D. (1992) *The Cognitive Neuropsychology of Schizophrenia*, Lawrence Erlbaum, Hove.

Frohman, L., Cameron, J. and Wise, P. (1999) Neuroendocrine systems II: Growth, reproduction, and lactation. In *Fundamental Neuroscience* (eds M.J. Zigmond, F.E. Bloom, S.C. Landis, J.L. Roberts and L.R. Squire), Academic Press, San Diego, pp. 1151–1187.

Fuchs, R.A., Tran-Nguyen, L.T.L., Specio, S.E., Groff, R.S. and Neisewander, J.L. (1998) Predictive validity of the extinction/reinstatement model of drug craving. *Psychopharmacology*, **135**, 151–160.

Fuller, J.L. (1986) Genetics and emotions. In *Emotion – Theory, Research and Experience*, Vol. 3, *Biological Foundations of Emotion* (eds R. Plutchik and H. Kellerman), Academic Press, Orlando, pp. 199–216.

Fuster, J.M. (1997) *The Prefrontal Cortex – Anatomy, Physiology and Neuropsychology of the Frontal Lobe*, Raven Press, New York.

Fuster, J.M. (1999) Synopsis of function and dysfunction of the frontal lobe. *Acta Psychiatrica Scandinavica*, **99** (Suppl. 395), 51–57.

Fuster, J.M. (2005) *Cortex and Mind: Unifying Cognition*, Oxford University Press, New York.

Gabriëls, L., Cosyns, P., Nuttin, B., Demeulemeester, H. and Gybels, J. (2003) Deep brain stimulation for treatment-refractory disorder: psychopathological and neuropsychological outcome in three cases. *Acta Psychiatrica Scandinavica*, **107**, 275–282.

Gallistel, C.R. (1980) *The Organization of Action – A New Synthesis*, Lawrence Erlbaum, Hillsdale.

Gallo, L.C. and Matthews, K.A. (2003) Understanding the association between socioeconomic status and physical health. *Psychological Bulletin*, **129**, 10–51.

Gallup, G.G. (1977) Self-recognition in primates. *American Psychologist*, **32**, 329–338.

Gandevia, S.C., Killian, K., McKenzie, D.K., Crawford, M., Allen, G.M., Gorman, R.B. and Hales, J.P. (1993) Respiratory sensations, cardiovascular control, kinesthesia and transcranial stimulation during paralysis in humans. *Journal of Physiology*, **470**, 85–107.

Gao, J-H., Parsons, L.M., Bower, J.M., Xiong, J., Li, J. and Fox, P.T. (1996) Cerebellum implicated in sensory acquisition and discrimination rather than motor control. *Science*, **272**, 545–547.

Garcia, J. (1989) Food for Tolman: cognition and cathexis in concert. In *Aversion, Avoidance and Anxiety – Perspectives on Aversively Motivated Behavior* (eds T. Archer and L.-G. Nilsson), Lawrence Erlbaum, Hillsdale, pp. 45–85.

Garcia-Reboll, L., Mulhall, J.P. and Goldstein, I. (1997) Drugs for the treatment of impotence. *Drugs and Aging*, **11**, 140–151.

Gardner, H. (1982) *Art, Mind, and Brain: A Cognitive Approach to Creativity*, Basic Books, New York.

Gardner, H. (1985) The centrality of modules. *Behavioral and Brain Sciences*, **8**, 12–14.

Garrard, P., Maloney, L.M., Hodges, J.R. and Patterson, K. (2005) The effects of very early Alzheimer's disease on the characteristics of writing by a renowned author. *Brain*, **128**, 250–260.

Gay, P. (1988) *Freud – A Life for our Time*, J.M. Dent, London.

Gazzaniga, M.S. (1993) Brain mechanisms and conscious experience. In *Experimental and Theoretical Studies of Consciousness* (eds G.R. Bock and J. Marsh), Wiley, Chichester, pp. 247–262.

Gazzaniga, M.S. (2004) *The Cognitive Neurosciences* (3rd edition), MIT Press, Cambridge.

Gazzaniga, M.S., Ivery, R.B. and Mangun, G.R. (1998) *Cognitive Neuroscience: The Biology of the Mind*, W.W. Norton, New York.

Geary, N. (2004) Endocrine controls of eating: CCK, leptin, and ghrelin. *Physiology and Behavior*, **81**, 719–733.

Geffen, G., Bradshaw, J.L. and Nettleton, N.C. (1972) Hemispheric asymmetry: verbal and spatial encoding of visual stimuli. *Journal of Experimental Psychology*, **95**, 25–31.

Gervais, R. (1993) Olfactory processing controlling food and fluid intake. In *Neurophysiology of Ingestion* (ed. D.A. Booth), Pergamon Press, Oxford, pp. 119–135.

Geschwind, N. (1972) Language and the brain. *Scientific American*, **226**, No. 4, 76–83.

Geschwind, N. (1979) Specializations of the human brain. *Scientific American*, **241**, No. 3, 158–168.

Geschwind, N. and Levitsky, W. (1968) Human brain: left–right asymmetries in temporal speech region. *Science*, **161**, 186–187.

Gessa, G., Melis, M., Muntoni, A. and Diana, M. (1998) Cannabinoids activate mesolimbic dopamine neurons by an action on cannabinoid CB_1 receptors. *European Journal of Pharmacology*, **341**, 39–44.

Geyer, M.A., Swerdlow, N.R., Mansbach, R.S. and Braff, D.L. (1990) Startle response models of sensorimotor gating and habituation deficits in schizophrenia. *Brain Research Bulletin*, **25**, 485–498.

Ghez, C. (1991a) Voluntary movement. In *Principles of Neural Science* (eds E.R. Kandel, J.H. Schwartz and T.M. Jessell), Appleton and Lange, Norwalk, pp. 609–625.

Ghez, C. (1991b) The cerebellum. In *Principles of Neural Science* (eds E.R. Kandel, J.H. Schwartz and T.M. Jessell), Appleton and Lange, Norwalk, pp. 626–646.

Gilbert, D.G., McClerlon, F.J. and Gilbert, B.O. (1997) The psychology of the smoker. In *The Tobacco Epidemic* (eds C.T. Bollinger and K.O. Fagerström), Karger, Basle, pp. 132–150.

Gilbert, P. (1998) Evolutionary psychopathology: why isn't the mind designed better than it is? *British Journal of Medical Psychology*, **71**, 353–373.

Gittelman-Klein, R. and Abikoff, H. (1989) The role of psycho-stimulants and psychosocial treatment in hyperkinesis. In *Attention Deficit Disorder: Clinical and Basic Research* (eds T. Sagvolden and T. Archer), Lawrence Erlbaum, Hillsdale, pp. 167–180.

Gladue, B.A. (1988) Hormones in relationship to homosexual/bisexual/heterosexual gender orientation. In *Handbook of Sexology*, Vol. 6, *The Pharmacology and Endocrinology of Sexual Function* (ed. J.M.A. Sitsen), Elsevier Science, Amsterdam, pp. 388–409.

Gladue, B.A. (1994) The biopsychology of sexual orientation. *Current Directions in Psychological Science*, **3**, 150–154.

Glickman, S.E. and Schiff, B.B. (1967) A biological theory of reinforcement. *Psychological Review*, **74**, 81–109.

Glickman, S.E. and Sroges, R.W. (1966) Curiosity in zoo animals. *Behaviour*, **26**, 151–188.

Glimcher, P.W. (1999) Eye movements. In *Fundamental Neuroscience* (eds M.J. Zigmond, F.E. Bloom, S.C. Landis, J.L. Roberts and L.R. Squire), Academic Press, San Diego, pp. 993–1010.

Gloor, P. (1986) Role of the human limbic system in perception, memory, and affect: lessons from temporal lobe epilepsy. In *The Limbic System: Functional Organization and Clinical Disorders* (eds B.K. Doane and K.E. Livingstone), Raven Press, New York, pp. 159–169.

Glover, S. (2004) Separate visual representations in the planning and control of action. *Behavioral and Brain Sciences*, **27**, 3–78.

Glucksberg, S. (1985) Modularity: contextual interactions and the tractability of nonmodular systems. *Behavioral and Brain Sciences*, **8**, 14–15.

Glue, P., Nutt, D. and Coupland, N. (1993) Stress and psychiatric disorder: reconciling social and biological approaches. In *Stress – From Synapse to Syndrome* (eds S.C. Stanford and P. Salmon), Academic Press, London, pp. 53–73.

Goldberg, J.M. and Fernández, C. (1984) The vestibular system. In *Handbook of Physiology. Section 1: The Nervous System*, Vol. III, Part 2 (ed. I. Darian-Smith), American Physiological Society, Bethesda, pp. 977–1022.

Goldman-Rakic, P.S. (1987) Circuitry of primate prefrontal cortex and regulation of behavior by representational memory. In *Handbook of Physiology. Section 1: The Nervous System*, Vol. V. *Higher Functions of the Brain*, Part 1 (eds V.B. Mountcastle, F. Plum and S.R. Geiger), American Physiological Society, Bethesda, pp. 373–417.

Goldman-Rakic, P.S. (1995) Toward a circuit model of working memory and the guidance of voluntary motor action. In *Models of Information Processing in the Basal Ganglia* (eds J.C. Houk, J.L. Davis and D.G. Beiser), MIT Press, Cambridge, pp. 131–148.

Goldstein, A. (2001) *Addiction: From Biology to Drug Policy*, Oxford University Press, New York.

Goldstein, I., Lue, T., Padma-Nathan, H., Rosen, R.C., Steers, W.D. and Wickler, P.A. (1998) Oral sildenafil in the treatment of erectile dysfunction. *New England Journal of Medicine*, **338**, 1397–1404.

Goodale, M.A. and Humphrey, G.K. (1998) The objects of action and perception. *Cognition*, **67**, 181–207.

Goodale, M.A. and Milner, A.D. (2004) *Sight Unseen: An Exploration of Conscious and Unconscious Vision*, Oxford University Press, Oxford.

Goodale, M.A., Milner, A.D., Jakobsen, L.S. and Carey, D.P. (1991) A neurological dissociation between perceiving objects and grasping them. *Nature*, **349**, 154–156.

Gordon, C.J. and Heath, J.E. (1986) Integration and central processing in temperature regulation. *Annual Review of Physiology*, **48**, 595–612.

Gordon, J. (1991) Spinal mechanisms of motor coordination. In *Principles of Neural Science* (eds E.R. Kandel, J.H. Schwartz and T.M. Jessell), Appleton and Lange, Norwalk, pp. 581–595.

Gordon, J. and Ghez, C. (1991) Muscle receptors and spinal reflexes: the stretch reflex. In *Principles of Neural Science* (eds E.R. Kandel, J.H. Schwartz and T.M. Jessell), Appleton and Lange, Norwalk, pp. 564–580.

Gorman, M.R. (1994) Male homosexual desire: neurological investigations and scientific bias. *Perspectives in Biology and Medicine*, **38**, 61–81.

Gossop, M. (2000) *Living with Drugs*, Ashgate Publishers, London.

Gottesman, I.I. and Moldin, S.O. (1998) Genotypes, genes, genesis, and pathogenesis in schizophrenia. In *Origins and Development of Schizophrenia* (eds M.F. Lenzenweger and R.H. Dworkin), American Psychological Association, Washington, pp. 5–26.

Gottlieb, G. (1973) B*ehavioral Embryology: I. Studies on the Development of Behavior and the Nervous System*, Academic Press, New York.

Gottlieb, G. (1997a) A systems view of psychobiological development. In *The Lifespan Development of Individuals: Behavioral, Neurobiological, and Psychosocial Perspectives. A Synthesis* (ed. D. Magnusson), Cambridge University Press, New York, pp. 76–103.

Gottlieb, G. (1997b) *Synthesizing Nature–Nurture: Prenatal Roots of Instinctive Behavior*, Lawrence Erlbaum, Mahwah.

Gottlieb, G. (1998) Normally occurring environmental and behavioral influences on gene activity: from central dogma to probabilistic epigenesis. *Psychological Review*, **105**, 792–802.

Goudriaan, A.E., Oosterlaan, J., de Beurs, E. and van den Brink, W. (2004) Pathological gambling: a comprehensive review of biobehavioural findings. *Neuroscience and Biobehavioral Reviews*, **28**, 123–141.

Gould, E., Woolley, C.S. and McEwen, B.S. (1991) The hippocampal formation: morphological changes induced by thyroid, gonadal and adrenal hormones. *Psychoneuroendocrinology*, **16**, 67–84.

Gould, S.J. and Vrba, E.S. (1982) Exaptation – a missing term in the science of form. *Paleobiology*, **8**, 4–15.

Grace, A.A. (2001) Psychostimulant actions on dopamine and limbic system function: relevance to the pathophysiology and treatment of ADHD. In *Stimulant Drugs and ADHD: Basic and Clinical Neuroscience* (eds M.V. Solanto, A.F.T. Arnsten and F.X. Castellanos), Oxford University Press, Oxford, pp. 134–157.

Grafman, J. (1989) Plans, actions, and mental sets: managerial knowledge units in the frontal lobes. In *Integrating Theory and Practice in Clinical Neuropsychology* (ed. E. Perecman), Lawrence Erlbaum, Hillsdale, pp. 93–138.

Grafton, S.T., Woods, R.P. and Tyszka, M. (1994) Functional imaging of procedural motor learning: relating cerebral blood flow with individual subject performance. *Human Brain Mapping*, **1**, 221–234.

Grammer, K., Fink, B. and Neave, N. (2005) Human pheromones and sexual attraction. *European Journal of Obstetrics and Gynecology and Reproductive Biology*, **118**, 135–142.

Grant, V.J. (1994a) Sex of infant differences in mother–infant interaction: a reinterpretation of past findings. *Developmental Review*, **14**, 1–26.

Grant, V.J. (1994b) Maternal dominance and the conception of sons. *British Journal of Medical Psychology*, **67**, 343–351.

Gray, J. (2004) *Consciousness: Creeping up on the Hard Problem*, Oxford University Press, Oxford.

Gray, J.A. (1987a) *The Psychology of Fear and Stress*, Cambridge University Press, Cambridge.

Gray, J.A. (1987b) The mind–brain identity as a scientific hypothesis: a second look. In *Mindwaves: Thoughts on Intelligence, Identity and Consciousness* (eds C. Blakemore and S. Greenfield), Basil Blackwell, Oxford, pp. 461–483.

Gray, J.A. (1993) Consciousness, schizophrenia and scientific theory. In *Experimental and Theoretical Studies of Consciousness* (eds G.R. Bock and J. Marsh), Wiley, Chichester, pp. 263–281.

Gray, J.A. (1995) The contents of consciousness: a neuropsychological conjecture. *Behavioral and Brain Sciences*, **18**, 659–722.

Gray, J.A., Feldon, J., Rawlins, J.N.P., Hemsley, D.R. and Smith, A.D. (1991) The neuropsychology of schizophrenia. *Behavioral and Brain Sciences*, **14**, 1–84.

Graybiel, A.M. (1997) The basal ganglia and cognitive pattern generators. *Schizophrenia Bulletin*, **23**, 459–469.

Graybiel, A.M., Aosaki, T., Flaherty, A.W. and Kimura, M. (1994) The basal ganglia and adaptive motor control. *Science*, **265**, 1826–1831.

Green, D.M. and Wier, C.C. (1984) Auditory perception. In *Handbook of Physiology. Section 1: The Nervous System*, Vol. III, Part 2 (ed. I. Darian-Smith), American Physiological Society, Bethesda, pp. 557–594.

Greenberg, G. and Haraway, M.M. (1998) *Comparative Psychology*, Garland Publishing, New York.

Greenberg, M.S. (1992) Olfactory hallucinations. In *Science of Olfaction* (eds M.J. Serby and K.L. Chobor), Springer-Verlag, New York, pp. 467–499.

Greene, J. (1990) Perception. In *Introduction to Psychology*, Vol. 2 (ed. I. Roth), Lawrence Erlbaum, Hove, pp. 475–527.

Greenfield, P.M. (1991) Language, tools and brain: the ontogeny and phylogeny of hierarchically organized sequential behaviour. *Behavioral and Brain Sciences*, **14**, 531–595.

Greenough, W.T. (1976) Enduring brain effects of differential experience and training. In *Neural Mechanisms of Learning and Memory* (eds M.R. Rosenzweig and E.L. Bennett), MIT Press, Cambridge, pp. 255–278.

Greenspan, J.D. and Bolanowski, S.J. (1996) The psychophysics of tactile perception and its peripheral basis. In *Pain and Touch* (ed. L. Kruger), Academic Press, San Diego, pp. 25–103.

Gregory, R.L. (1997) *Eye and Brain*, Oxford University Press, Oxford.

Gregory, R.L. (1998) *Eye and Brain: The Psychology of Seeing*, Oxford University Press, Oxford.

Griffiths, D., Dickinson, A. and Clayton, N. (1999) Episodic memory: what can animals remember about their past? *Trends in Cognitive Sciences*, **3**, 74–80.

Griffiths, M. (1999) Internet addiction: fact or fiction? *The Psychologist*, **12**, 246–250.

Griffiths, P.E. (1997) *What Emotions Really Are*, University of Chicago Press, Chicago.

Griffiths, R.R and Woodson, P.P. (1988) Caffeine physical dependence: a review of human and laboratory animal studies. *Psychopharmacology*, **94**, 437–451.

Griffiths, R.R., Brady, J.V. and Bradford, L.D. (1979) Predicting the abuse liability of drugs with animal drug self-administration procedures: psychomotor stimulants and hallucinogens. In *Advances in Behavioral Pharmacology*, Vol. 2 (eds T. Thompson and P.B. Dews), Academic Press, New York, pp. 163–208.

Grill, H.J. and Berridge, K.C. (1985) Taste reactivity as a measure of the neural plasticity of palatability. In *Progress in Psychobiology and Physiological Psychology*, Vol. 11 (eds J.M. Sprague and A.N. Epstein), Academic Press, Orlando, pp. 1–61.

Grill, H.J. and Kaplan, J.M. (1990) Caudal brainstem participates in the distributed neural control of feeding. In *Handbook of Behavioral Neurobiology*, Vol. 10 *Neurobiology of Food and Fluid Intake* (ed. E.M. Stricker), Plenum Press, New York, pp. 125–149.

Grobstein, P. (1988) On beyond neuronal specificity: problems in going from cells to networks and from networks to behaviour. In *Advances in Neural and Behavioral Development*, Vol. 3 (ed. P.G. Shinkman), Ablex Publishing, Norwood, pp. 1–58.

Gross, C.G. (1985) On Gall's reputation and some recent 'new phrenology'. *Behavioral and Brain Sciences*, **8**, 16–18.

Gross, C.G., Rodman, H.R., Gochin, P.M. and Colombo, M.W. (1993) Inferior temporal cortex as a pattern recognition device. In *Computational Learning and Cognition* (ed. E.B. Baum), Society for Industrial and Applied Mathematics, Philadelphia, pp. 44–73.

Grossman, M. (1980) A central processor for hierarchically structured material: evidence from Broca's aphasia. *Neuropsychologia*, **18**, 299–308.

Groves, P.M. and Thompson, R.F. (1970) Habituation: a dual process theory. *Psychological Review*, 77, 419–450.

Grunberg, N.E. (1985) Specific taste preferences: an alternative explanation for eating changes in cancer patients. In *Cancer, Nutrition, and Eating Behavior: A Biobehavioral Perspective* (eds T.G. Burish, S.M. Levy and B.E. Meyerowitz), Lawrence Erlbaum, Hillsdale, pp. 43–61.

Guisinger, S. (2003) Adapted to flee famine: adding an evolutionary perspective on anorexia nervosa. *Psychological Review*, **110**, 745–761.

Gulevich, G., Dement, W. and Johnson, L. (1966) Psychiatric and EEG observations on a case of prolonged (264 hours) wakefulness. *Archives of General Psychiatry*, **15**, 29–35.

Gunne, L.M., Änggård, E. and Jönsson, L.E. (1972) Clinical trials with amphetamine-blocking drugs. *Psychiatria, Neurologia and Neurochirurgia*, **75**, 225–226.

Guyton, A.C. (1991) *Textbook of Medical Physiology*, W.B. Saunders, Philadelphia.

Guzman-Marin, R., Suntsova, N., Methippara, M., Greiffenstein, R., Szymusiak, R. and McGinty, D. (2005) Sleep deprivation suppresses neurogenesis in the adult hippocampus of rats. *European Journal of Neuroscience*, **22**, 2111–2116.

Haberich, F.J. (1968) Osmoreception in the portal circulation. *Federation Proceedings*, **27**, 1137–1141.

Hagemann, E., Hay, D.A. and Levy, F. (2002) Cognitive aspects and learning. In *Hyperactivity and Attention Disorders of Childhood* (2nd edition) (ed. S. Sandberg), Cambridge University Press, Cambridge, pp. 214–241.

Halford, J.C.G., Harrold, J.A., Lawton, C.L. and Blundell, J.E. (2005) Serotonin (5-HT) drugs: effects on appetite expression and use for the treatment of obesity. *Current Drug Targets*, **6**, 201–213.

Hall, M. and Halliday, T. (1998) *Behaviour and Evolution*, Springer, Berlin.

Haller, J., Makara, G.B. and Kruk, M.R. (1998) Catecholaminergic involvement in the control of aggression: hormones, the peripheral sympathetic, and central noradrenergic systems. *Neuroscience and Biobehavioral Reviews*, **22**, 85–97.

Halliday, T. (1998) *The Senses and Communication*, Springer, Berlin.

Halligan, P.W. and Marshall, J.C. (1993) The history and clinical presentation of neglect. In *Unilateral Neglect: Clinical and Experimental Studies* (eds I.H. Robertson and J.C. Marshall), Lawrence Erlbaum, Hove, pp. 3–25.

Halmi, K. (1980) Gastric bypass for massive obesity. In *Obesity* (ed. A.J. Stunkard), W.B. Saunders, Philadelphia, pp. 388–394.

Hamburger, V. (1963) Some aspects of the embryology of behaviour. *Quarterly Review of Biology*, **38**, 342–365.

Hanin, I., Fisher, A. and Cacabelos, R. (2005) *Recent Progress in Alzheimer's and Parkinson's Diseases*. Taylor and Francis, London.

Harlow, H.F. and Harlow, M.K. (1962) Social deprivation in monkeys. *Scientific American*, **207**, No. 5, 136–146.

Harrington, M.E., Rusak, B. and Mistlberger, R.E. (1994) Anatomy and physiology of the mammalian circadian system. In *Principles and Practice of Sleep Medicine* (eds M.H. Kryger, T. Roth and W.C. Dement), Saunders, Philadelphia, pp. 286–300.

Harris, C.R. and Christenfeld, N. (1996) Gender, jealousy, and reason. *Psychological Science*, 7, 364–366.

Harris, G.C., Wimmer, M. and Aston-Jones, G. (2005) A role for lateral hypothalamic orexin neurons in reward seeking. *Nature*, **437**, 556–559.

Harris, J.A. (1996) Descending antinociceptive mechanisms in the brainstem: their role in the animal's defensive system. *Journal of Physiology (Paris)*, **90**, 15–25.

Harris, W.A. and Hartenstein, V. (1999) Cellular determination. In *Fundamental Neuroscience* (eds M.J. Zigmond, F.E. Bloom, S.C. Landis, J.L. Roberts and L.R. Squire), Academic Press, San Diego, pp. 481–517.

Harrop, C. and Trower, P. (2003) *Why Does Schizophrenia Develop at Late Adolescence?: A Cognitive–Developmental Approach to Psychosis*, Wiley, Chichester.

Hart, B.L. (1988) Biological basis of the behavior of sick animals. *Neuroscience and Biobehavioral Reviews*, **12**, 123–137.

Harvey, P.H. and Krebs, J.R. (1990) Comparing brains. *Science*, **249**, 140–146.

Hatfield, E., Cacioppo, J.T. and Rapson, R.L. (1993) Emotional contagion. *Current Directions in Psychological Science*, **2**, 96–99.

Healy, S. and Guilford, T. (1990) Olfactory-bulb size and nocturnality in birds. *Evolution*, **44**, 339–346.

Heath, R.G. (1986) The neural substrate for emotion. In *Emotion – Theory, Research and Experience*, Vol. 3, *Biological Foundations of Emotion* (eds R. Plutchik and H. Kellerman), Academic Press, Orlando, pp. 3–35.

Hebb, D.O. (1949) *The Organization of Behavior*, Wiley, New York.

Heilman, K.M. and Bowers, D. (1990) Neuropsychological studies of emotional changes induced by right and left hemispheric lesions. In *Psychological and Biological Approaches to Emotion* (eds N.L. Stein, B. Leventhal and T. Trabasso), Lawrence Erlbaum, Hillsdale, pp. 97–113.

Helfert, R.H., Snead, C.R. and Altschuler, R.A. (1991) The ascending auditory pathways. In *Neurobiology of Hearing: The Central Auditory System* (eds R.A. Altschuler, R.P. Bobbin, B.M. Clopton and D.W. Hoffman), Raven Press, New York, pp. 1–26.

Heller, H.C., Crawshaw, L.I. and Hammel, H.T. (1978) The thermostat of vertebrate animals. *Scientific American*, **239**, 88–96.

Heller, W. (1990) The neuropsychology of emotion: developmental patterns and implications for psychopathology. In *Psychological and Biological Approaches to Emotion* (eds N.L. Stein, B. Leventhal and T. Trabasso), Lawrence Erlbaum, Hillsdale, pp. 167–211.

Hemsley, D.R. (1996) Schizophrenia – a cognitive model and its implications for psychological intervention. *Behavior Modification*, **20**, 139–169.

Henderson, V.W. (1986) Anatomy of posterior pathways in reading: a reassessment. *Brain and Language*, **29**, 119–133.

Hendry, S.H.C., Hsiao, S.S. and Brown, M.C. (1999a) Fundamentals of sensory systems. In *Fundamental Neuroscience* (eds M.J. Zigmond,

F.E. Bloom, S.C. Landis, J.L. Roberts and L.R. Squire), Academic Press, San Diego, pp. 657–670.

Hendry, S.H.C., Hsaio, S.S. and Bushnell, M.C. (1999b) Somatic sensation. In *Fundamental Neuroscience* (eds M.J. Zigmond, F.E. Bloom, S.C. Landis, J.L. Roberts and L.R. Squire), Academic Press, San Diego, pp. 761–789.

Henningfield, J.E., Johnson, R.E. and Jasinski, D.I. (1987) Clinical procedures for the assessment of abuse potential. In *Methods of Assessing the Reinforcing Properties of Abused Drugs* (ed. M.A. Bozarth) Springer-Verlag, New York.

Henriksen, S.J. and Giacchino, J. (1993) Functional characteristics of nucleus accumbens neurons: evidence obtained from *in vivo* electrophysiological recordings. In *Limbic Motor Circuits and Neuropsychiatry* (eds P.W. Kalivas and C.D. Barnes), CRC Press, Boca Raton, pp. 101–124.

Henry, J.P. (1982) The relation of social to biological processes in disease. *Social Science and Medicine*, **16**, 369–380.

Henry, J.P. (1986) Neuroendocrine patterns of emotional response. In *Emotion – Theory, Research and Experience*, Vol. 3, *Biological Foundations of Emotion* (eds R. Plutchik and H. Kellerman), Academic Press, Orlando, pp. 37–60.

Herbert, J. (1995) Neuropeptides, stress and sexuality: towards a new psychopharmacology. In *The Pharmacology of Sexual Function and Dysfunction* (ed. J. Bancroft), Excerpta Medica, Amsterdam, pp. 77–96.

Herman, B.H. and Panksepp, J. (1978) Effects of morphine and naloxone on separation distress and approach attachment: evidence for opiate mediation of social affect. *Pharmacology Biochemistry and Behavior*, **9**, 213–220.

Herz, R.S. (1997) Emotion experienced during encoding enhances odor retrieval cue effectiveness. *American Journal of Psychology*, **110**, 489–505.

Hess, W.R. (1981) *Biological Order and Brain Organization: Selected Works of W.R. Hess* (ed. K. Akert), Springer-Verlag, Berlin.

Hickok, G. and Poeppel, D. (2004) Dorsal and ventral streams: a framework for understanding aspects of the functional anatomy of language. *Cognition*, **92**, 67–99.

Hilton, S.M. (1979) The defense reaction as a paradigm for cardiovascular control. In *Integrative Functions of the Autonomic Nervous System* (eds C.McC. Brooks, K. Koizumi and A. Sato), University of Tokyo Press/Elsevier, Amsterdam, pp. 443–449.

Hines, M. (2004) *Brain Gender*. Oxford University Press, New York.

Hines, M., Ahmed, S.F. and Hughes, I.A. (2003) Psychological outcomes and gender-related development in complete androgen insensitivity syndrome. *Archives of Sexual Behavior*, **32**, 93–101.

Hines, T. (1991) The myth of right hemisphere creativity. *Journal of Creative Behavior*, **25**, 223–226.

Hinke, R.M., Hu, X., Stillman, A.E., Kim, S-G., Merkle, H., Salmi, R. and Ugurbil, K. (1993) Functional magnetic resonance imaging of Broca's area during internal speech. *NeuroReport*, **4**, 675–678.

Hobson, J.A. (1988) *The Dreaming Brain*, Basic Books, New York.

Hobson, J.A. (1990) Activation, input source, and modulation: a neurocognitive model of the state of the brain–mind. In *Sleep and Cognition* (eds R.R. Bootzin, J.F. Kihlstrom and D.L. Schacter), American Psychological Association, Washington, pp. 25–40.

Hobson, J.A. (1996) Dreams and the brain. In *Neuroscience: Exploring the Brain* (eds M.F. Bear, B.W. Connors and M.A. Paradiso), Williams and Wilkins, Baltimore, p. 471.

Hobson, J.A. (1999) Sleep and dreaming. In *Fundamental Neuroscience* (eds M.J. Zigmond, F.E. Bloom, S.C. Landis, J.L. Roberts and L.R. Squire), Academic Press, San Diego, pp. 1207–1227.

Hobson, J.A. (2003) *Dreaming: An Introduction to the Science of Sleep*, Oxford University Press, Oxford.

Hobson, J.A. (2004) *13 Dreams Freud Never Had: A New Mind Science*, Pi Press, New York.

Hobson, J.A. and Pace-Schott, E.F. (2002) The cognitive neuroscience of sleep: neuronal systems, consciousness and learning. *Nature Reviews Neuroscience*, **3**, 679–693.

Hobson, J.A. and Stickgold, R. (1994) Dreaming a neurocognitive approach. *Consciousness and Cognition*, **3**, 1–15.

Hoebel, B.G. (1997) Neuroscience and appetitive behavior research: 25 years. *Appetite*, **29**, 119–133.

Hof, P.R., Trapp, B.D., de Vellis, J., Claudio, L. and Colman, D.R. (1999) The cellular components of nervous tissue. In *Fundamental Neuroscience* (eds M.J. Zigmond, F.E. Bloom, S.C. Landis, J.L. Roberts and L.R. Squire), Academic Press, San Diego, pp. 41–70

Hofbauer, K.G. (2004) *Pharmacotherapy of Obesity*, Taylor and Francis, London.

Hofer, M.A. (1988) On the nature and function of prenatal behavior. In *Behavior of the Fetus* (eds W.P. Smotherman and S.R. Robinson), Telford Press, Caldwell, pp. 3–18.

Hogan, J.A. (1980) Homeostasis and behaviour. In *Analysis of Motivational Processes* (eds F.M. Toates and T.R. Halliday), Academic Press, London, pp. 3–21.

Hogarth, L., Dickinson, A. and Duka, T. (2003) Discriminative stimuli that control instrumental tobacco-seeking by human smokers also command selective attention. *Psychopharmacology*, **168**, 435–445.

Hollis, K.L. (1997) Contemporary research on Pavlovian conditioning. *American Psychologist*, **52**, 956–965.

Holmes, G. (1939) The cerebellum of man. *Brain*, **62**, 1–30.

Holsboer, F. and Barden, N. (1996) Antidepressants and hypothalamic–pituitary–adrenocortical regulation. *Endocrine Reviews*, **17**, 187–205.

Holstege, G. and Georgiadis, J.R. (2004) Brain activation during orgasm is basically the same in men and women. *Hormones and Behavior*, **46**, 132.

Holstege, G., Georgiadis, J.R., Paans, A.M.J., Meiners, L.C., van der Graaf, F.H.C.E. and Reinders, A.A.T. (2003) Brain activation during human male ejaculation. *Journal of Neuroscience*, **23**, 9185–9193.

Hommet, C., Sauerwein, H.C., De Toffol, B., and Lassonde, M. (2005) Idiopathic epileptic syndromes and cognition. *Neuroscience and Biobehavioral Reviews*, **30**, 85–96.

Honjo, I. (1999) *Language Viewed from the Brain*, Karger, Basle.

Hooks, M.S. and Kalivas, P.W. (1995) The role of mesoaccumbens-pallidal circuitry in novelty-induced behavioural activation. *Neuroscience*, **64**, 587–597.

Hoon, P.W., Wincze, J.P. and Hoon, E.F. (1976) Physiological assessment of sexual arousal in women. *Psychophysiology*, **13**, 196–204.

Horn, S. and Munafo, M. (1997) *Pain: Theory, Research and Intervention*, Open University Press, Maidenhead.

Horne, J. (1988) *Why We Sleep*, Oxford University Press, Oxford.

Horne, J. (1992) Insomnia, *The Psychologist*, May, 216–218.

Horne, J.A. and Reyner, L.A. (1995) Sleep related vehicle accidents. *British Medical Journal*, **310**, 565–567.

Hosokawa, T., Rusakov, D.A., Bliss, T.V.P. and Fine, A. (1995) Repeated confocal imaging of individual dendritic spines in the living hippocampal slice: evidence for changes in length and orientation associated with chemically induced LTP. *Journal of Neuroscience*, **15**, 5560–5573.

Hsiao, S.S., O'Shaughnessy, D.M. and Johnson, K.O. (1993) Effects of selective attention on spatial form processing in monkey primary and secondary somatosensory cortex. *Journal of Neurophysiology*, **70**, 444–447.

Hsiao, S.S., Johnson, K.O., Twombly, A. and DiCarlo, J. (1996) Form processing and attention effects in the somatosensory system. In *Somesthesis and the Neurobiology of the Somatosensory Cortex* (eds O. Franzén, R. Johansson and L. Terenius), Birkhäuser Verlag, Basle, pp. 229–247.

Hubel, D.H. (1982) Exploration of the primary visual cortex, 1955–78. *Nature*, **299**, 515–524.

Hubel, D.H. and Wiesel, T.N. (1959) Receptive fields of single neurons in the cat's striate cortex. *Journal of Physiology (London)*, **148**, 574–591.

Hubel, D.H. and Wiesel, T.N. (1965) Binocular interaction in striate cortex of kittens reared with artificial squint. *Journal of Neurophysiology*, **28**, 1041–1059.

Hudspeth, A.J. and Konishi, M. (2000) Auditory neuroscience: development, transduction, and integration, *Proceedings of the National Academy of Sciences*, **97**, 11690–11691.

Hull, E.M. (1995) Dopaminergic influences on male rat sexual behavior. In *Neurobiological Effects of Sex Steroid Hormones* (eds P.E. Micevych and R.P. Hammer), Cambridge University Press, Cambridge, pp. 234–253.

Humphreys, G.W., Riddoch, M.J. and Price, C.J. (1997) Top-down processes in object identification: evidence from experimental psychology, neuropsychology and functional anatomy. *Philosophical Transactions of the Royal Society of London B*, **352**, 1275–1282.

Huttenlocher, P.R. (1994) Synaptogenesis in human cerebral cortex. In *Human Behavior and the Developing Brain* (eds G. Dawson and K.W. Fischer), Guilford Press, New York, pp. 137–152.

Huxley, A. (1972) *The Doors of Perception and Heaven and Hell*, Chatto and Windus, London.

Huxley, L.A. (1969) *This Timeless Moment: A Personal View of Aldous Huxley*, Chatto and Windus, London.

Hyde, J.S. (2005a) The genetics of sexual orientation. In *Biological Substrates of Human Sexuality* (ed. J.S. Hyde), American Psychological Association, Washington, pp. 9–20.

Hyde, J.S. (2005b) *Biological Substrates of Human Sexuality*, American Psychological Association, Washington.

Insel, T., Miller, L., Gelhard, R. and Hill, J. (1988) Rat pup ultrasonic isolation calls and the benzodiazepine receptor. In *The Physiological Control of Mammalian Vocalization* (ed. J.D. Newman), Plenum Press, New York, pp. 331–342.

Insel, T.R. and Young, L.J. (2001) The neurobiology of attachment. *Nature Reviews Neuroscience*, **2**, 129–136.

Ito, M. (1984) *The Cerebellum and Neural Control*, Raven Press, New York.

Jacob, F. (1977) Evolution and tinkering. *Science*, **196**, 1161–1166.

Jacobs, K.M., Mark, G.P. and Scott, T.R. (1988) Taste responses in the nucleus tractus solitarius of sodium-deprived rats. *Journal of Physiology*, **406**, 393–410.

Jacobsen, C.F. (1936) Studies of cerebral function in primates. *Comparative Psychology Monographs*, **13**, 1–68.

Jacobsen, E. (1931) Electrical measurements of neuromuscular states during mental activities. V. Variation of specific muscles contracting during imagination. *American Journal of Physiology*, **96**, 115–121.

Jahanshahi, M. and Frith, C.D. (1998) Willed action and its impairments. *Cognitive Neuropsychology*, **15**, 483–533.

Jahanshahi, M., Jenkins, I.H., Brown, R.G., Marsden, C.D., Passingham, R.E. and Brooks, D.J. (1995) Self-initiated versus externally triggered movements I. An investigation using measurement of regional cerebral blood flow with PET and movement-related potentials in normal and Parkinson's disease subjects. *Brain*, **118**, 913–933.

James, W. (1890/1950) *The Principles of Psychology*, Vol. 2, Dover Publications, New York.

Jarrard, L.E. (1993) On the role of the hippocampus in learning and memory in the rat. *Behavioral and Neural Biology*, **60**, 9–26.

Jeannerod, M. (1997) *The Cognitive Neuroscience of Action*, Blackwell, Oxford.

Jenkins, I.H., Brooks, D.J., Nixon, P.D., Frackowiak, R.S.J. and Passingham, R.E. (1994) Motor sequence learning. A study with positron emission tomography. *Journal of Neuroscience*, **14**, 3775–3790.

Jenkins, J. (1997) Pavlovian conditioning of sexual behavior in male three-spine stickleback (*Gasterosteus aculeatus*). *Behaviour*, **41**, 133–137.

Jerison, H.J. (1976) Principles of the evolution of the brain and behaviour. In *Evolution, Brain, and Behavior: Persistent Problems* (eds R.B. Masterton, W. Hodos and H. Jerison), Lawrence Erlbaum, Hillsdale, pp. 23–45.

Jerison, H.J. (1991a) *Brain Size and the Evolution of Mind*, American Museum of Natural History, New York.

Jerison, H.J. (1991b) Fossil brains and the evolution of the neocortex. In *The Neocortex: Ontogeny and Phylogeny* (eds B.L. Finlay, G. Innocenti and H. Scheich), Plenum, New York, pp. 5–19.

Jessell, T.M. and Kelly, D.D. (1991) Pain and analgesia. In *Principles of Neural Science* (eds E.R. Kandel, J.H. Schwartz and T.M. Jessell), Appleton and Lange, East Norwalk, pp. 385–399.

Johnson, A.K. and Thunhorst, R.L. (1997) The neuroendocrinology of thirst and salt appetite: visceral sensory signals and mechanisms of central integration. *Frontiers in Neuroendocrinology*, **18**, 292–353.

Johnson, M.H. (1997) *Developmental Cognitive Neuroscience – An Introduction*, Blackwell, Oxford.

Johnson, M.K. and Chalfonte, B.L. (1994) Binding complex memories: the role of reactivation and hippocampus. In *Memory Systems 1994* (eds D.L. Schacter and E. Tulving), MIT Press, Cambridge, pp. 311–350.

Johnson, M.K. and Multhaup, K.S. (1992) Emotion and MEM. In *The Handbook of Emotion and Memory – Research and Theory* (ed. S-A. Christianson), Lawrence Erlbaum, Hillsdale, pp. 33–66.

Johnston, T.D. (1987) The persistence of dichotomies in the study of behavioral development. *Developmental Review*, 7, 149–182.

Jones, E.G. and Friedman, D.P. (1982) Projection pattern of functional components of thalamic ventrobasal complex on monkey somatosensory cortex. *Journal of Neurophysiology*, 48, 521–544.

Jönsson, L-E., Änggård, E. and Gunne, L.-M. (1971) Blockade of intravenous amphetamine euphoria in man. *Clinical Pharmacology and Therapeutics*, 12, 889–896.

Jordan, D. (1990) Autonomic changes in affective behaviour. In *Central Regulation of Autonomic Functions* (eds A.D. Loewy and K.M. Spyer), Oxford University Press, New York, pp. 349–366.

Jouvet, M. (1975) The function of dreaming: a neurophysiologist's point of view. In *Handbook of Psychobiology* (eds M.S. Gazzaniga and C. Blakemore), Academic Press, New York, pp. 499–527.

Jouvet-Mounier, D., Astic, L. and Lacote, D. (1969) Ontogenesis of the states of sleep in rat, cat, and guinea pig during the first postnatal month. *Developmental Psychobiology*, 2, 216–239.

Jung, C.G. (1963) *Memories, Dreams, Reflections*, Collins and Routledge and Kegan Paul, London.

Jusczyk, P.W. and Cohen, A. (1985) What constitutes a module? *Behavioral and Brain Sciences*, 8, 20–21.

Kaas, J.H. (1996) The somatosensory cortex. In *Somesthesis and the Neurobiology of the Somatosensory Cortex* (eds O. Franzén, R. Johansson and L. Terenius), Birkhäuser Verlag, Basle, pp. 163–171.

Kagan, J. and Baird, A. (2004) Brain and behavioral development during childhood and adolescence. In *The Cognitive Neurosciences* (3rd edition) (ed. M.S. Gazzaniga), MIT Press, Cambridge, pp. 93–103.

Kaiyala, K.J., Woods, S.C. and Schwartz, M.W. (1995) New model for the regulation of energy balance and adiposity by the central nervous system. *American Journal of Clinical Nutrition*, 62 (suppl.), 1123S–1134S.

Kalat, J.W. (1998) *Biological Psychology*, 6th edn, Brooks/Cole, Pacific Grove.

Kalat, J.W. (2004) *Biological Psychology*, 8th edn, Brooks/Cole, Pacific Grove.

Kalin, N.H., Shelton, S.E. and Lynn, D.E. (1995) Opiate systems in mother and infant primates coordinate intimate contact during reunion. *Psychoneuroendocrinology*, 20, 735–742.

Kandel, E.R. (1976) *Cellular Basis of Behavior: An Introduction to Behavioral Neurobiology*, W.H. Freeman, San Francisco.

Kandel, E.R. (1991) Cellular mechanisms of learning and the biological basis of individuality. In *Principles of Neural Science* (eds E.R. Kandel, J.H. Schwartz and T.M. Jessell), Appleton and Lange, Norwalk, pp. 1009–1031.

Kandel, E.R. (2006) *Principles of Neural Science*, McGraw-Hill, New York

Kandel, E.R. and Jessell, T.M. (1991) Touch. In *Principles of Neural Science* (eds E.R. Kandel, J.H. Schwartz and T.M. Jessell), Appleton and Lange, Norwalk, pp. 367–384.

Kanwisher, N. and Wojciulik, E. (2000) Visual attention: insights from brain imaging. *Nature Reviews Neuroscience*, 1, 91–100.

Kaplan, E. (2004) The M, P, and K pathways of the primate visual system. In *The Visual Neurosciences* (Vol. 1) (eds L.M. Chalupa and J.S. Werner), MIT Press, Cambridge, pp. 481–493.

Kapur, S. (2003) Psychosis as a state of aberrant salience: a framework linking biology, phenomenology, and pharmacology in schizophrenia. *American Journal of Psychiatry*, 160, 13–23.

Karmiloff-Smith, A., Klima, E., Bellugi, U., Grant, J. and Baron-Cohen, S. (1995) Is there a social module? Language, face processing, and theory of mind in individuals with Williams syndrome. *Journal of Cognitive Neuroscience*, 7, 196–208.

Karnath, H-O., Ferber, S. and Himmelbach, M. (2001) Spatial awareness is a function of the temporal not the posterior parietal lobe. *Nature*, 411, 950–953.

Karnath, H-O., Himmelbach, M. and Rorden, C. (2002) The subcortical anatomy of human spatial neglect: putamen, caudate nucleus and Pulvinar. *Brain*, 125, 350–360.

Kassel, J.D. and Shiffman, S. (1992) What can hunger teach us about drug craving? A comparative analysis of the two constructs. *Advances in Behaviour Research and Therapy*, 14, 141–167.

Kavanau, J.L. (1994) Sleep and dynamic stabilization of neural circuitry: a review and synthesis. *Behavioural Brain Research*, 63, 111–126.

Kavanau, J.L. (1998) Vertebrates that never sleep: implications for sleep's basic function. *Brain Research Bulletin*, 46, 269–279.

Keefauver, S.P. and Guilleminault, C. (1994) Sleep terrors and sleep walking. In *Principles and Practice of Sleep Medicine* (eds M.H. Kryger, T. Roth and W.C. Dement), Saunders, Philadelphia, pp. 567–573.

Keefe, F.J., Abernethy, A.P. and Campbell, L.C. (2005) Psychological approaches to understanding and treating disease-related pain. *Annual Review of Psychology*, 56, 601–630.

Kellerman, H. (1987) *The Nightmare*, Columbia University Press, New York.

Keltner, D. and Buswell, B.N. (1997) Embarrassment: its distinct form and appeasement functions. *Psychological Bulletin*, 122, 250–270.

Kempermann, G. (2006) *Adult Neurogenesis: Stem Cells and Neuronal Development in the Adult Brain*. Oxford University Press, New York.

Kenshalo, D.R. and Douglass, D.K. (1995) The role of cerebral cortex in the experience of pain. In *Pain and the Brain: From Nociception to Cognition* (Advances in Pain Research and Therapy, Vol. 22) (eds B. Bromm and J.E. Desmedt), Raven Press, New York, pp. 21–34.

Keverne, E.B., Martensz, N.D. and Tuite, B. (1989) Beta-endorphin concentrations in cerebrospinal fluid of monkeys are influenced by grooming relationships. *Psychoneuroendocrinology*, 14, 155–161.

Kiecolt-Glaser, J.K., Page, G.G., Marucha, P.T., MacCallum, R.C. and Glaser, R. (1998) Psychological influences on surgical recovery: perspectives from psychoneuroimmunology. *American Psychologist*, 53, 1209–1218.

Kihlstrom, J.F. (1993) The psychological unconscious and the self. In *Experimental and Theoretical Studies of Consciousness* (eds G.R. Bock and J. Marsh), Wiley, Chichester, pp. 147–167.

Kim, J.J. and Diamond, D.M. (2002) The stressed hippocampus, synaptic plasticity and lost memories. *Nature Reviews Neuroscience*, 3, 453–462.

King, H.E. (1961) Psychological effects of excitation in the limbic system. In *Electrical Stimulation of the Brain* (ed. D.E. Sheer), University of Texas Press, Austin, pp. 477–486.

Kinsbourne, M. (1995) Septohippocampal comparator: consciousness generator or attention feedback loop? *Behavioral and Brain Sciences*, **18**, 687–688.

Kinsley, C.H. and Lambert, K.G. (2006) The maternal brain. *Scientific American*, **294**(1), 72–79.

Klee, H. and Morris, J. (1997) Amphetamine misuse: the effects of social context on injection related risk behaviour. *Addiction Research*, **4**, 329–342.

Klein, R. (1991) Is consciousness information processing? *Behavioral and Brain Sciences*, **14**, 683.

Klein, S.B., Cosmides, L., Tooby, J. and Chance, S. (2002a) Decisions and the evolution of memory: multiple systems, multiple functions. *Psychological Review*, **109**, 306–329.

Klein, S.B., Rozendal, K. and Cosmides, L. (2002b) A social-cognitive neuroscience analysis of the self. *Social Cognition*, **20**, 105–135.

Kleschevnikov, A.M., Belichenko, P.V., Villar, A.J., Epstein, C.J., Malenka, R.C. and Mobley, W.C. (2004) Hippocampal long-term potentiation suppressed by increased inhibition in Ts65Dn mouse, a genetic model of Down syndrome. *Journal of Neuroscience*, **24**, 8153–8160.

Kling, A.S. (1986) The anatomy of aggression and affiliation. In *Emotion – Theory, Research and Experience*, Vol. 3, *Biological Foundations of Emotion* (eds R. Plutchik and H. Kellerman), Academic Press, Orlando, pp. 237–264.

Klüver, H. and Bucy, P.C. (1939) Preliminary analysis of functions of the temporal lobes in monkeys. *Archives of Neurology and Psychiatry*, **42**, 979–1000.

Knibestol, M. and Vallbo, A. (1980) Intensity of sensation related to activity of slowly adapting mechanoreceptive units in the human hand, *Journal of Physiology* (London), **300**, 251–267.

Knutson, B. (2004) Sweet revenge? *Science*, **305**, 1246–1247.

Koepp, M.J., Gunn, R.N., Lawrence, A.D., Cunningham, V.J., Dagher, T., Jones, T., Brooks, D.J., Bench, C.J. and Grasby, P.M. (1998) Evidence for striatal dopamine release during a video game. *Nature*, **393**, 266–268.

Kohler, E., Keysers, C., Umiltà, M.A., Fogassi, L., Gallese, V. and Rizzolatti, G. (2002) Hearing sounds, understanding actions: action representation in mirror neurons. *Science*, **297**, 846–848.

Kohlert, J.G. and Meisel, R.L. (1999) Sexual experience sensitizes mating-related nucleus accumbens dopamine responses of female Syrian hamsters. *Behavioural Brain Research*, **99**, 45–52.

Kokkinidis, L. and Anisman, H. (1980) Amphetamine models of paranoid schizophrenia: an overview and elaboration of animal experimentation. *Psychological Bulletin*, **88**, 551–597.

Kolársky, A., Freund, K., Machek, J. and Polák, O. (1967) Male sexual deviation. *Archives of General Psychiatry*, **17**, 735–743.

Kolb, B. and Taylor, L. (1990) Neocortical substrates of emotional behaviour. In *Psychological and Biological Approaches to Emotion* (eds N.L. Stein, B. Leventhal and T. Trabasso), Lawrence Erlbaum, Hillsdale, pp. 115–144.

Kolb, B., Forgie, M., Gibb, R., Gorny, G. and Rowntree, S. (1998) Age, experience and the changing brain. *Neuroscience and Biobehavioral Reviews*, **22**, 143–159.

Komisaruk, B.R. and Whipple, B. (2005) Brain activity imaging during sexual response in women with spinal cord injury. In *Biological Substrates of Human Sexuality* (ed. J.S. Hyde), American Psychological Association, Washington, pp. 109–145.

Koob, G.F. (1999) Drug reward addiction. In *Fundamental Neuroscience* (eds M.J. Zigmond, F.E. Bloom, S.C. Landis, J.L. Roberts and L.R. Squire), Academic Press, San Diego, pp. 1261–1279.

Koob, G.F. and Le Moal, M. (2006) *Neurobiology of Addiction*, Elsevier, Amsterdam.

Korsakoff, S. (1889) Étude médico-psychologique sur une forme des maladies de la mémoire. *Revue Philosophique*, **28**, 501–530.

Kosfeld, M., Heinrichs, M., Zak, P.J., Fischbacher, U. and Fehr, E. (2005) Oxytocin increases trust in humans. *Nature*, **435**, 673–676.

Kosslyn, S.M. (1988) Aspects of a cognitive neuroscience of mental imagery. *Science*, **240**, 1621–1626.

Kosslyn, S.M., Gazzaniga, M.S., Galaburda, A.M. and Rabin, C. (1999) Hemispheric specialization. In *Fundamental Neuroscience* (eds M.J. Zigmond, F.E. Bloom, S.C. Landis, J.L. Roberts and L.R. Squire), Academic Press, San Diego, pp. 1521–1542.

Kozlowski, L.T., Wilkinson, A., Skinner, W., Kent, C., Franklin, T. and Pope, M. (1989) Comparing tobacco cigarette dependence with other drug dependencies. *Journal of the American Medical Association*, **261**, 898–901.

Kraepelin, E. (1919) *Dementia Praecox and Paraphrenia*, Livingstone, Edinburgh.

Kraly, F.S. (1991) Effects of eating on drinking. In *Thirst: Physiological and Psychological Aspects* (eds D.J. Ramsey and D. Booth), Springer-Verlag, London, pp. 297–312.

Krane, R.J., Goldstein, I. and Saenz de Tejada, I. (1989) Impotence. *New England Journal of Medicine*, **321**, 1648–1659.

Kropotov, J.D. and Etlinger, S.C. (1999) Selection of actions in the basal ganglia–thalamocortical circuits: review and model. *International Journal of Psychophysiology*, **31**, 197–217.

Krueger, J.M., Fang, J., Hansen, M.K., Zhang, J. and Obál, F. (1998) Humoral regulation of sleep. *News in Physiological Sciences*, **13**, 189–194.

Krupa, D.J., Thompson, J.K. and Thompson, R.F. (1993) Localization of a memory trace in the mammalian brain. *Science*, **260**, 989–991.

Kryger, M.H., Roth, T. and Dement, W.C. (2005) *Principles and Practice of Sleep Medicine*, 4th edition, Saunders, Philadelphia.

Kuffler, S.W. (1953) Discharge patterns and functional organization of mammalian retina. *Journal of Neurophysiology*, **16**, 37–68.

Kuffler, S.W. and Nicholls, J.G. (1976) *From Neuron to Brain*, Sinauer Associates, Sunderland.

Kurihara, K. and Kashiwayanagi, M. (2000) Physiological studies on umami taste. *Journal of Nutrition*, **130**, 931S–934S.

Lacquaniti, F., Grasso, R. and Zago, M. (1999) Motor patterns in walking. *News in Physiological Sciences*, **14**, 168–174.

Laing, R.D. (1960) *The Divided Self*, Tavistock Publications, London.

Lal, S.K.L., Henderson, R.J., Carter, N., Bath, A., Hart, M.G., Langeluddecke, P. and Hunyor, S.N. (1998) Effect of feedback signal and psychological characteristics on blood pressure self-manipulation capability. *Psychophysiology*, **35**, 405–412.

Lang, P.J., Bradley, M.M. and Cuthbert, B.N. (1990) Emotion, attention and the startle reflex. *Psychological Review*, **97**, 377–395.

Langhans, W. (1996) Role of the liver in the metabolic control of eating: what we know and what we do not know. *Neuroscience and Biobehavioral Reviews*, **20**, 145–153.

Langhans, W. and Scharrer, E. (1992) Metabolic control of eating. *World Review of Nutrition and Diatetics*, **70**, 1–67.

Larriva-Sahd, J., Rondán, A., Orozco-Estévez, H. and Sánchez-Robles, M.R. (1993) Evidence of a direct projection of the vomeronasal organ to the medial preoptic nucleus and hypothalamus. *Neuroscience Letters*, **163**, 45–49.

Larson, C.R., Ortega, J.D. and DeRosier, E.A. (1988) Studies on the relation of the midbrain periaqueductal gray, the larynx and vocalization in awake monkeys. In *The Physiological Control of Mammalian Vocalization* (ed. J.D. Newman), Plenum Press, New York, pp. 43–65.

Larson, S.J. (2002) Behavioral and motivational effects of immune-system activation. *Journal of General Psychology*, **129**, 401–414.

Laudenslager, M.L., Ryan, S.M., Drugan, R.C., Hyson, R.L. and Maier, S.F. (1983) Coping and immunosuppression: inescapable but not escapable shock suppresses lymphocyte proliferation. *Science*, **221**, 568–570.

Lazarus, R.S. (1984) On the primacy of cognition. *American Psychologist*, **39**, 124–129

Le Doux, J.E. (1989) Cognitive–emotional interactions in the brain. *Cognition and Emotion*, **3**, 267–289.

Le Doux, J.E. (1991) Emotion and the limbic system concept. *Concepts in Neuroscience*, **2**, 169–199.

Le Doux, J.E. (1992) Emotion as memory: anatomical systems underlying indelible neural traces. In *The Handbook of Emotion and Memory – Research and Theory* (ed. S-A. Christianson), Lawrence Erlbaum, Hillsdale, pp. 269–288.

Le Doux, J.E. (1994) Emotion, memory and the brain. *Scientific American*, **270**, 32–39.

Le Doux, J. (1998) *The Emotional Brain*, Weidenfeld and Nicolson, London.

Lee, A., Clancy, S. and Fleming, A.S. (2000) Mother rats bar-press for pups: effects of lesions of the mpoa and limbic sites on maternal behavior and operant responding for pup-reinforcement. *Behavioral Brain Research*, **108**, 215–231.

Lee, S.W. and Stanley, B.G. (2005) NMDA receptors mediate feeding elicited by neuropeptide Y in the lateral and perifornical hypothalamus. *Brain Research*, **1063**, 1–8.

Lehrner, J., Marwinski, G., Lehr, S., Johren, P. and Deecke, L. (2005) Ambient odors of orange and lavender reduce anxiety and improve mood in a dental office. *Physiology and Behavior*, **86**, 92–95.

Leiblum, S.R. and Rosen, R.C. (2000) *Principles and Practice of Sex Therapy*, Guilford Press, New York.

Leiblum, S., Bachmann, G., Kemmann, E., Colburn, D. and Swartzman, L. (1983) Vaginal atrophy in the postmenopausal woman. *Journal of the American Medical Association*, **249**, 2195–2198.

Le Magnen, J. (1967) Habits and food intake. In *Handbook of Physiology*, Section 6, *Alimentary Canal*, Vol. 1, American Physiological Society, Washington, pp. 11–30.

Le Magnen, J. (1981) The metabolic basis of dual periodicity of feeding in rats. *Behavioral and Brain Sciences*, **4**, 561–607.

Le Magnen, J., Devos, M., Gaudillière, J-P., Louis-Sylvestre, J. and Tallon, S. (1973) Role of a lipostatic mechanism in regulation by feeding of energy balance in rats. *Journal of Comparative and Physiological Psychology*, **84**, 1–23.

LeMay, M. (1976) Morphological cerebral asymmetries of modern man, fossil man, and nonhuman primate. *Annals of the New York Academy of Sciences*, **280**, 349–366.

Lenard, H.G. and Schulte, F.J. (1972) Polygraphic sleep study in craniopagus twins. (Where is the sleep transmitter?) *Journal of Neurology, Neurosurgery, and Psychiatry*, **35**, 756–762.

Lenneberg, E.H. (1967) *Biological Foundations of Language*, Wiley, New York.

Lenzenweger, M.F. and Dworkin, R.H. (1998) *Origins and Development of Schizophrenia*. American Psychological Association, Washington.

Leopold, D.A., Maier, A. and Logothetis, N.K. (2003) Measuring subjective visual perception in the nonhuman primate. *Journal of Consciousness Studies*, **10**, 115–130.

Leshem, M. (1998) Salt preference in adolescence is predicted by common prenatal and infantile mineralofluid loss. *Physiology and Behavior*, **63**, 699–704.

Leslie, A.M. (1999) 'Theory of mind' as a mechanism of selective attention. In *The New Cognitive Neurosciences* (ed. M.S. Gazzaniga), MIT Press, Cambridge, pp. 1235–1247.

LeVay, S. (1991) A difference in hypothalamic structure between heterosexual and homosexual men. *Science*, **253**, 1034–1037.

LeVay, S. (1993) *The Sexual Brain*, MIT Press, Cambridge.

LeVay, S. and Valentine, S.M. (2006) *Human Sexuality*. Sinauer Associates, Sunderland, MA.

Levenstein, S. (1998) Stress and peptic ulcer: life beyond *helicobacter*. *British Medical Journal*, **316**, 538–541.

Levitsky, D.A. (2005) The non-regulation of food intake in humans: hope for reversing the epidemic of obesity. *Physiology and Behavior*, **86**, 623–632.

Levy, F. and Hay, D.A. (2001) *Attention, Genes and ADHD*. Brunner-Routledge, Hove.

Lewis, D.J. (1979) Psychobiology of active and inactive memory. *Psychological Bulletin*, **86**, 1054–1083.

Lewis, M., Alessandri, S.M. and Sullivan, M.W. (1990) Violation of expectancy, loss of control and anger expressions in young infants. *Developmental Psychology*, **26**, 745–751.

Leyens, J-P. and Fraczek, A. (1986) Aggression as an interpersonal phenomenon. In *The Social Dimension. European Developments in Social Psychology*, Vol. 1 (ed. H. Tajfel), Cambridge University Press, Cambridge, pp. 184–203.

Lhermitte, F. (1983) 'Utilization behaviour' and its relation to lesions of the frontal lobes. *Brain*, **106**, 237–255.

Liberman, A.M. (1995) The relation of speech to reading and writing. In *Speech and Reading: A Comparative Approach* (eds B. de Gelder and J. Morais), Taylor and Francis, Hove, pp. 17–31.

Libet, B. (1993a) Discussion. In *Experimental and Theoretical Studies of Consciousness* (eds G.R. Bock and J. Marsh), Wiley, Chichester, p. 35.

Libet, B. (1993b) The neural time factor in conscious and unconscious events. In *Experimental and Theoretical Studies of Consciousness* (eds G.R. Bock and J. Marsh), Wiley, Chichester, pp. 123–146.

Libet, B. (2005) *Mind Time: The Temporal Factor in Consciousness*, Harvard University Press, Cambridge.

Libet, B., Pearl, D.K., Morledge, D.E., Gleason, C.A., Hosobuchi, Y. and Barbaro, N.M. (1991) Control of the transition from sensory detection to sensory awareness in man by the duration of a thalamic stimulus. *Brain*, **114**, 1731–1757.

Lichtman, J.W., Burden, S.J., Culican, S.M. and Wong, R.O.L. (1999) Synapse formation and elimination. In *Fundamental Neuroscience* (eds M.J. Zigmond, F.E. Bloom, S.C. Landis, J.L. Roberts and L.R. Squire), Academic Press, San Diego, pp. 547–580.

Lieberman, P. (1991) Speech and brain evolution. *Behavioral and Brain Sciences*, **14**, 566–568.

Lim, M.M., Wang, Z., Olazábal, D.E., Ren, X., Terwilliger, E.F. and Young, L.J. (2004) Enhanced partner preference in a promiscuous species by manipulating the expression of a single gene. *Nature*, **429**, 754–757.

Lipska, B.K., Khaing, Z.Z. and Weinberger, D.R. (1999) Neonatal hippocampal damage in the rat: a heuristic model of schizophrenia. *Psychiatric Annals*, **29**, 157–160.

Lisander, B. (1979) Somato-autonomic reactions and their higher control. In *Integrative Functions of the Autonomic Nervous System* (eds C.M. Brooks, K. Koizumi and A. Sato), University of Tokyo Press/Elsevier, Amsterdam, pp. 385–395.

Lisberger, S.G. (1988) The neural basis for learning of simple motor skills. *Science*, **242**, 728–735.

Lissauer, H. (1988) A case of visual agnosia with a contribution to theory. *Cognitive Neuropsychology*, **5**, 157–192.

Little, A.C., Penton-Voak, I.S., Burt, D.M. and Perrett, D.I. (2002) In *Facial Attractiveness: Evolutionary, Cognitive, and Social Perspectives* (eds G. Rhodes, and L.A. Zebrowitz) Ablex, Westpoint, pp. 59–90.

Liu, D., Diorio, J., Tannenbaum, B., Caldji, C., Francis, D., Freedman, A., Sharma, S., Pearson, D., Plotsky, P.M. and Meaney, M.J. (1997) Maternal care, hippocampal glucocorticoid receptors, and hypothalamic–pituitary–adrenal responses to stress. *Science*, **277**, 1659–1662.

Liu, G. and Rao, Y. (2004) Neuronal migration in the brain. In *The Cognitive Neurosciences* (3rd edition) (ed. M.S. Gazzaniga), MIT Press, Cambridge, pp. 93–103.

Livingstone, M. and Hubel, D. (1988) Segregation of form, colour, movement, and depth: anatomy, physiology, and perception. *Science*, **240**, 740–749.

Livingstone, M. and Hubel, D. (1995) Through the eyes of monkeys and men. In *The Artful Eye* (eds R. Gregory, J. Harris, P. Heard and D. Rose), Oxford University Press, Oxford, pp. 52–65.

Llinás, R.R. and Paré, D. (1991) Of dreaming and wakefulness. *Neuroscience*, **44**, 521–535.

Lloyd, D.M., Bolanowski, S.J., Howard, L. and McGlone, F. (1999) Mechanisms of attention in touch. *Somatosensory and Motor Research*, **16**, 3–10.

Loewy, A.D. (1990) Anatomy of the autonomic nervous system: an overview. In *Central Regulation of Autonomic Functions* (eds A.D. Loewy and K.M. Spyer), Oxford University Press, New York, pp. 3–16.

Logothetis, N.K. (1999) Vision: a window on consciousness. *Scientific American*, **281**, No. 5, 68–75.

Logue, A.W. (1991) *The Psychology of Eating and Drinking*. W.H. Freeman, New York.

Lopez, O.L. and Becker, J.T. (2004) The natural history of Alzheimer's disease. In *Cognitive Neuropsychology of Alzheimer's Disease* 2nd edition (eds R.G. Morris and J.T. Becker), Oxford University Press, Oxford, pp. 47–61.

Lorberbaum, J.P., Newman, J.D., Horwitz, A.R., Dubno, J.R., Lydiard, R.B., Hamner, M.B., Bohning, D.E. and George, M.S. (2002) A potential role for thalamocingulate circuitry in human maternal behaviour. *Biological Psychiatry*, **51**, 431–445.

Lorenz, K.Z. (1981) *The Foundations of Ethology*, Springer-Verlag, New York.

Lozano, A.M. and Kalia, S.K. (2005) New movements in Parkinson's disease. *Scientific American*, **293**(1), 68–75.

Luck, S.J., Chelazzi, L., Hillyard, S.A. and Desimone, R. (1997) Neural mechanisms of spatial selective attention in areas V1, V2, and V4 of Macaque visual cortex. *Journal of Neurophysiology*, **77**, 24–42.

Lundberg, P.O. (1992) Sexual dysfunction in patients with neurological disorders. *Annual Review of Sex Research*, **3**, 121–150.

Luria, A.R. (1966) *Higher Cortical Function in Man*, Tavistock Press, London.

Luria, A.R. (1973) *The Working Brain: An Introduction to Neuropsychology*, Penguin Books, Harmondsworth.

Luria, A.R. and Homskaya, E.D. (1964) Disturbance in the regulative role of speech with frontal lobe lesions. In *The Frontal Granular Cortex and Behavior* (eds J.M. Warren and K. Akert), McGraw-Hill, New York, pp. 353–371.

Luria, A.R., Pribram, K.H. and Homskaya, E.D. (1964) An experimental analysis of the behavioral disturbance produced by a left frontal arachnoidal endothelioma (meningioma). *Neuropsychologia*, **2**, 257–280.

McBride, W.J. and Li, T-K. (1998) Animal models of alcoholism: neurobiology of high alcohol-drinking behaviour in rodents. *Critical Reviews in Neurobiology*, **12**, 339–369.

McBurney, D.H. (1984) Taste and olfaction: sensory discrimination. In *Handbook of Physiology*. Section 1: The Nervous System, Vol. III, Part 2 (ed. I. Darian-Smith), American Physiological Society, Bethesda, pp. 1067–1086.

McCann, U.D., Szabo, Z., Scheffel, U., Dannals, R.F. and Ricaurte, G.A. (1998) Positron emission tomographic evidence of toxic effect of MDMA ('Ecstasy') on brain serotonin neurons in human beings. *The Lancet*, **352**, 1433–1437.

McCarley, R.W. (1995) Sleep, dreams and states of consciousness. In *Neuroscience in Medicine* (ed. P.M. Conn), J.B. Lippincott, Philadelphia, pp. 537–553.

McCarthy, M.M. and Albrecht, E.D. (1996) Steroid regulation of sexual behaviour. *Trends in Endocrinology and Metabolism*, **7**, 324–327.

McCaughey, S.A. and Scott, T.R. (1998) The taste of sodium. *Neuroscience and Biobehavioral Reviews*, **22**, 663–676.

McClintock, M.K. (1971) Menstrual synchrony and suppression. *Nature*, **229**, 244–245

McClintock, M.K. (1984) Estrous synchrony: modulation of ovarian cycle length by female pheromones. *Physiology and Behavior*, **32**, 701–705.

McDonald, M.P. and Overmier, J.B. (1998) Present imperfect: a critical review of animal models of the mnemonic impairments in Alzheimer's disease. *Neuroscience and Biobehavioral Reviews*, **22**, 99–120.

McDonald, R.J. and White, N.M. (1993) A triple dissociation of memory systems: hippocampus, amygdala and dorsal striatum. *Behavioral Neuroscience*, **107**, 3–22.

McDonnell, P.M. and Corkum, V.L. (1991) The role of reflexes in the patterning of limb movements in the first six months of life. In *The Development of Timing Control and Temporal Organization of Coordinated Action* (eds J. Fagard and P.H. Wolff), North-Holland, Amsterdam, pp. 151–173.

McDougall, W. (1923) *An Outline of Psychology*, Methuen, London.

McEwen, B.S. (2004) *The End of Stress as We Know It*, Joseph Henry Press, Washington.

McEwen, B.S., De Kloet, E.R. and Rostene, W. (1986) Adrenal steroid receptors and actions in the nervous system. *Physiological Reviews*, **66**, 1121–1188.

McFarland, D.J. (1999) *Animal Behaviour: Psychobiology, Ethology and Evolution*, Pearson Education, Harlow.

McGaugh, J.L. (1992) Affect, neuromodulatory systems and memory storage. In *The Handbook of Emotion and Memory – Research and Theory* (ed. S-A. Christianson), Lawrence Erlbaum, Hillsdale, pp. 245–268.

McGaugh, J.L. (2004) The amygdala modulates the consolidation of memories of emotionally arousing experiences. In *Annual Review of Neuroscience*, **27** (eds S.E. Hyman, T.M. Jessell, C.J. Shatz and C.F. Stevens), Annual Reviews, Palo Alto, pp. 1–28.

McGuffin, P. and Katz, R. (1993) Genes, adversity and depression. In *Nature, Nurture and Psychology* (eds R. Plomin and G.E. McClearn), American Psychological Association, Washington, pp. 217–230.

McGuire, P.K. and Shah, G.M.S. (1993) Increased blood flow in Broca's area during auditory hallucinations in schizophrenia. *Lancet*, **342**, 703–706.

McHugh, P.R. (1990) Clinical issues in food ingestion and body weight maintenance. In *Handbook of Behavioral Neurobiology*, Vol. 10, *Neurobiology of Food and Fluid Intake* (ed. E.M. Stricker), Plenum Press, New York, pp. 531–547.

Mackintosh, N. (1974) *The Psychology of Animal Learning*, Academic Press, London.

MacKay, D. (1987) Divided brains – divided minds? In *Mindwaves: Thoughts on Intelligence, Identity and Consciousness* (eds C. Blakemore and S. Greenfield), Basil Blackwell, Oxford, pp. 5–16.

MacKay, D.M. (1966) Cerebral organization and the conscious control of action. In *Brain and Conscious Experience* (ed. J.C. Eccles), Springer-Verlag, Berlin, pp. 422–445.

MacKay, D.M. (1974) *The Clockwork Image*, Inter-Varsity Press, London.

MacKay, W.A. (1991) Consciousness is king of the neuronal processors. *Behavioral and Brain Sciences*, **14**, 687–688.

McKee, D.P. and Quigley, E.M.M. (1993) Intestinal motility in irritable bowel syndrome: is IBS a motility disorder? Part 2. Motility of the small bowel, esophagus, stomach, and gall-bladder. *Digestive Diseases and Sciences*, **38**, 1773–1782.

MacLean, P.D. (1958) Contrasting functions of limbic and neocortical systems of the brain and their relevance to psychophysiological aspects of medicine. *American Journal of Medicine*, **25**, 611–626.

Macmillan, M.B. (1986) A wonderful journey through skull and brains: the travels of Mr. Gage's tamping iron. *Brain and Cognition*, **5**, 67–107.

McMurray, G.A. (1950) Experimental study of a case of insensitivity to pain. *Archives of Neurology and Psychiatry*, **64**, 650–667.

MacRae, J.R. and Siegel, S. (1997) The role of self-administration in morphine withdrawal in rats. *Psychobiology*, **25**, 77–82.

Madsen, P.L., Holm, S., Vorstrup, S., Friberg, L., Lassen, N.A. and Wildschiødtz, G. (1991) Human regional cerebral blood flow during rapid-eye-movement sleep. *Journal of Cerebral Blood Flow and Metabolism*, **11**, 502–507.

Maguire, E.A., Gadian, D.G., Johnsrude, I.S., Good, C.D., Ashburner, J., Frackowiak, R.S.J. and Frith, C.D. (2000) Navigation-related structural change in the hippocampi of taxi drivers. *Proceedings of the National Academy of Sciences*, **97**, 4398–4403.

Maier, S.F. and Watkins, L.R. (1998) Cytokines for psychologists: implications of bidirectional immune-to-brain communication for understanding behavior, mood, and cognition. *Psychological Review*, **105**, 83–107.

Maier, S.F., Watkins, L.R. and Fleshner, M. (1994) Psychoneuro-immunology. *American Psychologist*, **49**, 1004–1017.

Maldonado, R., Robledo, P., Chover, A.J., Caine, S.B. and Koob, G.F. (1993) D1 dopamine receptors in the nucleus accumbens modulate cocaine self-administration in the rat. *Pharmacology, Biochemistry and Behavior*, **45**, 239–242.

Mann, K., Klingler, T., Noe, S., Röschke, J., Müller, S. and Benkert, O. (1996) Effects of yohimbine on sexual experiences and nocturnal penile tumescence and rigidity in erectile dysfunction. *Archives of Sexual Behavior*, **25**, 1–16.

Marie, P. and Foix, C. (1917) Les aphasies de Guerre. *Revue Neurologique*, **1**, 53–87.

Marissen, M.A.E., Franken, I.H.A., Blanken, P., van den Brink, W. and Hendriks, V.M. (2005) Cue exposure therapy for opiate dependent clients, *Journal of Substance Use*, **10**, 97–105.

Mark, V.H. and Ervin, F.R. (1970) *Violence and the Brain*, Harper and Row, New York.

Markou, A., Kosten, T.R. and Koob, G.F. (1998) Neurobiological similarities in depression and drug dependence: a self-medication hypothesis. *Neuropsychopharmacology*, **18**, 135–174.

Markowitsch, H.J. (1995) Anatomical basis of memory disorders. In *The Cognitive Neurosciences* (ed. M.S. Gazzaniga), MIT Press, Cambridge, pp. 765–779.

Marmot, M.G. and Syme, S.L. (1976) Acculturation and coronary heart disease in Japanese-Americans. *American Journal of Epidemiology*, **104**, 225–247.

Marr, D. (1969) A theory of cerebellar cortex. *Journal of Physiology*, **202**, 437–470.

Marsden, C.D. (1984) Which motor disorder in Parkinson's disease indicates the true motor function of the basal ganglia? *CIBA Foundation Symposium*, **107**, 225–241.

Marsden, C.D. (1987) What do the basal ganglia tell premotor cortical areas? *CIBA Foundation Symposium*, **132**, 282–300.

Marsden, C.D., Rothwell, J.C. and Day, B.L. (1984) The use of peripheral feedback in the control of movement. *Trends in Neurosciences*, **7**, 253–257.

Marshall, B.J. (1995) *Helicobacter pylori* in peptic ulcer: have Koch's postulates been fulfilled? *Annals of Medicine*, **27**, 565–568.

Martin, G.N. (1996) Olfactory remediation: current evidence and possible applications. *Social Science and Medicine*, **43**, 63–70.

Martin, J.H. (1991) Coding and processing of sensory information. In *Principles of Neural Science* (eds E.R. Kandel, J.H. Schwartz and T.M. Jessell), Prentice Hall, Englewood Cliffs, pp. 329–340.

Martin, J.H. (1996) *Neuroanatomy: Text and Atlas*, Prentice Hall, London.

Martin, J.H. and Jessell, T.M. (1991) Anatomy of the somatic sensory system. In *Principles of Neural Science* (eds E.R. Kandel, J.H. Schwartz and T.M. Jessell), Appleton and Lange, Norwalk, pp. 353–366.

Martin, P.R. (1998) Colour processing in the primate retina: recent progress. *Journal of Physiology*, **513**, 631–638.

Martin, S.J., Grimwood, P.D. and Morris, R.G.M. (2000) Synaptic plasticity and memory: an evaluation of the hypothesis. *Annual Review of Neuroscience*, **23**, 649–711.

Martini, F.H., Timmons, M.J. and McKinley, M.P. (2000) *Human Anatomy*, Prentice Hall, Upper Saddle River.

Mashour, G.A., Walker, E.E. and Martuza, R.L. (2005) Psychosurgery: past, present, and future. *Brain Research Reviews*, **48**, 409–419.

Mason, G.J. (1991) Stereotypies: a critical review. *Animal Behaviour*, **41**, 1015–1037.

Mason, P. (1999) Central mechanisms of pain modulation. *Current Opinion in Neurobiology*, **9**, 436–441.

Mattson, B.J., Williams, S.E., Rosenblatt, J.S. and Morrell, J.I. (2003) Preferences for cocaine- or pup-associated chambers differentiates otherwise behaviorally identical postpartum maternal rats. *Psychopharmacology*, **167**, 1–8.

Maurer, K., Volk, S. and Gerbaldo, H. (1997) Auguste D and Alzheimer's disease. *The Lancet*, **349**, 1546–1549.

Mayr, E. (1974) Behavior programs and evolutionary strategies. *American Scientist*, **62**, 650–659.

Mazenod, B., Pugeat, M. and Forest, M.G. (1988) Hormones, sexual function and erotic behaviour in women. In *Handbook of Sexology*, Vol. 6, *The Pharmacology and Endocrinology of Sexual Function* (ed. J.M.A. Sitsen), Elsevier Science, Amsterdam, pp. 316–351.

Mazur, A. and Booth, A. (1998) Testosterone and dominance in men. *Behavioral and Brain Sciences*, **21**, 353–397.

Meana, M. (1998) The meeting of pain and depression: comorbidity in women. *Canadian Journal of Psychiatry*, **43**, 893–899.

Meaney, M.J., Diorio, J., Francis, D., Widdowson, J., LaPlante, P., Caldji, C., Sharma, S., Seckl, J.R. and Plotsky, P.M. (1996) Early environmental regulation of forebrain glucocorticoid receptor gene expression: implications for adrenocortical responses to stress. *Developmental Neuroscience*, **18**, 49–72.

Meddis, R. (1977) *The Sleep Instinct*, Routledge and Kegan Paul, London.

Meeter, M. and Murre, J.M.J. (2004) Consolidation of long-term memory: evidence and alternatives. *Psychological Bulletin*, **130**, 843–857.

Meï, N. (1993) Gastrointestinal chemoreception and its behavioural role. In *Neurophysiology of Ingestion* (ed. D.A. Booth), Pergamon Press, Oxford, pp. 47–56.

Meï, N. (1994) Role of digestive afferents in food intake regulation. In *Appetite: Neural and Behavioural Bases* (eds C.R. Legg and D. Booth), Oxford University Press, Oxford, pp. 86–97.

Melges, F.T. (1982) *Time and the Inner Future: A Temporal Approach to Psychiatric Disorders*, Wiley, New York.

Mellerio, J. (1966) Ocular refraction at low illuminations. *Vision Research*, **6**, 217–237.

Mellor, C.S. (1970) First rank symptoms of schizophrenia. *British Journal of Psychiatry*, **117**, 15–23.

Melzack, R. (1988) The tragedy of needless pain: a call for social action. In *Proceedings of the Vth World Congress on Pain* (eds R. Dubner, G.F. Gubner and M.R. Bond), Elsevier Science Publishers, Amsterdam, pp. 1–11.

Melzack, R. (1989) Phantom limbs, the self and the brain (The D.O. Hebb Memorial Lecture). *Canadian Psychology*, **30**, 1–16.

Melzack, R. (1993) Pain: past, present and future. *Canadian Journal of Experimental Psychology*, **47**, 615–629.

Melzack, R. and Scott, T.H. (1957) The effects of early experience on the response to pain. *Journal of Comparative and Physiological Psychology*, **50**, 155–161.

Melzack, R. and Wall, P.D. (1965) Pain mechanisms: a new theory. *Science*, **150**, 971–979.

Melzack, R. and Wall, P. (1996) *The Challenge of Pain*, Penguin Books, Harmondsworth.

Mendelson, W.B. (1990) Insomnia: the patient and the pill. In *Sleep and Cognition* (eds R.R. Bootzin, J.F. Kihlstrom and D.L. Schacter), American Psychological Association, Washington, pp. 139–147.

Menzel, E. (1978) Cognitive mapping in chimpanzees. In *Cognitive Processes in Animal Behavior* (eds S.H. Hulse, H. Fowler and W.K. Honig), Lawrence Erlbaum, Hillsdale, pp. 375–422.

Mercer, M.E. and Holder, M.D. (1997) Food cravings, endogenous opioid peptides and food intake: a review. *Appetite*, **29**, 325–352.

Merigan, W.H. and Maunsell, J.H.R. (1993) How parallel are the primate visual pathways? *Annual Review of Neuroscience*, **16**, 369–402.

Merzenich, M.M., Kaas, J.H., Wall, J.T., Sur, M., Nelson, R.J. and Felleman, D.J. (1983) Progression of change following median nerve section in the cortical representation of the hand in areas 3b and 1 in adult owl and squirrel monkeys. *Neuroscience*, **10**, 639–665.

Merzenich, M.M., Wang, X., Xerri, C. and Nudo, R. (1996) Functional plasticity of cortical representations of the hand. In *Somesthesis and the Neurobiology of the Somatosensory Cortex* (eds O. Franzén, R. Johansson and L. Terenius), Birkäuser Verlag, Basle, pp. 249–269.

Meyer, E.A. and Gebhart, G.F (1994) Basic and clinical aspects of visceral hyperalgesia. *Gastroenterology*, **107**, 271–293.

Michel, G.F. and Moore, C.L. (1995) *Developmental Psychobiology: An Interdisciplinary Science*, MIT Press, Cambridge.

Miller, B.L., Cummings, J.L., McIntyre, H., Ebers, G. and Grode, M. (1986) Hypersexuality or altered sexual preference following brain injury. *Journal of Neurology, Neurosurgery, and Psychiatry*, **49**, 867–873.

Miller, M.W. (2006) *Brain Development: Normal Processes and the Effects of Alcohol and Nicotine*. Oxford University Press, New York.

Miller, R.E., Caul, W.F. and Mirsky, I.A. (1967) Communication of affects between feral and socially isolated monkeys. *Journal of Personality and Social Psychology*, **7**, 231–239.

Milner, B. (1964) Some effects of frontal lobectomy in man. In *The Frontal Granular Cortex and Behavior* (eds J.M. Warren and K. Akert), McGraw-Hill, New York, pp. 313–334.

Milner, B. (1966) Amnesia following operation on the temporal lobes. In *Amnesia* (eds C.W.M. Whitty and O.L. Zangwill), Butterworths, London, pp. 109–133.

Milner, B. (1971) Interhemispheric differences in the localization of psychological processes in man. *British Medical Bulletin*, **27**, 272–277.

Milner, B. (1974) Hemispheric specialization: scope and limits. In *The Neurosciences. Third Study Program* (eds F.O. Schmitt and F.G. Worden), MIT Press, Cambridge, pp. 75–89.

Mineka, S. and Öhman, A. (2002) Phobias and preparedness: the selective, automatic, and encapsulated nature of fear. *Biological Psychiatry*, **52**, 927–937.

Mink, J.W. (1999) Basal ganglia. In *Fundamental Neuroscience* (eds M.J. Zigmond, F.E. Bloom, S.C. Landis, J.L. Roberts and L.R. Squire), Academic Press, San Diego, pp. 951–972.

Mishkin, M. (1982) A memory system in the monkey. *Philosophical Transactions of the Royal Society B*, **298**, 85–95.

Mishkin, M., Ungerleider, L.G. and Macko, K.A. (1983) Object vision and spatial vision: two cortical pathways. *Trends in Neurosciences*, **6**, 414–417.

Mistlberger, R.E. (2005) Circadian regulation of sleep in mammals: role of the suprachiasmatic nucleus. *Brain Research Reviews*, **49**, 429–454.

Mistlberger, R.E. and Rusak, B. (2005) Circadian rhythms in mammals: formal properties and environmental influences. In *Principles and Practice of Sleep Medicine,* 4th edition (eds M.H. Kryger, T. Roth and W.C. Dement), Saunders, Philadelphia, pp. 321–334.

Mistlberger, R.E. and Skene, D.J. (2004) Social influences on mammalian circadian rhythms: animal and human studies. *Biological Reviews*, **79**, 533–556.

Mitchell, A.J. (1998) The role of corticotropin releasing factor in depressive illness: a critical review. *Neuroscience and Biobehavioral Reviews*, **22**, 635–651.

Moberg, G.P. (1985) Biological response to stress: key to assessment of animal well-being. In *Animal Stress* (ed. G.P. Moberg), American Physiological Society, Bethesda, pp. 27–49.

Moberg, G.P. and Mench, J.A. (2000) *The Biology of Animal Stress*, CAB International, Wallingford.

Moerman, D.E. (2002) *Meaning, Medicine and the Placebo Effect*, Cambridge University Press, Cambridge.

Mogenson, G.J. (1984) Limbic–motor interaction – with emphasis on initiation of exploratory and goal directed locomotion. In *Modulation of Sensorimotor Activity During Alteration in Behavioral States* (ed. R. Bandler), A.R. Liss, New York, pp. 121–137.

Mogenson, G.J., Brudzynski, S.M., Wu, M., Yang, C.R. and Yim, C.C.Y. (1993) From motivation to action: a review of dopaminergic regulation of limbic → nucleus accumbens → ventral pallidum→ pedunculopontine nucleus circuitries involved in limbic–motor integration. In *Limbic Motor Circuits and Neuropsychiatry* (eds P.W. Kalivas and C.D. Barnes), CRC Press, Boca Raton, pp. 193–236.

Moles, A., Kieffer, B.L. and D'Amato, F.R. (2004) Deficit in attachment behavior in mice lacking the μ-opioid receptor gene. *Science*, **304**, 1983–1986.

Money, J. (1960) Phantom orgasm in the dreams of paraplegic men and women. *Archives of General Psychiatry*, **3**, 373–382.

Money, J., Leal, J. and Gonzalez-Heydrich, J. (1988) Aphrodisiology: history, folklore and efficacy. In *Handbook of Sexology*, Vol. 6, *The Pharmacology and Endocrinology of Sexual Function* (ed. J.M.A. Sitsen), Elsevier Science, Amsterdam, pp. 499–515.

Montgomery, K.C. (1952) A test of two explanations of spontaneous alternation. *Journal of Comparative and Physiological Psychology*, **45**, 287–293.

Monti-Bloch, L., Jennings-White, C., Dolberg, D.S. and Berliner, D.L. (1994) The human vomeronasal system. *Psychoneuroendocrinology*, **19**, 673–686.

Moorcroft, W.H. (2005) *Understanding Sleep and Dreaming*, Springer-Verlag, New York.

Moore, R.Y. (1999) Circadian timing. In *Fundamental Neuroscience* (eds M.J. Zigmond, F.E. Bloom, S.C. Landis, J.L. Roberts and L.R. Squire), Academic Press, San Diego, pp. 1189–1206.

Moore-Ede, M.C., Sulzman, F.M. and Fuller, C.A. (1982) *The Clocks that Time Us*, Harvard University Press, Cambridge.

Moran, J. and Desimone, R. (1985) Selective attention gates visual processing in the extrastriate cortex. *Science*, **229**, 782–784.

Moran, T.H. (2000) Cholecystokinin and satiety: current perspectives. *Nutrition*, **16**, 858–865.

Morris, J.A., Jordan, C.L. and Breedlove, S.M. (2004) Sexual differentiation of the vertebrate nervous system. *Nature Neuroscience*, **7**, 1034–1039.

Morris, J.S., Öhman, A. and Dolan, R.J. (1998) Conscious and unconscious emotional learning in the human amygdala. *Nature*, **393**, 467–470.

Morris, J.S., Öhman, A. and Dolan, R.J. (1999) A subcortical pathway to the right amygdala mediating 'unseen' fear. *Proceedings of the National Academy of Sciences USA*, **96**, 1680–1685.

Morris, R.G. (1996a) *The Cognitive Neuropsychology of Alzheimer-type Dementia*, Oxford University Press, Oxford.

Morris, R.G. (1996b) A cognitive neuropsychology of Alzheimer-type dementia. In *The Cognitive Neuropsychology of Alzheimer-type Dementia* (ed. R.G. Morris), Oxford University Press, Oxford, pp. 3–10.

Morris, R.G. (1996c) Neurobiological correlates of cognitive dysfunction. In *The Cognitive Neuropsychology of Alzheimer-type Dementia* (ed. R.G. Morris), Oxford University Press, Oxford, pp. 223–254.

Morris, R.G. (2004) Neurobiological abnormalities in Alzheimer's disease: structural, genetic, and functional correlates of cognitive dysfunction. In *Cognitive Neuropsychology of Alzheimer's Disease*, 2nd edition (eds R.G. Morris and J.T. Becker), Oxford University Press, Oxford, pp. 299–319.

Morris, R.G. and Becker, J.T. (2004) *Cognitive Neuropsychology of Alzheimer's Disease*, 2nd edition. Oxford University Press, Oxford.

Morris, R.G. and Hannesdottir, K. (2004) Loss of 'awareness' in Alzheimer's disease. In *Cognitive Neuropsychology of Alzheimer's Disease*, 2nd edition (eds R.G. Morris and J.T. Becker), Oxford University Press, Oxford, pp. 275–296.

Morris, R.G.M. (1981) Spatial localization does not require the presence of local cues. *Learning and Motivation*, **12**, 239–260.

Moruzzi, G. (1966) The functional significance of sleep with particular regard to the brain mechanisms underlying consciousness. In *Brain and Conscious Experience* (ed. J.C. Eccles), Springer-Verlag, Berlin, pp. 345–388.

Moruzzi, G. and Magoun, H.W. (1949) Brain stem reticular formation and activation of the EEG. *Electroencephalography and Clinical Neurophysiology*, 1, 455–473.

Moscovitch, M. (1994) Memory and working with memory: evaluation of a component process model and comparisons with other models. In *Memory Systems 1994* (eds D.L. Schacter and E. Tulving), MIT Press, Cambridge, pp. 269–310.

Moscovitch, M. and Umiltà, C. (1990) Modularity and neuropsychology: modules and central processes in attention and memory. In *Modular Deficits in Alzheimer-type Dementia* (ed. M.F. Schwartz), MIT Press, Cambridge, pp. 1–60.

Mountcastle, V.B. (1984) Central nervous mechanisms in mechanoreceptive sensibility. In *Handbook of Physiology, Section 1: The Nervous System*, Vol. III, Part 2 (ed. I. Darian-Smith), American Physiological Society, Bethesda, pp. 789–878.

Moyer, K.E. (1986) Biological bases of aggressive behaviour. In *Emotion – Theory, Research and Experience*, Vol. 3, *Biological Foundations of Emotion* (eds R. Plutchik and H. Kellerman), Academic Press, Orlando, pp. 219–236.

Mukhametov, L.M. (1984) Sleep in marine mammals. In *Sleep Mechanisms* (eds A. Borbély and J-L. Valatx), Springer-Verlag, Berlin, pp. 227–238.

Munakata, Y. and Johnson, M. (2006) *Processes of Change in Brain and Cognitive Development*. Oxford University Press, Oxford.

Munakata, Y., Casey, B.J. and Diamond, A. (2004) Developmental cognitive neuroscience: progress and potential. *Trends in Cognitive Sciences*, **8**, 122–128.

Murphy, M. (1993a) The neuroanatomy and neurophysiology of erection. In *Impotence: An Integrated Approach to Clinical Practice* (eds A. Gregoire and J.P. Pryor), Churchill Livingstone, Edinburgh, pp. 29–48.

Murphy, M. (1993b) The pharmacology of erection and erectile dysfunction. In *Impotence: An Integrated Approach to Clinical Practice* (eds A. Gregoire and J.P. Pryor), Churchill Livingstone, Edinburgh, pp. 55–77.

Murphy, M.R., Seckl, J.R., Burton, S., Checkley, S.A. and Lightman, S.L. (1987) Changes in oxytocin and vasopressin secretion during sexual activity in men. *Journal of Clinical Endocrinology and Metabolism*, **65**, 738–741.

Musselman, D.L., Evans, D.L. and Nemeroff, C.B. (1998) The relationship of depression to cardiovascular disease. *Archives of General Psychiatry*, **55**, 580–592.

Mutschler, N.H. and Miczek, K.A. (1998) Withdrawal from IV cocaine 'binges' in rats: ultrasonic distress calls and startle. *Psychopharmacology*, **135**, 161–168.

Myers, L.S. and Morokoff, P.J. (1986) Physiological and subjective sexual arousal in pre- and postmenopausal women and postmenopausal women taking replacement therapy. *Psychophysiology*, **23**, 283–292.

Myers, R., Spinks, T.J., Luthra, S.K. and Brooks, D.J. (1992) Positron-emission tomography. In *Quantitative Methods in Neuroanatomy* (ed. M. Stewart), Wiley, Chichester, pp. 117–161.

Nader, K. (2003) Memory traces unbound. *Trends in Neurosciences*, **26**, 65–72.

Nagel, T. (1974) What is it like to be a bat? *Philosophical Review*, **83**, 435–451.

Nagel, T. (1993) What is the mind–body problem? In *Experimental and Theoretical Studies of Consciousness* (eds G.R. Bock and J. Marsh), Wiley, Chichester, pp. 1–13.

Nelson, E. and Panksepp, J. (1996) Oxytocin mediates acquisition of maternally associated odor preferences in preweanling rat pups. *Behavioral Neuroscience*, **110**, 583–592.

Nelson, M.D., Saykin, A.J., Flashman, L.A. and Riordan, H.J. (1998) Hippocampal volume reduction in schizophrenia as assessed by magnetic resonance imaging. A meta-analytic study. *Archives of General Psychiatry*, **55**, 433–440.

Nesse, R.M. and Berridge, K.C. (1997) Psychoactive drug use in evolutionary perspective. *Science*, **278**, 63–66.

Nettle, D. (2004) Evolutionary origins of depression: a review and reformulation. *Journal of Affective Disorders*, **81**, 91–102.

Nettle, D. and Clegg, H. (2006) Schizotypy, creativity and mating success in humans. *Proceedings of the Royal Society B Biological Sciences*, **273**, 611–615.

Neve, R.L. and Robakis, N.K. (1998) Alzheimer's disease: a re-examination of the amyloid hypothesis. *Trends in Neurosciences*, **21**, 15–19.

Neville, H.J. (1991) Neurobiology of cognitive and language processing: effects of early experience. In *Brain Maturation and Cognitive Development: Comparative and Cross-cultural Perspectives* (eds K.R. Gibson and A.C. Petersen), Aldine de Gruyter, New York, pp. 355–380.

Newsome, W.T. and Salzman, C.D. (1993) The neuronal basis of motion perception. In *Experimental and Theoretical Studies of Consciousness* (eds G.R. Bock and J. Marsh), Wiley, Chichester, pp. 217–246.

Nielsen, J.M. (1958) *Memory and Amnesia*, San Lucus Press, Los Angeles.

Nielsen, E., Eison, M., Lyon, M. and Iversen, S. (1983) Hallucinatory behaviors in primates produced by around-the-clock amphetamine treatment for several days via implanted capsules. In *Ethopharmacology: Primate Models of Neuropsychiatric Disorders* (ed. K. Miczek), Alan Liss, New York, pp. 79–100.

Nishimura, H., Hashikawa, K., Doi, K., Iwaki, T., Watanabe, Y., Kusuoka, H., Nishimura, T. and Kubo, T. (1999) Sign language 'heard' in the auditory cortex. *Nature*, 397, 116.

Nolte, J. (2002) *The Human Brain: An Introduction to its Functional Anatomy*, Mosby, St. Louis.

Norgren, R. (1984) Central neural mechanisms of taste. In *Handbook of Physiology. Section 1: The Nervous System*, Vol. III, Part 2 (ed. I. Darian-Smith), American Physiological Society, Bethesda, pp. 1097–1128.

Norman, D.A. and Shallice, T. (1986) Attention to action – willed and automatic control of behaviour. In *Consciousness and Self-regulation: Advances in Research and Theory*, Vol. 4 (eds R.J. Davidson, G.E. Schwartz and D. Shapiro), Plenum Press, New York, pp. 1–18.

Norman, J. (2002) Two visual systems and two theories of perception: an attempt to reconcile the constructivist and ecological approaches. *Behavioral and Brain Sciences*, 25, 73–96.

Northcutt, R.G. and Kaas, J.H. (1995) The emergence and evolution of mammalian neocortex. *Trends in Neuroscience*, 18, 373–379.

Novin, D. (1993) Regulatory control of food and water intake and metabolism by the liver. In *Neurophysiology of Ingestion* (ed. D.A. Booth), Pergamon Press, Oxford, pp. 19–32.

Nowakowski, R.S. and Hayes, N.L. (1999) CNS development: an overview. *Development and Psychopathology*, 11, 395–417.

Numan, M. and Insel, T.R. (2003) *The Neurobiology of Parental Behavior*. Springer-Verlag, New York.

Oatley, K. (1988) On changing one's mind: a possible function of consciousness. In *Consciousness in Contemporary Science* (eds A.J. Marcel and E. Bisiach), Clarendon Press, Oxford, pp. 369–389.

Oatley, K. and Jenkins, J.M. (1996) *Understanding Emotions*, Blackwell Publishers, Oxford.

O'Craven, K.M. and Kanwisher, N. (2000) Mental imagery of faces and places activates corresponding stimulus-specific brain regions. *Journal of Cognitive Neuroscience*, 12, 1013–1023.

Ogden, J. (2002) *The Psychology of Eating. From Healthy to Disordered Behavior*. Blackwell Publishers, Oxford.

Öhman, A. (1986) Face the beast and fear the face: animal and social fears as prototypes for evolutionary analyses of emotion. *Psychophysiology*, 23, 123–145.

Öhman, A. (2005) The role of the amygdala in human fear: automatic detection of threat. *Psychoneuroendocrinology*, 30, 953–958.

Öhman, A. and Mineka, S. (2001) Fears, phobias, and preparedness: toward an evolved module of fear and fear learning. *Psychological Review*, 108, 483–522.

Öhman, A. and Mineka, S. (2003) The malicious serpent: snakes as a prototypical stimulus for an evolved module of fear. *Current Directions in Psychological Science*, 12, 5–9.

Ojemann, G.A. (1990) Organization of language cortex derived from investigations during neurosurgery. *Seminars in the Neurosciences*, 2, 297–305.

O'Keefe, J. and Dostrovsky, J. (1971) The hippocampus as a spatial map. Preliminary evidence from unit activity in the freely moving rat. *Brain Research*, 34, 171–175.

O'Keefe, J. and Nadel, L. (1978) *The Hippocampus as a Cognitive Map*, Clarendon Press, Oxford.

Olds, J. and Milner, P. (1954) Positive reinforcement produced by electrical stimulation of septal area and other regions of rat brain. *Journal of Comparative and Physiological Psychology*, 47, 419–427.

O'Leary, A. (1990) Stress, emotion and human immune function. *Psychological Bulletin*, 108, 363–382.

Olton, D.S., Becker, J.T. and Handelmann, G.E. (1979) Hippocampus, space and memory. *Behavioral and Brain Sciences*, 2, 313–365.

Oppenheim, R.W. (1999) Programmed cell death. In *Fundamental Neuroscience* (eds M.J. Zigmond, F.E. Bloom, S.C. Landris, J.L. Roberts and L.R. Squire), Academic Press, San Diego, pp. 581–609.

Orford, J. (2001) *Excessive Appetites: A Psychological View of Addictions*, Wiley, Chichester.

Orr, S.P., Lasko, N.B., Shalev, A.Y. and Pitman, R.K. (1995) Physiological responses to loud tones in Vietnam veterans with posttraumatic stress disorder. *Journal of Abnormal Psychology*, 104, 75–82.

Oscar-Berman, M., Kirkley, S.M., Gansler, D.A. and Couture, A. (2004) Comparisons of Korsakoff and non-Korsakoff alcoholics on neuropsychological tests of prefrontal brain imaging. *Alcoholism: Clinical and Experimental Research*, 28, 667–675.

Oswald, I., Taylor, A.M. and Treisman, M. (1960) Discriminative responses to stimulation during human sleep. *Brain*, 83, 440–453.

Ott, A., Breteler, M.M.B., van Harskamp, F., Claus, J.J., van der Cammen, T.J.M., Grobbe, D.E. and Hofman, A. (1995) Prevalence of Alzheimer's disease and vascular dementia: association with education. The Rotterdam study. *British Medical Journal*, 310, 970–973.

Ottesen, B., Wagner, G. and Fahrenkrug, J. (1988) Peptidergic innervation of the sexual organs. In *Handbook of Sexology*, Vol. 6: *The Pharmacology and Endocrinology of Sexual Function* (ed. J.M.A. Sitsen), Elsevier Science, Amsterdam, pp. 66–97.

Overmier, J.B. and Murison, R. (1997) Animal models reveal the 'psych' in the psychosomatics of peptic ulcers. *Current Directions in Psychological Science*, 6, 180–184.

Pace-Schott, E.F. and Hobson, J.A. (2002) The neurobiology of sleep: genetics, cellular physiology and subcortical networks. *Nature Reviews Neuroscience*, 3, 591–604.

Pace-Schott, E.F., Solms, M., Blagrove, M. and Harnad, S. (2003) *Sleep and Dreaming: Scientific Advances and Reconsiderations*, Cambridge University Press, Cambridge.

Packard, M.G., Hirsh, R. and White, N.M. (1989) Differential effects of fornix and caudate nucleus lesions on two radial maze tasks: evidence for multiple memory systems. *Journal of Neuroscience*, 9, 1465–1472.

Pallis, C.A. (1955) Impaired identification of faces and places with agnosia for colours. *Journal of Neurology, Neurosurgery and Psychiatry*, 18, 218–224.

Pallmeyer, T.P., Blanchard, E.B. and Kolb, L.C. (1986) The psychophysiology of combat-induced post-traumatic stress disorder in Vietnam veterans. *Behaviour Research and Therapy*, **24**, 645–652.

Panksepp, J. (1982) Toward a general psychobiological theory of emotions. *Behavioral and Brain Sciences*, **5**, 407–467.

Panksepp, J. (1986) The neural substrate for emotion. In *Emotion – Theory, Research and Experience*, Vol. 3, *Biological Foundations of Emotion* (eds R. Plutchik and H. Kellerman), Academic Press, Orlando, pp. 91–124.

Panksepp, J. (1994) Affective neuroscience: a paradigm to study the animate circuits for human emotions. In *Emotion: Interdisciplinary Perspectives* (eds R.D. Kavanaugh, B. Zimmerberg and S. Fein), Lawrence Erlbaum, Mahwah, pp. 29–60.

Panksepp, J. (1998a) *Affective Neuroscience*, Oxford University Press, New York.

Panksepp, J. (1998b) Attention deficit hyperactivity disorders, psychostimulants, and intolerance of childhood playfulness: a tragedy in the making? *Current Directions in Psychological Science*, **7**, 91–98.

Panksepp, J., Herman, B., Conner, R., Bishop, P. and Scott, J.P. (1978) The biology of social attachments: opiates alleviate separation distress. *Biological Psychiatry*, **9**, 213–220.

Panksepp, J., Normansell, L., Herman, B., Bishop, P. and Crepeau, L. (1988) Neural and neurochemical control of the separation distress call. In *The Physiological Control of Mammalian Vocalization* (ed. J.D. Newman), Plenum Press, New York, pp. 263–299.

Panksepp, J., Knutson, B. and Burgdorf, J. (2002) The role of brain emotional systems in addictions: a neuro-evolutionary perspective and new 'self-report' animal model. *Addiction*, **97**, 459–469.

Papanicolaou, A.C. (1998) *Fundamentals of Functional Brain Imaging: A Guide to the Methods and their Applications to Psychology and Behavioral Neuroscience*, Swets and Zeitlinger, Lisse.

Pappenheimer, J.R. (1983) Induction of sleep by muramyl peptides. *Journal of Physiology*, **336**, 1–11.

Parasuraman, R. (2004) Attentional functioning in Alzheimer's disease. In *Cognitive Neuropsychology of Alzheimer's Disease,* 2nd edition (eds. R.G. Morris and J.T. Becker), Oxford University Press, Oxford, pp. 81–102.

Paredes, R.G. and Ågmo, A. (2004) Has dopamine a physiological role in the control of sexual behavior? A critical review of the evidence. *Progress in Neurobiology*, **73**, 179–226.

Pavlov, I.P. (1935/1955) *Selected Works*, Foreign Languages Publishing House, Moscow.

Pear, J.J., Moody, J.E. and Persinger, M.A. (1972) Lever attacking by rats during free-operant avoidance. *Journal of the Experimental Analysis of Behavior*, **18**, 517–523.

Peciña, S. and Berridge, K.C. (2000) Opioid site in nucleus accumbens shell mediates eating and hedonic 'liking' for food: map based on microinjection Fos plumes. *Brain Research*, **863**, 71–86.

Peciña, S., Cagniard, B., Berridge, K.C., Aldridge J.W. and Zhuang, X. (2003) Hyperdopaminergic mutant mice have higher 'wanting' but not 'liking' for sweet rewards. *Journal of Neuroscience*, **23**, 9395–9402.

Peele, S. (1985) *The Meaning of Addiction*, Lexington Books, Lexington.

Peele, S. and Alexander, B.K. (1985) Theories of addiction. In *The Meaning of Addiction* (ed. S. Peele), Lexington Books, Lexington, pp. 47–72.

Peele, S. and Degrandpre, R.J. (1998) Cocaine and the concept of addiction: environmental factors in drug compulsions. *Addiction Research*, **6**, 235–263.

Penfield, W. (1966) Speech, perception and the cortex. In *Brain and Conscious Experience* (ed. J.C. Eccles), Springer-Verlag, Berlin, pp. 217–237.

Penfield, W. and Evans, J. (1935) The frontal lobe in man: a clinical study of maximum removals. *Brain*, **58**, 115–133.

Penfield, W. and Rasmussen, T. (1968) *The Cerebral Cortex of Man*, Hafner Publishing, New York.

Penrose, R. (1987) Minds, machines and mathematics. In *Mindwaves: Thoughts on Intelligence, Identity and Consciousness* (eds C. Blakemore and S. Greenfield), Basil Blackwell, Oxford, pp. 259–276.

Penrose, R. (1990) Précis of *The Emperor's New Mind: Concerning Computers, Minds, and The Laws of Physics. Behavioral and Brain Sciences*, **13**, 643–705.

Perrett, D.I., Burt, D.M., Penton-Voak, I.S., Lee, K.J., Rowland, D.A. and Edwards, R. (1999) Symmetry and human facial attractiveness. *Evolution and Human Behavior*, **20**, 295–307.

Perry, E., Walker, M., Grace, J. and Perry, R. (1999) Acetylcholine in mind: a neurotransmitter correlate of consciousness? *Trends in Neurosciences*, **22**, 273–280.

Perry, R.J. and Hodges, J.R. (1999) Attention and executive deficits in Alzheimer's disease. *Brain*, **122**, 383–404.

Pertwee, R.G. (2001) Cannabinoid receptors and pain. *Progress in Neurobiology*, **63**, 569–611.

Petersen, S.E., Fox, P.T., Posner, M.I., Mintun, M. and Raichle, M.E. (1988) Positron emission tomographic studies of the cortical anatomy of single-word processing. *Nature*, **331**, 585–589.

Petri, H.L. and Mishkin, M. (1994) Behaviorism, cognitivism and the neuropsychology of memory. *American Scientist*, **82**, 30–37.

Petrides, M. (1994) Frontal lobes and working memory: evidence from investigations of the effects of cortical excisions in nonhuman primates. In *Handbook of Neuropsychology*, Vol. 9 (eds F. Boller and J. Grafman), Elsevier, Amsterdam, pp. 59–82.

Petrovic, P., Kalso, E., Petersson, K.M. and Ingvar, M. (2002) Placebo and opioid analgesia – imaging a shared neuronal network. *Science*, **295**, 1737–1740.

Pfaff, D.W. (1989) Features of a hormone-driven defined neural circuit for a mammalian behavior. *Annals of the New York Academy of Sciences*, **563**, 131–147.

Pfaff, D.W. and Pfaffmann, C. (1969) Olfactory and hormonal influences on the basal forebrain of the male rat. *Brain Research*, **15**, 137–156.

Pfaff, D.W., Phillips, M.I. and Rubin, R.T. (2004) *Principles of Hormone Behavior Relations*, Elsevier Academic Press, Amsterdam.

Phelps, J.A., Davis, J.O. and Schartz, K.M. (1997) Nature, nurture, and twin research strategies. *Current Directions in Psychological Science*, **6**, 117–121.

Phillips-Bute, B.G. and Lane, J.D. (1998) Caffeine withdrawal symptoms following brief caffeine deprivation. *Physiology and Behavior*, **63**, 35–39.

Phoenix, C.H., Goy, R.W., Gerall, A.A. and Young, W.C. (1959) Organizing action of prenatally administered testosterone propionate on the tissues mediating mating behavior in the female guinea pig. *Endocrinology*, **65**, 369–382.

Piaget, J. (1954) *The Child's Construction of Reality*, Routledge and Kegan Paul, London.

Pierce, R.C. and Kalivas, P.W. (1997) A circuitry model of the expression of behavioral sensitization to amphetamine-like psychostimulants. *Brain Research Reviews*, **25**, 192–216.

Pierrot-Deseilligny, E. and Burke, D. (2005) *The Circuitry of the Human Spinal Cord: Its Role in Motor Control and Movement Disorders*, Cambridge University Press, Cambridge.

Pihl, R.O. and LeMarquand, D. (1998) Serotonin and aggression and the alcohol–aggression relationship. *Alcohol and Alcoholism*, **33**, 55–65.

Pillard, R.C. and Weinrich, J.D. (1986) Evidence of familial nature of male homosexuality. *Archives of General Psychiatry*, **43**, 808–812.

Pinker, S. and Bloom, P. (1990) Natural language and natural selection. *Behavioral and Brain Sciences*, **13**, 707–784.

Pitman, R.K., Orr, S.P. and Shalev, A.Y. (1993) Once bitten, twice shy: beyond the conditioning model of PTSD. *Biological Psychiatry*, **33**, 145–146.

Plomin, R. (1989) Environment and genes. *American Psychologist*, **44**, 105–111

Plomin, R. and Rutter, M. (1998) Child development, molecular genetics, and what to do with genes once they are found. *Child Development*, **69**, 1223–1242.

Plomin, R., DeFries, J.C., McClearn, G.E. and Rutter, M. (1997) *Behavioral Genetics*, W.H. Freeman, New York.

Ploog, D. (1986) Biological foundations of the vocal expressions of emotions. In *Emotion – Theory, Research and Experience, Vol. 3 Biological Foundations of Emotion* (eds R. Plutchik and H. Kellerman), Academic Press, Orlando, pp. 173–197.

Plutchik, R. (1980) *Emotion: A Psychoevolutionary Synthesis*, Harper and Row, New York.

Poeppel, D. and Hickok, G. (2004) Towards a new functional anatomy of language. *Cognition*, **92**, 1–12.

Pohl, W. (1973) Dissociation of spatial discrimination deficits following frontal and parietal lesions in monkeys. *Journal of Comparative and Physiological Psychology*, **82**, 227–239.

Poizner, H., Bellugi, U. and Klima, E.S. (1990) Biological foundations of language: clues from sign language. *Annual Review of Neurosciences*, **13**, 283–307.

Polosa, C., Mannard, A. and Laskey, W. (1979) Tonic activity of the autonomic nervous system: functions, properties, origins. In *Integrative Functions of the Autonomic Nervous System* (eds C.M. Brooks, K. Koizumi and A. Sato), University of Tokyo Press/Elsevier, Amsterdam, pp. 342–354.

Pomeranz, B., Wall, P.D. and Weber, W.V. (1968) Cord cells responding to fine myelinated afferents from viscera, muscle and skin. *Journal of Physiology*, **199**, 511–532.

Pomerleau, O.F. and Pomerleau, C.S. (1984) Neuroregulators and the reinforcement of smoking: towards a biobehavioral explanation. *Neuroscience and Biobehavioral Reviews*, **8**, 503–513.

Popper, K. and Eccles, J.C. (1977) *The Self and Its Brain*, Springer International, Berlin.

Posner, M.I. (1980) Orienting of attention. *Quarterly Journal of Experimental Psychology*, **32**, 3–25.

Posner, M.I. (1993) Interaction of arousal and selection in the posterior attention network. In *Attention: Selection, Awareness, and Control – A Tribute to Donald Broadbent* (eds A. Baddeley and L. Weiskrantz), Clarendon Press, Oxford, pp. 390–405.

Posner, M.I. and Petersen, S.E. (1990) The attention system of the human brain. *Annual Review of Neurosciences*, **13**, 25–42.

Povinelli, D.J. and Preuss, T.M. (1995) Theory of mind: evolutionary history of a cognitive specialization. *Trends in Neurosciences*, **18**, 418–424.

Powley, T.L. (1999) Central control of autonomic functions. In *Fundamental Neuroscience* (eds M.J. Zigmond, F.E. Bloom, S.C. Landis, J.L. Roberts and L.R. Squire), Academic Press, San Diego, pp. 1027–1050.

Powley, T.L. and Phillips, R.J. (2004) Gastric satiation is volumetric, intestinal satiation is nutritive. *Physiology and Behavior*, **82**, 69–74.

Prechtl, H.F.R. (1981) The study of neural development as a perspective of clinical problems. In *Maturation and Development: Biological and Psychological Perspectives* (eds K.J. Connolly and H.F.R. Prechtl), William Heinemann Medical Books, London, pp. 198–215.

Prechtl, H.F.R. (1982) Assessment methods for the newborn infant, a critical evaluation. In *Psychobiology of the Human Newborn* (ed. P. Stratton), Wiley, Chichester, pp. 21–52.

Prescott, T.J., Redgrave, P. and Gurney, K. (1999) Layered control architectures in robots and vertebrates. *Adaptive Behavior*, **7**, 99–127.

Preuss, T.M. and Kaas, J.H. (1999) Human brain evolution. In *Fundamental Neuroscience* (eds M.J. Zigmond, F.E. Bloom, S.C. Landis, J.L. Roberts and L.R. Squire), Academic Press, San Diego, pp. 1283–1311.

Pribram, K.H. (1986) The cognitive revolution and mind/brain issues. *American Psychologist*, **41**, 507–520.

Price, J., Sloman, L., Gardner, R., Gilbert, P. and Rohde, P. (1994) The social competition hypothesis of depression. *British Journal of Psychiatry*, **164**, 309–315.

Profet (1992) Pregnancy sickness as adaptation: a deterrent to maternal ingestion of teratogens. In *The Adapted Mind: Evolutionary Psychology and the Generation of Culture*, Oxford University Press, Oxford, pp. 327–365.

Provine, R.R. (1988) On the uniqueness of embryos and the difference it makes. In *Behavior of the Fetus* (eds W.P. Smotherman and S.R. Robinson), Telford Press, Caldwell, pp. 35–46.

Pulvermuller, F. (2003) *The Neuroscience of Language: On Brain Circuits of Words and Serial Order*, Cambridge University Press, Cambridge.

Purves, D. (1994) *Neural Activity and the Growth of the Brain*, Cambridge University Press, Cambridge.

Purves, D. and Lichtman, J.W. (1985) *Principles of Neural Development*, Sinauer Associates, Sunderland.

Purves, D., Augustine, G.J., Fitzpatrick, D., Katz, L.C., LaMantia, A-S. and McNamara, J.O. (1997) *Neuroscience*, Sinauer Associates, Sunderland.

Råberg, L., Grahn, M., Hasselquist, D. and Svensson, E. (1998) On the adaptive significance of stress-induced immunosuppression. *Proceedings of the Royal Society of London B*, **265**, 1637–1641.

Raichle, M.E., Fiez, J.A., Videen, T.O., MacLeod, A-M.K., Pardo, J.V., Fox, P.T. and Petersen, S.E. (1994) Practice-related changes in human brain functional anatomy during nonmotor learning. *Cerebral Cortex*, **4**, 8–26.

Raine, A., Buchsbaum, M. and LaCasse, L. (1997) Brain abnormalities in murderers indicated by positron emission tomography. *Biological Psychiatry*, **42**, 495–508.

Rainville, P., Duncan, G.H., Price, D.D., Carrier, B. and Bushnell, M.C. (1997) Pain affect encoded in human anterior cingulate but not somatosensory cortex. *Science*, **277**, 968–971.

Rakic, P. (1971) Guidance of neurons migrating to the fetal monkey neocortex. *Brain Research*, **33**, 471–476.

Rammsayer, T.H. (2004) Extraversion and the dopamine hypothesis. In *On the Psychobiology of Personality* (ed. R.M. Stelmack), Elsevier, pp. 411–430.

Ramos, A. and Mormède, P. (1998) Stress and emotionality: a multidimensional and genetic approach. *Neuroscience and Biobehavioral Reviews*, **22**, 33–57.

Ramsay, D.J. and Booth, D. (1991) *Thirst: Physiological and Psychological Aspects*, Springer-Verlag, London.

Ramsay, D.J. and Thrasher, T.N. (1990) Thirst and water balance. In *Handbook of Behavioral Neurobiology*, Vol. 10, *Neurobiology of Food and Fluid Intake* (ed. E.M. Stricker), Plenum Press, New York, pp. 353–386.

Randolph, M. and Semmes, J. (1974) Behavioral consequences of elective subtotal ablations in the postcentral gyrus of *Macaca mulatta*. *Brain Research*, **70**, 55–70.

Raper, J.A. and Tessier-Lavigne, M. (1999) Growth cones and axon pathfinding. In *Fundamental Neuroscience* (eds M.J. Zigmond, F.E. Bloom, S.C. Landis, J.L. Roberts and L.R. Squire), Academic Press, San Diego, pp. 519–546.

Ratcliffe, J.M., Fenton, M.B. and Galef, B.G. (2003) An exception to the rule: common vampire bats do not learn taste aversions. *Animal Behaviour*, **65**, 385–389.

Ravussin, E., Valencia, M.E., Esparza, J., Bennett, P.H. and Schulz, L.O. (1994) Effects of a traditional lifestyle on obesity in Pima Indians. *Diabetes Care*, **17**, 1067–1074.

Read, N.W. (1992) Role of gastrointestinal factors in hunger and satiety in man. *Proceedings of the Nutrition Society*, **51**, 7–11.

Reason, J. (1979) Actions not as planned: the price of automatization. In *Aspects of Consciousness*, Vol. 1 *Psychological Issues* (eds G. Underwood and R. Stevens), Academic Press, London, pp. 67–89.

Reason, J. (1984) Lapses of attention in everyday life. In *Varieties of Attention* (eds R. Parasuraman and D.R. Davies), Academic Press, Orlando, pp. 515–549.

Reber, A.S. (1992) The cognitive unconscious: an evolutionary perspective. *Consciousness and Cognition*, **1**, 93–133.

Rechtschaffen, A. (1998) Current perspectives on the function of sleep. *Perspectives in Biology and Medicine*, **41**, 359–390.

Rechtschaffen, A., Hauri, P. and Zeitlin, M. (1966) Auditory awakening threshold in REM and NREM sleep stages. *Perceptual and Motor Skills*, **22**, 927–942.

Redgrave, P. and Dean, P. (1991) Does the PAG learn about emergencies from the superior colliculus? In *The Midbrain Periaqueductal Gray Matter – Functional, Anatomical, and Neurochemical Organization* (eds A. Depaulis and R. Bandler), Plenum Press, New York, pp. 199–209.

Redgrave, P., Prescott, T.J. and Gurney, K. (1999) The basal ganglia: a vertebrate solution to the selection problem? *Neuroscience*, **89**, 1009–1023.

Reeve, J.M. (2004) *Understanding Motivation and Emotion*. Wiley, New York.

Reeves, A.G. and Plum, F. (1969) Hyperphagia, rage, and dementia accompanying a ventromedial hypothalamic neoplasm. *Archives of Neurology*, **20**, 616–624.

Reid, M.S., Mickalian, J.D., Delucchi, K.L., Hall, S.M. and Berger, S.P. (1998) An acute dose of nicotine enhances cue-induced cocaine craving. *Drug and Alcohol Dependence*, **49**, 95–104.

Reid, R.C. (1999) Vision. In *Fundamental Neuroscience* (eds M.J. Zigmond, F.E. Bloom, S.C. Landis, J.L. Roberts and L.R. Squire), Academic Press, San Diego, pp. 821–851.

Reiman, E.M., Caselli, R.J., Yun, L.S., Chen, K., Bandy, D., Minoshima, S., Thibodeau, S.N. and Osborne, D. (1996) Preclinical evidence of Alzheimer's disease in persons homozygous for the ε4 allele for apolipoprotein E. *New England Journal of Medicine*, **334**, 752–758.

Reimund, E. (1994) The free radical flux theory of sleep. *Medical Hypotheses*, **43**, 231–233.

Reiner, A., Medina, L. and Veenman, C.L. (1998) Structural and functional evolution of the basal ganglia in vertebrates. *Brain Research Reviews*, **28**, 235–285.

Reinisch, J.M. and Sanders, S.A. (1992) Prenatal hormonal contributions to sex differences in human personality development. In *Handbook of Behavioral Neurobiology*, Vol. 11, *Sexual Differentiation* (eds A.A. Gerall, H. Moltz and I.L. Ward), Plenum Press, New York, pp. 221–243.

Reisenzein, R. (1983) The Schachter theory of emotion: two decades on. *Psychological Bulletin*, **94**, 239–264.

Renner, M.J. and Rosenzweig, M.R. (1986) Object interactions in juvenile rats (*Rattus norvegicus*): effects of different experiential histories. *Journal of Comparative Psychology*, **100**, 229–236.

Rhodes, G. and Zebrowitz, L.A. (2002) *Facial Attractiveness: Evolutionary, Cognitive, and Social Perspectives*, Ablex, Westpoint.

Ribot, T.H. (1885) *Diseases of Memory*, Kegan Paul, Trench and Co., London.

Richards, G. (1987) *Human Evolution*, Routledge and Kegan Paul, London.

Richards, M. (1996) Neurobiological treatment of Alzheimer's disease. In *The Cognitive Neuropsychology of Alzheimer-type Dementia* (ed. R.G. Morris), Oxford University Press, Oxford, pp. 327–342.

Richardson, D.K. Reynolds, S.M., Cooper, S.J. and Berridge, K.C. (2005) Endogenous opioids are necessary for benzodiazepine palatability enhancement: naltrexone blocks diazepam-induced increase of sucrose 'liking'. *Pharmacology, Biochemistry and Behavior*, **81**(3), 657–663.

Rideout, H.J. and Parker, L.A. (1996) Morphine enhancement of sucrose palatability: analysis by the taste reactivity test. *Pharmacology Biochemistry and Behavior*, **53**, 731–734.

Ridley, R.M. and Baker, H.F. (1983) Is there a relationship between social isolation, cognitive inflexibility, and behavioral stereotypy? An analysis of the effects of amphetamine in the marmoset. In *Ethopharmacology: Primate Models of Neuropsychiatric Disorder*s (ed. K.A. Miczek), Alan R. Liss, New York, pp. 101–135.

Rivier, C. (1991) Neuroendocrine mechanisms of anterior pituitary regulation in the rat exposed to stress. In *Stress – Neurobiology and Neuroendocrinology* (eds M.R. Brown, G.F. Koob and C. Rivier), Marcel Dekker, New York, pp. 119–136.

Rizzo, T.A., Metzger, B.E., Dooley, S.L. and Cho, N.H. (1997) Early malnutrition and child neurobehavioral development: insights from the study of children of diabetic mothers. *Child Development*, **68**, 26–38.

Rizzolatti, G. (1983) Mechanisms of selective attention in mammals. In *Advances in Vertebrate Neuroethology* (eds J-P. Ewert, R.R. Capranica and D.J. Ingle), Plenum Press, New York, pp. 261–297.

Rizzolatti, G. and Berti, A. (1993) Neural mechanisms of spatial neglect. In *Unilateral Neglect: Clinical and Experimental Studies* (eds I.H. Robertson and J.C. Marshall), Lawrence Erlbaum, Hove, pp. 87–105.

Rizzolatti, G. and Craighero, L. (2004) The mirror-neuron system. In *Annual Review of Neuroscience*, Vol. 27 (eds S. E. Hyman, T.M. Jessell, C.J. Shatz and C.F. Stevens), Annual Reviews, Palo Alto, pp. 169–172.

Rizzolatti, G., Riggio, L., Dascola, I. and Umiltà, C. (1987) Reorienting attention across the horizontal and vertical meridians: evidence in favour of a premotor theory of attention. *Neuropsychologia*, **25**, 31–40.

Robbins, T.W. and Everitt, B.J. (1992) Functions of dopamine in the dorsal and ventral striatum. *Seminars in the Neurosciences*, **4**, 119–127.

Robbins, T.W. and Everitt, B.J. (1999) Motivation and reward. In *Fundamental Neuroscience* (eds M.J. Zigmond, F.E. Bloom, S.C. Landis, J.L. Roberts and L.R. Squire), Academic Press, San Diego, pp. 1245–1260.

Robbins, T.W. and Fray, P.J. (1980a) Stress-induced eating: fact, fiction or misunderstanding? *Appetite*, **1**, 103–133.

Robbins, T.W. and Fray, P.J. (1980b) Stress-induced eating; reply to Bolles, Rowland and Marques, and Herman and Polivy. *Appetite*, **1**, 231–239.

Robbins, T.W., Jones, G.H. and Sahakian, B.J. (1989) Central stimulants, transmitters and attentional disorder: a perspective from animal studies. In *Attention Deficit Disorder: Clinical and Basic Research* (eds T. Sagvolden and T. Archer), Lawrence Erlbaum, Hillsdale, pp. 199–222.

Robbins, T.W., McAlonan, G., Muir, J.L. and Everitt, B.J. (1997) Cognitive enhancers in theory and practice: studies of the cholinergic hypothesis of cognitive deficits in Alzheimer's disease. *Behavioural Brain Research*, **83**, 15–23.

Roberts, S.C., Havlicek, J., Flegr, J., Hruskova, M., Little, A.C., Jones, B.C., Perrett, D.I. and Petrie, M. (2004) Female facial attractiveness increases during the fertile phase of the menstrual cycle. *Proceedings of the Royal Society of London B* (Suppl.), **271**, S270–S272.

Roberts, W.C. (1996) Coronary atherosclerosis: description, manifestations, and prevention. In *Heart and Mind. The Practice of Cardiac Psychology* (eds R. Allan and S. Scheidt), American Psychological Association, Washington, pp. 147–177.

Robertson, L.C. and Delis, D.C. (1986) 'Part–whole' processing in unilateral brain-damaged patients: dysfunction of hierarchical organization. *Neuropsychologia*, **24**, 363–370.

Robertson, L.C., Lamb, M.R. and Knight, R.T. (1988) Effects of lesions of temporal–parietal junction on perceptual and attentional processing in humans. *Journal of Neuroscience*, **8**, 3757–3769.

Robins, L.N., Helzer, J.E. and Davis, D.H. (1975) Narcotic use in Southeast Asia and afterward. *Archives of General Psychiatry*, **32**, 955–961.

Robinson, P.H. (1989) Gastric function in eating disorders. *Annals of the New York Academy of Sciences*, **575**, 456–465.

Robinson, S.R. and Smotherman, W.P. (1988) Chance and chunks in the ontogeny of fetal behavior. In *Behavior of the Fetus* (eds W.P. Smotherman and S.R. Robinson), Telford Press, Caldwell, pp. 95–115.

Robinson, T.E. and Berridge, K.C. (1993) The neural basis of drug craving: an incentive-sensitization theory of addiction. *Brain Research Reviews*, **18**, 247–291.

Rodgers, R.J. and Randall, J.I. (1987) On the mechanisms and adaptive significance of intrinsic analgesia systems. *Reviews in the Neurosciences*, **1**, 185–200.

Rodin, J. (1980) The externality theory today. In *Obesity* (ed. A.J. Stunkard), W.B. Saunders, Philadelphia, pp. 226–239.

Rodriguez-Manzo, G. and Fernandez-Guasti, A. (1994) Reversal of sexual exhaustion by serotonergic and noradrenergic agents. *Behavioural Brain Research*, **62**, 127–134.

Roffwarg, H.P., Muzio, J.N. and Dement, W.C. (1966) Ontogenetic development of the human sleep–dream cycle. *Science*, **152**, 604–619.

Rogers, C.R. (1959) A theory of therapy, personality, and interpersonal relationships, as developed in the client-centered framework. In *Psychology: A Study of a Science*, Vol. 3 (ed. S. Koch), McGraw-Hill, New York, pp. 184–256.

Rogers, P.J. (1995) Food, mood and appetite. *Nutrition Research Reviews*, **8**, 243–269.

Rogers, P.J. and Smit, H.J. (2000) Food craving and food 'addiction': a critical review of the evidence from a biopsychosocial perspective. *Pharmacology Biochemistry and Behavior*, **66**, 3–14.

Roland, P.E. and Friberg, L. (1985) Localization of cortical areas activated by thinking. *Journal of Neurophysiology*, **53**, 1219–1243.

Rolls, B.J. (1991) Physiological determinants of fluid intake in humans. In *Thirst: Physiological and Psychological Aspects* (eds D.J. Ramsey and D. Booth), Springer-Verlag, London, pp. 391–399.

Rolls, E.T. (1993) The neural control of feeding in primates. In *Neurophysiology of Ingestion* (ed. D.A. Booth), Pergamon Press, Oxford, pp. 137–169.

Rolls, E.T. (1994) Neural processing related to feeding in primates. In *Appetite – Neural and Behavioural Bases* (eds C.R. Legg and D. Booth), Oxford University Press, Oxford, pp. 11–53.

Rolls, E.T. (2004) The functions of the orbitofrontal cortex. *Brain and Cognition*, **55**, 11–29.

Rolls, E.T. (2005) *Emotion Explained*, Oxford University Press, Oxford.

Roman, V., Walstra, I., Luiten, P.G.M. and Meerlo, P. (2005) Too little sleep gradually desensitizes the serotonin 1A receptor system. *Sleep*, **28**, 1505–1510.

Rose, J.E. and Corrigal, W.A. (1997) Nicotine self-administration in animals and humans: similarities and differences. *Psychopharmacology*, **130**, 28–40.

Rose, J.E., Hind, J.E., Anderson, D.J. and Brugge, J.F. (1971) Some effects of stimulus intensity on response of auditory nerve fibres in the squirrel monkey. *Journal of Neurophysiology*, **34**, 685–699.

Rose, R.M., Bernstein, I.S. and Gordon, T.P. (1975) Consequences of social conflict on plasma testosterone levels in rhesus monkeys. *Psychosomatic Medicine*, **37**, 50–61.

Rose, S. (1992) *The Making of Memory*, Bantam, London.

Rosen, J.B. and Schulkin, J. (1998) From normal fear to pathological anxiety. *Psychological Review*, **105**, 325–350.

Rosen, R.C. (1991) Alcohol and drug effects on sexual response: human experimental and clinical studies. In *Annual Review of Sex Research*, **2** (ed. J. Bancroft), Society for the Scientific Study of Sex, Allentown, pp. 119–179.

Rosenblatt, J.S. (1992) Hormone-behavior relations in the regulation of parental behavior. In *Behavioral Endocrinology* (eds J.B. Becker, S.M. Breedlove and D. Crews), MIT Press, Cambridge, pp. 219–259.

Rosenblueth, A., Wiener, N. and Bigelow, J. (1968) Behavior, purpose and teleology. In *Modern Systems Research for the Behavioral Scientist* (ed. W. Buckley), Aldine, Chicago, pp. 221–225.

Rosenzweig, M.R., Leiman, A.L. and Breedlove, S.M. (1996) *Biological Psychology*, 1st edn, Sinauer Associates, Sunderland.

Rosenzweig, M.R., Breedlove, S.M. and Watson, N.V. (2004) *Biological Psychology*, 4th edn, Sinauer Associates, Sunderland.

Rothwell, J. (1994) *Control of Human Voluntary Movement*, Chapman and Hall, London.

Rouby, C., Schaal, B., Dubois, D., Gervais, R. and Holley, A. (2005) *Olfaction, Taste and Cognition*, Cambridge University Press, Cambridge.

Rozin, P. (1976) The evolution of intelligence and access to the cognitive unconscious. In *Progress in Psychobiology and Physiological Psychology* (eds J.M. Sprague and A.N. Epstein), Academic Press, New York, pp. 245–280.

Rozin, P.N. and Schulkin, J. (1990) Food selection. In *Handbook of Behavioral Neurobiology*, Vol. 10, *Neurobiology of Food and Fluid Intake* (ed. E.M. Stricker), Plenum Press, New York, pp. 297–328.

Rubens, A.B. and Benson, D.F. (1971) Associative visual agnosia. *Archives of Neurology*, **24**, 305–316.

Rubia, K., Overmeyer, S., Taylor, E., Brammer, M., Williams, S.C.R., Simmons, A. and Bullmore, E.T. (1999) Hypofrontality in attention deficit hyperactivity disorder during higher-order motor control: a study with functional MRI. *American Journal of Psychiatry*, **156**, 891–896.

Rumelhart, D.E. and Norman, D.A. (1989) Introduction. In *Parallel Models of Associative Memory* (eds G.E. Hinton and J.A. Anderson), Lawrence Erlbaum, Hillsdale, pp. 15–21.

Rutter, M. (2001) Child psychiatry in the era following sequencing the genome. In *Attention, Genes and ADHD* (eds. F. Levy and D.A. Hay), Brunner-Routledge, Hove, pp. 225–248.

Sachs, B.D. (1995) Placing erection in context: the reflexogenic–psychogenic dichotomy reconsidered. *Neuroscience and Biobehavioral Reviews*, **19**, 211–224.

Sacks, O. (1982) *Awakenings*, Pan Books, London.

Saffran, E.M., Fitzpatrick-DeSalme, E.J. and Coslett, H.B. (1990) Visual disturbances in dementia. In *Modular Deficits in Alzheimer-type Dementia* (ed. M.F. Schwartz), MIT Press, Cambridge, pp. 297–328.

Sagvolden, T. (2000) Behavioral validation of the spontaneously hypertensive rat (SHR) as an animal model of attention-deficit/hyperactivity disorder (AD/HD). *Neuroscience and Biobehavioral Reviews*, **24**, 31–39.

Sagvolden, T., Johansen, E.B., Aase, H. and Russell, V.A. (2005) A dynamic developmental theory of attention-deficit/hyperactivity disorder (ADHD) predominantly hyperactive/impulsive and combined subtypes. *Behavioral and Brain Sciences*, **28**, 397–468.

Sahakian, B. (1978) Hyperactive children and the drug paradox. *New Scientist*, **80**, 350–352.

Sakakibara, M., Takeuchi, S. and Hayano, J. (1994) Effect of relaxation training on cardiac parasympathetic tone. *Psychophysiology*, **31**, 223–228.

Salamy, A. (1978) Commissural transmission: maturational changes in humans. *Science*, **200**, 1409–1411.

Salkovskis, P.M. (1985) Obsessional-compulsive problems: a cognitive–behavioural analysis. *Behavior Research and Therapy*, **23**, 571–583.

Salmond, C.H., Ashburner, J., Connelly, A., Friston, K.J., Gadian, D.G. and Vargha-Khadem, F. (2005) The role of the medial temporal lobe in autistic spectrum disorders. *European Journal of Neuroscience*, **22**, 764–772.

Salzinger, K. (1971) An hypothesis about schizophrenic behavior. *American Journal of Psychotherapy*, **25**, 601–614.

Sanes, J.N. and Evarts, E.V. (1985) Psychomotor performance in Parkinson's disease. In *Clinical Neurophysiology in Parkinsonism* (eds P.J. Delwaide and A. Agnoli), Elsevier, Amsterdam, pp. 117–132.

Sano, K., Mayanagi, Y., Sekino, H., Ogashiwa, M. and Ishijima, B. (1970) Results of stimulation and destruction of the posterior hypothalamus in man. *Journal of Neurosurgery*, **33**, 689–707.

Sapolsky, R. (2005) Sick of poverty. *Scientific American*, **293**(6), 92–99.

Sapolsky, R.M. (1990a) Adrenocortical function, social rank, and personality among wild baboons. *Biological Psychiatry*, **28**, 862–878.

Sapolsky, R.M. (1990b) Stress in the wild. *Scientific American*, **262**, No. 1, 106–113.

Sapolsky, R.M. (1992) Neuroendocrinology of the stress response. In *Behavioral Endocrinology* (eds J.B. Becker, S.M. Breedlove and D. Crews), MIT Press, Cambridge, pp. 287–324.

Sapolsky, R.M. (1997) The importance of the well-groomed child. *Science*, **277**, 1620–1621.

Sapolsky, R.M. (2004) *Why Zebras don't get Ulcers*, Saint Martin's Press, New York.

Sapolsky, R., Rivier, C., Yamamoto, G., Plotsky, P. and Vale, W. (1987) Interleukin-1 stimulates the secretion of hypothalamic corticotropin-releasing factor. *Science*, **238**, 522–524.

Sarter, M., Givens, B. and Bruno, J.P. (2001) The cognitive neuroscience of sustained attention: where top-down meets bottom-up. *Brain Research Reviews*, **35**, 146–160.

Satinoff, E. (1983) A reevaluation of the concept of the homeostatic organization of temperature regulation. In *Handbook of Behavioral Neurobiology*, Vol. 6: *Motivation* (eds E. Satinoff and P. Teitelbaum), Plenum Press, New York.

Schacter, D.L. (1997) False recognition and the brain. *Current Directions in Psychological Science*, **6**, 65–69.

Schacter, D.L. and Tulving, E. (1994a) *Memory Systems 1994*, MIT Press, Cambridge.

Schacter, D.L. and Tulving, E. (1994b) What are the memory systems of 1994? In *Memory Systems 1994* (eds D.L. Schacter and E. Tulving), MIT Press, Cambridge, pp. 1–38.

Schacter, S. (1975) Cognition and peripheralist–centralist controversies in motivation and emotion. In *Handbook of Psychobiology* (eds M.S. Gazzaniga and C. Blakemore), Academic Press, New York, pp. 529–564.

Schachter, S. and Singer, J.E. (1962) Cognitive, social and physiological determinants of emotional state. *Psychological Review*, **69**, 379–399.

Schanberg, S.M. and Field, T.M. (1987) Sensory deprivation stress and supplemental stimulation in the rat pup and preterm human neonate. *Child Development*, **58**, 1431–1447.

Scheib, J.E. (2001) Context-specific mate choice criteria: women's trade-offs in the contexts of long-term and extra-pair mateships. *Personal Relationships*, 8, 371–389.

Scheidt, S. (1996) A whirlwind tour of cardiology for the mental health professional. In *Heart and Mind. The Practice of Cardiac Psychology* (eds R. Allan and S. Scheidt), American Psychological Association, Washington, pp. 15–62.

Schenck, C.H., Bundlie, S.R., Ettinger, M.G. and Mahowald, M.W. (1986) Chronic behavioral disorders of human REM sleep: a new category of parasomnia. *Sleep*, **9**, 293–308.

Scherer, K.R. (1993) Neuroscience projections to current debates in emotion psychology. *Cognition and Emotion*, 7, 1–41.

Schieber, M.H. (1999) Voluntary descending control. In *Fundamental Neuroscience* (eds M.J. Zigmond, F.E. Bloom, S.C. Landis, J.L. Roberts and L.R. Squire), Academic Press, San Diego, pp. 931–949.

Schlemmer, R.F. and Davis, J.M. (1983) A comparison of three psychotomimetic-induced models of psychosis in nonhuman primate social colonies. In *Ethopharmacology: Primate Models of Neuropsychiatric Disorders* (ed. K.A. Miczek), Alan R. Liss, New York, pp. 33–78.

Schmajuk, N.A. and Tyberg, M. (1991) *The hippocampal-lesion model of schizophrenia*. In *Neuromethods*, Vol. 18, *Animal Models in Psychiatry I* (eds A. Boulton, G. Baker and M. Martin-Iverson), Humana Press, Totowa, pp. 67–102.

Schmidt, R.A. and Lee, T.D. (2005) *Motor Control and Learning*, Human Kinetics Europe Ltd, Leeds.

Schmolling, P. (1983) A systems model of schizophrenic dysfunction. *Behavioral Science*, **28**, 253–267.

Schneider, J. and Weiss, R. (2001) *Cybersex Exposed: Simple Fantasy or Obsession?*, Hazelden, Center City.

Schneider, W. and Shiffrin, R.M. (1977) Controlled and automatic human information processing: I. Detection, search and attention. *Psychological Review*, **84**, 1–66.

Schrödinger, E. (1958) *Mind and Matter*, Cambridge, Cambridge University Press.

Schulkin, J. (1994) Melancholic depression and the hormones of adversity: a role for the amygdala. *Current Directions in Psychological Science*, 3, 41–44.

Schulkin, J. (2005) *Sodium Hunger: The Search for a Salty Taste*, Cambridge University Press, Cambridge.

Schulte, F.J. (1974) The neurological development of the neonate. In *Scientific Foundations of Paediatrics* (eds J.A. Davis and J. Dobbing), William Heinemann, London, pp. 587–615.

Schultz, W., Apicella, P., Romo, R. and Scarnati, E. (1995) Context-dependent activity in primate striatum reflecting past and future behavioural events. In *Models of Information Processing in the Basal Ganglia* (eds J.C. Houk, J.L. Davis and D.G. Beiser), MIT Press, Cambridge, pp. 11–28.

Schwartz, J.M. (1996) *Brain Lock*, HarperCollins, New York.

Sclafani, A. (1997) Learned controls of ingestive behaviour. *Appetite*, **29**, 153–158.

Scott, T.R. (1990) Gustatory control of food selection. In *Handbook of Behavioral Neurobiology*, Vol. 10, *Neurobiology of Food and Fluid Intake* (ed. E.M. Stricker), Plenum Press, New York, pp. 243–263.

Scott, T.R. and Giza, B.K. (1993) Gustatory control of ingestion. In *Neurophysiology of Ingestion* (ed. D.A. Booth), Pergamon Press, Oxford, pp. 99–117.

Scoville, W.B. and Milner, B. (1957) Loss of recent memory after bilateral hippocampal lesions. *Journal of Neurology, Neurosurgery and Psychiatry*, **20**, 11–21.

Searle, J.R. (1993) The problem of consciousness. In *Experimental and Theoretical Studies of Consciousness* (eds G.R. Bock and J. Marsh), Wiley, Chichester, pp. 61–80.

Seeman, T.E. and Robbins, R.J. (1994) Aging and hypothalamic–pituitary–adrenal response to challenge in humans. *Endocrine Reviews*, **15**, 233–260.

Seitz, R.J. and Roland, P.E. (1992) Learning of sequential finger movements in man: a combined kinematic and positron emission tomography (PET) study. *European Journal of Neuroscience*, **4**, 154–165.

Seligman, M. (1975) *Helplessness*, W.H. Freeman, San Francisco.

Seligman, M.E.P. and Hager, J.L. (1972) *Biological Boundaries of Learning*, Appleton-Century-Crofts, New York.

Selikowitz, M. (2004) *ADHD: The Facts*, Oxford University Press, Oxford.

Selye, H. (1973) The evolution of the stress concept. *American Scientist*, **61**, 692–699.

Serper, M.R., Bergman, R.L. and Harvey, P.D. (1990) Medication may be required for the development of automatic information processing in schizophrenia. *Psychiatry Research*, **32**, 281–288.

Shaham, Y. and Stewart, J. (1995) Stress reinstates heroin-seeking in drug-free animals: an effect mimicking heroin, not withdrawal. *Psychopharmacology*, **119**, 334–341.

Shakow, D. (1963) Psychological deficit in schizophrenia. *Behavioral Science*, **8**, 275–305.

Shallice, T. (1981) Phonological agraphia and the lexical route in writing. *Brain*, **104**, 413–429.

Shallice, T. and Jackson, M. (1988) Lissauer on agnosia. *Cognitive Neuropsychology*, **5**, 153–156.

Sham, P.C., O'Callaghan, E., Takei, N., Murray, G.K., Hare, E.H. and Murray, R.M. (1992) Schizophrenia following pre-natal exposure to influenza epidemics between 1939 and 1960. *British Journal of Psychiatry*, **160**, 461–466.

Shankle, W.R., Landing, B.H., Rafii, M.S., Schiano, A., Chen, J.M. and Hara, J. (1998) Evidence for a postnatal doubling of neuron number in the developing human cerebral cortex between 15 months and 6 years. *Journal of Theoretical Biology*, **191**, 115–140.

Shapleske, J., Rossell, S.L., Woodruff, P.W.R. and David, A.S. (1999) The planum temporale: a systematic, quantitative review of its structural, functional and clinical significance. *Brain Research Reviews*, **29**, 26–49.

Sharma, T. and Harvey, P. (2006) *The Early Course of Schizophrenia*, Oxford University Press, Oxford.

Sharpless, S. and Jasper, H. (1956) Habituation of the arousal reaction. *Brain*, **79**, 655–680.

Shaw, W.A. (1940) The relation of muscular action potentials to imaginal weight lifting. *Archives of Psychology*, **35**, 5–50.

Shaywitz, S.E. and Shaywitz, B.A. (1989) Critical issues in attention deficit disorder. In *Attention Deficit Disorder: Clinical and Basic Research* (eds T. Sagvolden and T. Archer), Lawrence Erlbaum, Hillsdale, pp. 53–69.

Sherry, D.F. (1992) Memory, the hippocampus, and natural selection: studies of food-storing birds. In *Neuropsychology of Memory* (eds L.R. Squire and N. Butters), Guilford Press, New York, pp. 521–532.

Sherry, D.F. and Schacter, D.L. (1987) The evolution of multiple memory systems. *Psychological Review*, **94**, 439–454.

Sherry, D.F., Vaccarino, A.L., Buckenham, K. and Herz, R.S. (1989) The hippocampal complex of food-storing birds. *Brain Behavior and Evolution*, **34**, 308–317.

Sherwin, B.B. (1991) The psychoendocrinology of aging and female sexuality. In *Annual Review of Sex Research, 2* (ed. J. Bancroft), Society for the Scientific Study of Sex, Allentown, pp. 181–198.

Shoaib, M., Swanner, L.C., Yasar, S. and Goldberg, S.R. (1999) Chronic caffeine exposure potentiates nicotine self-administration in rats. *Psychopharmacology*, **142**, 327–333.

Shomstein, S. and Yantis, S. (2004) Control of attention shifts between vision and audition in human cortex. *Journal of Neuroscience*, **24**, 10702–10706.

Siebert, M., Markowitsch, H.J. and Bartel, P. (2003) Amygdala, affect and cognition: evidence from 10 patients with Urbach-Wiethe disease. *Brain*, **126**, 2627–2637.

Siegel, A. (2005) *The Neurobiology of Aggression and Rage*, CRC Press, Boca Raton.

Siegel, J.M. (1994) Brainstem mechanisms generating REM sleep. In *Principles and Practice of Sleep Medicine* (eds M.H. Kryger, T. Roth and W.C. Dement), Saunders, Philadelphia, pp. 125–144.

Siegel, J.M. (2001) The REM sleep-memory consolidation hypothesis. *Science*, **294**, 1058–1063.

Siegel, J.M. (2004) Hypocretin (orexin): role in normal behavior and neuropathology. *Annual Review of Psychology*, **55**, 125–148.

Siegel, J.M. (2005) The incredible, shrinking sleep-learning connection. *Behavioral and Brain Sciences*, **28**, 82–83.

Siegel, R.K. and Jarvik, M.E. (1980) DMT self-administration by monkeys in isolation. *Bulletin of the Psychonomic Society*, **16**, 117–120.

Siegel, S. (1984) Pavlovian conditioning and heroin overdose: reports by overdose victims. *Bulletin of the Psychonomic Society*, **22**, 428–430.

Siffre, M. (1965) *Beyond Time*, Chatto and Windus, London.

Silbersweig, D.A., Stern, E., Frith, C., Cahill, C., Holmes, A., Grootoonk, S., Seaward, J., McKenna, P., Chua, S.E., Schnorr, L., Jones, T. and Frackowiak, R.S.J. (1995) A functional neuroanatomy of hallucinations in schizophrenia. *Nature*, **378**, 176–179.

Singer, J.L. (1993) Experimental studies of ongoing conscious experience. In *Experimental and Theoretical Studies of Consciousness* (eds G.R. Bock and J. Marsh), Wiley, Chichester, pp. 100–122.

Singer, T., Seymour, B., O'Doherty, J., Kaube, H., Dolan, R.J. and Frith, C.D. (2004) Empathy for pain involves the affective but not sensory components of pain. *Science*, **303**, 1157–1162.

Singh, D. and Bronstad, P.M. (2001) Female body odour is a potential cue to ovulation. *Proceedings of the Royal Society of London B*, **268**, 797–801.

Sitsen, J.M.A. (1988) Prescription drugs and sexual function. In *Handbook of Sexology*, Vol. 6, *The Pharmacology and Endocrinology of Sexual Function* (ed. J.M.A. Sitsen), Elsevier Science Publishers, Amsterdam, pp. 425–461.

Skakkebaek, N.E., Bancroft, J., Davidson, D.W. and Warner, P. (1981) Androgen replacement with oral testosterone undecanoate in hypogonadal men: a double blind controlled study. *Clinical Endocrinology*, **14**, 49–61.

Skinner, B.F. (1957) *Verbal Behavior*, Appleton-Century-Crofts, New York.

Skinner, B.F. (1966) *The Behavior of Organisms*, Appleton-Century-Crofts, New York.

Skinner, B.F. (1971) *Beyond Freedom and Dignity*, Penguin, Harmondsworth.

Skinner, B.F. (1976) *Particulars of My Life*, Jonathan Cape, London.

Skinner, B.F. (1984) Behaviorism at fifty. *Behavioral and Brain Sciences*, **7**, 615–667.

Skoubis, P.D., Lam, H.A., Shoblock, J., Narayanan, S. and Maidment, N.T. (2005) Endogenous enkephalins, not endorphins, modulate basal hedonic state in mice. *European Journal of Neuroscience*, **21**, 1379–1384.

Small, B.J., Herlitz, A. and Bäckman, L. (2004) Preclinical Alzheimer's disease: Cognitive and memory functioning. In *Cognitive Neuropsychology of Alzheimer's Disease*, 2nd edition (eds R.G. Morris, and J.T. Becker), Oxford University Press, Oxford, pp. 63–77.

Small, D.M. and Prescott, J. (2005) Odor/taste integration and the perception of flavor. *Experimental Brain Research*, **166**, 345–357.

Small, S.A. (2005) Alzheimer disease, in living colour. *Nature Neuroscience*, **8**, 404–405.

Smith, A. (1966) Speech and other functions after left (dominant) hemispherectomy. *Journal of Neurology, Neurosurgery and Psychiatry*, **29**, 467–471.

Smith, A. and Sugar, O. (1975) Development of above normal language and intelligence 21 years after left hemispherectomy. *Neurology*, **25**, 813–818.

Smith, D.V. and Duncan, H.J. (1992) Primary olfactory disorders: anosmia, hyposmia and dysosmia. In *Science of Olfaction* (eds M.J. Serby and K.L. Chobor), Springer-Verlag, New York, pp. 439–466.

Smith, G.P. (1996) The direct and indirect controls of meal size. *Neuroscience and Biobehavioral Reviews*, **20**, 41–46.

Smith, G.P. and Epstein, A.N. (1969) Increased feeding in response to decreased glucose utilization in the rat and monkey. *American Journal of Physiology*, **217**, 1083–1087.

Smith, G.P. and Gibbs, J. (1994) Satiating effect of cholecystokinin. *Annals of the New York Academy of Sciences*, **713**, 236–240.

Smith, W.S. and Fetz, E.E. (1987) Noninvasive brain imaging and the study of higher brain function in humans. In *Higher Brain Functions: Recent Explorations of the Brain's Emergent Properties* (ed. S.P. Wise), Wiley, New York, pp. 311–346.

Snowdon, C.T. (1998) The nurture of nature: social, developmental and environmental controls of aggression. *Behavioral and Brain Sciences*, **21**, 384–385.

Snyder, S.H. (1996) *Drugs and the Brain*, Scientific American Library, New York.

Sobik, L., Hutchison, K. and Craighead, L. (2005) Cue-elicited craving for food: a fresh approach to the study of binge eating. *Appetite*, **44**, 253–261.

Södersten, P., Bergh, C. and Ammar, A. (2003) Anorexia nervosa: towards a neurobiologically based therapy. *European Journal of Pharmacology*, **480**, 67–74.

Solanto, M.V., Arnsten, A.F.T. and Castellanos, F.X. (2001) *Stimulant Drugs and ADHD: Basic and Clinical Neuroscience*, Oxford University Press, Oxford.

Solomon, P.R. and Staton, D.M. (1982) Differential effects of microinjections of d-Amphetamine into the nucleus accumbens or the caudate putamen on the rats' ability to ignore an irrelevant stimulus. *Biological Psychiatry*, **17**, 743–756.

Solomon, P.R., Crider, A., Winkelman, J.W., Turi, A., Kamer, R.M. and Kaplan, L.J. (1981) Disrupted latent inhibition in the rat with chronic amphetamine or haloperidol-induced supersensitivity: relationship to schizophrenic attention disorder. *Biological Psychiatry*, **16**, 519–537.

Solomon, R.L. and Corbit, J.D. (1974) The opponent-process theory of motivation. I. *Psychological Review*, **81**, 119–145.

Sorg, B.A. and Kalivas, P.W. (1995) Stress and neuronal sensitization. In *Neurobiological and Clinical Consequences of Stress. From Normal Adaptation to Post-traumatic Stress Disorder* (eds M.J. Friedman, D.S. Charney and A.Y. Deutch), Lippincott-Raven, Philadelphia, pp. 83–102.

Southwick, C.H. (1968) Effect of maternal environment on aggressive behavior of inbred mice. *Communications in Behavioral Biology*, Part A, **1**, 129–132.

Spangler, K.M. and Warr, W.B. (1991) The descending auditory system. In *Neurobiology of Hearing: The Central Auditory System* (eds R.A. Altschuler, R.P. Bobbin, B.M. Clopton and D.W. Hoffman), Raven Press, New York, pp. 27–46.

Spencer, N.A., McClintock, M.K., Sellergren, S.A., Bullivant, S., Jacob, S. and Mennella, J.A. (2004) Social chemosignals from breastfeeding women increase sexual motivation. *Hormones and Behavior*, **46**, 362–370.

Sperry, R. (1970) Perception in the absence of the neocortical commisures, *Perception and its Disorders*, Res. Publ. A.R.N.M.D. **48**, 123–38.

Sperry, R.W. (1969) Hemisphere deconnection and unity in conscious awareness. *American Psychologist*, **23**, 723–733.

Sperry, R.W. (1974) Lateral specialization in the surgically separated hemispheres. In *The Neurosciences. Third Study Program* (eds F.O. Schmitt and F.G. Worden), MIT Press, Cambridge, pp. 5–19.

Spoont, M.R. (1992) Modulatory role of serotonin in neural information processing: implications for human psychopathology. *Psychological Bulletin*, **112**, 330–350.

Spray, K.J. and Bernstein, I.L. (2004) Afferent and efferent connections of the parvicellular subdivision of iNTS: defining a circuit involved in taste aversion learning. *Behavioural Brain Research*, **154**, 85–97.

Sprich-Buckminster, S., Biederman, J., Milberger, S., Faraone, S.V. and Lehman, B.K. (1993) Are perinatal complications relevant to the manifestation of ADD? Issues of comorbidity and familiality. *Journal of American Academy of Child and Adolescent Psychiatry*, **32**, 1032–1037.

Spruijt, B.M., Van Hooff, J.A.R.A.M. and Gispen, W.H. (1992) Ethology and neurobiology of grooming behaviour. *Physiological Reviews*, **72**, 825–852.

Squire, L.R. (1994) Declarative and nondeclarative memory: multiple brain systems supporting learning and memory. In *Memory Systems 1994* (eds D.L. Schacter and E. Tulving), MIT Press, Cambridge, pp. 203–231.

Squire, L.R. and Zola-Morgan, S. (1991) The medial temporal lobe memory system. *Science*, **253**, 1380–1386.

Stahl, S.M. (1996) *Essential Psychopharmacology*, Cambridge University Press, Cambridge.

Stahl, S.M. (1997) Estrogen makes the brain a sex organ. *Journal of Clinical Psychiatry*, **58**, 421–422.

Stahl, S.M. (1998) Getting stoned without inhaling: anandamide is the brain's natural marijuana. *Journal of Clinical Psychiatry*, **59**, 566–567.

Stam, R., Akkermans, L.M.A. and Wiegant, V.M. (1997) Trauma and the gut: interactions between stressful experience and intestinal function. *Gut*, **40**, 704–709.

Stearns, S.C. and Hoekstra, R.F. (2000) *Evolution: An Introduction*, Oxford University Press, Oxford.

Stebbins, G.L. (1969) *The Basis of Progressive Evolution*, University of North Carolina Press, Chapel Hill.

Steele, T.D., McCann, U.D. and Ricaurte, G.A. (1994) 3,4–Methylenedioxymethamphetamine (MDMA, 'Ecstasy'): pharmacology and toxicology in animals and humans. *Addiction*, **89**, 539–551.

Stein, M., Miller, A.H. and Trestman, R.L. (1991) Depression, the immune system, and health and illness. *Archives of General Psychiatry*, **48**, 171–177.

Stein, N.L. and Jewett, J.L. (1986) A conceptual analysis of the meaning of negative emotions: implications for a theory of development. In *Measuring Emotions in Infants and Children*, Vol. II (eds C.E. Izard and P.B. Read), Cambridge University Press, Cambridge, pp. 238–267.

Stein, Z., Susser, M., Saenger, G. and Marolla, F. (1972) Nutrition and mental performance. *Science*, **178**, 708–713.

Steiner, J.E. (1979) Human facial expressions in response to taste and smell stimulation. *Advances in Child Development and Behavior*, **13**, 257–295.

Stellar, E. (1990) Brain and behaviour. In *Handbook of Behavioral Neurobiology*, Vol. 10, *Neurobiology of Food and Fluid Intake* (ed. E.M. Stricker), Plenum Press, New York, pp. 3–22.

Stepanski, E.J. (1994) Behavioral therapy for insomnia. In *Principles and Practice of Sleep Medicine* (eds M.H. Kryger, T. Roth and W.C. Dement), Saunders, Philadelphia, pp. 535–541.

Stephan, K.M., Fink, G.R., Passingham, R.E., Silbersweig, D., Ceballos-Baumann, A.O., Frith, C.D. and Frackowiak, R.S.J. (1995) Functional anatomy of the mental representation of upper extremity movements in healthy subjects. *Journal of Neurophysiology*, **73**, 373–386.

Steptoe, A. (1993) Stress and the cardiovascular system: a psychosocial perspective. In *Stress – From Synapse to Syndrome* (eds S.C. Stanford and P. Salmon), Academic Press, London, pp. 119–141.

Steriade, M. (1994) Brain electrical activity and sensory processing during waking and sleep states. In *Principles and Practice of Sleep Medicine* (eds M.H. Kryger, T. Roth and W.C. Dement), Saunders, Philadelphia, pp. 105–124.

Stern, J.M. (1997) Offspring-induced nurturance: animal–human parallels. *Developmental Psychobiology*, **31**, 19–37.

Stern, K. and McClintock, M.K. (1998) Regulation of ovulation by human pheromones. *Nature*, **392**, 177–179.

Sternbach, H. (1998) Age-associated testosterone decline in men: clinical issues for psychiatry. *American Journal of Psychiatry*, **155**, 1310–1318.

Stevens, R. (1990) Humanistic psychology. In *Introduction to Psychology*, Vol. 1 (ed. I. Roth), Lawrence Erlbaum, Hove, pp. 419–469.

Stewart, J. (1995) How does incentive motivational theory apply to sexual behaviour? In *The Pharmacology of Sexual Function and Dysfunction* (ed. J. Bancroft), Excerpta Medica, Amsterdam, pp. 3–14.

Stewart, J., de Wit, H. and Eikelboom, R. (1984) Role of unconditioned and conditioned drug effects in the self-administration of opiates and stimulants. *Psychological Review*, **91**, 251–268.

Stewart-Williams, S. and Podd, J. (2004) The placebo effect: dissolving the expectancy versus conditioning debate. *Psychological Bulletin*, **130**, 324–340.

Still, G.F. (1902) Some abnormal psychical conditions in children. *The Lancet*, April 12th, pp. 1008–1012.

Stocchi, F. (1998) Dopamine agonists in Parkinson's disease. *CNS Drugs*, **10**, 159–170.

Stolerman, I.P. and Jarvis, M.J. (1995) The scientific case that nicotine is addictive. *Psychopharmacology*, **117**, 2–10.

Strader, A.D. and Woods, S.C. (2005) Gastrointestinal hormones and food intake. *Gastroenterology*, **128**, 175–191.

Stratton, G.M. (1897) Vision without inversion of the retinal image. *Psychological Review*, **4**, 341–360.

Strayer, D.L., Drews, F.A. and Johnston, W.A. (2003) Cell phone-induced failures of visual attention during simulated driving. *Journal of Experimental Psychology, Applied*, **9**, 23–32.

Stricker, E.M. (1990) Homeostatic origins of ingestive behaviour. In *Handbook of Behavioral Neurobiology*, Vol. 10, *Neurobiology of Food and Fluid Intake* (ed. E.M. Stricker), Plenum Press, New York, pp. 45–60.

Stricker, E.M. and Sved, A.F. (2000) Thirst. *Nutrition*, **16**, 821–826.

Stricker, E.M. and Verbalis, J.G. (1999) Water intake and body fluids. In *Fundamental Neuroscience* (eds M.J. Zigmond, F.E. Bloom, S.C. Landis, J.L. Roberts and L.R. Squire), Academic Press, San Diego, pp. 1111–1126.

Stringer, C. and Gamble, C. (1993) In *Search of the Neanderthals*, Thames and Hudson, New York.

Stroop, J.R. (1935) Studies of interference in serial verbal reactions. *Journal of Experimental Psychology*, **18**, 643–662.

Strubbe, J.H. and Woods, S.C. (2004) The timing of meals. *Psychological Review*, **111**, 128–141.

Sufka, K. and Turner, D. (2005) An evolutionary account of chronic pain: integrating the natural method of evolutionary psychology. *Philosophical Psychology*, **18**, 243–257.

Sullivan, E.V. and Marsh, L. (2003) Hippocampal volume deficits in alcoholic Korsakoff's syndrome. *Neurology*, **61**, 1716–1719.

Sullivan, R.M. and Brake, W.G. (2003) What the rodent prefrontal cortex can teach us about attention-deficit/hyperactivity disorder: the critical role of early developmental events on prefrontal function. *Behavioural Brain Research*, **146**, 43–55.

Sulloway, F.J. (1979) *Freud – Biologist of the Mind*, Burnett Books, London.

Sutanto, W. and de Kloet, E.R. (1993) The role of GABA in the regulation of the stress response. In *Stress – From Synapse to Syndrome* (eds S.C. Stanford and P. Salmon), Academic Press, London, pp. 333–354.

Sutherland, N.S. (1975) Is the brain a physical system? In *Explanation in the Behavioural Sciences* (eds R. Borger and F. Cioffi), Cambridge University Press, Cambridge, pp. 97–138.

Sutton, J.P., Mamelak, A.N. and Hobson, J.A. (1992) Modelling states of waking and sleeping. *Psychiatric Annals*, **22**, 137–143.

Swaab, D.F. and Hofman, M.A. (1990) An enlarged suprachiasmatic nucleus in homosexual men. *Brain Research*, **537**, 141–148.

Szasz, T.S. (1971) *The Manufacture of Madness*, Routledge and Kegan Paul, London.

Szechtman, H. and Woody, E. (2004) Obsessive-compulsive disorder as a disturbance of security motivation. *Psychological Review*, **111**, 111–127.

Szuster, R.R., Pontius, E.B. and Campos, P.E. (1988) Marijuana sensitivity and panic attack. *Journal of Clinical Psychiatry*, **49**, 427–429.

Taberner, P.V. (1996) Sex and drugs: the search for aphrodisiacs. *Biologist*, **43**, 198–201.

Takahashi, H., Takada, Y., Nagai, N., Urano, T. and Takada, A. (1998) Effects of nicotine and footshock stress on dopamine release in the striatum and nucleus accumbens. *Brain Research Bulletin*, **45**, 157–162.

Tallis, F. (1995) *Obsessive Compulsive Disorder*, Wiley, Chichester.

Tanji, J. and Kurata, K. (1985) Contrasting neuronal activity in supplementary and precentral motor cortex of monkeys. I. Responses to instructions determining motor responses to forthcoming signals of different modalities. *Journal of Neurophysiology*, **53**, 129–141.

Taylor, J.R. and Jentsch, J.D. (2001) Stimulant effects on striatal and cortical dopamine systems involved in reward-related behavior and impulsivity. In *Stimulant Drugs and ADHD: Basic and Clinical Neuroscience* (eds M.V. Solanto, A.F.T. Arnsten and F.X. Castellanos), Oxford University Press, Oxford, pp. 104–133.

Taylor, S.E., Kemeny, M.E., Reed, G.M., Bower, J.E. and Gruenewald, T.L. (2000) Psychological resources, positive illusions, and health. *American Psychologist*, **55**, 99–109.

Teicher, M.H., Dumont, N.L., Ito, Y., Vaituzis, C., Giedd, J.N. and Andersen, S.L. (2004) Childhood neglect is associated with reduced corpus callosum area. *Biological Psychiatry*, **56**, 80–85.

Teitelbaum, P. (1977) Levels of integration of the operant. In *Handbook of Operant Behavior* (eds W.K. Honig and J.E.R. Staddon), Prentice Hall, Englewood Cliffs, pp. 7–27.

Temple, C.M. and Richardson, P. (2004) Developmental amnesia: a new pattern of dissociation with intact episodic memory. *Neuropsychologia*, **42**, 764–781.

Thach, W.T. (1998) What is the role of the cerebellum in motor learning and cognition? *Trends in Cognitive Sciences*, **2**, 331–337.

Thach, W.T., Goodkin, H.P. and Keating, J.G. (1992) The cerebellum and the adaptive coordination of movement. *Annual Review of Neuroscience*, **15**, 403–442.

Thewissen, R., van den Hout, M., Havermans, R.C. and Jansen, A. (2005) Context-dependency of cue-elicited urge to smoke. *Addiction*, **100**, 387–396.

Thompson, P.M., Vidal, C., Giedd, J.N., Gochman, P., Blumenthal, J., Nicolson, R., Toga, A.W. and Rapoport, J.L. (2001) Mapping adolescent brain change reveals dynamic wave of accelerated gray matter loss in very early-onset schizophrenia. *Proceedings of the National Academy of Sciences USA*, **98**, 11650–11655.

Thompson, R.F. (1990) Neural mechanisms of classical conditioning in mammals. *Philosophical Transactions of the Royal Society of London B*, **329**, 161–170.

Thorn, B.E. (2004) *Cognitive Therapy for Chronic Pain*, Guilford Press, New York.

Thornhill, N.W. (1991) An evolutionary analysis of rules regulating human inbreeding and marriage. *Behavioral and Brain Sciences*, **14**, 247–293.

Thrasher, T.N. (1991) Volume receptors and the stimulation of water intake. In *Thirst: Physiological and Psychological Aspects* (eds D.J. Ramsey and D. Booth), Springer-Verlag, London, pp. 93–109.

Tiffany, S.L. (1990) A cognitive model of drug urges and drug-use behaviour: role of autonomic and nonautonomic processes, *Psychological Review*, **97**, 147–168.

Tiggemann, M. and Kemps, E. (2005) The phenomenology of food cravings: the role of mental imagery. *Appetite*, **45**, 305–313.

Tinbergen, N. (1963) On aims and methods of ethology. *Zeitschrift für Tierpsychologie*, **20**, 410–433.

Toates, F. (1980) *Animal Behaviour – A Systems Approach*, Wiley, Chicester.

Toates, F. (1986) *Motivational Systems*. Cambridge University Press, Cambridge.

Toates, F. (1990) Biological perspectives. In *Introduction to Psychology*, Vol. 1 (ed. I. Roth), Lawrence Erlbaum, Hove, pp. 191–249.

Toates, F. (1992) *Control of Behaviour*, The Open University, Milton Keynes.

Toates, F. (1995) *Stress – Conceptual and Biological Aspects*, Wiley, Chichester.

Toates, F. (1997a) The control of movement. In *Growing and Responding* (SK220, Book 2) (ed. M. Stewart), The Open University, Milton Keynes, pp. 109–154.

Toates, F. (1997b) Pain. In *The Human Condition* (SK220, Book 4) (ed. F.M. Toates), The Open University, Milton Keynes, pp. 66–93.

Toates, F. (1997c) Human sexuality. In *The Human Condition* (SK220, Book 4) (ed. F. Toates), The Open University, Milton Keynes, pp. 43–65.

Toates, F. (1998a) The interaction of cognitive and stimulus–response processes in the control of behaviour. *Neuroscience and Biobehavioral Reviews*, **22**, 59–83.

Toates, F. (1998b) The biological bases of behaviour. In *Psychology – An Integrated Approach* (ed. M. Eysenck), Addison Wesley Longman, Harlow, pp. 23–67.

Toates, F. (1998c) Sensory systems. In *Psychology – An Integrated Approach* (ed. M. Eysenck), Addison Wesley Longman, Harlow, pp. 100–137.

Toates, F. (2004) Introduction to brains, mind and consciousness. In *From Cells to Consciousness*. Book 1 of Course SD226 *Biological Psychology: Exploring the Brain*, The Open University, Milton Keynes.

Toates, F. and Coschug-Toates, O. (2002) *Obsessive Compulsive Disorder*, Class Publishing, London.

Tobet, S.A. and Fox, T.O. (1992) Sex differences in neuronal morphology influenced hormonally throughout life. In *Handbook of Behavioral Neurobiology*, Vol. 11, *Sexual Differentiation* (eds A.A. Gerall, H. Moltz and I.L. Ward), Plenum Press, New York, pp. 41–83.

Tokar, J.T., Brunse, A.J., Stefflre, V.J., Sodergren, J.A. and Napior, D.A. (1975) Determining what heroin means to heroin addicts. *Diseases of the Nervous System*, **36**, 77–81.

Tolman, E.C. (1932) *Purposive Behavior in Animals and Men*, The Century Co., New York.

Tooby, J. and Cosmides, L. (1990) The past explains the present. *Ethology and Sociobiology*, **11**, 375–424.

Tranel, D., Damasio, A.R. and Damasio, H. (1988) Intact recognition of facial expression, gender, and age in patients with impaired recognition of face identity. *Neurology*, **38**, 690–696.

Tranel, D., Anderson, S.W. and Benton, A. (1994) Development of the concept of 'executive function' and its relationship to the frontal lobes. In *Handbook of Neuropsychology*, Vol. 9 (eds F. Boller and J. Grafman), Elsevier, Amsterdam, pp. 125–148.

Trevarthen, C. (1984) Hemispheric specialization. In *Handbook of Physiology. Section 1: The Nervous System*, Vol. III, Part 2 (ed. I. Darian-Smith), American Physiological Society, Bethesda, pp. 1129–1190.

Tronick, E.Z. (1989) Emotions and emotional communication in infants. *American Psychologist*, **44**, 112–119.

Trout, J.D. (2001) The biological basis of speech: what to infer from talking to the animals. *Psychological Review*, **108**, 523–549.

Tryon, R.C. (1940) X.III. Genetic differences in maze-learning ability in rats. *Yearbook for the National Society for the Study of Education*, **39**, 111–119.

Tsuchitani, C. and Johnson, D.H. (1991) Binaural cues and signal processing in the superior olivary complex. In *Neurobiology of Hearing: The Central Auditory System* (eds R.A. Altschuler, R.P. Bobbin, B.M. Clopton and D.W. Hoffman), Raven Press, New York, pp. 163–194.

Tucker, D.M. and Frederick, S.L. (1989) Emotion and brain lateralization. In *Handbook of Social Psychophysiology* (eds H. Wagner and A. Manstead), Wiley, Chichester, pp. 27–70.

Tucker, D.M. and Williamson, P.A. (1984) Asymmetric neural control systems in human self-regulation. *Psychological Review*, **91**, 185–215.

Tucker, D.M., Vannatta, K. and Rothlind, J. (1990) Arousal and activation systems and primitive adaptive controls on cognitive priming. In *Psychological and Biological Approaches to Emotion* (eds N.L. Stein, B. Leventhal and T. Trabasso), Lawrence Erlbaum, Hillsdale, pp. 145–166.

Tulving, E. (1972) Episodic and semantic memory. In *Organization of Memory* (ed. E. Tulving and W. Donaldson), Academic Press, New York, pp. 381–403.

Tulving, E. (1985a) How many memory systems are there? *American Psychologist*, **40**, 385–398.

Tulving, E. (1985b) Memory and consciousness. *Canadian Psychology*, **26**, 1–12.

Tulving, E. (1995) Introduction. In *The Cognitive Neurosciences* (ed. M.S. Gazzaniga), MIT Press, Cambridge, pp. 751–753.

Tulving, E. (1999) Study of memory: processes and systems. In *Memory: Systems, Process, or Function* (eds J.K. Foster and M. Jelicic), Oxford University Press, Oxford, pp. 11–30.

Ullman, M.T. (2004) Contributions of memory circuits to language: the declarative/procedural model. *Cognition*, **92**, 231–270.

Ulrich, R.E. and Favell, J.E. (1970) Human aggression. In *Behavior Modification in Clinical Psychology* (eds C. Neuringer and J.L. Michael), Appleton-Century-Crofts, New York, pp. 105–132.

Umiltà, C. and Zorzi, M. (1995) Consciousness does not seem to be linked to a single neural mechanism. *Behavioral and Brain Sciences*, **18**, 701–702.

Ungerleider, L.G. and Mishkin, M. (1982) Two cortical visual systems. In *Analysis of Visual Behavior* (eds D.J. Ingle, M.A. Goodale and R.J.W. Mansfield), MIT Press, Cambridge, pp. 549–586.

Uno, H., Tarara, R., Else, J.G., Suleman, M.A. and Sapolsky, R.M. (1989) Hippocampal damage associated with prolonged and fatal stress in primates. *Journal of Neuroscience*, **9**, 1705–1711.

Ur, E., White, P.D. and Grossman, A. (1992) Hypothesis: cytokines may be activated to cause depressive illness and chronic fatigue syndrome. *European Archives of Psychiatry and Clinical Neuroscience*, **241**, 317–322.

Ursin, H. and Olff, M. (1993) The stress response. In *Stress – From Synapse to Syndrome* (eds S.C. Stanford and P. Salmon), Academic Press, London, pp. 3–22.

Vahle-Hinz, C. Brüggemann, J. and Kniffki, K-D. (1995) Thalamic processing of visceral pain. In *Pain and the Brain: From Nociception to Cognition* (Advances in Pain Research and Therapy, Vol. 22) (eds B. Bromm and J.E. Desmedt), Raven Press, New York, pp. 125–141.

Vaidya, C.J., Austin, G., Kirkorian, G., Ridlehuber, H.W., Desmond, J.E., Glover, G.H. and Gabrieli, J.D.E. (1998) Selective effects of methylphenidate in attention deficit hyperactivity disorder: a functional magnetic resonance study. *Proceedings of the National Academy of Sciences USA*, **95**, 14494–14499.

Valenstein, E.S. (1969) Behavior elicited by hypothalamic stimulation – a prepotency hypothesis. *Brain Behavior and Evolution*, **2**, 295–316.

Valenstein, E.S. (1973) *Brain Control – A Critical Examination of Brain Stimulation and Psychosurgery*, Wiley, New York.

Valins, S. (1970) The perception and labelling of bodily changes as determinants of emotional behavior. In *Physiological Correlates of Emotion* (ed. P. Black), Academic Press, New York, pp. 229–243.

Vallbo, A.B. (1995) Single-afferent neurons and somatic sensation in humans. In *The Cognitive Neurosciences* (ed. M.S. Gazzaniga), MIT Press, Cambridge, pp. 237–252.

Vander, A.J., Sherman, J.H. and Luciano, D.S (1975) *Human Physiology*, McGraw-Hill, New York.

Vander, A.J., Sherman, J.H. and Luciano, D.S. (1994) *Human Physiology*, McGraw-Hill, New York.

Van der Loos, H. and Woolsey, T.A. (1973) Somatosensory cortex: structural alterations following early injury to sense organs. *Science*, **179**, 395–397.

Vanderschuren, L.J.M.J. and Everitt, B.J. (2004) Drug seeking becomes compulsive after prolonged cocaine self-administration. *Science*, **305**, 1017–1019.

Vanderschuren, L.J.M.J., Niesink, R.J.M. and Van Ree, J.M. (1997) The neurobiology of social play behavior in rats. *Neuroscience and Biobehavioral Reviews*, **21**, 309–326.

van Dijken, H.H., de Goeij, D.C.E., Sutanto, W., Mos, J., de Kloet, E.R. and Tilders, F.J.H. (1993) Short inescapable stress produces long-lasting changes in the brain–pituitary–adrenal axis of adult male rats. *Neuroendocrinology*, **58**, 57–64.

van Honk, J., Tuiten, A., van den Hout, M., Koppeschaar, H., Thijssen, J., de Haan, E. and Verbaten, R. (1998) Baseline salivary cortisol levels and preconscious selective attention for threat. A pilot study. *Psychoneuroendocrinology*, **23**, 741–747.

van Honk, J., Tuiten, A., Verbaten, R., van den Hout, M., Koppeschaar, H., Thijssen, J. and de Haan, E. (1999) Correlations among salivary testosterone, mood, and selective attention to threat in humans. *Hormones and Behavior*, **36**, 17–24.

van Honk, J., Tuiten, A., Hermans, E., Putman, P., Koppeschaar, H., Thijssen, J., Verbaten, R. and van Doornen, L. (2001) A single administration of testosterone induces cardiac accelerative responses to angry faces in healthy young women. *Behavioral Neuroscience*, **115**, 238–242.

VanItallie, T.B. and Kissileff, H.R. (1990) Human obesity – a problem in body energy economics. In *Handbook of Behavioral Neurobiology*, Vol. 10, *Neurobiology of Food and Fluid Intake* (ed. E.M. Stricker), Plenum Press, New York, pp. 207–240.

Van Lange, P.A.M. (2006) *Bridging Social Psychology: The Benefits of Transdisciplinary Approaches*, Erlbaum, Hillsdale.

Van Thiel, D.H., Gavaler, J.S. and Tarter, R.E. (1988) The effects of alcohol on sexual behaviour and function. In *Handbook of Sexology*, Vol. 6, *The Pharmacology and Endocrinology of Sexual Function* (ed. J.M.A. Sitsen), Elsevier Science Publishers, Amsterdam, pp. 478–498.

Vargha-Khadem, F., Isaacs, E. and Muter, V. (1994) A review of cognitive outcome after unilateral lesions sustained during childhood. *Journal of Child Neurology*, **9** (Suppl.), 2S67–2S73.

Velmans, M. (1991) Is human information processing conscious? *Behavioral and Brain Sciences*, **14**, 651–726.

Velmans, M. (2000) *Understanding Consciousness*, Taylor and Francis, London.

Verbalis, J.G. (1990) Clinical aspects of body fluid homeostasis in humans. In *Handbook of Behavioral Neurobiology*, Vol. 10, *Neurobiology of Food and Fluid Intake* (ed. E.M. Stricker), Plenum Press, New York, pp. 421–462.

Verbalis, J.G. (1991) Inhibitory controls of drinking: satiation of thirst. In *Thirst: Physiological and Psychological Aspects* (eds D.J. Ramsey and D. Booth), Springer-Verlag, London, pp. 313–334.

Verney, E.B. (1947) The anti-diuretic hormone and the factors which determine its release. *Proceedings of the Royal Society of London B*, **135**, 25–106.

Verry, Dr (1888) Hémiachromtopsic droite absolue – conservation partielle de la perception lumineuse et des formes. Ancien kyste hémorrhagique de la partie inférieure du lobe occipital gauche. *Archives d'Ophtalmologie*, **8**, 289–301.

Vessie, P.R. (1932) On the transmission of Huntington's chorea for 300 years – The Bures family group. *Journal of Nervous and Mental Disease*, **76**, 553–573.

Vingerhoets, J.J.M. (1985) The role of the parasympathetic division of the autonomic nervous system in stress and the emotions. *International Journal of Psychosomatics*, **32**, 28–33.

Volkow, N.D., Wang, G.-J., Fowler, J.S., Logan, J., Gatley, S.J., Hitzemann, R., Chen, A.D., Dewey, S.L. and Pappas, N. (1997) Decreased striatal dopaminergic responsiveness in detoxified cocaine-dependent subjects. *Nature*, **386**, 830–833.

Volkow, N.D., Fowler, J.S. and Wang, J-W. (2002) Role of dopamine in drug reinforcement and addiction in humans: results from imaging studies. *Behavioural Pharmacology*, **13**, 355–366

von Békésy, G. (1960) *Experiments in Hearing*, McGraw-Hill, New York.

von der Heydt, R. (1995) Form analysis in visual cortex. In *The Cognitive Neurosciences* (ed. M.S. Gazzaniga), MIT Press, Cambridge, pp. 365–382.

von der Heydt, R. and Peterhans, E. (1989) Mechanisms of contour perception in monkey visual cortex. I. Lines of pattern discontinuity. *Journal of Neuroscience*, **9**, 1731–1748.

von Holst, D. (1986) Vegetative and somatic components of tree shrews' behaviour. *Journal of the Autonomic Nervous System*, Suppl. 657–670.

von Holst, E. and Mittlestaedt, H. (1950) Das Reafferenzprinzip. *Naturwissenschaften*, **37**, 464–476. English translation in Gallistel, C.R. (1980) *The Organization of Action: A New Synthesis*, Lawrence Erlbaum, Hillsdale, pp. 176–209.

Waddington, C.H. (1936) *How Animals Develop*, W.W. Norton, New York.

Waddington, C.H. (1975) *The Evolution of an Evolutionist*, Edinburgh University Press, Edinburgh.

Wager, T.D., Rilling, J.K., Smith, E.E., Sokolik, A., Casey, K.L., Davidson, R.J., Kosslyn, S.M., Rose, R.M. and Cohen, J.D. (2004) Placebo-induced changes in fMRI in the anticipation and experience of pain. *Science*, **303**, 1162–1167.

Wagner, G. and Sjöstrand, N.O. (1988) Autonomic pharmacology and sexual function. In *Handbook of Sexology*, Vol. 6, *The Pharmacology and Endocrinology of Sexual Function* (ed. J.M.A. Sitsen), Elsevier Science Publishers, Amsterdam, pp. 32–43.

Waldman, I.D. and Rhee, S.H. (2002) Behavioural and molecular genetic studies. In *Hyperactivity and Attention Disorders of Childhood* (2nd edition) (ed. S. Sandberg), Cambridge University Press, Cambridge, pp. 290–335.

Walker, E.F., Baum, K.M. and Diforio, D. (1998) Developmental changes in the behavioral expression of vulnerability for schizophrenia. In *Origins and Development of Schizophrenia* (eds M.F. Lenzenweger and R.H. Dworkin), American Psychological Association, Washington, pp. 469–491.

Wall, P. (2002) Pain: *The Science of Suffering*, Columbia University Press, New York.

Wall, P.D. (1993) Pain and the placebo response. In *Experimental and Theoretical Studies of Consciousness* (eds G.R. Bock and J. Marsh), Wiley, Chichester, pp. 187–216.

Wall, P.D. and Egger, M.D. (1971) Formation of new connections in adult rat brains after partial deafferentation. *Nature*, **232**, 542–545.

Walsh, J.K., Hartman, P.G. and Kowall, J.P. (1994) Insomnia. In *Sleep Disorders Medicine: Basic Science, Technical Considerations and Clinical Aspects* (ed. S. Chokroverty), Butterworth-Heinemann, Boston, pp. 219–239.

Waltz, J.A., Knowlton, B.J., Holyoak, K.J., Boone, K.B., Mishkin, F.S., de Menezes Santos, M., Thomas, C.R. and Miller, B.L. (1999) A system for relational reasoning in human prefrontal cortex. *Psychological Science*, **10**, 119–125.

Wand, G.S., Mangold, D., El Deiry, S., McCaul, M.E. and Hoover, D. (1998) Family history of alcoholism and hypothalamic opioidergic activity. *Archives of General Psychiatry*, **55**, 1114–1119.

Wang, J.Q. and McGinty, J.F. (1999) Glutamate–dopamine interactions mediate the effects of psychostimulant drugs. *Addiction Biology*, **4**, 141–150.

Wang, S-H., Ostlund, S.B., Nader, K. and Balleine, B.W. (2005) Consolidation and reconsolidation of incentive learning in the amygdala. *Journal of Neuroscience*, **25**, 830–835.

Warr, W.B., Guinan, J.J. and White, J.S. (1986) Organization of the efferent fibers: the lateral and medial olivocochlear systems. In *Neurobiology of Hearing: The Cochlea* (eds R.A. Altschuler, D.W. Hoffman and R.P. Bobbin), Raven Press, New York, pp. 333–348.

Warrington, E.K. and Weiskrantz, L. (1970) Amnesic syndrome: consolidation or retrieval? *Nature*, **228**, 628–630.

Watson, P.J. and Andrews, P.W. (2002) Toward a revised evolutionary adaptationist analysis of depression: the social navigation hypothesis. *Journal of Affective Disorders*, **72**, 1–14.

Watts, F.N., East, M.P. and Coyle, K. (1995) Insomniacs' perceived lack of control over sleep. *Psychology and Health*, **10**, 81–95.

Waxham, M.N. (1999) Neurotransmitter receptors. In *Fundamental Neuroscience* (eds M.J. Zigmond, F.E. Bloom, S.C. Landis, J.L. Roberts and L.R. Squire), Academic Press, San Diego, pp. 235–267.

Wegner, D.M. (2003) *The Illusion of Conscious Will*, MIT Press, Cambridge.

Weinberger, D.R. (1987) Implications of normal brain development for the pathogenesis of schizophrenia. *Archives of General Psychiatry*, **44**, 660–669.

Weinberger, N.M. (1993) Learning-induced changes of auditory receptive fields. *Current Opinion in Neurobiology*, **3**, 570–577.

Weiner, H. (1996) Use of animal models in peptic ulcer disease. *Psychosomatic Medicine*, **58**, 524–545.

Weingarten, H.P. (1984) Meal initiation controlled by learned cues: basic behavioral properties. *Appetite*, **5**, 147–158.

Weinstein, A., Wilson, S., Bailey, J., Myles, J. and Nutt, D. (1997) Imagery of craving in opiate addicts undergoing detoxification. *Drug and Alcohol Dependence*, **48**, 25–31.

Weinstein, S. (1968) Intensive and extensive aspects of tactile sensitivity as a function of body part, sex and laterality. In *The Skin Senses* (ed. D.R. Kenshalo), C.C. Thomas, Springfield, pp. 195–222.

Weisenberg, M. (1994) Cognitive aspects of pain. In *Textbook of Pain* (eds P.D. Wall and R. Melzack), Churchill Livingstone, Edinburgh, pp. 275–289.

Weiskrantz, L. (1976) *Blindsight – A Case Study and Implications*, Clarendon Press, Oxford.

Weiskrantz, L. (1982) Comparative aspects of studies of amnesia. *Philosophical Transactions of the Royal Society B*, **298**, 97–109.

Weiskrantz, L. (1997) *Consciousness Lost and Found*, Oxford University Press, Oxford.

Weiskrantz, L. and Saunders, R.C. (1984) Impairments of visual object transforms in monkeys. *Brain*, **107**, 1033–1072.

Weiskrantz, L. and Warrington, E.K. (1979) Conditioning in amnesic patients. *Neuropsychologia*, **17**, 187–194.

Weiss, J.M. (1971) Effects of coping behaviour in different warning signal conditions on stress pathology in rats. *Journal of Comparative and Physiological Psychology*, **77**, 1–13.

Weiss, J.M. (1972) Psychological factors in stress and disease. *Scientific American*, **226**, No. 6, 104–113.

Weiss, J.M., Pohorecky, L.A., Salman, S. and Gruenthal, M. (1976) Attenuation of gastric lesions by psychological aspects of aggression in rats. *Journal of Comparative and Physiological Psychology*, **90**, 252–259.

Welker, W.I. (1961) An analysis of exploratory and play behavior in animals. In *Functions of Varied Experience* (eds D.W. Fiske and S.R. Maddi), Dorsey Press, Homewood, pp. 175–226.

Weller, A. (1998) Communication through body odour. *Nature*, **392**, 126–127.

Wernicke, C. (1874) *Der Aphasische Symptomenkomplex*, Cohn und Weigert, Breslau.

Wexler, B.E. (2006) *Brain and Culture: Neurobiology, Ideology, and Social Change*, MIT Press, Cambridge.

Whatson, T. and Sterling, V. (1998) *Development and Flexibility*, Springer (The Open University), Berlin.

Whipple, B. and Komisaruk, B.R. (1999) Beyond the G spot: recent research on female sexuality. *Psychiatric Annals*, **29**, 34–37.

Whitaker, H.A. (1983) Towards a brain model of automatization: a short essay. In *Memory and Control of Action* (ed. R.A. Magill), North-Holland, Amsterdam, pp. 199–214.

White, N.M. (1989) Reward or reinforcement: what's the difference? *Neuroscience and Biobehavioral Reviews*, **13**, 181–186.

White, N.M. and McDonald, R.J. (1993) Acquisition of a spatial conditioned place preference is impaired by amygdala lesions and improved by fornix lesions. *Behavioural Brain Research*, **55**, 269–281.

Wiepkema, P.R. (1987) Behavioural aspects of stress. In *Biology of Stress in Farm Animals: An Integrative Approach* (eds P.R. Wiepkema and P.W.M. Van Adrichem), Martinus Nijhoff, Dordrecht.

Wikler, A. (1965) Conditioning factors in opiate addiction and relapse. In *Narcotics* (eds D.I. Wilner and G.G. Kassanbaum), McGraw-Hill, New York, pp. 399–414.

Wilkins, L. and Richter, C.P. (1940) A great craving for salt by a child with cortico-adrenal insufficiency. *Journal of the American Medical Association*, **114**, 866–868.

Williams, C.L., Villar, R.G., Peterson, J.M. and Burks, T.F. (1988) Stress-induced changes in intestinal transit in the rat: a model for irritable bowel syndrome. *Gastroenterology*, **94**, 611–621.

Williams, R. (1989) *The Trusting Heart*, Times Books, New York.

Williamson, P. (2005) *Mind, Brain, and Schizophrenia*, Oxford University Press, Oxford.

Willingham, D. (2004) *Cognition: The Thinking Animal*, Allyn and Bacon, Boston.

Willingham, D.B. (1998) A neuropsychological theory of motor skill learning. *Psychological Review*, **105**, 558–584.

Willner, P. (1993) Animal models of stress: an overview. In *Stress – From Synapse to Syndrome* (eds S.C. Stanford and P. Salmon), Academic Press, London, pp. 145–165.

Willner, P., James, D. and Morgan, M. (2005) Excessive alcohol consumption and dependence are associated with parallel increases in subjective ratings of both 'wanting' and 'liking'. *Addiction*, **100**, 1487–1495.

Wilson, G. and Rahman, Q. (2004) *Born Gay?: The Psychobiology of Sex Orientation*, Peter Owen, London.

Windmann, S. and Krüger, T. (1998) Subconscious detection of threat as reflected by an enhanced response bias. *Consciousness and Cognition*, **7**, 603–633.

Winkielman, P., Berridge, K.C., and Wilbarger, J.L. (2005) Unconscious affective reactions to masked happy versus angry faces influence consumption behavior and judgments of value. *Personality and Social Psychology Bulletin*, **31**, 121–135.

Winn, P. (1995) The lateral hypothalamus and motivated behaviour: an old syndrome reassessed and a new perspective gained. *Current Directions in Psychological Science*, **4**, 182–187.

Winterer, G. and Weinberger, D.R. (2004) Genes, dopamine and cortical signal-to-noise ratio in schizophrenia. *Trends in Neuroscience*, **27**, 683–689.

Wise, R.A. (1982) Neuroleptics and operant behaviour: the anhedonia hypothesis. *Behavioral and Brain Sciences*, **5**, 39–87.

Wise, R.A. (1987) Sensorimotor modulation and the variable action pattern (VAP): toward a noncircular definition of drive and motivation. *Psychobiology*, **15**, 7–20.

Wise, R.A. (1988) The neurobiology of craving: implications for the understanding and treatment of addiction. *Journal of Abnormal Psychology*, **97**, 118–132.

Wise, R.A. and Bozarth, M.A. (1987) A psychomotor stimulant theory of addiction. *Psychological Review*, **94**, 469–492.

Wise, S.P. (1984) The nonprimary motor cortex and its role in the cerebral control of movement. In *Dynamic Aspects of Neocortical Function* (eds G.M. Edelman, W.E. Gall and W.M. Cowan), Wiley, New York, pp. 525–555.

Wolffgramm, J. and Heyne, A. (1991) Social behavior, dominance, and social deprivation of rats determine drug choice. *Pharmacology Biochemistry and Behavior*, **38**, 389–399.

Wong, A.H.C. and Van Tol, H.H.M. (2003) Schizophrenia: from phenomenology to neurobiology. *Neuroscience and Biobehavioral Reviews*, **27**, 269–306.

Wood, J.D. (1979) Neurophysiology of the enteric nervous system. In *Integrative Functions of the Autonomic Nervous System* (eds C.M. Brooks, K. Koizumi and A. Sato), University of Tokyo Press/Elsevier, Amsterdam, pp. 177–193.

Woodruff-Pak, D.S. (1999) New directions for a classical paradigm: human eyeblink conditioning. *Psychological Science*, **10**, 1–3.

Woodruff-Pak, D.S., Vogel, R.W., Ewers, M., Coffrey, J., Boyko, O.B. and Lemieux, S.K. (2001) MRI-assessed volume of cerebellum correlates with associative learning. *Neurobiology of Learning and Memory*, **76**, 342–357.

Woods, S.C. and Stricker, E.M. (1999) Food intake and metabolism. In *Fundamental Neuroscience* (eds M.J. Zigmond, F.E. Bloom, S.C. Landis, J.L. Roberts and L.R. Squire), Academic Press, San Diego, pp. 1091–1109.

Woods, S.C., Chaverz, M., Park, C.R., Reidy, C., Kaiyala, K., Richardson, R.D., Figlewicz, D.P., Schwartz, M.W., Porte, D. Jr and Seeley, R.J. (1996) The evolution of insulin as a metabolic signal influencing behaviour via the brain. *Neuroscience and Behavioral Reviews*, **20**, 139–144.

Woolsey, T.A. and Wann, J.R. (1976) Areal changes in mouse cortical barrels following vibrissal damage at different postnatal ages. *Journal of Comparative Neurology*, **170**, 53–66.

Workman, L. and Reader, W. (2004) *Evolutionary Psychology: An Introduction*, Cambridge University Press, Cambridge.

Wright, I. and Woodruff, P. (1995) Aetiology of schizophrenia – a review of theories and their clinical and therapeutic implications. *CNS Drugs*, **3**, 126–144.

Würbel, H., Freire, R. and Nicol, C.J. (1998) Prevention of stereotypic wire-gnawing in laboratory mice: effects on behaviour and implications for stereotypy as a coping response. *Behavioural Processes*, **42**, 61–72.

Wurtz, R.H., Goldberg, M.E. and Robinson, D.L. (1982) Brain mechanisms of visual attention. *Scientific American*, **246**, No. 6, 100–107.

Xerri, C., Stern, J.M. and Merzenich, M.M. (1994) Alterations of the cortical representation of the rat ventrum induced by nursing behavior. *Journal of Neuroscience*, **14**, 1710–1721.

Yates, B.J. and Stocker, S.D. (1998) Integration of somatic and visceral inputs by the brainstem. *Experimental Brain Research*, **119**, 269–275.

Yehuda, R., Giller, E.L., Levengood, R.A., Southwick, S.M. and Siever, L.J. (1995) Hypothalamic–pituitary–adrenal functioning in post-traumatic stress disorder. In *Neurobiological and Clinical Consequences of Stress. From Normal Adaptation to Post-traumatic Stress Disorder* (eds M.J. Friedman, D.S. Charney and A.Y. Deutch), Lippincott-Raven, Philadelphia, pp. 351–365.

Yeni-Komshian, G.H. and Benson, D.A. (1976) Anatomical study of cerebral asymmetry in the temporal lobe of humans, chimpanzees, and rhesus monkeys. *Science*, **192**, 387–389.

Yeomans, M.R. and Gray, R.W. (1997) Effects of naltrexone on food intake and changes in subjective appetite during eating: evidence for opioid involvement in the appetizer effect. *Physiology and Behavior*, **62**, 15–21.

Yirmiya, R. (1997) Behavioural and psychological effects of immune activation: implications for 'depression due to a general medical condition'. *Current Opinions in Psychiatry*, **10**, 470–476.

Young, A.M.J., Joseph, M.H. and Gray, J.A. (1993) Latent inhibition of conditioned dopamine release in rat nucleus accumbens. *Neuroscience*, **54**, 5–9.

Young, L.J. and Wang, Z. (2004) The neurobiology of pair bonding. *Nature Neuroscience*, **7**, 1048-1054.

Zaidel, E. and Iacoboni, M. (2003) *The Parallel Brain: The Cognitive Neuroscience of the Corpus Callosum*, MIT Press, Cambridge.

Zajonc, R.B. (1980) Feeling and thinking – preferences need no inferences. *American Psychologist*, **35**, 151–175.

Zangwill, O.L. (1974) Consciousness and the cerebral hemispheres. In *Hemisphere Function in the Human Brain* (eds S.J. Dimond and J.G. Beaumont), Elek Science, London, pp. 264–278.

Zarcone, V.P. (1994) Sleep hygiene. In *Principles and Practice of Sleep Medicine* (eds M.H. Kryger, T. Roth and W.C. Dement), Saunders, Philadelphia, pp. 542–546.

Zeki, S. (1993) *A Vision of the Brain*, Blackwell, Oxford.

Zigmond, M.J., Finlay, J.M. and Sved, A.F. (1995) Neurochemical studies of central noradrenergic responses to acute and chronic stress. In *Neurobiological and Clinical Consequences of Stress. From Normal Adaptation to Post-traumatic Stress Disorder* (eds M.J. Friedman, D.S. Charney and A.Y. Deutch), Lippincott-Raven, Philadelphia, pp. 45–60.

Zihl, J., von Cramon, D. and Mai, N. (1983) Selective disturbance of movement vision after bilateral brain damage. *Brain*, **106**, 313–340.

Zohar, D. (1990) *The Quantum Self*, Flamingo, London.

Zorick, F. (1994) Overview of insomnia. In *Principles and Practice of Sleep Medicine* (eds M.H. Kryger, T. Roth and W.C. Dement), Saunders, Philadelphia, pp. 483–485.

Zubin, J. and Spring, B. (1977) Vulnerability – A new view of schizophrenia. *Journal of Abnormal Psychology*, **86**, 103–126.

Zucker, R.S., Kullmann, D.M. and Bennett, M. (1999) Release of neurotransmitter. In *Fundamental Neuroscience* (eds M.J. Zigmond, F.E. Bloom, S.C. Landis, J.L. Roberts and L.R. Squire), Academic Press, San Diego, pp. 155–192.

Zuk, M. (2003) *Sexual Selections: What We Can and Can't Learn from Animals*, University of California Press, Berkeley.

Index

Note: Page references in *italics* refer to Figures

2-deoxy-D-glucose (2-DG) 140, 403–4, *404*

ablation 142
abnormal behaviour 28
absorption from gut 401, *401*
absorption, of light 194
absorptive state 401, *401*
accommodation 192, *193*
acetylcholine (ACh) 75, 77, 94, 257, 391, 437, 539
acetylcholinesterase (AChE) 171, 257
achromatopsia 212
across-fibre pattern coding 237
action 26, 206, 246–7, 488–515, 542
action potential 50, *50*, 63, 86–90, *87*, *88*, *89*,
    222, 224
    basis 86
    information carried by 184–6
    movement 88, 89
    triggering 87
activational effects, of hormones 163–4
activation–synthesis model of dreaming 484
active memory 284
active strategy 337–9
acuity
    spatial 231–2
    visual 197
acupuncture 360
adaptation 23, 185, 194, 228, 310
adaptive 4
adaptive orientation 461
addiction 363, 450, 459–60
adenosine 457, 481
adipose tissue 401, 402
adrenal cortex 334
adrenal gland 66, 70, 75, 334–5, 435
adrenal medulla 76, 334
adrenalin 57, 70, 325
adrenocorticotrophic hormone (ACTH) 70,
    171, 333, 334
affect 42, 303, 355, 362, 448, 461, 531
affective neuroscience 305–6
affective states 376–7
    model of 461, *461*
afferent neurons 64
after-image 194, 252
ageing 337
aggression 387–91
    genes and environment and 391
    hormonal factors 388–9
    learning and 388
    neural mechanisms 389–91
    restraint of 390–1
agnosia 210, 212
agonists 100–2, *101*

agraphia 507
akinesia 264
alcohol 446, 461–2
    addiction 457
    aggression and 391
    sexual behaviour and 440
alertness 128–9
alexia 507
alimentary tract 400
allele 39, *39*
alliesthesia 376
alpha activity 476
alpha motor neuron 258
altricial species 174, 482
Alzheimer's disease 242, 492, 536–40
    cellular changes 536, 538–9
    changes in gross brain structure 537–8
    cognitive deficit in 537
    genetics 36, 538
    neurotransmitter changes 539
ambiguous figures 180, 215–16
amino acids 29, 323–4
amnesia 284–5, 520
amnesic syndrome 287–9, 537
AMPA receptors 298
amphetamine 450, 452, 453, 461, 544, 546
amphetamine-induced effect 545, 546
amygdala 123, 385, 437
    damage to 320
    emotion and 318–20, *318*, 342
    fear and 318–20, 325, 326
    and incentive learning 379, 430
    role of 224
    sexual desire and 434, 436
analgesia 355, 367
    techniques of 363–5
analgesics 355, 363–5
analogies 12–13, 130, 147–8, 197, 513, 528, 531
androgen 164, *165*, 427, 435, 437
anger 313
angiotensin 418, 420, 421
anhedonia 381
animal models 16
anomalous phenomena, of pain 365
anorexia nervosa 413–14
anorexia, cancer-associated 414
anosmia 242
A-not-B test 169, 172
antagonist muscles 257, *257*
antagonists 100–2, *101*, 257
anterior cingulate cortex (ACC) 361, *362*, 368, 552
anterior commissure 109, 110, 441
anterograde amnesia 284
anterograde labelling 137
anti-androgens 430, 435
antidepressants 102, 323

anti-diuretic hormone (ADH) 67
anti-nociception 355, 356, 359, 369
antisocial behaviour 388
antithesis, principle of 304
anxiety 306
anxiogenics 323, 448
anxiolytics 323, 393
apathy 540
aphagia 410
aphasia 507–8
aphrodisiacs 433, 440
Aplysia 131–2, *131*
    habituation in 277, 296
    sensitization in 297
ApoE4 36, 538
apomorphine 440, 545
appetite 399
appetitive phase 375
    of sexual behaviour 430, 431
arcuate nucleus 410
arcuate fasciculus *507*, 508
arginine vasopressin (AVP) 67, 68, 128, 419,
    432–3, 436
aromatization 165
arousal 117, 331–2
ascending reticular activating system (ARAS)
    116–17, *116*, 478–9
as-if loop 315–16
aspirin 363, *364*
association cortex 129, 134
associative learning 277
associative visual agnosia 212
astonishing hypothesis 529
ataxia 267
atherosclerosis 335
attachment 312–13
attention 493–7
    in Alzheimer's disease 537
    brain regions and 495–7
    consciousness and 522
    cross-modal 494–5
    divided 493
    selective 493–5
    spotlight of 522
    sustained 493
    types of 493
attention deficit hyperactivity disorder 552–5
    animal model 554–5
    drug treatment 554
    environmental factors 555
    heredity 555
    social implications 555
    underlying disfunction 553–4
auditory cortex 115, *223*
auditory information, routes of 224, *224*
auditory system, anatomy *223*

Auguste, D. 536
autism 170, 491
autoaddiction 413
autoimmune disorders 340
automaticity 267
automatic processing 249–51, 521–2
automatic reactions 48, 249
autonomic ganglion 76
autonomic nervous system 54, *54*, 71–8, 162,
    192, 226, 270, 303, 313–14, 332, 351
    chemistry of 77
    definition 72
    divisions 72–5
    effectors 75–6
    global and local control 77
    parasympathetic branch 72, *74*, 75, 332, 334,
        437
    sensory feedback 76
    sexual behaviour and *425*, 426, 436
    stress and 333–4
    sympathetic branch 72, 73, 332, 333–4, 343,
        437, 439
autonomic neurons 72
aversion 375
axon hillock 96, *96*
axons 51, 63, 76

barbiturates 323
basal ganglia 122, *122*, 262, 264–6, 538, 550
    role of 264
    structure and connections 264
Bechara gambling task 504–5
behaviour therapy 415
behavioural embryology 149
behavioural indices 332
behavioural inhibition 391
behavioural satiety sequence 407, 415
belonging 349
benefits 24–5
benzodiazepine agonists 411
benzodiazepine receptors 323
benzodiazepines 323
beta activity 476
beta-amyloid 539
beta-blockers 315, 334
Beuren's syndrome 491
biaural processing 224
binding problem 526
binocular rivalry 215–16
biological clock 468
biology–psychology relationship 10–11, 12–14
bipolar cells 118, *119*, 194
blindsight 9, 524–5, 526, 527
blood–brain barrier 126, 266, 419, 420
blushing 54, 311
body fluids 416–17
bottom-up aspect 180, 190, 192, 213–16, 226,
    491, 493
bradykinesia 264
brain 3, *3*, 52
    action and 53–4
    anatomy 108–11, *109–14*
    attention and 495–7
    blood vessels 124–6
    consciousness and 523
    development 109, *110*, 147, 152, *154*, 168,

173–4, 543
    eating and 409–12
    environment 124–8
    growth spurt 173
    homosexuality and 441–2
    landmarks 108–11
    and mind 17–18
    orientation 107, *108*
    pain and 361–2
    planes of reference 107, *107*
    in sexual differentiation 165
    size 133, *133*
    stimulation 143, 381
    streaming 206–7, 511
brain damage 142, 287
    accidental 8, 9
    consciousness and 524–5
    experimental lesions 142–3
    selective, cognition and 500–1
brain lock 551
brain stem 108, *109*, 267–9
brain stimulation 143
Broca, Paul 507
Broca's aphasia 508, 513
Broca's area 507, 513, *514*, 543
Brodmann's areas 111, *113*
bulimia nervosa 413
Burt, Sir Cyril 525

caffeine 457–8, 459
cannabinoids 364, 415, 448, 457
cannabis 440
    see also marijuana
Capgras's syndrome 519
carbohydrates 400–1
cardiac muscle 71, 75
catastrophizing 366
catecholamines 57, 334, 338, 391, 554
caudal 107
caudate nucleus *122*, 264, 491, 550, 551
causal explanation 3, 5
cell body 51, 63, 76
cell death 157
cell life 157
cell migration *155*, 156
cell-adhesion molecules 157
cells 6, 6, 29, 400–1, *400*
    place 143
central executive system (CES) 284, *286*, 502,
    505, 520, 537–8
central nervous system 48
    control and 250
central pattern generators (CPGs) 261
central sulcus *113, 123*
centre–surround organization 195
cephalic phase 67, 402
cerebellum 108, *109*, 122, 262, 266–7, 522, 538
    damage to 267, 291–2
cerebral cortex 109, 262
cerebral hemispheres *109*, 110
cerebrospinal fluid (CSF) 125
cerebrum 108, *109*
characteristics, complex 36
Charles Bonnet syndrome 522
chemical senses 236–42

chemoattraction 156, 157
chemoreceptors 236
chemotropic factor 157
chlordiazepoxide 323
chlorpromazine 544
cholecystokinin (CCK) 360, 408
choline acetyltransferase (ChAT) 539
cholinergic hypothesis, of Alzheimer's disease 539
cholinergic systems in sleep 479
chromosomes 30, 149
cingulate cortex 111, 316
cingulate gyrus 111, *114, 123*, 316
circadian rhythms 468–71, 480
circumventricular organs 126, 420
Claparède, Edouard 287–8, 308, 320
classical conditioning 277–8, *278*, 291, 295, 311,
    326, 367, 375, 411, 429, 449–50, 545–6
classical hormones 66–9
classical neurotransmission 55–8
classical neurotransmitter 56, *57*
classical route 224
clomipramine 102, 440
closed programmes 174
cocaine 385, 440, 446, 450, 452–4, *453*, 462
cochlea *222, 223*
cognition 123, 308, 356, 360, 541, 554
    action and 488–515
    definition 490
    effect of emotion on 324
cognitive development, brain and 168–70
cognitive impulsiveness 555
cognitive mapping 290, 393
cognitive maps, forming 279–80
cognitive processing 129–30
cognitive targeting 366–7
cognitive therapy 43
cognitive unconscious 520
cold neurons 383
collateral 117
colocalization 95, *95*
colour constancy 212
colour perception 198–9, 212
command neurons 77
comorbidity 552
comparative approach 16, 130–6
complete androgen insensitivity syndrome
    (CAIS) 167
complex characteristics 36
complex cortical cells 202, *202*
computerized axial tomogram (CAT) 140
computerized tomography (CT) 140
concentration gradients 85–6, 416
concept-driven perception 180
concordance 151
conditional emotional response 311
conditional incentives 375, 385, 388, 426
conditional response 278
conditional stimuli (CS) 278, 310–11, 326, 426
conditioned place preference (CPP) 375, *375*,
    430, 452, 454, 456
conditioning
    classical 59, 277–8, 311, 375, 449–50
    drug taking and 449–50
    feeding and 406
    sexual motivation and 429–30

conduction aphasia 509
cones 193, 194, *194*, 198–9
confabulation 287, 296
congenital adrenal hyperplasia (CAH) 167
conscious awareness 240, 248, 517
conscious information processing 519–21
consciousness
    binding problem 526
    brain mechanisms of 521–6
    comparative issues 527
    definition 518
    function 526–7
    Libet's studies 524, 530
    linking psychology and biology 522–3
    memory and 524, 527
    neural systems 621–3
    Penfield's study 524
    phenomenal 518, 528, 531
    philosophical considerations 18, 528–32
conservation of organization 132–3
consolidation 283, 296
constancy 186, 209
consummatory phase 375, 380–1
    of sexual behaviour 430, 431
contextual factors 336–9
contralateral 107
controllability 336
controlled processing 249–51, 522
convergence 197, *197*
Coolidge effect 429
coping strategy 330
core sleep 473
corollary discharge 253
coronary heart disease (CHD) 345
corpus callosum *109*, 110, *123*, 150, 171 203,
    203, 525
cortex 134, 201–2, 262–3
    controlling input to 116–17
    defined by role 115–16, *115*
    emotion and 320–2
    memory and 286, 294
    sleep and 523
cortical development 168
cortical processing, sensory system 233–6
cortical streaming 206
cortical–thalamic interaction 523
corticospinal tract 269
corticosteroids 70, 172, 323, 325, 332, 335, *335*,
    337, 345
corticosterone 334
corticotropin releasing factor (CRF) 69–70,
    171–2, 333, 334, 340, 342–3, 345
    role as a neurotransmitter 345
corticotropin releasing hormone (CRH) *see*
    corticotropin releasing factor (CRF)
cortisol 334, 339
costs 24–5, 40
covert orientating 494, *494*
cranial nerves 65, *65*, 221
    development of 152, *154*
craving 415, 450, 454, 457, 462, *463*, 464
creativity 501, 521, 548
critical period 164
cross–talk avoidance 97–8, *98*

cultures 149–50, 307
    comparing, stress and 349–50
Cushing's disease 345
cytokines 340, 414

Dale's principle 94–5
d-amphetamine 554
dark adaptation 194
Darwin, Charles 4, 304, *305*, 306–7
data-driven perception 180
D.B. 9, 524
decerebrate 409
decision-making 503–5
declarative memory 282, 293
deep brain stimulation (DBS) 551
defeminization 166, *166*
delusions 537, 540
demasculinization 165, *166*
dementia 492, 536
dendrite 63
dendritic spines 63, 295
denervation 159
deoxyribonucleic acid (DNA) 33, *33*
depolarization 87
depression 36, 42–3, 321, 324, 435, 454, 518, 552
    stress and 344–5
deprivation effects 171
dermatomes 62, *62*
Descartes, René 50–1, 528
    see also mind–body dualism
descending, pathways 224, 362
design, metaphor of 39–40, 130, 404, 418, 432
desmethylclomipramine 102
determinism 12
development
    analogies 147–8
    auditory stimulation 225
    determinants 149, *150*
    length of 174
    motor systems 271
    sleep and 481–2
    somatosensory system 253
    stress and 337
developmental abnormalities 548
developmental/learning explanation 4, 5, 15, 38,
    42, 159
developmental time 150
diabetes 403
diazepam (Valium) 323, 324
DiCaprio, Leonardo 550
diencephalon 108, *109*
differentiation, cell 155, 156–7
digestion 400
digestive system 400
discrimination test 448
discriminative touch 226
dishabituation *296*, 297
display rules 307
distress vocalization (DV) 312, *312*, 323–4, 386,
    448
divided attention 493
dizygotic twins 151, 547
dominance 388–9
dopamine (DA) 57, 101, *101*, 379–81, 415, 431,

450, 458, 546, 548, 554
    disruption of 264, 266, 287
    role of, in development 169, 172
    in sexual behaviour 429, 431, 440
dopamine hypothesis, of schizophrenia 544–5
dorsal 61, 107
dorsal root (DRG) neurons 228, 232
dorsal root ganglion 61
dorsal stream 206, 511
    lesions in 208
double–blind study 367
double-dissociation effect 207, 285, 290–1, 320,
    492
down-regulation 102
Down's syndrome 35–6
dreaming 75, 483–4
    function 483–4
drinking 399, 415
    body fluids and 416–18
    neuroscience of 419–20
    normal 419
    sodium ingestion and 417–18
drug addiction 451
drug taking 363
    automatic and controlled intake 461–2
    characteristics of behaviour 448–52
    conditioning and 449–50
    contextual effects 451–2
    control 452
    evolutionary considerations 464
    relapse 463
    similarities and differences of drugs 458
    social dimensions 451
    therapy for 463
    types of drug 452–8
    withdrawal 448, 451, 455–6, 461, 463
dualism *see* mind–body dualism

ear, anatomy *220*
Ebbinghaus illusion *207*
Eccles, Sir John 521
echoic memory 283
ecstasy 447, 458
effectors 64
efference copy 253
efferent neurons 64
Einstein, Albert 91, 534
ejaculation 430, 433, 437
electrical stimulation of the brain 381
electrical synapse 99, *99*
electrically–induced behaviour 381
electrocortical mapping 510
electroencephalography (EEG) 138, *138,* 476
electromyogram 139
electron microscopy 138
embarrassment 311
embryo 146, 149, 152
emergent properties 12–13, 492, 529
emotion
    brain mechanisms and inputs 316–23, 342–3
    cognition and action 123
    definition 302–3
    development of 307
    evolutionary experience 306–7

emotion *continued*
  feedback 313–16, *314*
  genes and environment of expression 391
  James–Lange theory of 313, *314*
  learning and individual experience 305
  nature and function 304–9
  perception in others 321–2
  role in behaviour 321–2
  role of odour 241
  Schachter–Singer theory of 313–14, *314*
  structures concerned with *123*, 224, 316–23
  triggers for 310–13
  within an individual 305
empathy 10, 368
encephalization 133
endocrine system 48, 65–71
endogenous opioids (EOs) 415
endorphins 386, 413
engram 283
enkephalin 359, 360, *360*, 363
enrichment effects 171
enteric nervous system 77–8, *78*, 348
entorhinal cortex 37–8
entrainment 469, 470–1
environment
  enrichment of 147, 171
  genes and 37–9, *37*, 43
  womb as 151
enzymes 29
epilepsy 242, 434
epinephrine, *see* adrenalin
episodic memory 282–3, 292, 293, 492, 524,
    527, 536–8
equilibrium, ionic 416
  disturbances to, mechanical 258–9
erectile dysfunction 438–9
erectile function 426, 436–7
ethanol 323, 440, 457
ethology 17, 173–5
euphoria 454, 461
event-related potential (ERP) *see* evoked
    potential
evoked potential (ERP) 139, *139*
evolution 4, 23–5, 304–5
  brain and 130, 292–4
  emotion and 306–7
  genetics and 38–9
evolutionary explanation 4, 5, 130, 548
evolutionary psychology 39–42, 43, 130, 169,
    293, 299, 310, 357, 406, 408, 413, 414, 434,
    435, 442, 464
excitability 86
excitation 55–7
excitatory post-synaptic potential (EPSP) 96, *96*
experiential factor 303
explicit memory 282
exploration 392–4
exposure orientation 461
extension, of muscles 257
external ear, pressure 220
exteroceptive senses 179
extracellular fluid 83, 416
extrafusal muscle fibre 258
extrapyramidal pathways 269

eye 119, 191–200
  adaptation 194
  anatomy *192*
  attention and 494, *494*, 495, *496*
  movement relative to position of 252–3. *253*
  movements 192–3, 252–3, *252*
  optics 192
eye-blink conditioning 291, *292*
eye-blink reflex 291

face perception 168, 210, 491, 519
face–vase figure 180, *180*, 519, 520, 522, 528
Factor S 480
false memory 287
fasciculation 157
fear
  conditioned 310–11
  unconditioned 310–11, 325
feature detection 224
feedback 27, 181–2
feedback pathway *225*
feedforward control 248–9, 251–2, 417
feeding 398
  abnormalities of 412–15
  brain mechanisms 404–5, 409–12
  external stimuli 406
  fat and 405, 407
  internal cue for 402–5
  role of learning and cognition 405–7
  role of social factors and habits 407, 414
feminization 165, *166*
feminized behaviour 165
fight or flight strategy 337
filopodia 156
fissure 110
fitness 23, 548
flavour 242
  preference 405–6
Fletcher, Dee 208, *208*, 524
flexion, muscle 257
foetus 146
follicle stimulating hormone (FSH) 427, 428
food caching 16, 293
food cravings 415
foraging 289–92
forebrain 108
fornix 123, 290
fovea 119, 192, 197
free-will 48, 529–31
frequency coding 184, *184*
Freud, Sigmund 455, 484
frontal lobe *111*, 544
fronto-parietal system 497
frustration 311
functional explanation 4, 5, 23–4
functional imaging 140
functional lesion 510
functional magnetic resonance imaging (fMRI)
    141, 213, 368, 380, 436, 538, 554
functional specialization
  within perception 209–13
  in vision 204–8

Gage, Phineas *2*, 8–9, 321, 503, 530

gambling 460
gametes 30
gamma motor neuron 258
gamma-aminobutyric acid (GABA) 57, 323,
    411, 433
ganglion 61
ganglion cells 118, *119*, 194–7, 201, 205
Garcia effect 279, 406, 412, 414
Gardner, Randy 474
gate theory 359–60, *359*, 367
gay gene debate 442
gender identity 167
gene expression 156
gene knock-down 380
gene–environment interaction 33, 150
general emergency reaction 332
genes 4, 14–15, *15*, 29–31, 148
  environment and 36, 37–9, *37*, 43
  evolution and 38–9
  expression of 156
  role of 31, 547–8
  selfish 25
genetic condition 34
genetics, basics of 32–3
genotype 29
gestation 160
ghrelin 410
giant axons 131
glands 48
glial cells 91–3
globus pallidus *122*
glossopharyngeal nerve 65, *65*, 126
glucoreceptors 403
glucose 400
glucostatic theory 403
glutamate 323
glutamatergic transmission 539
gonadotropin releasing hormone (GnRH) 427,
    428
goal-directed behaviour 247, 490, 501–5,
    529–30, 541
goal setting 520
Golgi stain 137–8, *138*
gonadotropins 427
gonads 164
grandmother cell 203
grey matter 63, 91, 110, 543
growth cones 156, *156*
gustatory cortex *127*, 239
gut, stress and 348–9
gyrus 111, *113*, *114*, 537

habit formation 551
habituation 277, 296
haemorrhage 418
hair cells 221, 222, 226, *227*
hallucinations 522, 536–7, 540, 543–4, *544*
hallucinogens 457–8
hard problem of consciousness 528, 531
hard-wired systems 26, 59
hearing 179–88, 219–25
Hebb synapse 295
hedonic monitor 238
hedonic states 376–7, 461

hedonism 27, 380, 405
  drug taking and 461, 463, *463*
hemispheric asymmetry 321, 497–501, 538
  anatomical differences 498, *499*
  differential targeting 499–500
heredity, biological basis 33
heritability 37
heroin 446, 455
hierarchical control 77, 78
hierarchical processing 234
hindbrain 108
hippocampus 123, 164, 290, 317, *335*, 537
  exploration and 394
  memory and 285–6, 294, 320
  schizophrenia and 543
  size, comparative 134–5
  size, in taxi drivers 169
  sleep and 523
histology 137–8
H.M. 288, 320, 524
homeostasis 6–7, *7*, 27, 125, 382–4, 395
  drugs and 449
  sleep and 471–2
homology 130, 134, 513
homosexuality
  brain in 441
  genetics 442
homunculus fallacy 182, 530
homunculus, sensory 228
hormonal axis 427
hormone replacement therapy 435
hormones 3, 6, 10, 48, 66–9, 332, 388–90
  classical 66–9
  and development 163–7
  cf neurotransmitters 70–1
  sex 425–6, 435
HPA axis 344–5
Hubel, David 202
Hughes, Howard *534*, 550
Huntington's disease (HD) 35, 266
Huxley, Aldous 458
hyperalgesia 360
hyperphagia 410
hyperpolarization 96–7
hypnosis 362
hypocretin 485
hypokinesia 264
hypothalamic pituitary adrenocortical system
    (HPA system) 334–5
hypothalamic pituitary gonadal axis 427
hypothalamus 70, 109, *123*, 126–7, *127, 128,*
    317, 322
  drinking and 419–20
  emotion and 322
  feeding and 404, 409–11
  nuclei 128
  nuturance and 385
  sexual behaviour and 428, 430, 431, 441
  sleep and 480
  stimulation of 381
  temperature regluation and 383–4

iconic memory 283
illusion 181

visual 207, *207*
imaging techniques 9–10, 140–1, 530
imitation 270–1
immediacy hypothesis 541
immune system 12, 339–41
implicit memory 282
impoverished images 213–15, *213*
imprinting 174–5
incentive 375–6, 425, 461
incentive learning 379
incentive motivation theory 451
incentive salience 379, 463
incentive sensitization theory 462–3
identity theory 18
indirect agonists 101
indirect antagonists 101
induction 156
inertia 307
infant isolation call 323–4
inferior colliculus 109, *110, 122, 123*
inferotemporal cortex *214,* 286, 495
inflow theory 252, *253*
information encapsulation 491–2
inheritance 32–3
inherited disorders 34–6
inhibition 55–8
inhibitory neuron 55
inhibitory postsynaptic potential (IPSP) 96, *97*
innateness 37–8, 168, 169
inner ear, pressure 221
insomnia 485
instinct 37–8
instrumental conditioning 278–9, 450
insula cortex 315
insulin 66–7, *67,* 71, 402–4, *404,* 405, 407, 410,
    414
  feeding and 407
  in satiety 407
integrative nucleus 343
interhemispheric communication 203–4, 525–6
interleukin-1 (IL-1) 340, 414
  sleep and 481
intermittent explosive disorder 390–1
Internet addiction 459–60
interneurons 53
interoceptive cortex 315
intracellular fluid 83, 416
intracranial self–stimulation 381
intrafusal muscle fibre 258
invariance 181, 191, 209, 212
invertebrates 131–2
involuntary movement 249
involuntary reactions 249, 530
ions 83–4
Iowa gambling task 504–5
ipsilateral 107
irritable bowel syndrome 348
isolation 386–7
isolation syndrome 332

James–Lange theory of emotion 313, *314*
jealousy 40, 41

Kanizsa triangle 190, *191*

Klüver–Bucy syndrome 316–17
knee-jerk response 259, *259*
Korsakoff's syndrome 289
labelled-line coding 237
labelled-line principle183–4
language 506–14
  brain mechanisms of 507–11
  development and learning 512–13
  evolutionary and development perspectives
      506–7
  object manipulation and 513
  sign 513
large-diameter neurons 358, 363
latent inhibition 545–6, *547*
lateral geniculate nucleus (LGN) 109, *110,* 118,
    200, 201, 202, 205, *205*
lateral inhibition 196–7
lateral sulcus 111, *113*
lateralization 497
L-dopa 266, 440, 544
Le Doux, J. 325
learned helplessness 336
learning
  aggression and 388
  definition 276
  development and 148
  feeding and 406
  plasticity and 59
  types 277–80
lens *119*
leptin 405, 410, 414
lesion 142–3
  visual processing and 524–5
leucocytes 340
liability 548
light–dark cycle *401,* 468–9, 480
lignocaine 363, *364*
limbic system 316–18
limbic system theory of emotion 316–17, *317*
lipoproteins 350
Little Albert 311
liver 401, 404, 418, 420
localization, principle of 133, 286
lock and key principle 97, 239
locus coeruleus 343, *343*
locus, gene 38
Loewi, Otto 75
long-term memory (LTM) 283
long-term potentiation (LTP) 298, *298*
lordosis 68, *68,* 431, *431*
Lorenz, Konrad 174, 175
loudness 224
love 436
luteinizing hormone (LH) 427, *428*
lymphocyte 340
lysergic acid diethylamide (LSD) 447, 457, 484

Mach, Ernst 252
Madame R 212–13
Madame X 287–8, 308
magnetic resonance imaging (MRI) 140–1, 170,
    171, *214, 543, 543*
magno cells 205
magno system 205

malleability 147, 158
malnutrition, brain and 170–1
mammillary body *123, 128*
marijuana 440, 457
   see also cannabinoids; cannabis
masculinization 165, *166*
masculinized behaviour 166
maturation 148, 152, 174
McDougall, William 525
medial geniculate nucleus 109, *110, 223*
meditation 350
medulla 108, *109, 122, 344*
Meissner's corpuscle *229*
membrane potential 84–5
memory systems 293
memory
   in Alzheimer's disease 537
   brain mechanisms 285–92
   cellular mechanisms 294–8
   changes in neural activity 294–5
   criteria of 298
   classification 282–4, *282*
   definition 276
   disrupted 524
   emotion and 324–6
   sleep and 473
   structural changes 295–6
   temporal stages 283, *283*
   types of 282–4
menopause 438
menstrual cycles, synchronization of 241
mental illness 13
Merkel's disks 228, *229*
mescaline 457, 458
mesencephalon 108
mesolimbic dopamine pathway 378–9, *378*, 385,
   393, 456, 457, 543, 545
metabolic rate 400–1, *401*
metabolism 400
   of glucose 67, 401–2, 538
metabolites 98
metarepresentation 541, 542
methylphenidate 454, 554
microdialysis 141–2, *141*
microelectrode 143
midbrain 108
migration, of cells 155
mind 18, 518
mind–body dualism 18, 528–9
mind–body problem 528
mind, theory of 18, 134, 521
mirror neurons 270–1
modality segregation 228
modularity 491–2, 512
modules 41–2, 168, 310, 491, 512, 520
monoamines 57
monozygotic twins 151, 547
morphine 363, 455
Morris water maze apparatus 279–80, *280, 281*
motivation 27, 306
   definition 373
   brain and 381
   neuroscience of 378–81
   properties 374–7
   sexual incentive and 68, 425–6, *425*

sleep and 475–6
motor control 120, 261, *262*
motor cortex 120–2
motor homunculus 120, *121,* 263
motor imagery 270–1
motor learning 248
motor neurons 53, 64, 256, 258, *258,* 268–9
   types 258
motor potential 263
motor systems, development of 271–2
motor units 256, 2*56*
movement
   control of, by brain 261–8
   definition 247
   visual detection of 210
Muller–Lyer illusion *182,* 491
multiplier effect, of development 167
Murdoch, Iris 536, *536*
muscle spindle 258
muscles
   activity 139
   arrangement of 257, *257*
   cardiac 71, 75
   contraction 255
   eye 252–3
   fibres 255
   skeletal 255, *255,* 258–61, *259*
   smooth 75, 437, 440
   types 258, *258*
mutation 30, 33
myelin 91–2, 256
myelinated axons 91, 92, *92,* 131
myelination 91–3, 131, 150, 256, 271, 502

naloxone 368, 411, 448
narcolepsy 485–6
natural killer cells (NK) 341
natural selection 23
naturalistic fallacy 40
nature 4
negative affect 355
negative feedback 7, 248, 254, 417
negative reinforcement 279
   drug taking and 450
neglect syndrome 497
neocortex 134
nerve fibre 63
nerve growth factor (NGF) 157, 162
nerves *61,* 63
nervous system 3, 47–8
   development 152–7, 1*53*
   organization of 48, 61–5, *61*
neural correlations of consciousness 521, 524
neural encoding 183
neural mechanisms in hearing 223–4
neural tube 152
neuritic plaques 538–9
neuroanatomy 107
neurochemistry 54
neurofibrillary tangles 538
neurogenesis 155, 156
neurohormone 66, 69
neuroleptic drugs 544
neuromodulators 58, *58,* 69
neuromuscular control *247*

neuromuscular junction 93, 257
neuron–muscle connections, in development
   160–3
neuron–neuron connections, in development
   158–60
neurons 6, 48, 49–50
   adult 158
   afferent 64
   autonomic 72
   cold 384
   command 77
   communication between 52–3
   development of 158–63
   efferent 64
   inhibitory 55
   large-diameter 363
   learning and 59–60
   motor 53, 64, 256, 258, *258,* 268–9
   nociceptive 50, 181, *186,* 230, 357–8
   postsynaptic 52
   presynaptic 52
   sensory 50, 64, 237–9
   serotonergic 94, *94,* 479
   somatosensory 228, *229,* 229
   structure 63–4, *64*
   types 63–4, 95–6
   warm 383–4
neuropeptide Y 410
neuropeptides 312
neurotransmitters 52–3
   aggression and 391
   of autonomic nervous system 77
   cf hormones 70–1
   classical 56
   synapse and 93–100, *93*
neurotrophic factor 157
neutral stimulus 277
nicotine 440, 447, 456, 458, *459,* 461, 463
Nissl stain 137
NMDA receptors 298
nocebo effect 367
nociception 355
nociceptive information transfer 117, 1*17, 118*
nociceptive neuron 50, 181, *183,* 186, 230, 358,
   360
nociceptive reflex 2*60*
nociceptive system 355
nociceptors 357, 358
nodes of Ranvier 91–2
non-associative learning 277
non-corticospinal tracts 269
non-declarative memory 282, 293
non-rapid eye movement sleep (non-REM)
   476–7
non-specific cortex 134
noradrenalin 57, 70, 75, 77, 323, 332–4, 338,
   343, 391, 433, 544
noradrenergic systems 343
   in sleep 479
norepinephrine *see* noradrenalin
nose 240
noxious stimulus, reaction to 260
nucleus (nuclei) 29, 67, 128, 137
nucleus accumbens (N.acc) 378, *378,* 379,
   379, 393, 411, 429, 430, 432, 452,
   455, 458

nucleus of the solitary tract (NTS) 126–7, 1*27*, 238, 325, *344*, 404, 412, 414
nucleus of the tractus solitarius *see* nucleus of the solitary tract
nurturance 385–6
nurture 4
nutrition 170–1, 400–2

obesity 410, 414–15
object permanence task 169
object retrieval test 169
obsessive-compulsive disorder 103, 549–52
occipital cortex 208, 286
occipital lobe 111
odour, emotion, mood and 241–2
oestradiol 1*65*, 427
oestrogen 68, 165, 385, 427, 431, 435, 438
oestrous cycle 428
off centre cells 196
olfaction, disorders of 242
olfactory bulb 1*20*, 135–6, 240
olfactory hallucination (OH) 242
olfactory system 239–42, *240*
olfactory tract *123*
oligodendrocytes 91
on centre cells 195
ontogenetic hypothesis of REM sleep 482
ontogeny 15, 482
open programmes 174
operant conditioning 278
opiates 312, 363, *364*, 440, 448, 451, 455–6, *455*, 461–2
opioids 312, 363, 368, 385–6, 450, 461–2
    drug taking and 448, 455–6, 457
    feeding and 405, 411, 413, 415
    pain and 359, *360*
    role of 312
opponent-process coding 199
optic ataxia 208
optic nerve 65, 65, 118, *119*, 1*20*
optic tract 118, *120*
optional sleep 473
orbitofrontal cortex (OFC) *129*, 242, 368, 409, 503, 551, *551*
orexin 485
organic cause 439
organizational effects, of hormones 163–4
organs 6
orgasm 433, 440
    female 438
    male 437
orgasmic imagery 438
oscillations 468, *469*
osmoreceptor 418, 419, *419*, 420
outflow theory 252, 253
overt orienting 494
oxytocin 312, 385–7, 394, 432, *432*, 433, 436, 438

Pacinian corpuscle 228, 2*29*
pain 10, 26
    adaptive value 355–7
    analgesia and 363–5
    brain processes of 361–2
    brain and spinal pathways 357–8
    cognitive and social factors in 366–9

definition 355
gate theory of 359–61
sensory contribution 357–8
pain matrix 361–2
pain receptor 181, 358
pair bonding 432–3, 436
palatability 399, 411
palmar grasp reflex 271
Panksepp, Jaak 312
paradoxical sleep 477
parallel processing 204
paraventricular nucleus of the hypothalamus (PVN) 128, 334, *335*, *344*, 410, 438
parietal lobe *111*
Parkinson's disease (PD) 264–6, 379
parvo cells 205
parvo system 205
passive avoidance learning 297–8
passive strategy 336, 337–9
pathogen 339
Pavlov 59, 277
Pavlovian conditioning *see* classical conditioning
Penfield, Wilder 503
pentylenetetrazol (PTZ) 448
perception 179–82, 190, 206, 247
periaqueductal grey (PAG) 125, *126*, 322, 344, 362, 368, 385, 450, 456
period of rhythm 468
peripheral nervous system 48
permeability, of cell membrane 85
personal responsibility 14
personality 346, 380, 394
PGO system 479
phantom pain 365–6
phantosmia 242
phenomenal consciousness 518, 528, 531
phenotype 29
phenylketonuria (PKU) 34, 172–3
pheromones 180–1, 237, 241, 425, 429, 435
phonemes 506
phylogenetically old 168
phylogeny 4, 502
physiological effect 408
physiology 6–7
pioneer axons 157
pituitary adrenocortical system 334–5
pituitary gland *120*, *128*, *335*
place cells 143
place code 221, 223
placebo effect 367–9
placebo responder 368
planum temporale 498
plasticity 59, 147, 158, 263
    in *Aplysia* 296–7
    brain 472–3
    cognition and 159–70
    in somatosensory cortex 235–6
play 172
pleasure 27, 356
pleasure regions 306, 381
pons 108, *109*, *122*
population coding 184
positive psychology 349
positive reinforcement 27, 279

drug taking and 450
positron emission tomography (PET) 140, 168, 169, 171, 213, 250, 267, 379, 388, 437, 509, 538, 550
    of aggression 390
    of amygdala 324
post absorptive state 401, *402*, 404
postcentral gyrus 111, *113*, 120
posterior attention system (PAS) 497
postsynaptic neuron 52
post-synaptic potentials (PSP) 96–7
post-traumatic stress disorder 347
postural stability 254
precentral gyrus 111, *113*, 120
precocial species 174, 482
predatory aggression 387
predictability 336
prefrontal cortex (PFC) 127, 129, 134, *134*, *135*, 169, 207, 263, 286–7, 321, 369, 409, 435, 452, 496, 502–5, 542, 544, 550, 554
    damage to 462, 503
pregnancy sickness (PS) 406–7
premotor area (PMA) 262, *263*
prepulse inhibition 545, *546*
prestriate cortex 129, 201, 210, 215
presynaptic neuron 52
primary motor cortex 201, *262*, 263
primary visual areas 213
primary visual cortex 201, 213
primate 10
primates, stress in 338–9
priming 289
primitive reflexes 168
procedural memory 282, 292
proceptivity 431
processes, neural 63
progesterone 428, 431
programmed cell death (PCD) 157, 170
prolactin 385–6
proprioception 247
prosopagnosia 168, 210
prostaglandins 363
protein synthesis 297–8
proteins 15, 29
Prozac (fluoxetine) 102
psychedelic drugs 457–8
psychoactive drugs 447
psychoendoimmunology 339
psychogenic cause 439
psychogenic trigger 362
psychological distress syndrome 450
psychological factor 180
psychology–biology relationship 10–11, 12–14
psychoendoimmunology 339
psychoneuroimmunology (PNI) 339, 341
psychopharmacology 55
psychosis 537–8, 540, 545
pumps, metabolic 86
punishment 279
pupil, of eye *119*
Purkinje cell 291
putamen *122*, 264
pyramidal system 269
pyramidal tract 269

qualia 519, 528

radial maze 289, *290*
rage 322, 387
rapid eye movement sleep (REM) 477–8, 523
reaction 25, 246
reactive depression 42
readiness potential 263
receptive fields 186, *186*, 194–5, *195*, 196–7, *196*, 201, 228, *229*, 232, *233*, 234
receptivity 431
receptor cells 118, *119*, 193
receptors 50, 52, 193
reciprocal inhibition 259
reciprocal interaction model of sleep 480, *480*
recruitment 256
reductionism 12
referred pain 365, *365*
reflectance 191
reflex substitution 278, *278*
reflexes 25–6, 48, 49–50, 271
   interactions within spinal cord 260
   local autonomy 260
   modulation by the brain 260
   nociceptive *260*
   palmar grasp 271
   primitive 168
   spinal 50, 431, 437
   startle 260, 326
   stretch 258
   unconditional 277
   vestibulo-ocular 254, *254*, 267
   withdrawal 49–50, 132
refractory period 89
regional cerebral blood flow (rCBF) 125, 140, 250, 437–8, 544, 550
regularity, of stimuli 541
regulation, of nutrient 399
regulatory behaviour 27
reinforcement 27, 60, 278–9, 388, 450, 512, 553
replication 30, *31*
representations 169, 522
reproduction 30, *31*
resting potential 86
retained memories 288–9
reticular activating system (RAS) 116–17, *116*, 128, 478–9
reticular formation *122*
retina 118, *119*, 191, *192*, *193*
retrograde amnesia 284–5
retrograde labelling 137, *137*
reuptake 98, *99*, 380
reuptake inhibitor 102, 440, 554
reward 375
rhythms
   of movement 261
   sleep–waking 468–71
   terminology 468
rods 193–4, *194*, *198*
rostral 107
rubrospinal tract 269

saccadic eye movements 193
sagittal 108
salience 544–5
satiety 399, 404–5, 407–8
   feeding 407–9

sexual 433, 438
thirst 418–19, 420
Schacter–Singer theory of emotion 313–14
schedule-induced polydipsia 399
schizophrenia 540–9
   accounts of 540–1
   brain and 542–4
   evolution, genes and environment 547–50
   explanatory frameworks 541–2
Schwann cells 51
Schwartz, Jeffrey 550
scotoma 201
Seasonal Affective Disorder (SAD) 415
second messengers 98–9
selective attention 493
selective serotonin reuptake inhibitors (SSRIs) 440, 460, 551
self-concept 521, 527, 537, 541
self-mutilation 28
self-reflection 18
selfish gene 25, 40
Seligman, Martin 279
semantic memory 282–3, 292, 492, 537–8
semipermeable membrane 416, *416*
senile plaques 538
sensation-seeking 394
sensitive period 164, 166
sensitization 297, 336–7
sensory homunculus 117, *118*, 182, 228
sensory neglect 497
sensory neurons 50, 64, 228–30
   receptive fields 228, *229*, 230
   types 228
sensory regions 7
sensory receptors 183, 192–3
sensory systems 115
   definition 179
sensory threshold 186
sensory-specific satiety (SSS) 408
serotonergic neuron 94, *94*
serotonin 57, 94, 391, 457
   in feeding 415
   in sexual behaviour 440
   in sleep 472, 479
set-point 246, 382, 421
sex chromosomes 33, *34*
sex determinants 150
sex differences 40–1, 149, 164–6
sex in rats 430–3
sex-hormones 426
   control of secretion 427–8
sex-linked characteristics 33
sexual addiction 460
sexual arousal 426
sexual behaviour 27–8
   brain structures and 430–1
   comparative perspective on 429–33
   effects of chemicals on 440–3
   female 428, 431, 435, 437–8
   influences on 426, *427*
   male 428, 430–1, 435, 436–7
   novelty, role of 429
   physiology 436–9
   satiety 433

sexual desire 433–6
sexual development 150, 164–7, 426–7
sexual differentiation 164–6, *166*, 427
sexual motivation 425–6, *425*
sexual orientation 431, 441–3
sexually dimorphic nucleus 165
Shakespeare, William 440
shape constancy 209
shock, as aversive stimulus 311
short-term memory (STM) 283, 288
side-effects, drug 102, 412, 440, 539
sidepath control 254
Siffre, Michel 470
sign language 513
simple cortical cell 201–2, *202*
single-unit recording 143
size constancy 209
skeletal muscle 53, 255, *255*
   feedback control 258–61, *259*
skill learning 249, 250
skin conductance response 504–5
Skinner box 17, 27, *27*, 279, 393, 420, 452, 462
sleep 128–9, 467
   in animals 473–4
   behavioural disturbances during 485
   brain mechanisms 478–81
   core vs optional 473
   development and 481–2
   dreaming 483–4
   function of 471–4
   health and 484–6
   homeostasis and 471
   learning and memory and 473
   motivation 475–6
   neuropsychological model 484
   non-REM 477
   plasticity and 472, 473
   rhythmicity 468–71
   REM 477–8
   safety and inactivity 472
   slow-wave 477
   types 476–7
sleep deprivation 474
sleep factor 480–1
sleep–waking and consciousness 468–71, 523
slow-wave sleep 477
small-diameter fibres 358
smell 236, 239–42, 405
smooth muscles 54, 71, 75, 102, 437, 441
social attachment 385, 386–7, 448
social behaviour 385–7, 503–5
social constructivism 307
social interaction 10, 308–9
   adults 309
   development factors 171, 309
   stress and 349–50
social policy 13–14
social rejection 10, 362
social role theory 40
social stimuli 171–2
sodium appetite 420–1
sodium ingestion, drinking and 417–18, 420–1
sodium-potassium pump 86

soft-wired systems 59
solitary nucleus 1*27*
soma 63
somatic nervous system 53, *53*, 54, 72, 76, 315, 426
somatic-marker hypothesis 315–16, 503, 505
somatosensory cortex 115, 228, 234, *234*, *235*, 263, *263*, 361
  development and plasticity 235–6
  information processing in 234–5, *235*
somatosensory neurons 228, *229*, *230*, 230
somatosensory pathways 230–3
  processing within 232–3
somatosensory system 226–36
song learning 293
sonic shadow 224
sound production 179, *180*
spatial acuity 231–2
spatial summation 96
species-specific defence reaction (SSDR) 310
species-typical behaviour (STB) 38
Sperry, Roger 202
spinal cord 3, *3*, 49, *114*, 262
  interactions within 260
  organization 61–3, 255–6, *256*, 362, 431
spinal injury, erectile function and 439
spinal nerve 62, *62*
spinal reflex 50, 431, 437
spinothalamic tract (STT) *117*, 357, *358*, 361, *362*
split brains 203–4, 500–1, 525–6
  language and 510
spontaneous alternation 393
spontaneous background activity 194
stability, maintaining of 251–4, 258–60
staining 137
startle reflex 260, 326, 448, 545
stem cells 152
stereotaxic apparatus 142, *143*
stereotaxic atlas 142
stereotaxic surgery 142
stereotypies 28, 171
steroids 427
stimulants 554
stimulus–response (S–R)
  association 278, 290
stimulus–stimulus association 278
strains 38–9
Stratton, George 192
stress
  alcohol and 457
  brain mechanisms and 342–4
  cardiovascular systems and 345–7
  definition 330
  drugs and 463
  four criteria of 333
  gut and 348–9
  immune system and 339–42
  positive action for health 349–51
  schizophrenia and 548
stressors
  cognitive processes 332
  contextual factors and 336–9
  external stimuli 330–1, 332
  physiological stimuli 332
  types 330–1, 332

stretch receptor 258
stretch reflex 258
striate cortex 201
striatum 264, 554
stroke 142
Stroop test 251, *251*, 492, 520
structural imaging 140
subcortical pathway 200
subcortical systems 168
subjective experience 303, 306, 355, 528, 531
substance P 357
substantia nigra 264, *265*
suckling 151, 158, 405
sulcus 110, *113*, 537
superior colliculus 109, *110*, *122*, *206*
superior temporal polysensory area (STP) 210, *211*
supervisory attentional system (SAS) 502
supplementary motor area (SMA) 262, 263, *263*, 264
suprachiasmatic nucleus (SCN) *128*, 441, 480
sustained attention 493
Sylvian fissure 111, 498–9
synapse 52, 55–6
  classification 63
  chemical 99, *99*
  electrical 99, *99*
  learning and 59–60
  neurotransmitters and 93–9, *94*
  removal of transmitter from 97–8
  restructuring 155, 157
  strength, alterations in 100–2
synaptic cleft 93
synaptic delay 56
synaptic vesicles 93, 94
synaptogenesis *155*, 157
synchronized sleep 477
systems 6

T cells 357, *358*, 359
tactile stimuli 117, 171–2
Tan 507
taste 127, 236–9, *238–9*, 405–6, 411
taste buds 237–8, *238*
taste reactivity test 376–7, *376*, 379, 411,
taste-aversion learning 5, 279, 399, 406, 412, 414
telencephalon 108, *109*
temperature regulation 128, 382–4, 421
temporal cortex 286
temporal lobe 111, *113*, 316–17
temporal summation 96
testosterone 10, 14, 68–9, 164, 388–9, 428, 431, 433, 440, 441
thalamus 109, *110*, 117, *122*, 223, 523, *523*
theory of mind 134, 170, 518, 521, 541
theory of mind mechanism (ToMM) 170
theta waves 477
thirst
  extracellular stimulus 418
  satiety 418–19
threshold, of action potential 87
tissue 137–8
T-maze 379, 393, 394, 449
tolerance, drug 451

tongue 238–9
tonotopic representation 224
top-down control 180, 190, 192, 202, 213–16, 224, 226, 237, 271, 439, 492–3
  sensory system 235
topographical map 201
touch 226–36
Tourette's syndrome 552
tract 63
trait 24
transcutaneous electrical nerve stimulation (TENS) 363
transduction 183–4, 219, 220, *221*
transmitter *see* neurotransmitter
tree shrews, stress in 337–8
trust 312
tumour necrosis factor 414
twin studies 43, 146, 151, 547
two-point threshold 231
type A behaviour 346
type B behaviour 346

ulcers 348–9
umami 237
unconditional reflex 277
unconditional response 277
unconditional stimulus 277, 310, 326, 449
unconscious information 519–21
unmyelinated axons 91, *92*
up-regulation 102
utilization behaviour 263, 287

vagus nerve 65, *65*, 75, 76, 1*27*, 314
vasoactive intestinal polypeptide (VIP) 95, 437–8
ventral 61, 107
ventral bed nucleus of the stria terminalis (VBN) 385
ventral root 62
ventral stream 206, 215, 511
  lesions in 208
ventral tegmental area (VTA) 378, 432, 437, 450, 455
ventricles 125, 537, 542
ventromedial prefrontal cortex (VMPFC) 462, 503–5
vertebrates 131–2
vestibular apparatus 226, *227*, 252
vestibular system 226
vestibulo-ocular reflex 254, *254*, 267
Viagra 424, 441
vibrissae 235, *235*, *236*
viscera 71
visible spectrum 191, *191*
visual agnosia 208
visual association area 215
visual cortex 115
visual field 200, *201*
visual pathways 200–4
visual system 189, 200, *201*
  development of, 168
  neuron–neuron connections and development 158–60
visuomotor transformations 206
vocalization 322, 448

voltages 83–4, 86
vulnerability model 548
voluntary behaviour 26, 48, 54, 260–1, 271, 530
voluntary movement 53, 249–50
vomeronasal organ (VNO) 429
vomeronasal system 241

Wada technique 511, 513, 525
waking 128–9
wanting vs liking 379–80, 409, 411, 462–3, *463*
warm neurons 383–4
water
   deprivation 418, *418*
   distribution in body 416–17, *417*

Waterman, Ian 250
Watson, John 311
wavelength 179, 191, 198
Wernicke–Geschwind model 508–9, *508*
Wernicke's aphasia 508
Wernicke's area 507
wet dog shakes 488, 456
whisker barrel 235
white matter *61*, 63, 91, *112*
Whitman, Charles 390
Wiesel, Torsten 202
Williams syndrome 491
wind-up 366
win–shift 289–90, *290*

win–stay 290, *291*
Wisconsin card sorting test 173, *173*, 289, 544
withdrawal reflex 26, 132, 447
withdrawal symptoms 447–8, 451, 459
womb as environment 151
word-completion test 288–9
working memory 284, *284*, 462, 544

yohimbine 433

Zeitgeber 469, 470, 480
zygote 30, 146, 15